Today's most **popular authors** have collaborated on this exciting new series, which combines **great literature** with remarkably **effective instruction,** bringing real writers and real tools together for real results.

Give your students

Real writers

unprecedented access
to award-winning authors
(see page NC T2)

Real tools

remarkably effective tools
for differentiated instruction
(see page NC T4)

Real results

built-in benchmarking to guarantee
Standard Course of Study mastery and
North Carolina Writing Assessment
success (see page NC T6)

"**This project is what I wish I'd had when I was in school . . . a resource where I could not only read really good writing, but also get a sense about how the authors actually felt!**"

—Cornelius Eady
featured unit author

North Carolina
Professional Development Handbook

NORTH CAROLINA

TEACHER'S EDITION

NORTH CAROLINA
PRENTICE HALL LITERATURE

PENGUIN EDITION

PEARSON
Prentice Hall

Upper Saddle River, New Jersey
Boston, Massachusetts

GRADE TEN
VOLUME TWO

Copyright © 2007. by Pearson Education, Inc., publishing as Pearson Prentice Hall, Upper Saddle River, New Jersey 07458. All rights reserved. Printed in the United States of America. This publication is protected by copyright, and permission should be obtained from the publisher prior to any prohibited reproduction, storage in a retrieval system, or transmission in any form or by any means, electronic, mechanical, photocopying, recording, or likewise. For information regarding permission(s), write to: Rights and Permissions Department.

Pearson Prentice Hall™ is a trademark of Pearson Education, Inc.
Pearson® is a registered trademark of Pearson plc.
Prentice Hall® is a registered trademark of Pearson Education, Inc.

PEARSON
Prentice Hall

Upper Saddle River, New Jersey
Boston, Massachusetts

ISBN 0-13-190806-5

3 4 5 6 7 8 9 10   09 08 07 06

CONTRIBUTING AUTHORS

The contributing authors guided the direction and philosophy of *Prentice Hall Literature: Penguin Edition.* Working with the development team, they helped to build the pedagogical integrity of the program and to ensure its relevance for today's teachers and students.

Kate **Kinsella**

Kate Kinsella, Ed.D., is a teacher educator in the Department of Secondary Education at San Francisco State University. She teaches coursework addressing academic language and literacy development in linguistically and culturally diverse classrooms. Dr. Kinsella maintains secondary classroom involvement by teaching an academic literacy class for adolescent English learners through the University's Step to College Program. She publishes and provides consultancy and training nationally, focusing upon responsible instructional practices that provide second language learners and less proficient readers in grades 4–12 with the language and literacy skills vital to educational mobility.

Dr. Kinsella is the program author for *Reading in the Content Areas: Strategies for Reading Success,* published by Pearson Learning, and the lead program author for the 2002 Prentice Hall secondary language arts program *Timeless Voices: Timeless Themes.* She is the co-editor of the *CATESOL Journal* (California Association of Teachers of ESL) and serves on the editorial board for the *California Reader.* A former Fulbright scholar, Dr. Kinsella has received numerous awards, including the prestigious Marcus Foster Memorial Reading Award, offered by the California Reading Association in 2002 to a California educator who has made a significant statewide impact on both policy and pedagogy in the area of literacy.

Sharon **Vaughn**

Sharon Vaughn, Ph.D., is the H.E. Hartfelder/The Southland Corporation Regents Professor at the University of Texas and also director of the Vaughn Gross Center for Reading and Language Arts at the University of Texas (VGCRLA). As director of the VGCRLA, she leads more than five major initiatives, including The Central Regional Reading First Technical Assistance Center; the Three-Tier Reading Research Project; a bilingual-biliteracy (English/Spanish) intervention research study; the Grades 1–4 Teacher Reading Academies that have been used for teacher education throughout Texas and the nation; and the creation of online professional development in reading for teachers and other interested professionals.

Dr. Vaughn has published more than ten books and over one hundred research articles. She is Editor in Chief of the *Journal of Learning Disabilities* and serves on the editorial boards of more than ten research journals, including the *Journal of Educational Psychology,* the *American Educational Research Journal,* and the *Journal of Special Education.*

Kevin **Feldman**

Kevin Feldman, Ed.D., is the Director of Reading and Intervention for the Sonoma County Office of Education and an independent educational consultant. He publishes and provides consultancy and training nationally, focusing upon improving school-wide literacy skills as well as targeted interventions for struggling readers, special needs students, and second language learners. Dr. Feldman is the co-author of the California Special Education Reading Task Force report and the lead program author for the 2002 Prentice Hall secondary language arts program *Timeless Voices: Timeless Themes.* He serves as technical consultant to the California Reading and Literature Project and the CalSTAT State Special Education Improvement Project. Dr. Feldman has taught for nineteen years at the university level in Special Education and Masters' level programs for University of California, Riverside, and Sonoma State University.

Dr. Feldman earned his undergraduate degree in Psychology from Washington State University and has a Master's Degree from UC Riverside in Special Education, Learning Disabilities, and Instructional Design. He has an Ed.D. from the University of San Francisco in Curriculum and Instruction.

Differentiated Instruction Advisor
Don **Deshler**

Don Deshler, Ph.D, is the Director of the Center for Research on Learning (CRL) at the University of Kansas. Dr. Deshler's expertise centers on adolescent literacy, learning strategic instruction, and instructional strategies for teaching content-area classes to academically diverse classes. He is the author of *Teaching Content to All: Evidence-Based Inclusive Practices in Middle and Secondary Schools,* a text which presents the instructional practices that have been tested and validated through his research at CRL.

UNIT AUTHORS

An award-winning contemporary author hosts each unit in each level of *Prentice Hall Literature: Penguin Edition.* In the upper-level courses, some of these authors are renowned scholars or translators, while others are famous for their own contributions to literature. All serve as guides, helping to introduce a unit, discussing the work of a traditional author or their own work in a translation, and revealing their own writing processes. Following are the featured unit authors who guide students for *World Masterpieces.*

Coleman **Barks**

Coleman Barks, who serves as a guide for this unit, is a critically acclaimed and popular translator of one of the unit's major authors, the Persian poet Rumi. Professor Barks explains the cultural and religious context of Rumi's work.

Wendy **Doniger**

An authority on Hindu literature and a translator of the *Rig Veda*, Professor Wendy Doniger is the perfect choice for this unit's guide. Her books include *The Origins of Evil in Hindu Mythology*, and she is a distinguished professor at the University of Chicago.

Royall **Tyler**

Royall Tyler is highly qualified to be this unit's guide. He has taught Japanese literature, language, and culture at many universities. His acclaimed translations include *The Tale of Genji*, which is widely recognized as the world's first novel.

David **Mamet**

A major playwright and a brilliant student of the theater, David Mamet is well suited to introduce Greek drama. His works include the Pulitzer Prize-winning play *Glengarry Glen Ross* and *Three Uses of the Knife: On the Nature and Purpose of Drama.*

Marilyn **Stokstad**

Marilyn Stokstad, the guide for this unit, is the author of the widely used textbook *Art History* and a specialist in medieval art. She brings an art historian's perspective to medieval literature, helping students picture the grail castle in *Perceval.*

João **Magueijo**

João Magueijo is a theoretical physicist and author whose ideas challenge some cherished beliefs of science. As a contemporary rebel, he is ideally suited to help students understand that scientific rebel of the Renaissance, Galileo.

W. S. **Merwin**

One of the best poets now writing in English, W. S. Merwin has received the Pulitzer Prize and many other honors. He has been deeply influenced by the Romantic tradition, and as this unit's guide, comments on French Romantic poetry and two of his own poems.

Judith Ortiz **Cofer**

Poet, essayist, and novelist Judith Ortiz Cofer has won many awards for her work, including a nomination for the Pulitzer Prize. As this unit's guide, she describes her experiences with modern world literature and introduces "Ithaka" by Constantine Cavafy.

Jamaica **Kincaid**

A leading figure in world literature, Jamaica Kincaid is a natural choice to serve as a guide for this unit. She describes her sudden discovery of contemporary literature, at age nineteen, and she introduces an excerpt from her own book *Annie John*.

Chinua **Achebe**

Chinua Achebe, nominated for the Nobel Prize in Literature in 2000, introduces his story "Marriage Is a Private Affair." Mr. Achebe's novel *Things Fall Apart* is widely acknowledged as both an inaugurator and a classic of postcolonial African literature.

State of North Carolina
Program Advisors

Shanita Anderson
Grays Creek Middle School
Hope Hills, NC

Michael D. Blas
Lowe's Grove Middle School
Durham, NC

Karen C. Lilly-Bowyer
Winston-Salem/Forsyth County Schools
Winston-Salem, North Carolina

Amanda Grose
Lufkin Road Middle School
Apex, NC

Stephanie S. Kestner
Providence High School
Charlotte, NC

Mark Kozlowski
Winston-Salem/Forsyth County Schools
Winston-Salem, NC

Erin McDermott
Brogden Middle School
Durham, NC

Suzanne V. Micallef
John T. Hoggard High School
Wilmington, NC

Donna H. Morris
South Mecklenburg High School
Charlotte, North Carolina

Melaine Rickard
Alamance-Burlington Schools
Burlington, NC

Andrea Rumley
Alamance-Burlington Schools
Graham, NC

Tara Alexandra Thomas
South Mecklenburg High School
Charlotte, North Carolina

Betty S. Tunks
North Rowan High School
Spencer, North Carolina

Stephanie J. Wallace
East Forsyth High School
Kernersville, NC

Harriett Wilson
Vance High School,
Charlotte-Mecklenberg Schools
Charlotte, NC

Susanna Quick Winton
Lufkin Road Middle School
Apex, NC

North Carolina
Academic Achievement Handbook

Unit 1

Origins and Traditions
Ancient Worlds (c. 3000 B.C.–A.D. 1400)

NC   *All selections and workshops in this unit support your North Carolina standards.*

Skills Workshops

SAT's
PREP
ACT

Contents ■ *NC 9*

**All selections and workshops in this unit support your
North Carolina standards.**

Unit 3

Wisdom and Insight
Chinese and Japanese Literature (1000 B.C.–A.D. 1890)

From the Scholar's Desk
Royall Tyler

Chinese Literature

Comparing Literary Works

Connections: American Literature

Focus on Literary Forms: Poetry

Comparing Literary Works

Contents ■ *NC 11*

Japanese Literature

Skills Workshops

 All selections and workshops in this unit support your North Carolina standards.

Unit 4

Classical Civilizations
Ancient Greece and Rome (c. 800 B.C.–A.D. 500)

From the Scholar's Desk
David Mamet

Greek Literature

Comparing Literary Works

Connections: American Literature

Focus on Literary Forms: Drama

Reading Informational Materials: Web Research Sources

Skills Workshops

 All selections and workshops in this unit support your North Carolina standards.

Contents ■ *NC 15*

Unit 6

Rebirth and Exploration
The Renaissance and Rationalism (1300–1800)

From the Scholar's Desk
João Magueijo

Focus on Literary Forms: Sonnet

Comparing Literary Works

Connections: British Literature

Comparing Literary Works

All selections and workshops in this unit support your North Carolina standards.

Skills Workshops

SAT PREP ACT

Revolution and Reaction
Romanticism and Realism (1800–1890)

> *All selections and workshops in this unit support your North Carolina standards.*

Skills Workshops

SAT
PREP
ACT

Unit 8

From Conflict to Renewal
The Modern World (1890–1945)

From the Scholar's Desk
Judith Ortiz Cofer

Focus on Literary Forms: Short Story

Reading Informational Materials: Scientific Texts

Connections: American Literature

Comparing Literary Works

> **NC** *All selections and workshops in this unit support your North Carolina standards.*

Skills Workshops

SAT
PREP
ACT

Unit 9

Voices of Change
The Contemporary World (1945–Present)

***All selections and workshops in this unit support your
North Carolina standards.***

NC 22 ■ *Contents*

Skills Workshops

Resources

INFORMATIONAL TEXT AND OTHER NONFICTION

▪ Reading Informational Materials—Instructional Workshops

▪ Additional Nonfiction—Selections by Type

■ Historical and Literary Background

■ Themes in World Masterpieces—Reading in the Humanities

INFORMATIONAL TEXT AND OTHER NONFICTION (cont.)

■ Literature in Context—Reading in the Content Areas

■ A Closer Look

■ Focus on Literary Forms

SKILLS WORKSHOPS

■ Writing Workshops

SAT PREP ACT

SKILLS WORKSHOPS

■ Vocabulary Workshops

■ Assessment Workshops

■ Communications Workshops

■ Connections to Literature

Literature of the Americas

American Literature

British Literature

PRENTICE HALL
LITERATURE

WORLD MASTERPIECES

Batik Sarong, Javanese c. 1920, on glazed cotton: This image is a detail from a sarong, a traditional type of clothing consisting of a long strip of cloth worn like a skirt. This particular sarong hails from Java, an island in the Indonesian archipelago. The fabric features a design called *batik*, meaning "to dot" in Javanese. The herons featured in the design of this sarong have many symbolic meanings throughout Asia.

P E N G U I N E D I T I O N

PEARSON
Prentice Hall

Upper Saddle River, New Jersey
Boston, Massachusetts

ISBN 0-13-131737-7

1 2 3 4 5 6 7 8 9 10   09 08 07 06 05

Cover: A detail of the design on a batik sarong which incorporates herons and other birds, flowers and water plants. c. 1920. Javanese. Glazed cotton, Werner Forman/Art Resource, NY

ACKNOWLEDGMENTS

Grateful acknowledgement is made to the following for copyrighted material:

The American University in Cairo Press "Half a Day," extract from "The Time and Place" by Naguib Mahfouz, first published in Arabic in 1962 as "Nisf Yawm, in al-fajn al Kadhib (The False Dawn)". Copyright © 1991 by The American University in Cairo Press. Reprinted by permission of The American University in Cairo Press.

The Asia Society and Dr. Nguyen Ngoc Bich "Thoughts of Hanoi," by Nguyen Thi Vinh from *A Thousand Years of Vietnamese Poetry*, edited by Nguyen Ngoc Bich. Copyright © 1962, 1967, 1968, 1969, 1970, 1971, 1974 by The Asia Society and Nguyen Ngoc Bich. Reprinted by permission.

Georges Borchardt, Inc. "The Metamorphosis," by Franz Kafka, editor and translated by Stanley Corngold. Copyright © 1972 by Stanley Corngold. Reprinted by permission of Georges Borchardt, Inc.

The Citadel Press/Kensington Publishing Corp. "The Lorelei," by Heinrich Heine translated by Aaron Kramer from *The Poetry of Heinrich Heine*. Copyright © 1969 by Citadel Press, Inc. All rights reserved. Reprinted by permission of Citadel Press/Kensington Publishing Corp. www.kensingtonbooks.com

The Claredon Press, an imprint of Oxford University Press "African Proverbs: Tanzania and Kenya: The Masai: "We begin by being foolish . . :,"

"Do not repair another man's fence . . ."," "Nobody can say . . ."," "It is better to be poor . . ."," "Baboons do not go far . . ."," "The hyena said . . ."," "The zebra cannot do away . . ."," from The Masai: Their Language and Folklore by A.C. Hollis. Published in 1905 by The Claredon Press.

Ruth Harwood Cline and The University of Georgia Press "from Perceval: The Grail," by Chretien de Troyes from *Perceval or The Story of the Grail*, translated by Ruth Harwood Cline. Copyright © 1983 by Ruth Harwood Cline. Reprinted by permission of The University of Georgia Press.

Toby Cole, Actors & Authors Agency "War" from *The Medals and Other Stories* by Luigi Pirandello. © E.P. Dutton, NY, 1932, 1967. Reprinted by permission of Toby Cole, Agent for the Pirandello Estate. All rights reserved. For performance rights in all media apply to Toby Cole, Agent for the Pirandello Estate, 295 Derby Street, #225, Berkeley, CA 94705.

Copper Canyon Press c/o The Permissions Company T'ao Ch'ien, "Form, Shadow, Spirit," translated by David Hinton, from *Selected Poems of T'ao Ch'ien*. Copyright © 1993 by David Hinton. Reprinted with permission of Copper Canyon Press, P.O. Box 271, Port Townsend, WA 98368-0271, c/o The Permissions Company, High Bridge, New Jersey.

Darhansoff, Verrill, Feldman Literary Agents "I Am Not One of Those Who Left the Land," and

(Continued on page R55, which is hereby considered an extension of this copyright page.)

PRENTICE HALL
LITERATURE

PENGUIN EDITION

WORLD MASTERPIECES

VOLUME II

WL.1.03.2 Identify and analyze text components and evaluate impact on expressive text.

FA.3.03.1 Gather information to prove a point about issues in literature.

CT.4.03.1 Analyze how writers introduce and develop a main idea.

LT.5.01.1 Use strategies for preparation, engagement, and reflection on world literature.

Unit 6

Rebirth and Exploration

1300–1800

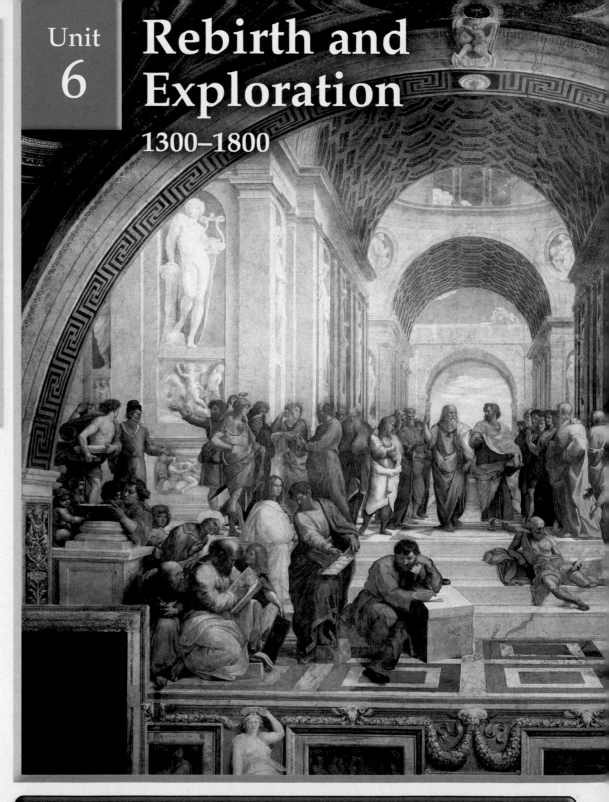

Unit Instructional Resources

In *Unit 6 Resources,* you will find materials to support students in developing and mastering the unit skills and to help you assess their progress.

▶ **Vocabulary and Reading**

Additional vocabulary and reading support, based on Lexile scores of vocabulary words, is provided for each selection or grouping.

- **Word Lists A and B** and **Practices A and B** provide vocabulary-building activities for students reading two grades or one grade below level, respectively.

- **Reading Warm-ups A and B**, for students reading two grades or one grade below level, respectively, consist of short readings and activities that provide a context and practice for newly learned vocabulary.

▶ **Selection Support**

- Reading Strategy
- Literary Analysis
- Vocabulary Builder
- Grammar and Style
- Support for Writing
- Support for Extend Your Learning
- Enrichment

TeacherEXPRESS™
Plan · Teach · Assess
You may also access these resources at TeacherExpress.

Assessment Resources

Listed below are the resources available to assess and measure students' progress in meeting the unit objectives and your state standards.

Skills Assessment

Unit 6 Resources
  Selection Tests A and B

TeacherExpress™
  ExamView® Test Bank
    Software

Adequate Yearly Progress Assessment

Unit 6 Resources
  Diagnostic Test 8
  Benchmark Test 7

Standardized Assessment

Standardized Test
  Preparation Workbook

The Renaissance and Rationalism

Standard Course of Study
In This Unit You Will

- Identify and analyze text components and evaluate impact on expressive text. (WL.1.03.2)
- Gather information to prove a point about issues in literature. (FA.3.03.1)
- Use specific references from texts to show theme. (CT.4.02.2)
- Analyze how writers introduce and develop a main idea. (CT.4.03.1)
- Use strategies for preparation, engagement, and reflection on world literature. (LT.5.01.1)
- Make connections between works, self and related topics in world literature. (LT.5.03.8)
- Employ varying sentence structures and sentence types. (GU.6.01.1)

◀ This painting by Raphael depicts philosophers and scholars such as Plato, Aristotle, Socrates, Pythagoras, Euclid, Ptolemy, and Zoroaster— and a portrait of Raphael himself.

The Renaissance and Rationalism ■ 713

Setting the Scene

The literature in Unit 6 springs from some of the greatest minds of the Renaissance and of the Age of Rationalism. One of those minds, that of Galileo Galilei, is the subject of author João Magueijo's essay in the introduction to this unit. Later, the literature of Unit 6 samples the brilliance of poets and scientists alike who wrote to inspire, to question, and to amuse.

João Magueijo

 From the Scholar's Desk
João Magueijo Talks About the Time Period

Introducing João Magueijo (b. 1967) Born in Portugal, Magueijo is currently a professor of theoretical physics at Imperial College, London. His ideas are often viewed as radical—his varying speed of light theory conflicts with long-standing theories of one of the world's most respected scientists, Albert Einstein.

The Father of Modern Science

Galileo Galilei is frequently credited as the father of modern science; yet some of his findings even today look like those of a magician. His hat tricks would, centuries later, make space travel possible. He made these curious discoveries against all odds, when common sense made everyone think they were nonsense. That he managed to break through the smokescreen is his incredible accomplishment.

Renaissance Science Was Ahead of Today's Science Fiction
Current science fiction films would have us believe a lot of junk about the dynamics of dog-fights in space. Invariably they portray spaceships grinding to a halt when their rockets malfunction or they are hit by enemy fire. Furious acceleration appears to be required just to maintain a respectable speed. It all makes sense. It's intuitive. It's just what happens with car chases on Earth—or horse chases, in Galileo's time.

But it's wrong.

Amazing as it might sound at first, if you turn off the engines of a spaceship, you just keep moving at the same speed—you get a free ride. The Pioneer spacecrafts ran out of fuel long ago but they're still moving out into deep space. Without fuel you don't accelerate, but neither do you stop. Magic at play? Not at all. That's how the world appears to work.

Which leaves us with a mystery. How did Galileo work this out without the benefit of televised space travel? Was he abducted by aliens?

▼ **Critical Viewing**
Which details in this portrait of Galileo suggest a scholarly, scientific gentleman? Explain. **[Analyze]**

714 ■ *The Renaissance and Rationalism*

Reading the Unit Introduction

Tell students that the terms and questions listed here are the key points in this introductory material. This information provides a context for the selections in this unit. Students should use the terms and questions as a guide to focus their reading of the unit introduction. When students have completed the unit introduction, they should be able to identify or explain each of these terms and answer or discuss the Focus Questions.

The answer is not quite so spectacular, but Galileo was indeed a man with a secret. He grew up reading the Greek classics, in particular two giants at odds with each other, Aristotle and Plato.

Two thousand years later, Aristotle, unknowingly, would act as a scientific adviser to misguided SciFi films. He's the man who proposed the notion that absence of a force means absence of motion. His philosophy is based upon experiment, but not of the sort you see present-day scientists perform in labs. For him experiment was human experience, our common sense.

The trouble is that our common sense is polluted by the pervasiveness of friction on Earth. Absence of force is never absence of friction. If we stop pushing a cart it grinds to a halt because the force of friction drives it to rest. In space, without friction, the cart would just go on forever.

Modern Science: Marrying Aristotle and Plato, and Going Beyond Them

Galileo didn't need to go to space to get this intuition. He applied Plato's philosophy instead: to seek mathematical perfection and idealized forms beyond our often confused senses. If you oil up the wheels of a cart, it takes longer to stop because you reduce friction. If you idealize perfectly oiled wheels, the cart would go on for ever. Just like in space.

So, here's Galileo's secret: to combine Aristotle's focus on sensory experience—without his trust in "common sense"—with Plato's search for perfection. He married Aristotle and Plato, in the process contradicting both and creating modern science and experimentation. As a famous astronomer admirably put it, "Galileo built a telescope from an iron tube, attaching to one side a very small one-inch lens, and to the other a very large brain."

Go Online
—Author Link

For: A video clip of João Magueijo
Visit: www.PHSchool.com
Web Code: ete-8601

For: More about João Magueijo
Visit: www.PHSchool.com
Web Code: ete-9610

Concept Connector

After students have read the unit introduction, return to the Focus Questions to review the main points. For key points, see p. 725.

Reading the Unit Introduction

Reading for Information and Insight Use the following terms and questions to guide your reading of the unit introduction on pages 718–725.

Names and Terms to Know
- Renaissance
- Black Death
- Humanism
- Reformation
- Rationalism
- Industrial Revolution

Focus Questions As you read this introduction, use what you learn to answer these questions:
- What factors contributed to the general feeling of insecurity during this period?
- In what ways did the Enlightenment change the folk wisdom of the past?
- What was the role of imitation in the literature of this period?

From the Scholar's Desk: João Magueijo ■ 715

Using the Timeline

The Timeline can serve a number of instructional purposes, as follows:

Getting an Overview

Use the Timeline to help students get a quick overview of themes and events of the period. This approach will benefit all students but may be especially helpful for Visual/Spatial Learners, English Learners, and Less Proficient Readers. (For strategies in using the Timeline as an overview, see the bottom of this page.)

Thinking Critically

Questions are provided on the facing page. Use these questions to have students review the events, discuss their significance, and examine the "so what" behind the "what happened."

Connecting to Selections

Have students refer to the Timeline when they begin to read individual selections. By consulting the Timeline regularly, they will gain a better sense of the period's chronology. In addition, they will appreciate world events that gave rise to these works of literature.

Projects

Students can use the Timeline as a launching pad for projects like these:

• **Literary Timeline** Have students create a literary timeline of the Renaissance in England and Italy. Have them begin with the birth of Petrarch and finish with the end of the Renaissance in England in 1625.

• **Reflections of a Life** Have students choose either the Renaissance period or the Age of Reason and play the role of an imaginary person who has lived through that period. Have students review the Timeline of that period and present an oral reflection of what took place during that person's life.

716

European and World Events

1300   1400   1500

EUROPEAN EVENTS

■ early 1300s The Renaissance begins in Italy.

■ 1304–1374 Petrarch, great Italian poet and Humanist, lives. ◀

■ 1313–1375 Boccaccio, author of the *Decameron*, lives.

■ 1300s Gunpowder is introduced into Europe.

■ 1347–1351 The Black Death ravages Europe, killing about 25 million people.

■ 1425 The artist Massaccio is the first to use perspective in a fresco.

■ 1450s Gutenberg uses his invention of movable type to print the Bible.

■ 1452 Leonardo da Vinci, great Italian Renaissance artist and inventor, is born. ▼

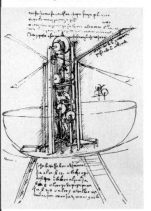

■ 1516 Christian Humanist Erasmus publishes his annotations of the Greek New Testament.

■ 1519 Magellan begins his voyage around the world.

■ 1524–1585 Pierre de Ronsard, French poet, lives.

■ 1527 Niccolò Machiavelli, author of *The Prince*, dies.

■ 1543 Polish astronomer Nicolaus Copernicus declares in print that Earth circles the sun.

■ 1546 Martin Luther, founder of the Protestant Reformation, dies.

■ c. 1550 Approximate date for the end of the Renaissance in Italy.

WORLD EVENTS

■ 1300s **(Japan)** First Nō dramas emerge.

■ 1300s **(West Africa)** The Mali empire controls the gold trade.

■ 1324 **(West Africa)** The Muslim emperor of Mali, Mansa Musa, makes a religious pilgrimage to Mecca.

■ 1328–1341 **(Russia)** Moscow emerges as an important city.

■ 1431 **(Southeast Asia)** Angkor, capital of Cambodia, is abandoned after being pillaged. ▼

■ 1453 **(Turkey)** Ottoman Turks conquer Constantinople.

■ 1462–1505 **(Russia)** During the reign of Ivan III, Moscow extends its power.

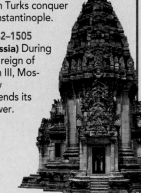

■ 1513 **(China)** The Portuguese arrive at Macau, a peninsula and islands off China's coast.

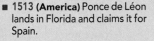

■ 1513 **(America)** Ponce de Léon lands in Florida and claims it for Spain.

■ 1517 **(Middle East)** Ottoman Turks conquer Syria and Egypt.

■ 1519–1521 **(Mexico)** ▲ Cortés conquers the Aztec empire.

716 ■ The Renaissance and Rationalism

Getting an Overview of the Period

Introduction To give students an overview of the period, indicate the span of dates in the title of the Timeline. Next, point out that the Timeline is divided into European Events (on the top) and World Events (on the bottom). Have students scan the Timeline, looking at both the European Events and the World Events. Finally, point out that the events in the Timeline often represent beginnings, turning points, and endings. (For example, Magellan began his voyage around the world in 1519.)

Key Events Ask students to identify key events related to the Renaissance and to Rationalism.
Possible response: Gutenberg used his printing press to print the Bible (1450s), and Copernicus declared in print that the Earth circles the sun (1543).

Ask students which events indicate progress in science.
Possible response: Galileo improved the telescope; the Royal Society was formed to promote science; and Newton published his work on the laws of gravity and motion (1609) / (1660) / (1687).

1600   **1700**   **1800**

- 1605 Cervantes publishes the first part of *Don Quixote*.
- 1608–1674 English poet John Milton lives.
- 1609 Galileo improves the telescope and begins observing the solar system with telescopes of increasing magnification.
- 1610 Galileo observes four moons orbiting around Jupiter. ▼

- 1625 The Renaissance in England ends.
- 1657 Pascal begins writing his *Pensées*.
- 1660 The Royal Society, a group formed to promote science, is founded in London, England.
- 1664–1666 There is an outbreak of plague in London, England.
- 1687 Sir Isaac Newton publishes a book describing the laws of gravity and motion.

- 1613 (Russia) The Time of Troubles, a fifteen-year period of political crisis, ends.
- 1633 (Japan) The Tokugawas close Japan to the rest of the world. ▼

- 1644 (China) The Ming dynasty is overthrown by armies from Manchuria.
- 1644–1694 (Japan) Haiku poet Matsuo Bashō lives.
- 1669 (Greece) The Ottoman empire seizes Crete.

Night of August 4, 1789, or "Patriotic Delirium," Bibliothèque Nationale, Paris, Giraudon

- 1702 First daily English newspaper appears.
- early 1700s Addison and Steele publish periodicals.
- 1744 English poet Alexander Pope dies.
- 1765 James Watt helps launch the Industrial Revolution by improving the steam engine.
- 1772 Diderot completes the *Encyclopedia*, a major achievement of the Enlightenment.
- 1778 Voltaire, author of *Candide*, dies.
- 1787–1799 The French Revolution is fought. ▲
- 1799 Napoleon Bonaparte assumes control in France.

- 1703 (Russia) Czar Peter the Great begins the construction of St. Petersburg. ▼
- 1776–1781 (America) The colonies defeat Great Britain in the American Revolution.

Introduction ■ 717

Critical Viewing

1. On the basis of the painting of Petrarch (1304–1374), how would you describe the poet's demeanor? **[Analyze]**
   Possible response: Petrarch appears serious but kind; his gesture indicates an openness and a desire to share his knowledge.

2. What does the drawing of the ornithopter in the center of the page (1452) indicate about Leonardo da Vinci? **[Infer]**

   Possible response: It shows da Vinci's interest in science, invention, and detail as well as his ability as an artist.

3. What does the picture from the French Revolution (1787–1799) indicate about that particular war? **[Generalize]**
   Possible response: It indicates that the middle class rose up against the monarchy of King Louis XIV.

Analyzing the Timeline

1. (a) When did Gutenberg first print the Bible using movable type? (b) What effect did the availability of movable type have on the accessibility of ideas? **[Analyze Cause and Effect]**
   Answer: (a) Gutenberg first used movable type to print the Bible in the 1450s. (b) Movable type provided printed materials so that more people could learn and share their ideas.

2. (a) What kinds of events were taking place in the world during the Italian Renaissance? (b) Compare and contrast the events in Europe with world events. **[Compare and Contrast]**
   Possible response: (a) There were many wars and conquests. (b) This was a time of intellectual and cultural growth for Europe. The rest of the world showed some intellectual and cultural growth, but growth seemed impeded by war and conquest.

3. (a) When was gunpowder introduced into Europe? (b) What effects might the availability of gunpowder have had on European explorers? **[Analyze Cause and Effect]**
   Answer: (a) Gunpowder was introduced in the 1300s. (b) The introduction of gunpowder made it easier for European explorers to conquer the areas they explored.

4. (a) When did the Renaissance end in Italy? (b) Why do you think it ended later in England? **[Speculate]**
   Answer: (a) The Renaissance ended in Italy around 1550. (b) The Renaissance began in Italy and then spread to England. Because the Renaissance came to England later, it may have ended later. Ideas traveled slowly, and England was not a part of the European continent.

5. (a) When was the Royal Society founded in London? (b) What events might have prompted the founding of the society? **[Analyze Cause and Effect]**
   Answer: (a) The Royal Society was founded in 1660. (b) The advances in science made scientific discovery a new priority for Europe.

Literature of the Period

- In "Federigo's Falcon," found on p. 744, students will find Boccaccio's tale of a man who parts with something of great value to him.

- In *Don Quixote,* by Miguel de Cervantes Saavedra, on p. 770, students will find one of the strangest and funniest characters in literature.

Themes in World Literature

Point/Counterpoint

Point out that the Renaissance was a time for great change. Invention, exploration, and rediscovery marked the time period, and many previous beliefs were altered. How the Renaissance affected the people of the time has been and still is a subject of debate among scholars.

Ask students the following questions:

1. What do these two viewpoints have in common?
   Possible response: Both viewpoints imply that great changes took place during the Renaissance and that these changes affected the individual.

2. In what ways do these viewpoints differ?
   Possible response: They differ in the degree of rebirth of human consciousness evident in the Renaissance. Rice believes that the age saw as much continuity and tradition as it did change and innovation. Burckhardt believes that during the Renaissance, man became a spiritual *individual.*

3. What are some current controversies about the effect of an intellectual movement on the people who experienced it?
   Possible response: People may debate the effects of the protests of the 1960s or the civil rights movement.

Historical Background

The Renaissance in Western Europe The Renaissance, which means "rebirth," is a period that saw many changes and innovations. Among them were the rediscovery of classical art and literature; the exploration of regions of the globe that were previously unknown in Europe; the discovery that Earth revolves around the sun; and an upsurge in trade and invention. This rebirth, which lasted in Italy from the early 1300s until 1550, gradually extended its influence northward. In England, it lasted from 1485 to 1625.

Status and Insecurity The Renaissance was a period during which rank and status mattered a great deal. For every social class, however, this era was a time of insecurity. The Black Death (see page 720) devastated Europe in the late 1340s, toward the beginning of the Italian Renaissance.

In addition to sickness, other disasters contributed to the insecurity of the times. With the exception of castles and churches, most buildings were built of wood, and fire in cities was a constant hazard.

Kings Up, Nobles Down Against this backdrop of general insecurity, the power of kings tended to increase during the Renaissance. This centralization of power helped create the nations that are familiar to us today.

Themes in World Masterpieces Point/Counterpoint

Was the Renaissance a Rebirth of Consciousness?

Did the Renaissance mark a complete rebirth of human consciousness? Two scholars—writing about a hundred years apart—disagree on this question.

Yes! In the Middle Ages both sides of human consciousness— that which was turned within as that which was turned without—lay dreaming or half awake beneath a common veil. The veil was woven of faith, illusion, and childish prepossession, through which the world and history were seen clad in strange hues. Man was conscious of himself only as a member of a race, people, party, family, or corporation—only through some general category. In Italy this veil first melted into air . . . man became a spiritual *individual,* . . .
— **Jacob Burckhardt, from *The Civilization of the Renaissance in Italy* (1860)**

No! Certainly the hundred years before and after 1450 were enormously fertile in innovation. But the great discoveries and historical mutations of the age were not confined to Italy; while even in Italy continuity and tradition mark the age as deeply as change and innovation. The history of discovery and novelty must be balanced by the equally interesting and important story of the survival and adaptation of traditional institutions, social distinctions, professional disciplines, and modes of thought.
—**Eugene F. Rice, Jr., from *The Columbia History of the World* (1972)**

Enrichment

The Role of Women

For the most part, women's lives changed little during the Renaissance. Many women still devoted themselves to raising a family. Some also worked outside their homes as servants or spinners and weavers. Others ran small businesses, selling their handiwork or the produce of their gardens.

A few women gained national or international prominence. Isabella d'Este (born 1474), for instance, was a brilliant woman and skillful diplomat. Her family ruled the wealthy Italian city-state of Ferrara. Isabella married the ruler of Mantua, established herself as a patron of the arts, and helped her husband govern.

Meanwhile, the great nobility were losing their importance. Their mighty castles, for instance, were threatened by the introduction of gunpowder into Europe in the 1300s. Castle walls became vulnerable to cannon shot, and even well-armored knights could be toppled by a well-placed bullet.

Humanism: Out of the "Dark" Ages The most important cultural movement of the Renaissance was Humanism, which advocated a return to classical studies and ideals. This movement began in fourteenth-century Italy, where the first Humanists were the famous writers Petrarch (pē´ trärk´) and Boccaccio (bō kä´ chô). For the first time in about a thousand years, the intellectual life of Western Europe was directly influenced by the works of classical writers known before only through inaccurate summaries or quotations. The Humanists viewed the classics as sources of moral and practical wisdom. Humanist ideals also influenced Italian Renaissance artists like Michelangelo (mī´ kel an´ jə lō´) and Leonardo da Vinci (də vin´ chē), who followed classical artists in portraying the beauty of the human form.

According to the Humanists, the Middle Ages were "dark" because the Germanic tribes that had invaded Rome, the Goths, had destroyed classical civilization. Humanists believed that with the rediscovery of classical learning, these "dark" times had given way to an age of "enlightenment." Today, scholars no longer accept this belief, which might be called the Humanist Myth, without qualifications. (See Point/Counterpoint on page 718.)

Humanism started in Italy, yet as it moved northward it changed somewhat in character. The enthusiasm for classical antiquity remained, but it was influenced by a Christian fervor. This slightly different movement, called Christian Humanism, tended to look back to early Christian as well as classical sources. Unlike medieval thinkers, Christian Humanists stressed the importance of the active life. They also ridiculed the performing of mechanical acts in the place of inner worship. In this way, Christian Humanism prepared for the more radical protests of the Reformation.

The Reformation: From Debate to Bloodshed In the early 1500s, an obscure German professor of theology, Martin Luther, protested against the corruption of the church. His key ideas—that salvation depends on one's faith, rather than one's actions, and that the priesthood and church ritual are less important than the truths of the Bible—launched the movement called the Reformation. This movement gave birth to new Protestant

Mona Lisa, Leonardo da Vinci, Louvre, Dep. des Peintures, Paris, France

▲ **Critical Viewing**
The *Mona Lisa* by Leonardo da Vinci is one of the most famous paintings of all time. Many critics and viewers have remarked on the "mystery" of the subject's smile. What, if anything, do you think is mysterious about her expression? Explain. **[Interpret]**

Introduction ■ 719

Humanities

Mona Lisa, by Leonardo da Vinci

In the early 1500s, Leonardo da Vinci (1452–1519) painted this portrait of Francesco del Giocondo's wife. The expression on her face has created curiosity among her viewers for centuries. The *Mona Lisa,* also known as *La Gioconda,* is displayed in Paris at the Louvre.

Use the following question for discussion.

- How is this painting an outstanding representation of the Renaissance? **Possible response:** Leonardo's painting captures the beauty of the human form; the painting also reflects Renaissance artists' interest in nature and perspective.

- Show students Art Transparency 6: *Mona Lisa* by Leonardo da Vinci in the **Fine Art Transparencies** booklet. Have them discuss ways in which Leonardo's painting demonstrates an interest in classical forms.

Critical Viewing

Possible response: It is difficult to tell whether the subject's expression is a true smile or whether it is her response to another emotion.

Background
Leonardo da Vinci

Although he is best known as a painter, Leonardo da Vinci was also an engineer and scientist. Because of his insatiable curiosity about the physical world, Leonardo experimented in geology, botany, hydraulics, and mechanics. His resulting drawings, rendered with scientific precision and artistry, range from flying machines to anatomical studies of people, animals, and plants.

Background
Martin Luther

German peasants greeted Luther's ideas enthusiastically. They resented the fact that they had to pay so much tax money to the Church. They also began to voice other long-suppressed complaints they had against the Church and the noble landlords. In 1524, their resentment flamed into a full-scale rebellion, known as the Peasants' Revolt. Peasants demanded not only the right to read the Bible and choose their own ministers but also an end to serfdom. At first, Luther supported this revolt. He withdrew his support, however, when he heard accounts of peasants looting and destroying property. Moreover, he sided with the nobles who stamped out the revolt, and he rejected political revolution once and for all.

Themes in World Literature
Close-up on History

Point out to students that the enlightenment of the Renaissance did not yet extend to medical science and that people had little defense against the plague.

- **Ask:** What conflicts made the plague worse?
  Possible response: People's dismay at why some were afflicted while others were not led to the ugly business of people looking for scapegoats to blame, such as Arabs, lepers, and Jews.

- **Ask:** What are current threats to world health?
  Possible response: Biochemical weapons, AIDS, flu viruses, bacteria from foods, and poverty that prevents people from accessing medical care.

Critical Viewing

Possible response: The skeleton's expansive gestures may indicate the wide-reaching effects of the plague. In addition, the skeleton—astride coffins and with arrows in hand—appears almost victorious, suggesting the triumph of death over life.

---

denominations, whose name comes from the term *to protest*. Protestants dominated in Switzerland, northern Germany, parts of France, and eventually in England and Scotland. The Catholic Church, on the other hand, was strong in Spain, Italy, most of France, and southern Germany. Religious debates soon escalated into war, and in France the civil conflict led to years of bloodshed.

The Globe Explored, the Earth Displaced Not only were religious truths being questioned, but the face of the globe was changing with each new voyage of discovery. (See the map on page 721.) In 1492, for instance, Columbus sailed to the West Indies; and in 1519, Magellan began a voyage around the world.

The image of the universe itself was changing. According to older views, Earth was the center of the universe. The astronomer Copernicus (1473–1543), however, argued that Earth revolved around the sun.

The Age of Rationalism: From Lore to Law The Renaissance ushered in the Age of Rationalism, or the Enlightenment, an era that spanned the seventeenth and eighteenth centuries. During this time, reason was accepted as the greatest authority in art, thought, and politics. Philosophers challenged folk wisdom, attempting to replace traditional lore with formal laws based on the analysis of natural phenomena.

Themes in World Masterpieces · Close-up on History

The Black Death

Between 1347 and 1351, a disease people called the Black Death, and which we know as the plague, ravaged Europe. It killed about one fourth of the population, perhaps 25 million people. Those afflicted with the disease developed fever and other symptoms, either swellings that turned into black spots or infected lungs together with weakness and loss of memory. Few recovered.

The plague was usually spread by fleas that lived on rodents—the rats that in fourteenth-century Europe were everywhere in the overcrowded and dirty cities and in the countryside as well. When a rat died, its fleas often migrated to a nearby person. To people of the time, however, it seemed a terrible mystery why some were spared and some perished.

Faced with this horrible and mysterious disease, people looked for someone to blame. Usually, outsiders of some kind—Arabs, lepers, or Jews—were chosen as scapegoats. Massacres of these groups only added to the sum of suffering.

Among the longer-lasting effects of the plague were a decrease in farmed land, an increase in wages for surviving workers, and—in northern Europe—a new obsession with death. Thomas Nashe, writing about a later outbreak of plague in England, expressed such a mood in his poem "Litany in Time of Plague": "Physic [the doctor] himself must fade, / all things to end are made."

▼ **Critical Viewing**
This image is a detail from a picture depicting the effects of the Great Plague of London in 1665. What do the gestures of the skeleton indicate about the outbreak of the plague? Why? **[Infer]**

Enrichment

Humors

Medieval and Renaissance medical science had no way of understanding the bacilli that caused the plague. The best medical opinion held that the body was dominated by four different fluid "humors"—blood, phlegm, yellow bile, and black bile—and that each of these humors had a different physical and psychological effect.

In the healthy individual, these humors were all in balance, each of them canceling out the bad effects of the others. Sickness consisted of an excess of one humor over another. The primary cure for such an excess was bleeding the patient to get rid of the excessive humor. Tragically, this bleeding weakened patients, making them more likely to die.

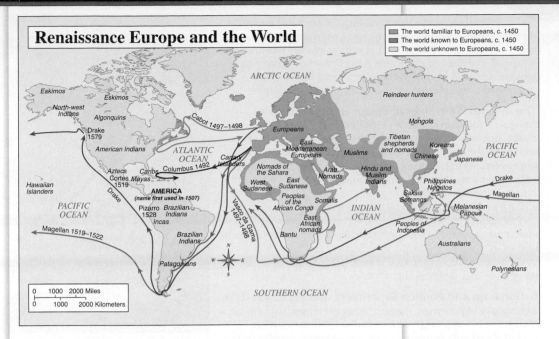

Renaissance Europe and the World

- The world familiar to Europeans, c. 1450
- The world known to Europeans, c. 1450
- The world unknown to Europeans, c. 1450

Rationalism and Nature: Mud Baths and Artful Foliage The application of reason to natural phenomena coincided with a renewed focus on nature throughout society. Notable painters, such as the French artist Jean-Antoine Watteau (wä tō´), for example, captured the beauty of outdoor scenes. In addition, people who could afford to do so made pilgrimages to spas and hot springs. There, nature could exert its healing influence as sufferers bathed in the waters and coated their limbs with medicinal mud. Nature could also delight the eye in formal gardens, whose symmetrical rows of plants showed that even foliage followed reason's laws.

The new interest in nature included human nature as well. The English Enlightenment philosopher John Locke described the human mind as a blank slate on which impressions are recorded. By denying the existence of prenatal, and therefore unlearned, ideas, Locke placed a stronger emphasis on experience and the satisfaction of natural curiosity.

Rationalism and Science: Falling Apples and Orbiting Planets In science, the delights of curiosity led to intellectual triumphs. Sir Isaac Newton, the greatest scientist of the age, discovered the laws of motion, the law of gravitation, and the mathematical system called calculus. By showing that gravity governed both apples and planets, Newton seemed to prove that the world was rational and that the mind could make sense of matter.

▲ **Critical Viewing**
Compare and contrast the world familiar or known to Europeans in 1450 with the world unknown to them.
[Read a Map]

Introduction ■ 721

Critical Viewing

Possible response: This telescope shows that Galileo and his Renaissance colleagues took scientific observation seriously. The telescope's graceful, detailed construction suggests that scientific observation—including the tools employed for that observation—was viewed as an art.

Historical Background
Comprehension Check

1. In what ways was the Renaissance a time of insecurity?
   Answer: The Black Death immediately preceded this era. Fires were also common because most buildings were made of wood.

2. How did the power of kings change during this period?
   Answer: Kings became more powerful because of the general insecurity of the times.

3. What is Humanism?
   Answer: Humanism is the most important cultural movement of the Renaissance. It encourages a return to the study of the classics and the ideals they embodied.

4. What beliefs held by Martin Luther led to the Reformation?
   Answer: Martin Luther believed in salvation by faith and in the importance of following the truths of the Bible rather than the priesthood and church ritual.

5. How did the ideas of Rationalism affect politics?
   Answer: John Locke declared that all people have a right to life, liberty, and property, and that government is a contract between the government and the governed. These ideas undermined the idea of the divine right of kings.

Critical Thinking

1. Compare the Renaissance and Rationalism. **[Compare and Contrast]**
   Possible response: The Renaissance was a period of great creativity and the rediscovery of classical art and literature. It also focused on exploration of the world and a new view of the relationship between the Earth and the sun. Rationalism emphasized reason as the greatest authority in art, thought, and politics.

While Newton was revealing the laws that controlled distant heavenly bodies, Antonie van Leeuwenhoek (lā' vən hōōk') used the microscope to study the miniature worlds that swarmed in a drop of rainwater. Also, Robert Boyle earned a reputation as the "father of chemistry," and Edward Jenner discovered a vaccination for the deadly disease smallpox.

The Industrial Revolution: Steam Flexes Its Muscles
Across a wide span of human activities, people were employing reason not only to advance theory but also to regulate and enhance their daily existence. James Watt's significant improvements to the steam engine in 1765 helped revolutionize industrial production and paved the way for steam-powered railroad engines and ships.

Further, inventions such as the syringe, air pump, mercury thermometer, mainspring clock, and cotton gin provided effective new ways of solving old problems. The establishment of the Greenwich Observatory in England (1675) led to the systematic use of astronomy for such practical purposes as navigation and timekeeping.

Rationalism and Politics: Experiment and Explosion Like a chemistry experiment, the application of reason to political discontent led to an explosion called revolution. John Locke declared that government was a contract between ruler and ruled and that all people had natural rights to life, liberty, and property. These two "rational" ideas undermined the notion that kings had a divine right to rule. In America, these ideas added to the dissatisfaction of colonists with British repression, a dissatisfaction that erupted into the American Revolution (1776–1781). After the colonists won, the ideas of Locke and other Enlightenment thinkers influenced the framers of the American Constitution.

The French Revolution (1787–1799) was also inspired by Enlightenment ideas, especially those of Jean-Jacques Rousseau (zhän zhäk rōō sō'). This philosopher wrote in *The Social Contract* (1762), "Man was born free, but he is everywhere in chains." In France, however, sharper differences between the rich and the poor made the conflict more of a war between classes than the American Revolution had been. The result was a Reign of Terror in the early 1790s during which the king and many aristocrats were executed. By 1799, the revolution yielded to the dictatorial rule of Napoleon Bonaparte.

These two "experiments" in revolution indicated two different ways in which the Age of Rationalism would influence politics in the following centuries: on the one hand, the "reasonableness" of democratic institutions; on the other, the use of "reason" to justify revolt or even repression.

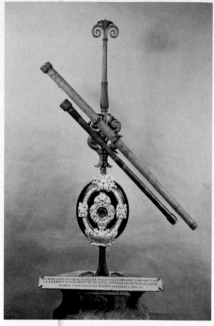

▲ **Critical Viewing**
This telescope belonged to Galileo, the Italian Renaissance scientist who pioneered astronomical studies. Galileo's observations helped dispel the belief that, in contrast to Earth, the heavens were a perfect, unchanging realm. What, if anything, does this telescope reveal about the attitudes of Galileo and his Renaissance colleagues toward scientific observation? Why? **[Infer]**

2. How did the Renaissance and Humanism help lead to the Reformation? **[Support]**
   Possible response: The spread of literacy and the return to the classics in Italy led to the spread of Christian Humanism. This movement encouraged its followers to study early Christian sources, which led to an emphasis on the Bible as the most important source of information for believers.

3. Evaluate the impact Rationalism had on science. **[Evaluate]**
   Possible response: People began to analyze what happened in the natural world, eliminating superstitions and traditional beliefs. Science provided an avenue for that analysis and for organizing the information gathered from that analysis.

Literature

Renaissance Literature: A Branch of Rhetoric During the years of the Renaissance, literature was classified as a branch of rhetoric—the art of using spoken language to teach, give pleasure, and persuade. Literature was therefore closely related to the art of speechmaking, and it is not surprising that Renaissance writing is full of elaborate speeches. As a branch of rhetoric, literature also had the function of persuading readers to do good. Its purpose was to train the will by increasing our horror of evil and by strengthening our resolve to act well.

Machiavelli: Do Well, Not Good One major exception to literature in the service of the good is *The Prince*, a book of political philosophy by Niccolò Machiavelli (nē kô lô´ mak´ ē ə vel´ ē). While other theorists said that public deeds should reflect private morality, Machiavelli insisted that personal morality has no place in politics. Rulers are saved not by their goodness but by their strength, cunning, and ability. Because he took this approach, the adjective *Machiavellian* has come to mean "crafty and deceitful."

Literature and the Vernacular In the Middle Ages, literature in native languages, or the vernacular, had already begun to emerge. The Renaissance, however, saw a new emphasis on Italian, French, Spanish, German, Dutch, and English. In this period of linguistic patriotism, many of the great works of the period were written in the vernacular: in Italian, the sonnets of Petrarch, Boccaccio's prose tales in the *Decameron*, and Machiavelli's *The Prince*; in French, the poetry of Pierre de Ronsard (pē er´ də rōn sár´); and in Spanish, the novel *Don Quixote* by Miguel de Cervantes (mē gel´ *the* ser vän´ tes).

Latin, however, still served an important function. The Dutch scholar Erasmus, who translated the New Testament into Latin, Sir Thomas More, and many of the great Humanists wrote primarily in Latin.

Originality Through Imitation: "as the bees make honey" Rather than inventing new stories or forms, Renaissance authors often altered old forms to give them new meanings. Many authors, for example, wrote epics modeled in part on Virgil's *Aeneid*, odes modeled on the odes of Horace, and histories modeled on the work of Pliny and Tacitus. Yet just as the Romans copied and changed the forms of Greek literature to fit their own

Lorenzo il Magnifico, G. Vasari, Scala

▼ **Critical Viewing**
Which details in this portrait of Lorenzo de' Medici, an Italian Renaissance merchant prince, suggest that he had the leadership qualities recommended by Machiavelli? Explain. **[Connect]**

Introduction ■ 723

Themes in World Masterpieces   Art in the Historical Context

The Invention of Perspective

You may assume that viewing a painting should always give you the illusion of looking into three-dimensional space. Yet it was Renaissance artists who invented perspective, the method for conveying this illusion. In the Middle Ages, paintings did not convey an accurate sense of depth. the Renaissance architect Brunellesschi (broo´ nel les k ē) devised the system by which lines of sight, perpendicular to the vertical plane of the picture, seem to converge at a vanishing point on the horizon within the picture.

TIn 1425, Masaccio (Mä säch´ ē ō) became the first artist to use perspective in a fresco, or wall painting. His work *The Holy Trinity with the Virgin and St. John* shows Jesus being crucified in a space that is truly three-dimensional. (See this painting to the right.) From this time on, flat surfaces could open into imaginary but realistic worlds. the scholar Eugene F. Rice, Jr., compares the invention of perspective in art to the newly acquired historical perspective by which Renaissance thinkers viewed classical antiquity as a separate period in history. Medieval scholars, says Rice, could not make such a distinction.

The Trinity (detail), Masaccio, Nicolo Orsi Battaglini

▲ **Critical Viewing**
Masaccio painted this picture on a church wall so that the platform supporting the cross is about at eye level. Where is the point at which all sightlines going "into" the picture seem to converge? Explain. **[Analyze]**

culture, so the writers of Renaissance Europe changed classical forms. Petrarch, for instance, asserted that "we must write just as the bees make honey, not keeping the flowers [works of other writers] but turning them into a sweetness all our own, blending many different flavors into one, which shall be unlike them all, and better."

The Classics in the Age of Reason Like Renaissance Humanists, Enlightenment writers admired ancient Greek and Roman literature. The English poet John Milton (1608–1674), for example, mastered Greek, Latin, and Hebrew, as well as several modern European languages. Not only was he widely read in the classics, but he used Homer's *Iliad* and *Odyssey* and Virgil's *Aeneid* as models for his own Christian epic, *Paradise Lost.*

The Classics Pay Alexander Pope (1688–1744), an English Neoclassical (or "new classical") poet, translated Homer's *Iliad* and *Odyssey* into elegant eighteenth-century verse. His efforts earned him the princely sum of £10,000 and assured his financial independence.

In France, Jean de La Fontaine (zhän´ də lä fōn ten´) based many of his fables in verse on the prose fables of the Greek author Aesop (ē´ səp). In addition, the grace and restraint of La Fontaine's style are qualities that mark his writing as classical in spirit.

Reason Rolls Up Its Sleeves Invention, the use of reason to solve life's problems, affected reading habits as well as navigation and industry. The creation of movable type by Johannes Gutenberg in the mid-1400s had

Enrichment

The *Encyclopedia*

Denis Diderot, a French philosopher and scholar, helped create the first encyclopedia. Originally the *Encyclopedia* was meant to be only a translation of Ephraim Chambers's *Cyclopaedia,* but Diderot and his coeditor, Jean Le Rond d'Alembert, decided to use the *Encyclopedia* for more drastic purposes. Their focus was to spread knowledge and further the minds of humans, going against the limitations imposed by government and the church.

The project, begun in 1745 and completed in 1772, provided a rational look at all the arts and sciences. Because the editors believed in man's ability to reason, Rationalism drove their task. In spite of much interference, including Diderot's imprisonment for some of his views as well as the censorship of the French government, the work continued. The first volume was published in 1751. Despite opposition, Diderot published more than seventeen volumes by the time the work was completed in 1772.

made possible the printing and widespread distribution of the Bible for the first time, paving the way for the Protestants' emphasis on biblical authority. Then, in the 1600s, the new methods of printing helped foster the growth of newspapers. The first English daily newspaper appeared in 1702, and a few years later, the English authors Addison and Steele founded *The Tatler* and *The Spectator*. These periodicals served up humorous essays and witty commentaries on current topics. The growth of newspapers and periodicals created a new entity called Public Opinion.

The Encyclopedia Is Born In France, Denis Diderot (dē′ də rō′) brought to a public hungry for knowledge the world's first *encyclopedia*—a word based on the Greek for "instruction in the circle of arts and sciences." Because its commentary often clashed with accepted principles, this multivolume work suffered repeated censorship. Yet upon its completion in 1772 after long years of toil, the *Encyclopedia* became a major achievement of the Enlightenment.

Pascal and Voltaire: Reason's Differing Children Finally, it is worth remembering that in an age of reason, not every thinker reasoned in the same way. Blaise Pascal (blez′ pas kal′), for example, was a French mathematician and physicist whose credentials as a rationalist were as good as anyone's. Yet in his book *Pensées* ("Thoughts"), he emphasizes human frailty and urges readers to approach God through feelings, not thought. His fellow Frenchman Voltaire (1694–1778), author of the novel *Candide*, disapproved of Pascal's concern with finding happiness in heaven. Voltaire stressed the use of reason to foster progress and happiness on Earth.

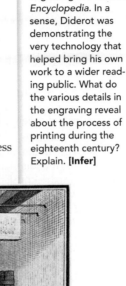

▼ **Critical Viewing**
This illustration, showing the composing room of a print shop, was an engraving in Diderot's *Encyclopedia*. In a sense, Diderot was demonstrating the very technology that helped bring his own work to a wider reading public. What do the various details in the engraving reveal about the process of printing during the eighteenth century? Explain. **[Infer]**

Concept Connector

Have students return to the Focus Questions on p. 715. Ask them to use these questions to orally summarize the main points in the Unit Introduction. Students' summaries should include the following points:

Factors contributing to the general feeling of insecurity during this period:
• The Black Death devastated Europe.
• Fires and other disasters contributed to people's insecurities.

Ways in which the Enlightenment changed the folk wisdom of the past:
• Reason was accepted as the greatest authority in art, thought, and politics.
• Explanations of phenomena that were based on folklore were rejected in favor of laws based on analyzing nature.

Role of imitation during this period:
• Writers were not interested in creating new masterpieces.
• Renaissance writers imitated stories written in classical Greece and Rome and transformed them to fit their needs.

Critical Viewing

Possible response: The work looks very labor intensive and time consuming, as the typesetting was done by hand and the printed sheets had to be hung to dry.

Literature of the Period
Comprehension Check

1. What effect did the Renaissance have on the language of writing?
   Answer: As a result of the Renaissance, people placed new emphasis on writing in the vernacular.

2. How did the printing press affect people during the Renaissance and the Age of Reason?
   Answer: The printing press made books and newspapers available to many more people, and people used these sources to become better informed.

Critical Thinking

1. Why would Alexander Pope's translation of the *Iliad* and *Odyssey* be so valuable during the Age of Reason? **[Draw Conclusions]**
   Possible response: The focus on the classics demanded that they be accessible to the public. Translating them into elegant verse provided a high quality version in English.

2. Speculate about why the French government would be so opposed to an encyclopedia. **[Speculate]**
   Possible response: The control the church had over the people and the government on the basis of the divine right of kings made people who used reason to evaluate and solve problems seem dangerous. Consequently, the government and the church did not want the encyclopedia published.

3. Evaluate the impact that the printing press had on European and English literacy. **[Evaluate]**
   Possible response: The availability of printed material increased the level of literacy among the population. As more people became literate, they created more demand for information; consequently, newspapers and magazines became popular.

Standard Course of Study

LT.5.01.2 Build knowledge of literary genres and explore how characteristics apply to literature of world cultures.

LT.5.01.3 Analyze literary devices and explain their effect on the work of world literature.

❶ Types of Sonnet

• Tell students that they will study sonnets in Unit 6. **Ask** students: How might the form of the sonnet make sonnets more difficult to write than some other types of poetry? **Possible response:** Students may say that following rigid rhyme schemes, examining a topic too thoroughly, and coming up with an idea for a poem that involves a question and its answer can be difficult.

• Encourage students to see that following a set length, rhyme scheme, meter, and content structure might make writing the sonnet more challenging than writing some other types of poetry.

• Review the types of sonnet with students.

❷ Characteristics of Sonnets

• Point out to students that sonnets use many of the same poetic devices found in other lyric poetry.

• Review the characteristics of sonnets. Clarify the information on these pages, and suggest that students use these pages as a reference as they read sonnets in Unit 6 and in other units.

Defining the Sonnet

A **sonnet** is a fourteen-line lyric poem that is written in rhymed iambic pentameter. This form of poetry developed in fourteenth-century Italy and emerged in English literature in the mid-sixteenth century. By the end of that century, the sonnet had become the leading form of love poetry.

*S*CORN NOT THE SONNET; CRITIC,

YOU HAVE FROWNED/MINDLESS

OF ITS JUST HONORS. . . *— William Wordsworth*

❶ Types of Sonnet

There are two major types of sonnet. The principal differences between these types involve rhyme scheme and structure.

• The **Italian**, or **Petrarchan, sonnet**—named for the fourteenth-century Italian poet Petrarch—consists of an *octave* (eight-line stanza) and a *sestet* (six-line stanza). The octave usually has the rhyme scheme *abba abba*, and the sestet has the rhyme scheme *cdecde, cdedce,* or *cdcdcd*. The octave states a theme or asks a question that the sestet then answers or resolves.

• The **English**, or **Shakespearean, sonnet** consists of three *quatrains* (four-line stanzas) and a final *couplet* (two lines), with the rhyme scheme *abab cdcd efef gg*. Each of the three quatrains explores a different aspect of the poem's subject, and the couplet presents a concluding comment.

❷ Characteristics of Sonnets

Most sonnets use the same kinds of poetic conventions as other lyric poems.

Common Themes

Love, lost love, and the admiration of a fair-haired beauty are a few of the more common themes in early sonnets. Over the centuries, however, sonnet themes have covered a wide and imaginative array of topics.

> *Example:* "Love is in all the water, earth, and air, / And love possesses every living thing." —*from* "Spring" by Petrarch, page 733

> **The Rhythm of Sonnets**
> Most sonnets use a rhythmic meter called an *iamb*, a two-part rhythm comprised of one unstressed (ᴗ) and one stressed (/) syllable. One iamb (ᴗ/) is called a *foot*.
> The length of a sonnet line is a pentameter, or five iambic feet.
>
> She used to let her golden hair fly down . . .

726 ■ *The Renaissance and Rationalism*

Extend the Lesson

Sonnet Rhythms

• Direct students' attentions to the side bar about the rhythm of sonnets.

• Review the sidebar with students, and ask them to consider how the example should be read.

• Write the line on the board or on a large sheet of paper, and mark the accents.

• Then have students stand up and read the line of poetry, but have them clap their hands or stamp their feet on each accented syllable.

• Then have students try the same exercise with the lines from "Spring" by Petrarch. Once they have clapped to the beat, have students mark the accents in the lines.

Literary Devices

As in other forms of lyric poems, literary devices appear in sonnets through the centuries. The following are a few key literary devices.

Device	Example
Alliteration: the repetition of initial consonant sounds	"For the wind to toy and tangle and molest . . . "
Consonance: the repetition of final consonant sounds in stressed syllables containing dissimilar vowel sounds	"Let me not to the marriage of true minds / Admit impediments . . . "
Personification: giving human characteristics to nonhuman subjects	"The rose / in her beautiful youth . . . "
Simile: using the words "like" or "as" to compare two dissimilar things	". . . in love's soft bands, / Like captives trembling at the victor's sight . . ."
Metaphor: speaking of a subject as though it were something else as a way to compare two dissimilar things	"The sky folds its wings over you, / Lifting you . . . "

Conceits

Many sonnets include *Petrarchan conceits.* A conceit is a startling and often elaborate comparison between two apparently different things. Often, this extended metaphor forms the controlling idea of an entire sonnet.

> *Example:* "For her who carried in her little hand/ my heart's key to her heavenly sojourn…" —*from* "Spring" by Petrarch, page 733

❸ Sonnet Sequences

In Elizabethan England, poets wrote **sonnet sequences**, or series of sonnets that allow the poet to trace the development of a relationship or examine different aspects of a single theme. Petrarch wrote a series of sonnets to a lifelong love named Laura. Shakespeare's 154 sonnets are the most famous sonnet sequences in the English language.

❹ Strategies for Reading Sonnets

Use these strategies as you read sonnets.

Focus on the Speaker Sonnets typically record the intensely personal feelings and thoughts of the speaker. As you read a sonnet, stay alert to clues to the speaker's identity, personality, and perspective.

Respond to Imagery and Figurative Language Sonnets are a highly compressed form in which sensory images and figurative language play a major role. Read slowly and imaginatively, noticing the poet's word choice and technique so that you can appreciate these features of the form.

Focus on Literary Forms: The Sonnet ■ 727

❸ Sonnet Sequences

- Review the information about sonnet sequences. Then **ask** students: What can a sonnet sequence show the reader about a poet that a single sonnet cannot reveal?

- Encourage students to look at the different ways in which a poet can address a topic and the ways in which the poet's relationship with or understanding of the topic has developed.

❹ Strategies for Reading Sonnets

- Remind students that the speaker in a poem is not the same persona as the author. The author can have the speaker be any personality that he or she chooses.

- As students read sonnets, remind them again to watch for punctuation so that they do not automatically stop at the end of each line. Because of the rhyme scheme in a sonnet, stopping at the end of each line can create a singsong effect.

Standard Course of Study

Goal 1: WRITTEN LANGUAGE

WL.1.03.2 Identify and analyze text components and evaluate impact on expressive text.

WL.1.03.4 Demonstrate comprehension of main idea and supporting details in personal reflection.

WL.1.03.6 Make inferences and draw conclusions based on personal reflection.

Goal 5: LITERATURE

LT.5.01.2 Build knowledge of literary genres, and explore how characteristics apply to literature of world cultures.

Goal 6: GRAMMAR AND USAGE

GU.6.01.2 Analyze author's use of language to demonstrate understanding of expression.

GU.6.02.1 Edit for agreement, tense choice, pronouns, antecedents, case, and complete sentences.

Step-by-Step Teaching Guide	Pacing Guide
PRETEACH	
• Administer Vocabulary and Reading Warm-ups as necessary.	5 min.
• Engage students' interest with the motivation activity.	5 min.
• Read and discuss author and background features. **FT**	10 min.
• Introduce the Literary Analysis Skill: The Sonnet. **FT**	5 min.
• Introduce the Reading Strategy: Reading in Sentences. **FT**	
• Prepare students to read by teaching the selection vocabulary. **FT**	10 min.
TEACH	
• Informally monitor comprehension while students read independently or in groups. **FT**	30 min.
• Monitor students' comprehension with the Reading Check notes.	as students read
• Reinforce vocabulary with Vocabulary Builder notes.	as students read
• Develop students' understanding of the sonnet with the Literary Analysis annotations. **FT**	5 min.
• Develop students' ability to read in sentences with the Reading Strategy annotations. **FT**	5 min.
ASSESS/EXTEND	
• Assess students' comprehension and mastery of the Literary Analysis and Reading Strategy by having them answer the Apply the Skills questions. **FT**	15 min.
• Have students complete the Vocabulary Lesson and the Grammar and Style Lesson. **FT**	15 min.
• Apply students' ability to incorporate details by using the Writing Lesson. **FT**	45 min. or homework
• Apply students' understanding by using one or more of the Extend Your Learning activities.	20–90 min. or homework
• Administer Selection Test A or Selection Test B. **FT**	15 min.

Resources

Print

Unit 6 Resources

Transparency

Graphic Organizer Transparencies

Print

Reader's Notebook [L2]

Reader's Notebook: Adapted Version [L1]

Reader's Notebook: English Learner's Version [EL]

Unit 6 Resources

Technology

Listening to Literature Audio CDs [L2, EL]

Print

Unit 6 Resources

General Resources

Technology

Go Online: Research **[L3]**
Go Online: Self-test **[L3]**
ExamView®, Test Bank **[L3]**

Choosing Resources for Differentiated Instruction

[L1] Special Needs Students

[L2] Below-Level Students

[L3] All Students

[L4] Advanced Students

[EL] English Learners

For Vocabulary and Reading Warm-ups and for Selection Tests, **A** signifies "less challenging" and **B** "more challenging." For Graphic Organizer transparencies, **A** signifies "not filled in" and **B** "filled in."

FT Fast Track Instruction: To move the lesson more quickly, use the strategies and activities identified with **FT**.

Scaffolding for Less Proficient and Advanced Students

The leveled Critical Thinking questions after selections progress in the levels of thinking required to answer them. To address the needs of your different students, you may use the (a) level questions for your less proficient students and the (b) level questions with your on-level and advanced students. The occasional (c) level questions are appropriate for your advanced students.

PRENTICE HALL

Teacher EXPRESS™ Use this complete
Plan · Teach · Assess suite of powerful
teaching tools to make lesson planning and testing quicker and easier.

PRENTICE HALL

Student EXPRESS™ Use the interactive
Learn · Study · Succeed textbook (online and on CD-ROM) to make selections and activities come alive with audio and video support and interactive questions.

 For: Information about Lexiles
Professional **Visit:** www.PHSchool.com
Development **Web Code:** eue-1111

Motivation

Tell students that they will read several love poems from the fourteenth and sixteenth centuries. Ask them to use what they know about contemporary love poems and songs to predict the kinds of statements and images they might encounter in these poems. Discuss students' responses, and suggest that they keep their predictions in mind as they read each poem.

❶ Background

More About the Authors

As an adolescent, Petrarch had already developed what he later described as "an unquenchable thirst for literature." His father, however, wanted him to be a lawyer and was afraid that literature would distract him from more profitable legal studies. According to a famous anecdote, Petrarch's father once hurled the boy's literary books into a fire. Petrarch pleaded with his father and finally persuaded him to retrieve copies of Cicero and Virgil from the flames.

During his long life, Pierre de Ronsard wrote sonnets to many different women. Of them, Helen was the last. Ronsard was already over fifty when he met her and wooed her, and while she seems to have enjoyed talking with him, she was not interested in his advances.

Geography Note

Draw students' attention to the map on this page. Point out Italy and France, the respective homes of Petrarch and Ronsard. Although Petrarch was from Italy and wrote much of his poetry in Italian, he first saw Laura, the subject of his love poetry, in the French city of Avignon.

Laura • The White Doe • Spring • To Hélène • Roses ❶

Petrarch (1304–1374)

Francesco Petrarca, whom the English called Petrarch (pē´ trärk´), was the greatest Italian poet of the fourteenth century. His talent set a pattern for lyric poetry over the next three centuries. Born in 1304, Petrarch traveled extensively throughout his life. While studying law, he began reading classical works and writing poetry. In 1327, in Avignon, France, he first saw the Laura whom he celebrates in his love poetry.

Literary Inspiration Little is known about the Laura who inspired Petrarch to write some of the world's greatest love poetry. She may have been Laura de Noyes, the wife of Hugues de Sade. Petrarch himself creates a picture of her as golden-haired, beautiful, and rich. Whoever she was, Petrarch loved her hopelessly for twenty years, and her beauty inspired the *Canzoniere* (kän tsô nyer´ ē), a vast collection of hundreds of love lyrics that Petrarch wrote and revised until the end of his life.

After his first trip to Rome in 1337, Petrarch composed two ambitious projects in Latin, leading a new Latin cultural flowering and prompting the city of Rome to crown him poet laureate. After years of travel through France and Italy, he finally completed his two major Italian works: the *Triumphs* and the *Canzoniere*.

Petrarch's prose—Latin letters, dialogues, and treatises—centers on himself, examining his own thoughts and emotions with extraordinary subtlety and depth, while his poetry exhaustively analyzes his uncertainties about love. It is this self-analysis and self-proclamation that made him a model for subsequent Renaissance writers.

Pierre de Ronsard (1524–1585)

Pierre de Ronsard (pē er´ də rōn sár´) was called the "Prince of Poets" by his contemporaries, and the title suited his range and ambition. He wrote verse of many different kinds— epics, satires, political commentaries, and the odes and sonnets for which he is famous.

A Poet's Career Ronsard was the youngest son of a noble French family. When illness ended his chances for a life of diplomatic service, he turned to writing. He was slow to publish his work, but in 1550 he released his first four books of odes, modeled on the works of the classical poets Pindar and Horace. In 1552, he published a book of love poetry addressed largely to a woman named Cassandre. From then on, he worked prolifically, writing books of odes, hymns, and love poetry alike. Ronsard saw poetry as a kind of inspired discipline, with the poet acting as a receiver and transmitter of divine energies. At times, this vision could lead to self-importance and heavy-handedness, but it often resulted in exciting and vibrant work. His verse is marked by intensity, energy, and deep feelings for the natural world.

In 1572, he published the first four books of his *Franciade*, a patriotic epic about France that he never completed. His last major sequence of love poems, the *Sonnets pour Hélène*, appeared in 1578. Ronsard's devotion to his calling made him an untiring reviser of his poetry. During his later years, he revised his collected works over and over, preparing a final edition just before his death in 1585.

Preview

Connecting to the Literature

Today, love is the subject of all genres of popular music, from country to rap to heavy metal. Despite the passage of centuries, the similarities you find between your favorite love songs and these poems may be striking.

❷ Literary Analysis

The Sonnet

Petrarch established the **sonnet** as the dominant form of lyric poetry during the Italian Renaissance. A sonnet is a fourteen-line poem focused on a single theme. The following characteristics are typical of the highly structured Petrarchan sonnet:

- It is divided into an eight-line *octave* followed by a six-line *sestet*.
- The octave usually has a rhyme scheme of *abba abba*.
- The sestet usually has one of three rhyme patterns: *cdecde, cdcdcd,* or *cdedce.*
- The octave often poses a question or makes a statement that is then brought to closure in the sestet.

Look for these characteristics as you read the poems in this grouping.

Comparing Literary Works

All five poems in this grouping are Petrarchan sonnets, and all share the subject of love, but the poets use a variety of images to describe their beloved. **Imagery** is descriptive language that re-creates sensory experiences. For example, Ronsard uses the image of a rose to describe his young beloved. Use a chart like the one shown to compare imagery in the five poems and to determine the overall effect the imagery produces.

❸ Reading Strategy

Reading in Sentences

Reading in sentences will help you understand the meaning of a poem. Although these poems are written in sentences, the end of each sentence does not always coincide with the end of the poetic line. A sentence may extend for several lines or end in the middle of a line. To read in sentences, notice the punctuation. Do not pause or make a full stop at the end of a line unless there is a period, comma, colon, semicolon, or dash.

Vocabulary Builder

sated (sāt′ ed) *v.* completely satisfied (p. 732)

exults (eg zults′) *v.* rejoices greatly (p. 733)

sojourn (sō′ jurn) *n.* visit (p. 733)

crone (krōn) *n.* very old woman (p. 734)

languishing (laŋ′ gwish iŋ) *v.* becoming weak (p. 736)

reposes (ri pōz′ ez) *v.* puts to rest (p. 736)

Senses	Image
Touch	
Sight	
Hearing	
Smell	
Taste	
Overall Effect of the Images	

NC Standard Course of Study

- Identify and analyze text components and evaluate impact on expressive text. (WL.1.03.2)
- Demonstrate comprehension of main idea and supporting details in personal reflection. (WL.1.03.4)
- Make inferences and draw conclusions based on personal reflection. (WL.1.03.6)

Laura / The White Doe / Spring / To Hélène / Roses ■ 729

❷ Literary Analysis
The Sonnet

- Read aloud the Petrarchan sonnet characteristics. Discuss and define each element.

- Tell students that the rhyme schemes of Petrarchan sonnets may vary slightly. Direct students to the poem "The White Doe" on p. 732. Have them read the last word of each line and write the rhyme scheme used in the poem. Then, have students **discuss** how the rhyme scheme varies from the usual rhyme scheme of a Petrarchan sonnet.
  Answer: The rhyme scheme is *abab, cddc, efefef.*

- Give students a copy of **Literary Analysis Graphic Organizer A,** p. 126 in *Graphic Organizer Transparencies.* Have them use it to compare imagery in the poems.

- Ask students to consider how imagery can create an overall effect in a work of literature. For example, ask what overall effect might be created by the image of an elderly woman sitting alone by a fire and reading old love letters. Discuss ways in which this image could appeal to the senses.

- Point out that in each of the following poems, the poet uses vivid imagery to create an overall effect regarding his beloved.

❸ Reading Strategy
Reading in Sentences

- Read aloud the Reading Strategy instruction. Point out that sometimes the entire stanza of a poem can be a single sentence.

- Explain that different stops, such as commas or periods, indicate longer or shorter pauses.

- Demonstrate the appropriate pauses by reading one or more lines from one of the poems.

Vocabulary Builder

- Pronounce each vocabulary word for students, and read the definitions as a class. Have students identify any words with which they are already familiar.

Differentiated Instruction   Solutions for All Learners

Support for Special Needs Students
Have students complete the **Preview** and **Build Skills** pages for these selections in the *Reader's Notebook: Adapted Version.* These pages provide a selection summary, an abbreviated presentation of the reading and literary skills, and the graphic organizer on the **Build Skills** page in the student book.

Support for Less Proficient Readers
Have students complete the **Preview** and **Build Skills** pages for these selections in the *Reader's Notebook.* These pages provide a selection summary, an abbreviated presentation of the reading and literary skills, and the graphic organizer on the **Build Skills** page in the student book.

Support for English Learners
Have students complete the **Preview** and **Build Skills** pages for these selections in the *Reader's Notebook: English Learner's Version.* These pages provide a selection summary, an abbreviated presentation of the reading and literary skills, additional contextual vocabulary, and the graphic organizer on the **Build Skills** page in the student book.

729

Facilitate Understanding

To help students understand "The White Doe," review the meaning of *allegory*. Have students explain how the speaker's experience with a doe could be an allegory for Petrarch and Laura.

❶ About the Selection

The earliest lyrics in Petrarch's *Canzoniere* were written in the 1320s. Although most of the collection concerns the poet's unrequited love for Laura, it also includes many sonnets on political and religious matters not directly related to Laura.

❷ Humanities

Detail from *Primavera* depicting the Three Graces, by Sandro Botticelli

The Three Graces are ancient Greek goddesses representing beauty, charm, and grace. They were associated with the Muses, the goddesses of art, and with Venus.

In *Primavera*, the Graces dance beside Venus, who is decorously clothed and wears the cap of a married Florentine woman. The scene is set in an orange grove, and the oranges in the trees could symbolize the coat of arms of the Medicis.

Botticelli is famous for the linear rhythms of his paintings. The vertical lines of the background make an excellent backdrop for the rhythmic curves of the dancers.

Use the following question for discussion:

How does Botticelli convey the feeling of a dance?
Possible response: The graceful positions of the women's arms suggest movement.

❸ Critical Viewing

Possible response: The golden hair and the "angelic progress" in which the three goddesses move recall the imagery in "Laura."

---

from CANZONIERE
by Petrarch

❶

Background Petrarch's *Canzoniere* features 366 poems dedicated to his beloved Laura. Although Petrarch gives no clue about her real identity, many scholars agree that Laura was a married woman whom he supposedly first saw on April 6, 1327. Even though she apparently gave his affection no encouragement, at least so far as he describes in his poetry, Petrarch loved Laura all his life—even after her death in 1348.

The *Canzoniere* is divided into two parts—those poems to Laura "in life" and those to her "in death." Her importance in the sequence of poems lies in her effect on the poet, whose desire for her is never fulfilled. This "Petrarchan" scenario, in which the lovers' relationship is never fully realized, would become a standard model for generations to come.

❷

Three Graces (detail), Botticelli, Giraudon

❸
◀ **Critical Viewing**
Compare the visual details in this painting with the imagery in "Laura."
[Compare]

730 ■ *The Renaissance and Rationalism*

Differentiated Instruction   Solutions for All Learners

Accessibility at a Glance

	Laura	The White Doe	Spring	To Hélène	Roses
Language	Evocative and descriptive	Visual imagery; symbolism	Vivid verbs, adjectives	Participial phrases	Syntax: Long sentences
Concept Level	Accessible (Love lasts.)	Accessible (Rejection of love hurts.)	Accessible (Love is like spring.)	Accessible (Love now.)	Accessible (Love is like a rose.)
Literary Merit	Petrarchan sonnet	Sonnet with allegory of love	Love sonnet	Love sonnet	Love sonnet
Lexile	NP	NP	NP	NP	NP
Overall Rating	Average	Challenging	Challenging	Challenging	Challenging

Laura

Petrarch

translated by Morris Bishop

She used to let her golden hair fly free
　For the wind to toy and tangle and molest;
　Her eyes were brighter than the radiant west.
　(Seldom they shine so now.) I used to see

5　Pity look out of those deep eyes on me.
　("It was false pity," you would now protest.)
　I had love's tinder[1] heaped within my breast;
　What wonder that the flame burned furiously?

She did not walk in any mortal way,
10　But with angelic progress; when she spoke,
　Unearthly voices sang in unison.

She seemed divine among the dreary folk
　Of earth. You say she is not so today?
　Well, though the bow's unbent,[2] the wound bleeds on.

1. **tinder** (tin′ dər) *n.* dry, easily flammable material used for starting a fire.
2. **though the bow's unbent** though she is older and does not have her original beauty; the bow is Cupid's.

Reading Strategy
Reading in Sentences
In the octave, which lines require you to read on to the next line without stopping? Why?

Reading Check

What emotion did Laura once feel for the speaker?

---

❹ About the Selection

In "Laura," Petrarch reverently describes his idealized beloved, noting that although time has passed and she may not be as beautiful or kind as he has always imagined—and although she has never loved him—he loves her still.

❺ Reading Strategy
Reading in Sentences

• Review with students the Reading Strategy information on p. 729. Remind them that reading in sentences will help them understand a poem's meaning.

• Have a student read aloud the bracketed passage and carefully follow the punctuation. Then, **ask** the Reading Strategy question: In the octave, which lines require you to read on to the next line without stopping? Why?
Answer: Line 1 and the last four words of line 4 require readers to go on to the next line without stopping; because those lines have no end punctuation.

• Point out the midline stops in lines 10 and 13. Note that the stops force the reader to emphasize the balance of the lines.

❻ Literary Analysis
The Sonnet

• Review with students the characteristics on p. 729 of the Petrarchan sonnet. Have them clarify the difference between an *octave* and a *sestet.*

• After students have finished reading the poem, have them **contrast** the speaker's description of Laura in the octave with the description of her in the sestet.
Possible response: In the octave, Laura is presented as a beautiful young woman; in the sestet, she is described as having been a divine creature who is now changed.

• **Ask** students: Do you think Petrarch presents a realistic portrait of Laura? Why or why not?
Possible response: The picture is not realistic because Petrarch is blinded by love.

❼ Reading Check

Answer: Laura used to pity the speaker.

"The White Doe" again explores the pain of Petrarch's love for Laura. The poem's speaker (Petrarch) finds the doe (Laura) so beautiful that he feels compelled to pursue her, though she wears a sign warning that she is not to be touched (she is unattainable). Focused on her, he falls into the stream (of love), and she vanishes.

9 **Themes in World Literature**

Allegory One of the greatest allegories in literature is *The Divine Comedy* by Dante Alighieri (1265–1321). The allegory is divided into three sections: *Inferno, Purgatorio,* and *Paradiso.* The poem describes the allegorical journey of the poet Dante from darkness and ignorance—the *Inferno*—to the light of the divine vision of God—*Paradiso.*

Connect to the Literature Caution students not to mistake fantasy for allegory. A fantasy is fiction characterized by dreamlike or supernatural elements, and an allegory requires that every detail, character, and plot point have a symbolic meaning. JRR Tolkien firmly stated that his *Lord of the Rings* was a fantasy with no allegorical elements; he wrote it simply to entertain. Ask students to identify allegorical films or plays.

Possible responses: Although it is not a love allegory, Arthur Miller's *The Crucible* (about the Salem witch trials) is an allegory for McCarthyism during the Red Scare of 1948–1956.

10 **Literary Analysis**

The Sonnet and Imagery

• Remind students that imagery is descriptive language that appeals to the senses.

• Have students respond to the Literary Analysis item: **Identify** two visual images in the octave. **Possible response:** Two visual images are the white doe and a green grove of trees.

The White Doe

Petrarch

translated by Anna Maria Armi

A pure-white doe in an emerald glade
Appeared to me, with two antlers of gold,
Between two streams, under a laurel's shade,
At sunrise, in the season's bitter cold.

5 Her sight was so suavely[1] merciless
That I left work to follow her at leisure,
Like the miser who looking for his treasure
Sweetens with that delight his bitterness.

Around her lovely neck "Do not touch me"
10 Was written with topaz[2] and diamond stone,
"My Caesar's will has been to make me free."

Already toward noon had climbed the sun,
My weary eyes were not <u>sated</u> to see,
When I fell in the stream and she was gone.

---

1. **suavely** (swäv´ lē) in a smoothly gracious manner.
2. **topaz** (tō´ paz) yellow gem.

Themes in World Masterpieces

9 **Allegory**

An **allegory** is an extended metaphor or a story line with both a literal and a symbolic level. "The White Doe," for example, is an allegory in which the speaker sees his beloved as "a pure-white doe in an emerald glade." Like his beloved Laura, Petrarch's doe is beautiful and untouchable. In the end, the doe disappears from sight, just as the real Laura disappears in death.

Italian poet Dante Alighieri wrote his famous allegory, the *Divine Comedy,* in the 1300s. In *Moby-Dick* (1851), American novelist Herman Melville incorporated allegorical elements concerning the human struggle against evil and fate. The message in Petrarch's "The White Doe" seems lighter in comparison with these other allegories, but the fleeting nature of love remains a powerful theme despite the passage of centuries.

Connect to the Literature

What modern-day allegories, in movies or plays, remind you of "The White Doe"?

Literary Analysis
The Sonnet and Imagery
Identify two visual images in the octave.

Vocabulary Builder
sated (sāt´ ed) *v.* completely satisfied

▶**Monitor Progress** Have students **identify** the characteristics of a Petrarchan sonnet that are found in "The White Doe."
Answer: "The White Doe" is divided into an eight-line octave and a six-line sestet; it presents the appearance of a deer and then brings it to closure by having the deer disappear.

▶**Reteach** To assist students' understanding of the sonnet form, use the **Literary Analysis** support, p. 8 in *Unit 6 Resources.*

(11)
(12)

Spring

Petrarch

translated by
Morris Bishop

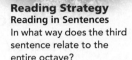

Zephyr[1] returns, and scatters everywhere
    New flowers and grass, and company does bring,
    Procne and Philomel,[2] in sweet despair,
    And all the tender colors of the Spring.
(13) 5 Never were fields so glad, nor skies so fair;
    And Jove <u>exults</u> in Venus'[3] prospering.
    Love is in all the water, earth, and air,
    And love possesses every living thing.
    But to me only heavy sighs return
10   For her who carried in her little hand
    My heart's key to her heavenly <u>sojourn.</u>
    The birds sing loud above the flowering land;
    Ladies are gracious now.—Where deserts burn
    The beasts still prowl on the ungreening sand.

---

1. **Zephyr** (zef´ ər) the west wind.
2. **Procne** (präk´ nē) **and Philomel** (fil´ ō mel´) In Greek mythology, Philomel was a princess of Athens who was raped by Tereus, husband of her sister Procne. The gods changed Philomel into a nightingale, Procne into a swallow, and Tereus into a hawk.
3. **Jove . . . Venus'** Jove was the chief god in Roman mythology, and Venus was the goddess of love.

Critical Reading

1. **Respond:** What do you imagine Petrarch's Laura was like?
2. **(a) Recall:** List four details about Laura that the speaker recalls in "Laura." **(b) Analyze:** What are the common qualities of the details that he remembers about her?
3. **(a) Recall:** In "The White Doe," which details of time does the speaker mention? **(b) Interpret:** What do you think these references to time mean? Explain.
4. **Interpret:** In "Spring," in what ways is the speaker's "heart's key" responsible for these contrasting images he sees?
5. **Relate:** Do you think the feelings or situations Petrarch describes in his poems are still relevant today? Why or why not?

Reading Strategy
Reading in Sentences
In what way does the third sentence relate to the entire octave?

Vocabulary Builder
exults (eg zults´) *v.* rejoices greatly

sojourn (sō´ jʉrn) *n.* visit

Go Online
Author Link
For: More about Petrarch
Visit: www.PHSchool.com
Web Code: ete-9601

Spring ■ 733

---

(11) About the Selection
In "Spring," the speaker acknowledges the beauty and joy of spring, observing that love "possesses" every living thing. However, he notes that his own possession by love is a source of suffering.

(12) Critical Thinking
Predict
• Have students consider how and why people often associate romantic love with the season of spring.
• **Ask** students to make predictions about the content of the poem. **Possible response:** "Spring" will compare spring's beauty with love's joy.

(13) Reading Strategy
Reading in Sentences
• Have a volunteer read aloud the octave. Point out that except for line 1, each line ends with a pause or a stop.
• Have a volunteer read aloud the sestet. Note how the last three lines differ in structure and rhythm.
• **Ask** students the Reading Strategy question.
Answer: The sentence sums up the idea that love is everywhere.

ASSESS

Answers

1. **Possible response:** Laura was a beautiful, elegant young woman.
2. **(a)** Laura had golden hair; deep, bright eyes; an angelic walk; and a beautiful voice. **(b)** The details portray her as beautiful.
3. **(a)** Time references include "at sunrise" and "toward noon." **(b) Possible response:** The time references symbolize stages in the speaker's love for Laura.
4. **Possible response:** He sees that spring has returned love to the world; however, because his love is gone, he sees desolation.
5. **Possible response:** Petrarch's poems are still relevant because people still fall in love and suffer without it.

Go Online For additional informa-
Author Link tion about Petrarch, have students type in the Web Code, then select *P* from the alphabet, and then select Petrarch.

733

Help students understand the difference between a translation, such as Norman Shapiro's translation of "To Hélène," and an adaptation, such as that by William Butler Yeats, which follows:

When You Are Old

When you are old and gray and full of sleep,

And nodding by the fire, take down this book,

And slowly read, and dream of the soft look

Your eyes had once, and of their shadows deep;

How many loved your moments of glad grace,

And loved your beauty with love false or true,

But one man loved the pilgrim soul in you,

And loved the sorrows of your changing face;

And bending down beside the glowing bars,

Murmur, a little sadly, how Love fled

And paced upon the mountains overhead

And hid his face amid a crowd of stars.

Here are the elements that make Yeats' poem an adaptation rather than a translation:

• Unlike the original, it has twelve lines and is not a sonnet.

• It omits the "servant."

• It contains "eye" imagery that is not in the original.

• Unlike the original, it contrasts love of the soul with love of the body.

• It ends with the image of Love hiding "his face amid a crowd of stars," rather than with the injunction to "Gather life's roses. . . ."

To Hélène

Pierre de Ronsard

translated by Norman Shapiro

Background The Latin phrase *carpe diem* means "seize the day"—in other words, make use of the present time and enjoy life while you can. This popular theme acknowledges the brevity and uncertainties of life and provides encouragement to grasp the good that the world has to offer. In "To Hélène," for example, the speaker urges his beloved to "Gather life's roses while still fresh they grow."

When you are very old, by candle's flame,
Spinning beside the fire, at end of day,
Singing my verse, admiring, you will say:
"When I was fair, Ronsard's muse I became."

⓯

5 Your servant then, some weary old beldame[1]—
Whoever she may be—nodding away,
Hearing "Ronsard," will shake off sleep, and pray
Your name be blessed, to live in deathless fame.

Buried, I shall a fleshless phantom be,
10 Hovering by the shadowed myrtle tree;
You, by the hearth, a pining <u>crone</u>, bent low,

Whose pride once scorned my love, much to your sorrow.
Heed me, live for today, wait not the morrow:
Gather life's roses while still fresh they grow.

Literary Analysis
The Sonnet What is the rhyme scheme of the octave?

Vocabulary Builder
crone (krōn) *n.* very old woman

---

1. **beldame** (bel´ dam) old woman.

734 ■ The Renaissance and Rationalism

Enrichment

Critical Evaluation of Ronsard

Literary critic Annette Elizabeth Armstrong has called Ronsard "The most eminent and prolific poet of the French Renaissance. . . . To the twentieth-century reader he is perhaps most appealing when celebrating his native countryside, reflecting on the brevity of youth and beauty, or voicing the various states of unrequited love. . . . He was a master of lyric themes and forms, and his poetry remains attractive to composers; some of his odes, such as 'Mignonne allons voir si la rose . . .' ["Mignonne, let us go to see if the rose . . ."], were set to music half a dozen times in the sixteenth century alone and have become as familiar to the general public in France as folk songs."

16

17 ▲ **Critical Viewing** Look closely at the expression on this woman's face. Compare and contrast her attitude with your perception of Hélène. **[Compare and Contrast]**

To Hélène ■ 735

15 **Literary Analysis**
The Sonnet

- Tell students that "To Hélène," like the previous poems in this grouping, is a Petrarchan sonnet.

- Have students read the poem in its entirety. Then, **ask** the Literary Analysis question: What is the rhyme scheme of the octave?
  Answer: The rhyme scheme is *abba, abba.*

- Discuss with students how the poet uses images to appeal to the senses. **Ask:** What overall effect does the imagery in this poem produce?
  Possible responses: The imagery gives readers a sense of sadness, regret, loneliness, or anger.

16 **Humanities**

The Nurse Resigning to Ursula's Decision (detail), by Vittore Carpaccio

Born in Venice, Italy, Vittore Carpaccio (1460–1526) is best known for his cycles of narrative paintings. This detail, taken from *Arrival of the English Ambassadors at the Court of Maurus, King of Brittany,* is part of *The Legend of Saint Ursula* cycle. The cycle consists of nine large paintings that tell the story of St. Ursula, a fourth-century British princess who was martyred by the Huns, nomadic invaders of southeastern Europe. It was completed between 1490 and 1495.

Use the following question for discussion:

What mood does the artist create?
Possible response: The painting conveys a gloomy, serious mood.

17 **Critical Viewing**

Possible response: The woman appears to be solemn, sad, and deep in thought, which is how Hélène is perceived.

Differentiated Instruction Solutions for All Learners

Strategy for Special Needs Students
As students read Ronsard's poetry, have them study the word choices he makes to create a mood and explore a theme. Organize students in groups, and have each group identify specific words in "To Hélène" and "Roses" that are particularly effective at evoking each poem's mood and theme.

Support for Less Proficient Readers
Point out that in "To Hélène," the speaker describes to the young woman what will happen if she does not accept and return his love. In "Roses," the speaker describes how his love dies when she is young and lovely. Discuss with students how this reflects the brevity and uncertainty of life.

Strategy for Gifted/Talented Students
Challenge students to write essays comparing and contrasting the treatment of the *carpe diem* theme in "To Hélène" and "Roses." Suggest that they consider the theme in terms of the particular effects of time on each of the women being addressed by the poems' speakers.

735

Roses

18

Pierre de Ronsard
translated by Vernon Watkins

As one sees on the branch in the month of May the rose
In her beautiful youth, in the dawn of her flower,
When the break of day softens her life with the shower,
Make jealous the sky of the damask[1] bloom she shows:
5   Grace lingers in her leaf and love sleeping glows
Enchanting with fragrance the trees of her bower,
But, broken by the rain or the sun's oppressive power,
<u>Languishing</u> she dies, and all her petals throws.
Thus in thy first youth, in thy awakening fair
10   When thy beauty was honored by lips of Earth and Air,
Atropos[2] has killed thee and dust thy form <u>reposes</u>.
O take, take for obsequies[3] my tears, these poor showers,
This vase filled with milk, this basket strewn with flowers,
That in death as in life thy body may be roses.

19

20

---

1. **damask** (dam´ əsk) deep pink or rose.
2. **Atropos** (a´ trə päs) in Greek and Roman mythology, the goddess who cuts the thread of life.
3. **obsequies** (äb´ si kwēz) funeral rites or ceremonies.

Critical Reading

1. **Respond:** How do you think Hélène might have responded to the poem about her? Explain.

2. **(a) Recall:** Describe the scene that the speaker presents in the octave of "To Hélène." **(b) Speculate:** What feelings might have prompted the speaker's emotions in this poem? Explain.

3. **(a) Recall:** Which phrases in the first six lines of "Roses" describe the gentleness of nature? **(b) Interpret:** What change has nature brought in line seven? **(c) Draw Conclusions:** What does this suggest about the well-being of the speaker's beloved?

4. **Hypothesize:** If Ronsard were alive today, what famous person might the poet immortalize in verse? Why?

736 ■ The Renaissance and Rationalism

Go Online
Author Link
For: More about Pierre de Ronsard
Visit: www.PHSchool.com
Web Code: ete-9602

Apply the Skills

Laura • The White Doe • Spring • To Hélène • Roses

Literary Analysis

The Sonnet

1. In what way does the two-part structure of the **sonnet** "Laura" reflect the speaker's recollections of Laura?
2. **(a)** What is the rhyme scheme of "The White Doe"? **(b)** In what ways does the pattern vary from that of a typical sonnet?
3. How do the poems "The White Doe" and "Roses" reflect the popular Petrarchan scenario in which the lovers' relationship will never be fully realized?

Comparing Literary Works

4. **(a)** List three **images** describing the doe in "The White Doe" that relate to images of Laura in "Laura." **(b)** Why might the speaker choose to associate Laura with a white doe?
5. **(a)** What is the condition of the speaker in "To Hélène"? **(b)** In what ways do the speaker and the object of his desire differ from those in the other poems in this grouping?
6. Which of Ronsard's two sonnets is most like Petrarch's three sonnets in imagery and feeling? Explain.

Reading Strategy

Reading in Sentences

7. **(a)** To analyze how **reading in sentences** affects the meaning in a poem, choose sentences from the poem "Spring" to complete the chart below. **(b)** Then, explain the meaning of each sentence and relate its meaning to the poem.

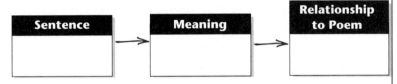

Sentence	Meaning	Relationship to Poem

8. **(a)** How many complete sentences are in "The White Doe"? **(b)** How does the arrangement of complete sentences in the poem reflect the imagery?

Extend Understanding

9. **Psychology Connection:** Do you think that writing these poems comforted the poets or caused them more suffering? Explain.

QuickReview

A **sonnet** is a fourteen-line poem focused on a single theme. A sonnet has two parts and a structured rhyme scheme.

Imagery is descriptive language that re-creates sensory experiences.

To **read in sentences**, note the punctuation in a poem, and stop at the end of a line only if there is a period, comma, semicolon, colon, or dash.

Assessment
For: Self-test
Visit: www.PHSchool.com
Web Code: eta-6601

Laura / The White Doe / Spring / To Hélène / Roses ■ 737

Answers

1. In the first section, the speaker remembers Laura the way she was when she was young and beautiful; in the second section, he is remembering her as older.

2. **(a)** The rhyme scheme is *abab, cddc, efefef.* **(b)** A typical sonnet has a rhyme scheme of *abba, abba, cdecde.*

3. In "The White Doe," the woman is unattainable and unreachable; in "Roses," the woman dies in her youth.

4. **(a)** Three images are the woman's ethereal appearance as a white doe with golden antlers; her "suavely merciless" look of disdain; and the sign "Do not touch me" around her neck. **(b) Possible response:** The white doe is beautiful, pure, and rare.

5. **(a)** The speaker is scornful. **(b)** The speaker is frustrated and irritated with the woman; she is not distant and unattainable; she simply rejects him.

6. "Roses" is similar to Petrarch's sonnets; it describes a beautiful young woman who dies young, like Laura, especially in "Spring," and it describes how the speaker will continue to mourn, as does the speaker in "Laura."

7. **Possible response: Sentence:** "But to me only heavy sighs return / For her who carried in her little hand / My heart's key to her heavenly sojourn." **Meaning:** The sentence means that when spring returns, the speaker feels only sadness and sighs as he mourns for his beloved who has died and taken his heart with her. **Relationship to Poem:** The sentence is in contrast to the first part of the poem in which the speaker describes the beauty and love that returns with the season of spring. Another sample answer can be found on **Reading Strategy Graphic Organizer B**, p. 129 in *Graphic Organizer Transparencies.*

8. **(a)** Four complete sentences are in "The White Doe." **(b)** Each sentence reflects a different image: the doe; the speaker leaving his work to follow her; the sign around her neck; and the speaker following her until her disappearance.

Answers continued

9. **Possible response:** Writing these poems might have comforted the poets because it helped them express their pain.

Go Online
Assessment Students may use the **Self-test** to prepare for **Selection Test A** or **Selection Test B.**

❶ Vocabulary Lesson

Related Words: *languish*

1. languid   3. languishing
2. languor

**Vocabulary Builder:
Sentence Completion**

1. sated   4. exults
2. reposes   5. languishing
3. crone   6. sojourn

Spelling Strategy

1. *wi*   3. *i*
2. *oo*

❷ Grammar and Style Lesson

1. Her <u>eyes</u> were *brighter* than the sun. (modifies <u>eyes</u>)

2. <u>She</u> seemed *divine* among the dreary folk of earth. (modifies <u>She</u>)

3. <u>I</u> was *fair,* [and] Ronsard's muse I became. (modifies <u>I</u>)

4. Her <u>sight</u> was so . . . *merciless* that I left work to follow her at leisure. (modifies <u>sight</u>)

5. <u>He</u> seems *languid* since her death. (modifies <u>He</u>)

Writing Application

Possible response:

1. Her <u>hair</u> is *golden.* (modifies <u>hair</u>)

2. Her <u>eyes</u> seem *brighter* than the stars. (modifies <u>eyes</u>)

3. Her <u>voice</u> sounds *musical,* like angels singing. (modifies <u>voice</u>)

4. <u>She</u> is *lovelier* than an angel. (modifies <u>She</u>)

*W*G **Writing and Grammar
Platinum Level**

For support in teaching the Grammar and Style Lesson, use Chapter 19, Section 4.

Build Language Skills

❶ Vocabulary Lesson

Related Words: *languish*

The word *languish* means "to become weak," or "to fail in vitality and health." Other words related to *languish* include the following:

languishing (participle and verb form): "becoming weak"

languor (noun): "the feeling of being weak"

languid (adjective): "weak; without energy or vitality"

Complete each of the following sentences with one of the related words listed above.

1. The deep sadness he felt at her death left him feeling _____.

2. His _____ prevents him from working on his poetry.

3. She is _____ and very near death.

Vocabulary Builder: Sentence Completion

Fill in the blanks below with the correct word from the vocabulary list on page 729.

1. He felt _____ after the great feast.

2. She _____ upon the satin pillows.

3. The old _____ sat knitting by the fire.

4. He _____ in knowing that she loves him.

5. He is _____ still, though the worst of his illness has passed.

6. A short _____ restored his spirits.

Spelling Strategy

The letters *ui* can represent several sounds: long *i* as in *guide;* short *i* as in *biscuit; oo* as in *fruit;* and *wi* as in *languish.* Indicate which sound is found in each of these words.

1. distinguish   2. suit   3. circuit

❷ Grammar and Style Lesson

Predicate Adjective

A **predicate adjective** appears only with a linking verb and describes the subject of a sentence. Common linking verbs include *is, am, are, was, were, sound, taste, appear, feel, look,* and *seem.*

<u>Ladies</u> are *gracious* now. (modifies <u>Ladies</u>)

Practice Underline the subject in each item below, and draw an arrow from the predicate adjective to the word it modifies.

1. Her eyes were brighter than the sun.

2. She seemed divine among the dreary folk of earth.

3. I was fair, [and] Ronsard's muse I became.

4. Her sight was so . . . merciless that I left work to follow her at leisure.

5. He seems languid since her death.

Writing Application Write four sentences describing a great beauty. In each sentence, underline the subject and draw an arrow from the predicate adjective to the word it modifies. Note that action verbs do not take predicate adjectives.

*W*G *Prentice Hall Writing and Grammar Connection: Platinum Level, Chapter 19, Section 4*

Assessment Practice

Evaluate and Make Judgments   (**For more practice, see** *Test Preparation Workbook,* **p. 32**)

The reading comprehension and vocabulary sections of standardized tests often require students to evaluate and make judgments about an author's word choice. Write the following lines of "Roses" on the board, along with the sample test item.

As one sees on the branch in the month of May the rose
In her beautiful youth, in the dawn of her flower . . .

In the poem, the word *dawn* means—

A the time of first daylight.
B to begin to be understood.
C first appearance.
D the beginning of history.

B is incorrect because it defines the use of the word as a verb. *A* and *D* do not fit with the rest of the phrase, "of her flower." Therefore, *C* is the best answer.

❸ Writing Lesson

Journal Passage

For Petrarch and Ronsard, writing poems was much like keeping a journal—the poetry preserved the thoughts and feelings each poet experienced. Write a journal passage responding to any of these poems, using the voice of the love object in the poem. Use details from the poem to establish the personality of the beloved.

Prewriting   Begin by choosing one of the poems. Then, list details that reveal both the relationship the speaker shared with his beloved and how the love object might respond to the poem.

Drafting   In the voice of the beloved, state your feelings about the poem and the poet. Add details from your list along with fictitious but logical encounters or conversations between the love object and the speaker.

Model: Incorporating Details

When I was young, I inspired every great poet I

though I am old,

knew. Even now,ᴧI am considered a great beauty.

> Adding details makes writing more interesting and provides a more complete picture.

Revising   Check your finished draft against the details in your list. Replace any vague words or phrases with concrete details that reflect the voice of the beloved.

 *Prentice Hall Writing and Grammar Connection: Platinum Level, Chapter 4, Section 3*

Extend Your Learning

❹ **Listening and Speaking** Working with a partner, perform a **dramatic reading** of "Laura" and "To Hélène." As you rehearse, consider these tips:

- Adjust your voice to reflect the speaker of each poem.
- Consider the emotions expressed in the poem, and try to reflect them in your voice.
- Remember to read in complete sentences.

Perform your reading for your class, and invite questions from the audience. **[Group Activity]**

Research and Technology Compose an **informative essay** on William Butler Yeats's poem "When You Are Old" using your library's Internet or electronic sources. Address the relationship between this poem and Ronsard's. Be sure to cite your sources and include Yeats's poem.

Go Online
Research
For: An additional research activity
Visit: www.PHSchool.com
Web Code: etd-7601

---

❸ Writing Lesson

- To give students guidance in writing this journal passage, give them the **Support for Writing Lesson,** p. 12 in *Unit 6 Resources.*
- Read aloud the Writing Lesson instruction. Have students work in small groups to reread each of the poems and discuss the relationship between the speaker and his beloved.
- Encourage students to visualize the love object of the poem they select and to imagine themselves as that person.
- Use the Narration: Autobiographical Narrative rubrics in *General Resources,* pp. 43–44, to evaluate students' journal passages.

WG Writing and Grammar Platinum Level

For support in teaching the Writing Lesson, use Chapter 4, Section 3.

❹ Listening and Speaking

- Have students independently read the Listening and Speaking instruction. Explain that a dramatic reading will help them understand and interpret a poem's meaning.
- Students may wish to record their readings and listen to their own performances before presenting the readings to the class.
- The **Support for Extend Your Learning** page (*Unit 6 Resources,* p. 13) provides guided note-taking opportunities to help students complete the Extend Your Learning activities.

Go Online Have students type in the **Research** Web Code for another research activity.

Assessment Resources

The following resources can be used to assess students' knowledge and skills.

Unit 6 Resources
Selection Test A, pp. 15–17
Selection Test B, pp. 18–20

General Resources
Rubrics for Narration: Autobiographical Narrative, pp. 43–44

Go Online Students may use the **Self-test** to **Assessment** prepare for **Selection Test A** or **Selection Test B.**

LT.5.01.2 Build knowledge of literary genres, and explore how characteristics apply to literature of world cultures.

LT.5.01.6 Make connections between historical and contemporary issues in world literature.

LT.5.03.9 Analyze and evaluate the effects of author's craft and style in world literature.

Connections

British Literature

Although the Petrarchan sonnet is slightly different from the Shakespearean sonnet in form and style, both types of sonnets address the emotions that are experienced by a speaker who is in love. Have students reread the Petrarchan sonnets on pp. 731–733 after they have read the Shakespearean sonnets. What similarities and differences do students notice between the two types of sonnets?

Love and the Sonnet

- Explain to students that the first sonnets were written, scholars believe, in the thirteenth century in Italy. About a hundred years later, Petrarch wrote so many beautiful sonnets that the Italian form (an octave followed by a sestet) was named after him.

- Explain the unique rhyme scheme of Petrarchan sonnets. Often the octave uses rhymes *abbaabba,* and the sestet uses rhymes *cdecde* or some combination of *cd* rhymes.

- Then, explain the rhyme scheme of the Shakespearean sonnet. Each of the three quatrains has a rhyme pattern of its own, followed by a rhymed couplet. A typical rhyme scheme would be *abab cdcd efef gg.*

- Point out that in a Shakespearean sonnet, each of the three quatrains usually explores a different variation of the main theme. The sonnet is usually not printed with the stanzas divided, but a reader can see distinct ideas in each.

CONNECTIONS
British Literature

England

Love and the Sonnet

The fourteen-line poem called the *sonnet* has traditionally been a poem of love. Petrarch, whose sonnets to Laura set the thematic course of the genre, uses an octave (eight lines) and a sestet (six lines) to give his poems a kind of statement/response structure: The octave often takes a position that the sestet contradicts or modifies. The Petrarchan sonnets in this unit are selected from a sonnet sequence charting the pangs of a speaker's unfulfilled love for an idealized lady.

Elizabethan Variations Shakespeare's sonnets 29 and 116 have also been selected from a sonnet sequence. Shakespeare uses a variation of Petrarch's sonnet form: three quatrains (four lines each) and a couplet (two lines), with the couplet often a dramatic statement that resolves, restates, or redefines the central problem of the sonnet. Shakespeare's speaker and beloved, however, are less ideal and more real than the lovers in Petrarch's sonnets. Though Petrarch wrote in fourteenth-century Italy and Shakespeare in sixteenth-century England, the joy and despair in their poetry will be familiar to anyone who has ever been in love.

Sonnet 29
William Shakespeare

When in disgrace with fortune and men's eyes,
I all alone beweep my outcast state,
And trouble deaf heaven with my bootless[1] cries,
And look upon myself and curse my fate,
5 Wishing me like to one more rich in hope,
Featured like him, like him with friends possessed
Desiring this man's art, and that man's <u>scope</u>,
With what I most enjoy contented least.
Yet in these thoughts myself almost despising,
10 Haply[2] I think on thee, and then my state,
Like to the lark at break of day arising
From <u>sullen</u> earth, sings hymns at heaven's gate;
    For thy sweet love remembered such wealth brings
    That then I scorn to change my state with kings.

---

1. **bootless** *adj.* futile.
2. **haply** *adv.* by chance.

Vocabulary Build

scope *n.* range of perce
tion or understanding

sullen *adj.* gloomy; dis

Enrichment

The Beloved in Shakespeare's Sonnets

Debate has long raged over the identity of the beloved in Shakespeare's sonnets. Whereas the traditional sonnet sequence is addressed to a single love object, some of Shakespeare's sonnets are clearly addressed to a Young Man and others are addressed to the famous "Dark Lady." Still other sonnets seem to be addressed to neither the Young Man nor the Lady, but to time, love itself, or the speaker's own soul. Various scholars have suggested that the Young Man was either the Earl of Pembroke or the Earl of Southampton, and the Dark Lady was one of the queen's maids of honor.

Sonnet 116

William Shakespeare

Let me not to the marriage of true minds
Admit <u>impediments</u>. Love is not love
Which <u>alters</u> when it alteration finds,
Or bends with the remover to remove.
5   O, no! It is an ever-fixèd mark
That looks on tempests and is never shaken;
It is the star to every wandering bark,[1]
Whose worth's unknown, although his height be taken.[2]
Love's not Time's fool, though rosy lips and cheeks
10   Within his bending sickle's compass[3] come;
Love alters not with his brief hours and weeks,
But bears it out even to the edge of doom.[4]
          If this be error, and upon me proved,
          I never writ, nor no man ever loved.

---

1. **star . . . bark** the star that guides every wandering ship: the North Star.
2. **Whose . . . be taken** whose value is unmeasurable, although navigators measure its
   height in the sky.
3. **compass** n. range; scope.
4. **doom** Judgment Day.

Connecting British Literature

1. Compare the speaker's attitude toward his beloved in "Laura" with the
   speaker's attitude in "Sonnet 29." **(a)** Which speaker is more optimistic?
   (b) Is the central figure in each poem the speaker or the beloved?
   (c) Indicate the specific lines that provide the information.
2. **(a)** In what way is the speaker's perspective on the inevitable changes
   of time in "Sonnet 116" similar to the perspective of the speaker in
   "Laura"? **(b)** In what way are the perspectives different?
3. Of the three poems by Petrarch and the two by Shakespeare, which one
   is your favorite? Explain.

Vocabulary Builder

impediments *n.* obstacles
alters *v.* changes

Shakespeare (1564–1616)

William Shakespeare was born in the country town of Stratford-on-Avon, England, and probably attended the town's free grammar school. Well known as an actor and a playwright, Shakespeare was part owner of a London theater, the Globe, where many of his plays were performed. From 1592 to 1594, London's theaters were closed because of the plague—this period may have provided an opportunity for Shakespeare to write some of his 154 sonnets.

Connections: Sonnets 29 and 116 ■ *741*

TIME AND RESOURCE MANAGER | *from the* **Decameron**

Goal 2: INFORMATIONAL READING

IR.2.01.8 Make connections between works, self and related topics in research texts.

IR.2.01.10 Analyze the connections between ideas, concepts, characters and experiences in research.

Goal 4: CRITICAL THINKING

CT.4.03.1 Analyze how writers introduce and develop a main idea.

CT.4.05.11 Identify and analyze elements of critical environment.

Goal 5: LITERATURE

LT.5.03.8 Make connections between works, self and related topics in world literature.

Goal 6: GRAMMAR AND USAGE

GU.6.01.1 Employ varying sentence structures and sentence types.

GU.6.01.4 Use vocabulary strategies to determine meaning.

Step-by-Step Teaching Guide	Pacing Guide
PRETEACH	
• Administer Vocabulary and Reading Warm-ups as necessary.	5 min.
• Engage students' interest with the motivation activity.	5 min.
• Read and discuss author and background features. **FT**	10 min.
• Introduce the Literary Analysis Skill: Novella. **FT**	5 min.
• Introduce the Reading Strategy: Identifying with Characters. **FT**	10 min.
• Prepare students to read by teaching the selection vocabulary. **FT**	
TEACH	
• Informally monitor comprehension while students read independently or in groups. **FT**	30 min.
• Monitor students' comprehension with the Reading Check notes.	as students read
• Reinforce vocabulary with Vocabulary Builder notes.	as students read
• Develop students' understanding of the novella with the Literary Analysis annotations. **FT**	5 min.
• Develop students' ability to identify with characters with the Reading Strategy annotations. **FT**	5 min.
ASSESS/EXTEND	
• Assess students' comprehension and mastery of the Literary Analysis and Reading Strategy by having them answer the Apply the Skills questions. **FT**	15 min.
• Have students complete the Vocabulary Lesson and the Grammar and Style Lesson. **FT**	15 min.
• Apply students' ability to use relevant citations by using the Writing Lesson. **FT**	45 min. or homework
• Apply students' understanding by using one or more of the Extend Your Learning activities.	20–90 min. or homework
• Administer Selection Test A or Selection Test B. **FT**	15 min.

Resources

Print

Unit 6 Resources

Transparency

Graphic Organizer Transparencies

Print

Reader's Notebook [L2]

Reader's Notebook: Adapted Version [L1]

Reader's Notebook: English Learner's Version [EL]

Unit 6 Resources

Technology

Listening to Literature Audio CDs [L2, EL]

Reader's Notebook: Adapted Version Audio CD [L1, L2]

Print

Unit 6 Resources

General Resources

Technology

Go Online: Research [L3]

Go Online: Self-test [L3]

ExamView®, **Test Bank [L3]**

Choosing Resources for Differentiated Instruction

[L1] Special Needs Students

[L2] Below-Level Students

[L3] All Students

[L4] Advanced Students

[EL] English Learners

For Vocabulary and Reading Warm-ups and for Selection Tests, **A** signifies "less challenging" and **B** "more challenging." For Graphic Organizer transparencies, **A** signifies "not filled in" and **B** "filled in."

FT Fast Track Instruction: To move the lesson more quickly, use the strategies and activities identified with **FT**.

Scaffolding for Less Proficient and Advanced Students

The leveled Critical Thinking questions after selections progress in the levels of thinking required to answer them. To address the needs of your different students, you may use the (a) level questions for your less proficient students and the (b) level questions with your on-level and advanced students. The occasional (c) level questions are appropriate for your advanced students.

PRENTICE HALL

TeacherEXPRESS™ Use this complete
Plan · Teach · Assess suite of powerful
teaching tools to make lesson planning and testing quicker and easier.

PRENTICE HALL

StudentEXPRESS™ Use the interactive
Learn · Study · Succeed textbook (online
and on CD-ROM) to make selections and activities come alive with audio and video support and interactive questions.

 For: Information about Lexiles
Professional **Visit:** www.PHSchool.com
Development **Web Code:** eue-1111

Motivation

Ask students whether they own a particular object or pet that has great value to them. Have them consider under what circumstances, if any, they might part with it. Use the phrase "not for love or money" in the discussion to underscore the attachment people sometimes have for an object or animal. Tell students that they are about to read a story that deals with such a strong attachment.

❶ Background

More About the Author

The whole direction of Boccaccio's career changed as a result of his meeting with Petrarch. Boccaccio no longer wrote in Italian, with the exception of one late work, and he rejected imaginative writing in favor of humanist scholarship. Until the final years of his life, Petrarch was not even aware that his younger friend had once written in Italian a work called the *Decameron*.

Geography Note

Draw students' attention to the map on this page. Point out that although Boccaccio lived most of his life in Italy, he also spent about eight years living in Paris. During this time, he first became acquainted with Petrarch's poetry, which would strongly influence his work for the rest of his life.

from the Decameron ❶

Giovanni Boccaccio
(1313–1375)

Born in 1313, Giovanni Boccaccio [bô kä´ chō] was the illegitimate son of a Florentine merchant, an associate of a well-known banking family. His father sent him at the age of ten to work in one of his firm's banks in Naples. This southern Italian city was ruled by the Frenchman Robert of Anjou, whose court was known for its splendor and sophistication. As a member of the banking firm that lent this ruler money, Boccaccio was able to attend court functions, and he later remembered this period of his life as a time of happiness and pleasure.

Boccaccio's father encouraged his son to become a businessman and, later, a lawyer specializing in church law; Boccaccio showed little interest in either field. He did, however, begin to write while at the Neapolitan court, and he continued to write prolifically for the rest of his life. His early works, written mostly in Italian, include several long narratives. One of them, *Filocolo*, demonstrates Boccaccio's deep insights into human motives and behaviors.

A Wider Worldview In 1340, financial problems caused Boccaccio's family to recall him to Florence, and he had to leave behind the cultivated court that he loved. His letters suggest that the return to what seemed at first a petty, middle-class, money-grubbing environment was difficult. However, this change provided essential experience for the future author of the *Decameron*, a book dealing with all kinds and classes of people. As time passed, Boccaccio became more sympathetic to Florence and its citizens—he actively engaged in Florentine politics, serving as an ambassador to other countries.

Scholar and Poet In 1350, Boccaccio met the celebrated Italian poet Francesco Petrarch, the only contemporary whose gifts matched his own. This meeting was the start of a lifelong friendship. Boccaccio admired Petrarch greatly, and Petrarch's example encouraged Boccaccio in his own writings. Boccaccio produced a series of scholarly Latin works arising out of his vast reading in classical literature. In addition, with the help of a Greek collaborator, he produced the first European translation of Homer's works into Latin. He also wrote a biography of poet Dante Alighieri. In Boccaccio's last year, he began an important commentary on Dante's great work, the *Divine Comedy*.

Greatest Achievements Although Boccaccio was famous for his Latin works—and he would have regarded them as his greatest achievement—the *Decameron* is a collection of amusing and artful stories that reveal Boccaccio's impressive literary versatility. Far from being a musty old classic, the *Decameron* has delighted readers and inspired writers for half a millennium. Like many best-selling novels of our own time, it has been the inspiration for numerous full-length film adaptations.

The men and women who narrate the tales within the *Decameron* share the harrowing experience of escaping an outbreak of bubonic plague, similar to the 1348 epidemic that killed Boccaccio's parents as well as more than half of Florence's population. Framed by their medieval setting, the narratives in the *Decameron* feature a multitude of characters representing an array of social classes. Boccaccio explores deeply human themes of love, loss, deception, fortune, and more, creating a work of universality and timelessness.

742 ■ *The Renaissance and Rationalism*

Preview

Connecting to the Literature

Cherished items are keepsakes, objects you might not willingly give away. In Boccaccio's story, the main character's generous sacrifice of such an item may seem noble to some readers but very foolish to others.

❷ Literary Analysis

Novella

A **novella** is a short prose tale. First written as early as the fourteenth century, the novella influenced the later development of the novel and the modern short story. Boccaccio's *Decameron* is a group of one hundred novellas, including "Federigo's Falcon." Like other short prose stories, these novellas share the following elements:

- a setting
- well-developed characters
- a plot that includes the main events, conflicts, a climax or turning point in the story, and a final resolution
- a theme, or a message about life

Use a chart like the one shown to identify details of these elements in "Federigo's Falcon."

Connecting Literary Elements

Rather than tell his stories directly, Boccaccio creates a fictional background, or **frame,** surrounding the novellas of the *Decameron.* In the frame, ten young people leave Florence to escape the bubonic plague. To pass the time, they tell each other stories—including "Federigo's Falcon"—that fit within the shared frame. As you read, look for characters and dialogue from the frame and watch for the transition into the novella itself.

❸ Reading Strategy

Identifying with Characters

Identifying with characters helps you connect to your reading. To identify with characters, put yourself into a character's place and relate his or her thoughts, feelings, and experiences to your own life. Note each character's situations and choices and consider the ways you might act in similar circumstances.

Vocabulary Builder

courtly (kôrt´ lē) *adj.* dignified; polite; elegant (p. 745)

sumptuous (sump´ chōō əs) *adj.* costly; lavish (p. 745)

frugally (frōō´ gə lē) *adv.* thriftily; economically (p. 745)

deference (def´ ər əns) *n.* courteous regard or respect (p. 748)

affably (af´ ə blē) *adv.* in a friendly manner (p. 748)

impertinence (im pʉrt´ 'n əns) *n.* insolence; impudence (p. 748)

despondent (di spän´ dənt) *adj.* dejected; hopeless (p. 749)

NC	Standard Course of Study

- Analyze how writers introduce and develop a main idea. (CT.4.03.1)
- Make connections between works, self and related topics in world literature. (LT.5.03.8)

Novella "Federigo's Falcon"
Setting:
Characters:
Plot:
Theme:

from the *Decameron* ■ 743

❷ Literary Analysis

Novella

- Read aloud the characteristics of a novella. Explain that the novella was a precursor to the short story and the novel.
- Give students a copy of **Literary Analysis Graphic Organizer A,** p. 130 in *Graphic Organizer Transparencies.* Have them complete it as they read this selection.
- Read aloud the Connecting Literary Elements text. Ask students to describe what they know about the collection of tales *The Thousand and One Nights.* Tell students that these tales are part of a larger frame story. In it, a young woman named Scheherazade postpones her execution by entertaining the king with her clever tales every night for a thousand and one nights.
- Then, point out that the story of the ten young people is the frame for the *Decameron.*

❸ Reading Strategy

Identifying With Characters

- Explain to students that identifying with characters means understanding and sympathizing with how the characters act and feel. Identifying with characters helps readers better understand a story.
- Point out that the main character in this story goes to extremes to impress the woman he loves. Ask students to put themselves in his place as they read. Encourage them to imagine what it feels like to try very hard to impress a loved one.

Vocabulary Builder

- Pronounce each vocabulary word for students, and read the definitions as a class. Have students identify any words with which they are already familiar.

Differentiated Instruction   Solutions for All Learners

Support for Special Needs Students	Support for Less Proficient Readers	Support for English Learners
Have students read the adapted version of "Federigo's Falcon" from the *Decameron* in the *Reader's Notebook: Adapted Version.* This version provides basic-level instruction in an interactive format with questions and write-on lines. Completing these pages will prepare students to read the selection in the Student Edition.	Have students read "Federigo's Falcon" from the *Decameron* in the *Reader's Notebook.* This version provides basic-level instruction in an interactive format with questions and write-on lines. After students finish the selection in the *Reader's Notebook,* have them complete the questions and activities in the Student Edition.	Have students read "Federigo's Falcon" from the *Decameron* in the *Reader's Notebook: English Learner's Version.* This version provides basic-level instruction in an interactive format with questions and write-on lines. Completing these pages will prepare students to read the selection in the Student Edition.

Facilitate Understanding

Students should not have much difficulty with this story. In order to motivate their interest, however, you might ask them to do further research on falconry.

❶ About the Selection

In "Federigo's Falcon," Federigo is an aristocratic young man known for his deeds of chivalry. From the beginning, he is willing to give up all his wealth in an attempt to win his beloved, Monna Giovanna. When all of his money is spent, Federigo shows no sign of bitterness, and his final act of generosity epitomizes his unhesitating devotion to his love.

❷ Critical Viewing

Possible response: A sharp beak and powerful claws enable falcons to capture quarry.

❸ Literary Analysis

Novella and Frame

• Read aloud the Background information. Emphasize that the "king" or "queen" presides over the storytelling.

• Then, have students independently read the bracketed passage. **Ask** them to identify the characters mentioned in the first paragraph of the story.
Answer: Three characters are mentioned: Filomena, the queen, and Dioneo.

• **Ask** students the Literary Analysis question: Which character from the frame is the narrator of the novella?
Answer: The queen is the narrator.

• **Ask** students what might be an advantage of having a frame story.
Possible response: A frame story allows a writer to weave a number of different stories into one long grouping.

from the
Decameron ❶
Giovanni Boccaccio

translated by G. H. McWilliam

Background In the *Decameron*, a group of ten young aristocrats—seven women and three men—take up residence at a country estate to wait out an outbreak of the plague. To entertain themselves, each of them tells one story a day for ten days—hence, the name *Decameron*, which means "ten days." Each day, they elect a "king" or "queen" from among their number to preside over the day's storytelling. "Federigo's Falcon" is told on the fifth day.

❷ ▲ Critical Viewing
What physical attributes enable falcons, like this one, to find and capture quarry such as rabbits and game birds? **[Analyze]**

Federigo's Falcon

❸ Once Filomena had finished, the queen, finding that there was no one left to speak apart from herself (Dioneo being excluded from the reckoning because of his privilege), smiled cheerfully and said:

It is now my own turn to address you, and I shall gladly do so, dearest ladies, with a story similar in some respects to the one we have just heard. This I have chosen, not only to acquaint you with the power of your beauty over men of noble spirit, but so that you may learn to choose for yourselves, whenever necessary, the persons on whom to bestow your largesse,[1] instead of always leaving these matters to be decided for you by Fortune, who, as it happens, nearly always scatters her gifts with more abundance than discretion.

You are to know, then, that Coppo di Borghese Domenichi, who once used to live in our city and possibly lives there still, one of the most highly respected men of our century, a person worthy of eternal fame, who achieved his position of pre-eminence by dint of his character and abilities rather than by his noble lineage, frequently took pleasure

Literary Analysis
Novella and Frame Which character from the frame is the narrator of the novella?

---

1. **largesse** (lär jes′) *n.* generous gifts.

744 ■ *The Renaissance and Rationalism*

Differentiated
Instruction   Solutions for All Learners

Accessibility at a Glance

	Federigo's Falcon
Context	Young Italian aristocrats escape the plague in a country estate where they entertain one another with stories.
Language	Syntax: long sentences with embedded clauses; challenging Italian names
Concept Level	Accessible (Good things can happen even after great loss.)
Literary Merit	Classic frame story that explores universal human themes
Lexile	1510L
Overall Rating	Challenging

during his declining years in discussing incidents from the past with his neighbors and other folk. In this pastime he excelled all others, for he was more coherent, possessed a superior memory, and spoke with greater eloquence. He had a fine repertoire, including a tale he frequently told concerning a young Florentine called Federigo, the son of Messer Filippo Alberighi, who for his deeds of chivalry and <u>courtly</u> manners was more highly spoken of than any other squire in Tuscany. In the manner of most young men of gentle breeding, Federigo lost his heart to a noble lady, whose name was Monna[2] Giovanna, and who in her time was considered one of the loveliest and most adorable women to be found in Florence. And with the object of winning her love, he rode at the ring, tilted, gave <u>sumptuous</u> banquets, and distributed a large number of gifts, spending money without any restraint whatsoever. But since she was no less chaste than she was fair, the lady took no notice, either of the things that were done in her honor, or of the person who did them.

In this way, spending far more than he could afford and deriving no profit in return, Federigo lost his entire fortune (as can easily happen) and reduced himself to poverty, being left with nothing other than a tiny little farm, which produced an income just sufficient for him to live very <u>frugally</u>, and one falcon of the finest breed in the whole world. Since he was as deeply in love as ever, and felt unable to go on living the sort of life in Florence to which he aspired, he moved out to Campi, where his little farm happened to be situated. Having settled in the country, he went hunting as often as possible with his falcon, and, without seeking assistance from anyone, he patiently resigned himself to a life of poverty.

Now one day, while Federigo was living in these straitened circumstances, the husband of Monna Giovanna happened to fall ill, and, realizing that he was about to die, he drew up his will. He was a very rich man, and in his will he left everything to his son, who was just growing up, further stipulating that, if his son should die without legitimate issue, his estate should go to Monna Giovanna, to whom he had always been deeply devoted.

Shortly afterward he died, leaving Monna Giovanna a widow, and every summer, in accordance with Florentine custom, she went away with her son to a country estate of theirs, which was very near Federigo's farm. Consequently this young lad of hers happened to become friendly with Federigo, acquiring a passion for birds and dogs; and, having often

2. **Monna** Lady.

8 Critical Viewing ▶ In what ways might this portrait be an accurate representation of Federigo? **[Analyze]**

Vocabulary Builder
courtly (kôrt′ lē) *adj.* dignified; polite; elegant

sumptuous (sump′ chōō əs) *adj.* costly; lavish

Literary Analysis
Novella Identify the setting of the novella.

Vocabulary Builder
frugally (frōō′ gə lē) *adv.* thriftily; economically

✔**Reading Check** **6**

What remains of Federigo's fortune after pursuing Monna Giovanna's affection?

7

Robert Cheseman, Hans Holbein the Younger, Scala

from the *Decameron* ■ 745

4 **Literary Analysis**
Novella
- Review with students the characteristics of the novella on p. 743.
- Ask a volunteer to read aloud the bracketed passage. Then, **ask** students to respond to the Literary Analysis item: Identify the setting of the novella.
Answer: The story is set in Florence and in Campi, where Federigo's farm is located.

5 **Reading Strategy**
Identifying With Characters
- **Ask** students how Federigo expresses his feelings about Monna Giovanna.
Answer: Federigo expresses his love by participating in tournaments, giving lavish banquets, spending money, and giving out gifts.
- **Ask** students: Can you identify with Federigo's futile efforts to win Monna Giovanna's heart? Why or why not?
Possible response: Some readers may identify with Federigo because they have tried to win someone's attention; others may not identify with Federigo, saying that he is foolish.

6 **Reading Check**
Answer: Federigo is left with a small farm and a falcon.

7 **Humanities**
Robert Cheseman,
by Hans Holbein the Younger
Holbein (c. 1498–1543) is considered one of the finest portrait painters of all time. In 1536, he became the court artist of King Henry VIII. Holbein's portraits of the royalty and nobility of England convey the flavor of court life.

Use the following question for discussion:
What does this portrait suggest about Cheseman?
Possible response: Cheseman appears to be a serious aristocrat with a passion for falconry.

8 **Critical Viewing**
Possible response: Like Cheseman, Federigo cherishes his falcon.

745

Identifying With Characters

- Have students independently read the bracketed passage. Then, ask whether any students have ever been seriously ill. Ask what their parents or caretakers did—or were willing to do—to help them feel better.

- Remind students that to identify with a character, they should relate the character's thoughts and feelings to their own experiences.

- **Ask** the Reading Strategy question: What might you be willing to do if you were in Monna Giovanna's place?
  Possible response: Most students will say that they would do anything to save the life of their child.

▶ **Reteach** To assist students in their efforts to identify with characters, use **Reading Strategy** support, p. 26 in *Unit 6 Resources*.

10 Humanities

Departure for the Hunt

Tapestry is a decorative fabric made by creating a design or picture through the process of weaving. Traditionally, tapestries were hung, often in sets, as decorative items on interior walls of homes or churches.

The art of tapestry flourished in Europe in the Middle Ages. During the sixteenth century, tapestries—such as the one shown here—changed to reflect the influence of Italian Renaissance art.

Use the following questions for discussion:

- Where are the events in this tapestry taking place?
  Answer: The events are taking place just outside the city.

- What are some of the small details in the foreground of this tapestry?
  Answer: Some small details of the tapestry include the birds, the dog, and the small flowers and plants.

11 Critical Viewing

Possible response: The tapestry depicts a story about young noblemen preparing to go on a hunt.

---

seen Federigo's falcon in flight, he became fascinated by it and longed to own it, but since he could see that Federigo was deeply attached to the bird, he never ventured to ask him for it.

And there the matter rested, when, to the consternation of his mother, the boy happened to be taken ill. Being her only child, he was the apple of his mother's eye, and she sat beside his bed the whole day long, never ceasing to comfort him. Every so often she asked him whether there was anything he wanted, imploring him to tell her what it was, because if it was possible to acquire it, she would move heaven and earth to obtain it for him.

After hearing this offer repeated for the umpteenth time, the boy said:

"Mother, if you could arrange for me to have Federigo's falcon, I believe I should soon get better."

On hearing this request, the lady was somewhat taken aback, and began to consider what she could do about it. Knowing that Federigo had been in love with her for a long time, and that she had never deigned to cast so much as a single glance in his direction, she said to herself: "How can I possibly go to him, or even send anyone, to ask him for this falcon, which to judge from all I have heard is the finest that ever flew, as well as being the only thing that keeps him alive? And how can I be so heartless as to deprive so noble a man of his one remaining pleasure?"

Departure for the Hunt, 16th century, Réunion des Musées Nationaux, Paris

746 ■ *The Renaissance and Rationalism*

Reading Strategy
Identifying With Characters What might you be willing to do if you were in Monna Giovanna's place?

11
◀ **Critical Viewing**
Medieval and Renaissance tapestries, like the one shown, often tell stories or depict specific events. What detailed story might this tapestry narrate?
[Speculate]

Enrichment

The Black Plague
The frame story of the *Decameron* is centered on young people who are fleeing the plague. In the introduction to the *Decameron,* Boccaccio describes the terrible plague, which probably killed a third of the population of Western Europe. In 1348, says Boccaccio, "the deadly plague broke out in the great city of Florence, . . ." The disease was called the Black Plague or Black Death, but we know it as the bubonic plague. Those afflicted with the disease were covered with swellings that grew to "the size of a common apple or egg."

Soon, those swellings gave way to "black or livid spots appearing on the arms, thighs, and the whole person." Few of the sick recovered; most died after the third day. The plague caused severe social breakdown. According to Boccaccio, "The calamity had instilled such horror into the hearts of men and women that . . . parents avoided visiting or nursing their very children, as though these were not their own flesh. . . ."

Her mind filled with reflections of this sort, she remained silent, not knowing what answer to make to her son's request, even though she was quite certain that the falcon was hers for the asking.

At length, however, her maternal instincts gained the upper hand, and she resolved, come what may, to satisfy the child by going in person to Federigo to collect the bird, and bring it back to him. And so she replied:

"Bear up, my son, and see whether you can start feeling any better. I give you my word that I shall go and fetch it for you first thing tomorrow morning."

Next morning, taking another lady with her for company,[3] his mother left the house as though intending to go for a walk, made her way to Federigo's little cottage, and asked to see him. For several days, the weather had been unsuitable for hawking, so Federigo was attending to one or two little jobs in his garden, and when he heard, to his utter astonishment, that Monna Giovanna was at the front door and wished to speak to him, he happily rushed there to greet her.

When she saw him coming, she advanced with womanly grace to meet him. Federigo received her with a deep bow, whereupon she said:

"Greetings, Federigo!" Then she continued: "I have come to make amends for the harm you have suffered on my account, by loving me more than you ought to have done. As a token of my esteem, I should like to take breakfast with you this morning, together with my companion here, but you must not put yourself to any trouble."

"My lady," replied Federigo in all humility, "I cannot recall ever having suffered any harm on your account. On the contrary I have gained so much that if ever I attained any kind of excellence, it was entirely because of your own great worth and the love I bore you. Moreover I can assure you that this visit which you have been generous enough to pay me is worth more to me than all the money I ever possessed, though I fear that my hospitality will not amount to very much."

So saying, he led her unassumingly into the house, and thence into his garden, where, since there was no one else he could call upon to chaperon her, he said:

"My lady, as there is nobody else available, this good woman, who is the wife of the farmer here, will keep you company whilst I go and see about setting the table."

Though his poverty was acute, the extent to which he had squandered his wealth had not yet been fully borne home to Federigo; but on this particular morning, finding that he had nothing to set before the lady for whose love he had entertained so lavishly in the past, his eyes were well and truly opened to the fact. Distressed beyond all measure, he silently cursed his bad luck and rushed all over the house like one possessed, but could find no trace of either money or valuables. By now the morning was well advanced, he was still

---

3. **taking . . . company** A young woman of the upper classes would not go out by herself.

Literary Analysis
Novella What fear motivates Monna Giovanna to ask Federigo for the falcon?

Reading Check

What does Monna Giovanna seek for her son?

Novella

• Have a volunteer read aloud the last paragraph on the previous page. **Ask** students to summarize the conflict that Monna Giovanna is experiencing.
  Answer: Monna Giovanna knows that Federigo will give her the falcon, but she fears that it will cause him great suffering to do so. She knows that she has no right to make the request but also believes that the health of her son hinges on whether he gets the falcon.

• Have a volunteer read aloud the rest of the bracketed passage. Then, **ask** the Literary Analysis question: What fear motivates Monna Giovanna to ask Federigo for the falcon?
  Answer: Monna Giovanna is motivated by the fear of losing her son.

⑬ **Reading Strategy**
Identifying With Characters

• Discuss with students Federigo's attitude toward Monna Giovanna revealed in the bracketed passage.

• **Ask** students: Can you identify with Federigo's feelings here? Why or why not?
  Possible response: Some readers may say that they can identify with Federigo and his pleasure at having the woman he loves finally take notice of him; others may say that they cannot identify with his feelings because they would probably feel angry or resentful toward her.

⑭ **Background**
Federigo's Generosity

This story is very much concerned with the aristocratic virtue of generosity. From the beginning, Federigo, known for his deeds of chivalry, is willing to give up all his wealth for Monna Giovanna. His lavishness has a positive side because it is part of a larger kind of generosity. Federigo is someone who holds back nothing. He "loses his heart" to the lady, and his subsequent actions simply elaborate this openness of spirit.

⑮ **Reading Check**
Answer: Monna Giovanna seeks Federigo's falcon for her son.

Differentiated
Instruction Solutions for All Learners

Enrichment for Advanced Readers
Tell students that Boccaccio lived at the beginning of the Italian Renaissance, a historical period of cultural rebirth and flowering that spanned from about 1340 to about 1550. During the Italian Renaissance, literature, art, and architecture flourished. The city of Florence, where the character of Federigo originally lived, was the center of the Renaissance during this period.

Have students research and prepare a multimedia report on the Italian Renaissance. Encourage them to focus on one element, such as art or architecture, or on one individual, such as Leonardo da Vinci, Michelangelo, or the architect Filippo Brunelleschi.

Have students present their reports to the class, displaying photocopies or sketches of paintings, sculpture, or architecture.

- Read aloud the bracketed passage.
- Then, **ask** students the Literary Analysis question: What does the phrase "without thinking twice" reveal about Federigo's character? **Answer:** The phrase reveals that Federigo is very generous.

▶ **Monitor Progress** Review with students the elements of a novella listed on p. 743. Have them give an example from "Federigo's Falcon" of each of the elements (with the exception of the theme).

17 **Vocabulary Builder**

Latin Suffix -ence

- Call students' attention to the word *deference,* its definition, and its use in the story. Explain that the Latin suffix -ence means "quality of" or "state of being."
- Tell students that they can change an adjective that ends in -ent to a noun by changing the word's suffix to -ence. Have students **brainstorm** for examples of these words. **Answer:** *Absence* and *silence* are possible suggestions.

18 **Humanities**

Girl at the Window,
by Nicolaes Maes

Nicolaes Maes (1634–1693) studied under Rembrandt, the great Dutch master. After Maes established his own studio, he turned to painting domestic scenes, primarily of women spinning or cooking.

Use the following question for discussion:

What is the effect of Maes's emphasis on the young woman's face and hands? **Possible response:** The emphasis draws the viewer's attention to the thoughtful look on the woman's face.

19 **Critical Viewing**

Possible response: The woman's pensive expression illustrates Monna Giovanna's dilemma.

determined to entertain the gentlewoman to some sort of meal, and, not wishing to beg assistance from his own farmer (or from anyone else, for that matter), his gaze alighted on his precious falcon, which was sitting on its perch in the little room where it was kept. And having discovered, on picking it up, that it was nice and plump, he decided that since he had nowhere else to turn, it would make a worthy dish for such a lady as this. So without thinking twice about it he wrung the bird's neck and promptly handed it over to his housekeeper to be plucked, dressed, and roasted carefully on a spit. Then he covered the table with spotless linen, of which he still had a certain amount in his possession, and returned in high spirits to the garden, where he announced to his lady that the meal, such as he had been able to prepare, was now ready.

The lady and her companion rose from where they were sitting and made their way to the table. And together with Federigo, who waited on them with the utmost <u>deference</u>, they made a meal of the prize falcon without knowing what they were eating.

On leaving the table they engaged their host in pleasant conversation for a while, and when the lady thought it time to broach the subject she had gone there to discuss, she turned to Federigo and addressed him <u>affably</u> as follows:

"I do not doubt for a moment, Federigo, that you will be astonished at my <u>impertinence</u> when you discover my principal reason for coming here, especially when you recall your former mode of living and my virtue, which you possibly mistook for harshness and cruelty. But if you had ever had any children to make you appreciate the power of parental love, I should think it certain that you would to some extent forgive me.

"However, the fact that you have no children of your own does not exempt me, a mother, from the laws common to all other mothers. And being bound to obey those laws, I am forced, contrary to my own wishes and to all the rules of decorum and propriety, to ask you for something to which I know you are very deeply attached—which is only natural, seeing that it is the only consolation, the only pleasure, the only recreation remaining to you in your present extremity of fortune. The gift I am seeking is your falcon, to which my son has taken so powerful a liking, that if I fail to take it to him I fear he will succumb to the illness from which he is suffering, and consequently I shall lose him. In imploring you to give me this falcon, I appeal, not to your love, for you are under no obligation to me on that account, but rather to your noble heart, whereby you have proved yourself superior to all others in the practice of courtesy. Do me this favor, then, so that I may claim that through your generosity I have saved my son's life, thus placing him forever in your debt."

Literary Analysis
Novella What does the phrase "without thinking twice" reveal about Federigo's character?

Vocabulary Builder
deference (def′ ər əns) *n.* courteous regard or respect
affably (af′ ə blē) *adv.* in a friendly manner
impertinence (im pʉrt′ 'n əns) *n.* insolence; impudence

19 ▼ **Critical Viewing** Which details from "Federigo's Falcon" are aptly represented in this painting? Explain. **[Interpret]**

Falconry
In Boccaccio's story, Federigo is extremely attached to his pet falcon. The sport of falconry was popular among the nobility in medieval and Renaissance Europe. (Actually, it was developed in ancient China, Persia, and Egypt and came to Western Europe by way of Eastern Europe.) This sport used falcons to hunt small birds. Peregrine falcons were taken from the nest when quite young and subjected to a rigorous course of training so that they would respond to the falconer's calls and perch quietly on the falconer's wrist when they were hooded. They were also trained to leave their prey untouched after it was killed.

Although falconry was often associated with the aristocracy, people in the lower classes also engaged in the sport for purposes of feeding their families. By the seventeenth century, people had developed faster and more efficient ways of obtaining food, and, as a result, falconry declined in popularity.

When he heard what it was that she wanted, and realized that he could not oblige her because he had given her the falcon to eat, Federigo burst into tears in her presence before being able to utter a single word in reply. At first the lady thought his tears stemmed more from his grief at having to part with his fine falcon than from any other motive, and was on the point of telling him that she would prefer not to have it. But on second thoughts she said nothing, and waited for Federigo to stop crying and give her his answer, which eventually he did.

"My lady," he said, "ever since God decreed that you should become the object of my love, I have repeatedly had cause to complain of Fortune's hostility towards me. But all her previous blows were slight by comparison with the one she has dealt me now. Nor shall I ever be able to forgive her, when I reflect that you have come to my poor dwelling, which you never deigned to visit when it was rich, and that you desire from me a trifling favor which she has made it impossible for me to concede. The reason is simple, and I shall explain it in few words.

"When you did me the kindness of telling me that you wished to breakfast with me, I considered it right and proper, having regard to your excellence and merit, to do everything within my power to prepare a more sumptuous dish than those I would offer to my ordinary guests. My thoughts therefore turned to the falcon you have asked me for and, knowing its quality, I reputed it a worthy dish to set before you. So I had it roasted and served to you on the trencher this morning, and I could not have wished for a better way of disposing of it. But now that I discover that you wanted it in a different form, I am so distressed by my inability to grant your request that I shall never forgive myself for as long as I live."

In confirmation of his words, Federigo caused the feathers, talons and beak to be cast on the table before her. On seeing and hearing all this, the lady reproached him at first for killing so fine a falcon, and serving it up for a woman to eat; but then she became lost in admiration for his magnanimity[4] of spirit, which no amount of poverty had managed to diminish, nor ever would. But now that her hopes of obtaining the falcon had vanished she began to feel seriously concerned for the health of her son, and after thanking Federigo for his hospitality and good intentions, she took her leave of him, looking all <u>despondent</u>, and returned to the child. And to his mother's indescribable sorrow, within the space of a few days, whether through his disappointment in not being able to have the falcon, or because he

---

4. **magnanimity** (mag´ nə nim´ ə tē) *n.* noble generosity.

Themes in World Masterpieces

Boccaccio's Influence on Geoffrey Chaucer

Boccaccio's *Decameron* became a model for many subsequent writers. The English poet Geoffrey Chaucer (1340?–1400) made use of this narrative model to write *The Canterbury Tales.*

Chaucer's frame features twenty-nine pilgrims who embark on a pilgrimage to the cathedral at Canterbury, England. To pass the time, the pilgrims agree to a storytelling contest in which each traveler tells two tales along the way to Canterbury and two more tales on the return journey. The winner will receive a free dinner at the Tabard Inn upon return. Like Boccaccio's *Decameron, The Canterbury Tales* features richly developed characters whose flaws and strengths make them very human.

Connect to the Literature

List two or three characteristics of Federigo that make him seem very human.

Literary Analysis
Novella In what way is Monna Giovanna's visit a deeply bittersweet occasion for Federigo?

Vocabulary Builder
despondent (di spän´ dent) *adj.* dejected; hopeless

 **Reading Check**

What emotional response does Federigo have to Monna Giovanna's request?

from the *Decameron* ■ 749

---

⑳ Literary Analysis
Novella
• Allow time for students to read the bracketed passage.
• Discuss with them the irony of the situation in which Federigo finds himself: He freely sacrifices his falcon to serve Monna Giovanna, only to learn that it is the one thing that she asks of him.
• **Ask** students the Literary Analysis question: In what way is Monna Giovanna's visit a deeply bittersweet occasion for Federigo?
Answer: Federigo still loves Monna Giovanna, so her visit brings him great happiness; however, this feeling is tempered by the knowledge that he has sacrificed the falcon that she wanted for her son.

㉑ Themes in World Literature
Boccaccio's Influence on Geoffrey Chaucer Like Boccaccio, Geoffrey Chaucer borrows from other sources for his *Canterbury Tales.* In fact, one of his stories in the collection, the "Knight's Tale," is adapted from Boccaccio's epic story of the Greek hero Theseus.

Chaucer develops his frame story more fully than does Boccaccio. Chaucer describes the pilgrims gathering at the Tabard Inn and agreeing to tell the stories. Most of the framework stories reflect the characters who tell them. For example, one of the pilgrims is a nun who tells a story about a saint.

Connect to the Literature Point out to students that Chaucer's frame characters—the pilgrims who narrate the tales—are developed in far more detail than are Boccaccio's characters. When Chaucer introduces these characters, he gives details about their appearance, personalities, and private lives. Some of the characters in the frames are more memorable than the characters in the framework stories themselves. Ask students to share their ideas on the qualities that make Federigo so real and appealing.
Possible responses: He is generous, hospitable, gracious, and thoughtful, and he has a close relationship with his pet falcon.

㉒ Reading Check
Answer: Federigo bursts into tears.

Infer

- Have students read the bracketed passage and note the comments that Monna Giovanna makes about marrying Federigo.

- **Ask** students: Do you think that Monna Giovanna loves Federigo? Explain.
Possible response: Although Monna Giovanna admires Federigo, she does not love him because she says that she would rather remain a widow.

ASSESS

Answers

1. **Possible responses:** Federigo was noble in so generously giving up all that he had without a thought for material goods; on the other hand he was foolish to impoverish himself without receiving any benefit from his generosity.

2. (a) Federigo spends all of his money on lavish banquets and expensive gifts, and he participates in tournaments. (b) Because of the customs of the time, it was considered unladylike to be influenced by such displays of affection.

3. (a) Federigo bows graciously; he makes sure that Monna Giovanna is comfortably seated, and he arranges for someone to be with her while he prepares the meal; he sacrifices his most precious possession for her meal. (b) Federigo is generous, thoughtful, and courteous. (c) **Possible response:** Monna Giovanna may have expected Federigo to be angry or hostile because he was impoverished by trying to win her love.

4. (a) At first, Monna Giovanna scolds Federigo for serving a fine bird as food, but then she admires his generosity. (b) She is kind, gracious, and noble.

5. **Possible response:** Young women are not compelled to ignore suitors today; young men usually do not expend so much effort to win the favor of a woman. Love is based on nobility of character, not current notions of romantic love.

750

---

was in any case suffering from a mortal illness, the child passed from this life.

After a period of bitter mourning and continued weeping, the lady was repeatedly urged by her brothers to remarry, since not only had she been left a vast fortune but she was still a young woman. And though she would have preferred to remain a widow, they gave her so little peace that in the end, recalling Federigo's high merits and his latest act of generosity, namely to have killed such a fine falcon in her honor, she said to her brothers:

"If only it were pleasing to you, I should willingly remain as I am; but since you are so eager for me to take a husband, you may be certain that I shall never marry any other man except Federigo degli Alberighi."

Her brothers made fun of her, saying:

"Silly girl, don't talk such nonsense! How can you marry a man who hasn't a penny with which to bless himself?"

"My brothers," she replied, "I am well aware of that. But I would sooner have a gentleman without riches, than riches without a gentleman."

Seeing that her mind was made up, and knowing Federigo to be a gentleman of great merit even though he was poor, her brothers fell in with her wishes and handed her over to him, along with her immense fortune. Thenceforth, finding himself married to this great lady with whom he was so deeply in love, and very rich into the bargain, Federigo managed his affairs more prudently, and lived with her in happiness to the end of his days.

Critical Reading

1. **Respond:** Do you think Federigo was noble or misguided in serving up the falcon? Explain.

2. **(a) Recall:** What early efforts does Federigo make to win Monna Giovanna's love? **(b) Infer:** What does the narrator mean when she says Monna Giovanna's chastity compelled her to take no notice of Federigo?

3. **(a) Recall:** What gestures of hospitality does Federigo make when Monna Giovanna visits? **(b) Connect:** In what ways do his efforts reflect his former life as a wealthy gentleman? **(c) Speculate:** Do you think Monna Giovanna expected such behavior from him? Why or why not?

4. **(a) Recall:** How does Monna Giovanna respond to the news of the falcon's death? **(b) Infer:** What does her response indicate about her character?

5. **Apply:** In what ways do the ideals of love expressed in this story differ from current notions of romantic love?

Go Online
Author Link
For: More about Giovanni Boccaccio
Visit: www.PHSchool.com
Web Code: ete-9603

Go Online For additional information about
Author Link Giovanni Boccaccio, have students type in the Web Code, then select *B* from the alphabet, and then select Giovanni Boccaccio.

Apply the Skills

from the *Decameron*

Literary Analysis

Novella

1. Do you think "Federigo's Falcon" contains all the elements of a **novella**? Why or why not?

2. How does the setting reflect Federigo's change of fortune?

3. What lesson about loss and restoration does this story teach? Use details from the tale to support your answer.

Connecting Literary Elements

4. **(a)** In the *Decameron*'s **frame,** what does the queen claim her story teaches? **(b)** Which details in the novella might her listening audience relate to their own lives? Explain.

5. **(a)** Who is Coppo di Borghese Domenichi? **(b)** What credibility does he add to the novella and its narrator?

Reading Strategy

Identifying With Characters

6. Using a chart like the one shown, choose two events involving Federigo and two involving Monna Giovanna. Then, **identifying with each character,** explain what your reaction might be if you experienced similar events.

	Their Experiences	**My Reactions**
Federigo	1. 2.	
Monna Giovanna	1. 2.	

7. **(a)** For which character do you feel the most sympathy? **(b)** In what way does identifying with the character influence your ability to sympathize? Explain.

Extend Understanding

8. **Cultural Connection:** What can you infer from the characters' behavior about love, marriage, and the status of women during this period? Explain.

QuickReview

A **novella** is a short prose tale.

A **frame** is a unifying background that links together a series of stories.

When you **identify with characters,** you relate to their thoughts and feelings and connect them to your own experiences.

Go Online
Assessment
For: Self-test
Visit: www.PHSchool.com
Web Code: eta-6602

from the *Decameron* ■ *751*

Answers continued

8. **Possible response:** Men idolized women. Women were expected to marry.

Go Online
Assessment Students may use the **Self-test** to prepare for **Selection Test A** or **Selection Test B.**

Answers

❶ Vocabulary Lesson

**Word Analysis:
Latin Suffix -ence**

1. turbulence
2. insistence
3. munificence

Spelling Strategy

1. affably
2. gently
3. sparkly

**Vocabulary Builder:
Synonym or Antonym?**

1. A   4. S   6. S
2. S   5. A   7. A
3. A

❷ Grammar and Style Lesson

1. <u>At his shocking request,</u> she gasped. (prepositional phrase)
2. <u>Shortly afterward,</u> he died, leaving Monna Giovanna a widow. (transition)
3. <u>When she saw him coming,</u> she advanced with womanly grace to meet him. (dependent clause)
4. <u>As a token of his esteem,</u> he took breakfast with her. (prepositional phrase)
5. <u>After dinner,</u> they had a pleasant conversation. (prepositional phrase)

Writing Application

Possible response: <u>Because we have become friends,</u> I would like to issue an invitation. (dependent clause) <u>Although I seldom celebrate my birthday,</u> I am having a party this year. (dependent clause) <u>In spite of the weather,</u> I am planning a picnic. (prepositional phrase) <u>Of course,</u> I know that you don't usually like picnics, but I think you'll enjoy this one. (transition)

Build Language Skills

❶ Vocabulary Lesson

Word Analysis: Latin Suffix -ence

The Latin suffix *-ence* means "quality of" or "state of being." To change an adjective ending in *-ent* to a noun, replace the *-ent* suffix with *-ence*. For example, the adjective *impertinent*, meaning "insolent or impudent," becomes *impertinence*, meaning "the quality of being impertinent."

Change the following adjectives to nouns by replacing the suffix *-ent* with *-ence*.

1. turbulent   2. insistent   3. munificent

Spelling Strategy

Many words end in an unstressed syllable spelled with a consonant + *-le*, as in *remarkable*. To add *-ly*, drop the *-le*: *remarkable* becomes *remarkably*. Rewrite these words, adding *-ly*.

1. affable   2. gentle   3. sparkle

Vocabulary Builder: Synonym or Antonym?

Review the vocabulary words on page 743 and notice the use of the words in context in the selections. Then, for each pair of words below, write *S* for *synonym* if the words have similar meanings or *A* for *antonym* if they have opposite meanings.

1. courtly, impolite
2. sumptuous, expensive
3. frugally, lavishly
4. deference, respect
5. affably, nastily
6. impertinence, rudeness
7. despondent, cheerful

❷ Grammar and Style Lesson

Varying Sentence Beginnings

By **varying sentence beginnings,** an author adds interest to the text and helps avoid repetition. In addition to starting sentences with a subject, writers can vary sentence beginnings by using prepositional phrases, transitions, or dependent clauses.

> **Prepositional Phrase:** *In due time,* Federigo lost his heart to a noble lady.
>
> **Transition:** *Now one day . . .* the husband of Monna Giovanna happened to fall ill.
>
> **Dependent Clause:** *Though his poverty was acute,* the extent of it was yet unknown.

Practice Revise the following sentences so they begin with a prepositional phrase, a transition, or a dependent clause. Underline your new sentence beginnings and identify each by type.

1. She gasped at his shocking request.
2. He died leaving Monna Giovanna a widow shortly afterward.
3. She advanced with womanly grace to meet him when she saw him coming.
4. He took breakfast with her as a token of his esteem.
5. They had a pleasant conversation after dinner.

Writing Application Write a short letter of invitation. Use a variety of sentence beginnings, underlining each and identifying its type.

W͏G Prentice Hall Writing and Grammar Connection: Platinum Level, Chapter 21, Section 3

Assessment Practice

Evaluate and Make Judgments   (For more practice, see *Test Preparation Workbook*, p. 33)

Standardized tests often require students to make judgments based on a passage. Use the following sample test item to help students practice this skill.

> Knowing that Federigo had been in love with her for a long time, and that she had never deigned to cast so much as a single glance in his direction, she said to herself: "How can I possibly . . . ask him for this falcon, which . . . is the finest that ever flew, as well as being the only thing that keeps him alive?"

Which of the following is the best description of the speaker in this passage?

A She is arrogant.
B She is cruel and heartless.
C She is kind and thoughtful.
D She is indifferent.

A, B, and *D* are incorrect because the speaker expresses concern about Federigo. *C* is the best answer.

❸ Writing Lesson

Timed Writing: Literary Analysis

One theme, or universal message, in "Federigo's Falcon" is that people should preserve their nobility of spirit at all costs. Write an essay supporting this theme, or choose a different one and defend its presence in the novella. *(40 minutes)*

Prewriting
(10 minutes)
Begin by explaining the theme you have chosen and the ways in which it relates to readers today. Reread the story, listing points and specific quotations that support your idea.

Drafting
(20 minutes)
In your introduction, include a statement of the theme and its meaning. Then, in the body of your essay, identify specific details from the novella and explain how each example supports your point.

Revising
(10 minutes)
Revise your draft to include enough evidence to defend your main point. Consider strengthening your point by adding relevant citations.

Model: Using Relevant Citations

Federigo shows remarkable nobility of spirit as he faces his dwindling wealth. He never complains about sacrificing his fortune in vain. ʌ *As the narrator describes, "he patiently resigned himself to a life of poverty."*

> One effective way to cite details from a literary work is to use a direct quotation.

𝒲𝒢 *Prentice Hall Writing and Grammar Connection: Platinum Level, Chapter 13, Section 3*

❹ Extend Your Learning

Listening and Speaking With a small group, organize a **storytelling circle.** Choose a central idea, such as generosity, love, or trickery. Have each group member create a story exemplifying this idea. Use the following tips as you prepare:

- Choose events that illustrate the theme.
- Add details to the story to make it vivid.
- Consider exaggerating the details to make your point more strongly.

Take turns telling your stories to the class. Then, invite the class to identify the central theme. **[Group Activity]**

Research and Technology Use library and Internet resources to research falconry. Find images from both Boccaccio's time and the present that show how falcons are handled and how they are used to hunt. Create a **classroom display** that compares or contrasts the use of falconry through the centuries, including captions that explain each image. Share your display with the class.

Go Online
Research
For: An additional research activity
Visit: www.PHSchool.com
Web Code: etd-7602

from the *Decameron* ■ 753

---

❸ Writing Lesson

You may use this Writing Lesson as a timed-writing practice, or you may allow students to develop the analytical essay as a writing assignment over several days.

- To give students guidance in writing this essay, give them the **Support for Writing Lesson**, p. 29 in *Unit 6 Resources.*

- Read aloud the Writing Lesson instruction. Remind students that a literary analysis closely examines and evaluates something specific in a literary work.

- Explain that a story can have more than one theme. Encourage students to think about a lesson or message from the story of Federigo.

- Use the Response to Literature rubrics in *General Resources,* pp. 55–56, to evaluate students' essays.

𝒲𝒢 **Writing and Grammar**
Platinum Level
For support in teaching the Writing Lesson, use Chapter 13, Section 3.

❹ Research and Technology

- Read aloud the Research and Technology instruction.

- Encourage students to brainstorm topics they want to cover in their classroom display. Then, organize students into small groups. Assign each group a particular topic to research.

- After the classroom display is completed, have each group present a report on their particular topic.

- Use the Research: Research Report rubrics in *General Resources,* pp. 51–52, to evaluate students' reports.

- The **Support for Extend Your Learning** page (*Unit 6 Resources,* p. 30) provides guided note-taking opportunities to help students complete the Extend Your Learning activities.

Go Online
Research
Have students type in the Web Code for another research activity.

Assessment Resources

The following resources can be used to assess students' knowledge and skills.

Unit 6 Resources
Selection Test A, pp. 32–34
Selection Test B, pp. 35–37

General Resources
Rubrics for Response to Literature, pp. 55–56
Rubrics for Research: Research Report, pp. 51–52

Go Online
Assessment
Students may use the **Self-test** to prepare for **Selection Test A** or **Selection Test B.**

Standard Course of Study

Goal 1: WRITTEN LANGUAGE

WL.1.02.1 Relate personal knowledge to textual information in a written reflection.

WL.1.03.4 Demonstrate comprehension of main idea and supporting details in personal reflection.

WL.1.03.11 Identify and analyze elements of expressive environment in personal reflections.

Goal 4: CRITICAL THINKING

CT.4.01.3 Distinguish fact from fiction and recognize personal bias in interpretation.

CT.4.03.4 Analyze how writers use effective word choice as a basis for coherence.

Goal 5: LITERATURE

LT.5.03.7 Analyze influences, contexts, or biases in world literature.

Goal 6: GRAMMAR AND USAGE

GU.6.01.4 Use vocabulary strategies to determine meaning.

Step-by-Step Teaching Guide	Pacing Guide	
PRETEACH		
• Administer Vocabulary and Reading Warm-ups as necessary.	5 min.	
• Engage students' interest with the motivation activity.	5 min.	
• Read and discuss author and background features. **FT**	10 min.	
• Introduce the Literary Analysis Skill: Narrative Accounts. **FT**	5 min.	
• Introduce the Reading Strategy: Breaking Down Long Sentences. **FT**	10 min.	
• Prepare students to read by teaching the selection vocabulary. **FT**		
TEACH		
• Informally monitor comprehension while students read independently or in groups. **FT**	30 min.	
• Monitor students' comprehension with the Reading Check notes.	as students read	
• Reinforce vocabulary with Vocabulary Builder notes.	as students read	
• Develop students' understanding of narrative accounts with the Literary Analysis annotations. **FT**	5 min.	
• Develop students' ability to break down long sentences with the Reading Strategy annotations. **FT**	5 min.	
ASSESS/EXTEND		
• Assess students' comprehension and mastery of the Literary Analysis and Reading Strategy by having them answer the Apply the Skills questions. **FT**	15 min.	
• Have students complete the Vocabulary Lesson and the Grammar and Style Lesson. **FT**	15 min.	
• Apply students' ability to revise with vivid words by using the Writing Lesson. **FT**	45 min. or homework	
• Apply students' understanding using one or more of the Extend Your Learning activities.	20–90 min. or homework	
• Administer Selection Test A or Selection Test B. **FT**	15 min.	

Resources

Print

Unit 6 Resources

Transparency

Graphic Organizer Transparencies

Technology

Print

Reader's Notebook [L2]

Reader's Notebook: Adapted Version [L1]

Reader's Notebook: English Learner's Version [EL]

Unit 6 Resources

Technology

Listening to Literature Audio CDs [L2, EL]

Reader's Notebook: Adapted Version Audio CD [L1, L2]

Print

Unit 6 Resources

General Resources

Technology

Go Online: Research [L3]

Go Online: Self-test [L3]

ExamView®, **Test Bank [L3]**

Choosing Resources for Differentiated Instruction

[**L1**] Special Needs Students

[**L2**] Below-Level Students

[**L3**] All Students

[**L4**] Advanced Students

[**EL**] English Learners

For Vocabulary and Reading Warm-ups and for Selection Tests, **A** signifies "less challenging" and **B** "more challenging." For Graphic Organizer transparencies, **A** signifies "not filled in" and **B** "filled in."

FT Fast Track Instruction: To move the lesson more quickly, use the strategies and activities identified with **FT**.

Scaffolding for Less Proficient and Advanced Students

The leveled Critical Thinking questions after selections progress in the levels of thinking required to answer them. To address the needs of your different students, you may use the (a) level questions for your less proficient students and the (b) level questions with your on-level and advanced students. The occasional (c) level questions are appropriate for your advanced students.

PRENTICE HALL

TeacherEXPRESS™ Use this complete

Plan · Teach · Assess   suite of powerful

teaching tools to make lesson planning and testing quicker and easier.

PRENTICE HALL

StudentEXPRESS™ Use the interactive

Learn · Study · Succeed   textbook (online

and on CD-ROM) to make selections and activities come alive with audio and video support and interactive questions.

 **For:** Information about Lexiles
Professional   **Visit:** www.PHSchool.com
Development   **Web Code:** eue-1111

- You might wish to have students read João Magueijo's introduction to the unit on pages 714–715.

- Show Segment 2 on João Magueijo on *From the Author's Desk DVD* to provide insight into Galileo and his impact on modern science. After students have watched the segment, **ask:** How was Galileo an important scientific figure to Magueijo?
Answer: Galileo was considered a heretic and a troublemaker, much as Magueijo is considered a trouble-maker today for his bold ideas.

The Anarchy of Science

- After students have read Magueijo's comments on these pages, have a student summarize the varying speed of light theory. Then **ask:** What was the reaction to the theory?
Answer: The scientific community was upset, and the press called his group the "punk rockers of physics."

- Point out to students that the nature of science requires that science be always in a state of change and uncertainty. Have students name contemporary changes in scientific views, such as improvements in cures for diseases and discoveries in space.

🐧 From the Scholar's Desk

JOÃO MAGUEIJO INTRODUCES
from "Astronomical Messages" and
from The Assayer *by Galileo Galilei*

João Magueijo

João Magueijo is an author and physicist whose theories challenge those of scientist Albert Einstein. In 2000, Magueijo appeared in the British television documentary "Einstein's Biggest Blunder." He currently teaches theoretical physics at Imperial College in London.

Challenging Einstein

A few years ago a group of physicists, including myself, came up with an idea that unceremoniously contradicted Albert Einstein's theory of relativity. We suggested that the speed of light might vary rather than be the constant of nature that provides the solid framework of Einstein's theory. Our proposal envisaged that such variations can only occur under very extreme circumstances—such as the flash at the beginning of the Universe (the so-called Big Bang), or the vicinity of cosmic black holes. VERY extreme circumstances. We never entertained the notion that the great Albert is wrong altogether—merely that his theory might show its limitations by fraying around the edges when things get too hot.

The Anarchy of Science Nevertheless our theory—the varying speed of light theory—caused consternation in part of the scientific community. The press reaction was even more dramatic. We were labeled—I quote—"the punk rockers of physics." I have to admit that I'm not offended by this description. Indeed it's not even completely incorrect. You may think that anarchy plays no role in science; but that's because . . . well, let me break the news to you—that's because the real world of science is not limited to what you've been taught in school. Science in the making is a world of chaos and uncertainty. It's a mad game of hit and miss, a continuous struggle against what has been said before. In this process scientists behave emotionally and irrationally, like grown-up kids. It's all most unbecoming. I chronicled this process, in reference to "the punk rockers of physics," in my book *Faster Than the Speed of Light*. But the story of this process is far from new. It's also the story of how past physicists were led to their own theories.

▶ **Critical Viewing** How might you describe Albert Einstein's character based solely on this photograph of him? **[Speculate]**

Teaching Resources

The following resources can be used to enrich or extend the instruction for From the Scholar's Desk.

Unit 6 Resources
　　Support for Penguin Essay, p. 38
　　Listening and Viewing, p. 39
From the Author's Desk DVD
　　João Magueijo, Segment 2

Discovering the Rules of Nature Science is always the result of an argumentative and emotional process in which whenever you propose something new, everyone thinks you've gone out of your mind. What distinguishes the scientific search for novelty, however, is that the scientist is ultimately humbled by Nature. At the end of the day, if experiments show that a groundbreaking new idea is wrong, then the game is over. Scientists have to accept defeat gracefully. They can't take themselves too seriously. This attitude was present right at the start of modern science, when Galileo rejected authority as a criterion for truth. He unveiled a new world because he had the guts to question what he'd been taught. Perhaps the best introduction to this idea is the fairy tale you're about to read in "The Assayer." In Galileo's time it was still considered respectable for a scientist to explain his views by means of fairy tales. Galileo's tale, these days, might get him labeled a punk rocker of science, too.

▶ **Critical Viewing** In what ways has the science of flu prevention changed or remained the same since this ad was run in 1918? **[Compare and Contrast]**

Thinking About the Commentary

1. **(a) Recall:** What is the idea behind the theory that Magueijo and his fellow physicists developed? **(b) Compare and Contrast:** What is the primary difference between Magueijo's theory and Einstein's? **(c) Infer:** Why might the scientific community be shocked by a challenge to Einstein's theroies?

2. **(a) Recall:** According to Magueijo, what response do many scientists receive when they propose new ideas? **(b) Draw Conclusions:** Besides humility, what qualities must scientists possess to manage both the discovery process and the criticism they may receive along the way? **(c) Make a Judgment:** Would you enjoy a career in science? Why or why not?

As You Read from "Astronomical Messages" and from The Assayer . . .

3. Consider ways in which Galileo struggled with the same scientific processes identified by Magueijo.

4. Be ready to explain how Galileo was a "punk rocker" in his own day.

Discovering the Rules of Nature

- **Ask:** What quality must good scientists have when testing a new theory?
  Answer: Good scientists must be humble; they must be willing to accept defeat gracefully and not take themselves too seriously.

ASSESS

Answers

1. (a) The idea behind Magueijo and his fellow physicists' theory is that the speed of light might vary under extreme circumstances. (b) While Magueijo and his fellow physicists believe that the speed of light might vary under extreme conditions, Einstein's theory claims that the speed of light is constant. (c) **Possible response:** Because Einstein's theory has been accepted as a basic tenet of physics, many people believe that it cannot be challenged.

2. (a) Scientists who propose new ideas are sometimes said to have gone out of their minds. (b) Besides humility, scientists must not take themselves too seriously and must be willing to experiment until they prove or disprove their theories. (c) **Possible response:** Students may say that they would enjoy a career in science because they like to test theories and work math problems.

3. **Possible response:** Magueijo received criticism for challenging Einstein's theory of relativity, which has great weight among scientists. In a similar way, Galileo received criticism for challenging the view that prevailed at the time about the revolution of the sun and its planets.

4. **Possible response:** Galileo could be considered a "punk rocker" in his day because, like what a punk rocker is known for doing, Galileo challenged authority, and his actions upset many people.

Motivation

Although Galileo's brilliance was noted early in his life, his scientific theories contradicted common belief, and he was eventually forced to renounce his own beliefs. Today we widely accept many of Galileo's theories, but he did not receive the acclaim he deserved in his own time. Ask students to explain the disadvantages of being the first to disprove what everyone has always believed true. Then have students discuss why people are often unwilling to accept new ideas.

❶ Background

More About the Author

When Galileo first learned of the instrument "that showed distant things as though they were nearby," he discerned how to make his own three-powered instrument. Galileo learned how to grind lenses so that he could increase the strength of his telescopes. Soon he was using 20 power telescopes and saw that Saturn looked different from the other planets, a phenomenon which was later discovered to be caused by rings. He learned that Venus has phases like the moon and revolves around the sun. In 1630, he discovered sunspots, which contradicted the belief that the sun was perfect.

from Starry Messenger: *from* Astronomical Message • *from* The Assayer ❶

Galileo Galilei
(1564–1642)

As a sixteenth-century philosopher, mathematician, and astronomer, Galileo Gallilei insisted that the proper language of science was mathematics and that the experimental method was the key to unlocking nature's secrets. These fundamental features of scientific study have remained constant over the past 400 years.

Early Life and Career Beginnings Born in Pisa in northern Italy, Galileo was the oldest son of a musician who shared with his son a curiosity about science. According to tradition, father and son may have performed some experiments on the connection between the tension of the strings of musical instruments and the pitch, or sounds, that the strings make. After attending the University of Pisa, where he shifted his studies from medicine to mathematics, Galileo became a private tutor for a few years in his early twenties. At the age of twenty-five, he took a professorship at the University of Pisa. In some of his important early experiments, conducted at the famous Leaning Tower of Pisa, Galileo demonstrated that the speed of a heavy falling object is not necessarily proportional to its weight. By challenging theories held for centuries, Galileo increased his reputation for brilliance. Discoveries like these, however, would make him a controversial figure both during his lifetime and later.

A Momentous Turn In his middle years, Galileo continued his studies on motion. He discovered the Law of Falling Bodies, which states that falling objects will accelerate at the same, constant rate as a result of gravity. He also demonstrated that the trajectory of a projectile—for example, a cannon ball—will always follow the same path, a geometric form called a parabola.

In the spring of 1609, momentous news of a new invention in Holland attracted Galileo's attention: a telescope, possibly first constructed by spectacle maker Hans Lippershey. Swiftly analyzing the instrument's design, Galileo constructed his own telescopes and demonstrated one of them to the Venetian Senate. The officials were so impressed that they gave him life tenure at the University of Pisa.

With increasingly powerful telescopes, Galileo discovered the craters of the moon's surface and four satellites on Jupiter. Galileo described his observations in a book entitled *Starry Messenger*, which he dedicated to Cosimo de Medici, the Grand Duke of Florence. Galileo was promptly rewarded with an appointment as mathematician and philosopher to the court.

Troubles With the Church Galileo was soon convinced that the Polish astronomer Nicolaus Copernicus (1473–1543) had been right: Earth revolves around the sun. While this truth seems self-evident today, Copernicus's theory was extremely controversial in Galileo's day. By 1613, Galileo had to confront questions from the office of the Inquisition in Rome. Two years later, Church authorities denounced the Copernican theory as heresy, and Copernicus's book was officially banned.

Over the next twenty years, Galileo and the Church authorities settled into an uneasy standoff. In his book *The Assayer* (1623), Galileo boldly described the new approach to science as a mathematical, objective enterprise. In 1632, he published his *Dialogue Concerning the Two Chief World Systems,* in which he championed Copernicus's theory. Summoned to Rome, Galileo was condemned to life imprisonment on suspicion of heresy. He was forced to renounce publicly his own scientific proofs and beliefs.

Galileo refused to be broken by this setback, however. For his ten remaining years, he continued to experiment and write on the sciences of motion.

Preview

Connecting to the Literature

In this age of modern technology, it is easy to take for granted the scientific advances that led to space exploration and travel. Centuries before any person could walk on the moon, however, one man saw its craters for the very first time.

❷ Literary Analysis

Narrative Accounts

A **narrative account** tells the story of real-life events and is usually written in prose. Typically, narrative accounts use the first-person point of view and focus on personal experience. In addition to their literary qualities, many narrative accounts are useful to historians and other researchers as primary or secondary sources. Because of the writer's firsthand involvement, however, these works are sometimes subjective, or limited by the feelings and experiences of the writer. As you read, notice clues in Galileo's writing that convey the thrill of discovery and his personal investment in his work.

Connecting Literary Elements

Narrative Style

Narrative accounts are often shaped in important ways by features of **narrative style**, or the distinctive ways in which an author chooses to tell his or her story.

- *Diction,* or word choice, and *syntax,* or word order, give a narrative account its unique flavor and tone.
- *Examples* of different types may affect the reader's response.
- *Sentence structure* may shape the total effect of a narrative account.

As you read Galileo's accounts, note both the content of his ideas and the narrative style he used.

❸ Reading Strategy

Breaking Down Long Sentences

You can analyze meaning by **breaking down long sentences** and considering one section at a time. Separate a sentence's key parts (the *who* and the *what*) from the difficult language to get to the main idea. Use a diagram like the one shown to analyze long sentences.

Vocabulary Builder

manifest (man´ ə fest) *adj.* clear; evident (p. 760)

conspicuous (kən spik´ yoo əs) *adj.* easy to see or perceive (p. 760)

multitude (mul´ tə tood) *n.* a great number (p. 762)

impelled (im peld´) *v. used here as adj.* pushed or driven forward (p. 762)

derive (di riv´) *v.* to get or receive from a source (p. 763)

diffidence (dif´ ə dəns) *n.* lack of confidence in oneself (p. 764)

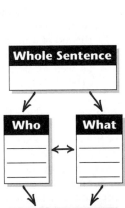

from *The Starry Messenger*/from *The Assayer* ■ 757

Standard Course of Study

- Identify and analyze elements of expressive environment in personal reflections. (WL.1.03.11)
- Distinguish fact from fiction and recognize personal bias in interpretation. (CT.4.01.3)

❷ Literary Analysis
Narrative Accounts

- Have a volunteer read aloud the instructions about narrative accounts. **Ask** students: How are narrative accounts affected by the writer's firsthand involvement? **Answer:** Narrative accounts are sometimes limited because they are subjective, or limited by the feelings or experiences of the writer.

- As they read each selection, have students look for the feelings and experiences of the writer that help the reader to feel what the writer has experienced. Point out that Galileo's writing shows the excitement that he felt as he discovered new things.

❸ Reading Strategy
Breaking Down Long Sentences

- Explain to students that this section contains selections with long sentences. Tell students that breaking down long sentences can help them understand these sentences.

- Point out the graphic organizer on this page. Write this sentence on the board: *Great indeed are the things which in this brief treatise I propose for observation and consideration by all students of nature.* **Ask** students to break this sentence down into the who, what, and central point. **Answer:** The *who* is things; the *what* is great; The *central point* is this: The things he wants people to look at and think about are great.

- Give students a copy of the **Reading Strategy Graphic Organizer A,** p. 134 in *Graphic Organizer Transparencies.* As they read the selections, remind students to break down the long, difficult sentences by analyzing them.

Vocabulary Builder

- Pronounce each vocabulary word for students, and read the definitions as a class. Have students identify any words with which they are already familiar.

❶ About the Selection

In this selection, Galileo describes his discovery of the surface of the moon and the nature of the Milky Way. He tells of learning about the telescope and of his excitement upon seeing celestial objects closer than ever before.

❷ Literary Analysis

Narrative Accounts

- Review with students the points of view an author can use: first person, limited third person, and omniscient.

- Have a volunteer read aloud the first paragraph. Then, **ask** students the Literary Analysis question: What point of view does Galileo use as he sets out to tell his story?
Answer: Galileo uses first person point of view.

❸ Reading Strategy

**Breaking Down
Long Sentences**

- Then **ask** the Reading Strategy question: What is the author's main idea in the sentence that begins, "Surely it is a great thing. . ."?
Answer: It is great to increase the number of stars people can see.

from
The Starry Messenger
Galileo Galilei
translated by Stillman Drake

❶

Background The astronomical discoveries that Galileo describes in his book *The Starry Messenger* were landmarks in the scientific revolution of the Renaissance. They confirmed the truth of the highly contested Copernican theory that the Earth revolves around the sun. Until Copernicus's time, two or three generations before Galileo, scientists believed in a cosmological assumption that dated back to the philosopher Aristotle (384–322 B.C.). According to this theory, all of the celestial bodies, including the sun, revolved around a motionless Earth, which was located at the center of the universe. With the help of a groundbreaking device called a telescope, Galileo and the scientific world stepped into the future of cosmology.

from ASTRONOMICAL MESSAGE,
Which contains and explains recent observations made with the aid of a new spyglass concerning the surface of the moon, the Milky Way, nebulous stars, and innumerable fixed stars, as well as four planets never before seen, and now named THE MEDICEAN STARS

❷   Great indeed are the things which in this brief treatise I propose for observation and consideration by all students of nature. I say great, because of the excellence of the subject itself, the entirely unexpected and novel character of these things, and finally because of the instrument by means of which they have been revealed to our senses.

❸   Surely it is a great thing to increase the numerous host of fixed stars previously visible to the unaided vision, adding countless more which have never before been seen, exposing these plainly to the eye in numbers ten times exceeding the old and familiar stars.

❹ ▶ **Critical Viewing** Use details from this image to defend Galileo's premise that a glance at the moon is "a great thing." **[Defend]**

Literary Analysis
Narrative Accounts
What point of view does Galileo use as he sets out to tell his story?

Reading Strategy
Breaking Down Long Sentences What is the author's main idea in the sentence that begins, "Surely it is a great thing . . . "?

758 ■ The Renaissance and Rationalism

from *Starry Messenger* 759

④ Critical Viewing

Possible Response: For Galileo, the chance to see the moon in greater detail is a great improvement in our understanding of its nature. This image of the moon reveals craters and mountains.

Differentiated Instruction   Solutions for All Learners

Support for English Learners
To help students break down and understand this selection, provide students with pictures of the solar system with labels for the planets, the moon, and the Milky Way. These may be available in their science books. As students read the selection, have them refer as necessary to the pictures to help them visualize what Galileo is describing. Point out that before the invention of the telescope, all of the universe was only visible through the naked eye.

Strategy for Advanced Learners
Have students research to find the diameter of Earth and calculate the moon's distance from Earth as Galileo estimated it. Then have students compare their naked eye view of the moon with telescopic photographs of the moon from the Internet or their science book and describe the differences. Have students write a paragraph, describing why many people of Galileo's time could not believe Galileo's observations and conclusions.

❺ Author's Insight

- **Ask:** What does the word *snipe* mean?
  Answer: *Snipe* means an attack.

- **Ask:** Why might Galileo use a snipe in his writings?
  Answer: He was pointing out to those who opposed his views another instance of their faulty views.

❻ Critical Viewing

Possible response: The telescope may not look advanced now, but at the time it was the newest development. It appears less significant to us because we have seen newer technology.

❼ Reading Strategy

Breaking Down Long Sentences

- Read aloud the sentence that begins, "Like Venus and Mercury."

- Then, **ask** students to respond to the Reading Strategy prompt: Identify the main subject and main verb of the sentence beginning, "Of this truly remarkable event . . ."
  Answer: Main subject: experiences; **Main verb:** were related

It is a very beautiful thing, and most gratifying to the sight to behold the body of the moon, distant from us almost sixty earthly radii, as if it were no farther away than two such measures—so that its diameter appears almost thirty times larger, its surface nearly nine hundred times, and its volume twenty-seven thousand times as large as when viewed with the naked eye. In this way one may learn with all the certainty of sense evidence that the moon is not robed in a smooth and polished surface but is in fact rough and uneven, covered everywhere, just like the earth's surface, with huge prominences, deep valleys, and chasms.

Again, it seems to me a matter of no small importance to have ended the dispute about the Milky Way by making its nature <u>manifest</u> to the very senses as well as to the intellect. Similarly it will be a pleasant and elegant thing to demonstrate that the nature of those stars which astronomers have previously called "nebulous" is far different from what has been believed hitherto. But what surpasses all wonders by far, and what particularly moves us to seek the attention of all astronomers and philosophers, is the discovery of four wandering stars not known or observed by any man before us. Like Venus and Mercury, which have their own periods about the sun, these have theirs about a certain star that is <u>conspicuous</u> among those already known, which they sometimes precede and sometimes follow, without ever departing from it beyond certain limits. All these facts were discovered and observed by me not many days ago with the aid of a spyglass which I devised, after first being illuminated by divine grace. Perhaps other things, still more remarkable, will in time be discovered by me or by other observers with the aid of such an instrument, the form and construction of which I shall first briefly explain, as well as the occasion of its having been devised. Afterwards I shall relate the story of the observations I have made.

About ten months ago a report reached my ears that a certain Fleming[1] had constructed a spyglass by means of which visible objects, though very distant from the eye of the observer, were distinctly seen as if nearby. Of this truly remarkable effect several experiences were related, to which some persons gave credence while others denied them. A few days later the report was confirmed to me in a letter from a noble Frenchman at Paris, Jacques Badovere, which caused me to apply myself wholeheartedly to inquire into the means by which I might arrive at the invention of a similar instrument. This I did shortly afterwards, my basis being the theory of refraction.[2] First I prepared a tube of lead, at the ends of which I fitted two glass lenses, both plane

---

1. **Fleming** Most likely Hans Lippershey, who patented a telescope in 1608.
2. **refraction** (ri frak′ shən) *n.* the bending of a ray of light as it passes through various mediums.

João Magueijo **Scholar's Insight** This is a snipe at the classical notion that the celestial objects are perfect, with all coarseness and roughness reserved for the Earth.

Vocabulary Builder **manifest** (man′ə fest) *adj.* clear, evident

Vocabulary Builder **conspicuous** (kən spik′ yōō əs) *adj.* easy to see or perceive

❻ ▲ Critical Viewing Do you think Galileo's telescope looks like a significant scientific advancement? Why or why not? **[Evaluate]**

Reading Strategy **Breaking Down Long Sentences** Identify the main subject and main verb of the sentence beginning, "Of this truly remarkable event . . ."

◄ **Critical Viewing ⑧**
What similarities exist
between Galileo's work
and that of the scientists
who operate modern
telescopes like the one
pictured here? **[Compare]**

on one side while on the other side one was spherically convex and the
other concave. Then placing my eye near the concave lens I perceived
objects satisfactorily large and near, for they appeared three times
closer and nine times larger than when seen with the naked eye alone.
Next I constructed another one, more accurate, which represented
objects as enlarged more than sixty times. Finally, sparing neither
labor nor expense, I succeeded in constructing for myself so excellent
an instrument that objects seen by means of it appeared nearly one
thousand times larger and over thirty times closer than when regarded
with our natural vision. . . .

⑨

⑩

Literary Analysis
Narrative Accounts and
Narrative Style What
transition words does the
writer use in this passage
to indicate time order?

João Magueijo
Author's Insight
To this day, the
repeatability of an
experiment and its
independent verification
by others are central
criteria in science.

from *Starry Messenger* ■ 761

⑧ Critical Viewing

Possible response: Galileo used
special tools to learn about the
cosmos, just as scientists do today.

⑨ Literary Analysis

Narrative Accounts and Narrative Style

• Review transition words with
students.

• **Ask** the Literary Analysis question:
What transition words does the
writer use in this passage to indicate
time order?
Answer: Transition words used
include *a few days later, shortly afterwards, first, then, next,* and *finally.*

⑩ Author's Insight

• Ask a volunteer to read the Author's
Insight. **Ask:** Why is it important
that a scientific experiment be done
by various scientists and give the
same result?
Possible response: If a scientific
experiment does not give the same
result regardless of who performs it,
the conclusions are questionable.

⓫ About the Selection

In this fable, Galileo relates the tale of a man who was sure that the source for all music was birds. As he traveled, he discovered more sources for song than he had imagined. He then became cautious about claiming much knowledge about the sources of songs. The point is that the more a person knows about a topic, the less willing the person is to pass judgment about anything new.

⓬ Literary Analysis

Narrative Accounts and Narrative Style

• Point out that authors can use different narrative styles within a narrative account.

• **Ask** students to respond to the Literary Analysis prompt: Identify two changes in Galileo's narrative style as he begins the second paragraph.
Answer: Galileo changes from first person to third person narration and moves from personal narrative to fiction, with the phrase "Once upon a time."

⓭ Reading Strategy

Breaking Down Long Sentences

• **Ask** students to respond to the Reading Strategy prompt: List the order of events in the last sentence of this paragraph.
Answer: He raised birds, he enjoyed their songs, and he observed how they sang.

from *The Assayer* ⓫
Galileo Galilei
translated by Stillman Drake

Long experience has taught me this about the status of mankind with regard to matters requiring thought: the less people know and understand about them, the more positively they attempt to argue concerning them, while on the other hand to know and understand a <u>multitude</u> of things renders men cautious in passing judgment upon anything new.

⓬ Once upon a time, in a very lonely place, there lived a man endowed by nature with extraordinary curiosity and a very penetrating mind. For a pastime he raised birds, whose songs he much enjoyed; and he observed with great admiration the happy contrivance by which they could transform at will the very air they breathed into a variety of sweet songs.

One night this man chanced to hear a delicate song close to his house, and being unable to connect it with anything but some small bird he set out to capture it. When he arrived at a road he found a shepherd boy who was blowing into a kind of hollow stick while moving his fingers about on the wood, thus drawing from it a variety of notes similar to those of a bird, though by quite a different method. Puzzled, but <u>impelled</u> by his natural curiosity, he gave the boy a calf in exchange for this flute and returned to solitude. But realizing that if he had not chanced to meet the boy he would never have learned of the existence ⓭ of a new method of forming musical notes and the sweetest songs, he decided to travel to distant places in the hope of meeting with some new adventure.

Vocabulary Builder
multitude (mul′ te tōōd) *n.* a great number

impelled (im peld′) *adj.* pushed or driven forward

Literary Analysis
Narrative Accounts and Narrative Style Identify two changes in Galileo's narrative style as he begins the second paragraph.

Reading Strategy
Breaking Down Long Sentences List the order of events in the last sentence of this paragraph.

Enrichment

Cicadas

Cicadas, medium to large insects that can range from 0.8 to two inches long, have two sets of wings. Cicadas that live in North America usually make rhythmical ticks or buzz or whine. About 1,500 species of cicadas exist, and some appear in hordes on a seventeen-year cycle. Male cicadas make three different sounds. These sounds can be influenced by weather and other males' songs, can be mating songs, and can indicate that the cicada has been captured or forced into flight. Vibrating membranes on the abdomen generate the sounds.

In various cultures cicadas serve as an ingredient in folk medicine, as a food source, and as monetary exchange. In China male cicadas were placed in cages and held for their songs.

The very next day he happened to pass by a small hut within which he heard similar tones; and in order to see whether this was a flute or a bird he went inside. There he found a small boy who was holding a bow in his right hand and sawing upon some fibers stretched over a hollowed piece of wood. The left hand supported the instrument, and the fingers of the boy were moving so that he drew from this a variety of notes, and most melodious ones too, without any blowing. Now you who participate in this man's thoughts and share his curiosity may judge of his astonishment. Yet finding himself now to have two unanticipated ways of producing notes and melodies, he began to perceive that still others might exist.

His amazement was increased when upon entering a temple he heard a sound, and upon looking behind the gates discovered that this had come from the hinges and fastenings as he opened it. Another time, led by curiosity, he entered an inn expecting to see someone lightly bowing the strings of a violin, and instead he saw a man rubbing his fingertip around the rim of a goblet and drawing forth a pleasant tone from that. Then he observed that wasps, mosquitoes, and flies do not form single notes by breathing, as did the birds, but produce their steady sounds by swift beating of their wings. And as his wonder grew, his conviction proportionately diminished that he knew how sounds were produced; nor would all his previous experiences have sufficed to teach him or even allow him to believe that crickets <u>derive</u> their sweet and sonorous shrilling by scraping their wings together, particularly as they cannot fly at all.

Well, after this man had come to believe that no more ways of forming tones could possibly exist—after having observed, in addition to all the things already mentioned, a variety of organs, trumpets, fifes, stringed instruments, and even that little tongue of iron which is placed between the teeth and which makes strange use of the oral cavity for sounding box and of the breath for vehicle of sound[3]—when, I say, this man believed he had seen everything, he suddenly found himself once more plunged deeper into ignorance and bafflement than ever. For having captured in his hands a cicada, he failed to diminish its strident noise either by closing its mouth or stopping its wings, yet he could not see it move the scales that covered its body, or any other thing. At last he lifted up the armor of its chest and there he saw some thin hard ligaments beneath; thinking the sound might come from their vibration, he decided to break them in order to silence it. But nothing happened until his needle drove too deep, and transfixing the creature he took away its life with its voice, so that he was still unable

---

3. **tongue . . . sound** Galileo describes an instrument called a jew's harp, in which a small metal frame held between the teeth is played by plucking a projecting metal piece with the thumb.

Literary Analysis
Narrative Accounts and Narrative Style
What examples in this paragraph support the main character's investigation?

Vocabulary Builder
derive (di riv´) v. to get or receive from a source

Reading Strategy
Breaking Down Long Sentences What is the central point of the long sentence that begins, "Well, after the man . . ."?

✓**Reading Check** ⑯
What instrument prompted the man to seek out more unusual sounds?

⑭ **Literary Analysis**
Narrative Accounts and Narrative Style

• Point out that the use of examples is important in building a narrative account.

• **Ask:** What is the main character investigating in this paragraph?
Answer: The main character is traveling to another place to investigate the source of a song not produced by his birds.

• **Ask** the Literary Analysis question: What examples in this paragraph support the main character's investigation?
Answer: The examples include the violin, the squeaking hinges, and the insects.

⑮ **Reading Strategy**
Breaking Down Long Sentences

• Ask a student volunteer to read the first sentence of the paragraph beginning, "Well, after this. . . ."

• **Ask:** What is the purpose of the information between the dashes?
Answer: The information between the dashes lists the types of musical instruments he had observed.

• Have students read the last part of the sentence. Then **ask** the Reading Strategy question: What is the central point of the long sentence that begins, "Well, after this man . . ."?
Answer: When the man thought he had seen everything, he was suddenly more confused than ever.

⑯ **Reading Check**
Answer: The violin sparked his interest.

Differentiated
Instruction   **Solutions for All Learners**

Strategy for Less Proficient Learners
To help students understand the last sentence in the second paragraph on p. 762, ask students to list the first action in the sentence: *he raised birds.* Then have students continue through the sentence, listing the actions. Provide students with dictionaries to check the meanings of unfamiliar words. Then have students write a summary of the sentence and a way in which humans can transform the air they breathe into song.

Strategy for English Learners
Have students read the last sentence in the second paragraph on p. 762. Ask students to write down any unfamiliar words and use their dictionaries to find the meanings. Clarify words as necessary. Have students break the sentence into a series of simple sentences. Then have students **explain** the meaning of the sentence.
Answer: The man raised birds, enjoyed their songs, and was intrigued by their ability to sing.

- Have a student volunteer read the Author's Insight.
- **Ask** students what they think the author means by this statement. **Possible response:** Students may say that the nature of the world unfolds as people discover new information. What may seem true today may be proved wrong tomorrow.

ASSESS

Answers

1. Students may respond that "Astronomical Message" conveys the excitement of scientific discovery because it shows how Galileo worked to develop the telescope. Others may choose the fable because it concretizes the search for knowledge.

2. (a) Galileo claims that the spyglass has enabled him to observe the surface of the moon, the Milky Way, nebulous stars, innumerable fixed stars, and four planets never seen before. (b) Most students will believe his claim because people now know that his claim is accurate.

3. (a) A report that a certain Fleming had constructed a spyglass that allowed him to see distant objects more distinctly motivated Galileo to build a telescope. (b) He may have wanted to make an even better telescope to outdo the Fleming and to see more, or to see how much he could see.

4. (a) Galileo characterizes the man as having extraordinary curiosity and a penetrating mind. (b) His decision to travel to distant lands displays his curiosity.

5. (a) He hears a man rubbing his fingertip around the rim of a goblet. (b) He learns that his wonder is undermining his conviction about his own knowledge. (c) Scientists have learned not to be satisfied with what they know but to try to learn and understand more, as they realize that there is always more to know.

6. Galileo draws a parallel between the man and his own situation by saying that if the man realized that he could not know everything about the source of music, Galileo should not be upset, as nature can create things that we cannot even begin to imagine.

764

---

to determine whether the song had originated in those ligaments. And by this experience his knowledge was reduced to <u>diffidence</u>, so that when asked how sounds were created he used to answer tolerantly that although he knew a few ways, he was sure that many more existed which were not only unknown but unimaginable.

I could illustrate with many more examples Nature's bounty in producing her effects, as she employs means we could never think of without our senses and our experiences to teach them to us—and sometimes even these are insufficient to remedy our lack of understanding. So I should not be condemned for being unable to ❶ determine precisely the way in which comets are produced, especially in view of the fact that I have never boasted that I could do this, knowing that they may originate in some manner that is far beyond our power of imagination. The difficulty of comprehending how the cicada forms its song even when we have it singing to us right in our hands ought to be more than enough to excuse us for not knowing how comets are formed at such immense distances. . . .

Critical Reading

1. **Respond:** Which essay better conveys to you the excitement of scientific discovery? Explain.

2. **(a) Recall:** In the opening paragraph of "Astronomical Message," what claim does Galileo make for the subject of his "brief treatise"? **(b) Evaluate:** Do you think his claim is exaggerated? Why or why not?

3. **(a) Recall:** According to "Astronomical Message," what report motivated Galileo to build a "spyglass," or telescope? **(b) Speculate:** What relationship might exist between the report and Galileo's excitement as he built a series of ever more powerful telescopes?

4. **(a) Recall:** How does Galileo characterize the man in the fable within *The Assayer?* **(b) Analyze:** In what ways does the man's decision to travel to distant places support this characterization?

5. **(a) Recall:** In *The Assayer,* what sound does the narrator hear at the inn that surprises him? **(b) Interpret:** After his visits to the temple and the inn, what does the man learn about the relationship between his wonder and his conviction about his own knowledge? **(c) Generalize:** How might this relationship apply more generally to the growth of knowledge in science?

6. **Analyze:** According to the final paragraph in *The Assayer,* what parallel does Galileo draw between the situation of the man in the fable and his own situation?

7. **Speculate:** Both the man in the fable and Galileo seem humbled by their inability to answer all of the new questions that their research reveals. Do you think such humility encourages the work of scientists or hinders it? Explain.

Vocabulary Builder

diffidence (dif' ə dəns) *n.* lack of confidence in oneself

João Magueijo
Author's Insight
The moral is clear and devastating: Science can never be right; it can at most be not too wrong.

Go Online
Author Link

For: More about Galileo Galilei
Visit: www.PHSchool.com
Web Code: ete-9608

Answers continued

7. Students may say that humility encourages the work of scientists as they recognize that they still have much more to learn. The humility would also encourage scientists to consider new ideas.

Go Online For additional information about Galileo
Author Link Galilei have students type in the Web Code, then select *G* from the alphabet, and then select Galileo Galilei.

Apply the Skills

from *The Starry Messenger*: from *Astronomical Message* • from *The Assayer*

Literary Analysis

Narrative Accounts

1. Use a chart like the one shown to find examples of the key features of **narrative accounts** in each of the selections.

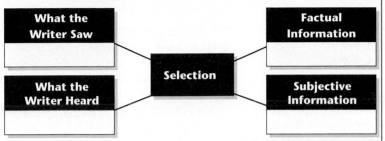

2. **(a)** What do you think was Galileo's purpose in writing *The Assayer?* **(b)** How do modern readers benefit from these primary sources?

Connecting Literary Elements

3. Galileo frequently uses transitions as a part of his **narrative style.** **(a)** Identify four transitional words or phrases in "Astronomical Message." **(b)** In what ways do these words help you understand a technical essay like this?

4. **(a)** In "Astronomical Message," why do you think Galileo included the detailed description of how he built a series of telescopes? **(b)** What does this aspect of his narrative style add to the total effect of the essay?

5. In *The Assayer,* in what way does the last paragraph both echo and extend Galileo's remarks in the introductory paragraph?

Reading Strategy

Breaking Down Long Sentences

6. Reread the third paragraph in "Astronomical Message," which begins "It is a very beautiful thing . . . " **(a)** Analyze the two sentences, separating the complex language from the essential parts (the *who* and the *what*) in each. **(b)** Then, write the meaning of the sentences as you understand them.

Extend Understanding

7. **Science Connection:** What are some of the ways in which a scientific account written today might differ from Galileo's accounts in these excerpts?

QuickReview

A **narrative account** tells the story of real-life events experienced by the writer.

Narrative style is the distinctive way in which an author chooses to tell his or her story.

When you **break down long sentences**, you separate a sentence's key parts (the *who* and the *what*) to get to the main idea.

Assessment
For: Self-test
Visit: www.PHSchool.com
Web Code: eta-6607

from *The Starry Messenger*/from *The Assayer* ■ 765

Answers continued

7. **Possible response:** A scientific account written today would have additional technical vocabulary, graphics and possibly images, less subjectivity, and shorter sentences; it probably would not contain the extended analogy of the fable.

Go Online Students may use the **Self-test** to **Assessment** prepare for **Selection Test A** or **Selection Test B.**

Answers

1. *Selection:* "Astronomical Message"
   What the writer saw: Milky Way, moon's surface, four new planets, and nebulous stars. *What the writer heard:* about Fleming's spyglass. *Factual information:* Galileo's spy-glass worked; universe was as he saw it; process of making telescope factual; *Subjective information:* information about Fleming's tele-scope; Galileo's view of the impor-tance and beauty of his discoveries. *Selection:* The Assayer
   What the writer saw: people less certain as they learn more. *What the writer heard:* condemnation for not knowing the origin of comets. *Factual information:* Comets are distant and hard to understand. *Subjective information:* Galileo's defense of science's inability to answer all questions

2. (a) Galileo's purpose may have been to explain why it is not possible to know everything and to encourage people to judge new ideas fairly. (b) **Possible response:** These sources show how people questioned, learned, and continued to explore ideas.

3. (a) Transitional words include *finally, again, all these facts, after-wards, first, then, next,* and *a few days later.* (b) These words show chronological order and relation-ships among ideas.

4. (a) The detailed description shows how he built success upon success, learning more as he explored fur-ther. (b) This aspect shows that the process took perseverance. It also shows his curiosity, with which readers can identify.

5. The introductory paragraph indi-cates what he has observed in the world. In the final paragraph, he applies that knowledge to himself and his scientific work.

6. (a) In the first sentence, *The moon is beautiful through a telescope* is essential; the information on size is nonessential. In the second sen-tence, *The moon does not have a smooth surface* is essential; all of the other details are nonessential. (b) The first sentence means that the moon is beautiful and huge when seen through a telescope. The second sentence means that the moon has an uneven surface like Earth's.

765

❶ Vocabulary Lesson

The Latin Word root -pel-

1. repel: to drive back
2. compel: to force or constrain
3. propel: to cause to move forward
4. expel: to force or drive out

Spelling Strategy

1. tanned   3. rapped
2. hopped

Vocabulary Builder

1. You could be conspicuous at a meeting if you did something to stand out or be noticed.
2. A multitude or large number of errors is not a good thing.
3. Holding back from a group, blushing, and waving someone away all indicate *diffidence.*
4. If it is *derived*, it is not original.
5. Providing an eye witness and evidence makes an argument *manifest.*
6. Horses *impelled* carriages forward.

❷ Grammar and Style Lesson

1. When we think of great scientists, Galileo is the name that most quickly comes to mind.
2. Of the many scientists who experimented with the telescope during the Renaissance, Galileo is often considered the most influential.
3. Many readers find Galileo's scientific treatises easier to read than those of Sir Isaac Newton.
4. Of the two examples, I find the scientific report the more persuasive.

Writing Application

Students' sentences should contain comparative or superlative adjectives in each sentence.

Build Language Skills

❶ Vocabulary Lesson

Word Analysis: Latin Root -pel-

The word root -pel- comes from a Latin verb meaning "to push into motion" or "to drive." Thus, the English word *impelled* means "pushed forward."

Write a definition for each word below. Confirm your answers with a dictionary.

1. repel   3. propel
2. compel   4. expel

Spelling Strategy

When adding -ed to a one-syllable word that ends in a single consonant preceded by a vowel, double the final consonant. For example, *stop* becomes *stopped*. Add -ed to each of the following words.

1. tan   2. hop   3. rap

❷ Grammar and Style Lesson

Comparative and Superlative Adjectives and Adverbs

The **comparative** form of adjectives and adverbs is used to compare two things or ideas. The **superlative** form compares more than two things or ideas. Many words follow the pattern below to indicate comparative and superlative degrees.

> **Regular form:** Reginald is *young*.
>
> **Comparative form:** Betsy is *younger*.
>
> **Superlative form:** Jamie is the *youngest*.

Other adjectives and adverbs use the words *more* and *most*, as in "Ann is *more athletic* than Joe. Tamara is the *most athletic*." Finally, some forms such as *good, better,* and *best* are irregular.

Vocabulary Builder: Words in Context

Explain your answers to each question.

1. In what way could you be *conspicuous* at a meeting?
2. Is a *multitude* of errors a good thing?
3. What gestures show someone's *diffidence?*
4. If a movie is *derived* from a novel, is the movie original?
5. What techniques can help a lawyer make an argument *manifest?*
6. Before the invention of the car, what *impelled* carriages forward?

Practice Rewrite the following sentences, correcting all errors in comparisons.

1. When we think of great scientists, Galileo is the name that quickliest comes to mind.
2. Of the many scientists who experimented with the telescope during the Renaissance, Galileo is often considered the more influential.
3. Many readers find Galileo's scientific treatises more easier to read than those of Sir Isaac Newton.
4. Of the two examples, I find the scientific report the most persuasive.

Writing Application Write five sentences about a field of science that interests you—for example, astronomy, biology, ecology, or geology. Use a comparative or superlative adjective or adverb in each sentence.

WG Prentice Hall Writing and Grammar Connection: Platinum Level, Chapter 25, Section 1

❸ Writing Lesson

Timed Writing: Response to Literature

Although it is basically a scientific essay, "Astronomical Message" reveals Galileo's personal enthusiasm for astronomy. In an essay, explain whether you think the inclusion of the author's emotions makes Galileo's writing—and his findings—more or less scientifically trustworthy. **(40 minutes)**

Prewriting
(10 minutes)

List examples of Galileo's reactions, emotions, or subjectivity. Determine whether the effect of each contributes to the scientific nature of the findings or weakens the writer's credibility. Use these examples to draw a final conclusion about the trustworthy nature of Galileo's writing.

Drafting
(20 minutes)

Using your notes, develop and present a central idea or thesis statement for your essay. Then, support your thesis with the specific examples from the text.

Revising
(10 minutes)

Review your paper, adding vivid words or substituting strong words for weak language.

Model: Revising to Add Vivid Words

conveys   meticulous
Galileo ~~gives~~ a sense of personal pride with his description of
how he built the telescopes.

Replacing a bland verb and including a vivid adjective adds precision to the sentence.

𝒲𝒢 *Prentice Hall Writing and Grammar Connection: Platinum Level, Chapter 6, Section 4*

❹ Extend Your Learning

Listening and Speaking With a partner, take turns performing **dramatic readings** of the fable in Galileo's *The Assayer*. As a listener, provide written feedback to the reader.

- Note both the strengths and weaknesses of the performance.
- Identify specific measures that would improve the performance.

Discuss your feedback with your partner.
[Group Activity]

Research and Technology Compile a list of the astronomical sights that Galileo describes in these selections. Then, using the Internet or other electronic sources, locate images of each item. Use these images to create a **scrapbook,** including a descriptive passage focusing on each image you select.

For: An additional research activity
Visit: www.PHSchool.com
Web Code: etd-7607

from Starry Messenger /from The Assayer ■ 767

Assessment Resources

The following resources can be used to assess students' knowledge and skills.

Unit 6 Resources
  Selection Test A, pp. 51–53
  Selection Test B, pp. 54–56

General Resources
  Rubrics for Response to Literature, pp. 55–56
  Rubrics for Research: Research Report, pp. 51–52

Go Online Students may use the **Self-test** to **Assessment** prepare for **Selection Test A** or **Selection Test B.**

---

❸ Writing Lesson

You may use this writing lesson as timed-writing practice, or you may allow students to develop this response to literature as a writing assignment over several days.

- To guide students in writing this response to literature, give them the **Support for Writing Lesson,** p. 48 in *Unit 6 Resources.*

- Students' essays should clearly state their central thesis explaining why Galileo's emotions increase or decrease the validity of his writings. Students need to use enough examples to fully support their thesis.

- Point out to students that they should indicate in which writing the quotes or paraphrases appear and the page number.

- Use the Response to Literature rubrics in *General Resources,* pp. 55–56, to evaluate students' work.

❹ Research and Technology

- Suggest reliable search engines to students. As students research the sights, remind them to record the sources and URLs for the pictures they use. Remind them that they need to cite print visuals as well as print sources.

- If the technology is available, have students work in pairs to compile a slide show presentation on the computer. Use the rubrics for Research: Research Report, pp. 51–52 in *General Resources* to evaluate students' work.

- The **Support for Extend Your Learning** page (*Unit 6 Resources,* p. 49) provides guided note-taking opportunities to help students complete the Extend Your Learning activities.

Go Online Have students type in the **Research** Web Code for another research activity.

Standard Course of Study

Goal 4: CRITICAL THINKING

CT.4.02.2 Use specific references from texts to show theme.

Goal 5: LITERATURE

LT.5.01.2 Build knowledge of literary genres, and explore how characteristics apply to literature of world cultures.

LT.5.01.6 Make connections between historical and contemporary issues in world literature.

Goal 6: GRAMMAR AND USAGE

GU.6.01.3 Use recognition strategies to understand vocabulary and exact word choice.

GU.6.01.5 Examine language for elements to apply effectively in own writing/speaking.

GU.6.01.7 Use language effectively to create mood and tone.

Step-by-Step Teaching Guide	Pacing Guide
PRETEACH	
• Administer Vocabulary and Reading Warm-ups as necessary.	5 min.
• Engage students' interest with the motivation activity.	5 min.
• Read and discuss author and background features. **FT**	10 min.
• Introduce the Literary Analysis Skill: Parody. **FT**	5 min.
• Introduce the Reading Strategy: Comparing and Contrasting. **FT**	10 min.
• Prepare students to read by teaching the selection vocabulary. **FT**	
TEACH	
• Informally monitor comprehension while students read independently or in groups. **FT**	30 min.
• Monitor students' comprehension with the Reading Check notes.	as students read
• Reinforce vocabulary with Vocabulary Builder notes.	as students read
• Develop students' understanding of parody with the Literary Analysis annotations. **FT**	5 min.
• Develop students' ability to compare and contrast with the Reading Strategy annotations. **FT**	5 min.
ASSESS/EXTEND	
• Assess students' comprehension and mastery of the Literary Analysis and Reading Strategy by having them answer the Apply the Skills questions. **FT**	15 min.
• Have students complete the Vocabulary Lesson and the Grammar and Style Lesson. **FT**	15 min.
• Apply students' ability to gather details by using the Writing Lesson. **FT**	45 min. or homework
• Apply students' understanding by using one or more of the Extend Your Learning activities.	20–90 min. or homework
• Administer Selection Test A or Selection Test B. **FT**	15 min.

Resources

Print

Unit 6 Resources

Transparency

Graphic Organizer Transparencies

Print

Reader's Notebook [L2]

Reader's Notebook: Adapted Version [L1]

Reader's Notebook: English Learner's Version [EL]

Unit 6 Resources

Technology

Listening to Literature Audio CDs [L2, EL]

Reader's Notebook: Adapted Version Audio CD [L1, L2]

Print

Unit 6 Resources

General Resources

Technology

Go Online: Research [**L3**]
Go Online: Self-test [**L3**]
ExamView®, Test Bank [**L3**]

Choosing Resources for Differentiated Instruction

[**L1**] Special Needs Students

[**L2**] Below-Level Students

[**L3**] All Students

[**L4**] Advanced Students

[**EL**] English Learners

For Vocabulary and Reading Warm-ups and for Selection Tests, **A** signifies "less challenging" and **B** "more challenging." For Graphic Organizer transparencies, **A** signifies "not filled in" and **B** "filled in."

FT Fast Track Instruction: To move the lesson more quickly, use the strategies and activities identified with **FT**.

Scaffolding for Less Proficient and Advanced Students

The leveled Critical Thinking questions after selections progress in the levels of thinking required to answer them. To address the needs of your different students, you may use the (a) level questions for your less proficient students and the (b) level questions with your on-level and advanced students. The occasional (c) level questions are appropriate for your advanced students.

PRENTICE HALL

TeacherEXPRESS™ Use this complete
Plan · Teach · Assess suite of powerful teaching tools to make lesson planning and testing quicker and easier.

PRENTICE HALL

StudentEXPRESS™ Use the interactive
Learn · Study · Succeed textbook (online and on CD-ROM) to make selections and activities come alive with audio and video support and interactive questions.

Benchmark

After students have completed reading these excerpts from *Don Quixote,* administer **Benchmark Test 7** *(Unit 6 Resources,* **pp. 74–79).** If the Benchmark Test reveals that some of the students need further work, use the **Interpretation Guide** to determine the appropriate reteaching page in the **Reading Kit** and on **Success Tracker.**

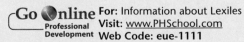 **For:** Information about Lexiles
Professional **Visit:** www.PHSchool.com
Development **Web Code:** eue-1111

Motivation

Ask students to describe some super-heroes they have seen in films. Then, invite them to brainstorm ideas for scenes in a new film they would create that makes fun of superheroes. Encourage them to use exaggeration and distortion to heighten the humor of their invented scenes. Finally, point out that these techniques are similar to those Cervantes uses in his parody of knights and chivalry.

❶ Background
More About the Author

In his personal life, Cervantes often exhibited the gallant traits and the adventuresome spirit of a knight-errant embodied in his character Don Quixote. Besides fighting in the Battle of Lepanto, Cervantes fought with the Spanish army in Italy. His travels took him to Italian cities such as Naples and Genoa. There he learned a great deal about Italian culture, no doubt familiarizing himself with Italian literature.

Cervantes made a name for himself as well when he was enslaved by the Algerians. He led several escape attempts with his fellow slaves, and when they were recaptured, he always took the blame upon himself. His bravery is mentioned in records written by other captives in Algiers.

Geography Note

Use the map on this page to identify Spain, the highlighted area. Point out central Spain, where Madrid is located and where Cervantes spent much of his life. Tell students that Madrid is known for its many impressive public squares, one of which is Plaza Mayor, adjacent to Calle Cervantes, the street named for the beloved author of *Don Quixote*.

Build Skills | *Fiction* |

❶ *from* Don Quixote

Miguel de Cervantes Saavedra
(1547–1616)

Miguel de Cervantes Saavedra (sər van′ tēz sä′ ə vä′ drə) led a life that was every bit as exciting as that of his famous character, the knight-errant Don Quixote (dän′ kē hōt′ ē). Cervantes himself also displayed, on occasion, the almost fool-hardy bravery that was so characteristic of his absurd knight.

Military Career Born into a poor family, Cervantes received little education. In 1570, he joined the Spanish army and shortly afterward fought in the battle of Lepanto against the Turks. This naval battle saw the destruction of the Turkish fleet by the combined forces of Spain and Italy.

Cervantes was among the 30,000 soldiers transported by the Spanish and Italian galleys. Although he was ill when the battle began, he plunged into the fighting and was wounded twice in the chest and once in the left arm. For the rest of his life, he regarded his maimed left arm as a badge of honor.

Cervantes went on to fight in a number of other battles, but he was captured by Barbary pirates while he was sailing home from the wars. Sold into slavery in Algiers, he repeatedly tried to escape. Although he was always recaptured, his bravery so impressed the Algerians that they did not put him to death. Believing that Cervantes was a citizen of great importance, his captors demanded a considerable ransom for his release. After he had been a prisoner for five years, the ransom was finally paid, and Cervantes was free to return to Madrid.

Difficult Times Back in Spain, Cervantes pursued an ambitious goal: to become Spain's most successful dramatist. Although he wrote prolifically, his significant collection of theatrical works was largely overlooked. Cervantes braved difficult economic circumstances during his years as a playwright and eventually found a bookkeeping job with the government to support his large household. Problems with his account books, however, led to his imprisonment on two occasions. According to legend, Cervantes began writing *Don Quixote* during one of these spells in prison.

A Wealth of Imagination When the first part of the novel appeared in 1605, it was a great success. Within only a few years, the novel had been translated into English, French, and a number of other European languages. When a false, or unauthorized, sequel to *Don Quixote* appeared on the market, Cervantes quickly embarked upon the continuation of his story—*Don Quixote, Part II*—which was published in 1615. Despite his appreciable success, Cervantes received only a small sum from his publisher for the works. At the time of his death in 1616, he was still a poor man.

It is clear that Cervantes invested his true wealth—his keen observation, playfulness, and imagination—in the creation of his novel. That is why it remains, as one translator called it, "one of the best adventure stories in the world." To date, Cervantes's masterpiece has been published in more than sixty languages, and the novel continues to be read, studied, critiqued, and debated by scholars all around the world.

768 ■ The Renaissance and Rationalism

Preview

Connecting to the Literature

Literature is filled with dreamers—people who hook their wagons to a star or try to lasso the moon. Perhaps the best-known dreamer of all is Don Quixote de la Mancha, an unlikely hero who gets swept away by the stories he reads and the dreams they inspire.

❷ Literary Analysis

Parody

A **parody** is a humorous imitation of another, usually serious, work. Most often, a parody uses exaggeration or distortion to ridicule the work, its style, or its author. *Don Quixote* affectionately parodies the literature of chivalry—elaborate stories about knights; their code of honor, courage, and chastity; and their adventures. The central character, for example, makes swords out of oak branches and helmets of cardboard, yet he considers himself a well-dressed knight. As you read, look for details that parody chivalric romances.

Connecting Literary Elements

Parodies lend themselves to discussions of **theme,** the central message or idea revealed through a literary work. *Don Quixote* uses parody to explore the idea of reality versus fantasy, prompting readers to ask:

- At what point do flights of fancy interfere with reality?
- Is a life of hard-nosed realism more rewarding than a life filled with fantastic adventures?

Note thematic questions like these as you read.

❸ Reading Strategy

Comparing and Contrasting

Comparing and contrasting an ideal knight and Don Quixote's version means looking for similarities and differences between the two. Before you read, use a chart like the one shown to list the details you know about an ideal knight, such as his armor, squire, horse, and adventures. Then, as you read, record the details from Don Quixote's world. Identify any conclusions you can draw from comparing and contrasting those details.

Vocabulary Builder

constitution (kän′ stə tōō′ shən) *n.* structure or makeup of a person or thing (p. 770)

conjectures (kən jek′ chərz) *n.* guesses (p. 770)

infatuation (in fach′ ōō ā′ shən) *n.* foolish or shallow feelings of affection (p. 772)

ingenuity (in′ jə nōō′ ə tē) *n.* cleverness; inventiveness (p. 774)

incongruous (in kän′ grōō əs) *adj.* inconsistent; lacking in harmony (p. 777)

appropriate (ə prō′ prē āt′) *v.* take for one's own use (p. 778)

illustrious (i lus′ trē əs) *adj.* distinguished or outstanding (p. 780)

NC **Standard Course of Study**

- Use specific references from texts to show theme. (CT.4.02.2)
- Make connections between historical and contemporary issues in world literature. (LT.5.01.6)

Ideal Knight
1.
2.

Don Quixote
1.
2.

Conclusion

from *Don Quixote* ■ 769

---

❷ Literary Analysis

Parody

- Tell students that a parody works best when the object of its ridicule is something that is taken seriously. Don Quixote entertains readers because his behavior exaggerates that of the traditional "knight in shining armor."
- Point out that characters in a parody take their actions seriously, even though their behavior may be quite funny or ridiculous.
- Tell students that Don Quixote believes he is part of the world of knights and chivalry. Remind them that the reader, not the characters, determines what is being ridiculed.

❸ Reading Strategy

Comparing and Contrasting

- Point out that much of the humor in *Don Quixote* comes from the sharp difference between the ideal knight and Don Quixote's version. Compare and contrast the two to highlight the humor of *Don Quixote*.
- Review with students the chart. Have them brainstorm details about an ideal knight. Encourage them to be precise.
- Give students a copy of **Reading Strategy Graphic Organizer A,** p. 138 in *Graphic Organizer Transparencies.* As students read, ask them to look for Don Quixote's version of each detail and add it to the chart.

Vocabulary Builder

- Pronounce each vocabulary word for students, and read the definitions as a class. Have students identify any words with which they are already familiar.

Differentiated Instruction   Solutions for All Learners

Support for Special Needs Students

Have students read the adapted version of these chapters for the excerpt from *Don Quixote* in the *Reader's Notebook: Adapted Version.* This version provides basic-level instruction in an interactive format with questions and write-on lines. Completing these pages will prepare students to read the selection in the Student Edition.

Support for Less Proficient Readers

Have students read these chapters for the excerpt from *Don Quixote* in the *Reader's Notebook.* This version provides basic-level instruction in an interactive format with questions and write-on lines. After students finish the selection in the *Reader's Notebook,* have them complete the questions and activities in the Student Edition.

Support for English Learners

Have students read these chapters for the excerpt from *Don Quixote* in the *Reader's Notebook: English Learner's Version.* This version provides basic-level instruction in an interactive format with questions and write-on lines. Completing these pages will prepare students to read the selection in the Student Edition.

Facilitate Understanding

Ask a student to look up the word *quixotic* in the dictionary. After he or she reads the definition aloud, tell students that this word was coined with Don Quixote in mind.

❶ About the Selection

Don Quixote ceaselessly reads tales of "enchantments, knightly encounters, battles, challenges, wounds, . . . of love and its torments" until, bedazzled by the romance of chivalry, he looks for knightly adventure in every corner of his own ordinary world.

❷ Literary Analysis

Parody

- Remind students that parodies assume that the audience has knowledge of the topic being mocked. **Ask** students to offer ideas about the average knight's financial situation.
  Possible response: Knights were able to provide well for themselves.

- **Ask** how Don Quixote's life parodies knighthood.
  Answer: Don Quixote barely manages to feed and clothe himself.

- **Ask** students the Literary Analysis question: In what way do Don Quixote's age and physical appearance parody the typical heroic knight?
  Answer: Don Quixote is older than the average knight and skinny.

❸ Vocabulary Builder

Latin Root -ject-

- Refer students to the word *conjectures* in the bracketed passage.

- Tell students that this word has the Latin root *-ject-*, which means "to throw."

- **Ask** students to offer ideas about the connection between "to throw" and *guesses,* the word's definition.
  Answer: Someone "throws in" a guess when he or she does not have an exact answer.

---

❶ from
Don Quixote

Miguel de Cervantes   *translated by Samuel Putnam*

Background In traditional courtly romances, a knight-errant is a great fighter who has earned renown in jousting and tournaments. He spends his life wandering the land, performing deeds of bravery in the name of a noble woman who can never return his affection. This impossible love and its accompanying code of honor justify the knight's death-defying adventures. Don Quixote sees himself as such a knight, and no reality can resist his fabulous imagination.

Chapter I

Which treats of the station in life and the pursuits of the famous gentleman, Don Quixote de la Mancha.

In a village of La Mancha[1] the name of which I have no desire to recall, there lived not so long ago one of those gentlemen who always have a lance in the rack, an ancient buckler, a skinny nag, and a greyhound for the chase. A stew with more beef than mutton in it, chopped meat for his evening meal, scraps for a Saturday, lentils on Friday, and ❷ a young pigeon as a special delicacy for Sunday, went to account for three-quarters of his income. The rest of it he laid out on a broadcloth greatcoat and velvet stockings for feast days, with slippers to match, while the other days of the week he cut a figure in a suit of the finest homespun. Living with him were a housekeeper in her forties, a niece who was not yet twenty, and a lad of the field and market place who saddled his horse for him and wielded the pruning knife.

This gentleman of ours was close on to fifty, of a robust <u>constitution</u> but with little flesh on his bones and a face that was lean and gaunt. He was noted for his early rising, being very fond of the hunt. They will try to tell you that his surname was Quijada or Quesada—there is some difference of opinion among those who have written on the sub- ❸ ject—but according to the most likely <u>conjectures</u> we are to understand

---

1. **La Mancha** province in south central Spain.

770 ■ The Renaissance and Rationalism

Literary Analysis
Parody In what way do Don Quixote's age and physical appearance parody the typical heroic knight?

Vocabulary Builder
constitution (kän´ stə too´ shən) *n.* structure or makeup of a person or thing

conjectures (kən jek´ chərz) *n.* guesses

Differentiated
Instruction   Solutions for All Learners

Accessibility at a Glance

	Don Quixote Chapter I	*Don Quixote* Chapter VII	*Don Quixote* Chapter VIII
Context	Quixote confuses stories with reality.	The mad Quixote finds a squire.	Quixote has a battle with windmill "giants."
Language	Syntax: long, complex sentences	Syntax: long, complex sentences	Syntax: dialogue of long, complex sentences
Concept Level	Accessible (role of imagination)	Accessible (effects of persuasion)	Accessible (effects of impulsive actions)
Literary Merit	Classic parody of medieval courtly romance	Builds suspense about the adventures ahead	"Tilting at windmills" scene famous in Western literature
Lexile	1520L	1520L	1520L
Overall Rating	Average	Average	Average

4

Don Quixote, Honoré Daumier, Scala

5 ⬛ **Critical Viewing** Which details from this painting match the description in Chapter I of *Don Quixote* and his horse? **[Analyze]**

from *Don Quixote* ■ 771

Caricaturist, painter, and sculptor Honoré Daumier (1808–1879) is best known for his cartoons satirizing the politics and society of nineteenth-century France. He found a wide audience for his cartoons attacking certain public figures and aspects of society. After 1850, Daumier produced a series of works based on *Don Quixote.* This image of Don Quixote on his horse is very loosely rendered and appears incomplete when compared to earlier, more detailed versions of the painting. Nevertheless, his lively use of line and texture captures the essence of the gentleman of La Mancha.

Use the following questions for discussion:

• Why do you think Daumier painted Don Quixote as a faceless figure?
Possible response: Don Quixote masquerades as a knight. By painting him as faceless, Daumier suggests that the "real" Don Quixote is unknown, despite his being a highly recognizable literary figure.

• **Ask** students to identify details from the painting that show Daumier's respect for Don Quixote.
Possible response: Don Quixote's good posture suggests confidence, as does the casual way he holds his shield. His lance looks serviceable.

⑤ Critical Viewing

Possible response: The man appears skinny; his horse is bony; he carries a lance; and he wears a helmet.

Differentiated Instruction Solutions for All Learners

Enrichment for Gifted/Talented Students

Point out to students the relation between parodies, such as this story of Don Quixote, and caricatures, or pictures of people that exaggerate certain physical attributes. Tell students that parodies and caricatures are both meant to create a humorous effect.

Most students will know caricature from political cartoons. Have them find examples of caricatures by classic or contemporary artists. Invite interested students to write short essays that explain the parody in the caricatures.

Other students may be interested in creating their own caricatures. Have each student choose a well-known figure, such as a movie or rock star, and draw a caricature of that person, exaggerating some physical attribute in a humorous way.

Have students read their parodies and display their caricatures to the class.

that it was really Quejana. But all this means very little so far as our story is concerned, providing that in the telling of it we do not depart one iota from the truth.

❻ You may know, then, that the aforesaid gentleman, on those occasions when he was at leisure, which was most of the year around, was in the habit of reading books of chivalry with such pleasure and devotion as to lead him almost wholly to forget the life of a hunter and even the administration of his estate. So great was his curiosity and <u>infatuation</u> in this regard that he even sold many acres of tillable land in order to be able to buy and read the books that he loved, and he would carry home with him as many of them as he could obtain.

Of all those that he thus devoured none pleased him so well as the ones that had been composed by the famous Feliciano de Silva, whose lucid prose style and involved conceits[2] were as precious to him as pearls; especially when he came to read those tales of love and amorous challenges that are to be met with in many places, such a passage as the following, for example: "The reason of the unreason that afflicts my reason, in such a manner weakens my reason that I with reason lament me of your comeliness." And he was similarly affected when ❼ his eyes fell upon such lines as these: ". . . the high Heaven of your divinity divinely fortifies you with the stars and renders you deserving of that desert your greatness doth deserve."

The poor fellow used to lie awake nights in an effort to disentangle the meaning and make sense out of passages such as these, although Aristotle himself would not have been able to understand them, even if he had been resurrected for that sole purpose. He was not at ease in his mind over those wounds that Don Belianís gave and received; for no matter how great the surgeons who treated him, the poor fellow must have been left with his face and his entire body covered with marks and scars. Nevertheless, he was grateful to the author for closing the book with the promise of an interminable adventure to come; many a time he was tempted to take up his pen and literally finish the tale as had been promised, and he undoubtedly would have done so, and would have succeeded at it very well, if his thoughts had not been constantly occupied with other things of greater moment.

2. **conceits** elaborate comparisons or metaphors.

❽ ▲ **Critical Viewing**
Which details in this picture might Don Quixote find fascinating? Explain. **[Speculate]**

Vocabulary Builder
infatuation (in fach´ o͞o a´ shən) *n.* foolish or shallow feelings of affection

Enrichment

Amadis of Gaul
Among the stories that Don Quixote reads voraciously is the chivalric romance *Amadis of Gaul*. The story dates to the late thirteenth century, but it was first published in Spain in 1508.

The story was so popular that its hero, Amadis, became the model for the perfect knight: brave, romantic, and chaste. Influenced by the Arthurian legends, it is the tale of the battles Amadis must fight to win the love of Oriana, an English princess.

Because *Amadis of Gaul* was so well known, the romance spawned many sequels and poor imitations. Cervantes was familiar with both the original and its derivatives, and he drew from them both in writing his parody, *Don Quixote*. This is particularly apparent in the quotation from "the famous Feliciano de Silva" on this page.

The 1605 publication of *Don Quixote* ended the popularity of the more serious chivalric romances.

He often talked it over with the village curate,[3] who was a learned man, a graduate of Sigüenza,[4] and they would hold long discussions as to who had been the better knight, Palmerin of England or Amadis of Gaul; but Master Nicholas, the barber of the same village, was in the habit of saying that no one could come up to the Knight of Phoebus, and that if anyone *could* compare with him it was Don Galaor, brother of Amadis of Gaul, for Galaor was ready for anything—he was none of your finical[5] knights, who went around whimpering as his brother did, and in point of valor he did not lag behind him.

In short, our gentleman became so immersed in his reading that he spent whole nights from sundown to sunup and his days from dawn to dusk in poring over his books, until, finally, from so little sleeping and so much reading, his brain dried up and he went completely out of his mind. He had filled his imagination with everything that he had read, with enchantments, knightly encounters, battles, challenges, wounds, with tales of love and its torments, and all sorts of impossible things, and as a result had come to believe that all these fictitious happenings were true; they were more real to him than anything else in the world. He would remark that the Cid Ruy Díaz[6] had been a very good knight, but there was no comparison between him and the Knight of the Flaming Sword, who with a single backward stroke had cut in half two fierce and monstrous giants. He preferred Bernardo del Carpio, who at Roncesvalles had slain Roland despite the charm the latter bore, availing himself of the stratagem which Hercules employed when he strangled Antaeus, the son of Earth, in his arms.

He had much good to say for Morgante who, though he belonged to the haughty, overbearing race of giants, was of an affable disposition and well brought up. But, above all, he cherished an admiration for Rinaldo of Montalbán, especially as he beheld him sallying forth from his castle to rob all those that crossed his path, or when he thought of him overseas stealing the image of Mohammed which, so the story has it, was all of gold. And he would have liked very well to have had his fill of kicking that traitor Galalón, a privilege for which he would have given his housekeeper with his niece thrown into the bargain.

At last, when his wits were gone beyond repair, he came to conceive the strangest idea that ever occurred to any madman in this world. It now appeared to him fitting and necessary, in order to win a greater amount of honor for himself and serve his country at the same time, to become a knight-errant and roam the world on horseback, in a suit of armor; he would go in quest of adventures, by way of putting into practice all that he had read in his books; he would right every manner of wrong, placing himself in situations of the greatest peril such as would

---

3. **curate** clergyman in charge of a parish.
4. **Sigüenza** (se gwän′ sä) one of a group of "minor universities" granting degrees that were often laughed at by Spanish humorists.
5. **finical** (fin′i kəl) finicky.
6. **Cid Ruy Díaz** (cĕd rōō′ ē dē′ äs) famous Spanish soldier Ruy Diaz de Vivar: called the Cid, a derivation of the Arabic word for *lord*.

Reading Strategy
Comparing and Contrasting Compare and contrast Don Quixote's current lifestyle with that of the knights described in this passage.

Reading Check

What activity consumes Don Quixote's time from dawn to dusk each day?

from Don Quixote ■ 773

Differentiated
Instruction　　Solutions for All Learners

Support for Special Needs Students
Students will have difficulty with the challenging vocabulary on these facing pages. Help students with context or definitions to assist their understanding of the following words: *aforesaid, tillable, devoured, lucid, amorous, fortifies, disentangle, interminable, immersed, stratagem, affable, beheld, sallying, conceive,* and *peril.* Encourage students to mention any other words with which

they have problems. Have students work in pairs to select five of the words listed above, and write a sentence for each word.

Then help students work through the **Vocabulary Warm-up List** and **Vocabulary Warm-up Practice,** pp. 57–58 in *Unit 6 Resources.*

❾ Critical Thinking
Relate
- Point out that in the bracketed passage, Cervantes is poking fun at certain aspects of the culture of the day. **Ask** students to identify what these might be.
  Answer: People invest much time and energy in thinking about stories that simply are meant to entertain them.
- **Ask** students to identify aspects of our culture that compare to the ones Cervantes mocks in this passage.
  Answer: This passage relates to contemporary people's tendency to talk hypothetically about characters from action and horror movies, telling what those characters could do in the "real" world, or to each other, if they should meet.

❿ Reading Strategy
Comparing and Contrasting
- Remind students that Don Quixote's interest in books about knights was not unique: many people enjoyed the same works. **Ask** students to compare his approach to his reading with that of other readers.
  Possible response: Most readers do not confuse stories with reality, no matter how much they enjoy reading them.
- Have students **respond** to the Reading Strategy item: Compare and contrast Don Quixote's current lifestyle with that of the knights described in this passage.
  Answer: Don Quixote is a poor and sedentary gentleman who spends his time reading, whereas the knights described in this passage pursue adventure and perform feats of valor.

⓫ Reading Check
Answer: Reading books about the adventures of knights consumes Don Quixote's time.

Comparing and Contrasting

- Have students read and discuss the bracketed passage. **Ask** students why they think Don Quixote refrains from testing the latest version of his helmet.
  Answer: Don Quixote wants to believe that this version, unlike his earlier attempts, will not fall apart.

- **Ask** students the Reading Strategy item: Compare and contrast Don Quixote's armor with that of a traditional knight.
  Answer: A traditional knight's helmet is polished, impressive-looking, fully closed, and able to withstand cuts and blows. Don Quixote's helmet is a crude and improvised piece of old armor with a cardboard visor.

▶ **Monitor Progress Ask** students to explain how Don Quixote's handling of the helmet confirms that he is not a real knight.
  Possible response: A real knight would hand his helmet over to his squire for any repairs that might be necessary. Protecting his head from harm would be the knight's first priority.

▶ **Reteach** If students have difficulty identifying the characteristics of a real medieval knight, use the **Reading Strategy** support, p. 62 in *Unit 6 Resources*.

13 **Critical Thinking**

Connect

- Refer students to the bracketed passage, and have them discuss the appearance of the horse. **Ask** students to draw conclusions about the condition of the animal.
  Answer: Descriptions of cracks in its hoof and blemishes, the use of the word *nag,* and the reference to skin and bones indicate that the horse is in poor condition.

- **Ask** students in what ways Don Quixote's approach to naming his horse is similar to his approach to outfitting himself with armor.
  Answer: In both cases, he uses his imagination to transform something shabby into something heroic; he does all he can to model himself on the famous knights whom he admires.

redound to the eternal glory of his name. As a reward for his valor and the might of his arm, the poor fellow could already see himself crowned Emperor of Trebizond[7] at the very least; and so, carried away by the strange pleasure that he found in such thoughts as these, he at once set about putting his plan into effect.

The first thing he did was to burnish up some old pieces of armor, left him by his great-grandfather, which for ages had lain in a corner, moldering and forgotten. He polished and adjusted them as best he could, and then he noticed that one very important thing was lacking: there was no closed helmet, but only a morion, or visorless headpiece, with turned up brim of the kind foot soldiers wore. His <u>ingenuity</u>, however, enabled him to remedy this, and he proceeded to fashion out of cardboard a kind of half-helmet, which, when attached to the morion, **12** gave the appearance of a whole one. True, when he went to see if it was strong enough to withstand a good slashing blow, he was somewhat disappointed; for when he drew his sword and gave it a couple of thrusts, he succeeded only in undoing a whole week's labor. The ease with which he had hewed it to bits disturbed him no little, and he decided to make it over. This time he placed a few strips of iron on the inside, and then, convinced that it was strong enough, refrained from putting it to any further test; instead, he adopted it then and there as the finest helmet ever made.

After this, he went out to have a look at his nag; and although the animal had more *cuartos,* or cracks, in its hoof than there are quarters in a real,[8] and more blemishes than Gonela's steed which *tantum pellis et ossa fuit,*[9] it nonetheless looked to its master like a far better horse than Alexander's Bucephalus or the Babieca of the Cid.[10] He spent all of four days in trying to think up a name for his mount; for—so he told himself—seeing that it belonged to so famous and worthy a knight, there was no reason why it should not have a name of equal renown. **13** The kind of name he wanted was one that would at once indicate what the nag had been before it came to belong to a knight-errant and what its present status was; for it stood to reason that, when the master's worldly condition changed, his horse also ought to have a famous, high-sounding appellation, one suited to the new order of things and the new profession that it was to follow.

After he in his memory and imagination had made up, struck out, and discarded many names, now adding to and now subtracting from the list, he finally hit upon "Rocinante," a name that impressed him as being sonorous and at the same time indicative of what the steed had

---

7. **Trebizond** (treb´ i zänd) in medieval times, a Greek empire off the southeast coast of the Black Sea.
8. **real** (rā äl´) former coin of Spain. In a real, there were eight *cuartos,* which means both "quarters" and "cracks."
9. ***tantum pellis et ossa fuit*** (tän´ tum pel´ is et äs´ə fōō´ it) Latin: "It was nothing but skin and bones."
10. **Alexander's Bucephalus** (byōō sef´ ə ləs) **or the Babieca** (bäb ē ā´kä) **of the Cid** Bucephalus was Alexander the Great's war horse; Babieca was the Cid's war horse.

774 ■ *The Renaissance and Rationalism*

Vocabulary Builder
ingenuity (in´je nōō´ ə tē) *n.* cleverness; inventiveness

Reading Strategy
Comparing and Contrasting Compare and contrast Don Quixote's armor with that of a traditional knight.

Enrichment

History of Armor
The first thing that Don Quixote does after deciding to become a knight-errant is to clean up some old and rusty armor that had belonged to his ancestors. The outfit that he restores would have dated from the period in which the manufacturing and use of armor reached its peak in Europe—the 1300s to the mid-1500s. After this time, gunpowder was increasingly used in battle and the production of armor, useful in hand-to-hand combat, declined.

Don Quixote Preparing His Armor; scene from the novel by Cervantes, Zacarías Velazquez Gonzalez, Caylus Anticuario, Madrid, Spain

◀ **Critical Viewing**
In most cases, only the wealthy could afford the costly armor, horse, and training necessary to become a knight. Which details in this painting suggest that Don Quixote did not possess such wealth? **[Interpret]**

 been when it was but a hack,[11] whereas now it was nothing other than the first and foremost of all the hacks in the world.

Having found a name for his horse that pleased his fancy, he then desired to do as much for himself, and this required another week, and by the end of that period he had made up his mind that he was henceforth to be known as Don Quixote, which, as has been stated, has led the authors of this veracious history to assume that his real name

---

11. **hack** horse used in all kinds of work and usually well worn out in service.

✔ **Reading Check**

Whose armor does Don Quixote use?

from *Don Quixote* ■ 775

⑭ Humanities

Don Quixote Preparing His Armour,
by Zacarías González Velázquez

Zacarías González Velázquez (1763–1834) belonged to the González Velázquez family of Spanish artists. His grandfather, father, uncles, and brothers were all artists.

In this painting, Velázquez portrays Don Quixote getting his armor ready for his great adventure. The plainness of the room, with its drab walls and sparse furnishings, contrasts with Don Quixote's dreams of becoming a magnificent knight-errant.

Use these questions for discussion:

• What items in the room show Don Quixote's interest in knighthood?
Answer: The pieces of armor, the sword, and the scroll on the wall all show interest in knighthood.

• What crucial part of his interest in knighthood is missing from the painting?
Answer: None of Quixote's many books of chivalry appear in the painting.

• How would you describe the attitude or pose of Don Quixote in this painting?
Answer: He appears to be full of energy, purposeful, and impatient to complete his work.

⑮ Critical Viewing

Answer: The rough, unfinished look of his door, window, and floor; his nearly unadorned walls; and his rustic furniture show that Don Quixote is not a wealthy man.

⑯ Reading Check

Answer: Don Quixote uses his great-grandfather's armor.

Dulcinea del Toboso,
by Charles Robert Leslie

Charles Robert Leslie (1794–1859) was born in London to American parents. Although he was raised and educated for the most part in the United States, he studied art in England.

Much of his work focused on scenes from literary works, such as this painting depicting Don Quixote's ladylove, Dulcinea.

Use these questions for discussion:

• According to this painting, what kind of person does Dulcinea appear to be?
Possible response: Some students will note that she appears to be innocent and have a sweet disposition; however, others may find her expression coy.

• How would you describe the expression on her face?
Answer: She appears thoughtful and not self-conscious, perhaps unaware that she is being observed.

⑱ Critical Viewing

Possible response: Although the young woman is pretty, her dress does not look like one worn by a princess or a great lady, nor is her casual gesture or facial expression commonly found in portraits of such women.

⑲ Literary Analysis

Parody

• Point out that the knight Amadis chose to take the name of Gaul, the ancient Roman province that was his "kingdom and fatherland."

• Have students note what name Don Quixote has chosen for himself. **Ask** them what makes this a humorous parody of the character Amadis of Gaul.
Answer: Don Quixote de la Mancha means Don Quixote *of* La Mancha and refers to an undistinguished province of south central Spain, not a "kingdom and fatherland."

▶ **Reteach** To assist students' understanding of parody, review the Literary Analysis instruction on p. 769.

⑰

◀ Critical Viewing ⑱
Do you think the woman in this painting conveys "the suggestion of a princess or a great lady" worthy of being Don Quixote's ladylove? Why or why not? [**Make a Judgment**]

must undoubtedly have been Quijada, and not Quesada as others would have it. But remembering that the valiant Amadis was not content to call himself that and nothing more, but added the name of his kingdom and fatherland that he might make it famous also, and thus ⑲ came to take the name Amadis of Gaul, so our good knight chose to add his place of origin and become "Don Quixote de la Mancha"; for by this means, as he saw it, he was making very plain his lineage and was conferring honor upon his country by taking its name as his own.

And so, having polished up his armor and made the morion over into a closed helmet, and having given himself and his horse a name, he naturally found but one thing lacking still: he must seek out a lady of

776 ■ *The Renaissance and Rationalism*

whom he could become enamored; for a knight-errant without a lady-love was like a tree without leaves or fruit, a body without a soul.

"If," he said to himself, "as a punishment for my sins or by a stroke of fortune I should come upon some giant hereabouts, a thing that very commonly happens to knights-errant, and if I should slay him in a hand-to-hand encounter or perhaps cut him in two, or, finally, if I should vanquish and subdue him, would it not be well to have someone to whom I may send him as a present, in order that he, if he is living, may come in, fall upon his knees in front of my sweet lady, and say in a humble and submissive tone of voice, 'I, lady, am the giant Caraculiambro, lord of the island Malindrania, who has been overcome in single combat by that knight who never can be praised enough, Don Quixote de la Mancha, the same who sent me to present myself before your Grace that your Highness may dispose of me as you see fit'?"

Oh, how our good knight reveled in this speech, and more than ever when he came to think of the name that he should give his lady! As the story goes, there was a very good-looking farm girl who lived near by, with whom he had once been smitten, although it is generally believed that she never knew or suspected it. Her name was Aldonza Lorenzo, and it seemed to him that she was the one upon whom he should bestow the title of mistress of his thoughts. For her he wished a name that should not be <u>incongruous</u> with his own and that would convey the suggestion of a princess or a great lady; and, accordingly, he resolved to call her "Dulcinea del Toboso," she being a native of that place. A musical name to his ears, out of the ordinary and significant, like the others he had chosen for himself and his appurtenances.

Literary Analysis
Parody List three details from chivalric romances that are parodied in this paragraph.

Vocabulary Builder
incongruous (in´ kän´ grōō əs) *adj.* inconsistent; lacking in harmony

Critical Reading

1. **Respond:** What do you find most humorous about Don Quixote's behavior? Why?
2. **(a) Recall:** What name does Don Quixote choose for his horse? **(b) Infer:** Identify two considerations Don Quixote makes as he chooses names. **(c) Speculate:** In what way might a simple change of name affect Don Quixote's entire world?
3. **(a) Recall:** Who is Aldonza Loreno? **(b) Analyze:** What role will she play in Don Quixote's adventures? **(c) Compare:** In what way does she fulfill the stereotype of a knight's ladylove?
4. **(a) Make a Judgment:** What theme do you think Don Quixote embodies? **(b) Support:** Which details in Chapter I reflect that theme?
5. **Evaluate:** Do you consider Don Quixote insane or the noble victim of an overactive imagination? Explain.

Go Online
Author Link

For: More about Miguel de Cervantes Saavedra
Visit: www.PHSchool.com
Web Code: ete-9605

from Don Quixote ■ 777

- Have students **respond** to the Literary Analysis item: List three details from chivalric romances that are parodied in this paragraph.
Possible response: Don Quixote refers to encounters with giants as "common occurrences" within such tales; he imitates the flowery style of speech in these tales when he imagines the dying words of the giant Caraculiambro, and he finds a pretext to refer to himself ridiculously as "that knight who never can be praised enough."

ASSESS

Answers

1. **Possible response:** Repairing his helmet by adding a cardboard visor is humorous; it shows Don Quixote's foolishness as the helmet could not withstand a blow.

2. (a) Don Quixote names his horse Rocinante. (b) Don Quixote wants the name to sound musical, pleasing, and noble. (c) Changing a name transforms Don Quixote's everyday world into a world of fantasy.

3. (a) Aldonza Lorenzo is Don Quixote's chosen ladylove, whom he renames Dulcinea. (b) She will be the lady to whom he dedicates his deeds of valor. (c) She is young and attractive.

4. (a) **Possible response:** Don Quixote embodies the theme that fantasy, or imagination, enriches a person's life. (b) Don Quixote takes ordinary things such as old, rusty armor; a broken-down nag; and a farm girl and places them in a fantasy world of knights and chivalry.

5. Don Quixote may be insane because he is out of touch with reality. He may simply have an overactive imagination, because he very carefully constructs the details of his fantasy world.

Go Online For additional informa-
Author Link tion about Miguel de Cervantes Saavedra, have students type in the Web Code, then select S from the alphabet, and then select Miguel de Cervantes Saavedra.

Differentiated Instruction   Solutions for All Learners

Support for Special Needs Students
Review with students the elements of the life of a "knight-errant" that Don Quixote has created so far. Help students review the story thus far by having them read along with *Listening to Literature Audio CDs* for this selection.

Support for Less Proficient Readers
To model the way to compare and contrast details in a parody, give students a copy of **Reading Strategy Graphic Organizer B**, p. 139 in **Graphic Organizer Transparencies**. The completed graphic organizer will give students insight into the process.

Support for English Learners
Review with students some of the difficult vocabulary words on this page, such as *vanquish, submissive, smitten, bestow,* and *appurtenances*. Ask students to describe the elements of a "knight errant" that Don Quixote has demonstrated so far. Have them review the story thus far by using the *Listening to Literature Audio CDs* for this selection.

Chapter VII

Of the second sally of our good knight, Don Quixote de la Mancha.

㉑ . . . He remained at home very tranquilly for a couple of weeks, without giving sign of any desire to repeat his former madness. During that time he had the most pleasant conversations with his two old friends, the curate and the barber, on the point he had raised to the effect that what the world needed most was knights-errant and a revival of chivalry. The curate would occasionally contradict him and again would give in, for it was only by means of this artifice that he could carry on a conversation with him at all.

In the meanwhile Don Quixote was bringing his powers of persuasion to bear upon a farmer who lived near by, a good man—if this title may be applied to one who is poor—but with very few wits in his head. The short of it is, by pleas and promises, he got the hapless rustic to agree to ride forth with him and serve him as his squire.[1] Among other things, Don Quixote told him that he ought to be more than willing to go, because no telling what adventure might occur which would win them an island, and then he (the farmer) would be left to be the governor of it. As a result of these and other similar assurances, Sancho ㉒ Panza forsook his wife and children and consented to take upon himself the duties of squire to his neighbor.

Next, Don Quixote set out to raise some money, and by selling this thing and pawning that and getting the worst of the bargain always, he finally scraped together a reasonable amount. He also asked a friend of his for the loan of a buckler and patched up his broken helmet as well as he could. He advised his squire, Sancho, of the day and hour when they were to take the road and told him to see to laying in a supply of those things that were most necessary, and, above all, not to forget the saddlebags. Sancho replied that he would see to all this and added that he was also thinking of taking along with him a very good ass that he had, as he was not much used to going on foot.

With regard to the ass, Don Quixote had to do a little thinking, trying to recall if any knight-errant had ever had a squire thus asininely mounted. He could not think of any but nevertheless he decided to take Sancho with the intention of providing him with a nobler steed as soon as occasion offered; he had but to <u>appropriate</u> the horse of the first dis-
㉓ courteous knight he met. Having furnished himself with shirts and all

---

1. **squire** (skwir) knight's attendant.

778 ■ *The Renaissance and Rationalism*

Literary Analysis
Parody In what ways is Sancho Panza a parody of an ideal knight's squire?

Vocabulary Builder
appropriate (ə prō′ prē āt′)
v. take for one's own use

23 the other things that the innkeeper had recommended, he and Panza rode forth one night unseen by anyone and without taking leave of wife and children, housekeeper or niece. They went so far that by the time morning came they were safe from discovery had a hunt been started for them.

25

Don Quixote and Sancho Panza Riding Clavileno, Zacarías Velazquez Gonzalez, Caylus Antiquario, Madrid, Spain

26 ▲ **Critical Viewing** Compare and contrast the preparations for knighthood that Don Quixote makes to the training depicted in this painting. **[Compare and Contrast]**

✔ **Reading Check** **24**

What service does Don Quixote persuade Sancho Panza to provide?

from Don Quixote ■ 779

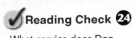

23 **Critical Thinking**
Infer
• Have students read the bracketed passage.
• **Ask** students why they think Sancho Panza and Don Quixote set out on their adventure in the night, without telling anyone.
Answer: Don Quixote and Sancho Panza do not want anyone to know they are leaving because they are afraid people might try to stop them.

24 **Reading Check**
Answer: Don Quixote persuades Sancho Panza to become his squire.

25 **Humanities**
Don Quixote and Sancho Panza Riding Clavileno,
by Zacarías González Velázquez

This painting illustrates an episode from Part II of *Don Quixote* in which Don Quixote and Sancho Panza ride the wooden horse, Clavileno. Don Quixote believes that the wooden horse is magical and was originally constructed by the magician Merlin.

In this painting, Don Quixote and Sancho Panza believe they are about to fly away on Clavileno to rescue the Princess Antonomasia.

Use this question for discussion:

What details of the painting capture the humor of the situation?
Answer: Don Quixote and Sancho Panza do not look like valiant knights as they perch awkwardly on the rough, wooden horse, which seems to lack magical potential.

26 **Critical Viewing**
Possible response: Real knights probably practice jousting with each other and use reliable armor, weapons, and horses as they learn battle maneuvers.

Chivalric Romances

Although little is known about the twelfth-century French writer, Chrétien de Troyes, the influence of his writings has lasted for more than eight centuries. Indeed, stories like the ones he wrote enchanted Don Quixote, a character invented four centuries later. Chrétien de Troyes did more than any other writer to introduce tales of King Arthur's knights to literature.

Connect to the Literature Point out to students that de Troyes' three major works, *Yvain, Lancelot,* and *Perceval,* are tales of the knights of King Arthur's Round Table. *Yvain* and *Lancelot* explore the conflict between love and the knight's chivalric duty to bring glory to himself or to his lord. *Perceval,* on the other hand, focuses on a knight's spiritual quest. Ask students to list three qualities that Don Quixote shares with the idealized knights of medieval romance.
Possible response: Quixote is idealistic, honorable, and fearless.

28 Reading Strategy

Comparing and Contrasting

• Point out that in the bracketed passage, Sancho Panza claims that he could govern any island that Don Quixote might give him. **Ask** students to compare Sancho Panza's confidence in himself with what they know about his abilities.
Possible response: Because Sancho Panza impulsively leaves his family and farm to be Don Quixote's squire, he seems to be more of a follower than a leader; he is dim-witted, gullible, and has no political experience, all of which further contradict his belief that he can successfully govern an island.

• **Ask** students to respond to the Reading Strategy item: Compare and contrast the promises Don Quixote makes with the actual abilities of a knight to grant such favors.
Answer: Knights are usually in the service of great lords or of the king; they do not have the power to give away kingdoms.

Mounted on his ass, Sancho Panza rode along like a patriarch, with saddlebags and flask, his mind set upon becoming governor of that island that his master had promised him. Don Quixote determined to take the same route and road over the Campo de Montiel[2] that he had followed on his first journey; but he was not so uncomfortable this time, for it was early morning and the sun's rays fell upon them slantingly and accordingly did not tire them too much.

"Look, Sir Knight-errant," said Sancho, "your Grace should not forget that island you promised me; for no matter how big it is, I'll be able to govern it right enough."

"I would have you know, friend Sancho Panza," replied Don Quixote, "that among the knights-errant of old it was a very common custom to make their squires governors of the islands or the kingdoms that they won, and I am resolved that in my case so pleasing a usage shall not fall into desuetude.[3] I even mean to go them one better; for they very often, perhaps most of the time, waited until their squires were old men who had had their fill of serving their masters during bad days and worse nights, whereupon they would give them the title of count, or marquis at most, of some valley or province more or less. But if you live and I live, it well may be that within a week I shall win some kingdom with others dependent upon it, and it will be the easiest thing in the world to crown you king of one of them. You need not marvel at this, for all sorts of unforeseen things happen to knights like me, and I may readily be able to give you even more than I have promised."

"In that case," said Sancho Panza, "if by one of those miracles of which your Grace was speaking I should become king, I would certainly send for Juana Gutiérrez, my old lady, to come and be my queen, and the young ones could be infantes."[4]

"There is no doubt about it," Don Quixote assured him.

"Well, I doubt it," said Sancho, "for I think that even if God were to rain kingdoms upon the earth, no crown would sit well on the head of Mari Gutiérrez,[5] for I am telling you, sir, as a queen she is not worth two maravedis.[6] She would do better as a countess, God help her."

"Leave everything to God, Sancho," said Don Quixote, "and he will give you whatever is most fitting; but I trust you will not be so pusillanimous[7] as to be content with anything less than the title of viceroy."

"That I will not," said Sancho Panza, "especially seeing that I have in your Grace so illustrious a master who can give me all that is suitable to me and all that I can manage."

---

2. **Campo de Montiel** (käm´ po dā mōn tyēl´) site of a major battle in Spain in 1369.
3. **desuetude** (des´ wi tood) *n.* disuse.
4. **infantes** (in fan´ tāz) sons of Spanish or Portuguese monarchs.
5. **Mari Gutiérrez** Sancho Panza's wife (also called Juana Gutiérrez).
6. **maravedis** (mar´ ə vä dēz) former Spanish coin of trivial monetary value.
7. **pusillanimous** (pyoo´ si lan´ ə məs) *adj.* cowardly.

780 ■ *The Renaissance and Rationalism*

---

27 **Chivalric Romances**

Stories of the legendary deeds of King Arthur's knights make up a genre called medieval romances. These romances typically feature idealized knights who are gentlemanly, courteous, and honorable men whose oaths bind them in fidelity to God, the king, and their ladyloves and whose journeys take them to distant ho lands.

Chivalric romances can be found throughout world literature. The *Song of Roland* recounts heroic deeds in the eighth-century court of Charlemagne. *Perceval,* by Chrétien de Troyes, features a quest for the Grail, or holy cup. Although *Don Quixote* parodies medieval romances like these, the novel nonetheless retains a strong connection to this rich literary heritage.

Connect to the Literature

What does Don Quixote have in common with the idealized knights of medieval romances?

Reading Strategy
Comparing and Contrasting Compare and contrast the promises that Don Quixote makes with the actual abilities of a knight to grant such favors.

Vocabulary Builder
illustrious (i lus´ trē əs) *adj.* distinguished or outstanding

---

Enrichment

Cervantes's Dream

Cervantes understood Don Quixote's desire to be something that he could not be. All through his life, Cervantes wanted to be a great poet. He wrote twenty to thirty plays in verse in the years immediately following 1585, but he was not pleased with them. By the time he wrote *Don Quixote,* he knew that he lacked poetic gifts. The absurdity and appeal of this great character at the center of a masterpiece derive not only from Cervantes's graceful style but also from his identification with his hero.

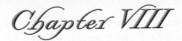

*Of the good fortune which the valorous Don Quixote had in the
terrifying and never-before-imagined adventure of the windmills,
along with other events that deserve to be suitably recorded.*

At this point they caught sight of thirty or forty windmills which were standing on the plain there, and no sooner had Don Quixote laid eyes upon them than he turned to his squire and said, "Fortune is guiding our affairs better than we could have wished; for you see there before you, friend Sancho Panza, some thirty or more lawless giants with whom I mean to do battle. I shall deprive them of their lives, and with the spoils from this encounter we shall begin to enrich ourselves; for this is righteous warfare, and it is a great service to God to remove so accursed a breed from the face of the earth."

"What giants?" said Sancho Panza.

"Those that you see there," replied his master, "those with the long arms some of which are as much as two leagues[8] in length."

"But look, your Grace, those are not giants but windmills, and what appear to be arms are their wings which, when whirled in the breeze, cause the millstone to go."

"It is plain to be seen," said Don Quixote, "that you have had little experience in this matter of adventures. If you are afraid, go off to one side and say your prayers while I am engaging them in fierce, unequal combat."

Saying this, he gave spurs to his steed Rocinante, without paying any heed to Sancho's warning that these were truly windmills and not giants that he was riding forth to attack. Nor even when he was close upon them did he perceive what they really were, but shouted at the top of his lungs, "Do not seek to flee, cowards and vile creatures that you are, for it is but a single knight with whom you have to deal!"

At that moment a little wind came up and the big wings began turning.

"Though you flourish as many arms as did the giant Briareus," said Don Quixote when he perceived this, "you still shall have to answer to me."

He thereupon commended himself with all his heart to his lady Dulcinea, beseeching her to succor him in this peril; and, being well covered with his shield and with his lance at rest, he bore down upon them at a full gallop and fell upon the first mill that stood in his way, giving a thrust at the wing, which was whirling at such a speed that his lance was broken into bits and both horse and horseman went rolling over the plain, very much battered indeed. Sancho upon his donkey came hurrying to his master's assistance as fast as he could, but when he reached the spot, the knight was unable to move, so great was the shock with which he and Rocinante had hit the ground.

8. **leagues** units of distance, each measuring approximately 3.5 miles.

Reading Strategy
Comparing and Contrasting Do you think that, as a knight, Don Quixote is an effective role model for his squire? Why or why not?

Reading Strategy
Comparing and Contrasting Do you think the outcome of Don Quixote's battle is different from that which a real knight would experience? Explain.

✓ **Reading Check** ③①

What are the giants that Don Quixote intends to fight?

from *Don Quixote* ■ 781

Differentiated Instruction   Solutions for All Learners

Enrichment for Gifted/Talented Students

Tell students that the scene described on p. 781—tilting at windmills—is not only the most famous from this novel, it is one of the most famous scenes in all of Western literature. The phrase itself—"tilting at windmills"—has entered the English language and refers to an act that is courageous but foolish or is based on an incomplete understanding of the situation.

Ask students to draw or paint an image of this scene, showing Don Quixote on Rocinante, "tilting at windmills." Refer students to the image on p. 783, which depicts the end of Quixote's "battle."

Suggest that students capture Don Quixote's earnest pursuit of defeating "giants" or the humor of the situation in their artwork. Have students display their completed work in the classroom.

㉙ Reading Strategy
Comparing and Contrasting

• Ask a volunteer to read the bracketed passage aloud. **Ask** students what Don Quixote means when he says that he is going to engage the "giants" in "unequal combat." **Answer:** He means that the contest is unequal because he is only one knight and there are many "giants."

• **Ask** students the first Reading Strategy question: Do you think that, as a knight, Don Quixote is an effective role model for his squire? Why or why not? **Answer:** Yes; Don Quixote is an effective role model because he is independent, fearless, and willing to confront what he perceives as evil, even when he is outnumbered. On the other hand, he is not an effective role model, because he behaves foolishly.

▶ **Monitor Progress Ask** students to point out the differences between the character of Don Quixote and the character of Sancho Panza. **Answer:** Don Quixote is a dreamer who does not comprehend reality; Sancho Panza is practical and sees the world for what it is.

㉚ Reading Strategy
Comparing and Contrasting

• Tell students that the "tilting at windmills" scene is the most famous episode of the novel.

• **Ask** students the second Reading Strategy question: Do you think the outcome of Don Quixote's battle is different from that which a real knight would experience? Explain. **Possible response:** Don Quixote's encounter with the windmill is not a real battle because the windmill is an inanimate object; however, a real knight might also find himself unhorsed and injured after a defeat.

㉛ Reading Check

Answer: The giants are actually windmills.

Infer

- Point out that the magician Frestón, to whom Don Quixote refers in the bracketed passage, was introduced in a chapter that precedes this episode.

- **Ask** students who they think Frestón might be.
  Possible response: Frestón might be an evil magician whom Don Quixote has invented, or he may be a real person who has taken Quixote's possessions because he has failed to fulfill his "real world" responsibilities.

33 **Literary Analysis**

Parody

- Read and discuss with students the bracketed passage.

- **Ask** students what aspects of knights' conduct is parodied in this passage.
  Possible response: Don Quixote's refusal to admit that he is injured makes him feel like a brave knight, but Sancho Panza cannot perform his duty as squire if he does not know his knight needs help.

- Have students **respond** to the Literary Analysis item: List three "things that are almost beyond belief" that Don Quixote has already experienced.
  Possible response: Don Quixote's renaming of the horse and Aldonza Lorenzo to make them appear to be figures of chivalry; the assembly of a suit of armor from old pieces of armor, cardboard, and scrap metal; and the battle with the windmills are almost beyond belief.

"God help us!" exclaimed Sancho, "did I not tell your Grace to look well, that those were nothing but windmills, a fact which no one could fail to see unless he had other mills of the same sort in his head?"

"Be quiet, friend Sancho," said Don Quixote. "Such are the fortunes of war, which more than any other are subject to constant change. What is more, when I come to think of it, I am sure that this must be the work of that magician Frestón, the one who robbed me of my study and my books, and who has thus changed the giants into windmills in order to deprive me of the glory of overcoming them, so great is the enmity that he bears me; but in the end his evil arts shall not prevail against this trusty sword of mine."

"May God's will be done," was Sancho Panza's response. And with the aid of his squire the knight was once more mounted on Rocinante, who stood there with one shoulder half out of joint. And so, speaking of the adventure that had just befallen them, they continued along the Puerto Lápice highway; for there, Don Quixote said, they could not fail to find many and varied adventures, this being a much traveled thoroughfare. The only thing was, the knight was exceedingly downcast over the loss of his lance.

"I remember," he said to his squire, "having read of a Spanish knight by the name of Diego Pérez de Vargas, who, having broken his sword in battle, tore from an oak a heavy bough or branch and with it did such feats of valor that day, and pounded so many Moors, that he came to be known as Machuca, and he and his descendants from that day forth have been called Vargas y Machuca. I tell you this because I too intend to provide myself with just such a bough as the one he wielded, and with it I propose to do such exploits that you shall deem yourself fortunate to have been found worthy to come with me and behold and witness things that are almost beyond belief."

"God's will be done," said Sancho. "I believe everything that your Grace says; but straighten yourself up in the saddle a little, for you seem to be slipping down on one side, owing, no doubt, to the shaking up that you received in your fall."

"Ah, that is the truth," replied Don Quixote, "and if I do not speak of my sufferings, it is for the reason that it is not permitted knights-errant to complain of any wound whatsoever, even though their bowels may be dropping out."

"If that is the way it is," said Sancho, "I have nothing more to say; but, God knows, it would suit me better if your Grace did complain when something hurts him. I can assure you that I mean to do so, over the least little thing that ails me—that is, unless the same rule applies to squires as well."

 Don Quixote laughed long and heartily over Sancho's simplicity, telling him that he might complain as much as he liked and where and when he liked, whether he had good cause or not; for he had read nothing to the contrary in the ordinances of chivalry.[9] Sancho then called

---

9. **ordinances of chivalry** codes, or rules, of knighthood.

782 ■ *The Renaissance and Rationalism*

Literary Analysis
Parody List three "things that are almost beyond belief" that Don Quixote has already experienced.

33

Strategy for English Learners

Have students discuss the conversation in which Sancho Panza urges Don Quixote to talk about the pain he is in. Ask students to discuss the main points each character makes and why he makes those points. Remind students that Sancho Panza, as a parent and a farmer, is accustomed to taking care of people and things that need his help, whereas Don Quixote wants to emulate a brave knight by keeping his pain a secret.

Have students work in pairs to role-play the parts of both characters. Encourage them also to use both facial expressions and gestures to help them communicate the personality traits of the characters.

Let students evaluate their own and their classmates' work. After each performance you might ask the following: Did the scene bring out the contrasts between the characters? How did it show these contrasts?

35 ◀ **Critical Viewing**
Based solely on this painting, predict the outcome of most of Don Quixote's adventures. **[Predict]**

34 his master's attention to the fact that it was time to eat. The knight replied that he himself had no need of food at the moment, but his squire might eat whenever he chose. Having been granted this permission, Sancho seated himself as best he could upon his beast, and, taking out from his saddlebags the provisions that he had stored there, he rode along leisurely behind his master, munching his victuals and taking a good, hearty swig now and then at the leather flask in a manner that might well have caused the biggest-bellied tavernkeeper of Málaga to envy him. Between drafts he gave not so much as a thought to any promise that his master might have made him, nor did he look upon it as any hardship, but rather as good sport, to go in quest of adventures however hazardous they might be.

36 The short of the matter is, they spent the night under some trees, from one of which Don Quixote tore off a withered bough to serve him as a lance, placing it in the lance head from which he had removed the broken one. He did not sleep all night long for thinking of his lady Dulcinea; for this was in accordance with what he had read in his books, of men of arms in the forest or desert places who kept a wakeful vigil, sustained by the memory of their ladies fair. Not so with Sancho, whose stomach was full, and not with chicory water. He fell into a dreamless slumber, and had not his master called him, he would not have been awakened either by the rays of the sun in his face or by the many birds who greeted the coming of the new day with their merry song.

Upon arising, he had another go at the flask, finding it somewhat more flaccid than it had been the night before, a circumstance which grieved his heart, for he could not see that they were on the way to remedying the deficiency within any very short space of time. Don Quixote did not wish any breakfast; for, as has been said, he was in the habit of nourishing himself on savorous memories. They then set out once more

Reading Strategy
Comparing and Contrasting In what ways do Don Quixote and Sancho Panza accurately imitate the lifestyle of a knight and his squire?

 **Reading Check** **37**

Where did Don Quixote spend the night?

from *Don Quixote* ■ 783

Infer

- Ask two volunteers to read aloud the bracketed passage, with one reading the part of Don Quixote and the other reading the part of Sancho Panza.

- Point out how readily Sancho Panza agrees with Don Quixote's request. **Ask** students why they think Sancho Panza complies so quickly. **Possible response:** Sancho Panza is happy to avoid putting himself at risk of physical harm.

ASSESS

Answers

1. **Possible response:** Don Quixote's endearing qualities are his optimism, his courage in facing his imaginary foes, and his devotion to upholding the "rules" he has read about in books, even though those books are fictional.

2. (a) Don Quixote promises to make him governor of an island. (b) **Possible response:** No; Don Quixote is irrational and will never conquer anything.

3. (a) Don Quixote believes that the windmills are "lawless giants" and that he must take their riches. (b) The wings of the windmill appear to be long arms that remind him of a giant he has read about in tales of knighthood. (c) Sancho Panza means that Don Quixote is unrealistic, or lives in a dream world, and is out of touch with reality.

4. (a) Seeing things as they are, Sancho Panza keeps his master from even greater danger, but he is mild-mannered enough neither to quit nor to stand in Don Quixote's way. (b) **Possible response:** Sancho Panza likes Don Quixote; he feels sorry for him and wants to protect him; he enjoys the game of playing "squire" to Don Quixote's "knight-errant."

5. **Possible response:** Don Quixote might make a good writer or movie director.

---

along the road to Puerto Lápice, and around three in the afternoon they came in sight of the pass that bears that name.

"There," said Don Quixote as his eyes fell upon it, "we may plunge our arms up to the elbow in what are known as adventures. But I must warn you that even though you see me in the greatest peril in the world, you are not to lay hand upon your sword to defend me, unless it be that those who attack me are rabble and men of low degree, in which case you may very well come to my aid; but if they be gentlemen, it is in no wise permitted by the laws of chivalry that you should assist me until you yourself shall have been dubbed a knight."

38 "Most certainly, sir," replied Sancho, "your Grace shall be very well obeyed in this; all the more so for the reason that I myself am of a peaceful disposition and not fond of meddling in the quarrels and feuds of others. However, when it comes to protecting my own person, I shall not take account of those laws of which you speak, seeing that all laws, human and divine, permit each one to defend himself whenever he is attacked."

"I am willing to grant you that," assented Don Quixote, "but in this matter of defending me against gentlemen you must restrain your natural impulses."

"I promise you I shall do so," said Sancho. "I will observe this precept as I would the Sabbath day."

Critical Reading

1. **Respond:** Which aspects of Don Quixote's appearance or behavior—if any—do you find endearing? Explain.

2. **(a) Recall:** What promise does Don Quixote make to convince Sancho Panza to be his squire? **(b) Speculate:** Do you think this promise will be fulfilled? Why or why not?

3. **(a) Recall:** What reasons does Don Quixote give for fighting the windmills? **(b) Infer:** What characteristics of the windmills convince him that they are worthy foes? **(c) Interpret:** What does Sancho Panza mean when he says Don Quixote has "other mills of the same sort in his head"?

4. **(a) Infer:** Why is Sancho Panza a particularly helpful squire to Don Quixote? **(b) Draw Conclusions:** Why do you think Sancho Panza stays with Don Quixote even after realizing that Don Quixote has lost touch with reality?

5. **Speculate:** For which careers might it be considered an asset to have a vivid imagination like that of Don Quixote?

Go Online
Author Link
For: More about Miguel de Cervantes Saavedra
Visit: www.PHSchool.com
Web Code: ete-9605

Go Online For additional information about Miguel
Author Link de Cervantes Saavedra, have students type in the Web Code, then select *S* from the alphabet, and then select Miguel de Cervantes Saavedra.

Apply the Skills

from *Don Quixote*

Literary Analysis
Parody

1. **(a)** List three characteristics of a medieval romance that *Don Quixote* parodies. **(b)** What details indicate that the parody is affectionate or gentle? **(c)** In what way does Cervantes suggest his admiration for chivalric tales? Explain.

2. Using the chart shown below, identify details from the selection that parody elements of a real knight's life. Indicate how Don Quixote's personality or circumstances influence the parody.

Real Knight	Details	Don Quixote's Influence
Training		
Weapons		
Ladylove		

Connecting Literary Elements

3. **(a)** Identify three events that suggest a struggle between reality and fantasy. **(b)** What **theme** or insight into life do these events reveal?

4. **(a)** In what ways does Don Quixote embody the theme that a vivid imagination makes a life richer? **(b)** Do you agree with this theme? Why or why not?

5. **(a)** List two ways in which Sancho Panza is a realist—someone who sees the world as it is. **(b)** What theme does he embody?

Reading Strategy
Comparing and Contrasting

6. **(a)** **Compare and contrast** the appearance, attitude, and motives of Don Quixote and Sancho Panza as they embark on their quest. **(b)** Do you think their personalities complement each other, or are their differences obstacles to be overcome? Explain.

7. In what ways is Don Quixote, at least in his own mind, similar to the knights of old?

Extend Understanding

8. **Career Connection:** What careers require the kind of determination Don Quixote needed to become a knight? Explain.

QuickReview

A **parody** is an imitation of another work of literature for amusement or for instruction.

A **theme** is a central message or idea revealed through a literary work.

To **compare and contrast**, note the similarities and differences between two things.

 Go Online
Assessment
For: Self-test
Visit: www.PHSchool.com
Web Code: eta-6604

from *Don Quixote* ■ 785

Answers continued

8. **Possible response:** Being a professional athlete or member of the armed forces requires determination.

Go Online Students may use the **Self-test** to pre-**Assessment** pare for **Selection Test A** or **Selection Test B.**

Answers

1. **(a)** Some characteristics include his armor, his horse, and his squire. **(b)** Cervantes portrays Don Quixote as courageous, idealistic, and committed to behaving honorably at all times. **(c)** Cervantes mentions many of the knights who were the heroes of these tales and includes details of their adventures; it is clear that he knows much about these writings.

2. **Possible response: Training: Details:** Don Quixote reads about the knight's code of honor in order to prepare. **Influence:** He takes his reading to extremes. **Weapons: Details:** He uses old, rusted armor; he repairs a helmet with cardboard. **Influence:** Don Quixote's imagination allows him to create equipment from cardboard. **Ladylove: Details:** Don Quixote knows that knights have noble women they idealize. **Influence:** His ladylove is a farm girl. Another sample answer can be found on **Literary Analysis Graphic Organizer B,** p. 141 in *Graphic Organizer Transparencies.*

3. **(a) Possible response:** Don Quixote chooses a broken-down nag for his horse; he chooses a farmer as his squire; he tilts at windmills. **(b)** These events reveal that a vivid imagination enriches life.

4. **(a)** He shows that he can take the mundane and create fantasy. **(b) Possible responses:** Yes; it is better to live a richer life through imagination. No; it is more important to be practical.

5. **(a)** He recognizes that Don Quixote can get hurt acting out his fantasies; he believes in tending to the needs of the body, such as food and sleep. **(b) Possible response:** One must be a realist to survive.

6. **(a)** Both Don Quixote and Sancho Panza are dressed poorly but are optimistic and have high expectations. Don Quixote lives in a fantasy world and is motivated by idealism; Sancho Panza lives in the real world and is motivated by the hope of material rewards. **(b) Possible response:** Don Quixote brings excitement to Sancho Panza who, in turn, helps protect Don Quixote.

7. **Possible response:** Don Quixote is well bred, honorable, and adventurous.

785

❶ Vocabulary Lesson

Word Analysis: Latin Root -ject-

1. b   3. a
2. d   4. c

Vocabulary Builder: Synonyms

1. conjectures   5. ingenuity
2. appropriate   6. illustrious
3. infatuation   7. incongruous
4. constitution

Spelling Strategy

1. irreverent   2. irrefutable

❷ Grammar and Style Lesson

1. Smashing; subject
2. ending; object of preposition *of*
3. attacking; direct object
4. Eating; subject
5. supporting; predicate nominative

Writing Application

Possible response: <u>Righting</u> wrongs is the usual practice of knights. (subject)

A knight leaves the task of <u>cleaning</u> the equipment to his squire. (object of preposition)

A chivalrous knight holds <u>serving</u> his lady uppermost in his mind. (direct object)

A knight's most important task is <u>defending</u> the weak. (predicate nominative)

<u>Fighting</u> dragons and giants can win fame for a knight. (subject)

ᏔᏀ Writing and Grammar
Platinum Level

For support in teaching the Grammar and Style Lesson, use Chapter 20, Section 1.

Build Language Skills

❶ Vocabulary Lesson

Word Analysis: Latin Root -ject-

The Latin root -ject- means "to throw." If you make a *conjecture,* you "throw in," or offer, a thought or a guess. Each numbered word below contains the root -ject-. Match each word with the letter of the correct definition.

1. rejection
   (*re-* = back)
2. inject
   (*in-* = to bring in)
3. project
   (*pro-* = before, or forward)
4. trajectory
   (*tra-* = across)

a. to throw forward
b. the condition of being thrown back
c. the path of something thrown through space
d. to throw or put into

Vocabulary Builder: Synonyms

Review the vocabulary list on page 769. Then, for each item below, identify the vocabulary word with the closest meaning.

1. theories   5. imagination
2. confiscate   6. famous
3. shallow affection   7. unsuitable
4. composition

Spelling Strategy

The prefix *im-* or *in-,* meaning "not," changes to *ir-* when it is added to words beginning with *r*: <u>irreparable</u> = not able to be repaired; <u>irregular</u> = not regular. Use the prefix *ir-* to write the words for each definition below.

1. not reverent   2. not refutable

❷ Grammar and Style Lesson

Gerunds

A **gerund** is a verb form ending in *-ing* that acts as a noun. Gerunds can perform all the roles of a noun in a sentence: subject, direct or indirect object, object of a preposition, and predicate nominative.

Subject: *Jousting* becomes a challenge, for he owns no lance.

Direct Object: Sancho Panza wants *fighting* the windmills to end peacefully.

Object of a Preposition: Don Quixote is an early riser and fond of *hunting*.

Predicate Nominative: Don Quixote's favorite pastime is *reading*.

Practice Identify each gerund below, and name its function in the sentence.

1. Smashing the makeshift armor with his sword gave Don Quixote no pleasure.
2. He commends the author's way of ending his books.
3. On his journey, Don Quixote tries attacking windmills.
4. Eating is one of Sancho's greatest pleasures.
5. The foremost goal of a squire is supporting his knight.

Writing Application Write four sentences describing the activities of a knight-errant. Use a gerund in each sentence, underlining the gerund and identifying its use in the sentence.

ᏔᏀ *Prentice Hall Writing and Grammar Connection: Platinum Level, Chapter 20, Section 1*

Assessment Practice

Evaluate and Make Judgments   **(For more practice, see *Test Preparation Workbook,* p. 34.)**

Standardized tests require students to make judgments about an author's meaning. Have students practice this skill by completing this item, which features a passage from an essay by Jorge Luis Borges:

Defeated by reality, by Spain, Don Quixote died in his native village around 1614.

Which best expresses Borges's view of Spanish culture in the early 1600s?

A Spanish people should have traveled more.
B Spanish people wanted to stay in their native village.
C Spain was a place that did not value imagination.
D Spain was a place where older people felt defeated.

Answer **C** is correct because it is the only one that makes a connection between Spain and the contrast between imagination and reality implied by the passage.

❸ Writing Lesson

Profile of a Comic Hero

A hero in literature is often a very serious character on an important quest. In *Don Quixote*, however, Cervantes reinvented this character by creating a comic hero. In the spirit of *Don Quixote*, create your own comic hero and write a profile of his or her idiosyncrasies and achievements.

Prewriting   Start by creating a chart like the one shown to categorize the traits of your comic hero. Then, give an example of each trait in action.

Model: Gathering Details

Trait	Trait in Action

Drafting   Begin your profile with a catchy introduction, such as a quotation or an anecdote that illustrates a humorous quality of your hero. Then, present the traits of your hero and specific examples of each.

Revising   Compare the details you gathered in your chart against your draft. Keep Cervantes's model in mind, and make sure that you have provided enough information to convey your hero's comic qualities. If necessary, add further details to develop those traits.

W͜G Prentice Hall Writing and Grammar Connection: Platinum Level, Chapter 6, Section 4

❹ Extend Your Learning

Listening and Speaking Work with a partner to **role-play** the scene in which Sancho Panza tries to talk Don Quixote out of attacking the windmills. Use the following tips to prepare your scene:

- Make a few notes to capture the personality of the character you will role-play.
- Adjust your voice and facial expressions to reflect the emotions being expressed.
- Decide how, if at all, you will refer to his transformation.
- Speak directly to your partner as if you are having a conversation.

Present the scene for the class. **[Group Activity]**

Research and Technology Create a **visual essay** on the subject of heroes. Use computer programs such as music or imaging software to enhance your essay. Include scanned or downloaded images, and write captions that illustrate how your examples relate to the central message about heroes. Display your essay for the class.

For: An additional research activity
Visit: www.PHSchool.com
Web Code: etd-7604

from Don Quixote ■ 787

❸ Writing Lesson

- To give students guidance in writing this profile, give them the **Support for Writing Lesson**, p. 65 in *Unit 6 Resources*.

- Explain that a profile, unlike a biography, does not tell the full story of a person's life but focuses on specific aspects of an individual. Tell students that they will write a profile that focuses on elements that make a character humorous and heroic.

- Tell students to choose traits that illustrate the humorous or heroic side of their characters.

- Use the Descriptive Essay rubrics in *General Resources*, pp. 67–68, to evaluate students' profiles.

W͜G Writing and Grammar
Platinum Level
For support in teaching the Writing Lesson, use Chapter 6, Section 4.

❹ Research and Technology

- Point out to students that as they begin to research the subject of heroes, they will encounter various types of heroes: knights, superheroes, and everyday heroes.

- Have students meet in small groups to brainstorm the heroes or types of heroes they would like to include in their essays.

- The **Support for Extend Your Learning** page (*Unit 6 Resources*, p. 66) provides guided note-taking opportunities to help students complete the Extend Your Learning activities.

Go Online Have students type in the Research Web Code for another research activity.

Assessment Resources

The following resources can be used to assess students' knowledge and skills.

Unit 6 Resources
    Selection Test A, pp. 68–70
    Selection Test B, pp. 71–73
    Benchmark Test 7, pp. 74–79

General Resources
    Rubrics for Descriptive Essay, pp. 67–68

Go Online Students may use the Self-test to Assessment prepare for **Selection Test A** or **Selection Test B**.

Benchmark
Administer **Benchmark Test 7**. If some students need further work, use the **Interpretation Guide** to determine the appropriate reteaching page in the **Reading Kit** and on **Success Tracker**.

Standard Course of Study

Goal 4: CRITICAL THINKING

CT.4.02.2 Use specific references from texts to show theme.

CT.4.03.5 Analyze how writers achieve a sense of completeness and closure.

Goal 5: LITERATURE

LT.5.01.2 Build knowledge of literary genres, and explore how characteristics apply to literature of world cultures.

LT.5.01.6 Make connections between historical and contemporary issues in world literature.

LT.5.03.6 Make inferences, predictions, and draw conclusions based on world literature.

Goal 6: GRAMMAR AND USAGE

GU.6.02.1 Edit for agreement, tense choice, pronouns, antecedents, case, and complete sentences.

Step-by-Step Teaching Guide	Pacing Guide
PRETEACH	
• Administer Vocabulary and Reading Warm-ups as necessary.	5 min.
• Engage students' interest with the motivation activity.	5 min.
• Read and discuss author and background features. **FT**	10 min.
• Introduce the Literary Analysis Skill: Fables. **FT**	5 min.
• Introduce the Reading Strategy: Drawing Conclusions. **FT**	10 min.
• Prepare students to read by teaching the selection vocabulary. **FT**	
TEACH	
• Informally monitor comprehension while students read independently or in groups. **FT**	30 min.
• Monitor students' comprehension with the Reading Check notes.	as students read
• Reinforce vocabulary with Vocabulary Builder notes.	as students read
• Develop students' understanding of fables with the Literary Analysis annotations. **FT**	5 min.
• Develop students' ability to draw conclusions with the Reading Strategy annotations. **FT**	5 min.
ASSESS/EXTEND	
• Assess students' comprehension and mastery of the Literary Analysis and Reading Strategy by having them answer the Apply the Skills questions. **FT**	15 min.
• Have students complete the Vocabulary Lesson and the Grammar and Style Lesson. **FT**	15 min.
• Apply students' ability to punctuate dialogue by using the Writing Lesson. **FT**	45 min. or homework
• Apply students' understanding by using one or more of the Extend Your Learning activities.	20–90 min. or homework
• Administer Selection Test A or Selection Test B. **FT**	15 min.

Resources

Print

Unit 6 Resources

Transparency

Graphic Organizer Transparencies

Print

Reader's Notebook [L2]

Reader's Notebook: Adapted Version [L1]

Reader's Notebook: English Learner's Version [EL]

Unit 6 Resources

Technology

Listening to Literature Audio CDs [L2, EL]

Print

Unit 6 Resources

General Resources

Technology

Go Online: Research [L3]

Go Online: Self-test [L3]

ExamView®, **Test Bank [L3]**

Choosing Resources for Differentiated Instruction

[**L1**] Special Needs Students

[**L2**] Below-Level Students

[**L3**] All Students

[**L4**] Advanced Students

[**EL**] English Learners

For Vocabulary and Reading Warm-ups and for Selection Tests, A signifies "less challenging" and B "more challenging." For Graphic Organizer transparencies, A signifies "not filled in" and B "filled in."

FT Fast Track Instruction: To move the lesson more quickly, use the strategies and activities identified with **FT**.

Scaffolding for Less Proficient and Advanced Students

The leveled Critical Thinking questions after selections progress in the levels of thinking required to answer them. To address the needs of your different students, you may use the (a) level questions for your less proficient students and the (b) level questions with your on-level and advanced students. The occasional (c) level questions are appropriate for your advanced students.

TeacherEXPRESS™ Use this complete suite of powerful teaching tools to make lesson planning and testing quicker and easier.

PRENTICE HALL

StudentEXPRESS™ Use the interactive textbook (online and on CD-ROM) to make selections and activities come alive with audio and video support and interactive questions.

Monitoring Progress

Before students read these selections, administer **Diagnostic Test 8** (*Unit 6 Resources*, **pp. 80–82**). This test will determine students' level of readiness for the reading and vocabulary skills.

Go Online **For:** Information about Lexiles
Professional **Visit:** www.PHSchool.com
Development **Web Code:** eue-1111

Motivation

Remind students that clichés are expressions that have become worn because of constant use. Moral clichés address issues of right and wrong or good character. Ask students to brainstorm a list of moral clichés. Record the clichés on the board, and add these to the list: *"A bird in the hand is worth two in the bush," "Haste makes waste," "The early bird catches the worm,"* and *"A stitch in time saves nine."* Then, lead students in a discussion about how moral clichés have become an important part of our culture. Use these questions to stimulate discussion: What role do moral clichés play in American culture? Why do they remain popular? Whose morality do they reflect? Are there such things as common moral values?

❶ Background

More About the Author

Relatively little is known about Jean de La Fontaine: He left no memoirs and few letters. The few documents that do survive provide tantalizing hints about his life, however. From a marriage contract, we know that twenty-six-year-old Jean married fourteen-year-old Marie Hericart on November 19, 1647. The couple had a son, but the marriage did not endure. They separated in 1658.

It appears that La Fontaine went to Limoges in 1663, voluntarily or by force, to prevent himself from becoming embroiled in his patron's disgrace. In 1664, he applied for a license in Paris to publish a book, indicating that his exile was relatively brief.

Geography Note

Use the map on this page to identify France. Tell students that La Fontaine spent much of his time in Paris in north central France but that later he was exiled to the city of Limoges in the west central part of the country.

Build Skills [Fables]

❶ The Fox and the Crow • The Oak and the Reed

Jean de La Fontaine (1621–1695)

An early French example of the somewhat absent-minded professor, Jean de La Fontaine (zhän də là fō*n* ten´) delighted his seventeenth-century audience, as well as later generations, with his outpouring of short stories, poems, and fables. While learning to compose verses, La Fontaine dabbled with the possibilities of studying law, entering the priesthood, or following his father's profession of forest ranger before he finally settled on a literary career. An admirer of ancient poets and playwrights, La Fontaine began publishing his own stories in his early thirties and continued to write for nearly forty years.

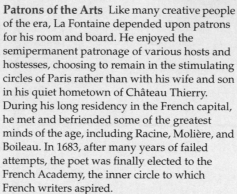

Patrons of the Arts Like many creative people of the era, La Fontaine depended upon patrons for his room and board. He enjoyed the semipermanent patronage of various hosts and hostesses, choosing to remain in the stimulating circles of Paris rather than with his wife and son in his quiet hometown of Château Thierry. During his long residency in the French capital, he met and befriended some of the greatest minds of the age, including Racine, Molière, and Boileau. In 1683, after many years of failed attempts, the poet was finally elected to the French Academy, the inner circle to which French writers aspired.

La Fontaine wrote in a variety of genres and styles, including prose tales, religious poetry, letters, and even an epitaph for his friend Molière. It is his vast collections of verse fables, however, for which La Fontaine is best remembered.

Words of Wisdom La Fontaine was a voracious reader of histories and literature. In fact, his own writings reflect the influences of Homer, Plato, and Boccaccio, among others. Many of La Fontaine's poems are adaptations of other works. Most contain quirky statements of ethics and philosophy, often in the form of homilies, or wise sayings. One of the major sources of his stories is Aesop, a sixth-century B.C. Greek storyteller of beast fables. A much-loved work by both authors, "The Ant and the Grasshopper," is a moralistic yet entertaining tale that contrasts the frolicsome grasshopper with the frugal, hard-working ant who collects stores of food to carry him through the winter.

Virtues and Vices La Fontaine's succinct, homespun animal stories address human idiosyncrasies, such as cowardice, curiosity, greed, and laziness. Stopping short of heavy-handed preaching, the stories contain common-sense reminders that delight as they instruct. La Fontaine used a wide range of nonhuman characters in his fables: ants, cats, wolves, trees, and mice are just a few. By putting animals in the place of humans, La Fontaine creates droll restatements of themes that continue to capture the imagination of his readers.

La Fontaine's 238 fables are so popular that French schoolchildren memorize them in their entirety and dramatize them as recital pieces. The French language is heavily salted with La Fontaine's witty aphorisms, such as "The sign brings customers," "A hungry stomach cannot hear," and "On the wings of Time grief flies away."

Preview

Connecting to the Literature

Winnie the Pooh, Snoopy, Garfield, Roadrunner, Wile E. Coyote, and the animal characters of Dr. Seuss—all figures from children's literature and cartoons—pass along useful bits of wisdom wrapped in laughter and entertainment. The seventeenth-century poetry of La Fontaine presents advice in a similar format.

❷ Literary Analysis

Fables

Whether in the form of a poem or a short story, a **fable** dramatizes a simple lesson or principle of behavior. Most fables share the following elements:

- creatures—animals or inanimate objects—who speak and interact as though they were human
- a clearly worded moral at either the beginning or the end
- a single compressed episode
- an implied frailty or fault of character that is often the object of satire

Look for these characteristics in the fables of La Fontaine.

Comparing Literary Works

Because many fables include creatures as main characters, these works often employ **personification,** a type of figurative language in which a nonhuman subject is given human characteristics. For example, in "The Oak and the Reed," the oak tree has a conversation with his neighbor, the reed. By giving human qualities to nonhumans, La Fontaine subtly charms his readers, teaching them valuable life lessons from the experiences of imaginary beings. As you read the poems in this grouping, note the variety and degree of human responses the creatures possess.

❸ Reading Strategy

Drawing Conclusions

La Fontaine does not directly state a moral or lesson to be learned from his fables. Instead, he allows readers to **draw conclusions** about the meaning of his works. To draw conclusions, consider the details of the fable, and use them to infer a larger message or meaning. Use a chart like the one shown to determine the moral, or general truth, that La Fontaine's fable teaches.

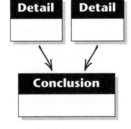

Vocabulary Builder

buffeted (buf´ it id) *v.* struck sharply (p. 793)

hazards (haz´ ərdz) *n.* dangers (p. 793)

impervious (im pʉr´ vē əs) *adj.* not affected by, or unable to be damaged (p. 794)

prone (prōn) *adj.* lying face downward (p. 794)

The Fox and the Crow / The Oak and the Reed ■ 789

NC Standard Course of Study

- Analyze how writers achieve a sense of completeness and closure. (CT.4.03.5)
- Make inferences, predictions, and draw conclusions based on world literature. (LT.5.03.6)

❷ Literary Analysis

Fables

- Tell students that Aesop, an ancient Greek, is credited with some of the most famous fables. Remind students of the fable about the tortoise and the hare: The hare challenges the tortoise to a race. Because the tortoise is slow, the hare believes that he will win easily. The hare, feeling secure about victory, stops to take a nap during the race, while the tortoise plods ahead and wins.

- Help students see the elements of fable found in "The Tortoise and the Hare": a fault of character, a clear moral, animals who act human, and a compressed episode.

- Point out that the two characters, the tortoise and the hare, are examples of personification.

❸ Reading Strategy

Drawing Conclusions

- Remind students that fables teach moral lessons.

- Refer students to the graphic organizer. **Tell** them to use the organizer to identify the moral of "The Tortoise and the Hare."
  Possible response: Detail: The tortoise walks slowly but keeps moving. **Detail:** The hare stops to take a nap and awakens to find that the tortoise has won the race. **Conclusion:** The moral of the fable is "Slow but steady wins the race."

- Give students a copy of **Reading Strategy Graphic Organizer A,** p. 142 in *Graphic Organizer Transparencies.* Have them use it to determine the moral in each of La Fontaine's fables.

Vocabulary Builder

- Pronounce each vocabulary word for students, and read the definitions as a class. Have students identify any words with which they are already familiar.

Differentiated Instruction Solutions for All Learners

Support for Special Needs Students

Have students complete the **Preview** and **Build Skills** pages for these selections in the *Reader's Notebook: Adapted Version.* These pages provide a selection summary, an abbreviated presentation of the reading and literary skills, and the graphic organizer on the **Build Skills** page in the student book.

Support for Less Proficient Readers

Have students complete the **Preview** and **Build Skills** pages for these selections in the *Reader's Notebook.* These pages provide a selection summary, an abbreviated presentation of the reading and literary skills, and the graphic organizer on the **Build Skills** page in the student book.

Support for English Learners

Have students complete the **Preview** and **Build Skills** pages for these selections in the *Reader's Notebook: English Learner's Version.* These pages provide a selection summary, an abbreviated presentation of the reading and literary skills, additional contextual vocabulary, and the graphic organizer on the **Build Skills** page in the student book.

Facilitate Understanding

Encourage students to brainstorm a list of characteristics that they associate with the fox and the crow. Record the associations on the board. After students have read "The Fox and the Crow," refer to the list on the board, and discuss why La Fontaine's choice of animals is suitable or unsuitable for the fable.

❶ About the Selection

In this fable, the cunning fox tricks the vain crow into giving up his cheese.

❷ Literary Analysis
Fables and Personification

• Remind students that personification is a type of figurative language that ascribes human characteristics to nonhuman beings and objects.

• **Ask** students the Literary Analysis question: What human traits does the fox possess?
Answer: The fox possesses cunning and speech.

❸ Reading Strategy
Drawing Conclusions

• Remind students that fables express morals, or universal truths about correct behavior.

• **Ask** students the Reading Strategy question: What general truth does the crow learn about pride?
Answer: The crow learns that the "flatterer lives at the flattered listener's cost."

▶ **Monitor Progress Ask** students to paraphrase the fox's message to the crow.
Possible response: A person who praises another insincerely does so to win favor at the listener's expense.

▶ **Reteach** If students are having difficulty drawing conclusions, use the **Reading Strategy** support, p. 88 in *Unit 6 Resources*.

---

❶ The **Fox** and the **Crow**

Jean de La Fontaine   *translated by Marianne Moore*

Background La Fontaine's fables were well suited to the Age of Reason. In them, he instructs the reader in prudent living, basing his aphorisms on the mind-over-emotions philosophy of seventeenth-century moralists. A key feature of these fables is the logical and carefully worded statement of advice—or moral—on such ethical issues as integrity, diligence, compromise, and pride. Although his poems seem simple and light, La Fontaine characteristically dwells on the dangers that lurk in seemingly innocent surroundings.

On his airy perch among the branches
    Master Crow was holding cheese in his beak.
Master Fox, whose pose suggested fragrances,[1]
    Said in language which of course I cannot speak,
5   "Aha, superb Sir Ebony, well met.
How black! who else boasts your metallic jet!
    If your warbling[2] were unique,
    Rest assured, as you are sleek,
One would say that our wood had hatched nightingales."
10 All aglow, Master Crow tried to run a few scales,
    Risking trills and intervals,
Dropping the prize as his huge beak sang false.
The fox pounced on the cheese and remarked, "My dear sir,
    Learn that every flatterer
15   Lives at the flattered listener's cost:
A lesson worth more than the cheese that you lost."
    The tardy learner, smarting under ridicule,
Swore he'd learned his last lesson as somebody's fool.

1. **fragrances** false and devious charm.
2. **warbling** melodious singing.

790 ■ *The Renaissance and Rationalism*

Literary Analysis
Fables and Personification What human traits does the fox possess?

Reading Strategy
Drawing Conclusions What general truth does the crow learn about pride?

Differentiated
Instruction   Solutions for All Learners

Accessibility at a Glance

	The Fox and the Crow	The Oak and the Reed
Language	Syntax: long sentences with embedded clauses and participial phrases	Syntax: long sentences with embedded clauses separated by semicolons
Concept Level	Accessible (the price of succumbing to flattery)	Accessible (the importance of adaptability to survival)
Literary Merit	Classic poetic fable with aphorisms	Classic poetic fable
Lexile	NP	NP
Overall Rating	Average	Average

"The Crow and the Fox", Félix Lorioux, illustration for "Fables" by Jean de La Fontaine, Private Collection/Roger Perrin, Copyright ©Artists Right Society (ARS), New York

⑤ ▲ Critical Viewing Identify details in this illustration that might interest young readers of La Fontaine's poems. **[Analyze]**

❹ Humanities

The Crow and the Fox,
by Félix Lorioux

This twentieth-century color engraving by French publicity and fashion designer Félix Lorioux (1872–1964) is characteristic of the artist's children's illustrations. Lorioux favors joyful images, mischievous animals and plants, and brilliant colors.

Use the following question for discussion:

What characteristics of the fox and the crow does this illustration capture?
Possible response: The illustration captures the expression of greed in the fox, with his upturned eyes and open mouth, and the foolishness of the crow, with his exuberant singing.

❺ Critical Viewing

Possible response: The umbrella hanging on the limb, the crow's necktie, the whimsical worms, the personified tree, and the falling cheese might interest young readers.

Differentiated
Instruction Solutions for All Learners

Strategy for Special Needs Students
Help students locate examples of visual art forms, like cartoons or video games, that use personified animals for amusing effect. Make sure that each student has an example to analyze. Ask each student to respond to the following items in writing: Describe one animal in this example. What human traits does this animal have? How does the artist convey these human traits to the viewer? How does the artist achieve a comic effect?

Enrichment for Gifted/Talented Students
Tell students that the critic David Lee Rubins laments that "La Fontaine's work runs a grave risk of being taken for granted, underread, misread, and finally misjudged" because many readers imagine his work is aimed primarily at children. Direct students to conduct research into Jean-Baptiste Oudry's illustrations for the 1755 edition of La Fontaine's *Fables.* Have them write an essay in which they analyze Oudry's work. Suggest that they bring copies of Oudry's work to class and share their analyses with their classmates.

⑥ Humanities

The oak tree is an important symbol in world literature. Generally, it represents strength and protection. The acorn, the seed of the oak tree, is recognized as a symbol of life.

The oak has traditionally played a part in different cultures. It is often associated with thunder gods and thunder. In Graeco-Roman culture, Zeus, the sky god, and Hera, his wife, are also the oak gods. Worshippers of Zeus and Hera wore oak leaf crowns. Christians see the oak tree as a symbol of Christ's strength in difficult times. The tree is sometimes thought to be the tree of the cross. In Judaism, the oak tree is a symbol of divine presence. On the other hand, the Chinese associate the oak tree with physical weakness because it does not bend with the wind.

Use the following questions for discussion:

• Why might the acorn have become a symbol of life?
  Possible response: In addition to their role in the propagation of oak trees, acorns provide food for animals and people.

• Why might not bending with the wind be a sign of weakness rather than strength?
  Possible response: Not bending with the wind might indicate stubbornness, inflexibility, and lack of awareness.

Enrichment

Fable in the Western World

The fable is a popular mainstay of literature. Permeating all levels of writing, it has influenced Western society through the works of Aesop and his Roman collector, Phaedrus, before being retold in the writings of La Fontaine. Other important fabulists include Horace, the Roman poet who relates the story of the city mouse and the country mouse; Chaucer, who incorporates the tale of Chanticleer and the fox in his *Canterbury Tales;* Rudyard Kipling, the author of *The Jungle Book* and *Just So Stories;* and Julius Lester who reclaimed Joel Chandler Harris's Uncle Remus stories. These stories, which originated with African slaves, emphasize the wisdom of weaker animals who must use their wits to survive the attacks of stronger, more ferocious beasts.

The Oak and the Reed

❼

Jean de La Fontaine
translated by **Marianne Moore**

❽

> The oak said to the reed, "You grow
> Too unprotectedly. Nature has been unfair;
> A tiny wren[1] alights, and you are bending low;
>   If a fitful breath of air
> 5   Should freshen till ripples show,
>   You heed her and lower your head;
> My form not only makes shade where the sun would play
> But like the Caucasus[2] it does not sway.
>   However it is <u>buffeted</u>.

❾

> 10 Your so-called hurricanes are too faint to fear.
> Would that you'd been born beneath this towering tent I've made,
>   Which could afford you ample shade;
>   Your <u>hazards</u> would not be severe:
>   I'd shield you when the lightning played;
> 15   But grow you will, time and again,
> On the misty fringe of the wind's domain.
> I perceive that you are grievously oppressed."

---

1. **wren** (ren) small, sparrowlike songbird.
2. **Caucasus** (kô′ kə səs) mountain range between southeastern Europe and western Asia.

⓫ ◀ **Critical Viewing** Which images in the poem match details visible in the photograph? Explain. **[Connect]**

Vocabulary Builder
buffeted (buf′ it id)
v. struck sharply
hazards (haz′ ərdz) *n.*
dangers

Literary Analysis
Fables What human
foible, or weakness, does
the oak possess?

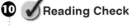

❿ ✔ **Reading Check**

From what would the
oak shield the reed?

The Oak and the Reed ■ 793

---

❼ About the Selection
In this fable, an oak tree brags about its superior size and strength and expresses pity for the reed, who the oak believes is oppressed. However, the oak quickly discovers which of the two is better able to survive.

❽ Critical Thinking
Make an Inference
• Ask a volunteer to read aloud the first three lines of "The Oak and the Reed."
• **Invite** students to make an inference about the oak tree on the basis of the opening three lines.
Possible response: The oak begins by criticizing the reed. Criticism often stems from one's feelings of superiority over another. Therefore, the oak probably feels superior.

❾ Literary Analysis
Fables
• Remind students that fables satirize human weakness. Then, read aloud the bracketed passage.
• **Ask** students whether they believe that the oak tree is genuinely concerned about the reed's welfare. Why or why not?
Possible response: The oak tree is not really concerned about the reed; it is simply bragging about its own perceived superiority.
• **Ask** students the Literary Analysis question: What human foible, or weakness, does the oak possess?
Answer: The oak tree is proud and believes itself superior to the reed.

❿ Reading Check
Answer: The oak tree would shield the reed from the sun and from lightning.

⓫ Critical Viewing
Answer: The details "makes shade," "towering tent," "ample shade," and "kingly height" are all visible in the photograph.

Differentiated
Instruction   Solutions for All Learners

Strategy for Less Proficient Readers	Suppport for English Learners	Enrichment for Gifted/Talented Students
Students may have difficulty with the vocabulary and the sentence structure of the fables. Have them read the fables aloud, reminding them to read according to sentence punctuation. Then, have students reenact the exchange between the fox and the crow or the oak and the reed, using the language of everyday conversation.	Students may have difficulty with the vocabulary and the sentence structure of the fables. Read the fables along with them, modeling how to read according to sentence punctuation. Explain difficult vocabulary or phrases. Then, have students reenact the exchange between the fox and the crow or the oak and the reed.	Encourage students to create original fables. Remind students that their fables must personify creatures, illustrate a moral, and revolve around a human weakness. Students should also compress their fables into a single episode. Encourage students to illustrate their fables as well.

793

Latin Prefix *im-*

- Call students' attention to the word *impervious* and its definition. Tell students that the prefix *im-* means "no, not, without."
- Have students **suggest** and **define** words that contain this prefix, and list them on the board.
Possible response: *Immature, immortal, impossible,* and *imprudent* are possible suggestions.

ASSESS

Answers

1. **Possible response:** "The Fox and the Crow" has the more useful moral. Although the crow's vanity makes him the victim of another character, he can control the situation in the future. The oak's sense of superiority, however, makes it the victim of the wind, over which he has no control.

2. (a) The crow has a piece of cheese that the fox wants. (b) The fox flatters the crow's appearance but questions his voice. (c) **Possible response:** Although he vows to relinquish his role as the fool, the crow, smarting from ridicule, does not learn the lesson of humility.

3. (a) The fox's pose, or body language, suggests that he has false and devious charm. (b) The fox uses his intelligence to take advantage of the crow's vanity. (c) **Possible response:** The fox is known as a symbol of cunning.

4. (a) The oak speaks more than the reed. (b) **Possible response:** The oak's sense of superiority is emphasized by its verbosity.

5. (a) The reed is better able to withstand the storm. (b) The reed can bend with the wind. (c) **Possible response:** Adaptability is essential for survival.

6. **Possible response:** The fables address human weaknesses of vanity and feelings of superiority.

The rush[3] said, "Bless you for fearing that I might be distressed;
It is you alone whom the winds should alarm.
20 I bend and do not break. You've seemed consistently
⓬   Impervious to harm—
    Erect when blasts rushed to and fro;
As for the end, who can foresee how things will go?"
Relentless wind was on them instantly—
25   A fury of destruction
Which the North had nursed in some haunt known to none.
    The bulrush bent, but not the tree.
    Confusion rose to a roar,
    Until the hurricane threw prone
30 That thing of kingly height whose head had all but touched God's
                throne—

Who had shot his root to the threshold of Death's door.

---

3. rush *n.* reed.

Critical Reading

1. **Respond:** Which of these fables do you think has the more important or useful moral? Why?

2. **(a) Recall:** What is the situation in "The Fox and the Crow"?
(b) Interpret: What is the fox's strategy for getting what he wants?
(c) Draw Conclusions: Do you think the crow learned the value of humility from his experience? Why or why not?

3. **(a) Recall:** Which of the fox's physical traits does the fable reveal?
(b) Interpret: Why is the fox's intelligence a featured characteristic?
(c) Speculate: Why do you think the speaker uses a fox in this fable?

4. **(a) Recall:** Which of the two characters in "The Oak and the Reed" speaks more? **(b) Infer:** What does this suggest about the character of the oak tree?

5. **(a) Recall:** Is the oak or the reed better able to withstand the storm?
(b) Analyze: What physical trait does the reed possess that the oak does not? **(c) Speculate:** What does this fable suggest about the traits necessary for survival in a harsh world?

6. **Connect:** In what ways do the morals of these two fables apply to readers' lives today?

Vocabulary Builder
impervious (im pʉr′ vē əs) *adj.* not affected by, or unable to be damaged

prone (prōn) *adj.* lying face downward

Go Online
—Author Link

For: More about Jean de La Fontaine
Visit: www.PHSchool.com
Web Code: ete-9606

Go Online For additional information about Jean
—Author Link de La Fontaine, have students type in the Web Code, then select *F* from the alphabet, and then select Jean de La Fontaine.

Apply the Skills

The Fox and the Crow • The Oak and the Reed

Literary Analysis

Fables

1. **(a)** Compare the elements of a **fable** found in each of the poems using a Venn diagram like the one shown below. **(b)** In what ways do the poems differ?

2. Which lines in "The Fox and the Crow" make it clear that the poem is a fable?

3. **(a)** Besides the oak and the reed, what nonhuman contributes to the moral in "The Oak and the Reed"? **(b)** What moral does this character teach?

Comparing Literary Works

4. **(a)** List three examples of **personification** in "The Fox and the Crow." **(b)** In what typically human way does the crow respond to the fox's flattery? **(c)** What type of person might the fox represent?

5. **(a)** Besides physical traits, what other methods of personification are used in "The Oak and the Reed"? **(b)** In what way is the sun personified?

6. In what ways does the use of personification help these fables teach ethical issues?

Reading Strategy

Drawing Conclusions

7. **(a)** Why does the crow consider himself "somebody's fool"? **(b)** What **conclusions** can you draw from his experience?

8. **(a)** What role does extreme weather play in the lesson the oak learns? **(b)** What conclusions can you draw from the fable about man's ability to withstand the forces of nature?

Extend Understanding

9. **Science Connection:** Like the reed, which plants possess highly specialized abilities to survive in difficult circumstances?

QuickReview

A **fable** is a brief work that dramatizes a simple lesson or principle of behavior.

Personification is the literary technique of applying human characteristics to nonhuman or inanimate objects.

To **draw conclusions,** note details in a work and infer a larger message or meaning from them.

Assessment
For: Self-test
Visit: www.PHSchool.com
Web Code: eta-6605

Go Online Students may use the **Self-test** to prepare for **Selection Test A** or **Selection Test B.**

Answers

1. (a) **Sample response: The Fox and the Crow:** animal characters; loss of possession; **Overlap:** personification of nonhuman characters; compressed episode; human weakness; moral; **The Oak and the Reed:** plant characters; loss of life. (b) "The Fox and the Crow" features animal characters in conflict over a possession. "The Oak and the Reed" features plant characters, one of whom does not survive.
   Another sample answer can be found on **Literary Analysis Graphic Organizer B**, p. 145 in *Graphic Organizer Transparencies*.

2. The last two lines state the moral, thus indicating that the poem is a fable.

3. (a) The wind contributes to the moral in "The Oak and the Reed." (b) **Possible response:** The wind teaches the oak that the inability to adapt to change will cause destruction.

4. (a) **Possible response:** Examples of personification include the following: the fox talks; the fox's pose suggests false and devious charm; and the crow sings musical scales. (b) The crow tries to elicit more flattery. (c) The fox might represent a con artist.

5. (a) **Possible response:** Other methods include the following: the reed lowers its head, and the North nurses the wind. (b) The sun plays.

6. **Possible response:** The use of personification distances the animal and plant characters from the reader so that the reader appreciates the lesson without feeling directly attacked for his or her own weaknesses.

7. (a) The crow allows the fox to manipulate him; as a result, he loses his cheese and is subjected to ridicule. (b) **Possible response:** Flattery should cause suspicion.

8. (a) The strong wind fells the oak. (b) **Possible response:** To withstand the forces of nature, humans must be adaptable.

9. **Possible response:** The cactus survives with very little water.

❶ Vocabulary Lesson

Word Analysis:
Latin Prefix im-

1. not mature or well developed
2. not subject to death
3. not prudent or wise
4. not keeping within normal bounds

Spelling Strategy

1. subterraneous   3. prodigious
2. delicious

Vocabulary Builder:
Sentence Completions

1. hazards   3. buffeted
2. impervious   4. prone

❷ Grammar and Style Lesson

1. who was as black as ebony; modifies *crow*
2. whom the crow never suspected of being sly and deceitful; modifies *fox*
3. whose slender form bent to the earth; modifies *reed*
4. whose fury blasted the tree and the tender reeds; modifies *gale*
5. who was once again standing straight; modifies *reed*

Writing Application

Possible response:

- The fox, whose stomach was growling with hunger, had a plan to steal the cheese. [modifies *fox*]
- The crow, who was especially vain, listened with pleasure to the flattery. [modifies *crow*]
- The tortoise, who refused to give up, won the race. [modifies *tortoise*]
- The grasshopper laughed at the hard-working ant, who was preparing for winter. [modifies *ant*]

Build Language Skills

❶ Vocabulary Lesson

Word Analysis: Latin Prefix *im-*

The word *impervious* contains the prefix *im-*, meaning "no, not, without." *Impervious*, therefore, means "not affected by." Use the meaning of this prefix to define the words below.

1. immature   3. imprudent
2. immortal   4. immoderate

Spelling Strategy

The ending *-ious* is used to form an adjective, like the word *impervious*. Although the spelling *ious* is more common, some adjectives are spelled with *eous*. Add *-ious* or *-eous* to each item below. Use a dictionary to check your work.

1. subterran-   2. delic-   3. prodig-

Vocabulary Builder: Sentence Completions

Review the words from the vocabulary list on page 789. Then, copy each sentence below, filling in the blanks with the appropriate vocabulary word.

1. The old tree had faced many _____, yet it remained strong.
2. The tree seemed _____ to the forces of nature.
3. Despite being _____ by the wind and rain, the oak stood straight and tall.
4. The delicate reeds, however, were often laid _____ by the gales, but their resilient stems soon straightened again.

❷ Grammar and Style Lesson

Adjective Clauses Using *who, whom,* and *whose*

Subordinate clauses contain a subject and a verb, and they act as a single part of speech. **Adjective clauses** are subordinate clauses that modify nouns or pronouns. They are often introduced by the relative pronouns *who, whom,* and *whose*.

> **Example:** Master Fox, *whose pose suggested fragrances,* said in language which of course I cannot speak . . . (modifies "Master Fox")

Practice Identify the adjective clause and the word it modifies in each of the following sentences.

1. The crow, who was as black as ebony, sat holding cheese in his beak.

2. The crow was flattered by the fox, whom the crow never suspected of being sly and deceitful.

3. The reed, whose slender form bent to the earth, waited for the storm to pass.

4. The mighty gale, whose fury blasted the tree and the tender reeds, finally destroyed the great oak.

5. After the storm passed, the reed, who was once again standing straight, saw that the tree had fallen.

Writing Application Write four sentences about animals. Include an adjective clause in each sentence, and identify both the clause and the noun it modifies.

WG Prentice Hall Writing and Grammar Connection: Platinum Level, Chapter 20, Section 2

796 ■ *The Renaissance and Rationalism*

Assessment Practice

Distinguish Between Fact and Nonfact (For more practice, see *Test Preparation Workbook*, p. 35.)

Present students with this sample test item from La Fontaine's "The Oak and the Reed," in which the oak first addresses and is then answered by the rush:

["I] perceive that you are grievously oppressed."
The rush said, "Bless you for fearing that I might be distressed;
   It is you alone whom the wind should alarm.
I bend and do not break. You've seemed consistently

Impervious to harm—
   Erect when beasts rushed to and fro.
As for the end, who can foresee how
   things will go?"

Which is an OPINION expressed in the passage?
   A The rush bends but does not break.
   B The rush is uncertain about the future.
   C The rush blesses the oak.
   D The rush is grievously oppressed.

The oppression of the rush is a perception of the oak, so *D* is the correct answer.

❸ Writing Lesson

A Children's Story

Fables and stories with animal characters have always been popular with children. Use one of La Fontaine's poems as a basis for a fully developed children's story that teaches the same lesson as the original poem. Use additional characters if you wish.

Prewriting Start by writing an outline of the plot, or main events, of La Fontaine's fable. Then, jot down notes about his characters, adding your own ideas to describe how they sound, look, and move.

Drafting As you draft, use vivid details and dialogue to make your story entertaining. Include descriptions of each character.

Revising Compare your draft with the original poem to be sure the moral of the story is clear. Make certain that all the dialogue is set in quotation marks and that other punctuation in your fable is used correctly.

Writing Model: Punctuating for Dialogue

"I see you have a lovely piece of cheese," said the Fox in a greasy voice. "It must surely be delicious!"

"Grt hgach tuk," garbled the crow, whose beak was full of cheddar.

"Tell me, Sir Ebony," said the fox, "was that your beautiful warbling I heard this morning?"

> To make dialogue clear, all punctuation that is part of the dialogue is set inside the quotation marks.

 Prentice Hall Writing and Grammar Connection: Platinum Level, Chapter 28, Section 4

❹ Extend Your Learning

Listening and Speaking Work with a partner to prepare a **dramatic reading** of one of La Fontaine's poems. Use these storytelling strategies to enliven your reading:

- Sit at eye level with your audience.
- Adjust your voice and your facial expressions to reflect the characters.
- Use props, such as plants or stuffed animals, to add interest.

Present the reading to the kindergarten class at a local school. **[Group Activity]**

Research and Technology Use the Internet or library resources to compose a **research report** on fables. Describe the types of animals that the stories feature and the lessons that they teach. Compare your findings with La Fontaine's pieces.

Go **Online**
Research

For: An additional research activity
Visit: www.PHSchool.com
Web Code: etd-7605

Assessment Resources

The following resources can be used to assess students' knowledge and skills.

Unit 6 Resources
Selection Test A, pp. 94–96
Selection Test B, pp. 97–99

General Resources
Rubrics for Narration: Short Story, pp. 63–64
Rubric for Speaking: Narrative Account, p. 88

Go **Online**
Assessment
Students may use the **Self-test** to prepare for **Selection Test A** or **Selection Test B.**

---

❸ Writing Lesson

- To give students guidance in writing this story, give them the **Support for Writing Lesson**, p. 91 in *Unit 6 Resources.*
- Remind students that stories for children should focus on simple plots with a great deal of action.
- Tell students to use effective methods of characterization when describing characters: what the narrator says about a character; what a character says about himself or herself; what a character does; and what other characters say about a character.
- Remind each student to verify that the moral of the story is directly stated or clearly implied.
- Use the Narration: Short Story rubrics in *General Resources*, pp. 63–64, to evaluate students' stories.

Writing and Grammar
Platinum Level
For support in teaching the Writing Lesson, use Chapter 28, Section 4.

❹ Listening and Speaking

- Instruct students to practice eye contact by rehearsing their performances in front of a mirror.
- Encourage students to develop different voices for each of the characters.
- Help students locate or design props for their performances.
- Use the Speaking: Narrative Account rubric in *General Resources*, p. 88, to evaluate students' performances.
- The **Support for Extend Your Learning** page (*Unit 6 Resources*, p. 92) provides guided note-taking opportunities to help students complete the Extend Your Learning activities.

Go **Online**
Research
Have students type in the Web Code for another research activity.

Standard Course of Study

IR.2.03.2 Prioritize and organize information to construct an explanation to answer a question.

FA.3.04.10 Analyze connections between ideas, concepts, characters and experiences in argumentative work.

LT.5.03.8 Make connections between works, self and related topics in world literature.

Background
Niccolò Machiavelli

Niccolò Machiavelli has often been characterized as cool, skeptical, and cautious. He was, however, passionate and patriotic on behalf of his native city of Florence. When Florence went to war with Pisa, for example, Machiavelli was asked to remain at headquarters and not take part in the fighting. However, he insisted on commanding the troops he had trained and declared that if he were kept out of the battle, he would die of sadness.

Background
Pascal's Calculator

In 1642, when Blaise Pascal was nineteen, he built a calculator to help his father in his work as a customs officer. Pascal's calculator—a wooden box with six wheels—allowed the user to deal with numbers up to 999,999. In order to add numbers, the user would dial digits into the device and view the resulting sum in the machine's six windows. Later, Pascal developed a calculator made of brass with eight dials. This version, however, was a commercial failure because it was so expensive.

Great Minds Do Not Think Alike

Toward the end of the sixteenth century, the French essayist Michel de Montaigne created a medallion with a motto encapsulating his life and work: *Que scay-je?* or "What do I know?" His question is the central theme of his time—the Age of Rationalism.

During the Renaissance, artists and thinkers celebrated human potential. By the seventeenth and eighteenth centuries, Europeans recognized the vast power of the mind itself. The power of thought forced tradition and complacency deeper into the shadows.

> **❝** *Montaigne's question, "What do I know?" is the central theme of his time — the Age of Rationalism.* **❞**

Niccolo Machiavelli—The Mind as a Weapon The idea of the mind as a political tool found practical expression in the writings of Niccolo Machiavelli (1469–1527). As a diplomat for the Florentine republic, Machiavelli observed firsthand how governments should, and should not, be run. After enduring prison and exile, he wrote one of the world's most influential books of political theory—*The Prince*.

In Machiavelli's view, a ruler maintains control not with goodness but with strength and mental agility. A Machiavellian ruler must possess both force and cunning without sentiment. Rather than loving his subjects and cherishing peace, Machiavelli's prince seeks first and foremost to retain and extend his power. He is wily, aggressive, and ruthless, and his greatest weapon is his mind.

Blaise Pascal—The Dialogue of Reason and Religion Blaise Pascal (1623–1662), French mathematician, physicist, and religious philosopher, pondered problems both earthly and heavenly. At the age of twelve he independently rediscovered Euclid's first thirty-two propositions of geometry. He later engineered the world's first calculator.

Pascal sought harmony between mathematical certainty and moral truth. In 1657, he began writing his *Penseés,* short philosophical "thoughts" that integrate science and spirituality. Some of Pascal's *penseés* reveal his logical mind, while others reveal his more poetic side. All argue his fundamental idea that the human nature is a paradox—a logical contradiction.

Pascal's paradox is that the mind has vast power but is virtually powerless in comparison with the infinite. Human beings are, therefore, "incapable of absolute ignorance and of certain knowledge."

798 ■ *The Renaissance and Rationalism*

Enrichment

The Age of Rationalism
The late seventeenth and eighteenth centuries were a time of concern for truth as revealed through reason. Philosophers of the Age of Rationalism challenged traditions, folk wisdom, and other unscientific beliefs and attempted to replace them with laws derived from contemplation and analysis of natural phenomena. During this time of enlightenment, reason was accepted as the greatest authority in matters of art and the intellect.

Leaning on the structure of arithmetic, algebra, geometry, and the newly evolved study of calculus, the application of rationalism required considerable training. As Galileo, a forerunner of the rationalist movement, pointed out, "Truth is written in the great book of Nature, but only he can read it who can decipher the letters in which it is written." Rationalism soon came to be connected with great depth of thought, maturity, and scholarly training.

As if to answer Montaigne's "What do I know?" Pascal believed that we do know many things, and yet we do not really know much at all.

John Locke—Reason and Revolution To the English philosopher John Locke (1632–1704), the human mind is a blank slate. Locke believed that everything we experience make impressions on that blank slate. In this approach, called empiricism, the consciousness of every human being develops according to personal experience, reflections, and decisions.

Locke was also a highly influential political philosopher. In his *Two Treatises of Government* (1690), Locke argued that people are free to choose their own government. Locke reasoned that the government has a rational purpose—to protect life, liberty, and property. If it fails, it may be overthrown. Thomas Jefferson and other founders of the American Republic were deeply influenced by Locke's ideas.

Jean-Jacques Rousseau—The Social Contract The most extraordinarily multifaceted mind to emerge during the Age of Rationalism was that of Jean-Jacques Rousseau (1712–1778). Orphan, footman, music teacher, tutor, encyclopedic writer, political philosopher, social critic, novelist, autobiographer, wanderer, radical, free spirit—Rousseau was all of these and more. For Rousseau, civilization corrupted humanity's natural goodness. He believed that people are fundamentally good, but society has made it impossible for the best in human nature to flourish; therefore, a new social order needs to be created. In *The Social Contract* (1762), Rousseau described a society in which a ruler leads at the will of the people, who can revoke their support if they wish. The social contract achieved its most complete embodiment in American democracy. Rousseau's devotion to nature and his belief in the unique and passionate individual make him the intellectual bridge to the Age of the Romantics.

▼ **Critical Viewing**
In what way does this portrait of Rousseau reflect the philosopher's ideas?
[Connect]

Activity

Machiavelli Today

Machiavelli's *The Prince* has never gone out of print. To this day, it is required reading for anyone with an interest in government, politics, or leadership. With a group, discuss the relevance of Machiavelli's theories in today's world. Use these questions to guide your discussion:

- Machiavelli wrote that it is better for a ruler to be feared than loved. Do you agree or disagree? Explain.
- Do Machiavelli's notions of leadership apply to America's current political leaders? Cite specific examples to support your answer.

Choose a point person to share your ideas with the class.

Great Minds Do Not Think Alike ■ 799

Activity

Have students form groups, and have group members choose a point person to present their findings. Suggest that pairs of students take responsibility for choosing examples of feared leaders throughout history, while other pairs choose examples of beloved leaders.

Then point out to students that any discussion about current government leaders in the United States can be colored by political party leanings.

Advise students to be tolerant of these differences. Encourage them to offer specific examples that support their opinions.

Have students in each group organize their examples and opinions for the presentation.

Standard Course of Study

Goal 3: FOUNDATIONS OF ARGUMENT

FA.3.04.9   Analyze and evaluate the effects of author's craft and style in argument.

FA.3.04.11   Analyze elements of argumentative environment.

Goal 4: CRITICAL THINKING

CT.4.05.4   Comprehend main idea and supporting details in critical text.

Goal 5: LITERATURE

LT.5.01.6   Make connections between historical and contemporary issues in world literature.

Goal 6: GRAMMAR AND USAGE

GU.6.01.1   Employ varying sentence structures and sentence types.

GU.6.02.3   Edit for parallel structure.

Step-by-Step Teaching Guide	Pacing Guide
PRETEACH	
• Administer Vocabulary and Reading Warm-ups as necessary.	5 min.
• Engage students' interest with the motivation activity.	5 min.
• Read and discuss author and background features. **FT**	10 min.
• Introduce the Literary Analysis Skill: Satire. **FT**	5 min.
• Introduce the Reading Strategy: Connecting to Historical Context. **FT**	
• Prepare students to read by teaching the selection vocabulary. **FT**	10 min.
TEACH	
• Informally monitor comprehension while students read independently or in groups. **FT**	30 min.
• Monitor students' comprehension with the Reading Check notes.	as students read
• Reinforce vocabulary with Vocabulary Builder notes.	as students read
• Develop students' understanding of satire with the Literary Analysis annotations. **FT**	5 min.
• Develop students' ability to connect to historical context with the Reading Strategy annotations. **FT**	5 min.
ASSESS/EXTEND	
• Assess students' comprehension and mastery of the Literary Analysis and Reading Strategy by having them answer the Apply the Skills questions. **FT**	15 min.
• Have students complete the Vocabulary Lesson and the Grammar and Style Lesson. **FT**	15 min.
• Apply students' ability to organize details by using the Writing Lesson. **FT**	45 min. or homework
• Apply students' understanding by using one or more of the Extend Your Learning activities.	20–90 min. or homework
• Administer Selection Test A or Selection Test B. **FT**	15 min.

Resources

Print

Unit 6 Resources

Transparency

Graphic Organizer Transparencies

Print

Reader's Notebook [**L2**]

Reader's Notebook: Adapted Version [**L1**]

Reader's Notebook: English Learner's Version [**EL**]

Unit 6 Resources

Technology

Listening to Literature Audio CDs [**L2, EL**]

Print

Unit 6 Resources

General Resources

Technology

Go Online: Research [L3]

Go Online: Self-test [L3]

ExamView®, **Test Bank [L3]**

Choosing Resources for Differentiated Instruction

[**L1**] Special Needs Students

[**L2**] Below-Level Students

[**L3**] All Students

[**L4**] Advanced Students

[**EL**] English Learners

For Vocabulary and Reading Warm-ups and for Selection Tests, **A** signifies "less challenging" and **B** "more challenging." For Graphic Organizer transparencies, **A** signifies "not filled in" and **B** "filled in."

FT Fast Track Instruction: To move the lesson more quickly, use the strategies and activities identified with **FT**.

Scaffolding for Less Proficient and Advanced Students

The leveled Critical Thinking questions after selections progress in the levels of thinking required to answer them. To address the needs of your different students, you may use the (a) level questions for your less proficient students and the (b) level questions with your on-level and advanced students. The occasional (c) level questions are appropriate for your advanced students.

PRENTICE HALL

TeacherEXPRESS Use this complete suite of powerful

Plan · Teach · Assess

teaching tools to make lesson planning and testing quicker and easier.

PRENTICE HALL

StudentEXPRESS Use the interactive

Learn · Study · Succeed textbook (online

and on CD-ROM) to make selections and activities come alive with audio and video support and interactive questions.

 **Go Online** For: Information about Lexiles
Professional Visit: www.PHSchool.com
Development Web Code: eue-1111

Motivation

Tell students that stories about the adventures of young people in search of some special dream are plentiful in world literature and film. If possible, summarize excerpts from such novels as *The Adventures of Huckleberry Finn* or *Great Expectations*. Lead students in a discussion about the popularity of this plot.

Use the following questions to stimulate discussion:

- Why is this plot appealing to readers and viewers?
- Why does this plot remain popular across time and cultures?
- Can you name other stories or films that make use of this plot?

❶ Background

More About the Author

During Voltaire's exile in England, he learned to speak the English language. He met such important English writers and thinkers as Alexander Pope, Jonathan Swift, William Congreve, and the philosopher George Berkeley. Voltaire was particularly impressed by the freedom of the English to discuss openly religion and philosophy. He believed that this freedom was responsible for the advances in thought exemplified by English scientists such as Sir Isaac Newton and John Locke.

Geography Note

Draw students' attention to the map of France on this page. Point out that Voltaire's estate in Ferney, France, is near the Swiss border.

from Candide ❶

Voltaire
(1694–1778)

A lifelong social critic and champion of liberty, tolerance, and truth, François-Marie Arouet—who wrote under the pen name Voltaire (vôl ter´)—often invited trouble by questioning authority. Although he was imprisoned twice and spent many years in exile from his native land, he is still regarded as one of France's greatest writers and thinkers.

Man-About-Paris Voltaire grew up in the French capital of Paris in the waning years of King Louis XIV's reign. Although his family expected him to study law, he was more interested in literature and the theater. Clever and witty, he was an immediate success when his godfather introduced him to the best of Paris society after he left school. He attended all the trendy gatherings, and his short satirical poems were much quoted by fashionable Parisians.

Fame—and Prison In 1715, Louis XIV died, and his five-year-old great-grandson came to the French throne as Louis XV. Two years later, Voltaire was accused of penning satirical barbs criticizing the late king and the Duc d'Orléans, who was serving as regent, or acting ruler, for young Louis XV. As punishment, Voltaire was at first exiled, and then he was sent to the Bastille, the notorious Paris prison, for nearly a year.

He made the most of his prison stay by completing *Oedipe,* the first of his many tragic dramas, and beginning work on the *Henriade,* his epic poem in tribute to Henry IV. After Voltaire's release from prison, *Oedipe* was staged in Paris to much acclaim. It was also around this time that Voltaire adopted his famous pen name.

Voltaire's favor in Paris was short-lived, however. In 1725, never one to hold his tongue, he made the mistake of quarreling with the powerful Chevalier de Rohan. When Voltaire challenged Rohan to a duel, Voltaire was sent briefly to the Bastille again and then into exile from his homeland.

The English Influence Voltaire spent his exile in England, a nation he found more tolerant and open-minded than the France of his day. He especially admired the achievements of English scientist Sir Isaac Newton and the ideas of English philosopher John Locke, whose principles of liberty had helped justify England's Glorious Revolution of 1688. Voltaire concluded that the freedom of thought he found in England encouraged scientific advancement and thus helped the nation prosper. When he was allowed to return home, he produced his *Lettres philosophiques,* in which he compared England favorably to France. With its emphasis on reason, religious tolerance, and freedom of thought, the work is considered a landmark of the eighteenth-century Age of Enlightenment.

Later Years Voltaire considered himself an enemy of injustice; his determination to help others, his strong opinions, and his argumentative disposition caused him trouble throughout his life. In 1750, he was invited to Berlin by the Prussian leader Frederick the Great, but three years later he angered Frederick by mocking one of Prussia's leading scientists. In Geneva, Switzerland, the Calvinist religious leaders who at first welcomed him as a champion of religious tolerance were disturbed by some of his more radical ideas.

In 1758, just after writing his best-known work, the satirical novel *Candide,* Voltaire retired to Ferney, a property he had bought near Geneva. There, he lived in semiretirement for the last two decades of his life—writing, running the estate, instituting agricultural reforms, and, of course, getting into arguments with the locals.

800 ■ *The Renaissance and Rationalism*

Preview

Connecting to the Literature

Moviemakers and authors entertain the public with wildly comedic characters. *Candide* features such personalities, yet they serve a higher purpose: to expose social inequities and to suggest a means of escaping them.

❷ Literary Analysis

Satire

Satire is writing that uses humor to expose and ridicule human foolishness. Although satirists take aim at individuals, institutions, types of behavior, or humanity in general, the ultimate goal of a satirical piece is to inspire positive change. *Candide* prompts readers to question the conditions of their lives by calling attention to social injustices such as corrupt political systems. As you read this selection, note cases of injustice or inhumanity just under the humorous surface of this work.

Connecting Literary Elements

Satirists ridicule their subjects by using tools such as **exaggeration or hyperbole, understatement,** and **faulty logic.** Consider these examples from the selection:

- *Exaggeration or Hyperbole:* "... The Baron's castle was the best of castles...."
- *Understatement:* "... the next day he drilled not so badly and received only twenty strokes [of the lash]."
- *Faulty logic:* "Observe that noses were made to wear spectacles: and so we have spectacles."

As you read, notice how the repeated use of these tools contributes to the humor and persuades a reader toward the speaker's point of view.

❸ Reading Strategy

Connecting to Historical Context

When you **connect a work to its historical context,** you identify the ideas and events in a piece that may be responses to its era. To make the connection, use a chart like the one shown to list details from the story that reflect the time period. Then, consider the way the details connect to history.

Vocabulary Builder

endowed (en doud´) *v.* given, or provided with (p. 802)

candor (kan´ dər) *n.* open honesty and frankness (p. 803)

vivacity (vī vas´ ə tē) *n.* liveliness or animation (p. 804)

prodigy (präd´ ə jē) *n.* person of very great ability (p. 805)

clemency (klem´ ən sē) *n.* mercy toward an enemy or offender (p. 806)

from *Candide* ■ 801

NC Standard Course of Study

- Analyze and evaluate the effects of author's craft and style in argument. (FA.3.04.9)
- Comprehend main idea and supporting details in critical text. (CT.4.05.4)

❷ Literary Analysis
Satire

- Read aloud the Literary Analysis instruction. Tell students that satire pokes fun at situations, ideas, or people, through the use of exaggeration, understatement, and faulty logic.

- Review with students the examples. Then, encourage student pairs to construct an original example of each satiric strategy. Invite students to share their examples with the class.

- Instruct students to note examples of each satiric strategy as they read the excerpt from *Candide.*

❸ Reading Strategy
Connecting to Historical Context

- Tell students that many works of literature bear a direct relation to the time and place in which they were written. For example, Voltaire was shocked by the terrible earthquake that struck Lisbon, Portugal, in 1755, claiming nearly 25,000 lives. Voltaire uses this event in satirizing the philosophic idea that this is "the best of all possible worlds."

- Give students a copy of **Reading Strategy Graphic Organizer A,** p. 146 in *Graphic Organizer Transparencies.* Direct them to use the chart to record details regarding political situations, wars, or other events in *Candide.* Help students research Voltaire's time to locate the historical context for these details.

Vocabulary Builder

- Pronounce each vocabulary word for students, and read the definitions as a class. Have students identify any words with which they are already familiar.

Differentiated Instruction   Solutions for All Learners

Support for Special Needs Students	Support for Less Proficient Readers	Support for English Learners
Have students complete the **Preview** and **Build Skills** pages for the excerpt from *Candide* in the *Reader's Notebook: Adapted Version.* These pages provide a selection summary, an abbreviated presentation of the reading and literary skills, and the graphic organizer on the **Build Skills** page in the student book.	Have students complete the **Preview** and **Build Skills** pages for the excerpt from *Candide* in the *Reader's Notebook.* These pages provide a selection summary, an abbreviated presentation of the reading and literary skills, and the graphic organizer on the **Build Skills** page in the student book.	Have students complete the **Preview** and **Build Skills** pages for the excerpt from *Candide* in the *Reader's Notebook: English Learner's Version.* These pages provide a selection summary, an abbreviated presentation of the skills, additional contextual vocabulary, and the graphic organizer on the **Build Skills** page in the student book.

Facilitate Understanding

Students are likely to have recently studied William Shakespeare's *Romeo and Juliet* and possibly *West Side Story*. Students should therefore identify with the young Candide and his girlfriend Cunegonde and the problems they have with her father. After students have read Chapter 1, encourage them to state what seems realistic about the Baron's reaction to the young lovers and what is purely satirical.

❶ About the Selection

In this story, the adolescent Candide and his girlfriend Cunegonde have been taught to believe in the innocence and goodness of all things by the famous Doctor Pangloss. But misfortune soon arrives when Cunegonde's father catches her kissing Candide and throws him off the estate. So begins an intercontinental whirlwind that will take Candide around the world, surviving disasters, tortures, mayhem, and massacres in an attempt to become reunited with Cunegonde.

❷ Literary Analysis

Satire

- Remind students that satirists make use of tools such as faulty logic and exaggeration. To help students recognize instances of faulty logic, instruct them to look for stated or implied thinking verbs that serve as clue words to a character's thought process.

- Read aloud the bracketed passage. Then, **ask** students to respond to the Literary Analysis item: Identify two tools of satire in the first paragraph.

Possible response: Voltaire uses faulty logic ("His judgment was quite honest and he was extremely simple-minded; and this was the reason, I think, that he was named Candide.") and exaggeration ("this young lady would never marry because he could only prove seventy-one quarterings").

---

❶ from

Candide

Voltaire *translated by Richard Aldington*

Background Subtitled "Optimism," *Candide* is deeply rooted in historical events and ideas close to Voltaire's heart. For example, his work alludes to a devastating earthquake in Lisbon in 1755 and to a popular philosophy claiming that this world is the best of all possible worlds.

Candide is an innocent youth who suffers severe hardships as he searches for his beloved, Cunegonde. Along the way, Candide learns firsthand that life is often shaped by incomprehensible forces and by the cruelty and frivolity of the ruling classes.

CHAPTER I

*How Candide was brought up in a noble castle
and how he was expelled from the same*

❷ In the castle of Baron Thunder-ten-tronckh in Westphalia[1] there lived a youth, <u>endowed</u> by Nature with the most gentle character. His face was the expression of his soul. His judgment was quite honest and he was extremely simple-minded; and this was the reason, I think, that he was named Candide. Old servants in the house suspected that he was the son of the Baron's sister and a decent honest gentleman of the neighborhood, whom this young lady would never marry because he could only prove seventy-one quarterings[2] and the rest of his genealogical tree was lost, owing to the injuries of time.

The Baron was one of the most powerful lords in Westphalia, for his castle possessed a door and windows. His Great Hall was even decorated with a piece of tapestry. The dogs in his stable-yards formed a pack of hounds when necessary; his grooms were his huntsmen; the village curate was his Grand Almoner. They all called him "My Lord," and laughed heartily at his stories.

The Baroness weighed about three hundred and fifty pounds, was therefore greatly respected, and did the honors of the house with a dignity which rendered her still more respectable. Her daughter Cunegonde, aged seventeen, was rosy-cheeked, fresh, plump and tempting. The Baron's son appeared in every respect worthy of his father. The tutor Pangloss was the oracle of the house, and little Candide followed his lessons with all the <u>candor</u> of his age and character.

---

1. **Baron . . . Westphalia** The Baron is a lesser member of nobility in a historic region of northwestern Germany.
2. **quarterings** divisions on a coat-of-arms indicating generations of noble or distinguished ancestry.

---

802 ■ The Renaissance and Rationalism

Vocabulary Builder
endowed (en doud´) *v.* given, or provided with

Literary Analysis
Satire Identify two tools of satire in the first paragraph.

Vocabulary Builder
candor (kan´ dər) *n.* open honesty and frankness

Differentiated Instruction   Solutions for All Learners

Accessibility at a Glance

	from **Candide** Chapter I	*from* **Candide** Chapter II
Context	Candide's expulsion from the Castle	Candide's suffering in Bulgaria
Language	Exaggeration, understatement, and faulty logic	Syntax: dialogue and long sentences with embedded clauses and phrases
Concept Level	Accessible (value of equality)	Accessible (value of freedom and merciful leadership)
Literary Merit	Classic fictional satire of the French aristocracy	Classic fictional satire of the Prussian Army
Lexile	1000L	1000L
Overall Rating	Average	Average

Pangloss taught metaphysico-theologo-cosmolonigology.[3] He proved admirably that there is no effect without a cause and that in this best of all possible worlds, My Lord the Baron's castle was the best of castles and his wife the best of all possible Baronesses.

"'Tis demonstrated," said he, "that things cannot be otherwise; for, since everything is made for an end, everything is necessarily for the best end. Observe that noses were made to wear spectacles; and so we have spectacles. Legs were visibly instituted to be breeched, and we have breeches. Stones were formed to be quarried and to build castles; and My Lord has a very noble castle; the greatest Baron in the province should have the best house; and as pigs were made to be eaten, we eat pork all the year round; consequently, those who have asserted that all is well talk nonsense; they ought to have said that all is for the best."

Candide listened attentively and believed innocently; for he thought Mademoiselle Cunegonde extremely beautiful, although he was never bold enough to tell her so. He decided that after the happiness of being born Baron of Thunder-ten-tronckh, the second degree of happiness was to be Mademoiselle Cunegonde; the third, to see her every day; and the fourth to listen to Doctor Pangloss, the greatest philosopher of the province and therefore of the whole world.

One day when Cunegonde was walking near the castle, in a little wood which was called The Park, she observed Doctor Pangloss in the bushes, giving a lesson in experimental physics to her mother's waiting-maid, a very pretty and docile brunette. Mademoiselle Cunegonde had a great inclination for science and watched breathlessly the reiterated experiments she witnessed; she observed clearly the Doctor's sufficient reason, the effects and the causes, and returned home very much excited, pensive, filled with the desire of learning, reflecting that she might be the sufficient reason of young Candide and that he might be hers.

On her way back to the castle she met Candide and blushed; Candide also blushed. She bade him good-morning in a hesitating voice; Candide replied without knowing what he was saying. Next day, when they left the table after dinner, Cunegonde and Candide found themselves behind a

---

3. **metaphysico-theologo-cosmolonigology** Voltaire satirizes philosophical studies by inventing an entirely fake school of thought.

5 ▲ **Critical Viewing**
Which details in this engraving illustrate action from the story? **[Connect]**

Reading Check 6

What service does Pangloss provide to Candide and the Baron's family?

from Candide ■ *803*

3 Literary Analysis
Satire
- Ask a student to read aloud the bracketed passage.
- **Ask** students to identify the satirical tool illustrated in the passage.
  Answer: Faulty logic is illustrated in Pangloss' "proofs."

4 Humanities
***Illustration from* Candide,**
by Jean-Michel Moreau le Jeune
Jean-Michel Moreau le Jeune (1741–1814) was an illustrator, painter, and engraver. He was known as Moreau le Jeune to distinguish him from his brother who was also an artist.

The son of a wigmaker, Moreau made a name for himself as the illustrator of a costume book. The book remains today one of the finest records of the manners and tastes of the French nobility.

Although Moreau studied painting and engraving, he eventually concentrated on illustrating. He illustrated a number of literary works, including the collected works of Voltaire, from which this image is taken.

Moreau was known for his talent for capturing fine details of gesture, pose, and light.

Use the following questions for discussion:
- Which characters are portrayed in this illustration?
  Answer: This illustration portrays Candide, the Baron, Cunegonde, and the Baroness.
- What emotions does the artist portray in the characters in this illustration?
  Possible response: The illustration captures the emotions of anger from the Baron, excitement from the Baroness, and despair from Cunegonde.

5 Critical Viewing
Answer: Candide and Cunegonde are behind a screen, where the Baron discovers them. The Baron kicks Candide, while Cunegonde faints.

6 Reading Check
Answer: Pangloss is a tutor.

Differentiated
Instruction   Solutions for All Learners

Enrichment for Gifted/Talented Students
Direct students to continue the list of philosophical inquiries noted in the Advanced Readers box. Then, instruct students to create a book with a question on the left-hand page and multiple responses to the question on the right-hand page. Require that students include a response to the question from a film, a historical text, and a religious text in addition to both a literary and philosophical text. Students may also want to include a visual response to the question, such as a painting or sculpture.

Enrichment for Advanced Readers
Voltaire's *Candide* leaves important questions unanswered: What place has fortune in life? Why do the innocent suffer unfairly? Are people never constant enough to be reliable? Is it possible to find some escape from a fate that seems haphazard? Direct students to continue this list of inquiries. Then, instruct students to create a book with a question on the left-hand page and a response from a poet, writer, or philosopher on the right-hand page.

Latin Suffix *-ity*

- Draw students' attention to the word *vivacity,* and read its definition. Tell students that the word combines the Latin suffix *-ity,* which means "quality or state of," with the root *-viv-* which means "life."

- **Encourage** students to brainstorm for other words that use the suffix *-ity.* Write students' suggestions on the board.
Possible response: *Veracity, opacity,* and *prosperity* are possible suggestions.

- Then, tell students to write a short satire of a current issue in popular culture using some of the suggested words.

8 Literary Analysis

Satire and Exaggeration

- Read aloud the bracketed passage. Have students discuss whether they find humor in the scene and, if they do, why.

- **Ask** students the Literary Analysis question: Which details in the paragraph might be exaggerations? Why?
Possible response: The Baron's castle is referred to as an earthly paradise, but it clearly is not perfect; The noble castles are associated with Heaven, but they are built by humans; Candide calls Cunedgonde the most beautiful of baronesses, but this is an opinion; The town is called Waldberghoff-trarbk-dikdorff, a ridiculously long name that is difficult to pronounce.

▶ **Monitor Progress Ask** students to cite one example of each of the tools of satire they have seen in Chapter 1.
Possible response: Exaggeration: "The Baroness weighed about three hundred and fifty pounds" (p. 802). **Understatement:** The Great Hall was "even decorated with a piece of tapestry" (p. 802). **Faulty Logic:** "As pigs were made to be eaten, we eat pork" (p. 803).

▶ **Reteach** If students continue to have difficulty with the tools of satire, use the **Literary Analysis** support, p. 104 in *Unit 6 Resources.*

---

screen; Cunegonde dropped her handkerchief, Candide picked it up; she innocently held his hand; the young man innocently kissed the young **7** | lady's hand with remarkable <u>vivacity</u>, tenderness and grace; their lips met, their eyes sparkled, their knees trembled, their hands wandered. Baron Thunder-ten-tronckh passed near the screen, and, observing this cause and effect, expelled Candide from the castle by kicking him in the backside frequently and hard. Cunegonde swooned; when she recovered her senses, the Baroness slapped her in the face; and all was in consternation in the noblest and most agreeable of all possible castles.

CHAPTER II

What happened to Candide among the Bulgarians

8 Candide, expelled from the earthly paradise, wandered for a long time without knowing where he was going, turning up his eyes to Heaven, gazing back frequently at the noblest of castles which held the most beautiful of young Baronesses; he lay down to sleep supperless between two furrows in the open fields: it snowed heavily in large flakes. The next morning the shivering Candide, penniless, dying of cold and exhaustion, dragged himself towards the neighboring town, which was called Waldberghoff-trarbk-dikdorff. He halted sadly at the door of an inn. Two men dressed in blue noticed him.

"Comrade," said one, "there's a well-built young man of the right height." They went up to Candide and very civilly invited him to dinner.

"Gentlemen," said Candide with charming modesty, "you do me a great honor, but I have no money to pay my share."

"Ah, sir," said one of the men in blue, "persons of your figure and merit never pay anything; are you not five feet five tall?"

"Yes, gentlemen," said he, bowing, "that is my height."

"Ah, sir, come to table; we will not only pay your expenses, we will never allow a man like you to be short of money; men were only made to help each other."

"You are in the right," said Candide, "that is what Doctor Pangloss was always telling me, and I see that everything is for the best."

They begged him to accept a few crowns,[4] he took them and wished to give them an IOU, they refused to take it and all sat down to table.

"Do you not love tenderly . . ."

"Oh, yes," said he. "I love Mademoiselle Cunegonde tenderly."

"No," said one of the gentlemen." "We were asking if you do not tenderly love the King of the Bulgarians."

"Not a bit," said he, "for I have never seen him."

"What! He is the most charming of Kings, and you must drink his health."

"Oh, gladly, gentlemen."

And he drank.

---

4. **crowns** monetary units.

Vocabulary Builder
vivacity (vī vas´ ə tē) *n.* liveliness or animation

Literary Analysis
Satire and Exaggeration
Which details in the paragraph might be exaggerations? Why?

Enrichment

Gottfried Wilhelm Leibniz

Author Gottfried Wilhelm Leibniz (1646–1716) was one of the great philosophers of the Age of Rationalism. He was a brilliant mathematician (he invented infinitesimal calculus), as well as a diplomat, historian, and court librarian. His primary contribution was in the field of logic. To him, logic was a kind of mathematics. In his words, "True reasoning depends upon necessary or eternal truths, such as those of logic, numbers, [and] geometry, which establish an indubitable connection of ideas and unfailing consequences."

For Leibniz, this world is the "best" even though it has evil, because God had a "sufficient reason" to choose to create this world above all others. Other worlds would have evils even greater than this one. Therefore, God created this "best of all possible worlds."

It is this idea that Voltaire satirizes in *Candide.*

"That is sufficient," he was told. "You are now the support, the aid, the defender, the hero of the Bulgarians, your fortune is made and your glory assured."

They immediately put irons on his legs and took him to a regiment. He was made to turn to the right and left, to raise the ramrod[5] and return the ramrod, to take aim, to fire, to march double time, and he was given thirty strokes with a stick; the next day he drilled not quite so badly, and received only twenty strokes; the day after, he only had ten and was looked on as a <u>prodigy</u> by his comrades.

Candide was completely mystified and could not make out how he was a hero. One fine spring day he thought he would take a walk, going straight ahead, in the belief that to use his legs as he pleased was a

---
5. **ramrod** long rod used to tamp the charge of a muzzle-loading firearm.

9

Reading Strategy
Connecting to Historical Context In what way is bitterness toward Prussia reflected in this characterization of Prussia's military training?

Vocabulary Builder
prodigy (präd´ ə jē) *n.* person of very great ability.

✔ **Reading Check** **10**

Which army does Candide join?

12 ▼ **Critical Viewing**
Why might Candide consider it the best of all worlds to live in a castle such as this one? **[Speculate]**

11

from Candide 805

---

9 Reading Strategy
Connecting to Historical Context

- Have students read the bracketed passage independently. Tell students that the Bulgarians that Voltaire refers to in this passage represent the Prussians. France fought against Prussia during the Seven Years' War (1756–1763).

- **Ask** students the Reading Strategy question: In what way is bitterness toward Prussia reflected in this characterization of Prussia's military training?
Answer: The Bulgarians call Candide a hero, but they put him in leg irons and force him to stay in the army against his will. Voltaire portrays the Prussians as brutal and authoritarian.

10 Reading Check

Answer: Candide joins the Bulgarian army.

11 Humanities
Neuschwanstein Castle

Neuschwanstein Castle in the Bavarian Alps was begun in 1869 by Bavaria's King Louis II (sometimes called "Mad Ludwig") and was meant to imitate the "old German Knightly fortresses." This magnificent building—of the sort that Candide might refer to as "the best of all possible castles"—gives the appearance of a romantic medieval castle, built in the Romanesque style of the early thirteenth century, with spires, towers, and a walled courtyard. It sits on a rock ledge overlooking the Pöllat Gorge, offering a spectacular view of the Bavarian Alps.

The castle was left unfinished upon the death of King Louis in 1886, and it has since become a popular tourist attraction. It may seem familiar to American viewers, because it served as the model for Sleeping Beauty's castle in Disneyland.

12 Critical Viewing

Possible response: This castle looks magical and is picturesque.

Use the following question for discussion:

Which of the castles' architectural details do you find most striking?
Possible response: The tremendous spires are quite striking.

Differentiated
Instruction   Solutions for All Learners

Strategy for Special Needs Students
Have students make a two-column chart in which they contrast positive and negative aspects of Candide's experience with the Bulgarian army. Ask students to discuss Voltaire's use of this contrast for sarcastic or ironic effect. Then, provide students with brief background on the Seven Years' War. Have them draw a conclusion about Voltaire's attitude toward the war, given his ironic presentation of Candide's experience.

Strategy for Less Proficient Readers
Help students conduct research on the Seven Years' War. Then, have them make a two-column chart in which they draw lines connecting events in *Candide* with facts about the war. For example, they should draw a line connecting Candide's leg irons with facts about forced conscription. Then, have them draw a conclusion about Voltaire's attitude toward the war, given his ironic presentation of Candide's experience.

Connect

- Read the bracketed passage aloud. Draw students' attention to the footnoted definition of the word *metaphysician*.

- **Ask** students to name writers whose works they have read who would fit the definition of a metaphysician. **Possible response:** Lao Tzu and Confucius both fit the definition of a metaphysician.

ASSESS

Answers

1. **Possible response:** Candide's world is not "the best of all possible worlds" because of the injustices and suffering Candide encounters.

2. (a) Details include the Baron who is the "most powerful lord in Westphalia" because his castle has a door and window; the Baroness, who weighs three hundred and fifty pounds and is therefore "greatly respected"; the Baron's son, who is "in every respect worthy of his father." (b) **Possible response:** Pangloss is the perfect tutor for the Baron's family because his logic supports their superiority.

3. (a) The men are recruiters for the Bulgarian army. (b) **Possible response:** Candide believes that they are just being nice to him when they buy him food and give him money, and he attempts to give them an IOU. (c) **Possible response:** Candide accepts without question the teachings of people who outrank him socially and educationally. His role as a simpleton emphasizes for the reader the ridiculousness of this blind acceptance of authority.

4. **Possible response:** Contemporary authors use essays, editorials, and novels to illustrate injustices.

Go Online For additional informa-
Author Link tion about Voltaire, have students type in the Web Code, then select *V* from the alphabet, and then select Voltaire.

806

---

privilege of the human species as well as of animals. He had not gone two leagues when four other heroes, each six feet tall, fell upon him, bound him and dragged him back to a cell. He was asked by his judges whether he would rather be thrashed thirty-six times by the whole regiment or receive a dozen lead bullets at once in his brain. Although he protested that men's wills are free and that he wanted neither one nor the other, he had to make a choice; by virtue of that gift of God which is called *liberty*, he determined to run the gauntlet[6] thirty-six times and actually did so twice. There were two thousand men in the regiment. That made four thousand strokes which laid bare the muscles and nerves from his neck to his backside. As they were about to proceed to a third turn, Candide, utterly exhausted, begged as a favor that they would be so kind as to smash his head; he obtained this favor; they bound his eyes and he was made to kneel down. At that moment the King of the Bulgarians came by and inquired the victim's crime, and as this King was possessed of a vast genius, he perceived from what he learned about Candide that he was a young metaphysician[7] very ignorant in worldly matters, and therefore pardoned him with a <u>clemency</u> which will be praised in all newspapers and all ages. An honest surgeon healed Candide in three weeks with the ointments recommended by Dioscorides.[8] He had already regained a little skin and could walk when the King of the Bulgarians went to war with the King of the Abares.[9]

6. **gauntlet** (gônt´ lit) double row of soldiers armed with clubs or weapons used to strike an individual who ran between them.
7. **metaphysician** one who studies worldly matters, such as the order and nature of the universe.
8. **Dioscorides** (dī´ əs kor´ ə dēz´) Greek physician (c. 40–c. 90) and author of *De materia medica*, the definitive text about botany and pharmacology for more than 1500 years.
9. **Bulgarians . . . Abares** (ab ar ās´) In *Candide*, the Bulgarians are Frederic the Great's Prussian army, and the Abares are the French.

Critical Reading

1. **Respond:** Do you think that Candide's world is "the best of all possible worlds"? Why or why not?

2. **(a) Recall:** What details concerning the Baron and his family have earned them great respect? **(b) Analyze:** In what ways is Pangloss the perfect tutor for this family?

3. **(a) Recall:** Who are the "men dressed in blue" whom Candide meets at the inn? **(b) Analyze:** In what ways does Candide reveal his innocence as he speaks with them? **(c) Evaluate:** Why do you think Candide is made to look like such a simpleton?

4. **Apply:** What kinds of writing do authors use today to address social injustices like those satirized in *Candide*?

Vocabulary Builder
clemency (klem´ ən sē) *n.* mercy toward an enemy or offender

Go Online
Author Link
For: More about Voltaire
Visit: www.PHSchool.com
Web Code: ete-9607

Apply the Skills

from *Candide*

Literary Analysis

Satire

1. **(a)** Identify two kinds of social injustices that are **satirized** in *Candide*. **(b)** What types of social reform do you think the work attempts to inspire? Explain.
2. What attitude is satirized in the statement, ". . . Doctor Pangloss, the greatest philosopher of the province and therefore of the whole world"?
3. What satirical message about political freedom does Candide reveal by choosing to run the gauntlet rather than be shot for deserting the Bulgarian army?

Connecting Literary Elements

4. **(a)** Use a chart like the one shown to identify at least one example of each of the tools of satire—**exaggeration or hyperbole, understatement**, and **faulty logic**—used in *Candide*.

Detail from *Candide*	Tool of Satire Used

   (b) What conclusions can you draw about the use of satirical tools in this work?
5. **(a)** Describe the ways in which humor is used as a tool of satire in this selection. **(b)** What risks do you think satirists take when using this tool to address serious issues? Explain.

Reading Strategy

Connecting to Historical Context

6. Connect two details about the Baron's family to the **historical context** of Voltaire's era.
7. **(a)** What philosophy of the day does Pangloss teach? **(b)** What effect might this philosophy have on a society that practices it over time? Explain.
8. Why do you think the Bulgarian army is represented in a critical light?

Extend Understanding

9. **Social Studies Connection:** In what ways is a satire such as *Candide* similar to political cartoons you might find in today's newspapers and magazines?

QuickReview

Satire uses humor to ridicule or criticize a specific subject and to inspire change.

To create satire, authors use various tools, such as **exaggeration or hyperbole, understatement,** and **faulty logic.**

To **connect works to their historical contexts,** note ideas, assumptions, and events that are specific to the selection's era.

Go Online
Assessment
For: Self-test
Visit: www.PHSchool.com
Web Code: eta-6606

from *Candide* ■ 807

Answers continued

9. **Possible response:** *Candide* uses humor to address serious social and political issues and injustices, just as political cartoons do, in the hope that people will think about the issues and attempt to change the situations.

Go Online Students may use the **Self-test** to pre-
Assessment pare for **Selection Test A** or **Selection Test B.**

Answers

1. **(a) Possible response:** Two injustices are the inability of a young woman to choose to marry a man who is not a nobleman and the forced conscription of young men into the army. **(b) Possible response:** The work attempts to inspire the values of equality and liberty.

2. **Possible response:** The attitude satirized is the belief that one's own province is the most important in the world.

3. **Possible response:** Candide reveals that a so-called free choice amounts to nothing but a choice between two evils.

4. **(a) Possible responses: Exaggeration:** "the greatest philosopher of the province and therefore of the whole world." **Understatement:** "One fine spring day he thought he would take a walk. . . ." **Faulty Logic:** "Legs were visibly instituted to be breeched, and we have breeches." **(b)** Voltaire makes heavy use of satirical tools to convey his messages.
   Another sample answer can be found on **Literary Analysis Graphic Organizer B**, p. 149 in *Graphic Organizer Transparencies.*

5. **(a) Possible response:** Voltaire uses Dr. Pangloss' humorous "proofs" to satirize philosophers; he uses the humorous exaggeration of Candide's punishment to satirize the Prussian army. **(b)** Satirists risk making the subject seem light or frivolous by using humor.

6. **Possible response:** The Baron is a nobleman, and his family lives in a castle. During Voltaire's time, most countries in Europe were ruled by an aristocracy, frequently living in castles.

7. **(a)** Pangloss teaches the philosophy of Leibniz, which states that this is the best of all possible worlds. **(b) Possible response:** A society that practices this philosophy may ignore the sufferings of people, reasoning that because this is the best of all possible worlds, suffering does not need to be addressed.

8. **Possible response:** Voltaire presents the Bulgarian army, which represents the Prussian army, in a critical light because the Prussians were at war with France.

❶ Vocabulary Lesson

Word Analysis: Latin Suffix -ity

1. the quality of being unknown
2. the quality of inventiveness
3. the quality acquired by length of service
4. the quality of being genuine

Spelling Strategy

1. exhibitor
2. traitor
3. chamber
4. manner

Vocabulary Builder: Sentence Completion

1. vivacity
2. candor
3. clemency
4. prodigy
5. endowed

❷ Grammar and Style Lesson

1. the best of castles; the best of Baronesses
2. noses were made to wear glasses; legs were made to wear breeches
3. to take aim; to fire; and to double up
4. the support; the aid; the defender; the hero
5. Your fortune is made; your glory is assured

Writing Application

Possible response: Candide is <u>the most innocent</u>, <u>the most naïve</u>, and <u>the most simple-minded</u> of characters. Candide believes that the castle is <u>the best of all castles</u> and that Cunegonde is <u>the best of all Baronesses</u>. The <u>father is a powerful lord</u>, and the <u>mother is a respected Baroness</u>. Cunegonde is <u>rosy-cheeked</u>, <u>fresh</u>, and <u>lovely</u>.

Build Language Skills

❶ Vocabulary Lesson

Word Analysis: Latin Suffix -ity

The Latin suffix -ity means "quality or state of." For example, the word *vivacity* means "a quality or state of liveliness." Use your understanding of this suffix to define the following words:

1. anonymity
2. ingenuity
3. seniority
4. authenticity

Spelling Strategy

Although the word ending -er is more common, words that name a quality or a role, such as *candor* and *juror,* usually end in -or. Add the correct word ending to each item below. Use a dictionary to check your answers.

1. exhibit-
2. trait-
3. chamb-
4. mann-

Vocabulary Builder: Sentence Completion

Review the words from the vocabulary list on page 801. Then, complete each sentence below with the correct word from the vocabulary list.

1. The volunteers' enthusiasm and _____ make difficult work more enjoyable.
2. She spoke with _____ about her hurt feelings.
3. The judge granted _____ to the remorseful offender.
4. The piano, flute, and violin were a few of the instruments mastered by the child _____.
5. Little money remained in the trust fund _____ by her parents.

❷ Grammar and Style Lesson

Parallel Structure

Parallel structure, or parallelism, is the repetition of equal ideas in a similar grammatical form. Parallelism can involve the repeated use of words, phrases, clauses, or sentences.

> *Their* lips met, *their* eyes sparkled, *their* knees trembled. . . .
>
> Candide *listened attentively* and *believed innocently.* . . .

Practice Identify the parallel structures in the following sentences.

1. The Baron's castle was the best of castles and his wife, the best of Baronesses.

2. According to Dr. Pangloss, noses were made to wear glasses and legs were made to wear breeches.

3. While he was in the army, he learned to take aim, to fire, and to double up.

4. You are now the support, the aid, the defender, the hero of Bulgarians.

5. Your fortune is made and your glory is assured.

Writing Application Write four sentences describing your impression of Candide and Cunegonde, using parallel structures in each one. Then, identify the parallelism in your sentences.

WG Prentice Hall Writing and Grammar Connection: Platinum Level, Chapter 7, Section 4

Assessment Practice

Distinguish Between Fact and Nonfact

Standardized tests often require students to distinguish between fact and nonfact. Use the following sample test item to demonstrate.

Candide, expelled from the earthly paradise, wandered for a long time . . . gazing back frequently at the noblest of castles which held the most beautiful of young Baronesses; he lay down to sleep supperless between two furrows in the open fields: it snowed heavily in large flakes.

—from *Candide,* Chapter II

(For more practice, see *Test Preparation Workbook*, p. 36.)

Which of the following is an OPINION expressed in the passage?

A Candide . . . wandered for a long time . . .
B it snowed heavily in large flakes.
C the most beautiful of young Baronesses . . .
D He lay down to sleep supperless . . .

Responses A, B, and D are facts expressed in the passage. Beauty is subjective. Therefore, the correct answer is C.

❸ Writing Lesson

Short Satirical Story

Satirists write about something they would like to change in the world. Choose a foolish behavior, a social injustice, or an institution you believe worthy of reform, and write a **short satirical story** that encourages people to bring about change.

Prewriting   Use a chart like the one shown to organize your story. Start by identifying a subject. Then, list specific details that you want to satirize. Finally, state the suggested reform you hope your satire will inspire.

Writing Model: Organizing Details

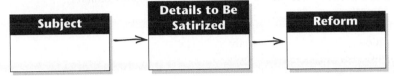

Subject	Details to Be Satirized	Reform

Drafting   As you draft your satire, use a variety of tools, such as exaggeration, faulty logic, and understatement. Remember that to be effective, the satire should be humorous.

Revising   Check your finished draft against your prewriting chart, noting any details you may have omitted. Be sure that your story ends in a way that supports the purpose of your satire. Add more details or alter the ending if necessary.

W̶G Prentice Hall Writing and Grammar Connection: Platinum Level, Chapter 5, Section 2

❹ Extend Your Learning

Listening and Speaking Listen to selections from a musical version of *Candide*. Then, participate in a **group discussion** to determine the ways in which the music reflects Voltaire's written work. Be sure to address these questions:

- Does the music add to or detract from the story?
- Do the lyrics accurately represent the characters and events?

Compare your group's reactions to other groups' opinions. **[Group Activity]**

Research and Technology Find three political cartoons that use satire to make a point. You might check the editorial pages of major newspapers or some online magazines that cover politics and world events. Use the cartoons to create a **visual report** that explains what satire is and what is satirized in the cartoons.

Go Online
Research

For: An additional research activity
Visit: www.PHSchool.com
Web code: etd-7607

from Candide ■ 809

---

❸ Writing Lesson

- To give students guidance in writing this story, give them the **Support for Writing Lesson**, p. 108 in *Unit 6 Resources.*

- Suggest that students meet in small groups to brainstorm topics for their satires. Ask group members to continue to work together to help one another develop humorous details.

- Give students a copy of the **Plot Diagram Graphic Organizer**, p. 280 in *Graphic Organizer Transparencies*, to help them develop their stories. Encourage students to make notes about details, characters, and satirical tools.

- Use the Narration: Short Story rubrics in *General Resources*, pp. 63–64, to evaluate students' stories.

W̶G **Writing and Grammar Platinum Level**
For support in teaching the Writing Lesson, use Chapter 5, Section 2

❹ Research and Technology

- Tell students that most major newspapers can be found online. Students may find not only current issues but archives as well.

- Suggest that students write a caption for each cartoon, explaining what is being satirized and what satirical tool is being used.

- Suggest that students share their reports with the class.

- The **Support for Extend Your Learning** page (*Unit 6 Resources*, p. 109) provides guided note-taking opportunities to help students complete the Extend Your Learning activities.

Go Online Have students type in the
Research Web Code for another
research activity.

Assessment Resources

The following resources can be used to assess students' knowledge and skills.

Unit 6 Resources
Selection Test A, pp. 111–113
Selection Test B, pp. 114–116

General Resources
Rubrics for Narration: Short Story,
pp. 63–64

Go Online Students may use the Self-test to
Assessment prepare for **Selection Test A** or
Selection Test B.

WL.1.02.5 Demonstrate an understanding of media's
impact on analyses and
personal reflection.

IR.2.01.10 Analyze the connections
between ideas, concepts,
characters and experi-
ences in research.

CT.4.04.1 Identify clear criteria for
evaluation of work of
others.

*See **Teacher Express™/Lesson View**
for a detailed lesson for Reading
Informational Material.*

About Feature Articles

• Have students read "About Feature
Articles." Then, **ask** them to name
types of feature articles that they
have read in newspapers.
Possible responses: Movie
reviews, restaurant reviews, interviews with sports figures, and profiles of interesting people are types
of feature articles.

• If possible, bring several newspapers
to class and have students look
through them for feature articles.
Discuss how these feature articles
differ from news articles.

• **Ask** why it is important to know the
difference between a news article
and a feature article.
Possible response: Knowing the
difference between the two is
important because feature articles
are not objective; they contain a
mix of facts and opinions.

Reading Strategy

Evaluating Support

• Have students read the information
about the Reading Strategy.

• Explain that students evaluate support for opinions in everyday life,
such as when they hear advertisements and political speeches.

• **Ask** students why it is important to
evaluate support for an opinion in a
feature article.
Answer: By evaluating the support
for an opinion, the reader can tell
whether the support is reliable and
sufficient.

• Point out the chart. Have students
copy the chart and list as they read
the article each opinion, its support,
and their evaluation of the support.

Feature Articles
About Feature Articles

Most people turn to newspapers for current information about recent
events. Daily papers include news articles on local and world events,
but they also include a variety of other types of information. For example,
feature articles showcase various topics of interest and are written to inform and entertain the public. Unlike news articles that present information formally and objectively, features can be written in a more informal
style. In addition, feature articles often include the opinion of the writer.

Because they are meant to entertain, feature articles usually present the
lighter side of life, and they address topics that are less time-sensitive than
those found in straightforward news articles. Here are some common
topics for feature writers:

• The Arts
• Fashion
• Health
• Entertainment

• Unusual occurrences
• Family
• Leisure
• People

"Leonardo: The Eye, The Hand, The Mind" is a feature on an exhibit of the
works of Leonardo da Vinci, one of the great masters of art in Renaissance
Italy.

Reading Strategy
Evaluating Support

In addition to the information they showcase, feature articles often
present a writer's opinion or evaluation of a topic. These opinions must
be supported with evidence such as facts, statistics, observations, and
examples. To determine whether you agree with the writer's opinions,
evaluate the support, deciding whether or not the evidence is persuasive
and valid. Use a chart like the one shown to list each opinion in the
following feature. For each one, identify the details that support that
opinion. Then, evaluate the support to decide whether the writer's
opinion is valid.

Opinion	Support	Evaluation of Support
Cotter says Leonardo's strengths lie in art, science, engineering, and aesthetic theory.	Cotter lists Leonardo's accomplishments in hydrodynamics, anatomy, physics, astronomy, invention, and art.	The list of accomplishments supports Cotter's opinion that Leonardo's strengths lie in many areas.

Differentiated
Instruction   Solutions for All Learners

Reading Support
Give students reading support with the appro-
priate version of the **Reader's Notebooks:**
   Reader's Notebook: [L2, L3]
   **Reader's Notebook: Adapted Version
      [L1, L2]**
   **Reader's Notebook: English Learner's
      Version [EL]**

January 24, 2003

The New York Times

Leonardo: The Eye, the Hand, the Mind

By Holland Cotter

LEONARDO DA VINCI (1452–1519) is the Great Oz of European art. At least that's the way he sometimes seems, glimpsed through the fogs and fumes of history: a cultural force more than a man, a colossal brain and a sovereign hand at the controls of a multidisciplinary universe.

Where did his supreme gift lie? In art? Science? Engineering? Aesthetic theory? All of the above. We all have our strengths; I have mastered MetroCard dispensers and a home computer. Yet Leonardo understood, described and illustrated the principles of hydrodynamics, gross anatomy, physics and astronomy. He invented the helicopter, the armored tank and the submarine. He painted like an angel and despite being phobic about deadlines, wrote often and well. In addition, according to Vasari, he was drop-dead gorgeous.

And, perhaps most confounding, he generated all this near-magical accomplishment from behind a curtain of personal discretion so dense and insulating that no historian or psychologist—and dozens, maybe hundreds, have tried—has been able to pull it aside to reveal the person behind the personage.

"Leonardo da Vinci, Master Draftsman" at the Metropolitan Museum of Art also tries, and manages to part the curtain just a crack. We may not learn exactly what made this artist tick, but we can see him ticking away, at length and in some depth.

Naturally, the show had blockbuster written all over it from the word go. With 118 Leonardo drawings, it is the largest gathering of his work in America. The lending institutions are a super-

A Rider on a Rearing Horse in a Profile View,
Leonardo da Vinci, Fitzwilliam Museum, University of Cambridge, England

> In the opening sentence, the writer expresses an opinion, an element that is often found in a feature article.

> This paragraph introduces an opinion about Leonardo da Vinci's accomplishments and supports it with examples.

Reading Feature Articles

- Tell students that this feature article about Leonardo da Vinci is the type of article that might appear as an arts feature in a newspaper.
- Have students read "Leonardo: The Eye, the Hand, the Mind" and the notes that identify the elements of this article.
- Direct students' attention to the first paragraph. Have them **summarize** the author's opinion about Leonardo da Vinci.
  Possible response: The author sees Leonardo da Vinci as an intellectual and artistic giant who could do almost anything.
- Call students' attention to the second paragraph. **Ask:** What support does Cotter provide to show that Leonardo da Vinci is not like most people?
  Answer: Cotter is proud to have mastered MetroCard dispensers and a home computer; Leonardo da Vinci, on the other hand, invented the helicopter, the armored tank, and the submarine; explained and illustrated complicated scientific topics; and painted and wrote prolifically and beautifully.

Humanities

A Rider on a Rearing Horse in a Profile View,
by Leonardo da Vinci

The Italian Renaissance painter, scientist, and inventor Leonardo da Vinci (1452–1519) was also an insatiable draftsman; some four thousand of his drawings, many preserved in his notebooks, still survive. This body of work has been preserved in part because collectors avidly sought Leonardo's drawings even in his own lifetime.

This sketch of a horseman is executed using a metalpoint stylus on treated paper. (In this medium, the stylus is used to etch away the prepared surface of the paper, revealing color beneath.) Sophisticated shading techniques flesh out the horse's torso and chest. Leonardo often drew to test ideas, as is suggested by the alternative placements of the horse's rear legs and the vague presentation of the rider.

continued on p. 812

Differentiated Instruction — Solutions for All Learners

Strategy for Less Proficient Readers
As students read, have them independently fill out the first two columns of the chart. In addition, tell them to record the page on which they found each piece of information that they have entered. After students have finished reading the article, have them work in pairs to evaluate the support for each opinion that they identified.

Strategy for English Learners
You may wish to show students pictures of some of Leonardo da Vinci's creations to give students an idea of his genius. If possible, obtain copies of the drawings specifically mentioned in the article. Then, as students read, have them compare the author's descriptions of Leonardo's work with the images.

Enrichment for Advanced Readers
To demonstrate the difference between a feature article and a news article, have students read an encyclopedia article on Leonardo da Vinci. Tell students to list the similarities and differences between the two articles and then report their findings to the class.

- Point out the first full paragraph on this page. **Ask** students to identify which phrases in the paragraph make the article both informative and entertaining.

  Possible response: Informal language—"a few are just weird, so weird you find yourself wondering: what planet was this guy from?"—is followed by descriptive information about drawing.

- If students have trouble identifying informal language, point out the second call-out note. Read aloud the examples such as "hit parade" and "they've created something like." Then, **ask** students how this informal language affects the article.

  Possible response: The informal language makes the article interesting and easy to read.

- Draw students' attention to the evaluation of Leonardo's work pattern. **Ask:** How does the author lead up to this evaluation?

  Answer: The author provides information on Leonardo's training, background, and first important job.

January 24, 2003

starry lot: the Uffizi, the Louvre, the Vatican, the Royal Library at Windsor Castle. And the Met has given it the imperial treatment: crimson walls, acres of space, a catalog as thick as *The Physician's Desk Reference.*

> *The language the writer uses makes this article both informative and entertaining.*

Are the drawings worth the fuss? In a word, totally. Individually, many are glorious; some are workmanlike; a few are just weird, so weird you find yourself wondering: what planet was this guy from? As a package, though, as the datastream output of a single sensibility, they're huge. They are also very alive. People always say that you can't know painting from a book, that you have to experience it. This is at least as true of drawing, a profoundly physical medium, where a smudge or erasure can be a heart-catching event, and a pen stroke can leap like a solar flare.

The show comes with some fresh scholarship, not blindingly revealing, but solid and worthwhile. The curators Carmen C. Bambach and George R. Goldner, both of the Met's department of drawings and prints, have avoided a hit parade approach in their some less familiar material. They've also brought related drawings—10 studies for the Florentine mural "The Battle of Anghiari" alone—together, in some cases for the first time. Finally, by arranging the work chronologically, they've created something like an organic picture of the history of one man's polymathic life.

> *The informal language in this paragraph is characteristic of feature articles.*

Leonardo was born in 1452 and started life with certain disadvantages. He was a small-town kid, . . . indifferently educated and—a liability for an artist, you would think—left-handed. But he also had luck. His supportive father took him to Florence, by then a major node on the information highway of Renaissance Europe. There he was apprenticed to Andrea del Verrocchio, a leading sculptor but also a painter (five gorgeous drawings of his open the show) from whom Leonardo learned much.

For one thing, he learned to draw sculpturally. This meant drawing with a command of volume, as several early drapery studies demonstrate. It also meant executing fleet, notational sketches to capture the look of real things viewed from many angles in actual space, as seen in Leonardo's serial depictions of squirming babies and wide-awake cats. From Verrocchio he also learned to carry a notebook with him at all times and to use it, so that whatever went in through the eye came out through his hand.

In 1481, he landed a substantial job, an altarpiece painting of "The Adoration of the Magi." And at that point, he seemed to have settled on a work pattern that, for better or worse, he would follow thereafter. Basically, it entailed conceiving pictorial designs so complex and technically demanding that he would never complete them.

> *Here the writer offers an evaluation of da Vinci's work pattern.*

For "The Adoration," for example, he planned to place more than 60 figures in an elaborate perspective setting. He drew and drew; several well-known studies, one of them madly complicated, are in the

Head of the Virgin, Leonardo da Vinci, The Metropolitan Museum of Art

> In this paragraph, the writer provides support for his evaluation of da Vinci's work pattern.

show. But the ideas never really gelled, and he eventually headed to Milan in search of different work, leaving an unfinished painting behind.

He stayed in Milan, employed by the city's ruler, Ludovico Sforza, for 15 years, which were among the most productive of his life. His first commission—he proposed it himself—was an outsize equestrian monument to Ludovico's father. Again, he produced studies galore, dashed off and spirited, fastidious and polished. But the monument never materialized, and the plans were abandoned.

In any case, Leonardo was, as usual, working on several other things. One was the unfinished painting, now owned by the Vatican, titled "St. Jerome in the Wilderness." It's at the Met and gives a stark, almost agonizing sense of how he carried his obsessive, draftsmanlike self-

correction right into what should have been the final stages of a painting.

And there was "The Last Supper," painted from 1493 to 1498 in the refectory of Santa Maria della Grazie. One renowned sheet from Windsor carries what could be a preliminary sketch of that painting's composition, mixed in with geometric and architectural designs. And from the Albertina in Vienna comes a powerfully resolved drawing on blue paper of an old man who is sometimes identified as St. Peter. Whatever his identity, he is animated by the tense, urgent gravitas of the painting itself.

When French troops invaded Milan in 1499, Leonardo made his way back to Florence. There he whipped up a large-scale drawing titled "Virgin and Child With Saint Anne" and gave himself a one-man show. The drawing—now lost, though later versions on the same theme

Reading Informational Materials: Feature Articles ■ 813

Reading Feature Articles (cont.)

- Read aloud the call-out note. Then, have students read independently the bracketed passage and the following paragraph.
- Have students **discuss** the support the writer provides to justify the opinion that Leonardo conceived "pictorial designs so complex and technically demanding that he would never complete them." **Answer:** Details concerning the equestrian monument and the unfinished painting *St. Jerome in the Wilderness* serve as support.

Humanities

Head of the Virgin in Three-Quarter View Facing to the Right,
by Leonardo da Vinci

Leonardo was notorious for his difficulty in finishing projects. Only fifteen finished paintings survive, and it is thought that none of his sculptural projects were completed. Yet even his preparatory sketches for works excited admiration. According to a traditional biography, admirers turned out in droves to view Leonardo's cartoon, or large sketch, for *Virgin and Child with Saint Anne,* a painting Leonardo completed between 1508 and 1513.

Although *Head of the Virgin* is one of a number of studies for this painting, the drawing is a polished work in its own right. Working in charcoal and red and black chalks, Leonardo achieves the effect known as *sfumato.* This softening of focus, as though the figure were seen through a mist, is achieved by blending tones in "the manner of smoke" (as Leonardo himself described it). Leonardo, a scientist and inventor as well as a great artist, had performed extensive observations of the behavior of light and shadow, and his scientific observations informed his artistic technique. Like a number of Leonardo's women, the Virgin in this drawing bears a gentle, somewhat enigmatic smile.

continued on p. 814

Differentiated Instruction   Solutions for All Learners

Strategy for Special Needs Students
Students may have difficulty sorting out the order of events in Leonardo da Vinci's life discussed in the article. As they read, have students create timelines to help track the main events of Leonardo's life and his major works. Then, have students work in pairs to compare their timelines.

Enrichment for Gifted/Talented Students
Encourage students to create collages to represent Leonardo da Vinci's impact on art or science. Have students begin by researching Leonardo's achievements; as they learn more, students may wish to narrow their focus (his major achievements, for example, or his contributions to future generations). Ask volunteers to discuss the elements of their collages and explain to the class what those elements represent.

- Allow students to review the writer's evaluation of Leonardo da Vinci's work pattern on p. 812.

- Then, have a student read aloud the first full paragraph on this page. **Ask** students whether the writer has provided enough support for this evaluation.
Possible response: Yes; the writer has supported his evaluation. Drawing conclusions from established facts is adequate support for the opinion.

- Have students reread the last paragraph of the article. Draw their attention to the informal wording in this paragraph. **Ask:** How does this language add to the article?
Possible response: Informal language such as "for me" and the last sentence of the paragraph makes the article more personal and appealing.

January 24, 2003

exist—was rapturously received and resulted in a commission from the city government for the Battle of Anghiari mural, to be painted in the Palazzo della Signoria. Its subject was a Florentine military victory.

Details in this paragraph continue to support the writer's evaluation of da Vinci's work pattern.

The assignment was a very big, very public deal; Michelangelo, the local reigning prince of art, was to paint the opposite wall. Once more, Leonardo feverishly poured out ideas on paper, and the studies in the show are fantastic, from an explosive drawing of a horse in motion (several legs, many heads) to a hyperrealistic depiction of a screaming soldier. As for the mural, Leonardo designed a cartoon and expensive scaffolding, then left town, heading back to Milan.

Once there, he did what he had always done: many things simultaneously. He painted; he taught; he studied anatomy and geometry. He designed maps, architectural plans and stage sets. He conducted scientific experiments and recorded his findings in notebooks, writing from right to left and in mirror image, which, as a lefty, he had always done.

And he sketched. Small drawings of grotesque human heads flowed from his hand like telephone pad doodles. His famous "Deluge" pictures date to this time. Imaginary scenes of tidal waves overwhelming minute towns, they are both aquatic studies and apocalyptic visions. In 1516, the French king Francis I, who

collected trophy artists as well as art, invited him to live at his court. Leonardo, old at 64, moved to France and died there three years later.

He left behind a godlike reputation, worshipful disciples, a scant handful of paintings—about 15 survive—and the 4,000 works on paper that are his primary visual legacy. Some of his drawings are art historical icons; the face of Mary in a study for the painting of "The Virgin and Child With St. Anne," now in the Louvre, is one. He invented this expressive type, with its interior smile and apparitional draftsmanship, and with it a Western ideal of human perfection.

My favorite drawings, though, are of a different kind. They're ones where everything is happening, nonlinearly, all at once, and anything goes: double-sided sheets filled with animals, armaments, allegorical scenes, geometrical diagrams, exploding buildings, . . . dissected muscles, wheels and bridges, flowing water, reminder notes, sums, scratches, spots and stains.

In these, for me, the curtain parts that little bit, to reveal an artist who always preferred to dream and draw rather than to do, who remained at some level a venturesome child controlling his world by taking it apart, piece by piece, to see how the whole thing worked. By thinking big, Leonardo became big; illusions sometimes work that way. And the neat thing is that in his company, we get to think big, too.

The language of this conclusion reflects the informal style of a feature article.

Reading: Evaluating Support

Directions: *Choose the letter of the best answer to each question about the article.*

1. What support does Cotter give to prove that da Vinci did not always finish a commission?
   A Da Vinci stayed in Milan for fifteen years to work for Ludovico Sforza.
   B Da Vinci always carried a notebook with him in order to sketch.
   C Da Vinci left behind 4,000 works on paper as a visual legacy.
   D Da Vinci left Florence without completing the "Adoration" altarpiece.

2. Which of the following best supports Cotter's point that da Vinci preferred dreaming to doing?
   A Da Vinci created innumerable small doodles that were never developed.
   B Da Vinci conducted experiments and recorded his findings.
   C Da Vinci was apprenticed to painter Andrea del Verrocchio.
   D Da Vinci was commissioned to paint "The Adoration of the Magi."

3. When Cotter describes da Vinci's work as "spirited," "fastidious," and "polished," what kind of support would be best to prove that Cotter's opinion is truly valid?
   A supporting facts and statistics by experts on Italian art
   B more of Cotter's personal experiences with da Vinci's works
   C second opinions by other reporters
   D persuasive devices meant to convince readers of da Vinci's talents

Reading: Comprehension and Interpretation

Directions: *Write your answers on a separate sheet of paper.*

4. According to Cotter, what are Leonardo da Vinci's supreme gifts?
5. **(a)** What three things did da Vinci invent? **(b)** How are these things important in today's world?

Timed Writing: Description

Using the information in Cotter's article, describe the Met's da Vinci show. Address the works presented in the show, the organization of the show, and the qualities of the show. **(25 minutes)**

ASSESS

Answers

Reading: Evaluating Support
1. D
2. A
3. A

Reading: Comprehension and Interpretation
4. **Answer:** Leonardo da Vinci's supreme gifts are art, science, engineering, and aesthetic theory.
5. **Possible response:** (a) Da Vinci invented the helicopter, the armored tank, and the submarine. (b) All three are still used in warfare. Helicopters are also used by corporations and private businesses, as well as for recreational flying.

Timed Writing Description

• Encourage students to reread the article to collect and organize their details before writing.

• Suggest that students plan their time to give 10 minutes to planning, 10 minutes to writing, and 5 minutes to revising and editing.

Extend the Lesson

Conducting a Survey on Newspaper Reading
Have students form groups to design and conduct a survey to find out how people get their news. Show examples of a few survey questionnaires. Point out that questionnaires should provide space for an adult to fill in occupation and for his or her student to identify his or her grade level in school. Suggest that groups also include the following questions in their survey:
1. How often do you read a newspaper? Check one. (less than once a week; 1–2 times a week; 3–5 times a week; every day)

2. What sections of the newspaper do you regularly read? (Tell students to list all newspaper sections, including the classified advertisements.)

Advise students to decide whom their surveys will target and how each group will administer the survey. Point out that a long survey will discourage people from responding. Have students create the survey on a word-processing program, distribute the surveys, and compile the answers. Ask students to draw conclusions from the information they gather and share these with the class.

WL.1.02.2 Show awareness of culture in personal reflections.

CT.4.02.1 Show an understanding of cultural context in analyzing thematic connections.

LT.5.02.1 Explore works which relate to an issue, author, or theme and show increasing comprehension.

Prewriting

- To guide students in developing this assignment, give them the **Writing About Literature** support, pp. 117–118 in *Unit 6 Resources.*

- Have students work independently to review the Unit Opener. Then, ask them to define the terms *humanism, Renaissance,* and *Rationalism.*

- After students have identified the authors and selections about which they will write, encourage them to review the selections to renew their familiarity with them. Then, have students answer the bulleted questions.

- Explain the use of the model chart. Then give students a copy of the **Three-column Chart** in *Graphic Organizer Transparencies,* p. 282. Guide students as they begin to fill in their charts for the selections they have chosen.

- Have students use the details they have gathered to draft their working theses. Point out that when drafting their thesis statements, students should focus on one or two characteristics of humanism—its return to classical texts, for example, or its emphasis on education and human perfectibility.

Tips for Test Taking

A writing prompt on the SAT or ACT test may assess students' ability to analyze literary periods, state a point of view regarding the topic, and support the point of view with examples from literary texts. When writing under timed circumstances, students will need to quickly clarify a point of view (the thesis statement) and the evidence that supports it. Because they will not be able to refer to a text, their evidence must be based on their own experiences, readings, or observations.

816

SAT PREP ACT

Analyze Literary Periods

The literature of the Renaissance and the Age of Rationalism was influenced by the cultural movement known as humanism. During the Renaissance, humanists celebrated the rediscovered ideals of classical antiquity. Scholars studied the classics in their original languages: Greek, Latin, and Hebrew. The humanist belief in the value of an active life of involvement with the world overtook the medieval ideal of a contemplative life devoted to God. Humanity's achievements and faculties—knowledge, love, and reason—took center stage. The arts and sciences took on new life, while traditional religious authority was questioned.

To explore the influences of humanism on the selections in this unit, complete the assignment described in the box at right.

Prewriting

Find a focus. Begin by reviewing the discussion of humanism and rationalism in the Unit Introduction on pages 718–725. Then, review the literature in this unit and relate it to humanism. Fill out a chart similar to the one shown below, using these questions as a guide:

- What is the theme of the selection?
- How do the characters and plot reveal the theme?
- How does the theme relate to humanism?

Model: Charting Humanism in Renaissance and Rationalist Literature

Selection	Characteristic of Humanism	Example/Quote
"The White Doe"	speaker's ideals are	"A pure-white doe in an
	expressed in a vision of his	emerald glade/Appeared
	human beloved, not in a	to me . . ."
	religious vision	

Gather evidence. After you have filled in the chart, review the chart carefully. Choose those examples you have listed that most strongly express characteristics of humanism. Then, look for other examples illustrating the same characteristics.

Write a working thesis. After you have decided which characteristics of humanism will be the focus of your paper, write a working thesis. Introduce the characteristics you will discuss, and explain why they were central to the selections.

816 ■ The Renaissance and Rationalism

Assignment: Humanism in the Literature of the Renaissance and the Age of Rationalism

Write an analytical essay that traces the influence of humanism on the writings of the Renaissance authors—Petrarch, Boccaccio, Ronsard, and Cervantes—or the Rationalist authors—La Fontaine and Voltaire—whose works are excerpted in this unit.

Criteria:
- Include a thesis statement that defines humanism and explains its influence on the works you discuss.
- Support your thesis with detailed analyses of the works.
- Cite examples from each work you explore.
- Approximate length: 700 words

Read to Write

As you reread the texts, keep in mind that the writer may be reacting against the values of humanism. Look for both positive and negative influences of humanism in the selections.

Teaching Resources

The following resources can be used to extend or enrich the instruction for Writing About Literature.

Unit 6 Resources
Writing About Literature, pp. 117–118

General Resources
Response to Literature rubrics, pp. 55–56

Graphic Organizer Transparencies
Three-column Chart, p. 282

Drafting

Clarify your thesis statement. As you write your first draft, make sure that your thesis statement explains clearly the characteristics of humanism that you are discussing in your paper.

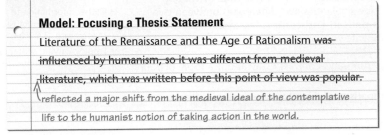

Model: Focusing a Thesis Statement

~~Literature of the Renaissance and the Age of Rationalism was~~ ~~influenced by humanism, so it was different from medieval~~ ~~literature, which was written before this point of view was popular.~~

reflected a major shift from the medieval ideal of the contemplative life to the humanist notion of taking action in the world.

Choose examples for maximum effect. Illustrate the characteristics of humanism that you discuss with specific quotations from the selections. For each example, ask yourself whether it clearly supports the point you are making. Use only examples that give strong support.

Revising and Editing

Review content: Check connections. Underline each example you use, and draw an arrow to the general point it illustrates. For any example that does not clearly support a general point, either replace it with a stronger example or add a sentence clarifying the connection.

Review style: Combine sentences and use transition words. Review your draft for choppy passages made up of short sentences. Revise these passages by combining sentences and adding transitions.

Original: Petrarch's "Spring" shows the influence of humanism. Humanism looks for inspiration in classical antiquity. This poem includes several references to Greek and Roman mythology. It mentions Zephyr, Procne, Jove, and Venus.

Revised: Petrarch's "Spring" shows the influence of humanism, which looks for inspiration in classical antiquity. Petrarch emphasizes this inspiration with references to characters of Greek and Roman myths: Zephyr, Procne, Jove, and Venus.

Publishing and Presenting

Present an informal summary. List the main points of your paper, and explain each in an informal talk to your classmates. Encourage the audience to ask questions.

W̶G Writing and Grammar Connection: Platinum Level, Chapter 13

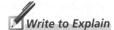 **Write to Learn**
If you have difficulty writing a thesis statement, you may need to do some additional research on the values and characteristics of humanism. The more you know about this cultural movement, the easier it will be to write your thesis statement.

Write to Explain
To make every example and quotation in your paper count, directly connect these details to the point you are trying to make about humanism. Don't expect your readers to infer connections that you don't explain clearly.

Drafting

- Tell students to underline the characteristics of humanism identified in their thesis statements. If students have difficulty completing this step, the thesis statements should be clarified. In the model, the humanist characteristic is the "notion of taking action in the world."

- Remind students that within each paragraph, examples should be connected to one another with transition words, phrases, sentences, and explanations.

Revising and Editing

- If students find it difficult to find examples that support the general point they are making, suggest that they revise their thesis statements.

- As they combine sentences, encourage students to experiment with punctuation marks such as semicolons, colons, and dashes.

Publishing and Presenting

Have students who wrote about Renaissance authors give their talks first, followed by those who wrote about Rationalist authors.

W̶G Writing and Grammar Platinum Level
Students will find additional instruction on writing an analytical essay in Chapter 13.

Writing and Grammar Interactive Textbook CD-ROM

Students can use the following tools as they complete their analytical essays:

- Comparatives
- KWL Chart

Six Traits Focus

✓	Ideas	✓	Word Choice
✓	Organization	✓	Sentence Fluency
	Voice	✓	Conventions

Assessing the Essay

To evaluate students' essays, use the Response to Literature rubrics in *General Resources,* pp. 55–56.

Differentiated Instruction — Solutions for All Learners

Support for Less Proficient Writers
Work with students to identify characteristics of humanism, and list these on the board. Then, have each student select a single characteristic about which to write. Help students identify selections that reflect the chosen characteristics, and then instruct them to locate other selections on their own.

Support for English Learners
Before students begin prewriting, write the word *humanism* on the board. Circle the root *human,* and ask students to discuss what this word means. Point out that humanism is a way of thinking that emphasizes the accomplishments and abilities of human beings.

Enrichment for Advanced Writers
Have students trace the evolution of one humanist idea over the course of the Renaissance and the Age of Rationalism. (To achieve balance, students may want to discuss two selections from each period.) Does the idea strengthen or weaken over time? What historical events may have influenced each writer's thinking?

Standard Course of Study

IR.2.01.10	Analyze the connections between ideas, concepts, characters and experiences in research.
CT.4.05.8	Make connections between works, self and related topics in critical texts.
LT.5.01.6	Make connections between historical and contemporary issues in world literature.

From the Scholar's Desk

João Magueijo

Show students Segment 3 on João Magueijo on *From the Author's Desk DVD.* Discuss the importance of his research and his methods of implementing the writing process.

Writing Genres

Using the Form Point out to students that comparison-and-contrast writing is often incorporated into other types of writing in addition to those mentioned on the student page. Point out these examples:

- Comparison and contrast may provide the center of a report explaining why a certain process or piece of equipment is superior to another in the workplace.

- Comparison and contrast may support persuasive writing.

- An employer may need to compare and contrast the qualifications of two candidates before hiring one of them.

Online Essay Scorer

A writing prompt for this mode of writing can be found on the *PH Online Essay Scorer* at PHSuccessNet.com.

Exposition:
Comparison-and-Contrast Essay

World literature offers many opportunities for comparison and contrast. Petrarch and Shakespeare, for example, both use the sonnet form, and the exuberant tone of Boccaccio contrasts with the ironic tone of Voltaire. Expository essays that describe similarities and differences between two or more items are called **comparison-and-contrast essays.** Follow the steps outlined in this workshop to write your own comparison-and-contrast essay.

Assignment Write a comparison-and-contrast essay about a topic of your choice.

What to Include Your comparison-and-contrast essay should feature the following elements:

- a purpose for comparing and contrasting two or more items
- a clearly focused thesis statement
- evidence to support the thesis, consisting of descriptions of similarities and differences among the items
- a logical organizational plan suited to the topic
- focused paragraphs that feature effective transitions

To preview the criteria on which your comparison-and-contrast essay may be assessed, see the rubric on page 825.

Standard Course of Study

- Analyze the connections between ideas, concepts, characters and experiences in research. (IR.2.01.10)
- Gather information to prove a point about issues in literature. (FA.3.03.1)
- Employ varying sentence structures and sentence types. (GU.6.01.1)

Using the Form
You may use elements of a comparison-and-contrast essay in these types of writing:

- consumer reports
- comparative reviews
- essays on historic figures or events
- comparisons of literary works

Reading Writing Connection

To get a feel for comparison-and-contrast writing, read "Great Minds Do Not Think Alike" on page 798.

Teaching Resources

The following resources can be used to enrich or extend the instruction for the Writing Workshop.

Unit 6 Resources
Writing Workshop: Comparison-and-Contrast Essay, pp. 119–120

General Resources
Rubrics for Exposition: Comparison-and-Contrast Essay, pp. 53–54

Graphic Organizer Transparencies
Venn Diagram, p. 286

From the Author's Desk DVD
João Magueijo, Segments 3 and 4

Prewriting

Choosing Your Topic

To write a strong comparison-and-contrast essay, you need a topic about two or more items with clear similarities or differences. Use one of the following strategies to choose a topic.

Brainstorm a list. First, choose a general subject area that interests you, such as music, sports, presidents, or novels. Next, brainstorm the issues that intrigue you within this broad area. Choose a topic for your essay from your list.

Respond to ideas. Work with a partner to generate a list of pairs. Your pairs might be opposites or closely related subjects. Take turns suggesting a person, character, place, subject, idea, or product, and challenge your partner to respond with the first related idea that comes to mind. Record your ideas on a chart like the one shown. Choose the pair that interests you most to compare or contrast in your essay.

Idea	Response
London	Paris
Frankenstein	Dracula
sonnet	soliloquy
satire	parody
La Fontaine	Voltaire

Narrowing Your Topic

Choose subjects that have sufficient points of comparison for an effective comparison-and-contrast essay. Check your topic by using a Venn diagram like the one shown. If your diagram suggests too few connections, consider choosing a richer topic.

Homer's Sirens — **Margaret Atwood's Sirens**

- romantic, alluring
- "ravishing" harmonies

- deadly
- effective

- unromantic, ungainly
- "bird suit," "squatting"

Gathering Details

Identify your purpose. You should have a focused purpose for your essay. Think about the value or importance of comparing the items you have chosen. You may write to achieve one of these purposes:

- to advocate one item over the other
- to show connections
- to show what causes the similarities and differences

Identify points of comparison and contrast. Focus on gathering details that develop the comparisons that you want to draw. You may need to conduct research or rely on your own knowledge or experience to identify key elements. As you gather information, focus on points of similarity and difference between your subjects.

Prewriting

- Have students suggest general areas of interest, and list these on the board. Students can then brainstorm independently within one of these areas.

- Limit student pairs to five minutes to help them stay on task and to encourage them to work quickly.

- Within a given area, encourage students to choose two or more items that have a strong commonality. For example, if comparing and contrasting movies, students should choose films of the same genre—not, for example, an adventure film and a romantic comedy.

- Remind students that they need a purpose for writing any essay. **Ask** students to identify some other reasons for writing a comparison-and-contrast essay. **Possible response:** Reasons for writing a comparison-and-contrast essay might be to examine similarities and differences or to evaluate the quality of similar items.

- Clarify that in establishing the purpose for this essay, students should go beyond mere superficial similarities and differences.

- Emphasize the importance of researching and gathering details. The more details students gather now, the easier their drafting process will be.

- Before students begin their drafts, have them review the Rubric for Self-Assessment, p. 825, so that they know what is expected of their essays.

Six Traits Focus

✓	Ideas		Word Choice
✓	Organization		Sentence Fluency
	Voice		Conventions

Tips for Using Rubrics

- Before students begin work on this assignment, have them preview the Rubric for Self-Assessment, p. 825, to know what is expected.

- Review the Assessment criteria in class. Before students use the Rubric for Self-Assessment, work with them to rate the student model by applying one or two criteria to it.

- If you wish to assess students' comparison-and-contrast essays, with a 4-point, 5-point, or 6-point scoring rubric, see *General Resources*, pp. 53 and 54.

𝒲ℊ Writing and Grammar Platinum Level

Students will find additional instruction on prewriting for a comparison-and-contrast essay in Chapter 9, Section 2.

Writing and Grammar Interactive Textbook CD-ROM

- Venn Diagram
- Topic Bank
- Transition Words Revising Tools

Drafting

- To help students distinguish between the two types of organization, write the following values on the board: Subject A = Pizza World pizza; Subject B = Pizza Time pizza; Point 1 = crust; Point 2 = sauce; Point 3 = toppings.

- Have students plug these values into the model outlines on this page.

- Then, have students write two more outlines, this time using subjects and points of their choice.

- Finally, have them decide which outline better suits their needs. Use the **Outline** organizer in *Graphic Organizer Transparencies,* p. 248.

- Challenge students to use each kind of evidence (examples, facts, and quotations) at least once. For more on providing evidence, see João Magueijo's comments on p. 821.

Six Traits Focus

✓	Ideas		Word Choice
✓	Organization		Sentence Fluency
	Voice		Conventions

Writing and Grammar
Platinum Level
Students will find additional instruction on drafting a comparison-and-contrast essay in Chapter 9, Section 3.

Drafting

Shaping Your Writing

Organize your essay. Comparison-and-contrast essays are generally organized in one of two ways: subject by subject or point by point.

- To use **subject-by-subject organization,** first discuss all the features of one item and then discuss all the features of the second, the third, and so on. This format allows you to focus your full attention on one subject at a time. Be careful to address the same features and devote equal time to each subject.

- To use **point-by-point organization,** begin by discussing the same point about all of the items and then move on to the second, third, and subsequent points. This plan allows you to move back and forth between subjects as you discuss each point of comparison, allowing you to sharpen the similarities and differences. It also makes it easy for you to make sure that you address each feature for both subjects.

The outlines shown illustrate these two methods of organization.

Organizational Plans

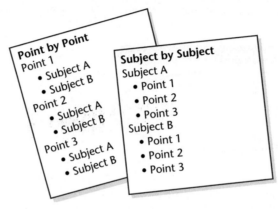

Providing Elaboration

Support your position. Provide evidence to support all of the important points you make in your essay. Supporting evidence may take any or all of the following forms:

- **Examples:** Use examples that illustrate the similarities and differences between the items.
- **Facts:** Whenever possible, use detailed, factual evidence that will help readers gain a clear understanding of each item.
- **Quotations:** Quotations from original texts or from experts on your topic lend authority to your arguments.

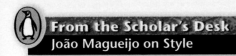

João Magueijo

I'm a scientist before I'm a writer. Writing about science, for me, has been a matter of mental sanity. It has kept another stereotype at bay—that of becoming a mad scientist. Perhaps for this reason my style is not very subtle. I benefited from a great editor. When you're a scientist you use jargon even without noticing it. Cutting it out was essential in cleaning the book.

"I didn't revise my book much."
—— João Magueijo

Professional Model:

from *Faster Than the Speed of Light*

But it was not until I was well into my own career as a physicist that I realized that most problems in physics are not approached in a coolly rational manner; at least not initially. Before we are scientists we are Homo sapiens, a species that, despite its pompous name, is more often driven by emotion than by reason. We don't always carefully sort out false clues and bad assumptions, nor do we limit ourselves to the most rational techniques of problem solving.

During the early development of a new idea we behave rather more like artists, driven by temperament and matters of taste. In other words, we start off with a hunch, a feeling, even a desire that the world be one way, and then proceed from that presentiment, often sticking with it long after data suggests we may be leading ourselves and those who trust us down a blind alley. What ultimately saves us is that at the end of the day, experiment acts as the ultimate referee, settling all disputes. No matter how strong our hunch is, and how well it is articulated, at some point we will have to prove it with hard, cold facts. Or our hunches, no matter how strongly held, will remain just that.

Starting a phrase with "but" or "or" is not exactly perfect grammar—but it's conversational. Also, breaking a sentence with a semi-colon introduces a break in rhythm, a bit like what we find in oral speech.

One bit was changed in this piece from first to final draft. The original read, "...we will have to prove it with the hard, cold data of experimentation."

- Show students Segment 4 on João Magueijo on *From the Author's Desk DVD.* Discuss what keeps him motivated to try new ideas and why he thinks it is important for young people to read literature about science.

- Point out that João Magueijo depends on a good editor to keep him from using scientific language and jargon that many people would not understand.

- Tell students that many professional authors have an editor or another person read their work to provide feedback. This process helps make their work more readable. An editor can point out the areas that are unclear to the average reader but that might be perfectly clear to the writer.

- Review João Magueijo's comments about his revision to **from Faster Than the Speed of Light. Ask** students to explain how the change in wording makes the passage more accessible to the average reader. **Possible response:** The changes make the passage sound more like conversation.

Tips for
Improving Word Choice

Give students these suggestions for revising for word choice:

1. Look for places in your draft where the wording sounds too technical or uses jargon, and replace or revise that wording. If you are not sure, ask a person less familiar than you are with your topic to read your essay and tell you whether your information and language is clear.

2. To add variety to your sentences, revise long, compound sentences by inserting a semi-colon in place of the coordinating conjunction *and.*

3. When writing for a general audience, choose words that seem more conversational rather than stiff and formal. For example, replace *data* with *facts.*

Revising

- Explain that strong topic sentences in paragraphs help make writing clear. Explain that topic sentences within an essay are like road signs for the reader. They tell what is being left behind and what is coming up. To make the point, read aloud the second paragraph of the model on p. 824 without the first sentence and then with the first sentence. Discuss how the first sentence of this paragraph tells the reader what the rest of the paragraph is about.

- Have students underline—or, if missing, supply—a topic sentence for each paragraph in the essay. Then, have them verify that each topic sentence clearly identifies the subject or point being discussed.

- Point out that evidence should be balanced not only in quantity but in kind. To make sure that students have provided similar kinds of support for each major point, have them label each highlighted piece of evidence E (example), F (fact), or Q (quotation), and then check for overall balance.

- On the board, write the following sentences: *Pizza Time's pizza sauce is rich and robust. Pizza World's toppings are the freshest in town.*

- **Ask** students to establish a relationship between the two sentences by using as many different transition words or phrases as they can. Write their responses on the board. **Possible responses:** Pizza Time's pizza sauce is rich and robust, but Pizza World's . . . ; although Pizza Time's . . . , Pizza World's . . . ; Pizza Time's pizza sauce. . . . By contrast, Pizza World's . . . ; Pizza Time's pizza sauce. . . On the other hand, Pizza World's . . . .

Six Traits Focus

✓	Ideas	✓	Word Choice
✓	Organization	✓	Sentence Fluency
	Voice	✓	Conventions

Writing and Grammar
Platinum Level
Students will find additional guidance for revising a comparison-and-contrast essay in Chapter 9, Section 4.

Writing Workshop

Revising

Revising Your Overall Structure
Check for clarity. Because a comparison-and-contrast essay covers two or more items, a clear organization is essential. The reader must know which item is the focus in which part of the essay, so revise your essay to achieve this clarity. Reorder details if necessary, grouping related points or adding transitions as needed.

To read the complete student model, see page 824.

> **Student Model: Revising for Clarity**
>
> Immune to the Sirens' feminine allure, Atwood takes a tersely unromantic approach. By adopting the perspective of a Siren, she portrays the creatures, not as deadly beauties, but as helpless victims. The ^Atwood's narrator presents herself as trapped in a "bird suit" and "squatting" on an island, depictions that strip away dignity and beauty.

Adding the author's name reinforces the subject of this paragraph—the poem by Margaret Atwood.

Revise for balance. Review your draft and highlight your supporting evidence, using a different color for each item that you compare and contrast. Check your essay for balance by determining whether you have included approximately the same amount of detail for every item. If not, add or delete examples, facts, quotations, statistics, expert testimony, and other supporting details.

Revising Your Sentences
Create effective transitions. Make sure that you have used logical, smooth transitions between sentences and paragraphs. Use words and phrases that signal and clarify transitions, such as *similarly*, *in contrast*, and *on the other hand*.

Choppy: The theme of the first story emphasizes acceptance of one's lot in life. The theme of the second focuses on struggling against one's fate.

Smooth: The theme of the first story emphasizes acceptance of one's lot in life. *In contrast*, the theme of the second focuses on struggling against one's fate.

Peer Review: Ask a partner to review your draft and mark places in your writing where sentences seem choppy or where the movement between topics seems awkward. Together, discuss ways to improve these points in your writing. Evaluate the revisions suggested by your partner and make those that will improve your draft.

Tips for
Using Technology in Writing

Have students put their drafts into a word-processing software program. As they revise, encourage them to use the program's Font Color function to check for balanced evidence. Have students apply different colors to different pieces of evidence. Next, using the Find function, students can search for and count pieces of evidence they have formatted in different colors.

Developing Your Style
Introductions and Conclusions

Improve your beginnings and endings. Just as entrances and exits are important for actors, beginnings and endings present important challenges to writers. Your introduction is your chance to grab the reader's attention. In your conclusion, you can make a final—and memorable—impression on your audience. Polish your beginnings and endings so that they become more than just a summary or a repetition of your main ideas. Use one or more of the following strategies:

- Instead of beginning with a declarative sentence, consider starting with a question, an exclamation, or a command—or even a deliberately provocative sentence fragment.

  Example: Does Machiavelli's philosophy still hold true today?

- Try quotations, brief anecdotes, or surprising facts for attention-grabbing lead-ins to an essay.

  Example: Machiavelli believed that "a prince never lacks legitimate reasons to break his promise."

- In your conclusion, do not merely restate your thesis or your research results. Instead, add a thought-provoking final comment that inspires your readers to go beyond your essay to think about the broader impact of the topic.

  Example: Ask yourself whether Machiavelli would support or criticize the behaviors of our federal, state, or local lawmakers.

Find It in Your Reading Read or review Chapter 1 from *Don Quixote,* by Miguel de Cervantes, on page 770.

1. Notice the ways in which the details in the first sentence of the chapter grab your attention.
2. Identify the features of the last sentence that make it an appropriate and satisfying conclusion for the chapter.

Apply It to Your Writing Review the draft of your comparison-and-contrast essay.

- Experiment with variations for your introduction by altering the sentence structure or substituting new details.
- Review your conclusion for conciseness and impact.
- Challenge yourself to find a different way to leave your reader with a memorable final impression.

WG Prentice Hall Writing and Grammar Connection: Platinum Level, Chapter 13, Section 4

Developing Your Style

- Point out to students that they have only a few seconds to catch their reader's interest. This tiny time frame is why their introductions are critical to the success of their essays. Similarly, tell students that an audience will remember their main points best if they write an effective conclusion.

- Caution students against beginning with a yes/no question such as "Have you ever wondered why the sky is dark at night?" Have students speculate about why such a question might turn away readers. Make sure students realize that if readers answer "no," they probably will not read more of the essay.

- Have students look at the suggestions for introductions. Ask them what type of essay might best fit each idea for introductions.

- As students work on **Find It in Your Reading,** have them discuss the ways the details of the first sentence grab their attention and why the features in the last sentence create an effective conclusion.

- After students have reviewed their drafts and revised their introductions and conclusions, have them share their papers with a partner and provide each other with feedback on the effectiveness of their revisions.

WG Writing and Grammar Platinum Level
Students will find additional instruction on creating introductions and conclusions in Chapter 3, Section 2 and Chapter 10, Section 4.

Differentiated Instruction — Solutions for All Learners

Strategy for Less Proficient Writers	Vocabulary for English Learners	Strategy for Advanced Writers
As students develop their thesis statements, have them use the following sentence patterns: Both item A and item B _____. However, item A _____, whereas item B _____. Students can use these sentences as a drafting guide and revise them for clarity and interest later.	Encourage students to choose concrete objects rather than abstract ideas to compare and contrast. Before students begin writing, tell them to use a Venn diagram to brainstorm descriptive words that apply to each object.	Point out that the writer of the model essay takes a particular critical approach to her subjects—a feminist approach. Have students identify some other critical vantage points, such as socioeconomic, historical, and cultural views. Encourage students to adopt one of these approaches in their own writing.

Student Model

- Explain that the Student Model is a sample and that students' own essays may be longer.

- Ask a volunteer to read aloud the first paragraph. **Ask** students to identify the two subjects that will be compared and contrasted in the essay.
  Answer: The two subjects to be compared and contrasted are Homer's portrayal of the Sirens and Atwood's portrayal of the Sirens.

- After students read the second paragraph silently, point out that it addresses only Homer's representation of the Sirens.

- Read aloud the third paragraph. Then, **ask** how it is similar to and different from the second paragraph.
  Possible responses: Each paragraph focuses mainly on a single writer. However, the third paragraph, which addresses Atwood's viewpoint, briefly refers to the discussion of Homer in the preceding paragraph.

- Have students finish reading the essay. Then, **ask** them at what point in the essay the writer identifies a similarity between the two subjects.
  Answer: The fourth paragraph shows a similarity between the two subjects.

- Point out that the differences between two subjects are usually more interesting than the similarities, and so may warrant more attention.

- Have students offer personal responses to the essay's conclusion. Explain that strong, even debatable, language piques the reader's interest and creates a lasting impression.

Writing Genres

Comparison-and-Contrast Essays in the Workplace Explain that business professionals often perform comparative analyses on competitors' products or services. Point out that such analyses can help a company develop new products or services or improve the quality of existing ones. Point out that a student may want to make a comparative analysis of two or more products before purchasing an item. Have students imagine that they are looking to purchase a stereo system. What features might they want to compare and contrast before they make their purchase? Ask students to share their ideas.

Writing Workshop

Student Model: Anna Lvovsky
Rockville, Maryland

Sirens: His and Hers

Femininity in classical myth has been treated differently by men and women. Men tend to romanticize mythic females, while women tend to reject such fictionalization. These divergent viewpoints are exemplified by Homer's and Margaret Atwood's portrayals of the legendary Sirens. Homer's *Odyssey* relays an idealized vision of alluring, powerful females, whereas Atwood's "Siren Song" bluntly depicts the Sirens as miserable victims of their own condition.

The *Odyssey* is narrated from a masculine perspective and presents a romantic but superficial impression of the Sirens. The speaker remarks on the "ravishing" quality of their harmonies, suggesting their power to overcome. His reference to "honeyed" voices evokes sweetness and appeal. The creatures' very song is stirring; the speaker refers to the music as "thrilling." As a man, the speaker of the poem responds in the expected fashion to these stimuli: He is seduced. His reaction completes an image of the Sirens as powerful, enthralling creatures, capable of manipulating all men. Homer's creatures compel a reader's awed respect.

Immune to the Sirens' feminine allure, Atwood takes a tersely unromantic approach. By adopting the perspective of a Siren, she portrays the creatures, not as deadly beauties, but as helpless victims. Atwood's narrator presents herself as trapped in a "bird suit" and "squatting" on a island, depictions that strip away dignity and beauty. "Beached skulls" convey the destructiveness and barrenness of her occupation. Whereas Homer's narrator finds the song exciting, she herself dismisses it as "boring."

Exciting or boring, the song's lethal efficiency does provide one point of agreement between Homer and Atwood: The song induces men to leap to their deaths and, as Atwood writes, "it works every time." Ultimately, though, Atwood conjures an image diametrically opposed to Homer's idealized suggestion of alluring women. Her Sirens are dejected creatures who merit not our awe or respect but our pity.

It is unsurprising that men of traditional literature judge women entirely by external attributes. Homer's *Odyssey* epitomizes this tendency, representing the Sirens as powerful, desirable creatures on the basis of a brief impression. It is up to Margaret Atwood in "Siren Song" to rebut such a shallow interpretation and portray the true vulnerability of these idealized figures.

> In her introduction, Anna identifies the subjects she will compare.

> Anna uses a subject-by-subject organization and begins by discussing Homer.

> The essay offers equivalent depth and detail in discussing the second subject.

> Anna acknowleges a similarity between her subjects; then, she sharpens the contrast between them.

> The essay ends with a strong conclusion. (See *Developing Your Style*, p. 823)

824 ■ *The Renaissance and Rationalism*

Tips for Test Taking

Tell students that scorers of the SAT writing portion look for a well-supported and well-written essay. They realize that students are under time constraints and may not get to finish their work. Therefore, suggest to students when they take the test that they spend more time on their introductions and on balanced support for their theses rather than concentrate on a well-developed conclusion. An essay with an engaging introduction and strong conclusion—but little support in the body—will not score well, whereas an essay with a strong introduction and support will score higher than one with a weak or less developed conclusion.

Editing and Proofreading

Review your essay to eliminate errors in grammar, punctuation, capitalization, and spelling.

Focus on Commas: Check to be sure that you have used commas correctly in compound and complex sentences. Use a comma before the conjunction separating two independent clauses in a compound sentence. Also use a comma after an introductory adverb clause in a complex sentence.

> **Compound sentence:** The students wanted to play soccer, but the hailstorm made it impossible to play.
> **Complex sentence:** Although the students wanted to play soccer, the hailstorm made it impossible to play.

Publishing and Presenting

Consider these ways to share your comparison-and-contrast writing.

Give an oral presentation. Outline your essay, and then present the main points to the class. Use charts, diagrams, or other visual aids to clarify your ideas. Encourage questions and discussion after your presentation.

Publish your essay electronically. Post your essay on your school's Web site, or upload it to a classroom computer.

Reflecting on Your Writing

Writer's Journal Jot down your thoughts on the experience of writing a comparison-and-contrast essay. Begin by answering these questions:

- What have you learned in this workshop about organizing your material logically and clearly?
- What insights have you gained about how to make your writing more interesting and accessible to your audience?

W̶G̶ Prentice Hall Writing and Grammar Connection: Platinum Level, Chapter 9

Rubric for Self-Assessment

Evaluate your comparison-and-contrast essay using the following criteria and rating scale, or, with your classmates, determine your own reasonable evaluation criteria.

Criteria	Rating Scale
	not very very
Focus: How clear is the purpose for your comparison and contrast?	1 2 3 4 5
Organization: How logical is your organization for comparison?	1 2 3 4 5
Support/Elaboration: How well do you use evidence to support similarities and differences in your comparison?	1 2 3 4 5
Style: How smooth are the transitions between sentences and paragraphs?	1 2 3 4 5
Conventions: How correct is your grammar, especially your use of commas?	1 2 3 4 5

Writing Workshop ■ 825

- Remind students not to confuse compound predicates with compound sentences. In a compound sentence, the clauses on either side of the comma and coordinating conjunction can stand alone as complete sentences. In compound predicates at least one cannot. Commas often appear mistakenly between two parts of a long compound predicate.

- Mention that an adverb clause introducing a complex sentence does contain a subject and a verb.

Six Traits Focus

Ideas		Word Choice	
Organization		Sentence Fluency	
Voice		✓	Conventions

ASSESS

Publishing and Presenting

- Use the rubrics for Exposition: Comparison-and-Contrast Essays, pp. 53 and 54 in **General Resources**, to evaluate students' presentations.

- Suggest that students model their charts and diagrams after the outlines that appear on p. 820.

- If groups of students have written on similar topics, have them post their essays on the same Web site. Encourage them to compose an introduction welcoming visitors to the site, giving an overview of its content, and introducing its authors.

Reflecting on Your Writing

- When students have finished writing their reflections, ask volunteers to share and discuss them.

- To make sure that students understand the rubric, have them use it to score the Student Model on p. 824. Discuss the scoring process as a class. Then have students justify their scores by citing particular passages from the model.

W̶G̶ Writing and Grammar Platinum Level
Students will find additional guidance for editing and proofreading, publishing and presenting, and reflecting on a comparison-and-contrast essay in Chapter 9, Sections 5 and 6.

Tips for
Test Taking

Explain to students that comparison-and-contrast writing prompts often appear on standardized tests. Point out that it is tempting to read the prompt and begin writing immediately. Remind students, though, that about one-quarter of the total time allotted (or, if open-ended, about 15 minutes) should be used to plan and organize the essay. In most comparison-and-contrast prompts, the objects or ideas to be compared will be provided. Therefore, suggest that students use their planning time for these purposes:

- to decide their position in regard to each object or idea (1–2 minutes)

- to decide on the type of organization they will use—point-by-point or subject-by-subject (1–2 minutes)

- to brainstorm possible details and pieces of evidence, and then select the strongest and most relevant (5 minutes)

- to write a rough outline (5 minutes)

Know Your Terms: Interpreting Information

Explain that the terms listed under Terms to Learn will be used in standardized-test-taking situations when students are asked to interpret information from a reading passage.

Terms to Learn

- Review *illustrate*. Point out that *illustrate* means that the writer draws the picture with words. When students are asked to give examples that illustrate information from a reading passage, have students ask themselves, "How does the author show what . . . is in the passage?" The reading sample should provide sufficient material for students to give examples that illustrate the concept.

- Review *interpret*. Point out that language frequently has more than one meaning, or its meaning is not always obvious. The passage should include multiple clues to help students discern the underlying meaning. Students need to examine these clues to interpret the passage correctly.

ASSESS

Answers

1. Two examples that illustrate the reason for the youth's name are that his face is the expression of his soul and that his judgment is quite honest.

2. The description of the Baron's house can be interpreted as an exaggeration because even the houses of the poor most likely had doors and windows; these things alone do not make one powerful.

826

 **Vocabulary Workshop**

High-Frequency Academic Words

High-frequency academic words are words that appear often in textbooks and on standardized tests. Although you may already know the meaning of many of these words, they usually have a more specific meaning when they are used in textbooks and on tests.

Know Your Terms: Interpreting Information

Each of the terms listed below is a verb that prompts you to use examples to show your understanding. The terms indicate the specific kinds of details and information that you should include in your answer.

Terms to Learn

Illustrate Give examples that show what the information means.

> Sample test item: Give two examples that *illustrate* Shakespeare's use of metaphor in Sonnet 116.

Interpret Examine words, images, and events for their underlying meaning.

> Sample test item: Do you *interpret* the language of La Fontaine's fable "The Fox and the Crow" as lightly amusing or as bitterly satirical?

Practice

Directions: *Read the passage from* Candide, *by Voltaire. Then, on a separate sheet of paper, answer questions 1–2.*

In the castle of Baron Thunder-ten-tronckh of Westphalia there lived a youth, endowed by Nature with the most gentle character. His face was the expression of his soul. His judgment was quite honest, and he was extremely simple-minded; and this was the reason, I think, that he was named Candide. . . .

The Baron was one of the most powerful lords in Westphalia, for his castle possessed a door and windows. His Great Hall was even decorated with a piece of tapestry. The dogs in his stable-yards formed a pack of hounds when necessary; his grooms were his huntsmen; the village curate was his Grand Almoner. They all called him "My Lord," and laughed heartily at his stories.

1. Give two examples that *illustrate* the reasons for the youth's name, Candide.

2. How do you *interpret* the description of the Baron's house in the second paragraph?

826 ■ The Renaissance and Rationalism

Tips for Test Taking

When students are asked to select the best interpretation of a passage on a multiple-choice standardized test, they must carefully read the question first to find what they are asked to interpret. Then they must use the clues provided in the passage to help to answer the question. For example, the author's choice of language provides hints about the underlying meaning of the text. The author's selection and description of the events can provide insight about how the material should be interpreted.

Once students have an idea of the interpretation, they need to look at the answer choices and select the best one.

Go Online For: An Interactive Crossword Puzzle
Vocabulary Visit: www.PHSchool.com
Web Code: etj-5601

This crossword puzzle contains vocabulary that reflects the concepts in Unit 6. After students have completed Unit 6, give students the Web Code and have them complete the crossword puzzle.

Assessment Workshop

Critical Reading:
Critical Reasoning

In the reading sections of many tests, you may be required to use critical reasoning skills. Use these strategies to answer questions testing these skills.

- Identify and interpret a writer's implicit assumptions. Ask yourself what else must be true for the writer's claims to be true.

- Read actively, making inferences based on the passage and testing those inferences against your own knowledge.

Practice

Directions: *Read the passages, and then answer the questions that follow.*

Passage A.
A pure white doe in an emerald glade
Appeared to me, with two antlers of gold,
Between two streams, under a laurel's shade,
At sunrise, in the season's bitter cold.

• • •

Around her lovely neck "Do not touch me"
Was written with topaz and diamond stone,
"My Caesar's will has been to make me free."

—Petrarch, from "The White Doe"

1. The poet assumes that the reader will

  A recognize the poem as an allegory.

  B have seen all the things the speaker mentions.

  C know about the behavior of deer.

  D all of the above

Passage B.
Zephyr returns, and scatters everywhere
  New flowers and grass, and company does bring,
  Procne and Philomel, in sweet despair,
  And all the tender colors of the Spring.
5 Never were fields so glad, nor skies so fair;
  And Jove exults in Venus' prospering.

—Petrarch, from "Spring"

2. Which adjective best describes the speaker's feelings about spring?

  A delighted   **C** curious

  B indifferent   **D** bitter

3. "Venus' prospering" refers to

  A spring growth.   **C** fall leaves.

  B summer heat.   **D** winter cold.

Assessment Workshop ■ *827*

 Standard Course of Study

- WL.1.03.6
- CT.4.02.1
- CT.4.02.3

Test-Taking Strategies

- Read the test questions before you read the passage.

- After you have read the passage, jot down a sentence summarizing the main idea.

- Illustrate the main idea with specific examples.

Standard Course of Study

WL.1.03.6 Make inferences and draw conclusions based on personal reflection.

CT.4.02.1 Show an understanding of cultural context in analyzing thematic connections.

CT.4.02.3 Examine how elements such as irony and symbolism impact theme.

Critical Reading

- Remind students that *implicit* means implied or understood but not directly stated.

- Point out that *inferences* are conclusions that readers draw from indirect or limited evidence given in the passage. Point out that many authors expect readers to draw inferences as they read.

- After students have read the Practice passages and have answered the questions, point out that A is the correct answer to question 1 because the poem compares the doe to the lady whom the speaker loves. B and C are not relevant to the poem's meaning, so D must also be incorrect.

- Point out that in question 2 the poem does not describe A, C, or D. Although the speaker recognizes the beauty of spring, he seems indifferent to it; therefore B is the correct answer.

ASSESS

Answers

1. A
2. B
3. C

Tips for
Test Taking

Students often perform poorly on standardized-test questions based on reading passages because students fail to identify a writer's assumptions or do not make inferences correctly or when required. Tell students that they must read passages critically, asking questions such as, "Does the writer offer support for this idea anywhere in the passage, or does the writer simply assume that this idea is true?" Answering these questions will help students identify assumptions.

Explain that writers frequently withhold details from a passage and expect readers to make inferences in order to understand the text. Remind students that an inference is a conclusion that a reader draws based on information. Therefore, answer choices that are not based on text information must be incorrect.

827

 Standard Course of Study

FA.3.03.2 Use reason and evidence to prove a given point.

LT.5.01.1 Use strategies for preparation, engagement, and reflection on world literature.

LT.5.02.1 Explore works which relate to an issue, author, or theme and show increasing comprehension.

Plan Your Content

- Ask students to tell about some "Wow!" moments they have had while reading specific passages of stories, novels, or poems. Encourage them to pinpoint what in the passage inspired their awe. Then, use a favorite piece of literature to model a "Wow!" moment of your own.

- Next, have each student consider how the passage that he or she identified relates to the work as a whole: Does it capture a character's essence? Does it express a central theme? Then, ask each student to draft a thesis statement stating why the selected passage is important.

- Finally, have each student look for other passages in the work—or in other sources—that support his or her thesis statement. Remind students to use only the most interesting or relevant evidence in their drafts.

Prepare Your Presentation

- During a first practice session with partners or groups, have students devise hand signals to use while listening; for example, a lowered hand might mean *slow down*. Speakers can then adjust their volume and pace according to their classmates' signals.

- During a second practice session, have partners or group members fill out Feedback Forms for speakers to use as they make final revisions to their presentations.

Assess the Activity

To evaluate students' interpretations, use the Speaking: Presenting an Oral Response to Literature rubric, p. 91 in *General Resources.*

Presenting a Literary Interpretation

In a **literary interpretation**, a speaker analyzes an element of a work of literature such as theme, characterization, language, or plot, persuading an audience to accept his or her views. Use the strategies on this page to develop and deliver an effective literary interpretation.

Plan Your Content

Analyze literature that intrigues you and about which you have strong feelings or ideas. An interpretation that shows a work in a dramatically new light is sure to pique your audience's interest.

Choose a topic. Ask yourself: What have I read recently that made my mind race? Which selections raised the most questions in my mind? Which ones generated the liveliest discussions? Choose your topic from among those works that come to mind.

Formulate a thesis statement. Your presentation should focus on a strong thesis, or a central point. Start by reviewing the features—or the questions—that led you to select the work. Formulate your main point about the work in a clear sentence, and build your talk around this thesis statement.

Gather ammunition. As with all persuasive presentations, rely on supporting details to make your case. For most literary presentations, you will rely on the work under discussion, though you may want to cite other sources about the author. Select quotes and specific references. Be accurate!

Prepare Your Presentation

Use these speaking techniques to make sure your presentation is a success.

- **Control volume and pace.** Your most important responsibility for any oral presentation is to speak clearly and slowly enough so that everyone can hear you and understand what you say. Vary your volume and pace to emphasize key points.

- **Practice your presentation.** Practice often to avoid stagefright. Experiment with tone and inflection of voice, pacing, gestures, and eye contact. Develop confidence as you rehearse. Memorize your talk, or use notes for the main points and improvise.

Activity ▶ **Presentation and Feedback** ▶ Select one or more works of literature to interpret that most of your audience has read, and prepare a three-minute presentation. Practice with a partner or in a small group, videotaping the practice sessions if possible. Have your partners fill out a Feedback Form like the one above to use as a basis for discussing your content and delivery.

828 ■ *The Renaissance and Rationalism*

 Standard Course of Study

- Use reason and evidence to prove a given point. (FA.3.03.2)

- Use strategies for preparation, engagement, and reflection. (LT.5.01.1)

Feedback Form for Literary Interpretation

Rating System
+ = Excellent   ✓ = Average   − = Wea[k]

Content
Organization _____
Appeal to reason _____
Appeal to emotion _____
Addresses counterarguments _____
Evaluate the quality of the supporting eviden[ce]
_____

Delivery
Volume _____
Pacing _____
Eye contact _____
Body language _____

Suggestions for improvement: _____
_____

Differentiated Instruction — Solutions for All Learners

Strategy for Less Proficient Readers
Have students practice their presentations, using sticky notes to identify any difficult or confusing passages. Students can then revisit these passages and rephrase lines they find long-winded or unclear.

Strategy for English Learners
Encourage students who are intimidated by speaking in front of a group of peers to read their presentations several times before delivering them. Tell them that by practicing repeatedly in front of friends, family members, and even a mirror, and repeating any words that give them difficulty, students will build confidence.

Suggestions for Further Reading

Featured Titles:

The Prince
Niccolò Machiavelli, *translated by George Bull, Penguin Classic, 2003*

Philosophical Text In *The Prince,* a book about statecraft, Italian Renaissance author Machiavelli stresses the degree to which his views of political morality differ from those of previous writers. Where other theorists discuss how rulers ought to act, Machiavelli says that he deals with how rulers do act. Where others say that public deeds should reflect private morality, Machiavelli insists that personal morality has no place in politics. Rulers do not survive by their goodness but by their strength, cunning, and ability. Machiavelli's success can be measured by the enduring appeal of his work and by the continued use of his name as an adjective to denote craftiness and deceit: *Machiavellian.*

Tartuffe and Other Plays
Jean-Baptiste Molière, *translated by Donald M. Frame, Signet Classic, 1960*

Drama In Molière's comedy *Tartuffe,* religiously devout but gullible Orgon opens his home to a stranger—Tartuffe—who poses as a pious, generous humanitarian. Unbeknownst to Orgon, however, Tartuffe is a con artist and hypocrite, a trickster who is both the creator and victim of schemes and lies that draw Orgon's seventeenth-century household into riotous chaos. Along with *Tartuffe,* this edition includes additional Molière comedies such as *The Ridiculous Précieuses* and *School for Husbands.* In general, these plays feature such character types as the hypocrite, the misanthrope, and the hypochondriac, all of whom serve to expose the absurdities of the playwright's society.

Works Presented in Unit Six:
If sampling a portion of the following texts has built your interest, treat yourself to the full works.

Candide
Voltaire, *translated by John Butt, Penguin Classic, 1950*

Don Quixote
Miguel de Cervantes, *translated by John Rutherford, Penguin Classic, 2003*

Related British Literature:
The Tempest
William Shakespeare, *Pearson Prentice Hall, 2000*

In his final play, England's greatest author says farewell to the theater and explores Renaissance ideas concerning savagery and civilization.

Related American Literature:
The Falcon
John Tanner, *Penguin, 2003*

The author was captured as a boy by Ojibwa Indians, and his autobiography is the story of the encounter between white and Indian cultures.

Galileo's Daughter
Dava Sobell, *Penguin, 2003*

This biography of a great scientist's daughter explores religion, science, and family relations during the Renaissance.

Many of these titles are available in the Prentice Hall/Penguin Literature Library. Consult your teacher before choosing one.

The Falcon by John Tanner

The writer's difficult and dangerous life includes the constant threat of hunger and violence. Polygamy, magical totems, and the brutal treatment of women, children, and animals are part of the book's cultural landscape.

Lexile: Appropriate for high school students

Galileo's Daughter by Dava Sobel

This book makes frequent references to religious rituals and includes references to conflicts between science and religion. Galileo's illegitimate children are also discussed. To prepare students to read this work, discuss the cultural context of Galileo's thought.

Lexile: Appropriate for high school students

Planning Students' Further Reading

Discussions of literature can raise sensitive and often controversial issues. Before you recommend further reading to your students, consider the values and sensitivities of your community as well as the age, ability, and sophistication of your students. It is also good policy to preview literature before you recommend it to students. The notes below offer some guidance on specific titles.

The Prince by Niccolò Machiavelli

Lexile: Appropriate for high school students

Tartuffe and Other Plays
by Jean-Baptiste Molière

Several aspects of these plays may benefit from mature discussion with students. *Religious Piety* As Molière makes clear, Tartuffe is not intended to deride religion or religious piety. On the contrary, Molière attacks the hypocritical use of religious piety by a confidence man. *Parental Authority* Remind students that Orgon's obsession with Tartuffe leads him to abuse his parental authority in extreme ways—for example, he capriciously disinherits his son and orders his daughter to marry a man whom she detests. Molière thus depicts Orgon as distorting the proper application of parental authority. *Lust and Avarice* Molière depicts Tartuffe's hypocrisy primarily in connection with the vices of lust and avarice. Whereas Tartuffe pretends to be modest and virtuous, he is really so lustful as to propose an adulterous relationship with Elmire, and although he pretends to be unworldly, he is all too ready to deprive Orgon and his family of their possessions when he is given the chance.

Lexile: Appropriate for high school students

Candide by Voltaire

This great satire of human philosophy and foibles contains lighthearted references to violence, sexual acts, drunkenness, and slavery and refers to numerous cultures as primitive or barbarous.
Lexile: 1000L

Don Quixote by Miguel de Cervantes

Sensitive issues include ethnic labels and sexual promiscuity. Lower-class women are treated very poorly.
Lexile: 1520L

The Tempest by William Shakespeare
Lexile: Appropriate for high school students

Standard Course of Study

WL.1.03.11 Identify and analyze elements of expressive environment in personal reflections.

IR.2.03.2 Prioritize and organize information to construct an explanation to answer a question.

LT.5.01.4 Analyze the importance of tone and mood in world literature.

LT.5.01.6 Make connections between historical and contemporary issues in world literature.

LT.5.03.10 Analyze connections between ideas, concepts, characters and experiences in world literature.

Unit Instructional Resources

In *Unit 7 Resources,* you will find materials to support students in developing and mastering the unit skills and to help you assess their progress.

▶ **Vocabulary and Reading**

Additional vocabulary and reading support, based on Lexile scores of vocabulary words, is provided for each selection or grouping.

- **Word Lists A and B** and **Practices A and B** provide vocabulary-building activities for students reading two grades or one grade below level, respectively.

- **Reading Warm-ups A and B,** for students reading two grades or one grade below level, respectively, consist of short readings and activities that provide a context and practice for newly learned vocabulary.

▶ **Selection Support**

- Reading Strategy
- Literary Analysis
- Vocabulary Builder
- Grammar and Style
- Support for Writing
- Support for Extend Your Learning
- Enrichment

Teacher EXPRESS PRENTICE HALL
Plan · Teach · Assess
You may also access these resources at TeacherExpress.

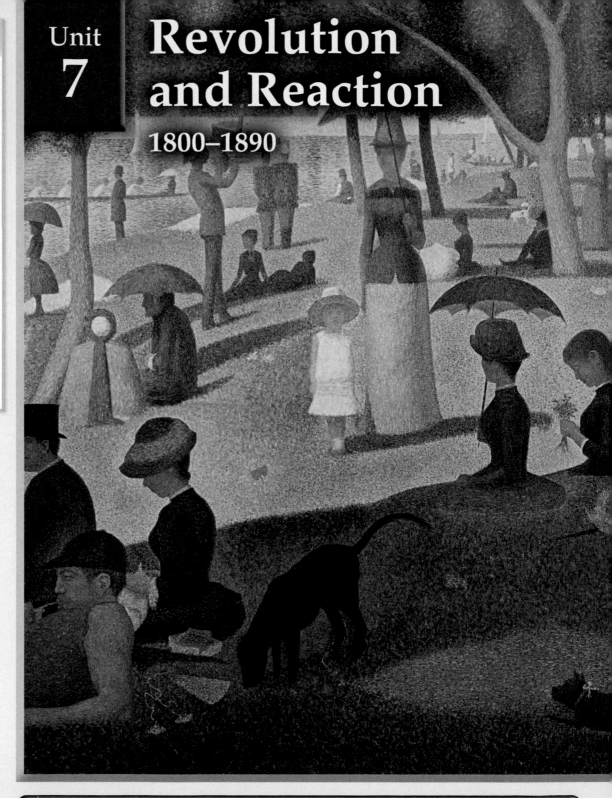

Unit 7
Revolution and Reaction
1800–1890

Assessment Resources

Listed below are the resources available to assess and measure students' progress in meeting the unit objectives and your state standards.

Skills Assessment

Unit 7 Resources
   Selection Tests A and B

TeacherExpress™
   ExamView® Test Bank
      Software

Adequate Yearly Progress Assessment

Unit 7 Resources
   Diagnostic Test 9
   Benchmark Tests 8 and 9

Standardized Assessment

Standardized Test
   Preparation Workbook

Romanticism
and Realism

 Standard Course of Study
In This Unit You Will

- Identify and analyze elements of expressive environment in personal reflections. (WL.1.03.11)
- Use transitions to make logical connections. (IR.2.02.3)
- Use specific references from texts to show theme. (CT.4.02.2)
- Identify clear criteria for evaluation of work of others. (CT.4.04.1)
- Make connections between historical and contemporary issues in world literature. (LT.5.01.6)
- Summarize key events and points from world literature. (LT.5.03.5)
- Analyze connections between ideas, concepts, characters and experiences in world literature. (LT.5.03.10)
- Examine language for elements to apply effectively in own writing/speaking. (GU.6.01.5)

◀ Painter George Seurat developed a technique called Pointillism, which relies on the observer's eyes to blend colors.

Romanticism and Realism ■ 831

Introduce Unit 7

- Direct students' attention to the title and time period of this unit. Have a student read the quotation. **Ask** students: What does this quotation suggest about the spirit of this time in history?
Possible response: The quotation suggests a strong commitment to change. It views the future with optimism.

- Have students look at the art. Read the Humanities note to them and ask the discussion question.

- Then **ask:** What themes in literature might typify this period in literary history?
Possible response: Romantic writers rejected Neoclassical order and explored nature. They were influenced by the revolutionary spirit of their time. The Realists examined the effects of industrialization on people. Themes might include progress, humanity's relationship with nature, and the painful realities of city life.

Humanities

Sunday Afternoon on the Island of La Grande Jatte, by Georges Pierre Seurat

Georges Pierre Seurat (1859-1891) was a French painter who founded Neo-Impressionism. This school became known for Pointillism, which used tiny dots of contrasting colors to portray the play of light. The dots blend together when viewers look at the paintings as a whole. Seurat spent much time vacationing or working on La Grande Jatte, and this painting is considered one of his masterpieces.

Use the following question for discussion.

How does Seurat's painting make use of light?
Possible response: The painting clearly shows sunlight and shadows. The water shimmers. Even the trees that face the sun reflect light.

Unit Features

W. S. Merwin
Each unit features commentary by a contemporary writer or scholar under the heading "From the Author's Desk." Author W. S. Merwin introduces Unit 7 in Setting the Scene, in which he discusses the role of time and place in Romantic poetry. Later in the unit, he introduces his poems, "Ancestral Voices" and "Substance." In the Writing Workshop, he discusses the process of revising poetry.

Connections
Every unit contains a feature that connects literature to a related topic, such as art, science, or history. In this unit, students will read a selection from Christopher Marlowe's *Doctor Faustus* on pp. 866–871.

Use the information and questions on the Connections page to help students enrich their understanding of the selections presented in the unit.

Reading Informational Materials
These selections will help students learn to analyze and evaluate informational texts, such as workplace documents, technical directions, and consumer materials. They will expose students to the organization and features unique to nonnarrative texts.

In this unit, the focus is on Critical Reviews. *CurtainUp* Review: *A Doll's House* and "A Lot of Baggage for Nora to Carry" are on pp. 1029–1031.

Introduce W. S. Merwin

- W. S. Merwin, a poet, playwright, and translator, introduces the unit and provides insight into the romantic sense of other times and places and their relationship to the here and now. His commentary on his selections, "Substance" and "Ancestral Voices," appears later in the unit on pages 898–900.

- Have students read the introductory paragraph about W. S. Merwin. Point out that he has won the Pulitzer Prize for Poetry and since his early twenties has spent periods of his life living in southwest France.

- Use *From the Author's Desk DVD* to introduce W. S. Merwin. Show Segment 1 to provide insight into his writing career. After students have watched the segment, **ask:** How has Merwin's passion for nature affected his writing?
  Answer: Nature represents freedom, beauty, and exhilaration, and he uses these themes in his writing.

A Romantic Sense of Time and Place

- After students have read Merwin's commentary on Romantic poetry, **ask:** How does Merwin explain that our present is made up of other times and places?
  Answer: He says that our perception of the "present" involves skills or abilities, such as languages and the ability to read, that we learned in the past, or we may be thinking of things that will take place in the future.

- **Ask:** How does Merwin explain the importance to Romantic writers of their projections of other times and places?
  Answer: The projections were important to the present time and enabled the writers to explore their feelings.

- Tell students that they will also read W. S. Merwin's introduction to his poems, "Substance" and "Ancestral Voices" later in the unit. Merwin will also explain his writing of those pieces.

Critical Viewing

Possible response: Papers and personal pictures still might be found at a desk today. Although quill pens are no longer used, modern pens serve the same purposes. The purpose of the workspace as well as its order and simplicity are timeless.

832

Setting the Scene

The literature in Unit 7 illustrates a sort of soul-searching, a yearning on the part of writers and readers to explain how their individual sense of self fits into the world around them. The Romantic poets explored time and place as a means of justifying their emotions, as poet W. S. Merwin explains in his essay below. The unit introduction and the literature in this unit trace the changes in literature from the Romantics to the age of Realism.

From the Author's Desk
W. S. Merwin Talks About the Time Period

W. S. Merwin

Introducing W. S. Merwin (b. 1927) Born in New York, W. S. Merwin is primarily a poet, but he is also a playwright and translator. Rich in imagery, Merwin's verse focuses on the condition of modern humanity and its separation from the natural world.

A Romantic Sense of Time and Place

In this unit, you will be reading poems written more than a hundred years ago in other countries and translated out of other languages, and now I would like you to think for a moment about two words. First, the "present." And then "romantic," both with a small "r," with all that it may mean to you, and with a capital "R," referring to the characteristics of the period of literature when these poems were written.

Our "Present" Is Made Up of Other Times and Places The "present," first. You know what day of the week it is, what classroom you are in, what you are studying. You can tell me something of what you feel about those. But in this "present" you may be thinking about somewhere else, somebody else, somewhere you remember, something you hope will happen. This language, your understanding of it, and the ability to read, are remembered from earlier times, and the words you are reading were written some time ago, in another place, by someone you've never met. So the "present" is made up of other times and places, including an imperfectly remembered past, a future that may never come to be, and desires that may owe part of their attraction to their very impossibility.

Previewing Romantic Poetry

Baudelaire's Voyage to Paradise The Romantic desire for other times or places is easy to recognize in the French poet

▼ **Critical Viewing**
In what ways is poet Robert Burns's workspace both antiquated and timeless? **[Analyze]**

Teaching Resources

The following resources can be used to enrich or extend the instruction for Unit 7 Introduction.

Unit 7 Resources
   Setting the Scene, p. 49
   Unit Introduction: Names and Terms to Know, p. 2
   Unit Introduction: Focus Questions, p. 3
   Listening and Viewing, p. 50
From the Author's Desk DVD
   W. S. Merwin, Segment 1

Charles Baudelaire's "Invitation to the Voyage." This is one of the most romantic poems ever written, and if you like it in this translation by Richard Wilbur, which I think is as true as a translation of this poem can be, maybe you can get someone to read it to you in the original, so you can hear its seductive sound, and listen to the beautiful musical setting of it by Duparc. Baudelaire keeps equating the person he is "inviting" on the voyage to the paradise to which he wants them to go. He wants to believe in her, and in their love, in the same way that he longs to believe in that impossibly happy place.

Painful Reality and Worlds Out of Reach Baudelaire's "The Albatross" works differently, depicting the painful distance between the freedom and beauty that are the true life of the bird named in the title, and of the imagination represented by the poet, and the cruelty and mockery of the world in which both are caught and will be killed.

Two planes, again, occupy Rimbaud's "The Sleeper in the Valley." What appears to be a peaceful, beautiful pastoral scene with a figure lying asleep is really a face of death, the utterly unknown. And Rimbaud does this in "Ophelia," too, where death, veiled by false hopes and hidden in flower-like appearances, floats through imagery.

In Verlaine's "Autumn Song" the place that is out of reach is the world of memory, the past, and grief for its loss carries away with it the poet who remembers it.

For the Romantics, Other Times and Places Fill the "Now" with Feeling In the Romantic period there was a recognition that these projections of other times and places are important to the "here and now," and are where our feelings can be recognized. The Romantics did not invent these other planes of our experience but they accorded them, and our feelings about them, a vital respect.

Go **Online**
Author Link
For: A video clip of W. S. Merwin
Visit: www.PHSchool.com
Web Code: ete-8701

For: More about W. S. Merwin
Visit: www.PHSchool.com
Web Code: ete-9711

Reading the Unit Introduction

Reading for Information and Insight Use the following terms and questions to guide your reading of the unit introduction on pages 836–843.

Names and Terms to Know	**Focus Questions** As you read this introduction, use what you learn to answer these questions:
John Locke	• What was the impact of the Industrial Revolution on daily life in this period?
Jean-Jacques Rousseau	
Napoleon	• What were the benefits and the problems of the Industrial Revolution?
Battle of Waterloo	
Charles Darwin	• In what ways does Romanticism differ from Realism?
Romanticism	
Realism	

Reading the Unit Introduction

Tell students that the terms and questions listed here are the key points in this introductory material. This information provides a context for the selections in this unit. Students should use the terms and questions as a guide to focus their reading of the unit introduction. When students have completed the unit introduction, they should be able to identify or explain each of these terms and answer or discuss the Focus Questions.

Concept Connector

After students have read the unit introduction, return to the Focus Questions to review the main points. For key points, see p. 843.

Go **Online** Typing in the Web Codes
Author Link when prompted will bring students to a video clip and more information on W. S. Merwin.

Using the Timeline

The Timeline can serve a number of instructional purposes, as follows:

Getting an Overview

Use the Timeline to help students get a quick overview of themes and events of the period. This approach will benefit all students but may be especially helpful for Visual/Spatial Learners, English Learners, and Less Proficient Readers. (For strategies in using the Timeline as an overview, see the bottom of this page.)

Thinking Critically

Questions are provided on the facing page. Use these questions to have students review the events, discuss their significance, and examine the "so what" behind the "what happened."

Connecting to Selections

Have students refer to the Timeline when they begin to read individual selections. By consulting the Timeline regularly, they will gain a better sense of the period's chronology. In addition, they will appreciate world events that gave rise to these works of literature.

Projects

Students can use the Timeline as a launching pad for projects like these:

- **Focused Timeline** Have students research the events leading up to an item on the Timeline and create a smaller, more focused timeline on which to record them. For example, students can use a biography of Johann Wolfgang von Goethe on p. 844, as well as other sources, to show the events leading to the publication of Part I of *Faust* in 1808.

- **Additional Illustrations** Have students search for additional illustrations for items in the Timeline. They can find such illustrations in biographies of the figures mentioned in the Timeline, encyclopedias, books on world history, and books on the history of technology. Students should be prepared to justify each new illustration they suggest.

European and World Events

1800   1820   1840

EUROPEAN EVENTS

- **1800** Wordsworth and Coleridge publish *Lyrical Ballads*, 2ⁿᵈ edition.

- **1804** Napoleon declares himself emperor. ◄
- **1804** Beethoven completes Symphony No. 3, the first Romantic symphony.
- **1808** Goethe publishes Part I of *Faust*.
- **1812** Napoleon invades Russia.

- **1825** In Russia, the forces of the czar crush an uprising by army officers.
- **1827** Heinrich Heine publishes *The Book of Songs*.
- **1829** In England, George Stephenson creates a better steam locomotive.
- **1831** Victor Hugo publishes his novel *Notre-Dame de Paris*. ▼

- **1848** Insurrections break out across Europe; the Second French Republic is declared.
- **1849** Gustave Courbet paints *The Stone Breakers*, a Realist work. ▼

- **1852** Second French Republic ends; the Second Empire begins.
- **1856** In England, Robert Bessemer develops process for mass-producing steel.
- **1857** Flaubert publishes *Madame Bovary*, a masterpiece of Realist fiction.

WORLD EVENTS

- **1803 (United States)** The Louisiana Purchase doubles the size of the country. ▼
- **1808 (Sierra Leone)** Britain acquires Sierra Leone as a colony; goes on to acquire Gambia (1816) and Gold Coast (1874).

- **1818 (India)** British control most of India.

- **1820–1821 (Egypt)** Muhammad Ali, ruler of Egypt, begins creating an African empire.
- **1825 (United States)** Erie Canal opens.
- **1825 (United States)** An organized baseball club exists in upstate New York.
- **1828 (Japan)** Poet Kobayashi Issa dies.

- **1842 (China)** China loses to Western powers in the Opium War.
- **1842 (United States)** Dr. Crawford Long begins using ether as an anesthetic.
- **1853–1854 (Japan)** Commander Matthew Perry forces Japan to trade with the West. ◄

834 ■ *Romanticism and Realism*

Getting an Overview of the Period

Introduction To give students an overview of the period, have them indicate the span of dates in the title of the Timeline. Next, point out that the Timeline is divided into European Events (on the top) and World Events (on the bottom). Have students scan the Timeline, looking at both the European Events and the World Events. Finally, point out that the events in the Timeline often represent beginnings, turning points, and endings (for example, Napoleon declared himself emperor in 1804).

Key Events Have students identify key events related to political and industrial change.

Possible response: In the United States, the Civil War begins (1861); in England, Robert Bessemer develops process for mass-producing steel (1856).

What events indicate the growing dominance of Europe and the United States?

Possible response: The Louisiana Purchase doubles the size of the United States (1803); British control most of India (1818).

1860   1880   1900

- **1861** In Russia, the serfs are freed.
- **1861** A united Italy is established.
- **1864** Fyodor Dostoyevsky publishes *Notes from the Underground*.
- **1867** Karl Marx publishes the first volume of *Das Kapital*, a criticism of capitalism.
- **1869** Leo Tolstoy completes his novel *War and Peace*.
- **1870** The Franco-Prussian War begins.
- **1871** The Franco-Prussian War ends with France's defeat; the Third French Republic is established.
- **1871** The German empire begins.
- **1873** Arthur Rimbaud stops writing poetry, at the age of 19.

- **1880s** Swedish chemist Alfred Nobel builds dynamite factories.
- **1881** In Russia, Czar Alexander II is assassinated.
- **1885** Émile Zola publishes the novel *Germinal*, which depicts life in a mining town. ◄
- **1896** Alfred Nobel's will endows the Nobel Prizes.

- **1861 (United States)** The American Civil War begins.
- **1864 (China)** A destructive civil war ends.
  - **1865 (United States)** The Civil War ends; President Lincoln is assassinated.
  - **1869 (Egypt)** Suez Canal opens.
  - **1876 (United States)** Alexander Graham Bell invents the telephone. ◄

- **1883 (Tunisia)** France gains control over Tunisia. ►
- **c. 1884 (United States)** Hiram Stevens Maxim uses smokeless powder in a new type of machine gun.
- **1886 (United States)** John Pemberton invents Coca-Cola.
- **1890 (United States)** In the West, fenced pasture has largely replaced range land.
- **1898 (Palestine)** Theodor Herzl visits Palestine to look into setting up a Jewish state.

Introduction ■ 835

Critical Viewing

1. What does the portrait of Napoleon (1804) suggest about the emperor's character? Explain. **[Analyze]**
   Possible response: Napoleon appears confident and proud in the portrait.

2. What attitude about exploration does the sign for the Lewis and Clark Trail (1803) suggest? **[Infer]**
   Possible response: The United States is ready to be explored by ambitious people.

3. What mood does the picture of Alexander Graham Bell with the first telephone (1876) convey? **[Analyze]**
   Possible response: The crowd conveys a mood of excitement, expectation, and an awareness of the significance of the invention.

Analyzing the Timeline

1. (a) Which two entries in European events mention Napoleon? (b) What do these entries reveal about Napoleon's attitudes? **[Infer]**
   Answer: (a) In 1804, Napoleon declares himself emperor; in 1812, Napoleon invades Russia. (b) He believed that he had a right to assert his rule over France and Russia.

2. (a) According to the Timeline, What happened in France in 1848 and 1871? (b) What do these events suggest about the political climate in France during this time? **[Connect]**
   Answer: (a) In 1848, the Second French Republic is declared; in 1871, the Franco-Prussian War ends with France's defeat, and the Third French Republic is established. (b) These events suggest that the political climate in France was turbulent.

3. (a) What events occurred in Russia and in the United States in 1861? (b) What do these events suggest about changing world attitudes toward the individual? **[Generalize]**
   Answer: (a) In Russia, the serfs are freed, and in the United States, the Civil War begins. (b) These events suggest awareness of the importance of individual freedom.

4. (a) How are the facts about the United States in 1825 and Egypt in 1869 related? (b) What do these facts indicate about trade and transportation? **[Synthesize]**
   Answer: (a) In these years, both countries opened canals. (b) These facts indicate a growing worldwide interest in trade and transportation.

5. (a) Which events in the 1880s relate to the development of weapons? (b) How did these events change the face of war? **[Deduce]**
   Answer: (a) In the 1880s, Alfred Nobel built dynamite factories, and c. 1884, Hiram Stevens Maxim used smokeless powder in a new type of machine gun. (b) Dynamite and machine guns increased the efficiency of weapons.

Literature of the Period

- For a view of life in Paris during the Franco-Prussian War, students can read the story "Two Friends" by Guy de Maupassant, p. 906.

- To get a greater understanding of Realism in literature, students can read Leo Tolstoy's story "How Much Land Does a Man Need?" on p. 913.

- For a taste of realistic prose drama, students can read Henrik Ibsen's *A Doll House*, p. 942.

Themes in World Literature

Point/Counterpoint

Do people have a right to revolt against their rulers? Emphasize to students that the rights we take for granted in the United States were not always so well accepted. In the aristocratic societies of England and France in the late eighteenth century, the idea that people could self-govern was widely debated.

1. What right does Burke deny people?
   Answer: Burke denies the right to share in the power and authority of the state.

2. How does Paine's view differ from Burke's?
   Answer: Paine says that no group in any country is entitled to control the state to the "end of time."

3. Identify and explain ways in which the United States today reflects the ideas of both Burke and Paine.
   Possible response: People in the United States today have the right to inherit property, and all children are entitled to an education, as Burke argues. In keeping with Paine's ideas, the United States has no formal aristocracy with the power to rule the country politically.

Historical Background

Throughout Europe, the nineteenth century was marked by political and industrial revolutions, progress, and hope for the future. Yet it was also an era characterized by unfulfilled expectations and by the emergence of new problems.

The Seeds of Revolution Inspired by the ideas of political and social philosophers such as John Locke (1632–1704) and Jean-Jacques Rousseau (zhän zhäk′ roo sō′) (1712–1778), the American colonists revolted against British rule and declared their independence in 1776. The success of the American Revolution helped stir up political unrest throughout Europe, especially in France. There, revolutionary activities that had begun in 1787 reached their first high point in 1789 when a Paris mob attacked and destroyed the prison known as the Bastille. In the years that followed, the monarchy was abolished, and France was declared a republic. On January 21, 1793, the leaders of the newly established French republican government executed the king. Then, from September 5, 1793, to July 27, 1794, there was a period in France known as the Reign of Terror, during which the revolutionary government executed 17,000 people.

Themes in World Masterpieces — Point/Counterpoint

Do people have a right to revolt against their rulers?
Stirred by the French Revolution (1787–1799), two important thinkers of the time expressed opposing views on this question.

No! Men have a right . . . to justice. . . . They have a right to the fruits of their industry; . . . They have a right to the acquisitions of their parents; to the nourishment and improvement of their offspring; to instruction in life, and to consolation in death. . . . [A]nd as to the share of power, authority, and direction which each individual ought to have in the management of the state, that I must deny to be amongst the direct original rights of man in civil society. . . .
—from *Reflections on the Revolution in France* by Edmund Burke

Yes! There never did, there never will, and there never can exist a parliament, or any description of men, or any generation of men, in any country, possessed of the right or the power of binding and controlling posterity to the "end of time," or of commanding for ever how the world shall be governed, or who shall govern it; and therefore, all such clauses, . . . are . . . null and void. . . . Man has no property in man. . . .
—from *Rights of Man: Being an Answer to Mr. Burke's Attack on the French Revolution* by Thomas Paine

836 ■ *Romanticism and Realism*

Enrichment

Europe at War
In 1814, the allied armies of Britain, Austria, Russia, and Prussia captured Paris. Forced to abdicate the throne, Napoleon went into exile on the island of Elba, off the coast of Italy. He returned to Paris a year later and again proclaimed himself emperor, but his second reign was short-lived.

One hundred days after his reemergence, he was easily defeated at Waterloo by the allied forces commanded by the Duke of Wellington. Napoleon was forced back into exile on the island of St. Helena, where he died in 1821.

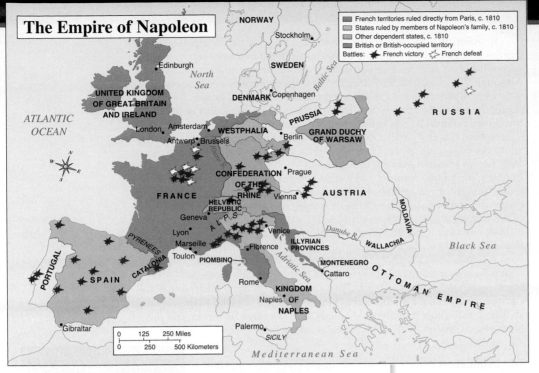

The Empire of Napoleon

French territories ruled directly from Paris, c. 1810
States ruled by members of Napoleon's family, c. 1810
Other dependent states, c. 1810
British or British-occupied territory
Battles: ★ French victory ☆ French defeat

Napoleon In 1799, a successful and popular young general, Napoleon Bonaparte (nə pō′ lē ən bō′ nə pärt′), assumed political power in France. Five years later, he made himself emperor. Although in many respects Napoleon ruled as a military dictator, he did accomplish many domestic reforms. In addition, he aroused a strong sense of nationalism among the French people.

Europe at War Between 1792 and 1815, France was almost constantly at war with other nations. At first, France defended itself against monarchies that were frightened by the Revolution and hoped to destroy it. Later, as Napoleon came to power, France embarked on a series of military conquests in which it seized control of nearly all of Europe as far east as the Russian border (see map above).

In 1812, however, Napoleon overextended himself by invading Russia. There, his army suffered a disastrous defeat. Napoleon's final defeat came in 1815 at the Battle of Waterloo, when his forces were overpowered by an allied army led by Great Britain.

Although Napoleon dominated Europe for only a brief period, his conquests had lasting effects. His armies spread many of the achievements of the French Revolution throughout Europe.

While such reforms were welcomed by many, public opinion turned against Napoleon when his occupying forces began assessing high taxes and conscripting local men into his armies.

▲ **Critical Viewing**
In 1810, which countries or territories were part of the French empire, dependent on it, or ruled by members of Napoleon's family? Explain. **[Read a Map]**

Critical Viewing
The countries or territories that were part of the French empire, dependent on it, or ruled by members of Napoleon's family in 1810 were Spain, Catalonia, France, Piombino, the Kingdom of Naples, the Helvetic Republic, the Confederation of the Rhine, Westphalia, the Illyrian Provinces, and the Grand Duchy of Warsaw.

Background
Napoleon Bonaparte

Napoleon Bonaparte—Napoleon I—crowned himself emperor of France in 1804. During his ten-year reign, "the Little Corporal" created an empire that spanned most of central and western Europe. Napoleon's downfall resulted in part from his pride and stubbornness and from his betrayal of many people.

Toward the end of his rule, people around him began to desert him. Finally, his commanders insisted he give up the throne. The French crowned Louis XVIII king and exiled Napoleon to Elba in 1814.

The following year Napoleon escaped and returned to France. During the Hundred Days—the period from his escape to his final defeat at Waterloo—Napoleon ruled once again. After Waterloo, Napoleon was once again exiled, this time to the barren island of St. Helena, off the coast of west Africa, where he died of cancer in 1821.

Introduction ■ *837*

Revolutions and Reactions Following the collapse of Napoleon's empire, a large group of national delegates gathered in Vienna to reestablish the traditions that had existed before the French Revolution. Although they were able to restore royal authority throughout Europe, they were unable to erase the desire for political and social justice. As a result, the rest of the century was marked by an ongoing conflict between traditional political beliefs and democratic ideals.

Nowhere was this conflict more apparent than in France. In the aftermath of Napoleon's downfall, royal rule had been reestablished. In 1830, however, when the king took measures to restrict the people's freedom, the people revolted and forced him out of power. Although this revolt brought about a number of important reforms, it did not bring an end to the monarchy. The new king, however, was a member of the upper middle class rather than the aristocracy. When another revolution occurred in 1848, however, a second French republic was established. Yet the Second Republic lasted only four years, and it was not until 1871 that the Third French Republic was born.

The French uprising of 1848 was one of several armed rebellions breaking out in Europe that year. Others took place in Italy, Austria, and Germany, but unlike the rebellion in France, they did not lead to the abolition of absolute monarchy. Meanwhile, in Denmark, Belgium, and the Netherlands, the spirit of the age manifested itself in reform rather than armed revolt.

The Unification of Germany Also in 1848, a movement arose among the German people that was aimed at unifying the many German states into a single nation controlled by a democratic government. Like the revolts in the other European nations, this movement was thwarted. In 1871, however, after Prussia defeated France in the Franco-Prussian War, the Prussian prime minister, Otto von Bismarck (biz′ märk′), did succeed in unifying the German states. While the newly established German empire was a source of pride for nationalists, it was a major disappointment for reformers.

Similarly, Russian reformers had little success in bringing about political and social changes. Russia remained a repressive, autocratic state throughout the nineteenth century.

The Industrial Revolution Like the French Revolution, the Industrial Revolution took shape in the 1700s. In the British textile industry, inventors produced new machines that reduced the time needed to spin and weave cloth. The new machines led to the growth of the factory system, which brought workers and machinery together in one place to manufacture goods.

Industry got a further boost with the invention of the steam engine. By the 1850s, steam was the main source of power, not only in factories but also in new means of transportation such as the railroad and the steamship.

By the end of the century, the Industrial Revolution had transformed Europe's entire way of life. Scientists and inventors had developed

▼ **Critical Viewing**
Does this portrait of Bismarck offer any evidence that his government was authoritarian and militaristic? Why or why not? **[Interpret]**

Prince Otto von Bismarck in uniform with Prussian helmet,
Franz von Lenbach

838 ■ *Romanticism and Realism*

countless new products, including the first automobiles. Electricity became an important new source of power.

Industrial Hardships The Industrial Revolution brought many benefits. It created millions of new jobs and produced a variety of goods more cheaply than ever before. At the same time, the rise of industry brought new problems. Early industrial workers often faced great hardships. Pay was low, hours were long, and working conditions were often dangerous. As people moved from the countryside to the growing industrial cities, they crowded into unhealthy urban slums.

By the end of the century, reformers were at work to raise wages, outlaw child labor, and win better conditions in factories and slums. Gradually, the standard of living for workers and their families improved.

Gare Saint-Lazare, Claude Oscar Monet

The Middle Class and Women's Rights Industry and the growth of cities sparked the rise of a new middle class. The values of this new class—values that influenced all of society—included duty, thrift, honesty, hard work, and, above all, respectability.

By the middle of the century, some reformers had begun to protest restrictions on women. Even in the most democratic nations, such as Britain, women could not vote. They were banned from most schools, and married women could not legally control their own property.

A Controversial New Idea In the mid-nineteenth century, the theories of British biologist Charles Darwin created a tremendous uproar that shook the entire Western world. According to Darwin, all forms of life evolve, or change, over a long period of time. Simpler forms of life evolve into more complex forms, and new forms evolve out of older ones. Some people attacked Darwin's theories, believing that they contradicted the Bible. Today, however, evolution is (according to the *Encyclopedia Britannica*) "one of the fundamental keystones of modern biological theory."

▲ **Critical Viewing**
Which details in this picture reveal the influence of the Industrial Revolution? Explain. **[Infer]**

Introduction ■ 839

Answers continued

2. In what ways did the Industrial Revolution encourage the growth of cities? **[Analyze Causes and Effects]**
Possible response: New machines led to the growth of the factory system, which relied on the need for a large number of workers. These workers tended to live near the factory, resulting in the growth of cities around the factories.

3. Do you think the Industrial Revolution was more of a benefit or a detriment to humanity?

Explain your answer. **[Make a Judgment]**
Possible response: Some students may say that it was a benefit because as more goods were cheaply produced, many jobs were created and cities grew. Others may say that it was a detriment because of the tedium of factory work, the decline of the craftsman's role in the production of goods, and the polluting effects of big cities and industry on the environment.

Possible response: The details that reveal the influence of the Industrial Revolution include the train, the train tracks, smoke, steam, and the factory.

Historical Background

Comprehension Check

1. Between 1792 and 1815, which country was almost continually at war with the other European nations?
Answer: France was almost continually at war.

2. (a) Which European country became a unified nation in 1871? (b) Under whose leadership did this happen?
Answer: (a) Germany became a unified nation. (b) Germany was unified under Bismark.

3. What were some of the benefits of the Industrial Revolution?
Answer: The Industrial Revolution created millions of new jobs and allowed a variety of goods to be produced more cheaply than ever before.

4. What were some of the problems caused by the Industrial Revolution?
Answer: Workers faced great hardships, such as low pay, long hours, and dangerous working conditions. They also crowded into unhealthy urban slums.

5. How did the Industrial Revolution change the structure of European society?
Answer: The Industrial Revolution resulted in the emergence of a new middle class whose values included duty, thrift, honesty, hard work, and respectability.

Critical Thinking

1. Ralph Waldo Emerson referred to the opening shot of the Revolutionary War as "the shot heard round the world." In what way do the events in Europe following the American Revolution reflect this view? **[Connect]**
Possible response: The success of the American revolutionaries inspired Europeans, especially the French, to rebel against monarchic rule.

Humanities

The Wanderer Above the Sea of Fog, by Caspar David Friedrich

Primarily self-taught, Friedrich (1774–1840) was one of a group of artists in the early nineteenth-century German Romantic movement. The works of this circle of writers and artists are characterized by their studies of nature and their symbolic and mysterious representations of the natural world. Friedrich's early drawings gained the notice and approval of the poet Goethe and were awarded a prize from the Weimar Art Society in 1805. Friedrich painted *The Wanderer Above the Sea of Fog* in 1818.

Use the following question for discussion:

What is the most unusual aspect of the painting that is representative of the Romantic period?
Possible response: The man appears to be walking in the clouds and is at the same height as the mountains. This composition suggests that the relationship between the individual and nature has a magical quality.

Background

The French Revolution

The French people overthrew their ancient monarchy. They wanted to stop the inequality they saw in their government, including exclusion of the nobility and clergy from paying taxes. The revolutionaries wanted everyone treated equally before the law. In Paris on July 14, 1789, a group of revolutionaries stormed the Bastille prison and freed the prisoners; then, the revolutionaries established a committee of middle-class citizens to govern Paris. Other provinces joined in the revolution and elevated average citizens to government posts throughout France.

Critical Viewing

Possible response: Romantic elements include the individual at the center of the painting and the wild, untamed scene over which he is looking. These details illustrate the Romantic elevation of the individual and love of wild nature.

Literature

Shaped by the major events and developments of the time, four major artistic movements dominated nineteenth-century literature: Romanticism, Realism, Naturalism, and Symbolism.

Romanticism: The French Revolution on a Page The first of these movements, Romanticism, rejected the objectivity, rationality, and harmony that many eighteenth-century writers admired in ancient Greek and Roman artists. Romantic writers, painters, and musicians responded not to an idealized image of ancient civilization but to the real unrest of their own times: the fervor of political revolution and the squalor of the Industrial Revolution. Rebelling against Neoclassical values, they prized subjectivity, the imagination, and the wildness associated with untamed nature.

Although there were many differences in the concerns and approaches of the various writers associated with this movement, they generally shared a desire to discard the dominant forms and approaches of the eighteenth century and to forge a new type of literature. In this sense, Romanticism might be called the French Revolution carried over to the literary page. The English poet William Wordsworth, a pioneer of literary Romanticism, was at first inspired by the French Revolution and its emphasis on the worth of the ordinary person. Later, when he became disillusioned with the violence in France, he began plotting the literary revolution known as Romanticism. He would uphold the dignity of ordinary people by writing about them with imagination and respect.

In his preface to *Lyrical Ballads* (1798), a collection of poetry he co-authored with his friend Samuel Taylor Coleridge, Wordsworth outlined the dominant principles of Romanticism. He stressed the need to employ "language really used by men" in describing "situations from common life," emphasized the role of nature as a source of inspiration, and asserted that poetry should be a "spontaneous overflow of powerful feelings." These principles contrasted with the practice of eighteenth-century Neoclassical writers, who used witty language to portray upper-class people in social rather than natural settings.

The Lure of the Exotic and the Supernatural Among the other important characteristics of the Romantics were their fascination with folklife in general and the folklore of the Middle Ages specifically, their attraction to exotic cultures and the supernatural, their sense of optimism, their emphasis on individualism, their refusal to accept human limitations, and their desire for social change. Again, most of these characteristics contrast with those of Neoclassical writers.

In addition to Wordsworth and Coleridge, the Romantic movement included the German poet and dramatist Johann Wolfgang von Goethe (yō′ hän vôlf′ gäŋ fôn gō′ tə), the Russian poet Alexander Pushkin, the German poet Heinrich Heine (hīn′ riH hī′ nə), and the French author Victor Hugo (hyōō′ gō).

840 ■ *Romanticism and Realism*

▼ **Critical Viewing**
Which details in this painting suggest that it is a Romantic work? Explain. **[Connect]**

The Wanderer Above the Sea of Fog, 1818, Caspar David Friedrich, Kunsthalle, Hamburg

---

Enrichment

Charles Darwin

From 1831 to 1836, Charles Darwin (1809–1882) served as a naturalist with a British scientific expedition aboard the H.M.S. *Beagle.* Scientists on the expedition studied plants and animals throughout the world. Darwin's studies aboard the *Beagle* convinced him that through millions of years all species of plants and animals evolved, or developed gradually, from a few common ancestors. He documented his theories and presented them at a meeting of scientists in 1858. Although Darwin's theories of evolution and natural selection are widely accepted by scientists today, they also created a wave of controversy because of the perception that they challenge the biblical account of the Creation.

Themes in World Masterpieces — Music in the Historical Context

Beethoven Writes the First Romantic Symphony

It is 1802 and the virtuoso pianist and promising composer Ludwig von Beethoven (lōōt′ viH vän bā′ tō′ vən) can no longer deny that he is growing deaf. He retreats to a country village to write a confession of his deepest fears: ". . . reflect now that for six years I have been in a hopeless case, made worse by ignorant doctors, yearly betrayed in the hope of getting better, finally forced to face the prospect of a permanent malady. . . ." He will soon have to end his career as a pianist, focusing more and more on composing.

It is 1802 and Napoleon, commanding the armies of the French Revolution, has recently defeated the Austrians and forced a peace treaty with the British. At home, a grateful populace votes him consul, or ruler, for life.

Soon, Beethoven begins working on his Symphony No. 3, which will inaugurate a musical revolution. It will be the first Romantic symphony, an expression of thought and feeling on a more ambitious scale than can be found in symphonies of the previous century. Unlike these classical works, it will have an audience wider than a small circle of aristocrats. Beethoven labors on this composition in his sketchbooks, leaving empty spaces where he will fill in melodies later. Heroic in defiance of his "malady," the composer will dedicate his work to the hero who is bringing freedom to all of Europe: Napoleon.

It is 1804 and Napoleon's agents have just discovered an assassination plot against him. An influential adviser whispers that by making himself emperor, Napoleon will discourage future conspiracies. The consul agrees. The empire begins.

It is 1804 and Symphony No. 3 is complete. When he learns that Napoleon has declared himself emperor, Beethoven angrily strikes the leader's name from the dedication. This will be the Eroica ("Heroic") Symphony, dedicated not to a great man but, in disillusionment and defiance, to "the memory of a great man."

Ludwig von Beethoven, Joseph Karl Stieler, 1820, Beethoven-Haus, Bonn

▲ **Critical Viewing**
Which details in this portrait of Beethoven suggest aspects of the new Romantic music—for example, the powerful expression of emotion and the heroic stature of the composer? Explain. **[Interpret]**

Realism: The Discovery of Contemporary Life During the middle of the nineteenth century in France, a new literary movement known as Realism emerged, partly as a reaction against Romanticism and partly as a result of the industrial and scientific developments that were transforming society. Just as the Romantics had focused on humble people ignored by the Neoclassicists, Realists sought to portray previously ignored figures in con-temporary life, such as middle- and working-class city dwellers.

The French writer Honoré de Balzac (ô nô rā′ dae bäl zäk′) (1799–1850) anticipated Realism in scores of novels that give a vast and detailed picture of nineteenth-century French society, from criminals and lowlifes to upper-class women. Balzac's compatriot Gustave Flaubert (güs täv′ flō ber′) (1821–1880) wrote the classic Realist novel, *Madame Bovary*, which dissects the life of an unhappy middle-class woman. Other Realists were the English novelist Charles Dickens (1812–1870) and the Russian novelists Feodor Dostoyevsky (fyô′ dôr dôs′ tô yef′ skē) (see below) and Leo Tolstoy. In the latter part of the century, Henrik Ibsen wrote the first realistic prose dramas.

Introduction ■ 841

Enrichment

Realism in America
The harsh reality of American frontier life, coupled with reaction to the Civil War gave rise to a new movement in American literature called Realism. Realism in literature began after the Civil War. Although the outcome of the war had given the nation a hard-won sense of unity, the enormous cost of human life had shattered the nation's idealism. Young writers turned away from the Romanticism that was popular before the war. Instead, writers began to focus on portraying "real life" as ordinary people lived it, and attempted to show characters and events in an honest, objective, almost factual way. Willa Cather, for example, was a Realist noted for her unflinching portrayal of the loneliness and cultural isolation of life on the prairie. Edith Wharton wrote fiction in the Realist vein about the Eastern high society into which she had been born.

Background

Ralph Ellison

Ralph Ellison developed a new type of black protaganist in reaction to the characters of Richard Wright, a popular African American writer of the mid-1900s. Wright's characters, victims of societal oppression, typically were enraged and lacked education. In contrast, Ellison's Invisible Man was schooled and introspective. Ellison did not believe that blacks were victims of white America but rather participants in cultural creation. Ellison saw the affirmation of black culture—its songs, folktales, and rituals—as a path to freedom. Raised in Oklahoma, a state without a history of slavery, Ellison navigated the borders between white and black America. *Invisible Man* is a novel that asserts black identity but also offers guidance to a person of any color or gender who feels "invisible." Ellison said that it is the job of the writer to "tell us about the unity of American experience beyond all considerations of class, of race, of religion." Ellison saw America as a place where anyone could forge an identity. He viewed the racial divide in America as a microcosm of the larger human struggle to find individual meaning in a world of chaos.

Themes in World Literature

A Living Tradition

Point out that one of the effects of the literary movement known as Naturalism is that today, readers of novels that emerged at that time can learn more about the history of the industrial revolution from the portrayal of middle-class characters struggling with the grim political, social, and economic forces of that period. A further benefit is the work of major American Naturalist authors, and later, of Ralph Ellison, who was less pessimistic.

Ask: What does Ellison's narrator, the invisible man, complain about?

Answer: He feels invisible because white people do not acknowledge his existence but rather walk past him as though he were not there. However, he offers advice to those who feel like him, rather than feed his anger.

Naturalism and Greek Tragedy Realism eventually gave birth to the literary movement known as Naturalism. One of the leaders of this movement was the French writer Émile Zola (ā mēl′ zō′ lä′) (1840–1902). Like realists, Naturalists attempted to depict life accurately, but Naturalists were even more pessimistic than their forebears. They were reacting to the worst excesses of the Industrial Revolution and to misinterpretations of Darwinian theory that viewed society as a jungle in which only the fittest survived. As a result, they believed that the scientific laws governing heredity and society, like the Fates in ancient Greek mythology, determined the course of a person's life. Characters in naturalistic novels are therefore shaped by forces they can neither understand nor control. In a sense, these novels are like Greek tragedies rendered in prose, with characters who live in slums, not palaces, and with scientific laws replacing the decrees of the gods.

The Symbolist Movement Throughout the nineteenth century, literary movements reacted to previous movements as well as to social conditions: Realism was a response to Romanticism, and Naturalism grew out of Realism. The Symbolist movement, proclaimed in an 1886 manifesto in France but based on the work of earlier writers, followed this same pattern. It rejected the fate-driven world of the Naturalist novel and the Realist drama. In a sense, it was a rebellion of poets against novelists and dramatists.

Themes in
World Masterpieces — A Living Tradition

Feodor Dostoyevsky and Ralph Ellison

One nineteenth-century work with many literary descendants is *Notes from the Underground* (1864) by Russian author Feodor Dostoyevsky. In this novel, a nameless first-person narrator begins by announcing, "I am a sick man. . . . I am a spiteful man." This narrator is an angry stepchild of the Industrial Revolution, a nasty disbeliever in the progress of science and reason.

A literary descendant of this character is the narrator of Ralph Ellison's novel *Invisible Man*, written nearly 100 years after *Notes*. Ellison, who had been studying Dostoyevsky's work, created an African American protagonist who feels "invisible" in white society and therefore does not share that society's belief in progress:

> I am an invisible man. No, I am not a spook like those who haunted Edgar Allan Poe; nor am I one of your Hollywood-movie ectoplasms. I am a man of substance, of flesh and bone, fiber and liquids—and I might even be said to possess a mind. I am invisible, understand, simply because people refuse to see me. Like the bodiless heads you see sometimes in circus sideshows, it is as though I have been surrounded by mirrors of hard, distorting glass. When they approach me they see only my surroundings, themselves, or figments of their imagination—indeed, everything and anything except me.

842 ■ *Romanticism and Realism*

Enrichment

Naturalism Around the World

Naturalism flourished in Europe during the late nineteenth and early twentieth centuries. In fact, scholars point to France as the birthplace of the movement. The writer Émile Zola was its leading practitioner. His approach to literature was similar to a scientist's approach to an experiment. Characters should be subjected to tests, Zola suggested, and the author should record their reactions objectively.

Overall, Naturalism drew on advances in the world of science. Scientific principles were imported into literature, and writers created characters whose lives were shaped and whose actions were dictated by powerful forces—heredity and nature, but also social and economic pressure—entirely beyond their control. Major American Naturalist authors include Jack London, Stephen Crane, Frank Norris, and Theodore Dreiser.

Led by Stéphane Mallarmé (stā fån' má lár mā') (1842–1898), these poets were looking for an exit from the materialistic nineteenth century. Dismayed by the drabness of everyday life and the vulgar taste of the rising middle class, they searched for an otherworldly spiritual reality. Taking the earlier French poet Charles Baudelaire (shårl bōd ler') as their guide, Symbolist poets sought to suggest this reality through musical phrasing and unusual figurative language.

In addition to Baudelaire, poets who anticipated this movement were Paul Verlaine (pôl ver len') and Arthur Rimbaud (år tür' ram bō'). Verlaine, famous for the musicality of his verse, expressed a Symbolist credo when he wrote in "The Art of Poetry," "Let there be music, again and forever!" Rimbaud, a visionary poet who believed he could create a new world and a new language in his verse, stopped writing poetry when he was still a teenager!

On the Bank of the Seine, Bennecourt, 1868, Claude Monet, The Art Institute of Chicago

The Visual Arts: From Splendor to Strangeness Some of the same movements influencing literature affected the visual arts, as well. Romantic painters like Caspar David Friedrich (frē' driH) (page 840) depicted mysterious, lonely views of natural splendor. Then, as in literature, Realists rebelled against Romantics. Gustave Courbet (güs tåv' kōōr be'), for example, painted such gritty subjects as laborers breaking stones (page 834). He declared, "I cannot paint an angel because I have never seen one." In their turn, Impressionists rebelled against Realists. Trying to capture fleeting impressions of shimmering light and color, they treated their paintings less like windows onto reality and more like colorful flat surfaces. Still later, Symbolists like Odilon Redon (ô dē lōn' rə dōń) painted such strange and unreal subjects as a drifting balloon in the form of a gigantic eyeball.

▲ **Critical Viewing**
In what ways might this Impressionist painting by Monet differ from a photograph of the same scene? Explain. **[Compare and Contrast]**

Introduction ■ 843

Literature of the Period
Comprehension Check

1. What are some characteristics of Romanticism?
   Answer: Characteristics include an emphasis on subjectivity, the imagination, and untamed nature.

2. (a) During the middle of the nineteenth century, what literary movement emerged in Europe? (b) What type of characters were portrayed in this literature?
   Answer: (a) Realism emerged at this time. (b) Middle- and working-class people were portrayed.

3. (a) What literary movement followed Realism in Europe? (b) What are its characteristics?
   Answer: (a) Naturalism followed Realism. (b) It portrays individuals who are shaped by uncontrollable forces.

4. (a) What literary movement was a reaction to Naturalism and Realism in Europe? (b) What was its goal?
   Answer: (a) Symbolism was a reaction to these movements. (b) Its goal was to escape from the drabness of everyday life to find an otherworldly spiritual reality.

Critical Thinking

Why do you think the nineteenth century produced four distinct literary styles, whereas the previous 150 years—the Age of Rationalism—saw only one? **[Analyze]**
Possible response: Rapid political, social, and economic changes affected people's lives and the literature.

Critical Viewing

Possible response: The painting shows the artist's impression of light and color; a photograph might be more realistic.

Concept Connector

Have students return to the Focus Questions on page 833. Ask them to summarize the main points in the Unit Introduction. Their summaries should include the following points:

Impact of the Industrial Revolution:
- New products, such as the automobile, changed the way people lived.
- A new middle class developed, which valued hard work and respectability.
- People became concerned about society's restrictions on women.

Pros and cons of the Industrial Revolution:
- Goods were produced cheaper and faster than ever before.

- Millions of new jobs were created.
- Early industrial workers faced low pay, long hours, and dangerous working conditions.
- Unhealthy urban slums resulted from people crowding into industrial cities.

Ways Romanticism differs from Realism:
- Romantic writers were interested in the common people, political revolution, and squalid cities, and valued subjectivity, imagination, and nature.
- Realism reacted against Romanticism. It portrayed previously ignored figures, such as middle- and working-class city dwellers.

Standard Course of Study

Goal 1: WRITTEN LANGUAGE

WL.1.03.6 Make inferences and draw conclusions based on personal reflection.

Goal 4: CRITICAL THINKING

CT.4.03.1 Analyze how writers introduce and develop a main idea.

CT.4.03.2 Analyze how writers choose and incorporate significant supporting details.

CT.4.03.3 Analyze how writers relate the organization to the ideas.

Goal 5: LITERATURE

LT.5.03.6 Make inferences, predictions, and draw conclusions based on world literature.

LT.5.03.10 Analyze connections between ideas, concepts, characters and experiences in world literature.

Goal 6: GRAMMAR AND USAGE

GU.6.01.2 Analyze author's use of language to demonstrate understanding of expression.

Step-by-Step Teaching Guide	Pacing Guide
PRETEACH	
• Administer Vocabulary and Reading Warm-ups as necessary.	5 min.
• Engage students' interest with the motivation activity.	5 min.
• Read and discuss author and background features. **FT**	10 min.
• Introduce the Literary Analysis Skill: Romanticism. **FT**	5 min.
• Introduce the Reading Strategy: Drawing Inferences. **FT**	10 min.
• Prepare students to read by teaching the selection vocabulary. **FT**	
TEACH	
• Informally monitor comprehension while students read independently or in groups. **FT**	30 min.
• Monitor students' comprehension with the Reading Check notes.	as students read
• Reinforce vocabulary with Vocabulary Builder notes.	as students read
• Develop students' understanding of Romanticism with the Literary Analysis annotations. **FT**	5 min.
• Develop students' ability to draw inferences with the Reading Strategy annotations. **FT**	5 min.
ASSESS/EXTEND	
• Assess students' comprehension and mastery of the Literary Analysis and Reading Strategy by having them answer the Apply the Skills questions. **FT**	15 min.
• Have students complete the Vocabulary Development Lesson and the Grammar and Style Lesson. **FT**	15 min.
• Apply students' ability to write stage directions by using the Writing Lesson. **FT**	45 min. or homework
• Apply students' understanding by using one or more of the Extend Your Learning activities.	20–90 min. or homework
• Administer Selection Test A or Selection Test B. **FT**	15 min.

Resources

Print

Unit 7 Resources

Transparency

Graphic Organizer Transparencies

Print

Reader's Notebook [L2]

Reader's Notebook: Adapted Version [L1]

Reader's Notebook: English Learner's Version [EL]

Unit 7 Resources

Technology

Listening to Literature Audio CDs [L2, EL]

Reader's Notebook: Adapted Version Audio CD [L1, L2]

Print

Unit 7 Resources

General Resources

Technology

Go Online: Research [L3]

Go Online: Self-test [L3]

ExamView®, **Test Bank [L3]**

Choosing Resources for Differentiated Instruction

[**L1**] Special Needs Students

[**L2**] Below-Level Students

[**L3**] All Students

[**L4**] Advanced Students

[**EL**] English Learners

For Vocabulary and Reading Warm-ups and for Selection Tests, **A** signifies "less challenging" and **B** "more challenging." For Graphic Organizer transparencies, **A** signifies "not filled in" and **B** "filled in."

FT Fast Track Instruction: To move the lesson more quickly, use the strategies and activities identified with **FT**.

Scaffolding for Less Proficient and Advanced Students

The leveled Critical Thinking questions after selections progress in the levels of thinking required to answer them. To address the needs of your different students, you may use the (a) level questions for your less proficient students and the (b) level questions with your on-level and advanced students. The occasional (c) level questions are appropriate for your advanced students.

PRENTICE HALL

TeacherEXPRESS™ Use this complete
Plan · Teach · Assess   suite of powerful
teaching tools to make lesson planning and testing quicker and easier.

PRENTICE HALL

StudentEXPRESS™ Use the interactive
Learn · Study · Succeed   textbook (online
and on CD-ROM) to make selections and activities come alive with audio and video support and interactive questions.

 For: Information about Lexiles
Professional **Visit:** www.PHSchool.com
Development **Web Code:** eue-1111

Motivation

Have students discuss stories, tales, or poems they have read in which a character makes a bargain with the Devil. Then, have students explore reasons that such stories recur throughout world literature. Ask: Why are people so fascinated by the idea of a person making a pact with the Devil?

❶ Background

More About the Author

Goethe was greatly influenced by two of his friends, Johann von Herder and Friedrich von Schiller. Goethe was still a young man when he met the older Herder, whom he came to regard as the most brilliant person he had known. "If I am destined to be your satellite," wrote Goethe, "then I will be, gladly and faithfully." To some degree, Goethe was Herder's satellite, becoming part of Herder's *Sturm und Drang* movement and embracing Herder's appreciation for Shakespeare. Many years later, when Goethe was middle-aged and losing the poetic drive, he met the young Schiller, whose enthusiasm for Goethe's work revitalized the older author. Yet their friendship did not always go smoothly. Although Goethe insisted on deference, Schiller was not about to become Goethe's satellite.

Geography Note

Draw students' attention to the map on this page and identify Germany. Remind students that Goethe spent most of his life in Weimar, in central Germany. Tell students that Goethe and Friedrich von Schiller are buried together in Weimar, in a mausoleum in the ducal cemetery.

---

from Faust ❶

Johann Wolfgang von Goethe (1749–1832)

Because of the tremendous diversity of his talents and interests, Johann (yō hän′) Wolfgang von Goethe (gö′ tə) is best described as a true Renaissance man. He was not only a gifted writer but also a scientist, a painter, a statesman, a philosopher, and an educator.

The son of a wealthy lawyer, Goethe was born in the German town of Frankfurt am Main. After receiving a thorough education from private tutors, he was sent to the University of Leipzig to study law. More interested in the arts than in law, Goethe spent most of his free time writing poetry, studying art, and attending concerts. Nonetheless, he finished his legal studies in 1771.

A Developing Novelist Goethe practiced law for a brief period, during which he wrote *The Sorrows of Young Werther* (1774), an autobiographical novel inspired by an unhappy love affair and the suicide of one of his friends. One of the most important novels of the eighteenth century, *The Sorrows of Young Werther* earned Goethe international fame.

A year after the novel's publication, Goethe accepted an invitation to the court of the reigning duke of Weimar, Charles Augustus. Developing a close friendship with the duke, Goethe lived in Weimar for the rest of his life, and for ten years he served as the duke's chief minister. In 1786, he traveled to Italy in an effort to dedicate time and energy to his writing. He remained there for two years, writing, traveling, painting, and studying classical culture.

Shortly after returning to Weimar, Goethe fell in love with Christiane Vulpius, whom he later married. He also became the director of the court theater and began devoting much of his energy to scientific studies. Through a close friendship with the noted German writer Friedrich von Schiller (1759–1805), Goethe gained valuable guidance and advice concerning his writing and assistance in revising a number of his important works.

A Legendary Figure Probably the most notable of these works was *Faust*. With Schiller's advice and direction, Goethe revised an early draft of the play, adding a prologue. Unfortunately, Schiller died three years before *Faust, Part I* (1808) was published.

The final and greatest achievment of Goethe's literary career was the completion of *Faust, Part II*. The poet's vision of the legendary Faust transformed the traditional character into a newer, more sympathetic one that has fascinated readers and scholars for centuries. Goethe had begun his work on *Part II* while still a young man; because he contributed to the piece throughout his life, *Faust, Part II* ultimately reflects the deep philosophy of life and wry wisdom of the poet's mature years. Goethe never knew of the success of *Faust, Part II*, as it was published late in 1832, a few months after his death.

Faust was by no means the only literary work that Goethe completed. Among his other notable works are his novels—*Wilhelm Meister's Apprenticeship* (1795), *Elective Affinities* (1809), and *Wilhelm Meister's Travels* (1821–1829)—and his autobiographical work *Poetry and Truth* (1811–1832). By the time of his death, Goethe had become a legendary figure throughout the Western world.

844 ■ *Romanticism and Realism*

Preview

Connecting to the Literature

The Devil lurks in many forms in literature across time and cultures, often trying to convince victims to sell their souls in exchange for their heart's desire. Compare Faust's dilemma to the situation of other characters from books or movies who were tempted by the Devil.

❷ Literary Analysis

Romanticism

Romanticism is a literary and artistic movement that is characterized by the following elements:

- The Romantics favored emotion over reason, intuition over intellect, the subjective over the objective.
- They celebrated creativity, individuality, and imagination.
- Their writings reflect nature, self-knowledge, folklore, and the mysterious and exotic.

Look for these characteristics of Romanticism in *Faust*.

Connecting Literary Elements

A **legend** is a traditional story, handed down through many generations. It usually deals with a hero, a saint, or a national leader. Often, legends reflect a people's cultural values. Notice how Goethe uses facts from the real Faust's life to develop his story.

❸ Reading Strategy

Drawing Inferences

Drawing inferences means making educated guesses based on specific details the author provides.

- Read between the lines to look for any implied meaning.
- Explore passages for clues about characters, setting, plot, and mood.
- Examine significant word choices, patterns of events, and other clues to help you understand the writer's implied message.

Use an organizer like the one shown as you read.

Vocabulary Builder

envoys (än′ voiz′) *n.* messengers (p. 847)

fervent (fur′ vənt) *adj.* intensely devoted or earnest (p. 848)

primal (prī′ məl) *adj.* original; fundamental (p. 849)

obstinate (äb′ stə nət) *adj.* determined to have one's way; stubborn (p. 853)

fetters (fet′ ərz) *n.* shackles; chains (p. 858)

tenacity (tə nas′ ə tē) *n.* persistence; stubbornness (p. 861)

insatiableness (in sā′ shə bəl nəs) *n.* the quality of being impossible to fill (p. 862)

Standard Course of Study

- Make inferences, predictions, and draw conclusions based on world literature. (LT.5.03.6)
- Analyze connections between ideas, concepts, characters and experiences in world literature. (LT.5.03.10)

Passage

"I work as the cat does with the mouse."

↓

What Can Be Inferred

Mephistopheles is sly, using man's weaknesses and catching man when he's unaware of his predicament.

---

from *Faust* ■ 845

❷ Literary Analysis

Romanticism

- Explain to students that they will focus on the elements of Romanticism that are exhibited in each selection.
- As a class, **read** the list of characteristics of Romanticism. Point out that although elements of Romanticism appear in the literature of many ages, including ours, Romanticism as a prevailing movement began in the eighteenth century and flourished during the nineteenth.
- Tell students that Goethe's *Faust* is an excellent example of Romanticism. Because Romanticism was later replaced by two contrasting literary movements—Realism and Naturalism—Goethe's work is in many ways different from the literary works of the later part of the century.

❸ Reading Strategy

Drawing Inferences

- Ask students to describe the mood you are projecting when you fold your arms across your chest and frown. When students say that you look angry, tell them that they have just drawn an inference on the basis of your body language. Remind them that they can use the same skill to draw inferences as they read, using clues in the text to infer the writer's meaning.
- Explain the use of the graphic organizer. Then give students a copy of **Reading Strategy Graphic Organizer A**, p. 151 in *Graphic Organizer Transparencies.* Have them use it to draw inferences as they read.

Vocabulary Builder

- Pronounce each vocabulary word for students, and read the definitions as a class. Have students identify any words with which they are already familiar.

Differentiated Instruction   Solutions for All Learners

Support for Special Needs Students

Have students read the support pages for these selections in the *Reader's Notebooks.* Completing these pages will prepare students to read the selections in the Student Edition.

Support for Less Proficient Readers

Have students read the support pages for these selections in the *Reader's Notebooks.* After students finish each selection in the *Reader's Notebooks,* have them complete the questions and activities in the Student Edition.

Support for English Learners

Have students read the support pages for these selections in the *Reader's Notebooks: English Learner's Version.* Completing these pages will prepare students to read the selections in the Student Edition.

Facilitate Understanding

Have students silently read "Prologue in Heaven" and the excerpt from "The First Part of the Tragedy." Then, have students summarize the events that Goethe dramatizes in the selections.

❶ About the Selection

"Prologue in Heaven" opens with the angels praising God's creation. This dialogue is followed by a scene in which God (the Lord) and the Devil (Mephistopheles) have a discussion about humanity in general and Faust in particular. Mephistopheles asks for permission to try to steer Faust down the path of evil, and God grants it, saying that he never hated the Devil.

❷ Literary Analysis

Romanticism

- Point out to students that the Romantics had a deep love and appreciation for nature and were most concerned with the thoughts and emotions that nature aroused in them.

- Have a volunteer read aloud the bracketed passage.

- Then, **ask** students how these lines reflect elements of Romanticism. **Answer:** This description of nature creates a mysterious and awe-inspiring portrait of the universe. Goethe even has the angels acknowledge the beauty of the sun and "his brother spheres" (the stars) as they move through the universe.

from Faust.❶

JOHANN WOLFGANG VON GOETHE
translated by Louis MacNeice

Background Few historical figures have fueled the imagination of the Western world as much as the German scholar and traveling magician Georg Faust (or Faustus), who lived from about 1480 to 1540. According to legend, Faust sold his soul to the Devil in exchange for youth, knowledge, and magical powers. At the time of its origin, the Faust legend was widely thought to be true. In contrast, when Goethe's *Faust* was published, few people believed that the type of events it depicted could actually happen.

Many versions of the Faust legend portray Faust as a man with an unquenchable thirst for knowledge. In Faust's time, only the very wealthy could afford to dedicate their lives to learning. Faust's quest, though noble in theory, drives him into a contract with the Devil. Goethe's version transforms Faust into something of a Romantic hero, embodying the ideal of limitless spiritual aspirations.

Prologue in Heaven

The LORD. *The* HEAVENLY HOSTS. MEPHISTOPHELES[1] *following.*
The THREE ARCHANGELS[2] *step forward.*

RAPHAEL: The chanting sun, as ever, rivals
　　　　　The chanting of his brother spheres
　　　　　And marches round his destined circuit—
　　　　　A march that thunders in our ears.
5　　　His aspect cheers the Hosts of Heaven
　　　　　Though what his essence none can say;
　　　　　These inconceivable creations

---

1. **Mephistopheles** (mef′ ə stäf′ ə lēz′) the Devil.
2. **three archangels** the three chief angels—Raphael, Gabriel, and Michael.

Differentiated Instruction   Solutions for All Learners

Accessibility at a Glance

	from Faust Prologue in Heaven	*from* Faust The First Part of the Tragedy
Context	God permits the Devil to compete for Faust's soul.	Faust agrees to sell his soul to the Devil in exchange for knowledge.
Language	Words of emotional intensity in rhyming verses	Syntax: exclamatory sentences
Concept Level	Accessible (The choice between loyalty to God or the Devil)	Accessible (The price of always yearning for more in life)
Literary Merit	Classic drama	Classic drama
Lexile	NP	NP
Overall Rating	Challenging	Challenging

Keep the high state of their first day.

GABRIEL: And swift, with inconceivable swiftness,
10   The earth's full splendor rolls around,
     Celestial radiance alternating
     With a dread night too deep to sound;
     The sea against the rocks' deep bases
     Comes foaming up in far-flung force,
15   And rock and sea go whirling onward
     In the swift spheres' eternal course.

MICHAEL: And storms in rivalry are raging
     From sea to land, from land to sea,
     In frenzy forge the world a girdle
20   From which no inmost part is free.
     The blight of lightning flaming yonder
     Marks where the thunder-bolt will play;
     And yet Thine <u>envoys</u>, Lord, revere
     The gentle movement of Thy day.

25   CHOIR OF ANGELS: Thine aspect cheers the Hosts of Heaven
     Though what Thine essence none can say,
     And all Thy loftiest creations
     Keep the high state of their first day.

     [*Enter* MEPHISTOPHELES.]

MEPHISTOPHELES: Since you, O Lord, once more approach and ask
30   If business down with us be light or heavy—
     And in the past you've usually welcomed me—
     That's why you see me also at your levee.[3]

---

3. **levee** (lev′ ē) *n.* morning reception held by a person of high rank.

❸ ▲ Critical Viewing
Which of the archangels' words could describe the scene in this photograph? **[Connect]**

Literary Analysis
Romanticism Which words in Michael's dialogue are charged with emotional intensity?

Vocabulary Builder
envoys (än′ vȯiz′) *n.* messengers

❺ ✓ Reading Check
According to Michael, what girdles, or imprisons, the earth?

from *Faust* ■ 847

---

❸ Critical Viewing

Answer: In lines 21–22 of the play, Michael says: "The blight of lightning flaming yonder / Marks where the thunder-bolt will play."

❹ Literary Analysis
Romanticism

• Review with students the defining characteristics of Romanticism listed on p. 845. Emphasize that the expression of heightened emotion is one of these defining characteristics.

• Have students review lines 1–28, and then **ask** them to comment on the emotions the angels are expressing here.
  Answer: The angels are expressing wonder at the beauty, excitement, and wildness of nature; they are also expressing reverence at the gentleness of the day.

• **Ask** students the Literary Analysis question: Which words in Michael's dialogue are charged with emotional intensity?
  Answer: Words such as *storms, rivalry, raging, frenzy, forge, blight, lightning* and *flaming* are charged with emotional intensity.

❺ Reading Check

Answer: According to Michael, storms girdle the earth.

Drawing Inferences

- **Ask** students to summarize how readers can determine an author's intended meaning when the message is conveyed indirectly.
  Answer: The reader must draw inferences after taking note of textual details, especially the writer's use of description and dialogue. In a play, description is often included in the dialogue.

- Ask a volunteer to read aloud lines 38–50. Then, **ask** students the Reading Strategy question: What does Mephistopheles imply that Faust is unable to accomplish with his ability to reason?
  Possible response: Mephistopheles implies that Faust, like all other men, has been unable to rise above the level of the beasts. Even with the ability to reason, he makes no progress.

❼ Literary Analysis

Romanticism

- Have students read and then **paraphrase** the bracketed lines. Make sure that they understand the meaning of such phrases as "the ferment in him" and "the deep-sea swell of his breast."
  Possible response: By "the ferment in him," Mephistopheles means that Faust is agitated by the quest for knowledge; by "the deep-sea swell of his breast," Mephistopheles means that Faust's desire is so vast that it will never be satisfied.

- Then, **ask** students the Literary Analysis question: Explain how these lines reflect the Romantics' attitude toward the importance of the individual and the value of unbounded spiritual aspirations.
  Possible response: These lines describe Faust's own passionate quest for knowledge and experience. They suggest that this quest is for spiritual rather than physical fulfillment, because he "has no earthly habits in meat and drink." The line "He serves you oddly enough, I think" indicates that this quest is unusual or "odd," thus defining Faust as an individual.

Excuse me, I can't manage lofty words—
Not though your whole court jeer and find me low;
35 My pathos[4] certainly would make you laugh
Had you not left off laughing long ago.
Your suns and worlds mean nothing much to me;
How men torment themselves, that's all I see.
The little god of the world, one can't reshape, reshade him;
40 He is as strange to-day as that first day you made him.
His life would be not so bad, not quite,
Had you not granted him a gleam of Heaven's light;
He calls it Reason, uses it not the least
Except to be more beastly than any beast.
45 He seems to me—if your Honor does not mind—
Like a grasshopper—the long-legged kind—
That's always in flight and leaps as it flies along
And then in the grass strikes up its same old song.
I could only wish he confined himself to the grass!
50 He thrusts his nose into every filth, alas.

LORD: Mephistopheles, have you no other news?
Do you always come here to accuse?
Is nothing ever right in your eyes on earth?

MEPHISTOPHELES: No, Lord! I find things there as downright bad
        as ever.
55 I am sorry for men's days of dread and dearth;
Poor things, *my* wish to plague 'em isn't <u>fervent</u>.

LORD: Do you know Faust?

MEPHISTOPHELES: The Doctor?[5]

LORD: Aye, my servant.

MEPHISTOPHELES: Indeed! He serves you oddly enough, I think.
The fool has no earthly habits in meat and drink.
60 The ferment in him drives him wide and far,
That he is mad he too has almost guessed;
He demands of heaven each fairest star
And of earth each highest joy and best,
And all that is new and all that is far
65 Can bring no calm to the deep-sea swell of his breast.

LORD: Now he may serve me only gropingly,
Soon I shall lead him into the light.
The gardener knows when the sapling first turns green
That flowers and fruit will make the future bright.

---

4. **pathos** (pā´ thäs) *n.* suffering.
5. **Doctor** Doctor of Philosophy.

Reading Strategy
Drawing Inferences
What does Mephistopheles imply that mankind is unable to accomplish with his ability to reason?

Vocabulary Builder
fervent (fur´ vənt) *adj.* intensely devoted or earnest

Literary Analysis
Romanticism Explain how these lines reflect the Romantics' attitude toward the importance of the individual and the value of unbounded spiritual aspirations.

Enrichment

Georg Faust

In the Middle Ages, the story of Georg Faust, the man who was the historical basis for the literary character Faust, spread far and wide and became part of folk legend. In 1587, *Faustbuch*— a crude, loosely organized narrative about the life of Faust—was published in Germany. Written by an anonymous author, the book not only drew upon the existing tales about Faust, but

it also attributed to Faust numerous stories about other legendary magicians, such as Merlin. Concluding with Faust's death and descent into Hell, the book had a major impact on readers throughout Europe. The book was first translated into English in 1592 under the title *The History of the Damnable Life and Deserved Death of Doctor John Faustus.*

8

70   **MEPHISTOPHELES:** What do you wager?
      You will lose him yet,
    Provided *you* give *me* permission
    To steer him gently the course I set.

LORD: So long as he walks the earth alive,
    So long you may try what enters your head;
75   Men make mistakes as long as they strive.

MEPHISTOPHELES: I thank you for that; as regards the dead,
    The dead have never taken my fancy.
    I favor cheeks that are full and rosy-red;
    No corpse is welcome to my house;
80   I work as the cat does with the mouse.

LORD: Very well; you have my full permission.
    Divert this soul from its <u>primal</u> source
    And carry it, if you can seize it,
    Down with you upon your course—
85   And stand ashamed when you must needs admit:
    A good man with his groping intuitions
    Still knows the path that is true and fit.

MEPHISTOPHELES: All right—but it won't last for long.
    I'm not afraid my bet will turn out wrong.
90   And, if my aim prove true and strong,
    Allow me to triumph wholeheartedly.
    Dust shall he eat—and greedily—
    Like my cousin the Snake[6] renowned in tale and song.

---

6. **my cousin the Snake** In Genesis, the devil assumes the form of a serpent in order to tempt Eve to eat from the Tree of Knowledge.

Mephistopheles, 1863, Eugène Delacroix, Giraudon

9 ▲ **Critical Viewing**
What impression of Mephistopheles does the artist convey? **[Explain]**

Vocabulary Builder
primal (prī′ məl) *adj.*
original; fundamental

 Reading Check
What wager has Mephistopheles made with the Lord?

from *Faust* ■ 849

8 **Humanities**
Mephistopheles,
by Eugène Delacroix
Eugène Delacroix (1798–1863) is widely regarded as the greatest of the French Romantic painters. Three of his main sources of inspiration were literature, music, and history. In fact, many of his works were interpretations of scenes from history or literature. This depiction of Mephistopheles is one of seventeen bizarre and intriguing lithographs that Delacroix produced for a French edition of Goethe's *Faust*.

Use the following question for discussion:
  Would this lithograph be more or less effective if it were in color? Explain.
  Answer: This lithograph would be less effective in color because the use of only white and black suggests the seriousness of the struggle between good and evil.

9 **Critical Viewing**
Possible response: The artist conveys the impression that Mephistopheles is a fallen angel. The weight of his body seems to pull him down. The darkness and shading of the art suggest evil.

10 **Vocabulary Builder**
Related Words: *prime*
• Draw students' attention to the word *primal* and its definition.
• Tell students that *primal* is related to the word *prime*, which comes from a Latin root meaning "first."
• Invite students to **suggest words** related to *prime*, and list the words on the board.
  Possible responses: Students may suggest *primate, primarily,* and *primordial.*
• Then, have students use dictionaries to find the meanings of these words and write a short paragraph for each word, describing how the meaning "first" contributes to the word's definition.

11 **Reading Check**
Answer: The Lord has wagered that Mephistopheles will not be able to win Faust over to the side of evil, and Mephistopheles has wagered that he will.

⑫ Reading Strategy
Drawing Inferences

- Have students discuss their impressions of the relationships between the Lord and Mephistopheles, between the Lord and humanity, and between Mephistopheles and humanity.

- Read aloud the bracketed passage. Then, **ask** students the Reading Strategy question: What can you infer about the purpose of the Devil from the Lord's words?

Possible response: One might infer that the Devil's purpose is to keep man from relaxing too much.

ASSESS

Answers

1. **Possible response:** Some students might imagine that Mephistopheles will win the wager because he knows how to tempt Faust in a way that Faust will find difficult to resist. Others might imagine that the Lord will win the wager because it has already been established that Faust is basically a good man.

2. (a) Mephistopheles is shrewd and cynical and has a surprising sense of humor. (b) Mephistopheles has little respect for or faith in humanity.

3. (a) Mephistopheles says that Faust has an insatiable quest for knowledge that cannot be satisfied. As a result, Faust is extremely agitated and nearly mad. (b) **Possible response:** Faust is a restless seeker of knowledge and experience and does not indulge in earthly pleasures.

4. (a) The Lord is tolerant of Mephistopheles and understands Mephistopheles's role in the cosmos. (b) The Lord says that he has never hated Mephistopheles and allows him to compete for Faust's soul.

5. **Possible responses:** Yes; making mistakes is part of being human. No; humans should strive to be perfect.

Go Online For additional information
Author Link about Johann Wolfgang von Goethe, have students type in the Web Code, then select *G* from the alphabet, and then select Johann Wolfgang von Goethe.

850

LORD: That too you are free to give a trial;
95   I have never hated the likes of you.
  Of all the spirits of denial
  The joker is the last that I eschew.
  Man finds relaxation too attractive—
  Too fond too soon of unconditional rest;
⑫ 100   Which is why I am pleased to give him a companion
  Who lures and thrusts and must, as devil, be active.
  But ye, true sons of Heaven, it is your duty
  To take your joy in the living wealth of beauty.
  The changing Essence which ever works and lives
105   Wall you around with love, serene, secure!
  And that which floats in flickering appearance
  Fix ye it firm in thoughts that must endure.

CHOIR OF ANGELS: Thine aspect cheers the Hosts of Heaven
  Though what Thine essence none can say,
110   And all Thy loftiest creations
  Keep the high state of their first day.

[*Heaven closes.*]

MEPHISTOPHELES [*alone*]: I like to see the Old One now and then
  And try to keep relations on the level.
  It's really decent of so great a person
115   To talk so humanely even to the Devil.

Reading Strategy
Drawing Inferences
What can you infer about the purpose of the Devil from the Lord's words?

Critical Reading

1. **Respond:** What do you imagine will be the outcome of Mephistopheles's wager with the Lord? Explain your answer.

2. **(a) Recall:** How would you characterize Mephistopheles as he appears in "Prologue in Heaven"? **(b) Infer:** What is his attitude toward humanity?

3. **(a) Recall:** How does Mephistopheles describe Faust?
   (b) Deduce: Based on Mephistopheles's description, what type of person do you imagine Faust to be?

4. **(a) Recall:** What is the Lord's attitude toward Mephistopheles?
   (b) Support: How is this attitude conveyed?

5. **Take a Position:** Do you agree with the Lord's statement that "Men make mistakes as long as they strive" (line 75)? Explain.

Go Online
Author Link
For: More about Johann Wolfgang von Goethe
Visit: www.PHSchool.com
Web Code: ete-9701

from Faust ⑬

Background In "Prologue in Heaven," Mephistopheles and the Lord disagree about Faust's true soul, and the Lord gives Mephistopheles permission to compete for Faust's soul. Only a great test will determine whether Faust recognizes the value of the life he currently lives or whether greed and irrationality will drive him to sell his soul to the Devil. Mephistopheles knows Faust's weakness—an unquenchable desire for knowledge—and seeks to use it as his means of luring Faust into a high-stakes bargain. Will Faust be tempted? Will Mephistopheles be forced to admit that Faust is like other good men who know "the path that is true and fit"? Look for the answers to these questions in "The First Part of the Tragedy."

from The First Part of the Tragedy

NIGHT

In a high-vaulted narrow Gothic[1] room FAUST, *restless, in a chair at his desk.*

⑮

FAUST: Here stand I, ach, Philosophy
    Behind me and Law and Medicine too
    And, to my cost, Theology—
    All these I have sweated through and through
5   And now you see me a poor fool
    As wise as when I entered school!
    They call me Master, they call me Doctor,
    Ten years now I have dragged my college
    Along by the nose through zig and zag

---

1. **Gothic** (gäth´ ik) *adj.* of a style of architecture characterized by the use of ribbed vaulting, flying buttresses, pointed arches, and steep, high roofs.

⑭ **Reading Check**

Why does Faust consider himself a "poor fool"?

from Faust ■ 851

⓯ Literary Analysis
Romanticism and Legends

- Have a volunteer read aloud Faust's opening monologue beginning on p. 851.

- **Ask** students the Literary Analysis question: How does Faust's speech reflect what you know about the real Faust from the Background on p. 846?

Answer: According to Faust's speech, he, like the real Faust, is a scholar who is also very interested in magic.

⓰ Humanities

Martin Luther at Erfurt, 1861
by Sir Joseph Noel Paton

Although Scottish painter Paton (1821–1901) was never a member of the Pre-Raphaelites, many of his works, with their attention to detail and concern with Romantic themes, clearly reflect the movement's influence.

Use the following question to initiate a discussion:

Do you think that this piece of art is a good or poor choice for an illustration of this selection? Explain.

Possible responses: It is a good choice because the man in the painting is consumed with his studies, just as Faust is consumed with his quest for knowledge. The painting's Gothic setting is similar to the setting of Faust's room. However, the man in the painting is too devout to consider bargaining with the Devil.

⓱ Critical Viewing

Answer: Faust might sympathize with the man in the painting because it appears that the man shares many of Faust's interests. He is obviously interested in learning and spends a great deal of time pursuing knowledge.

10 Through up and down and round and round
And this is all that I have found—
The impossibility of knowledge!
It is this that burns away my heart;
Of course I am cleverer than the quacks,
15 Than master and doctor, than clerk and priest,
I suffer no scruple or doubt in the least,
I have no qualms about devil or burning,
Which is just why all joy is torn from me,
I cannot presume to make use of my learning,
20 I cannot presume I could open my mind
To proselytize² and improve mankind.

Besides, I have neither goods nor gold,
Neither reputation nor rank in the world;
No dog would choose to continue so!
25 Which is why I have given myself to Magic
To see if the Spirit may grant me to know
Through its force and its voice full many a secret,
May spare the sour sweat that I used to pour out
In talking of what I know nothing about,
30 May grant me to learn what it is that girds
The world together in its inmost being,
That the seeing its whole germination, the seeing
Its workings, may end my traffic in words.

ⓕ

After summoning the Earth Spirit and finding it unwilling to assist him in his quest for knowledge, Faust lapses into a state of despair. He decides to end his life by drinking a cup of poison but abruptly changes his mind when he hears the tolling of church bells and the singing of choruses, celebrating the arrival of Easter. Setting out on a walk through the countryside with Wagner, his assistant, Faust is inspired by the beauty of spring and soothed by the peasants' expressions of admiration and affection for him. When he returns to his study, however, his sense of contentment quickly dissipates. Alerted by the growling of his dog, Faust becomes aware of another presence in the room. When Faust threatens to use magic to defend himself against the unseen intruder, Mephistopheles comes forward from behind the stove, disguised as a traveling scholar. Faust soon becomes aware of Mephistopheles's true identity, and he is intrigued by the possibility of establishing a contract with the devil. However, Faust falls asleep before the two can reach an agreement. In the following scene, Mephistopheles returns to the study to resume his discussion with Faust.

---

2. **proselytize** (präs´ ə li tīz´) *v.* to try to convert.

852 ■ *Romanticism and Realism*

Literary Analysis
Romanticism and Legends How does Faust's speech reflect what you know about the real Faust from the Background on page 846?

⓱ ▼ **Critical Viewing**
Why might Faust sympathize with the man in this painting?
[Hypothesize]

⓰

[*The same room. Later.*]

FAUST: Who's knocking? Come in! *Now* who wants to annoy me?

35 **MEPHISTOPHELES** [*outside door*]: It's I.

FAUST: Come in!

MEPHISTOPHELES [*outside door*]:
    You must say "Come in" three times.

FAUST: Come in then!

18

MEPHISTOPHELES [*entering*]:
                    Thank you; you overjoy me.
    We two, I hope, we shall be good friends;
40   To chase those megrims[3] of yours away
    I am here like a fine young squire to-day,
    In a suit of scarlet trimmed with gold
    And a little cape of stiff brocade,
    With a cock's feather in my hat
45   And at my side a long sharp blade,
    And the most succinct advice I can give
    Is that you dress up just like me,
    So that uninhibited and free
    You may find out what it means to live.

50 **FAUST:** The pain of earth's constricted life, I fancy,
    Will pierce me still, whatever my attire;
    I am too old for mere amusement,
    Too young to be without desire,
    How can the world dispel my doubt?
55   You must do without, you must do without!
    That is the everlasting song
    Which rings in every ear, which rings,
    And which to us our whole life long
    Every hour hoarsely sings.
60   I wake in the morning only to feel appalled,
    My eyes with bitter tears could run
    To see the day which in its course
    Will not fulfil a wish for me, not one;
    The day which whittles away with obstinate carping
65   All pleasures—even those of anticipation,
    Which makes a thousand grimaces to obstruct
    My heart when it is stirring in creation.
    And again, when night comes down, in anguish
    I must stretch out upon my bed

---

3. **megrims** (mē′ grəmz) *n.* low spirits.

Reading Strategy
Drawing Inferences Why has Mephistopheles changed his costume from that of a traveling scholar to "a suit of scarlet trimmed with gold"?

Vocabulary Builder
obstinate (äb′ stə nət) *adj.* determined to have one's way; stubborn

19 Reading Check
What torments Faust every day?

from *Faust* ■ 853

---

18 **Reading Strategy**
Drawing Inferences

• Have a pair of students read aloud the opening exchange between Faust and Mephistopheles, acting it out with appropriate expression.

• Then, **ask** students the Reading Strategy question: Why has Mephistopheles changed his costume from that of a traveling scholar to "a suit of scarlet trimmed with gold"?
Answer: Mephistopheles has changed his costume in order to demonstrate to Faust that dressing in a certain way can help change one's attitude.

▶ **Reteach** If students are having difficulty answering the Reading Strategy question, use the **Reading Strategy** support, page 9 in *Unit 7 Resources*.

19 **Reading Check**

Answer: Faust is tormented by "the pain of earth's constricted life." He believes he is "too old for mere amusement" yet "Too young to be without desire." He is tired of having to "do without" and defeated in knowing that none of his wishes will be fulfilled.

Differentiated
Instruction   Solutions for All Learners

Support for Less Proficient Readers
Have pairs of students read aloud the opening dialogue between Faust and Mephistopheles, as suggested in the Reading Strategy note. Students may find it difficult to capture a natural rhythm when reading the dialogue. To model appropriate rhythm and tone, read aloud one or two sections of dialogue.

Support for English Learners
Have pairs of students read aloud the opening dialogue between Faust and Mephistopheles, as suggested in the Reading Strategy note. Pair students with more proficient partners, and have those partners model the pronunciation of unfamiliar words. Students can keep track of new words by keeping a vocabulary journal.

Enrichment for Advanced Readers
Before students perform the opening dialogue, have them analyze the language in Faust's opening speech, noting the rhyme scheme and looking for examples of alliteration, parallel structure, repetition, and other poetic devices. Challenge students to write a similar statement about themselves, in which they imitate Goethe's style.

70   And again no rest is granted me,
      For wild dreams fill my mind with dread.
      The God who dwells within my bosom
      Can make my inmost soul react;
      The God who sways my every power
75   Is powerless with external fact.
      And so existence weighs upon my breast
      And I long for death and life—life I detest.

MEPHISTOPHELES: Yet death is never a wholly welcome guest.

FAUST: O happy is he whom death in the dazzle of victory
80   Crowns with the bloody laurel in the battling swirl!
      Or he whom after the mad and breakneck dance
      He comes upon in the arms of a girl!
      O to have sunk away, delighted, deleted,
      Before the Spirit of the Earth, before his might!

⓴ 85   **MEPHISTOPHELES:** Yet I know someone who failed to drink
      A brown juice on a certain night.

FAUST: Your hobby is espionage—is it not?

MEPHISTOPHELES: Oh I'm not omniscient[4]—but I know a lot.

FAUST: Whereas that tumult in my soul
90   Was stilled by sweet familiar chimes
      Which cozened the child that yet was in me
      With echoes of more happy times,
      I now curse all things that encompass
      The soul with lures and jugglery
95   And bind it in this dungeon of grief
      With trickery and flattery.
      Cursed in advance be the high opinion
      That serves our spirit for a cloak!
㉑ Cursed be the dazzle of appearance
100   Which bows our senses to its yoke!
      Cursed be the lying dreams of glory,
      The illusion that our name survives!
      Cursed be the flattering things we own,
      Servants and ploughs, children and wives!
105   Cursed be Mammon[5] when with his treasures
      He makes us play the adventurous man
      Or when for our luxurious pleasures
      He duly spreads the soft divan![6]

---

4. **omniscient** (äm nish′ ent) *adj.* knowing all things.
5. **Mammon** (mam′ en) Generally, Mammon refers to riches regarded as an object of worship and greedy pursuit; here, the word is used to refer to the Devil, as an embodiment of greed.
6. **divan** (di van′) *n.* large, low couch or sofa, usually without armrests or a back.

854 ■ *Romanticism and Realism*

Literary Analysis
Romanticism In what way does this passage exhibit the Romantics' interest in emotion and the individual?

◀ **Critical Viewing**
How does the study portrayed here fit Faust's personality? **[Connect]**

A curse on the balsam of the grape!
110 A curse on the love that rides for a fall!
A curse on hope! A curse on faith!
And a curse on patience most of all!

[*The* INVISIBLE SPIRITS *sing again.*]

SPIRITS: Woe! Woe!
You have destroyed it,
115   The beautiful world;
By your violent hand
'Tis downward hurled!
A half-god has dashed it asunder!
From under
120   We bear off the rubble to nowhere
And ponder
Sadly the beauty departed.
Magnipotent
One among men,

Reading Strategy
Drawing Inferences
Which details help you determine whether these invisible spirits are on the side of good or evil?

 **Reading Check**
What has Faust destroyed?

from *Faust* ■ *855*

㉒ Humanities

Faust and Mephistopheles,
by Alfred Louis Vigny Jacomin

Jacomin created this gravure reproduction in 1869 after an oil on canvas.

Use the following question for discussion:

Do you think this image accurately captures the relationship between Mephistopheles and Faust? Explain. **Possible response:** Yes; the art shows Faust as weary, but intrigued by Mephistopheles. Mephistopheles is shown as a suave, yet imposing, figure.

㉓ Critical Viewing

Answer: The study portrayed here fits Faust's personality because the room seems to be littered with the kinds of objects he would use in his studies and perhaps in his magic.

㉔ Reading Strategy
Drawing Inferences

• Remind students that the theme of a literary work is often implied rather than stated directly. To determine the theme, students must draw inferences from details in the text.

• Ask a small group to read aloud the bracketed passage. Make sure students understand that the Spirits are talking to Faust, responding to his speech in which he curses so many things that most people find enjoyable and valuable.

• **Ask** students the Reading Strategy question: Which details help you determine whether these invisible spirits are on the side of good or evil?
Answer: The fact that the spirits are sad about Faust's negativism and mourn the loss of beauty puts them in a positive light.

㉕ Reading Check

Answer: Faust has destroyed "the beautiful world"; that is, his rejection of the world causes its beauty to vanish for him.

Differentiated Instruction Solutions for All Learners

Support for Special Needs Students
Remind students that a contraction is a word made up of two words with an apostrophe taking the place of the missing letters. Explain to students that the word *'Tis* (line 117) is a contraction meaning "it is." Then, call students' attention to the contraction *it's* (line 35) on page 853. Tell students that this contraction also means "it is." On the board, show students how each contraction is formed, demonstrating which letter the apostrophe replaces in each case.

Support for English Learners
Call students' attention to the use of the word *'Tis* in line 117. Explain that this word is a contraction meaning "it is." Ask students to read the entire sentence in which the word appears, and then point out that the *it* in *'Tis* refers to "the beautiful world." A more common way to express the thought would be: "By your violent hand, the beautiful world is hurled downward."

• Have students read the bracketed passage independently. **Ask** them how they would characterize the method Mephistopheles is using to get Faust to accept Mephistopheles' offer.
Answer: First, Mephistopheles minimizes the importance of the invisible spirits. Then, he flatters Faust by saying that he doesn't really belong with the common men. Finally, he offers his services to help Faust in his "career through life."

• **Ask** students the Literary Analysis question: In what ways does Mephistopheles's speech reflect the Romantics' interest in emotions?
Answer: Mephistopheles's speech plays on Faust's emotions. He mentions Faust's grief and tells him that it acts like a vulture on his life and mind. He also appeals to Faust's desire to have a partner through life who can help him achieve his goals of acquiring knowledge and experience.

27 Reading Strategy
Drawing Inferences

• Direct students' attention to the bracketed line.

• **Ask** students the Reading Strategy question: What does Faust mean when he refers to Mephistopheles as "a servant like you"?
Answer: Faust means that he recognizes Mephistopheles's "servitude" as potentially dangerous.

---

125   Magnificent
    Build it again,
    Build it again in your breast!
    Let a new course of life
    Begin
130   With vision abounding
    And new songs resounding
    To welcome it in!

MEPHISTOPHELES: These are the juniors
    Of my faction.
    Hear how precociously[7] they counsel
135   Pleasure and action.
    Out and away
    From your lonely day
    Which dries your senses and your juices
    Their melody seduces.

140   Stop playing with your grief which battens
    Like a vulture on your life, your mind!
    The worst of company would make you feel
    That you are a man among mankind.
    Not that it's really my proposition
145   To shove you among the common men;
    Though I'm not one of the Upper Ten,
    If you would like a coalition
    With me for your career through life,
    I am quite ready to fit in,
150   I'm yours before you can say knife.
    I am your comrade;
    If you so crave,
    I am your servant, I am your slave.

FAUST: And what have I to undertake in return?

155 **MEPHISTOPHELES:** Oh it's early days to discuss what that is.

FAUST: No, no, the devil is an egoist
    And ready to do nothing gratis
    Which is to benefit a stranger.
    Tell me your terms and don't prevaricate![8]
160   A servant like you in the house is a danger.

MEPHISTOPHELES: I will bind myself to your service in this world,
    To be at your beck and never rest nor slack;

---

7. **precociously** (pri kō′ shəs lē) *adv.* exhibiting maturity to a point beyond that which is normal for the age.
8. **prevaricate** (pri var′ i kāt) *v.* to tell an untruth.

856 ■ *Romanticism and Realism*

Literary Analysis
Romanticism In what ways does Mephistopheles's speech reflect the Romantics' interest in emotions?

Reading Strategy
Drawing Inferences What does Faust mean when he refers to Mephistopheles as "a servant like you"?

Enrichment

Rousseau and Kant

The French Revolution and the Industrial Revolution, along with the ideas of eighteenth-century philosophers Jean-Jacques Rousseau (1712–1778) and Immanuel Kant (1724–1804), gave rise to a variety of new European cultural attitudes and beliefs, including those Romantic attitudes expressed in *Faust.* Influenced by the French revolutionary spirit and by the writings of Rousseau, who argued that society must respect but typically infringes on personal liberty, many writers and thinkers of the early nineteenth century stressed the need for freedom and equality. These beliefs were accompanied by an emphasis on individuality and the fundamental power of the imagination, which reflected the teachings of Kant. The early nineteenth-century writers and thinkers were also influenced by industrialization, which prompted them to emphasize the importance of nature and the need to return to a simpler way of life.

When we meet again on the other side,
In the same coin you shall pay me back.

165 **FAUST:** The other side gives me little trouble;
First batter this present world to rubble,
Then the other may rise—if that's the plan.
This earth is where my springs of joy have started,
And this sun shines on me when broken-hearted;
170 If I can first from them be parted,
Then let happen what will and can!
I wish to hear no more about it—
Whether there too men hate and love
Or whether in those spheres too, in the future,
175 There is a Below or an Above.

MEPHISTOPHELES: With such an outlook you can
        risk it.
Sign on the line! In these next days you will get
Ravishing samples of my arts;
I am giving you what never man saw yet.

180 **FAUST:** Poor devil, can *you* give anything ever?
Was a human spirit in its high endeavor
Even once understood by one of your breed?
Have you got food which fails to feed?
Or red gold which, never at rest,
185 Like mercury runs away through the hand?
A game at which one never wins?
A girl who, even when on my breast,
Pledges herself to my neighbor with her eyes?
The divine and lovely delight of honor
190 Which falls like a falling star and dies?
Show me the fruits which, before they are plucked,
        decay
And the trees which day after day renew their green!

MEPHISTOPHELES: Such a commission doesn't
        alarm me,
I have such treasures to purvey.
195 But, my good friend, the time draws on when we
Should be glad to feast at our ease on something good.

FAUST: If ever I stretch myself on a bed of ease,
Then I am finished! Is that understood?
If ever your flatteries can coax me
200 To be pleased with myself, if ever you cast
A spell of pleasure that can hoax me—
Then let *that* day be my last!
That's my wager!

The Terrible Bargain

Over the years, the Faust legend has appeared in many variations. Each retelling involves a person who trades his soul for experience, knowledge, or treasure. "The Devil and Tom Walker" by Washington Irving is just one of these variations. Set in colonial Massachusetts, the short story features the miser Tom Walker. Wishing for untold wealth, Tom makes a pact with the Devil, whom he encounters in a swampy forest, and obtains his heart's desire in exchange.

Adaptations do not share the same ending—in some, such as "The Devil and Tom Walker," the protagonist is doomed; in others, such as "The Devil and Daniel Webster" by Stephen Vincent Benét, he is redeemed. Variations of the legend appear across genres and generations as well. In Oscar Wilde's novel *A Picture of Dorian Gray* (1891), Gray trades his soul for perpetual youth. In *Bedazzled*, a Hollywood film released in 2000, the terrible bargain is reinvented when a man trades his soul to the Devil—who appears in the form of a beautiful woman—in exchange for seven wishes.

Connect to the Literature

What techniques does Mephistopheles use to persuade Faust to sell his soul?

29 ✓ **Reading Check**

What will Mephistopheles show Faust when he signs the agreement?

from *Faust* ■ 857

28 **Themes in World Literature**

The Terrible Bargain Washington Irving traveled extensively and learned about European customs, traditions, and folklore. Inspired by the European folk heritage, Irving created two of his most famous stories, "The Legend of Sleepy Hollow" and "Rip Van Winkle." Both stories transform traditional German tales into distinctly American narratives set in the Hudson Valley. While living in Europe, Irving completed *Tales of a Traveler,* which contains "The Devil and Tom Walker." Irving's adaptation of the Faust legend is set in New England during the 1720s, a time when the Puritan belief in devoting one's life to God was being replaced by materialism and the desire for personal gain.

Connect to the Literature Note the widespread attraction to tales of interaction between man and the devil. Suggest that the human desire for attaining what one doesn't have and the lure of "The grass is greener on the other side" seem to motivate artists and writers to continue working on this theme of man's willingness to sell one's soul to the devil. Ask students how Mephistopheles manages to persuade Faust to sell his soul.
Answer: He appeals to Faust's vanity by offering to be his constant partner and friend and by cautioning him to stop nurturing his grief like a common man. He also promises to show Faust "ravishing samples of his arts," thus giving him everything he wants from life.

29 **Reading Check**

Answer: Mephistopheles will show Faust "ravishing samples" of his arts, things that no other man has ever seen.

Differentiated Instruction — Solutions for All Learners

Support for Special Needs Students
Draw students' attention to lines 197–202. To check comprehension, discuss with students what will happen to Faust if he loses his bet and whether Mephistopheles will lose his bet with the Lord even if he wins his bet with Faust.

Support for Less Proficient Readers
Check students' comprehension by asking them what Faust means in lines 156–160. Make sure they understand that Faust is fully aware that the devil is not his friend and does not intend to reward him without exacting a heavy price.

Vocabulary for English Learners
Draw students' attention to the phrase "at your beck" in line 162. Tell them that this is a shortened version of the idiom "at your beck and call," which means "ready and willing to do whatever you ask."

MEPHISTOPHELES: Done!

FAUST: Let's shake!
205   If ever I say to the passing moment
      "Linger a while! Thou art so fair!"
      Then you may cast me into <u>fetters</u>,
      I will gladly perish then and there!
      Then you may set the death-bell tolling,
210   Then from my service you are free,
      The clock may stop, its hand may fall,
      And that be the end of time for me!

MEPHISTOPHELES: Think what you're saying, we shall not
      forget it.

FAUST: And you are fully within your rights;
215   I have made no mad or outrageous claim.
      If I stay as I am, I am a slave—
      Whether yours or another's, it's all the same.

MEPHISTOPHELES: I shall this very day at the College Banquet⁹
      Enter your service with no more ado,
220   But just one point—As a life-and-death insurance
      I must trouble you for a line or two.

FAUST: So you, you pedant, you too like things in writing?
      Have you never known a man? Or a man's word? Never?
      Is it not enough that my word of mouth
225   Puts all my days in bond for ever?
      Does not the world rage on in all its streams
      And shall a promise hamper *me*?
      Yet this illusion reigns within our hearts
      And from it who would be gladly free?
230   Happy the man who can inwardly keep his word;
      Whatever the cost, he will not be loath to pay!
      But a parchment, duly inscribed and sealed,
      Is a bogey¹⁰ from which all wince away.
      The word dies on the tip of the pen
235   And wax and leather lord it then.
      What do you, evil spirit, require?
      Bronze, marble, parchment, paper?
      Quill or chisel or pencil of slate?
      You may choose whichever you desire.

240   **MEPHISTOPHELES:** How can you so exaggerate
      With such a hectic rhetoric?

---

9. **the College Banquet** the *Doctorschmaus*, a dinner given by a successful candidate for a Ph.D. degree.
10. **bogey** (bō′ gē) *n.* anything one especially, and often needlessly, fears.

858 ■ *Romanticism and Realism*

Enrichment

The Romantic "Love of Life"
In an essay written in 1910, George Santayana, an American philosopher and poet, discussed the qualities that make Faust a work of Romantic literature. He wrote that Faust is the drama of a philosophical adventure; a rebellion against convention; a flight to nature, to tenderness, to beauty; and then a return to convention again, with a feeling that nature, tenderness, and beauty, unless found there, will not be found at all. Goethe never depicts, as Dante does, the object his hero is pursuing; he is satisfied with depicting the pursuit. . . . [When Goethe wrote *Faust*] the love of life, primal and adventurous, was gathering head in many an individual. In the Romantic movement and in the French Revolution, this love of life freed itself from the political compromises and conventions that had been stifling it for two hundred years. Goethe's hero embodies this. . . romantic emancipation of the mind. . . . He cries for air, for nature, and for experience.

Any little snippet is quite good—
And you sign it with one little drop of blood.

FAUST: If that is enough and is some use,
245   One may as well pander to your fad.

MEPHISTOPHELES: Blood is a very special juice.

FAUST: Only do not fear that I shall break this contract.
What I promise is nothing more
Than what all my powers are striving for.
250   I have puffed myself up too much, it is only
Your sort that really fits my case.
The great Earth Spirit has despised me
And Nature shuts the door in my face.
The thread of thought is snapped asunder,
255   I have long loathed knowledge in all its fashions.
In the depths of sensuality

Reading Check

Why does Mephistopheles want Faust to sign the agreement in blood?

Dunstanburgh Castle in a Thunderstorm, Thomas Girtin, Ashmolean Museum, Oxford, UK

---

32 Reading Check

Answer: Mephistopheles wants Faust to sign the agreement in blood because "Blood is a very special juice," a vital life force with symbolic overtones, and Faust will presumably be unable to escape any agreement signed in blood.

33 Humanities

Dunstanburgh Castle in a Thunderstorm, by Thomas Girtin

By creating dramatic depictions of light effects and natural phenomena, watercolorist Thomas Girtin (1775–1802) presented an alternative to the standard tinted drawing, revolutionizing the watercolor genre in the process.

Use the following questions to stimulate discussion:

• Imagine that a person lives in the castle shown in this painting. How do you think that person would feel upon seeing this scene?
Possible response: The person would feel frightened because of the castle's isolated location and the severity of the raging storm. Because the person would be sheltered within the castle's wall, he or she would feel safe from the elements.

• Describe the mood of this painting. What details and elements contribute to the mood?
Answer: The mood of this painting is tumultuous and ominous. Details that contribute to the mood include the crashing waves; the lightning; the looming, rocky cliffs; and the dark, billowing clouds.

Differentiated Instruction   Solutions for All Learners

Vocabulary for Less Proficient Readers
Post the meaning of the word *loathed* (line 255). Then, have students list on the board synonyms for *loathed*. Ask volunteers to read line 255, substituting a different synonym for *loathed* with each reading. Lead students in a discussion about which word choice is the most powerful and why.

Support for English Learners
Draw students' attention to line 254: "The thread of thought is snapped asunder." Explain to students that this line contains a metaphor, or a figure of speech. In this example, thought is compared to a thread, which can be broken or "snapped." Have students skim the selection for examples of metaphor, and help them understand the comparisons.

Vocabulary for Advanced Readers
Draw students' attention to the word *fad* in line 245. Ask them to research its etymology and meaning. Then, have them find words with meanings similar to that of *fad* but with positive or neutral, rather than negative, connotations.

859

34 **Literary Analysis**

Romanticism

- Review with students the characteristics of Romanticism listed on p. 845. Then, have students read aloud the bracketed passage starting on the previous page.

- **Ask** students to respond to the Literary Analysis item: Identify two characteristics of Romanticism in lines 256–265.
  Answer: Faust emphasizes the Romantic concern with emotion in the lines, "In the depths of sensuality/Let us now quench our glowing passions." The reference to "unpenetrated sorcery" reveals the Romantic interest in the mysterious and the exotic.

35 **Humanities**

Vanitas, by Edwaert Collier

Vanitas still-life paintings depict objects that function symbolically to represent fleeting earthly pleasures.

Use the following questions for discussion:

- Why is this painting an appropriate choice to accompany this selection?
  Answer: The painting depicts the vanity of knowledge, represented by the various books and the globe.

- The Latin word *vanitas* refers to the vanity of indulging in these pleasures, such as music, knowledge, and riches. How does Faust exhibit vanity in his own search for knowledge and in his dealings with Mephistopheles?
  Answer: Faust is vain in thinking he's worthy of knowing all there is to know. He also exhibits vanity by underestimating Mephistopheles and the pact they have made.

36 **Critical Viewing**

Answer: Because Faust is on a quest for knowledge in general, he would find all the arts and sciences—including geography (represented by the globe), music (represented by the recorder), and literature (represented by the books)—interesting.

860

34

260

265

> Let us now quench our glowing passions!
> And at once make ready every wonder
> Of unpenetrated sorcery!
> Let us cast ourselves into the torrent of time,
> Into the whirl of eventfulness,
> Where disappointment and success,
> Pleasure and pain may chop and change
> As chop and change they will and can;
> It is restless action makes the man.

MEPHISTOPHELES: No limit is fixed for you, no bound;
If you'd like to nibble at everything
Or to seize upon something flying round—
Well, may you have a run for your money!
270   But seize your chance and don't be funny!

FAUST: I've told you, it is no question of happiness.
The most painful joy, enamored hate, enlivening
Disgust—I devote myself to all excess.
My breast, now cured of its appetite for knowledge,
275   From now is open to all and every smart,
And what is allotted to the whole of mankind
That will I sample in my inmost heart,
Grasping the highest and lowest with my spirit,
Piling men's weal and woe upon my neck,
280   To extend myself to embrace all human selves
And to founder in the end, like them, a wreck.

MEPHISTOPHELES: O believe *me,* who have been
                    chewing
These iron rations many a thousand year,
No human being can digest
285   This stuff, from the cradle to the bier[11]
This universe—believe a devil—
Was made for no one but a god!
He exists in eternal light
But *us* he has brought into the darkness
290   While *your* sole portion is day and night.

FAUST: I will all the same!

MEPHISTOPHELES: That's very nice.
There's only one thing I find wrong;
Time is short, art is long.
You could do with a little artistic advice.
295   Confederate with one of the poets
And let him flog his imagination

---

11. **bier** (bir) *n.* coffin and its supporting platform.

860 ■ *Romanticism and Realism*

Literary Analysis
Romanticism Identify two characteristics of Romanticism in lines 256–265.

36 ▼ **Critical Viewing**
What arts and sciences represented in this still life would Faust find interesting? **[Speculate]**

35

Vanitas, Edwaert Collier, Johnny van Haeften Gallery, London, UK

Enrichment

Common Quotations
Tell students that certain quotations recur throughout the literary works of different cultures and eras. The line "Time is short, art is long" (line 293) is an example of such a quotation. Four hundred years before Christ, Hippocrates wrote, "Art is long, life is short" (quoted in Latin as "Ars longa, vita brevis").

In the fourteenth century, Geoffrey Chaucer wrote, "The lyf so short, the craft so long to lerne." During the nineteenth century, Robert Browning wrote, "Art's long, though time is short," and Henry Wadsworth Longfellow wrote, "Art is long, and Time is fleeting."

To heap all virtues on your head,
A head with such a reputation:
Lion's bravery,
300 Stag's velocity,
Fire of Italy,
Northern tenacity.
Let *him* find out the secret art
Of combining craft with a noble heart
305 And of being in love like a young man,
Hotly, but working to a plan.
Such a person—*I'd* like to meet him;
"Mr. Microcosm"¹² is how I'd greet him.

FAUST: What am I then if fate must bar
310 My efforts to reach that crown of humanity
After which all my senses strive?

MEPHISTOPHELES: You are in the end . . . what you are.
You can put on full-bottomed wigs with a million locks,
You can put on stilts instead of your stocks,
315 You remain for ever what you are.

FAUST: I feel my endeavors have not been worth a pin
When I raked together the treasures of the human mind,
If at the end I but sit down to find
No new force welling up within.
320 I have not a hair's breadth more of height,
I am no nearer the Infinite.

MEPHISTOPHELES: My very good sir, you look at things
Just in the way that people do;
We must be cleverer than that
325 Or the joys of life will escape from you.
Hell! You have surely hands and feet,
Also a head and you-know-what;
The pleasures I gather on the wing,
Are they less mine? Of course they're not!
330 Suppose I can afford six stallions,
I can add that horse-power to my score
And dash along and be a proper man
As if my legs were twenty-four.
So good-bye to thinking! On your toes!
335 The world's before us. Quick! Here goes!
I tell you, a chap who's intellectual
Is like a beast on a blasted heath
Driven in circles by a demon
While a fine green meadow lies round beneath.

---

12. **Mr. Microcosm** man regarded as the epitome of the world.

Vocabulary Builder
tenacity (tə nas′ ə tē) *n.* persistence; stubborness

Reading Strategy
Drawing Inferences
What can you infer about Faust from line 312?

Literary Analysis
Romanticism and Legends Do you think Faust hopes to become a legendary figure? Explain.

 **Reading Check**
After all Faust's efforts to gain knowledge, what will he become in the end?

from Faust ■ *861*

37 Reading Strategy
Drawing Inferences
• Read aloud the bracketed line. **Ask** students the Reading Strategy question: What can you infer about Faust from line 312?
Answer: Mephistopheles implies that Faust has been trying to disguise or escape his true nature and that Faust perhaps has been aiming for a goal that is higher than he is capable of attaining.

▶ **Monitor Progress Ask** students what wigs and stilts have in common.
Answer: They both change a person's appearance. Guide students to see that Mephistopheles is implying that for all of Faust's striving, Faust will be unable to change himself.

• Then, **ask** students to explain Mephistopheles's attitude toward Faust.
Possible response: As described in the *Prologue,* Mephistopheles believes that men are "always in flight." Mephistopheles believes that Faust is no different from other men because Faust cannot be content with his station in life.

38 Literary Analysis
Romanticism and Legends
• Read aloud the bracketed passage. Have students **answer** the Literary Analysis question: Do you think Faust hopes to become a legendary figure? Explain.
Answer: Faust's yearning for a "new force welling up within," more "height," and closeness to "the Infinite" indicates that he hopes to achieve more than the ordinary person and hopes to be remembered after his death.

• Then, **ask** students whether Faust would be content merely with external fame.
Answer: No, Faust's reference to a "force welling up within" suggests that he desires inspiration and the ability to create something new.

39 Reading Check
Answer: According to Mephistopheles, Faust will become simply what he is: "You are in the end . . . what you are."

Drawing Inferences

• Read aloud the bracketed passage.

• Then **ask** students the Reading Strategy question: What does Mephistopheles mean by "meat and drink"?

Answer: He refers not to physical meat and drink, but to joy, satisfaction and a feeling of accomplishment.

ASSESS

Answers

1. **Possible response:** Faust's feelings of accomplishing so little despite being an honored and respected scholar might have surprised some students.

2. (a) Faust is in a state of deep despair. (b) **Possible response:** Despite his learning, Faust believes he knows nothing of real value.

3. (a) Mephistopheles will serve Faust until the day on which Faust becomes pleased with himself. On that day, Faust will die and be given over to Mephistopheles. (b) **Possible response:** Mephistopheles has the better bargain because he will serve Faust only until Faust dies, but Faust will serve Mephistopheles for eternity.

4. (a) Faust uses his own blood to sign the agreement. (b) Faust may not believe in an afterlife or he would not sign such an agreement.

5. **Possible response:** Faust would be no happier in today's world because he would still be unable to answer life's ultimate questions.

Go Online For additional information **Author Link** about Johann Wolfgang von Goethe, have students type in the Web Code, then select *G* from the alphabet, and then select Johann Wolfgang von Goethe.

---

340 **FAUST:** How do we start?

MEPHISTOPHELES: We just say go—and skip.
But please get ready for this pleasure trip.

[*Exit* FAUST.]

    Only look down on knowledge and reason,
    The highest gifts that men can prize,
345 Only allow the spirit of lies
    To confirm you in magic and illusion,
    And then I have you body and soul.
    Fate has given this man a spirit
    Which is always pressing onward, beyond control,
350 And whose mad striving overleaps
    All joys of the earth between pole and pole.
    Him shall I drag through the wilds of life
    And through the flats of meaninglessness,
    I shall make him flounder and gape and stick
355 And to tease his <u>insatiableness</u>
    Hang meat and drink in the air before his watering lips;
    In vain he will pray to slake his inner thirst,
    And even had he not sold himself to the devil
    He would be equally accursed.

Reading Strategy
Drawing Inferences
What does Mephistopheles mean by "meat and drink"?

Vocabulary Builder
insatiableness (in sā′ shə bəl nəs) *n.* the quality of being impossible to fill

Critical Reading

1. **Respond:** Which of Faust's feelings in the selection, if any, surprised you? Explain.

2. **(a) Recall:** What is Faust's state of mind in the opening scene? **(b) Deduce:** What does Faust mean when he says that he has discovered "the impossibility of knowledge"?

3. **(a) Recall:** What are the terms of the agreement between Faust and Mephistopheles? **(b) Evaluate:** Which character has the better part of the bargain?

4. **(a) Recall:** What does Faust use to sign his agreement with Mephistopheles? **(b) Infer:** What can you infer about Faust's attitude regarding the afterlife from his willingness to sign the agreement?

5. **Hypothesize:** Would Faust be a more satisfied person if he were living in today's world? Explain.

Go Online
Author Link
For: More about Johann Wolfgang von Goethe
Visit: www.PHSchool.com
Web Code: ete-9701

Apply the Skills

from *Faust*

Literary Analysis

Romanticism

1. Use a chart like the one shown to cite passages from *Faust* that demonstrate key features of **Romanticism.**

Features of Romanticism	Passage from *Faust*
favoring emotion over reason	
favoring intuition over intellect	
favoring the subjective over the objective	
celebrating the individual	

2. **(a)** Identify three details from *Faust* that express the Romantics' love of the mysterious and exotic. **(b)** Why is this characteristic of Romantic writing particularly suitable for *Faust*?

3. In what way does the treatment of Mephistopheles reflect the idealism and optimism of the Romantics? Explain.

Connecting Literary Elements

4. Which details in *Faust* point to the fact that Goethe embellishes the truth about the real Faust and adds to the **legend** about him?

5. What does this version of *Faust* tell you about the values and beliefs of Goethe's society?

Reading Strategy

Drawing Inferences

6. By **drawing inferences** from lines 10–24 of "The First Part of the Tragedy," explain why Faust makes a pact with the Devil.

7. In lines 180–192, what crucial knowledge does Faust imply is missing in Mephistopheles?

8. What can you infer about Mephistopheles's true character from lines 343–359, lines that are spoken after Faust has exited?

Extend Understanding

9. **Cultural Connection:** In Goethe's *Faust,* the Devil offers the temptation of knowledge. **(a)** Do you think this offer would be valuable in all cultures? **(b)** What other prizes might tempt people?

Romanticism is a literary and artistic movement characterized by imagination, emotion, nature, individuality, and the exotic.

A **legend** is a traditional story, usually based on a hero, a saint, or a national leader.

To **draw inferences,** use a variety of clues to interpret the author's message.

Go Online
Assessment
For: Self-test
Visit: www.PHSchool.com
Web Code: eta-6701

from *Faust* ■ 863

Go Online Students may use the **Self-test** to
Assessment prepare for **Selection Test A** or
Selection Test B.

Answers

1. **Possible response:** favoring emotion over reason: "And this is all that I have found— / The impossibility of knowledge! / It is this that burns away my heart. . . ." ("The First Part of the Tragedy," lines 11–13); **favoring intuition over intellect:** "A good man with his groping intuitions / Still knows the path that is true and fit." ("Prologue in Heaven," lines 86–87); **favoring the subjective over the objective:** "How can the world dispel my doubt?" ("The First Part of the Tragedy," line 54); **celebrating the individual:** "You are in the end . . . what you are." ("The First Part of the Tragedy," line 312) Another sample answer can be found on **Literary Analysis Graphic Organizer B,** p. 154 in *Graphic Organizer Transparencies.*

2. (a) References to magic, conversations in Heaven, and bargains with the devil all add to the mystery and exoticism of *Faust.* (b) Faust's quest is for something beyond the ordinary human experience.

3. Romantics believed that the Devil could be dealt with, bargained with, and maybe even thwarted.

4. Goethe has embellished the truth about the real Faust with details of his conversations and his bargain with the Devil.

5. Goethe's society believed in the struggle between good and evil, believed that people deserved fulfillment, and believed in the value of knowledge.

6. Faust is so weary of his present life that he is willing to wager everything.

7. Faust believes that the Devil has no appreciation for human yearning and striving.

8. Lines 343–359 reveal that Mephistopheles is cunning and evil and plans to torment Faust for the rest of his life.

9. (a) **Possible responses:** Yes; this offer would be valuable in all cultures. No; some cultures might value wealth or fame over knowledge. (b) Other prizes that might tempt people include material wealth, beauty, strength, power, family, love, admiration, and athletic ability.

❶ Vocabulary Lesson

Related Words: *prime*

1. b
2. a
3. d
4. c

Vocabulary Builder: Synonyms

1. e
2. d
3. b
4. f
5. a
6. g
7. c

Spelling Strategy

1. tenacity
2. scarcity
3. possibility

❷ Grammar and Style Lesson

1. who; subject
2. who; subject of clause
3. whom; object of preposition *upon*
4. who; subject of clause
5. whom; direct object of *meets*

Writing Application

Sample sentences: I predict that Mephistopheles, with whom Faust has made a wager, will torment the scholar. As to who will win the wager, I believe Faust will keep his soul.

𝒲G Writing and Grammar Platinum Level
For support in teaching the Grammar and Style Lesson, use Chapter 23, Section 2.

Build Language Skills

❶ Vocabulary Lesson

Related Words: *prime*

The word *prime*, from a Latin root meaning "first," is the basis for many related words.

From the following list, choose the related word that best completes each sentence below. Use a dictionary to check your responses.

   a. primal **b.** primitive **c.** primary **d.** primeval

1. She is held back by the ___ nature of the technology she uses.
2. One of our ___ instincts is the need to protect our young.
3. He lives on one hundred acres of ___ forest, untouched by an ax.
4. The doctor's ___ concern is for the health of his patients.

Vocabulary Builder: Synonyms

Match each vocabulary word on the left to the word on the right that has a similar meaning.

1. envoys	**a.** shackles
2. fervent	**b.** basic
3. primal	**c.** greediness
4. obstinate	**d.** eager
5. fetters	**e.** messengers
6. tenacity	**f.** stubborn
7. insatiableness	**g.** persistence

Spelling Strategy

In English, the suffix *-ity,* as used in the word *laity,* is more common than the suffix *-ety.* For each of the following words, write its noun form ending in *-ity.*

   1. tenacious   **2.** scarce   **3.** possible

❷ Grammar and Style Lesson

Usage: *who* and *whom*

The words *who* and *whom* are often used incorrectly. *Who,* like *he* or *she,* is used as a subject or subject complement. *Whom,* like *him* or *her,* is used as a direct object or as an object of a preposition. Study these examples:

> "The God <u>who</u> dwells within my bosom . . ."
>
> "Happy is he <u>whom</u> death . . . Crowns with the bloody laurel . . ."

Practice Copy each item below, adding *who* or *whom* as needed. Then, identify the word's function in the phrase or sentence.

1. "*Now* ___ wants to annoy me?"
2. "The God ___ sways my every power /Is powerless with external fact."
3. "O happy is he . . . ___ after the mad and breakneck dance / He comes upon . . ."
4. "Yet I know someone ___ failed to drink / A brown juice on a certain night."
5. It is the Devil ___ Faust meets in the study.

Writing Application Write a paragraph in which you predict how this play might end. Include two sentences in which you use *who* and *whom* correctly.

𝒲G Prentice Hall Writing and Grammar Connection: Platinum Level, Chapter 23, Section 2

864 ■ *Romanticism and Realism*

Assessment Practice

Distinguish Between Fact and Nonfact

Use the sample test item to show students how to distinguish between fact and nonfact.

   I am here like a fine young squire to-day, / In a suit of scarlet trimmed with gold / And a little cape of stiff brocade, / With a cock's feather in my hat / And at my side a long sharp blade, / And the most succinct advice I can give / Is that you dress up just like me, / So that uninhibited and free / You may find out what it means to live.

   — *Faust,* "The First Part of the Tragedy," lines 41–49

(For more practice, see *Test Preparation Workbook,* p. 37.)

Which of the following is an OPINION?

  A Mephistopheles is carrying a sword.
  B Mephistopheles is a better dresser than Faust.
  C Mephistopheles offers Faust advice.
  D Mephistopheles is wearing a cape.

Choices *A, C,* and *D* are facts from the passage. Only choice *B* is a personal belief that cannot be proved. The correct answer is *B.*

❸ Writing Lesson

Writing a Film Script

Imagine that you are a screenwriter who has been hired to create a film adaptation of Goethe's *Faust*. Think about the ways in which the original text should be expanded in preparation for filming. Your script should focus only on the parts of Goethe's poetic drama that you have read.

Prewriting   Begin by imagining what the scene would look like on a movie screen. List any special effects that you would expect to see, such as lighting, sound effects, and camera angles.

Drafting   Once you have a good idea of the adaptations that should be made, begin writing your screenplay. Format the script like the model below.

Model: Writing Stage Directions

[*Camera on Faust, deep in study. Candlelight on him and his books.*
Sound of knocking on door.]

Faust: Who's knocking? [*Camera close-up on Faust's face as he*
looks up.] Come in! *Now who wants to annoy me?*

Mephistopheles: [*Camera shot of Mephistopheles.*] It's I.

> Stage directions describe actions, camera angles, sound effects, lighting, and special effects.

Revising   Ask a classmate to read your finished screenplay to see if your stage directions are clear. Finally, keeping your classmate's comments in mind, revise your screenplay, and prepare a final copy.

W͟G Prentice Hall Writing and Grammar Connection: Platinum Level, Chapter 2, Section 2

❹ Extend Your Learning

Listening and Speaking With a partner, rehearse and present a **brief dialogue** based on the play. As you rehearse, keep the following elements consistent:

- the tone and mood of the work
- the character development
- the culture in which the dialogue is set

As you prepare your presentation, be sure to use your voice and facial expressions effectively. **[Group Activity]**

Research and Technology Using a video camera, make a **film** version of a segment from the play. Your short film might include unusual camera angles, sound effects, planned lighting, and other special effects.

 Go Online Research

For: An additional research activity
Visit: www.PHSchool.com
Web Code: etd-7701

from Faust ■ 865

---

❸ Writing Lesson

- To give students guidance in writing this script, give them the **Support for Writing Lesson**, p. 12 in *Unit 7 Resources*.

- Tell students that a film script is the written version of a film that the directors, actors, and other personnel follow as they make a film.

- Remind students that an effective film script has detailed stage directions. These directions guide the people involved in the film in how to act and deliver lines, hold the camera, and arrange and execute the lighting, sound, and other special effects.

W͟G **Writing and Grammar Platinum Level**

For support in teaching the Writing Lesson, use Chapter 2, Section 2.

❹ Listening and Speaking

- Have partners discuss the scene or scenes from the play on which they will base their dialogue. Students should understand the scene thoroughly before they develop the dialogue.

- Remind students to pay attention to the listed elements as they rehearse.

- Allow enough time for students to rehearse with partners before their presentations.

- Adapt the Speaking: Narrative Account rubric in *General Resources*, p. 88, to evaluate students' work.

- The **Support for Extend Your Learning** page (*Unit 7 Resources*, p. 13) provides guided note-taking opportunities to help students complete the Extend Your Learning activities.

Go Online Research Have students type in the Web Code for another research activity.

Assessment Resources

The following resources can be used to assess students' knowledge and skills.

Unit 7 Resources
    Selection Test A, pp. 15–17
    Selection Test B, pp. 18–20

General Resources
    Rubric for Speaking: Narrative Account,
      p. 88

Go Online Assessment Students may use the **Self-test** to prepare for **Selection Test A** or **Selection Test B.**

FA.3.04.8	Make connections between works, self, and related topics in argument.
LT.5.01.5	Analyze archetypal characters, themes, and settings in world literature.
GU.6.01.2	Analyze author's use of language to demonstrate understanding of expression.

Connections
British Literature

The Faust legend, in which a learned scholar sells his soul to the devil in exchange for worldly gain, is but one of the many legends of the devil that have appeared in literature. Have students reread the excerpts from Goethe's *Faust,* pp. 846–862, after they have read the excerpt from Marlowe's *The Tragical History of Doctor Faustus.* Ask students what similarities and differences they notice between the two plays.

Legends of the Devil

- Ask students to discuss whether they have ever read a story or seen a movie in which a character makes a bargain with the devil to get something he or she wants very much, such as "The Devil and Daniel Webster" by Stephen Vincent Benét. Then, guide a discussion in which students consider the similarities between these stories or movies.

- Point out to students that Marlowe's Doctor Faustus is a brilliant man with a gift for powerful and challenging speech. When he invokes the devil, however, he is out of his depth. He believes that giving up his soul will give him a godlike power to satisfy all of his wishes.

- **Ask** students to use what they already know about Goethe's Faust and Marlowe's Doctor Faustus to comment on the character of these two men. Are these men admirable? Are they ignorant? Are they arrogant?
Possible response: The determination and chutzpah of both men are admirable. However, both men are ultimately arrogant and foolish.

CONNECTIONS
British Literature

England
Legends of the Devil

Great literature often grows from legendary events and characters. Goethe's *Faust,* for example, was inspired by the folk legend of an actual person: Johann Faust (or Faustus), who lived in Wittenberg, Germany, from 1480 to 1540. According to the legend, Faust had sold his soul to the devil for youth, knowledge, and magical powers. Like the real person, Goethe's Faust willingly sacrifices his soul and risks eternal damnation to have all his wishes fulfilled.

Doomed Forever Christopher Marlowe's *The Tragical History of Doctor Faustus* was written in the sixteenth century, not long after the death of the real Johann Faust. Like Goethe's Faust, Marlowe's Doctor Faustus learns the awful majesty and inevitable doom of the bargain he makes with the devil.

The Tragical History of DOCTOR FAUSTUS

CHRISTOPHER MARLOWE

Enrichment

Marlowe's Dramas
Clifford Leech declared that Marlowe "is historically important for his achievement in stimulating the astonishingly rapid growth of drama in Elizabethan England. Before him, dramatic blank verse had been wooden: he made it triumphantly flexible. His *Tamburlaine* and his *Doctor Faustus* were the first truly tragic plays in English."

ACT I. SCENE III. IN A GROVE.

Enter FAUSTUS.

FAUSTUS: Now that the gloomy shadow of the earth,
 Longing to view Orion's drizzling look,
 Leaps from th' antarctic world unto the sky,
 And dims the welkin[1] with her pitchy breath,
5 Faustus, begin thine incantations,
 And try if devils will obey thy hest,
 Seeing thou hast pray'd and sacrific'd to them.
 Within this circle is Jehovah's name,
 Forward and backward anagrammatiz'd,[2]
10 The breviated names of holy saints,
 Figures of every adjunct to the heavens,
 And characters of signs and erring stars,
 By which the spirits are enforc'd to rise:
 Then fear not, Faustus, but be resolute,
15 And try the uttermost magic can perform.—
  Sint mihi dei Acherontis propitii! Valeat numen
 triplex Jehovoe! Ignei, aërii, aquatani spiritus, salvete!
 Orientis princeps Belzebub, inferni ardentis monarcha, et
 Demogorgon, propitiamus vos, ut appareat et surgat
 Mephistophilis: quid tu moraris? Per Jehovam, Gehennam,
20 *et consecratam aquam quam nunc spargo, signumque*
 crucis quod nunc facio, et per vota nostra, ipse nunc surgat
 nobis dicatus Mephistophilis![3]

Enter MEPHISTOPHILIS.

 I charge thee to return, and change thy shape;
 Thou art too ugly to attend on me:
25 Go, and return an old Franciscan friar;
 That holy shape becomes a devil best.

Exit MEPHISTOPHILIS.

---

1. **welkin** sky or vault of heaven.
2. **Jehovah's name . . . anagrammatiz'd** (an´ ə gram´ ə tizd) Jehovah, the holy name of God in the Old Testament, has been spelled backward and forward in a magical rite.
3. **Sint . . . Mephistophilis** May the gods of the underworld (Acheron) be kind to me! May the triple deity of Jehovah be gone! To the spirits of fire, air, and water, greetings. Prince of the east, Beelzebub, monarch of the fires below, and Demogorgon, we appeal to you, so that Mephistophilis may appear and rise: why do you delay? By Jehovah, hell, and the hallowed water which I now sprinkle, and the sign of the cross which I now make, and by our vows, let Mephistophilis himself now arise to serve us!

Thematic Connection
Why do you think the physical appearance of Mephistophilis is important to Faustus?

Connections: The Tragical History of Doctor Faustus ■ 867

Background
Latin
Tell students that the language used in lines 16–22 is Latin. Point out that Latin was a spoken language during the time of the Holy Roman Empire. After the fall of that empire, Latin slowly became a "dead" language, used only in certain academic and religious applications. As a medieval scholar, Faust would have been familiar with the language. His use of Latin as he addresses the gods of the underworld follows the tradition of magicians and sorcerers using mysterious-sounding words in their incantations. Such language seems to add to the solemnity of the moment.

Thematic Connection
Possible response: Doctor Faustus is concerned with all that is sensory, therefore, he wants to look upon something pleasing, or at least bearable.

Differentiated Instruction   Solutions for All Learners

Strategy for Special Needs Students
Students may have difficulty with Marlowe's style of language. Have partners read the selection, helping each other decode difficult words. If necessary, partners should read the play aloud. To increase student comprehension, have students stop frequently to paraphrase sections of the play and clarify the language with a partner.

Enrichment for Gifted/Talented Students
Have students create visual interpretations of this excerpt from Marlowe's play. Students should include in their artwork some kind of interpretation of both Mephistophilis and Faustus and something that indicates the setting of the play. Encourage students to think about how they will portray the characters' facial expressions and body language, as well as the theme of the selection. When students have finished their visual interpretations, ask volunteers to present and explain their work to the class.

I see there's virtue[4] in my heavenly words:
Who would not be proficient in this art?
How pliant is this Mephistophilis,
30   Full of obedience and humility!
Such is the force of magic and my spells:
Now, Faustus, thou art conjuror laureat,[5]
That canst command great Mephistophilis:
Quin regis Mephistophilis fratris imagine.[6]

Enter MEPHISTOPHILIS *(like a Franciscan friar).*

35   **MEPHISTOPHILIS:** Now, Faustus, what wouldst thou have me do?

FAUSTUS: I charge thee wait upon me whilst I live,
To do whatever Faustus shall command,
Be it to make the moon drop from her sphere,
Or the ocean to overwhelm the world.

40   **MEPHISTOPHILIS:** I am a servant to great Lucifer,
And may not follow thee without his leave:
No more than he commands must we perform.

FAUSTUS: Did not he charge thee to appear to me?

MEPHISTOPHILIS: No, I came hither of mine own accord.

45   **FAUSTUS:** Did not my conjuring speeches raise thee? speak.

MEPHISTOPHILIS: That was the cause, but yet *per accidens:*[7]
For, when we hear one rack the name of God,
Abjure[8] the Scriptures and his Savior Christ,
We fly, in hope to get his glorious soul;
50   Nor will we come, unless he use such means
Whereby he is in danger to be damn'd.
Therefore the shortest cut for conjuring
Is stoutly to abjure the Trinity,
And pray devoutly to the prince of Hell.

55   **FAUSTUS:** So Faustus hath
Already done; and holds this principle,
There is no chief but only Belzebub;[9]
To whom Faustus doth dedicate himself.

---

4. **virtue** power, as well as goodness.
5. **conjuror laureat** the greatest magician.
6. *Quin . . . imagine* Why do you not return, Mephistophilis, in the appearance of a friar?
7. *per accidens* by the immediate, not the ultimate, cause.
8. **abjure** (ab jŏŏr´) *v.* give up; renounce.
9. **Belzebub**, variant spelling of **Beelzebub** (bē el´ zə bub´) the chief devil, whose name means "god of flies" in Hebrew.

868 ■ Romanticism and Realism

Humanities

Mephistopheles Appears Before Faust,
by Eugène Delacroix

A great French Romantic painter, Delacroix (1798–1863) was inspired by literature, art, and music. This lithograph is one of seventeen he made to illustrate a French edition of Goethe's *Faust*. In making a lithograph, an artist carves an image on a flat surface such as a smooth stone or a metal plate. The surface is then inked (the image absorbs the ink and the blank area repels it) and used to print paper.

Use the following questions for discussion:

• Which elements in this scene are dramatic?
  Possible response: Faust's uplifted right hand and Mephistopheles's hand poised on his sword create drama. In addition, Delacroix's use of dark reds creates a feeling of tension and drama.

• This picture was painted more than two hundred years after Marlowe lived, and it was meant to illustrate Goethe's *Faust*. Does it go well with Marlowe's play? Explain.
  Possible response: The general mood of the painting goes with Marlowe's play, but the depiction of Mephistopheles does not. In Marlowe's play, Mephistophilis appears as a friar.

Connections: The Tragical History of Doctor Faustus ■ 869

Differentiated
Instruction   Solutions for All Learners

Vocabulary for Less Proficient Readers
Students may have difficulty with words such as *thou, art,* and *hither.* Have students find synonyms for these words and replace the words with the synonyms. For example, students can replace *thou* with *you, art* with *are,* and *hither* with *here.*

Vocabulary for English Learners
Students may find the language in this selection difficult, especially because much of it is obsolete. Help them by defining unfamiliar or difficult words and phrases. Have students write down unfamiliar words and their definitions to create a glossary of terms to use as a reference as they read.

Vocabulary for Advanced Readers
Have students create word webs or synonym lists based on words in this selection. For example, the word *abjure* might inspire a word web with the following words: *renounce, disown, disavow, deny, forswear, recant, retract.* Encourage students to note the connotations of each synonym.

Thematic Connection

Answer: Mephistophilis says that hell is the mental torment he feels because he is deprived of God's presence.

Legends of the Devil

- **Ask** students to read and paraphrase lines 83–86.
  Possible response: Mephistophilis, do you have such strong feelings because you're not in heaven? Watch me, and you'll learn to be stronger and more manly and be able to turn your back on those joys you can never have.
- **Ask** students to consider how these lines are similar to Faustus's speeches in lines 27–33 and in lines 36–39.
  Answer: In each speech, Faustus asserts his strength and importance.

60 This word "damnation" terrifies not him,
For he confounds hell in Elysium:
His ghost be with the old philosophers![10]
But, leaving these vain trifles of men's souls,
Tell me what is that Lucifer, thy Lord?

MEPHISTOPHILIS: Arch-regent and commander of all spirits.

65 **FAUSTUS:** Was not that Lucifer an angel once?

MEPHISTOPHILIS:
Yes, Faustus, and most dearly lov'd of God.

FAUSTUS:
How comes it, then, that he is prince of devils?

MEPHISTOPHILIS:
O, by aspiring pride and insolence;
For which God threw him from the face of heaven.

70 **FAUSTUS:** And what are you that live with Lucifer?

MEPHISTOPHILIS: Unhappy spirits that fell with Lucifer,
Conspir'd against our God with Lucifer,
And are for ever damn'd with Lucifer.

FAUSTUS: Where are you damn'd?

75 **MEPHISTOPHILIS:** In hell.

FAUSTUS: How comes it, then, that thou art out of hell?

MEPHISTOPHILIS: Why this is hell, nor am I out of it;
Think'st thou that I, who saw the face of God,
And tasted the eternal joys of heaven,
Am not tormented with ten thousand hells,
80 In being depriv'd of everlasting bliss?
O Faustus, leave these frivolous[11] demands,
Which strike a terror to my fainting soul!

FAUSTUS: What, is great Mephistophilis so passionate
For being deprivèd of the joys of heaven?
85 Learn thou of Faustus manly fortitude,
And scorn those joys thou never shalt possess.

---

10. For he . . . philosophers He thinks that hell is really Elysium. In Greek mythology, Elysium was the dwelling place of the virtuous after death. In Dante's *Inferno*, it is a pleasant abode for righteous pagans in a special part of hell.
11. frivolous (friv′ ə ləs) *adj.* of little value, trifling.

870 ■ *Romanticism and Realism*

Thematic Connection
What is Mephistophilis's definition of hell?

Enrichment

Where Is Hell?
Faustus wishes to think of hell as a particular place, but the truth is worse. Marlowe portrays hell as a state of mind; it exists in the terrible absence of God's love.

In the first book of John Milton's *Paradise Lost,* Satan is portrayed as haunted by the same incompleteness that bedevils Marlowe's Faustus. Satan, adopting something like Faustus's position, boasts that the hell that surrounds him is not going to destroy his inner fortitude:

The mind is its own place, and in itself
Can make a heav'n of hell, a hell of heav'n.
What matter where, if still I be the same. . . .
Later, when Satan flies to Paradise and realizes that he cannot enjoy it, he sees that what he said is true in a way he never meant. If the mind is its own "place," then there is no escape from oneself: "Which way I fly is hell; myself am hell."

Go bear these tidings to great Lucifer:
Seeing Faustus hath incurr'd eternal death
By desperate thoughts against Jove's deity,
90　Say, he surrenders up to him his soul,
So he will spare him four and twenty years,
Letting him live in all voluptuousness;[12]
Having thee ever to attend on me,
To give me whatsoever I shall ask,
95　To tell me whatsoever I demand,
To slay mine enemies, and aid my friends,
And always be obedient to my will.
Go and return to mighty Lucifer,
And meet me in my study at midnight,
100　And then resolve me of thy master's mind.

MEPHISTOPHILIS: I will, Faustus.

Exit MEPHISTOPHILIS.

FAUSTUS: Had I as many souls as there be stars,
I'd give them all for Mephistophilis.
By him I'll be great emperor of the world,
105　And make a bridge thorough the moving air,
To pass the ocean with a band of men;
I'll join the hills that bind the Afric[13] shore,
And make that country continent to Spain,
And both contributory to my crown:
110　The Emperor shall not live but by my leave,
Nor any potentate of Germany.
Now that I have obtain'd what I desire,
I'll live in speculation of this art,[14]
Till Mephistophilis return again.

Exit FAUSTUS.

---

12. **voluptuousness** (və lup′ choo əs nis) *n.* indulgence in sensual delights and pleasures.
13. **Afric** African.
14. **speculation of this art** deep study of this art.

Connecting British Literature

1. What universal human temptations are at the heart of both Faust and *The Tragical History of Doctor Faustus*?
2. **(a)** In what ways is Faustus in *The Tragical History of Doctor Faustus* like Faust in Goethe's *Faust*? **(b)** In what ways are these two characters different?
3. Which of these two characters do you find more sympathetic? Explain.

Connections: The Tragical History of Doctor Faustus ■ *871*

Christopher Marlowe (1564–1593)

Born the son of a shoemaker in Canterbury, England, Christopher Marlowe earned B.A. and M.A. degrees from Cambridge University and later moved to London, where he wrote a series of plays. Marlowe was unorthodox in his opinions and his life. His plays treat controversial topics, and he had a reputation for heretical opinions. In 1593, he was brought before a government council on charges of speaking against the doctrines of the Church of England. Before the case was resolved, however, he was killed in a tavern brawl.

Background
Christopher Marlowe

Marlowe's murder in a tavern brawl is still a disturbing case, more than three hundred years later. Marlowe had just been arrested by the Privy Council (a government body) and then, somewhat suspiciously, released. On the day he was killed, May 30, 1593, he had been drinking in a tavern with three dubious characters. Two of these companions were known spies and plotters. The third man claimed that he killed Marlowe in self-defense when Marlowe drew a knife.

Was Marlowe killed by agents of the Privy Council? This august body may have believed that as a former spy, Marlowe knew too much about them. Or was he killed by friends who feared that, under torture, he would implicate them in seditious plots? This fear was not unrealistic. The dramatist Thomas Kyd had just been tortured and had accused his friend Marlowe of treason.

ASSESS
Answers

Connecting British Literature

1. The universal human temptations that are at the heart of both *Faust* and *The Tragical History of Doctor Faustus* include the desire to be powerful, respected, and wealthy; and the opportunity and ability to live according to one's deepest wishes.

2. **(a)** Faustus in *The Tragical History of Doctor Faustus* is like Faust in Goethe's *Faust* in that he is willing to give up his soul in exchange for temporal rewards. **(b)** The two characters are different in that Doctor Faustus is interested in power and sensual pleasure, whereas Faust is obsessed with his quest for knowledge.

3. **Possible response:** Faust is more sympathetic because his desire for knowledge is more admirable than Doctor Faustus's desire for sensual pleasures.

NC **Standard Course of Study**

LT.5.01.2 Build knowledge of literary genres and explore how characteristics apply to literature of world cultures.

LT.5.01.3 Analyze literary devices and explain their effect on the work of world literature.

❶ Elements of Lyric Poetry

- Tell students that that they will study lyric poetry in Unit 7. Point out Shelley's quotation, and **ask** students how lyric poetry helps "lift the veil of hidden beauty. . . ." **Possible response:** The musical feeling and song-like structure of lyric poetry and the deep feelings that lyric poets convey can help readers appreciate beauty that they might otherwise overlook.

- Review the elements of lyric poetry with students. Clarify the information available on these pages, and suggest that students use these pages as a reference as they read lyric poetry in Unit 7 and in other units.

- Explain that devices such as onomatopoeia help bring out the full flavor of words. **Ask** students to name examples of onomatopoeia. **Possible responses:** Students may give the following examples: *buzz, purr, hiss, clang,* or *whirr.*

- Point out that many of the same elements of lyric poetry are found in other types of poetry.

Defining Lyric Poetry

Lyric poetry expresses the personal thoughts and feelings of a single speaker. Lyric poems, or lyrics, originated with the people of ancient Greece, who sang them to the accompaniment of a stringed instrument called a lyre. Although lyric poetry is no longer sung, such poems retain their musical feeling and a songlike structure. They are usually relatively short and focused on creating a single, unifying, emotional effect.

*P*OETRY LIFTS THE VEIL FROM THE HIDDEN BEAUTY OF THE WORLD. . . . —*Percy Bysshe Shelley*

❶ Elements of Lyric Poetry
Writers of lyric poetry employ a variety of poetic elements, including *sound devices, imagery,* and *figurative language* to achieve a desired effect.

Sound Devices

Sound devices use the sound of language to create a musical quality in poetry.

- Repetition: repeated use of sounds, words, phrases, or sentences. Repetition can be used to provide emphasis and to create a musical effect. The following popular devices rely on repetition:
  - Alliteration is the repetition of initial consonant sounds.
  - Consonance is the repetition of final consonant sounds.
  - Assonance is the repetition of similar vowel sounds.
- Rhyme: repetition of sounds at the ends of words
  - End rhyme is the most common type of rhyme. It occurs when rhyming words appear at the ends of lines.
- Onomatopoeia: use of words that imitate sounds

Some sound elements may be lost as poems are translated. For example, alliteration and onomatopoeia may not translate well from the original language. Most translators attempt to preserve the original rhyme scheme, or pattern of end rhymes, as they work.

Imagery

Imagery is descriptive language that appeals to the senses of sight, hearing, touch, taste, or smell. Some imagery is literal, but other imagery uses figurative language to evoke sensory impressions:
> *Example:* ". . . proud sunlight slants / Within a valley thick with beams like moss" —"The Sleeper in the Valley" by Rimbaud, page 889

872 ■ *Romanticism and Realism*

Most poems fall into one of three main categories:

- **Lyric poetry** expresses a speaker's personal thoughts and feelings.
- **Narrative poetry** tells a story.
- **Dramatic poetry** uses the techniques of drama to present the voice of one or more characters.

Differentiated Instruction   Solutions for All Learners

Vocabulary for Less Proficient Readers
Review the sound devices in this section. Have students make a flash card for each sound device. On the front of each card, have students write the name of the device; on the back of each card, have them write the definition of the device. Have students study in pairs to recognize the devices and give examples.

Vocabulary for English Learners
Review the sound devices in this section. Have students make flash cards for each sound device. Have them write an example of the device on one side of the card and the term on the back. Then, work with students, showing them the example and having them respond with the correct sound device.

Figurative Language

Figurative language is language that is used imaginatively rather than literally, and it contains one or more figures of speech—expressions not meant to be taken literally Figurative language is often used to make unexpected comparisons or to change the usual meanings of words. Common figures of speech include the following:

- A simile compares two apparently unlike things by using *like* or *as*.
    Example: "O pale Ophelia! fair as snow!"
    — "Ophelia" by Rimbaud, page 890

- A metaphor compares two apparently unlike things without using *like* or *as*.
    Example: "the voice of mad seas. . . Bruised your child's heart."
    — "Ophelia" by Rimbaud, page 890

- Personification gives human traits to something nonhuman.
    Example: "Violins complain. They sob and moan."
    — "Autumn Song" by Verlaine, page 894

- An oxymoron juxtaposes two opposite or contradictory words that together reveal an interesting truth.
    Example: "All my sour-sweet days / I will lament with love."
    — "Bittersweet" by George Herbert

❷ Romanticism and Lyric Poetry

Romanticism was a literary and artistic movement of the late eighteenth century and early nineteenth centuries. Poets of the Romantic Movement rebelled against the rationality, logic, and objectivity that earlier writers prized. The Romantics embraced new values in their poetry, emphasizing personal, emotional, and imaginative aspects of experience. The lyric poem was the perfect vehicle for this new breed of poet.

Romantic poetry tends to celebrate the following themes:

- emotion
- individuality
- imagination
- untamed nature
- the exotic
- freedom

❸ Strategies for Reading Lyric Poetry

Use these strategies as you read lyric poetry.
Use Your Senses Imagery appeals to your senses. As you read lyric poetry, experience the images with all five senses. For example, as you read "Autumn Song," listen for the violins' "sob and moan." Note other examples of imagery as you read.
Read Verse for Meaning As you read, focus on sentences, not line breaks. Follow the punctuation, pausing at commas and stopping at periods.

Focus on Literary Forms: Lyric Poetry ■ 873

Standard Course of Study

Goal 1: WRITTEN LANGUAGE

WL.1.03.4 Demonstrate comprehension of main idea and supporting details in personal reflection.

WL.1.03.11 Identify and analyze elements of expressive environment in personal reflection.

Goal 2: INFORMATIONAL READING

IR.2.03.2 Prioritize and organize information to construct an explanation to answer a question.

Goal 5: LITERATURE

LT.5.01.2 Build knowledge of literary genres, and explore how characteristics apply to literature of world cultures.

LT.5.03.2 Analyze text structure and components and evaluate impact.

Step-by-Step Teaching Guide	Pacing Guide
PRETEACH	
• Administer Vocabulary and Reading Warm-ups as necessary.	5 min.
• Engage students' interest with the motivation activity.	5 min.
• Read and discuss author and background features. **FT**	10 min.
• Introduce the Literary Analysis Skill: Lyric Poetry. **FT**	5 min.
• Introduce the Reading Strategy: Reading Between the Lines. **FT**	
• Prepare students to read by teaching the selection vocabulary. **FT**	10 min.
TEACH	
• Informally monitor comprehension while students read independently or in groups. **FT**	30 min.
• Monitor students' comprehension with the Reading Check notes.	as students read
• Reinforce vocabulary with Vocabulary Builder notes.	as students read
• Develop students' understanding of lyric poetry with the Literary Analysis annotations. **FT**	5 min.
• Develop students' ability to read between the lines with the Reading Strategy annotations. **FT**	5 min.
ASSESS/EXTEND	
• Assess students' comprehension and mastery of the Literary Analysis and Reading Strategy by having them answer the Apply the Skills questions. **FT**	15 min.
• Have students complete the Vocabulary Development Lesson and the Grammar and Style Lesson. **FT**	15 min.
• Apply students' ability to clarify meaning by using the Writing Lesson. **FT**	45 min. or homework
• Apply students' understanding by using one or more of the Extend Your Learning activities.	20–90 min. or homework
• Administer Selection Test A or Selection Test B. **FT**	15 min.

Resources

Print
Unit 7 Resources

Transparency
Graphic Organizer Transparencies

Print
Reader's Notebook [L2]

Reader's Notebook: Adapted Version [L1]

Reader's Notebook: English Learner's Version [EL]

Unit 7 Resources

Technology
Listening to Literature Audio CDs [L2, EL]

Print
Unit 7 Resources

General Resources

Technology
Go Online: Research **[L3]**

Go Online: Self-test **[L3]**

ExamView®, Test Bank **[L3]**

Choosing Resources for Differentiated Instruction

[L1] Special Needs Students

[L2] Below-Level Students

[L3] All Students

[L4] Advanced Students

[EL] English Learners

For Vocabulary and Reading Warm-ups and for Selection Tests, **A** signifies "less challenging" and **B** "more challenging." For Graphic Organizer transparencies, **A** signifies "not filled in" and **B** "filled in."

FT Fast Track Instruction: To move the lesson more quickly, use the strategies and activities identified with **FT**.

Scaffolding for Less Proficient and Advanced Students

The leveled Critical Thinking questions after selections progress in the levels of thinking required to answer them. To address the needs of your different students, you may use the (a) level questions for your less proficient students and the (b) level questions with your on-level and advanced students. The occasional (c) level questions are appropriate for your advanced students.

PRENTICE HALL

TeacherEXPRESS™ Use this complete
Plan · Teach · Assess suite of powerful
teaching tools to make lesson planning and testing quicker and easier.

PRENTICE HALL

StudentEXPRESS™ Use the interactive
Learn · Study · Succeed textbook (online
and on CD-ROM) to make selections and activities come alive with audio and video support and interactive questions.

 For: Information about Lexiles
Professional **Visit:** www.PHSchool.com
Development **Web Code:** eue-1111

Motivation

Tell students that today's pop songs have their roots in lyric poetry, and enumerate the fundamental similarities between pop songs and early lyric poems: Both are verbal expressions of personal thoughts and feelings, and both are accompanied by music. Pop songs are often written out of romantic love for another person or as a tribute to a person or a place. Similarly, these poems by Pushkin and Heine express emotions directed toward people and places.

❶ Background

More About the Authors

Alexander Pushkin's experiences in exile may seem curious to modern students. For three years, he lived in the city of Kishinyov (also spelled *Kishinev*), near the Romanian border, under the supervision of a kindly general. When he was transferred to a post in Odessa, he paid too much attention to his new superior's wife. He was then exiled to his own home, the family estate near Pskov. Pushkin's father was supposed to act as his supervisor this time, but the two quarreled so much that his father moved away, taking the rest of the family with him.

Throughout his life, Heinrich Heine felt like an outsider. According to the critic S. S. Prawer, Heine considered himself "a Jew among Germans, a German among Frenchmen, a Hellene [one loyal to classical Greek ideals] among Jews, a rebel among the bourgeois, and a conservative among revolutionaries."

Geography Note

Draw students' attention to the map on this page. Remind them that geography helped define Pushkin and Heine as outsiders. Born in the urban center of Moscow, Russia, Pushkin was exiled to the provinces. Heine, born in Düsseldorf, Germany, was also banished for political reasons and lived as a German exile in Paris, France.

Build Skills [Poems]

❶ I Have Visited Again • The Lorelei • The Lotus Flower

Alexander Pushkin
(1799–1837)

Russian author Alexander Pushkin was born in Moscow into an aristocratic family. As a youth, he led a life of relative privilege and wrote with a skill that would hint at his eventual fame. While working in government service in St. Petersburg, he aroused suspicion by associating with political rebels and writing poems advocating government changes. In 1820, the government acted upon its suspicions by reappointing Pushkin to a post in a remote province in southern Russia. During the five years Pushkin spent there, he enhanced his reputation as a writer and began working on his masterpiece, the verse novel *Yevgeny Onegin* (1833). Unfortunately, his unrestrained and sometimes violent behavior resulted in his dismissal from civil service in 1824 and banishment to his family's estate.

Though isolated and unhappy on the estate, Pushkin channeled most of his energy into his writing. He spent much of his time interacting with the peasants who lived on the estate, learning about their lifestyles and incorporating their legends and folklore into a number of his finest poems.

Acts of Rebellion Pushkin was allowed to return to Moscow in 1826. Yet again, he became the object of political distrust and was eventually put under police surveillance. Despite limited freedoms, Pushkin produced some of his finest works during this time, including his collection of prose tales *Tales of the Late I.P. Belkin* (1831).

After marrying Natalya Goncharova in 1831, Pushkin grudgingly returned to government service. In a final act of rebellion, Pushkin entered into a duel that cost him his life. Despite the pointless ending of his brief life, Pushkin is now regarded as the finest poet Russia has ever produced.

Heinrich Heine
(1797–1856)

German poet Heinrich Heine [hīn´ rik hī´ nə] wrote brilliant love poems that have been set to music by various composers. Yet he was also a gifted satirist and political writer, and his fierce attacks on repression and prejudice made him a highly controversial figure.

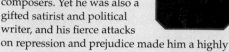

Born and raised in Düsseldorf, Heine earned a law degree in 1825 but abandoned it to pursue a career as a writer. In 1827, he gained prominence as a poet with *The Book of Songs* (1827), a collection regarded by many as his finest work. Influenced by the Romantic poets, these love poems were inspired by Heine's unrequited attachment to his cousin, Amalie.

A Controversial Poet Heine moved to Paris in 1831, and from this vantage point he wrote scathing criticisms of the political and social situation in Germany. After his views were published in *The Romantic School* (1833–1835) and "On the History of Religion and Philosophy in Germany" (1834–1835), his popularity was soon overshadowed by outrage. The German government banned all his books and made it clear that he was no longer welcome in his homeland.

Even after his death in 1856, Heine remained controversial. Riots broke out in several German cities when attempts were made to erect monuments in his honor, and when the Nazis assumed power in the 1930s, many of his works were suppressed. After World War II, Heine became a controversial figure in other countries, including the United States, because his political beliefs resembled Marxism. Despite such controversy, Heine is still generally regarded as one of the finest writers of the nineteenth century.

874 ■ Romanticism and Realism

Preview

Connecting to the Literature

Elements of nature, such as trees, rivers, flowers, and the night sky, often have an emotional effect on us. As you read, think about how you would feel if you were standing with the speaker, looking at the same sights.

❷ Literary Analysis

Lyric Poetry

Lyric poetry, or lyrics, are brief poems that express a speaker's personal thoughts and feelings. Many early lyrics were written to be sung to the accompaniment of a lyre, which looks much like a small, modern-day harp. Most of these poems still tend to be melodic, like songs, and generally focus on producing a single, unified effect. In these lines from "The Lotus Flower," notice the melancholy effect of the words.

> With sunken head and sadly
> She dreamily waits for the night.

As you read these poems, use a chart like the one shown to record the words and phrases that contribute to a single unifying effect.

Comparing Literary Works

Each of these poems uses **symbols** to achieve a desired effect. A symbol is a person, place, or object that has its own meaning but also suggests a larger or secondary meaning. For example, in "I Have Visited Again," the growing trees symbolize the passing of time and inspire the speaker to reflect on his mortality. As you read, compare the way each speaker uses symbols to express observations and emotions.

❸ Reading Strategy

Reading Between the Lines

Reading between the lines reveals different or deeper meanings in poems, meanings that clarify a speaker's words, a character's actions, and even a poem's relevance to readers of all backgrounds. To read between the lines:

- Make inferences, or educated guesses, about the meanings of whole lines or passages.
- Find clues about the characters, setting, mood, and symbolism.
- Examine specific word choices, including words in the title.

Vocabulary Builder

painstakingly (pānz′ tāk iŋ lē) *adv.* using great diligence or care (p. 876)

fathomless (fa*th*′ əm les) *adj.* immeasurably deep (p. 877)

ancestral (an ses′ trəl) *adj.* inherited, as from an ancestor (p. 877)

morose (mə rōs′) *adj.* gloomy; in a bad or sullen mood (p. 878)

resplendent (ri splen′ dənt) *adj.* brightly shining; dazzling (p. 880)

mutely (myo͞ot′ lē) *adv.* silently; without the capacity to speak (p. 880)

I Have Visited Again / The Lorelei / The Lotus Flower ■ 875

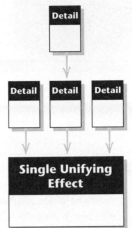

Standard Course of Study

- Identify and analyze elements of expressive environment in personal reflections. (WL.1.03.11)
- Prioritize and organize information to construct an explanation to answer a question. (IR.2.03.2)

❷ Literary Analysis
Lyric Poetry

- Read the definition of lyric poetry together with the class. If students have difficulty with the definition, point out that the term as it is used today is very broad. Almost any poem that is fairly short and is not a narrative or an exercise in wit, such as a limerick, can be classified as a lyric. Have students keep this broad definition in mind as they name lyric poems they have read in previous literature courses.

- After discussing the Literary Analysis instruction, have students preview the selections for words that evoke emotion, such as *embrace, scarred,* and *trembles.* Then, explain the use of the graphic organizer. Give students a copy of **Literary Analysis Graphic Organizer A**, p. 155 in *Graphic Organizer Transparencies.* Have them use it to identify words and phrases that create a single, unifying effect in the poems they read.

❸ Reading Strategy
Reading Between the Lines

- Tell students that reading a poem can be like solving a mystery. Few poets simply state outright what they want the reader to know. Instead, they give the reader details about characters, setting, and mood. When a reader puts these details together, he or she is able to read between the lines and discover the poem's deeper meaning.

- Tell students to focus on specific words, lines, and passages that reveal the poems' deeper meanings.

Vocabulary Builder

- Pronounce each vocabulary word for students, and read the definitions as a class. Have students identify any words with which they are already familiar.

Differentiated Instruction   Solutions for All Learners

Support for Special Needs Students

Have students complete the **Preview** and **Build Skills** pages for these selections in the *Reader's Notebook: Adapted Version.* These pages provide a selection summary, an abbreviated presentation of the reading and literary skills, and the graphic organizer on the **Build Skills** page in the student book.

Support for Less Proficient Readers

Have students complete the **Preview** and **Build Skills** pages for these selections in the *Reader's Notebook.* These pages provide a selection summary, an abbreviated presentation of the reading and literary skills, and the graphic organizer on the **Build Skills** page in the student book.

Support for English Learners

Have students complete the **Preview** and **Build Skills** pages for these selections in the *Reader's Notebook: English Learner's Version.* These pages provide a selection summary, an abbreviated presentation of the reading and literary skills, additional contextual vocabulary, and the graphic organizer on the **Build Skills** page in the student book.

Facilitate Understanding

Invite students to share their experiences of leaving a familiar place, such as moving to a new city or changing schools. Ask them to imagine how it would feel to revisit a place where they had spent some time in the past. How might the place have changed? How might they react to the changes?

❶ About the Selection

In "I Have Visited Again," the speaker recounts his return to his family home after being away for ten years. As he remembers people and events from the past, he compares his memories to the current appearance of the land.

❷ Background
Russian Writers

Critic Edmund Wilson called Pushkin the "great fountainhead of Russian literature," the writer from whom Turgenev, Chekhov, Tolstoy, Dostoevsky "in more or less degree derive."

❸ Literary Analysis
Lyric Poetry

- As students read the bracketed passage, have them consider what the speaker is saying about the passage of time.
  Answer: The speaker is saying that the changes that occurred during the last ten years seem immaterial now that he has returned home.

- **Ask** students to respond to the Literary Analysis item: Explain how Pushkin achieves a single, unifying effect in this stanza.
  Answer: Pushkin refers to the passage of time repeatedly in such phrases as "two / Unnoticed, exiled years," "Ten years have passed," and "only yesterday."

I Have Visited. Again

Alexander Pushkin
translated by **D.M. Thomas**

❷ Background
Initially, Alexander Pushkin found the inspiration to write in the politics of his homeland. His rebellious writings, as well as his unruly behavior, resulted in banishment to his family estate. Such a personality seems distantly related to the speaker of the gentle words and images in "I Have Visited Again." In this poem, the speaker revisits the estate to find that time and nature have hardly stood still in the intervening years.

> . . . I have visited again
> That corner of the earth where I spent two
> Unnoticed, exiled years. Ten years have passed
> Since then, and many things have changed for me,
> 5 And I have changed too, obedient to life's law—
> But now that I am here again, the past
> Has flown out eagerly to embrace me, claim me,
> And it seems that only yesterday I wandered
> Within these groves.
>
>   Here is the cottage, sadly
> 10 Declined now, where I lived with my poor old nurse.
> She is no more. No more behind the wall
> Do I hear her heavy footsteps as she moved
> Slowly, <u>painstakingly</u> about her tasks.

Literary Analysis
Lyric Poetry Explain how Pushkin achieves a single, unifying effect in this stanza.

Vocabulary Builder
painstakingly (pānz′ tāk iŋ lē) *adv.* using great diligence or care

876 ■ *Romanticism and Realism*

Differentiated
Instruction   Solutions for All Learners

Accessibility at a Glance

	I Have Visited Again	The Lorelei	The Lotus Flower
Language	Syntax: long sentences with embedded clauses	Words conveying strong emotions	Symbolic words for personification of nature
Concept Level	Accessible (Effects of time's passing)	Accessible (Lure of the unattainable)	Accessible (Sorrows of unrequited love)
Literary Merit	Classic lyric poem of nostalgia	Classic lyric poem about a famous legend	Classic lyric poem personifying a flower and the moon
Lexile	NP	NP	NP
Overall Rating	Average	Average	Average

Here are the wooded slopes where often I
15 Sat motionless, and looked down at the lake,
Recalling other shores and other waves . . .
It gleams between golden cornfields and green meadows,
A wide expanse; across its <u>fathomless</u> waters
A fisherman passes, dragging an ancient net.
20 Along the shelving banks, hamlets are scattered
—Behind them the mill, so crooked it can scarcely
Make its sails turn in the wind . . .

On the bounds
Of my <u>ancestral</u> acres, at the spot
Where a road, scarred by many rainfalls, climbs
25 The hill, three pine-trees stand—one by itself,
The others close together. When I rode
On horseback past them in the moonlit night,
The friendly rustling murmur of their crowns
Would welcome me. Now, I have ridden out
30 Upon that road, and seen those trees again.

8 ▼ **Critical Viewing** Which details in this landscape could serve to illustrate
Pushkin's poem? **[Support]**

Lake Scene in France, Josephine Bowes, The Bowes Museum, Barnard Castle, County Durham, UK

I Have Visited Again ■ 877

Apply

- Read aloud the bracketed line.

- **Ask:** To what universal human desire does the poem's final line appeal?
Possible response: The poem's final line appeals to the desire to be remembered after death.

ASSESS

Answers

1. **Possible response:** The poem conveys feelings of melancholy with its use of words such as *declined, painstakingly, crooked, scarred, solitary,* and *morose.* Or the poem may create a feeling of hope with words such as *eagerly, embrace, golden, green, friendly, welcome,* and *children.*

2. (a) Four familiar landmarks that have changed are the cottage, the mill, the road, and the old trees. (b) The speaker, like these landmarks, has aged.

3. (a) The speaker would sit on the slopes and think of "other shores and other waves." (b) By "other shores," the speaker means other places he has visited. (c) **Possible response:** The speaker might have yearned to be in another place because the estate, as the location of his exile, was a place of isolation.

4. (a) The "unknown tribe of pine-trees" grows around the aging roots of the older pine trees. (b) In the future, the new pines will shield the older trees "from the gaze / Of passers-by." These young trees may also provide someone comfort, as the older trees have provided the speaker comfort. (c) The new pines symbolize the continuity of life.

5. **Possible response:** Most readers will probably agree with Thomas Wolfe's comment. Often when people do return home, they are made instantly aware of how both they and the environments have changed.

⌐Go ●nline For additional information
└**Author Link** about Alexander Pushkin, have students type in the Web Code, then select *P* from the alphabet, and then select Alexander Pushkin.

878

They have remained the same, make the same murmur—
But round their ageing roots, where all before
Was barren, naked, a thicket of young pines
Has sprouted; like green children round the shadows
35 Of the two neighboring pines. But in the distance
Their solitary comrade stands, <u>morose</u>,
Like some old bachelor, and round its roots
All is barren as before.

　　　　　　　　　　I greet you, young
And unknown tribe of pine-trees! I'll not see
40 Your mighty upward thrust of years to come
When you will overtop these friends of mine
And shield their ancient summits from the gaze
Of passers-by. But may my grandson hear
Your welcome murmur when, returning home
45 From lively company, and filled with gay
And pleasant thoughts, he passes you in the night,
❾ | And thinks perhaps of me . . .

Critical Reading

1. **Respond:** What single effect does the entire poem convey to you? Identify words that Pushkin used to evoke this feeling.

2. **(a) Recall:** Identify four familiar landmarks in the poem that have changed over the years. **(b) Infer:** How has the speaker changed in a similar fashion?

3. **(a) Recall:** In stanza three, what thoughts occupied the speaker while he looked down at the lake? **(b) Infer:** What does the speaker mean by "other shores"? **(c) Hypothesize:** Why might the speaker have yearned to be in another place?

4. **(a) Recall:** Where does the "unknown tribe of pine-trees" grow? **(b) Speculate:** What role will those pines play in the future? **(c) Interpret:** What do those pines symbolize?

5. **Apply:** Novelist Thomas Wolfe commented on how our lives change by saying that we "can't go home again," a theme shared by "I Have Visited Again." Do you agree or disagree with such a claim? Explain your answer.

⌐Go ●nline
└**Author Link**
For: More about
　Alexander Pushkin
Visit: www.PHSchool.com
Web Code: ete-9702

Enrichment

Pushkin and Mozart
The distinguished American critic Edmund Wilson wrote: "The Russians are in the habit of comparing Pushkin with Mozart, and this is perhaps the nearest one can come to a simple comparison. Pushkin does, through both his career and his qualities, somewhat recall Mozart: He is able to express through an art that is felicitous and formal a feeling that is passionate and exquisite; he has a wide range of moods and emotions, yet he handles them all with precision. . . ."

The Lorelei

Heinrich Heine ❿
translated by Aaron Kramer

Background The lorelei is a legendary sea nymph whose irresistible singing from the rocks in the Rhine River lured unsuspecting sailors to shipwrecks. Both this poem and "The Lotus Flower" seem to be inspired by Heine's deep attachment to his cousin Amalie. Fearing her father's reaction, Amalie did not return Heine's affection. While lyric poetry often explores the joys of love, "The Lorelei" and "The Lotus Flower" focus on love's difficulties.

> I cannot explain the sadness
> That's fallen on my breast.
> An old, old fable haunts me,
> And will not let me rest.
>
> 5 The air grows cool in the twilight,
> And softly the Rhine[1] flows on;
> The peak of a mountain sparkles
> Beneath the setting sun.
>
> More lovely than a vision,
> 10 A girl sits high up there;
> Her golden jewelry glistens,
> She combs her golden hair.
>
> With a comb of gold she combs it,
> And sings an evensong;
> 15 The wonderful melody reaches
> A boat, as it sails along.
>
> The boatman hears, with an anguish
> More wild than was ever known;
> He's blind to the rocks around him;
> 20 His eyes are for her alone.
>
> —At last the waves devoured
> The boat, and the boatman's cry;
> And this she did with her singing,
> The golden Lorelei.

❶

Literary Analysis
Lyric Poetry Which words convey strong emotions in the poem?

1. **Rhine** (rīn) river in western Europe.

The Lorelei ■ 879

⓬ **About the Selection**

The lotus flower is bothered by the light of the sun, so she waits for the night. When the "moon appears as her wooer," the lotus flower wakes and opens up to him. As the lotus flower gazes at the moon, she cries and "trembles with love and the sorrows of love."

⓭ **Reading Strategy**

Reading Between the Lines

• Read aloud the first stanza.

• **Ask** the Reading Strategy question: What kind of person does Heine describe as "the sun"?
Answer: The sun has "resplendent light," so the sun may represent an outgoing, joyous personality.

ASSESS

Answers

1. **Possible response:** The lorelei is beautiful, with golden jewelry, golden hair, a golden comb, and a lovely singing voice. The lorelei's beauty, voice, and unattainable quality are alluring and haunting.

2. (a) The boatman is drawn to the lorelei so strongly that he becomes agitated. (b) Heine believed that his uncle's daughter lured him as the lorelei lured sailors; like the lorelei, she was unattainable.

3. (a) The words *troubled, sunken head, sadly, dreamily waits, wakes, kindly uncovers, sweetly flowering face, mutely, gazes, weeps, exhales,* and *trembles* give human traits to the lotus flower; the words *wooer* and *fond embrace* give human traits to the moon. (b) The moon might symbolize a secret lover. (c) **Possible response:** On a symbolic level, the lotus flower sees her wooer only at night because the moon might represent a forbidden love.

4. (a) The speaker links the ideas of love and sorrow. (b) The speaker is referring to the pain of unrequited or forbidden love.

5. **Possible response:** The legend could apply to any situation in which a person feels a strong desire that turns out to be his or her ruin.

The Lotus Flower

Heinrich Heine
translated by Edgar Alfred Bowring

⓭

The lotus flower is troubled
    At the sun's <u>resplendent</u> light;
With sunken head and sadly
    She dreamily waits for the night.

5 The moon appears as her wooer,
    She wakes at his fond embrace;
For him she kindly uncovers
    Her sweetly flowering face.

She blooms and glows and glistens,
10   And <u>mutely</u> gazes above;
She weeps and exhales and trembles
    With love and the sorrows of love.

Critical Reading

1. **Respond:** How do you envision the lorelei in Heine's "The Lorelei"? Explain. What is it about this vision that would seem so alluring and haunting to the boatman?

2. **(a) Recall:** What effect does the lorelei have on the boatman?
(b) Interpret: What similarities do you see between the legend of the lorelei and Heine's situation with his uncle's daughter?

3. **(a) Recall:** What words does the speaker use in "The Lotus Flower" to give human traits to both the lotus flower and the moon?
(b) Interpret: Whom might the moon symbolize? **(c) Apply:** Why does the lotus flower see her wooer only at night?

4. **(a) Recall:** In "The Lotus Flower," what two ideas does the speaker link in the last line? **(b) Infer:** What does the speaker mean when he refers to the "sorrows of love"?

5. **Apply:** To what types of situations in real life could you relate the legend of the lorelei? Explain your answer.

880 ■ *Romanticism and Realism*

Vocabulary Builder

resplendent (ri splen′ dent) *adj.* brightly shining; dazzling

Reading Strategy
Reading Between the Lines What kind of person does Heine describe as "the sun"?

Vocabulary Builder

mutely (myσ̄ot′ lē) *adv.* silently; without capacity to speak

Go Online
Author Link
For: More about Heinrich Heine
Visit: www.PHSchool.com
Web Code: ete-9703

Go Online For additional information about
Author Link Heinrich Heine, have students type in the Web Code, then select *H* from the alphabet, and then select Heinrich Heine.

Apply the Skills

I Have Visited Again • *The Lorelei* • *The Lotus Flower*

Literary Analysis

Lyric Poetry

1. Which specific emotions expressed in "I Have Visited Again" qualify it as a **lyric poem**?

2. **(a)** What words in "The Lorelei" refer to sounds? **(b)** How do these words reflect the original purpose of many lyric poems?

3. What is the single effect produced in "The Lotus Flower"?

Comparing Literary Works

4. **(a)** Complete a chart like the one shown to analyze the **symbols** in "I Have Visited Again." Begin by listing persons, places, or objects and the words the speaker uses to describe them. **(b)** In the last column, use the speaker's description to determine what the symbols mean.

Person, Place or Object	Words Describing the Image	Symbolic Meaning of the Image

5. In "The Lorelei," the girl is wearing golden jewelry, and she combs her "golden hair" with a "comb of gold." **(a)** What does the girl have in common with gold? **(b)** What does this suggest about what the girl symbolizes?

Reading Strategy

Reading Between the Lines

6. By **reading between the lines**, what deeper understanding of the speaker can you discover in the fifth stanza of "I Have Visited Again"?

7. **(a)** According to the first stanza of "The Lorelei," what haunts the speaker? **(b)** What connection might exist between the sadness he feels and the lorelei?

Extend Understanding

8. **Science Connection:** In what ways are modern ships equipped to prevent the kinds of shipwrecks described in "The Lorelei"?

QuickReview

Lyric poems are brief poems that express a speaker's personal thoughts and feelings and create a unified effect.

A **symbol** is a person, place, or object that stands for or represents something else.

When you **read between the lines**, you use clues in the text to discover deeper meaning in literature.

Go Online
Assessment
For: Self-test
Visit: www.PHSchool.com
Web Code: eta-6702

I Have Visited Again / The Lorelei / The Lotus Flower ■ 881

Go Online Students may use the **Self-test** to **Assessment** prepare for **Selection Test A** or **Selection Test B.**

Answers

1. The emotions expressed in "I Have Visited Again" that qualify it as a lyric poem include sorrow, nostalgia, and hope.

2. (a) The words in "The Lorelei" that refer to sounds are *sings, evensong, melody, hears, cry,* and *singing.* (b) Because ancient lyric poems were devised to be sung to the accompaniment of a lyre, the musicality of these words would lend themselves to singing.

3. The single effect produced in "The Lotus Flower" is a feeling of dreamy, sorrowful romance.

4. **Possible response: Person, Place, or Object:** cottage; **Words Describing the Image:** "sadly / Declined"; **Symbolic Meaning of the Image:** the toll time takes; **Person, Place, or Object:** nurse; **Words Describing the Image:** "poor," "old," "moved slowly," "painstakingly"; **Symbolic Meaning of the Image:** the toll time takes; **Person, Place, or Object:** mill; **Words Describing the Image:** "so crooked it can scarcely / Make its sails turn"; **Symbolic Meaning of the Image:** the toll time takes; **Person, Place, or Object:** young pines; **Words Describing the Image:** "like green children"; **Symbolic Meaning of the Image:** the continuity of life.

5. (a) Like gold, the girl is beautiful and costly. (b) These similarities suggest that the girl symbolizes anything in life that is alluring, costly, and out of reach.

6. The predictions about the trees and grandchild suggest that the speaker thinks being part of a family is a happier, friendlier, and more productive way of life than remaining solitary, like the lone pine tree.

7. (a) An old fable haunts the speaker in "The Lorelei." (b) The sadness the speaker feels and the legend of the lorelei might be connected in that the speaker's sadness, like that of the boatman, may be caused by a longing for something unattainable.

8. Modern ships have the means to track weather and avoid bad storms; they have sonar to detect underwater hazards; they have global positioning technology to stay precisely on course.

881

❶ Vocabulary Lesson

Word Analysis: Anglo-Saxon Suffix -less

1. fathomless   3. pitiless
2. guileless   4. sunless

Spelling Strategy

1. scarcely   3. tuneful
2. lovely

Vocabulary Builder

1. mutely   4. fathomless
2. ancestral   5. morose
3. painstakingly 6. resplendent

❷ Grammar and Style Lesson

1. They (trees)
2. its (pine)
3. They (bracelet, necklace)
4. him (boatman)
5. It (boat)

Writing Application

Possible response: The <u>mountains</u> rise to the west; <u>they</u> are dusted with white. At the foot of the mountains runs a <u>fence</u>, and around <u>it</u> grow yellow asters. The yellow <u>asters</u> sway in the breeze; <u>they</u> dance left and then right. In the wind, the wire <u>fence</u> squeaks; <u>its</u> sound keeps a beat for the dancing asters. The <u>horses</u> in the pasture at the base of the mountain stomp on the ground; <u>they</u> keep time with nature's song, too.

𝒲 Writing and Grammar
Platinum Level

For support in teaching the Grammar and Style Lesson, use Chapter 24, Section 2.

Build Language Skills

❶ Vocabulary Lesson

Word Analysis: Anglo-Saxon Suffix -less

The suffix -less, which means "without," "not able to," or "not able to be," can be added to many nouns to form an adjective. Use your understanding of -less to write the word that means the same as each of the following phrases.

1. not able to be fathomed
2. without guile
3. without pity
4. without sun

Spelling Strategy

When adding a suffix that begins with a consonant to a word that ends with a silent e, retain the silent e. On a separate piece of paper, add -ly or -ful to each of the following words.

1. scarce   2. love   3. tune

Vocabulary Builder: Clarify Word Meaning

Select the word from the vocabulary list on page 875 that matches or best relates to each description below.

1. How you might respond to a surprise that left you speechless
2. The land from which your great-grandparents came
3. The way you might walk across a rocky field in the dark
4. The deepest lake ever discovered
5. A very sad child
6. A dazzling display of gold

❷ Grammar and Style Lesson

Pronouns and Antecedents

A **pronoun** must agree with its **antecedent**—the word to which it refers—in the following ways:

- in number—singular or plural
- in gender—masculine or feminine

> ANTECEDENT   PRONOUN
> . . . my poor old *nurse*. *She* is no more.
> (**feminine, singular**)

Practice For each item that follows, choose the correct pronoun. Then, identify its antecedent.

1. I saw those trees again. (It, They) remained the same.
2. The solitary pine stands alone, and around (its, their) roots are no young pines.
3. A lovely girl wore a gold bracelet and necklace. (It, They) sparkled in the twilight.
4. The boatman hears the lorelei singing. The song lures (him, her) to the rocks.
5. At last the waves devoured the boat. (It, They) sank beneath the surface of the river.

Writing Application Write five sentences describing scenes in nature. In each, use a pronoun that correctly matches its antecedent.

𝒲 *Prentice Hall Writing and Grammar Connection: Platinum Level, Chapter 24, Section 2*

Assessment Practice

Recognize Forms of Propaganda   (For more practice, see *Test Preparation Workbook*, p. 38.)

Many tests require students to recognize forms of rhetorical manipulation. Use the following item to practice the skill.

In the aftermath of World War II, Heinrich Heine became a controversial figure in Europe and in the United States because of the similarities of his political beliefs to Marxism. Certain literary critics were perhaps blinded by the political prejudices of the day. The fact remains that Heine is one of the finest writers of the nineteenth century.

Which word in the passage is used to sway readers?

A *aftermath*

B *controversial*

C *similarities*

D *blinded*

Answer *D* is correct. The word *blinded* is used to imply that those critical of Heine were not judging rationally.

❸ Writing Lesson

Timed Writing: Analytical Essay

Pushkin reflects on the passing of time in "I Have Visited Again." In the poem, the speaker relies on images from nature to mark the passing stages of his life. Write an essay in which you analyze the treatment of time in this poem. *(40 minutes)*

Prewriting
(10 minutes)
Begin by rereading the poem and taking notes about how time progresses. You might make an informal outline with headings such as "past," "present," and "future." Under each heading, write phrases used in the poem.

Drafting
(20 minutes)
Use your informal outline or your notes as you begin writing your analytical essay.

Revising
(10 minutes)
After completing the first draft of your essay, trade papers with a partner and read each other's essay. Circle any points that lack support or seem vague, and suggest clarifying details that will strengthen each point in your partner's essay.

Model: Clarifying Meaning

The speaker sees the effects of time in the old cottage,

which has "sadly / Declined" and deteriorated∧ in the ten

years since his exile there.

> Specific examples or illustrations can clarify the writer's points.

𝒲𝒢 Prentice Hall Writing and Grammar Connection: Platinum Level, Chapter 10, Section 4

❹ Extend Your Learning

Listening and Speaking Lyric poems have often been set to music. With a partner, find appropriate background music for either "The Lorelei" or "The Lotus Flower." As you choose the music, keep these questions in mind:

- Does the music express the same mood as the poem?
- Does the music enhance the poem's meaning?

Then, prepare and perform an **oral interpretive reading** of the poem for your classmates, using the music to enrich the performance. **[Group Activity]**

Research and Technology The term *siren* has a special meaning in literature. Use the Internet and electronic encyclopedias to research this term, and prepare a **museum exhibit** of images and artifacts related to literary sirens. Write placards that connect your findings to "The Lorelei."

For: An additional research activity
Visit: www.PHSchool.com
Web Code: etd-7702

I Have Visited Again / The Lorelei / The Lotus Flower ■ 883

Assessment Resources

The following resources can be used to assess students' knowledge and skills.

Unit 7 Resources
Selection Test A, pp. 32–34
Selection Test B, pp. 35–37

General Resources
Rubrics for Response to Literature,
pp. 55–56

Go Online Students may use the **Self-test** to
Assessment prepare for **Selection Test A** or
Selection Test B.

---

❸ Writing Lesson

You may use this Writing Lesson as a timed-writing practice, or you may allow students to develop the analytical essay as a writing assignment over several days.

- To give students guidance in writing this essay, give them **Support for Writing Lesson,** p. 29 in *Unit 7 Resources.*

- Tell students that in an analytical essay, a writer interprets various smaller elements of a topic. By examining smaller parts, a writer can develop conclusions about the whole.

- Tell students that a good analytical essay begins with a strong thesis statement that establishes the purpose and parameters of the analysis.

- Use the Writing Lesson to guide students in developing their essays.

- Use the Response to Literature rubrics in *General Resources,* pp. 55–56, to evaluate students' work.

𝒲𝒢 **Writing and Grammar**
Platinum Level
For support in teaching the Writing Lesson, use Chapter 10, Section 4.

❹ Listening and Speaking

- Have partners choose a poem and determine the mood that is expressed in the poem.

- Remind students that the mood, or atmosphere, of a literary work is the feeling created in the reader. Elements that can influence mood include setting, tone, and events.

- Once students have selected their music and prepared their interpretive readings, allow time for presentations.

- The **Support for Extend Your Learning** page (*Unit 7 Resources,* p. 30) provides guided note-taking opportunities to help students complete the Extend Your Learning activities.

Go Online Have students type in the
Research Web Code for another
research activity.

Standard Course of Study

Goal 1: WRITTEN LANGUAGE

WL.1.03.2 Identify and analyze text components and evaluate impact on expressive text.

WL.1.03.9 Analyze effects of author's craft and style in reflection.

Goal 4: CRITICAL THINKING

CT.4.03.1 Analyze how writers introduce and develop a main idea.

Goal 5: LITERATURE

LT.5.03.10 Analyze connections between ideas, concepts, characters and experiences in world literature.

Goal 6: GRAMMAR AND USAGE

GU.6.01.2 Analyze author's use of language to demonstrate understanding of expression.

GU.6.01.4 Use vocabulary strategies to determine meaning.

Step-by-Step Teaching Guide	Pacing Guide
PRETEACH	
• Administer Vocabulary and Reading Warm-ups as necessary.	5 min.
• Engage students' interest with the motivation activity.	5 min.
• Read and discuss author and background features, including From the Author's Desk. **FT**	10 min.
• Introduce the Literary Analysis Skill: Romantic Poetry. **FT**	5 min.
• Introduce the Reading Strategy: Judging a Poet's Message. **FT**	10 min.
• Prepare students to read by teaching the selection vocabulary. **FT**	
TEACH	
• Informally monitor comprehension while students read independently or in groups. **FT**	30 min.
• Monitor students' comprehension with the Reading Check notes.	as students read
• Reinforce vocabulary with Vocabulary Builder notes.	as students read
• Develop students' understanding of Romantic poetry with the Literary Analysis annotations. **FT**	5 min.
• Develop students' ability to judge a poet's message with the Reading Strategy annotations. **FT**	5 min.
ASSESS/EXTEND	
• Assess students' comprehension and mastery of the Literary Analysis and Reading Strategy by having them answer the Apply the Skills questions. **FT**	15 min.
• Have students complete the Vocabulary Development Lesson and the Grammar and Style Lesson. **FT**	15 min.
• Apply students' ability to outline an essay by using the Writing Lesson. **FT**	45 min. or homework
• Apply students' understanding by using one or more of the Extend Your Learning activities.	20–90 min. or homework
• Administer Selection Test A or Selection Test B. **FT**	15 min.

Resources

Print

Unit 7 Resources

Transparency

Graphic Organizer Transparencies

Technology

From the Author's Desk DVD .... W. S. Merwin, Segment 2

Print

Reader's Notebook [L2]

Reader's Notebook: Adapted Version [L1]

Reader's Notebook: English Learner's Version [EL]

Unit 7 Resources

Technology

Listening to Literature Audio CDs [L2, EL]

Reader's Notebook: Adapted Version Audio CD [L1, L2]

Print

Unit 7 Resources

General Resources

Technology

Go Online: Research **[L3]**

Go Online: Self-test **[L3]**

ExamView®, **Test Bank [L3]**

Choosing Resources for Differentiated Instruction

[L1] Special Needs Students

[L2] Below-Level Students

[L3] All Students

[L4] Advanced Students

[EL] English Learners

For Vocabulary and Reading Warm-ups and for Selection Tests, **A** signifies "less challenging" and **B** "more challenging." For Graphic Organizer transparencies, **A** signifies "not filled in" and **B** "filled in."

FT Fast Track Instruction: To move the lesson more quickly, use the strategies and activities identified with **FT**.

Scaffolding for Less Proficient and Advanced Students

The leveled Critical Thinking questions after selections progress in the levels of thinking required to answer them. To address the needs of your different students, you may use the (a) level questions for your less proficient students and the (b) level questions with your on-level and advanced students. The occasional (c) level questions are appropriate for your advanced students.

PRENTICE HALL

TeacherEXPRESS™ Use this complete
Plan · Teach · Assess suite of powerful teaching tools to make lesson planning and testing quicker and easier.

PRENTICE HALL

StudentEXPRESS™ Use the interactive
Learn · Study · Succeed textbook (online and on CD-ROM) to make selections and activities come alive with audio and video support and interactive questions.

 For: Information about Lexiles
Professional **Visit:** www.PHSchool.com
Development **Web Code:** eue-1111

Motivation

Have students discuss their perceptions of poets. Do students believe that poets are somehow different from other people? If so, why? Explain that a number of nineteenth-century poets—including Baudelaire, Rimbaud, and Verlaine—felt alienated from the rest of society. Ask students to discuss how a poet might express this sense of alienation.

❶ Background

More About the Authors

Charles Baudelaire was one of the most inventive poets of his time. A Romantic in his taste for what was remote and mysterious, he went beyond Romanticism in his accurate portrayal of the modern city. He pioneered a new type of writing called Symbolism—viewing things in the visible world as symbols of a greater spiritual reality.

When Arthur Rimbaud was sixteen, he wrote a letter to his friend Paul Demeny in which he spoke of the poet as a visionary who "searches his soul, inspects it, tries it, learns it," and who virtually creates a new language.

While in prison for attempting to murder Arthur Rimbaud, Paul Verlaine returned to Roman Catholicism. His renewed religious faith, at first, seemed to change his life. However, his failure to reconcile with his wife and Rimbaud and the deaths of both Verlaine's mother and his star pupil finally caused him to return to his former life of debauchery.

Geography Note

Draw students' attention to the map on this page, and tell them that France was home to Baudelaire, Rimbaud, and Verlaine. It was here that the poets participated in the bohemian lifestyle of the Parisian artistic community.

Build Skills | Poems

❶ Invitation to the Voyage • The Albatross • The Sleeper in the Valley • Ophelia • Autumn Song

Charles Baudelaire
(1821–1867)

Charles Baudelaire (shärl bōd ler´) was one of the most colorful, startling, and innovative poets of the nineteenth century. Attempting to break away from the Romantic tradition, Baudelaire created poems that are objective rather than sentimental. Many of his works celebrate the city and the artificial rather than nature.

As a youth, Baudelaire rebelled against his family to pursue a career as a writer. To dissuade him from such a dissolute life, they sent him on an ocean voyage to India. Instead of completing the voyage, he returned to France to claim his share of his late father's fortune. Soon, extravagant living drove him into debt, a problem that would plague him for the rest of his life.

Baudelaire published short stories, translated works by Edgar Allan Poe into French, and both wrote and collected poems for *Flowers of Evil* (1857), which would become his signature work. Although his talents were not widely recognized during his lifetime, Baudelaire's reputation blossomed posthumously, and he came to be considered one of the finest nineteenth-century poets.

Arthur Rimbaud
(1854–1891)

Arthur Rimbaud (är tür´ ran bō´) earned recognition for his poetry at the age of eight, was first published at age fifteen, and stopped writing altogether at nineteen. Renowned French poet Paul Verlaine introduced Rimbaud to many of the most prominent poets of the day and encouraged Rimbaud as he wrote some of his finest poetry. Unfortunately, Verlaine and Rimbaud quarreled frequently; ultimately, Verlaine attempted to murder his young friend. After serving a two-year prison sentence for his crime, Verlaine published Rimbaud's collection of poetry, *Illuminations* (1886). The collection earned widespread acclaim among critics and writers and was applauded as the work of a mature and remarkably talented poet. By the time of his death in 1891, Rimbaud's poetry had already begun to influence other writers; during the twentieth century, his lifestyle became a model for such vagabond writers, artists, and musicians as Jack Kerouac and Bob Dylan.

Paul Verlaine
(1844–1896)

Like many of his fellow poets, Paul Verlaine (ver lān´) was an accomplished writer at a very young age; his body of work includes exquisitely musical lyrics, religious verse, and sonnets. Verlaine benefited from associations with renowned authors such as Baudelaire, Rimbaud, and novelist Victor Hugo. In particular, Verlaine shared a tumultuous friendship with Rimbaud that ended badly—Verlaine shot his friend in a murder attempt that landed him in prison for two years.

Through the success of his poems, Verlaine brought early attention to the Symbolists, an emerging group of writers whose works relied on complex patterns of symbols to convey deeply personal themes.

Like so many of his fellow poets, Verlaine craved a bohemian lifestyle. Though the last years of his life were spent in poverty and dissolution, Verlaine was honored as Prince of Poets in 1895 and given a public funeral in Paris upon his death in 1896.

Preview

Connecting to the Literature

Baudelaire, Rimbaud, and Verlaine believed that personal, immediate, and emotional responses were valid subjects for poetry. Pay attention to the emotion in these poems, and notice the part nature plays in those feelings.

❷ Literary Analysis

Romantic Poetry

Romantic poetry is part of a literary and artistic movement called Romanticism. While earlier poems often relied on wit and stylish pretense, Romantic works placed a premium on elements closer to the heart:

- imagination
- nature
- the exotic
- emotion
- individuality

As you read, notice how these elements guide a reader's imagination toward an emotional response, and identify the emotions you feel.

Comparing Literary Works

All the poems in this grouping use nature as a subject or as a way to communicate a message. Consider these questions as you read:

- Is nature something to interact with, wonder at, fear, or appreciate?
- Is nature indifferent to human suffering or sympathetic toward it?
- Is nature—especially its colors and seasons—used symbolically?

Look for the poets' attitudes toward nature and contrast the messages these poems communicate.

❸ Reading Strategy

Judging a Poet's Message

As a reader, your job is not only to discover the point a poet is making but also to weigh what the poet says against your own experiences and past readings. When you **judge a poet's message,** you assess the validity of the poet's ideas and decide whether you agree or disagree with them.

As you read these poems, use a chart like the one shown to identify and judge the message each poet expresses.

Vocabulary Builder

proffering (präf′ ər iŋ) *v.* offering (p. 887)

nonchalantly (nän′ shə länt′ lē) *adv.* in a casually indifferent manner (p. 888)

sovereign (säv′ rən) *n.* monarch or ruler (p. 888)

adroit (ə droit′) *adj.* skillful in a physical or mental way (p. 888)

flourish (flʉ′ ish) *n.* fanfare, as of trumpets (p. 891)

strains (strānz) *n. pl.* passages of music; tunes; airs (p. 892)

monotone (män ə tōn) *n.* sound or song that repeats a single note (p. 894)

Poet's Message

Experiences I Share With the Poet

My Unique Experiences

My Conclusions

NC Standard Course of Study

- Identify clear criteria for evaluation of work of others. (WL.1.03.2)
- Analyze how writers introduce and develop a main idea. (CT.4.03.1)

Invitation to the Voyage / The Albatross / The Sleeper in the Valley / Ophelia / Autumn Song ■ 885

Differentiated Instruction — Solutions for All Learners

Support for Special Needs Students

Have students use the support pages for these selections in the *Reader's Notebooks.* Completing these pages will prepare students to read the selections in the Student Edition.

Support for Less Proficient Readers

Have students use the support pages for these selections in the *Reader's Notebooks.* After students finish each selection in the *Reader's Notebooks,* have them complete the questions and activities in the Student Edition.

Support for English Learners

Have students use the support pages for these selections in the *Reader's Notebooks: English Learner's Version.* Completing these pages will prepare students to read the selections in the Student Edition.

---

❷ Literary Analysis
Romantic Poetry

- Read aloud the list of elements found in Romantic poetry. Discuss and define each element.

- Then, ask students to give an example of how each element might be conveyed poetically. For example, imagination and nature might be conveyed through a description of a beautiful, idyllic landscape.

- Read with the class the questions in the Comparing Literary Works instruction. Point out that each of the poems in this grouping contains a reference to nature, one of the elements of Romantic poetry.

- Encourage students to identify other elements of Romantic poetry as they read the poems.

❸ Reading Strategy
Judging a Poet's Message

- Point out that identifying imagery and using the questions in the Comparing Literary Works instruction can help students understand a poem's message.

- Guide students to understand how to judge a poet's message by using the graphic organizer. Suggest the following poetic message: Modern society has lost touch with the power and mystery of nature. Ask students to suggest some of their experiences that either support or contradict this message. Then, have students draw a conclusion about, or judge, the validity of the message.

- Give students a copy of **Reading Strategy Graphic Organizer A,** p. 159 in *Graphic Organizer Transparencies.* Have them use it to judge each poet's message as they read the poems in this grouping.

Vocabulary Builder

- Pronounce each vocabulary word for students, and read the definitions as a class. Have students identify any words with which they are familiar.

Facilitate Understanding

Explain to students that the albatross is a bird found mainly in the South Pacific. With a wingspan that extends up to nine feet, it excels at flying and gliding. During the 1800s, albatrosses were often slaughtered for their feathers and wings.

❶ About the Translation

Richard Wilbur, the translator of Baudelaire's "Invitation to the Voyage," is an important poet and a superb translator of French poetry. In this translation, Wilbur is faithful to the original while moving beyond a literal translation. To appreciate his achievement, consider the refrain (lines 13 and 14). This is the literal translation of the couplet: "There, all is only order and beauty, / Luxury, calm, and voluptuousness." Wilbur has rendered this "There, there is nothing else but grace and measure, / Richness, quietness, and pleasure."

❷ Literary Analysis

Romantic Poetry

- Direct students' attention to the Literary Analysis instruction on p. 885, and read aloud the elements of Romantic poetry.

- Then, **ask** students to respond to the Literary Analysis item: List three characteristics of Romantic poetry in lines 8–11.

Possible response: The poem shows a concern with nature with its description of the "cloud-disheveled air." The exotic and the imaginative are reflected in the "mystery" of "those other skies." The description of "treacherous eyes" evokes the Romantic interest in emotion.

❸ Critical Viewing

Possible response: The stormy sky, the rough waves, and the beauty and grace of the ship's sails might inspire poets.

❶ Invitation to the Voyage

Charles Baudelaire
translated by Richard Wilbur

Background   There is little doubt that Charles Baudelaire's ocean voyage to India was a significant event in his life. Although the journey was cut short—lasting only eight months instead of eighteen—the experience clearly inspired him as a poet. The voyage, his desire for a life of ease and luxury, and his yearning to escape reality all find expression in his poems "Invitation to the Voyage" and "The Albatross."

My child, my sister, dream
How sweet all things would seem
Were we in that kind land to live together
And there love slow and long,
5   There love and die among
Those scenes that image you, that sumptuous[1] weather.
Drowned suns that glimmer there
Through cloud-disheveled[2] air
Move me with such a mystery as appears
10   Within those other skies
Of your treacherous eyes
When I behold them shining through their tears.

There, there is nothing else but grace and measure,
Richness, quietness, and pleasure.

15   Furniture that wears
The luster of the years
Softly would glow within our glowing chamber,

---

1. **sumptuous** (sump′ chōō əs) *adj.* magnificent or splendid.
2. **disheveled** (di shev′ əld) *adj.* disarranged and untidy.

---

886 ■ *Romanticism and Realism*

Literary Analysis
Romantic Poetry List three characteristics of Romantic poetry in lines 8–11.

❸ **Critical Viewing** ▶
Which details in this seascape might inspire a poet? **[Interpret]**

Differentiated
Instruction   Solutions for All Learners

Accessibility at a Glance

	Invitation to the Voyage	The Albatross	The Sleeper in the Valley	Ophelia	Autumn Song
Language	Descriptive words for nature and emotion	Syntax: Long sentences with embedded clauses	Colorful adjectives	Emotive words and phrases	Vivid verbs expressing intense emotion
Concept Level	Accessible	Accessible	Accessible	Accessible	Accessible
Literary Merit	Classic Romantic poem celebrates a graceful life	Romantic poem with a central simile	Romantic poem with a touching image of death	Romantic poem with personification of nature	Romantic poem equates grief with autumn
Lexile	NP	NP	NP	NP	NP
Overall Rating	More challenging	More challenging	More challenging	More challenging	More challenging

Flowers of rarest bloom
<u>Proffering</u> their perfume
20 Mixed with the vague fragrances of amber;
    Gold ceilings would there be,
    Mirrors deep as the sea,
The walls all in an Eastern splendor hung—
    Nothing but should address
25   The soul's loneliness,
Speaking her sweet and secret native tongue.

❹ There, there is nothing else but grace and measure,
Richness, quietness, and pleasure.

    See, sheltered from the swells
30   There in the still canals
Those drowsy ships that dream of sailing forth;
    It is to satisfy
❺   Your least desire, they ply
Hither through all the waters of the earth.
35   The sun at close of day
    Clothes the fields of hay,
Then the canals, at last the town entire
    In hyacinth and gold:
    Slowly the land is rolled
40 Sleepward under a sea of gentle fire.

There, there is nothing else but grace and measure,
Richness, quietness, and pleasure.

Vocabulary Builder
proffering (präf´ ər iŋ) *v.*
offering

Reading Strategy
Judging a Poet's Message What message is the speaker determined to communicate through these repeated lines?

Literary Analysis
Romantic Poetry Explain how individuality is presented in lines 32–34.

Erminia in the Rough Sea, 1869, National Trust Photographic Library

Invitation to the Voyage ■ 887

❹ Reading Strategy
Judging a Poet's Message
- Remind students that a reader cannot judge a poet's message until he or she identifies the message.
- Have a volunteer read aloud the bracketed passage. Then, **ask** students the Reading Strategy question: What message is the speaker determined to communicate through these repeated lines?
Possible response: Through repetition, the speaker is trying to reinforce the pleasurable qualities of the voyage. He may also be trying to convince his beloved to join him on the voyage or trying to reassure himself that the voyage does indeed have these qualities.

❺ Literary Analysis
Romantic Poetry
- Remind students that individuality is often a theme of Romantic poetry. Then, have a volunteer read aloud the bracketed passage.
- **Ask** students to respond to the Literary Analysis item: Explain how individuality is presented in lines 32–34.
Possible response: Lines 32–34 describe the ships as sailing to fulfill an individual's personal desire.

❻ Humanities
Erminia in the Rough Sea, 1869
The artist created this nineteenth-century English painting using gouache, which is a type of thick and opaque watercolor paint.

Use the following question for discussion:
What details in this painting illustrate ideas similar to the poet's message?
Possible response: The vibrant colors and darkening sky reflect the exotic and mysterious qualities of the poem.

Differentiated
Instruction   Solutions for All Learners

Support for Special Needs Students
Students may have difficulty with the vocabulary in this poem. Work with them to complete Vocabulary Warm-up List and Vocabulary Warm-up Practice, pp. 38–39 in *Unit 7 Resources.* Then post the meanings of the words *treacherous, luster, splendor,* and *ply* on these pages, and assist students with additional synonyms. Tell students to read "Invitation to the Voyage," replacing the difficult words with synonyms. Encourage them to use this strategy as they read other poems in this grouping.

Enrichment for Gifted/Talented Students
If any students are currently studying French, ask them to obtain the text of "Invitation to the Voyage" in French. Then, have students read the poem in French to their classmates. This should help give students a sense of how the poem sounds in its original language, and it will remind students that this poem, as well as the other poems in the grouping, were translated from French.

❼ The Albatross

Charles Baudelaire *translated by* Richard Howard

Often, to pass the time on board, the crew
will catch an albatross, one of those big birds
which <u>nonchalantly</u> chaperone a ship
across the bitter fathoms of the sea.

5   Tied to the deck, this <u>sovereign</u> of space,
as if embarrassed by its clumsiness,
pitiably lets its great white wings
drag at its sides like a pair of unshipped oars.

How weak and awkward, even comical
10 this traveler but lately so <u>adroit</u>—
one deckhand sticks a pipestem in its beak,
another mocks the cripple that once flew!

The Poet is like this monarch of the clouds
riding the storm above the marksman's range;
15 exiled on the ground, hooted and jeered,
he cannot walk because of his great wings.

Vocabulary Builder

nonchalantly (nän´shə länt´ lē) *adv.* in a casually indifferent manner

sovereign (säv´ rən) *n.* monarch or ruler

adroit (ə droit´) *adj.* skillful in a physical or mental way

Reading Strategy

Judging a Poet's Message What message does the speaker convey about the albatross in its natural setting?

Critical Reading

1. **Respond:** Would you like to experience the type of voyage that the speaker describes in "Invitation to the Voyage"? Why or why not?

2. **(a) Recall:** Which details describe the "kind land" in "Invitation to the Voyage"? **(b) Interpret:** What impression of the land do these details convey?

3. **(a) Interpret:** What message about the life of a poet does the speaker convey in "The Albatross"? **(b) Evaluate:** Do you think this message can be applied to contemporary poets? Why or why not?

4. **(a) Connect:** Explain whether the world described in "Invitation to the Voyage" is enticing to you. **(b) Compare:** How does this place compare to your ideal world?

888 ■ Romanticism and Realism

Critical Viewing ▶ ❾
Which images in Rimbaud's poem describe the scene in this landscape? **[Connect]**

Go Online
Author Link

For: More about Charles Baudelaire
Visit: www.PHSchool.com
Web Code: ete-9704

The Sleeper in the Valley

Arthur Rimbaud *translated by* William Jay Smith

This is the green wherein a river chants
Whose waters on the grasses wildly toss
Its silver tatters, where proud sunlight slants
Within a valley thick with beams like moss.

5 A youthful soldier, mouth agape, head bare,
And nape where fresh blue water cresses drain
Sleeps stretched in grass, beneath the cloud, where
On abundant green the light descends like rain.

His feet on iris roots, smiling perhaps
10 As would some tiny sickly child, he naps.
O nature, he is cold: make warm his bed.

This quiver of perfume will not break his rest;
In the sun he sleeps, his hand on quiet breast.
Upon one side there are two spots of red.

Literary Analysis
Romantic Poetry List four
visual images of nature in
the first stanza.

Reading Strategy
Judging a Poet's Message
What philosophy about
death does the speaker
imply by referring to the
soldier as being in a bed?

The Sleeper in the Valley ■ *889*

Ophelia

Arthur Rimbaud
translated by Daisy Aldan

Ophelia, John Everett Millais; Tate Gallery, London

▲ **Critical Viewing** What emotions do the colors and images in this painting evoke in you? **[Respond]**

890   *Romanticism and Realism*

⓱ Background Arthur Rimbaud's rare talent for poetry came at an early age. He wrote "Ophelia," for example, at age fifteen. Many critics consider it a remarkable piece—not only because of the author's youth but also because of the poem's quality as a literary piece. By the time Rimbaud's brief career ended at nineteen, novice poets were crafting their own poems in imitation of his widely recognized lyrical style.

In his poem "Ophelia," Rimbaud borrows a character from *Hamlet*. In Shakespeare's play, Ophelia is a beautiful, innocent, impressionable young maiden who is in love with Hamlet, the play's protagonist. Confused by Hamlet's sudden rejection of her, and grief-stricken by her father's death, Ophelia spirals into depression and insanity. The poem "Ophelia" presents one interpretation of Ophelia's life, the troubled relationship she endures with Hamlet, and the way in which her life ends.

I

On the calm black wave where the stars sleep
Floats white Ophelia like a great lily,
Floats very slowly, lying in her long veils . . .
—From the distant woods, the <u>flourish</u> of the kill.

5 For more than a thousand years sad Ophelia
White phantom, passes, on the long black river.
For more than a thousand years her sweet obsession
Whispers her love to the evening breeze.

The wind embraces her breasts and unfolds her great veils
10 In a corolla[1] gently rocked by the waters;
Trembling willows weep on her shoulder,
Reeds lean on her lofty pensive[2] brow.

---

1. **corolla** (kə räl′ ə) *n.* the petals, or inner floral leaves, of a flower.
2. **pensive** (pen′ siv) *adj.* thinking deeply or seriously, often of sad or melancholy things.

Vocabulary Builder
flourish (flur′ ish) *n.* fanfare, as of trumpets

Literary Analysis
Romantic Poetry What comparison is the speaker making through the use of phrases such as "the wind embraces" and "willows weep"?

⓳ Reading Check
How long has the spirit of Ophelia passed on the dark river?

Ophelia ■ 891

891

❷⓿ Humanities

Ophelia Among the Flowers,
by Odilon Redon

Odilon Redon (1840–1916) was a
French painter and graphic artist
associated with the art movement
known as Symbolism. Redon began
his career making black and white
charcoal drawings and lithographs,
which were heavily influenced by the
words of poet and author Edgar Allan
Poe. Later in his career, Redon turned
to painting and color drawing, creating imaginative, sensitive works of
radiant color, featuring mythological
scenes and delicate flowers, such as
those shown in this painting.

Use the following question for
discussion:

Which painting of Ophelia—
John Everett Millais' or Odilon
Redon's—do you think more
accurately portrays the
scene in Rimbaud's poem?
Possible response: Millais'
painting is the more accurate
because it is detailed and realistic;
however, Redon's impressionistic
depiction more accurately evokes
the eerie, ethereal quality of
Rimbaud's poem.

❷❶ Critical Viewing

Possible response: The details of
the painting show Ophelia floating in
the water surrounded by flowers, as
described in the poem. However, the
water of the river is blue, not black as
in the poem; the painting does not
show Ophelia's veils; nor does it
capture nature mourning her death.

❷❷ Critical Thinking

Infer

- Read aloud the bracketed passage.
  Ask students to focus on the natural
  images.

- **Ask:** On the basis of these images,
  what can you infer about Ophelia's
  relationship with nature?
  Possible response: The images
  suggest that Ophelia, while alive,
  was especially attuned to nature and
  that it had a haunting effect on her.
  Rimbaud depicts nature as speaking
  or appealing to Ophelia's very soul.

Ophelia Among the Flowers, Odilon Redon

❷⓿

Bruised water lilies sigh about her;
Sometimes in a sleeping alder tree she awakens
15 A nest; a tiny wing-flutter escapes;
Mysterious sounds fall from the golden stars.

II

O pale Ophelia! fair as snow!
You died, child, yes, carried off by a river!
Because the winds falling from the great cliffs of Norway
20 Spoke low to you of fierce freedom;

❷❷

Because a wind, tearing your long hair,
Bore strange shouts to your dreaming spirit;
Because your heart listened to the <u>strains</u> of Nature
In the wails of the tree and the sighs of the nights.

892 ■ Romanticism and Realism

❷❶ ▲ Critical Viewing
How do details in this
painting compare and
contrast with images in
the poem? **[Compare
and Contrast]**

Vocabulary Builder
strains (strānz) *n.* passages
of music; tunes; airs

25   Because the voice of mad seas, immense rattle,
Bruised your child's heart, too sweet and too human;
Because on an April morning, a handsome pale courtier,
A sorry fool, sat mutely at your feet!

Heaven! Love! Freedom! What a dream, O Foolish girl!
30   You melted toward him as snow near flame:
Your words were strangled by your great visions
—And the terrible Infinite frightened your blue eyes!

III

And the Poet says you come at night
To gather flowers in the rays of the stars;
35   And he has seen on the water, lying in her long veils,
White Ophelia floating, like a great lily.

Reading Strategy
Judging a Poet's Message What does the speaker seem to say about people who seek nature, love, and freedom?

Critical Reading

1. **Respond:** What are your impressions of Ophelia after reading Rimbaud's poem? How do you feel about the choices she made? Explain.
2. **(a) Recall:** In "The Sleeper in the Valley," who appears to be sleeping? **(b) Draw Conclusions:** What evidence in the poem suggests that the sleeper is not really asleep?
3. **(a) Recall:** Identify three words or phrases the speaker uses to describe the gentle qualities of nature in "The Sleeper in the Valley." **(b) Compare and Contrast:** How does the speaker's depiction of nature contrast with the actual events that took place there? Refer to specific lines and details to support your answers.
4. **(a) Recall:** In "Ophelia," what colors are mentioned in the first four lines? **(b) Analyze:** How are these colors used to establish Ophelia's purity and innocence?
5. **(a) Apply:** In what way is nature indifferent to human affairs? **(b) Speculate:** How does nature affect people emotionally?

For: More about
Arthur Rimbaud
Visit: www.PHSchool.com
Web Code: ete-9705

Ophelia ■ 893

㉓ Reading Strategy
Judging a Poet's Message
• Have a volunteer read aloud the bracketed passage.
• **Ask** students the Reading Strategy question.
Possible response: The speaker seems to say that those who seek nature, love, and freedom are foolish for thinking that these things are attainable.

Monitor Progress If students have difficulty judging the speaker's message, encourage them to weigh this message against their own experiences.

Reteach Help students judge the speaker's message by having them use the **Reading Strategy** support, page 43 in *Unit 7 Resources.*

ASSESS

Answers

1. **Possible response:** Ophelia is gentle, sensitive, and vulnerable. Her choice was foolish; she let herself be swept away by "A sorry fool."
2. (a) A young soldier appears to be sleeping. (b) The descriptions of the sleeper as a "sickly child," as cold, and as having two spots of red on his side are evidence that he is not really asleep.
3. (a) The gentle qualities of nature are suggested by "abundant green," "the light descends like rain," and "this quiver of perfume." (b) The descriptions of the beautiful, scenic valley contrast with the sleeper's apparent violent encounter with death.
4. (a) The colors mentioned in the first four lines are black and white. (b) Ophelia's whiteness contrasts with the black water on which she floats, emphasizing her purity.
5. (a) Nature, as an entity, takes no notice of human suffering or vulnerability. (b) **Possible response:** Weather has the power to make people melancholy or happy.

Go Online For additional information **Author Link** about Arthur Rimbaud, have students type in the Web Code, then select *R* from the alphabet, and then select Arthur Rimbaud.

Autumn Song

Paul Verlaine *translated by* Louis Simpson

25

Violins complain
Of autumn again,
    They sob and moan.
And my heartstrings ache
5 Like the song they make,
    A <u>monotone</u>.   **26**

Suffocating, drowned,
And hollowly, sound
    The midnight chimes.
10 Then the days return
I knew, and I mourn
    For bygone times.

And I fall and drift
With the winds that lift
15   My heavy grief.
Here and there they blow,
And I rise and go
    Like a dead leaf.

Literary Analysis

Romantic Poetry What comparison in the first stanza helps the reader understand the intense emotion the speaker feels?

Vocabulary Builder

monotone (män´ ə tōn´) *n.* sound or song that repeats a single note

Critical Reading

1. **Respond:** What advice would you give to the speaker in "Autumn Song"? Why?

2. **(a) Recall:** Identify four verbs in lines 1–12. **(b) Analyze:** What overall feeling is created by these verbs?

3. **(a) Recall:** What is the speaker mourning? **(b) Speculate:** What events or conditions in the speaker's past might be worth mourning?

4. **(a) Make a Judgment:** In what ways would this poem be different if it were called "Summer Song"? **(b) Extend:** Compose three lines of this new poem.

Go Online
Author Link

For: More about Paul Verlaine
Visit: www.PHSchool.com
Web Code: ete-9706

Apply the Skills

Invitation to the Voyage • *The Albatross* • *The Sleeper in the Valley* • *Ophelia* • *Autumn Song*

Literary Analysis

Romantic Poetry

1. For each poem in this grouping, complete an organizer like the one below, noting details that are typical of **Romantic poetry**.

Imagination	Emotion	Nature	Individuality	The Exotic

2. In "Invitation to the Voyage," how do the images of the "kind land" in line 3 relate to the ideas expressed in the poem's refrain?

3. **(a)** In line 26 of "Ophelia," what does the speaker mean when he says that Ophelia was "too human"? **(b)** What element of Romantic poetry does this sentiment evoke?

Comparing Literary Works

4. **(a)** Compare the ways in which "Invitation to the Voyage" and "Autumn Song" express the emotion of longing. **(b)** In what ways is nature used to express this longing? Explain.

5. **(a)** What images from nature are associated with Ophelia in "Ophelia" and the soldier in "The Sleeper in the Valley"? **(b)** Identify three factors contributing to the perception that these characters deserve sympathy.

Reading Strategy

Judging a Poet's Message

6. **(a)** Explain how the desire to escape to an ideal or imaginary world is a message in "Invitation to the Voyage." **(b)** **Judge the poet's message** by explaining the possible benefits of escapism. **(c)** What negative consequences result from escapist behavior?

7. **(a)** Which details in "The Albatross" best communicate the speaker's attitude toward the crew? **(b)** Do you agree with this attitude? Explain.

Extend Understanding

8. **Science Connection:** How might a naturalist react to the treatment of the bird in "The Albatross"?

Invitation to the Voyage / The Albatross / The Sleeper in the Valley / Ophelia / Autumn Song ■ 895

QuickReview

Romantic poetry focuses on imagination, emotion, nature, individuality, and the exotic.

To **judge a poet's message**, test the message against your own experiences, assess the validity of the message, and decide whether you agree or disagree with it.

Assessment

For: Self-test
Visit: www.PHSchool.com
Web Code: eta-6703

Answers continued

7. (a) Details such as "another mocks the cripple" and the hoots and jeers of the crew communicate the speaker's attitude of disapproval. (b) **Possible response:** It is cruel to torment the bird.

8. **Possible response:** A naturalist probably would be horrified at the abuse of the bird.

Go **Online** Students may use the **Self-test** to **Assessment** prepare for **Selection Test A** or **Selection Test B.**

Answers

1. **Sample response: Imagination:** the simile of the poet and the albatross; **Emotion:** "embarrassed . . ."; **Nature:** the albatross; **Individuality:** "The Poet is like this monarch . . ."; **The Exotic:** the albatross. Another sample answer can be found on **Literary Analysis Graphic Organizer B,** p. 162 in *Graphic Organizer Transparencies.*

2. The refrain serves to reinforce and summarize the details provided about the "kind land."

3. (a) By saying that Ophelia was "too human," the speaker means that she was too sensitive. (b) This sentiment evokes the element of emotion.

4. (a) "Invitation to the Voyage" expresses longing for a place of ease and comfort; "Autumn Song" expresses longing for "bygone times." (b) **Possible response:** In "Invitation to the Voyage," nature imagery such as "vague fragrances of amber," and a sunset that "Clothes the fields of hay, /. . . / In hyacinth and gold," making "a sea of gentle fire," creates a drowsy yet overheated atmosphere, conveying a sense of sultry passion. In "Autumn Song," autumn is reflected in violins that "sob and moan," conveying the longing of regret.

5. (a) **Possible response:** "Ophelia": **touch details**—wind "embracing," wind "tearing" Ophelia's hair; **sound details**—sweet obsession whispering, wing-flutter, mysterious sounds, wind speaking low. "**The Sleeper in the Valley**": **smell details**—"this quiver of perfume"; **sound details**—river chanting. (b) The speaker refers to Ophelia's "bruised" child's heart; the speaker of "The Sleeper in the Valley" compares the soldier with a "tiny sickly child." By comparing these characters with children, the speaker suggests that they did not deserve the fates that befell them.

6. (a) The refrain demonstrates the speaker's desire for the ideal world described in the poem. (b) The benefits of escapism include peace and freedom from stress and responsibility. (c) Negative consequences include an inability to face and so fix problems.

Answers

❶ Vocabulary Lesson

Word Analysis: Greek Prefix *mono-*

1. monotone: repetition of the same sound
2. monologue: a long speech by a single speaker
3. monopoly: the control of something by a single person or company

Spelling Strategy

1. one sound   3. one sound
2. two sounds   4. one sound

Vocabulary Builder: Analogies

1. proffering   5. nonchalantly
2. flourish   6. sovereign
3. strains   7. adroit
4. monotone

❷ Grammar and Style Lesson

1. "Drowned suns <u>that glimmer there</u> . . ."; modifies *suns*
2. "The Poet is <u>like this monarch</u> . . ."; modifies *Poet*
3. "Because a wind, <u>tearing your long hair,</u> . . ."; modifies *wind*
4. "This is the green <u>wherein a river chants</u> . . ."; modifies *green*
5. "With the winds <u>that lift / My heavy grief</u> . . ."; modifies *winds*

Writing Application

Possible response: We'll sail on waves <u>of golden water</u> (modifies *waves*); We'll visit lands <u>that are fragrant with spices and flowers</u> (modifies *lands*).

𝒲𝒢 Writing and Grammar Platinum Level

For support in teaching the Grammar and Style Lesson, use Chapter 20, Sections 1 and 2.

Build Language Skills

❶ Vocabulary Lesson

Word Analysis: Greek Prefix *mono-*

The Greek prefix *mono-* means "alone," "one," or "single." Add the prefix *mono-* to each of the roots given below. Use your understanding of the prefix and the clues provided to define the new word.

1. _____tone (sound)
2. _____logue (speaking)
3. _____poly (commerce)

Spelling Strategy

In words like *indignant,* the *g* and the *n* each stand for a separate sound. Sometimes, *gn* stands for only the *n* sound, as in *sign.* In these cases, it usually follows the letters *ai, ei,* or *i.* For each word below, identify whether *gn* stands for two separate sounds or just one sound.

1. sovereign   3. arraign
2. malignant   4. sovereignty

❷ Grammar and Style Lesson

Adjectival Modifiers

An **adjectival modifier** is a phrase or clause that describes a noun or pronoun. Adjectival modifiers can come in many different forms. Study the examples provided below.

> **Prepositional Phrase:** "Flowers of *rarest bloom* . . ." (modifies *Flowers*)
>
> **Partical Phrase:** ". . .When I behold them *shining through their tears.* " (modifies *them*)
>
> **Adjective Phrase:** " . . . drowsy ships that *dream of sailing forth* . . . " (modifies *ships*)

𝒲𝒢 *Prentice Hall Writing and Grammar Connection: Platinum Level, Chapter 20, Sections 1 and 2*

896 ■ *Romanticism and Realism*

Vocabulary Builder: Analogies

An *analogy* compares the relationship between word meanings. For example, in analogies, word pairs often represent these common relationships:

synonym:	*talk* is to *chat*
antonym:	*noise* is to *silence*
degree:	*cold* is to *freezing*
part to whole:	*clarinet* is to *orchestra*

Review the vocabulary list on page 885. Then, choose the word from that list that best completes each analogy below.

1. *Wanting* is to *desiring* as *offering* is to ___.
2. *Noisy* is to *loud* as *fanfare* is to ___.
3. *Fiddle* is to *violin* as *tunes* is to ___.
4. *Felicitous* is to *felicity* as *monotonous* is to ___.
5. *Elegant* is to *refined* as *casually* is to ___.
6. *Student* is to *teacher* as *subject* is to ___.
7. *Plain* is to *beautiful* as *incapable* is to ___.

Practice For each item below, underline the adjectival modifier. Then, circle the word that the adjectival modifier describes.

1. "Drowned suns that glimmer there . . ."
2. "The Poet is like this monarch . . ."
3. "Because a wind, tearing your long hair, . . ."
4. "This is the green wherein a river chants . . ."
5. "With the winds that lift / My heavy grief . . ."

Writing Application Write two sentences about a journey, using adjectival modifiers. In each sentence, underline the adjectival modifier and circle the word it describes.

Assessment Practice

Distinguish Between Fact and Nonfact

(For more practice, see *Test Preparation Workbook,* **p. 40.)**

Many tests require students to distinguish between fact and nonfact. Use the following sample test item to demonstrate how students can use this skill when reading.

> Charles Baudelaire was the most inventive poet of his time. He was born in France in 1821. A rebellious young man, Baudelaire was expelled from school in 1839. He then moved to Paris. A Romantic in taste, he went beyond Romanticism to accurately portray the modern city. He died in 1867.

Which of the following is an opinion from the passage?

A Baudelaire was born in France in 1821.
B Baudelaire was expelled from school.
C Baudelaire was the most inventive poet of his time.
D Baudelaire died in 1867.

Lead students to recognize that the correct answer is *C.* Choices *A, B,* and *D* can be proved, and *C* cannot.

❸ Writing Lesson

Timed Writing: Comparison-and-Contrast Essay

In all of the poems within this grouping, nature significantly affects both the speakers and the events in the poems. Write an essay in which you compare and contrast the treatment of nature in three of the poems you have read. *(40 minutes)*

Prewriting
(10 minutes) Choose three poems and take note of how nature is depicted in each one. Make an outline of the similarities and differences, organizing your observations into points you want to make.

Model: Making an Outline

I. Comparisons between "Invitation to the Voyage"
  and "The Albatross"

  A. Nature is presented positively in both.

  B. Examples: "Flowers of rarest bloom," albatross
    as "monarch of the clouds"

> An outline for your own use can be formal, with numerals and letters as shown here, or informal, using bullets.

Drafting
(20 minutes) Using the words and details in your outline, write your essay. Address each of the points you have outlined.

Revising
(10 minutes) Compare your finished draft to your outline. Revise your essay to add any details that were missed.

WG Prentice Hall Writing and Grammar Connection: Platinum Level, Chapter 9, Section 3

❹ Extend Your Learning

Listening and Speaking Read Queen Gertrude's monologue in *Hamlet* at the end of Act IV, Scene vii. Then, read section II of Rimbaud's "Ophelia." In a **discussion** with a partner:

1. Consider each speaker and each audience.
2. Note the passage of time in each.
3. Evaluate how each speaker feels about Ophelia's death.

Draw conclusions about the differences you find. **[Group Activity]**

Research and Technology Build a **multimedia travelogue** illustrating Baudelaire's sea voyage to India. Select images and music or sounds that connect to his poem. You may also be able to include scents and items to touch. Present your travelogue to the class.

For: An additional research activity
Visit: www.PHSchool.com
Web Code: etd-7703

Invitation to the Voyage / The Albatross / The Sleeper in the Valley / Ophelia / Autumn Song ■ 897

---

❸ Writing Lesson

You may use this Writing Lesson as a timed-writing practice, or you may allow students to develop the comparison-and-contrast essay as a writing assignment over several days.

- To give students guidance in writing this essay, give them the **Support for Writing Lesson,** p. 46 in *Unit 7 Resources.*

- Before students create their outlines, have them refer to the graphic organizer that they completed for question 1 on p. 895.

- Students can use the **Outline** in *Graphic Organizer Transparencies,* p. 279, to help them complete their outlines.

- After students have finished their essays, use the Exposition: Comparison-and-Contrast Essay rubrics in *General Resources,* pp. 53–54, to evaluate their work.

WG Writing and Grammar
Platinum Level
For support in teaching the Writing Lesson, use Chapter 9, Section 3.

❹ Research and Technology

- Encourage students to consult maps or a globe to find the sea route from France to India.

- Suggest that students use travel brochures from cruise lines, Internet resources, and print resources to locate images.

- Have students consult their local library's music collection for suitable music or sound effects to accompany their presentations.

- The **Support for Extend Your Learning** page (*Unit 7 Resources,* p. 47) provides guided note-taking opportunities to help students complete the Extend Your Learning activities.

Go Online
Research Have students type in the Web Code for another research activity.

Assessment Resources

The following resources can be used to assess students' knowledge and skills.

Unit 7 Resources
  Selection Test A, pp. 51–53
  Selection Test B, pp. 54–56

General Resources
  Rubrics for Exposition: Comparison-and-Contrast Essay, pp. 53–54

Go Online
Assessment Students may use the **Self-test** to prepare for **Selection Test A** or **Selection Test B.**

W. S. Merwin

- You might wish to have students read W. S. Merwin's introduction to the unit on pages 832–833.

- Show Segment 2 on W. S. Merwin on *From the Author's Desk DVD* to provide insight into his views on poetry, particularly French poetry. **Ask:** How has Merwin's poetry changed over time?
  Answer: His poetry has changed from "tight and traditional" to more abstract and experimental.

- Have students read Merwin's comments on these pages.

- **Ask** students what Merwin means by his statement that his poetry is "physical."
  Answer: His poems have long lines without punctuation, as in speech, so it is necessary to use the sense of hearing to understand his poetry.

Elegies

- Point out to students that elegies are poems written to remember with sadness someone who has died. **Ask** students: What does Merwin mean when he writes "All of the past experience a word has carried flows into today's usage."
  Answer: A word's meaning has a history that has shaped the word's current meaning.

Critical Viewing

Possible response: Sentiments that a poet might include in an elegy are nostalgia for Greece's past greatness and sadness over monuments that are in ruins.

 From the Author's Desk

W. S. MERWIN INTRODUCES
"Ancestral Voices" and "Substance"

W. S. Merwin

W. S. Merwin won the Pulitzer Prize for Poetry for *The Carrier of Ladders*. His most recent collection is entitled *The Ends of the Earth: Essays.*

Poetic Forms

My poems "Ancestral Voices" and "Substance" are both from a book called *The Vixen*, published in 1996. The poems have the same form: a long line close to the rhythms of speech, and without punctuation, like our speech. That makes it important to hear the words in order to "get" what they mean. It gives the writing a physical dimension, which I think is something essential to poetry: it must be taken in by one of the senses, hearing. And each of these poems can be read as a single sentence. The variation of the lines on the page, with alternate lines indented, is meant to direct and contribute to the current of the sentence.

Elegies, Linked to Romantic Poetry and the Classical World

The form suggests that these poems are, in some sense, elegies. It is also a deliberate reminder of a literary ancestor from the ancient, classical world: the elegies of Greece and Rome. You may wonder what point there is in such a reminder, when even among people who read poetry many probably do not know that there were ancient poems of that kind. But we use the word "elegiac" in English, to refer to something we remember fondly and are sad to have lost. (In the elegies, classical literature approaches the concerns of the Romantics, centuries later.)

All of our language is like that. Any word can be traced back to a point where its earlier meanings are unknown to us, yet all of the past experience a word has carried flows into today's usage.

▶ **Critical Viewing**
What sentiments might a poet include in an elegy—or mourning poem—to Greece's age of the Parthenon, pictured here? **[Speculate]**

898 ■ *Romanticism and Realism*

Teaching Resources

The following resources can be used to enrich or extend the instruction for From the Author's Desk.

Unit 7 Resources
    Support for Penguin Essay, p. 49
    Listening and Viewing, p. 50

From the Author's Desk DVD
    W. S. Merwin, Segment 2

- Point out to students that their memories of the past are shaded or influenced by what has happened since then and what influence the memories have had on them. For example, what once was a neutral, unimportant place for someone may forever hold great meaning if later the place is the setting where the person falls in love.

- Remind students that while many towns and villages in the United States are relatively young, similar places in Europe have existed for many hundreds of years.

- **Ask** students to explain how Merwin sees the link between memory and one's identity.
  Possible response: Merwin writes that "we are made of memory," and he understands that his life is part of the "current" of the events and people of the past, who once inhabited the place in France where he lived.

Critical Viewing

Possible response: The painting is similar to the landscape that Merwin describes. The house in the painting could be a farmhouse. Although the house does not appear to sit on a high ridge, there seems to be a valley in the background.

"We Are Made of Memory and It Has Many Depths" All of the poems in *The Vixen* are about a region deep in the country in southwest France, where I have spent parts of my life since I was in my early twenties, living in a small, very old, stone farmhouse, on a high ridge looking out over a wide valley. The poems shift in time, as though we were looking at a series of photographic negatives through each other. You look at images of the past as you recall it now, and you see them through other moments that you have lived through since then. We are made of memory and it has many depths. We are not even aware of some of them.

As in Romantic Poetry, "A Current of Loss and Memory and Affection" In our time the world around us encourages us to suppose that the past is really a very brief period, a few years in our own lives. But in the place these poems were written about, the human past is immensely deep. I loved that when I found it, as a young man. I lived in a tiny farming village where many things, from farming customs and wedding ceremonies to some of the tools and clothes, had been unchanged for as long as anyone could remember. Before that there was the French Revolution, and before that the age of the castles and the

▲ **Critical Viewing**
Compare this painting to the landscape Merwin describes in his essay.
[Compare]

The Vixen

- **Ask** students how Merwin understands the present moment.
Answer: The present moment is elusive and mysterious. Merwin says that we can never look directly at it because it is gone as soon as we find it.

ASSESS

Answers

1. (a) Merwin says that it is important to hear the words of his poems because they are like speech, and it is important to hear the words to "get" what they mean. (b) **Possible response:** Students may say that physically experiencing the poem forces them to look at the poem differently than they would otherwise and to become more involved in it.

2. (a) *The Vixen* takes place in a region deep in the country in southwest France. (b) **Possible response:** This place has had such a profound impact on Merwin because it has a long, continuous history and because he has spent parts of his life there since his early twenties.

3. **Possible response:** Merwin's poetry is similar to "Autumn Song," by Paul Verlaine because both poets are concerned with the loss of the past. Merwin's poetry is different from the poetry of Heinrich Heine because Merwin's poetry resembles spoken conversation while Heine's poetry has punctuation and meter.

4. **Possible response:** In "Ancestral Voices," Merwin describes the past as night and our ancestors as singing birds whose "voices were lifted here long before the first / of our kind had come to be able to listen . . ."

5. **Possible answer:** Students may say that reading this commentary helped them understand the power that the past and memory can exercise on people's lives.

Middle Ages, and before that the Romans, and before them the Gauls, and before them the hunters of the Ice Age who left great paintings on the cave walls, and before them the earlier hunters who buried their chiefs facing east, toward the dawn, thirty-five thousand years ago. Eventually I would look back at my own past there as part of that same current of loss and memory and affection, and write these poems.

The Vixen The title of the book is a word for an animal whose experience of the world is older than that of humanity, yet exemplifies for me the elusive, mysterious nature of the present moment, which disappears when we try to look straight at it. In these poems I consider the consciousness of the animals, and realize that it was they who inhabited the moment in a clear and absolute sense, without our idea of time.

But then, I am disturbed by an assumption that I see all around me, that the world really began with us human beings. I do not think it is a hopeful point of view.

Thinking About the Commentary

1. **(a) Recall:** Why does Merwin say that it is important to hear the words of his poems? **(b) Speculate:** In what ways might experiencing the poem physically enhance your enjoyment of it?

2. **(a) Recall:** What location is the subject of all of the poems in Merwin's *The Vixen*? **(b) Infer:** Why do you think this specific place had such a profound impact on Merwin?

As You Read the Poetry of W. S. Merwin . . .

3. Consider the ways in which Merwin's poetry is similar to and different from the other poetry in this unit.

4. Look for ways that layers of "the immensely deep past" are reflected in the language and imagery of Merwin's poems.

5. Think about the ways in which reading this commentary enriched your understanding of Merwin's poems.

SUBSTANCE
W. S. Merwin

I could see that there was a kind of distance lighted
    behind the face of that time in its very days
as they appeared to me but I could not think of any
    words that spoke of it truly nor point to anything
5 except what was there at the moment it was beginning
    to be gone and certainly it could not have been proven
nor held however I might reach toward it touching
    the warm lichens[1] the features of the stones the skin
of the river and I could tell then that it was
10   the animals themselves that were the weight and place
of the hour as it happened and that the mass of the cow's neck
    the flash of the swallow the trout's flutter were
where it was coming to pass they were bearing the sense of it
    without questions through the speechless cloud of light

---

1. **lichens** (lī′ kenz) algae or fungus that attaches patchlike onto rocks, wood, or soil.

W. S. Merwin
Author's Insight
The poem has form: a long line close to the rhythms of speech, and without punctuation, like our speech.

❸ **W. S. Merwin**
Author's Insight
The poem shifts in time and exemplifies the elusive, mysterious nature of the present moment, which disappears when we try to look straight at it.

Substance ■ 901

902

❹ About the Selection

This selection explores memory. The poet speaks of the birds, which simply sing their songs automatically as part of their existence. He also states that these songs and behaviors existed long before people existed to hear them. Merwin stresses the idea that animals are unaware of time and live life engaged in the present moment.

❺ Author's Insight

• Have a student volunteer read lines 11–15. **Ask:** What is Merwin saying about the birds in this passage? **Answer:** He is saying that the animals existed long before humans did.

• Direct students' attention to the Author's Insight. **Ask:** What does Merwin mean when he says, "it is they who inhabited the moment in a clear and absolute sense"? **Possible response:** Animals are not conscious of time; they simply live, following what they have done for as long as animals have existed.

❻ Author's Insight

• Have students read line 19 silently. **Ask:** What is the poet saying in this line? **Answer:** The key word is *remember.* Merwin is saying that the birds, without realizing it, know themselves through remembering the songs of their ancestors; their songs are automatic.

• Have a student volunteer read the Author's Insight. **Ask:** What is Merwin saying about people? **Answer:** He is saying that people, as in birds, are made of memory, even though people sometimes are unaware of it.

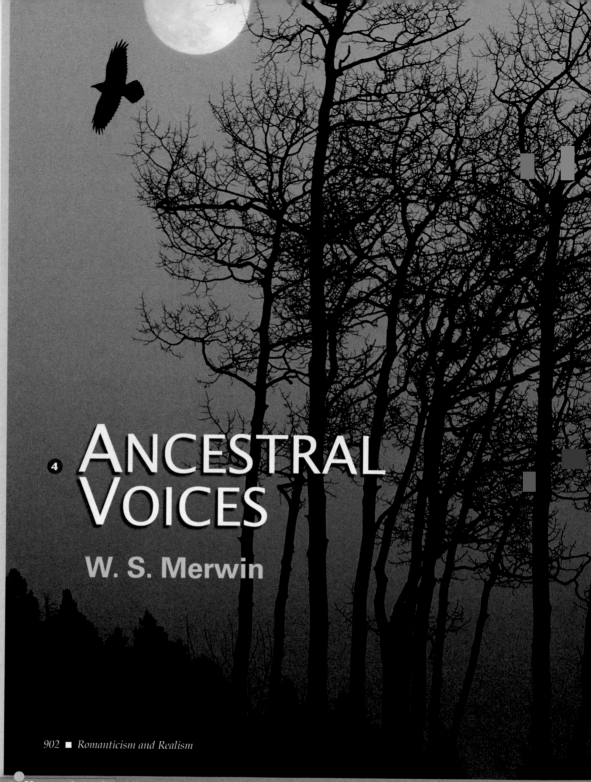

❹ ANCESTRAL VOICES

W. S. Merwin

902 ■ Romanticism and Realism

Differentiated Instruction   Solutions for All Learners

Strategy for Less Proficient Readers
Students may find "Ancestral Voices" difficult to understand due to the lack of punctuation and the content. To help students understand the sentences, provide each student with a disposable copy of the poem. Then, read the poem aloud with students. Ask them where they need to pause for the poem to make sense. Draw their attention to the subjects and verbs of each sentence. Then, as a group, mark the punctuation on the disposable copies. Once students can see the sentences in the poem, have them read and discuss the poem.

Strategy for English Learners
Students may have difficulty understanding this poem. Provide students with a disposable copy of the poem that is double-spaced. Have students read the poem and highlight words that they do not understand. Either discuss the words' definitions or have students use their dictionaries to find the meanings. Then have students write the definitions in the space above the confusing words. Once students understand the language, use an overhead transparency to help students determine the punctuation breaks and mark them in the poem. Then have students read and discuss the poem.

In the old dark the late dark the still deep shadow
      that had traveled silently along itself all night
while the small stars of spring were yet to be seen and the few
      lamps burned by themselves with no expectations
5 far down through the valley then suddenly the voice
      of the blackbird came believing in the habit
of the light until the torn shadows of the ridges
      that had gone out one behind the other into the darkness
began appearing again still asleep surfacing in their
10   dream and the stars all at once were gone and instead the
      song
of the blackbird flashed through the unlit boughs and far
      out in the oaks a nightingale went on echoing

5

itself drawing out its own invisible starlight
      these voices were lifted here long before the first
15 of our kind had come to be able to listen
      and with the faint light in the dew of the infant
leaves goldfinches flew out from their nests in the brambles
      they had chosen their colors for the day and they sang

6

of themselves which was what they had wakened to remember

Critical Reading

1. **Respond:** What tone, or mood, does Merwin create in his poetry?
2. **(a) Recall:** What three physical gestures does the speaker make in "Substance"? **(b) Interpret:** Why does he make these gestures?
3. **(a) Recall:** In "Substance," what are two things the speaker says about the animals? **(b) Compare and Contrast:** In what ways were the animals' reactions to passing time different from those of the speaker? **(c) Connect:** How does the title of the poem relate to the description of the animals?
4. **(a) Recall:** What occurs in the poem "Ancestral Voices"? **(b) Infer:** To what "voices" does the title refer? **(c) Interpret:** Why are these voices called "ancestral"?
5. **(a) Recall:** What kinds of punctuation appear in these poems? **(b) Evaluate:** Do the style of punctuation and the long lines give the poems the feeling of spoken language, as Merwin asserts in his commentary? Why or why not?
6. **(a) Recall:** What tense do the speakers use in these poems—present, past, or future? **(b) Analyze:** In each poem, how does the speaker suggest both a personal memory and a time older than human memory? **(c) Speculate:** In each poem, how much time separates the speaker's "present" from the past he remembers? Explain.
7. **Speculate:** Imagine you are an architect. Using hints from these poems, write a brief proposal for a house and plot of land for your client W. S. Merwin.

Ancestral Voices ■ 903

W. S. Merwin
Author's Insight

In this poem I consider the consciousness of the animals, and realize that it is they who inhabited the moment in a clear and absolute sense.

W. S. Merwin
Author's Insight

We are made of memory and it has many depths. We are not even aware of some of them.

Answers

1. Merwin creates a dreamlike, thoughtful, meditative tone.
2. (a) He touches the lichens, stones, and river. (b) He is trying to touch the present moment.
3. (a) The animals "were the weight and place of the hour," meaning that their bodies or movements marked the present moment and the passing of time; the animals "were bearing the sense of" passing time without being conscious of time. (b) Unlike the speaker, the animals did not ask questions or think about the passing of time. (c) The animals are the "substance" that bears and reflects the mystery of passing time.
4. (a) Sometime before dawn breaks, a blackbird starts to sing and a nightingale continues singing. Later, when light begins to appear, goldfinches fly out and sing. (b) The title refers to the "voices" of these birds. (c) The birds' voices are "ancestral" because they are birds of long past.
5. (a) Each poem uses an initial capital letter to begin the first line, a capital for the pronoun "I," and apostrophes to show possession. (b) **Possible response:** Some students may argue that the poems flow seamlessly, like spoken language. Other students may feel that the lack of punctuation makes the poems seem more artificial and less like speech.
6. (a) The speakers use the past tense. (b) In "Substance," the speaker refers to "that time," meaning a specific period in his past, but the way in which the animals related to the passing time suggests a type of existence older than human memory. In "Ancestral Voices," the speaker is remembering an experience, unique or repeated, of hearing birds sing at night and at dawn. However, he also declares that such singing predates humans. (c) In "Ancestral Voices," the wording of the poem could describe the passage of one night; the phrase "before the first of our kind had come to be able to listen," however, suggests that the separation of time could be the time before humans existed. The phrase "that time" in "Substance" suggests a considerable gap in time, perhaps 20 years or more.

Answers continued

7. **Possible response:** Students should refer to specific passages to support their ideas but also should let their imaginations rove freely. For example, some students might propose ways to design the house around such natural features as streams or trees. Tools, appliances, technology, and other human-made equipment should be hidden or not emphasized in the house's layout.

Go **Online** For additional information about **Author Link** Merwin, have students type in the Web Code, then select *M* from the alphabet, and then select W. S. Merwin.

903

Standard Course of Study

Goal 2: INFORMATIONAL READING

IR.2.03.2 Prioritize and organize information to construct an explanation to answer a question.

Goal 3: FOUNDATIONS OF ARGUMENT

FA.3.01.5 Present data about controversial issues in multiple forms.

FA.3.04.2 Analyze text components and evaluate their impact on argumentative texts.

Goal 5: LITERATURE

LT.5.01.2 Build knowledge of literary genres, and explore how characteristics apply to literature of world cultures.

LT.5.03.10 Analyze connections between ideas, concepts, characters and experiences in world literature.

Goal 6: GRAMMAR AND USAGE

GU.6.01.4 Use vocabulary strategies to determine meaning.

Step-by-Step Teaching Guide	Pacing Guide
PRETEACH	
• Administer Vocabulary and Reading Warm-ups as necessary.	5 min.
• Engage students' interest with the motivation activity.	5 min.
• Read and discuss author and background features. **FT**	10 min.
• Introduce the Literary Analysis Skill: Dynamic and Static Characters. **FT**	5 min.
• Introduce the Reading Strategy: Evaluating Characters' Decisions. **FT**	
• Prepare students to read by teaching the selection vocabulary. **FT**	10 min.
TEACH	
• Informally monitor comprehension while students read independently or in groups. **FT**	30 min.
• Monitor students' comprehension with the Reading Check notes.	as students read
• Reinforce vocabulary with Vocabulary Builder notes.	as students read
• Develop students' understanding of dynamic and static characters with the Literary Analysis annotations. **FT**	5 min.
• Develop students' ability to evaluate characters' decisions with the Reading Strategy annotations. **FT**	5 min.
ASSESS/EXTEND	
• Assess students' comprehension and mastery of the Literary Analysis and Reading Strategy by having them answer the Apply the Skills questions. **FT**	15 min.
• Have students complete the Vocabulary Development Lesson and the Grammar and Style Lesson. **FT**	15 min.
• Apply students' ability to use transitions for coherence by using the Writing Lesson. **FT**	45 min. or homework
• Apply students' understanding by using one or more of the Extend Your Learning activities.	20–90 min. or homework
• Administer Selection Test A or Selection Test B. **FT**	15 min.

Resources

Print

Unit 7 Resources

Transparency

Graphic Organizer Transparencies

Print

Reader's Notebook [L2]

Reader's Notebook: Adapted Version [L1]

Reader's Notebook: English Learner's Version [EL]

Unit 7 Resources

Technology

Listening to Literature Audio CDs [L2, EL]

Reader's Notebook: Adapted Version Audio CD [L1, L2]

Print

Unit 7 Resources

General Resources

Technology

Go Online: Research [**L3**]

Go Online: Self-test [**L3**]

ExamView®, Test Bank [**L3**]

Choosing Resources for Differentiated Instruction

[**L1**] Special Needs Students

[**L2**] Below-Level Students

[**L3**] All Students

[**L4**] Advanced Students

[**EL**] English Learners

For Vocabulary and Reading Warm-ups and for Selection Tests, **A** signifies "less challenging" and **B** "more challenging." For Graphic Organizer transparencies, **A** signifies "not filled in" and **B** "filled in."

FT Fast Track Instruction: To move the lesson more quickly, use the strategies and activities identified with **FT**.

Scaffolding for Less Proficient and Advanced Students

The leveled Critical Thinking questions after selections progress in the levels of thinking required to answer them. To address the needs of your different students, you may use the (a) level questions for your less proficient students and the (b) level questions with your on-level and advanced students. The occasional (c) level questions are appropriate for your advanced students.

PRENTICE HALL

Teacher EXPRESS™ Use this complete
Plan · Teach · Assess suite of powerful teaching tools to make lesson planning and testing quicker and easier.

PRENTICE HALL

Student EXPRESS™ Use the interactive
Learn · Study · Succeed textbook (online and on CD-ROM) to make selections and activities come alive with audio and video support and interactive questions.

Benchmark

After students have completed reading these selections, administer **Benchmark Test 8** (*Unit 7 Resources,* **pp. 74–79**). If the Benchmark Test reveals that some of the students need further work, use the **Interpretation Guide** to determine the appropriate reteaching page in the **Reading Kit** and on **Success Tracker.**

 Go Online For: Information about Lexiles
Professional Visit: www.PHSchool.com
Development Web Code: eue-1111

Motivation

Have students discuss some of the potential dangers of making foolish, spur-of-the-moment decisions. Ask whether they have ever made a decision that was foolish or too hasty. If so, what were the consequences?

❶ Background

More About the Authors

Maupassant's first short story, "Ball of Fat," won praise from the great French realist Gustave Flaubert, who wrote in a letter to Maupassant: "I consider 'Ball of Fat' a *masterpiece*."

During Tolstoy's childhood, 800 serfs lived on the Tolstoy estate of Yasnaya Polyana ("Clear Glade"). When he inherited the estate at the age of nineteen, he tried to make a better life for them.

When Chekhov was an adolescent, his parents moved to Moscow, leaving him to finish school in his hometown of Taganrog. Living essentially on his own for three years, Chekhov completed high school, attended the theater, read widely, and began writing.

Geography Note

Use the map on this page to identify Russia, the native country of both Tolstoy and Chekhov. Explain that during the authors' lifetimes, millions of peasants were required to work the land for wealthy, often brutal, landowners. The peasants, or serfs, were freed in 1861 but were still subject to restrictions.

Build Skills | Short Stories |

❶ Two Friends • How Much Land Does a Man Need? • A Problem

Guy de Maupassant (1850–1893)

Guy de Maupassant (gē də mō′ pä sän) first wrote under the guidance of famous French writers Gustave Flaubert and Émile Zola. Encouraged by Zola, Maupassant published his first short story in 1880. The story earned him immediate fame, establishing his career as a prolific and extremely popular writer. The royalties from his first volume of short stories, *Madame Tellier's Establishment* (1881), and his novels *A Woman's Life* (1883) and *Bel-Ami* (1885) enabled him to live a life of luxury. He traveled extensively, incorporating his recollections into his early works. Maupassant's later stories, however, reflect his growing inner turmoil, often presenting an uncomplimentary but realistic portrait of the world. In "Two Friends," for example, Maupassant presents a graphic depiction of the violence and destruction of war.

Health problems and bouts of depression plagued Maupassant. Finally, Maupassant was committed to an asylum, where he died in 1893.

Leo Tolstoy (1828–1910)

Leo Tolstoy (tŏl′ stŏĭ) was born at his family's estate near Moscow. The tragic loss of his parents and a beloved aunt affected him profoundly, leading to a lifelong obsession with the inevitability of death. Tolstoy's first novel was published in 1852, followed by a collection of stories in 1856. *War and Peace* (1869), a novel about Napoleon's invasion of Russia in 1812, was immediately regarded as a masterpiece for its graphic depiction of war, its insights into Russian culture, and its exploration into the meaning of life. The deeply tragic novel confirmed Tolstoy's already lofty reputation as a writer.

Struggling through a spiritual crisis, Tolstoy created his own religious faith that emphasized a natural existence, universal love, equality, and nonviolence. In accordance with his beliefs, Tolstoy renounced the rights to his works published after 1881 and gave his property to his family. In 1910, shortly after leaving his wife and family, Tolstoy died in an obscure railroad station.

Anton Chekhov (1860–1904)

Anton Chekhov (chek′ôf) is one of only a few major writers who also studied and practiced medicine. Despite the demands of a medical career, Chekhov published a substantial body of work, including both scientific pieces and great literary works. One of his finest plays, *The Seagull* (1896), focuses on intergenerational conflict.

Toward the end of the nineteenth century, declining health forced Chekhov to move to the warmer climate of Yalta. Illness did not impair his literary output, however, and in his last years he produced two critically acclaimed plays, *The Sisters* (1901) and *The Cherry Orchard* (1904). When Chekhov finally succumbed to tuberculosis in 1904, his literary reputation had not yet extended beyond Russia. Since World War I, however, he has come to be regarded as one of the finest short-story writers the world has ever produced.

Preview

Connecting to the Literature

Sometimes, even the smallest decision can be difficult to make. The protagonists in these stories are forced to make important choices that have disastrous consequences. Look for the challenges the characters face as they make their decisions, and imagine what you might have done in their place.

❷ Literary Analysis

Dynamic and Static Characters

Like people in life, characters in literature can change as a story progresses. A **dynamic character** experiences a change or shift in attitude and behavior during the course of a literary work. However, a **static character's** attitudes and behavior remain essentially stable throughout.

As you become acquainted with the characters in these stories, create a chart like the one shown to identify each of the characters as either dynamic or static. Consider how the contrasts between these character types add tension within each story.

Comparing Literary Works

These short stories feature characters making decisions that direct the outcomes of their lives. Every decision brings consequences—some good, some bad. These anticipated consequences often drive the choices characters make. Look at the way each character approaches his or her choices, and compare the factors each one considers before he or she acts.

❸ Reading Strategy

Evaluating Characters' Decisions

Evaluate characters' decisions just as you would assess your own. Follow these steps to critically consider a choice and its effect on future actions:

- Consider whether the character benefits from the decision the way he or she imagined.
- Analyze the effect each decision has on other characters.
- Finally, judge whether the decision turns out to be good or bad.

Use this process to evaluate characters' decisions in each story you read.

Vocabulary Builder

pillaging (pil´ ij iŋ) *v.* plundering; looting (p. 908)

superimposed (sōō´ pər im pōzd´) *v.* placed on top of something else (p. 908)

placidly (plas´ id lē) *adv.* calmly (p. 911)

discord (dis´ kôrd) *n.* dissension; conflict (p. 915)

prostrate (präs´ trāt) *adj.* lying with one's face down (p. 923)

taciturn (tas´ ə tʉrn) *adj.* almost always silent (p. 930)

benevolent (bə nev´ ə lənt) *adj.* doing or inclined to do good; kindly; charitable (p. 930)

Two Friends / How Much Land Does a Man Need? / A Problem ■ 905

NC Standard Course of Study

- Analyze connections between ideas, concepts, characters and experiences in world literature. (LT.5.03.10)
- Analyze elements of literary environment in world literature. (LT.5.03.11)

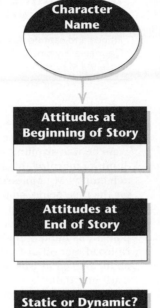

Character Name

↓

Attitudes at Beginning of Story

↓

Attitudes at End of Story

↓

Static or Dynamic?

❷ Literary Analysis
Dynamic and Static Characters

- Point out that dynamic characters usually learn something as a result of the events of a story. Static characters remain the same no matter what happens to them. Tell students that the interaction of dynamic and static characters often creates conflict in a story.

- Review with students the chart. Model the use of the chart with a character familiar to the students. Then give students a copy of **Literary Analysis Graphic Organizer A**, p. 163 in *Graphic Organizer Transparencies*. Suggest students use the chart to examine each character they encounter in the following stories.

❸ Reading Strategy
Evaluating Characters' Decisions

- Tell students that the decisions characters make move the plot of a story forward.

- Discuss with students what might constitute a good or bad decision. Give the example of a character who, under pressure from his family, decides to cheat on a college entrance exam. Explain that in order to evaluate the decision, students must consider how the decision affects the character and others around him.

- Remind students that sometimes the consequences of a decision are not explicitly stated in the story; they must be inferred.

Vocabulary Builder

- Pronounce each vocabulary word for students, and read the definitions as a class. Have students identify any words with which they are already familiar.

Differentiated Instruction   Solutions for All Learners

Support for Special Needs Students
Have students use the support pages for these selections in the *Reader's Notebooks*. Completing these pages will prepare students to read the selections in the Student Edition.

Support for Less Proficient Readers
Have students use the support pages for these selections in the *Reader's Notebooks*. After students finish each selection in the *Reader's Notebooks*, have them complete the questions and activities in the Student Edition.

Support for English Learners
Have students use the support pages for these selections in the *Reader's Notebooks: English Learner's Version*. Completing these pages will prepare students to read the selections in the Student Edition.

❶

Two Friends

Guy de Maupassant *translated by* Gordon R. Silber

Background The backdrop for "Two Friends" is the Franco-Prussian War, also called the Franco-German War. In this ten-month conflict in 1870–71, a coalition of German states known as Prussia fought to defeat France and capture its emperor, Napoleon III. In one military strategy, the German army blockaded Paris, starving the city's inhabitants into compliance. As Maupassant's story begins, Paris is on the verge of surrender.

Paris was blockaded, starved, in its death agony. Sparrows were becoming scarcer and scarcer on the rooftops and the sewers were being depopulated. One ate whatever one could get.

As he was strolling sadly along the outer boulevard one bright January morning, his hands in his trousers pockets and his stomach empty, M.[1] Morissot, watchmaker by trade but local militiaman for the time being, stopped short before a fellow militiaman whom he recognized as a friend. It was M. Sauvage, a riverside acquaintance.

Every Sunday, before the war, Morissot left at dawn, a bamboo pole in his hand, a tin box on his back. He would take the Argenteuil railroad, get off at Colombes, and walk to Marante Island. As soon as he arrived at this ideal spot he would start to fish; he fished until nightfall.

Every Sunday he would meet a stout, jovial little man, M. Sauvage, a haberdasher[2] in Rue Notre-Dame-de-Lorette, another ardent fisherman. Often they spent half a day side by side, line in hand and feet dangling above the current. Inevitably they had struck up a friendship.

❸

Some days they did not speak. Sometimes they did; but they understood one another admirably without saying anything because they had similar tastes and responded to their surroundings in exactly the same way.

❷ **Critical Viewing** ▶
What might Sauvage and Morissot find enticing about the setting of this landscape? **[Speculate]**

---

1. **M.** abbreviation for French title *Monsieur* (mə syö´), equivalent to *Mister* or *Sir*.
2. **haberdasher** (hab´ ər dash´ ər) *n.* person who is in the business of selling men's clothing.

906 ■ *Romanticism and Realism*

On a spring morning, toward ten o'clock, when the young sun was drawing up from the tranquil stream wisps of haze which floated off in the direction of the current and was pouring down its vernal warmth on the backs of the two fanatical anglers,[3] Morissot would sometimes say to his neighbor, "Nice, isn't it?" and M. Sauvage would answer, "There's nothing like it." And that was enough for them to understand and appreciate each other.

On an autumn afternoon, when the sky, reddened by the setting sun, cast reflections of its scarlet clouds on the water, made the whole river crimson, lighted up the horizon, made the two friends look as ruddy as fire, and gilded the trees which were already brown and beginning to tremble with a wintery shiver, M. Sauvage would look at Morissot with a smile and say, "Fine sight!" And Morissot, awed, would answer, "It's better than the city, isn't it?" without taking his eyes from his float.

As soon as they recognized one another they shook hands energetically, touched at meeting under such changed circumstances. M. Sauvage, with a sigh, grumbled, "What goings-on!" Morissot groaned dismally, "And what weather! This is the first fine day of the year."

The sky was, in fact, blue and brilliant.

---

3. **anglers** (aŋ′ glərz) *n.* people who fish.

Literary Analysis
Dynamic and Static Characters In what way do these opening paragraphs prepare you for changes that may occur in the main characters?

Reading Check
What hobby do Sauvage and Morissot have in common?

Les Maisons Cabassud à la Ville d'Avray, Camille Corot, The Louvre, Paris

Two Friends ■ 907

❸ Literary Analysis

Dynamic and Static Characters

- **Ask** students to describe what they have learned about Morissot and Sauvage from their reading.
  Answer: The characters are both pleasant, friendly men who enjoy fishing, the country, and each other's company.

- Call students' attention to the bracketed passage. **Ask** them to describe the friendship between the two characters.
  Possible response: The characters understand each other and appreciate each other's company.

- **Ask** students the Literary Analysis question: In what way do these opening paragraphs prepare you for changes that may occur in the main characters?
  Possible response: The two friends have not been fishing since before the war began. The men may try to find a way to fish because the hobby brings so much pleasure.

❹ Reading Check

Answer: Sauvage and Morissot have fishing in common.

❺ Humanities

Les Maisons Cabassud à la Ville d'Avray (The Cabassud Houses in the Town of Avray), by Jean-Baptiste-Camille Corot

A predecessor of the Impressionists, Jean-Baptiste-Camille Corot (1796–1875) was one of the first French painters devoted to capturing the vitality and freshness of nature. One of Corot's favorite painting sites was northern France, especially the town of Avray, which is the subject of this painting.

Use the following question for discussion:

What elements in the painting convey a sense of harmony and peacefulness?
Possible response: The small, unhurried human figures convey a sense of harmony. The rural buildings and open countryside convey a sense of peace.

Differentiated Instruction   Solutions for All Learners

Support for Less Proficient Readers
The early part of the narrative of "Two Friends" moves back and forth in time. Help students identify the flashbacks by calling their attention to such signal phrases as "some days," "On a spring morning," and "On an autumn afternoon." Students may wish to mark the flashbacks with sticky notes.

Support for English Learners
To help clarify challenging vocabulary, especially in Maupassant's descriptions of nature, pair students with native English speakers. Have partners work together to use context clues to determine the meanings of such words as *scarlet, ruddy,* and *gilded.*

Enrichment for Gifted/Talented Students
Tell students that friendship is a universal theme in literature around the world. Have them brainstorm words and images that call to mind the friendship between Sauvage and Morissot. Suggest that students use magazines to make collages illustrating the characters' relationship.

⑥ Literary Analysis
Dynamic and Static Characters

- Review with students the definitions of dynamic and static characters on p. 905.
- Read aloud the bracketed passage. Then, discuss with students the characters' behavior. **Ask:** Why do the men stop at the cafe? How do they feel after they stop?
Answer: The men stop at the cafe to have a drink. Afterward, they feel giddy and do not appear to be thinking clearly.
- **Ask** students the Literary Analysis question: What is changing in the relationship between the characters?
Answer: The characters discover that they like to spend time with each other outside of fishing.

⑦ Reading Strategy
Evaluating Characters' Decisions

- Remind students that evaluating characters' decisions leads to a deeper understanding of a story. Review the steps on p. 905 for making an evaluation.
- Ask a volunteer to read aloud the bracketed passage. Then, **ask** students what influences the characters' decision to go fishing.
Answer: The alcohol and warm weather influence the characters' decision.
- **Ask** students the Reading Strategy question: Which details prove that the decision to go to the island is a dangerous one?
Possible response: The existence of an outpost, the emptiness and silence of the towns and country-side, the nearby presence of Prussians, the description of the Prussians' pillaging and massacring, and the two men's fear that they may meet the Prussians all indicate that the decision to go to the island is a dangerous one.

They started to walk side by side, absent-minded and sad. Morissot went on, "And fishing! Ah! Nothing but a pleasant memory."

"When'll we get back to it?" asked M. Sauvage.

They went into a little café and had an absinthe,[4] then resumed their stroll along the sidewalks.

⑥ Morissot stopped suddenly. "How about another, eh?" M. Sauvage agreed, "If you want." And they entered another wine shop.

On leaving they felt giddy, muddled, as one does after drinking on an empty stomach. It was mild. A caressing breeze touched their faces.

The warm air completed what the absinthe had begun. M. Sauvage stopped. "Suppose we went?"

"Went where?"

"Fishing, of course."

"But where?"

"Why, on our island. The French outposts are near Colombes. I know Colonel Dumoulin; they'll let us pass without any trouble."

Morissot trembled with eagerness: "Done! I'm with you." And they went off to get their tackle.

An hour later they were walking side by side on the highway. They reached the villa which the Colonel occupied. He smiled at their request and gave his consent to their whim. They started off again, armed with a pass.

⑦ Soon they passed the outposts, went through the abandoned village of Colombes, and reached the edge of the little vineyards which slope toward the Seine. It was about eleven.

Opposite, the village of Argenteuil seemed dead. The heights of Orgemont and Sannois dominated the whole countryside. The broad plain which stretches as far as Nanterre was empty, absolutely empty, with its bare cherry trees and its colorless fields.

Pointing up to the heights, M. Sauvage murmured, "The Prussians are up there!" And a feeling of uneasiness paralyzed the two friends as they faced this deserted region.

"The Prussians!" They had never seen any, but for months they had felt their presence—around Paris, ruining France, <u>pillaging</u>, massacring, starving the country, invisible and all-powerful. And a kind of superstitious terror was <u>superimposed</u> on the hatred which they felt for this unknown and victorious people.

Morissot stammered, "Say, suppose we met some of them?"

His Parisian jauntiness coming to the surface in spite of everything, M. Sauvage answered, "We'll offer them some fish."

But they hesitated to venture into the country, frightened by the silence all about them.

---

4. **absinthe** (ab′ sinth) *n.* bitter, anise-flavored liqueur.

908 ■ Romanticism and Realism

Literary Analysis
Dynamic and Static Characters What is changing in the relationship between the characters?

Reading Strategy
Evaluating Characters' Decisions Which details prove that the decision to go to the island is a dangerous one?

Vocabulary Builder
pillaging (pil′ ij iŋ) *v.* plundering; looting

superimposed (soo′ pər im pōzd′) *v.* placed on top of something else

---

Enrichment

A Closer Look at the City of Paris

"Two Friends" is set in Paris, France, in the 1870s. Many important water and land routes in Europe cross Paris. Under the ancient Romans, the city was the capital of the Parisii tribe, from which the city took its name. In the late 900s, the city became the focal point for what was becoming modern France. The historical city of Paris is situated on the river Seine and is divided into three main parts: the Île de la Cité (the word *île* means "island," and *cité* refers to the center of the ancient city); the left bank, which has been considered the artistic and intellectual center of Paris; and the right bank, which is the city's economic center.

The early city was circular in shape; it has generally retained that shape as it has grown over the centuries. From its early beginnings on an island in the Seine, the city has grown to include neighboring towns.

Finally M. Sauvage pulled himself together: "Come on! On our way! But let's go carefully." And they climbed over into a vineyard, bent double, crawling, taking advantage of the vines to conceal themselves, watching, listening.

A stretch of bare ground had to be crossed to reach the edge of the river. They began to run, and when they reached the bank they plunged down among the dry reeds.

Morissot glued his ear to the ground and listened for sounds of anyone walking in the vicinity. He heard nothing. They were indeed alone, all alone.

Reassured, they started to fish.

Opposite them Marante Island, deserted, hid them from the other bank. The little building which had housed a restaurant was shut up and looked as if it had been abandoned for years.

M. Sauvage caught the first gudgeon,[5] Morissot got the second, and from then on they pulled in their lines every minute or two with a silvery little fish squirming on the end, a truly miraculous draught.

Skillfully they slipped the fish into a sack made of fine net which they had hung in the water at their feet. And happiness pervaded their whole being, the happiness which seizes upon you when you regain a cherished pleasure of which you have long been deprived.

The good sun was pouring down its warmth on their backs. They heard nothing more; they no longer thought about anything at all; they forgot about the rest of the world—they were fishing!

But suddenly a dull sound which seemed to come from under ground made the earth tremble. The cannon were beginning.

Morissot turned and saw, over the bank to the left, the great silhouette of Mount Valérien wearing a white plume on its brow, powdersmoke which it had just spit out.

And almost at once a second puff of smoke rolled from the summit, and a few seconds after the roar still another explosion was heard.

Then more followed, and time after time the mountain belched forth death-dealing breath, breathed out milky-white vapor which rose slowly in the calm sky and formed a cloud above the summit.

M. Sauvage shrugged his shoulders. "There they go again," he said.

As he sat anxiously watching his float bob up and down, Morissot was suddenly seized by the wrath which a peace-loving man will feel toward madmen who fight, and grumbled, "Folks sure are stupid to kill one another like that."

M. Sauvage answered, "They're worse than animals."

And Morissot, who had just pulled in a bleak, went on, "And to think that it will always be like this as long as there are governments."

M. Sauvage stopped him: "The Republic[6] wouldn't have declared war—"

---

5. **gudgeon** (guj´ ən) *n.* small European freshwater fish.
6. **The Republic** the provisional republican government that assumed control when Napoleon III was captured by the Prussians.

✔ **Reading Check** ❿
Why are Sauvage and Morissot anxious while approaching their favorite spot?

Two Friends ■ 909

❽ Reading Strategy
Evaluating Characters' Decisions

• Review the bracketed passage with students. **Ask** students: Which of the men's actions suggests that their decision to go fishing is a foolhardy one?
Answer: Morissot's attempt to listen for sounds of someone approaching by pressing his ear to the ground suggests that the men's decision to go fishing is foolhardy.

• **Ask:** Do you think the men believe at this point that their decision is foolhardy? Why or why not?
Possible response: The men probably realize that their decision is foolhardy, but they quickly forget their nervousness as they begin to fish.

❾ Critical Thinking
Analyze

• Have a volunteer read aloud the bracketed passage. Invite students to **comment** on the description of the two men fishing.
Answer: The description shows fishing as a delightful and peaceful pleasure of life.

• **Ask:** How does this passage help readers understand why the men decide to go fishing?
Possible response: To the men, fishing represents one of the simple and precious pleasures of life. They are unwilling to give up that pleasure despite the risks.

❿ Reading Check

Answer: Sauvage and Morissot are afraid of being seen by the Prussians.

Differentiated Instruction   Solutions for All Learners

Support for Special Needs Students
Some readers tend to skip passages of description. Tell students that because Maupassant's stories tend to be very spare, it is important for them to read his descriptions carefully. Point out that the descriptions on these pages highlight the lifelessness of the countryside. Lead a discussion about how the lifelessness of the countryside shows that the men are in a dangerous area.

Strategy for Advanced Readers
Encourage students to read the descriptions on these pages carefully. Have them contrast the lifeless countryside with the "truly miraculous draught" of fishes that the men catch. Ask them to speculate on the symbolism behind the juxtaposition of lifelessness and abundant life. What message is Maupassant trying to convey through this juxtaposition? Have volunteers share their speculations with the class.

⑪ Literary Analysis
Dynamic and Static Characters

• Direct students to the bracketed passage that begins on p. 909. Ask one student to read Sauvage's lines and another student to read Morissot's lines.

• Have students **summarize** the men's conversation.
Answer: The men oppose killing people in war, but they decide that war seems an inevitable part of human affairs.

• **Ask** students the Literary Analysis question: In what way does the characters' conversation show that the men have changed?
Possible response: Their conversation shows that the men have grown closer as friends because they are comfortable talking about their political beliefs.

⑫ Critical Viewing

Possible response: The grand and imposing details of the uniforms—such as the epaulets and tail hats—as well as the soldiers' weapons might intimidate citizens like the two friends.

Morissot interrupted: "Under kings you have war abroad; under the Republic you have war at home."

And they started a leisurely discussion, unraveling great political problems with the sane reasonableness of easy-going, limited individuals, and found themselves in agreement on the point that men would never be free. And Mount Valérien thundered unceasingly, demolishing French homes with its cannon, crushing out lives, putting an end to the dreams which many had dreamt, the joys which many had been waiting for, the happiness which many had hoped for, planting in wives' hearts, in maidens' hearts, in mothers' hearts, over there, in other lands, sufferings which would never end.

"That's life for you," opined M. Sauvage.

"You'd better say 'That's death for you,'" laughed Morissot.

But they shuddered in terror when they realized that someone had just come up behind them, and looking around they saw four men standing almost at their elbows, four tall men, armed and bearded, dressed like liveried[7] servants, with flat caps on their heads, pointing rifles at them.

The two fish lines dropped from their hands and floated off down stream.

In a few seconds they were seized, trussed up, carried off, thrown into a rowboat and taken over to the island.

And behind the building which they had thought deserted they saw a score of German soldiers.

A kind of hairy giant who was seated astride a chair smoking a porcelain pipe asked them in excellent French: "Well, gentlemen, have you had good fishing?"

Then a soldier put down at the officer's feet the sack full of fish which he had carefully brought along. The Prussian smiled: "Aha! I see that it didn't go badly. But we have to talk about another little matter. Listen to me and don't get excited.

"As far as I am concerned, you are two spies sent to keep an eye on me. I catch you and I shoot you. You were pretending to fish in order to conceal your business. You have fallen into my hands, so much the worse for you. War is like that.

---

7. liveried (liv´ ər ēd) *adj.* uniformed.

910 ■ *Romanticism and Realism*

Literary Analysis
Dynamic and Static Characters In what way does the characters' conversation show that the men have changed?

⑫ ▼ Critical Viewing
Which details of these Prussian officers' uniforms might intimidate citizens like the two friends? **[Analyze]**

Enrichment

The Prussian Army

The Prussian forces in "Two Friends" are portrayed as heartless and cruel. The Prussian army, under the leadership of General Helmuth von Moltke (1800–1891), was arguably the most formidable army of the nineteenth century. Many military historians consider von Moltke a master of military strategy.

Under his leadership, the Prussian army defeated the French in the Franco-Prussian War, the period in which "Two Friends" is set.

Von Moltke was a brilliant leader and molded the army into a well-disciplined fighting machine. He was one of the first generals to use the telegraph and train to communicate and move troops. This gave his forces an enormous advantage.

"But—since you came out past the outposts you have, of course, the password to return. Tell me that password and I will pardon you."

The two friends, side by side, pale, kept silent. A slight nervous trembling shook their hands.

The officer went on: "No one will ever know. You will go back placidly. The secret will disappear with you. If you refuse, it is immediate death. Choose."

They stood motionless, mouths shut.

13 The Prussian quietly went on, stretching out his hand toward the stream: "Remember that within five minutes you will be at the bottom of that river. Within five minutes! You have relatives, of course?"

Mount Valérien kept thundering.

The two fishermen stood silent. The German gave orders in his own language. Then he moved his chair so as not to be near the prisoners and twelve men took their places, twenty paces distant, rifles grounded.

The officer went on: "I give you one minute, not two seconds more."

Then he rose suddenly, approached the two Frenchmen, took Morissot by the arm, dragged him aside, whispered to him, "Quick, the password? Your friend won't know. I'll pretend to relent."

Morissot answered not a word.

The Prussian drew M. Sauvage aside and put the same question.

M. Sauvage did not answer.

They stood side by side again.

And the officer began to give commands. The soldiers raised their rifles.

Then Morissot's glance happened to fall on the sack full of gudgeons which was lying on the grass a few steps away.

A ray of sunshine made the little heap of still squirming fish gleam. And he almost weakened. In spite of his efforts his eyes filled with tears.

He stammered, "Farewell, Monsieur Sauvage."

M. Sauvage answered, "Farewell, Monsieur Morissot."

14 They shook hands, trembling from head to foot with a shudder which they could not control.

The officer shouted, "Fire!"

The twelve shots rang out together.

M. Sauvage fell straight forward, like a log. Morissot, who was taller, tottered, half turned, and fell crosswise on top of his comrade, face up, as the blood spurted from his torn shirt.

The German gave more orders.

His men scattered, then returned with rope and stones which they tied to the dead men's feet. Then they carried them to the bank.

Mount Valérien continued to roar, its summit hidden now in a mountainous cloud of smoke.

Two soldiers took Morissot by the head and the feet, two others seized M. Sauvage. They swung the bodies for a moment then let go.

Vocabulary Builder
placidly (plas´ id lē)
adv. calmly

Reading Strategy
Evaluating Characters' Decisions What will be the consequences for Paris if the two men reveal the password?

Reading Strategy
Evaluating Characters' Decisions Do you think the fate of the two friends would have been different if they had revealed the password? Explain.

15  **Reading Check**

What does the Prussian officer demand of Sauvage and Morissot?

Two Friends ■ *911*

---

13 **Reading Strategy**

Evaluating Characters' Decisions

• Remind students that when they evaluate a character's decision, they should consider the effects the decision has on the character and others around him or her.

• Read aloud the bracketed passage. Then, **ask** the first Reading Strategy question: What will be the consequences for Paris if the two men reveal the password?
Possible response: With the password, soldiers in disguise could enter Paris and sabotage its defenses, causing the city to fall to its enemies.

▶ **Monitor Progress** Encourage students to speculate about the final decision these two men have to make. Lead a discussion about what students might do in such circumstances and how difficult it would be to face this decision.

▶ **Reteach** If students have difficulty mastering the Reading Strategy, have them use the **Reading Strategy** support, p. 62 in *Unit 7 Resources,* to examine the men's decisions.

14 **Reading Strategy**

Evaluating Characters' Decisions

• Read aloud the bracketed passage. **Discuss** what might have motivated the two men's decision.
Possible response: The men felt a sense of honor and duty to their city.

• **Ask** the second Reading Strategy question: Do you think the fate of the two friends would have been different if they had revealed the password? Explain.
Possible response: Revealing the password would have made no difference because the Prussians would probably have executed the friends anyway.

15 **Reading Check**

Answer: The officer wants the men to reveal a password that would allow passage through the French outpost.

1. **Possible response:** The execution of the two men and the disposal of their bodies were especially disturbing because the friends are stripped of their humanity by the Prussians. Their deaths as well as their "catch" simply feed the machine that is war.

2. (a) The men's similar way of thinking, their mutual enjoyment of fishing, and their loyalty to Paris are characteristics of their friendship. (b) Giddiness from the absinthe and the warm weather motivate them to try fishing again.

3. (a) The villages and surrounding areas are deserted because the Prussians have seized control of the region. (b) The emptiness reflects the fact that the Prussians are in control of the region, and the Prussians pose a great danger to the two friends.

4. (a) The men think war is ignorant but inevitable, regardless of whether a country is a republic or a monarchy. (b) Their comments reveal that the men dislike war but have accepted it as a harsh reality of life. (c) These attitudes affect the outcome because although the men see war as inevitable, they do what they can to lessen its effects on others.

5. (a) The soldiers are tall, bearded, wearing flat caps, and carrying weapons; the two men are "seized, trussed up, carried off, and thrown into" a boat. (b) The forces are described as cold-blooded and callous; they act "worse than animals," as the two men had observed earlier.

6. (a) The officer threatens the friends' lives; he separates the men and offers each one freedom for the information. (b) **Possible responses:** Trying to get the men to turn on each other is unethical. Or, a soldier's duty is to get the information, by duplicity, if necessary.

They described an arc and plunged into the river feet first, for the weights made them seem to be standing upright.

There was a splash, the water trembled, then grew calm, while tiny wavelets spread to both shores.

A little blood remained on the surface.

The officer, still calm, said in a low voice: "Now the fish will have their turn."

And he went back to the house.

And all at once he caught sight of the sack of gudgeons in the grass. He picked it up, looked at it, smiled, shouted, "Wilhelm!"

A soldier in a white apron ran out. And the Prussian threw him the catch of the two and said: "Fry these little animals right away while they are still alive. They will be delicious."

Then he lighted his pipe again.

Critical Reading

1. **Respond:** What did you find especially shocking or disturbing about this story? Explain.

2. (a) **Recall:** List three characteristics of the friendship between M. Morissot and M. Sauvage. (b) **Infer:** What motivates the two men to go fishing?

3. (a) **Recall:** Why are the villages of Colombes and Argenteuil and the surrounding areas deserted? (b) **Connect:** How does the emptiness of the landscape foreshadow, or hint at, the events that occur later in the story?

4. (a) **Recall:** What do the two men say about war in relation to republics and monarchies? (b) **Draw Conclusions:** What do their comments reveal about their own attitudes? (c) **Connect:** In what way do these attitudes affect the outcome of the story?

5. (a) **Recall:** Which words describe the physical appearance and actions of the Prussian soldiers? (b) **Support:** How does this description support the two men's earlier impressions of the Prussian forces?

6. (a) **Recall:** What strategies does the Prussian officer use to force the password from the two friends? (b) **Judge:** Would you describe the Prussian officer as an ethical soldier? Explain.

7. (a) **Relate:** If you were in the place of one of the two friends in Maupassant's story, would you have gone fishing? Why or why not? (b) **Take a Position:** Should the two friends be blamed for their own deaths? Why or why not?

Go Online
Author Link
For: More about Guy de Maupassant
Visit: www.PHSchool.com
Web Code: ete-9707

Answers continued

7. (a) **Possible responses:** Some readers may say that they would not have gone because of the danger of war; others may say they would have gone to prove that they could have some kind of a normal life in the midst of war. (b) **Possible responses:** The men should be blamed because it was silly for them to leave the safety of Paris just to fish. Or, the men should not be blamed for the brutality of the Prussian soldiers.

Go Online For additional information about
Author Link Guy de Maupassant, have students type in the Web Code, then select *M* from the alphabet, and then select Guy de Maupassant.

HOW MUCH LAND DOES A MAN NEED?

Leo Tolstoy
translated by **Louise and Aylmer Maude**

Background From the sixteenth century to the mid-nineteenth century, Russian peasants were bound by law to work land they could rent but not own. They grew food meant to feed others, cultivated crops that others would sell, and worked to exhaustion to make a profit for the land-owner. Peasants could even be bought and sold with the land they worked. This story takes place after the laws were changed to allow ordinary people to purchase land. To those who had never owned it, land represented the ability to control one's destiny. Tolstoy uses land, an image close to the heart of every Russian, to explore the age-old question, "How much is enough?"

I

An elder sister came to visit her younger sister in the country. The elder was married to a tradesman in town, the younger to a peasant in the village. As the sisters sat over their tea talking, the elder began to boast of the advantages of town life: saying how comfortably they lived there, how well they dressed, what fine clothes her children wore, what good things they ate and drank, and how she went to the theater, promenades,[1] and entertainments.

The younger sister was piqued, and in turn disparaged the life of a tradesman, and stood up for that of a peasant.

"I would not change my way of life for yours," said she. "We may live roughly, but at least we are free from anxiety. You live in better style than we do, but though you often earn more than you need, you are very likely to lose all you have. You know the proverb, 'Loss and gain are brothers twain.'[2] It often happens that people who are wealthy one day are begging their bread the next. Our way is safer. Though a peasant's life is not a fat one, it is a long one. We shall never grow rich, but we shall always have enough to eat."

---

1. **promenades** (präm´ ə nädz) *n.* balls or formal dances.
2. **twain** (twān) *n.* two.

 **Reading Check**
Which sister lives the life of a country peasant?

How Much Land Does a Man Need? ■ 913

The elder sister said sneeringly:

"Enough? Yes, if you like to share with the pigs and the calves! What do you know of elegance or manners! However much your goodman may slave, you will die as you are living—on a dung heap—and your children the same."

"Well, what of that?" replied the younger. "Of course our work is rough and coarse. But, on the other hand, it is sure, and we need not bow to any one. But you, in your towns, are surrounded by temptations; today all may be right, but tomorrow the Evil One may tempt your husband with cards, wine, or women, and all will go to ruin. Don't such things happen often enough?"

Pakhom, the master of the house, was lying on the top of the stove and he listened to the women's chatter.

"It is perfectly true," thought he. "Busy as we are from childhood tilling mother earth, we peasants have no time to let any nonsense settle in our heads. Our only trouble is that we haven't land enough. If I had plenty of land, I shouldn't fear the Devil himself!"

The women finished their tea, chatted a while about dress, and then cleared away the tea-things and lay down to sleep.

But the Devil had been sitting behind the stove, and had heard all that was said. He was pleased that the peasant's wife had led her husband into boasting, and that he had said that if he had plenty of land he would not fear the Devil himself.

> **Literary Analysis**
> **Dynamic and Static Characters** In what ways does Pakhom think his life would change if he had enough land?

The Village of Andreikovo (detail), 1958, Vladimir Stozharov, The Tretyakov Gallery, Moscow
© Estate of Vladimir Stozharov/Licensed by VAGA, New York, NY

㉑ ▲ **Critical Viewing** Does this painting suggest that Pakhom will remain a peasant forever? Read the story, then confirm your prediction. **[Predict]**

914 ■ *Romanticism and Realism*

"All right," thought the Devil. "We will have a tussle. I'll give you land enough; and by means of that land I will get you into my power."

II

Close to the village there lived a lady, a small landowner who had an estate of about three hundred acres. She had always lived on good terms with the peasants until she engaged as her steward an old soldier, who took to burdening the people with fines. However careful Pakhom tried to be, it happened again and again that now a horse of his got among the lady's oats, now a cow strayed into her garden, now his calves found their way into her meadows—and he always had to pay a fine.

Pakhom paid up, but grumbled, and, going home in a temper, was rough with his family. All through that summer, Pakhom had much trouble because of this steward, and he was even glad when winter came and the cattle had to be stabled. Though he grudged the fodder when they could no longer graze on the pasture-land, at least he was free from anxiety about them.

In the winter the news got about that the lady was going to sell her land and that the keeper of the inn on the high road was bargaining for it. When the peasants heard this they were very much alarmed.

"Well," thought they, "if the innkeeper gets the land, he will worry us with fines worse than the lady's steward. We all depend on that estate."

So the peasants went on behalf of their commune, and asked the lady not to sell the land to the innkeeper, offering her a better price for it themselves. The lady agreed to let them have it. Then the peasants tried to arrange for the commune to buy the whole estate, so that it might be held by them all in common. They met twice to discuss it, but could not settle the matter; the Evil One sowed <u>discord</u> among them and they could not agree. So they decided to buy the land individually, each according to his means; and the lady agreed to this plan as she had to the other.

Presently Pakhom heard that a neighbor of his was buying fifty acres, and that the lady had consented to accept one half in cash and to wait a year for the other half. Pakhom felt envious.

"Look at that," thought he, "the land is all being sold, and I shall get none of it." So he spoke to his wife.

"Other people are buying," said he, "and we must also buy twenty acres or so. Life is becoming impossible. That manager is simply crushing us with his fines."

So they put their heads together and considered how they could manage to buy it. They had one hundred rubles[3] laid by. They sold a colt and one half of their bees, hired out one of their sons as a laborer and took his wages in advance, borrowed the rest from a brother-in-law, and so scraped together half the purchase money.

---

3. **rubles** (rōō′ bəlz) *n.* Russian money.

Vocabulary Builder
discord (dis′ kôrd) *n.*
dissension; conflict

 **Reading Check**
What motivates Pakhom and the villagers to buy land?

How Much Land Does a Man Need? ■ 915

㉒ Critical Thinking
Speculate
• Read aloud the bracketed passage with students. Point out how the landowner's actions affect Pakhom and his family.
• **Ask** students to speculate about how this experience with the landowner will affect Pakhom if he acquires more land.
Possible response: Pakhom will be a more understanding landowner because he remembers the anxiety he felt as a peasant paying rent.

㉓ Vocabulary Builder
Latin Prefix *dis-*
• Direct students' attention to the word *discord,* its definition, and its use in the story. Explain that the prefix *dis-* can mean "apart" or "not." It often changes the meaning of a word to its opposite.
• **Ask** students to name words that use this prefix. Write their suggestions on the board.
Possible response: *Disobey, disuse,* and *disarray* all use the prefix *dis-*.
• Have students suggest definitions for the words on the board and then use dictionaries to check those definitions.
• Encourage students to write a short summary of "Two Friends" using at least three words with the prefix *dis-*.

㉔ Reading Check
Answer: Pakhom and the villagers are afraid that the new landowner of the estate will burden them with heavy fines.

Differentiated Instruction   Solutions for All Learners

Strategy for English Learners
Some of the longer sentences in this story may be confusing for students. Choose some of the longer sentences, and model the process of breaking a sentence into its main subject and action to determine its basic meaning. Have students answer these questions: Who or what is this sentence about? What is happening to the subject of the sentence? Advise students to use this strategy as they read.

Enrichment for Advanced Readers
Suggest that students meet in a group to compare and contrast Tolstoy's style in this parable with the writing style of other works they have recently read. Encourage them to discover the relationship between an author's style and the central message of the story. Of the works they analyze, students should select a story style that fits its message and then explain their choice.

- Remind students that the Devil has a hand in Pakhom's decision to buy the land by sowing discord among the commune members who want to buy it.

- **Ask** students what financial arrangement makes it easier for Pakhom to buy the land.
Answer: Although Pakhom initially has to pay half the money for the land, he has two years to pay the remainder.

- Read aloud the bracketed passage. Then, **ask** students the first Reading Strategy question: Considering the costs of purchasing the land, do you think Pakhom made the right decision? Explain.
Possible responses: On the one hand, Pakhom made the right decision because he needed the land and had time to pay it off. On the other hand, it was too risky to go so heavily in debt for the land.

26 Reading Strategy

Evaluating Characters' Decisions

- Tell students to read the first paragraph in the bracketed passage independently.

- **Ask** the second Reading Strategy question: Which of Pakhom's past experiences may have influenced his decision to overlook his neighbors' behavior?
Answer: Pakhom's experience of being fined by the landowner may have influenced his decision to overlook his neighbors' behavior.

- Have students read the rest of the bracketed passage. Then, discuss as a class whether Pakhom is being reasonable in teaching a lesson to the peasants.

---

25 Having done this, Pakhom chose a farm of forty acres, some of it wooded, and went to the lady to bargain for it. They came to an agreement, and he shook hands with her upon it and paid her a deposit in advance. Then they went to town and signed the deeds; he paying half the price down, and undertaking to pay the remainder within two years.

So now Pakhom had land of his own. He borrowed seed, and sowed it on the land he had bought. The harvest was a good one, and within a year he had managed to pay off his debts both to the lady and to his brother-in-law. So he became a landowner, plowing and sowing his own land, making hay on his own land, cutting his own trees, and feeding his cattle on his own pasture. When he went out to plow his fields, or to look at his growing corn, or at his grass-meadows, his heart would fill with joy. The grass that grew and the flowers that bloomed there seemed to him unlike any that grew elsewhere. Formerly, when he had passed by that land, it had appeared the same as any other land, but now it seemed quite different.

III

So Pakhom was well-contented, and everything would have been right if the neighboring peasants would only not have trespassed on his corn-fields and meadows. He appealed to them most civilly, but they still went on: now the communal herdsmen would let the village cows stray into his meadows, then horses from the night pasture would get among his corn. **26** Pakhom turned them out again and again, and forgave their owners, and for a long time he forbore to prosecute anyone. But at last he lost patience and complained to the district court. He knew it was the peasants' want of land, and no evil intent on their part, that caused the trouble, but he thought:

"I cannot go on overlooking it or they will destroy all I have. They must be taught a lesson."

So he had them up, gave them one lesson, and then another, and two or three of the peasants were fined. After a time Pakhom's neighbors began to bear him a grudge for this, and would now and then let their cattle on to his land on purpose. One peasant even got into Pakhom's wood at night and cut down five young lime trees for their bark. Pakhom, passing through the wood one day, noticed something white. He came nearer and saw the stripped trunks lying on the ground, and close by stood the stumps where the trees had been. Pakhom was furious.

"If he had only cut one here and there it would have been bad enough," thought Pakhom, "but the rascal has actually cut down a whole clump. If I could only find out who did this, I would pay him out."

He racked his brains as to who it could be. Finally he decided: "It must be Simon—no one else could have done it." So he went to Simon's homestead to have a look round, but he found nothing, and only had an angry scene. However, he now felt more certain than ever that Simon had done it, and he lodged a complaint. Simon was summoned. The case was tried, and retried, and at the end of it all Simon was

916 ■ *Romanticism and Realism*

Reading Strategy
Evaluating Characters' Decisions Considering the costs of purchasing the land, do you think Pakhom made the right decision? Explain.

Reading Strategy
Evaluating Characters' Decisions Which of Pakhom's past experiences may have influenced his decision to overlook his neighbors' behavior?

Enrichment

Mortgages

Pakhom buys his forty-acre farm by scraping together half the purchase price and agreeing to pay the remainder within two years. Today, most home buyers apply to a local bank for a mortgage. The buyer pays a certain amount of the total asking price up front—for example, ten or fifteen percent—and the bank lends the buyer the money for the rest of the payment. The buyer repays the remainder to the bank with interest over a period of years (usually longer than Pakhom's two-year period).

Have students inquire at local banks or lending agencies about current interest rates for loans to purchase real estate. Have them find out the total cost of a specified mortgage— say, $50,000 or $100,000—over several time periods, including twenty-five, thirty, and forty years. Students may be interested in finding out how amortization rates are calculated, discovering the incremental benefits of repaying a loan in a shorter period of time.

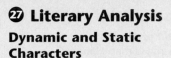

acquitted, there being no evidence against him. Pakhom felt still more aggrieved, and let his anger loose upon the elder and the judges.

"You let thieves grease your palms," said he. "If you were honest folk yourselves you would not let a thief go free."

So Pakhom quarreled with the judges and with his neighbors. Threats to burn his building began to be uttered. So though Pakhom had more land, his place in the commune was much worse than before.

About this time a rumor got about that many people were moving to new parts.

"There's no need for me to leave my land," thought Pakhom. "But some of the others may leave our village and then there would be more room for us. I would take over their land myself and make my estate a bit bigger. I could then live more at ease. As it is, I am still too cramped to be comfortable."

One day Pakhom was sitting at home when a peasant, passing through the village, happened to call in. He was allowed to stay the night, and supper was given him. Pakhom had a talk with this peasant and asked him where he came from. The stranger answered that he came from beyond the Volga,[4] where he had been working. One word led to another, and the man went on to say that many people were settling in those parts. He told how some people from his village had settled there. They had joined the commune, and had had twenty-five acres per man granted them. The land was so good, he said, that the rye sown on it grew as high as a horse, and so thick that five cuts of a sickle made a sheaf. One peasant, he said, had brought nothing with him but his bare hands, and now he had six horses and two cows of his own.

Pakhom's heart kindled with desire. He thought:

"Why should I suffer in this narrow hole, if one can live so well elsewhere? I will sell my land and my homestead here, and with the money I will start afresh over there and get everything new. In this crowded place one is always having trouble. But I must first go and find out all about it myself."

Toward summer he got ready and started. He went down the Volga on a steamer to Samara,[5] then walked another three hundred miles on foot, and at last reached the place. It was just as the stranger had said. The peasants had plenty of land: every man had twenty-five acres of communal land given him for his use, and any one who had money could buy, besides, at two shillings an acre as much good freehold land[6] as he wanted.

Having found out all he wished to know, Pakhom returned home as autumn came on, and began selling off his belongings. He sold his land at a profit, sold his homestead and all his cattle, and withdrew from

---

4. **Volga** (väl′ gə) the major river in western Russia.
5. **Samara** (Sə ma′ rə) city in eastern Russia.
6. **freehold land** privately owned land that the owner can lease to others for a fee.

   **Reading Check**
What does Pakhom think he can find beyond the Volga River?

How Much Land Does a Man Need? ■ 917

---

(27) Literary Analysis
Dynamic and Static Characters

• Discuss with students whether at this point in the story they think Pakhom is changing or the people around him are changing.

• Remind them that a character who changes is a dynamic character; a character who remains the same is a static character.

• Then, read aloud the bracketed passage. **Ask** students: What new challenges plague Pakhom now that he is a landowner?
Answer: Pakhom quarrels with his neighbors and the judges, and he receives threats against his property.

(28) Critical Thinking
Infer

• Have students read aloud the bracketed passage. Discuss the description the peasant gives about the land beyond the Volga.

• Guide students to see that the Devil may be playing a role in this passage. **Ask:** Do you think the description about the land is truthful? If not, why is the man telling Pakhom about the land?
Possible response: The man, who may be the Devil in disguise, is exaggerating, trying to tempt Pakhom to buy more land.

(29) Background
Geography

Samara is a river that rises in the Ural Mountains and flows west-northwest into the Volga. At the time of the story, Samara was also the name of a city at the junction of the Volga and Samara Rivers.

(30) Reading Check
Answer: Pakhom thinks he can get more and better land as well as freedom from the problems he is having with the peasants in his village.

Differentiated Instruction Solutions for All Learners

Background for Special Needs Students
Tell students that the use of communal land, like that mentioned in the passage above, is typical of many agrarian societies. Usually, a section of land is set aside on which everyone in a village may graze cattle or plant a garden. Discuss with students the pros and cons of the communal land system.

Strategy for Less Proficient Readers
Organize students into small groups. Have them discuss the decisions that Pakhom has made so far. Urge students to offer their opinions about whether these decisions have been good for Pakhom and his family. Explain that this information will help them evaluate Pakhom's decisions throughout the story.

Support for English Learners
Students may have difficulty with some of the vocabulary in this selection. Help them complete Vocabulary Warm-up List and Vocabulary Warm-up Practice pages 57–58 in *Unit 7 Resources.* Then post meanings for land-related words they encounter, such as *fallow, sheaf,* and *arable* and help them with pronunciations.

31 Humanities

Cornfield at Ewell,
by William Holman Hunt

This landscape depicts a large field of grain similar to those Pakhom would have cultivated in Russia. The artist, William Holman Hunt, was a member of the Pre-Raphaelite Brotherhood in England, a group of artists and poets who held to pre- and early-Renaissance standards and ideals in art. They strove to portray nature in a way that demonstrated both its detail and its simplicity.

Use the following questions for discussion:

• What quality does this field have that might appeal to Pakhom?
Possible response: The field is vast and potentially productive.

• Do you think this is an appropriate illustration for this story? Explain.
Possible response: The image of a lone man in a vast expanse of land suits the story well. It illustrates Pakhom's desire for more and more land.

32 Critical Viewing

Possible response: The vast expanse in the painting is a large amount of land for one man to manage. Should Pakhom be hurt or sick, he stands to lose a great deal.

membership of the commune. He only waited till the spring, and then started with his family for the new settlement.

IV

As soon as Pakhom and his family reached their new abode, he applied for admission into the commune of a large village. He stood treat to the elders and obtained the necessary documents. Five shares of communal land were given him for his own and his sons' use: that is to say—125 acres (not all together, but in different fields) besides the use of the communal pasture. Pakhom put up the buildings he needed, and bought cattle. Of the communal land alone he had three times as

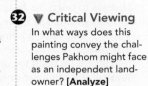

32 ▼ Critical Viewing
In what ways does this painting convey the challenges Pakhom might face as an independent landowner? **[Analyze]**

Cornfield at Ewell, William Holman Hunt

918 ■ *Romanticism and Realism*

Crop Rotation
Pakhom mentions the practices of rotating crops and of sowing wheat for one or two years and then allowing the field to lie fallow until it is covered with grass. This process has a scientific justification. Certain crops, such as wheat and corn, leach nutrients from the soil. Other crops, such as alfalfa or soybeans, can reconstitute the soil, making it ready for planting grain again. By rotating crops from year to year, farmers can increase the productivity of their cropland.

Sometimes, farmers let the land "rest": They do not plant it but let it lie fallow.

Students might like to speculate on how greed might make a farmer sacrifice productivity over time. If a farmer were shortsighted and planted grain year after year in hopes of making the best profit, eventually the grain crop would fail because the soil would be barren.

much as at his former home, and the land was good corn-land. He was ten times better off than he had been. He had plenty of arable land and pasturage, and could keep as many head of cattle as he liked.

At first, in the bustle of building and settling down, Pakhom was pleased with it all, but when he got used to it he began to think that even here he had not enough land. The first year, he sowed wheat on his share of the communal land and had a good crop. He wanted to go on sowing wheat, but had not enough communal land for the purpose, and what he had already used was not available; for in those parts wheat is only sown on virgin soil or on fallow land. It is sown for one or two years, and then the land lies fallow till it is again overgrown with prairie grass. There were many who wanted such land and there was not enough for all; so that people quarreled about it. Those who were better off wanted it for growing wheat, and those who were poor wanted it to let to dealers, so that they might raise money to pay their taxes. Pakhom wanted to sow more wheat, so he rented land from a dealer for a year. He sowed much wheat and had a fine crop, but the land was too far from the village—the wheat had to be carted more than ten miles. After a time Pakhom noticed that some peasant-dealers were living on separate farms and were growing wealthy; and he thought:

"If I were to buy some freehold land and have a homestead on it, it would be a different thing altogether. Then it would all be nice and compact."

The question of buying freehold land recurred to him again and again.

He went on in the same way for three years, renting land and sowing wheat. The seasons turned out well and the crops were good, so that he began to lay money by. He might have gone on living contentedly, but he grew tired of having to rent other people's land every year, and having to scramble for it. Wherever there was good land to be had, the peasants would rush for it and it was taken up at once, so that unless you were sharp about it you got none. It happened in the third year that he and a dealer together rented a piece of pasture land from some peasants; and they had already plowed it up, when there was some dispute and the peasants went to law about it and things fell out so that the labor was all lost.

Reading Strategy
Evaluating Characters' Decisions What happiness have Pakhom's decisions brought him?

Reading Check 35
What thought continues to bother Pakhom?

How Much Land Does a Man Need? ■ 919

920

920

36 Background

Pakhom's Travels

The Bashkirs live "far away" from Pakhom's present home, but their land is still in Europe, not Asia. Pakhom is moving eastward (somewhat like America's westward-moving pioneers) in search of cheaper and more abundant land.

37 Critical Thinking

Analyze

• Have a volunteer read aloud the bracketed passage. Point out Pakhom's interest in obtaining thousands of acres of land.

• Remind students that Pakhom once told his wife that he needed only twenty acres of land. **Ask** why he now chooses to pass up acquiring "only thirteen hundred acres" to try to acquire even more land? **Answer:** Pakhom is becoming increasingly greedy for land.

38 Critical Viewing

Possible response: Pakhom's desire for more land seems foolish because it would be extremely difficult to tend such a large amount of land with hand tools.

"If it were my own land," thought Pakhom, "I should be independent, and there would not be all this unpleasantness."

So Pakhom began looking out for land which he could buy; and he came across a peasant who had bought thirteen hundred acres, but having got into difficulties was willing to sell again cheap. Pakhom bargained and haggled with him, and at last they settled the price at 1,500 rubles, part in cash and part to be paid later. They had all but clinched the matter when a passing dealer happened to stop at Pakhom's one day to get a feed for his horses. He drank tea with Pakhom and they had a talk. The dealer said that he was just returning from the land of the Bashkirs,[7] far away, where he had bought thirteen thousand acres of land, all for 1,000 rubles. Pakhom questioned him further, and the tradesman said:

"All one need do is to make friends with the chiefs. I gave away about one hundred rubles' worth of silk robes and carpets, besides a case of tea, and I gave wine to those who would drink it; and I got the land for less than a penny[8] an acre." And he showed Pakhom the title-deeds, saying:

"The land lies near a river, and the whole prairie is virgin soil."

Pakhom plied him with questions, and the tradesman said:

"There is more land there than you could cover if you walked a year, and it all belongs to the Bashkirs. They are as simple as sheep, and land can be got almost for nothing."

"There, now," thought Pakhom, "with my 1,000 rubles, why should I get only thirteen hundred acres, and saddle myself with a debt besides? If I take it out there, I can get more than ten times as much for the money."

V

Pakhom inquired how to get to the place, and as soon as the tradesman had left him, he prepared to go there himself. He left his wife to look after the homestead, and started on his journey taking his man with him. They stopped at a town on their way and bought a case of tea, some wine, and other presents, as the trademan had advised. On and on they went until they had gone more than three hundred miles, and on the seventh day they came to a place where the Bashkirs had pitched their tents. It was all just as the tradesman had said. The people lived on the steppes,[9] by a river, in felt-covered tents. They neither tilled the ground, nor ate bread. Their cattle and horses grazed in herds on the steppe. The colts were tethered behind the tents, and the mares were driven to them twice a day. The mares were milked, and from the milk kumiss[10] was made. It was the women who prepared kumiss, and they also made cheese. As far as the men were concerned,

▲ Critical Viewing 38

An iron sickle such as this might be used to clear fields of tall weeds and grasses. With this information in mind, does Pakhom's desire for more land seem foolish? Explain. **[Criticize]**

---

7. **Bashkirs** (bash kirz´) nomadic people who live in the plains of southwestern Russia.
8. **penny** here, one hundredth of a ruble.
9. **steppe** (step) *n.* high grassland of central Asia.
10. **kumiss** (koo´ mis) *n.* mare's milk that has been fermented and is used as a drink.

drinking kumiss and tea, eating mutton, and playing on their pipes, was all they cared about. They were all stout and merry, and all the summer long they never thought of doing any work. They were quite ignorant, and knew no Russian, but were good-natured enough.

As soon as they saw Pakhom, they came out of their tents and gathered round their visitor. An interpreter was found, and Pakhom told them he had come about some land. The Bashkirs seemed very glad; they took Pakhom and led him into one of the best tents, where they made him sit on some down cushions placed on a carpet, while they sat round him. They gave him some tea and kumiss, and had a sheep killed, and gave him mutton to eat. Pakhom took presents out of his cart and distributed them among the Bashkirs, and divided the tea amongst them. The Bashkirs were delighted. They talked a great deal among themselves, and then told the interpreter to translate.

"They wish to tell you," said the interpreter, "that they like you, and that it is our custom to do all we can to please a guest and to repay him for his gifts. You have given us presents, now tell us which of the things we possess please you best, that we may present them to you."

"What pleases me best here," answered Pakhom, "is your land. Our land is crowded and the soil is exhausted; but you have plenty of land and it is good land. I never saw the like of it."

The interpreter translated. The Bashkirs talked among themselves for a while. Pakhom could not understand what they were saying, but saw that they were much amused and that they shouted and laughed. Then they were silent and looked at Pakhom while the interpreter said:

"They wish me to tell you that in return for your presents they will gladly give you as much land as you want. You have only to point it out with your hand and it is yours."

The Bashkirs talked again for a while and began to dispute. Pakhom asked what they were disputing about, and the interpreter told him that some of them thought they ought to ask their chief about the land and not act in his absence, while others thought there was no need to wait for his return.

VI

While the Bashkirs were disputing, a man in a large fox-fur cap appeared on the scene. They all became silent and rose to their feet. The interpreter said, "This is our chief himself."

Pakhom immediately fetched the best dressing-gown and five pounds of tea, and offered these to the chief. The chief accepted them, and seated himself in the place of honor. The Bashkirs at once began telling him something. The chief listened for a while, then made a sign with his head for them to be silent, and addressing himself to Pakhom, said in Russian:

"Well, let it be so. Choose whatever piece of land you like; we have plenty of it."

Literary Analysis
Dynamic and Static Characters Which elements of the Bashkirs' lifestyle has Pakhom sought for himself since his days as a peasant farmer?

 **Reading Check** **40**

What generosities do the Bashkirs show Pakhom?

---

39 Literary Analysis

Dynamic and Static Characters

- Have students read the bracketed passage describing the lifestyle of the Bashkirs.

- Then, have them discuss how the Bashkir way of life differs from Pakhom's way of life.

- **Ask** students the Literary Analysis question: Which elements of the Bashkirs' lifestyle has Pakhom sought for himself since his days as a peasant farmer?
  Possible response: Pakhom has sought to have an easy, comfortable life and not have to work very hard. Similarly, the Bashkirs spend their days eating, drinking, and playing music instead of working.

▶ **Monitor Progress** Review with students the differences between dynamic and static characters. Then ask them to explain which type of character Pakhom is and why.

▶ **Reteach** If students have difficulty determining whether Pakhom is a dynamic or static character, have them use the **Literary Analysis** support, page 61 in *Unit 7 Resources*.

40 Reading Check

Answer: The Bashkirs treat Pakhom as an honored guest, give him food and drink, and offer to give him land.

Differentiated Instruction   Solutions for All Learners

Strategy for Special Needs Students	**Support for Less Proficient Readers**
Students may enjoy looking at a topographical map of Russia to get a sense of the vast distances Pakhom covers in his quest for land. Ask them to find some of the points of reference in the story: the Volga, the Samara, and the steppes or plains of southwestern Russia.	The conversation between Pakhom and the Bashkirs demonstrates Pakhom's obsessive nature. Point out specific context clues in this section that show Pakhom's obsession with acquiring land. Discuss with students how Pakhom's tense feelings contrast with the carefree attitude of the Bashkirs.

Evaluating Characters' Decisions

- Have a volunteer read aloud the bracketed passage in which Pakhom asks for a deed. Remind students that the Bashkirs are nomadic herders. Discuss how the Bashkirs might view the land differently than farmers such as Pakhom view it.

- **Ask** students the Reading Strategy question: What past experiences might have influenced Pakhom's decision to obtain a deed from the Bashkirs?
  Answer: Pakhom's previous experience of buying land and obtaining a deed, as well as his experience of renting land and not having a deed, might have influenced his decision to request a deed from the Bashkirs.

42 Critical Thinking

Speculate

- Have students read aloud the bracketed passage. Then, have them discuss what might be going through Pakhom's mind when he hears that, for one price, he can get as much land as he can walk around in a day.

- **Ask** students to speculate about how this chance of getting land might be Pakhom's downfall and the fulfillment of the Devil's plan.
  Possible response: In his greed, Pakhom will try to take too much land and something bad will happen as a result.

"How can I take as much as I like?" thought Pakhom. "I must get a deed to make it secure, or else they may say, 'It is yours,' and afterward may take it away again."

"Thank you for your kind words," he said aloud. "You have much land, and I only want a little. But I should like to be sure which bit is mine. Could it not be measured and made over to me? Life and death are in God's hands. You good people give it to me, but your children might wish to take it away again."

"You are quite right," said the chief. "We will make it over to you."

"I heard that a dealer had been here," continued Pakhom, "and that you gave him a little land, too, and signed title-deeds to that effect. I should like to have it done in the same way."

The chief understood.

"Yes," replied he, "that can be done quite easily. We have a scribe, and we will go to town with you and have the deed properly sealed."

"And what will be the price?" asked Pakhom.

"Our price is always the same: one thousand rubles a day."

Pakhom did not understand.

"A day? What measure is that? How many acres would that be?"

"We do not know how to reckon it out," said the chief. "We sell it by the day. As much as you can go around on your feet in a day is yours, and the price is one thousand rubles a day."

Pakhom was surprised.

"But in a day you can get around a large tract of land," he said.

The chief laughed.

"It will all be yours!" said he. "But there is one condition: If you don't return on the same day to the spot whence you started, your money is lost."

"But how am I to mark the way that I have gone?"

"Why, we shall go to any spot you like, and stay there. You must start from that spot and make your round, taking a spade with you. Wherever you think necessary, make a mark. At every turning, dig a hole and pile up the turf; then afterward we will go round with a plow from hole to hole. You may make as large a circuit as you please, but before the sun sets you must return to the place you started from. All the land you cover will be yours."

Pakhom was delighted. It was decided to start early next morning. They talked a while, and after drinking some more kumiss and eating some more mutton, they had tea again, and then the night came on. They gave Pakhom a feather-bed to sleep on, and the Bashkirs dispersed for the night, promising to assemble the next morning at daybreak and ride out before sunrise to the appointed spot.

VII

Pakhom lay on the feather-bed, but could not sleep. He kept thinking about the land.

"What a large tract I will mark off!" thought he. "I can easily do thirty-five miles in a day. The days are long now, and within a circuit of thirty-

Reading Strategy
Evaluating Characters' Decisions What past experiences might have influenced Pakhom's decision to obtain a deed from the Bashkirs?

Enrichment

The Bashkirs

The Bashkirs that Pakhom deals with have lived in what is now the eastern part of European Russia since the thirteenth century. Their lands came under Russian control in the sixteenth century, and the Russians began colonizing the land, gradually pushing the Bashkirs out. Angry and resentful of the colonists, the Bashkirs staged many uprisings, but they were harshly repressed by the Russian government.

Originally, the Bashkirs were nomadic herders who raised horses, sheep, goats, cattle, and at one time, camels. By the end of the nineteenth century, pressure from colonization forced the Bashkirs to give up their nomadic way of life and become farmers living in settled villages.

five miles what a lot of land there will be! I will sell the poorer land, or let it to peasants, but I'll pick out the best and farm it. I will buy two ox-teams, and hire two more laborers. About a hundred and fifty acres shall be plowland, and I will pasture cattle on the rest."

Pakhom lay awake all night, and dozed off only just before dawn. Hardly were his eyes closed when he had a dream. He thought he was lying in that same tent and heard somebody chuckling outside. He wondered who it could be, and rose and went out, and he saw the Bashkir chief sitting in front of the tent holding his sides and rolling about with laughter. Going nearer to the chief, Pakhom asked: "What are you laughing at?" But he saw that it was no longer the chief, but the dealer who had recently stopped at his house and had told him about the land. Just as Pakhom was going to ask, "Have you been here long?" he saw that it was not the dealer, but the peasant who had come up from the Volga, long ago, to Pakhom's old home. Then he saw that it was not the peasant either, but the Devil himself with hoofs and horns, sitting there and chuckling, and before him lay a man barefoot, <u>prostrate</u> on the ground, with only trousers and a shirt on. And Pakhom dreamt that he looked more attentively to see what sort of a man it was that was lying there, and he saw that the man was dead, and that it was himself! He awoke horror-struck.

"What things one does dream," thought he.

Looking round he saw through the open door that the dawn was breaking.

"It's time to wake them up," thought he. "We ought to be starting."

He got up, roused his man (who was sleeping in his cart), bade him harness; and went to call the Bashkirs.

"It's time to go to the steppe to measure the land," he said.

The Bashkirs rose and assembled, and the chief came too. Then they began drinking kumiss again, and offered Pakhom some tea, but he would not wait.

"If we are to go, let us go. It is high time," said he.

VIII

The Bashkirs got ready and they all started; some mounted on horses, and some in carts. Pakhom drove in his own small cart with his servant and took a spade with him. When they reached the steppe, the morning red was beginning to kindle. They ascended a hillock (called by the Bashkirs a *shikhan*) and, dismounting from their carts and their horses, gathered in one spot. The chief came up to Pakhom and stretching out his arm toward the plain;

Themes in World Masterpieces

43 The Parable

A **parable** is a story used to teach a lesson. Generally, parables focus on one or two characters and on a specific circumstance that motivates their actions. In addition, the outcome of a parable seems inevitable. The lessons reflect moral choices motivated by ambition, greed, or wisdom. Since the aim of most parables is to reach many people, the stories tend to be simple and brief.

Many cultures use parables to teach values specific to their culture, but the similarities in stories from all over the world are striking. For example, the Lenape, a Native American people, use the story "The Greedy Maiden" to answer the same question posed by Tolstoy: How much is enough?

Critics have noted that Tolstoy's story echoes the biblical parable of the rich fool (Luke 12:16–20), the story of a wealthy farmer who incurs the wrath of God by tearing down his barns and building larger ones.

Connect to the Literature

In what ways might Pakhom's dream be a sort of parable—and a preview of events to come?

Vocabulary Builder
prostrate (präs´ trāt) *adj.*
lying with one's face down

 Reading Check 45
How many miles does Pakhom plan to walk?

How Much Land Does a Man Need? ■ 923

---

43 Themes in World Literature

The Parable The following biblical parable of the rich fool (Luke 12: 16–20, King James Version) is similar to Pakhom's tale:

16 And he spake a parable unto them, saying, The ground of a certain rich man brought forth plentifully:

17 And he thought within himself, saying, What shall I do, because I have no room where to bestow my fruits?

18 And he said, This will I do: I will pull down my barns, and build greater; and there will I bestow all my fruits and my goods.

19 And I will say to my soul, Soul, thou have much goods laid up for many years; take thine ease, eat, drink, and be merry.

20 But God said unto him, Thou fool, this night thy soul shall be required of thee: then whose shall those things be, which thou has provided?

Connect to the Literature Point out to students that a fable is also a story used to teach a moral, but usually features animal characters. Ask students to share parables from their native cultures to determine what similarities they share. Then, ask students to discuss Pakhom's dream and ask what it might preview.
Possible response: The dream is a parable because despite the appearance of each of the three men, all change into one another until only the Devil is left. Furthermore, the sight of Pakhom's corpse foreshadows what will happen to him as he continues pursuing his greed for land.

44 Critical Thinking
Speculate
- Have students read the bracketed passage independently. Discuss what the dream says about the Devil's role in Pakhom's life.
- **Ask** students to speculate about the outcome of the story on the basis of Pakhom's dream.
Possible response: Pakhom will die in the end.

45 Reading Check
Answer: Pakhom plans to walk thirty-five miles.

46 Literary Analysis
Dynamic and Static Characters

- Direct students' attention to the bracketed passage.
- Remind students that years have passed since Pakhom first set out to increase his land holdings. Have them note how much land Pakhom is now considering.
- Then, **ask** students the Literary Analysis question: In what ways has ambition changed Pakhom?
Answer: Pakhom has become greedy for land. He is no longer striving to have a life of ease; he wants only to acquire as much land as possible, even though one man could not work it all.

47 Humanities

Field, Moscow, Idaho,
by David Brookover

This photograph illustrates the principle of *linear perspective*. Objects appear smaller as they recede into the distance, and lines that seem parallel actually converge at a vanishing point on the horizon. This vision of land as far as the eye can see would have tempted Pakhom.

Use the following questions for discussion:

- How do you think this scene would have made Pakhom feel?
Possible response: Pakhom would have become excited at the prospect of buying this land, or he would have felt envy because he did not own it.
- How would you react to owning such a vast tract of land?
Possible response: Some viewers may think they would enjoy the experience of ownership; others may think life would be lonely.

48 Critical Viewing

Possible response: Pakhom might imagine all the land planted with his own grain.

---

46 "See," said he, "all this, as far as your eye can reach, is ours. You may have any part of it you like."

Pakhom's eyes glistened: it was all virgin soil, as flat as the palm of your hand, as black as the seed of a poppy, and in the hollows different kinds of grasses grew breast high.

The chief took off his fox-fur cap, placed it on the ground and said:

"This will be the mark. Start from here, and return here again. All the land you go round shall be yours."

Pakhom took out his money and put it on the cap. Then he took off his outer coat, remaining in his sleeveless under-coat. He unfastened his girdle[11] and tied it tight below his stomach, put a little bag of bread into the breast of his coat, and tying a flask of water to his girdle, he drew up the tops of his boots, took the spade from his man, and stood ready to start. He considered for some moments which way he had better go—it was tempting everywhere.

"No matter," he concluded, "I will go toward the rising sun."

He turned his face to the east, stretched himself, and waited for the sun to appear above the rim.

"I must lose no time," he thought, "and it is easier walking while it is still cool."

The sun's rays had hardly flashed above the horizon, before Pakhom, carrying the spade over his shoulder, went down into the steppe.

Pakhom started walking neither slowly nor quickly. After having gone a thousand yards he stopped, dug a hole, and placed pieces of turf one on another to make it more visible. Then he went on; and now that he had walked off his stiffness he quickened his pace. After a while he dug another hole.

Pakhom looked back. The hillock could be distinctly seen in the sunlight, with the people on it, and the glittering tires of the cartwheels. At a rough guess Pakhom concluded that he had walked three miles. It was growing warmer; he took off his under-coat, flung it across his

---

11. **girdle** (gurd´ əl) *n.* belt or sash.

47

924 ■ *Romanticism and Realism*

Literary Analysis
Dynamic and Static Characters In what ways has ambition changed Pakhom?

48 ▼ **Critical Viewing**
What might Pakhom imagine for himself while looking at land such as this? **[Speculate]**

shoulder, and went on again. It had grown quite warm now; he looked at the sun, it was time to think of breakfast.

"The first shift is done, but there are four in a day, and it is too soon yet to turn. But I will just take off my boots," said he to himself.

He sat down, took off his boots, stuck them into his girdle, and went on. It was easy walking now.

"I will go on for another three miles," thought he, "and then turn to the left. This spot is so fine, that it would be a pity to lose it. The further one goes, the better the land seems."

He went straight on for a while, and when he looked round, the hillock was scarcely visible and the people on it looked like black ants, and he could just see something glistening there in the sun.

"Ah," thought Pakhom, "I have gone far enough in this direction, it is time to turn. Besides I am in a regular sweat, and very thirsty."

He stopped, dug a large hole, and heaped up pieces of turf. Next he untied his flask, had a drink, and then turned sharply to the left. He went on and on; the grass was high, and it was very hot.

Pakhom began to grow tired: he looked at the sun and saw that it was noon.

"Well," he thought, "I must have a rest."

He sat down, and ate some bread and drank some water; but he did not lie down, thinking that if he did he might fall asleep. After sitting a little while, he went on again. At first he walked easily: the food had strengthened him; but it had become terribly hot and he felt sleepy. Still he went on, thinking: "An hour to suffer, a lifetime to live."

He went a long way in this direction also, and was about to turn to the left again, when he perceived a damp hollow: "It would be a pity to leave that out," he thought. "Flax would do well there." So he went on past the hollow and dug a hole on the other side of it before he turned the corner. Pakhom looked toward the hillock. The heat made the air hazy: it seemed to be quivering, and through the haze the people on the hillock could scarcely be seen.

Reading Strategy
Evaluating Characters' Decisions What are the possible implications of Pakhom's decision to "go on for another three miles"?

✓ **Reading Check** 50

What obstacles does Pakhom encounter as he walks?

How Much Land Does a Man Need? ■ 925

49 **Reading Strategy**
Evaluating Characters' Decisions

• Have a student read aloud the bracketed passage. **Ask:** What does Pakhom mean when he says "The first shift is done, but there are four in a day"?
Answer: Pakhom means that he has gone one quarter of the square, or one side of the square, he plans to walk.

• **Ask** students the Reading Strategy question: What are the possible implications of Pakhom's decision to "go on for another three miles"?
Possible response: By going that far, Pakhom may not be able to get back to the starting point before sunset.

▶ **Monitor Progress** Review with students the decisions Pakhom has made up to this point. Have students discuss at what point they think Pakhom began to make bad decisions.

▶ **Reteach** To clarify the Reading Strategy for students, review with them the instruction on p. 905 before they evaluate Pakhom's decisions.

50 **Reading Check**

Answer: Pakhom encounters extreme heat, thirst, hunger, and fatigue.

Differentiated Instruction Solutions for All Learners

Strategy for Less Proficient Readers
As students read the account of Pakhom's walk, tell them to use sticky notes to mark when Pakhom turns the three corners to form the sides of his new property. This will help them keep track of his decisions and his progress and give clues about what will happen in the story.

Support for English Learners
Make sure that students understand that the words in quotation marks above are words that Pakhom is thinking. Point out that Pakhom is alone and is not having a conversation with anyone. Have students review the selection and identify other examples of this technique.

Enrichment for Gifted/Talented Students
Remind students that as Pakhom walks, the Bashkirs are watching him from where they are waiting on a hill. Suggest that students write a brief dialogue between the Bashkir chief and the other tribesmen as they watch Pakhom walk the land. Have students share their dialogues with the class.

⑤ Literary Analysis
Dynamic and Static Characters

- Remind students of Pakhom's growing ambition and his eventual discontent each time he acquires additional land. Then, read aloud the bracketed section.

- **Ask** the Literary Analysis question: Do you think Pakhom will be satisfied with his new tract of land? Explain.
  Answer: Pakhom is never satisfied with his acquisitions, and he will eventually become dissatisfied with this amount of land as well.

- At this point, you may want to discuss how Pakhom's changing character affects his decisions. Have students explain how Pakhom's greed has influenced the decisions he has made so far.

⑤ Reading Strategy
Evaluating Characters' Decisions

- Discuss the image of Pakhom described in the opening of Section IX. Point out that he is on the last leg of his walk but still far from the end.

- **Ask** the Reading Strategy question: Why do you think Pakhom did not prepare for his exhaustion as the day progressed?
  Possible response: In Pakhom's greed, he did not want to slow down or shorten the distance that he walked, and so he became exhausted.

"Ah!" thought Pakhom, "I have made the sides too long; I must make this one shorter." And he went along the third side, stepping faster. He looked at the sun: it was nearly half-way to the horizon, and he had not yet done two miles of the third side of the square. He was still ten miles from the goal.

"No," he thought, "though it will make my land lop-sided, I must hurry back in a straight line now. I might go too far, and as it is I have a great deal of land."

So Pakhom hurriedly dug a hole, and turned straight toward the hillock.

IX

Pakhom went straight toward the hillock, but he now walked with difficulty. He was exhausted from the heat, his bare feet were cut and bruised, and his legs began to fail. He longed to rest, but it was impossible if he meant to get back before sunset. The sun waits for no man, and it was sinking lower and lower.

"Oh, dear," he thought, "if only I have not blundered trying for too much! What if I am too late?"

He looked toward the hillock and at the sun. He was still far from his goal, and the sun was already near the rim.

Pakhom walked on and on; it was very hard walking but he went quicker and quicker. He pressed on, but was still far from the place. He began running, threw away his coat, his boots, his flask, and his cap, and kept only the spade which he used as a support.

"What shall I do?" he thought again. "I have grasped too much and ruined the whole affair. I can't get there before the sun sets."

And this fear made him still more breathless. Pakhom went on running, his soaking shirt and trousers stuck to him and his mouth was parched. His breast was working like a blacksmith's bellows, his heart was beating like a hammer, and his legs were giving way as if they did not belong to him. Pakhom was seized with terror lest he should die of the strain.

Though afraid of death, he could not stop. "After having run all that way they will call me a fool if I stop now," thought he. And he ran on and on, and drew near and heard the Bashkirs yelling and shouting to him, and their cries inflamed his heart still more. He gathered his last strength and ran on.

The sun was close to the rim, and cloaked in mist looked large, and red as blood. Now, yes now, it was about to set! The sun was quite low, but he was also quite near his aim. Pakhom could already see the people on the hillock waving their arms to hurry him up. He could see the fox-fur cap on the ground and the money on it, and the chief sitting on the ground holding his sides. And Pakhom remembered his dream.

"There's plenty of land," thought he, "but will God let me live on it? I have lost my life, I have lost my life! I shall never reach that spot!"

Pakhom looked at the sun, which had reached the earth: one side of it had already disappeared. With all his remaining strength he rushed

Literary Analysis
Dynamic and Static Characters Do you think Pakhom will be satisfied with his new tract of land? Explain.

Reading Strategy
Evaluating Characters' Decisions Why do you think Pakhom did not prepare for his exhaustion as the day progressed?

Enrichment

The Image of the Sun
In his critical biography of Tolstoy, William W. Rowe applauds the effectiveness of the ending of Tolstoy's story:

The image of the sun (which "will not wait") is particularly successful, as it races in its arching journey across the sky against the wide curve of Pakhom's greed upon the ground. The fact that Pakhom's heart pounds like a hammer while the sun turns blood-red is a grimly apt anticipation of the blood that will issue from his mouth when he dies. . . .

At the end, both Pakhom and the sun disappear beneath the ground after tracing their curving courses above the earth—a focus that appropriately reinforces the deadly playfulness of the story's title.

on, bending his body forward so that his legs could hardly follow fast enough to keep him from falling. Just as he reached the hillock it suddenly grew dark. He looked up—the sun had already set! He gave a cry: "All my labor has been in vain," thought he, and was about to stop, but he heard the Bashkirs still shouting, and remembered that though to him, from below, the sun seemed to have set, they on the hillock could still see it. He took a long breath and ran up the hillock. It was still light there. He reached the top and saw the cap. Before it sat the chief laughing and holding his sides. Again Pakhom remembered his dream, and he uttered a cry: his legs gave way beneath him, he fell forward and reached the cap with his hands.

"Ah, that's a fine fellow!" exclaimed the chief. "He has gained much land!"

Pakhom's servant came running up and tried to raise him, but he saw that blood was flowing from his mouth. Pakhom was dead!

The Bashkirs clicked their tongues to show their pity.

His servant picked up the spade and dug a grave long enough for Pakhom to lie in, and buried him in it. Six feet from his head to his heels was all he needed.

Critical Reading

1. **Respond:** If you were in Pakhom's place, at what point might you be satisfied with your property? Explain.

2. **(a) Recall:** What does the younger sister say about peasant life and city life? **(b) Connect:** Considering the outcome of the story, what is ironic, or surprising, about the younger sister's comments?

3. **(a) Recall:** What changes Pakhom's attitude toward his first plot of land? **(b) Speculate:** Explain whether you think that Pakhom's attitude would have remained the same if he had not had difficulties with his neighbors.

4. **(a) Recall:** Besides Pakhom, who is featured in his dream? **(b) Infer:** What does the dream suggest about the Devil's role in the story?

5. **(a) Recall:** In the end, how much land did Pakhom need? **(b) Analyze:** What is ironic about the final line? **(c) Criticize:** Did you find the ending satisfying? Why or why not?

6. **(a) Apply:** Greek playwright Socrates wrote, "He is richest who is content with the least. He who has little and wants less is richer than he that has much and wants more." Apply this sentiment to the story. **(b) Take a Stand:** Do you agree with Socrates? Why or why not?

Go Online
Author Link
For: More about Leo Tolstoy
Visit: www.PHSchool.com
Web Code: ete-9708

How Much Land Does a Man Need? ■ 927

53 *A Problem*

Anton Chekhov *translated by* Constance Garnett

The Library at Windsor Castle, Joseph Nash, National Trust Photographic Library

55 ▲ **Critical Viewing** In what ways is family honor reflected in a formal study like this one? **[Analyze]**

928 ■ *Romanticism and Realism*

Background

In the nineteenth century, members of the Russian aristocracy lived on wealth that had been accumulated generations earlier. For this class, honor meant more than displays of good behavior. Honor required preserving the reputation and heritage of a long-standing family name. When good fortunes changed and money became unavailable, a family name and its history of prosperity suggested the promise of stability to come. Such a promise was often all the aristocrats could rely on to save them from imminent financial disaster.

The strictest measures were taken that the Uskovs' family secret might not leak out and become generally known. Half of the servants were sent off to the theater or the circus; the other half were sitting in the kitchen and not allowed to leave it. Orders were given that no one was to be admitted. The wife of the Colonel, her sister, and the governess, though they had been initiated into the secret, kept up a pretense of knowing nothing; they sat in the dining-room and did not show themselves in the drawing-room or the hall.

Sasha Uskov, the young man of twenty-five who was the cause of all the commotion, had arrived some time before, and by the advice of kind-hearted Ivan Markovitch, his uncle, who was taking his part, he sat meekly in the hall by the door leading to the study, and prepared himself to make an open, candid explanation.

The other side of the door, in the study, a family council was being held. The subject under discussion was an exceedingly disagreeable and delicate one. Sasha Uskov had cashed at one of the banks a false promissory note[1] and it had become due for payment three days before, and now his two paternal uncles and Ivan Markovitch, the brother of his dead mother, were deciding the question whether they should pay the money and save the family honor, or wash their hands of it and leave the case to go to trial.

Literary Analysis
Dynamic and Static Characters Which clues about the character of Sasha Uskov does this paragraph present?

 ✓ **Reading Check**
Who is at the center of the Uskov family's secret?

---

1. **promissory note** written promise to pay a certain sum of money on demand; an IOU.

A Problem ■ *929*

Dynamic and Static Characters

• Have several volunteers take turns reading aloud the bracketed passage.

• Have students note that the author is giving clues about the characters of the three uncles. Point out that the first paternal uncle was a colonel in the army. **Ask** students how this fact affects his attitude and character. **Possible response:** The Colonel is firm and believes that being honorable means being honest.

• Have students discuss the differences in temperament of each uncle.

60 **Reading Strategy**

Evaluating Characters' Decisions

• Call students' attention to the bracketed passage.

• Remind students that each of the three uncles has his own reason for urging his solution to the problem. Furthermore, each uncle's opinion is grounded in his own character and personality.

• Have students **explain** how the two paternal uncles disagree about the solution. **Answer:** The Colonel believes that Sasha should be forced to accept the punishment for his behavior. The other paternal uncle simply wants the affair kept out of the papers, presumably by paying the money.

• **Ask** students the Reading Strategy question: With which paternal uncle do you agree? Explain. **Possible responses:** Some readers may agree with the Colonel, saying that Sasha should accept responsibility for his behavior; others may agree with the other paternal uncle, saying that it is important to keep family secrets private.

To outsiders who have no personal interest in the matter such questions seem simple; for those who are so unfortunate as to have to decide them in earnest they are extremely difficult. The uncles had been talking for a long time, but the problem seemed no nearer decision.

"My friends!" said the uncle who was a colonel, and there was a note of exhaustion and bitterness in his voice. "Who says that family honor is a mere convention? I don't say that at all. I am only warning you against a false view; I am pointing out the possibility of an unpardonable mistake. How can you fail to see it? I am not speaking Chinese; I am speaking Russian!"

"My dear fellow, we do understand," Ivan Markovitch protested mildly.

"How can you understand if you say that I don't believe in family honor? I repeat once more; fa-mil-y ho-nor false-ly un-der-stood is a prejudice! Falsely understood! That's what I say: whatever may be the motives for screening a scoundrel, whoever he may be, and helping him to escape punishment, it is contrary to law and unworthy of a gentleman. It's not saving the family honor; it's civic cowardice! Take the army, for instance. . . . The honor of the army is more precious to us than any other honor, yet we don't screen our guilty members, but condemn them. And does the honor of the army suffer in consequence? Quite the opposite!"

The other paternal uncle, an official in the Treasury, a <u>taciturn</u>, dull-witted, and rheumatic man, sat silent, or spoke only of the fact that the Uskovs' name would get into the newspapers if the case went for trial. His opinion was that the case ought to be hushed up from the first and not become public property; but, apart from publicity in the newspapers, he advanced no other argument in support of this opinion.

The maternal uncle, kind-hearted Ivan Markovitch, spoke smoothly, softly, and with a tremor in his voice. He began with saying that youth has its rights and its peculiar temptations. Which of us has not been young, and who has not been led astray? To say nothing of ordinary mortals, even great men have not escaped errors and mistakes in their youth. Take, for instance, the biography of great writers. Did not every one of them gamble, drink, and draw down upon himself the anger of right-thinking people in his young days? If Sasha's error bordered upon crime, they must remember that Sasha had received practically no education; he had been expelled from the high school in the fifth class; he had lost his parents in early childhood, and so had been left at the tenderest age without guidance and good, <u>benevolent</u> influences. He was nervous, excitable, had no firm ground under his feet, and, above all, he had been unlucky. Even if he were guilty, anyway he deserved indulgence and the sympathy of all compassionate souls. He ought, of course, to be punished, but he was punished as it was by his conscience and the agonies he was enduring now while awaiting the sentence of his relations. The comparison with the army made by the Colonel was

Vocabulary Builder

taciturn (tas´ ə tʉrn) *adj.* almost always silent

Reading Strategy
Evaluating Characters'
Decisions With which paternal uncle do you agree? Explain.

Vocabulary Builder

benevolent (bə nev´ ə lənt) *adj.* doing or inclined to do good; kindly; charitable

---

Enrichment

A Critic's View of Chekhov's Style
"When I write," Chekhov once noted, "I rely fully on the reader, presuming that he himself will add the subjective elements missing in my story."

In *The Russian Short Story: 1880–1917*, the critic Julian W. Connolly adds:

Chekhov's observation points to a fundamental principle of his narrative art: by declining to mold his reader's attitudes through traditional methods of authorial omniscience, he requires the reader to work at extracting meaning from his stories.

Structurally, Chekhov eliminated much of the expository material that earlier writers used to establish a background for their characters and plots. Paring descriptions of people and settings to a minimum, Chekhov relied on the use of a few details chosen for their suggestive potential. In many stories an internal conflict engenders expectations that are never met. Chekhov's plots have been compared to gradual curves that start out in one direction and gently arc to end up in an entirely unexpected place.

59
60

delightful, and did credit to his lofty intelligence; his appeal to their feeling of public duty spoke for the chivalry of his soul, but they must not forget that in each individual the citizen is closely linked with the Christian. . . .

"Shall we be false to civic duty," Ivan Markovitch exclaimed passionately, "if instead of punishing an erring boy we hold out to him a helping hand?"

Ivan Markovitch talked further of family honor. He had not the honor to belong to the Uskov family himself, but he knew their distinguished family went back to the thirteenth century; he did not forget for a minute, either, that his precious, beloved sister had been the wife of one of the representatives of that name. In short, the family was dear to him for many reasons, and he refused to admit the idea that, for the sake of a paltry fifteen hundred rubles[2] a blot should be cast on the escutcheon[3] that was beyond all price. If all the motives he had brought forward were not sufficiently convincing, he, Ivan Markovitch, in conclusion, begged his listeners to ask themselves what was meant by

---

2. **rubles** (roo′ bəlz) *n.* Russian unit of currency.
3. **escutcheon** (e skuch′ ən) *n.* shield on which a coat of arms is displayed.

61  **Reading Check**

Which uncle defends the mistakes made by all men in their youth?

62

Ball at the Moulin de la Galette, 1876, Pierre Auguste Renoir

63 ▲ **Critical Viewing** What do you think Sasha might find attractive about the lifestyle captured in this painting? **[Speculate]**

A Problem ■ 931

Differentiated Instruction   Solutions for All Learners

Support for Special Needs Students

Draw a web diagram on the board, and use it to help students understand the problem and the decision that has to be made in the story. Explain that the web will illustrate the problem and the reasons for the possible solutions. In the center, write *Problem: Sasha has written a bad note. The bank demands the money.* Draw two circles from the center for the two solutions:

Pay the money; Let Sasha go to jail. From each solution circle, draw circles showing the consequences: (1) *Pay the money: The family honor is preserved; Sasha does not get his just punishment and shirks responsibility.* (2) *Let Sasha go to jail: The family is humiliated; Sasha is punished for what could be considered a youthful mistake.*

---

61 Reading Check

Answer: Ivan Markovitch defends the mistakes made by all men in their youth.

62 Humanities

Ball at the Moulin de la Galette, by Pierre Auguste Renoir

Sasha Uskov might well have enjoyed a gathering such as depicted in this painting by Renoir (1841–1919). *Ball at the Moulin de la Galette* is one of the most important and popular examples of the school of painting known as Impressionism, and Renoir was one of the most famous Impressionist painters. Impressionism is noted for the use of light and color to portray life accurately. This work, for example, captures the dramatic play of light on the dancers as they move to the music. The Moulin de la Galette was a place where workers, young women, and artists gathered to dance and enjoy themselves in the garden. Renoir's biographer, Georges Rivière, claims that Renoir probably painted the entire work on the spot, rather than finishing it in the studio, as was the common practice.

Use the following questions for discussion:

- How would you describe this scene?
  Possible response: The scene is lively and shows people enjoying themselves.

- How does this painting differ from the painting on p. 928? Which setting do you think Sasha would find more appealing?
  Possible response: This painting is more energetic and dynamic than the painting on p. 928. The action here takes place outdoors, and people are enjoying themselves. The library scene is static and austere. Sasha would probably find Renoir's setting more appealing than the library.

63 Critical Viewing

Possible response: Sasha would be drawn to the carefree, lively, and fun-loving lifestyle that this painting captures.

Literary Analysis

Dynamic and Static Characters

- Remind students that Sasha is waiting outside the study while the three uncles argue. Have a student read aloud the bracketed passage.

- **Ask** students the Literary Analysis question: What is Sasha's attitude toward his misdeed at this point? **Answer:** Sasha feels neither ashamed nor guilty about cashing the false promissory note.

▶ **Monitor Progress** Remind students that a static character does not change during the course of a story. Ask students to name the qualities that Sasha demonstrates so far (obedience to his uncle's summons, patiently and "meekly" waiting outside the study, willingness to accept whatever happens).

▶ **Reteach** If students still have difficulty determining whether a character is static or dynamic, review the Literary Analysis instruction on p. 905.

65 Humanities

E. Duranty, by Edgar Degas

Along with artists such as Monet and Renoir, Edgar Degas (1834–1917) was one of the Impressionist painters in France during the latter half of the nineteenth century. Degas's work focused on the complexity of human expression as found in daily life.

Use the following question for discussion:

What do you think the man in this portrait is thinking?
Possible response: The man is puzzling over a problem presented in the papers on his desk; he may be worrying about family or financial problems.

66 Critical Viewing

Possible response: The man's earnest and serious expression matches what Ivan Markovitch might be feeling.

---

crime? Crime is an immoral act founded upon ill-will. But is the will of man free? Philosophy has not yet given a positive answer to that question. Different views were held by the learned. The latest school of Lombroso,[4] for instance, denies the freedom of the will, and considers every crime as the product of the purely anatomical peculiarities of the individual.

"Ivan Markovitch," said the Colonel, in a voice of entreaty, "we are talking seriously about an important matter, and you bring in Lombroso, you clever fellow. Think a little, what are you saying all this for? Can you imagine that all your thunderings and rhetoric will furnish an answer to the question?"

Sasha Uskov sat at the door and listened. He felt neither terror, shame, nor depression, but only weariness and inward emptiness. It seemed to him that it made absolutely no difference to him whether they forgave him or not; he had come here to hear his sentence and to explain himself simply because kind-hearted Ivan Markovitch had

---

4. **Lombroso** Cesare Lombroso (1835–1909), an Italian physician and criminologist who believed that a criminal was a distinct human type, with specific physical and mental deviations, and that a criminal tendency was the result of hereditary factors.

E. Duranty, 1879, Edgar Degas, Glasgow Museums

932 ■ *Romanticism and Realism*

Literary Analysis
Dynamic and Static Characters What is Sasha's attitude toward his misdeed at this point?

66 ◀ Critical Viewing In what way does the expression on this man's face match what Ivan Markovitch might be feeling? **[Connect]**

Enrichment

Criminology

While arguing for leniency for Sasha, Ivan Markovitch brings up the latest theories of *criminology*—the scientific study of crime and criminal behavior. Although the particular ideas that this Chekhov character cites have long been out of fashion, criminology remains an important field of social science.

Among the questions that modern criminologists study are the causes of crime, the nature

of criminal organizations, the prevention of crime, and the rehabilitation of convicted criminals. Criminologists may work within the criminal justice system, or they may teach and conduct studies within a college or university setting.

64 begged him to do so. He was not afraid of the future. It made no difference to him where he was: here in the hall, in prison, or in Siberia.

"If Siberia, then let it be Siberia, damn it all!"

He was sick of life and found it insufferably hard. He was inextricably involved in debt; he had not a farthing⁵ in his pocket; his family had become detestable to him; he would have to part from his friends and his women sooner or later, as they had begun to be too contemptuous of his sponging on them. The future looked black.

Sasha was indifferent, and was only disturbed by one circumstance; the other side of the door they were calling him a scoundrel and a criminal. Every minute he was on the point of jumping up, bursting into the study and shouting in answer to the detestable metallic voice of the Colonel:

"You are lying!"

"Criminal" is a dreadful word—that is what murderers, thieves, robbers are; in fact, wicked and morally hopeless people. And Sasha was very far from being all that. . . . It was true he owed a great deal and did not pay his debts. But debt is not a crime, and it is unusual for a man not to be in debt. The Colonel and Ivan Markovitch were both in debt. . . .

"What have I done wrong besides?" Sasha wondered.

67
68 He had discounted a forged note. But all the young men he knew did the same. Handrikov and Von Burst always forged IOU's from their parents or friends when their allowances were not paid at the regular time, and then when they got their money from home they redeemed them before they became due. Sasha had done the same, but had not redeemed the IOU because he had not got the money which Handrikov had promised to lend him. He was not to blame; it was the fault of circumstances. It was true that the use of another person's signature was considered reprehensible; but, still, it was not a crime but a generally accepted dodge, an ugly formality which injured no one and was quite harmless, for in forging the Colonel's signature Sasha had had no intention of causing anybody damage or loss.

"No, it doesn't mean that I am a criminal . . . " thought Sasha. "And it's not in my character to bring myself to commit a crime. I am soft, emotional. . . . When I have the money I help the poor. . . . "

Sasha was musing after this fashion while they went on talking the other side of the door.

70 "But, my friends, this is endless," the Colonel declared, getting excited. "Suppose we were to forgive him and pay the money. You know he would not give up leading a dissipated life, squandering money, making debts, going to our tailors and ordering suits in our names! Can you guarantee that this will be his last prank? As far as I am concerned, I have no faith whatever in his reforming!"

The official of the Treasury muttered something in reply; after him Ivan Markovitch began talking blandly and suavely again. The Colonel moved his chair impatiently and drowned the other's words with his

---

5. **farthing** (fär′ *th*iŋ) *n.* coin of little value.

Reading Strategy
Evaluating Characters'
Decisions Do you think that Sasha's line of reasoning adequately excuses the decision he made to discount the note? Explain.

✓**Reading Check** **69**

What terrible wrong has Sasha committed?

A Problem ■ 933

Differentiated
Instruction   Solutions for All Learners

Support for Special Needs Students
To help students understand the characters and their decisions, have them use the Literary Analysis support, page 61, and the Reading Strategy support, page 62 in *Unit 7 Resources.* Work with students to help them understand what decisions Sasha has made and what decisions the uncles will make. Have them identify the characters' traits and understand how these traits influence the characters' decisions.

Background for English Learners
Point out that the consequences of actions can vary according to the rules of a person's culture. In "A Problem," Sasha's uncles have gathered to determine how to deal with the decision Sasha made to cash an IOU dishonestly. Ask students to share their own knowledge of the consequences that would come from such actions in their own and other cultures.

Dynamic and Static Characters

- Read aloud the bracketed passage. Point out the stance and attitude of each uncle.

- Remind students that the family council has been going on for several hours and still no decision has been reached—the uncles are holding their positions.

- **Ask** students the first Literary Analysis question: Which details suggest that the Colonel and Ivan Markovitch are static characters? **Answer:** Ivan Markovitch and the Colonel do not show changes in personality traits, attitudes, or beliefs. Therefore, they are static characters.

71 **Literary Analysis**

Dynamic and Static Characters

- Refer students to the bracketed passage.

- **Ask** students the second Literary Analysis question: Do you think Sasha's unemotional response to his aunt is consistent with his character? Why or why not? **Possible response:** Sasha's unemotional response is consistent with his character, as earlier in the story he is described as being "indifferent" and "sick of life."

---

70 detestable metallic voice. At last the door opened and Ivan Markovitch came out of the study; there were patches of red on his lean shaven face.

"Come along," he said, taking Sasha by the hand. "Come and speak frankly from your heart. Without pride, my dear boy, humbly and from your heart."

Sasha went into the study. The official of the Treasury was sitting down; the Colonel was standing before the table with one hand in his pocket and one knee on a chair. It was smoky and stifling in the study. Sasha did not look at the official or the Colonel; he felt suddenly ashamed and uncomfortable. He looked uneasily at Ivan Markovitch and muttered:

"I'll pay it . . . I'll give it back. . . ."

"What did you expect when you discounted the IOU?" he heard a metallic voice.

"I . . . Handrikov promised to lend me the money before now."

Sasha could say no more. He went out of the study and sat down again on the chair near the door. He would have been glad to go away altogether at once, but he was choking with hatred and he awfully wanted to remain, to tear the Colonel to pieces, to say something rude to him. He sat trying to think of something violent and effective to say to his hated uncle, and at that moment a woman's figure, shrouded in the twilight, appeared at the drawing-room door. It was the Colonel's wife. She beckoned Sasha to her, and, wringing her hands, said, weeping:

"*Alexandre*, I know you don't like me, but . . . listen to me; listen, I beg you. . . . But, my dear, how can this have happened? Why, it's awful, awful! For goodness' sake, beg them, defend yourself, entreat them."

71 Sasha looked at her quivering shoulders, at the big tears that were rolling down her cheeks, heard behind his back the hollow, nervous voices of worried and exhausted people, and shrugged his shoulders. He had not in the least expected that his aristocratic relations would raise such a tempest over a paltry fifteen hundred rubles! He could not understand her tears nor the quiver of their voices.

An hour later he heard that the Colonel was getting the best of it; the uncles were finally inclining to let the case go for trial.

"The matter's settled," said the Colonel, sighing. "Enough."

After this decision all the uncles, even the emphatic Colonel, became noticeably depressed. A silence followed.

"Merciful Heavens!" sighed Ivan Markovitch. "My poor sister!"

And he began saying in a subdued voice that most likely his sister, Sasha's mother, was present unseen in the study at that moment. He felt in his soul how the unhappy, saintly woman was weeping, grieving, and begging for her boy. For the sake of her peace beyond the grave, they ought to spare Sasha.

The sound of a muffled sob was heard. Ivan Markovitch was weeping and muttering something which it was impossible to catch

Literary Analysis
Dynamic and Static Characters Which details suggest that the Colonel and Ivan Markovitch are static characters?

Literary Analysis
Dynamic and Static Characters Do you think Sasha's unemotional response to his aunt is consistent with his character? Why or why not?

through the door. The Colonel got up and paced from corner to corner. The long conversation began over again.

But then the clock in the drawing-room struck two. The family council was over. To avoid seeing the person who had moved him to such wrath, the Colonel went from the study, not into the hall, but into the vestibule. . . . Ivan Markovitch came out into the hall. . . . He was agitated and rubbing his hands joyfully. His tear-stained eyes looked good-humored and his mouth was twisted into a smile.

"Capital," he said to Sasha. "Thank God! You can go home, my dear, and sleep tranquilly. We have decided to pay the sum, but on condition that you repent and come with me tomorrow into the country and set to work."

A minute later Ivan Markovitch and Sasha in their great coats and caps were going down the stairs. The uncle was muttering something edifying. Sasha did not listen, but felt as though some uneasy weight were gradually slipping off his shoulders. They had forgiven him; he was free! A gust of joy sprang up within him and sent a sweet chill to his heart. He longed to breathe, to move swiftly, to live! Glancing at the street lamps and the black sky, he remembered that Von Burst was celebrating his name-day[6] that evening at the "Bear," and again a rush of joy flooded his soul. . . .

"I am going!" he decided.

But then he remembered he had not a farthing, that the companions he was going to would despise him at once for his empty pockets. He must get hold of some money, come what may!

"Uncle, lend me a hundred rubles," he said to Ivan Markovitch.

His uncle, surprised, looked into his face and backed against a lamppost.

"Give it to me," said Sasha, shifting impatiently from one foot to the other and beginning to pant. "Uncle, I entreat you, give me a hundred rubles."

His face worked; he trembled, and seemed on the point of attacking his uncle. . . .

"Won't you?" he kept asking, seeing that his uncle was still amazed and did not understand. "Listen. If you don't, I'll give myself up tomorrow! I won't let you pay the IOU! I'll present another false note tomorrow!"

---

6. **name-day** feast day of the saint after whom a person is named.

▲ Critical Viewing
In what way are Russian rubles like these at the heart of this story's conflict? **[Analyze]**

Reading Strategy
Evaluating Characters' Decisions What consequences might occur if Ivan Markovitch gives the hundred rubles to Sasha?

✓ Reading Check
Who agrees to pay Sasha's debt?

A Problem ■ 935

72 Critical Thinking
Infer
• Have students read the bracketed passage, focusing on the different attitudes of the two men. Discuss why the Colonel walks through the vestibule to avoid seeing Sasha and why Ivan Markovitch seems joyful.
• Then, **ask** students how they think each of the men expects Sasha to behave.
   Answer: The Colonel expects Sasha to continue in his irresponsible ways; Ivan Markovitch expects Sasha to reform and not repeat his bad behavior.

73 Critical Viewing
Answer: Sasha cashed the IOU to get money to pursue his carefree and idle lifestyle.

74 Reading Strategy
Evaluating Characters' Decisions
• Read aloud the bracketed passage. Tell students to pay special attention to the uncle's horror and to Sasha's attitude.
• Then, **ask** the Reading Strategy question: What consequences might occur if Ivan Markovitch gives the hundred rubles to Sasha?
   Answer: Sasha will probably spend it all and possibly forge another IOU, realizing that his uncle will once again get him out of trouble.

▶ **Reteach** If students have difficulty evaluating characters' decisions, suggest they use the **Reading Strategy** support, page 62 in *Unit 7 Resources.*

75 Reading Check
Answer: Sasha's uncles agree to pay Sasha's debt.

Differentiated
Instruction   Solutions for All Learners

Strategy for Less Proficient Readers
To help students summarize the events in the story and relate them to their lives, help them conduct a roundtable discussion to address the following questions:
• What choices does Sasha make in the story? What are the possible consequences of these choices?
• What choices do his family members make?
• What kind of person would be the modern equivalent of Sasha?

Point out that students need to provide specific examples to support the answers to the discussion questions. Have students explore these questions and present a summary of their discussion to the class.

1. **Possible response:** Some readers may sympathize with Ivan Markovitch because his trust and kindness are betrayed by his nephew. Others may think that Sasha is deeply troubled and needs help.

2. (a) Sasha has forged an IOU and cashed it. (b) **Possible response:** Sasha takes his offense lightly because his friends forge and cash IOUs.

3. (a) The relatives want Sasha to face the consequences. (b) Sasha has been irresponsible before, and they have grown tired of it.

4. (a) Ivan Markovitch wants to forgive Sasha and pay the money. (b) **Possible response:** His attitude is harmful because Sasha will not have to reform his dishonest ways.

5. (a) Ivan Markovitch argues that they should spare Sasha to give peace to his dead mother. (b) Ivan Markovitch is clever, kind, tolerant, and forgiving. (c) **Possible response:** The Colonel, who has previously appeared unyielding, is surprisingly affected by Ivan Markovitch's emotional plea. His willingness to reopen negotiations adds depth to his character and forces readers to reevaluate their assessments of him.

6. (a) Ivan Markovitch is horrified. (b) He realizes that Sasha really is a criminal with no morals or conscience.

7. **Possible response:** Letting Sasha go to trial would have done him the most good because he would have faced the consequences of his behavior.

Go Online For additional information
—Author Link about Anton Chekhov, have students type in the Web Code, then select C from the alphabet, and then select Anton Chekhov.

Petrified, muttering something incoherent in his horror, Ivan Markovitch took a hundred-ruble note out of his pocket-book and gave it to Sasha. The young man took it and walked rapidly away from him. . . .

Taking a sledge,[7] Sasha grew calmer, and felt a rush of joy within him again. The "rights of youth" of which kind-hearted Ivan Markovitch had spoken at the family council woke up and asserted themselves. Sasha pictured the drinking party before him, and, among the bottles, the women, and his friends, the thought flashed through his mind:

"Now I see that I am a criminal; yes, I am a criminal."

---

7. **sledge** (slej) *n.* strong, heavy sled.

Critical Reading

1. **Respond:** With which character in "A Problem" do you sympathize most? Why?

2. **(a) Recall:** What has Sasha done that has so upset the family? **(b) Infer:** Why do you think Sasha takes his offense so lightly?

3. **(a) Recall:** What do most of the relatives want to do about Sasha and the problem he has created? **(b) Speculate:** How has Sasha's past behavior influenced his relatives' attitude toward his current situation?

4. **(a) Recall:** What does Ivan Markovitch want to do about the problem? **(b) Make a Judgment:** Do you think Uncle Ivan's attitude helps or harms Sasha?

5. **(a) Recall:** What is Ivan Markovitch's most important, and ultimately most convincing, point in his defense of Sasha? **(b) Infer:** What inferences can you make about Ivan Markovitch's character based on his tearful speech to the uncles? **(c) Analyze Cause and Effect:** Does the Colonel's reaction to the speech change your impression of him? Why or why not?

6. **(a) Recall:** What is Ivan Markovitch's emotional reaction to Sasha's final request? **(b) Interpret:** Why does Ivan Markovitch react this way?

7. **Evaluate:** Of the two choices facing the family—to let the case go to trial or to pay Sasha's debt—which would have done Sasha the most good? Why?

Go Online
—Author Link

For: More about Anton Chekhov
Visit: www.PHSchool.com
Web Code: ete-9709

Apply the Skills

Two Friends • How Much Land Does a Man Need? • A Problem

Literary Analysis

Dynamic and Static Characters

1. Are the main characters in "Two Friends" **dynamic or static characters**? Use details from the story to support your response.
2. In "How Much Land Does a Man Need?" which details suggest that Pakhom is a static character in spite of the changes he experiences?
3. Which details in "A Problem" suggest that the character of Sasha Uskov will never change?

Comparing Literary Works

4. **(a)** How much consideration did Pakhom give to his family each time he decided to buy more land? **(b)** In what way does Pakhom's attitude compare with Sasha's in "A Problem"?
5. Do the main characters in "Two Friends" and "A Problem" pass a point of no return? Explain.

Reading Strategy

Evaluating Characters' Decisions

6. **Evaluate the characters' decisions** in the three stories by completing a chart like the one shown. Criteria for evaluating their choices are provided.

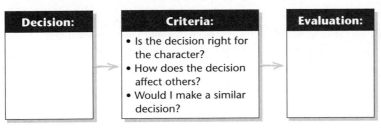

Decision:	Criteria:	Evaluation:
	• Is the decision right for the character? • How does the decision affect others? • Would I make a similar decision?	

7. Choose one character who, in your opinion, makes a bad decision. **(a)** What good or harmless intentions might have been at the heart of the decision? **(b)** Does having such good intentions make the character's behavior forgivable? Explain.

Extend Understanding

8. **Psychology Connection:** In Pakhom's culture, land is a status symbol indicating wealth, power, and social rank. What kinds of status symbols do people crave today? Explain.

QuickReview

A **dynamic character** experiences changes in behavior and attitude throughout a story.

A **static character** stays the same.

To **evaluate characters' decisions,** make judgments as to whether their decisions are good or bad.

Go Online
Assessment
For: Self-test
Visit: www.PHSchool.com
Web Code: eta-6704

Two Friends / How Much Land Does a Man Need? / A Problem ■ 937

 Go Online Students may use the **Self-test** to
Assessment prepare for **Selection Test A** or
Selection Test B.

Answers

1. The two friends are dynamic; they evolve from acquaintances to friends; they begin meek and accepting of war, and they end with a heroic decision that protects their city.

2. Pakhom maintains his desire for more and more land, even when he sees that his greed is killing him.

3. Sasha never accepts responsibility for his acts; instead, he blames others. When he is finally forgiven, he demands more money to continue his dissolute lifestyle.

4. (a) Pakhom never consulted his family and assumed that they would move whenever he wanted. (b) **Possible response:** Both men are self-centered.

5. **Possible response:** The two friends pass a point of no return when they are accosted by the Prussian soldiers. In "A Problem," Sasha passes a point of no return when he threatens Ivan Markovitch.

6. **Possible response: Decision:** The two friends refuse to give the password; **Evaluation:** The decision costs them their lives but, heroically, saves the lives of other Parisians. **Decision:** Pakhom buys a forty-acre farm; **Evaluation:** Pakhom becomes a landowner, but, in so doing, greed takes over his life. **Decision:** Sasha forges an IOU; **Evaluation:** The decision benefits Sasha but hurts Sasha's credibility with his family.
Another sample answer can be found on **Reading Strategy Graphic Organizer B,** p. 166 in *Graphic Organizer Transparencies.*

7. (a) **Possible response:** When Sasha forges the IOU, he probably wants to have fun with his friends and does not think about the consequences of his actions. (b) **Possible response:** Sasha's family should forgive him; however, they should make him learn from his mistakes instead of covering for him.

8. **Possible response:** Expensive cars, homes, and clothing, as well as high-tech gadgets are status symbols. Acquiring them is proof of wealth, power, or social rank.

❶ Vocabulary Lesson

Word Analysis: Latin Prefix dis-

1. disgrace: to lose respect
2. disclaim: to renounce
3. disorient: to confuse

Spelling Strategy

1. violent, violently
2. absent, absently
3. prudent, prudently

Vocabulary Builder: Synonyms

1. b   5. d
2. g   6. c
3. a   7. f
4. e

❷ Grammar and Style Lesson

1. restrictive; *anyone*
2. restrictive; *escutcheon*
3. restrictive; *land*
4. nonrestrictive; *sun*
5. nonrestrictive; *soldier*

Writing Application

Possible response:

Nonrestrictive: My (friend), *who is on the team,* is going to the movies with us.

Restrictive: We're going to see the new action (movie) *that opened today.*

W𝒢 Writing and Grammar Platinum Level

For support in teaching the Grammar and Style Lesson, use Chapter 20, Section 2.

Build Language Skills

❶ Vocabulary Lesson

Word Analysis: Latin Prefix dis-

The Latin prefix *dis-* can mean "apart" or "not," changing the meaning of a word to its opposite. Add the prefix *dis-* to each word below, and define the new words you create.

1. grace   **2.** claim   **3.** orient

Spelling Strategy

Nouns ending in *-ence* usually end in *-ent* and *-ently* in their adjective and adverb forms. Write the adjective and adverb forms of each of the following nouns.

1. violence   **2.** absence   **3.** prudence

Vocabulary Builder: Synonyms

Choose the word from the list on the right that is closest in meaning to each vocabulary word below.

1. benevolent   **a.** looting
2. discord   **b.** charitable
3. pillaging   **c.** over
4. placidly   **d.** face down
5. prostrate   **e.** calmly
6. superimposed   **f.** silent
7. taciturn   **g.** conflict

❷ Grammar and Style Lesson

Restrictive and Nonrestrictive Adjective Clauses

Restrictive—essential—**adjective clauses** limit, or restrict, the meaning of the nouns they modify. They identify and define, and they are necessary to the meaning.

> **Restrictive:** "[He] sowed it on the land *he had bought.*" (modifies *land*)

Nonrestrictive—nonessential—**adjective clauses** give additional information about nouns. They describe, but they are not necessary to the noun's meaning. Use commas to set off these clauses.

> **Nonrestrictive:** Sasha Uskov, *who was the cause of all the trouble . . .* (modifies *Sasha Uskov*)

Practice Identify each italicized clause that follows as restrictive or nonrestrictive. Then, circle the word it modifies.

1. Anyone *who had money* could buy . . . as much freehold land as he wanted.
2. . . . a blot should be cast on the escutcheon *that was beyond all price.*
3. He borrowed seed and sowed it on the land *he had bought.*
4. Pakhom looked at the sun, *which had reached the earth.*
5. She engaged . . . an old soldier, *who took to burdening the people with fines.*

Writing Application Write two sentences about a friend. Use a restrictive clause in one sentence and a nonrestrictive clause in the other. Identify each clause and circle the word it modifies.

W𝒢 *Prentice Hall Writing and Grammar Connection: Platinum Level, Chapter 20, Section 2*

Assessment Practice

Analyzing Literary Language   (For more practice, see *Test Preparation Workbook*, p. 41.)

Many standardized tests require students to analyze the literary language of texts. Use the following sample test item to give students practice with the skill.

Opposite, the village of Argenteuil seemed dead. The heights of Orgemont and Sannois dominated the whole countryside. The broad plain which stretches as far as Nanterre was empty, absolutely empty, with its bare cherry trees and its colorless fields.

—"Two Friends" by Guy de Maupassant

What kind of mood is set by this passage?

A danger
B joy
C romance
D humor

Students should recognize that words such as "dead," "empty," "bare," and "colorless" lend a mood of danger to the passage; therefore, *A* is the correct answer.

❸ Writing Lessson

Timed Writing: Analyzing a Character's Decision

For many of the characters in these stories, changing one critical decision would create an entirely new ending to the story. Write an essay analyzing a character's decision at such a major turning point. *(40 minutes)*

Prewriting
(10 minutes)
Choose a character from one of the stories you have read, and identify a key decision. Then, brainstorm for a plausible alternative decision and a new, logical ending to the story.

Drafting
(20 minutes)
As you write, refer to specific moments in the text to support your new ending, and address any other characters in the story who might be affected by your character's decision.

Revising
(10 minutes)
Review your essay, identifying sentences that do not connect logically. Use transitions to build a flowing, coherent paragraph.

Model: Using Transitions for Coherence

Ivan Markovitch forgot that Sasha had never worked

For his nephew's own good,

for anything in life. Ivan Markovitch should force

Sasha to recognize his errors.

> Transitional words and phrases build paragraph coherence and establish a clear line of reasoning.

🆆🅖 *Prentice Hall Writing and Grammar Connection: Platinum Level, Chapter 3, Section 2*

❹ Extend Your Learning

Listening and Speaking Create a **monologue** in which Sasha speaks to Uncle Ivan five years after the events in "A Problem." In your monologue, address the following topics:

- how Sasha's life progressed after the events of the story
- what Sasha has learned about himself since taking the hundred rubles from Uncle Ivan
- what kind of relationship Sasha would like to have with Uncle Ivan and the family

Perform your monologue for your class.

Research and Technology With a partner, use library or Internet sources to research the topic of heraldry. Build a **coat of arms** for a character in the story based on the examples you find. Include a brief report explaining how the parts of the heraldic shield apply to the character. **[Group Activity]**

Go Online
Research
For: An additional research activity
Visit: www.PHSchool.com
Web Code: etd-7704

Two Friends / How Much Land Does a Man Need? / A Problem ■ 939

Assessment Resources

The following resources can be used to assess students' knowledge and skills.

Unit 7 Resources
Selection Test A, pp. 68–70
Selection Test B, pp. 71–73
Benchmark Test 8, pp. 74–79

General Resources
Rubrics for Narration: Short Story, pp. 63–64
Rubric for Speaking: Narrative Account, p. 88

Go Online Students may use the **Self-test** to
Assessment prepare for **Selection Test A** or **Selection Test B**.

Benchmark
Administer **Benchmark Test 8.** If some students need further work, use the **Interpretation Guide** to determine the appropriate reteaching page in the **Reading Kit** and on **Success Tracker.**

---

❸ Writing Lesson

You may use this Writing Lesson as a timed-writing practice, or you may allow students to develop the analytical essay as a writing assignment over several days.

- To give students guidance in writing this essay, give them the **Support for Writing Lesson**, p. 65 in *Unit 7 Resources.*
- Suggest that after students choose a story, they work in pairs or small groups to brainstorm plausible new decisions and new endings.
- Use the Writing Lesson to guide students in developing their analyses. Have students use the Plot Diagram in *Graphic Organizer Transparencies*, p. 280, to organize details for the story ending.
- Use the Narration: Short Story rubrics in *General Resources*, pp. 63–64, to evaluate students' story endings.

🆆🅖 **Writing and Grammar**
Platinum Level
For support in teaching the Writing Lesson, use Chapter 3, Section 2.

❹ Listening and Speaking

- Encourage students to review the ending of the story and to keep in mind Sasha's character traits as described in the story.
- Suggest that students brainstorm what might have happened after the events in the story.
- Use the Speaking: Narrative Account rubric in *General Resources*, p. 88, to evaluate students' monologues.
- The **Support for Extend Your Learning** page (*Unit 7 Resources*, p. 66) provides guided note-taking opportunities to help students complete the Extend Your Learning activities.

Go Online Have students type in the
Research Web Code for another research activity.

Standard Course of Study

Goal 1: WRITTEN LANGUAGE

WL.1.03.9   Analyze effects of author's craft and style in reflection.

Goal 2: INFORMATIONAL READING

IR.2.01.10   Analyze the connections between ideas, concepts, characters and experiences in research.

Goal 5: LITERATURE

LT.5.01.3   Analyze literary devices and explain their effect on the work of world literature.

LT.5.02.1   Explore works which relate to an issue, author, or theme and show increasing comprehension.

Goal 6: GRAMMAR AND USAGE

GU.6.01.3   Use recognition strategies to understand vocabulary and exact word choice.

GU.6.02.1   Edit for agreement, tense choice, pronouns, antecedents, case, and complete sentences.

Step-by-Step Teaching Guide	Pacing Guide
PRETEACH	
• Administer Vocabulary and Reading Warm-ups as necessary.	5 min.
• Engage students' interest with the motivation activity.	5 min.
• Read and discuss author and background features. **FT**	10 min.
• Introduce the Literary Analysis Skill: Modern Realistic Drama. **FT**	5 min.
• Introduce the Reading Strategy: Reading Drama. **FT**	10 min.
• Prepare students to read by teaching the selection vocabulary. **FT**	
TEACH	
• Informally monitor comprehension while students read independently or in groups. **FT**	30 min.
• Monitor students' comprehension with the Reading Check notes.	as students read
• Reinforce vocabulary with Vocabulary Builder notes.	as students read
• Develop students' understanding of modern realistic drama with the Literary Analysis annotations. **FT**	5 min.
• Develop students' ability to read drama with the Reading Strategy annotations. **FT**	5 min.
ASSESS/EXTEND	
• Assess students' comprehension and mastery of the Literary Analysis and Reading Strategy by having them answer the Apply the Skills questions. **FT**	15 min.
• Have students complete the Vocabulary Development Lesson and the Grammar and Style Lesson. **FT**	15 min.
• Apply students' ability to analyze words by using the Writing Lesson. **FT**	45 min. or homework
• Apply students' understanding by using one or more of the Extend Your Learning activities.	20–90 min. or homework
• Administer Selection Test A or Selection Test B. **FT**	15 min.

Resources

Choosing Resources for Differentiated Instruction

[L1] Special Needs Students

[L2] Below-Level Students

[L3] All Students

[L4] Advanced Students

[EL] English Learners

For Vocabulary and Reading Warm-ups and for Selection Tests, **A** signifies "less challenging" and **B** "more challenging." For Graphic Organizer transparencies, **A** signifies "not filled in" and **B** "filled in."

FT Fast Track Instruction: To move the lesson more quickly, use the strategies and activities identified with **FT**.

Scaffolding for Less Proficient and Advanced Students

The leveled Critical Thinking questions after selections progress in the levels of thinking required to answer them. To address the needs of your different students, you may use the (a) level questions for your less proficient students and the (b) level questions with your on-level and advanced students. The occasional (c) level questions are appropriate for your advanced students.

Teacher**EXPRESS**™ Use this complete suite of powerful teaching tools to make lesson planning and testing quicker and easier.

Student**EXPRESS**™ Use the interactive textbook (online and on CD-ROM) to make selections and activities come alive with audio and video support and interactive questions.

Monitoring Progress

Before students read *A Doll House,* administer **Diagnostic Test 9** (*Unit 7 Resources,* **pp. 80–82**). This test will determine students' level of readiness for the reading and vocabulary skills.

 For: Information about Lexiles
Professional **Visit:** www.PHSchool.com
Development **Web Code:** eue-1111

Motivation

Refer students to the title of this play, and ask them what associations they have with the idea of a dollhouse. Students may suggest that a dollhouse is a toy, a miniature house where children like to play. Then, ask them to make inferences about the play on the basis of its title. Have students keep their inferences in mind as they read the play to see how accurate they are.

❶ Background

More About the Author

Visitors to Ibsen's tomb in Oslo, Norway, will find the image of an arm holding a hammer. Ibsen had this image placed on his tomb to symbolize the way in which his plays shattered illusions about life. In later years, Ibsen turned the focus away from the world and onto himself. His last play, *When We Dead Awaken,* written in 1899, is the most autobiographical play Ibsen wrote. It is a monologue (a speech by one character) by an aging playwright who questions the path he took during his life as a writer and as a human being.

Geography Note

Have students look at the map on this page. Students should understand that Norway is so far north that nearly half of the country is situated above the Arctic Circle. Ibsen describes his native land and its people as follows: "The magnificent, but severe, natural environment surrounding people up there in the north . . . forces them to . . . become introspective and serious. . . . At home every other person is a philosopher!"

Build Skills   *Drama*

❶ A Doll House

Henrik Ibsen
(1828–1906)

When the drama *Ghosts* by Henrik Ibsen (hen´ rik ib´ sən) was first performed in 1881, one critic attacked the play, calling it "an open drain, a loathsome sore, an abominable piece, a repulsive and degrading work." Critics and even audiences of his day sometimes responded negatively to Ibsen's works because he was a literary pioneer. He was not only the creator of the modern realistic prose drama but also one of the first modern writers to make drama a vehicle for social commentary by exploring issues considered socially unacceptable. Because of his bold innovation and his extraordinary talent, Ibsen is widely regarded as the greatest and most influential dramatist of the nineteenth century.

Difficult Beginnings Ibsen was born in Skien, Norway. Although his father had once been a successful merchant, bankruptcy reduced his family to poverty and social rejection. When he was fifteen, Ibsen became a druggist's apprentice. He hated the work and chose to live in virtual isolation, writing poetry in his spare time. After failing a university entrance examination, he became determined to forge a living as a writer. With two finished plays to his credit— *Catiline* (1850) and *The Burial Mound* (1850)— Ibsen was hired as a playwright by the National Theater in the city of Bergen, where he remained for six years.

A Career in Theater In 1857, Ibsen accepted an opportunity to manage a new theater. The theater went bankrupt in 1862, however, leaving Ibsen deeply in debt and in a state of despair. Two years later, he left Norway for Italy, where he wrote most of his finest plays.

With the completion of *Brand* (1866), the tragedy of a misunderstood idealist, and *Peer Gynt* (1867), a dramatic fantasy based on Norwegian folklore, he established himself as a popular playwright among both critics and theatergoers.

Controversial Art Ibsen's talent blossomed, though his plays were not always greeted enthusiastically by the public. *A Doll House* (1879), for example, aroused controversy because it portrayed a woman whose actions were unacceptable for that time. In response to the public's hostile reception of *Ghosts* (1881), Ibsen wrote *An Enemy of the People* (1882), which portrays a man who comes into conflict with the inhabitants of a village.

The Problem Plays Ibsen's later work defied the prevailing tastes in theater of the day. The typical dramatic style was modeled after the Romantic movement, with plot-heavy, idealized storylines whose endings were unfailingly happy. Ibsen eventually departed completely from such a style to create psychological dramas in which the conflict is internal and the plot's action is limited. Although Ibsen's later works often earned scathing reviews from critics and even from his audiences, emerging and notable playwrights like George Bernard Shaw embraced Ibsen's talent and defended his work. Ibsen's innovative pieces, often called "Problem Plays," constitute serious drama in which the problems of human life caused by society and its accepted practices are presented as such and are not masked by unrelated details.

Ibsen wrote prolifically through the nineteenth century, completing such well-known plays as *The Wild Duck* (1884) and *Hedda Gabler* (1890). When Ibsen died in 1906, it was already clear that his controversial work challenged the traditional expectations of theater. Only later in the twentieth century did it become obvious that Isben's contributions to dialogue, plot, set design, and acting style forged an entirely new form of modern theater.

940 ■ *Romanticism and Realism*

Preview

Connecting to the Literature

A nickname meant to express affection can sometimes offend or create a false impression. In Act One of *A Doll House*, Torvald has pet names for his wife, Nora, that reflect his impression of her personality and behavior.

❷ Literary Analysis

Modern Realistic Drama

Ibsen developed the **modern realistic drama**—a type of play unlike anything audiences had seen before—which included these characteristics:
- To reflect ordinary language, it is written in prose, not verse.
- It depicts characters and situations as they really are.
- It addresses controversial issues and society's assumptions.

A Doll House (1879) focuses on the role and status of women in the late nineteenth century. As you read Act One, notice Nora's subordinate role.

Connecting Literary Elements

Like real life, modern realistic dramas include **conflict,** the struggle between two opposing forces. Conflict can be either **internal,** occurring within the mind of a character, or **external,** occurring between a character and society, nature, another person, God, or fate.

In *A Doll House*, Nora faces both internal and external conflicts as she struggles to live life by her own rules.

❸ Reading Strategy

Reading Drama

A drama is written to be performed by actors. When **reading drama,** imagine how the scenes would look on stage, how the dialogue would sound, and how the characters would move. To get the most out of your reading:
- Picture the setting described in the stage directions.
- Imagine voice and tone as you read dialogue.
- Picture characters' gestures and movements.

Look for details in *A Doll House* that will help you envision the drama. Then, use a chart like the one shown to help you form mental images.

Vocabulary Builder

spendthrift (spend´ thrift´) *n.* person who spends money carelessly (p. 943)

squandering (skwän´ dər iŋ) *v.* spending money wastefully (p. 943)

prodigal (präd´ i gəl) *n.* person who spends money wastefully (p. 945)

indiscreet (in´ di skrēt´) *adj.* unwise or not careful (p. 953)

frivolous (friv´ ə ləs) *adj.* silly and light-minded; not sensible (p. 953)

contraband (kän´ trə band´) *n.* unlawful or forbidden goods (p. 958)

subordinate (sə bôr´ də nit) *adj.* inferior; ranking under or below (p. 963)

Standard Course of Study

- Analyze literary devices and explain their effect on the work of world literature. (LT.5.01.3)
- Explore works which relate to an issue, author, or theme and show increasing comprehension. (LT.5.02.1)

Detail From the Play

Torvald's nicknames for Nora: *squirrel, skylark*

↓

Mental Image

Nora should move as though she were a small animal, with quick, skipping steps.

A Doll House ■ 941

---

❷ Literary Analysis
Modern Realistic Drama

- Tell students that Ibsen was one of the first playwrights to use ordinary people as characters and to allow them to speak in everyday language. For many years, in Norway and Europe, plays were based on myth or highly romanticized stories about kings and queens. The language was usually poetic, and the themes of the plays had little to do with ordinary life.

- Read the three changes that Ibsen brought to drama. Point out that theatergoers of Ibsen's time might have been insulted by the changes. Many thought he had demeaned the theater. Point out that rather than ruining theater, Ibsen revitalized it.

❸ Reading Strategy
Reading Drama

- Remind students that dramas are meant to be heard and seen, not just read. Ask students to compare their experiences of reading and seeing plays.

- Explain the use of the graphic organizer. Remind students that in both the dialogue and the stage directions, playwrights often include clues about their characters' actions, tone of voice, and appearance. Give students a copy of **Reading Strategy Graphic Organizer A**, p. 167 in *Graphic Organizer Transparencies.* Have them use it to collect details that help them envision the drama.

Vocabulary Builder

- Pronounce each vocabulary word for students, and read the definition as a class. Have students identify any words with which they are already familiar.

Differentiated Instruction — Solutions for All Learners

Support for Special Needs Students

Have students complete the **Preview** and **Build Skills** pages for *A Doll House*, Act One in the *Reader's Notebook: Adapted Version.* These pages provide a selection summary, an abbreviated presentation of the reading and literary skills, and the graphic organizer on the **Build Skills** page in the student book.

Support for Less Proficient Readers

Have students complete the **Preview** and **Build Skills** pages for *A Doll House*, Act One in the *Reader's Notebook.* These pages provide a selection summary, an abbreviated presentation of the reading and literary skills, and the graphic organizer on the **Build Skills** page in the student book.

Support for English Learners

Have students complete the **Preview** and **Build Skills** pages for *A Doll House*, Act One in the *Reader's Notebook: English Learner's Version.* These pages provide a selection summary, an abbreviated presentation of the skills, additional contextual vocabulary, and the graphic organizer on the **Build Skills** page in the student book.

Facilitate Understanding

Start a discussion with students about how a society shapes the people who live in it. Ask students to identify and evaluate some ways that American society has shaped them. For example, American society values education, so many students probably will go to college.

❶ About the Translation

A Doll's House or A Doll House

An important issue in translation is the rendering of a literary work's title. The translated title will be the name of the work in the second language, and it will generate expectations about how the work is read and understood.

In English, the title has been traditionally rendered *A Doll's House.* Rolf Fjelde, the translator of this version of the play and the founder of the Ibsen Society of America, takes issue with the title. In the Foreword to his translation, he comments:

"There is certainly no sound justification for perpetuating the awkward and blindly traditional misnomer of *A Doll's House:* the house is not Nora's, as the possessive implies; the familiar children's toy is called a doll house; and one can make a reasonable supposition that Ibsen . . . at least partially includes Torvald with Nora in the original title . . . for the two of them at the play's opening are still posing like the little marzipan bride and groom atop the wedding cake."

❷ Humanities

Have students notice the doll pictured here. Its costume is from the period in which the play is set, and its face, hands, and feet are probably made of porcelain.

Use the following question for discussion:

What words would you use to describe this doll?

Possible response: The doll is delicate, breakable, lovely, and fragile.

A Doll House

Henrik Ibsen
translated by **Rolf Fjelde**

Background Critics regard Nora Helmer, one of the main characters in *A Doll House,* as among the most remarkable women characters in drama, primarily because of the personal journey she experiences in the play. As the drama opens, she appears to be a picture-perfect nineteenth-century wife to her husband, Torvald. The Helmers belonged to the upper middle class, and the elaborately decorated set would represent a typical wealthy home in the Victorian period. Like most other married women of her day, Nora would have made certain that every aspect of her home reflected the Helmers' social class and supported the comfortable, almost lavish lifestyle they enjoyed.

THE CHARACTERS

TORVALD HELMER, a lawyer	**THE HELMERS' THREE SMALL CHILDREN**
NORA, his wife	**ANNE-MARIE,** their nurse
DR. RANK	**HELENE,** a maid
MRS. LINDE	**A DELIVERY BOY**
NILS KROGSTAD, a bank clerk	

The action takes place in HELMER's *residence.*

942 ■ *Romanticism and Realism*

Differentiated Instruction   Solutions for All Learners

Accessibility at a Glance

	A Doll House, Act One
Context	Nineteenth-century upper-middle class Norwegian household
Language	Conversational dialogue
Concept Level	Accessible (Deceitfulness is not the best way to solve a problem.)
Literary Merit	Breakthrough realistic drama that focuses on an ordinary marriage and explores the theme of women's rights
Lexile	NP
Overall Rating	Average

ACT ONE

A comfortable room, tastefully but not expensively furnished. A door to the right in the back wall leads to the entryway; another to the left leads to HELMER's *study. Between these doors, a piano. Midway in the left-hand wall a door, and farther back a window. Near the window a round table with an armchair and a small sofa. In the right-hand wall, toward the rear, a door, and nearer the foreground a porcelain stove with two armchairs and a rocking chair beside it. Between the stove and the side door, a small table. Engravings on the walls. An* étagère[1] *with china figures and other small art objects; a small bookcase with richly bound books; the floor carpeted; a fire burning in the stove. It is a winter day.*

A bell rings in the entryway; shortly after we hear the door being unlocked. NORA *comes into the room humming happily to herself; she is wearing street clothes and carries an armload of packages, which she puts down on the table to the right. She has left the hall door open; and through it a* DELIVERY BOY *is seen, holding a Christmas tree and a basket, which he gives to the* MAID *who let them in.*

NORA: Hide the tree well, Helene. The children mustn't get a glimpse of it till this evening, after it's trimmed. [*To the* DELIVERY BOY, *taking out her purse*:] How much?

DELIVERY BOY: Fifty, ma'am.

NORA: There's a crown.[2] No, keep the change. [*The* BOY *thanks her and leaves.* NORA *shuts the door. She laughs softly to herself while taking off her street things. Drawing a bag of macaroons from her pocket, she eats a couple, then steals over and listens at her husband's study door.*] Yes, he's home. [*Hums again as she moves to the table right.*]

HELMER [*from the study*]: Is that my little lark twittering out there?

NORA [*busy opening some packages*]: Yes, it is.

HELMER: Is that my squirrel rummaging around?

NORA: Yes!

HELMER: When did my squirrel get in?

NORA: Just now. [*Putting the macaroon bag in her pocket and wiping her mouth.*] Do come in, Torvald, and see what I've bought.

HELMER: Can't be disturbed. [*After a moment he opens the door and peers in, pen in hand.*] Bought, you say? All that there? Has the little <u>spendthrift</u> been out throwing money around again?

NORA: Oh, but Torvald, this year we really should let ourselves go a bit. It's the first Christmas we haven't had to economize.

HELMER: But you know we can't go <u>squandering</u>.

NORA: Oh yes, Torvald, we can squander a little now. Can't we?

---

1. **étagère** (ā tà zher´) *n.* stand with open shelves for displaying small art objects and ornaments.
2. **crown** basic monetary unit of Norway; *krone* (krō´ nə) in Norwegian.

❸ Reading Strategy
Reading Drama List four details in the stage directions that indicate the Helmers' social standing.

Vocabulary Builder
spendthrift (spend´ thrift´) *n.* person who spends money carelessly
squandering (skwän´ dər iŋ) *v.* spending money wastefully

❺ ✔ Reading Check
What surprise is Nora preparing for her children?

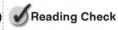

A Doll House, Act One ■ 943

---

❸ Reading Strategy
Reading Drama
- Have students read the first bracketed passage.
- Make sure students notice that stage directions do two things: They describe the set and the wordless actions of the characters as the play begins.
- **Ask** students to identify what they learn about the play even before a character has spoken.
  Possible response: The play is set in a well-appointed home, in a cold climate, at Christmas time.
- Have students **respond** to the Reading Strategy item: List four details in the stage directions that indicate the Helmers' social standing.
  Possible response: A piano, engravings on the walls, small art objects, books, a thick carpet, and a roaring fire all suggest that the Helmers are educated and have money to spend on comfort and decorative objects.

❹ Vocabulary Builder
Word Analysis: Coined Words
- Read aloud the sentence that includes the word *spendthrift,* and have students read the definition of the word that appears in the margin.
- Point out to students that *spendthrift* is a compound word—two or more words joined together. Ask students to identify the two words (*spend* and *thrift*) that make up this compound.
- Invite students to think of other compound words and to watch for others in the play.

❺ Reading Check
Answer: The surprise is a Christmas tree with all the trimmings.

---

❻ Literary Analysis

Modern Realistic Drama

- Have students read the first brack-eted passage.

- **Ask** students to respond to the Literary Analysis item: Identify two of Nora's words that reflect everyday, informal speech. **Answer:** Two words that reflect informal speech are "wee" and "pooh."

- Then, tell students that Nora will prove herself to be much more complex than she appears here.

❼ Critical Thinking

Analyze

- Have a volunteer read aloud the second bracketed passage. **Ask** students to list the nicknames Torvald calls Nora. **Answer:** Torvald calls Nora "little lark" and "squirrel."

- **Ask** students to explain what initial impression of Torvald the use of these names suggests about him and his relationship with Nora. **Possible response:** Torvald's use of the names gives a negative impression of him and makes Nora appear stupid and childlike. The balance of power in Nora and Torvald's relationship is unequal, with Torvald the dominant figure.

❽ Critical Viewing

Answer: This image suggests that the characters are happy because they are holding hands and smiling. They seem close to and interested in each other.

Just a tiny, wee bit. Now that you've got a big salary and are going to make piles and piles of money.

❻ **HELMER:** Yes—starting New Year's. But then it's a full three months till the raise comes through.

NORA: Pooh! We can borrow that long.

HELMER: Nora! [*Goes over and playfully takes her by the ear.*] Are your scatterbrains off again? What if today I borrowed a thousand crowns, and you squandered them over Christmas week, and then on New Year's Eve a roof tile fell on my head, and I lay there—

NORA [*putting her hand on his mouth*]: Oh! Don't say such things!

HELMER: Yes, but what if it happened—then what?

NORA: If anything so awful happened, then it just wouldn't matter if I had debts or not.

HELMER: Well, but the people I'd borrowed from?

NORA: Them? Who cared about them! They're strangers.

HELMER: Nora, Nora, how like a woman! No, but seriously, Nora, you know what I think about that. No debts! Never borrow! Something of freedom's lost—and something of beauty, too—from a home that's founded on borrowing and debt. We've made a brave stand up to now, the two of us; and we'll go right on like that the little while we have to.

NORA [*going toward the stove*]: Yes, whatever you say, Torvald.

❼ **HELMER** [*following her*]: Now, now, the little lark's wings mustn't droop. Come on, don't be a sulky squirrel. [*Taking out his wallet.*] Nora, guess what I have here.

NORA [*turning quickly*]: Money!

HELMER: There, see. [*Hands her some notes.*] Good grief, I know how costs go up in a house at Christmastime.

NORA: Ten—twenty—thirty—forty. Oh, thank you, Torvald; I can manage no end on this.

HELMER: You really will have to.

NORA: Oh yes, I promise I will! But come here so I can show you everything I bought. And so cheap! Look, new clothes for Ivar here—and a sword. Here a horse and a trumpet for Bob. And a doll and a doll's bed here for Emmy; they're nothing much, but she'll tear them to bits in no time anyway. And here I have

Literary Analysis
Modern Realistic Drama
Identify two of Nora's words that reflect every-day, informal speech.

❽ ▼ **Critical Viewing**
Can you tell that Nora and Torvald share a troubled relationship? Why or why not? [**Interpret**]

Enrichment

Banking Then and Now

Banking now is different from the way it was in Torvald Helmer's day. Banks were subject to far fewer laws and regulations in the nineteenth and early twentieth centuries than they are today. Also, bankers did not go to business school or study finance before starting their jobs. As you learn in the play, Torvald was a lawyer before going into banking.

In spite of the portrayal of Torvald Helmer in *A Doll House,* bankers do much more than read newspapers and order people around. Bankers play a very important role in modern society, whether at the international or local level. The kind of bank with which most students will be familiar is the commercial bank. These are the local banks that offer savings and checking accounts; make loans for cars, homes, college educations, and other purposes; and provide many other services.

dress material and handkerchiefs for the maids. Old Anne-Marie really deserves something more.

HELMER: And what's in that package there?

NORA [*with a cry*]: Torvald, no! You can't see that till tonight!

HELMER: I see. But tell me now, you little <u>prodigal</u>, what have you thought of for yourself?

NORA: For myself? Oh, I don't want anything at all.

HELMER: Of course you do. Tell me just what—within reason—you'd most like to have.

NORA: I honestly don't know. Oh, listen, Torvald—

HELMER: Well?

NORA [*fumbling at his coat buttons, without looking at him*]: If you want to give me something, then maybe you could—you could—

HELMER: Come on, out with it.

NORA [*hurriedly*]: You could give me money, Torvald. No more than you think you can spare; then one of these days I'll buy something with it.

HELMER: But Nora—

NORA: Oh, please, Torvald darling, do that! I beg you, please. Then I could hang the bills in pretty gilt paper on the Christmas tree. Wouldn't that be fun?

HELMER: What are those little birds called that always fly through their fortunes?

NORA: Oh yes, spendthrifts; I know all that. But let's do as I say, Torvald; then I'll have time to decide what I really need most. That's very sensible, isn't it?

HELMER [*smiling*]: Yes, very—that is, if you actually hung onto the money I give you, and you actually used it to buy yourself something. But it goes for the house and for all sorts of foolish things, and then I only have to lay out some more.

NORA: Oh, but Torvald—

HELMER: Don't deny it, my dear little Nora. [*Putting his arm around her waist.*] Spendthrifts are sweet, but they use up a frightful amount of money. It's incredible what it costs a man to feed such birds.

NORA: Oh, how can you say that! Really, I save everything I can.

HELMER [*laughing*]: Yes, that's the truth. Everything you can. But that's nothing at all.

NORA [*humming, with a smile of quiet satisfaction*]: Hm, if you only knew what expenses we larks and squirrels have, Torvald.

HELMER: You're an odd little one. Exactly the way your father was. You're never at a loss for scaring up money; but the moment you have it, it runs right out through your fingers; you never know what you've

Vocabulary Builder
prodigal (präd′ i gəl) *n.* person who spends money wastefully

Literary Analysis
Modern Realistic Drama
Explain how Torvald and Nora manage the family's money.

Reading Check
What is Torvald's attitude toward borrowing money?

A Doll House, Act One ■ 945

Strategy for Less Proficient Readers
By this point in the play, students should begin to appreciate the differences between the two main characters. Students may benefit from creating a two-column chart, with one column labeled *Nora* and one labeled *Torvald.* Have students jot down the identifying characteristics of each character. Then, challenge students to identify the points on which Torvald and Nora disagree, such as their ideas about money. Tell students that more points of disagreement will appear later in the play.

Background for English Learners
The whole class may be interested to know that there is no single English word for "little birds . . . that always fly through their fortunes." The translator chose the word *spendthrift* to convey the meaning of one Norwegian word. Have English learners tell how they translate English ideas and phrases into their native languages and vice versa. Ask volunteers to share examples of difficult translations with the class. As a class, talk about how ideas are lost or enhanced when translated into another language.

---

⑨ Critical Thinking
Connect
- Have a volunteer read aloud the bracketed sentence, and point out the word *prodigal.*
- Students may be familiar with the parable of the prodigal son told by Jesus in Luke 15:11–32. Have students review the definition of the term.
- Then, **ask** them to explain the parable and how its meaning relates to Nora in *A Doll House.*
  Possible response: The prodigal son in the Bible squanders all his possessions. Signs in the play indicate that Nora may be a spendthrift; Torvald already considers her one.

⑩ Literary Analysis
Modern Realistic Drama
- Remind students that Ibsen's play was one of the first to focus on an ordinary marriage, with its strengths and its flaws.
- **Ask** students to identify the strengths and flaws of the marriage as they see them now.
  Possible response: The marriage gets its strength from the man and the woman playing clear roles. However, Torvald talks down to Nora and does not trust her with money.
- **Ask** students to respond to the Literary Analysis item: Explain how Torvald and Nora manage the family's money.
  Answer: Nora spends the money that Torvald gives her in small amounts.

⑪ Background
Foreshadowing
This remark of Nora's is an example of foreshadowing, the literary technique by which authors use clues to suggest events that have yet to occur in the story. By using foreshadowing, Ibsen is creating suspense. Other examples of foreshadowing appear throughout the act.

⑫ Reading Check
Answer: Torvald disapproves of borrowing money because it eliminates the borrower's sense of freedom.

- Remind students that stage directions tell actors how to say their lines and which gestures to use.

- Call students' attention to the bracketed passage, and ask two volunteers to read it aloud, one volunteer assuming the role of Torvald and the other that of Nora.

- **Ask** the Reading Strategy question: What do the stage directions suggest about Torvald's attitude toward Nora?
  Answer: By shaking his finger at Nora, Torvald is acting like a parent who is scolding a child.

▶ **Monitor Progress** Ask students what other exchange between Nora and Torvald indicates the imbalance of their relationship, such as the recent discussion about money.

▶ **Reteach** Have students reread the dialogue on pp. 944–945. Lead them to understand that Torvald considers Nora extravagant and distrusts her with money.

❹ **Critical Thinking**

Analyze

- Read aloud the bracketed passage. **Ask** students how Torvald might have known that Nora has eaten some macaroons.
  Possible response: He might have seen crumbs on her face or clothing or heard her crumpling the bag earlier when he entered the room.

- Next, **ask** students what this exchange tells them about Nora, Torvald, and their relationship.
  Possible response: Nora is willing to lie to her husband, and Torvald thinks he has the right to forbid Nora to do certain things. Their relationship is based on unequal power and deceit.

❺ **Critical Viewing**

Possible response: The bird is delicate and sings beautifully. Torvald sees these traits in Nora.

---

done with it. Well, one takes you as you are. It's deep in your blood. Yes, these things are hereditary, Nora.

NORA: Ah, I could wish I'd inherited many of Papa's qualities.

HELMER: And I couldn't wish you anything but just what you are, my sweet little lark. But wait; it seems to me you have a very—what should I call it?—a very suspicious look today—

NORA: I do?

HELMER: You certainly do. Look me straight in the eye.

NORA [*looking at him*]: Well?

HELMER [*shaking an admonitory³ finger*]: Surely my sweet tooth hasn't been running riot in town today, has she?

❸ **NORA:** No. Why do you imagine that?

HELMER: My sweet tooth really didn't make a little detour through the confectioner's?

NORA: No, I assure you, Torvald—

HELMER: Hasn't nibbled some pastry?

❹ **NORA:** No, not at all.

HELMER: Not even munched a macaroon or two?

NORA: No, Torvald, I assure you, really—

---

3. **admonitory** (ad män′ i tôr′ ē) *adj.* warning.

❺ ◀ **Critical Viewing**
Which characteristics of a lark, like the one shown, does Torvald see in Nora? **[Connect]**

A Lark, Archibald Thorburn, John Spike Fine Watercolours, London, UK

946 ■ *Romanticism and Realism*

The Real Nora
Like many writers, Henrik Ibsen based some of his characters on real people. The real-life model for Nora Helmer in *A Doll House* was a friend of the writer, a woman named Laura Kieler. She was extremely displeased at the way she was portrayed in the play. One biographer of Ibsen wrote, "It is ironical that the play which established Ibsen as the champion of women should have been so deeply resented by the woman who had inspired it."

Ask students to discuss which aspects of the portrayal might have upset Laura Kieler, as well as situations in which a living person might resent being used as the model for a fictional character.

HELMER: There, there now. Of course I'm only joking.

NORA [*going to the table, right*]: You know I could never think of going against you.

HELMER: No, I understand that; and you *have* given me your word. [*Going over to her.*] Well, you keep your little Christmas secrets to yourself, Nora darling. I expect they'll come to light this evening, when the tree is lit.

NORA: Did you remember to ask Dr. Rank?

HELMER: No. But there's no need for that; it's assumed he'll be dining with us. All the same, I'll ask him when he stops by here this morning. I've ordered some fine wine. Nora, you can't imagine how I'm looking forward to this evening.

NORA: So am I. And what fun for the children, Torvald!

HELMER: Ah, it's so gratifying to know that one's gotten a safe, secure job, and with a comfortable salary. It's a great satisfaction, isn't it?

NORA: Oh, it's wonderful!

HELMER: Remember last Christmas? Three whole weeks before, you shut yourself in every evening till long after midnight, making flowers for the Christmas tree, and all the other decorations to surprise us. Ugh, that was the dullest time I've ever lived through.

NORA: It wasn't at all dull for me.

HELMER [*smiling*]: But the outcome *was* pretty sorry, Nora.

NORA: Oh, don't tease me with that again. How could I help it that the cat came in and tore everything to shreds.

HELMER: No, poor thing, you certainly couldn't. You wanted so much to please us all, and that's what counts. But it's just as well that the hard times are past.

NORA: Yes, it's really wonderful.

HELMER: Now I don't have to sit here alone, boring myself, and you don't have to tire your precious eyes and your fair little delicate hands—

NORA [*clapping her hands*]: No, is it really true, Torvald, I don't have to? Oh, how wonderfully lovely to hear! [*Taking his arm.*] Now I'll tell you just how I've thought we should plan things. Right after Christmas—[*The doorbell rings.*] Oh, the bell. [*Straightening the room up a bit.*] Somebody would have to come. What a bore!

HELMER: I'm not at home to visitors, don't forget.

MAID [*from the hall doorway*]: Ma'am, a lady to see you—

NORA: All right, let her come in.

MAID [*to* HELMER]: And the doctor's just come too.

HELMER: Did he go right to my study?

MAID: Yes, he did.

Reading Strategy
Reading Drama What mental image do you have of the Helmers as Torvald makes this speech? Explain.

---

17 **Reading Check**
Who will join the Helmers for dinner in the evening?

A Doll House, Act One ■ 947

---

16 Reading Strategy
Reading Drama

• Have two students read the bracketed passage.

• **Ask** students to track the moods Nora exhibits here.
Possible response: Nora is unhappy or even peeved as Torvald teases her; then, she becomes happy, as she claps her hands and realizes her troubles are over; then, she becomes irritated again when the doorbell rings.

• **Ask** students to read the Reading Strategy question: What mental image do you have of the Helmers as Torvald makes this speech? Explain.
Possible response: Torvald is talking down to his wife as she sits in a childlike way. Nora's eyes might be averted as Torvald paints an image of Nora slaving away in a dark room.

• Remind students to return to this moment in the play after Nora admits to Mrs. Linde what she was really working on last Christmas.

17 Reading Check
Answer: Dr. Rank is expected to join the Helmers for dinner.

Differentiated Instruction   Solutions for All Learners

Strategy for Less Proficient Readers
Help students track Ibsen's foreshadowing by creating a two-column chart. Have students label one column *Before Mrs. Linde* and the other column *After Mrs. Linde.* In the first column, students should jot down all the information they know about Nora. Make sure that they mention Nora's thoughts about money and last Christmas. Then, after they read pp. 948–960, have them jot down what they have learned about Nora in her conversation with Mrs. Linde. Students should realize that Nora has secrets.

Strategy for Advanced Readers
Advanced readers already will probably be suspicious of Nora, thinking that she is not what she seems. Invite students to make a list of predictions about Nora—what will happen to her and what her secrets might be. Students should be able to support their predictions with lines of dialogue from the play. Allow students to compare predictions and notes and to update and change them as they continue to read the play.

[HELMER *goes into his room. The* MAID *shows in* MRS. LINDE, *dressed in traveling clothes, and shuts the door after her.*]

MRS. LINDE [*in a dispirited and somewhat hesitant voice*]: Hello, Nora.

NORA [*uncertain*]: Hello—

MRS. LINDE: You don't recognize me.

⑱ **NORA:** No, I don't know—but wait, I think— [*Exclaiming.*] What! Kristine! Is it really you?

MRS. LINDE: Yes, it's me.

NORA: Kristine! To think I didn't recognize you. But then, how could I? [*More quietly.*] How you've changed, Kristine!

MRS. LINDE: Yes, no doubt I have. In nine—ten long years.

NORA: Is it so long since we met! Yes, it's all of that. Oh, these last eight years have been a happy time, believe me. And so now you've come in to town, too. Made the long trip in the winter. That took courage.

MRS. LINDE: I just got here by ship this morning.

⑲ **NORA:** To enjoy yourself over Christmas, of course. Oh, how lovely! Yes, enjoy ourselves, we'll do that. But take your coat off. You're not still cold? [*Helping her.*] There now, let's get cozy here by the stove. No, the easy chair there! I'll take the rocker here. [*Seizing her hands.*] Yes, now you have your old look again; it was only in that first moment. You're a bit more pale, Kristine—and maybe a bit thinner.

MRS. LINDE: And much, much older, Nora.

NORA: Yes, perhaps a bit older; a tiny, tiny bit; not much at all. [*Stopping short; suddenly serious.*] Oh, but thoughtless me, to sit here, chattering away. Sweet, good Kristine, can you forgive me?

MRS. LINDE: What do you mean, Nora?

NORA [*softly*]: Poor Kristine, you've become a widow.

MRS. LINDE: Yes, three years ago.

NORA: Oh, I knew it, of course; I read it in the papers. Oh, Kristine, you must believe me; I often thought of writing you then, but I kept postponing it, and something always interfered.

MRS. LINDE: Nora dear, I understand completely.

NORA: No, it was awful of me, Kristine. You poor thing, how much you must have gone through. And he left you nothing?

MRS. LINDE: No.

NORA: And no children?

MRS. LINDE: No.

NORA: Nothing at all, then?

MRS. LINDE: Not even a sense of loss to feed on.

NORA [*looking incredulously at her*]: But Kristine, how could that be?

Enrichment

Norway

Henrik Ibsen's homeland, Norway, is one of the northernmost countries in the world. It lies on the western half of the Scandinavian peninsula, which it shares with its neighbor, Sweden. Norway is about the size of New Mexico and is home to about 4.5 million people. In spite of its northern location, warm ocean currents give most of the country a relatively mild climate, although winters are long and cold and summers are short. About two thirds of the country is covered by mountains. Norway's most famous geographic features are the many *fjords,* or long narrow inlets of sea water surrounded by steep, rocky cliffs. The coastline is also dotted by around 50,000 islands of all sizes. Norway's important natural resources include wood and paper products, oil and natural gas, and fish. Because of its many waterfalls and dammable rivers, Norway is a world leader in the production of hydroelectric power.

MRS. LINDE [*smiling wearily and smoothing her hair*]: Oh, sometimes it happens, Nora.

NORA: So completely alone. How terribly hard that must be for you. I have three lovely children. You can't see them now; they're out with the maid. But now you must tell me everything—

MRS. LINDE: No, no, no, tell me about yourself.

NORA: No, you begin. Today I don't want to be selfish. I want to think only of you today. But there *is* something I must tell you. Did you hear of the wonderful luck we had recently?

MRS. LINDE: No, what's that?

NORA: My husband's been made manager in the bank, just think!

MRS. LINDE: Your husband? How marvelous!

NORA: Isn't it? Being a lawyer is such an uncertain living, you know, especially if one won't touch any cases that aren't clean and decent. And of course Torvald would never do that, and I'm with him completely there. Oh, we're simply delighted, believe me! He'll join the bank right after New Year's and start getting a huge salary and lots of commissions. From now on we can live quite differently—just as we want. Oh, Kristine, I feel so light and happy! Won't it be lovely to have stacks of money and not a care in the world?

MRS. LINDE: Well, anyway, it would be lovely to have enough for necessities.

NORA: No, not just for necessities, but stacks and stacks of money!

MRS. LINDE [*smiling*]: Nora, Nora, aren't you sensible yet? Back in school you were such a free spender.

NORA [*with a quiet laugh*]: Yes, that's what Torvald still says. [*Shaking her finger.*] But "Nora, Nora" isn't as silly as you all think. Really, we've been in no position for me to go squandering. We've had to work, both of us.

MRS. LINDE: You too?

NORA: Yes, at odd jobs—needlework, crocheting, embroidery, and such—[*Casually.*] and other things too. You remember that Torvald left the department when we were married? There was no chance of promotion in his office, and of course he needed to earn more money. But that first year he drove himself terribly. He took on all kinds of extra work that kept him going morning and night. It wore him down, and then he fell deathly ill. The doctors said it was essential for him to travel south.

MRS. LINDE: Yes, didn't you spend a whole year in Italy?

NORA: That's right. It wasn't easy to get away, you know. Ivar had just been born. But of course we had to go. Oh, that was a beautiful trip, and it saved Torvald's life. But it cost a frightful sum, Kristine.

MRS. LINDE: I can well imagine.

Literary Analysis
Modern Realistic Drama
Identify three ways that Nora's and Mrs. Linde's social situations differ.

✓**Reading Check** 22
What loss did Kristine suffer three years ago?

A Doll House, Act One ■ 949

---

⑳ Literary Analysis
Modern Realistic Drama

• Remind students that Torvald and Nora are living a little beyond their means but still have a comfortable home. Explain that Mrs. Linde represents a different economic bracket here. She is a poor working widow.

• **Ask** students to respond to the Literary Analysis item: Identify three ways that Nora's and Mrs. Linde's social situations differ.
Possible response: Mrs. Linde is widowed and childless; her thin and haggard appearance suggests that she has seen hard times. Nora, on the other hand, is married, has children, and lives in a comfortable home.

㉑ Background
Health

Make sure students understand that Nora and her husband traveled to Italy because Torvald's illness made it necessary for him to recuperate in a warmer climate.

㉒ Reading Check

Answer: Kristine's husband died three years ago.

Modern Realistic Drama

- **Ask** students what turning point in her life Mrs. Linde is describing in the first bracketed passage and whether they think she made the right decision.
  Answer: Mrs. Linde is describing how she decided to marry her husband. She seems to think it was the right decision but not a happy one.

- Next, **ask** students the Literary Analysis question: What factors motivated Mrs. Linde to marry someone she did not love?
  Answer: Mrs. Linde had a sick mother and two brothers who needed support. She probably needed the husband's financial support to help her family.

24 Reading Strategy

Reading Drama

- Point out that Mrs. Linde has financial and family problems that many people face every day. Remind students that a character with ordinary problems was an innovation in theater when Ibsen was writing.

- **Ask** students to answer the Reading Strategy question: What might Mrs. Linde's voice sound like in these lines?
  Answer: Her voice might sound tired, flat, shaky, or distant.

NORA: Four thousand, eight hundred crowns it cost. That's really a lot of money.

MRS. LINDE: But it's lucky you had it when you needed it.

NORA: Well, as it was, we got it from Papa.

MRS. LINDE: I see. It was just about the time your father died.

NORA: Yes, just about then. And, you know, I couldn't make that trip out to nurse him. I had to stay here, expecting Ivar any moment, and with my poor sick Torvald to care for. Dearest Papa, I never saw him again, Kristine. Oh, that was the worst time I've known in all my marriage.

MRS. LINDE: I know how you loved him. And then you went off to Italy?

NORA: Yes. We had the means now, and the doctors urged us. So we left a month after.

MRS. LINDE: And your husband came back completely cured?

NORA: Sound as a drum!

MRS. LINDE: But—the doctor?

NORA: Who?

MRS. LINDE: I thought the maid said he was a doctor, the man who came in with me.

NORA: Yes, that was Dr. Rank—but he's not making a sick call. He's our closest friend, and he stops by at least once a day. No, Torvald hasn't had a sick moment since, and the children are fit and strong, and I am, too. [*Jumping up and clapping her hands.*] Oh, dear God, Kristine, what a lovely thing to live and be happy! But how disgusting of me—I'm talking of nothing but my own affairs. [*Sits on a stool close by* KRISTINE, *arms resting across her knees.*] Oh, don't be angry with me! Tell me, is it really true that you weren't in love with your husband? Why did you marry him, then?

MRS. LINDE: My mother was still alive, but bedridden and helpless— and I had my two younger brothers to look after. In all conscience, I didn't think I could turn him down.

23 **NORA:** No, you were right there. But was he rich at the time?

MRS. LINDE: He was very well off, I'd say. But the business was shaky, Nora. When he died, it all fell apart, and nothing was left.

NORA: And then—?

MRS. LINDE: Yes, so I had to scrape up a living with a little shop and a little teaching and whatever else I could find. The last three years have been like one endless workday without a rest for me. Now it's over, Nora. My poor mother doesn't need me, for she's passed on. Nor the boys, either; they're working now and can take care of themselves.

NORA: How free you must feel—

MRS. LINDE: No—only unspeakably empty. Nothing to live for now. [*Standing up anxiously.*] That's why I couldn't take it any longer out in

950 ■ *Romanticism and Realism*

Literary Analysis
Modern Realistic Drama
What factors motivated Mrs. Linde to marry someone she did not love?

Reading Strategy
Reading Drama What might Mrs. Linde's voice sound like in these lines?

Enrichment

Progress in Nineteenth-Century Medicine

The nineteenth century was a time of great innovation and progress, particularly in the field of medicine. For hundreds of years, European medicine was largely a matter of superstition and luck. It was not until the mid-1800s that scientists agreed that health was not dictated by a balance of mysterious forces in the body called humors.

By the early 1800s, doctors had developed a more accurate physiology of the body (the major organs, muscles, and bones and where they are located). More importantly, doctors began to accept the idea that microscopic organisms, such as viruses and germs, were responsible for illnesses and infections.

The nature of Torvald's illness is not made clear in the play. Patients with illnesses such as tuberculosis, which would not have reliable treatment or prevention until the next century, were often sent to milder climates to recover.

that desolate hole. Maybe here it'll be easier to find something to do and keep my mind occupied. If I could only be lucky enough to get a steady job, some office work—

NORA: Oh, but Kristine, that's so dreadfully tiring, and you already look so tired. It would be much better for you if you could go off to a bathing resort.

MRS. LINDE [*going toward the window*]: I have no father to give me travel money, Nora.

NORA [*rising*]: Oh, don't be angry with me.

MRS. LINDE [*going to her*]: Nora dear, don't you be angry with me. The worst of my kind of situation is all the bitterness that's stored away. No one to work for, and yet you're always having to snap up your opportunities. You have to live; and so you grow selfish. When you told me the happy change in your lot, do you know I was delighted less for your sakes than for mine?

NORA: How so? Oh, I see. You think maybe Torvald could do something for you.

MRS. LINDE: Yes, that's what I thought.

NORA: And he will, Kristine! Just leave it to me; I'll bring it up so delicately—find something attractive to humor him with. Oh, I'm so eager to help you.

MRS. LINDE: How very kind of you, Nora, to be so concerned over me—double kind, considering you really know so little of life's burdens yourself.

NORA: I—? I know so little—?

MRS. LINDE [*smiling*]: Well, my heavens—a little needlework and such—Nora, you're just a child.

NORA [*tossing her head and pacing the floor*]: You don't have to act so superior.

MRS. LINDE: Oh?

NORA: You're just like the others. You all think I'm incapable of anything serious.

MRS. LINDE: Come now—

NORA: That I've never had to face the raw world.

MRS. LINDE: Nora dear, you've just been telling me all your troubles.

NORA: Hm! Trivia! [*Quietly*.] I haven't told you the big thing.

MRS. LINDE: Big thing? What do you mean?

▲ Critical Viewing
What type of household might pay Nora to complete needlework like that on the chair in this photograph? **[Connect]**

✔ Reading Check
What does Mrs. Linde hope to gain by visiting the Helmers?

A Doll House, Act One ■ 951

㉕ Critical Thinking

Speculate

• Have students read the bracketed passage.

• Then, have students **speculate** about whether Torvald will give Mrs. Linde a job. On what do they base their speculations?
Possible response: Torvald will give Mrs. Linde a job because Nora seems able to make her husband do what she wants him to do.

• Later, when students reach the end of this page, **ask** them to speculate about what Nora's secret is.
Possible response: The secret probably has to do with money.

• Indicate to students that this point in the play is crucial to the plot and to Nora's development as a character.

㉖ Critical Viewing

Possible response: A wealthy household would probably pay Nora for such needlework. The needlework itself is elaborate and detailed. It would take much time and effort to complete and would be worth a great deal of money.

㉗ Reading Check

Answer: Mrs. Linde hopes to gain a job.

Differentiated Instruction   Solutions for All Learners

Strategy for Special Needs Students
To help students follow the development of the characters, suggest that they create a sunburst diagram. Have students draw circles with lines radiating from them. Have students write the name of a character inside each circle. As they read the play, they should write down lines of dialogue or descriptive words that reveal information about the character's personality. These quotations and words should be written on the radiating lines.

Strategy for English Learners
Ask students to draw circles with lines radiating from them. Next, they should write the name of a character inside each circle. As they read, they should write down words or bits of dialogue that reveal something about each character's personality. These words or lines of dialogue should be written on the radiating lines. Encourage students to translate or use words from their native languages to help them get a better sense of the characters. Allow students to work in pairs.

Reading Drama

- Have two volunteers read aloud the dialogue between Nora and Mrs. Linde. **Ask** the first Reading Strategy question: Why do you think the stage direction specifies that Nora draw Mrs. Linde down onto the sofa?
  Answer: By drawing Mrs. Linde onto the sofa, Nora builds suspense and gives both Mrs. Linde and the audience a sense that she is going to say something important.

- As students read this passage, have them **identify** the different moods or tones of voice that Nora is suggesting by her actions and gestures.
  Answer: Nora shifts from plainly smiling to speaking disdainfully to humming and smiling mysteriously.

29 Background

Law

Students should understand the importance of Mrs. Linde's comment here. According to Norwegian law at the time, Nora had no legal right to borrow money without her husband's approval. Students should suspect that Nora has done something wrong.

30 Reading Strategy

Reading Drama

- Ask students to read the bracketed passage independently and then **describe** Nora's actions.
  Answer: She tosses her head and throws herself on the sofa.

- Next, **ask** students the second Reading Strategy question: What do the stage directions suggest about Nora's attitude toward her money scheme?
  Possible response: Nora is proud and pleased, in a childlike way, by the success of her scheme.

- Lead students in a discussion about whether a person has the right to be proud of making sacrifices for others. If appropriate, have students describe how they, or someone they know, felt after making a sacrifice for someone else.

NORA: You look down on me so, Kristine, but you shouldn't. You're proud that you worked so long and hard for your mother.

MRS. LINDE: I don't look down on a soul. But it *is* true: I'm proud—and happy, too—to think it was given to me to make my mother's last days almost free of care.

NORA: And you're also proud thinking of what you've done for your brothers.

MRS. LINDE: I feel I've a right to be.

NORA: I agree. But listen to this, Kristine—I've also got something to be proud and happy for.

MRS. LINDE: I don't doubt it. But whatever do you mean?

NORA: Not so loud. What if Torvald heard! He mustn't, not for anything in the world. Nobody must know, Kristine. No one but you.

MRS. LINDE: But what is it, then?

NORA: Come here. [*Drawing her down beside her on the sofa.*] It's true— I've also got something to be proud and happy for. I'm the one who saved Torvald's life.

MRS. LINDE: Saved—? Saved how?

NORA: I told you about the trip to Italy. Torvald never would have lived if he hadn't gone south—

MRS. LINDE: Of course; your father gave you the means—

NORA [*smiling*]: That's what Torvald and all the rest think, but—

MRS. LINDE: But—?

NORA: Papa didn't give us a pin. I was the one who raised the money.

MRS. LINDE: You? That whole amount?

NORA: Four thousand, eight hundred crowns. What do you say to that?

MRS. LINDE: But Nora, how was it possible? Did you win the lottery?

NORA [*disdainfully*]: The lottery? Pooh! No art to that.

MRS. LINDE: But where did you get it from then?

NORA [*humming, with a mysterious smile*]: Hmm, tra-la-la-la.

MRS. LINDE: Because you couldn't have borrowed it.

NORA: No? Why not?

MRS. LINDE: A wife can't borrow without her husband's consent.

NORA [*tossing her head*]: Oh, but a wife with a little business sense, a wife who knows how to manage—

MRS. LINDE: Nora, I simply don't understand—

NORA: You don't have to. Whoever said I *borrowed* the money? I could have gotten it other ways. [*Throwing herself back on the sofa.*] I could have gotten it from some admirer or other. After all, a girl with my ravishing appeal—

Reading Strategy
Reading Drama Why do you think the stage direction specifies that Nora draws Mrs. Linde down onto the sofa?

Reading Strategy
Reading Drama What do the stage directions suggest about Nora's attitude toward her money scheme?

Enrichment

Women's Rights

A Doll House explores the theme of women's rights through the story of one particular family in one country. In Europe and the United States, women lobbied for their economic and political rights for many decades. Women in Norway received the right to vote in 1913, thirty-four years after Ibsen's play was published. Norwegian women received the right to vote five years before women (aged 30 and older) in Great Britain and seven years before women in the United States. Women's struggle to obtain rights equal to those of men has been occurring throughout the world for more than a century.

Have students research and prepare a presentation on the status of women in a particular country today. Countries of particular interest that students may wish to study include Iran, India, Afghanistan, China, Russia, Mexico, Ireland, South Africa, Sweden, Denmark, and the Netherlands.

Critical Viewing
Which details in this photo suggest that Kristine and Nora enjoy each other's company? [Interpret]

MRS. LINDE: You lunatic.

NORA: I'll bet you're eaten up with curiosity, Kristine.

MRS. LINDE: Now listen here, Nora—you haven't done something <u>indiscreet</u>?

NORA [*sitting up again*]: Is it indiscreet to save your husband's life?

MRS. LINDE: I think it's indiscreet that without his knowledge you—

NORA: But that's the point: he mustn't know! My Lord, can't you understand? He mustn't ever know the close call he had. It was to *me* the doctors came to say his life was in danger—that nothing could save him but a stay in the south. Didn't I try strategy then! I began talking about how lovely it would be for me to travel abroad like other young wives; I begged and I cried; I told him please to remember my condition, to be kind and indulge me; and then I dropped a hint that he could easily take out a loan. But at that Kristine, he nearly exploded. He said I was <u>frivolous</u>, and it was his duty as man of the house not to indulge me in whims and fancies—as I think he called them. Aha, I thought, now you'll just have to be saved—and that's when I saw my chance.

MRS. LINDE: And your father never told Torvald the money wasn't from him?

NORA: No, never. Papa died right about then. I'd considered bringing him into my secret and begging him never to tell. But he was too sick at the time—and then, sadly, it didn't matter.

MRS. LINDE: And you've never confided in your husband since?

Vocabulary Builder
indiscreet (in′ di skrēt′) *adj.* unwise or not careful

Vocabulary Builder
frivolous (friv′ ə ləs) *adj.* silly and light-minded; not sensible

✔ **Reading Check** ㉝
What secret does Nora share with Kristine?

A Doll House, Act One ■ 953

㉛ Critical Viewing
Possible response: Nora appears excited or happy to talk to Kristine; Kristine, although serious, seems eager to know what Nora has to tell her.

㉜ Critical Thinking
Evaluate
- Ask students to **summarize** Nora's strategies for getting Torvald to go to Italy.
  Answer: Nora tried reasoning, begging and crying, and finally scheming.
- Next, **ask** students whether Nora should have told Torvald that his life was in danger, and have them explain their answers.
  Possible responses: Those who think she should have told him may say that honesty is an absolute necessity in a relationship. Those who say that she should not have told him may claim that Nora withheld the truth out of love and concern for Torvald's well-being.

㉝ Reading Check
Answer: Nora tells Kristine that she did not get the money she needed from her father, as everyone believes.

Enrichment for Advanced Readers
In the more than 120 years since *A Doll House* was written, the lives of women have changed in many important ways. Students can understand these changes in a more personal way by arranging to interview older women in their community about the changes they have seen in their own lifetimes. Students may wish to interview older relatives, friends, residents of retirement homes, or people active in senior centers or other activities. Have students arrange interviews, prepare interview questions, conduct the interviews, organize their information, and present their findings to the class. If appropriate, students may record their interviews on audiotape or videotape.

Encourage students to prepare questions about different types of change that have occurred in the status and condition of women, including economic, social, political, and psychological factors. It is recommended that you preview students' questions before the interviews.

- Read aloud the first bracketed passage.
- Then, **ask** the first Literary Analysis question: Do you think the Helmers' "beautiful, happy home" is built on the foundation of a lie? Why or why not?
  Possible responses: Yes; the Helmers' finances and marriage are secure only because of Nora's debt. No; *lie* is too harsh a word for Nora's self-sacrifice, which she made out of love.

▶ **Monitor Progress** After students read Nora's words here, **ask** them to review how her character fits the mold of the modern realistic drama.
  Possible response: Nora is an ordinary person; she has flaws and can be, in turn, silly, loving, arrogant, and patronizing. She has ordinary problems; she does not understand money; and she lies to her husband. The character is a lens through which readers and theatergoers can see the life of an ordinary nineteenth-century wife and mother.

▶ **Reteach** If necessary, have students revisit the characteristics of modern realistic drama. Ask students for examples of each of the characteristics found in the play so far.

35 Literary Analysis

Modern Realistic Drama and Conflict

- **Ask** students to comment on Nora's idea that it will be safe to tell Torvald her secret when she is older and unattractive. What does it say about her?
  Possible response: Nora has a shallow idea of marriage. She expects her husband to lose interest in her when she is older and will not be so angry or disappointed in her.

- **Ask** students the second Literary Analysis question: What type of conflict motivates Nora to maintain her house allowance? Explain.
  Answer: Nora must maintain her house allowance so that no one is uncomfortable or suspects that the family is in financial trouble.

NORA: For heaven's sake, no! Are you serious? He's so strict on that subject. Besides—Torvald, with all his masculine pride—how painfully humiliating for him if he ever found out he was in debt to me. That would just ruin our relationship. Our beautiful, happy home would never be the same.

MRS. LINDE: Won't you ever tell him?

NORA [*thoughtfully, half smiling*]: Yes—maybe sometime, years from now, when I'm no longer so attractive. Don't laugh! I only mean when Torvald loves me less than now, when he stops enjoying my dancing and dressing up and reciting for him. Then it might be wise to have something in reserve—[*Breaking off.*] How ridiculous! That'll never happen—Well, Kristine, what do you think of my big secret? I'm capable of something too, hm? You can imagine, of course, how this thing hangs over me. It really hasn't been easy meeting the payments on time. In the business world there's what they call quarterly interest and what they call amortization,[4] and these are always so terribly hard to manage. I've had to skimp a little here and there, wherever I could, you know. I could hardly spare anything from my house allowance, because Torvald has to live well. I couldn't let the children go poorly dressed; whatever I got for them, I felt I had to use up completely—the darlings!

MRS. LINDE: Poor Nora, so it had to come out of your own budget, then?

NORA: Yes, of course. But I was the one most responsible, too. Every time Torvald gave me money for new clothes and such, I never used more than half; always bought the simplest, cheapest outfits. It was a godsend that everything looks so well on me that Torvald never noticed. But it did weigh me down at times, Kristine. It *is* such a joy to wear fine things. You understand.

MRS. LINDE: Oh, of course.

NORA: And then I found other ways of making money. Last winter I was lucky enough to get a lot of copying to do. I locked myself in and sat writing every evening till late in the night. Ah, I was tired so often, dead tired. But still it was wonderful fun, sitting and working like that, earning money. It was almost like being a man.

MRS. LINDE: But how much have you paid off this way so far?

NORA: That's hard to say, exactly. These accounts, you know, aren't easy to figure. I only know that I've paid out all I could scrape together. Time and again I haven't known where to turn. [*Smiling.*] Then I'd sit here dreaming of a rich old gentleman who had fallen in love with me—

MRS. LINDE: What! Who is he?

NORA: Oh, really! And that he'd died, and when his will was opened, there in big letters it said, "All my fortune shall be paid over in cash, immediately, to that enchanting Mrs. Nora Helmer."

---

4. **amortization** (am′ ər ti zā′ shən) *n.* putting aside money at intervals for gradual payment of a debt.

Literary Analysis
Modern Realistic Drama
Do you think the Helmers' "beautiful, happy home" is built on the foundation of a lie? Why or why not?

Literary Analysis
Modern Realistic Drama and Conflict What type of conflict motivates Nora to maintain her house allowance? Explain.

MRS. LINDE: But Nora dear—who *was* this gentleman?

NORA: Good grief, can't you understand? The old man never existed; that was only something I'd dream up time and again whenever I was at my wits' end for money. But it makes no difference now; the old fossil can go where he pleases for all I care; I don't need him or his will—because now I'm free. [*Jumping up.*] Oh, how lovely to think of that, Kristine! Carefree! To know you're carefree, utterly carefree; to be able to romp and play with the children, and to keep up a beautiful, charming home—everything just the way Torvald likes it! And think, spring is coming, with big blue skies. Maybe we can travel a little then. Maybe I'll see the ocean again. Oh yes, it *is* so marvelous to live and be happy!

[*The front doorbell rings.*]

MRS. LINDE [*rising*]: There's the bell. It's probably best that I go.

NORA: No, stay. No one's expected. It must be for Torvald.

MAID [*from the hall doorway*]: Excuse me, ma'am—there's a gentleman here to see Mr. Helmer, but I didn't know—since the doctor's with him—

NORA: Who is the gentleman?

KROGSTAD [*from the doorway*]: It's me, Mrs. Helmer.

[MRS. LINDE *starts and turns away toward the window.*]

NORA [*stepping toward him, tense, her voice a whisper*]: You? What is it? Why do you want to speak to my husband?

KROGSTAD: Bank business—after a fashion. I have a small job in the investment bank, and I hear now your husband is going to be our chief—

NORA: In other words, it's—

KROGSTAD: Just dry business, Mrs. Helmer. Nothing but that.

NORA: Yes, then please be good enough to step into the study. [*She nods indifferently as she sees him out by the hall door, then returns and begins stirring up the stove.*]

MRS. LINDE: Nora—who was that man?

NORA: That was a Mr. Krogstad—a lawyer.

MRS. LINDE: Then it really was him.

NORA: Do you know that person?

MRS. LINDE: I did once—many years ago. For a time he was a law clerk in our town.

NORA: Yes, he's been that.

36 Cultural Connection
The Norwegian Krone

The krone, or crown, is a unit of Norwegian currency. Today, the forty kroner [plural form] that Torvald gives Nora would be worth only about five dollars and fifty cents, less than half the price of a typical compact disc. In 1879, however, the year *A Doll House* was first produced, those forty kroner would have bought considerably more. At that time, a pound of bacon cost about eight cents in the United States; a skilled laborer brought home about ten dollars a week. So, while forty kroner does not sound like a significant sum, Torvald was being rather generous. On a larger scale, Nora would need to devote considerable time and effort to paying back four thousand eight hundred crowns. Its current equivalent is more than six hundred American dollars.

Connect to the Literature

What does Nora's attitude toward her debt tell you about her?

Reading Strategy
Reading Drama How does the atmosphere onstage change when Krogstad enters?

✔ **Reading Check** 38
What kind of work did Nora perform to pay off her debt?

A Doll House, Act One ■ 955

---

36 Literature in Context

The Norwegian Krone Unlike many European nations, Norway still uses its traditional kroner as money. Many European countries, in joining the European Union (EU), have given up their individual currencies and use the euro instead. In 1992, the Norwegian government applied for a place in the EU, but two years later, in 1994, the voters of Norway rejected the idea of joining. Norway is one of the few developed European nations that has refused to join.

Connect to the Literature Note that the issue of personal debt is one of the urgent concerns of people around the world and that Ibsen was very savvy to depict an ordinary marriage with this specific conflict because it is meaningful to so many people. Ask students to comment on how Nora's attitude toward her debt affects her character.

Possible response: Even though she is anxious about her secret, Nora feels a certain sense of power knowing that Torvald is in her debt. She does show responsibility about repaying her debt by secretly working at home and enjoys making money because she feels like a man. Nora also fantasizes about inheriting money, paying off the debt, and being totally carefree. She is naïve about the seriousness of her problem.

37 Reading Strategy
Reading Drama

- Make sure that students notice the emotional ebb and flow in the play.
- Ask volunteers to read the bracketed dialogue among Nora, Krogstad, and Mrs. Linde.
- **Ask** students the Reading Strategy question: How does the atmosphere onstage change when Krogstad enters?
  Answer: Nora appears uneasy around him. Mrs. Linde seems surprised to see him. The atmosphere becomes tense and awkward.
- Challenge students to predict why the two women react as they do upon seeing Krogstad. Explain that his relationship with Nora will become clearer later in the act.

38 Reading Check
Answer: Nora copied documents by hand to make money to pay off her debt.

Enrichment for Gifted/Talented Students
Have students identify a favorite protagonist from another work of literature or from a movie, television, or video. Invite students to work in groups to role-play a panel discussion featuring Nora and at least two other protagonists. In character, students should discuss their characters' goals, as well as their problems and how they solved them. Have students perform their panel discussion for the class. Ask another student to serve as moderator to lead the discussion and take questions from the students in the audience.

Enrichment for Advanced Readers
Have students consider leading female protagonists they have encountered and admired in other works of literature or in film, video, or television. Ask them to write a brief comparison of one of those protagonists and Nora. Students should identify the two characters' conflicts, flaws, and goals. If students read ahead, they can also compare the two characters' solutions to their problems. Invite students to share their comparisons with the class, without revealing the ending of the play.

MRS. LINDE: How he's changed.

NORA: I understand he had a very unhappy marriage.

MRS. LINDE: He's a widower now.

NORA: With a number of children. There now, it's burning. [*She closes the stove door and moves the rocker a bit to one side.*]

MRS. LINDE: They say he has a hand in all kinds of business.

NORA: Oh? That may be true; I wouldn't know. But let's not think about business. It's so dull.

[DR. RANK *enters from* HELMER'*s study.*]

RANK [*still in the doorway*]: No, no, really—I don't want to intrude, I'd just as soon talk a little while with your wife. [*Shuts the door, then notices* MRS. LINDE.] Oh, beg pardon. I'm intruding here too.

NORA: No, not at all. [*Introducing him.*] Dr. Rank, Mrs. Linde.

RANK: Well now, that's a name much heard in this house. I believe I passed the lady on the stairs as I came.

MRS. LINDE: Yes, I take the stairs very slowly. They're rather hard on me.

RANK: Uh-hm, some touch of internal weakness?

MRS. LINDE: More overexertion, I'd say.

RANK: Nothing else? Then you're probably here in town to rest up in a round of parties?

MRS. LINDE: I'm here to look for work.

RANK: Is that the best cure for overexertion?

MRS. LINDE: One has to live, Doctor.

RANK: Yes, there's a common prejudice to that effect.

NORA: Oh, come on, Dr. Rank—you really do want to live yourself.

RANK. Yes, I really do. Wretched as I am, I'll gladly prolong my torment indefinitely. All my patients feel like that. And it's quite the same, too, with the morally sick. Right at this moment there's one of those moral invalids in there with Helmer—

MRS. LINDE [*softly*]: Ah!

NORA: Who do you mean?

RANK: Oh, it's a lawyer, Krogstad, a type you wouldn't know. His character is rotten to the root—but even he began chattering all-importantly about how he had to *live.*

NORA: Oh? What did he want to talk to Torvald about?

RANK: I really don't know. I only heard something about the bank.

 NORA: I didn't know that Krog—that this man Krogstad had anything to do with the bank.

RANK: Yes, he's gotten some kind of berth down there. [*To* MRS. LINDE.] I don't know if you also have, in your neck of the woods, a type of person who scuttles about breathlessly, sniffing out hints of moral corruption, and then maneuvers his victim into some sort of key position where he can keep an eye on him. It's the healthy these days that are out in the cold.

MRS. LINDE: All the same, it's the sick who most need to be taken in.

RANK [*with a shrug*]: Yes, there we have it. That's the concept that's turning society into a sanatorium.

[NORA, *lost in her thoughts, breaks out into quiet laughter and claps her hands.*]

RANK: Why do you laugh at that? Do you have any real idea of what society is?

Literary Analysis
Modern Realistic Drama
In what ways do Dr. Rank's words reflect characteristics of modern realistic drama?

✔ Reading Check
What does Dr. Rank know of Krogstad's personality?

A Doll House, Act One ■ 957

44 Literary Analysis
Modern Realistic Drama

- Have students read the first bracketed passage and **examine** it for signs that Nora has reached some kind of turning point.
  Answer: Nora laughs, smiles, hums, and pulls out the bag of macaroons.

- Then, **ask** students what the information might be that has made her so happy.
  Possible response: The idea that the bank employees, including Krogstad, are now under Torvald's control makes her happy.

- **Ask** students the first Literary Analysis question: What social benefits might Nora gain from Torvald's "power now over all those people"?
  Possible response: Nora may gain prestige and respect in the community. Also, the Helmers will have enough money, and Nora will be able to pay off her debt.

45 Literary Analysis
Modern Realistic Drama

- Have three volunteers read aloud the second bracketed passage.

- Then, **ask** students the second Literary Analysis question: Why are Mrs. Linde and Dr. Rank so shocked by Nora's words?
  Possible response: Nora's words are not something a proper middle-class woman would say. Mrs. Linde and Dr. Rank are shocked only in the way parents are shocked when a child says something inappropriate.

- Finally, point out to students that despite Nora's daring vocabulary, she does not say the words to Torvald and in fact hides her forbidden bag of macaroons when he enters the room.

NORA: What do I care about dreary old society? I was laughing at something quite different—something terribly funny. Tell me, Doctor—is everyone who works in the bank dependent now on Torvald?

44 RANK: Is that what you find so terribly funny?

NORA [*smiling and humming*]: Never mind, never mind! [*Pacing the floor.*] Yes, that's really immensely amusing: that we—that Torvald has so much power now over all those people. [*Taking the bag out of her pocket.*] Dr. Rank, a little macaroon on that?

RANK: See here, macaroons! I thought they were <u>contraband</u> here.

NORA: Yes, but these are some that Kristine gave me.

MRS. LINDE: What? I—?

NORA: Now, now, don't be afraid. You couldn't possibly know that Torvald had forbidden them. You see, he's worried they'll ruin my teeth. But hmp! Just this once! Isn't that so, Dr. Rank? Help yourself. [*Puts a macaroon in his mouth.*] And you too, Kristine. And I'll also have one, only a little one—or two, at the most. [*Walking about again.*] Now I'm really tremendously happy. Now there's just one last thing in the world that I have an enormous desire to do.

RANK: Well! And what's that?

NORA: It's something I have such a consuming desire to say so Torvald could hear.

RANK: And why can't you say it?

NORA: I don't dare. It's quite shocking.

MRS. LINDE: Shocking?

45 RANK: Well, then it isn't advisable. But in front of us you certainly can. What do you have such a desire to say so Torvald could hear?

NORA: I have such a huge desire to say—to hell and be damned!

RANK: Are you crazy?

MRS. LINDE: My goodness, Nora!

RANK: Go on, say it. Here he is.

NORA [*hiding the macaroon bag*]: Shh, shh, shh!

[HELMER *comes in from his study, hat in hand, overcoat over his arm.*]

Vocabulary Builder
contraband (kän´ trə band´) *n.* unlawful or forbidden goods

Literary Analysis
Modern Realistic Drama
What social benefits might Nora gain from Torvald's "power now over all those people"?

Literary Analysis
Modern Realistic Drama
Why are Mrs. Linde and Dr. Rank so shocked by Nora's words?

Enrichment

Norwegian Food for Thought
A macaroon is a small chewy cookie made of a few simple ingredients, including flour, sugar, egg white, almond paste, and coconut. Macaroons are often flavored with vanilla or liqueurs and decorated with whole nuts or dried fruit. They are not a traditional Norwegian food, however, and Nora's fondness for them suggests that she is being extravagant in buying them.

Norwegians eat a wide array of sweets at Christmastime, including gingersnap cookies, doughnuts, and cakes. People in different regions may eat fish, lamb, or pork for their Christmas meals. Some eat a special rice porridge for their Christmas lunch and then have rice cream and red fruit sauce as their Christmas dinner dessert.

NORA [*going toward him*]: Well, Torvald dear, are you through with him?

HELMER: Yes, he just left.

NORA: Let me introduce you—this is Kristine, who's arrived here in town.

HELMER: Kristine—? I'm sorry, but I don't know—

NORA: Mrs. Linde, Torvald dear. Mrs. Kristine Linde.

HELMER: Of course. A childhood friend of my wife's, no doubt?

MRS. LINDE: Yes, we knew each other in those days.

NORA: And just think, she made the long trip down here in order to talk with you.

HELMER: What's this?

MRS. LINDE: Well, not exactly—

NORA: You see, Kristine is remarkably clever in office work, and so she's terribly eager to come under a capable man's supervision and add more to what she already knows—

HELMER: Very wise, Mrs. Linde.

NORA: And then when she heard that you'd become a bank manager—the story was wired out to the papers—then she came in as fast as she could and—Really, Torvald, for my sake you can do a little something for Kristine, can't you?

HELMER: Yes, it's not at all impossible. Mrs. Linde, I suppose you're a widow?

MRS. LINDE: Yes.

HELMER: Any experience in office work?

MRS. LINDE: Yes, a good deal.

HELMER: Well, it's quite likely that I can make an opening for you—

NORA [*clapping her hands*]: You see, you see!

HELMER: You've come at a lucky moment, Mrs. Linde.

MRS. LINDE: Oh, how can I thank you?

HELMER: Not necessary. [*Putting his overcoat on.*] But today you'll have to excuse me—

RANK: Wait, I'll go with you. [*He fetches his coat from the hall and warms it at the stove.*]

NORA: Don't stay out long, dear.

HELMER: An hour; no more.

NORA: Are you going too, Kristine?

MRS. LINDE [*putting on her winter garments*]: Yes, I have to see about a room now.

HELMER: Then perhaps we can all walk together.

Reading Strategy
Reading Drama In what ways might Nora's determination to help Mrs. Linde be apparent in Nora's body language? Explain.

Reading Check ④⑧
What contraband does Nora hide from Torvald?

A Doll House, Act One ■ *959*

Modern Realistic Drama

- Tell students to pay attention to the small talk in the hallway as the adults are leaving and the children enter. **Ask** students what each character's contribution to the small talk says about him or her.

Possible response: Each character is true to himself or herself here. Nora sounds like an enthusiastic and proud young mother; Dr. Rank is worried about standing in a draft; Torvald is eager to leave the scene and let the children be with their mother.

- **Ask** students the Literary Analysis question: Judging by Torvald's comment, what role did men of that time seem to have in raising children?

Answer: Men seem to have had little interest or involvement in raising children. Torvald seems eager to leave Nora with the children.

50 **Reading Strategy**

Reading Drama

- Point out that the children do not have any written dialogue in this scene with Nora, and the actors who play the children must think of things to say that mesh with Nora's dialogue.

- Next, **ask** students the Reading Strategy question: How do the stage directions help clarify the relationship Nora has with her children?

Answer: The stage directions show that Nora is actively playing with the children by hiding under furniture and crawling around on the floor with them. These directions clarify Nora's own childishness.

960

NORA [*helping her*]: What a shame we're so cramped here, but it's quite impossible for us to—

MRS. LINDE: Oh, don't even think of it! Good-bye, Nora dear, and thanks for everything.

NORA: Good-bye for now. Of course you'll be back this evening. And you too, Dr. Rank. What? If you're well enough? Oh, you've got to be! Wrap up tight now.

[*In a ripple of small talk the company moves out into the hall; children's voices are heard outside on the steps.*]

NORA: There they are! There they are! [*She runs to open the door. The children come in with their nurse,* ANNE-MARIE.] Come in, come in! [*Bends down and kisses them.*] Oh, you darlings—! Look at them, Kristine. Aren't they lovely!

49

RANK: No loitering in the draft here.

HELMER: Come, Mrs. Linde—this place is unbearable now for anyone but mothers.

[DR. RANK, HELMER, *and* MRS. LINDE *go down the stairs.* ANNE-MARIE *goes into the living room with the children.* NORA *follows, after closing the hall door.*]

NORA: How fresh and strong you look. Oh, such red cheeks you have! Like apples and roses. [*The children interrupt her throughout the following.*] And it was so much fun? That's wonderful. Really? You pulled both Emmy and Bob on the sled? Imagine, all together! Yes, you're a clever boy, Ivar. Oh, let me hold her a bit, Anne-Marie. My sweet little doll baby! [*Takes the smallest from the nurse and dances with her.*] Yes, yes, Mama will dance with Bob as well. What? Did you throw snowballs? Oh, if I'd only been there! No, don't bother, Anne-Marie—I'll undress them myself. Oh yes, let me. It's such fun. Go in and rest; you look half frozen. There's hot coffee waiting for you on the stove. [*The nurse goes into the room to the left.* NORA *takes the children's winter things off, throwing them about, while the children talk to her all at once.*] Is that so? A big dog chased you? But it didn't bite? No, dogs never bite little, lovely doll babies. Don't peek in the packages, Ivar! What is it? Yes, wouldn't you like to know. No, no, it's an ugly something. Well? Shall we play? What shall we play? Hide-and-seek? Yes, let's play hide-and-seek. Bob must hide first. I must? Yes, let me hide first. [*Laughing and shouting, she and the children play in and out of the living room and the adjoining room to the right. At last* NORA *hides under the table. The children come storming in, search, but cannot find her, then hear her muffled laughter, dash over to the table, lift the cloth up and find her. Wild shouting. She creeps forward as if to scare them. More shouts. Meanwhile, a knock at the hall door; no one has noticed it. Now the door half opens, and* KROGSTAD *appears. He waits a moment; the game goes on.*]

50

KROGSTAD: Beg pardon, Mrs. Helmer—

NORA [*with a strangled cry, turning and scrambling to her knees*]: Oh! What do you want?

Literary Analysis
Modern Realistic Drama
Judging by Torvald's comment, what role did men of that time seem to have in raising children?

Reading Strategy
Reading Drama How do the stage directions help clarify the relationship Nora has with her children?

Enrichment

Contemporary Criticism: Shaw Looks at Ibsen

In his book *The Quintessence of Ibsenism,* Irish playwright George Bernard Shaw, a great follower of Ibsen, describes the Helmer household.

In the famous *Doll's House,* the pillar of the society who owns the doll is a model husband. In his little household, with the three darling children and the affectionate little wife, all on the most loving terms with one another, we have the sweet home, the womanly woman, the happy family life of

the idealist's dream. Mrs. Nora Helmer is happy in the belief that she has attained a valid realization of all these illusions that she is an ideal wife and mother; and that Helmer is an ideal husband who would, if the necessity arose, give his life to save her reputation.

Challenge students to explain why Shaw uses such a dark tone. They may suggest that his tone helps convey the dark side of the play and the characters.

51 Critical Viewing

Possible response: The children appear warmly and fashionably dressed. They have on warm coats, hats, and gloves. They appear happy and comfortable.

51 ▲ Critical Viewing Which details in this photograph support Nora's assertions that her children did not "go poorly dressed" as she paid her debt to Krogstad? **[Connect]**

A Doll House, Act One ■ 961

Differentiated Instruction Solutions for All Learners

Strategy for Less Proficient Readers
Allow students to work in pairs to select a line or two of dialogue from the play to accompany the photograph. Have students write the dialogue on a sticky note and place the note on the corner of the page. As a class, discuss students' choices. Students should be able to explain the connections they made among the image, the characters' expressions and body language, and the dialogue they selected. Discuss why their choices work.

Strategy for English Learners
Have students work in pairs to write a description of the photograph. Ask students to use complete sentences to identify the objects and people they see in the photograph and to write a sentence or two explaining what is happening in the photograph and what the characters may be saying. Discuss students' descriptions as a group. If time allows, repeat this activity with the photographs of characters that appear on previous pages.

Reading Drama

- Have students notice that Nora speaks both to her children and to Krogstad here. **Ask:** What different tones of voice do you think she would use?
Possible response: Nora switches from a guarded or flat tone with Krogstad to a soft, calming tone with the children.

- Point out that the children suspect Nora is afraid of Krogstad because one of them prompts her to say "No, the strange man won't hurt Mama."

- **Ask** students to read the first Reading Strategy question: What gestures might Nora use to convey her "tense and nervous" emotions?
Possible response: Nora might clench or wring her hands or hold her arms tightly across her body.

53 **Reading Strategy**

Reading Drama

- Have students notice how Nora's answers to Krogstad's questions are short and to the point. **Ask** students what Nora's short answers suggest about her relationship with Krogstad.
Possible response: Nora is keeping her answers short because she does not want to talk to him.

- **Ask** a volunteer to read aloud the second Reading Strategy question: What tone of voice do you think Nora uses in these lines? Explain.
Answer: Nora probably uses a haughty or arrogant tone of voice here. She is suggesting to Krogstad that she is above him, one of her husband's employees.

- **Ask** students to explain the irony in Nora's warning to Krogstad about being in a subordinate position.
Possible response: Although she is referring to Krogstad's inferior position at the bank, she herself is in a subordinate position in her marriage.

KROGSTAD: Excuse me. The outer door was ajar; it must be someone forgot to shut it—

NORA [*rising*]: My husband isn't home, Mr. Krogstad.

KROGSTAD: I know that.

52 **NORA:** Yes—then what do you want here?

KROGSTAD: A word with you.

NORA: With—? [*To the children, quietly.*] Go in to Anne-Marie. What? No, the strange man won't hurt Mama. When he's gone, we'll play some more. [*She leads the children into the room to the left and shuts the door after them. Then, tense and nervous:*] You want to speak to me?

KROGSTAD: Yes, I want to.

NORA: Today? But it's not yet the first of the month—

KROGSTAD: No, it's Christmas Eve. It's going to be up to you how merry a Christmas you have.

NORA: What is it you want? Today I absolutely can't—

KROGSTAD: We won't talk about that till later. This is something else. You do have a moment to spare, I suppose?

NORA: Oh, yes, of course—I do, except—

KROGSTAD: Good. I was sitting over at Olsen's Restaurant when I saw your husband go down the street—

NORA: Yes?

KROGSTAD: With a lady.

NORA: Yes. So?

KROGSTAD: If you'll pardon my asking: wasn't that lady a Mrs. Linde?

NORA: Yes.

KROGSTAD: Just now come into town?

53 **NORA:** Yes, today.

KROGSTAD: She's a good friend of yours?

NORA: Yes, she is. But I don't see—

KROGSTAD: I also knew her once.

NORA: I'm aware of that.

KROGSTAD: Oh? You know all about it. I thought so. Well, then let me ask you short and sweet: is Mrs. Linde getting a job in the bank?

NORA: What makes you think you can cross-examine me, Mr. Krogstad—you, one of my husband's employees? But since you ask, you might as well know—yes, Mrs. Linde's going to be taken on at the bank. And I'm the one who spoke for her, Mr. Krogstad. Now you know.

KROGSTAD: So I guessed right.

Reading Strategy
Reading Drama What gestures might Nora use to convey her "tense and nervous" emotions?

Reading Strategy
Reading Drama What tone of voice do you think Nora uses in these lines? Explain.

NORA [*pacing up and down*]: Oh, one does have a tiny bit of influence, I should hope. Just because I am a woman, don't think it means that— When one has a <u>subordinate</u> position, Mr. Krogstad, one really ought to be careful about pushing somebody who—hm—

KROGSTAD: Who has influence?

NORA: That's right.

KROGSTAD [*in a different tone*]: Mrs. Helmer, would you be good enough to use your influence on my behalf?

NORA: What? What do you mean?

KROGSTAD: Would you please make sure that I keep my subordinate position in the bank?

NORA: What does that mean? Who's thinking of taking away your position?

KROGSTAD: Oh, don't play the innocent with me. I'm quite aware that your friend would hardly relish the chance of running into me again; and I'm also aware now whom I can thank for being turned out.

NORA: But I promise you—

KROGSTAD: Yes, yes, yes, to the point: there's still time, and I'm advising you to use your influence to prevent it.

NORA: But Mr. Krogstad, I have absolutely no influence.

KROGSTAD: You haven't? I thought you were just saying—

NORA: You shouldn't take me so literally. I! How can you believe that I have any such influence over my husband?

KROGSTAD: Oh, I've known your husband from our student days. I don't think the great bank manager's more steadfast than any other married man.

NORA: You speak insolently about my husband, and I'll show you the door.

KROGSTAD: The lady has spirit.

NORA: I'm not afraid of you any longer. After New Year's, I'll soon be done with the whole business.

KROGSTAD [*restraining himself*]: Now listen to me, Mrs. Helmer. If necessary, I'll fight for my little job in the bank as if it were life itself.

NORA: Yes, so it seems.

KROGSTAD: It's not just a matter of income; that's the least of it. It's something else—All right, out with it! Look, this is the thing. You know, just like all the others, of course, that once, a good many years ago, I did something rather rash.

NORA: I've heard rumors to that effect.

KROGSTAD: The case never got into court; but all the same, every door was closed in my face from then on. So I took up those various

---

Vocabulary Builder
subordinate (sə bôr′ də nit) *adj.* inferior; ranking under or below

Literary Analysis
Modern Realistic Drama and Conflict What conflicts have troubled Krogstad for many years?

Reading Check
What favor does Krogstad ask of Nora?

A Doll House, Act One ■ 963

Analyze

- Point out to students that Nora calls her secret her pride and joy. **Ask** them what she means by this. **Possible response:** Nora sees her secret (obtaining money for a trip to Italy) as an accomplishment; she credits herself with saving her family.

- Next, make sure students are aware that Nora believes that should Krogstad tell Torvald about the loan, Torvald would save her.

- Hint that Nora is misguided on both of these points by asking students to predict what will happen.

58 Literary Analysis

Modern Realistic Drama

- Tell students to be aware that the play is leading up to another turning point and that they will learn that Nora has not been as clever as she thinks.

- Read aloud the second bracketed passage.

- **Ask** students the Literary Analysis question: In what way does this passage indicate that women in nineteenth-century Norway could not legally get loans on their own? **Possible response:** Krogstad had to leave lines for Nora's father's signature. Even though she was a married woman, Nora needed the signature of a man to whom she was related in order to get the loan.

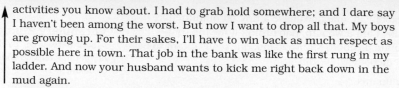

activities you know about. I had to grab hold somewhere; and I dare say I haven't been among the worst. But now I want to drop all that. My boys are growing up. For their sakes, I'll have to win back as much respect as possible here in town. That job in the bank was like the first rung in my ladder. And now your husband wants to kick me right back down in the mud again.

NORA: But for heaven's sake, Mr. Krogstad, it's simply not in my power to help you.

KROGSTAD: That's because you haven't the will to—but I have the means to make you.

NORA: You certainly won't tell my husband that I owe you money?

KROGSTAD: Hm—what if I told him that?

NORA: That would be shameful of you. [*Nearly in tears.*] This secret—my joy and my pride—that he should learn it in such a crude and disgusting way—learn it from you. You'd expose me to the most horrible unpleasant-ness—

KROGSTAD: Only unpleasantness?

NORA [*vehemently*]: But go on and try. It'll turn out the worse for you, because then my husband will really see what a crook you are, and then you'll never be able to hold your job.

KROGSTAD: I asked if it was just domestic unpleasantness you were afraid of?

NORA: If my husband finds out, then of course he'll pay what I owe at once, and then we'd be through with you for good.

KROGSTAD [*a step closer*]: Listen, Mrs. Helmer—you've either got a very bad memory, or else no head at all for business. I'd better put you a little more in touch with the facts.

NORA: What do you mean?

KROGSTAD: When your husband was sick, you came to me for a loan of four thousand, eight hundred crowns.

NORA: Where else could I go?

KROGSTAD: I promised to get you that sum—

NORA: And you got it.

KROGSTAD: I promised to get you that sum, on certain conditions. You were so involved in your husband's illness, and so eager to finance your trip, that I guess you didn't think out all the details. It might just be a good idea to remind you. I promised you the money on the strength of a note I drew up.

NORA: Yes, and that I signed.

KROGSTAD: Right. But at the bottom I added some lines for your father to guarantee the loan. He was supposed to sign down there.

964 ■ Romanticism and Realism

Literary Analysis
Modern Realistic Drama
In what way does this passage indicate that women in nineteenth-century Norway could not legally get loans on their own?

Enrichment

Forgery and Counterfeiting

Forgery is the use of false writing in a document that is used to mislead or defraud others. Nora's form of forgery was to falsify her father's signature in order to secure a loan, but there are other kinds of forgery.

Entering false information on a form or document and then signing it is one form of forgery. Another is creating a document, such as a letter of recommendation, and signing another person's name without his or her knowledge. Forgery also covers altering or falsifying information on documents of personal identification, such as passports, driver's licenses, and birth certificates.

Artworks such as paintings, etchings, and drawings can also be forged; some artists train themselves to copy valuable artworks and then sell them as if they were the originals. Another form of forgery is counterfeiting, the making and using of fake money.

NORA: Supposed to? He did sign.

KROGSTAD: I left the date blank. In other words, your father would have dated his signature himself. Do you remember that?

NORA: Yes, I think—

KROGSTAD: Then I gave you the note for you to mail to your father. Isn't that so?

NORA: Yes.

KROGSTAD: And naturally you sent it at once—because only some five, six days later you brought me the note, properly signed. And with that, the money was yours.

NORA: Well, then; I've made my payments regularly, haven't I?

KROGSTAD: More or less. But—getting back to the point—those were hard times for you then, Mrs. Helmer.

NORA: Yes, they were.

KROGSTAD: Your father was very ill, I believe.

NORA: He was near the end.

KROGSTAD: He died soon after?

NORA: Yes.

KROGSTAD: Tell me, Mrs. Helmer, do you happen to recall the date of your father's death? The day of the month, I mean.

NORA: Papa died the twenty-ninth of September.

KROGSTAD: That's quite correct; I've already looked into that. And now we come to a curious thing— [*Taking out a paper.*] which I simply cannot comprehend.

NORA: Curious thing? I don't know—

KROGSTAD: This is the curious thing: that your father co-signed the note for your loan three days after his death.

NORA: How—? I don't understand.

KROGSTAD: Your father died the twenty-ninth of September. But look. Here your father dated his signature October second. Isn't that curious, Mrs. Helmer? [NORA *is silent.*] Can you explain it to me? [NORA *remains silent.*] It's also remarkable that the words "October second" and the year aren't written in your father's hand, but rather in one that I think I know. Well, it's easy to understand. Your father forgot perhaps to date his signature, and then someone or other added it, a bit sloppily, before anyone knew of his death. There's nothing wrong in that. It all comes down to the signature. And there's no question about that, Mrs. Helmer. It really *was* your father who signed his own name here, wasn't it?

NORA [*after a short silence, throwing her head back and looking squarely at him*]: No, it wasn't. *I* signed Papa's name.

Reading Strategy
Reading Drama In what ways might stage directions indicating movements or gestures add tension to this dialogue?

Literary Analysis
Modern Realistic Drama and Conflict Identify three sources of external conflict against which Nora is struggling.

Reading Check

For whose sake does Krogstad wish to build a better life?

A Doll House, Act One ■ 965

59 Reading Strategy
Reading Drama
- Have two volunteers read aloud the first bracketed passage.
- **Ask** students of what the short question-answer format of this passage reminds them. Remind students that Krogstad was trained as a lawyer.
  Answer: The dialogue is similar to the cross-examination stage of a legal trial, familiar from television shows and movies.
- Next, **ask** students the Reading Strategy question: In what ways might stage directions indicating movements or gestures add tension to this dialogue?
  Answer: Stage direction might help readers picture how the characters interact. For example, stage directions might have Nora move away from or toward Krogstad, or they might identify how Krogstad changes his tone.

60 Literary Analysis
Modern Realistic Drama and Conflict
- Have the same volunteers continue reading the second bracketed passage.
- **Ask** students to explain why Nora's forgery was a turning point in her life.
  Possible response: By committing a crime, Nora placed herself in the power of an unethical person. The action will affect the rest of the play.
- **Ask** a student to respond to the Literary Analysis item: Identify three sources of external conflict against which Nora is struggling.
  Answer: Nora is struggling against Krogstad's attempts to get her to save his job, Krogstad's threat to reveal her secret to Torvald, and the law she has broken in order to get the loan.

61 Reading Check
Answer: Krogstad wishes to build a better life for his sons.

₆₂ Literary Analysis

Modern Realistic Drama and Conflict

- Have two volunteers read aloud the bracketed dialogue between Nora and Krogstad.

- **Ask** students to describe Nora's feelings about Krogstad.
  Possible response: She believes that he is cold-hearted and dislikes him.

- Have students **respond** to the first Literary Analysis item: List three points of conflict for Nora in this scene.
  Answer: The scene touches on conflicts Nora has had involving Krogstad, her husband, and her father.

₆₃ Literary Analysis

Modern Realistic Drama

- Make sure that students understand the distinction between Krogstad's common language and his gentlemanly gesture of bowing before leaving the room.

- Read the second bracketed passage aloud.

- Next, **ask** the second Literary Analysis question: In what two ways are Krogstad's words characteristic of modern realistic drama?
  Answer: Krogstad speaks in incomplete sentences, uses common language, and interrupts himself.

▶ **Monitor Progress** Ask students what characteristics of realistic drama this scene between Nora and Krogstad displays. (It shows both characters' flaws and addresses controversial societal issues, such as the law and women's rights at that time.)

▶ **Reteach** If students have difficulty identifying characteristics of realistic drama, have them use the **Literary Analysis** support, page 87 in *Unit 7 Resources*.

KROGSTAD: Wait, now—are you fully aware that this is a dangerous confession?

NORA: Why? You'll soon get your money.

KROGSTAD: Let me ask you a question—why didn't you send the paper to your father?

NORA: That was impossible. Papa was so sick. If I'd asked him for his signature, I also would have had to tell him what the money was for. But I couldn't tell him, sick as he was, that my husband's life was in danger. That was just impossible.

KROGSTAD: Then it would have been better if you'd given up the trip abroad.

NORA: I couldn't possibly. The trip was to save my husband's life. I couldn't give that up.

KROGSTAD: But didn't you ever consider that this was a fraud against me?

NORA: I couldn't let myself be bothered by that. You weren't any concern of mine. I couldn't stand you, with all those cold complications you made, even though you knew how badly off my husband was.

KROGSTAD: Mrs. Helmer, obviously you haven't the vaguest idea of what you've involved yourself in. But I can tell you this: it was nothing more and nothing worse that I once did—and it wrecked my whole reputation.

NORA: You? Do you expect me to believe that you ever acted bravely to save your wife's life?

KROGSTAD: Laws don't inquire into motives.

NORA: Then they must be very poor laws.

KROGSTAD: Poor or not—if I introduce this paper in court, you'll be judged according to law.

NORA: This I refuse to believe. A daughter hasn't a right to protect her dying father from anxiety and care? A wife hasn't a right to save her husband's life? I don't know much about laws, but I'm sure that somewhere in the books these things are allowed. And you don't know anything about it—you who practice the law? You must be an awful lawyer, Mr. Krogstad.

KROGSTAD: Could be. But business—the kind of business we two are mixed up in—don't you think I know about that? All right. Do what you want now. But I'm telling you *this*: if I get shoved down a second time, you're going to keep me company. [*He bows and goes out through the hall.*]

NORA [*pensive⁵ for a moment, then tossing her head*]: Oh, really! Trying to frighten me! I'm not so silly as all that. [*Begins gathering up the*

---

5. **pensive** (pen′ siv) *adj.* thinking deeply or seriously, often of sad or melancholy things.

Literary Analysis
Modern Realistic Drama and Conflict List three points of conflict for Nora in this scene.

Literary Analysis
Modern Realistic Drama In what two ways are Krogstad's words characteristic of modern realistic drama?

children's clothes, but soon stops.] But—? No, but that's impossible! I did it out of love.

THE CHILDREN [*In the doorway, left*]: Mama, that strange man's gone out the door.

NORA: Yes, yes, I know it. But don't tell anyone about the strange man. Do you hear? Not even Papa!

THE CHILDREN. No, Mama. But now will you play again?

NORA: No, not now.

THE CHILDREN. Oh, but Mama, you promised.

NORA: Yes, but I can't now. Go inside; I have too much to do. Go in, go in, my sweet darlings. [*She herds them gently back in the room and shuts the door after them. Settling on the sofa, she takes up a piece of embroidery and makes some stitches, but soon stops abruptly.*] No! [*Throws the work aside, rises, goes to the hall door and calls out.*] Helene! Let me have the tree in here. [*Goes to the table, left, opens the table drawer, and stops again.*] No, but that's utterly impossible!

MAID [*with the Christmas tree*]: Where should I put it, ma'am?

NORA: There. The middle of the floor.

MAID: Should I bring anything else?

NORA: No, thanks. I have what I need.

[*The* MAID, *who has set the tree down, goes out.*]

NORA [*absorbed in trimming the tree*]: Candles here—and flowers here. That terrible creature! Talk, talk, talk! There's nothing to it at all. The tree's going to be lovely. I'll do anything to please you, Torvald. I'll sing for you, dance for you—

[HELMER *comes in from the hall, with a sheaf of papers under his arm.*]

NORA: Oh! You're back so soon?

HELMER: Yes. Has anyone been here?

NORA: Here? No.

HELMER: That's odd. I saw Krogstad leaving the front door.

NORA: So? Oh yes, that's true. Krogstad was here a moment.

HELMER: Nora, I can see by your face that he's been here, begging you to put in a good word for him.

NORA: Yes.

HELMER: And it was supposed to seem like your own idea? You were to hide it from me that he'd been here. He asked you that, too, didn't he?

NORA: Yes, Torvald, but—

HELMER: Nora, Nora, and you could fall for that? Talk with that sort of person and promise him anything? And then in the bargain, tell me an untruth.

Reading Strategy
Reading Drama What tone of voice do you think Nora uses here? Explain.

**Reading Check**
What kind of lawyer does Nora believe Krogstad to be?

A Doll House, Act One ■ 967

967

67 ▲ Critical Viewing Which details in this illustration depict the perfect Christmas that Nora hopes to provide for her family? **[Speculate]**

968 ■ Romanticism and Realism

NORA: An untruth—?

HELMER: Didn't you say that no one had been here? [*Wagging his finger.*] My little songbird must never do that again. A songbird needs a clean beak to warble with. No false notes. [*Putting his arm about her waist.*] That's the way it should be, isn't it? Yes, I'm sure of it. [*Releasing her.*] And so, enough of that. [*Sitting by the stove.*] Ah, how snug and cozy it is here. [*Leafing among his papers.*]

NORA [*busy with the tree, after a short pause*]: Torvald!

HELMER: Yes.

NORA: I'm so much looking forward to the Stenborgs' costume party, day after tomorrow.

HELMER: And I can't wait to see what you'll surprise me with.

NORA: Oh, that stupid business!

HELMER: What?

NORA: I can't find anything that's right. Everything seems so ridiculous, so inane.[6]

HELMER: So my little Nora's come to *that* recognition?

NORA [*going behind his chair, her arms resting on his back*]: Are you very busy, Torvald?

HELMER: Oh—

NORA: What papers are those?

HELMER: Bank matters.

NORA: Already?

HELMER: I've gotten full authority from the retiring management to make all necessary changes in personnel and procedure. I'll need Christmas week for that. I want to have everything in order by New Year's.

NORA: So that was the reason this poor Krogstad—

HELMER: Hm.

NORA [*still leaning on the chair and slowly stroking the nape of his neck*]: If you weren't so very busy, I would have asked you an enormous favor, Torvald.

HELMER: Let's hear. What is it?

NORA: You know, there isn't anyone who has your good taste—and I want so much to look well at the costume party. Torvald, couldn't you take over and decide what I should be and plan my costume?

HELMER: Ah, is my stubborn little creature calling for a lifeguard?

NORA: Yes, Torvald, I can't get anywhere without your help.

HELMER: All right—I'll think it over. We'll hit on something.

---

6. **inane** (in ān´) *adj.* foolish; silly.

Literary Analysis
Modern Realistic Drama and Conflict What conflict makes everything else in Nora's life seem unimportant to her?

70 ✓ **Reading Check**
What changes at the bank is Torvald planning to make during Christmas week?

A Doll House, Act One ■ 969

68 Literary Analysis
Modern Realistic Drama and Conflict

• Have two students read aloud the first bracketed passage.

• Point out that this section of dialogue begins with a pair of seemingly happy observations by Nora and Torvald, but the reality of Nora's conflict soon intrudes.

• **Ask** the Literary Analysis question: What conflict makes everything else in Nora's life seem unimportant to her?
Answer: Nora's conflict with Krogstad over the forgery makes everything else seem unimportant.

69 Critical Thinking
Interpret

• Ask two students to read aloud the second bracketed passage. Suggest that the student reading Nora's lines exaggerate them.

• **Ask** students what Nora may be doing by showing affection toward Torvald and praising him.
Possible response: Nora may be trying to flatter her husband in order to get him to do what she wants later.

• Ask students to predict what Nora might want Torvald to do for her.

70 Reading Check
Answer: Torvald is going to fire people during Christmas week.

Differentiated Instruction Solutions for All Learners

Strategy for Special Needs Students
Pair students and assign each pair half a page of dialogue. Ask students to reread the assigned dialogue and then work together to write a two- or three-sentence summary of what happened. If students need help, ask them to identify which characters were speaking and what, in general, they discussed. Ask pairs to share their summaries. Students should feel free to make corrections to their summaries.

Enrichment for Gifted/Talented Students
Challenge students to create a soundtrack for Act 1 of *A Doll House*. Students may work alone or with a partner to find appropriate recordings that suit the mood, characters, and plot developments of the first act. Students should find at least three songs to match three points in the act. Also, challenge students to find a theme song for Nora. Allow students to play their selections in class and explain their choices.

❼❶ Reading Strategy

Reading Strategy
Reading Drama

- Ask two students to read aloud the first bracketed passage.

- Have students **explain** why Torvald's comments about children might hit Nora especially hard.
Possible response: Nora considers herself a good mother and does not want to believe that her illegal actions, done out of love, could create an "atmosphere of lies" that could infect her home.

- **Ask** students the Reading Strategy question: What emotions is Torvald experiencing as he says these lines? Explain.
Possible response: Torvald is probably experiencing feelings of moral outrage. He is offended and disgusted by Krogstad's deceit.

- Encourage students to **predict** how Torvald will react if he learns that Nora, too, has committed forgery.
Possible response: He will not be forgiving of Nora.

❼❷ Literary Analysis

Modern Realistic Drama and Conflict

- Ask students to read the second bracketed passage.

- **Ask** students the Literary Analysis question: In what ways might Torvald's words cause Nora more inner conflict?
Possible response: His comments about poisoning children with lies are particularly difficult for Nora because she loves her children and would never wish for her actions to harm them. His comments about feeling physically revolted by Krogstad make Nora suspect that he would feel the same about her if he knew her secret.

NORA: Oh, how sweet of you. [*Goes to the tree again. Pause.*] Aren't the red flowers pretty—? But tell me, was it really such a crime that this Krogstad committed?

HELMER: Forgery. Do you have any idea what that means?

NORA: Couldn't he have done it out of need?

HELMER: Yes, or thoughtlessness, like so many others. I'm not so heartless that I'd condemn a man categorically for just one mistake.

NORA: No, of course not, Torvald!

HELMER: Plenty of men have redeemed themselves by openly confessing their crimes and taking their punishment.

NORA: Punishment—?

HELMER: But now Krogstad didn't go that way. He got himself out by sharp practices, and that's the real cause of his moral breakdown.

NORA: Do you really think that would—?

HELMER: Just imagine how a man with that sort of guilt in him has to lie and cheat and deceive on all sides, has to wear a mask even with the nearest and dearest he has, even with his own wife and children. And with the children, Nora—that's where it's most horrible.

NORA: Why?

HELMER: Because that kind of atmosphere of lies infects the whole life of a home. Every breath the children take in is filled with the germs of something degenerate.

NORA [*coming closer behind him*]: Are you sure of that?

HELMER: Oh, I've seen it often enough as a lawyer. Almost everyone who goes bad early in life has a mother who's a chronic liar.

NORA: Why just—the mother?

HELMER: It's usually the mother's influence that's dominant, but the father's works in the same way, of course. Every lawyer is quite familiar with it. And still this Krogstad's been going home year in, year out, poisoning his own children with lies and pretense; that's why I call him morally lost. [*Reaching his hands out toward her.*] So my sweet little Nora must promise me never to plead his cause. Your hand on it. Come, come, what's this? Give me your hand. There, now. All settled. I can tell you it'd be impossible for me to work alongside of him. I literally feel physically revolted when I'm anywhere near such a person.

NORA [*withdraws her hand and goes to the other side of the Christmas tree*]: How hot it is here! And I've got so much to do.

HELMER [*getting up and gathering his papers*]: Yes, and I have to think about getting some of these read through before dinner. I'll think about your costume, too. And something to hang on the tree in gilt paper, I may even see about that. [*Putting his hand on her head.*] Oh you, my darling little songbird. [*He goes into his study and closes the door after him.*]

Reading Strategy
Reading Drama What emotions is Torvald experiencing as he says these lines? Explain.

Literary Analysis
Modern Realistic Drama and Conflict In what ways might Torvald's words cause Nora more inner conflict?

Assessment Practice

Comparing and Contrasting Texts (For more practice, see *Test Preparation Workbook*, p. 42.)

Some tests require students to compare and contrast two or more texts. Read the following excerpts from Ibsen. One is from a speech. The other is from *A Doll House*.

> I am not afraid of these so-called unpractical women; women have something in common with the true artist, just as young people have.
> **HELMER:** Nora! Are your scatterbrains off again? What if today I borrowed a thousand crowns, and you squandered them . . . Nora, Nora, how like a woman!

From the texts, one can tell that men in the nineteenth century often viewed women as—

A heroic.
B childlike.
C generous.
D irresponsible.

Lead students to recognize that both Ibsen and Helmer recognize that women had a reputation for being impractical, or irresponsible. The answer is *D*.

NORA [*softly, after a silence*]: Oh, really! It isn't so. It's impossible. It must be impossible.

ANNE-MARIE [*in the doorway, left*]: The children are begging so hard to come in to Mama.

NORA: No, no, no, don't let them in to me! You stay with them, Anne-Marie.

ANNE-MARIE: Of course, ma'am. [*Closes the door.*]

NORA [*pale with terror*]: Hurt my children—? Poison my home? [*A moment's pause; then she tosses her head.*] That's not true. Never in all the world.

Critical Reading

1. **Respond:** Considering the Helmers' current situation, do you feel more sympathy for Torvald or for Nora? Explain.

2. **(a) Recall:** What are some of the pet names Torvald uses for Nora? **(b) Infer:** What does Torvald's use of these pet names suggest about his attitude toward his wife? **(c) Assess:** Do you think these nicknames represent Nora's entire personality? Explain.

3. **(a) Recall:** What lie concerning the macaroons does Nora tell Torvald? **(b) Interpret:** How would you describe Torvald's treatment of Nora as he questions her about the macaroons? **(c) Draw Conclusions:** What does Torvald's attitude reveal about the relationship he has with his wife?

4. **(a) Recall:** How does Nora behave toward her husband? **(b) Compare and Contrast:** How is Nora's behavior different when she is around Krogstad? **(c) Make a Judgment:** Do you think Nora is "just a child" and "incapable of anything serious," as others seem to believe? Explain.

5. **(a) Recall:** Which details in the first act indicate that Nora and her husband do not know each other very well? **(b) Interpret:** What is ironic about Nora's comment that if Torvald found out her secret, it "would just ruin [their] relationship"?

6. **Draw Conclusions:** What developments in Act One suggest that Nora is in trouble? Explain.

7. **Relate:** Based on the behavior of the characters during Act One, what differences can you see between our society and the one depicted in the play?

Go Online
Author Link

For: More about Henrik Ibsen
Visit: www.PHSchool.com
Web Code: ete-9710

A Doll House, Act One ■ 971

Go Online For additional information about
Author Link Henrik Ibsen, have students type in
the Web Code, then select *I* from the alphabet, and
then select Henrik Ibsen.

Answers

1. **Possible response:** Ordinary language: informal language such as "pooh" and "wee"; characters changing train of thought in mid-sentence or letting ideas trail off **Realistic characters:** the bitter Dr. Rank, the hard-working Mrs. Linde **Controversial issues:** women taking financial matters into their own hands; marital relationships

2. (a) Nora is frustrated by having so few ways to make the money she needs. (b) She pretends to be doing housework when she is earning money doing copying; she flatters her husband into giving her money. (c) Her strategies seem realistic, especially for the time period.

3. (a) Nora has owed Krogstad money for several years. (b) Krogstad threatens to tell Torvald about the debt and Nora's forgery if she does not help him keep his job at Torvald's bank.

4. (a) Torvald believes that an "atmosphere of lies" will poison a family and harm the children. (b) Nora would lose Torvald's love, respect, financial support, and probably her children as well.

5. (a) Stage directions help a reader understand the physical relationships between the characters onstage. They also give hints about how certain lines are said. (b) For example, when Nora pulls Mrs. Linde down onto the sofa next to her, the reader can tell something important is going to be said.

6. On p. 966, when Nora says "This I refuse to believe . . . ," she might be standing with her hands on her hips and speaking angrily. She might point at Krogstad when she calls him "an awful lawyer."

7. **Possible response:** A counselor might suggest that they be honest with each other, express feelings, and avoid falling into parent and child roles.

Go **Online** Students may use the **Assessment Self-test** to prepare for **Selection Test A** or **Selection Test B**.

972

Apply the Skills

A Doll House, Act One

Literary Analysis
Modern Realistic Drama

1. Use an organizer like this one to record details that establish *A Doll House* as a **modern realistic drama**.

2. **(a)** What limitations on women does Nora find especially frustrating? **(b)** What strategies does she use to break through these restrictions? **(c)** Do you find her methods realistic? Explain.

Connecting Literary Elements

3. **(a)** **What conflict** has existed between Krogstad and Nora for the past few years? **(b)** What new circumstances does Krogstad introduce that intensify this conflict?

4. **(a)** What is Torvald's attitude about an "atmosphere of lies" in the home? **(b)** What would Nora lose if he discovered her secrets?

Reading Strategy
Reading Drama

5. **(a)** Explain how stage directions help clarify the relationships between characters when **reading a drama**. **(b)** Identify one example from the play that supports your response.

6. Select a passage in Act One that has no stage directions, and then add directions that make the passage easier to visualize.

Extend Understanding

7. **Psychology Connection:** What advice might a relationship expert offer Nora and Torvald?

QuickReview

Modern realistic drama reflects the way people actually talk and depicts characters and situations as they really are. It often addresses controversial issues and questions society's assumptions.

Conflict, which can be internal or external, is the struggle between two opposing forces.

When you **read drama,** use stage directions to help you picture the play as it would be performed on stage.

For: Self-test
Visit: www.PHSchool.com
Web Code: eta-6705

Build Language Skills

Vocabulary Lesson

Word Analysis: Coined Words

Coined words are manufactured, often by combining existing words. *Spendthrift* combines *spend* and *thrift* in a new word meaning "one who spends money carelessly." Replace each phrase with a lively coined word.

1. snow-covered trees   2. someone who gossips

Spelling Strategy

Adding a prefix to a word never changes the spelling of the base word. For each item, combine the prefix and the root to form an existing word.

1. *mis-* + understand   2. *dis-* + honest

Grammar and Style Lesson

Compound Predicates

A predicate states the action or condition of the subject. A **compound predicate** has two or more verbs or verb phrases that relate to the same subject. Compound predicates are usually connected by a conjunction, such as *and* or *or*.

S	V	V

"The *cat* **came** in and **tore** everything to shreds. . . ."

Practice Copy the examples below. In each one, circle the subject and underline the verbs or verb phrases in each compound predicate.

1. *The maid shows in Mrs. Linde . . . and shuts the door after her.*

Vocabulary Builder: Antonyms

Choose the letter of the word in each item below that is opposite in meaning to the first word.

1. spendthrift: **(a)** miser, **(b)** shopper
2. squandering: **(a)** spending, **(b)** saving
3. prodigal: **(a)** penny-pincher, **(b)** party-giver
4. indiscreet: **(a)** shocking, **(b)** prudent
5. frivolous: **(a)** wise, **(b)** foolish
6. contraband: **(a)** loot, **(b)** imports
7. subordinate: **(a)** superior, **(b)** inferior

2. "He'll join the bank right after New Year's and start getting a huge salary. . . ."

3. ". . . [he] scuttles about breathlessly . . . and then maneuvers his victims into some sort of key position. . . ."

4. *. . . she takes up a piece of embroidery and makes some stitches, but soon stops abruptly.*

5. *Nora . . . breaks out into quiet laughter and claps her hands.*

Writing Application Write two sentences about Nora's situation in *A Doll House*. Use compound predicates in each sentence, circling the subject and underlining the verbs or verb phrases.

Extend Your Learning

Writing Write a **monologue** in which Nora confesses her secrets to Torvald. Use details that reflect her personality and experiences. Rehearse your piece and present it to your class.

Research and Technology With a partner, make a **rendering of the set** from Act One using art supplies or computer software. Display your work for the class. **[Group Activity]**

WG Prentice Hall Writing and Grammar Connection: Platinum Level, Chapter 19, Section 1

Assessment Resources

The following resources can be used to assess students' knowledge and skills.

Unit 7 Resources
　Selection Test A, pp. 93–95
　Selection Test B, pp. 96–98

General Resources
　Rubrics for Response to Literature, pp. 55–56

Go Online Students may use the Self-test to
—Assessment prepare for Selection Test A or
Selection Test B.

Answers

❶ Vocabulary Lesson

Word Analysis: Coined Words

1. Snowshoulders   2. yakspreader

Spelling Strategy

1. Misunderstand   2. dishonest

Vocabulary Builder: Antonyms

1. a   2. b   3. a   4. b
5. a   6. b   7. a

❷ Grammar and Style Lesson

1. (maid)shows, shuts
2. (He)will join, will start
3. (he)scuttles, maneuvers
4. (she)takes, makes, stops
5. (Nora)breaks, claps

Writing Application

Possible response:

(Nora)takes sewing and copying jobs and pays her debt.(Torvald)works in his study and has no idea of Nora's problems.

WG **Writing and Grammar Platinum Level**

For support in teaching the Grammar and Style Lesson, use Chapter 19, Section 1.

❸ Writing

• Have students attempt to capture Nora's rhythm, vocabulary, and style, and urge them to rehearse.

• Use the Response to Literature rubrics in *General Resources*, pp. 55–56, to evaluate students' work.

• The **Support for Extend Your Learning** page (*Unit 7 Resources*, p. 91) provides guided note-taking opportunities to help students complete the Extend Your Learning activities.

Go Online Have students type in the
—Research Web Code for another research activity.

Standard Course of Study

Goal 5: LITERATURE

LT.5.01.2 Build knowledge of literary genres, and explore how characteristics apply to literature of world cultures.

LT.5.01.6 Make connections between historical and contemporary issues in world literature.

LT.5.01.7 Understand the cultural and historical impact on world literature texts.

LT.5.03.7 Analyze influences, contexts, or biases in world literature.

Goal 6: GRAMMAR AND USAGE

GU.6.01.3 Use recognition strategies to understand vocabulary and exact word choice.

GU.6.02.2 Edit for appropriate and correct mechanics.

Step-by-Step Teaching Guide	Pacing Guide
PRETEACH	
• Administer Vocabulary and Reading Warm-ups as necessary.	5 min.
• Engage students' interest with the motivation activity.	5 min.
• Read and discuss background features. **FT**	10 min.
• Introduce the Literary Analysis Skill: Characterization in Drama. **FT**	5 min.
• Introduce the Reading Strategy: Inferring Beliefs of the Period. **FT**	10 min.
• Prepare students to read by teaching the selection vocabulary. **FT**	
TEACH	
• Informally monitor comprehension while students read independently or in groups. **FT**	30 min.
• Monitor students' comprehension with the Reading Check notes.	as students read
• Reinforce vocabulary with Vocabulary Builder notes.	as students read
• Develop students' understanding of characterization in drama with the Literary Analysis annotations. **FT**	5 min.
• Develop students' ability to infer beliefs of the period with the Reading Strategy annotations. **FT**	5 min.
ASSESS/EXTEND	
• Assess students' comprehension and mastery of the Literary Analysis and Reading Strategy by having them answer the Apply the Skills questions. **FT**	15 min.
• Have students complete the Vocabulary Development Lesson and the Grammar and Style Lesson. **FT**	15 min.
• Apply students' ability to analyze by using the Writing Lesson. **FT**	45 min. or homework
• Apply students' understanding by using one or more of the Extend Your Learning activities.	20–90 min. or homework
• Administer Selection Test A or Selection Test B. **FT**	15 min.

Resources

Print

Unit 7 Resources

Transparency

Graphic Organizer Transparencies

Print

Reader's Notebook [L2]

Reader's Notebook: Adapted Version [L1]

Reader's Notebook: English Learner's Version [EL]

Unit 7 Resources

Technology

Listening to Literature Audio CDs [L2, EL]

Print

Unit 7 Resources

General Resources

Technology

Go Online: Research **[L3]**
Go Online: Self-test **[L3]**
ExamView®, **Test Bank [L3]**

Choosing Resources for Differentiated Instruction

[L1] Special Needs Students

[L2] Below-Level Students

[L3] All Students

[L4] Advanced Students

[EL] English Learners

For Vocabulary and Reading Warm-ups and for Selection Tests, **A** signifies "less challenging" and **B** "more challenging." For Graphic Organizer transparencies, **A** signifies "not filled in" and **B** "filled in."

FT Fast Track Instruction: To move the lesson more quickly, use the strategies and activities identified with **FT**.

Scaffolding for Less Proficient and Advanced Students

The leveled Critical Thinking questions after selections progress in the levels of thinking required to answer them. To address the needs of your different students, you may use the (a) level questions for your less proficient students and the (b) level questions with your on-level and advanced students. The occasional (c) level questions are appropriate for your advanced students.

PRENTICE HALL

Teacher EXPRESS™ Use this complete
Plan · Teach · Assess suite of powerful teaching tools to make lesson planning and testing quicker and easier.

PRENTICE HALL

Student EXPRESS™ Use the interactive
Learn · Study · Succeed textbook (online and on CD-ROM) to make selections and activities come alive with audio and video support and interactive questions.

 Go Online **For:** Information about Lexiles
Professional **Visit:** www.PHSchool.com
Development **Web Code:** eue-1111

Motivation

Act One ends with Nora afraid to see her children in case she "poisons" them or her home. Have students brainstorm a list of Nora's priorities, and write their suggestions on the board (for example, happy children, healthy husband, festive Christmas). Discuss conflicts of interest that Nora faces in Act One to secure these priorities.

❶ Literary Analysis

Characterization in Drama

• To illustrate the role stage directions can play in characterization, have students reread the scene on p. 960 in which Nora plays hide-and-seek with her children.

• Discuss how the stage directions show Nora's vigor and vitality.

❷ Reading Strategy

Inferring Beliefs of the Period

• Explain that to infer beliefs of nineteenth-century Europeans, readers must focus on the clues in the play. Tell students that in this play, characters' ideas about money, women's roles, respectability, and love affect their actions.

• Give students a copy of **Reading Strategy Graphic Organizer A,** p. 171 in *Graphic Organizer Transparencies.* Have them use it to help them focus on details that reveal characters' values.

Vocabulary Builder

• Pronounce each vocabulary word for students, and read the definitions as a class. Have students identify any words with which they are already familiar.

Build Skills | *Drama*

A Doll House, Act Two

❶ Literary Analysis

Characterization in Drama

Characterization is the means by which a writer reveals a character's personality. In most fiction, characterization is developed through one or more of the following methods:

• direct statements about a character
• a character's actions, thoughts, or comments
• comments about a character made by other characters

Along with these methods, **characterization in drama** uses the additional elements of stage directions and dialogue. Look for these methods as you read Act Two of *A Doll House.*

Connecting Literary Elements

In a literary work, the main character, called the **protagonist**, is central to the action and often the one with whom the audience sympathizes. The **antagonist** is the character or force in conflict with the protagonist.

In *A Doll House*, Nora Helmer is the protagonist. Instead of a single antagonist, however, Nora encounters various adversaries. Note Nora's many antagonists as you read.

❷ Reading Strategy

Inferring Beliefs of the Period

Inferring beliefs of the period means observing how social, religious, and cultural practices of a time period affect the characters and their choices. To infer the beliefs of the period as you read:

• Notice how husbands and wives relate to each other.
• Pay attention to the role of women in society.
• Look for clues to social, religious, or cultural practices.

Use an organizer like the one shown to infer the beliefs of a period.

Vocabulary Builder

proclaiming (prō klām´ iŋ) *v.* announcing publicly and loudly (p. 978)

intolerable (in täl´ ər ə bəl) *adj.* unbearable; painful; cruel (p. 979)

impulsive (im pul´ siv) *adj.* sudden and unthinking (p. 982)

tactless (takt´ lis) *adj.* unskilled in dealing with people (p. 982)

excruciating (eks krōō´ shē āt´ iŋ) *adj.* causing intense mental or bodily pain (p. 982)

retribution (re´ trə byōō´ shən) *n.* punishment; revenge (p. 985)

disreputable (dis rep´ yōō tə bəl) *adj.* not fit to be seen or approved (p. 992)

• Make connections between historical and contemporary issues in world literature. (LT.5.01.6)

• Understand the cultural and historical impact on world literature texts. (LT.5.01.7)

• Analyze influences, contexts, or biases in world literature. (LT.5.03.7)

What a Character Says or Does

Anne-Marie had given her daughter up for adoption.

↕

Inferred Beliefs of the Period

Society provided little or no assistance to young, unmarried mothers.

974 ■ *Romanticism and Realism*

Differentiated Instruction   Solutions for All Learners

Support for Special Needs Students

Have students complete the **Preview** and **Build Skills** pages for *A Doll House,* Act Two in the *Reader's Notebook: Adapted Version.* These pages provide a selection summary, an abbreviated presentation of the reading and literary skills, and the graphic organizer on the **Build Skills** page in the student book.

Support for Less Proficient Readers

Have students complete the **Preview** and **Build Skills** pages for *A Doll House,* Act Two in the *Reader's Notebook.* These pages provide a selection summary, an abbreviated presentation of the reading and literary skills, and the graphic organizer on the **Build Skills** page in the student book.

Support for English Learners

Have students complete the **Preview** and **Build Skills** pages for *A Doll House,* Act Two in the *Reader's Notebook: English Learner's Version.* These pages provide a selection summary, an abbreviated presentation of the skills, additional contextual vocabulary, and the graphic organizer on the **Build Skills** page in the student book.

❶ Review and Anticipate

Years ago, Nora secretly borrowed money from Krogstad to help her husband Torvald recover from a serious illness. Desperate for a signature to guarantee the loan but reluctant to disturb her dying father, she forged her father's name on the document. In Act One, Nora shares her secret with Mrs. Linde, her childhood friend who hopes to get a position at Torvald's bank. Nora persuades Torvald to hire Mrs. Linde, but he can do so only by firing Krogstad. Now Krogstad threatens to expose Nora's secret if she does not urge Torvald to keep him employed at the bank. Will Krogstad expose Nora's secrets to Torvald? Will Nora buy herself enough time to solve her dilemma without involving Torvald? Find the answers to these questions in Act Two.

ACT TWO

Same room. Beside the piano the Christmas tree now stands stripped of ornament, burned-down candle stubs on its ragged branches. NORA's *street clothes lie on the sofa.* NORA, *alone in the room, moves restlessly about; at last she stops at the sofa and picks up her coat.*

NORA [*dropping the coat again*]: Someone's coming! [*Goes toward the door, listens.*] No—there's no one. Of course—nobody's coming today, Christmas Day—or tomorrow, either. But maybe—[*Opens the door and looks out.*] No, nothing in the mailbox. Quite empty. [*Coming forward.*] What nonsense! He won't do anything serious. Nothing terrible could happen. It's impossible. Why, I have three small children.

[ANNE-MARIE, *with a large carton, comes in from the room to the left.*]

ANNE-MARIE: Well, at last I found the box with the masquerade clothes.

NORA: Thanks. Put it on the table.

ANNE-MARIE [*does so*]: But they're all pretty much of a mess.

NORA: Ahh! I'd love to rip them in a million pieces!

ANNE-MARIE: Oh, mercy, they can be fixed right up. Just a little patience.

NORA: Yes, I'll go get Mrs. Linde to help me.

ANNE-MARIE: Out again now? In this nasty weather? Miss Nora will catch cold—get sick.

NORA: Oh, worse things could happen— How are the children?

Literary Analysis
Characterization in Drama What does Nora's comment to herself reveal about her character?

❸ ✔**Reading Check**
What is in the box Anne-Marie brings to Nora?

A Doll House, Act Two ■ 975

- Review with students the Reading Strategy instruction on p. 974.
- Then, read aloud the bracketed passage.
- Explain that this kind of frank talk between two female characters would have scandalized the audiences of Ibsen's time, as would Anne-Marie's matter-of-factness about having had a child outside of marriage and keeping in touch with her.
- **Ask** students the Reading Strategy question: In what ways does Anne-Marie imply that religion and marriage were significant social concerns at this time?
  Answer: Although Anne-Marie gave up her child in order to keep her job, she is proud that her daughter has been confirmed and has married.

❺ Literary Analysis

Characterization in Drama

- Point out to students that Nora's speeches will sound a bit more erratic than in the previous act. She talks at length to herself and interrupts herself.
- Have students silently read the bracketed passage. Then, **ask** students to respond to the Literary Analysis item: Identify three of Nora's thoughts that reveal her anxiety over her situation.
  Possible response: Nora is full of nervous wishing ("Oh, if only . . ."); she calls her thoughts "craziness" because she wants to deny the possibility that her worries may come true; she tells herself to "let it go" in an attempt to relax.

ANNE-MARIE: The poor mites are playing with their Christmas presents, but—

NORA: Do they ask for me much?

ANNE-MARIE: They're so used to having Mama around, you know.

NORA: Yes, but Anne-Marie, I *can't* be together with them as much as I was.

ANNE-MARIE: Well, small children get used to anything.

NORA: You think so? Do you think they'd forget their mother if she was gone for good?

ANNE-MARIE: Oh, mercy—gone for good!

NORA: Wait, tell me, Anne-Marie—I've wondered so often—how could you ever have the heart to give your child over to strangers?

ANNE-MARIE: But I had to, you know, to become little Nora's nurse.

NORA: Yes, but how could you *do* it?

ANNE-MARIE: When I could get such a good place? A girl who's poor and who's gotten in trouble is glad enough for that. Because that slippery fish, he didn't do a thing for me, you know.

❹ NORA: But your daughter's surely forgotten you.

ANNE-MARIE: Oh, she certainly has not. She's written to me, both when she was confirmed and when she was married.

NORA [*clasping her about the neck*]: You old Anne-Marie, you were a good mother for me when I was little.

ANNE-MARIE: Poor little Nora, with no other mother but me.

NORA: And if the babies didn't have one, then I know that you'd— What silly talk! [*Opening the carton.*] Go in to them. Now I'll have to—Tomorrow you can see how lovely I'll look.

ANNE-MARIE: Oh, there won't be anyone at the party as lovely as Miss Nora. [*She goes off into the room, left.*]

NORA [*begins unpacking the box, but soon throws it aside*]: Oh, if I dared to go out. If only nobody would come. If only nothing would happen here while I'm out. What craziness—nobody's coming. Just don't think. This
❺ muff—needs a brushing. Beautiful gloves, beautiful gloves. Let it go. Let it go! One, two, three, four, five, six— [*With a cry.*] Oh, there they are! [*Poises to move toward the door, but remains irresolutely standing.* MRS. LINDE *enters from the hall, where she has removed her street clothes.*]

NORA: Oh, it's you, Kristine. There's no one else out there? How good that you've come.

❽ MRS. LINDE: I hear you were up asking for me.

NORA: Yes, I just stopped by. There's something you really can help me with. Let's get settled on the sofa. Look, there's going to be a costume party tomorrow evening at the Stenborgs' right above us, and now

Reading Strategy
Inferring Beliefs of the Period In what way does Anne-Marie imply that religion and marriage were significant social concerns at this time?

Literary Analysis
Characterization in Drama Identify three of Nora's thoughts that reveal her anxiety over her situation.

Enrichment

Ibsen's Method
Ibsen once offered the following explanation of how he developed characters for his plays:

> Before I write down one word, I have to have the character in mind through and through. I must penetrate into the last wrinkle of his soul. I always proceed from the individual; the stage setting, the dramatic ensemble, all that comes naturally and does not cause me any worry, as soon as I am certain of the individual in every aspect of his humanity. But I have to have

his exterior in mind also, down to the last button, how he stands and walks, how he conducts himself, what his voice sounds like. Then I do not let him go until his fate is fulfilled.

Tell students to keep this method of creating characters in mind as they read the second act. Have them evaluate how successful Ibsen has been in capturing his characters "down to the last button."

❻

❼ Critical Viewing ▷
In what ways might
Nora dress like the
woman in this painting?
[Interpret]

Lady with a Fur Muff, Theodor Bruckner, Whitford & Hughes, London, UK

A Doll House, Act Two ■ 977

❻ **Humanities**

Lady with a Fur Muff,
by Theodor Bruckner

A painter of frescoes, portraits, and
genre subjects, Theodor Bruckner
(1870–1921) lived most of his life in
his native Vienna. His best works were
his portraits of ordinary people, but
he was also well known for the theatrical stage sets he designed and
painted. Bruckner's works were popular enough in his day to be displayed
in exhibits in Europe's capital cities.

Use the following questions for
discussion:

• How would you characterize the
mood of this painting?
Possible response: The mood of
the painting is dark and somber.

• Why is this painting an appropriate
illustration for Act Two of A *Doll
House?*
Possible responses: The subject
of the painting—a richly dressed
woman—appears serious, as if contemplating something important.
The painting itself is dark, which is
appropriate because the play takes a
darker turn in Act Two.

❼ **Critical Viewing**

Possible response: Nora lives in a
cold climate, so she probably wears
warm clothes similar to those shown
in the painting. Nora also likes herself
and her family to be well dressed, so
her clothing might look similar to the
elegant attire of the woman in the
painting.

Differentiated
Instruction Solutions for All Learners

**Vocabulary for
Less Proficient Readers**
Read aloud the vocabulary
words on p. 974 to demon-
strate correct pronunciation.
Ask volunteers to read aloud
the definitions. Guide students
toward understanding that the
words refer to punishment,
pain, and sudden action.
Challenge students to predict
how Act Two will unfold, given
the vocabulary words.

**Vocabulary for
English Learners**
Review with students the list
of vocabulary words on p. 974.
Read aloud the words and
their definitions. Point out that
all the words have suffixes and
all but *tactless* have prefixes.
Allow students time to use a
dictionary to identify the
meanings of the prefixes, roots,
and suffixes of the words.

**Vocabulary for
Advanced Readers**
Have students review the
vocabulary words on p. 974.
Challenge them to use all the
words to write short vignettes
or scenes. The scene may take
place anywhere and may be
in narrative play form. Tell
students to notice how the
vocabulary words affect their
scenes' settings, characteriza-
tions, and moods.

⑧ Critical Thinking

Infer

- Have two students read aloud the bracketed passage beginning on p. 976; one student should read Nora's lines, and one student should read Mrs. Linde's lines.

- Then, **ask** why Nora relies on Mrs. Linde to sew her costume.
Answer: Mrs. Linde has had to work at such jobs as sewing, so she is probably quite good at it.

- **Ask:** What do these circumstances reveal about the women's respective abilities and lifestyles?
Answer: Nora and Mrs. Linde are in different social positions. Nora, as a woman of the upper-middle class, has not needed to earn a living. Mrs. Linde has had to work to survive.

⑨ Reading Strategy

Inferring Beliefs of the Period

- Ask students to review the bracketed passage.

- Then, have them **respond** to the Reading Strategy item: Identify two talents or accomplishments that upper-class society of that time expected of women like Nora.
Possible response: Upper-class women were expected to have at least one musical talent, such as singing or dancing, and they were expected to run their households efficiently and tastefully. Women were also expected to have a few children.

- Discuss with students whether Nora has met these expectations, and encourage them to predict what may change as the story progresses.

⑩ Background

Careful Language

Women, and many men, in the 1800s used careful, roundabout language when talking about sexual matters. According to Nora, Dr. Rank's condition was inherited from his loose-living father.

Torvald wants me to go as a Neapolitan[1] peasant girl and dance the tarantella that I learned in Capri.[2]

MRS. LINDE: Really, are you giving a whole performance?

⑧ NORA: Torvald says yes, I should. See, here's the dress. Torvald had it made for me down there; but now it's all so tattered that I just don't know—

MRS. LINDE: Oh, we'll fix that up in no time. It's nothing more than the trimmings—they're a bit loose here and there. Needle and thread? Good, now we have what we need.

NORA: Oh, how sweet of you!

MRS. LINDE [*sewing*]: So you'll be in disguise tomorrow, Nora. You know what? I'll stop by then for a moment and have a look at you all dressed up. But listen, I've absolutely forgotten to thank you for that pleasant evening yesterday.

⑨ NORA [*getting up and walking about*]: I don't think it was as pleasant as usual yesterday. You should have come to town a bit sooner, Kristine— Yes, Torvald really knows how to give a home elegance and charm.

MRS. LINDE: And you do, too, if you ask me. You're not your father's daughter for nothing. But tell me, is Dr. Rank always so down in the mouth as yesterday?

NORA: No, that was quite an exception. But he goes around critically ill all the time—tuberculosis of the spine, poor man. You know, his father was a disgusting thing who kept mistresses and so on—and that's why the son's been sickly from birth.

⑩ MRS. LINDE [*lets her sewing fall to her lap*]: But my dearest Nora, how do you know about such things?

NORA [*walking more jauntily*]: Hmp! When you've had three children, then you've had a few visits from—from women who know something of medicine, and they tell you this and that.

MRS. LINDE [*resumes sewing; a short pause*]: Does Dr. Rank come here every day?

NORA: Every blessed day. He's Torvald's best friend from childhood, and *my* good friend, too. Dr. Rank almost belongs to this house.

MRS. LINDE: But tell me—is he quite sincere? I mean, doesn't he rather enjoy flattering people?

NORA: Just the opposite. Why do you think that?

MRS. LINDE: When you introduced us yesterday, he was <u>proclaiming</u> that he'd often heard my name in this house; but later I noticed that your husband hadn't the slightest idea who I really was. So how could Dr. Rank—?

---

1. **Neapolitan** (nē ə päl′ ət 'n) of Naples, a seaport in southern Italy.
2. **Capri** (kä prē′) island near the entrance to the Bay of Naples.

978 ■ *Romanticism and Realism*

Reading Strategy
Inferring Beliefs of the Period Identify two talents or accomplishments that upper-class society of that time expected of women like Nora.

Vocabulary Builder
proclaiming (prō klām′ iŋ)
v. announcing publicly and loudly

Enrichment

Dr. Rank's Illness: Real or Symbolic?

Ibsen has given the character of Dr. Rank a fatal disease, which he and the characters call spinal tuberculosis. Spinal tuberculosis is a condition caused by tubercular bacteria. It is also called Pott's disease after the English doctor who studied it. Spinal tuberculosis affects a person's spine by attacking the vertebrae; it causes great pain and, in some cases, a deforming hunch-backed condition in the patient. The disease can also cause paralysis. Today, chemotherapy is used to treat spinal tuberculosis, but no effective treatments existed in the nineteenth century.

Dr. Rank's disease, however, is probably not tuberculosis. Both he and Nora talk about how he might have gotten the disease from his father, but tuberculosis is not inherited; it is caused by bacteria. Students should understand that the true nature of Dr. Rank's illness is not very important. The illness is really a symbol. It is another example of what Torvald was talking about in Act One—how the errors of the parents cause misfortune and pain for the children.

NORA: But it's all true, Kristine. You see, Torvald loves me beyond words, and, as he puts it, he'd like to keep me all to himself. For a long time he'd almost be jealous if I even mentioned any of my old friends back home. So of course I dropped that. But with Dr. Rank I talk a lot about such things, because he likes hearing about them.

MRS. LINDE: Now listen, Nora; in many ways you're still like a child. I'm a good deal older than you, with a little more experience. I'll tell you something: you ought to put an end to all this with Dr. Rank.

NORA: What should I put an end to?

MRS. LINDE: Both parts of it, I think. Yesterday you said something about a rich admirer who'd provide you with money—

NORA: Yes, one who doesn't exist—worse luck. So?

MRS. LINDE: Is Dr. Rank well off?

NORA: Yes, he is.

MRS. LINDE: With no dependents?

NORA: No, no one. But—?

MRS. LINDE: And he's over here every day?

NORA: Yes, I told you that.

MRS. LINDE: How can a man of such refinement be so grasping?

NORA: I don't follow you at all.

MRS. LINDE: Now don't try to hide it, Nora. You think I can't guess who loaned you the forty-eight hundred crowns?

NORA: Are you out of your mind? How could you think such a thing! A friend of ours, who comes here every single day. What an <u>intolerable</u> situation that would have been!

MRS. LINDE: Then it really wasn't him.

NORA: No, absolutely not. It never even crossed my mind for a moment— And he had nothing to lend in those days; his inheritance came later.

MRS. LINDE: Well, I think that was a stroke of luck for you, Nora dear.

NORA: No, it never would have occurred to me to ask Dr. Rank— Still, I'm quite sure that if I had asked him—

MRS. LINDE: Which you won't, of course.

NORA: No, of course not. I can't see that I'd ever need to. But I'm quite positive that if I talked to Dr. Rank—

MRS. LINDE: Behind your husband's back?

NORA: I've got to clear up this other thing; *that's* also behind his back. I've got to clear it all up.

MRS. LINDE: Yes, I was saying that yesterday, but—

NORA [*pacing up and down*]: A man handles these problems so much better than a woman—

MRS. LINDE: One's husband does, yes.

Reading Strategy
Inferring Beliefs of the Period What does Nora suggest about Torvald's personality?

Vocabulary Builder
intolerable (in tä´ ər ə bəl) *adj.* unbearable; painful; cruel

Reading Check 🔢

From what illness is Dr. Rank suffering?

A Doll House, Act Two ■ 979

⓫ Reading Strategy

Inferring Beliefs of the Period

- Read aloud Nora's lines at the top of the page.

- As a class, summarize the situation that Nora describes to Mrs. Linde. **Ask** students what Nora lost when she stopped mentioning her friends to her husband.
  Possible response: By talking less about her old friends, Nora lost the chance to remember her past and who she was before becoming Torvald's wife.

- **Ask** students the Reading Strategy question: What does Nora suggest about Torvald's personality?
  Answer: Torvald is jealous and controlling.

- **Ask** students whether they think such behavior from husbands is outdated or whether it still happens.
  Possible response: Husbands, and wives, still get jealous. However, most people do not get so jealous that they force their spouses not to mention people from their past, as Torvald expects from Nora.

⓬ Reading Strategy

Inferring Beliefs of the Period

- Have two volunteers read aloud the bracketed passage as the other students follow along in their textbooks.

- Make sure students realize that Mrs. Linde is more concerned than curious about the possibility of Nora's talking to Dr. Rank behind Torvald's back.

- **Ask** students what Mrs. Linde's questions reveal about relationships between unmarried men and women in the nineteenth century.
  Possible response: It was probably considered improper for men and women who were not related or married to one another to spend time alone together talking.

- Help students understand that even Nora's ease with Dr. Rank in public could be seen as improper behavior because it suggests familiarity.

⓭ Reading Check

Answer: Dr. Rank is suffering from tuberculosis of the spine.

Strategy for Special Needs Students

Ask each student to keep an informal journal in which to respond to the play. Encourage students to respond on a personal level, rather than on a literary level. To help them begin, ask students to address what they hope or fear will happen. Allow students time throughout the act to write their responses to the events. After students finish the play, have volunteers summarize their reactions over the course of the play.

Strategy for English Learners

Point out to students that they already know a good deal about Nora, Torvald, Mrs. Linde, and Krogstad from the first act. Have them suggest adjectives that describe each of these characters. List the suggestions on the board under each name, and have students give reasons for assigning each adjective, on the basis of what they learned in Act One.

980

⑭ Critical Viewing

Possible response: The adoring expression on the actress's face conveys Nora's great pride in and admiration for Torvald. The way she stands so close to Torvald and rests her hand on his shoulder shows how much Nora cares for him and trusts in him.

⑮ Literary Analysis

Characterization in Drama

• Remind students that stage directions can help reveal a character's thoughts and feelings.

• Read aloud the bracketed passage, and then point out the stage directions for Mrs. Linde. **Ask** students why Mrs. Linde looks "hard" at Nora.
  Answer: Mrs. Linde suspects that Nora's debt is not her only problem.

• **Ask** students what this reveals about Mrs. Linde's character.
  Possible response: Mrs. Linde is observant, sharp, and concerned about Nora's situation.

▶ **Monitor Progress Ask** students: In addition to stage directions, how else can character be revealed in a drama?
  Answer: Character can be revealed through direct statements or physical descriptions of a character; a character's actions, thoughts, or comments; or comments that other characters make about a character.

▶ **Reteach** Help students find an example from the text for each method of characterization. Encourage them to refer to these examples as they explore the concept of characterization throughout the play.

NORA: Nonsense. [*Stopping.*] When you pay everything you owe, then you get your note back, right?

MRS. LINDE: Yes, naturally.

NORA: And can rip it into a million pieces and burn it up—that filthy scrap of paper!

MRS. LINDE [*looking hard at her, laying her sewing aside, and rising slowly*]: Nora, you're hiding something from me.

⑮ NORA: You can see it in my face?

MRS. LINDE: Something's happened to you since yesterday morning. Nora, what is it?

NORA [*hurrying toward her*]: Kristine! [*Listening.*] Shh! Torvald's home. Look, go in with the children a while. Torvald can't bear all this snipping and stitching. Let Anne-Marie help you.

⑭ ▲ Critical Viewing
In what ways does the actress portraying Nora show the faith Nora has in her husband? **[Analyze]**

980 ■ *Romanticism and Realism*

MRS. LINDE [*gathering up some of the things*]: All right, but I'm not leaving here until we've talked this out. [*She disappears into the room, left, as* TORVALD *enters from the hall.*]

NORA: Oh, how I've been waiting for you, Torvald dear.

HELMER: Was that the dressmaker?

NORA: No, that was Kristine. She's helping me fix up my costume. You know, it's going to be quite attractive.

HELMER: Yes, wasn't that a bright idea I had?

16 | **NORA:** Brilliant! But then wasn't I good as well to give in to you?

HELMER: Good—because you give in to your husband's judgment? All right, you little goose, I know you didn't mean it like that. But I won't disturb you. You'll want to have a fitting, I suppose.

NORA: And you'll be working?

HELMER: Yes. [*Indicating a bundle of papers.*] See. I've been down to the bank. [*Starts toward his study.*]

NORA: Torvald.

HELMER [*stops*]: Yes.

NORA: If your little squirrel begged you, with all her heart and soul, for something—?

HELMER: What's that?

NORA: Then would you do it?

HELMER: First, naturally, I'd have to know what it was.

17 **NORA:** Your squirrel would scamper about and do tricks, if you'd only be sweet and give in.

HELMER: Out with it.

NORA: Your lark would be singing high and low in every room—

HELMER: Come on, she does that anyway.

NORA: I'd be a wood nymph and dance for you in the moonlight.

HELMER: Nora—don't tell me it's that same business from this morning?

NORA [*coming closer*]: Yes, Torvald, I beg you, please!

HELMER: And you actually have the nerve to drag that up again?

NORA: Yes, yes, you've got to give in to me; you *have* to let Krogstad keep his job in the bank.

HELMER: My dear Nora, I've slated his job for Mrs. Linde.

NORA: That's awfully kind of you. But you could just fire another clerk instead of Krogstad.

HELMER: This is the most incredible stubbornness! Because you go

---

Reading Strategy

Inferring Beliefs of the Period What common social beliefs about men and women can you infer from Nora's comment? Explain.

Reading Strategy

Inferring Beliefs of the Period Why does Nora compare herself to a squirrel as she pleads with Torvald?

 **Reading Check** **18**

What does Nora call "that filthy scrap of paper"?

A Doll House, Act Two ■ 981

---

16 **Reading Strategy**

Inferring Beliefs of the Period

• As a class, list the stresses Nora must address at this point in the play (for example, making her husband's money last through the Christmas season and performing well at the masquerade). **Ask** students why Nora wants to meet these challenges.
Answer: Nora wants to do these things to please her husband and to keep him from being suspicious about her spending.

• Read aloud the bracketed line. Then, **ask** the first Reading Strategy question: What common social beliefs about men and women can you infer from Nora's comment? Explain.
Possible response: Nora suggests that she had a right to reject her husband's "bright idea." Torvald's response, however, indicates that this rejection is unacceptable.

• Encourage students to look for clues that indicate Nora's changing attitude toward her husband. Tell students that they will begin to see increasing signs that Nora is actually disenchanted with her dollhouse marriage.

17 **Reading Strategy**

Inferring Beliefs of the Period

• Have two volunteers read aloud the bracketed passage. Then, **ask** the second Reading Strategy question: Why does Nora compare herself to a squirrel as she pleads with Torvald?
Answer: Nora's childish flirtations with Torvald cater to his idea of her as helpless. By portraying herself as such, she hopes to manipulate his decisions and actions.

• Explain that Nora is playing her familiar game of flirting with Torvald to get him to do what she wants. **Ask** students whether they believe that such behavior would be successful today. Why or why not?
Possible response: Nora is being too obvious; few probably would be fooled by her flattery and flirting today.

18 **Reading Check**

Answer: The scrap of paper is the loan agreement on which Nora's forged signature appears.

981

Make a Judgment

• Read aloud the first bracketed passage. Remind students that in the first act, Torvald speaks almost fondly of Nora's father's inability to handle money. Here, though, Torvald is clearly judgmental.

• **Ask** students: Do you find it surprising that Nora does not seem bothered by Torvald's attitude about her father? Why or why not? **Possible response:** It is not surprising; Nora is used to accepting Torvald's opinions without question. She is also preoccupied with Krogstad's threat.

• Guide students to recognize that Torvald's comments support the recurring idea that parents' immoral behavior affects their children. Torvald believes that Nora has inherited her father's immoral approach to business.

⑳ Literary Analysis

Characterization in Drama

• Point out that until now, Torvald has come across as proud, stubborn, and self-righteous. **Ask** students to explain what seems to bother Torvald most about Krogstad. **Answer:** Torvald is annoyed that his old friend calls him by his first name at the office.

• Discuss with students what this attitude reveals about Torvald's character. Point out that Torvald apparently has never bothered to ask Krogstad not to address him familiarly. Instead, he has decided that the only solution is to fire Krogstad.

• **Ask** students the Literary Analysis question: What do Torvald's real reasons for firing Krogstad reveal about Torvald's personality? **Possible response:** Torvald is petty, small-minded, insecure, and preoccupied with how his coworkers perceive him.

---

and give an <u>impulsive</u> promise to speak up for him, I'm expected to—

NORA: That's not the reason, Torvald. It's for your own sake. That man does writing for the worst papers; you said it yourself. He could do you any amount of harm. I'm scared to death of him—

HELMER: Ah, I understand. It's the old memories haunting you.

NORA: What do you mean by that?

HELMER: Of course, you're thinking about your father.

NORA: Yes, all right. Just remember how those nasty gossips wrote in the papers about Papa and slandered him so cruelly. I think they'd have had him dismissed if the department hadn't sent you up to investigate, and if you hadn't been so kind and open-minded toward him.

⑲ **HELMER:** My dear Nora, there's a notable difference between your father and me. Your father's official career was hardly above reproach. But mine is; and I hope it'll stay that way as long as I hold my position.

NORA: Oh, who can ever tell what vicious minds can invent? We could be so snug and happy in our quiet, carefree home—you and I and the children, Torvald! That's why I'm pleading with you so—

HELMER: And just by pleading for him you make it impossible for me to keep him on. It's already known at the bank that I'm firing Krogstad. What if it's rumored around now that the new bank manager was vetoed by his wife—

NORA: Yes, what then—?

HELMER: Oh yes—as long as our little bundle of stubbornness gets her way—! I should go and make myself ridiculous in front of the whole office—give people the idea I can be swayed by all kinds of outside pressure. Oh, you can bet I'd feel the effects of that soon enough! Besides— there's something that rules Krogstad right out at the bank as long as I'm the manager.

NORA: What's that?

HELMER: His moral failings I could maybe overlook if I had to—

NORA: Yes, Torvald, why not?

⑳ **HELMER:** And I hear he's quite efficient on the job. But he was a crony of mine back in my teens—one of those rash friendships that crop up again and again to embarrass you later in life. Well, I might as well say it straight out: we're on a first-name basis. And that <u>tactless</u> fool makes no effort at all to hide it in front of others. Quite the contrary—he thinks that entitles him to take a familiar air around me, and so every other second he comes booming out with his "Yes, Torvald!" and "Sure thing, Torvald!" I tell you, it's been <u>excruciating</u> for me. He's out to make my place in the bank unbearable.

NORA: Torvald, you can't be serious about all this.

HELMER: Oh no? Why not?

NORA: Because these are such petty considerations.

982 ■ *Romanticism and Realism*

Vocabulary Builder

impulsive (im pul′ siv) *adj.* sudden and unthinking

Literary Analysis

Characterization in Drama What do Torvald's real reasons for firing Krogstad reveal about Torvald's personality?

Vocabulary Builder

tactless (takt′ lis) *adj.* unskilled in dealing with people

excruciating (eks krōō′ shē āt′ iŋ) *adj.* causing intense mental or bodily pain

---

Enrichment

Ibsen's Politics

Shortly before he finished writing *A Doll House*, Ibsen received a letter from an old friend, Bjornstjerne Bjornson. The letter urged Ibsen to join the fight to free Norway from Swedish influence. Ibsen had no sympathy for this cause. He responded:

> I have not much sympathy for symbols. . . . I regard it as a sin against our people to make an issue burningly important when it is not. . . . We have only one thing which I

think worth fighting for, and that is the introduction of up-to-date education for our children. . . . It is quite immaterial whether our politicians bring about isolated reforms if they do not achieve liberty for the individual. . . . [T]ake away the mark of prejudice and narrow-mindedness and short-sightedness and subservience and unthinking trust in authority, so that every individual can sail under his own flag. . . .

HELMER: What are you saying? Petty? You think I'm petty!

NORA: No, just the opposite, Torvald dear. That's exactly why—

HELMER: Never mind. You call my motives petty; then I might as well be just that. Petty! All right! We'll put a stop to this for good. [*Goes to the hall door and calls.*] Helene!

NORA: What do you want?

HELMER [*searching among his papers*]: A decision. [*The* MAID *comes in.*] Look here; take this letter; go out with it at once. Get hold of a messenger and have him deliver it. Quick now. It's already addressed. Wait, here's some money.

MAID: Yes, sir. [*She leaves with the letter.*]

HELMER [*straightening his papers*]: There, now, little Miss Willful.

NORA [*breathlessly*]: Torvald, what was that letter?

HELMER: Krogstad's notice.

NORA: Call it back, Torvald! There's still time. Oh, Torvald, call it back! Do it for my sake—for your sake, for the children's sake! Do you hear, Torvald; do it! You don't know how this can harm us.

HELMER: Too late.

NORA: Yes, too late.

HELMER: Nora dear, I can forgive you this panic, even though basically you're insulting me. Yes, you are! Or isn't it an insult to think that *I* should be afraid of a courtroom hack's revenge? But I forgive you anyway, because this shows so beautifully how much you love me. [*Takes her in his arms.*] This is the way it should be, my darling Nora. Whatever comes, you'll see: when it really counts, I have strength and courage enough as a man to take on the whole weight myself.

NORA [*terrified*]: What do you mean by that?

HELMER: The whole weight, I said.

NORA [*resolutely*]: No, never in all the world.

HELMER: Good. So we'll share it, Nora, as man and wife. That's as it should be. [*Fondling her.*] Are you happy now? There, there, there—not these frightened dove's eyes. It's nothing at all but empty fantasies—Now you should run through your tarantella and practice your tambourine. I'll go to the inner office and shut both doors, so I won't hear a thing; you can make all the noise you like. [*Turning in the doorway.*] And when Rank comes, just tell him where he can find me. [*He nods to her and goes with his papers into the study, closing the door.*]

Literary Analysis
Characterization in Drama Does Torvald's decision to send the maid with Krogstad's notice reveal a cowardly personality? Explain.

Reading Check ㉓
Why does Torvald fire Krogstad?

A Doll House, Act Two ■ 983

㉑ **Literary Analysis**
Characterization in Drama

- Choose three volunteers to read aloud the bracketed lines for Torvald, the maid, and Nora.

- Help students understand that Torvald has sent the letter in part because he is insulted by Nora's suggestion that he is being petty.

- **Ask** students the Literary Analysis question: Does Torvald's decision to send the maid with Krogstad's notice reveal a cowardly personality? Explain.
  Possible response: It is cowardly to send a letter rather than tell Krogstad the news in person. Torvald does this to avoid an unpleasant situation.

- Point out the irony in Torvald's claiming to have "strength and courage"; Torvald says this just after he sends the letter, which allows him to avoid a possible confrontation with Krogstad.

㉒ **Critical Thinking**
Predict

- Discuss with students how Torvald's decision to send the letter firing Krogstad is a turning point in the play that reaffirms gender roles and seals Nora's fate.

- Challenge students to **predict** what will happen now that Torvald has sent the letter.
  Possible response: Krogstad may ruin Nora's reputation, which will end her marriage and destroy her family. Nora may find a way to intercept Krogstad's letter. Nora may finally convince her husband to change his mind about firing Krogstad.

㉓ **Reading Check**
Answer: Torvald fires Krogstad because Krogstad calls him by his first name at the office.

Differentiated Instruction   Solutions for All Learners

Strategy for Special Needs Students
Have students work in pairs to follow the development of Torvald's character. Have them reread Act Two to this point and use sticky notes wherever there is a direct statement about Torvald, an example of his own actions or comments, and any comments about him made by other characters. Advise them to label each sticky note with the method of characterization used by Ibsen. Suggest these labels: DSAT, ETA/C, and OC'sC. Then give students a copy of the Character Wheel organizer in *Graphic Organizer Transparencies*, p. 276. Have them work together to fill out the wheel for Torvald's character. Tell students to continue to use sticky notes and to add to the Character Wheel throughout Act Two and Act Three.

Finally, have students write a descriptive paragraph summarizing their findings about Torvald so far and share their paragraphs with the class.

984

24 **Critical Thinking**

Interpret

- Point out the last sentence of the stage directions: "During the following scene, it begins getting dark."

- **Ask** students to interpret the significance of this stage direction.
  Answer: As it grows dark outside, the atmosphere in the apartment is getting darker. The plot is closing in on Nora, and more dark news is about to be announced.

- **Brainstorm** as a class how the set might reflect this stage direction.
  Possible response: The windows in the set could turn dark as if the sun were setting, or the stage lights could dim slightly every time a significant line is spoken.

25 **Literary Analysis**

Characterization in Drama

- Ask students to read the bracketed passage silently, focusing on the stage directions for Nora. Then, **ask** why Nora breathes easier when she learns that Dr. Rank is dying.
  Answer: Nora is relieved that Dr. Rank is not referring to Nora's situation with Krogstad.

- Next, **ask** the Literary Analysis question: What do the stage directions reveal about Nora's concern for Dr. Rank?
  Possible response: Nora is more concerned about her own problems than she is about the health of Dr. Rank.

- **Ask** students what this passage reveals about Nora's friendship with Dr. Rank.
  Possible response: Nora apparently does not value Dr. Rank's friendship as much as she claims she does. On the other hand, her problem with Krogstad is so overwhelming that she cannot spare thoughts for another person's problems.

NORA [*standing as though rooted, dazed with fright, in a whisper*]: He really could do it. He will do it. He'll do it in spite of everything. No, not that, never, never! Anything but that! Escape! A way out— [*The doorbell rings.*] Dr. Rank! Anything but that! *Anything*, whatever it is! [*Her hands pass over her face, smoothing it; she pulls herself together, goes over and opens the hall door.* DR. RANK *stands outside, hanging his fur coat up. During the following scene, it begins getting dark.*]

NORA: Hello, Dr. Rank. I recognized your ring. But you mustn't go in to Torvald yet; I believe he's working.

RANK: And you?

NORA: For you, I always have an hour to spare—you know that. [*He has entered, and she shuts the door after him.*]

RANK: Many thanks. I'll make use of these hours while I can.

NORA: What do you mean by that? While you can?

RANK: Does that disturb you?

NORA: Well, it's such an odd phrase. Is anything going to happen?

RANK: What's going to happen is what I've been expecting so long—but I honestly didn't think it would come so soon.

NORA [*gripping his arm*]: What is it you've found out? Dr. Rank, you have to tell me!

RANK [*sitting by the stove*]: It's all over with me. There's nothing to be done about it.

NORA [*breathing easier*]: Is it you—then—?

RANK: Who else? There's no point in lying to one's self. I'm the most miserable of all my patients, Mrs. Helmer. These past few days I've been auditing my internal accounts. Bankrupt! Within a month I'll probably be laid out and rotting in the churchyard.

NORA: Oh, what a horrible thing to say.

RANK: The thing itself is horrible. But the worst of it is all the other horror before it's over. There's only one final examination left; when I'm finished with that, I'll know about when my disintegration will begin. There's something I want to say. Helmer with his sensitivity has such a sharp distaste for anything ugly. I don't want him near my sickroom.

NORA: Oh, but Dr. Rank—

RANK: I won't have him in there. Under no condition. I'll lock my door to him— As soon as I'm completely sure of the worst, I'll send you my calling card marked with a black cross, and you'll know then the wreck has started to come apart.

NORA: No, today you're completely unreasonable. And I wanted you so much to be in a really good humor.

RANK: With death up my sleeve? And then to suffer this way for somebody else's sins. Is there any justice in that? And in every single family,

984 ■ *Romanticism and Realism*

Literary Analysis
Characterization in Drama What do the stage directions reveal about Nora's concern for Dr. Rank?

Enrichment

Symbolism and Figurative Language in Ibsen's Writing

Ibsen first gained recognition as a poet. In fact, he was once considered Norway's leading poet. He wrote his early plays in verse, and after his "realistic period" (which included *A Doll House*), he wrote a number of plays that some critics think contain an excess of symbolism.

During the period in which Ibsen concentrated on prose realism, he tried to portray his characters precisely—their words, actions, attitudes, and beliefs. His literary technique at the time prevented him from using much figurative language or overt symbolism because they would have detracted from the realism. Consequently, the figures of speech in the dialogue of *A Doll House* are mostly clichéd metaphors from everyday life.

For example, Torvald calls Nora a "lark," a "goose," a "squirrel," and so on. These are the words of a narrow-minded lawyer, not of a poet. Similarly, the play's realistic quality prevents Ibsen from including many symbols, aside from Nora's beloved macaroons.

26 | in some way or another, this inevitable <u>retribution</u> of nature goes on—

NORA [*her hands pressed over her ears*]: Oh, stuff! Cheer up! Please—be gay!

RANK: Yes, I'd just as soon laugh at it all. My poor, innocent spine, serving time for my father's gay army days.

NORA [*by the table, left*]: He was so infatuated with asparagus tips and *pâté de foie gras,*[3] wasn't that it?

27 **RANK:** Yes—and with truffles.

NORA: Truffles, yes. And then with oysters, I suppose?

RANK: Yes, tons of oysters, naturally.

NORA: And then the port and champagne to go with it. It's so sad that all these delectable things have to strike at our bones.

RANK: Especially when they strike at the unhappy bones that never shared in the fun.

NORA: Ah, that's the saddest of all.

RANK [*looks searchingly at her*]: Hm.

NORA [*after a moment*]: Why did you smile?

RANK: No, it was you who laughed.

NORA: No, it was you who smiled, Dr. Rank!

RANK [*getting up*]: You're even a bigger tease than I'd thought.

NORA: I'm full of wild ideas today.

RANK: That's obvious.

NORA [*putting both hands on his shoulders*]: Dear, dear Dr. Rank, you'll never die for Torvald and me.

RANK: Oh, that loss you'll easily get over. Those who go away are soon forgotten.

NORA [*looks fearfully at him*]: You believe that?

RANK: One makes new connections, and then—

NORA: Who makes new connections?

RANK: Both you and Torvald will when I'm gone. I'd say you're well under way already. What was that Mrs. Linde doing here last evening?

NORA: Oh, come—you can't be jealous of poor Kristine?

RANK: Oh yes, I am. She'll be my successor here in the house. When I'm down under, that woman will probably—

NORA: Shh! Not so loud. She's right in there.

RANK: Today as well. So you see.

---

3. *pâté de foie gras* (pä tä′ də fwä′ grä′) paste or spread made of the livers of fattened geese.

Vocabulary Builder
retribution (re′ trə byoo′ shən) *n.* punishment; revenge

Reading Strategy
Inferring Beliefs of the Period What modern knowledge of health and heredity does Rank imply when he refers to his father's lavish lifestyle?

28 **Reading Check**
What will Dr. Rank send the Helmers when his death becomes imminent?

A Doll House, Act Two ■ 985

Inferring Beliefs of the Period

- Review with students the Reading Strategy instruction on p. 974.

- Have students independently read the bracketed passage. Then, explain that Nora's showing her stockings to Dr. Rank might have been scandalous to audiences of Ibsen's time. In the nineteenth century, most European cultures considered it improper for a married woman to show her legs or stockings to any man other than her husband. Once again, Nora behaves improperly by her society's standards.

- **Ask** students what is ironic when Nora says "Shame on you" to Dr. Rank.
Answer: Nora has initiated this flirtation by showing Dr. Rank the stockings, so she is the one who should feel ashamed according to the dictates of society.

30 Critical Viewing

Possible response: The sewing kit would be valued because part of a woman's reputation in nineteenth-century society was based on her ability to sew. In addition, some women earned a living by sewing.

31 Critical Thinking

Speculate

- Have students read the bracketed passage independently. Then, **ask** them to identify the "exceptionally big favor" that Nora is about to ask of Dr. Rank.
Possible response: Nora probably will ask Dr. Rank for the money to pay off her debt.

- Remind students that on p. 979 Nora tells Mrs. Linde that it never occurred to her originally to ask Dr. Rank for the forty-eight hundred crowns.

- Have students **speculate** on why Nora may be about to ask him for money.
Possible response: Nora is growing increasingly desperate. She hopes that Dr. Rank will pay off her debt for the sake of her and her family.

NORA: Only to sew on my dress. Good gracious, how unreasonable you are. [*Sitting on the sofa.*] Be nice now, Dr. Rank. Tomorrow you'll see how beautifully I'll dance; and you can imagine then that I'm dancing only for you—yes, and of course for Torvald, too—that's understood. [*Takes various items out of the carton.*] Dr. Rank, sit over here and I'll show you something.

RANK [*sitting*]: What's that?

NORA: Look here. Look.

RANK: Silk stockings.

29 **NORA:** Flesh-colored. Aren't they lovely? Now it's so dark here, but tomorrow— No, no, no, just look at the feet. Oh well, you might as well look at the rest.

RANK: Hm—

NORA: Why do you look so critical? Don't you believe they'll fit?

RANK: I've never had any chance to form an opinion on that.

NORA [*glancing at him a moment*]: Shame on you. [*Hits him lightly on the ear with the stockings.*] That's for you. [*Puts them away again.*]

RANK: And what other splendors am I going to see now?

NORA: Not the least bit more, because you've been naughty. [*She hums a little and rummages among her things.*]

RANK [*after a short silence*]: When I sit here together with you like this, completely easy and open, then I don't know—I simply can't imagine—whatever would have become of me if I'd never come into this house.

NORA [*smiling*]: Yes, I really think you feel completely at ease with us.

RANK [*more quietly, staring straight ahead*]: And then to have to go away from it all—

NORA: Nonsense, you're not going away.

RANK [*his voice unchanged*]: —and not even be able to leave some poor show of gratitude behind, scarcely a fleeting regret—no more than a vacant place that anyone can fill.

NORA: And if I asked you now for—? No—

31 **RANK:** For what?

NORA: For a great proof of your friendship—

RANK: Yes, yes?

NORA: No, I mean—for an exceptionally big favor—

30 ▲ **Critical Viewing**
Why might a lady's sewing kit be a valued piece of property for women like Nora and Mrs. Linde? **[Hypothesize]**

Enrichment

More About the Real Nora

In his biography of Ibsen, Halvdan Koht offers some information about Laura Kieler, the young and vivacious woman who served as Ibsen's model for Nora Helmer (see ATE, p. 946).

Mrs. Kieler had a tendency to color facts with imagination. It was this very quality that made her so valuable to Ibsen. She had a warm heart and a desire to help all that suffered. And although she had a sense of the beautiful and a genuine sense of justice, she had no comprehension of the letter of the law and no consideration for the simple facts. In copies of Ibsen's letters that she sent to the author of this book [Koht] there appeared statements that did not correspond to the given dates. When he inquired about this, she answered in all innocence that she had simply exchanged something in one letter with a passage in another letter that she thought was better expressed. She did not understand that it could make any difference.

RANK: Would you really, for once, make me so happy?

NORA: Oh, you haven't the vaguest idea what it is.

RANK: All right, then tell me.

NORA: No, but I can't, Dr. Rank—it's all out of reason. It's advice and help, too—and a favor—

RANK: So much the better. I can't fathom what you're hinting at. Just speak out. Don't you trust me?

NORA: Of course. More than anyone else. You're my best and truest friend, I'm sure. That's why I want to talk to you. All right, then, Dr. Rank: there's something you can help me prevent. You know how deeply, how inexpressibly dearly Torvald loves me; he'd never hesitate a second to give up his life for me.

RANK [*leaning close to her*]: Nora—do you think he's the only one—

NORA [*with a slight start*]: Who—?

RANK: Who'd gladly give up his life for you.

NORA [*heavily*]: I see.

RANK: I swore to myself you should know this before I'm gone. I'll never find a better chance. Yes, Nora, now you know. And also you know now that you can trust me beyond anyone else.

NORA [*rising, natural and calm*]: Let me by.

RANK [*making room for her, but still sitting*]: Nora—

NORA [*in the hall doorway*]: Helene, bring the lamp in. [*Goes over to the stove.*] Ah, dear Dr. Rank, that was really mean of you.

RANK [*getting up*]: That I've loved you just as deeply as somebody else? Was *that* mean?

NORA: No, but that you came out and told me. That was quite unnecessary—

RANK: What do you mean? Have you known—?
[*The MAID comes in with the lamp, sets it on the table, and goes out again.*]

RANK: Nora—Mrs. Helmer—I'm asking you: have you known about it?

NORA: Oh, how can I tell what I know or don't know? Really, I don't know what to say— Why did you have to be so clumsy, Dr. Rank! Everything was so good.

RANK: Well, in any case, you now have the knowledge that my body and soul are at your command. So won't you speak out?

NORA [*looking at him*]: After that?

RANK: Please, just let me know what it is.

NORA: You can't know anything now.

RANK: I have to. You mustn't punish me like this. Give me the chance to do whatever is humanly possible for you.

**Literary Analysis
Characterization in Drama** Why do you think Nora is willing to ask Dr. Rank for money in spite of his impending bankruptcy?

**Literary Analysis
Characterization in Drama** What does Nora's refusal to ask Dr. Rank for money suggest about her personality?

**Reading Check**
What does Dr. Rank claim he would give up for Nora?

A Doll House, Act Two ■ 987

- Have two students read aloud the lines for Dr. Rank and Nora in the bracketed passage. **Ask** students why Dr. Rank has decided to declare his love for Nora.
  Possible response: Dr. Rank knows he will die soon. He may want Nora to know how he feels before she asks a favor.

- **Ask** students the first Literary Analysis question: Why do you think Nora is willing to ask Dr. Rank for money in spite of his impending bankruptcy?
  Answer: Nora is concerned only with obtaining the money to pay her debt.

- **Ask** students whether they are surprised by Nora's actions. Have them consider how she has been characterized thus far in the play.
  Possible response: Nora has grown increasingly unstable and distraught.

33 Literary Analysis
Characterization in Drama

- With a volunteer, read aloud the lines for Dr. Rank and Nora.

- Then, **ask** students the second Literary Analysis question: What does Nora's refusal to ask Dr. Rank for money suggest about her personality?
  Possible responses: Now that Nora knows Dr. Rank loves her, she does not think it would be right to take advantage of him, especially because the money would save her marriage to Torvald. Or, Nora is offended by Dr. Rank's proclamation of love and is punishing them both.

- Review with students the Connecting Literary Elements instruction on p. 974. **Ask:** After this exchange, would you consider Dr. Rank an antagonist? Why or why not?
  Answer: Dr. Rank is an antagonist because his declaration of love prevents Nora from solving her problem.

34 Reading Check

Answer: Dr. Rank claims that he would give up his life for Nora.

Differentiated Instruction Solutions for All Learners

Strategy for Special Needs Students
To help students see the connections between characters' actions and the consequences of those actions, have them use the Cause-and-Effect Flowchart organizer in *Graphic Organizer Transparencies,* p. 275. Work with students to identify key events and their consequences so far. For example, the effect of Dr. Rank's declaration of love is that Nora refuses to ask him for a favor. Challenge students to predict the next consequence of this refusal.

Enrichment for Advanced Readers
Ask students to compare the scene between Nora and Dr. Rank with scenes from other books, plays, stories, or poems. For example, how are Dr. Rank and Nora similar to Shakespeare's Romeo and Juliet? Allow students to meet in small groups to discuss love in literature and to make generalizations about the topic from their comparisons. List each group's generalizations on the board, and discuss how literature reflects society's changing ideologies.

Interpret

- Have two volunteers read aloud the bracketed passage, and then lead a discussion about Nora's hazy concept of love. Note that Nora seems to be saying that although she likes Dr. Rank and the maids in her father's house, she cannot love them.

- **Ask** students why society might dictate Nora's emotions regarding these people.
  Possible response: Nora feels bound by duty to love the people society thinks she is supposed to love, first her father and then her husband. These men take care of her and are responsible for her social status. Society, however, frowns upon a woman loving another man or people of a lower class; thus, Nora is discouraged from loving Dr. Rank and the maids with whom she has lived.

36 **Reading Strategy**

Inferring Beliefs of the Period

- **Ask** students to explain how stage directions might enhance a play's real-life quality.
  Possible response: Stage directions tell actors and actresses how to react to dialogue and how to move on stage. Such actions can enhance a play's real-life quality.

- Have students read the bracketed passage, paying special attention to the stage directions. Then, **ask** students the Reading Strategy question: What common cultural practices are revealed in the stage directions?
  Answer: Visitors did not just enter a house. They waited while a maid took their calling cards to the person they wanted to see.

- To help students realize the impact realistic stage directions have on a scene, list modern-day equivalents for "She whispers to Nora and hands her a calling card." For example, "He heard the doorbell ring, looked through the peephole, and then opened the front door."

NORA: Now there's nothing you can do for me. Besides, actually, I don't need any help. You'll see—it's only my fantasies. That's what it is. Of course! [*Sits in the rocker, looks at him, and smiles.*] What a nice one you are, Dr. Rank. Aren't you a little bit ashamed, now that the lamp is here?

RANK: No, not exactly. But perhaps I'd better go—for good?

NORA: No, you certainly can't do that. You must come here just as you always have. You know Torvald can't do without you.

RANK: Yes, but *you?*

NORA: You know how much I enjoy it when you're here.

RANK: That's precisely what threw me off. You're a mystery to me. So many times I've felt you'd almost rather be with me **35** than with Helmer.

NORA: Yes—you see, there are some people that one loves most and other people that one would almost prefer being with.

RANK: Yes, there's something to that.

NORA: When I was back home, of course I loved Papa most. But I always thought it was so much fun when I could sneak down to the maids' quarters, because they never tried to improve me, and it was always so amusing, the way they talked to each other.

RANK: Aha, so it's *their* place that I've filled.

NORA [*jumping up and going to him*]: Oh, dear, sweet Dr. Rank, that's not what I meant at all. But you can understand that with Torvald it's just the same as with Papa—

[*The* MAID *enters from the hall.*]

36 **MAID:** Ma'am—please! [*She whispers to* NORA *and hands her a calling card.*]

NORA [*glancing at the card.*]: Ah! [*Slips it into her pocket.*]

RANK: Anything wrong?

NORA: No, no, not at all. It's only some—it's my new dress—

RANK: Really? But—there's your dress.

NORA: Oh, that. But this is another one—I ordered it—Torvald mustn't know—

RANK: Ah, now we have the big secret.

NORA: That's right. Just go in with him—he's back in the inner study. Keep him there as long as—

RANK: Don't worry. He won't get away. [*Goes into the study.*]

37 **NORA** [*to the* MAID]: And he's standing waiting in the kitchen?

Reading Strategy
Inferring the Beliefs of the Period What common cultural practices are revealed in the stage directions?

Enrichment

The Norwegian Language
Henrik Ibsen's native Norwegian is one of the North Germanic family of languages, along with Danish, Swedish, and Icelandic. This makes it a close relative of the English language, which, along with Dutch, is a member of the West Germanic family. Norwegian is descended from Old Norse, the language of the Vikings. Because Denmark controlled Norway from 1380 until 1814, Danish heavily influences one version of Norwegian.

Another, newer, version of Norwegian was created in the mid-1800s as an expression of nationalism. Both versions are characterized by a pleasant, singsong quality.

Show students a map of northern Europe, and point out the proximity of the countries whose people speak North and West Germanic languages. If possible, find a recording of Norwegian being spoken, and play it for students.

MAID: Yes, he came up by the back stairs.

NORA: But didn't you tell him somebody was here?

MAID: Yes, but that didn't do any good.

NORA: He won't leave?

MAID: No, he won't go till he's talked with you, ma'am.

NORA: Let him come in, then—but quietly. Helene, don't breathe a word about this. It's a surprise for my husband.

MAID: Yes, yes, I understand— [*Goes out.*]

NORA: This horror—it's going to happen. No, no, no, it can't happen, it mustn't. [*She goes and bolts* HELMER's *door. The* MAID *opens the hall door for* KROGSTAD *and shuts it behind him. He is dressed for travel in a fur coat, boots, and a fur cap.*]

NORA [*going toward him*]: Talk softly. My husband's home.

KROGSTAD: Well, good for him.

NORA: What do you want?

KROGSTAD: Some information.

NORA: Hurry up, then. What is it?

KROGSTAD: You know, of course, that I got my notice.

NORA: I couldn't prevent it, Mr. Krogstad. I fought for you to the bitter end, but nothing worked.

KROGSTAD: Does your husband's love for you run so thin? He knows everything I can expose you to, and all the same he dares to—

NORA: How can you imagine he knows anything about this?

KROGSTAD: Ah, no—I can't imagine it either, now. It's not at all like my fine Torvald Helmer to have so much guts—

NORA: Mr. Krogstad, I demand respect for my husband!

KROGSTAD: Why, of course—all due respect. But since the lady's keeping it so carefully hidden, may I presume to ask if you're also a bit better informed than yesterday about what you've actually done?

NORA: More than you ever could teach me.

KROGSTAD: Yes, I *am* such an awful lawyer.

NORA: What is it you want from me?

KROGSTAD: Just a glimpse of how you are, Mrs. Helmer. I've been thinking about you all day long. A cashier, a night-court scribbler, a—well, a type like me also has a little of what they call a heart, you know.

NORA: Then show it. Think of my children.

KROGSTAD: Did you or your husband ever think of mine? But never mind. I simply wanted to tell you that you don't need to take this thing too seriously. For the present, I'm not proceeding with any action.

Literary Analysis

Characterization in Drama What do Nora's instructions to Helene suggest about Nora's desperation?

Reading Check

Who waits for Nora in the kitchen?

A Doll House, Act Two ■ 989

Differentiated Instruction   Solutions for All Learners

Strategy for Special Needs Students

Remind students that Torvald believes that he has strength and courage, and Nora believes that Torvald will act nobly when he learns of the forgery. Above, Krogstad expresses a lower opinion of Torvald. Have students work in pairs to complete three-column charts, with the headings *Torvald, Nora,* and *Krogstad.* Under the character's name, students should write the person's opinion of Torvald (including Torvald's of himself). Have students revise their charts as they read.

Enrichment for Gifted/Talented Students

Ask each student to write a short monologue from the point of view of Dr. Rank at the moment he goes into the study to see Torvald. Have students consider how Dr. Rank must feel about his approaching death and his declaration of love for Nora. Also, challenge students to use language that sounds like Dr. Rank's speech. Ask volunteers to share their monologues with the class.

---

37 Literary Analysis
Characterization in Drama

• Have two volunteers read aloud the bracketed passage. **Ask** what this exchange makes clear about Krogstad's character.
Answer: Even though Krogstad appears proper, he is improper because he enters the house by the back stairs and refuses to leave without seeing Nora.

• **Ask** students the Literary Analysis question: What do Nora's instructions to Helene suggest about Nora's desperation?
Answer: Nora must be desperate if she talks to a man who behaves rudely.

▶ **Monitor Progress** Have students **identify** the main method of characterization employed in the bracketed passage.
Answer: Comments by Nora and the maid help reveal Krogstad's character.

▶ **Reteach** If students have difficulty understanding methods of characterization, have them use the **Literary Analysis** support, page 103 in *Unit 7 Resources.*

38 Critical Thinking
Analyze

• Tell students to read the bracketed passage independently. Point out that Krogstad initially believes Nora has told her husband about the loan. He apparently reasoned that when Torvald was faced with the possible revelation of Nora's crime, Torvald would keep Krogstad at the bank to avoid scandal.

• **Ask** students what assumption Krogstad must have made when he received his notice.
Answer: Krogstad must have assumed that Torvald did not care what happened to Nora.

• Invite students to **explain** how Ibsen develops Torvald's character in this conversation.
Possible response: Krogstad's perception of Torvald as a man who would sacrifice his wife's reputation suggests that Torvald is not the devoted husband that he and Nora portray him to be.

39 Reading Check

Answer: Krogstad waits for Nora.

40 Critical Thinking

Interpret

- Ask two students to read aloud the lines for Nora and Krogstad in the bracketed passage. Make sure students understand that the "something worse" being discussed is suicide.

- Have students **discuss** whether they think Nora will choose suicide as the way out of her dilemma. Would this choice be consistent with her character? Why or why not? **Possible response:** Nora loves her children too much to commit suicide. On the other hand, Nora is impetuous and misguided enough to commit suicide.

41 Background

Playwriting

People often use sentence fragments, or incomplete sentences, in their everyday conversations. Consequently, the dialogue in a realistic prose drama is likely to be filled with sentence fragments. For example, notice the sentence fragments in the bracketed passages on these facing pages.

If Ibsen had written this dialogue without sentence fragments, characters would not interrupt each other, and the language would have sounded formal and contrived.

42 Critical Viewing

Possible response: The two characters are standing far apart and not facing each other. Both seem very serious.

NORA: Oh no, really! Well—I knew that.

KROGSTAD: Everything can be settled in a friendly spirit. It doesn't have to get around town at all; it can stay just among us three.

NORA: My husband must never know anything of this.

KROGSTAD: How can you manage that? Perhaps you can pay me the balance?

NORA: No, not right now.

KROGSTAD: Or you know some way of raising the money in a day or two?

NORA: No way that I'm willing to use.

KROGSTAD: Well, it wouldn't have done you any good, anyway. If you stood in front of me with a fistful of bills, you still couldn't buy your signature back.

NORA: Then tell me what you're going to do with it.

KROGSTAD: I'll just hold onto it—keep it on file. There's no outsider who'll even get wind of it. So if you've been thinking of taking some desperate step—

NORA: I have.

KROGSTAD: Been thinking of running away from home—

NORA: I have!

KROGSTAD: Or even of something worse—

NORA: How could you guess that?

KROGSTAD: You can drop those thoughts.

NORA: How could you guess I was thinking of *that*?

40 KROGSTAD: Most of us think about *that* at first. I thought about it too, but I discovered I hadn't the courage—

NORA [*lifelessly*]: I don't either.

KROGSTAD [*relieved*]: That's true, you haven't the courage? You too?

NORA: I don't have it—I don't have it.

41 KROGSTAD: It would be terribly stupid, anyway. After that first storm at home blows out, why, then— I have here in my pocket a letter for your husband—

NORA: Telling everything?

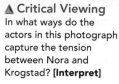

42 ▲ Critical Viewing
In what ways do the actors in this photograph capture the tension between Nora and Krogstad? **[Interpret]**

990 ■ *Romanticism and Realism*

41 ↑

KROGSTAD: As charitably as possible.

NORA [*quickly*]: He mustn't ever get that letter. Tear it up. I'll find some way to get money.

KROGSTAD: Beg pardon, Mrs. Helmer, but I think I just told you—

NORA: Oh, I don't mean the money I owe you. Let me know how much you want from my husband, and I'll manage it.

KROGSTAD: I don't want any money from your husband.

NORA: What do you want, then?

43 ↓

KROGSTAD: I'll tell you what. I want to recoup, Mrs. Helmer; I want to get on in the world—and there's where your husband can help me. For

44 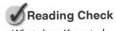 **Reading Check**

What does Krogstad plan to do with the signature Nora forged?

A Doll House, Act Two ■ 991

---

43 Literary Analysis

Characterization in Drama

- Read aloud the bracketed passage. **Ask** students to make a general statement about what the passage reveals about Krogstad's character. **Possible response:** The passage indicates that Krogstad is not the one-dimensional character he at first appears to be.

- Encourage students to **discuss** how their feelings about Krogstad have changed, if at all, after reading this passage. **Possible response:** Krogstad may inspire sympathy after readers learn that he has feelings, goals, and fears as any other person does.

44 Reading Check

Answer: Krogstad plans to keep Nora's forged signature so that he can use it to blackmail Torvald.

Differentiated Instruction Solutions for All Learners

Support for Less Proficient Readers
In scenes where key plot developments take place, students will benefit from hearing a recording of the play. Have them follow along in their textbooks as they listen to the **Listening to Literature Audio CDs.** Then, have students work in pairs or small groups to summarize key scenes throughout the play.

Background for English Learners
Tell students that Ibsen uses many sentence fragments, or incomplete sentences, to make his dialogue more realistic. Remind students that a sentence fragment is a sentence that lacks a subject, a verb, or both. Challenge each student to find at least two examples of sentence fragments in the dialogue in Act Two. Then, have students work alone or in pairs to rewrite the fragments as complete sentences. Ask students to share their work in small groups.

• Remind students that Krogstad
  recently revealed his desire for a
  better position at the bank, not
  money from Nora.

• Have a volunteer read aloud the
  bracketed passage. Point out that,
  at this point, readers know Torvald
  almost as well as Krogstad does.
  Ask students whether they agree
  with Krogstad's assessment that
  Torvald will not protest Krogstad's
  appointment at the bank.
  Possible response: Torvald may
  protest because he dislikes Krogstad
  and wants to maintain control at the
  bank; however, Torvald is probably
  not brave enough to stand up to a
  blackmailer and may agree to
  Krogstad's demands.

• Have students **respond** to the
  Literary Analysis question: Does
  knowing Krogstad's past and his
  plans for the future make him seem
  more or less villainous? Explain.
  Possible response: Krogstad's
  troubled past makes him more
  sympathetic, but his plans, which
  involve blackmailing Torvald and
  Nora, make him more villainous.

46 Critical Thinking
Evaluate

• Remind students that in order to
  evaluate a statement or an action,
  a reader must judge whether the
  statement or action is valid—that is,
  whether it makes sense and is well
  supported.

• Have students independently read
  the bracketed passage. Then, **ask:**
  Do you agree that Torvald has
  forced Krogstad "back to [his]
  own ways"? Why or why not?
  Possible response: Krogstad is
  free to make his own choices in life.
  However, Krogstad would not be
  doing this if Torvald had not
  fired him.

43 a year and a half I've kept myself clean of anything <u>disreputable</u>—all that time struggling with the worst conditions; but I was satisfied, working my way up step by step. Now I've been written right off, and I'm just not in the mood to come crawling back. I tell you, I want to move on. I want to get back in the bank—in a better position. Your husband can set up a job for me—

NORA: He'll never do that!

45 **KROGSTAD:** He'll do it. I know him. He won't dare breathe a word of protest. And once I'm in there together with him, you just wait and see! Inside of a year, I'll be the manager's right-hand man. It'll be Nils Krogstad, not Torvald Helmer, who runs the bank.

NORA: You'll never see the day!

KROGSTAD: Maybe you think you can—

NORA: I have the courage now—for *that.*

KROGSTAD: Oh, you don't scare me. A smart, spoiled lady like you—

NORA: You'll see; you'll see!

KROGSTAD: Under the ice, maybe? Down in the freezing, coal-black water? There, till you float up in the spring, ugly, unrecognizable, with your hair falling out—

NORA: You don't frighten me.

KROGSTAD: Nor do you frighten me. One doesn't do these things, Mrs. Helmer. Besides, what good would it be? I'd still have him safe in my pocket.

NORA: Afterwards? When I'm no longer—?

46 **KROGSTAD:** Are you forgetting that *I'll* be in control then over your final reputation? [NORA *stands speechless, staring at him.*] Good; now I've warned you. Don't do anything stupid. When Helmer's read my letter, I'll be waiting for his reply. And bear in mind that it's your husband himself who's forced me back to my old ways. I'll never forgive him for that. Good-bye, Mrs. Helmer. [*He goes out through the hall.*]

NORA [*goes to the hall door, opens it a crack, and listens*]: He's gone. Didn't leave the letter. Oh no, no, that's impossible too! [*Opening the door more and more.*] What's that? He's standing outside—not going downstairs. He's thinking it over? Maybe he'll—? [*A letter falls in the mailbox; then* KROGSTAD'*s footsteps are heard, dying away down a flight of stairs.* NORA *gives a muffled cry and runs over toward the sofa table. A short pause.*] In the mailbox. [*Slips warily over to the hall door.*] It's lying there. Torvald, Torvald—now we're lost!

MRS. LINDE [*entering with the costume from the room, left*]: There now, I can't see anything else to mend. Perhaps you'd like to try—

NORA [*in a hoarse whisper*]: Kristine, come here.

MRS. LINDE [*tossing the dress on the sofa*]: What's wrong? You look upset.

Vocabulary Builder
disreputable (dis rep′ yōō tə
bəl) *adj.* not fit to be seen
or approved

Literary Analysis
**Characterization in
Drama** Does knowing
Krogstad's past and his
plans for the future make
him seem more or less
villainous? Explain.

Enrichment

"National" Writers and Poets

To many Norwegians, the plays of Henrik Ibsen are a source of great national pride. He is one of the authors who are considered "national" writers because, in the opinion of many of his fellow Norwegians, he expressed the hopes, fears, and characters of his fellow citizens better than anyone else.

Other countries also have national writers. Perhaps some of the best known are William Shakespeare and Charles Dickens in England, James Joyce and William Butler Yeats in Ireland,

Rabindranath Tagore in India, Honoré de Balzac and Victor Hugo in France, Dante in Italy, Nazlm Hikmet in Turkey, Johann Wolfgang von Goethe in Germany, Pablo Neruda in Chile, and Leo Tolstoy and Anton Chekhov in Russia.

Ask students which writers might best be called national writers in the United States. Have them give reasons for their choices. Students may suggest Emily Dickinson, Mark Twain, Walt Whitman, Toni Morrison, or William Faulkner.

NORA: Come here. See that letter? *There!* Look—through the glass in the mailbox.

MRS. LINDE: Yes, yes, I see it.

NORA: That letter's from Krogstad—

MRS. LINDE: Nora—it's Krogstad who loaned you the money!

NORA: Yes, and now Torvald will find out everything.

MRS. LINDE: Believe me, Nora, it's best for both of you.

NORA: There's more you don't know. I forged a name.

MRS. LINDE: But for heaven's sake—?

NORA: I only want to tell you that, Kristine, so that you can be my witness.

MRS. LINDE: Witness? Why should I—?

NORA: If I should go out of my mind—it could easily happen—

MRS. LINDE: Nora!

NORA: Or anything else occurred—so I couldn't be present here—

MRS. LINDE: Nora, Nora, you aren't yourself at all!

(47) NORA: And someone should try to take on the whole weight, all of the guilt, you follow me—

MRS. LINDE: Yes, of course, but why do you think—?

NORA: Then you're the witness that it isn't true, Kristine. I'm very much myself; my mind right now is perfectly clear; and I'm telling you: nobody else has known about this; I alone did everything. Remember that.

MRS. LINDE: I will. But I don't understand all this.

NORA: Oh, how could you ever understand it? It's the miracle now that's going to take place.

MRS. LINDE: The miracle?

NORA: Yes, the miracle. But it's so awful, Kristine. It mustn't take place, not for anything in the world.

MRS. LINDE: I'm going right over and talk with Krogstad.

(48) NORA: Don't go near him; he'll do you some terrible harm!

MRS. LINDE: There was a time once when he'd gladly have done anything for me.

NORA: He?

MRS. LINDE: Where does he live?

NORA: Oh, how do I know? Yes. [*Searches in her pocket.*] Here's his card. But the letter, the letter—!

HELMER [*from the study, knocking on the door*]: Nora!

NORA [*with a cry of fear*]: Oh! What is it? What do you want?

Reading Strategy
Inferring Beliefs of the Period What social realities of the time would keep Mrs. Linde from mentioning her prior relationship with Krogstad?

(49) ✓ **Reading Check**
What does Krogstad leave for Torvald?

A Doll House, Act Two ■ 993

---

50 **Literary Analysis**

Characterization in Drama

• Have students read the bracketed passage. Explain that mailboxes at the time of the play often had locks on them, even though the mailboxes were not in public spaces.

• **Ask** students the Literary Analysis question: Why might Torvald carry the mailbox key instead of Nora? **Answer:** Torvald is responsible for household business and financial matters, so the mail would be most relevant to him.

• Ask students whether they think that had Nora wanted a key for the mailbox, she might have been able to get one. Guide students to see that Ibsen probably gave the only key to Torvald to show his role as the controlling adult in the household.

51 **Critical Thinking**

Analyze

• Read aloud the bracketed passage. Guide students to realize that Nora is once again flattering Torvald—this time in order to keep him away from the mailbox.

• **Ask** students to discuss why Nora is so easily able to convince Torvald that she is nervous about the party. **Possible response:** Nora is a good actress, as well as desperate, and the physical symptoms of fear and nervousness look the same; Torvald is so self-absorbed and confident in his own observations that he is willing to believe her when what she says matches his own beliefs.

HELMER: Now, now, don't be so frightened. We're not coming in. You locked the door—are you trying on the dress?

NORA: Yes, I'm trying it. I'll look just beautiful, Torvald.

MRS. LINDE [*who has read the card*]: He's living right around the corner.

NORA: Yes, but what's the use? We're lost. The letter's in the box.

50 **MRS. LINDE:** And your husband has the key?

NORA: Yes, always.

MRS. LINDE: Krogstad can ask for his letter back unread; he can find some excuse—

NORA: But it's just this time that Torvald usually—

MRS. LINDE: Stall him. Keep him in there. I'll be back as quick as I can. [*She hurries out through the hall entrance.*]

NORA [*goes to* HELMER'*s door, opens it, and peers in*]: Torvald!

HELMER [*from the inner study*]: Well—does one dare set foot in one's own living room at last? Come on, Rank, now we'll get a look— [*In the doorway.*] But what's this?

NORA: What, Torvald dear?

HELMER: Rank had me expecting some grand masquerade.

RANK [*in the doorway*]: That was my impression, but I must have been wrong.

NORA: No one can admire me in my splendor—not till tomorrow.

HELMER: But Nora, dear, you look so exhausted. Have you practiced too hard?

NORA: No, I haven't practiced at all yet.

HELMER: You know, it's necessary—

NORA: Oh, it's absolutely necessary, Torvald. But I can't get anywhere without your help. I've forgotten the whole thing completely.

HELMER: Ah, we'll soon take care of that.

51 **NORA:** Yes, take care of me, Torvald, please! Promise me that? Oh, I'm so nervous. That big party— You must give up everything this evening for me. No business—don't even touch your pen. Yes? Dear Torvald, promise?

HELMER: It's a promise. Tonight I'm totally at your service—you little helpless thing. Hm—but first there's one thing I want to— [*Goes toward the hall door.*]

NORA: What are you looking for?

HELMER: Just to see if there's any mail.

NORA: No, no, don't do that, Torvald!

994 ■ *Romanticism and Realism*

Enrichment

Ibsen's Influence on James Joyce

James Joyce had great admiration for Ibsen's plays. In fact, Joyce's play *Exiles* (1918) reflects the influence of Ibsen. In *Joyce and Ibsen,* critic B. J. Tysdahl writes:

In appearance *Exiles* is like one of Ibsen's realistic dramas from beginning to end. Joyce's stage directions begin, as if copied from *A Doll's House* . . . , with a minute description of the drawing room; then follows, in a new paragraph, a sketch of the persons we see on stage.

Throughout the play, stage directions are frequent, often in the form of an adverb to indicate the tone of speech. Behind these outer resemblances lies the fact that, like Ibsen, Joyce deliberately chose the present time and the ordinary parlor as a setting. . . . Joyce had praised the Norwegian dramatist for his courage to put life—real life—on the stage, without the conventions or embellishments that had often served to veil reality.

HELMER: Now what?

NORA: Torvald, please. There isn't any.

HELMER: Let me look, though. [*Starts out.* NORA, *at the piano, strikes the first notes of the tarantella.* HELMER, *at the door, stops.*] Aha!

NORA: I can't dance tomorrow if I don't practice with you.

HELMER [*going over to her*]: Nora dear, are you really so frightened?

NORA: Yes, so terribly frightened. Let me practice right now; there's still time before dinner. Oh, sit down and play for me, Torvald. Direct me. Teach me, the way you always have.

HELMER: Gladly, if it's what you want. [*Sits at the piano.*]

NORA [*snatches the tambourine up from the box, then a long, varicolored shawl, which she throws around herself, where-upon she springs forward and cries out*]: Play for me now! Now I'll dance! [HELMER *plays and* NORA *dances.* RANK *stands behind* HELMER *at the piano and looks on.*]

HELMER [*as he plays*]: Slower. Slow down.

NORA: Can't change it.

HELMER: Not so violent, Nora!

NORA: Has to be just like this.

HELMER [*stopping*]: No, no, that won't do at all.

NORA [*laughing and swinging her tambourine*]: Isn't that what I told you?

RANK: Let me play for her.

HELMER [*getting up*]: Yes, go on. I can teach her more easily then. [RANK *sits at the piano and plays;* NORA *dances more and more wildly.* HELMER *has stationed himself by the stove and repeatedly gives her directions; she seems not to hear them; her hair loosens and falls over her shoulders; she does not notice, but goes on dancing.* MRS. LINDE *enters.*]

MRS. LINDE [*standing dumbfounded at the door*]: Ah—!

NORA [*still dancing*]: See what fun, Kristine!

HELMER: But Nora darling, you dance as if your life were at stake.

NORA: And it is.

HELMER: Rank, stop! This is pure madness. Stop it, I say! [RANK *breaks off playing, and* NORA *halts abruptly.*]

HELMER [*going over to her*]: I never would have believed it. You've forgotten everything I taught you.

NORA [*throwing away the tambourine*]: You see for yourself.

Literature in Context

52 History Connection

The Tarantella

Henrik Ibsen had important dramatic reasons for choosing this specific dance for Nora to perform. Both the dance and the tarantula spider were named for the southern Italian city of Taranto. In the 1400s, it was believed that the bite of the taran-tula was deadly, and the only way to counteract its fatal bite was to dance wildly to distribute the poi-son throughout the body and sweat it out. The folk dance itself features quick steps, teasing behavior, and a tambourine.

Associated with the tarantella was tarantism, a form of mass hys-teria in which the victims, thought to be bitten by the tarantula, danced themselves into a frenzy. Two other forms of this hysteria were the St. Vitus dance, a bizarre twitching of seemingly possessed people, and the dance of death, in which a skeleton led a line of danc-ers across the countryside. Histori-ans believe all three dances may have been a response to the hor-rors of the Black Death, the plague that killed a third of all people in Europe in the 1300s. For Nora, the frenetic dancing of the tarantella releases the fear and desperation that torture her as Torvald comes closer to discovering her secrets.

Connect to the Literature

Why do you think Nora insists that she cannot slow her dancing down?

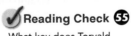

Reading Check 55

What key does Torvald always carry?

A Doll House, Act Two ■ 995

Characterization in Drama

- Have two volunteers read aloud the lines for Nora and Torvald in the bracketed passage.

- Then, **ask** students to respond to the Literary Analysis item: Explain how Nora's urgent pleading reflects her attitude toward her present situation.
  Answer: Nora believes that she is losing control of her life, so her behavior is becoming increasingly desperate.

- Point out that Dr. Rank is the one who finally persuades Torvald to leave the letter in the mailbox until tomorrow when he says, "You shouldn't deny her."

- **Ask** students what Dr. Rank's comment says about him and his feelings for Nora.
  Possible response: Dr. Rank wants to indulge Nora because he loves her. Also, he may be concerned, as a doctor, about Nora's frantic state.

57 **Critical Thinking**

Interpret

- Have a volunteer read aloud the bracketed passage.

- Have students respond to the sudden change in Nora's disposition. **Ask:** What does this change reveal about Nora's emotional state?
  Possible response: The sudden change reveals the instability and fragility of Nora's emotional state.

HELMER: Well, there's certainly room for instruction here.

NORA: Yes, you see how important it is. You've got to teach me to the very last minute. Promise me that, Torvald?

HELMER: You can bet on it.

NORA: You mustn't, either today or tomorrow, think about anything else but me; you mustn't open any letters—or the mailbox—

56 **HELMER:** Ah, it's still the fear of that man—

NORA: Oh yes, yes, that too.

HELMER: Nora, it's written all over you—there's already a letter from him out there.

NORA: I don't know. I guess so. But you mustn't read such things now; there mustn't be anything ugly between us before it's all over.

RANK [*quietly to* HELMER]: You shouldn't deny her.

HELMER [*putting his arm around her*]: The child can have her way. But tomorrow night, after you've danced—

NORA: Then you'll be free.

MAID [*in the doorway, right*]: Ma'am, dinner is served.

NORA: We'll be wanting champagne, Helene.

MAID: Very good, ma'am. [*Goes out.*]

HELMER: So—a regular banquet, hm?

NORA: Yes, a banquet—champagne till daybreak! [*Calling out.*] And some macaroons, Helene. Heaps of them—just this once.

HELMER [*taking her hands*]: Now, now, now—no hysterics. Be my own little lark again.

NORA: Oh, I will soon enough. But go on in—and you, Dr. Rank. Kristine, help me put up my hair.

RANK [*whispering, as they go*]: There's nothing wrong—really wrong, is there?

HELMER: Oh, of course not. It's nothing more than this childish anxiety I was telling you about. [*They go out, right.*]

NORA: Well?

MRS. LINDE: Left town.

NORA: I could see by your face.

MRS. LINDE: He'll be home tomorrow evening. I wrote him a note.

57 **NORA:** You shouldn't have. Don't try to stop anything now. After all, it's a wonderful joy, this waiting here for the miracle.

Assessment Practice

Analyzing Literary Language

(For more practice, see *Test Preparation Workbook*, p. 43.)

Many standardized tests require students to analyze the literary language of a text. To help students practice this skill, use the following sample test item.

> Poor *little* Nora, with no other mother but me.

The word *little* reveals the speaker's desire to—

A make fun of Nora's height.

B make Nora unhappy.

C comfort Nora.

D insult Nora's real mother.

The correct response is **C**. The person who speaks this sentence describes herself as Nora's mother, so she is probably not trying to make fun of Nora, make her unhappy, or insult her real mother. Also, because *poor* precedes *little*, the word *little* probably refers to Nora's emotional state, not her height.

MRS. LINDE: What is it you're waiting for?

NORA: Oh, you can't understand that. Go in to them; I'll be along in a moment. [MRS. LINDE *goes into the dining room.* NORA *stands a short while as if composing herself; then she looks at her watch.*]

NORA: Five. Seven hours to midnight. Twenty-four hours to the midnight after, and then the tarantella's done. Seven and twenty-four? Thirty-one hours to live.

HELMER [*in the doorway, right*]: What's become of the little lark?

NORA [*going toward him with open arms*]: Here's your lark!

Critical Reading

1. **Respond:** What would you advise Nora to do about her dilemma? Why?
2. **(a) Recall:** How does Nora describe her relationship with Dr. Rank? **(b) Recall:** What role did Anne-Marie fulfill for Nora in the past? **(c) Analyze:** What do Dr. Rank and Anne-Marie offer Nora that Torvald does not?
3. **(a) Recall:** What does Dr. Rank confess to Nora? **(b) Speculate:** What favor do you think Nora might have asked of Dr. Rank? **(c) Analyze:** Why do you think she changes her mind? **(d) Take a Stand:** Do you think Nora made the right decision? Why or why not?
4. **(a) Recall:** What does Krogstad say about Torvald? **(b) Infer:** What opinion of Torvald does Krogstad seem to have?
5. **(a) Interpret:** What does Nora mean when she says she has thirty-one hours left to live? **(b) Speculate:** What "miracle" do you think Nora hopes for at the end of the act? Explain.
6. **(a) Compare and Contrast:** Compare and contrast the situations of Dr. Rank, Krogstad, Torvald, and Nora as Act Two ends. **(b) Assess:** Of these four characters, which one seems most likely to experience an improved situation in the near future? **(c) Support:** Identify details in Act Two that help explain your answer.
7. **(a) Make a Judgment:** Is Mrs. Linde a loyal friend to Nora? **(b) Support:** Support your answer with evidence from the play.
8. **Extend:** What lessons can be learned about personal relationships from the problems facing Nora and Torvald?

Go Online
Author Link

For: More about Henrik Ibsen
Visit: www.PHSchool.com
Web Code: ete-9710

A Doll House, Act Two ■ 997

Go Online For additional information about
Author Link Henrik Ibsen, have students type in
the Web Code, then select *I* from the alphabet, and
then select Henrik Ibsen.

Apply the Skills

A Doll House, Act Two

Literary Analysis
Characterization in Drama

1. (a) Using a chart like the one below, track the **characterization** of Nora through descriptions of her behavior, the comments she makes, and comments made about her by other characters.

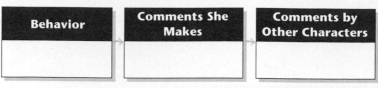

(b) Based on your findings, what conclusions can you draw about Nora?

2. When Dr. Rank says, "Those who go away are soon forgotten," what do we learn about his character?

3. Identify three details in Act Two that suggest that Krogstad was once a decent man.

Connecting Literary Elements

4. Which details in the play—or in your response to it—confirm that Nora is the **protagonist** of this work?

5. (a) In what way does Nora act as an **antagonist** to herself? (b) Does this dual nature make her character more or less realistic? Explain.

6. (a) Besides money, what does Krogstad want from the Helmers? (b) Is Krogstad a threat to Nora physically, mentally, or emotionally? Explain.

Reading Strategy
Inferring Beliefs of the Period

7. Based on the type of work that Mrs. Linde, Anne-Marie, and Nora are qualified to do, what can you **infer about beliefs of the period** regarding the importance of educating women?

8. (a) What does Nora see as her most important role in life? (b) How does this reflect the attitudes of her time?

Extend Understanding

9. **Career Connection:** If you were a judge, whom would you punish more severely—Nora, for forging her father's signature, or Krogstad, for blackmailing the Helmers? Why?

998 ■ *Romanticism and Realism*

Build Language Skills

Vocabulary Lesson

Word Analysis: Latin Prefix *re-*

The prefix *re-*, which means "again" or "back," can help you define many words. For example, the Latin word *tribuere* means "to pay," and *retribution* can be defined as "payback for evil done." Match each word in the left column with its definition in the right column.

1. reproach   **a.** to restore
2. reinstate   **b.** to accuse

Spelling Strategy

The long *a* sound can be spelled in several different ways—for example, *ei (deign)*, *ai (train)*, *ey (they)*, *a (apron)*, and *ay (essay)*. Complete the spelling of each word below.

1. ob___   2. del___   3. b___by

Vocabulary Builder: Context

Explain why each statement is true or false.

1. An *impulsive* shopper buys without first considering his or her budget.
2. An employee seeks *retribution* when awarded a day off from work.
3. A library is a place for *proclaiming* your thoughts to all of the patrons.
4. For their *disreputable* behavior, criminals are sent to prison.
5. A sleepy child finds a warm bed *intolerable*.
6. Many consider it *tactless* to compliment a friend on her new clothes.
7. *Excruciating* pain in a tooth would need a dentist's immediate care.

Grammar and Style Lesson

Commas After Introductory Words

Use commas to set off a mild interjection or another interrupter that introduces a sentence.

Examples: "Oh, of course not. . . ."

"Now, now, don't be frightened. . . ."

Practice Add commas to set off introductory words. If a sentence is correct as is, write *Correct*.

1. Hey did you ever see *A Doll House*?
2. Yes I saw a film version of the stage play.
3. Well which actors played the major roles?
4. I must say I found the play very disturbing.
5. Perhaps but you could learn a great deal from the play.

Writing Application Using dialogue, write a brief scene that involves two or more characters. Use commas to set off at least three introductory words.

Extend Your Learning

Writing Put yourself in Krogstad's place and write the **letter** that he mailed to Torvald. Proofread your letter, prepare a final copy, and share it with your classmates.

Listening and Speaking With a group, prepare a **radio play** based on a scene from Act Two. Use language that is appropriate to each character. **[Group Activity]**

WG Prentice Hall Writing and Grammar Connection: Platinum Level, Chapter 28, Section 2

A Doll House, Act Two ■ 999

Assessment Resources

The following resources can be used to assess students' knowledge and skills.

Unit 7 Resources
   Selection Test A, pp. 109–111
   Selection Test B, pp. 112–114

General Resources
   Rubric for Speaking: Narrative Account, p. 88

Go Online Students may use the **Self-test** to Assessment prepare for **Selection Test A** or **Selection Test B**.

---

❶ Vocabulary Lesson

Word Analysis: Latin Prefix *re-*

1. b   2. a

Spelling Strategy

1. obey   2. delay   3. baby

Vocabulary Builder: Context

1. True. Impulsive shoppers act suddenly without thinking.
2. False. An employee seeks retribution when treated badly.
3. False. One is quiet in a library.
4. True. Such behavior is punished.
5. False. A warm bed is cozy.
6. False. Complimenting is polite.
7. True. Severe pain needs attention.

❷ Grammar and Style Lesson

1. Hey, did you ever see . . . ?
2. Yes, I saw a film version. . . .
3. Well, which actors . . . ?
4. Correct
5. Perhaps, but you could learn. . . .

Writing Application

Possible response:

Mrs. Linde: Oh, Nora. You look lovely.
Nora: Really, you're so kind. Well, let's go.

WG Writing and Grammar Platinum Level

For support in teaching the Grammar and Style Lesson, use Chapter 28, Section 2.

❸ Listening and Speaking

- Tell students that radio plays include many sound effects.
- Use the Speaking: Narrative Account rubric in *General Resources*, p. 88, to evaluate students' work.
- The **Support for Extend Your Learning** page (*Unit 7 Resources*, p. 107) provides guided note-taking opportunities to help students complete the Extend Your Learning activities.

Go Online Have students type in the Research Web Code for another research activity.

Standard Course of Study

Goal 3: FOUNDATIONS OF ARGUMENT

FA.3.01.5   Present data about controversial issues in multiple forms.

FA.3.03.2   Use reason and evidence to prove a given point.

Goal 4: CRITICAL THINKING

CT.4.02.2   Use specific references from texts to show theme.

Goal 5: LITERATURE

LT.5.01.3   Analyze literary devices and explain their effect on the work of world literature.

LT.5.03.5   Summarize key events and points from world literature.

Goal 6: GRAMMAR AND USAGE

GU.6.01.3   Use recognition strategies to understand vocabulary and exact word choice.

Step-by-Step Teaching Guide	Pacing Guide
PRETEACH	
• Administer Vocabulary and Reading Warm-ups as necessary.	5 min.
• Engage students' interest with the motivation activity.	5 min.
• Read and discuss background features. **FT**	10 min.
• Introduce the Literary Analysis Skill: Theme. **FT**	5 min.
• Introduce the Reading Strategy: Recognizing Dramatic Tension. **FT**	
• Prepare students to read by teaching the selection vocabulary. **FT**	10 min.
TEACH	
• Informally monitor comprehension while students read independently or in groups. **FT**	30 min.
• Monitor students' comprehension with the Reading Check notes.	as students read
• Reinforce vocabulary with Vocabulary Builder notes.	as students read
• Develop students' understanding of theme with the Literary Analysis annotations. **FT**	5 min.
• Develop students' ability to recognize dramatic tension with the Reading Strategy annotations. **FT**	5 min.
ASSESS/EXTEND	
• Assess students' comprehension and mastery of the Literary Analysis and Reading Strategy by having them answer the Apply the Skills questions. **FT**	15 min.
• Have students complete the Vocabulary Lesson and the Grammar and Style Lesson. **FT**	15 min.
• Apply students' ability to revise to remove unnecessary words and phrases by using the Writing Lesson. **FT**	45 min. or homework
• Apply students' understanding by using one or more of the Extend Your Learning activities.	20–90 min. or homework
• Administer Selection Test A or Selection Test B. **FT**	15 min.

Resources

Print

Unit 7 Resources

Transparency

Graphic Organizer Transparencies

Print

Reader's Notebook [L2]

Reader's Notebook: Adapted Version [L1]

Reader's Notebook: English Learner's Version [EL]

Unit 7 Resources

Technology

Listening to Literature Audio CDs [L2, EL]

Print

Unit 7 Resources

General Resources

Technology

Go Online: Research [L3]
Go Online: Self-test [L3]
ExamView®, **Test Bank [L3]**

Choosing Resources for Differentiated Instruction

[L1] Special Needs Students

[L2] Below-Level Students

[L3] All Students

[L4] Advanced Students

[EL] English Learners

For Vocabulary and Reading Warm-ups and for Selection Tests, **A** signifies "less challenging" and **B** "more challenging." For Graphic Organizer transparencies, **A** signifies "not filled in" and **B** "filled in."

FT Fast Track Instruction: To move the lesson more quickly, use the strategies and activities identified with **FT**.

Scaffolding for Less Proficient and Advanced Students

The leveled Critical Thinking questions after selections progress in the levels of thinking required to answer them. To address the needs of your different students, you may use the (a) level questions for your less proficient students and the (b) level questions with your on-level and advanced students. The occasional (c) level questions are appropriate for your advanced students.

Teacher EXPRESS — PRENTICE HALL — **Plan · Teach · Assess** Use this complete suite of powerful teaching tools to make lesson planning and testing quicker and easier.

Student EXPRESS — PRENTICE HALL — **Learn · Study · Succeed** Use the interactive textbook (online and on CD-ROM) to make selections and activities come alive with audio and video support and interactive questions.

Benchmark

After students have completed reading *A Doll House,* administer **Benchmark Test 9** (*Unit 7 Resources,* **pp. 139–144**). If the Benchmark Test reveals that some of the students need further work, use the **Interpretation Guide** to determine the appropriate reteaching page in the **Reading Kit** and on **Success Tracker.**

 Go Online **Professional Development** **For:** Information about Lexiles **Visit:** www.PHSchool.com **Web Code:** eue-1111

❶ Literary Analysis

Theme

- Ask students to discuss the plots of their favorite books or movies. Tell them to explain what lessons or insights the work tries to get readers or viewers to consider in their own lives or apply to the world in general.

- Tell students that these universal ideas are called themes and that themes help readers think and talk about works. Give them the example of *A Doll House,* and **ask** them to identify general points the play raises about families and marriage.
  Possible response: Themes include the following: parents' sins and mistakes affect children; honesty is important in relationships; good intentions have limits.

- Tell students that foreshadowing can often help them identify themes; a suggested event or condition may emerge as a theme.

❷ Reading Strategy

Recognizing Dramatic Tension

- Explain the difference between suspense and dramatic tension: readers feel suspense when something frightening or damaging is about to happen. They feel dramatic tension as concern about what may eventually happen.

- Give students a copy of **Reading Strategy Graphic Organizer A,** p. 175 in *Graphic Organizer Transparencies.* Have them use it to record moments of conflict or mystery as they read Act Three.

Vocabulary Builder

- Pronounce each vocabulary word for students, and read the definition as a class. Have students identify any words with which they are already familiar.

Build Skills | *Drama*

A Doll House, Act Three

❶ Literary Analysis

Theme

A **theme** is a central message, idea, or insight into life that is revealed by a literary work. In a drama, a theme may be stated directly or suggested through dialogue and actions. A complex play like *A Doll House* may have several themes:

- Real love has little to do with physical beauty or social status.
- A successful relationship is based on trust, equality, individuality.
- Every person has the right to individuality.

As you read Act Three, pay close attention to how the characters' actions or dialogue convey the theme.

Connecting Literary Elements

To prepare readers to recognize key themes, Ibsen uses **foreshadowing,** a technique of incorporating details that suggest events or conditions to come. In Act Two, for example, Nora tells Torvald that he will soon be free, but she does not indicate from what he will be free. The outcome is revealed in Act Three. Note how foreshadowing keeps you guessing.

❷ Reading Strategy

Recognizing Dramatic Tension

Dramatic tension is the sense of suspense that an audience feels while watching a drama unfold. To **recognize dramatic tension,** monitor the anticipation you feel while reading each scene. Ask questions such as these:

- Why are these characters in conflict with one another?
- In what way are the stakes being raised, making it clear that the protagonist stands to lose more and more as the play progresses?

Record moments of conflict or mystery in a chart like the one shown. For each one, write a question to reflect the suspense you experience in that moment.

Vocabulary Builder

calculating (kal´ kyoo lāt´ iŋ) *adj.* shrewd or cunning (p. 1002)

evasions (ē vā´ zhənz) *n.* attempts to avoid duties or questions (p. 1004)

naturalistic (nach´ ər əl is´ tik) *adj.* faithful to nature (p. 1006)

proprieties (prō prī´ ə tēz) *n.* conformities with what is considered fitting, suitable, or proper (p. 1006)

hypocrite (hip´ ə krit´) *n.* someone who merely pretends to be virtuous (p. 1013)

grafter (graft´ ər) *n.* someone who takes advantage of his or her position to gain money or property dishonestly (p. 1013)

bewildered (bē wil´ dərd) *adj.* puzzled; confused (p. 1015)

Standard Course of Study
- Analyze literary devices and explain their effect on the work of world literature. (LT.5.01.3)
- Summarize key events and points from world literature. (LT.5.03.5)

Moment of Conflict or Mystery
Mrs. Linde asks Krogstad to speak with her about Nora's debt.

↓

Question
Will Mrs. Linde reveal Nora's desperation?

1000 ■ Romanticism and Realism

Differentiated Instruction — Solutions for All Learners

Support for Special Needs Students

Have students complete the **Preview** and **Build Skills** pages for *A Doll House,* Act Three in the *Reader's Notebook: Adapted Version.* These pages provide a selection summary, an abbreviated presentation of the reading and literary skills, and the graphic organizer on the **Build Skills** page in the student book.

Support for Less Proficient Readers

Have students complete the **Preview** and **Build Skills** pages for *A Doll House,* Act Three in the *Reader's Notebook.* These pages provide a selection summary, an abbreviated presentation of the reading and literary skills, and the graphic organizer on the **Build Skills** page in the student book.

Support for English Learners

Have students complete the **Preview** and **Build Skills** pages for *A Doll House,* Act Three in the *Reader's Notebook: English Learner's Version.* These pages provide a selection summary, an abbreviated presentation of the skills, additional contextual vocabulary, and the graphic organizer on the **Build Skills** page in the student book.

Review and Anticipate

In Act Two, Torvald's misgivings prompt him to fire Krogstad in spite of Nora's pleas to retain him. Not to be bested, Krogstad arrives with a letter for Torvald that reveals Nora's deception. Krogstad plans to blackmail Torvald into giving him back his job at the bank and leaves the letter in the Helmers' locked mailbox.

Desperate to protect her home and marriage, Nora exhausts every available tactic to change Krogstad's mind and to prevent Torvald from reading the letter. Will Nora salvage Torvald's good name or allow him to take the blame for her actions? What, if anything, will she learn from her mistakes? As you read, look for answers to these questions in the conclusion to Ibsen's *A Doll House*.

❶ ACT THREE

Same scene. The table, with chairs around it, has been moved to the center of the room. A lamp on the table is lit. The hall door stands open. Dance music drifts down from the floor above. MRS. LINDE *sits at the table, absently paging through a book, trying to read, but apparently unable to focus her thoughts. Once or twice she pauses, tensely listening for a sound at the outer entrance.*

MRS. LINDE [*glancing at her watch*]: Not yet—and there's hardly any time left. If only he's not—[*Listening again.*] Ah, there he is. [*She goes out in the hall and cautiously opens the outer door. Quiet footsteps are heard on the stairs. She whispers.*] Come in. Nobody's here.

KROGSTAD [*in the doorway*]: I found a note from you at home. What's back of all this?

MRS. LINDE: I just *had* to talk to you.

KROGSTAD: Oh? And it just *had* to be here in this house?

MRS. LINDE: At my place it was impossible; my room hasn't a private entrance. Come in; we're all alone. The maid's asleep, and the Helmers are at the dance upstairs.

KROGSTAD [*entering the room*]: Well, well, the Helmers are dancing tonight? Really?

MRS. LINDE: Why not?

KROGSTAD: How true—why not?

MRS. LINDE: All right, Krogstad, let's talk.

Reading Strategy
Recognizing Dramatic Tension What effect does time have on the dramatic tension in this scene?

❸ ✔ **Reading Check**
Who left a note for Krogstad at his home?

A Doll House, Act Three ■ 1001

TEACH

Facilitate Understanding

To help students understand and appreciate the play, highlight the difference between the status of women today and their status at the time the play was written. Tell students that the women of Nora's time had fewer opportunities than women have today. Women like Nora were expected to devote their lives to their husbands and families. After you have provided students with a sense of the changes in the status of women, have the class discuss how the play might be different had it been written today.

❶ About the Selection

As the events of the final act unfold, the approaching catastrophe comes nearer. Torvald's reaction to Nora's crime, long hinted at, is revealed; and Nora's response will surprise many readers.

❷ Reading Strategy

Recognizing Dramatic Tension

• Tell students that several clues in the stage directions suggest Mrs. Linde's anxiety. **Challenge** students to identify them.
Possible response: Mrs. Linde is distracted from her reading; she listens for someone at the door; when Krogstad arrives, she speaks in a whisper.

• **Ask** students the Reading Strategy question: What effect does time have on the dramatic tension in this scene?
Answer: Because Mrs. Linde and Krogstad have only a few minutes to talk, their conversation seems urgent.

❸ Reading Check

Answer: Mrs. Linde left a note at Krogstad's home.

Differentiated Instruction Solutions for All Learners

Accessibility at a Glance

	A Doll House, Act Three
Context	Torvald reacts to Nora's deception and crime, and she makes a life-changing decision.
Language	Syntax: sentence fragments, exclamatory and interrogative sentences
Concept Level	Accessible (Every person has a right to individuality. Trust and equality are important to relationships.)
Literary Merit	Act Three presents superb dramatic tension and Nora's metamorphosis.
Lexile	NP
Overall Rating	Average

Make a Judgment

- Read aloud the bracketed passage.
- Make sure that students understand the meaning of the vocabulary word *calculating*. Have them read the definition in the margin.
- Then, **ask:** Do you think Mrs. Linde's behavior can be characterized as calculating?
  Possible response: Some students may think that Mrs. Linde has been calculating in the way she appeared at the Helmers' house and obtained a job, but others might claim that she is simply trying to provide for herself.

❺ Literary Analysis

Theme and Foreshadowing

- Have two volunteers read aloud the bracketed passage.
- Challenge students to see that Mrs. Linde's story reinforces one of the themes Ibsen has revealed in early acts: that women must make sacrifices for their families, often at the expense of their own happiness.
- **Ask** students to explain what Mrs. Linde sacrificed to save her family.
  Possible response: She gave up her attachment to Krogstad to marry a man who could support her family.
- Point out that Mrs. Linde's past feelings for Krogstad may affect or foreshadow her actions now.
- Then, **ask** the Literary Analysis question: What action on Mrs. Linde's part might these words foreshadow?
  Possible response: Mrs. Linde's statement that "help may be near" may foreshadow an arrangement with Krogstad.

KROGSTAD: Do we two have anything more to talk about?

MRS. LINDE: We have a great deal to talk about.

KROGSTAD: I wouldn't have thought so.

MRS. LINDE: No, because you've never understood me, really.

❹ **KROGSTAD:** Was there anything more to understand—except what's all too common in life? A <u>calculating</u> woman throws over a man the moment a better catch comes by.

MRS. LINDE: You think I'm so thoroughly calculating? You think I broke it off lightly?

KROGSTAD: Didn't you?

MRS. LINDE: Nils—is that what you really thought?

KROGSTAD: If you cared, then why did you write me the way you did?

MRS. LINDE: What else could I do? If I had to break off with you, then it was my job as well to root out everything you felt for me.

KROGSTAD [*wringing his hands*]: So that was it. And this—all this, simply for money!

MRS. LINDE: Don't forget I had a helpless mother and two small brothers. We couldn't wait for you, Nils; you had such a long road ahead of you then.

KROGSTAD: That may be; but you still hadn't the right to abandon me for somebody else's sake.

❺ **MRS. LINDE:** Yes—I don't know. So many, many times I've asked myself if I did have that right.

KROGSTAD [*more softly*]: When I lost you, it was as if all the solid ground dissolved from under my feet. Look at me; I'm a half-drowned man now, hanging onto a wreck.

MRS. LINDE: Help may be near.

KROGSTAD: It was near—but then you came and blocked it off.

MRS. LINDE: Without my knowing it, Nils. Today for the first time I learned that it's you I'm replacing at the bank.

KROGSTAD: All right—I believe you. But now that you know, will you step aside?

MRS. LINDE: No, because that wouldn't benefit you in the slightest.

KROGSTAD: Not "benefit" me, hm! I'd step aside anyway.

MRS. LINDE: I've learned to be realistic. Life and hard, bitter necessity have taught me that.

KROGSTAD: And life's taught me never to trust fine phrases.

MRS. LINDE: Then life's taught you a very sound thing. But you do have to trust in actions, don't you?

KROGSTAD: What does that mean?

1002 ■ *Romanticism and Realism*

Vocabulary Builder
calculating (kal′ kyo͞o lāt′ in)
adj. shrewd or cunning

Literary Analysis
Theme and Foreshadowing What action on Mrs. Linde's part might these words foreshadow?

Enrichment

Spotlight on Two Characters

Ibsen scholar Keith M. May wrote this about the significance of Krogstad and Mrs. Linde:

> Krogstad's role is plainly necessary, for by sending his letter to Torvald . . . he precipitates the final disclosures and Nora's metamorphosis. But apart from that Krogstad is an interesting and indeed necessary figure of frustration and embitterment, the perfect though surprising partner for Mrs. Linde. In addition to aiding the mechanics of the plot these two enrich the theme, for they have

both suffered in humiliating ways, as the relatively comfortable Helmers have not. At the end there is an appropriate kind of ripening for them both.

There is a touch of seediness about both of them: the self-sacrificing, mildly represented Mrs. Linde, plain as well as spirited; Krogstad hitherto steeped in malice. And they come together tragically, which is to say with no higher hopes for a happy future than their pasts will allow.

MRS. LINDE: You said you were hanging on like a half-drowned man to a wreck.

KROGSTAD: I've good reason to say that.

MRS. LINDE: I'm also like a half-drowned woman on a wreck. No one to suffer with; no one to care for.

KROGSTAD: You made your choice.

MRS. LINDE: There wasn't any choice then.

KROGSTAD: So—what of it?

MRS. LINDE: Nils, if only we two shipwrecked people could reach across to each other.

KROGSTAD: What are you saying?

MRS. LINDE: Two on one wreck are at least better off than each on his own.

KROGSTAD: Kristine!

MRS. LINDE: Why do you think I came into town?

KROGSTAD: Did you really have some thought of me?

MRS. LINDE: I have to work to go on living. All my born days, as long as I can remember, I've worked, and it's been my best and my only joy. But now I'm completely alone in the world; it frightens me to be so empty and lost. To work for yourself—there's no joy in that. Nils, give me something—someone to work for.

KROGSTAD: I don't believe all this. It's just some hysterical feminine urge to go out and make a noble sacrifice.

MRS. LINDE: Have you ever found me to be hysterical?

KROGSTAD: Can you honestly mean this? Tell me—do you know everything about my past?

MRS. LINDE: Yes.

KROGSTAD: And you know what they think I'm worth around here.

MRS. LINDE: From what you were saying before, it would seem that with me you could have been another person.

KROGSTAD: I'm positive of that.

MRS. LINDE: Couldn't it happen still?

KROGSTAD: Kristine—you're saying this in all seriousness? Yes, you are! I can see it in you. And do you really have the courage, then—?

MRS. LINDE: I need to have someone to care for; and your children need a mother. We both need each other. Nils, I have faith that you're good at heart—I'll risk everything together with you.

KROGSTAD [*gripping her hands*]: Kristine, thank you, thank you— Now I know I can win back a place in their eyes. Yes—but I forgot—

MRS. LINDE [*listening*]: Shh! The tarantella. Go now! Go on!

Reading Strategy
Recognizing Dramatic Tension If Krogstad rejects Mrs. Linde, will it raise the dramatic tension in this scene? Why or why not?

 Reading Check ❽
What information has Mrs. Linde learned about her position at the bank?

A Doll House, Act Three ■ 1003

---

❻ **Critical Thinking**
Interpret
- Ask two volunteers to read aloud the bracketed passage. **Ask** students why Mrs. Linde picks up on Krogstad's metaphor of being shipwrecked as she explains why she rejected his marriage proposal.
Possible response: She feels shipwrecked now that she is alone and unneeded.

- **Ask** students what Mrs. Linde suggests and whether this suggestion surprises them.
Possible response: Mrs. Linde's suggestion that she and Krogstad marry may surprise students who think Krogstad may still harbor bitter feelings toward Mrs. Linde. Others may not find this suggestion surprising, citing the romantic history the two share.

❼ **Reading Strategy**
Recognizing Dramatic Tension
- Remind students that dramatic tension arises when readers feel the pressure characters put on one another to make certain decisions.

- **Ask** students to consider what motivation Mrs. Linde and Krogstad have for marrying each other.
Possible response: Mrs. Linde is lonely, and because she is used to working for others, her life is empty without someone to work and care for. Krogstad needs someone to help raise his children.

- Have students read the bracketed passage independently. **Ask** students the Reading Strategy question: If Krogstad rejects Mrs. Linde, will it raise the dramatic tension in this scene? Why or why not?
Answer: The dramatic tension will increase if Krogstad rejects Mrs. Linde because it will lead to more questions, such as "What will happen to Mrs. Linde?" and "If she is angered by the rejection, what will she do?"

❽ **Reading Check**
Answer: Mrs. Linde has learned that Krogstad will lose his position at the bank so that she can work there.

1003

Recognizing Dramatic Tension

- Before a pair of students read the passage, tell students that dramatic tension can be created by elements in the setting as well as by the actors onstage.
- Draw students' attention to the bracketed passage, and then **ask** students the Reading Strategy question: In what way does the music of the tarantella affect the dramatic tension in this scene?
  Possible response: The tarantella reminds the characters and the audience that time is running out.

10 Literary Analysis

Theme

- Have two students read aloud the bracketed passage. Make sure students realize that this is an important turning point in the play: Mrs. Linde declines Krogstad's offer to retrieve his letter so that Nora and Torvald learn from the experience.
- **Ask** students the Literary Analysis question: What general theme about people or life does Mrs. Linde express?
  Possible response: Mrs. Linde's actions reflect the theme that although truth can sometimes be difficult to take, it can be a powerful teaching tool.

11 Background

Krogstad's Character

This is Krogstad's last appearance onstage. During this scene he has undergone an amazingly rapid transformation from a miserable man whose life is about to collapse to someone who has "never been so happy." Many critics have objected to this transformation. One calls Krogstad "the only exonerated black-mailer [he] can think of in fiction."

KROGSTAD: Why? What is it?

MRS. LINDE: Hear the dance up there? When that's over, they'll be coming down.

KROGSTAD: Oh, then I'll go. But—it's all pointless. Of course, you don't know the move I made against the Helmers.

MRS. LINDE: Yes, Nils, I know.

KROGSTAD: And all the same, you have the courage to—?

MRS. LINDE: I know how far despair can drive a man like you.

KROGSTAD: Oh, if I only could take it all back.

MRS. LINDE: You easily could—your letter's still lying in the mailbox.

KROGSTAD: Are you sure of that?

MRS. LINDE: Positive. But—

KROGSTAD [*looks at her searchingly*]: Is that the meaning of it, then? You'll save your friend at any price. Tell me straight out. Is that it?

MRS. LINDE: Nils—anyone who's sold herself for somebody else once isn't going to do it again.

KROGSTAD: I'll demand my letter back.

MRS. LINDE: No, no.

KROGSTAD: Yes, of course. I'll stay here till Helmer comes down; I'll tell him to give me my letter again—that it only involves my dismissal—that he shouldn't read it—

MRS. LINDE: No, Nils, don't call the letter back.

KROGSTAD: But wasn't that exactly why you wrote me to come here?

MRS. LINDE: Yes, in that first panic. But it's been a whole day and night since then, and in that time I've seen such incredible things in this house. Helmer's got to learn everything; this dreadful secret has to be aired; those two have to come to a full understanding; all these lies and <u>evasions</u> can't go on.

KROGSTAD: Well, then, if you want to chance it. But at least there's one thing I can do, and do right away—

MRS. LINDE [*listening*]: Go now, go quick! The dance is over. We're not safe another second.

KROGSTAD: I'll wait for you downstairs.

MRS. LINDE: Yes, please do; take me home.

KROGSTAD: I can't believe it; I've never been so happy. [*He leaves by way of the outer door; the door between the room and the hall stays open.*]

MRS. LINDE [*straightening up a bit and getting together her street clothes*]: How different now! How different! Someone to work for, to live for—a home to build. Well, it is worth the try! Oh, if they'd only come! [*Listening.*] Ah, there they are. Bundle up. [*She picks up her hat and coat.* NORA's *and* HELMER's *voices can be heard outside; a key turns in*

Reading Strategy
Recognizing Dramatic Tension In what way does the music of the tarantella affect the dramatic tension in this scene?

Literary Analysis
Theme What general theme about people or life does Mrs. Linde express?

Vocabulary Builder
evasions (ē vā′ zhənz) *n.* attempts to avoid duties or questions

---

Enrichment

August Strindberg

Another great author who helped create modern drama was the Swedish playwright August Strindberg (1849–1912), who was born in Stockholm. Strindberg joined the realistic style of Ibsen to the intense examination of inner psychological realities and sometimes disordered imaginations. From this style developed the Expressionist drama, focused more on characters' inner states than on external reality.

Strindberg's childhood was unhappy. After trying several different careers, he settled on journalism and began to publish novels and short stories. His first play, strongly influenced by Ibsen's *Brand,* was *Master Olaf* (1872). Its rejection was deeply wounding. His intense but unhappy marriage led him to the subject he is most identified with—the conflict between men and women.

His best-known works are *The Father* (1887), *Miss Julie* (1888), *Creditors* (1890), *A Dream Play* (1902), and *The Ghost Sonata* (1907). Most of Strindberg's plays present dark views of humanity.

the lock, and HELMER brings NORA *into the hall almost by force. She is wearing the Italian costume with a large black shawl about her; he has on evening dress, with a black domino[1] open over it.*]

NORA [*struggling in the doorway*]: No, no, no, not inside! I'm going up again. I don't want to leave so soon.

HELMER: But Nora dear—

NORA: Oh, I beg you, please, Torvald. From the bottom of my heart, *please*— only an hour more!

HELMER: Not a single minute, Nora darling. You know our agreement. Come on, in we go; you'll catch cold out here. [*In spite of her resistance, he gently draws her into the room.*]

MRS. LINDE: Good evening.

NORA: Kristine!

HELMER: Why, Mrs. Linde—are you here so late?

MRS. LINDE: Yes, I'm sorry, but I did want to see Nora in costume.

NORA: Have you been sitting here, waiting for me?

MRS. LINDE: Yes. I didn't come early enough; you were all upstairs; and then I thought I really couldn't leave without seeing you.

HELMER [*removing NORA's shawl*]: Yes, take a good look. She's worth looking at, I can tell you that, Mrs. Linde. Isn't she lovely?

MRS. LINDE: Yes, I should say—

HELMER: A dream of loveliness, isn't she? That's what everyone thought at the party, too. But she's horribly stubborn—this sweet little thing. What's to be done with her? Can you imagine, I almost had to use force to pry her away.

NORA: Oh, Torvald, you're going to regret you didn't indulge me, even for just a half hour more.

HELMER: There, you see. She danced her tarantella and got a tumultuous[2] hand—which was well earned, although the performance may have

---

1. **domino** (däm´ ə nō´) *n.* loose cloak or robe with wide sleeves and hood, worn with a mask at masquerades.
2. **tumultuous** (to͞o mul´ cho͞o əs) *adj.* wild and noisy.

▲ **Critical Viewing** ⓬
In what way does Nora's attitude in Act Three match the expression of the actress in this picture? **[Connect]**

 ⓮ **Reading Check**

What does Mrs. Linde want Krogstad to do with the letter to Torvald?

A Doll House, Act Three ■ 1005

⓬ Critical Viewing

Possible response: In Act Three, Nora realizes that her life is about to fall apart. She is full of apprehension. Similarly, the actress looks thoughtful and apprehensive. Nora is contemplating the changes she faces as she waits for her secret to be discovered.

⓭ Critical Thinking

Analyze Causes and Effects

• Have a volunteer read aloud the bracketed passage. **Ask** students why Nora does not want to leave the party.
Answer: She knows that Torvald will read Krogstad's letter and that her life will change forever.

• Then, **ask** students what Torvald must be thinking about Nora's refusal to leave.
Answer: Torvald thinks that Nora is being stubborn and unreasonable, like a child who does not want to go home, although he may also be secretly pleased that his wife is "the life of the party" because it brings more attention to him.

⓮ Reading Check

Answer: Mrs. Linde wants Krogstad to leave the letter so that Nora and Torvald can deal with Nora's secret.

Differentiated Instruction Solutions for All Learners

Vocabulary for English Learners
Point out the first stage direction on p. 1004 and the use of the word *searchingly.* Explain that this is one of many adverbs formed by adding the suffix *-ly* to an adjective to give more specific meaning to the verb it modifies. Have students supply a definition for *searchingly* (in a searching manner) and list other adverbs formed in the same way. Some examples include *angrily, proudly, happily, sadly, willingly,* and *cheerfully.*

Enrichment for Gifted/Talented Students
Remind students that the play revolves around a lack of communication among its characters. Have students work in pairs or groups to identify at least one passage in the play in which Nora could have confessed her crime to Torvald. Then, have them work together to write additional dialogue for that scene in which Nora confesses and Torvald reacts. Have students read or act out their dialogues in class.

• Ask a volunteer to read aloud the bracketed passage. Tell students that Torvald's tendency to offer his unsolicited opinion is obvious in this passage.

• **Challenge** students to make an inference about Torvald's character on the basis of his conversational style.

Possible response: Torvald is very concerned about what other people think, finding himself more interested in the impression Nora made on the audience than on her actual dancing.

⑯ Reading Strategy

Recognizing Dramatic Tension

• Read aloud the second bracketed passage. Remind students that the letter holds the potential of elevating the play's dramatic tension.

• **Ask** students the Reading Strategy question: If Krogstad is no longer a threat to Nora, why does the letter continue to be a cause of dramatic tension?

Answer: The letter is still a threat because Torvald will find out that his wife has deceived him.

---

been a bit too <u>naturalistic</u>—I mean it rather overstepped the <u>proprieties</u> of art. But never mind—what's important is, she made a success, an overwhelming success. You think I could let her stay on after that and spoil the effect? Oh no; I took my lovely little Capri girl—my capricious[3] little Capri girl, I should say—took her under my arm; one quick tour of the ballroom, a curtsy to every side, and then—as they say in novels—the beautiful vision disappeared. An exit should always be effective, Mrs. Linde, but that's what I can't get Nora to grasp. Phew, its hot in here. [*Flings the domino on a chair and opens the door to his room.*] Why's it dark in here? Oh, yes, of course. Excuse me. [*He goes in and lights a couple of candles.*]

NORA [*in a sharp, breathless whisper*]: So?

MRS. LINDE [*quietly*]: I talked with him.

NORA: And—?

MRS. LINDE: Nora—you must tell your husband everything.

NORA [*dully*]: I knew it.

MRS. LINDE: You've got nothing to fear from Krogstad, but you have to speak out.

NORA: I won't tell.

MRS. LINDE: Then the letter will.

NORA: Thanks, Kristine. I know now what's to be done. Shh!

HELMER [*reentering*]: Well, then, Mrs. Linde—have you admired her?

MRS. LINDE: Yes, and now I'll say good night.

HELMER: Oh, come, so soon? Is this yours, this knitting?

MRS. LINDE: Yes, thanks. I nearly forgot it.

HELMER: Do you knit, then?

MRS. LINDE: Oh yes.

HELMER: You know what? You should embroider instead.

MRS. LINDE: Really? Why?

HELMER: Yes, because it's a lot prettier. See here, one holds the embroidery so, in the left hand, and then one guides the needle with the right—so—in an easy, sweeping curve—right?

MRS. LINDE: Yes, I guess that's—

HELMER: But, on the other hand, knitting—it can never be anything but ugly. Look, see here, the arms tucked in, the knitting needles going up and down, there's something Chinese about it. Ah, that was really a glorious champagne they served.

---

3. **capricious** (kə prish′ əs) *adj.* erratic; flighty.

Vocabulary Builder
naturalistic (nach′ər əl is′ tik) *adj.* faithful to nature
proprieties (prō prī′ə tēz) *n.* conformities with what is considered fitting, suitable, or proper

Reading Strategy
Recognizing Dramatic Tension If Krogstad is no longer a threat to Nora, why does the letter continue to be a cause of dramatic tension?

Differentiated

Instruction   Solutions for All Learners

Support for Less Proficient Readers
To model how to recognize dramatic tension, give students a copy of Reading Strategy Graphic Organizer B in *Graphic Organizer Transparencies,* p. 176. The completed graphic organizer will give students insight into the process of recognizing dramatic tension. They can use it as a model for making their own observations about dramatic tension as they read.

Enrichment for Advanced Readers
Ask students to review all of what they have read so far and then write these notes: a plot outline, a short description of the setting, and brief character sketches of Nora, Torvald, Mrs. Linde, Dr. Rank, and Krogstad. Have students write a short story based on the play and their notes. Because students have not yet finished reading the play, ask them to write an ending of their own without reading ahead.

MRS. LINDE: Yes, good night, Nora, and don't be stubborn anymore.

HELMER: Well put, Mrs. Linde!

MRS. LINDE: Good night, Mr. Helmer.

HELMER [*accompanying her to the door*]: Good night, good night. I hope you get home all right. I'd be very happy to—but you don't have far to go. Good night, good night. [*She leaves. He shuts the door after her and returns.*] There, now, at last we got her out the door. She's a deadly bore, that creature.

NORA: Aren't you pretty tired, Torvald?

HELMER: No, not a bit.

NORA: You're not sleepy?

HELMER: Not at all. On the contrary, I'm feeling quite exhilarated. But you? Yes, you really look tired and sleepy.

NORA: Yes, I'm very tired. Soon now I'll sleep.

HELMER: See! You see! I was right all along that we shouldn't stay longer.

NORA: Whatever you do is always right.

18 **HELMER** [*kissing her brow*]: Now my little lark talks sense. Say, did you notice what a time Rank was having tonight?

NORA: Oh, was he? I didn't get to speak with him.

HELMER: I scarcely did either, but it's a long time since I've seen him in such high spirits. [*Gazes at her a moment, then comes nearer her.*] Hm— it's marvelous, though, to be back home again—to be completely alone with you. Oh, you bewitchingly lovely young woman!

NORA: Torvald, don't look at me like that!

HELMER: Can't I look at my richest treasure? At all that beauty that's mine, mine alone—completely and utterly.

NORA [*moving around to the other side of the table*]: You mustn't talk to me that way tonight.

HELMER [*following her*]: The tarantella is still in your blood, I can see— and it makes you even more enticing. Listen. The guests are beginning to go. [*Dropping his voice.*] Nora—it'll soon be quiet through this whole house.

NORA: Yes, I hope so.

19 **HELMER:** You do, don't you, my love? Do you realize—when I'm out at a party like this with you—do you know why I talk to you so little, and keep such a distance away; just send you a stolen look now and then—you know why I do it? It's because I'm imagining then that you're my secret darling, my secret young bride-to-be, and that no one suspects there's anything between us.

NORA: Yes, yes; oh, yes, I know you're always thinking of me.

Theme What does Mrs. Linde suggest about everyone's right to become an individual when she tells Nora not to be stubborn?

Literary Analysis
Theme In what way is Torvald preventing Nora from finding happiness in their marriage?

 Reading Check

What advice does Mrs. Linde give Nora regarding Torvald?

A Doll House, Act Three ■ 1007

Theme

- Read aloud the bracketed line. Point out Mrs. Linde's echoing Torvald in calling Nora "stubborn." **Ask** students to explain what Mrs. Linde means by this characterization of Nora.
  Possible response: Mrs. Linde is reminding Nora to tell Torvald her secret and stop being stubborn about withholding it.

- **Ask** the first Literary Analysis question: What does Mrs. Linde suggest about everyone's right to become an individual when she tells Nora not to be stubborn?
  Possible response: Mrs. Linde suggests that people cannot be independent if they are dishonest.

18 **Background**

Torvald as Caricature

Some critics have observed that Torvald can be viewed almost as a caricature. Throughout the play, he lacks even a hint of self-awareness. In his own eyes he is the perfect husband, which means that in regard to his wife, he is infallible. Most husbands would immediately detect the sarcasm in the line, "Whatever you do is always right." Torvald, on the other hand, replies, "Now my little lark talks sense."

19 **Literary Analysis**

Theme

- Have two volunteers read the bracketed passage aloud. Make sure that students understand the nature of Torvald's advances and Nora's negative response.

- **Ask** students the second Literary Analysis question: In what way is Torvald preventing Nora from finding happiness in their marriage?
  Possible response: Torvald does not recognize Nora's need to find fulfillment in life beyond receiving compliments from other people.

20 **Reading Check**

Answer: Mrs. Linde tells Nora to be honest with Torvald.

Differentiated
Instruction Solutions for All Learners

Strategy for Less Proficient Readers
Ask students to choose two characters and make a word web for each that includes both good qualities and faults. As students read further, encourage them to note on the web additional personality traits and brief quotations that support them. Then, use these graphic organizers to generate a discussion about the characters. As a follow-up, have students discuss what this mix of good and bad in each character suggests about the play's major themes.

Strategy for Advanced Readers
Ask students to classify the play's characters as major (those who take a prominent part in the action) and minor (those who have relatively few lines and play a small part in the action). Remind students that even characters with relatively few lines can have a profound impact on the play. Have students work in small groups to decide how important each character is and why. Challenge students to create a pie chart that shows the percentages of each character's importance to the play.

㉑ Literary Analysis
Theme and Foreshadowing

- Point out to students that this line contains Nora's first open expression of irritation with Torvald. **Ask** students to connect her reaction to the theme that self-expression is a basic human right.
  Possible response: Faced with real problems, Nora finally objects to Torvald's seeing her as a character he has created.

- **Ask** students the Literary Analysis question: What personality change in Nora might be foreshadowed when she speaks up to Torvald?
  Possible response: This utterance may be Nora's first step toward honesty, especially in defining herself as an individual.

㉒ Reading Strategy
Recognizing Dramatic Tension

- Read aloud the bracketed passage. Then, point out to students how Dr. Rank's knock at the door immediately changes the mood onstage. **Ask** students to explain why a knock at the door has this power.
  Possible response: The reader knows that Nora is distressed; the knock at the door means her distress will be prolonged or even made worse, depending on the visitor and the purpose for the visit.

- **Ask** students the Reading Strategy question: What effect does Torvald's irritation have on the dramatic tension in this scene?
  Possible response: Torvald's annoyance with Nora may reveal itself as annoyance with Dr. Rank, a mistake that may lead to more problems.

▶ **Monitor Progress** **Ask** students what dramatic tension is brewing when Torvald says he isn't tired and starts to flirt with Nora.
  Answer: Nora already has decided she needs time away from Torvald. She resents his possessiveness and the way he speaks to and about her. The more unaware Torvald is, the more the tension rises.

▶ **Reteach** If students need help with identifying dramatic tension, have them use **Reading Strategy** support, p. 120 in *Unit 7 Resources.*

HELMER: And then when we leave and I place the shawl over those fine young rounded shoulders—over that wonderful curving neck—then I pretend that you're my young bride, that we're just coming from the wedding, that for the first time I'm bringing you into my house—that for the first time I'm alone with you—completely alone with you, your trembling young beauty! All this evening I've longed for nothing but you. When I saw you turn and sway in the tarantella—my blood was pounding till I couldn't stand it—that's why I brought you down here so early—

㉑ | **NORA:** Go away, Torvald! Leave me alone. I don't want all this.

HELMER: What do you mean? Nora, you're teasing me. You will, won't you? Aren't I your husband—?

[*A knock at the outside door.*]

NORA [*startled*]: What's that?

HELMER [*going toward the hall*]: Who is it?

㉒
RANK [*outside*]: It's me. May I come in a moment?

HELMER [*with quiet irritation*]: Oh, what does he want now? [*Aloud.*] Hold on. [*Goes and opens the door.*] Oh, how nice that you didn't just pass us by!

RANK: I thought I heard your voice, and then I wanted so badly to have a look in. [*Lightly glancing about.*] Ah, me, these old familiar haunts. You have it snug and cozy in here, you two.

HELMER: You seemed to be having it pretty cozy upstairs, too.

RANK: Absolutely. Why shouldn't I? Why not take in everything in life? As much as you can, anyway, and as long as you can. The wine was superb—

HELMER: The champagne especially.

RANK: You noticed that too? It's amazing how much I could guzzle down.

NORA: Torvald also drank a lot of champagne this evening.

RANK: Oh?

NORA: Yes, and that always makes him so entertaining.

RANK: Well, why shouldn't one have a pleasant evening after a well-spent day?

HELMER: Well spent? I'm afraid I can't claim that.

RANK [*slapping him on the back*]: But I can, you see!

NORA: Dr. Rank, you must have done some scientific research today.

RANK: Quite so.

HELMER: Come now—little Nora talking about scientific research!

NORA: And can I congratulate you on the results?

RANK: Indeed you may.

Literary Analysis
Theme and Foreshadowing What personality change in Nora might be foreshadowed when she speaks up to Torvald?

Reading Strategy
Recognizing Dramatic Tension What effect does Torvald's irritation have on the dramatic tension in this scene?

Enrichment

A Moral Disease?
The critic John Northam has explored the parallels between Nora's "moral disease" and Dr. Rank's physical illness:

Ibsen also emphasizes the climax of the disease and death theme by bringing on Rank. Nora has danced her tarantella at the party upstairs—her last fling. At the same party, Rank has been enjoying his last fling—at the champagne—before retiring to his deathbed. The last link which Ibsen forges between the two victims of the poison and corruption is that their death warrants share the same letterbox. Rank leaves behind him a visiting card marked with a black cross, a sign that he has crawled away to die; the card lies beside Krogstad's letter to Torvald, and when Torvald reads that, Nora must die so as not to inflict her moral disease on others; physical and moral corruption burn themselves out together.

NORA: Then they were good?

RANK: The best possible for both doctor and patient—certainty.

NORA [*quickly and searchingly*]: Certainty?

RANK: Complete certainty. So don't I owe myself a gay evening afterwards?

NORA: Yes, you're right, Dr. Rank.

HELMER: I'm with you—just so long as you don't have to suffer for it in the morning.

RANK: Well, one never gets something for nothing in life.

NORA: Dr. Rank—are you very fond of masquerade parties?

RANK: Yes, if there's a good array of odd disguises—

NORA: Tell me, what should we two go as at the next masquerade?

HELMER: You little featherhead—already thinking of the next!

RANK: We two? I'll tell you what: you must go as Charmed Life—

HELMER: Yes, but find a costume for *that*!

RANK: Your wife can appear just as she looks every day.

HELMER: That was nicely put. But don't you know what you're going to be?

RANK: Yes, Helmer, I've made up my mind.

HELMER: Well?

RANK: At the next masquerade I'm going to be invisible.

HELMER: That's a funny idea.

RANK: They say there's a hat—black, huge—have you never heard of the hat that makes you invisible? You put it on, and then no one on earth can see you.

HELMER [*suppressing a smile*]: Ah, of course.

㉓ ✓ Reading Check
What does Dr. Rank tell Nora regarding the results of his scientific research?

㉕ Critical Viewing ▶
What information has Dr. Rank learned that might explain the serious demeanor of the actor in this picture? [**Connect**]

A Doll House, Act Three ■ 1009

Recognizing Dramatic Tension

- Have volunteers read aloud the bracketed passage. Tell students that there is nothing particularly dramatic about Dr. Rank's request for a cigar, but that he asks for a specific type of cigar and then bids his friends farewell suggests that this is his last request, a revelation that adds tension to this scene.

- **Ask** students the Reading Strategy question: Do you think Dr. Rank's secrecy about his illness creates dramatic tension in this scene? Why or why not?
  Possible response: Because this is Dr. Rank's last chance to share his secret, his silence creates dramatic tension. Nora knows the secret, so there is also suspense about whether she will reveal it.

27 **Literary Analysis**

Theme and Foreshadowing

- Point out that in this passage Nora seems to have forgotten that her own troubles will begin once Torvald goes to the mailbox.

- Then, **ask** students the Literary Analysis question: What possible confrontation might be foreshadowed when Torvald goes to the mailbox?
  Answer: The final confrontation between Nora and Torvald is foreshadowed.

▶ **Reteach** To assist students who have trouble identifying the connection between foreshadowing and key themes, use the **Literary Analysis** support, p. 119 in *Unit 7 Resources.*

RANK: But I'm quite forgetting what I came for. Helmer, give me a cigar, one of the dark Havanas.

HELMER: With the greatest pleasure. [*Holds out his case.*]

RANK: Thanks. [*Takes one and cuts off the tip.*]

NORA [*striking a match*]: Let me give you a light.

26 **RANK:** Thank you. [*She holds the match for him; he lights the cigar.*] And now good-bye.

HELMER: Good-bye, good-bye, old friend.

NORA: Sleep well, Doctor.

RANK: Thanks for that wish.

NORA: Wish me the same.

RANK: You? All right, if you like— Sleep well. And thanks for the light. [*He nods to them both and leaves.*]

HELMER [*his voice subdued*]: He's been drinking heavily.

NORA [*absently*]: Could be. [HELMER *takes his keys from his pocket and goes out in the hall.*] Torvald—what are you after?

27 **HELMER:** Got to empty the mailbox; it's nearly full. There won't be room for the morning papers.

NORA: Are you working tonight?

HELMER: You know I'm not. Why—what's this? Someone's been at the lock.

NORA: At the lock—?

HELMER: Yes, I'm positive. What do you suppose—? I can't imagine one of the maids—? Here's a broken hairpin. Nora, it's yours—

NORA [*quickly*]: Then it must be the children—

HELMER: You'd better break them of that. Hm, hm—well, opened it after all. [*Takes the contents out and calls into the kitchen.*] Helene! Helene, would you put out the lamp in the hall. [*He returns to the room, shutting the hall door, then displays the handful of mail.*] Look how it's piled up. [*Sorting through them.*] Now what's this?

NORA [*at the window*]: The letter! Oh, Torvald, no!

HELMER: Two calling cards—from Rank.

NORA: From Dr. Rank?

HELMER [*examining them*]: "Dr. Rank, Consulting Physician." They were on top. He must have dropped them in as he left.

NORA: Is there anything on them?

HELMER: There's a black cross over the name. See? That's a gruesome notion. He could almost be announcing his own death.

NORA: That's just what he's doing.

1010 ■ *Romanticism and Realism*

Differentiated

Instruction ▸ Solutions for All Learners

Strategy for English Learners
Check comprehension and help maintain interest by asking students to draft a list of questions they would like to ask the characters at this point in the play. Have students work in pairs to answer each other's questions. If students have trouble preparing questions, offer them the following question and answer to get them started: **Question:** Mrs. Linde, why did you want Torvald to read Krogstad's letter? Don't you care about Nora? **Possible answer:** I wanted Torvald to know the truth.

Strategy for Gifted/Talented Students
Ask students to list questions they would like to ask the characters at this point in the play. After students have generated lists for Nora, Torvald, Mrs. Linde, Krogstad, and Dr. Rank, assign these "parts" to students who will appear in character during mock interviews conducted by other students.

HELMER: What! You've heard something? Something he's told you?

NORA: Yes. That when those cards came, he'd be taking his leave of us. He'll shut himself in now and die.

HELMER: Ah, my poor friend! Of course I knew he wouldn't be here much longer. But so soon— And then to hide himself away like a wounded animal.

NORA: If it has to happen, then it's best it happens in silence—don't you think so, Torvald?

HELMER [*pacing up and down*]: He'd grown right into our lives. I simply can't imagine him gone. He with his suffering and loneliness—like a dark cloud setting off our sunlit happiness. Well, maybe it's best this way. For him, at least. [*Standing still.*] And maybe for us too, Nora. Now we're thrown back on each other, completely. [*Embracing her.*] Oh you, my darling wife, how can I hold you close enough? You know what, Nora—time and again I've wished you were in some terrible danger, just so I could stake my life and soul and everything, for your sake.

NORA [*tearing herself away, her voice firm and decisive*]: Now you must read your mail, Torvald.

HELMER: No, no, not tonight. I want to stay with you, dearest.

NORA: With a dying friend on your mind?

HELMER: You're right. We've both had a shock. There's ugliness between us—these thoughts of death and corruption. We'll have to get free of them first. Until then—we'll stay apart.

NORA [*clinging about his neck*]: Torvald—good night! Good night!

HELMER [*kissing her on the cheek*]: Good night, little songbird. Sleep well, Nora. I'll be reading my mail now. [*He takes the letters into his room and shuts the door after him.*]

NORA [*with bewildered glances, groping about, seizing HELMER's domino, throwing it around her, and speaking in short, hoarse, broken whispers*]: Never see him again. Never, never. [*Putting her shawl over her head.*] Never see the children either—them, too. Never, never. Oh, the freezing black water! The depths—down—Oh, I wish it were over—He has it now; he's reading it—now. Oh no, no, not yet. Torvald, good-bye, you and the children—[*She starts for the hall; as she does, HELMER throws open his door and stands with an open letter in his hand.*]

HELMER: Nora!

NORA [*screams*]: Oh—!

HELMER: What is this? You know what's in this letter?

NORA: Yes, I know. Let me go! Let me out!

HELMER [*holding her back*]: Where are you going?

NORA [*struggling to break loose*]: You can't save me, Torvald!

Literary Analysis
Theme and Foreshadowing Do you think Torvald's lines foreshadow that he will take the blame for Nora? Explain.

 **Reading Check**
What discovery does Torvald make when he empties the mailbox?

A Doll House, Act Three ■ 1011

HELMER [*slumping back*]: True! Then it's true what he writes? How horrible! No, no it's impossible—it can't be true.

NORA: It *is* true. I've loved you more than all this world.

HELMER: Ah, none of your slippery tricks.

NORA [*taking one step toward him*]: Torvald—!

HELMER: What is this you've blundered into!

NORA: Just let me loose. You're not going to suffer for my sake. You're not going to take on my guilt.

HELMER: No more playacting. [*Locks the hall door.*] You stay right here and give me a reckoning. You understand what you've done? Answer! You understand?

32 | **NORA** [*looking squarely at him, her face hardening*]: Yes. I'm beginning to understand everything now.

31 ▲ Critical Viewing
In what ways does this photograph capture the change in the relationship between Torvald and Nora? **[Interpret]**

33 | **HELMER** [*striding about*]: Oh, what an awful awakening! In all these eight years—she who was my pride and joy—a <u>hypocrite</u>, a liar—worse, worse—a criminal! How infinitely disgusting it all is! The shame! [NORA *says nothing and goes on looking straight at him. He stops in front of her.*] I should have suspected something of the kind. I should have known. All your father's flimsy values— Be still! All your father's flimsy values have come out in you. No religion, no morals, no sense of duty—Oh, how I'm punished for letting him off! I did it for your sake, and you repay me like this.

NORA: Yes, like this.

HELMER: Now you've wrecked all my happiness—ruined my whole future. Oh, it's awful to think of. I'm in a cheap little <u>grafter</u>'s hands; he can do anything he wants with me, ask for anything, play with me like a puppet—and I can't breathe a word. I'll be swept down miserably into the depths on account of a featherbrained woman.

NORA: When I'm gone from this world, you'll be free.

HELMER: Oh, quit posing. Your father had a mess of those speeches too. What good would that ever do me if you were gone from this world, as you say? Not the slightest. He can still make the whole thing known; and if he does, I could be falsely suspected as your accomplice. They

34 | might even think that I was behind it—that I put you up to it. And all that I can thank you for—you that I've coddled the whole of our marriage. Can you see now what you've done to me?

NORA [*icily calm*]: Yes.

HELMER: It's so incredible, I just can't grasp it. But we'll have to patch up whatever we can. Take off the shawl. I said, take it off! I've got to appease him somehow or other. The thing has to be hushed up at any cost. And as for you and me, it's got to seem like everything between us is just as it was—to the outside world, that is. You'll go right on living in this house, of course. But you can't be allowed to bring up the children; I don't dare trust you with them— Oh, to have to say this to someone I've loved so much! Well, that's done with. From now on happiness doesn't matter; all that matters is saving the bits and pieces, the appearance— [*The doorbell rings.* HELMER *starts.*] What's that? And so late. Maybe the worst—? You think he'd—? Hide, Nora! Say you're sick. [NORA *remains standing motionless.* HELMER *goes and opens the door.*]

MAID [*half dressed, in the hall*]: A letter for Mrs. Helmer.

HELMER: I'll take it. [*Snatches the letter and shuts the door.*] Yes, it's from him. You don't get it; I'm reading it myself.

NORA: Then read it.

35 | **HELMER** [*by the lamp*]: I hardly dare. We may be ruined, you and I. But—I've got to know. [*Rips open the letter, skims through a few lines, glances at an enclosure, then cries out joyfully.*] Nora! [NORA *looks inquiringly at him.*] Nora! Wait!—better check it again— Yes, yes, it's true. I'm saved. Nora, I'm saved!

36 ✓ **Reading Check**
Other than Krogstad, whom does Torvald now consider a criminal and a grafter?

A Doll House, Act Three ■ 1013

1013

③⑦ Reading Strategy

Recognizing Dramatic Tension

- Read aloud the bracketed passage. Point out that in burning these papers, Torvald seems to think he has also erased the things he has said to Nora. **Ask** students to identify the dramatic tension in this passage.
  Possible response: As Torvald speaks at length, the audience must wait to learn Nora's reaction, wondering whether she will back down from the assertive stance she took earlier.

- **Ask** students the Reading Strategy question: In what ways does Torvald change when the dramatic tension breaks?
  Possible response: Torvald realizes that he can control the situation again and becomes his old self again, acting like Nora's protector.

③⑧ Literary Analysis

Theme and Foreshadowing

- Have a volunteer read aloud the bracketed passage. **Ask** students to discuss how Nora may feel as Torvald attempts to comfort her.
  Possible response: Nora likely doubts Torvald's sincerity because just a moment earlier, he told her that she was unfit to care for their children.

- **Ask** students the Literary Analysis question: Do you think Torvald recognizes his wife's individuality? Explain.
  Possible response: No; Torvald sees Nora as little more than a part of his public image.

③⑨ Background

Sign of the Times

Modern audiences often think that Torvald is impossibly ignorant and insensitive at this point in the play. However, Torvald's behavior was completely realistic to Ibsen's audiences. In fact, Laura Kieler, the model for Nora, was committed to an insane asylum by her husband after a series of events similar to those in the play.

NORA: And I?

HELMER: You too, of course. We're both saved, both of us. Look. He's sent back your note. He says he's sorry and ashamed—that a happy development in his life—oh, who cares what he says! Nora, we're saved! No one can hurt you. Oh, Nora, Nora—but first, this ugliness all has to go. Let me see— [*Takes a look at the note.*] No, I don't want to see it; I want the whole thing to fade like a dream. [*Tears the note and both letters to pieces, throws them into the stove and watches them burn.*] There—now there's nothing left— He wrote that since Christmas Eve you— Oh, they must have been three terrible days for you, Nora.

NORA: I fought a hard fight.

HELMER: And suffered pain and saw no escape but— No, we're not going to dwell on anything unpleasant. We'll just be grateful and keep on repeating: it's over now, it's over! You hear me, Nora? You don't seem to realize—it's over. What's it mean—that frozen look? Oh, poor little Nora, I understand. You can't believe I've forgiven you. But I have Nora; I swear I have. I know that what you did, you did out of love for me.

NORA: That's true.

HELMER: You loved me the way a wife ought to love her husband. It's simply the means that you couldn't judge. But you think I love you any the less for not knowing how to handle your affairs? No, no—just lean on me; I'll guide you and teach you. I wouldn't be a man if this feminine helplessness didn't make you twice as attractive to me. You mustn't mind those sharp words I said—that was all in the first confusion of thinking my world had collapsed. I've forgiven you, Nora; I swear I've forgiven you.

NORA: My thanks for your forgiveness. [*She goes out through the door, right.*]

HELMER: No, wait— [*Peers in.*] What are you doing in there?

NORA [*inside*]: Getting out of my costume.

HELMER [*by the open door*]: Yes, do that. Try to calm yourself and collect your thoughts again, my frightened little songbird. You can rest easy now; I've got wide wings to shelter you with. [*Walking about close by the door.*] How snug and nice our home is, Nora. You're safe here; I'll keep you like a hunted dove I've rescued out of a hawk's claws. I'll bring peace to your poor, shuddering heart. Gradually it'll happen, Nora; you'll see. Tomorrow all this will look different to you; then everything will be as it was. I won't have to go on repeating I forgive you; you'll feel it for yourself. How can you imagine I'd ever conceivably want to disown you—or even blame you in any way? Ah, you don't know a man's heart, Nora. For a man there's something indescribably sweet and satisfying in knowing he's forgiven his wife—and forgiven her out of a full and open heart. It's as if she belongs to him in two ways now: in a sense he's given her fresh into the world again, and she's become his wife and his child as well. From now on that's what you'll be to me—you little,

Reading Strategy

Recognizing Dramatic Tension In what ways does Torvald change when the dramatic tension breaks?

Literary Analysis

Theme and Foreshadowing Do you think Torvald recognizes his wife's individuality? Explain.

bewildered, helpless thing. Don't be afraid of anything, Nora; just open your heart to me, and I'll be conscience and will to you both—[NORA *enters in her regular clothes.*] What's this? Not in bed? You've changed your dress?

40 NORA: Yes, Torvald, I've changed my dress.

HELMER: But why now, so late?

NORA: Tonight I'm not sleeping.

HELMER: But Nora dear—

NORA [*looking at her watch*]: It's still not so very late. Sit down, Torvald; we have a lot to talk over. [*She sits at one side of the table.*]

HELMER: Nora—what is this? That hard expression—

NORA: Sit down. This'll take some time. I have a lot to say.

HELMER [*sitting at the table directly opposite her*]: You worry me, Nora. And I don't understand you.

NORA: No, that's exactly it. You don't understand me. And I've never understood you either—until tonight. No, don't interrupt. You can just listen to what I say. We're closing out accounts, Torvald.

HELMER: How do you mean that?

41 NORA [*after a short pause*]: Doesn't anything strike you about our sitting here like this?

HELMER: What's that?

NORA: We've been married now eight years. Doesn't it occur to you that this is the first time we two, you and I, man and wife, have ever talked seriously together?

HELMER: What do you mean—seriously?

NORA: In eight whole years—longer even—right from our first acquaintance, we've never exchanged a serious word on any serious thing.

HELMER: You mean I should constantly go and involve you in problems you couldn't possibly help me with?

NORA: I'm not talking of problems. I'm saying that we've never sat down seriously together and tried to get to the bottom of anything.

HELMER: But dearest, what good would that ever do you?

NORA: That's the point right there: you've never understood me. I've been wronged greatly, Torvald—first by Papa, and then by you.

HELMER: What! By us—the two people who've loved you more than anyone else?

NORA [*shaking her head*]: You never loved me. You've thought it fun to be in love with me, that's all.

HELMER: Nora, what a thing to say!

Vocabulary Builder
bewildered (bē wil′dərd)
adj. puzzled; confused

Literary Analysis
Theme and Foreshadowing What do you think Nora's change of dress foreshadows? Explain.

Literary Analysis
Theme In what way do these lines reflect the theme that a successful relationship is based on equality and partnership?

✔ **Reading Check** **42**

According to Torvald, what motivated Nora to get involved with Krogstad?

A Doll House, Act Three ■ 1015

Differentiated Instruction Solutions for All Learners

Strategy for English Learners
Explain to students that beginning here, Nora's character changes dramatically and what she has to say is the message of the play. Allow students to work in pairs or small groups, stopping after every half-page or so to review and summarize what Nora and Torvald have said. Allow students to ask questions to clarify the characters' meanings. If possible, ask a student who is proficient in English to participate in order to help with questions students might have.

Enrichment for Gifted/Talented Students
Invite students to write a song from Nora or Torvald's point of view or to write a duet that incorporates both. Tell students to make their songs entertaining, but to make sure that the lyrics remain true to the characters as revealed in the play. Have students write their own music or use the tune of a popular song and then perform their songs for the class.

---

40 **Literary Analysis**
Theme and Foreshadowing

• Read aloud the bracketed passage. Remind students that Nora's costume has also served as a symbol of her playacting. **Ask** students to offer ideas about the costume's symbolic meaning.
Possible response: By changing out of the costume, Nora sheds the role she has been playacting—that of Torvald's dutiful wife.

• **Ask** students the first Literary Analysis question: What do you think Nora's change of dress foreshadows? Explain.
Possible response: Nora does not plan to stay. She is getting dressed so that she can leave.

41 **Literary Analysis**
Theme

• Have two volunteers read aloud the bracketed passage. Point out Nora's use of banking language in this passage when she says, "We're closing out accounts." Help students understand that Nora chooses language that Torvald will understand easily and quickly because the points she is about to raise are important to her.

• **Ask** students with what Torvald equates serious conversation and how this attitude fits one of the play's themes.
Possible response: Torvald believes that serious conversations have to do with solving problems, not discussing ideas.

• **Ask** students the second Literary Analysis question: In what ways do these lines reflect the theme that a successful relationship is based on equality and partnership?
Possible response: Torvald's belief that Nora cannot help him with his problems indicates that he does not view their marriage as a partnership between equals; that Nora has never spoken about this rift between them also confirms that she does not share power with Torvald in their relationship.

42 **Reading Check**
Answer: Torvald believes that Nora got involved with Krogstad because she did not know any better.

Literary Analysis
Theme

- Have students read the bracketed passage independently. Point out to students how Torvald responds to Nora's realization that she has been treated like a doll, not an equal.

- **Ask** students the Literary Analysis question: Which of the play's themes is Nora stating in these lines? Explain.

  Possible response: Nora furthers the theme that a successful relationship is based on trust, equality, and individuality; she realizes that she has not been an equal in her marriage, and she is no longer willing to participate in a marriage that is not a partnership.

44 Reading Strategy
Recognizing Dramatic Tension

- Read the bracketed passage aloud. Before asking students the Reading Strategy question, **ask** them to review what Nora has meant to Torvald.

  Answer: Nora has been a comfort, a source of entertainment, a prize, and a sign of respectability.

- **Ask** students the Reading Strategy question: What does Torvald stand to lose if Nora leaves him?

  Possible response: Torvald loses not only his wife but also his respectability in the community. He loses the comfort of his home and his self-esteem.

NORA: Yes, it's true now, Torvald. When I lived at home with Papa, he told me all his opinions, so I had the same ones too; or if they were different I hid them, since he wouldn't have cared for that. He used to call me his doll-child, and he played with me the way I played with my dolls. Then I came into your house—

HELMER: How can you speak of our marriage like that?

NORA [*unperturbed*]: I mean, then I went from Papa's hands into yours. You arranged everything to your own taste, and so I got the same taste as you—or I pretended to; I can't remember. I guess a little of both, first one, then the other. Now when I look back, it seems as if I'd lived here like a beggar—just from hand to mouth. I've lived by doing tricks for you, Torvald. But that's the way you wanted it. It's a great sin what you and Papa did to me. You're to blame that nothing's become of me.

HELMER: Nora, how unfair and ungrateful you are! Haven't you been happy here?

NORA: No, never. I thought so—but I never have.

HELMER: Not—not happy!

43 **NORA:** No, only lighthearted. And you've always been so kind to me. But our home's been nothing but a playpen. I've been your doll-wife here, just as at home I was Papa's doll-child. And in turn the children have been my dolls. I thought it was fun when you played with me, just as they thought it fun when I played with them. That's been our marriage, Torvald.

HELMER: There's some truth in what you're saying—under all the raving exaggeration. But it'll all be different after this. Playtime's over; now for the schooling.

NORA: Whose schooling—mine or the children's?

HELMER: Both yours and the children's, dearest.

NORA: Oh, Torvald, you're not the man to teach me to be a good wife to you.

HELMER: And you can say that?

NORA: And I—how am I equipped to bring up children?

HELMER: Nora!

NORA: Didn't you say a moment ago that that was no job to trust me with?

HELMER: In a flare of temper! Why fasten on that?

44 **NORA:** Yes, but you were so very right. I'm not up to the job. There's another job I have to do first. I have to try to educate myself. You can't help me with that. I've got to do it alone. And that's why I'm leaving you now.

HELMER [*jumping up*]: What's that?

1016 ■ *Romanticism and Realism*

Literary Analysis
Theme Which of the play's themes is Nora stating in these lines? Explain.

Reading Strategy
Recognizing Dramatic Tension What does Torvald stand to lose if Nora leaves him?

Differentiated
Instruction   Solutions for All Learners

Enrichment for Gifted/Talented Students
Ask students to create a daytime talk-show skit that features visits from characters in *A Doll House.* Students can pattern the show after sit-down formats or choose the audience-participation style. Encourage them to make their skits entertaining, but remind them that the guests must remain true to their characters as revealed in the play. Have groups present their skits to the class. Discuss issues that arise during the presentations.

Enrichment for Advanced Readers
Have students research the evolution of laws protecting and providing for women in Norway in 1879, the time in which the play was written. Ask students to present short reports to the class and then speculate on what Nora's life will be like if she leaves Torvald. Make sure that they mention how she will earn income, who will likely have custody of the children, and so on.

NORA: I have to stand completely alone, if I'm ever going to discover myself and the world out there. So I can't go on living with you.

HELMER: Nora, Nora!

NORA: I want to leave right away. Kristine should put me up for the night—

HELMER: You're insane! You've no right! I forbid you!

NORA: From here on, there's no use forbidding me anything. I'll take with me whatever is mine. I don't want a thing from you, either now or later.

HELMER: What kind of madness is this?

NORA: Tomorrow I'm going home—I mean, home where I came from. It'll be easier up there to find something to do.

HELMER: Oh, you blind, incompetent child!

NORA: I must learn to be competent, Torvald.

HELMER: Abandon your home, your husband, your children! And you're not even thinking what people will say.

NORA: I can't be concerned about that. I only know how essential this is.

HELMER: Oh, it's outrageous. So you'll run out like this on your most sacred vows.

NORA: What do you think are my most sacred vows?

HELMER: And I have to tell you that! Aren't they your duties husband and children?

NORA: I have other duties equally sacred.

HELMER: That isn't true. What duties are they?

NORA: Duties to myself.

HELMER: Before all else, you're a wife and a mother.

NORA: I don't believe in that anymore. I believe that, before all else, I'm a human being, no less than you—or anyway, I ought to try to become one. I know the majority thinks you're right, Torvald, and plenty of books agree with you, too. But I can't go on believing what the majority says, or what's written in books. I have to think over these things myself and try to understand them.

HELMER: Why can't you understand your place in your own home? On a point like that, isn't there one everlasting guide you can turn to? Where's your religion?

NORA: Oh, Torvald, I'm really not sure what religion is.

HELMER: What—?

NORA: I only know what the minister said when I was confirmed. He told me religion was this thing and that. When I get clear and away by myself,

Literature in Context

45 History Connection

Independent Women, 1879

A Doll House shocked its original audience because it addressed a controversial issue: the status of women. In 1879, when the play was written, it was virtually unthinkable in Europe and America that a middle-class wife could be a wholly independent person. Few women were highly educated or had careers of their own. Women in Norway could not vote until 1913—in the United States and Britain, women did not win full voting rights until 1920 and 1928, respectively.

When Nora tells Torvald she is leaving him and her children, they both recognize the difficulties she will face on her own. Torvald—and Ibsen's audience—would find Nora's choice shocking, and perhaps even foolhardy.

Connect to the Literature

Identify one reason why Nora is willing to risk the difficulties she will face.

Literary Analysis
Theme Who or what is the "majority" whose opinion Nora questions?

47  **Reading Check**

What decision has Nora made about her life with Torvald?

A Doll House, Act Three ■ 1017

45 Literature in Context

Independent Women, 1879 At the time Ibsen was writing *A Doll House*, women activists in the United States had already been lobbying for the right to vote for more than thirty years. The first women's rights convention had been held in Seneca Falls, New York, in 1848. At the convention, leading women's rights proponents presented their own version of the Declaration of Independence, called the Declaration of Sentiments. Using the language that appeared in the original declaration, the writers, who included Elizabeth Cady Stanton and Lucretia Mott, pointed out the inequalities women historically had faced.

Connect to the Literature Point out that the most striking lines in the Declaration of Sentiments was the simple addition of the two words "and women" to the most important sentence in the original Declaration of Independence: "We hold these truths to be self-evident: that all men and women are created equal." Ask students to discuss why Nora is willing to leave, given the difficulties ahead. **Possible response:** Nora is determined to break free from her role as a childish, incompetent, adoring wife to be her own person and to learn how to survive on her own. She is willing to pay any price for such independence.

46 Literary Analysis
Theme

• Remind students of the theme "Every person has a right to individuality." Point out that society is a strong force that sometimes tries to coerce individuals to act or think a certain way.

• **Ask** students the Literary Analysis question: Who or what is the "majority" whose opinion Nora questions? **Answer:** The majority is probably society.

47 Reading Check

Answer: Nora has decided that she must leave Torvald.

- Help students understand that this deeper side of Nora shows her development as a character, and it foreshadows even more changes ahead for her.

- **Ask** students the Literary Analysis question: What future conflicts might Nora's lines foreshadow? **Possible response:** Nora will have to learn to make her own way in the world.

49 **Reading Strategy**

Recognizing Dramatic Tension

- Point out that Nora has clearly thought about the consequences of leaving and that her certainty creates concern that Torvald may prevent her from leaving.

- Have students **identify** what each character stands to lose if Nora leaves. **Possible response:** Nora stands to lose her children, her financial security, and her respectability; Torvald stands to lose his comfort and standing in the community.

- **Ask** the Reading Strategy question: In what ways does Nora raise the stakes, making it clear that she and Torvald may lose more than Torvald imagined? **Possible response:** Nora suggests that Torvald lost her belief in him when he automatically turned against her; witnessing his behavior may have taken away Nora's belief in love.

I'll go into that problem too. I'll see if what the minister said was right, or, in any case, if it's right for me.

HELMER: A young woman your age shouldn't talk like that. If religion can't move you, I can try to rouse your conscience. You do have some moral feeling? Or, tell me—has that gone too?

48 **NORA:** It's not easy to answer that, Torvald. I simply don't know. I'm all confused about these things. I just know I see them so differently from you. I find out, for one thing, that the law's not at all what I'd thought—but I can't get it through my head that the law is fair. A woman hasn't a right to protect her dying father or save her husband's life! I can't believe that.

HELMER: You talk like a child. You don't know anything of the world you live in.

NORA: No, I don't. But now I'll begin to learn for myself. I'll try to discover who's right, the world or I.

HELMER: Nora, you're sick; you've got a fever. I almost think you're out of your head.

NORA: I've never felt more clearheaded and sure in my life.

HELMER: And—clearheaded and sure—you're leaving your husband and children?

NORA: Yes.

HELMER: Then there's only one possible reason.

NORA: What?

HELMER: You no longer love me.

NORA: No. That's exactly it.

HELMER: Nora! You can't be serious!

NORA: Oh, this is so hard, Torvald—you've been so kind to me always. But I can't help it. I don't love you anymore.

HELMER [struggling for composure]: Are you also clearheaded and sure about that?

NORA: Yes, completely. That's why I can't go on staying here.

49 **HELMER:** Can you tell me what I did to lose your love?

NORA: Yes, I can tell you. It was this evening when the miraculous thing didn't come—then I knew you weren't the man I'd imagined.

HELMER: Be more explicit; I don't follow you.

NORA: I've waited now so patiently eight long years—for, my Lord, I know miracles don't come every day. Then this crisis broke over me, and such a certainty filled me: *now* the miraculous event would occur. While Krogstad's letter was lying out there, I never for an instant dreamed that you could give in to his terms. I was so utterly sure you'd

1018 ■ *Romanticism and Realism*

Literary Analysis
Theme and Foreshadowing What future conflicts might Nora's lines foreshadow?

Reading Strategy
Recognizing Dramatic Tension In what way does Nora raise the stakes, making it clear that she and Torvald may lose more than Torvald imagined?

Enrichment

Norway's Modern Social Welfare System

If Nora Helmer were living in Norway today, chances are that she would be much better prepared for a life on her own than she was in the 1870s. In fact, she would be among the most fortunate women in the world.

Today's Norway is one of the world's richest countries, with 100 percent literacy (compared with 97 percent in the United States) and almost universal free education and health care. Norwegians live, on the average, several years longer than Americans. Fewer Norwegian babies die at birth than do those in the United States.

Also, Norwegians receive a variety of social benefits unknown in the United States. These include, in addition to free medical care and college education, cash benefits during pregnancy, free dental care for children, a generous pension, state-financed home loans for most people, and a minimum of four weeks of paid vacation for every worker. In return for these benefits, Norwegians pay very high taxes.

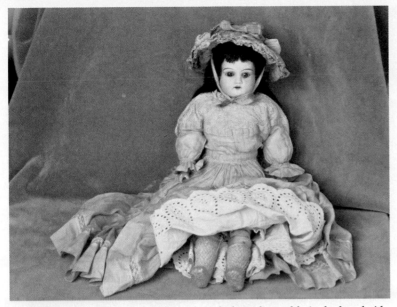

◀ Critical Viewing **50**
What characteristics does Nora share with this china doll? In what ways is Nora very different? [**Compare and Contrast**]

say to him: go on, tell your tale to the whole wide world. And when he'd done that—

HELMER: Yes, what then? When I'd delivered my own wife into shame and disgrace—!

NORA: When he'd done that, I was so utterly sure that you'd step forward, take the blame on yourself and say: I am the guilty one.

HELMER: Nora—!

NORA: You're thinking I'd never accept such a sacrifice from you? No, of course not. But what good would my protests be against you? That was the miracle I was waiting for, in terror and hope. And to stave that off, I would have taken my life.

HELMER: I'd gladly work for you day and night, Nora—and take on pain and deprivation. But there's no one who gives up honor for love.

NORA: Millions of women have done just that.

HELMER: Oh, you think and talk like a silly child.

NORA: Perhaps. But you neither think nor talk like the man I could join myself to. When your big fright was over—and it wasn't from any threat against me, only for what might damage you—when all the danger was past, for you it was just as if nothing had happened. I was exactly the same, your little lark, your doll, that you'd have to handle with double care now that I'd turned out so brittle and frail. [*Gets up.*] Torvald—in that instant it dawned on me that for eight years I've been living here with a stranger, and that I'd even conceived three children—oh, I can't stand the thought of it! I could tear myself to bits.

Reading Strategy
Recognizing Dramatic Tension In what ways does Nora's speech explain the increasing dramatic tension throughout the play?

 **Reading Check 53**

How long has Nora waited for some "miraculous" change to occur in her life?

A Doll House, Act Three ■ 1019

---

50 Critical Viewing
Possible response: Like the doll, Nora is pretty, well dressed, and subject to other's wishes. Unlike the doll, Nora is a real person who comes to realize that she has made mistakes and can take steps to improve herself and her life.

51 Reading Strategy
Recognizing Dramatic Tension
• Point out to students that Nora's expectation that Torvald would act nobly has been a source of dramatic tension throughout the play.
• **Ask** students the Reading Strategy question: In what ways does Nora's speech explain the increasing dramatic tension throughout the play?
Possible response: Nora's response clarifies that she has been waiting throughout the play for Torvald to act nobly.

52 Critical Thinking
Relate
• Have students read the bracketed passage.
• **Ask** students: Do you agree with Nora that millions of women have sacrificed honor for love?
Possible response: Marriages or relationships require some sacrifice, although it is possible to have both honor and love.
• **Ask:** Is this sacrifice more or less common today than in the 1870s?
Possible response: Because women have many more rights today, such a sacrifice is less common.

53 Reading Check
Answer: Nora has waited eight years.

Differentiated Instruction Solutions for All Learners

Enrichment for Gifted/Talented Students
Invite students to write an alternative ending to *A Doll House*. Ask students either to maintain Ibsen's realism and keep to the characters' personalities or to take the play and characters in a different direction. Ask volunteers to read aloud or act out their alternative endings for the class. Ask the listeners for their reactions.

Enrichment for Advanced Readers
Ask students to write a paragraph or two predicting what will happen to the characters after the ending of the play. Encourage students to base their predictions on their understanding of the characters and of the nineteenth-century world. Ask students to share their predictions with the class for discussion. Talk about why students think the way they do about the characters' chances after the play.

54 Humanities

The Customs, by Antonio Mancini

Italian painter Antonio Mancini (1852–1930) began his formal training as an artist at age twelve. After graduating from the Institute of Fine Art in Naples, he joined artists such as Vincenzo Gemito in creating a style of painting called Verismo (Italian for *Realism*). The paintings of the Verismo style depicted real people, particularly working-class people, in their own environment without idealizing them. Mancini's subjects included street people and artists, and his paintings of them tended to be dark and somber.

In 1875, Mancini traveled to Paris, where he met the leading painters of the day, Manet and Degas, who influenced his style. *The Customs* (1877) reflects a change. Although the painting has shadows and is dark overall, the gold of the walls adds a lightness and richness to the scene and sets off the woman's dark figure.

Use the following question for discussion:

What does the painting tell you about life for women in the nineteenth century?
Possible response: The woman may be waiting for something or someone to help her. She seems hemmed in by her clothes and the luggage at her feet. One can infer that women in the nineteenth-century were restricted in many ways beyond what appears here in this painting.

55 Critical Viewing

Possible response: Like the woman in the painting, Nora is about to embark on a journey. Unlike the woman in the painting, however, Nora tries to free herself rather than remain trapped by her status and belongings.

The Customs, National Gallery, London

55 ▲ **Critical Viewing** Which details in this painting suit this final scene of *A Doll House*? **[Interpret]**

1020 ■ *Romanticism and Realism*

Enrichment

Translations Are Not All the Same
This translation of *A Doll House* by Rolf Fjelde is so clear and informal in tone that a reader might easily forget that it is a translation from the Norwegian. Not every translation is as good as Fjelde's. Here are some excerpts from an English translation made by a Danish teacher.
Helmer: Don't utter such stupid shuffles. . . . From this moment it depends no longer on felicity; it depends on saving the rests, remnants, and the appearance.
(Compare with text on p. 1013.)

Nora: As I am now, I am no wife to you.
Helmer: I have the power to grow another. (Compare with text on p. 1021.)
Helmer: Change yourself in such a manner that—
Nora: —cohabitation between you and me might become a matrimony. Good-bye.
(Compare with text on p. 1022.)

HELMER [*heavily*]: I see. There's a gulf that's opened between us—that's clear. Oh, but Nora, can't we bridge it somehow?

NORA: The way I am now, I'm no wife for you.

HELMER: I have the strength to make myself over.

NORA: Maybe—if your doll gets taken away.

HELMER: But to part! To part from you! No, Nora, no—I can't imagine it.

NORA [*going out, right*]: All the more reason why it has to be. [*She reenters with her coat and a small overnight bag, which she puts on a chair by the table.*]

HELMER: Nora, Nora, not now! Wait till tomorrow.

NORA: I can't spend the night in a strange man's room.

HELMER: But couldn't we live here like brother and sister—

NORA: You know very well how long that would last. [*Throws her shawl about her.*] Good-bye, Torvald. I won't look in on the children. I know they're in better hands than mine. The way I am now, I'm no use to them.

HELMER: But someday, Nora—someday—?

NORA: How can I tell? I haven't the least idea what'll become of me.

HELMER: But you're my wife, now and wherever you go.

NORA: Listen, Torvald—I've heard that when a wife deserts her husband's house just as I'm doing, then the law frees him from all responsibility. In any case, I'm freeing you from being responsible. Don't feel yourself bound, any more than I will. There has to be absolute freedom for us both. Here, take your ring back. Give me mine.

HELMER: That too?

NORA: That too.

HELMER: There it is.

NORA: Good. Well, now it's all over, I'm putting the keys here. The maids know all about keeping up the house—better than I do. Tomorrow, after I've left town, Kristine will stop by to pack up everything that's mine from home. I'd like those things shipped up to me.

HELMER: Over! All over! Nora, won't you ever think about me?

NORA: I'm sure I'll think of you often, and about the children and the house here.

HELMER: May I write you?

NORA: No—never. You're not to do that.

HELMER: Oh, but let me send you—

NORA: Nothing. Nothing.

HELMER: Or help you if you need it.

Reading Strategy
Recognizing Dramatic Tension Which of Nora's words in this line best reveals the dramatic tension in the scene?

Literary Analysis
Theme and Foreshadowing Identify three details in Acts One and Two that foreshadow Nora's realization that she knows very little about her own home.

 Reading Check
From what is Nora freeing Torvald?

---

56 Reading Strategy
Recognizing Dramatic Tension
- Students should notice that Torvald is increasing the dramatic tension by refusing to let Nora go and offering her options that she does not want.
- Point out that Torvald's suggestions show that he no longer knows his wife.
- Have students **answer** the Reading Strategy question: Which of Nora's words in this line best reveals the dramatic tension in the scene? **Answer:** The word *strange* reveals the tension; Nora realizes that she barely knows her husband.

57 Literary Analysis
Theme and Foreshadowing
- Remind students that throughout the play, Nora has appeared helpless. **Review** the areas in her life where she has needed help. **Possible response:** Nora has needed help raising her children, maintaining the house, dealing with money, and even selecting a costume.
- **Ask** students to respond to the Literary Analysis item: Identify three details in Acts One and Two that foreshadow Nora's realization that she knows very little about her own home. **Possible responses:** In both acts it is clear that Nora is ignorant of situations within her home. On a literal level, Nora has little involvement with household activities; she has a nursemaid to care for her children and a maid to accept deliveries and admit visitors. More significant, however, is her ignorance of the people who are part of her home. Thinking that Krogstad's revelation of her secret to Torvald will cause mere "unpleasantness," assuming Torvald capable of change, and obliviousness to Dr. Rank's love for her, despite his daily visits, might foreshadow Nora's realization that she knows very little about her home and the nature of those who are part of it.

58 Reading Check
Answer: Nora is freeing Torvald from responsibility for her or her actions.

Differentiated Instruction Solutions for All Learners

Strategy for Less Proficient Readers
Ask students to write a short review of *A Doll House*. Remind them that a review should include their opinions about the plot, characters, or themes in the play and support for those opinions with words or ideas from the play. Finally, students should recommend or not recommend the play and give a reason why. If students need help getting started, allow them to look at reviews of movies, plays, or musical performances that have appeared in local newspapers. Encourage students to share their reviews with the class.

Enrichment for Advanced Readers
Ask students to write a review of *A Doll House* from the viewpoint of a nineteenth-century audience member. Students should give their opinions about the plot, characters, and themes from the perspective (and, if possible, in the language) of a nineteenth-century person. If students wish, they may research how early audiences responded to the play. Invite students to share their reviews with the class.

1. Many students will be sympathetic with Nora's decision because they believe that she deserves a better life. Others may fear that she does not realize what she is getting into or may find her selfish.

2. (a) Mrs. Linde proposes that she and Krogstad marry. (b) Mrs. Linde is no longer lonely. Krogstad is so happy that he drops his plans to blackmail the Helmers. (c) **Possible response:** Unlike Nora and Torvald, Mrs. Linde and Krogstad are honest in their relationship and understand each other's flaws.

3. (a) Torvald is furious with Nora when he reads the first letter. He fears for his reputation. (b) **Possible response:** His behavior proves that he is not noble and that he is more concerned about the appearance of his honor than his love for Nora.

4. (a) Nora agrees to accept nothing from Torvald in the future. (b) **Possible response:** Nora has grown up and wants to be responsible for herself alone; she does not want help from anyone. (c) **Possible response:** Torvald does not understand. Even as Nora leaves him, he talks about transforming himself and has a sudden hope for "the greatest miracle."

5. (a) Nora's marriage to Torvald has been like living in a doll house. She has been like a toy or a source of amusement for him, not his equal. His love for her has been like a child's for a doll. When Nora realizes this situation, she decides that she must leave in order to become an individual. (b) **Possible response:** It may be possible for Nora to find happiness later, in an equal partnership, after she has discovered more about herself.

6. **Possible response:** Nora's desire to be in an honest and equal relationship is relevant today, as is her awareness that people can change their lives when necessary.

NORA: No. I accept nothing from strangers.

HELMER: Nora—can I never be more than a stranger to you?

NORA [*picking up the overnight bag*]: Ah, Torvald—it would take the greatest miracle of all—

HELMER: Tell me the greatest miracle!

NORA: You and I both would have to transform ourselves to the point that— Oh, Torvald, I've stopped believing in miracles.

HELMER: But I'll believe. Tell me! Transform ourselves to the point that?

NORA: That our living together could be a true marriage. [*She goes out down the hall.*]

HELMER [*sinks down on a chair by the door, face buried in his hands*]: Nora! Nora! [*Looking about and rising.*] Empty. She's gone. [*A sudden hope leaps in him.*] The greatest miracle—?

[*From below, the sound of a door slamming shut.*]

Critical Reading

1. **Respond:** What is your response to Nora's decision to leave her husband and children? Explain.

2. **(a) Recall:** What plan does Mrs. Linde propose for herself and Krogstad? **(b) Analyze:** How does Mrs. Linde manage to solve several problems at once with this plan? **(c) Compare and Contrast:** What advantages do Mrs. Linde and Krogstad have over Torvald and Nora?

3. **(a) Recall:** What is Torvald's reaction when he reads the first letter from Krogstad? **(b) Draw Conclusions:** What does Torvald's reaction indicate to Nora about her husband's personality?

4. **(a) Recall:** What help does Nora agree to accept from Torvald in the future? **(b) Speculate:** Why do you think Nora refuses his help? **(c) Make a Judgment:** Do you think Torvald truly understands Nora's reasons for leaving? Why or why not?

5. **(a) Synthesize:** In what way does the play's title relate to Nora's discoveries about Torvald and to her decision to leave him? **(b) Speculate:** Do you think Nora might find happiness in another relationship in the future? Explain.

6. **Relate:** Which of Nora's experiences are still relevant today? Explain.

⌐Go **O**nline
└─**Author Link**
For: More about Henrik Ibsen
Visit: www.PHSchool.com
Web Code: ete-9710

⌐Go **O**nline For additional information about Henrik
└─**Author Link** Ibsen, have students type in the Web
Code, then select *I* from the alphabet, and then select
Henrik Ibsen.

Apply the Skills

A Doll House, Act Three

Literary Analysis

Theme

1. **(a)** One **theme** of *A Doll House* relates to discovering the keys to a successful relationship. Use a chart like the one shown to cite three examples of dialogue from Act Three that relate to this theme.

Character	Dialogue	Keys to a Successful Relationship

   (b) What conclusions about a successful relationship can you draw from the dialogue you noted?

2. Identify three details supporting the theme that society and authority hinder the development of the individual.

3. Which characters embody the theme that all people must live their lives according to their convictions? Explain.

Connecting Literary Elements

4. Mrs. Linde says to Krogstad, "Anyone who's sold herself for somebody else once isn't going to do it again." In what way does this comment **foreshadow** Nora's decision to leave Torvald?

5. **(a)** What events are foreshadowed when Torvald remarks that "an exit should always be effective, Mrs. Linde, but that's what I can't get Nora to grasp"? **(b)** What is ironic or unexpected about Torvald's statement?

Reading Strategy

Recognizing Dramatic Tension

6. **(a)** Which moment in Act Three marks the height of **dramatic tension? (b)** Which conflicts are resolved when the dramatic tension breaks? **(c)** Which conflicts remain unresolved?

7. **(a)** What is at stake for Nora if she remains with Torvald? **(b)** List three lines in Act Three that show the extent to which Torvald fails to understand what Nora stands to lose. **(c)** Explain the way in which those lines increase the dramatic tension.

Extend Understanding

8. **Career Connection:** Consider the résumé Nora might build. What marketable skills has Nora acquired during her years with Torvald that will allow her to support herself without his help?

QuickReview

A drama's **theme** is its central message, idea, or insight.

Foreshadowing is the use of details or clues that hint at events or conditions to come.

To **recognize dramatic tension,** look for moments of conflict and mystery that build suspense and anticipation.

Go Online
Assessment
For: Self-test
Visit: www.PHSchool.com
Web Code: eta-6707

A Doll House, Act Three ■ 1023

Answers continued

8. Nora can sew and copy manuscript. She knows something about raising children.

Go Online Students may use the **Self-test** to pre-
Assessment pare for **Selection Test A** or Selection
Test B.

Answers

1. **Possible response:** (a) **Character:** Mrs. Linde **Dialogue:** "We both need each other. Nils, I have faith that you're good at heart—I'll risk everything together with you." **Key:** Partners should have faith in each other. **Character:** Nora **Dialogue:** "I'm saying that we've never sat down seriously together and tried to get to the bottom of anything." **Key:** Communication is important to a relationship. **Character:** Nora **Dialogue:** "You never loved me. You've thought it fun to be in love with me, that's all." **Key:** A good relationship should be based on authentic love. (b) A good relationship is based on faith, open communication, honesty, respect, and love. Another sample answer can be found on **Literary Analysis Graphic Organizer B,** p. 178 in *Graphic Organizer Transparencies.*

2. **Possible response:** Mrs. Linde married unhappily to save her family; now she is able to make a choice as an individual. Torvald is so afraid of losing his respectability that he shows himself to be a coward. Nora has been kept like a doll in a doll house, so she must leave her marriage to become an individual.

3. Dr. Rank lives in the moment because he knows that he will die soon. Nora learns that she must leave her home and family to develop.

4. Like Mrs. Linde, Nora has "sold herself" in marriage, and she is not going to compromise herself by staying with Torvald.

5. (a) His remark foreshadows Nora's exit at the end of the play. (b) The irony is that Nora's exit will be more effective than any Torvald could imagine.

6. (a) Torvald reads Krogstad's letter. (b) The conflicts between Torvald and Nora, Krogstad and the Helmers, and within Nora are resolved. (c) The conflict between Nora and society is unresolved.

7. (a) Nora's ability to become an individual is at stake. (b) "But someday, Nora—someday—?"; "Over! All over! Nora, won't you ever think about me?"; "The greatest miracle—?" (c) The lines increase the dramatic tension by confirming Torvald's inability to understand Nora's feelings and thus prolonging the conflict.

1023

❶ Vocabulary Lesson

Word Analysis:
Greek Prefix *hypo-*

1. b   2. a

Spelling Strategy

1. hypocrite   3. trilogy
2. mystery   4. vicarious

Vocabulary Builder: Context

1. grafter   5. evasions
2. calculating   6. hypocrite
3. proprieties   7. naturalistic
4. bewildered

❷ Grammar and Style Lesson

1. to talk about; adjective (modifies *anything*)

2. to abandon me; adjective (modifies *right*)

3. to be realistic; noun (direct object of *learned*)

4. to see Nora in costume; noun (direct object of *did want*)

5. to sit with me; adverb (modifies *brought*)

Writing Application

Sample response: When she sees Torvald open the mailbox, Nora plans to drown herself. (noun; direct object of *plans*) Torvald needs someone to blame. (adjective; modifies *someone*) Nora feels ready to become an individual. (adverb; modifies *ready*)

𝒲𝒢 **Writing and Grammar**
Platinum Level

For support in teaching the Grammar and Style Lesson, use Chapter 20, Section 1.

Build Language Skills

❶ Vocabulary Lesson

Word Analysis: Greek Prefix *hypo-*

The Greek prefix *hypo-* means "under," "less than," or "slightly." Use your understanding of the meaning of *hypo-* to identify the word that best completes each sentence below.

    a. hypocrite   **b.** hypothermia

    1. After being rescued from the cold river, she suffered from ___.
    2. The ___ pretended to be someone that he was not.

Spelling Strategy

Both the letter *i* and the letter *y* can represent either the short or long *i* sound in words. Complete each word below with either the letter *i* or the letter *y*.

    1. h___pocrite   **3.** tr___logy
    2. m___stery   **4.** v___carious

Vocabulary Builder: Context

Review the vocabulary words on page 1000. Then, complete each of the following sentences.

    1. The ____ looted a local business.
    2. She used her___ ways to convince her brother to finish her chores.
    3. By paying attention to social ___, he earned a spotless reputation.
    4. The child seemed ___ by the unjust punishment.
    5. The suspect responded with ___ to all questions.
    6. The lawyer was branded a ___ when he committed perjury on the witness stand.
    7. The audience was shocked by the ___ appearance of the robot.

❷ Grammar and Style Lesson

Infinitives and Infinitive Phrases

An **infinitive** is a verb form consisting of the base form of a verb, usually with the word *to*. An **infinitive phrase** combines an infinitive plus its complements or modifiers to act as a single part of speech. Infinitive phrases function as nouns, adjectives, or adverbs.

> **As a Noun:** "Life's taught me <u>never to trust fine phrases</u>. . . ." (direct object of the verb *taught*)
>
> **As an Adjective:** "Someone <u>to work for</u>, <u>to live for</u>. . . ." (modifying the pronoun *someone*)
>
> **As an Adverb:** "How am I equipped <u>to bring up children</u>?" (modifying the verb *equipped*)

Practice Copy each item below, underlining the infinitive phrase and identifying its function in the sentence.

    1. "Do we two have anything more to talk about?"
    2. ". . . you hadn't the right to abandon me for somebody else's sake."
    3. "I've learned to be realistic."
    4. ". . . I did want to see Nora in costume."
    5. "That is why I brought you down to sit with me."

Writing Application Write a paragraph about Nora in which you use three infinitive phrases. Underline each phrase, and identify its function.

𝒲𝒢 *Prentice Hall Writing and Grammar Connection: Platinum Level, Chapter 20, Section 1*

Assessment Practice

Analyzing Literary Language   (For more practice, see *Test Preparation Workbook*, p. 44.)

Students must analyze the literary language of texts, including what the author's word choice reveals about a character. Use this sample test item.

> I have to work to go on living. All my born days, as long as I can remember, I've worked, and it's been my best and my only joy. But now I'm completely alone in the world; it frightens me to be so empty and lost. To work for yourself—there's no joy in that. Nils, give me something—someone to work for.
>
> —from *A Doll House*, Act Three

The series of sentences about work emphasizes that for Mrs. Linde working for others represents—

    A an intolerable burden.
    B a way to pass the time.
    C a way to establish independence.
    D an unselfish purpose for living.

Help students see that Mrs. Linde begins with a few general statements about working and then moves to her specific desire. The correct response is *D*.

❸ Writing Lesson

Timed Writing: Writing a Persuasive Essay

When one is faced with a difficult choice, it can be extremely hard to make the right decision. Write a persuasive essay in which you argue for or against Nora's decision to leave Torvald, basing your arguments on events or lines from the play. **(40 minutes)**

Prewriting
(10 minutes) Review the play and decide whether or not you agree with Nora's decision. Create an outline, listing points that confirm your opinion and including references to the play that support each point.

Drafting
(20 minutes) As you write, anticipate your readers' objections to the position you are taking. For example, if you think Nora's decision is the right one, you might consider who will take care of Nora's children or how she might support herself. Answer each objection, and write your counterarguments clearly and effectively.

Revising
(10 minutes) Review your draft, removing any empty or unnecessary words or phrases that do not add to your argument.

Model: Removing Unnecessary Words or Phrases

~~It seems to me that~~ Nora could never be happy if her marriage continued in the same pattern. Her husband's weaknesses and her own shortcomings force her to seek ~~a sense of~~ independence.

> Removing unnecessary words and phrases focuses your sentences and makes them more effective.

WG Prentice Hall Writing and Grammar Connection: Platinum Level, Chapter 7, Section 4

❹ Extend Your Learning

Listening and Speaking In a small group, participate in a **round-table discussion** of the themes in *A Doll House.* Follow these rules of courtesy:

1. Pay attention as others speak.
2. Do not interrupt.
3. Speak clearly.

Compare the opinions shared in the discussion with those of other groups in your class.
[Group Activity]

Research and Technology Choose one character and scene from *A Doll House* and develop a **costume design display.** Begin by researching the dress of the time. Make a sketch of the character wearing a costume appropriate for the scene. Choose fabric swatches and include them in a display that you share with your class.

Go Online
Research

For: An additional research activity
Visit: www.PHSchool.com
Web Code: etd-7705

A Doll House ■ 1025

Assessment Resources

The following resources can be used to assess students' knowledge and skills.

Unit 7 Resources
  Selection Test A, pp. 126–128
  Selection Test B, pp. 129–131
  Benchmark Test 9, pp. 139–144

General Resources
  Rubrics for Persuasion: Persuasive Essay, pp. 47–48
  Rubric for Listening: Evaluating a Persuasive Presentation, p. 83

Go Online
Assessment Students may use the **Self-test** to prepare for **Selection Test A** or **Selection Test B.**

Benchmark
Administer **Benchmark Test 9.** If some students need further work, use the **Interpretation Guide** to determine the appropriate reteaching page in the **Reading Kit** and on **Success Tracker.**

---

❸ Writing

You may use this Writing Lesson as a timed-writing practice, or you may allow students to develop the persuasive essay as a writing assignment over several days.

- To give students guidance in writing this essay, give them the **Support for Writing Lesson,** p. 123 in *Unit 7 Resources.*

- Tell students that a persuasive essay is a written statement that presents a position and tries to persuade readers to accept or support that position.

- Remind students that a good essay has an introduction with a strong opinion statement, a body that presents evidence, and a conclusion that sums up the argument. Tell students to use transition words to help readers follow the flow of their ideas.

- Use the Persuasion: Persuasive Essay rubrics in *General Resources,* pp. 47–48, to evaluate students' work.

WG **Writing and Grammar Platinum Level**
For support in teaching the Writing Lesson, use Chapter 7, Section 4.

❹ Listening and Speaking

- Have students use the themes listed on p. 1000 to begin their discussion. Students should use their discussion time to review the details of the play that support the different themes.

- Challenge students to identify the theme that they consider the most dominant or important in the play.

- Ask one student to take notes during the discussion and one to moderate and make sure that each student in the group contributes to the discussion.

- Use the Listening: Evaluating a Persuasive Presentation rubric in *General Resources,* p. 83, to evaluate students' work.

- The **Support for Extend Your Learning** page (*Unit 7 Resources,* p. 124) provides guided note-taking opportunities to help students complete the Extend Your Learning activities.

Go Online
Research Have students type in the Web Code for another research activity.

Standard Course of Study

WL.1.02.4 Explain how culture affects personal responses.

FA.3.02.1 State position or proposed solution in an editorial or response.

CT.4.05.4 Comprehend main idea and supporting details in critical text.

Background

George Bernard Shaw and Henrik Ibsen

Many later playwrights, including the great Irish playwright George Bernard Shaw, were influenced by Henrik Ibsen. Commenting on Ibsen's impact on the theater, Shaw wrote: "When Ibsen began to make plays, the art of the dramatist had shrunk into the art of contriving a situation. And it was held that the stranger the situation, the better the play. Ibsen saw that, on the contrary, the more familiar the situation, the more interesting the play."

Shaw greatly admired Ibsen's interest in social reform but acknowledged that after the reforms addressed in a play had taken place, the play might become outdated. Shaw wrote: "*A Doll House* will be as flat as ditchwater when *A Midsummer Night's Dream* will still be as fresh as paint; but it will have done more work in the world, and that is enough for the highest genius, which is always intensely utilitarian."

Background

The Nineteenth Amendment

In most American states, women did not gain the right to vote until the early 1900s. In fact, no state allowed women to vote until Wyoming entered the Union in 1890. Three decades later, however, the nineteenth Amendment to the United States Constitution was ratified, giving all American women the right to vote. The amendment reads: "The right of citizens of the United States to vote shall not be denied or abridged by the United States or by any state on account of sex."

A Closer Look

The Slamming of the Door

The last words of Henrik Ibsen's play *A Doll House* are not spoken by any of the characters. Rather, they are a single stage direction: "From below, the sound of a door slamming shut."

In 1879, when the play was first performed, that sound—a symbol of Nora's escape from her constrictive marriage—represented a direct challenge to society's views of men and women. In the decades that followed, the status of women in Western society began undergoing a dramatic transformation. Today, many scholars view Nora's slamming of the door as a pivotal point in the modern feminist movement. In fact, as the great Irish playwright George Bernard Shaw wrote, the slamming of the door can be regarded as "the end of a chapter in human history."

> **❝** *The slamming of the door at the end of A Doll House was a sound heard 'round the world.* **❞**

Women in the Nineteenth Century When Ibsen wrote *A Doll House*, the idea that a woman might choose to leave her family in order to live independently was not merely unacceptable—it was inconceivable for most people. Common belief suggested that women were inferior to men, a notion that was supported by the laws of that time. As a result, women did not enjoy the same rights and privileges as men. Few women were educated. They could not own property. They could not vote. They had severely limited career opportunities. Women were expected to marry, to raise their children, and to obey their husbands without question.

Nora's Rebellion When Nora leaves Torvald and her children in order to educate herself and seek her own fulfillment, she rebels not only against Torvald's authority but also against the expectations of society as a whole. She first tells Torvald that she is leaving, and he forbids her to go. Then, he warns her that she is "not even thinking about what people will say." Nora responds that she is not concerned with other people's opinions, adding that her duty to herself is more important than her duties as a wife and mother. She declares, "I'm a human being, no less than you— or anyway, I ought to try to become one. I know the majority thinks you're right, Torvald, and plenty of books agree with you, too. But I can't go on believing what the majority says, or what's written in books."

The Impact of Nora's Rebellion When Nora finally leaves Torvald and slams the door shut behind her, Ibsen's first audiences were shocked and dismayed. Yet, this sense of shock forced many people to reevaluate their ideas about men and women; in the years that followed the play's first

1026 ■ *Romanticism and Realism*

Enrichment

Ibsen's Modern Dramas

Prior to Henrik Ibsen's time, dramas, known as "well-made plays," were meant to entertain audiences by appealing to people's imaginations. Consequently, dramatists generally did not depict events in an accurate manner but instead wove together intricate plots filled with coincidences that would be unlikely to occur in real life and offered tidy resolutions to "unravel" these plots. In addition, characters often revealed their inner thoughts directly to the audience.

In contrast, Ibsen sought to depict life accurately and realistically in his plays, while delving into the types of conflicts and dilemmas that he viewed as characteristic of his time. He focused on situations that could easily occur in real life, and he patterned his dialogue after real-life conversations. Just as in a typical discussion between friends or family, emotions and inner thoughts unfold between Ibsen's characters. According to critic John Gassner, it was with this dramatic technique—the discussion— "that the distinctly modern drama was born."

performances, women began to gain some of the rights and privileges that they had previously been denied.

During the course of the twentieth century, women in many countries gained the right to vote and to own property. The educational and professional opportunities available to women expanded tremendously. Many women became involved in politics; in Great Britain, Pakistan, and the Philippines, women were elected to the highest government posts.

Ibsen and Feminism Because of the stories he tells in *A Doll House* and other works, Ibsen is often regarded as one of the pioneering spirits in the feminist movement. Although Ibsen himself might have rejected this label, it cannot be denied that he was one of the first men to openly express concern about the status of women. Ibsen's notes to *A Doll House* clearly indicate that he wanted the play to capture the ways in which society restricted women's freedom and growth. He wrote, "There are two kinds of spiritual law, two kinds of conscience, one in man and another, altogether different, in women. A woman cannot be herself in the society of the present day, which is exclusively a masculine society. . . . "

Today, many questions about gender remain unanswered. For example, are the psyches of men and women fundamentally different, as Ibsen suggests? Yet, even without answers to these questions, common attitudes and laws no longer support the notion that women are inferior. Nora's slamming of the door may no longer shock, but the echoes it created continue to resonate.

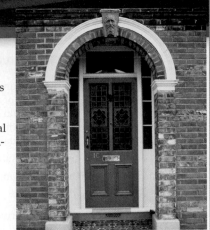

▲ **Critical Viewing**
In what ways can doors, like those shown above, serve as symbols for ideas or emotions? **[Generalize]**

Activity

Gender Roles Today

Few people would disagree that women's place in Western society has changed significantly since Ibsen wrote *A Doll House* in 1897. How widespread the changes are and whether more change is needed are questions that many believe are still open for debate.

With a group, discuss your thoughts about the roles of women and men in our society. Use these questions to guide your discussion:
- From your experience, are the values and attitudes of men and women fundamentally different, as Ibsen suggests?
- **(a)** In what ways do differences between men and women affect gender roles in our society? **(b)** Do other factors in society affect gender roles? Explain.
- What changes would you still like to see, if any, for women in our society?

Choose a point person to share your ideas with the class.

The Slamming of the Door ■ 1027

Activity

Have students form small groups with equal representation of males and females. In the values discussion, urge students to maintain respect for one another's opinions, and observe courtesy.

For the discussion on gender roles, suggest that some individuals research on the Internet for answers to questions such as these: How many women serve in your state legislature, in the U.S. Congress, and in the Supreme Court? How many women are CEOs in major U.S. corporations? How does the average hourly wage women receive compare with that of men? When this information is collected, organize it for the group's presentation.

Background

Ibsen and Women's "Instinctive Genius"

At the time Henrik Ibsen was writing *A Doll House,* he delivered a speech to the Scandinavian Club in which he proposed that women should be allowed to vote. He remarked: "I am not afraid of these so-called impractical women; women have something in common with the true artist, just as young people in general have—something that is a good substitute for worldly understanding. Look at our student societies in Norway! Matters are decided there which are ten times more complicated than ours; yet do they not manage well, although youth, untried, unpracticed and unpractical youth there enjoys an overwhelming majority? And why? Because youth has an instinctive genius which unconsciously hits upon the right answer. And it is precisely this instinct which women share with youth, and with the true artist."

Critical Viewing

Possible response: Doors, like ideas and emotions, can be open or closed, large or small, colorful or dull. An open door can be seen as an invitation to enter, explore, and see what exists on the other side. A closed door can be seen as an obstacle, a barrier, and a challenge to the adventurous spirit.

Critical Thinking

1. **Explain** why Nora's actions at the end of *A Doll House* would or would not be considered acceptable in contemporary American society. **[Make a Judgment]**
   Possible response: Nora's actions would not be considered surprising in contemporary American society but would generally be considered unacceptable because she essentially is abandoning her children.

2. Do you agree with Ibsen that the psyches of men and women are fundamentally different? Why or why not? **[Defend]**
   Possible responses: Men may be more aggressive and less nurturing than women. However, their apparent differences may also be merely the result of training and society's gender expectations.

NC Standard Course of Study

CT.4.05.3 Provide evidence to support understanding of and response to critical interpretation.

CT.4.05.5 Summarize key events and points from critical text.

CT.4.05.9 Analyze and evaluate the effects of craft and style in critical text.

See Teacher Express™/Lesson View for a detailed lesson for Reading Informational Material.

About Critical Reviews

- After students read "About Critical Reviews", **ask** them to name products or performances about which they have read critical reviews. **Possible responses:** Television shows, films, plays, musical groups, and restaurants are all reviewed.

- **Ask** students what they expect to learn when reading a critical review. **Possible response:** Students may expect to learn opinions about various aspects of the item being reviewed. Critical reviews often make recommendations.

- Discuss the terms *argumentative presentations* and *powerful language.* Emphasize that effective reviews use assertive words rather than noncommittal language such as *sort of* and *kind of.*

Reading Strategy
Comparing and Contrasting Critical Reviews

- Have a volunteer read aloud the information about the Reading Strategy. Remind students that a good critical review is a judgment based on established criteria. A reviewer must carefully select criteria against which to measure the subject of the review.

- Point out that reviewers may use different criteria in their reviews. However, in reviews of a certain genre—in this case, theatrical performance—reviewers often consider the same criteria. Draw students' attention to the Critical Reviews chart. Explain that the labels down the left side list criteria addressed in all three reviews.

Critical Reviews
About Critical Reviews

A critical review analyzes and evaluates a product, an artistic performance, or even the behavior of a person or group. As the name suggests, critical reviews usually contain strong opinions. In this context, however, the word *critical* can mean either a positive or a negative judgment. Most critical reviews will contain the following:

- a brief summary of the subject matter
- a carefully thought-out and stated opinion
- supporting evidence

Because the purpose of a critical review is often to persuade, expect to find argumentative presentations and powerful language.

Reading Strategy
Comparing and Contrasting Critical Reviews

Opinions can vary greatly from person to person. For objectivity, you should read multiple critical reviews on a single subject to arrive at the "big picture" of what is being reviewed. Compare the reviews to determine areas where critics share the same point of view. Then, note the contrasts—points where the critics' opinions differ. Making these comparisons and contrasts will help you evaluate both the critical reviews and their subject matter.

As critics, the writers of the following critical reviews saw the same performance of Ibsen's *A Doll's House.* Yet their impressions of the show—particularly the performance of the leading actress—range from glowing praise to lukewarm acceptance. To determine an overall impression of the show, complete a chart like the one shown by filling in the critics' names and opinions as you read the reviews.

Use the information you have gathered and your Overall Evaluation to determine whether you would be interested in seeing these productions.

Critical Reviews			
Critic			
Lead Actress's Performance			
Director and/or Script			
Overall Evaluation (+ or –)			

1028 ■ Romanticism and Realism

Differentiated Instruction   Solutions for All Learners

Reading Support
Give students reading support with the appropriate version of the **Reader's Notebooks:**
   Reader's Notebook: **[L2, L3]**
   Reader's Notebook: Adapted Version **[L1, L2]**
   Reader's Notebook: English Learner's Version **[EL]**

Curtain Up Review:

A Doll's House

by Judd Hollander & Sue Feinberg

> This critical review begins with a brief summary of the subject matter.

From the moment she steps onto the stage of the Belasco Theater, Janet McTeer delivers a riveting performance as Nora Helmer, the heroine of Henrik Ibsen's *A Doll's House,* currently playing at the Belasco Theatre.

Set in a small Norwegian town during Christmas 1879 (and inspired by actual events), the play tells the story of a young wife (McTeer) and mother who's still pretty much a child herself. This time out, however, the 118-year-old work has been given a 1990s feel. McTeer's Nora is a whirling dervish, full of life and laughter, a woman who would be more at home on the stage of an English Music Hall than with her husband Torvald (Owen Teale) and three children. (Her idea of a perfect life is having "pots and pots and pots of money.")

After years of struggle, the couple has finally achieved a measure of financial security, thanks to Torvald's new job as a bank manager. But then a ghost from Nora's past appears in the form of Nils Krogstad (Peter Gowen). Several years earlier, Nora secretly borrowed money for a trip to a warmer climate to allow her desperately ill husband to recover. In order to guarantee the loan, she forged a signature on a contract. Krogstad wants his money back and Nora, not able to give it, is terrified that Torvald will learn the truth.

As events unfold, Nora slowly comes to realize that the "perfect" life she has led is nothing but a fairy tale. Her life has been that of a doll to be pampered and protected, first by her father and then by her husband. But even as she's forced to face reality, she tries to do the right thing, only to realize that what she loves the most is the biggest lie of all.

Ibsen's work caused quite a shock when it first premiered in 1879 and was heralded as one of the first modern, post-Shakespeare "women's plays." McTeer takes the role of Ibsen's

---

* CurtainUp.com is an online theater magazine. URL: www.curtainup.com

Reading Informational Materials: Critical Reviews ■ 1029

Reading Critical Reviews

- Explain to students that critical reviews appear in a variety of publications, including newspapers and magazines.
- **Ask** students to identify the reviewers and the publication that features this review.
  Answer: Judd Hollander and Sue Feinberg are the reviewers. The review appeared in CurtainUp.com, an online theater magazine.
- Call students' attention to the first call-out note. Point out that the brief summary of the subject matter helps readers immediately identify the reviewer's position. **Ask** students: Will this review of Janet McTeer's performance be positive or negative? Explain.
  Answer: The use of the word *riveting* reveals that this will be a positive review of the performance.

continued on p. 1030

Differentiated Instruction Solutions for All Learners

Vocabulary for Less Proficient Readers
Students may have difficulty with the following words and phrases: *riveting, whirling dervish, forged,* and *heralded.* Have students work in pairs to use dictionaries to find the definitions for these words and phrases. Encourage students to use dictionaries to define other troublesome words or phrases encountered in the critical reviews and to begin a vocabulary journal in which they record these words and phrases.

Vocabulary for English Learners
Students may have difficulty with the description of Nora as a "whirling dervish," the reference to "a ghost from Nora's past," and the assertion that Nora's life has been a "fairy tale." Help students understand the figurative nature of these phrases by explaining that they are not meant to be taken literally. Then, guide a discussion in which students consider the meanings of these phrases and what the author wants to express through their use.

1029

- Direct students' attention to the first call-out note. Remind them that a reviewer must establish the criteria he or she will consider in the review. In a review of a stage performance, the director, the actors, the producers, and the script are the criteria evaluated.

- **Ask** students to list other criteria a reviewer might consider when evaluating a stage performance.
  Possible response: Costumes, lighting, set design, and musical accompaniment are other criteria a reviewer might consider.

- Read aloud the second call-out note and the paragraph to which it refers. Remind students that this paragraph functions as a conclusion, summing up the opinions presented in the review.

- **Ask** students to identify those words and phrases in the last paragraph that support a positive recommendation.
  Answer: The words *intense* and *compelling* and the phrase *well worth the trip* indicate that the recommendation is positive.

doll wife and brilliantly makes it her own. Her Nora runs the gamut of emotions from fear to rage to loathing to desperation. Even her demeanor and manner alter and she seems to age before our eyes, gaining not experience or wisdom, but the understanding that these are the qualities she must find. Just before the show ends, there's a scene where she mocks her former "sing-song" persona. That Nora is light-years removed from the one we first met only three hours or, according to the play's time frame, three days before.

While McTeer is the play's linchpin, she does not have the toughest role in the piece. That honor goes to Owen Teale. His Torvald at first glance seems the stereotypical nineteenth-century husband, a man with a keen sense of propriety who knows that a man is ruler

of his home. He unquestionably loves Nora, and Teale lets us see and feel the passion beneath the propriety of the character—as well as a mean streak that makes him dangerous if crossed.

Many of Teale's lines, which would not have raised an eyebrow in 1879 Norway, drew roars of contemptuous laughter from the 1997 audience. Yet when his whole world comes crashing down and he's forced (after much prodding) to confront the lie his life has become, he makes a subtle, almost unnoticed, transformation. Slowly he begins to understand his wife's pain and the role he has played in letting it continue. When he says to Nora "I have the strength in me to become another man," we're seeing a soul laid bare in a way that's totally convincing.

Director Anthony Page keeps the pace moving during the more active scenes, and he and the actors managed to hold the audience's interest even during the slow sections, which consist of lengthy, two-person conversations with very little action (though they do provide vital plot information). The script, taken from a literal translation of the work, could probably have been cut by a half-hour. However, the cast and producers seemed more interested in presenting a definitive version of the Ibsen work rather than adapting it to suit a 90s audience. And in this, they have succeeded admirably. Despite its wordiness, the play gradually draws you into its emotional web and delivers a knockout punch of a payoff.

Quibbles about slow-pacing aside, *A Doll's House* is an intense and compelling journey through the human spirit and well worth the trip.

A thorough critical review covers all the parts of what is being reviewed. Here, the critics discuss the director, the actors, the producers, and the script.

The review ends with a positive recommendation to potential theatergoers.

Sunday, April 20, 1997

A Lot of Baggage for Nora to Carry

After a History of Misinterpretation, Ibsen's Leave-Taking Heroine Finally Gets Her Due

By Lloyd Rose
Washington Post Staff Writer

As Nora in the London-produced *A Doll's House* now playing on Broadway, the tall, rangy Janet McTeer is as gawkily graceful as a young swan. This Nora is a six-foot bundle of adorability—and she knows it. Everything in her movement and manner—especially her hoarse, self-conscious giggle—says to the men in her life, "Aren't I silly, aren't I scatterbrained, aren't I helpless, don't you adore me?" And they do.

A Doll's House, the story of a pampered bourgeois wife who rebelliously leaves her domineering husband, has a problematic reputation. . . . At least one reviewer felt constrained to point out that the New York production is more than "a feminist screed." Henrik Ibsen . . . has been getting bopped with accusations of feminism since the play's debut in 1880. When Nora realized her life was a lie and walked out on her husband and children, nineteenth-century audiences were scandalized.

McTeer and director Anthony Page bring this production very close to what I've always thought is the essential truth of A Doll's House. . . .

McTeer's Nora doesn't realize so much that Torvald is a cad (Owen Teale's honorable, grounded performance makes that impossible anyway) as that she has constructed a fantasy about his being a hero. The mistake is hers, for being a grown woman who believes in a fairy tale.

This discovery doesn't put Nora in a lecturing mood. She's staggered, a little dazed, as if she'd been punched in the head by reality.

As McTeer plays it, the last speech isn't superior and scolding; she doesn't even don her coat until toward the end. Her Nora is tentative, feeling her way through the revelations that have been forced upon her, realizing what she has done. As a result, the character is fascinating, surprising, disturbing, instead of being all dreary and moral and right.

This production doesn't go quite as far as it could—Nora still scores some too-easy points over Torvald—but it goes a long, brave way. In London McTeer won an Olivier Award for her performance, beating out such powerhouse talents as Diana Rigg and Vanessa Redgrave, and you certainly see why. She's not as luminous as Redgrave. She's not as witty and fierce as Rigg. But she is certainly, as Ralph Richardson used to say of Laurence Olivier, "bold . . . very, very bold."

A subhead gives readers a preview of the opinion to follow.

Rose states his opinion and then supports his point of view with evidence from the performance.

Reading Critical Reviews (cont.)

- Draw students' attention to the first call-out note here. **Ask** students to predict what the reviewer's opinion will be, on the basis of the headline and subhead.
  Possible response: The headline, with its mention of "baggage," indicates that this performance is burdened by past interpretations and by social commentary on the play as a whole. The subhead, however, indicates that despite this burden, the performance is a successful one.

- Point out to students that in his review, Rose acknowledges other dramatic interpretations as well as other critical discussions of *A Doll House.* These interpretations and discussions become part of the criteria against which Rose weighs this particular performance.

- Read aloud the third paragraph of the review. Make sure that students understand that Rose is considering the intentions of Ibsen's play itself.

- Draw students' attention to the second call-out note. **Ask** students to restate Rose's opinion.
  Answer: Rose believes that this performance captures the essence of Ibsen's play: McTeer's Nora understands that her life is an illusion and that she is at fault for creating such an illusion.

- Then, have students read the remainder of the text independently. **Ask:** What evidence does Rose use to support his opinion?
  Answer: Rose says that McTeer's Nora is not "superior and scolding," but "tentative." This characterization supports Rose's interpretation of Nora as feeling foolish when her fantasies crumble.

continued on p. 1032

Differentiated Instruction — Solutions for All Learners

Vocabulary for Special Needs Students

Students may have difficulty with words such as *gawkily, adorability, bourgeois, domineering,* and *cad.* Have students use thesauruses to find synonyms for these words. Then, encourage students to reread the selection, replacing the difficult words with the synonyms. For example, students might replace *gawkily* with *awkwardly, adorability* with *cuteness, bourgeois* with *middle-class, domineering* with *controlling,* and *cad* with *rascal.*

Enrichment for Gifted/Talented Students

Pair students, and have them perform the final scene of *A Doll House,* first portraying Nora as "superior and scolding . . . dreary and moral and right" and then as "tentative." When students have finished their performances, ask them how these two dramatic interpretations change the meaning of the play. Which characterization of Nora do students think Ibsen intended? Which characterization do students prefer?

- Read the review's title and subtitle for students. Then, discuss with students what the subtitle "A New Version by Frank McGuiness" might mean. Tell students that plays, especially those written in earlier times, are often reinterpreted or rewritten for modern audiences.

- Ask a volunteer to read aloud the first two sentences of the selection. Then, **ask:** On the basis of these sentences, how would you characterize David Spencer's attitude toward this "new" version of Ibsen's play? Explain.
  Answer: Spencer seems wary of this version, made evident by the fact that he begins the review with an explanation of the performance's "newness." He wants the reader to realize that his review considers the performance in relation to other, more traditional interpretations of the play.

- Draw students' attention to the first call-out note. Remind students that reviewers use powerful language to convince the audience that their opinions are valid. The tone of a review should be confident. If a reviewer questions his or her own assessments, the reader will, too.

- Then, draw students' attention to the last call-out note. Explain that this last paragraph offers an overall assessment of McTeer's performance and McGuiness's version of the play. **Ask** students to summarize this assessment.
  Answer: Overall, Spencer expresses a positive opinion of McTeer's performance, calling her a "magnificent actress." However, in Spencer's opinion, McGuiness's version as a whole leaves much to be desired.

A Doll's House

By Henrik Ibsen
A New Version by Frank McGuiness

Reviewed by David Spencer

The first thing you have to understand about this so-called revival of A Doll's House—which comes to Broadway by way of London—is that it's not a revival at all. It follows the general outline of Ibsen's famous drama about a woman's coming of age—it contains the same characters and the same events—but it's essentially a new play by Frank ("Someone Who'll Watch over Me") McGuiness. Note his credit: not "translation by" but "a new version by." It's a credit I note with particular emphasis because I have one such on my own resumé. . . . So as you read all the pæans to Janet McTeer's performance as a devastating "new" Nora, keep in mind that a new Nora is precisely, literally, what's on offer. And it starts not with the actress, but with the script—whose spin on Ibsen is both compelling and subversive.

That [Janet McTeer] is vivacious, sensual, charismatic, explosive—everything you want a "star" to be—is undeniable. Her Nora trembles with suppressed giggles, bursts with surprise, teases mercilessly, touches, hugs, whispers conspiratorially, revels in her own outrageousness. In the play's first act, this electrifies the audience—palpably. At first, it all but overwhelms Owen Teale's performance as her husband Torvald (a portrayal of a vigorously insecure martinet wannabe) . . . but it creates a buzz of excitement and discovery.

It's not a buzz that sustains, though. Because after intermission, with Acts Two and Three (performed in one stretch), the vivacity turns to a jittery desperation and finally to out-and-out hysteria. It seems like a perfectly logical progression: once the tight rein on Nora's sense of stability is released by the threat of blackmail and ruination, her energy would fly out of control, she would find herself without moorings. But in the playing, it is merely relentless.

Happily, in Acts Two and Three, with the shock of the new Nora no longer a novelty, we do get to concentrate on the others in the ensemble—and they are fine within the parameters of the script.

They don't, however, bring the audience closer to the play. Yes, with this Doll's House being so different, so modern of intent, it is endlessly fascinating—but it's a fascination experienced from a distance. You are always aware of the revisionist take on things, always pausing to note the controversial new choices, to compare them to Ibsen's original . . . rather than just experiencing them on a visceral level.

I don't mean to condemn this production—or, for that matter, Ms. McTeer. McGuiness' revisionist take is a fine and noble experiment, and his Nora is clearly a magnificent actress. I just feel as if—in the final analysis, in the grand karmic sweep of the universe—this A Doll's House is not the be-all, end-all revelation the hype would have you believe, but rather an intermediary step.

> Notice the powerful words Spencer uses to communicate his opinion of the performance.

> The writer identifies both positive and negative aspects of the production.

Differentiated Instruction — Solutions for All Learners

Support for Special Needs Students
Revisit the Critical Reviews charts, making sure that students have completed each column. If students have difficulty assessing the reviews, guide them with the following questions: Would you see this performance? Why or why not? Which reviews would help you make your decision?

Strategy for Less Proficient Readers
Review the Reading Strategy instruction on p. 1028 and help students complete the Critical Reviews charts. Then, tell students to choose the review they most enjoyed and write a summary that identifies that review's main ideas and supporting details.

Enrichment for Advanced Readers
Lead a panel discussion in which students consider the advantages and disadvantages of revising classic works. Begin the discussion by brainstorming a list of revised works. Include movie revisions of literary works, such as Baz Luhrmann's modern take on Shakespeare's *Romeo and Juliet*.

Assessment Practice

Reading: Comparing and Contrasting Critical Reviews

Directions: *Choose the letter of the best answer to each question about the critical reviews.*

1. Which critic is **most** likely to agree with the *CurtainUp* assessment that this production of *A Doll's House* had a "1990s feel to it"?
   A Henrik Ibsen
   B Frank McGuiness
   C Lloyd Rose
   D David Spencer

2. Which review might state that this production of *A Doll's House* deserved the 1997 Tony Award for Best Revival of a Play?
   A the *CurtainUp* review
   B the *Washington Post* review
   C David Spencer's review
   D Lloyd Rose's review

3. Which critic might disagree with the awarding of the Best Revival Tony Award to this production of *A Doll's House*?
   A Judd Hollander
   B Sue Feinberg
   C David Spencer
   D Lloyd Rose

4. Which is an opinion that David Spencer and Lloyd Rose share?
   A Janet McTeer does not have the toughest role in the play.
   B Janet McTeer performs well as Nora.
   C Janet McTeer's Nora is hysterical and jittery.
   D Janet McTeer's acting overwhelms Owen Teale on stage.

Reading: Comprehension and Interpretation

Directions: *Write your answers on a separate sheet of paper.*

5. According to critic David Spencer, why is the 1997 production of *A Doll's House* "not the be-all, end-all" version of the play?
6. What evidence do the *CurtainUp* critics use to prove that the role of Torvald is the toughest one to portray in *A Doll's House*?
7. What words or phrases from these reviews would be effective in an advertisement for this production of *A Doll's House*?

Timed Writing: Evaluation

Write a critical review of a movie or television show that you have seen recently. Evaluate the quality of elements such as acting, costumes, script, and sets. Support your opinions with examples from the show. *(30 minutes)*

Reading Informational Materials: Critical Reviews ■ 1033

Reading: Comparing and Contrasting Critical Reviews

1. D
2. D
3. C
4. B

Reading: Comprehension and Interpretation

5. **Possible response:** Even though Spencer finds this revision of *A Doll House* "a fine and noble experiment," he does not think that it reaches the heights of the more traditional interpretations of the play.

6. **Possible response:** The critics point out that the role of Torvald is tough because the actor must show stereotypical aspects of Torvald's personality but at the same time show passion beneath his rigid behavior. Since modern audiences laugh contemptuously at many of Torvald's lines, the actor must convince the audience that he does finally feel pain at Nora's discomfort and anger about his treatment of her.

7. **Possible response:** The advertisement should contain positive language such as *riveting performance; keeps the pace moving; delivers a knockout punch of a payoff; an intense and compelling journey through the human spirit and well worth the trip; a six-foot bundle of adorability; character is fascinating, surprising, disturbing, vivacious, sensual, charismatic, explosive; electrifies the audience; creates a buzz of excitement and discovery.*

Timed Writing Evaluation

- Point out that critical reviews rely on opinions that are supported with convincing evidence. Remind students to include a brief summary of the show's subject matter.

- Suggest that students plan their time to give 15 minutes to planning, 10 minutes to writing, and 5 minutes to reviewing and revising.

Extend the Lesson

Writing an Advertisement

- Tell students that critical reviews share several elements with advertisements. In fact, it is a common practice in the theater to incorporate statements from critical reviews into a play's advertisements. Have students use the three critical reviews to create a print advertisement for this production of *A Doll House.*
- Students' advertisements should contain the basic facts about the production, such as the title, cast, director, and playwright, along with review quotations that encourage attendance. All quotations should be attributed to a reviewer and publication. To assist students, post this information:
  1. Ads should contain persuasive language and opinions about the performance.
  2. An ad would not include negative opinions about the performance.
  3. Powerful, positive language would be effective in an ad.
- Encourage students to use color and a variety of print styles in order to command the attention of their readers. When they have finished writing their ads, have students display them for the class.

Standard Course of Study

WL.1.02.3 Exhibit an awareness of cultural context of text in a personal reflection.

CT.4.02.2 Use specific references from texts to show theme.

GU.6.02.3 Edit for parallel structure.

Prewriting

- To give students guidance in developing this assignment, give them the **Writing About Literature** support, pp. 132–133 in *Unit 7 Resources.*

- Have students list a few selections they have particularly enjoyed from previous units. Then, have them review the introductions to those units.

- Point out the chart. Then give students a copy of the Three-column Chart (*Graphic Organizer Transparencies,* p. 251). Have them use it to select their works and take notes.

- Remind students as they gather details to provide sufficient evidence to support their essays. If students cannot find sufficient support, ask them to select different works.

- Have students meet in peer groups to review their thesis statements. If their statements are not clear or are too long, ask students to revise them. If necessary, explain the difference between a topic sentence and a thesis statement.

Tips for Test Taking

A writing prompt on the SAT or ACT test may assess students' ability to analyze a topic such as comparing and contrasting literary periods, state a point of view regarding the topic, and support the point of view with evidence. When writing under timed circumstances, students will need to quickly clarify a point of view (their thesis statement) and the evidence that supports it. Since they will not be able to refer to a text, their evidence must be based on their own experiences, readings, or observations.

1034

Compare and Contrast Literary Periods

Two movements, Romanticism and Realism, define the literature of the nineteenth century. Romantic writers—often inspired by nature—turned inward to tap spontaneous emotions. At the same time, they turned outward to celebrate the lives, language, and folklore of ordinary people. Realism, which emerged later, continued the Romantics' interest in ordinary life, but the Realists' pessimistic view of the suffering of the working class contrasted sharply with the Romantic vision of simple, contented folk.

Write an essay comparing Romantic and Realist literature with the literature of another literary period of your choice. See the box at the right for details of the assignment.

Prewriting

Find a focus. Review the literature both in this unit and in the unit against which you will compare these selections. For an overview of the periods, read the Unit Introduction for each unit as well. Use a chart similar to the one below to take notes. As you review selections, consider these questions to narrow your focus:

- Which aspects of a literary movement does this work reflect?
- Which parts of the work illustrate these aspects?
- What historical developments influenced this work?
- Which other works or literary trends influenced this work?

Model: Focus to Compare and Contrast Literary Periods

Selection	Literary Period	Evidence
"The Lorelei"	Romantic	Influence of folklore;
"The Fox and the Crow"	Age of Reason	irrational power of desire
		Rational analysis of motives;
		teaches a lesson

Review your chart, and select two works from each period on which you will focus. In making your choice, consider interesting contrasts as well as similarities between works.

Gather details. Go back to each work you have chosen and gather specific details of plot, setting, and characterization for comparison.

Write a working thesis. Write a single sentence summing up the main points of comparison and contrast between the work of the 1800s that you will discuss and the ones you have chosen from another literary era.

1034 ■ Romanticism and Realism

Assignment: Different Times, Different Literature

Write an analytical essay that compares and contrasts Romantic and Realist works of the nineteenth century with works of another literary period. Suggest how events of the period and reactions to other literary works influenced the works you analyze.

Criteria:
- Include a thesis statement drawn from your analysis of the works of two different literary eras.
- Support your thesis with detailed analyses of at least two works from each era.
- Highlight likenesses and differences among the works of different periods.
- Approximate length: 700 words

Read to Write
As you reread the texts, identify the themes and decide how these themes reflect the interests and values of the era in which the works were written.

Teaching Resources

The following resources can be used to extend or enrich the instruction for Writing About Literature.

Unit 7 Resources
    Writing About Literature, pp. 132–133

General Resources
    Rubrics for Exposition: Comparison-and-Contrast Essay, pp. 53–54

Graphic Organizer Transparencies
    Three-column Chart, p. 282
    Outline, p. 279

Drafting

Write an outline. Preparing a detailed outline will help you organize your thoughts and will guide you as you draft. Each main heading of the outline indicated by a capital letter will become a paragraph. Numbered subheadings indented under each heading will be supporting sentences.

> **Model: Making a Detailed Outline**
>
> **B.** Elements of Realism in Tolstoy story
>
>   1. simple language
>
>   2. main character is a peasant
>
>   3. realistic details about Russia
>
> **C.** Comparison to elements in Romantic story
>
>   1. courtly language
>
>   2. main characters are aristocrats
>
>   3. some realistic details

Revising and Editing

Review content: Eliminate unnecessary details. Identify the main idea in each paragraph. No matter how "interesting" they might be, details in a paragraph that do not support the main idea should be eliminated.

Review style: Strengthen word choice. Alter dull sentences to make them more interesting, replacing vague words with ones that are more expressive and words you use repeatedly with synonyms.

Original: Pakhom's enemy is his greed. He doesn't get greedy all at once—he becomes greedy little by little. When he has some land, he wants more. When he gets more land, he wants even more. His greed makes the devil happy.

Revised: Pakhom's enemy is his greed. His avarice doesn't sweep over him all at once—it creeps up on him little by little. When he has a modest amount of land, he craves more. His dissatisfaction delights the devil.

Publishing and Presenting

Submit your essay to a literary magazine. Revise your essay, adding necessary background to help a general audience who may be unfamiliar with your topic. Then, submit your essay to the school literary magazine.

WG Writing and Grammar Connection: Platinum Level, Chapter 9

Writing About Literature ■ 1035

✎ Write to Learn

Each time you reread the selections that you are analyzing in your paper, you will find additional nuances of meaning. Don't hesitate to add more information to your essay as your understanding of the works deepens.

✎ Write to Explain

Make sure that you have a good reason for including the details and quotations that you use in your essay. Explain those reasons clearly to your readers.

Drafting

- Point out the outline format. Tell students that each main heading listed should support their thesis statements and that they need sufficient support for each heading.
- Have students use their notes to develop a detailed outline. If they lack sufficient support, have them return to the texts to find more information or revise their thesis statements.

Revising and Editing

- Have students highlight or underline the main idea in each of their paragraphs. Then, have them evaluate whether the main ideas support their thesis statements.
- Review the style models. Then, have students work in peer groups to look at word choice and point out for one another overused words and expressions that weaken the essay.

Publishing and Presenting

- Have students check the submission guidelines for the literary magazine.
- Then, ask students to use a word processing program to create their submission copies. Remind them to follow all of the requirements, to proofread carefully, and to save their work on disks. Then, have students submit their work.

WG Writing and Grammar Platinum Level

Students will find additional instruction on writing a comparison-and-contrast essay in Chapter 9.

Writing and Grammar Interactive Textbook CD-ROM

Students can use the following tools as they complete their essays

- Word Bins: Descriptive
- Revising Tools: Language Variety

Six Traits Focus

✓	Ideas	✓	Word Choice
✓	Organization		Sentence Fluency
	Voice	✓	Conventions

Assessing the Essay

To evaluate students' essays, use the Exposition: Comparison-and-Contrast Essay rubrics in *General Resources*, pp. 53–54.

Differentiated Instruction   Solutions for All Learners

Support for Less Proficient Writers

Work with students to help them select suitable works, or assign selections instead. Then, guide students to help them find details, develop their thesis statements, and create their outlines. If students lack sufficient support for their thesis statements, help them search for details or allow them to work in pairs.

Support for English Learners

Review the terms *literary movement, analysis, formal outline,* and *literary trends*. Review thesis statements, including their purpose, structure, and content. Have students work with a partner to draft clear thesis statements. Partners should also help to make sure that thesis statements have enough support.

Strategy for Advanced Writers

Encourage students to select challenging works for their essays. Point out that challenging works provide better preparation for future writing assignments and are likely to provide more points of comparison for the essay. Have students work with partners to identify selections that will challenge them.

Writing Workshop

Standard Course of Study

FA.3.03.1 Gather information to prove a point about issues in literature.

CT.4.02.2 Use specific references from texts to show theme.

LT.5.02.1 Explore works which relate to an issue, author, or theme and show increasing comprehension.

Exposition:
Response to Literature

The writers in this unit undoubtedly expected their readers to respond to their writing. Henrik Ibsen, in particular, must have anticipated a strong reaction from the audiences of his play *A Doll House*—and he certainly got it. In fact the play continues to spark controversy today. A written **response to literature** may be personal and informal, or it may be formal and academic. Follow the steps outlined in this workshop to write your own response to literature.

Assignment Write a response to a work of literature you have recently read and enjoyed.

What to Include Your response to literature should feature the following elements:

- a discussion of the themes or significant ideas of a literary work
- accurate references to the text, including examples, quotations, and allusions
- a personal response drawn from your ideas and experience
- a logical organizational plan
- a thesis statement, an introduction, and a conclusion

To preview the criteria on which your response to literature may be assessed, see the rubric on page 1043.

Standard Course of Study

- Provide textual evidence to support understanding and response to personal reflection. (WL.1.03.3)
- Use specific references from texts to show theme. (CT.4.02.2)
- Document the reading of student-chosen works. (LT.5.02.2)

Using the Form
You may use elements of a response to literature in these types of writing:

- reading journals
- character analyses
- book reviews
- literary analyses

1036 ■ *Romanticism and Realism*

From the Author's Desk

W. S. Merwin

Show students Segment 3 on W. S. Merwin on *From the Author's Desk DVD*. Discuss the importance of Merwin's writing routine and process. Also, discuss the idea of saving work that one has started and may finish or use later.

Writing Genres

Using the Form Point out to students that a response to literature may be incorporated into other types of writing. Mention these examples:

- Professional reviewers, other writers, or experts in certain fields often write critiques of new books or other pieces of writing.
- Workers may need to write a response to a new policy.
- Teachers may need to write a critique of a new textbook that they are recommending for purchase.

  Online Essay Scorer

A writing prompt for this mode of writing can be found on the **PH Online Essay Scorer** at PHSuccessNet.com.

Reading → ← *Writing*
Connection

To get a feel for responses to literature, read the critical reviews of *A Doll House,* page 1029.

Teaching Resources

The following resources can be used to enrich or extend the instruction for the Writing Workshop.

Unit 7 Resources
Writing Workshop: Response to Literature, pp. 134–135

General Resources
Rubrics for Response to Literature, pp. 55 and 56

Graphic Organizer Transparencies
Rubric for Self-Assessment, p. 179

From the Author's Desk DVD
W. S. Merwin, Segments 3 and 4

Prewriting

Choosing Your Topic

The best topic for a response to literature is a work about which you have strong feelings. Use the following strategies to come up with a topic for your response to literature:

- **Make a list.** Begin by listing works of literature you have read recently that fully engaged your attention or related strongly to your own life. List also works that raised many questions for you. Alternatively, flip through this textbook to remind yourself of literature you have recently read. Choose as a topic the work that sparks the most ideas, or the one that you would most like to explore in depth.

- **Review your journal.** In your reading journal, you may have recorded quotations from literature—or themes, plots, or imagery that intrigued you. Look through your journal and put self-sticking notes on pages that contain interesting ideas. Then, revisit the pages that you marked, and choose one entry for your response to literature.

Narrowing Your Topic

Use hexagonal writing. To narrow your topic, allow yourself to consider a piece of literature from several angles. Use hexagonal writing to explore six aspects—one per side—of a piece of literature. Make a chart like the one shown here, and follow the directions in the example to analyze your topic. Then, review your writing to choose one aspect of the literary work to address.

Gathering Details

When you have a clear idea of what you want to discuss, generate a list of the kinds of details you need. Summarize your purpose in one sentence. Then, review the literature to back it up.

| **What I Want to Show:** | Oedipus was a character whose rash impulses led to his downfall. |
| **What Details I Need to Include:** | Examples of rash behavior; description of the effects of this behavior; how other characters tried to advise Oedipus. |

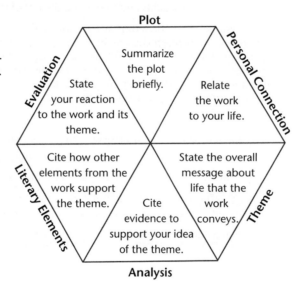

Writing Workshop ■ 1037

Tips for
Using Rubrics

- Before students begin work on this assignment, have them preview the Rubric for Self-Assessment, p. 1043, to know what is expected.

- Review the Assessment criteria in class. Before students use the Rubric for Self-Assessment, work with them to rate the student model by applying one or two criteria to it.

- If you wish to assess students' response-to-literature essays with a 4-point, 5-point, or 6-point scoring rubric, see *General Resources,* pp. 55–56.

Prewriting

- As a class, have students list works they have recently read. Then, ask students to select those works that they found most enjoyable or most engaging. Suggest that students use their reading journals as they choose their topics.

- Ask each student to select one work. Point out the hexagonal diagram on this page, and model its use with one aspect of a work. Then, have students copy the diagram onto their papers and complete the hexagon for their own topics.

- Point out that their audience may affect their choice of a selection. If they use a selection covered in class, they can assume that the audience is familiar with the work. If they choose another piece of literature, they will need to tailor their essays to the background of the audience.

- Point out to students that if they lack details to back up their topic, they will need to readjust the focus of their paper.

- Before students draft their essays, have them review the Rubric for Self-Assessment on p. 1043 so that they know what is expected of them.

Six Traits Focus

✓	Ideas		Word Choice
✓	Organization		Sentence Fluency
	Voice		Conventions

WG **Writing and Grammar** Platinum Level

Students will find additional instruction on prewriting for a response to literature in Chapter 13, Section 2.

Writing and Grammar Interactive Textbook CD-ROM

Students can use the following tools as they complete their responses to literature:

- Hexagonal Organizer
- Audience Profile Organizer
- Character Trait Word Bin
- Editing Revising Tool

Drafting

- Remind students that they can revise their thesis statements if the statements lack sufficient support.

- As students begin to organize their essays, point out the **Organization of a Response to Literature** chart on this page. Tell students that this chart indicates the basic information that they should include in each part of their essay.

- Emphasize that the strongest essays generally contain the most developed support in all three categories. Advise students not to focus on only one type.

- Encourage students to use an informal outline based on the points included in the organizational chart.

- Remind students that they must provide relevant and sufficient evidence to support their thesis statements and to cite information from outside sources.

- Tell students to single space citations in paragraph format.

Six Traits Focus

✓	Ideas		Word Choice
✓	Organization		Sentence Fluency
	Voice		Conventions

Writing and Grammar
Platinum Level

Students will find additional instruction on drafting a response to literature in Chapter 13, Section 3.

Drafting

Shaping Your Writing

Draft a thesis statement. The thesis statement is the main message of your essay, which you will support with various kinds of details. To develop a thesis statement, review your notes and decide which critical point you want to make about the piece of literature. Then, write a sentence that states your idea. Include the thesis statement in your introductory paragraph.

Organize your essay. Refer to your prewriting notes, and list the major details that help support your thesis statement. When the list is complete, decide on an organizational plan for your response to literature. Consider the basic three-part organization shown here.

Providing Elaboration

Be specific. When writing a response to literature, support your ideas with specific examples and allusions. The more specific you are, the more effective your point will be. Start with a statement, and then elaborate with examples.

> **Statement:** Many great playwrights have used art as a way to exemplify themes in their work.
>
> **Examples:** Many great playwrights have used the performing arts as a way to exemplify themes in their work. Shakespeare, for example, uses a play within *Hamlet* to reveal the guilt of Claudius and to deplore the evil of regicide.

Cite passages from the work. As you write, cite words, lines, or passages from the work to which you are responding. Enclose cited passages within quotation marks, and indicate where the passage is found in the literature. If you are citing a large passage of the work, place the excerpt in a separate paragraph, and indent the left and right margins. Quotation marks are not necessary when excerpts are set off this way.

Organization of a Response to Literature

Introduction
- State thesis.
- Introduce work of literature, theme, and response.

Body
- Elaborate on thesis statement.
- Provide evidence: examples, quotations, personal reactions.

Conclusion
- Summarize main ideas and provide final insight.

Reading ⟷ Writing Connection

To read the complete student model, see page 1042.

Student Model: Elaborating by Citing Passages

As he instructs Nora, Helmer shows that he views his wife as a "doll," a performing toy to be played with and shown off to his friends. Among his significant remarks: "you little helpless thing"; "Be my own little lark again"; "It's nothing more than this childish anxiety I was telling you about."

Quotations from the play support the writer's point.

From the Author's Desk
W. S. Merwin on the Process of Revision

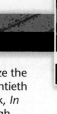
W. S. Merwin

Here is a passage in which I tried recently to summarize the achievement of a great, but somewhat neglected, twentieth century Welsh poet, David Jones. His best known work, *In Parenthesis*, and his writing as a whole surfaced through many revisions, from a profound sense of the roots of what he was trying to say.

"I can scarcely think of writing and revision as different activities."
——— W. S. Merwin

Professional Model:
from Foreword to *In Parenthesis*

The imposing echo of . . . ancient sources pervades passage after passage of *In Parenthesis,* perhaps nowhere so clearly as in the Welshman's boast in Part 4 . . . The boast, indeed, embodies just what Jones is doing in the whole work: it declares that the experience of the present terrible circumstance bears within it the experience of such circumstances that have returned again and again through the past. It says "I was there, I was there": "I was with Abel when his brother found him, / under the green tree . . . / I took the smooth stones of the brook, / I was with Saul / playing before him . . . / I saw cock-robin gain / His rosy breast. / I heard Him cry / *Apples ben ripe in my gardayne* / I saw Him die . . ."

Jones tells us . . . that he associates the boast directly with the poet Taliesin's boast at the court of Maelggwn, and indirectly with other boasts in several literatures. . . In Jones's use of it, it acquires once again the quality of poetry, that power that makes *In Parenthesis* not simply a great poem about war but a compelling reiteration of the terror and sadness and beauty of life."

I can remember few writings that I simply wrote down as they occurred to me and that was that. I revise as I go and usually the writing I hope for emerges through a cloud of possibilities until I hear bits of something clearer here and there, and draw them out and together.

Revisions and various possibilities arise from other parts of the mind from the first impulse, very often, and bring with them other overtones and meanings, besides focusing and clarifying what was at first dubious and unformed.

Writing Workshop ■ *1039*

Tips for
Improving Word Choice

Give students these suggestions for revising word choice.

1. Do not settle for wording that does not express what you want to say. Continue looking for options until you feel that you have expressed your thoughts exactly as you wish to.

2. Avoid words that you are unfamiliar with. Using a thesaurus to pick out "big, impressive words" backfires if you are not familiar enough with the word to know precisely how it should be used. In addition, using words that you really do not know and have not assimilated into your vocabulary may give your writing an artificial and awkward voice.

3. Try revising for word choice as you write. Reread earlier sentences or paragraphs and determine whether they use the right words to convey the meaning you want them to convey.

Revising

- Point out to students that one way to tell whether they have stayed on topic is to see whether the introduction and conclusion fit together or whether the conclusion wanders in a different direction. If it wanders, it needs revision.

- Direct students' attention to the revised conclusion in the Model. **Ask** students how this revision improves the essay.
  Possible response: In the revision, Nick addresses all three points of his thesis statement and provides examples of each.

- Provide students with highlighters for peer revision. Have partners highlight material that is unclear or confusing.

- After students revise, have partners reread each other's work to check whether the revisions are helpful or whether more revision is still needed.

Six Traits Focus

	Ideas	✓	Word Choice
✓	Organization	✓	Sentence Fluency
✓	Voice	✓	Conventions

W/G Writing and Grammar
Platinum Level

Students will find additional guidance for revising a response to literature in Chapter 4, Section 4.

Writing Workshop

Revising

Revising Your Overall Structure
Link the introduction and conclusion. Read through the introduction and conclusion of your essay. Check that the ideas in these key paragraphs are tightly related and not contradictory. If necessary, revise so that the conclusion restates or further explains the main points of the introduction in an interesting way.

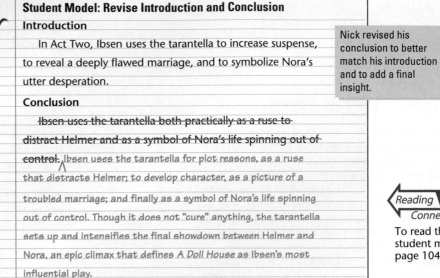

Student Model: Revise Introduction and Conclusion

Introduction

In Act Two, Ibsen uses the tarantella to increase suspense, to reveal a deeply flawed marriage, and to symbolize Nora's utter desperation.

Conclusion

~~Ibsen uses the tarantella both practically as a ruse to distract Helmer and as a symbol of Nora's life spinning out of control.~~ Ibsen uses the tarantella for plot reasons, as a ruse that distracts Helmer; to develop character, as a picture of a troubled marriage; and finally as a symbol of Nora's life spinning out of control. Though it does not "cure" anything, the tarantella sets up and intensifies the final showdown between Helmer and Nora, an epic climax that defines A Doll House as Ibsen's most influential play.

Nick revised his conclusion to better match his introduction and to add a final insight.

Reading → Writing
Connection

To read the complete student model, see page 1042.

Revising Your Paragraphs
Revise for clarity. Remember that your readers are most likely not as familiar as you are with the literature you discuss. Provide enough background information to help all of your readers follow your essay.

Peer Review: Have a classmate read a draft of your essay and mark words or phrases that make assumptions about the reader's knowledge of the literature. Ask your classmate to write questions and note places that are confusing or unclear. Revise as needed, providing enough background information to help all of your readers understand the important characters, events, or themes in the literature.

Tips for
Using Technology in Writing

Explain to students using word processing software that although programs that check spelling can be helpful, they do not take the place of proofreading. These programs check only for correct spelling, not correct usage. Nor do they check spelling for many types of proper nouns. The only way that students can be sure their papers are correct is to read them carefully.

Students can also use features of the Writing and Grammar Interactive Textbook CD-ROM to revise their essays.

Developing Your Style

Stating Your Opinion

Take a stand. A response to literature should be a forceful expression of a writer's ideas and opinions. Express your opinion confidently, using vivid and exact language, and support your opinion with specific details from the literature.

Learn to state your opinion without relying on phrases like *I think* and *in my opinion*. Follow these tips:

- Be specific.
- Use vivid language.
- State your opinion as if it were a fact.
- Prove your points with details, facts, and examples.

Weak: In my opinion, Janet McTeer seems very graceful in the role of Nora.

Confident: As Nora, the tall, rangy Janet McTeer is as gawkily graceful as a young swan.

Find It in Your Reading. Read one of the reviews of *A Doll House* on pages 1029–1032.

1. Find three statements of opinion in the review. For each, identify the words and phrases that convey the author's opinion.
2. Explain the ways in which the author makes his or her statements of opinion forceful and convincing.

Example: from "A Lot of Baggage for Nora to Carry," page 1031 "[Janet] McTeer and director Anthony Page bring this production very close to what I've always thought is the essential truth of *A Doll's House*..."

- Author Lloyd Rose uses a statement of opinion: "What I've always thought...."
- Rose uses vivid language: "the essential truth of *A Doll's House*...."
- Rose continues his article with statements that support his opinion.

Apply It to Your Writing. Review the draft of your response to literature. For each paragraph in your draft:

- Underline statements of opinion.
- Circle words and phrases that convey your opinion.
- Review circled phrases such as "in my opinion," "I think," and "it seems." Consider whether they are necessary. If you are in doubt, read the sentence aloud without the phrase. Deleting such phrases will usually strengthen your writing.
- Make sure that you have supported your opinion with evidence.

WG Prentice Hall Writing and Grammar Connection: Platinum Level, Chapter 31, Section 2

Developing Your Style

- Point out to students that words such as *it seems* or *maybe* also weaken their essays.
- Remind students that the support they offer for their opinions is what makes their opinions valid. Add that the phrase "In my opinion" is redundant and to avoid it; obviously what students write is their opinion.
- Direct students to **Find It in Your Reading.** With the class, find the first example from the reading and write it on the board. Then have students find two more examples independently.

Possible responses:
1. from "A Lot of Baggage for Nora to Carry," p. 1031 "This Nora is a six-foot bundle of adorability—and she knows it"; "This Nora is" and "and she knows it" make claims about the actress who plays Nora.
2. The use of the metaphor "a six-foot bundle of adorability" is a vivid image that makes the critic's review forceful.

- When students work on **Apply It to Your Writing,** provide them with colored pencils to mark statements of opinion and evidence. This strategy will help students see the balance between evidence and opinion.

WG Writing and Grammar Platinum Level

Students will find additional examples on stating their opinions in Chapter 31, Section 2.

Differentiated Instruction   Solutions for All Learners

Strategy for Less Proficient Writers

Using a copy of the Student Model on an overhead transparency, help students see the organization of the essay by using different colored markers to mark the main points and the support for each. Then have students do the same activity on their essays.

Strategy for English Learners

Review the terms on each side of the hexagon on p. 1037. Have students write the terms in their notebooks for future use. Then, guide them through the use of the hexagon with the selections they have chosen for their essays.

Student Model

- Explain that the Student Model is a sample and that student essays may be longer.

- **Ask** students to identify the thesis statement in Nick's essay.
  Answer: The thesis statement is "In Act Two, Ibsen uses the tarantella to increase suspense, to reveal a deeply flawed marriage, and to symbolize Nora's utter desperation."

- Discuss the importance of using direct quotations to support a point. Ask students to note that Nick cites the act from which he draws the quotations.

- **Ask** students how Nick's discussion of the essential background information about the tarantella supports his thesis.
  Possible response: The background information about the tarantella helps Nick prove that Ibsen utilizes the dance as a symbol of Nora's plight.

- Direct students' attention to the final paragraph. Have students **evaluate** the paragraph as a conclusion and **explain** how it supports the thesis statement.
  Possible response: It is an effective conclusion because it restates Nick's main points and ties together the support he has provided for his thesis statement.

Writing Genres

Responses to Literature in the Workplace Explain that a response to literature or other art is a type of writing a journalist might use. Point out that teachers and librarians may use this type of writing as well. Students in literature or history classes frequently will have to respond to literature or other writing. In addition, every time people discuss a movie or television show that they liked or disliked, they are responding to a form of literature. Other people who may need to write responses in the workplace are workers who are asked to respond to a new policy or procedure. Although not a direct response to literature, any type of written response requires a thesis statement with main points and support for those points.

Student Model: Nick Groesch
Decatur, Illinois

The Tarantella in Ibsen's *A Doll House*

Many great playwrights have used performing arts as a way to exemplify themes in their works. Shakespeare, for example, uses a play within *Hamlet* to reveal the guilt of Claudius and to deplore the evil of regicide. In *A Doll House*, Ibsen makes use of the tarantella, an Italian folk dance, in several dramatic ways. In Act Two, Ibsen uses the tarantella to increase suspense, to reveal a deeply flawed marriage, and to symbolize Nora's utter desperation.

> Nick's thesis statement clearly defines the scope of his response essay.

On a practical level, Nora's dancing serves as a distraction. By deliberately dancing badly, Nora draws Helmer's attention away from the arrival of Krogstad's letter, which will shatter her world. "Yes, you see how important [the tarantella] is. You've got to teach me to the very last minute" (Act Two). Nora successfully delays the reading of the letter, increasing the play's suspense.

On another level, Ibsen uses the tarantella rehearsal to reveal problems in the Helmers' marriage. As he instructs Nora, Helmer shows that he views his wife as a "doll," a performing toy to be played with and shown off to his friends. Among his significant remarks: "you little helpless thing"; "Be my own little lark again"; "It's nothing more than this childish anxiety I was telling you about." By showing Helmer's patronizing attitude in this scene, Ibsen prepares the viewer for Nora's explosion of resentment and rebellion.

> Nick accurately quotes lines of dialogue from the play to support his points. (See *Drafting*, p. 1038.)

Finally, Nora's wild dancing is a symbol of her desperation. The tarantella was believed to cure its dancer from the poison of a tarantula. Krogstad's threats and letter are poison to Nora's happiness and marriage. Nora takes it upon herself to practice the tarantella because she wishes to rid herself of this "poison." Unfortunately, the tarantella does not cure poison, nor does Nora's dance solve her problems. She realizes this and, at the end of Act Two, she says, "Seven hours to midnight. Twenty-four hours to the midnight after, and then the tarantella's done. Seven and twenty-four? Thirty-one hours to live."

> Nick gives essential background information in order to explore the tarantella as a symbol.

Ibsen uses the tarantella for plot reasons, as a ruse that distracts Helmer; to develop character, as a picture of a troubled marriage; and finally as a symbol of Nora's life spinning out of control. Though it does not "cure" anything, the tarantella sets up and intensifies the final showdown between Helmer and Nora, an epic climax that defines *A Doll House* as Ibsen's most influential play.

> Nick concludes his response with a summary and a forceful statement on the importance of the scene to Ibsen's play.

1042 ■ *Romanticism and Realism*

Editing and Proofreading

Review your essay to eliminate errors in grammar, spelling, or punctuation.

Focus on References and Citations: Review all references to literary works in your essay. Make sure that you spell, capitalize, and style the titles and names of authors correctly. Proofread all cited passages, comparing them with the source, and correct any errors.

Publishing and Presenting

Consider one of the following ways to share your response to literature.

Present to a book group. Invite a group of classmates or friends to read the work of literature that is the topic of your essay. After everyone has read the work, present a summary of your essay. Then, in a discussion, invite group members to compare their own reactions to the work with yours.

Publish an online review of the work. Post your response to literature on a student or bookstore Web site. To be sure that your submission is accepted and posted, follow all submission requirements for the site.

Reflecting on Your Writing

Writer's Journal Jot down your thoughts on the experience of writing a response to literature. Begin by answering these questions:

- How useful was the hexagonal writing strategy to your writing process? Explain.
- How did writing about a literary work affect your opinion of it?

WG *Prentice Hall Writing and Grammar Connection: Platinum Level, Chapter 13*

Rubric for Self-Assessment

Evaluate your response to literature *using the following criteria and rating scale or, with your classmates, determine your own reasonable evaluation criteria.*

Criteria	Rating Scale
	not very *very*
Focus: How clear is your thesis statement?	1 2 3 4 5
Organization: How logical is your organization?	1 2 3 4 5
Support/Elaboration: How well do you use examples and quotations from the literary works?	1 2 3 4 5
Style: How well do you use your own ideas and experience to craft a personal response?	1 2 3 4 5
Conventions: How accurate are your citations and references to literary works?	1 2 3 4 5

Tips for Test Taking

When taking a test that requires a response to literature, students should read the question before reading the literature. Then, when they read the literature, they can identify and underline specific information that relates to the question. When students begin to write, they already will have labeled supporting information for their essays. This strategy will save time.

Editing and Proofreading

- Remind students that their citations should follow the MLA format, which is used for English papers. If you or your school prefers another format, acquaint students with which format to follow.
- Remind students that punctuation is important in citing sources. Punctuation must be correct for the citation to be correct.

Six Traits Focus

Ideas		Word Choice	
Organization		Sentence Fluency	
Voice		✓	Conventions

ASSESS

Publishing and Presenting

- If some students have written about the same selection, have them form a group to discuss their reactions to the literature. Students can use their essays as a basis for discussion.
- Point out that many online book-stores have a place for comments about literary selections. Remind students that when they enter their essays on the Web site, correct grammar and punctuation are still important because these help give credibility to their opinions.

Reflecting on Your Writing

- When students write in their journals, have them include their thoughts on how writing about the selection affected their understanding of the piece and what they learned about the piece through the process.
- Review the assessment criteria in class.
- Encourage students to use the assessment rubric to evaluate the Student Model. Then, have them use the rubric to assess their own essays.

WG **Writing and Grammar Platinum Level**

Students will find additional guidance for editing and proofreading, publishing and presenting, and reflecting on a response to literature in Chapter 13, Section 5.

Know Your Terms: Analyzing Information

Explain that the terms listed under Terms to Learn will be used in standardized-test situations when students are asked to analyze information from a reading passage.

Terms to Learn

• Review *demonstrate*. Tell students that *demonstrate* means to show clearly and deliberately that they know the material. When students demonstrate that they understand something from a passage, have them ask themselves, "What example will show best that I know the information?" Tell students to select the example that most clearly demonstrates their understanding.

• Review *analyze*. Tell students that analyzing requires taking something apart and looking at the parts. When students are analyzing a situation, suggest that they ask themselves, "What are the parts of this issue, and how can I explain what each of them means?"

ASSESS

Answers

1. The elder sister boasts of comfortable living, fine clothes and food, and entertainment unavailable to those living in the country.

2. The older sister feels superior to the younger sister, who is defensive about her life.

Go Online **For:** An Interactive **Vocabulary** Crossword Puzzle
Visit: www.PHSchool.com
Web Code: etj-5701
This crossword puzzle contains vocabulary that reflects the concepts in Unit 7. After students have completed Unit 7, give students the Web Code and have them complete the crossword puzzle.

1044

High-Frequency Academic Words

High-frequency academic words are words that appear often in textbooks and on standardized tests. Although you may already know the meaning of many of these words, they usually have a more specific meaning when they are used in textbooks and on tests.

Know Your Terms: Analyzing Information

Each of the words listed is a verb that tells you to show that you recognize the significance of the text details and the relationships among them. The words indicate the kinds of details and information you should include in your answer.

Terms to Learn

Demonstrate Use examples to show that you understand the information.

> Sample test item: Give an example from *Faust* that ***demonstrates*** a characteristic of Romanticism.

Analyze Break down a topic or issue into parts and explain them.

> Sample test item: ***Analyze*** the use of the supernatural in literature of the Romantic period.

Practice

Directions: *Read the passage shown from "How Much Land Does a Man Need?" by Leo Tolstoy. Then, answer questions 1–2.*

An elder sister came to visit her younger sister in the country. The elder was married to a tradesman in town, the younger to a peasant in the village. As the sisters sat over their tea talking, the elder began to boast of the advantages of town life: saying how comfortably they lived there, how well they dressed, what fine clothes her children wore, what good things they ate and drank, and how she went to the theater, promenades, and entertainments.

The younger sister was piqued, and in turn disparaged the life of a tradesman, and stood up for that of a peasant.

"I would not change my way of life for yours," said she.

1. Give an example from the passage that *demonstrates* the elder sister's attitude towards her sister's life in the country.

2. Use the passage to *analyze* the relationship between the two sisters.

1044 ■ *Romanticism and Realism*

Tips for
Test Taking

• When students are asked to analyze a topic or demonstrate that they understand an idea on a standardized test, explain that they can make short notes in the margin as they read to help them track important ideas.

• Emphasize that notes should be short and to the point because students have limited time to complete standardized tests and should not spend excessive time writing notes. In addition, if they make too many notes, students may needlessly spend time trying to find the correct note when they try to answer a test question.

Critical Reading:
Strategy, Organization, and Style

On some tests, you may be required to read a passage with numbered sentences or paragraphs and to answer questions about its organization and use of language. Use these strategies to help you answer such questions.

- Summarize, in logical order, the events or ideas in the passage. Next to each event or idea, write the number of the sentence or paragraph in which it appears. Use your outline to help you answer questions about reordering parts of the passage.

- Analyze the passage to infer the author's purpose—to persuade readers to hold an opinion, to inform them about a topic, or to entertain them. Recall this purpose when answering questions about main ideas, supporting details, and irrelevant sentences.

Practice

Directions: *Read the passages, and then answer questions 1 and 2.*

Passage A. (1) In five years the plague, which had no cure, caused a gruesome death for 25 million people—one third of Europe's population. (2) The fleas on rodents soon carried the plague from China throughout Europe. (3) Smaller outbreaks of the plague continued until the 1600s. (4) In the 1330s, China was stricken by the bubonic plague, which got its name from buboes, the swellings of the lymph glands.

Passage B. (1) Beginning in the late ninth century, Viking raids from the north, Magyar raids from the east, and Muslim raids from the south endangered Europe. (2) After Charlemagne's death in 814, Europe once again faced the threat of invasion. (3) As a result of these attacks, the feudal system was born: a system of mutual defense pacts between lords and vassals. (4) The Holy Roman Empire, ruled by Charlemagne, returned some semblance of security to Europe. (5) The Roman Empire was overrun by Germanic tribes in the fifth century A.D., and its fall left Europe vulnerable to more invaders.

1. In Passage A, which sentence sequence makes the most sense?

A 4, 2, 1, 3

C 3, 1, 2, 4

B 2, 4, 3, 1

D 1, 2, 3, 4

2. Which sentence sequence makes the most sense in Passage B?

A 1, 3, 2, 5, 4

C 4, 1, 3, 2, 5

B 5, 4, 2, 1, 3

D 2, 1, 3, 5, 4

Assessment Workshop ■ 1045

Tips for
Test Taking

In order to find the most logical sequence for sentences in a passage on a standardized test, students should first try to identify which sentence belongs first or last in the sequence. Usually, tests have a variety of sentence sequences as answer choices. After students clearly decide which sentence should be first or last in the sequence, they can eliminate all of the answer choices that do not begin or end with that sentence. If only one choice begins or ends with that sentence, students can answer the question without determining the sequence of the rest of the sentences, thus saving time.

Standard Course of Study

WL.1.03.8 Make connections between works, self and related topics in response and reflection.

FA.3.01.1 Share and evaluate initial personal response to a controversial issue.

GU.6.01.5 Examine language for elements to apply effectively in own writing/speaking.

Prepare Your Content

- Remind students to select a topic that interests them. When a speaker is enthusiastic about a topic, it is likely that the audience will share that enthusiasm.

- Point out to students that if their focus is too broad, they will lose the interest of their audience. Also, remind them that a focused idea is far more effective and easy to support than one that is too broad.

- Remind students that their audience may determine the level of support required in their presentations. If an audience is likely to disagree with their ideas, students must provide more convincing support.

Prepare Your Delivery

- Have students look at the content of their responses. Discuss what types of content work best with which organizational strategies. For example, if students are responding to changes in a character, guide them to understand that chronological order may be the best way to organize the response.

- Have students discuss ways to create effective openings and conclusions. Point out that action, dialogue, or reactions are ways to create effective openings.

- Have students complete the Activity on the student page. Allow students time to rehearse their presentations. Have students work with partners who will complete the feedback forms. Then, have students revise their work and present their responses to the class.

Assess the Activity

To evaluate students' delivery, use the Speaking: Presenting an Oral Response to Literature rubric, p. 91 in *General Resources.*

Delivering an Oral Response to Literature

An **oral response to literature** might be an offhand comment to a friend about a bestseller you read, a panel discussion about the relevance of literature to the critical issues of the day, or a formal presentation on a theme in the work of a great author. The following strategies will help you prepare and present an effective formal oral response to a work.

Prepare Your Content

Choose a work that excites you or makes you angry, puzzled, or elated. That piece would make an excellent subject for your presentation.

Narrow your focus. What will be the main idea or theme of your talk? Keep that idea in mind as you prepare your presentation. Assume that you must persuade your audience to accept your viewpoint. Anticipate and address potential objections.

Support your ideas. Your ideas will be most convincing if they are supported with quotations from and references to the text under discussion. Read over the work several times. Then, carefully choose evidence that supports your viewpoint.

Prepare Your Delivery

Use the following techniques to prepare your presentation of a response to literature:

- **Choose a logical structure.** Which structure will work most effectively for your presentation: chronological order, order of importance, part to whole, comparison and contrast? Select a specific pattern and use it consistently throughout your talk.

- **Develop an effective opening and conclusion.** The impact of your talk as a whole is only as strong as its introduction and conclusion. An intriguing beginning snares the attention of the audience, and a dramatic conclusion leaves your main point etched in the audience's memory. Revise the opening and conclusion of your presentation until they are effective.

- **Rehearse your presentation.** Practice to make your delivery conversational and comfortable. Try to avoid reading an essay word for word. Instead, use your notes as a guide.

Activity ▶ **Presentation and Feedback** ▶ Prepare a three-minute oral response to a work of nonfiction. With a partner, use the feedback form to listen for inconsistencies and ambiguities, and to evaluate each other's preparation. Revise your work based on your partner's observations. Present your response to your class.

Standard Course of Study

- Make connections between works, in response and reflection. (WL.1.03.8)

- Examine language for elements to apply effectively in own writing/speaking. (GU.6.01.5)

Feedback Form for Oral Response to Literature

Rating System
+ = Excellent ✓ = Average – = Wea[k]

Content
Clarity of main idea _____
Persuasiveness of viewpoint _____
Supporting evidence _____

Suggestions for improvement: _____
_____

Delivery
Organization _____
Opening _____
Conclusion _____

Other comments on delivery: _____
_____

Differentiated Instruction — Solutions for All Learners

Support for Less Proficient Readers

Remind students that they must indicate to the reader when they are using a direct quotation. Have students provide the writer or character's name and tell the listener that the material is a direct quotation. Students may also say, "This passage can be found on page 94," for example.

Support for English Learners

Show students how to support their ideas with direct quotations and references to the text. Point out that only a short quotation may be needed for support. Ask students to have their partners give them feedback on their use of quotations and help them revise as necessary.

Support for Advanced Readers

Encourage students to find other resources for support as well as their own in response to the selection. Ask students to use library resources or the Internet to find additional responses. Students should include at least one of these additional resources in their presentations. They must be sure to cite this material correctly.

Suggestions for Further Reading

Featured Titles:

The Hunchback of Notre-Dame
Victor Hugo, *translated by Walter J. Cobb, Signet Classic, 2001*

Fiction This novel is set in medieval Paris in the shadow of the majestic Notre-Dame cathedral. Its main characters are Quasimodo, an orphaned hunchback who serves as the cathedral bell-ringer; Claude Frollo, the priest who has adopted Quasimodo; and Esmerelda, the gypsy dancer to whom Frollo is desperately attracted. The story, which begins with Quasimodo being shamefully crowned the Pope of Fools by the Parisian mob, is a tragic tale of love, loyalty, and betrayal. It is filled with unforgettable images, such as the description of a mob's assault on Notre-Dame as "a layer of living monsters crawling over the stone monsters of the façade." The story also vividly conveys two of Hugo's most important Romantic beliefs—the essential value of the outcast or outsider and the close relationship between beauty and ugliness.

Diary of a Madman and Other Stories
Nikolai Gogol, *translated by Ronald Wilks, Penguin Classic, 1973*

Short Stories Trudging through the mists of nineteenth-century St. Petersburg, mumbling to themselves as they go, the harried nobodies of Nikolai Gogol's stories reflect the new sorrow of the modern world—the life of the anonymous. Gogol's faceless clerks and petty bureaucrats battle their own insignificance. His genius is to make their struggle against erasure both deeply sad and outrageously funny. "The Nose" is the grotesque tale of a man who must pursue through the city his own nose, grown into a haughty official. In "The Overcoat," a poor clerk is broken and dies after he is robbed of his expensive new overcoat. In "The Diary of a Madman," an obscure bureaucrat descends into comical madness, but his delusion rescues him from insignificance—he realizes that he is the king of Spain! In these absurd yet moving tales, society's forgettable "little people" become literature's unforgettable characters.

Work Presented in Unit Seven:
If sampling a portion of the following text has built your interest, treat yourself to the full work.

Faust, Part One
Faust, Part Two
Johann Wolfgang von Goethe, *translated by Philip Wayne, Penguin Classic, 1950 and 1960*

Related British Literature:
Wuthering Heights
Emily Brontë, *Pearson Prentice Hall, 2000*

Set in the wild moors of northern England, this Romantic novel tells about the love between Catherine Earnshaw and the mysterious outsider Heathcliff.

Related American Literature:
The Science Fiction of Edgar Allan Poe
Edgar Allan Poe, *Penguin Classic, 1976*

These tales of time travel, hypnotism, and electromagnetism reveal that Poe was not only the inventor of the detective story, but also a pioneer of science fiction.

Many of these titles are available in the **Prentice Hall/Penguin Literature Library.**
Consult your teacher before choosing one.

The Science Fiction of Edgar Allan Poe
by Edgar Allan Poe

Poe is a master of horror and speculative fiction, and his stories contain gruesome scenes, as well as philosophical discussions about death and God. Other sensitive issues include references to mesmerism, suicide, and controlled substances. To prepare students, discuss reasons writers and readers are attracted to the "unimaginable"—the horrible, grotesque, or degraded.

Lexile: Appropriate for high school students

Planning Students' Further Reading

Discussions of literature can raise sensitive and often controversial issues. Before you recommend further reading to your students, consider the values and sensitivities of your community as well as the age, ability, and sophistication of your students. It is also good policy to preview literature before you recommend it to students. The notes below offer some guidance on specific titles.

The Hunchback of Notre Dame
by Victor Hugo

False accusations of witchcraft, defamation of gypsies, the suicide of Quasimodo, the murder of Claude Frollo, physical torture, the seduction of Esmeralda, and the inhumane treatment of the mentally ill might be disturbing.
Lexile: 1340L

Diary of a Madman and Other Stories
by Nikolai Gogol

This book contains derogatory references to Jews, brutal war scenes ("Taras Bulba"), and excessive drinking ("The Carriage" and "Taras Bulba").
Lexile: 1060L

Faust, Part One and Faust, Part Two
by Johann Wolfgang von Goethe

Faust's deep questions about life lead him to bargain with the devil; this work refers frequently to Hell and damnation and includes derogatory comments about Christians. Violent events are depicted, and there is some insensitive labeling of people with disabilities.

Lexile: Appropriate for high school students

Wuthering Heights by Emily Brontë

The character of Heathcliff personifies darkness and evil. His description as not being human, his violent and abusive behavior, and his need to seek revenge on others are all troubling, as is the notion that because he is adopted, he possesses some sort of evil influence on the family circle. Hindley Earnshaw's violent behavior and excessive drinking are also troublesome. Images of animals, especially dogs, being tortured may greatly disturb some students. Finally, the notion of ghosts, as well as Heathcliff's wandering the moors and digging up Catherine's coffin, will likely disturb many students.
Lexile: 880L

WL.1.02.5 Demonstrate an understanding of media's impact on analyses and personal reflection.

WL.1.03.8 Make connections between works, self and related topics in response and reflection.

IR.2.02.1 Summarize situations to examine cause/effect relationships.

LT.5.02.1 Explore works which relate to an issue, author, or theme and show increasing comprehension.

GU.6.01.3 Use recognition strategies to understand vocabulary and exact word choice.

Unit Instructional Resources

In *Unit 8 Resources,* you will find materials to support students in developing and mastering the unit skills and to help you assess their progress.

▶ **Vocabulary and Reading**

Additional vocabulary and reading support, based on Lexile scores of vocabulary words, is provided for each selection or grouping.

• **Word Lists A and B** and **Practices A and B** provide vocabulary-building activities for students reading two grades or one grade below level, respectively.

• **Reading Warm-ups A and B,** for students reading two grades or one grade below level, respectively, consist of short readings and activities that provide a context and practice for newly learned vocabulary.

▶ **Selection Support**

• Reading Strategy
• Literary Analysis
• Vocabulary Builder
• Grammar and Style
• Support for Writing
• Support for Extend Your Learning
• Enrichment

PRENTICE HALL
Teacher EXPRESS™
Plan · Teach · Assess
You may also access these resources at TeacherExpress.

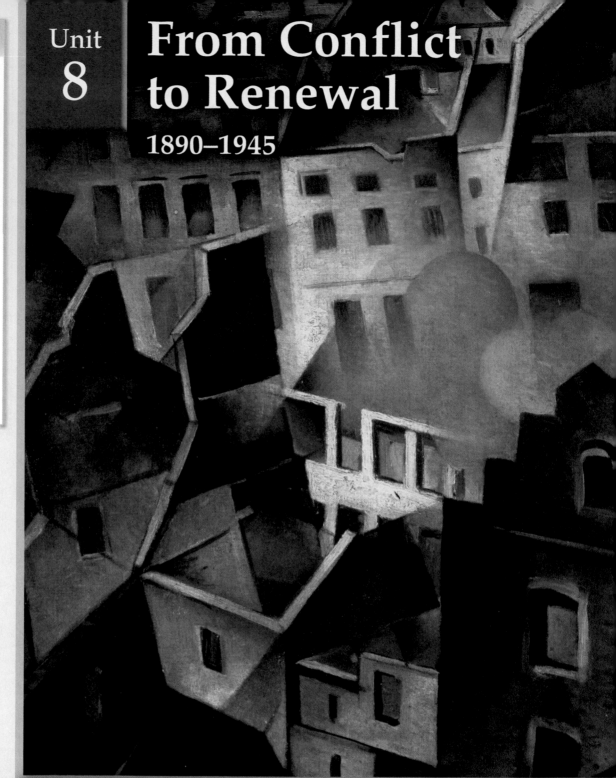

Unit 8
From Conflict to Renewal
1890–1945

Assessment Resources

Listed below are the resources available to assess and measure students' progress in meeting the unit objectives and your state standards.

Skills Assessment

Unit 8 Resources
  Selection Tests A and B

TeacherExpress™
  ExamView® Test Bank
    Software

Adequate Yearly Progress Assessment

Unit 8 Resources
  Diagnostic Test 10
  Benchmark Test 10

Standardized Assessment

Standardized Test
  Preparation Workbook

The Modern World

Standard Course of Study
In This Unit You Will

- Make connections between works, self and related topics in response and reflection. (WL.1.03.8)
- Summarize situations to examine cause/effect relationships. (IR.2.02.1)
- Present data about controversial issues in multiple forms. (FA.3.01.5)
- Distinguish fact from fiction and recognize personal bias in interpretation. (CT.4.01.3)
- Analyze how writers choose and incorporate significant, supporting details. (CT.4.03.2)
- Analyze elements of literary environment in world literature. (LT.5.03.11)
- Use recognition strategies to understand vocabulary and exact word choice. (GU.6.01.3)

◀ Artist Christopher Richard Wynne Nevinson became Britain's official war artist in 1917. *Ypres After First Bombardment* reflects his observations during World War I.

The Modern World ■ 1049

Introduce Unit 8

- Direct students' attention to the title of this unit and the art on this spread. **Ask** students: What does this painting suggest about the modern period of history?
  Possible response: It suggests that the modern world was a time of war and fear.

- Have students look at the quotation. **Ask:** In light of the painting, what does the line "we do not know what will be born . . ." mean?
  Possible response: The line might mean that people do not know what will be born, or come next, from those who destroyed the city. Read the Humanities note to students, and ask the discussion question.

- Then **ask:** What kinds of literature or themes in literature do you think might come out of this period in literary history?
  Possible response: Themes in modern literature might include uncertainty and the inability of tradition to answer modern questions.

Humanities

Ypres after First Bombardment, by Christopher Richard Wynne Nevinson

When Nevinson (1889–1946) studied art, a teacher told him that he would never be an artist. In 1911, he became aware of Cubism. Cubism used a two-dimensional viewpoint instead of perspective and influenced Nevinson's work. Nevinson was a pacifist and served as a Red Cross volunteer in World War I. Many of his paintings reflect his war experiences.

Use the following question for discussion:

What impression does the painting depict of war?
Possible response: The impression is one of partially destroyed buildings. The flames create a sense of recent destruction.

Unit Features

🐧 Judith Ortiz Cofer
Each unit features commentary by a contemporary writer or scholar under the heading "From the Author's Desk." Scholar Judith Ortiz Cofer introduces Unit 8 in Setting the Scene, in which she discusses how modern literature reflects the tensions and questions of the twentieth century. Later in the unit, she introduces the poem, "Ithaka" by Constantine P. Cavafy. In the Writing Workshop, she shows how she uses words to express powerful emotions and to help readers visualize a scene.

Connections
Every unit contains a feature that connects literature to a related topic, such as art, science, or history. In this unit, students will read **The Corn Planting** by Sherwood Anderson on pp. 1136–1141.

Use the information and questions on the Connections pages to help students enrich their understanding of the selections presented within the unit.

Reading Informational Materials
These selections will help students learn to analyze and evaluate informational texts, such as workplace documents, technical directions, and consumer materials. They will expose students to the organization and features unique to nonnarrative texts.

In this unit, the focus is on Scientific Texts. **What Is an Insect?** is on pp. 1112–1115.

Introduce Judith Ortiz Cofer

- Judith Ortiz Cofer, a poet, essayist, and novelist, introduces the unit and provides insight into the dramatic changes in the world in the twentieth century and how those changes have affected literature.

- Have students read the introductory paragraph about Judith Ortiz Cofer. Tell them that she has won numerous awards for her work, including the O. Henry Prize for short story. She is currently a professor of English at the University of Georgia.

- Use the *From the Author's Desk DVD* to introduce Judith Ortiz Cofer. Show Segment 1 to provide insight into her writing career. After students have watched the segment, **ask:** Why does Judith Ortiz Cofer believe that it is necessary to focus on universal themes in her writing? **Answer:** She believes that it is important for writers to attempt to relate to readers with themes that all people experience.

Changes in Modern Literature

- Have students read Cofer's commentary on changes in modern literature.

- Cofer explains how events during the twentieth century have formed modern literature. **Ask:** How does modern literature reflect the feelings and perceptions of people in the modern world? **Answer:** Modern literature reflects the radical changes in living that resulted from technology. It expresses the lost sense of safety that resulted from the First and Second World Wars.

- Tell students that they will read Judith Ortiz Cofer's introduction to and commentary on "Ithaka" by Constantine P. Cavafy on pages 1142–1143 later in this unit.

Critical Viewing

Possible response: Readers might find the change itself shocking. They may be shocked by the idea of a giant insect with human consciousness.

Setting the Scene

The literature of Unit 8 spans an era of dramatic change, of two world wars, and of a growing community of writers of world literature. In her essay, author Judith Ortiz Cofer describes her experiences with world literature and the way writers from around the world inspire her own work. In the unit introduction and the selections that follow, challenge yourself to participate in the richness of modern world literature.

From the Scholar's Desk
Judith Ortiz Cofer Talks About the Time Period

Judith Ortiz Cofer

Introducing Judith Ortiz Cofer (b. 1952) Born in Puerto Rico, Cofer writes literature that often addresses the experiences common to Puerto Rican Americans. A poet, an essayist, and a novelist, Cofer wrote the Pulitzer Prize-nominated novel *The Line of the Sun* (1989). Her recent works include *Woman in Front of the Sun: On Becoming a Writer* (2003) and *The Meaning of Consuelo* (2003).

Change in Modern Literature

At the beginning of the twentieth century, the world changed abruptly and radically. Technology such as the telephone and the car changed the way people lived even more than the Internet has done in our time. But the greatest shock of all was the First World War (1914–1918). After such slaughter, people realized that the world would never be the same again.

Later in the century, my father served in the navy during the Cuban Missile Crisis in 1962: When he returned, he no longer believed in a safe world. In the same way, those who have lived through 9/11 can understand how suddenly the world can be so fragmented. These are the kinds of feelings and perceptions that formed modern literature.

The Virtual Reality of Literature Works that became known as "modern literature" reflected the modern world in literary styles that began to change completely. The Irish novelist James Joyce rocked the foundation of narrative with *Ulysses* in 1922, a book that told a story in a totally new way. The British-American poet T. S. Eliot changed forever what poetry would look like and sound like. Modern artists seemed to be saying, "We have no easy answers. We have only new images and sounds. You, the reader or the audience member, need to help create their meaning."

▼ **Critical Viewing**
What might readers find suprising about a man turning into a cockroach? **[Speculate]**

1050 ■ *The Modern World*

Teaching Resources

The following resources can be used to enrich or extend the instruction for Unit 8 Introduction.

From the Author's Desk DVD
   Judith Ortiz Cofer, Segment 1

Unit 8 Resources
   Names and Terms to Know, p. 5
   Focus Questions, p. 6
   Listening and Viewing, p. 59

From Conflict to Renewal

In *Ulysses*, we wander through the streets of Dublin, experiencing the stream of consciousness, or flowing thoughts, of the main characters. We enter a "virtual reality" in which we learn the rules by playing the game. The Austrian-Czech writer Franz Kafka also created a game-like world. I loved his *Metamorphosis* because the idea of a guy waking up as a giant cockroach suited me just fine. I was modern enough to deal with that, and I think readers today have no problem understanding a story of transformation, of morphing.

Two Personal Favorites: Mistral and García Lorca When I was in high school, I read Dante, Shakespeare, Cervantes, and of course the *Odyssey*, but the great Spanish poets Juan Ramón Jiménez and Federico García Lorca were considered way too contemporary. I do remember thinking about Gabriela Mistral because it was such an astonishing thing for a woman and a Latin American to have won the Nobel Prize. She was inspiring to me in that way.

With García Lorca I have a close connection. He has always been special to me, reminding me of the American poet Walt Whitman in his celebrations of life. When the Lorca family invited me to Spain about ten years ago, I heard a gypsy singer like the ones that inspired Lorca, and he made me cry. That sound is like the gospel music of the African American tradition—soulful, beautiful, passionate, and so Lorca to me.

Reading Modern Literature My advice as you read this unit is to remember that human nature is both ancient and contemporary. If you say, "Why should I read Cavafy? He died in the 1930s," I would say, "Well, have you ever felt lonely? Have you ever wondered what the world contains for you?" The fact is that a light comes on when you read a great work of art. It has survived time with its meaning intact. So my advice is allow time. Literature is not mind candy. It has to be given time and effort.

Go Online
Author Link
For: A video clip of Judith Ortiz Cofer
Visit: www.PHSchool.com
Web Code: ete-8801

For: More on Judith Ortiz Cofer
Visit: www.PHSchool.com
Web Code: ete-9810

Reading the Unit Introduction

Reading for Information and Insight Use the following terms and questions to guide your reading of the unit introduction on pages 1054–1061.

Names and Terms to Know
Marie and Pierre Curie
Albert Einstein
Sigmund Freud
World War I
The Great Depression
World War II
The Holocaust
Modernism

Focus Questions As you read this introduction, use what you learn to answer these questions:
- In what ways did science and technology change lives in this period?
- What was the impact of two world wars on Europe?
- In what ways does the literature of this period reflect its turbulence and violence?

From the Scholar's Desk: Judith Ortiz Cofer ■ 1051

Reading the Unit Introduction

Tell students that the terms and questions listed here are the key points in this introductory material. This information provides a context for the selections in this unit. Students should use the terms and questions as a guide to focus their reading of the unit introduction. When students have completed the unit introduction, they should be able to identify or explain each of these terms and answer or discuss the Focus Questions.

Concept Connector

After students have read the unit introduction, return to the Focus Questions to review the main points. For key points, see p. 1061.

Go Online Typing in the Web Codes
Author Link when prompted will bring students to a video clip and more information on Judith Ortiz Cofer.

Using the Timeline

The Timeline can serve a number of instructional purposes, as follows:

Getting an Overview

Use the Timeline to help students get a quick overview of themes and events of the period. This approach will benefit all students but may be especially helpful for Visual/Spatial Learners, English Learners, and Less Proficient Readers. (For strategies in using the Timeline as an overview, see the bottom of this page.)

Thinking Critically

Questions are provided on the facing page. Use these questions to have students review the events, discuss their significance, and examine the "so what" behind the "what happened."

Connecting to Selections

Have students refer to the Timeline when they begin to read individual selections. By consulting the Timeline regularly, they will gain a better sense of the period's chronology. In addition, they will appreciate world events that gave rise to these works of literature.

Projects

Students can use the Timeline as a launching pad for projects like these:

- **Letter to the Editor** Have students study the Timeline events leading up to World War II. Then, have students write a letter to the editor attempting to persuade readers that the entry of the United States into the war was inevitable. Students should use Timeline events for support.

- **Technology Timeline** Have students study the Timeline and select events that show technological advancements. Then, have students create a poster-sized timeline, showing the technological advances that took place from 1890 to 1945. Ask students to illustrate their timelines and display them in the classroom.

World Events

1890 1900 1910

HISTORICAL AND CULTURAL EVENTS

- 1890 Ohio inventor builds first internal combustion automobile in the United States.
- 1899 Sigmund Freud publishes *The Interpretation of Dreams.* ▼

- 1901 Marconi sends a message across the Atlantic via wireless telegraphy.
- 1903 Orville Wright makes the first successful flight in an airplane. ▼

- 1911 Marie Curie wins second Nobel Prize, for isolating pure radium.
- 1914–1918 World War I is fought, killing millions. ▼
- 1917 Communists seize power in Russia.
  - 1919 U. S. Senate rejects League of Nations.

- 1903 Henri Becquerel and Pierre and Marie Curie win a Nobel Prize for work on radioactivity.
- 1905 Einstein proposes his theory of special relativity.
- 1907 Pablo Picasso completes *The Young Women of Avignon.*
- 1907 Tungsten filament lamps first used in the United States.
- 1908 Henry Ford starts producing standardized Model T automobiles.

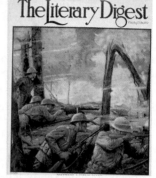

LITERARY EVENTS

- 1890 Japanese author Mori Ōgai publishes his story "The Dancing Girl."
- 1893 Nicaraguan poet Rubén Darío becomes Colombian consul in Buenos Aires, Argentina.
- 1896 Alfred Nobel dies; his will endows the Nobel Prize in Literature.
- 1896 French author Paul Valéry publishes *An Evening With Monsieur Teste.*

- 1900 French novelist Colette publishes *Claudine at School.*
- 1900 Spanish poet Juan Ramón Jiménez comes to Madrid at the invitation of Rubén Darío.
- 1907–1908 Austro-German poet Rainer Maria Rilke publishes *New Poems.*

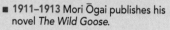

- 1911–1913 Mori Ōgai publishes his novel *The Wild Goose.*
  - c. 1912 Ezra Pound and others create the Imagist movement. ◄
- 1913 Rabindranath Tagore receives the Nobel Prize in Literature.
- 1913 Marcel Proust publishes the first volume of *Remembrance of Things Past.*
- 1913 French poet Guillaume Apollinaire publishes *Alcools.*

Getting an Overview of the Period

Introduction To give students an overview of the period, have them indicate the span of dates in the title of the Timeline. Next, point out that the Timeline is divided into Historical and Cultural Events (on the top) and Literary Events (on the bottom). Have students scan the Timeline, looking at both the Historical and Cultural Events and the Literary Events. Finally, point out that the events in the Timeline often represent beginnings, turning points, and endings (for example, the start of World War II in 1939).

Key Events Have students **identify** key events of the Modern World.

Possible response: Key events are the first successful airplane flight and the use of the atomic bomb.

   Ask students to describe the impact of these key events.

Possible response: Flight essentially reduced the size of the world, and the atomic bomb increased the destructive power of human beings.

1920　1930　1940　1950

- 1927 Charles Lindbergh makes a successful solo flight across the Atlantic.
- 1928 Stalin begins forcing peasants onto collective farms, killing those who resist.
- 1929 Great Depression begins, lasting until about 1939. ▼

- 1931 Japan seizes Manchuria from China.
- 1932 Franklin Roosevelt elected President of the U. S. (serves 1932–1945). ▼

- 1933 Hitler becomes chancellor of Germany.
- 1934 Stalin begins a campaign of terror against those who are "disloyal."
- 1937 Japan launches a full-scale war against China.
- 1939 Hitler invades Poland, starting World War II.

- 1940 Churchill becomes Prime Minister of Great Britain.
- 1940 Japanese enter the war on the side of the Axis Powers.
- 1941 Germany invades the Soviet Union.
- 1941 The United States enters the war on the side of the Allies.
- 1945 America drops two atom bombs on Japan. ▶
- 1945 The Allies defeat the Axis Powers, ending World War II.

- 1921 André Breton meets Sigmund Freud.
- 1921 Italian author Luigi Pirandello publishes the play *Six Characters in Search of an Author*.
- 1922 James Joyce publishes *Ulysses*.
- 1922 Russian poet Boris Pasternak publishes *My Sister—Life*.
- 1923 Rainer Maria Rilke publishes *Duino Elegies* and *Sonnets to Orpheus*.
- 1924 Franz Kafka dies of tuberculosis.

- 1935–1940 Anna Akhmatova composes *Requiem*.
- 1936 Federico García Lorca (portrayed here by actor Andy Garcia) is assassinated by fascists. ▼

- 1942 Albert Camus publishes his novel *The Stranger*.
- 1944 Colette publishes her novel *Gigi*.
- 1945 Gabriela Mistral becomes the first Latin American to win the Nobel Prize in Literature.

Introduction ■ 1053

Critical Viewing

1. On the basis of the illustration of Orville Wright's first airplane (1903), what can you deduce about his first flight? **[Deduce]**
   Possible response: The plane does not look sturdy enough to fly for very long. Therefore, the flight was probably dangerous and short.

2. What does the cover of the *Literary Digest* (1914–1918) imply about the fighting in World War I? **[Infer]**
   Possible response: The cover suggests that the fighting was difficult and primarily hand-to-hand.

3. What does the illustration of the atomic bomb blast (1945) suggest about its power? **[Analyze]**
   Possible response: The illustration suggests that the blast was extremely powerful, destructive, and visible from a great distance.

Analyzing the Timeline

1. (a) When did Marconi send a message across the Atlantic via wireless telegraphy? (b) How might this action eventually have affected the entry of the United States into World War I? **[Analyze Causes and Effects]**
   Answer: (a) Marconi sent the message in 1901. (b) Communication between the United States and Europe became faster. Consequently, people became more aware of what was happening in Europe.

2. (a) When did Charles Lindbergh make his successful solo flight across the Atlantic? (b) What advances in aviation must have taken place between Lindbergh's flight and World War II? **[Synthesize]**
   Answer: (a) Charles Lindbergh made his flight in 1927. (b) In the years between Lindbergh's flight and World War II, aviation improved significantly.

3. (a) When did Henri Becquerel and Pierre and Marie Curie win a Nobel Prize for their work on radioactivity? (b) What later event was an eventual outgrowth of their work? **[Deduce]**
   Answer: (a) Becquerel and the Curies won the Nobel Prize in 1903. (b) Their discovery led to the development and use of the atomic bomb in 1945.

4. (a) When did the United States enter World War II? (b) Why did the United States enter the war two years after it had begun in Europe? **[Infer]**
   Answer: (a) The United States entered World War II in 1941. (b) The late entry of the United States into the war demonstrates an isolationist policy.

5. (a) When did Japan seize Manchuria from China? (b) How might this action influence Japan's future relationship with China? **[Speculate]**
   Answer: (a) Japan seized Manchuria in 1931. (b) It would lead to poor relations between the countries. In fact, Japan invaded China in 1937.

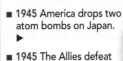

Literature of the Period

- In Franz Kafka's "The Metamorphosis," p. 1010, students will meet a character who wakes up to find that he has been transformed into a giant insect. This selection exemplifies the Modernist theme of alienation.

- As they read "The Bracelet" by Colette, p. 1118, students will find a Modernist nontraditional plot structure that deals with memories of a lost childhood gift, one as inexpensive as it was priceless.

- In Rabindranath Tagore's "The Artist," p. 1162, students will find a character who personifies the importance of creativity over modern materialistic values.

Background
Marie Curie

Marie Curie was born in Poland in 1867. As a child, Curie had an exceptional memory. She completed her secondary education at the age of sixteen but was forced to find work because her father's poor investing left the family with little money. Marie took jobs as a teacher and a governess to pay for her sister's education. Curie left for Paris in 1891, where she studied physics. She married Pierre Curie in 1895. The Curies became known throughout the world because of their work with radium and radioactivity. Marie Curie received the 1911 Nobel Prize in Chemistry for her work with radium, which she discovered in 1898. She died from leukemia in 1934.

Critical Viewing

Possible response: Nuclear power, radiation treatments for cancer, and other scientific advances are considered to be positive results; nuclear weapons and nuclear accidents are considered to be negative results.

Historical Background

Breakthroughs in Technology and Science Sparked by the efforts of brilliant scientists and inventors, major technological advances began occurring in the late nineteenth and early twentieth centuries that would permanently alter the ways in which people lived. Within a period of just a few decades, the airplane, the automobile, the radio, and the telephone were introduced, making travel and communication faster and easier than ever before. At the same time, other discoveries and inventions, such as electricity, central heating, movies, and new medical remedies, were improving the quality of people's lives. Still other advances, such as the development of the machine gun and the tank, made it easier for people to destroy one another.

Scientific breakthroughs rivaled these technological advances. The husband and wife team of Marie and Pierre Curie, for example, pioneered in studying radioactivity. Then, in 1905, German-born physicist Albert Einstein proposed his special theory of relativity, showing that calculations of time and motion depend on an observer's relative position. Einstein also proved that energy and matter can be converted into each other, as expressed by the famous formula $E = mc^2$.

Understanding Human Behavior Austrian psychiatrist Sigmund Freud (froid) proposed an equally radical theory of human behavior. Using a method of gathering information about mental processes known as psychoanalysis, Freud concluded that people's behavior is largely shaped by unconscious influences stemming from experiences during infancy and early childhood. Because Freud's theories challenged the belief that human activity sprang from rational thought, they initially sparked controversy. Yet as time passed, his ideas gained increasing acceptance. World War I itself seemed the greatest proof that humans were basically irrational!

World War I Encouraged by advances in science and technology, many people became increasingly optimistic about the future of humanity. To some, it even seemed possible that people could ultimately solve all their problems and establish lasting peace. This sense of optimism was utterly shattered, however, by the horrifying realities of World War I.

Beginning late in the summer of 1914, the war was a conflict between the Allies (France, Russia, Great Britain, Italy, and Japan, joined later by the United States) and the Central Powers (Germany, Austria-Hungary, and Turkey). This war eventually involved much of the world.

▼ **Critical Viewing**
This photograph shows Marie Curie in her laboratory, where she studied radioactivity. What positive and negative results have come from the study of radioactivity? Explain. **[Draw Conclusions]**

Enrichment

Albert Einstein and the Theory of Relativity
Albert Einstein (1879–1955), who was born in Germany, is known as the greatest physicist of all time. He is best known for his theory of relativity.

Einstein argued that because all matter is in constant motion, there is no fixed point from which to measure motion. The motion of one object can be measured only by comparing it with the motion of another. All measurements are therefore relative. This theory is called the theory of relativity.

In 1921, Einstein won the Nobel Prize in Physics for his work on photoelectric effect. He became an American citizen in 1940.

Themes in World Masterpieces

Art in the Historical Context

The Art of Colonized Lands Conquers the West

In the late nineteenth and early twentieth centuries, Western colonizers sought new markets and mineral wealth in Africa, the Pacific Islands, and other so-called primitive places. Western artists sought a different kind of wealth in these same lands. They realized how much they could learn from the art of tribal peoples, from sculptures and masks that broke up the human figure and face in startling ways. Instead of imitating nature as Western works did, tribal art used abstractions—geometric shapes and fantastic forms—to convey spiritual realities.

In 1906–7, Pablo Picasso incorporated the abstractions of tribal art in a painting that made people gasp, *Les Demoiselles d'Avignon* ("The Young Women of Avignon"). Picasso himself was so uncertain about the canvas that he put it aside for a while. Today, it is recognized as the work that revolutionized Western art. With his slashing lines, Picasso attacked ideals of beauty and techniques of perspective that dated back to the Renaissance.

Throughout most of the conflict, neither side was able to make any significant advances. Having reached a stalemate early in the war, the opposing armies settled into trenches protected by mines and barbed wire. For the next few years, the two sides took turns rushing the opposing trenches. With each of these charges, hundreds of soldiers would be mowed down by machine-gun fire. By the time the war ended in 1918 with the Allies victorious, about eight and a half million soldiers had died of wounds or disease and about thirteen million civilians had lost their lives from a variety of war-related causes.

The Rise of Nazism In the aftermath of the war, the Allies drafted a treaty that required Germany to accept full blame and pay reparations for the total cost of the war. Germany signed the treaty, but its harsh terms created strong feelings of resentment among the German people. These feelings, coupled with the inflation caused by war reparations that Germany had to pay, generated unrest that plagued the nation throughout the 1920s.

The Great Depression In 1929, a severe economic slump hit the United States and, soon afterward, other industrialized nations such as Germany. Known as the Great Depression, it lasted through the 1930s and contributed to the rise of Hitler and other political extremists. In the early 1930s, the Nazis exploited the turmoil resulting from political unrest and economic decline to seize control of Germany.

Persecution of Jews Hitler quickly molded the nation into a totalitarian state, brutally suppressing all dissent. The word *totalitarian* refers to "a state in which one party or group retains total authority under a dictator."

Les Demoiselles d'Avignon (detail), 1907, Pablo Picasso, The Museum of Modern Art, ©2004 Estate of Pablo Picasso; Artists Rights Society (ARS), NY.

▲ **Critical Viewing**
Compare and contrast this mask from the South Pacific island of New Britain (top) with the head of a young woman in Picasso's painting (bottom). Use details from each work to support your points. **[Compare and Contrast]**

Introduction ■ 1055

Themes in World Literature

Art in the Historical Context
Note that abstract art still thrives today, even without artists' intentions to convey spiritual values. Some architects use fantastic geometric shapes and other abstractions in their building designs. **Ask** students to give examples of abstract art that has impressed them.
Possible response: Students may suggest the work of Joan Miró, Salvador Dali, Wassily Kandinsky, Jackson Pollack, and the surrealist René Magritte.

Humanities

Les Demoiselles d'Avignon,
by Pablo Picasso

This famous painting by Picasso (1881–1973) exemplifies an extreme change in the type of art being produced in the early 1900s. Picasso uses asymmetrical shapes; sharp, uneven lines; and African masks to portray a group of women. Picasso uses the masks in the painting to show magical protection from dangerous spirits.

Use the following question for discussion:

How does Picasso's painting indicate a new direction in art?
Possible response: Unlike most nineteenth-century artists, Picasso is not concerned here with imitating reality.

Critical Viewing

Possible response: The mask and the young woman share some features such as almond-shaped eyes and a sharp nose, but the mask from New Britain is recognizably shaped like a human head; whereas in Picasso's painting, the young woman's head is fragmented.

Humanities
Show students *Le Tourangeau (The Man from Tours)* by Juan Gris, on Transparency 20 in **Fine Art Transparencies.** Use the image to help students understand the importance of multiple perspectives in both modern art and literature.

1055

Background

The Attack on Pearl Harbor

On December 7, 1941, Japanese carrier planes swept in over Pearl Harbor without warning. The raid on the United States Pacific Fleet damaged or destroyed eight American battleships, including the *U.S.S. Tennessee,* the *U.S.S. West Virginia,* and the *U.S.S. Arizona.* On December 8, 1941, the United States declared war on Japan.

Background

Hitler's Power

When Hitler's power was at its height, the Axis nations controlled much of Europe, including Sweden and Spain. Switzerland remained neutral and never fought the Axis powers. In the east, Germany held Austria, Czechoslovakia, western Poland, Hungary, Romania, and Bulgaria.

Background

Japan

During this period, Japan was also undergoing a period of rapid change. After reestablishing ties with the Western world during the mid-1800s, Japan had begun a program of modernization and militarization. Japan's newly acquired military strength first became evident in 1904, when it easily defeated the Russian navy in the Russo-Japanese War.

Critical Viewing

Possible response: The people standing at attention as Hitler passes and the swastika-emblazoned flags held at attention show Hitler's charismatic power.

The Nazis assumed control of every aspect of German life, including religion, schools, and the press. They burned books and destroyed works of art they judged to be "un-German," and they forced radio stations to play military music and Nazi speeches. At the same time, they began ruthlessly persecuting German Jews, stripping them of their citizenship and expelling them from government posts and teaching positions.

Other Totalitarian Regimes Hitler's government was only one of a number of totalitarian regimes to emerge during the first half of the twentieth century. In Russia, where communists had seized power in the November Revolution of 1917, a totalitarian state was established after Joseph Stalin rose to power in the early 1920s. Like Hitler, Stalin brutally suppressed all dissent, executing millions of people who resisted his policies. Another totalitarian ruler, Benito Mussolini, gained control of Italy and later became one of Hitler's chief allies. In Spain, Francisco Franco established a fascist regime after winning a bloody civil war.

The German Invasion of Poland During the Spanish Civil War (1936–1939), both the Germans and the Italians provided Franco with military support. Pablo Picasso's famous painting *Guernica* is a reaction to news of a German bombing raid on the Spanish city of Guernica in 1937. Because the democratic powers did little to discourage German and Italian involvement in Spain, Hitler and Mussolini did not hesitate to engage in further acts of military aggression. On September 1, 1939, German forces invaded Poland, subduing the country in little over a month. Britain and France responded by declaring war on Germany. Another world conflict had begun.

World War II pitted the Axis Powers (led by Germany, Italy, and Japan) against the Allies (led by Britain, France, the Soviet Union, and the United States). It is important to remember, however, that France was under German Occupation from 1940 to 1944, the Soviet Union was originally on Germany's side, Japan did not join the Axis immediately, and the United States did not enter the war until late in 1941.

The Russian Campaign Only weeks before the German invasion of Poland, Hitler had signed a Nonaggression Pact with the Soviet Union. On June 22, 1941, this famous "friendship" of dictators ended as German forces staged a surprise invasion of the Soviet Union.

▲ **Critical Viewing**
Which details in these pictures suggest the charismatic power that Hitler exercised over the German people? Explain. **[Interpret]**

Enrichment

The Soviet Union

Although the Soviet Union eventually fought with the Allies, it was not a free country. In the 1920s, under Joseph Stalin, the Soviet Union underwent a rapid process of industrialization. In addition, Stalin took extreme measures designed to improve the productivity of the Soviet agricultural system. He ordered all peasants to give up their land and farm animals.

The seized lands were combined into large collective farms that were run by the government. Millions of peasants resisted forced collectivization and were either executed or sent to labor camps in Siberia. In fact, it has been estimated that over ten million people lost their lives during the process of collectivization.

German forces advanced rapidly at first but could not achieve victory by the winter of 1941. Like Napoleon, Hitler would pay dearly for hurling his armies eastward. The German dictator would not be able to contend with the huge reserves of Soviet manpower or with the icy assaults of "General Winter," as historians have sometimes called the Russian winter.

The Attack on Pearl Harbor On July 27, 1940, the Japanese aligned themselves with the Germans and the Italians. At the time the Japanese officially entered the war, the United States had not become directly involved in the conflict. On December 7, 1941, however, the Japanese drew the United States into the war by launching a surprise air attack on the American naval base at Pearl Harbor in Hawaii.

The End of the War and the Beginning of the Atomic Age In May of 1945, after years of savage fighting, the Nazis surrendered to the Allies. About three months later, Japan also surrendered, after the United States had dropped atomic bombs on the Japanese cities of Hiroshima and Nagasaki. With the defeat of Japan, peace had finally arrived. Yet so had the atomic age.

The destruction caused by World War II was staggering. It is estimated that some 50 million people lost their lives as a result of the war. In addition, bombing raids reduced much of Europe and Japan to rubble, and millions of people were uprooted from their homes.

The Holocaust One of the most shocking aspects of the war was not fully discovered until the Allied forces marched into Germany. In response to Hitler's diabolical plan to exterminate the Jewish people, the Nazis had imprisoned and executed about six million Jews in concentration camps. They had also executed millions of others, including people of Slavic descent and Gypsies. This systematic slaughter of Jews and others is one of the most tragic events in human history. It has come to be known as the Holocaust, from the Greek *holokauston*, a translation of the Hebrew *'olah*, meaning "burnt sacrifice offered to God." Jews also refer to this event as the Shoah, a Hebrew word meaning "catastrophe."

▼ **Critical Viewing**
This view of the Nazis' Terezin concentration camp was painted by an inmate who suffered its horrors. Does anything in the painting reveal the harsh realities of the camp? Why or why not?
[Interpret]

View of Terezin, Hanus Weinberg, State Jewish Museum, Prague

Introduction ■ 1057

Answers continued

2. How did the Great Depression help lead to the rise of Hitler? **[Analyze Causes and Effects]**
Possible response: Difficult economic conditions in Germany added to the resentment the Germans felt after World War I. Because of this dissatisfaction, the Germans were more willing to elect political extremists to try to alleviate their problems.

3. In what ways can you support the conclusion that World War II might have lasted much longer if Hitler had not sent his troops to attack the Soviet Union? **[Support]**

Possible response: Invading the Soviet Union tied up a large number of German troops. Had Hitler concentrated his forces against Western Europe, the war probably would have lasted much longer.

Critical Viewing
Possible response: The sharp lines of the image exemplify the harshness of the camp. That no humans are depicted could symbolize the deaths that took place there.

Historical Background
Comprehension Check

1. According to Sigmund Freud, what shapes human behavior?
Answer: Freud believed that unconscious influences coming from experiences in infancy and early childhood—not from rational thought—shape human behavior.

2. What generated unrest in Germany throughout the 1920s?
Answer: The harsh terms of the treaty after World War I and the costly reparations caused resentment among the German people.

3. Why did Britain and France declare war on Germany in 1939?
Answer: Britain and France declared war on Germany because Germany invaded Poland.

4. What ended the "friendship" between Germany and the Soviet Union?
Answer: In 1941, German forces invaded the Soviet Union in spite of Germany's signing of a Nonaggression Pact with the Soviets.

5. What did the Allied forces find when they marched into Germany?
Answer: The Allied forces found that Hitler had carried out a plan to exterminate the Jewish population and had executed over six million Jews as well as millions of others.

Critical Thinking

1. Compare and contrast an optimistic view of humanity's future with the realities of World War I. **[Compare and Contrast]**
Possible response: The rapid advances in technology led people to believe that technological advances could solve humankind's problems and lead to a bright future. When World War I broke out, people saw eight and a half million soldiers and about thirteen million civilians killed. The optimistic view of humanity's future faded quickly in light of the war.

Background

Gabriela Mistral

As Gabriela Mistral stated in her Nobel address, she devoted her life to improving the position and education of women and children. As a young poet and schoolteacher, Mistral wrote poems to help children learn to read. As her reputation as a poet grew, so did her status and reputation as an educator. During her career, Mistral initiated what were then progressive methods of education, which included visual aids, extracts from literature, and games in place of textbooks.

Mistral's efforts to help children extended beyond her own country. In 1938, Mistral published *Tala,* her third collection of poetry, in Buenos Aires. At the time of this publication, Spain was in civil war. Mistral donated the proceeds from her book to the orphans living in children's camps in Catalonia and in France.

When the news reached her homeland that Mistral had died, Chilean president Ibañez decreed three days of national mourning.

Themes in World Literature

Close-up on Culture Tell students that university professors and other members of academic institutions around the world submit nominations for candidates for the various Nobel Prizes. Students can find out more about this process on pp. 1158–1159. **Ask** students to give examples of writers from a variety of cultures who have won the Nobel Prize.

Possible responses: Austria: Elfriede Jelinek; China: Gao Xingjian; Columbia: Gabriel García Marquez; Egypt: Naguib Mahfouz; England: Winston Churchill; Germany: Elie Weisel; Ireland: Seamus Heaney; Italy: Dario Fo; Japan: Kenzaburo Oe; Portugal: José Saramago; Poland: Wislawa Szymborska; Russia: Aleksandr Solzhenitsyn; South Africa: John Maxwell Coetzee; Spain: Juan Ramón Jiménez; United States: Toni Morrison

Literature

The modern age was one of the most turbulent and violent periods of human history. Yet it was also an era of tremendous artistic and literary achievement. Responding to the events and developments of their time and experimenting with new literary forms and approaches, modern writers from across the world created a fresh and remarkably diverse body of literature.

Worldwide Literary Connections With the advances in travel and communication, the various regions of the world became increasingly intertwined during the modern age. Consequently, the literary world became more interconnected than ever before, as writers from all countries were exposed to the literary movements and traditions of other cultures.

For the first time, writers from non-Western and less developed countries began to receive worldwide attention. The modern Indian writer Rabindranath Tagore (rə bēn′ drə nät′ tə gôr′), for example, earned a Nobel Prize in Literature. The Chilean poet Gabriela Mistral (gä brē ā′ lä mēs träl′) also won a Nobel Prize in Literature, after the Nicaraguan poet Rubén Darío (rōō ben′ dä rē′ ō) had drawn the attention of the literary world to Latin America. Darío not only received worldwide acclaim but also influenced a number of important European poets.

The Birth of Modernism The term *Modernism* refers to a movement or group of movements in all the arts that occurred in the late nineteenth and early twentieth centuries. Modernist writers, painters, and composers sensed that dramatic changes in society—advances in transportation and

Themes in World Masterpieces   Close-up on Culture

Nobel Launches "World Literature" With a Bang!

Alfred Nobel (1833–1896), the Swedish inventor of dynamite, was also the founder of the famous Nobel Prizes. One of these, the Nobel Prize in Literature, helped launch the modern idea of "World Literature." This world-class prize confirmed that writers were part of an international fellowship of the imagination, whether they worked in Chile or Nigeria, France or Australia.

Nobel had invented dynamite to serve peaceful uses, but it was later used to kill people in wars. Not wanting to be associated with death and destruction, the Swedish inventor set up a fund in his will to endow five Nobel Prizes (more were added later). One of the original five, the Nobel Prize in Literature is awarded by the Swedish Academy. Each winner receives a gold medal, a diploma, and a sum of money—by 1996, it was more than one million dollars! Not only has the prize established a standard by which all writers can be judged equally, but it has also helped publicize individual authors and groups of authors. For example, the 2002 prize awarded to Hungarian author Imre Kertész brought renewed attention to Holocaust literature.

1058 ■ *The Modern World*

Enrichment

Pablo Picasso

Pablo Picasso (1881–1973), one of the greatest painters of the twentieth century, had a long career that can be divided into several stages. Born in Malaga, Spain, Picasso demonstrated his artistic gift at an early age. After abandoning Realism as a young man, he entered a phase of his career known as the Blue Period. During this period, he produced works that featured many shades of blue and evoked feelings of loneliness and despair. When this stage of his career came to an end, he began creating paintings that contained startling combinations of jagged and often distorted images. These paintings gave birth to a major artistic movement known as Cubism. The next stage of his career was marked by his use of colorful, dreamlike images. In the 1920s and 1930s, he focused on expressing his reactions to current events in his works. Finally, as his career drew to a close, he produced paintings and sculptures with a more relaxed, gentle feeling.

communication, the growth of cities, devastating new modes of warfare—
were calling into question the values and traditions of the past. In response,
these artists began to question artistic traditions as well. They wanted to
create works of art that expressed the radically
different *modern* world in which they lived.

The first flowering of Modernism was in pre-
World War I Paris and London. Paris especially
was a laboratory for artistic experimentation.
There, in 1906, the young Spanish painter Pablo
Picasso looked to primitive art as a means of
challenging Western traditions (see page 1055).

Art That Provoked Riots If Picasso's work
caused astonishment, the music of Russian-born
composer Igor Stravinsky provoked riots. In
1913, the performance of his ballet piece *The Rite
of Spring* at a Paris theater caused an uproar in
the audience that drowned out the music. The
audience was reacting to the changing rhythms
and the lack of traditional harmony in a work
that, like Picasso's, drew on primitive sources
for inspiration.

In the field of literature, two great experi-
menters were the poet Guillaume Apollinaire
(gē yōm´ á pô lē ner´) (1880–1918) and the novelist
Marcel Proust (mär sel´ prōōst´) (1871–1922).
Apollinaire astonished readers with unexpected
associations, and Proust explored the meaning of
time and memory in his multivolume novel
Remembrance of Things Past (1913–1927).

An Imagist's Marching Orders Meanwhile,
across the Channel in London, a group of poets that included the American
Ezra Pound were struggling to make poetry in English more colloquial and
concrete. In a literary manifesto expressing the beliefs of this new Imagist
movement, Pound gave twentieth-century poets their marching orders: In
presenting images or clear pictures, he commanded, "Use no superfluous
word, . . . Go in fear of abstractions. . . . Don't make each line stop dead at
the end . . . "

The War and a Second Flowering of Modernism The unprecedented
destruction during World War I finally proved—to anyone who still
doubted—that a new historical age had arrived. The war forever divided
what came to seem like an innocent time from a modern era whose
innocence was another battlefield casualty.

To many artists who participated in the second flowering of Modernism
during the 1920s, the war was the ultimate proof of human irrationality. It
seemed to verify Freud's theories about the irrational motivations of human
behavior, and these theories gained in influence during the postwar period.

▲ **Critical Viewing**
This illustration for the
bound sheet music of
Stravinsky's ballet
Pétrouchka contains
Russian words because
the dance was
performed by the
Russian Ballet. Which
visual details suggest
that the dance will be
new and boldly
imaginative? Explain.
[Interpret]

Introduction ■ 1059

Background
Igor Stravinsky
Igor Stravinsky, born June 17, 1882,
near St. Petersburg, Russia, wrote in
the Modernist, or Neoclassic, style.
He came from a musical and theatrical
family and was tutored by composer
Nikolay Rimsky-Korsakov. His works
were revolutionary, and his ballet *The
Firebird*, which opened in Paris in 1910,
made him an overnight success. His
work *The Rite of Spring* was far different from the types of music and
dance to which audiences were accustomed. Stravinsky was considered a
major force in Modernism.

Critical Viewing
Possible response: The juxtaposition of the sword, the jester, and the
rose indicate a theme that may be
nontraditional.

Background

André Breton

André Breton was born in 1896 in France. During medical school, Breton studied the writings of Sigmund Freud because of his interest in mental illness. In the early 1900s, Breton started the Surrealist movement with Philippe Soupault in their work titled *"Les Champs magnétiques"* ("Magnetic Fields"). Breton was able to escape from France during the German occupation; in exile in the United States from 1941 to 1946, Breton organized a Surrealist exhibition at Yale University in 1942. He eventually returned to France and continued to write. Breton died in Paris in 1966.

Themes in World Literature

A Living Tradition Point out to students that Joyce became famous for the style of interior monologue that he used to portray his characters Leopold and Molly Bloom. That technique, now called stream-of-consciousness, created an uproar in society because of Molly's and Leopold's many controversial thoughts. Even though the novel was published in 1922, it was not legally available in England or the United States until 1933. Today, however, James Joyce is an icon in the literary world. Many writers use the stream-of-consciousness technique. **Ask** students to suggest another work that mirrors a classic source.

Possible response: Students' suggestions may include Tennyson's *Idylls of the King,* based on Arthurian legend, and Washington Irving's "The Devil and Tom Walker," based on the Faust legend.

For example, they were the basis for the literary and artistic movement called Surrealism, which viewed the unconscious as a source of inspiration. The French poet André Breton (än drä′ brə tôn′) (1896–1966), who led the movement, advocated writing quickly and without thinking. This technique would enable authors to bypass the rational mind and write directly from the unconscious.

Eliminating the Traditional Links Other great Modernists of the 1920s, while not Surrealists themselves, shared the Surrealists' tendency to remove connecting language and structures from their work—all the expositions, transitions, resolutions, and explanations that readers had come to expect. To reflect the disjointedness and irrationality of the modern world, they often built their work from fragments. James Joyce, for example, used a stream-of-consciousness narration to immerse readers in the flow of a character's fragmentary thoughts. Yet even as he did so, he created a new type of structure (see page 1060).

Themes in
World Masterpieces   A Living Tradition

James Joyce's *Ulysses* and Homer's *Odyssey*

In searching for new techniques to record modern realities, twentieth-century writers often returned to age-old sources. Irishman James Joyce, for example, went as far back as ancient Greece. In his novel *Ulysses*, besides pioneering a stream-of-consciousness narrative that reveals characters' thoughts directly, Joyce organizes events according to the episodes of Homer's ancient epic the *Odyssey*. (Ulysses is the Roman name of that epic's hero, Odysseus.) The epic describes the ten-year homeward journey of Odysseus from the Trojan War and his reunion with his son, Telemachus, and his faithful wife, Penelope.

Joyce's book follows two characters—young Irishman Stephen Dedalus and middle-aged Jew Leopold Bloom—as they traverse Dublin on June 16, 1904. Following in Odysseus' footsteps, Bloom goes on a one-day journey to meet his spiritual son, Stephen, and reunite with his wife, Molly. His thoughts and adventures humorously parallel the Greek hero's encounters with mythological characters. The result is a detailed realistic narrative with mythological dimensions.

For example, Bloom's casual thoughts as he passes a tea-merchant's window recall the lotus-eaters, who tempt Odysseus' men to taste the sleep-inducing lotus plant and forget their homeward journey:

> . . . The far east. Lovely spot it must be: the garden of the world, big lazy leaves to float about on, cactuses, flowery meads, snaky lianas they call them. Wonder is it like that. Those Cinghalese [people of Sri Lanka] lobbing around in the sun, in dolce far niente [Italian for "sweet doing nothing"]. Not doing a hand's turn all day. Sleep six months out of twelve. . . .

Enrichment

The Human Mind

Austrian psychiatrist Sigmund Freud (1856–1939) is the founder of psychoanalysis. Psychoanalysis, one type of psychotherapy used in psychiatry, has had great influence on child rearing, education, the cultural and social sciences, medicine, and the arts. Freud's theories of a dynamic unconscious and dreams as key to the unconscious were instrumental in influencing André Breton's Surrealism Manifesto and the subsequent Surrealist movement in literature.

Sigmund Freud believed that the human mind could be divided into three parts: the id, the ego, and the superego. The id includes the most basic human drives, such as the drive to satisfy thirst and hunger. The ego, on the other hand, connects the internal mind to the outside environment. Finally, the superego is the part of the mind that governs moral behavior.

Implied Themes, Elusive Realities In keeping with the uncertainties of modern life, Modernist writers tended to imply, rather than directly state, the themes of their works. This approach forced readers to draw their own conclusions. For example, at the beginning of Franz Kafka's novel *The Trial*, a man named Joseph K. (his last name is never more than an initial) wakes up one morning to find that he has been accused of a crime. Neither he nor the reader ever discovers the reason for the accusation. What is even stranger, this Austrian novelist describes the most bizarre events using prose suitable for a bland business report.

As Kafka's novel suggests, Modernists questioned the nature of reality itself. They no longer assumed that it was comprehensible, let alone comforting. In Luigi Pirandello's drama *Six Characters in Search of an Author*, for example, fictional characters that the author has discarded take over the stage.

"'Can you describe this?'...'I can.'" The turbulent events of the first half of the twentieth century directly affected the lives of many writers. It made them both victims and witnesses, falling prey to wars and the persecutions of tyrants but also nobly recording injustices. The Spanish poet Federico García Lorca (fe´ de rē´ kô gär sē´ ə lôr´ kə) was murdered by supporters of Franco during the early stages of the Spanish Civil War. The Russian poet Anna Akhmatova (ukh mät´ ə və), like many of her compatriots, suffered grievously at the hands of Stalin. In the poem *Requiem*, she laments the dictator's imprisonment of her son but also bears witness to the pain of all oppressed Russians. Likewise, her introduction to the poem could serve as a testament for all modern writers who battled injustice with their pens. In it, she describes how another woman waiting to see an imprisoned relative asks her, "Can you describe this?" She answers, "I can."

Beyond the Modern Age Although the end of World War II marks the official close of the modern age, the literary innovations and accomplishments of this era did not end in 1945. Many modern writers, including Albert Camus (ka mōō´), Gabriela Mistral, Boris Pasternak (pas´ tər nak´), and Anna Akhmatova remained productive long after the end of the war. At the same time, a new generation of talented writers arose across the globe, bringing with them fresh ideas and approaches.

La condition humaine (The Human Condition), 1933, René Magritte, National Gallery of Art, Washington; ©1998 C. Herscovici, Brussels/Artists Rights Society (ARS), New York

▲ **Critical Viewing**
Belgian artist René Magritte often painted scenes as strange as those evoked by authors like Kafka and Pirandello. Which details in this painting are strangely unreal? Why? **[Interpret]**

Introduction ■ 1061

❶ Elements of the Short Story

• Review the elements of the short story. Ask students what they like best about stories, and write their responses on the board. Then, ask students to tell whether each response is an example of one of the narrative elements listed on this page in the student book and which element the response is. Ask students to explain how their responses exemplify narrative elements.

• **Ask:** Are all of these narrative elements necessary? How would stories be different, better, or worse without some of these elements?
Possible response: Yes, these elements are necessary. Although a story could have different types of conflict or characterization, for instance, stories without conflict would lack the drama that makes reading them interesting; stories without characterization would be flat and uninteresting.

• Point out that Edgar Allan Poe wrote many short stories, including detective stories and gothic tales.

Defining the Short Story

A short story is a brief work of fiction that usually features a plot with a distinct beginning, middle, and end. There is no set length for a short story, but most are between five hundred words and fifty pages in length, or brief enough to read in one sitting. The American short story writer Edgar Allan Poe defined the genre as "a short prose narrative requiring from a half-hour to one or two hours in its perusal." He also explained that all of the details in a short story should achieve a single, unifying effect.

A GOOD SHORT STORY IS A WORK OF ART WHICH DAUNTS US IN PROPORTION TO ITS BREVITY. . . . — *Elizabeth Stuart Phelps*

❶ Elements of the Short Story
The short story and the novel share the same basic narrative elements:

• **Plot:** a sequence of events that explores characters in conflict.

• **Conflict:** a struggle between two opposing forces. There are two main types of conflict in literature:

  • **Internal conflict:** occurs within the mind of a character. It involves a struggle with attitudes, ideas, or emotions.

  • **External conflict:** takes place between a character and an outside force, such as another person, society, nature, fate, or God.

• **Setting:** the time and place of the action in a story. A short story often has a single setting.

> **Characters in Conflict**
> In a traditional short story plot, one main character—or *protagonist*—encounters a conflict that is resolved by the story's end. In many modern stories, the plot builds to a crucial moment in which the conflict is altered in some way, but not necessarily resolved.

• **Character:** a person or creature that participates in the action of a story. Short stories generally have fewer characters than novels do, and those characters must be depicted believably yet concisely. The way a writer creates and develops characters is called *characterization*.

  • **Direct characterization:** The writer states what a character is like.

  • **Indirect characterization:** The writer reveals what a character is like by describing his or her physical appearance; by presenting the character's words, actions, and thoughts; or by showing other characters' reactions to him or her. Readers can deduce what a character is like from such clues offered by the writer.

• **Theme:** the central idea, message, or insight of the story. A short story usually has a single theme, which may be revealed either in a crucial moment of insight or in clues that must be pieced together.

Extend the Lesson

Activity
• Have students write a brief first-person account of a conflict that they have encountered.
• Then have students change the narration to a third-person omniscient account.
• Finally, ask students to write the account a third time, using third-person limited.

• Ask students to compare what details they included in each type of narration and what details they had to eliminate as they changed points of view.
• Point out that the type of narration determines what authors can include and how they must develop a story.

❷ Narrating a Short Story

Like novels, short stories are narrated from a specific perspective, or vantage point, called *point of view*. Point of view is determined by what type of narrator, or voice, is telling the story. The writer's choice of narrator determines what information is revealed to the reader—and what information is left out of the telling. The three commonly used points of view are *first person, third-person omniscient,* and *third-person limited.*

- **First person:** The narrator is a character who speaks in the first person, using such first-person pronouns as *I, me,* and *we.* The reader learns only what the character sees, hears, and knows, and then learns only what the character chooses to reveal.

- **Third person:** The narrator is not a character in the story, but a voice outside the action that speaks by using third-person pronouns such as *he, she, it,* or *they.* A third-person narrator may be either *omniscient* or *limited*:

  - **Third-person omniscient:** an all-knowing narrator who can describe everything that happens and may reveal all of the characters' thoughts and feelings.

  - **Third-person limited:** a narrator who sees the world through a single character's eyes and reveals only what that character is experiencing, thinking, and feeling.

> **First Person Point of View**
> "I proceeded alongside my father, clutching his right hand, running to keep up with the long strides he was taking." —"Half a Day" by Naguib Mahfouz, page 1302
>
> **Third-Person Omniscient Point of View**
> "The main obstacle to the boy's initiation was his mother, Satyabati. She said nothing outright; her opposition showed in her behavior." —"The Artist" by Rabindranath Tagore, page 1162
>
> **Third-Person Limited Point of View**
> "She felt restless, both terribly hungry and sick to her stomach, like a convalescent whose appetite the fresh air has yet to restore." —"The Bracelet" by Colette, page 1118

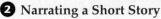

❸ Strategies for Reading a Short Story

Use these strategies as you read short stories.

Identify With a Character Identifying with a character—putting yourself in that character's place in order to understand his or her feelings, needs, problems, and goals—can help you understand the theme of a work. To identify with a character, look for similarities between yourself and the character, and ask yourself what you might do in the character's situation.

Make Inferences Because writers rarely tell everything, readers must often make inferences to fill in gaps in a writer's explanations. An inference is an educated guess based on details that are presented. To make an inference, notice what is said and unsaid, and look for clues to implied meanings. Use logic, context, and your own knowledge to make inferences about characters, setting, and plot.

Focus on Literary Forms: Short Story ■ 1063

Standard Course of Study

Goal 1: WRITTEN LANGUAGE

WL.1.03.9 Analyze effects of author's craft and style in reflection.

Goal 3: FOUNDATIONS OF ARGUMENT

FA.3.03.3 Emphasize culturally significant events.

Goal 4: CRITICAL THINKING

CT.4.04.2 Apply criteria to evaluate others using reasoning and substantiation.

Goal 5: LITERATURE

LT.5.01.7 Understand the cultural and historical impact on world literature texts.

LT.5.02.1 Explore works which relate to an issue, author, or theme and show increasing comprehension.

Goal 6: GRAMMAR AND USAGE

GU.6.01.4 Use vocabulary strategies to determine meaning.

Step-by-Step Teaching Guide	Pacing Guide
PRETEACH	
• Administer Vocabulary and Reading Warm-ups as necessary.	5 min.
• Engage students' interest with the motivation activity.	5 min.
• Read and discuss author and background features. **FT**	10 min.
• Introduce the Literary Analysis Skill: Modernism. **FT**	5 min.
• Introduce the Reading Strategy: Applying the Author's Biography. **FT**	10 min.
• Prepare students to read by teaching the selection vocabulary. **FT**	
TEACH	
• Informally monitor comprehension while students read independently or in groups. **FT**	30 min.
• Monitor students' comprehension with the Reading Check notes.	as students read
• Reinforce vocabulary with Vocabulary Builder notes.	as students read
• Develop students' understanding of Modernism with the Literary Analysis annotations. **FT**	5 min.
• Develop students' ability to apply the author's biography with the Reading Strategy annotations. **FT**	5 min.
ASSESS/EXTEND	
• Assess students' comprehension and mastery of the Literary Analysis and Reading Strategy by having them answer the Apply the Skills questions. **FT**	15 min.
• Have students complete the Vocabulary Lesson and the Grammar and Style Lesson. **FT**	15 min.
• Apply students' ability to use quotations to support a position by using the Writing Lesson. **FT**	45 min. or homework
• Apply students' understanding by using one or more of the Extend Your Learning activities.	20–90 min. or homework
• Administer Selection Test A or Selection Test B. **FT**	15 min.

Resources

Print
Unit 8 Resources

Transparency
Graphic Organizer Transparencies

Print
Reader's Notebook [L2]

Reader's Notebook: Adapted Version [L1]

Reader's Notebook: English Learner's Version [EL]

Unit 8 Resources

Technology
Listening to Literature Audio CDs [L2, EL]

Print
Unit 8 Resources

General Resources

Technology
Go Online: Research [**L3**]
Go Online: Self-test [**L3**]
ExamView®, Test Bank [**L3**]

Choosing Resources for Differentiated Instruction

[**L1**] Special Needs Students

[**L2**] Below-Level Students

[**L3**] All Students

[**L4**] Advanced Students

[**EL**] English Learners

For Vocabulary and Reading Warm-ups and for Selection Tests, **A** signifies "less challenging" and **B** "more challenging." For Graphic Organizer transparencies, **A** signifies "not filled in" and **B** "filled in."

FT Fast Track Instruction: To move the lesson more quickly, use the strategies and activities identified with **FT**.

Scaffolding for Less Proficient and Advanced Students

The leveled Critical Thinking questions after selections progress in the levels of thinking required to answer them. To address the needs of your different students, you may use the (a) level questions for your less proficient students and the (b) level questions with your on-level and advanced students. The occasional (c) level questions are appropriate for your advanced students.

PRENTICE HALL
TeacherEXPRESS™ Use this complete
Plan · Teach · Assess   suite of powerful
teaching tools to make lesson planning and testing quicker and easier.

PRENTICE HALL
StudentEXPRESS™ Use the interactive
Learn · Study · Succeed   textbook (online
and on CD-ROM) to make selections and activities come alive with audio and video support and interactive questions.

Monitoring Progress

Before students read *The Metamorphosis,* administer **Diagnostic Test 10** (*Unit 8 Resources,* **pp. 2–4**). This test will determine students' level of readiness for the reading and vocabulary skills.

 Go Online For: Information about Lexiles
Professional   Visit: www.PHSchool.com
Development Web Code: eue-1111

Motivation

Point out to students that myths, legends, and science fiction are filled with stories of metamorphosis, or transformation. An amorous god becomes a swan; a resentful girl becomes a spider; a vain man becomes a flower. Sailors become pigs; a scientist becomes a fly. Have students describe their favorite transformation from literature or film. Point out that modern movies often use elaborate computer-generated effects to create dramatic transformations. Tell them that in the story they are about to read, Franz Kafka accomplishes a shocking transformation in his first twenty-one words.

❶ Background
About the Author

To his co-workers in the insurance business, Franz Kafka must have seemed like a thoroughly modern man. They might have described him as bright, hard-working, and ambitious. Personally, he was a humorous and charming companion. Because of the demands of his work, writing could not be given his full or even primary attention; it was something he did in the evenings after work. Nonetheless, Kafka produced a large volume of work during his short life. He published only a few pieces while still living—"The Metamorphosis" was one of them—and those only because certain avant-garde publishers actively sought him out.

Geography Note

Draw students' attention to the map on this page, and help them identify the Czech Republic. Explain that at the time of Kafka's birth, Prague was part of the Austro-Hungarian Empire, not the capital of Czechoslovakia.

Build Skills [*Short Story*]

The Metamorphosis ❶

Franz Kafka
(1883–1924)

In a letter to a friend, Franz Kafka once wrote, "I think we ought to read only the kind of books that wound and stab us.... We need the books that affect us like a disaster, that grieve us deeply, like the death of someone we loved more than ourselves, like being banished into forests far from everyone.... A book must be the axe for the frozen sea inside us." Although he was not discussing his own writing at the time, Kafka's description of a book's potential power probably fits his own fiction better than that of any other writer. In fact, few writers have created literary works more tragic, disturbing, and unsettling than Kafka's.

The Writer's Beginnings Born in Prague, which is now the capital of the Czech Republic, Kafka was one of four children and the only son. His father was a successful and domineering businessman, and Kafka spent a good part of his life alternately longing for his father's approval and resenting his strictness. Kafka lived with his family until he was thirty-one, and his relationship with his father, along with his feelings of familial obligation, guilt, and duty, are reflected in much of his writing. In *Letter to My Father* (1919) Kafka wrote: "My writing was all about you; all I did there, after all, was to bemoan what I could not bemoan upon your breast. It was an intentionally long-drawn-out leave-taking from you."

Kafka began writing short stories and plays at a very young age. Despite his interest in writing, however, he chose to study law at the University of Prague. After serving a legal internship, he took a job as a lawyer with an Italian insurance company. A year later, he was offered a position with the state Worker's Accident Insurance Institute, where he remained employed until 1922. Kafka's career never hindered his writing. In fact, the bureaucratic chaos that he observed in the business world actually served as an inspiration for his fiction.

Being an Outsider As a German-speaking Jew in a country inhabited mainly by Czech-speaking gentiles, Kafka knew what it meant to be an outsider. His sense of alienation is apparent in nearly all his fiction. In his early works, including "The Metamorphosis" (1915), he explored the awful consequences of ignoring one's true desires and aspirations and living according to the expectations of others. During the later stages of his career, Kafka depicted the conflict of the individual who rejects society yet truly longs for its acclaim. In his story "A Hunger Artist" (1924), for example, the protagonist attracts the attention of the public by sitting in a cage and refusing to eat. Eventually, however, people lose interest in him, and he starves to death in obscurity and despair.

Posthumous Acclaim In 1917, Kafka was diagnosed with tuberculosis. Shortly before his death in 1924, he told his friend Max Brod to destroy all his papers and personal documents, as well as his unfinished and unpublished works. Brod did not believe that Kafka had truly wanted his work destroyed, so he ignored the request. Instead, he arranged for the publication of Kafka's unfinished novels, *The Trial*, *The Castle*, and *America*, along with his personal diaries, *Letter to My Father*, and a number of unpublished short stories. The publication of these works earned Kafka critical acclaim and public acceptance, neither of which he had known during his lifetime. Kafka's reputation continued to grow, and he is now widely recognized as one of the finest and most influential writers of the twentieth century.

Preview

Connecting to the Literature

Imagine that when you woke up one day, your friends did not recognize you, found you repulsive, and could not understand you when you spoke. In this story, the main character experiences just such a terrible transformation.

 Standard Course of Study

• Explore works which relate to an issue, author, or theme and show increasing comprehension. (LT.5.02.1)

❷ Literary Analysis

Modernism

In the late nineteenth and early twentieth centuries, many writers began turning away from the style, form, and content of nineteenth-century literature in favor of new themes and techniques. While this movement, known as **Modernism,** encompassed a vast number of smaller literary movements, most Modernist works share certain characteristics:

• They attempt to capture the realities of modern life.
• They express a sense of uncertainty and alienation.
• They leave readers to draw their own conclusions.

Consider how these and other Modernist views and techniques are at work in Kafka's story.

Connecting Literary Elements

The first paragraph of this story drops you into a world in which something impossible has happened. The presence of this imaginative element in an otherwise realistic story makes "The Metamorphosis" an example of **literature of the fantastic,** a genre that mixes imagination and reality to entertain and challenge readers. As you read, note the presence of both imaginative and realistic details, and think about the effects they create.

❸ Reading Strategy

Applying the Author's Biography

"The Metamorphosis" is not an autobiography, but **applying the author's biography**—making connections to Kafka's life—can shed light on its meaning. For example, Kafka's troubled relationship with his father probably helped him write realistically about the father and son in this story. Use a diagram like the one shown to record facts from Kafka's life that you think shed light on "The Metamorphosis."

Vocabulary Builder

impracticable (im prak′ ti kə bəl) *adj.* not capable of being put into practice (p. 1066)

obstinacy (äb′ stə nə sē) *n.* stubbornness (p. 1073)

exuded (ig zōōd′ id) *v.* discharged a liquid through the skin (p. 1074)

rectify (rek′ tə fī′) *v.* to set things right or restore balance (p. 1076)

imminent (im′ ə nənt) *adj.* ready to happen at any moment (p. 1077)

gyration (jī rā′ shən) *n.* circular or spiral motion (p. 1078)

pallid (pal′ id) *adj.* pale (p. 1080)

debacle (di bäk′ əl) *n.* overwhelming failure or defeat (p. 1103)

The Metamorphosis ■ 1065

---

❷ Literary Analysis
Modernism

• Tell students that Modernism was an extremely broad and diverse movement. Although there were significant differences in their interests and approaches, all Modernists shared the desire to create literature that was new and different.

• With the class, read the three characteristics of Modernism listed. Explain that Modernists often set their characters free in a fragmented, confusing, and unpredictable world and gave them the task of making sense of it. For example, in "The Metamorphosis," a man lives in a seemingly ordinary modern world until he wakes one morning to discover that he has been transformed into an insect.

❸ Reading Strategy
Applying the Author's Biography

• Remind students that most authors draw upon personal experiences when creating fictional worlds. Kafka was no different. Therefore, clues to the meaning of "The Metamorphosis" may be found in his biography. Emphasize that, as discussed in the biography, Kafka's relationship with his own father left him yearning for his father's approval. Ask students to take note of the relationship between father and son in the story as they read.

• Explain the use of the diagram. Then distribute copies of **Reading Strategy Graphic Organizer A,** p. 180 in **Graphic Organizer Transparencies.** As they read, have students use the organizer to record facts from Kafka's life that shed light on *The Metamorphosis.*

Vocabulary Builder

• Pronounce each vocabulary word for students, and read the definitions as a class. Have students identify any words with which they are already familiar.

1065

Facilitate Understanding

Remind students that a metamorphosis is a transformation, or change, from one form of existence to another. Have students discuss metamorphoses they have studied in science class. Then, ask students to consider the type of metamorphosis that might occur in a modern story.

❶ About the Selection

In this haunting Modernist tale, Gregor Samsa, a traveling salesman, wakes up one morning to find that he has metamorphosed into a giant insect. Both Gregor and his family struggle as they try to cope with the horror of the situation. As students read, they will realize that this story describes not only a physical transformation but also several psychological ones.

❷ Literary Analysis

Modernism

- Remind students that the Modernists wanted to discard traditional forms of literature and adopt new ways of looking at the world.

- **Ask** students the Literary Analysis question: From the very first paragraph, what seems new or different about Kafka's approach to telling this story?
Answer: Kafka challenges the logic of modern life. Clearly, a man cannot turn into an insect, yet Gregor Samsa does.

❶ THE Metamorphosis

FRANZ KAFKA   *translated by Stanley Corngold*

Background Many authors produce great writing that moves, challenges, and inspires readers. Only a few, however, make such distinctive contributions that their names become synonymous with specific literary qualities. Such is the case with Kafka. The term *kafkaesque* describes a nightmarish mood—specifically, the feeling that one is trapped in an intense, distorted world and that danger or doom is close at hand. As you read "The Metamorphosis," decide how well the adjective *kafkaesque* describes this tale, which many scholars consider one of the greatest stories of the twentieth century.

Part I

❷ When Gregor Samsa woke up one morning from unsettling dreams, he found himself changed in his bed into a monstrous vermin. He was lying on his back as hard as armor plate, and when he lifted his head a little, he saw his vaulted brown belly, sectioned by arch-shaped ribs, to whose dome the cover, about to slide off completely, could barely cling. His many legs, pitifully thin compared with the size of the rest of him, were waving helplessly before his eyes.

"What's happened to me?" he thought. It was no dream. His room, a regular human room, only a little on the small side, lay quiet between the four familiar walls. Over the table, on which an unpacked line of fabric samples was all spread out—Samsa was a traveling salesman—hung the picture which he had recently cut out of a glossy magazine and lodged in a pretty gilt frame. It showed a lady done up in a fur hat and a fur boa, sitting upright and raising up against the viewer a heavy fur muff in which her whole forearm had disappeared.

Gregor's eyes then turned to the window, and the overcast weather—he could hear raindrops hitting against the metal window ledge—completely depressed him. "How about going back to sleep for a few minutes and forgetting all this nonsense," he thought, but that was completely <u>impracticable</u>, since he was used to sleeping on his right side and in his present state could not get into that position. No matter

1066 ■ The Modern World

Literary Analysis
Modernism From the very first paragraph, what seems new or different about Kafka's approach to telling this story?

Vocabulary Builder
impracticable (im prak´ ti kə bəl) *adj.* not capable of being put into practice

---

how hard he threw himself onto his right side, he always rocked onto his back again. He must have tried it a hundred times, closing his eyes so as not to have to see his squirming legs, and stopped only when he began to feel a slight, dull pain in his side, which he had never felt before.

"Oh God," he thought, "what a grueling job I've picked. Day in, day out—on the road. The upset of doing business is much worse than the actual business in the home office, and besides, I've got the torture of traveling, worrying about changing trains, eating miserable food at all hours, constantly seeing new faces, no relationships that last or get more intimate. To the devil with it all!" He felt a slight itching up on top of his belly; shoved himself slowly on his back closer to the bedpost, so as to be able to lift his head better; found the itchy spot, studded with small white dots which he had no idea what to make of; and wanted to touch the spot with one of his legs but immediately pulled it back, for the contact sent a cold shiver through him.

He slid back again into his original position. "This getting up so early," he thought, "makes anyone a complete idiot. Human beings have to have their sleep. Other traveling salesmen live like harem women. For instance, when I go back to the hotel before lunch to write up the business I've done, these gentlemen are just having breakfast. That's all I'd have to try with my boss; I'd be fired on the spot. Anyway, who knows if that wouldn't be a very good thing for me. If I didn't hold back for my parents' sake, I would have quit long ago, I would have marched up to the boss and spoken my piece from the bottom of my heart. He would have fallen off the desk! It is funny, too, the way he sits on the desk and talks down from the heights to the employees, especially when they have to come right up close on account of the boss's being hard of hearing. Well, I haven't given up hope completely; once I've gotten the money together to pay off my parents' debt to him—that will probably take another five or six years—I'm going to do it without fail. Then I'm going to make the big break. But for the time being I'd better get up, since my train leaves at five."

And he looked over at the alarm clock, which was ticking on the chest of drawers. "God Almighty!" he thought. It was six-thirty, the hands were

Reading Strategy
Applying the Author's Biography In what ways might Kafka's career as an accident-insurance lawyer have helped him to write this scene?

 **Reading Check**
Into what kind of creature has Gregor Samsa been transformed?

The Metamorphosis, Part 1 ■ 1067

❸ **Reading Strategy**
Applying the Author's Biography

• Have a volunteer read the bracketed passage. Then, have the class discuss the frustrations of a job like Gregor's.

• **Ask** students to name aspects of Kafka's own job that might have involved the need to "hold back" experienced by Gregor.
Possible response: Kafka would have been accountable to managers and clients, with whom he could not always share his true feelings.

• **Ask** students the Reading Strategy question: In what ways might Kafka's career as an accident-insurance lawyer have helped him to write this scene?
Possible response: As a lawyer dealing with workers, Kafka would have been familiar with complaints such as Gregor's. As a worker answerable to a manager, Kafka might have experienced similar frustrations himself. He probably drew on such experiences to describe Gregor's dissatisfaction.

❹ **Reading Check**

Answer: Gregor has become an insect of some sort, possibly a beetle.

Differentiated
Instruction   Solutions for All Learners

Support for Special Needs Students
Organize the class into reading groups of three or four students. Have them read aloud these pages, taking each paragraph in turn, as you monitor their progress. Stop the reading at the end of each paragraph to ask a comprehension question and to help students clarify any points of confusion. In particular, help students define words that might be unfamiliar, such as *vermin, gilt, boa,* and *studded.*

Support for Less Proficient Readers
To give students a context for the story and to model how to apply the author's biography, distribute copies of **Reading Strategy Graphic Organizer B** (*Graphic Organizer Transparencies,* p. 181). The completed graphic organizer will give students insight into the process of determining which of the author's personal experiences shed light on the story. As they read, students can use the organizer as a model for making connections between the author's biography and details in the story.

- Read the bracketed passage aloud. Then, tell students that as an accident-insurance lawyer in an organization for workers, Kafka was sympathetic to his clients and worked hard to win claims for injured workers.

- **Ask** students how knowing this information about Kafka changes the way they understand this passage.
  Answer: Knowing this information reveals Kafka's tongue-in-cheek attitude. He is poking fun at himself and people in his business.

❻ **Critical Viewing**

Answer: The image of the jangling alarm clock reflects the frantic atmosphere in which Gregor is immersed. He cannot get up, and he is late for work. People are going to be checking on him, and he does not know what to do or what to tell them.

❼ **Literary Analysis**

Modernism

- Review with students the characteristics of Modernist works listed on p. 1065. Emphasize that alienation is a key Modernist theme.

- Read aloud the bracketed passage. Then, **ask** students the Literary Analysis question: In what ways does the change in Gregor's voice suggest the Modernist theme of alienation?
  Answer: Gregor can no longer communicate with his family because his voice has become unintelligible. Gregor can still understand what his family is saying, however.

- Have students **identify** other details in the conversation that suggest alienation or isolation.
  Answer: Gregor is surprised by his mother's soft voice; he is surprised by his own voice; he speaks briefly because he cannot explain in detail; Gregor's failure to respond incites his father's anger.

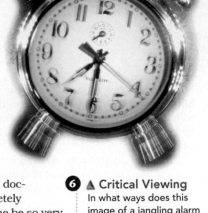

quietly moving forward, it was actually past the half-hour, it was already nearly a quarter to. Could it be that the alarm hadn't gone off? You could see from the bed that it was set correctly for four o'clock; it certainly had gone off, too. Yes, but was it possible to sleep quietly through a ringing that made the furniture shake? Well, he certainly hadn't slept quietly, but probably all the more soundly for that. But what should he do now? The next train left at seven o'clock; to make it, he would have to hurry like a madman, and the line of samples wasn't packed yet, and he himself didn't feel especially fresh and ready to march around. And even if he did make the train, he could not avoid getting it from the boss, because the messenger boy had been waiting at the five-o'clock train and would have long ago reported his not showing up. He was a tool of the boss, without brains or backbone. What if he were to say he was sick? But that would be extremely embarrassing and suspicious because during his five years with the firm Gregor had not been sick even once. The boss would be sure to come with the health-insurance doctor, blame his parents for their lazy

❺ son, and cut off all excuses by quoting the health-insurance doctor, for whom the world consisted of people who were completely healthy but afraid to work. And, besides, in this case would he be so very wrong? In fact, Gregor felt fine, with the exception of his drowsiness, which was really unnecessary after sleeping so late, and he even had a ravenous appetite.

Just as he was thinking all this over at top speed, without being able to decide to get out of bed—the alarm clock had just struck a quarter to seven—he heard a cautious knocking at the door next to the head of his bed. "Gregor," someone called—it was his mother—"it's a quarter to seven. Didn't you want to catch the train?" What a soft voice! Gregor was shocked to hear his own voice answering, unmistakably his own voice, true, but in which, as if from below, an insistent distressed chirping intruded, which left the clarity of his words intact only for a moment really, before so badly garbling them as they carried that no one could be sure if he had heard right. Gregor had wanted to answer in detail and to explain everything, but, given the circumstances, con-

❼ fined himself to saying, "Yes, yes, thanks, Mother, I'm just getting up." The wooden door must have prevented the change in Gregor's voice from being noticed outside, because his mother was satisfied with this explanation and shuffled off. But their little exchange had made the rest of the family aware that, contrary to expectations, Gregor was still in the house, and already his father was knocking on one of the side doors, feebly but with his fist. "Gregor, Gregor," he called, "what's going on?" And after a little while he called again in a deeper, warning voice, "Gregor! Gregor!" At the other side door, however, his sister moaned gently, "Gregor? Is something the matter with you? Do you want anything?" Toward both sides Gregor answered: "I'm all ready," and made

❻ ▲ **Critical Viewing**
In what ways does this image of a jangling alarm clock reflect the urgency of Gregor's situation? **[Connect]**

Literary Analysis
Modernism In what ways does the change in Gregor's voice suggest the Modernist theme of alienation?

Enrichment

Kafka's Familial Relationships
The Samsas' complicated familial relationships reflect the complexity of Kafka's own family life. Kafka himself could never really resolve his ambivalent feelings about his own family. In many of his stories, a son is destroyed by his rebellion against his family's wishes; in others, a son lovingly sacrifices himself for the family's good. In discussing how Kafka's relationship with his family influenced his writing, the critic

Michael Carrouges wrote: "His art flows out of the conflict with his father, it manifests that conflict and re-creates it all over again. . . . If Kafka's short stories and novels are reread in the light of this perspective, one will see that apart from any other significant aspects, they conceal with them first of all a significant familial and, more especially, a paternal orientation that is central to them. . . ."

an effort, by meticulous pronunciation and by inserting long pauses between individual words, to eliminate everything from his voice that might betray him. His father went back to his breakfast, but his sister whispered, "Gregor, open up, I'm pleading with you." But Gregor had absolutely no intention of opening the door and complimented himself instead on the precaution he had adopted from his business trips, of locking all the doors during the night even at home.

First of all he wanted to get up quietly, without any excitement; get dressed; and the main thing, have breakfast, and only then think about what to do next, for he saw clearly that in bed he would never think things through to a rational conclusion. He remembered how even in the past he had often felt some kind of slight pain, possibly caused by lying in an uncomfortable position, which, when he got up, turned out to be purely imaginary, and he was eager to see how today's fantasy would gradually fade away. That the change in his voice was nothing more than the first sign of a bad cold, an occupational ailment of the traveling salesman, he had no doubt in the least.

It was very easy to throw off the cover; all he had to do was puff himself up a little, and it fell off by itself. But after this, things got difficult, especially since he was so unusually broad. He would have needed hands and arms to lift himself up, but instead of that he had only his numerous little legs, which were in every different kind of perpetual motion and which, besides, he could not control. If he wanted to bend one, the first thing that happened was that it stretched itself out; and if he finally succeeded in getting this leg to do what he wanted, all the others in the meantime, as if set free, began to work in the most intensely painful agitation. "Just don't stay in bed being useless," Gregor said to himself.

First he tried to get out of bed with the lower part of his body, but this lower part—which by the way he had not seen yet and which he could not form a clear picture of—proved too difficult to budge; it was taking so long; and when finally, almost out of his mind, he lunged forward with all his force, without caring, he had picked the wrong direction and slammed himself violently against the lower bedpost, and the searing pain he felt taught him that exactly the lower part of his body was, for the moment anyway, the most sensitive.

He therefore tried to get the upper part of his body out of bed first and warily turned his head toward the edge of the bed. This worked easily, and in spite of its width and weight, the mass of his body finally followed, slowly, the movement of his head. But when at last he stuck his head over the edge of the bed into the air, he got too scared to continue any further, since if he finally let himself fall in this position, it would be a miracle if he didn't injure his head. And just now he had better not for the life of him lose consciousness; he would rather stay in bed.

But when, once again, after the same exertion, he lay in his original position, sighing, and again watched his little legs struggling, if possible more fiercely, with each other and saw no way of bringing peace and

Literary Analysis
Modernism and Literature of the Fantastic In what ways does this scene combine realistic details with fantastic ones in order to express a Modernist sense of alienation?

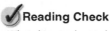**Reading Check**
What does each member of Gregor's family urge him to do?

The Metamorphosis, Part 1 ■ 1069

8 Literary Analysis
Modernism and Literature of the Fantastic

• Tell students that Gregor, despite knowing that he has turned into an insect, is determined to go to work. **Ask** students why Gregor is in denial of his situation.
Answer: Gregor is in denial because he probably believes that carrying on his daily routine will restore normalcy.

• **Ask** students the Literary Analysis question: In what ways does this scene combine realistic details with fantastic ones in order to express a Modernist sense of alienation?
Answer: Despite his transformation into an insect, Gregor remains somewhat calm, continues to have rational thoughts, and attempts to complete "normal" activities. This disconnection between Gregor's physical and mental reality creates alienation: He still has human thoughts and feelings, yet he is unwelcome in the human realm.

9 Critical Thinking
Deduce

• Read aloud the bracketed passage. **Ask:** Why can't Gregor control his legs?
Answer: Gregor's insect body is still unfamiliar to him. The legs work differently from his human legs, so he will have to learn how to use them.

• **Ask:** How long do you think it will take Gregor to master his new legs?
Possible response: He will learn to walk quickly once he is on his feet, the usual position for an insect, rather than lying on his back.

10 Reading Check
Answer: Gregor's mother urges him to get up and go to work; his father demands an explanation; his sister urges him to open the door.

⑪ Literary Analysis

Modernism

- Review with students the second bulleted characteristic of Modernist works listed on p. 1065. Emphasize the Modernist themes of uncertainty and alienation.

- Read aloud the bracketed passage. Then, **ask** students the Literary Analysis question: In what ways does the view from Gregor's window reflect a Modernist perception of twentieth-century life?
  Answer: The fog reflects a Modernist view by concealing the other side of the street, creating, for Gregor, a sense of isolation and disallowing a feeling of well-being.

- **Ask** students to discuss how Gregor's comment about the fog and the time of day reflects a Modernist view.
  Answer: Gregor notes a discrepancy between what is and what should be. In his mind, the fog should have burned off, yet it remains. This disparity indicates Gregor's alienation from reality and reflects the Modernist concern with uncertainty.

⑫ Humanities

Walking Man, by Rick Amor

Born in Frankston, Victoria, Australia, a suburb of Melbourne, Rick Amor (b. 1948) is an award-winning painter, printmaker, and sculptor. In 1999, the Australia War Memorial appointed Amor Official War Artist to document Australia's involvement in East Timor.

  Use the following activity to stimulate discussion:

- Have students **list** adjectives they would use to describe the feelings and movement conveyed by this figure.
  Possible response: Adjectives such as *defeated* and *sad* describe the feelings conveyed, and adjectives such as *trudging* and *slouching* describe the movement.

- Then, ask students to use the adjectives they have listed in brief stories about the man depicted.

⑬ Critical Viewing

Possible response: The man's shoulders are slouched, his head is bent, and he walks with resignation but determination. As a salesman, Gregor shared these feelings, knowing he had to work, but dreading every day of it.

---

9 ↑ order into this mindless motion, he again told himself that it was impossible for him to stay in bed and that the most rational thing was to make any sacrifice for even the smallest hope of freeing himself from the bed. But at the same time he did not forget to remind himself occasionally that thinking things over calmly—indeed, as calmly as possible—was much better than jumping to desperate decisions. At such moments he fixed his eyes as sharply as possible on the window, but unfortunately there was little confidence and cheer to be gotten from the view of the morning fog, which shrouded even the other side of the narrow street. "Seven o'clock already," he said to himself as the alarm clock struck again, "seven o'clock already and still such a fog." And for a little while he lay quietly, breathing shallowly, as if expecting, perhaps, from the complete silence the return of things to the way they really and naturally were.

  But then he said to himself, "Before it strikes a quarter past seven, I must be completely out of bed without fail. Anyway, by that time someone from the firm will be here to find out where I am, since the office opens before seven." And now he started rocking the complete length of his body out of the bed with a smooth rhythm. If he let himself topple out of bed in this way, his head, which on falling he planned to lift up sharply, would presumably remain unharmed. His back seemed to be hard; nothing was likely to happen to it when it fell onto the carpet. His biggest misgiving came from his concern about the loud crash that was bound to occur and would probably create, if not terror, at least anxiety behind all the doors. But that would have to be risked.

  When Gregor's body already projected halfway out of bed—the new method was more of a game than a struggle, he only had to keep on rocking and jerking himself along—he thought how simple everything would be if he could get some help. Two strong persons—he thought of his father and the maid—would have been completely sufficient; they would only have had to shove their arms under his arched back, in this way scoop him off the bed, bend down with their burden, and then just be careful and patient while he managed to swing himself down onto the floor, where his little legs would hopefully acquire some purpose. Well, leaving out the fact that the doors were locked, should he really call for help? In spite of all his miseries, he could not repress a smile at this thought.

  He was already so far along that when he rocked more strongly he could hardly keep his balance, and very soon he would have to commit himself, because in five minutes it would be a quarter past seven—

Literary Analysis

Modernism In what ways does the view from Gregor's window reflect a Modernist perception of twentieth-century life?

⑬ ▼ Critical Viewing Which elements of this sculpture of a business-man seem to express an attitude toward work that is similar to Gregor's? Explain. **[Analyze]**

Walking Man, bronze statue 150 x 60 x 133 cm, Rick Amor, Niagara Galleries

14 when the doorbell rang. "It's someone from the firm," he said to himself and almost froze, while his little legs only danced more quickly. For a moment everything remained quiet. "They're not going to answer," Gregor said to himself, captivated by some senseless hope. But then, of course, the maid went to the door as usual with her firm stride and opened up. Gregor only had to hear the visitor's first word of greeting to know who it was—the office manager himself. Why was only Gregor condemned to work for a firm where at the slightest omission they immediately suspected the worst? Were all employees louts without exception, wasn't there a single loyal, dedicated worker among them who, when he had not fully utilized a few hours of the morning for the firm, was driven half-mad by pangs of conscience and was actually unable to get out of bed? Really, wouldn't it have been enough to send one of the apprentices to find out—if this prying were absolutely necessary—did the manager himself have to come, and did the whole innocent family have to be shown in this way that the investigation of this suspicious affair could be entrusted only to the intellect of the manager? And more as a result of the excitement produced in Gregor by these thoughts than as a result of any real decision, he swung himself out of bed with all his might. There was a loud thump, but it was not a real crash. The fall was broken a little by the carpet, and Gregor's back was more elastic than he had thought, which explained the not very noticeable muffled sound. Only he had not held his head carefully enough and hit it; he turned it and rubbed it on the carpet in anger and pain.

"Something fell in there," said the manager in the room on the left. Gregor tried to imagine whether something like what had happened to him today could one day happen even to the manager; you really had to grant the possibility. But, as if in rude reply to this question, the manager took a few decisive steps in the next room and made his patent leather boots creak. From the room on the right his sister whispered, to inform Gregor, "Gregor, the manager is here." "I know," Gregor said to himself; but he did not dare raise his voice enough for his sister to hear.

16 "Gregor," his father now said from the room on the left, "the manager has come and wants to be informed why you didn't catch the early train. We don't know what we should say to him. Besides, he wants to speak to you personally. So please open the door. He will certainly be so kind as to excuse the disorder of the room." "Good morning, Mr. Samsa," the manager called in a friendly voice. "There's something the matter with him," his mother said to the manager while his father was still at the door, talking. "Believe me, sir, there's something the matter with him. Otherwise how would Gregor have missed a train? That boy has nothing on his mind but the business. It's almost begun to rile me that he never goes out nights. He's been back in the city for eight days now, but every night he's been home. He sits there with us at the table, quietly reading the paper or studying timetables. It's already a distraction for him when he's busy working with his fretsaw.[1] For instance, in

---

1. **fretsaw** (fret´ sô) *n.* saw with a long, narrow, fine-toothed blade.

Reading Strategy
Applying the Author's Biography Do you think Gregor's anger toward his employers may reflect Kafka's work experiences? Explain.

Reading Check 15

Who arrives to speak with Gregor?

The Metamorphosis, Part 1 ■ 1071

14 Reading Strategy

Applying the Author's Biography

• Have a volunteer read the bracketed passage aloud.

• Then, **ask** students the Reading Strategy question: Do you think Gregor's anger toward his employers may reflect Kafka's work experiences? Explain.

Answer: Gregor's anger may reflect Kafka's experiences. The description of Gregor's anger is realistic and detailed, indicating that it may have been based on personal experience or on attitudes Kafka encountered among workers in his job as an accident-insurance lawyer.

▶ **Monitor Progress** Ask students which details from these facing pages may reflect Kafka's work experience. Have them add these to their graphic organizers. (the alarm clock striking again at 7 A.M.; his expectation that someone from the office would arrive at his home; the arrival of the office manager; Gregor's annoyance at the manager's insistence on speaking to him; his mother's defense of him and reference to his passion for work)

▶ **Reteach** If students are having difficulty seeing connections between Kafka's biography and the story, have them use the **Reading Strategy** support, p. 12 in *Unit 8 Resources.*

15 Reading Check

Answer: The office manager arrives to speak with Gregor.

Differentiated Instruction Solutions for All Learners

Support for Special Needs Students
Kafka sometimes uses long sentence structures with multiple punctuation marks. The first bracketed passage above contains several examples. Work with students to break apart these complex sentences by identifying the main subjects and verbs. Then, have students explain how the other groups of words in the sentences relate to the main subjects and verbs.

Strategy for Less Proficient Readers
Read aloud the first full paragraph above. Ask students to consider what they know about the manager from the details Kafka provides. For example, have students discuss what they can tell about the manager's personality from the fact that he walks with "decisive steps." Then have students look for other details on the page about the manager and discuss what they can tell about him from these clues.

16 the span of two or three evenings he carved a little frame. You'll be amazed how pretty it is; it's hanging inside his room. You'll see it right away when Gregor opens the door. You know, I'm glad that you've come, sir. We would never have gotten Gregor to open the door by ourselves; he's so stubborn. And there's certainly something wrong with him, even though he said this morning there wasn't." "I'm coming right away," said Gregor slowly and deliberately, not moving in order not to miss a word of the conversation. "I haven't any other explanation myself," said the manager. "I hope it's nothing serious. On the other hand, I must say that we businessmen—fortunately or unfortunately, whichever you prefer—very often simply have to overcome a slight indisposition[2] for business reasons." "So can the manager come in now?" asked his father, impatient, and knocked on the door again. "No," said Gregor. In the room on the left there was an embarrassing silence; in the room on the right his sister began to sob.

Why didn't his sister go in to the others? She had probably just got out of bed and not even started to get dressed. Then what was she crying about? Because he didn't get up and didn't let the manager in, because he was in danger of losing his job, and because then the boss would start hounding his parents about the old debts? For the time being, certainly, her worries were unnecessary. Gregor was still here and hadn't the slightest intention of letting the family down. True, at the moment he was lying on the carpet, and no one knowing his condition could seriously have expected him to let the manager in. But just because of this slight discourtesy, for which an appropriate excuse would easily be found later on, Gregor could not simply be dismissed. And to Gregor it seemed much more sensible to leave him alone now than to bother him with crying and persuasion. But it was just the uncertainty that was tormenting the others and excused their behavior.

"Mr. Samsa," the manager now called, raising his voice, "what's the matter? You barricade yourself in your room, answer only 'yes' and 'no,' cause your parents serious, unnecessary worry, and you neglect—I mention this only in passing—your duties to the firm in a really shocking manner. I am speaking here in the name of your par-

---

2. **indisposition** (in´ dis pə zish´ ən) *n.* slight illness.

Literary Analysis
Modernism Why do Gregor's parents try to impress the office manager with a sense of Gregor's individuality?

17 ▼ **Critical Viewing**
What mood do you think this image of a traveling salesman conveys? Explain. **[Interpret]**

Enrichment

Kafka's Influence in America
In discussing Kafka's influence on twentieth-century American writers, the critic Leo Hamalian notes:

> Kafka became something of a vogue among intellectuals and the avant-garde in America shortly after the end of World War II, but those special states of mind conveyed in his writing did not attract a wider audience until the 1950s, that age of anxiety in which the events of the McCarthy era overtook fiction.

As Americans began to discover that mass society had neuroses of its own, they consumed in paperback and anthology the man who prophesied the ailments of our age. . . .

ents and of your employer and ask you in all seriousness for an immediate, clear explanation. I'm amazed, amazed. I thought I knew you to be a quiet, reasonable person, and now you suddenly seem to want to start strutting about, flaunting strange whims. The head of the firm did suggest to me this morning a possible explanation for your tardiness—it concerned the cash payments recently entrusted to you—but really, I practically gave my word of honor that this explanation could not be right. But now, seeing your incomprehensible <u>obstinacy</u>, I am about to lose even the slightest desire to stick up for you in any way at all. And your job is not the most secure. Originally I intended to tell you all this in private, but since you make me waste my time here for nothing, I don't see why your parents shouldn't hear too. Your performance of late has been very unsatisfactory; I know it is not the best season for doing business, we all recognize that; but a season for not doing any business, there is no such thing, Mr. Samsa, such a thing cannot be tolerated."

"But sir," cried Gregor, beside himself, in his excitement forgetting everything else, "I'm just opening up, in a minute. A slight indisposition, a dizzy spell, prevented me from getting up. I'm still in bed. But I already feel fine again. I'm just getting out of bed. Just be patient for a minute! I'm not as well as I thought yet. But really I'm fine. How something like this could just take a person by surprise! Only last night I was fine, my parents can tell you, or wait, last night I already had a slight premonition.[3] They must have been able to tell by looking at me. Why didn't I report it to the office! But you always think that you'll get over a sickness without staying home. Sir! Spare my parents! There's no basis for any of the accusations that you're making against me now; no one has ever said a word to me about them. Perhaps you haven't seen the last orders I sent in. Anyway, I'm still going on the road with the eight o'clock train; these few hours of rest have done me good. Don't let me keep you, sir. I'll be at the office myself right away, and be so kind as to tell them this, and give my respects to the head of the firm."

And while Gregor hastily blurted all this out, hardly knowing what he was saying, he had easily approached the chest of drawers, probably as a result of the practice he had already gotten in bed, and now he tried to raise himself up against it. He actually intended to open the door, actually present himself and speak to the manager; he was eager to find out what the others, who were now so anxious to see him, would say at the sight of him. If they were shocked, then Gregor had no further responsibility and could be calm. But if they took everything calmly, then he, too, had no reason to get excited and could, if he hurried, actually be at the station by eight o'clock. At first he slid off the polished chest of drawers a few times, but at last, giving himself a final push, he stood upright; he no longer paid any attention to the pains in his abdomen, no matter how much they were burning. Now he let himself fall against the back of a nearby chair, clinging to its slats with his

---

3. **premonition** (prēm′ ə nish′ ən) *n.* a warning in advance of an event.

The Metamorphosis, Part 1 ■ 1073

Vocabulary Builder
obstinacy (äb′ stə nə sē) *n.*
stubbornness

Literary Analysis
Modernism According to the office manager, how is Gregor's odd behavior alienating him from daily life?

Literary Analysis
Modernism In opening the door and showing himself, what does Gregor hope to learn about his own state of mind?

**Reading Check** ❷⓪
What is the warning the office manager gives Gregor about his job?

---

❶⓼ **Literary Analysis**
Modernism

• Remind students that Modernist characters are usually isolated, alienated figures. Discuss the office manager's behavior. **Ask:** Does he seem to be an appropriate character for a Modernist story? Why or why not?
Answer: The manager is both alienated and alienating. Because he represents the outside world, the manager is alienated from the Samsa family. His lack of concern for Gregor's condition and his unreasonable response alienate Gregor and Mr. and Mrs. Samsa.

• Read aloud the bracketed passage. **Ask** students the first Literary Analysis question: According to the office manager, how is Gregor's odd behavior alienating him from daily life?
Answer: According to the manager, Gregor is becoming proud and stubborn, which prevents him from functioning as a member of modern society.

❶⓽ **Literary Analysis**
Modernism

• Read the bracketed passage aloud. Point out that Gregor is now eager to let the others see him. **Ask** students: How does this attitude demonstrate Gregor's struggle against feelings of alienation?
Answer: Gregor's eagerness to be seen demonstrates his desire to make contact and be accepted by his family.

• Then, **ask** students the second Literary Analysis question: In opening the door and showing himself, what does Gregor hope to learn about his own state of mind?
Answer: Gregor wants to know whether he really has turned into an insect or is imagining it. If the others are shocked, Gregor will know that the transformation is real but that he is not responsible for it. If the others are calm, Gregor will know that the transformation is not real, and he will resume normal activities.

❷⓪ **Reading Check**

Answer: The office manager warns Gregor to get up, get to work, stop being stubborn, and improve his sales performance.

Possible response: Yes; the performer playing Gregor has assumed an awkward physical posture to suggest a physical transformation. The walls are extremely close to Gregor, emphasizing his isolation, and the family and the manager listening in on him with confused expressions reveal their uncertainty.

㉒ Literary Analysis

Modernism

• **Ask** students to identify a phrase in the bracketed passage that indicates that Gregor's confidence in the doctor and the locksmith is based on an emotional need to believe in authority and expertise.
Possible response: The phrase "felt integrated into human society once again" reveals Gregor's confidence in authority and expertise.

• **Ask** students the Literary Analysis question: In what ways might Gregor's confidence in the locksmith and the doctor reflect society's misplaced faith in both technology and medicine?
Answer: Gregor does not focus on his dire situation, but instead assumes that the "experts" will be able to solve all problems. This attitude reflects society's reliance on medicine and technology for quick and easy solutions.

little legs. But by doing this he had gotten control of himself and fell silent, since he could now listen to what the manager was saying.

"Did you understand a word?" the manager was asking his parents. "He isn't trying to make fools of us, is he?" "My God," cried his mother, already in tears, "maybe he's seriously ill, and here we are, torturing him. Grete! Grete!" she then cried. "Mother?" called his sister from the other side. They communicated by way of Gregor's room. "Go to the doctor's immediately. Gregor is sick. Hurry, get the doctor. Did you just hear Gregor talking?" "That was the voice of an animal," said the manager, in a tone conspicuously soft compared with the mother's yelling. "Anna!" "Anna!" the father called through the foyer into the kitchen, clapping his hands, "get a locksmith right away!" And already the two girls were running with rustling skirts through the foyer—how could his sister have gotten dressed so quickly?—and tearing open the door to the apartment. The door could not be heard slamming; they had probably left it open, as is the custom in homes where a great misfortune has occurred.

But Gregor had become much calmer. It was true that they no longer understood his words, though they had seemed clear enough to him, clearer than before, probably because his ear had grown accustomed to them. But still, the others now believed that there was something the matter with him and were ready to help him. The assurance and confidence with which the first measures had been taken did him good. He felt integrated into human society once again and hoped for marvelous, amazing feats from both the doctor and the locksmith, without really distinguishing sharply between them. In order to make his voice as clear as possible for the crucial discussions that were approaching, he cleared his throat a little—taking pains, of course, to do so in a very muffled manner, since this noise, too, might sound different from human coughing, a thing he no longer trusted himself to decide. In the next room, meanwhile, everything had become completely still. Perhaps his parents were sitting at the table with the manager, whispering; perhaps they were all leaning against the door listening.

Gregor slowly lugged himself toward the door, pushing the chair in front of him, then let go of it, threw himself against the door, held himself upright against it—the pads on the bottom of his little legs exuded a little sticky substance—and for a moment rested there from the exertion. But then he got started turning the key in the lock with his mouth. Unfortunately it seemed that he had no real teeth—what was he supposed to grip the key with?—but in compensation his jaws, of course, were very strong; with their help he actually got the key moving and paid no attention to the fact that he was undoubtedly hurting himself in some way, for a brown liquid came out of his mouth, flowed over the key, and dripped onto the floor. "Listen," said the manager in the next room, "he's turning the key." This was great encouragement to Gregor; but everyone should have cheered him on, his father and mother too. "Go, Gregor," they should have called, "keep going, at that lock, harder, harder!" And in the delusion that they were all following his efforts with suspense, he clamped his jaws madly on the key with all the strength he could muster.

1074 ■ *The Modern World*

Critical Viewing ▶ ㉑
Does this image from a dramatic adaptation of "The Metamorphosis" effectively capture both Gregor's physical transformation and his social alienation? Explain. **[Evaluate]**

Literary Analysis
Modernism In what ways might Gregor's confidence in the locksmith and the doctor reflect society's misplaced faith in both technology and medicine?

Vocabulary Builder
exuded (ig zood′ id) v. discharged a liquid through the skin

Enrichment

Kafkaesque
When a person has exhibited and achieved notoriety for special characteristics, his or her name is sometimes associated with and used as an adjective for those characteristics. The adjective might end with *-esque,* a suffix meaning "in the style of" or "like." For example, the word *Jordanesque* might be used to describe special skills or achievements related to the basketball star Michael Jordan. Franz Kafka is so well known for his novels and stories about fantastic, surreal dreams and looming danger that the term *Kafkaesque* is often used to describe works or situations with the same qualities.

Depending on the progress of the key, he danced around the lock; holding himself upright only by his mouth, he clung to the key, as the situation demanded, or pressed it down again with the whole weight of his body. The clearer click of the lock as it finally snapped back literally woke Gregor up. With a sigh of relief he said to himself, "So I didn't need the locksmith after all," and laid his head down on the handle in order to open wide one wing of the double doors.

Since he had to use this method of opening the door, it was really opened very wide while he himself was still invisible. He first had to edge slowly around the one wing of the door, and do so very carefully if he was not to fall flat on his back just before entering. He was still busy with this difficult maneuver and had no time to pay attention to anything else when he heard the manager burst out with a loud "Oh!"—it sounded like a rush of wind—and now he could see him, standing closest to the door, his hand pressed over his open mouth, slowly backing away, as if repulsed by an invisible, unrelenting force. His mother—in spite of the manager's presence she stood with her hair still unbraided from the night, sticking out in all directions—first looked at his father with her hands clasped, then took two steps toward Gregor, and sank down in the midst of her skirts spreading out around her, her face completely hidden on her breast. With a hostile expression his father clenched his fist, as if to drive Gregor back into his room, then looked

Literary Analysis
Modernism How do his parents' reactions to seeing Gregor underscore key Modernist ideas?

✓ **Reading Check** **25**
What does Gregor finally succeed in doing after great effort?

The Metamorphosis, Part 1 ■ 1075

23 Background
Metamorphosis

Steven Berkoff's dramatic adaptation of Kafka's story was first produced in 1969 in London. This scene from *Metamorphosis* is from the 1989 Broadway production starring Mikhail Baryshnikov. Baryshnikov earned a Tony nomination and a Drama Critics Award for his performance as Gregor.

24 Literary Analysis
Modernism

• **Ask** students to imagine for a moment that they have been transformed into monstrous creatures. Ask them how they might feel if friends and family failed to recognize them and even recoiled in shock.
Possible response: Students may say that they would react with hurt, confusion, or anger.

• Explain to students that these reactions are central to the idea of alienation, a condition in which one fails to recognize others or to be acknowledged by them, precisely when one expects or relies on mutual acknowledgement.

• Read aloud the bracketed passage.

• **Ask** students the Literary Analysis question: How do his parents' reactions to seeing Gregor underscore key Modernist ideas?
Answer: Gregor's parents' reactions reflect uncertainty and alienation. Mrs. Samsa collapses in despair. Mr. Samsa is angry and then begins to sob.

25 Reading Check

Answer: Gregor gets the door open.

Differentiated Instruction   Solutions for All Learners

Strategy for English Learners
Have students look at the photograph on this page and note key details that help them understand the story. Students might point out the narrow room that closes in on Gregor, the family and the manager listening at both sides, the confused look on Gregor's face, and the overall gloomy mood. Tell students that the other images that accompany the story can provide information about characters, plot, mood, and tone. Have students preview the images in the selection, and ask volunteers to discuss their observations with the class.

Enrichment for Gifted/Talented Students
Help students locate a copy of Steven Berkoff's stage play *Metamorphosis*. Encourage them to read the play and to note the similarities and differences between the play and Kafka's short story. Direct students to write literary analysis essays in which they discuss how the transformation from narrative to stage changes the original story. Students should consider whether Berkoff's transformation of Kafka's work helps reinforce the Modernist characteristics of the original or mutates the story in subtle or obvious ways.

26 Literary Analysis
Modernism and Literature of the Fantastic

- Review with students the Connecting Literary Elements instruction on p. 1065.

- Read the bracketed passage aloud. **Ask:** How does the photograph of Gregor compare with his current situation?
  Answer: The photo shows Gregor as a "carefree" lieutenant, "demanding respect" for his status. In contrast, Gregor as an insect is confined to an alien body and receives no respect.

- **Ask** students the Literary Analysis question: In what ways does the realistic description of Gregor in uniform emphasize the horror of his transformation?
  Answer: The description of the photograph humanizes Gregor and makes the reader realize how drastic Gregor's transformation is. The reader sees Gregor's "human" past, not just the insect that he has become.

▶ **Monitor Progress Ask** students how the realistic description of the photograph compares and contrasts with the Modernist themes in the story and Gregor's current transformation.
  Answer: In the photograph, Gregor demands respect for his bearing and rank as a member of a highly regimented group. There is an acute contrast between the Gregor in the photograph and the Gregor who is now alienated from participation in any human group. In his current state as an insect, Gregor belongs to a group that is almost uniformly disrespected by the human community.

---

24 ↑ uncertainly around the living room, shielded his eyes with his hands, and sobbed with heaves of his powerful chest.

Now Gregor did not enter the room after all but leaned against the inside of the firmly bolted wing of the door, so that only half his body was visible and his head above it, cocked to one side and peeping out at the others. In the meantime it had grown much lighter; across the street one could see clearly a section of the endless, grayish-black building opposite—it was a hospital—with its regular windows starkly piercing the façade; the rain was still coming down, but only in large, separately visible drops that were also pelting the ground literally one at a time. The breakfast dishes were laid out lavishly on the table; since for his father breakfast was the most important meal of the day, which he would prolong for hours while reading various newspapers. On the wall directly opposite hung a photograph of Gregor from his army days, in a lieutenant's uniform, his hand on his sword, a carefree smile on his lips, demanding respect for his bearing and his rank. The door to the foyer was open, and since the front door was open too, it was possible to see out onto the landing and the top of the stairs going down.

26 "Well," said Gregor—and he was thoroughly aware of being the only one who had kept calm—"I'll get dressed right away, pack up my samples, and go. Will you, will you please let me go? Now, sir, you see, I'm not stubborn and I'm willing to work; traveling is a hardship, but without it I couldn't live. Where are you going, sir? To the office? Yes? Will you give an honest report of everything? A man might find for a moment that he was unable to work, but that's exactly the right time to remember his past accomplishments and to consider that later on, when the obstacle has been removed, he's bound to work all the harder and more efficiently. I'm under so many obligations to the head of the firm, as you know very well. Besides, I also have my parents and my sister to worry about. I'm in a tight spot, but I'll also work my way out again. Don't make things harder for me than they already are. Stick up for me in the office, please. Traveling salesmen aren't well liked there, I know. People think they make a fortune leading the gay life. No one has any particular reason to <u>rectify</u> this prejudice. But you, sir, you have a better perspective on things than the rest of the office, an even better perspective, just between the two of us, than the head of the firm himself, who in his capacity as owner easily lets his judgment be swayed against an employee. And you also know very well that the traveling salesman, who is out of the office practically the whole year round, can so easily become the victim of gossip, coincidences, and unfounded accusations, against which he's completely unable to defend himself, since in most cases he knows nothing at all about them except

1076 ■ *The Modern World*

Literary Analysis
Modernism and Literature of the Fantastic In what ways does the realistic description of Gregor in uniform emphasize the horror of his transformation?

Vocabulary Builder
rectify (rek´ tə fī´) v. to set things right or restore balance

Enrichment

Freud
Explain that Sigmund Freud was doing his work on human psychology in the early 1900s, during the time when Kafka was writing. At the foundation of many of Freud's theories is his claim that there are no accidents, only events resulting from unconscious motives. This theory may explain Gregor's transformation in "The Metamorphosis." Gregor felt trapped in a job he hated. He could not quit or get fired because his family depended upon him. He could not even pretend to be sick; he would simply be fired. However, he *could* turn into an insect. Hence, Gregor's transformation is not "random," but rather a manifestation of his unconscious desire to escape the confinements of modern life.

when he returns exhausted from a trip, and back home gets to suffer on his own person the grim consequences, which can no longer be traced back to their causes. Sir, don't go away without a word to tell me you think I'm at least partly right!"

But at Gregor's first words the manager had already turned away and with curled lips looked back at Gregor only over his twitching shoulder. And during Gregor's speech he did not stand still for a minute but, without letting Gregor out of his sight, backed toward the door, yet very gradually, as if there were some secret prohibition against leaving the room. He was already in the foyer, and from the sudden movement with which he took his last step from the living room, one might have thought he had just burned the sole of his foot. In the foyer, however, he stretched his right hand far out toward the staircase, as if nothing less than an unearthly deliverance were awaiting him there.

Gregor realized that he must on no account let the manager go away in this mood if his position in the firm were not to be jeopardized in the extreme. His parents did not understand this too well; in the course of the years they had formed the conviction that Gregor was set for life in this firm; and furthermore, they were so preoccupied with their immediate troubles that they had lost all consideration for the future. But Gregor had this forethought. The manager must be detained, calmed down, convinced, and finally won over; Gregor's and the family's future depended on it! If only his sister had been there! She was perceptive; she had already begun to cry when Gregor was still lying calmly on his back. And certainly the manager, this ladies' man, would have listened to her; she would have shut the front door and in the foyer talked him out of his scare. But his sister was not there, Gregor had to handle the situation himself. And without stopping to realize that he had no idea what his new faculties of movement were, and without stopping to realize either that his speech had possibly—indeed, probably—not been understood again, he let go of the wing of the door; he shoved himself through the opening, intending to go to the manager, who was already on the landing, ridiculously holding onto the banisters with both hands; but groping for support, Gregor immediately fell down with a little cry onto his numerous little legs. This had hardly happened when for the first time that morning he had a feeling of physical well-being; his little legs were on firm ground; they obeyed him completely, as he noted to his joy; they even strained to carry him away wherever he wanted to go; and he already believed that final recovery from all his sufferings was <u>imminent</u>. But at that very moment, as he lay on the floor rocking with repressed motion, not far from his mother and just opposite her, she, who had seemed so completely self-absorbed, all at once jumped up, her arms stretched wide, her fingers spread, and cried, "Help, for God's sake, help!" held her head bent as if to see Gregor better, but inconsistently darted madly backward instead; had forgotten that the table laden with the breakfast dishes stood behind her; sat down on it hastily, as if her thoughts were elsewhere, when she

27

28

Reading Strategy
Applying the Author's Biography How might Gregor's reactions reflect Kafka's feelings about his financial responsibilities for his family?

Vocabulary Builder
imminent (im′ ə nənt) adj. ready to happen at any moment

 **Reading Check 29**
Once his door is open, what does Gregor insist he be permitted to do?

The Metamorphosis, Part 1 ■ 1077

---

27 Reading Strategy

Applying the Author's Biography

• Ask a volunteer to read aloud the bracketed passage.

• **Ask** students the Reading Strategy question: How might Gregor's reactions reflect Kafka's feelings about his financial responsibilities for his family?
Answer: As Gregor witnesses the manager's reaction to his new insect form, Gregor is struck with a sense of panic about the security of his job. Like Kafka, Gregor is responsible for his family's financial security, so Gregor wants to secure his position with his employer.

28 Vocabulary Builder

Latin Prefix im-

• Draw students' attention to the word *imminent,* and read its definition.

• Tell students that the prefix *im-* means "not," "into," or "toward."

• Have students **suggest** other words that contain the prefix *im-.*
Possible response: *Immigrant, immediate, immense, immerse, important, impossible,* and *impression* all contain the prefix *im-.*

• Ask students to use dictionaries to research each suggested word's etymology and explain how the prefix *im-* contributes to each word's meaning.

29 Reading Check

Answer: Gregor insists on talking to the manager to prevent him from leaving the house.

Differentiated
Instruction   **Solutions for All Learners**

Support for Less Proficient Readers
Read aloud the passage near the bottom of the page that describes how Gregor feels when he discovers the use of his legs. Call students' attention to the line "he already believed that final recovery from all his sufferings was imminent." Initiate a discussion about what Gregor has been through, both before and since his metamorphosis. Then, help students recognize that Gregor is feeling a sense of liberty that he has not felt all morning.

Enrichment for Gifted/Talented Students
Ask students to imagine that they have arrived at school one morning and no one recognizes them or understands a thing they say. Ask students to write journal entries in which they describe how it might feel to suddenly find themselves in this situation. Encourage students to provide details about how they might be treated and their responses to this treatment.

Applying the Author's Biography

- Read the bracketed passage aloud.
  Ask: What details bring this portrait of a powerful, dominating, yet subtly ridiculous, father alive?
  Answer: Kafka provides several sensory details to help the reader picture the father as an authority figure. We see Mr. Samsa wielding a cane and newspaper, and we hear him stamping his feet and "hissing like a wild man."

- Remind students that Kafka's father was a strict, domineering figure, and emphasize that Kafka incorporated these qualities into his characterization of Mr. Samsa.

- Then, **ask** students the Reading Strategy question: In what ways does this description of Gregor's father reflect your knowledge about Kafka's father?
  Answer: The description of Mr. Samsa as an intimidator reflects what we know about Kafka's own domineering father. If faced with the same situation, Kafka's father, like Mr. Samsa, might have tried to regain control of his household.

31 **Critical Thinking**

Analyze

- Discuss Mrs. Samsa's actions while this wild scene is taking place. **Ask** students what they think she is feeling.
  Possible response: She is probably feeling despair, panic, and confusion.

- **Ask:** Why has Mrs. Samsa thrown open the window?
  Possible response: She may feel unable to breathe as a result of anxiety caused by the realization of what has happened to her son and may be trying to get more air. She may have put her head out the window to escape the scene taking place in the apartment.

reached it; and did not seem to notice at all that near her the big coffeepot had been knocked over and coffee was pouring in a steady stream onto the rug.

"Mother, Mother," said Gregor softly and looked up at her. For a minute the manager had completely slipped his mind; on the other hand at the sight of the spilling coffee he could not resist snapping his jaws several times in the air. At this his mother screamed once more, fled from the table, and fell into the arms of his father, who came rushing up to her. But Gregor had no time now for his parents; the manager was already on the stairs; with his chin on the banister, he was taking a last look back. Gregor was off to a running start, to be as sure as possible of catching up with him; the manager must have suspected something like this, for he leaped down several steps and disappeared; but still he shouted "Agh," and the sound carried through the whole staircase. Unfortunately the manager's flight now seemed to confuse his father completely, who had been relatively calm until now, for instead of running after the manager himself, or at least not hindering Gregor in his pursuit, he seized in his right hand the manager's cane, which had been left behind on a chair with his hat and overcoat, picked up in his left hand a heavy newspaper from the table, and stamping his feet, started brandishing the cane and the newspaper to drive Gregor back into his room. No plea of Gregor's helped, no plea was even understood; however humbly he might turn his head, his father merely stamped his feet more forcefully. Across the room his mother had thrown open a window in spite of the cool weather, and leaning out, she buried her face, far outside the window, in her hands. Between the alley and the staircase a strong draft was created, the window curtains blew in, the newspapers on the table rustled, single sheets fluttered across the floor. Pitilessly his father came on, hissing like a wild man. Now Gregor had not had any practice at all walking in reverse, it was really very slow going. If Gregor had only been allowed to turn around, he could have gotten into his room right away, but he was afraid to make his father impatient by this time-consuming gyration, and at any minute the cane in his father's hand threatened to come down on his back or his head with a deadly blow. Finally, however, Gregor had no choice, for he noticed with horror that in reverse he could not even keep going in one direction; and so, incessantly throwing uneasy side-glances at his father, he began to turn around as quickly as possible, in reality turning only very slowly. Perhaps his father realized his good intentions, for he did not interfere with him; instead, he even now and then directed the maneuver from afar with the tip of his cane. If only his father did not keep making this intolerable hissing sound! It made Gregor lose his head completely. He had almost finished the turn when— his mind continually on this hissing—he made a mistake and even started turning back around to his original position. But when he had at last successfully managed to get his head in front of the opened door, it turned out that his body was too broad to get through as it was. Of course in his father's present state of mind it did not even remotely occur to him

Reading Strategy
Applying the Author's Biography In what ways does this description of Gregor's father reflect your knowledge about Kafka's father?

Vocabulary Builder
gyration (jī rā′ shən) *n.* circular or spiral motion

1078 ■ *The Modern World*

to open the other wing of the door in order to give Gregor enough room to pass through. He had only the fixed idea that Gregor must return to his room as quickly as possible. He would never have allowed the complicated preliminaries Gregor needed to go through in order to stand up on one end and perhaps in this way fit through the door. Instead he drove Gregor on, as if there were no obstacle, with exceptional loudness; the voice behind Gregor did not sound like that of only a single father; now this was really no joke anymore, and Gregor forced himself—come what may—into the doorway. One side of his body rose up, he lay lop-sided in the opening, one of his flanks was scraped raw, ugly blotches marred the white door, soon he got stuck and could not have budged anymore by himself, his little legs on one side dangled tremblingly in midair, those on the other were painfully crushed against the floor—when from behind his father gave him a hard shove, which was truly his salvation, and bleeding profusely, he flew far into his room. The door was slammed shut with the cane, then at last everything was quiet.

Critical Reading

1. **Respond:** In what ways, if any, did the characters in this story remind you of people whom you have met?

2. **(a) Recall:** What is Gregor's first reaction to his transformation? **(b) Generalize:** How does Gregor's family react to his transformation? **(c) Analyze:** In what ways do the differences in their reactions set up a challenge for this family?

3. **(a) Recall:** Who visits Gregor on the first morning of his transformation? **(b) Generalize:** How would you describe Gregor's relationship to this person? Explain. **(c) Analyze:** Was Gregor happy in his life before his transformation? Explain.

4. **(a) Recall:** In what ways are Gregor's parents indebted to Gregor's boss? **(b) Analyze Cause and Effect:** What does Gregor seem to fear will happen to his family if he loses his job?

5. **(a) Speculate:** Why do you think neither his family nor the office manager ever questions whether the creature before them is actually Gregor? **(b) Support:** Which details, if any, in Part I suggest that Gregor's physical transformation is an outward expression of an alienation he has already experienced both at home and at work? Explain.

6. **Analyze:** Do you think Gregor's inner sense of self has changed as a result of his physical transformation? Explain.

Go Online
Author Link

For: More about Franz Kafka
Visit: www.PHSchool.com
Web Code: ete-9801

The Metamorphosis, Part 1 ■ 1079

1079

Review and Anticipate

Part I of "The Metamorphosis" ends with Gregor being driven back into his room by his cane-wielding father. The office manager has fled in horror, the family is in shock, and Gregor himself is wounded and bloody. Do you think Gregor will be able to overcome his family's revulsion? Do you think he will become normal and human again, or will he grow increasingly alienated and different? Read Part II to see what happens as the first day of Gregor's strange transformation continues.

Part II 32

It was already dusk when Gregor awoke from his deep, comalike sleep. Even if he had not been disturbed, he would certainly not have woken up much later, for he felt that he had rested and slept long enough, but it seemed to him that a hurried step and a cautious shutting of the door leading to the foyer had awakened him. The light of the electric street-lamps lay in pallid streaks on the ceiling and on the upper parts of the furniture, but underneath, where Gregor was, it was dark. Groping clumsily with his antennae, which he was only now beginning to appreciate, he slowly dragged himself toward the door to see what had been happening there. His left side felt like one single long, unpleasantly tautening scar, and he actually had to limp on his two rows of legs. Besides, one little leg had been seriously injured in the course of the morning's events—it was almost a miracle that only one had been injured—and dragged along lifelessly.

Only after he got to the door did he notice what had really attracted him—the smell of something to eat. For there stood a bowl filled with fresh milk, in which small slices of white bread were floating. He could almost have laughed for joy, since he was even hungrier than he had been in the morning, and he immediately dipped his head into the milk, almost to over his eyes. But he soon drew it back again in disappointment; not only because he had difficulty eating on account of the soreness in his left side—and he could eat only if his whole panting body cooperated—but because he didn't like the milk at all, although it used to be his favorite drink, and that was certainly why his sister had put it in the room; in fact, he turned away from the bowl almost with repulsion and crawled back to the middle of the room.

In the living room, as Gregor saw through the crack in the door, the gas had been lit, but while at this hour of the day his father was in the habit of reading the afternoon newspaper in a loud voice to his mother and sometimes to his sister too, now there wasn't a sound. Well, perhaps this custom of reading aloud, which his sister was always telling

Vocabulary Builder
pallid (pal´ id) *adj.* pale

Literary Analysis
Modernism In what ways does Gregor's rejection of the food brought by Grete symbolize his growing alienation?

1080 ■ *The Modern World*

him and writing him about, had recently been discontinued altogether. But in all the other rooms too it was just as still, although the apartment certainly was not empty. "What a quiet life the family has been leading," Gregor said to himself, and while he stared rigidly in front of him into the darkness, he felt very proud that he had been able to provide such a life in so nice an apartment for his parents and his sister. But what now if all the peace, the comfort, the contentment were to come to a horrible end? In order not to get involved in such thoughts, Gregor decided to keep moving, and he crawled up and down the room.

During the long evening first one of the side doors and then the other was opened a small crack and quickly shut again; someone had probably had the urge to come in and then had had second thoughts. Gregor now settled into position right by the living-room door, determined somehow to get the hesitating visitor to come in, or at least to find out who it might be; but the door was not opened again, and Gregor waited in vain. In the morning, when the doors had been locked, everyone had wanted to come in; now that he had opened one of the doors and the others had evidently been opened during the day, no one came in, and now the keys were even inserted on the outside.

It was late at night when the light finally went out in the living room, and now it was easy for Gregor to tell that his parents and his sister had stayed up so long, since, as he could distinctly hear, all three were now retiring on tiptoe. Certainly no one would come in to Gregor until the morning; and so he had ample time to consider undisturbed how best to rearrange his life. But the empty high-ceilinged room in which he was forced to lie flat on the floor made him nervous, without his being able to tell why—since it was, after all, the room in which he had lived for the past five years—and turning half unconsciously and not without a slight feeling of shame, he scuttled under the couch where, although his back was a little crushed and he could not raise his head anymore, he immediately felt very comfortable and was only sorry that his body was too wide to go completely under the couch.

There he stayed the whole night, which he spent partly in a sleepy trance, from which hunger pangs kept waking him with a start, partly in worries and vague hopes, all of which, however, led to the conclusion that for the time being he would have to lie low and, by being patient and showing his family every possible consideration, help them bear

FRANZ KAFKA
DIE VERWANDLUNG

DER JÜNGSTE TAG ∗ 22/23
KURT WOLFF VERLAG · LEIPZIG
1916

▲ **Critical Viewing** 35
Why do you think Kafka insisted that the illustration for the cover of the first edition of "The Metamorphosis," shown above, not depict the insect itself? **[Speculate]**

✔ **Reading Check** 36
Where have the keys to Gregor's room been moved?

The Metamorphosis, Part II ■ 1081

34
35
36
37

34 **Humanities**

Front Cover of *Die Verwandlung*, by Ottomar Starke

When "The Metamorphosis" (called *Die Verwandlung* in German) was to be published as a book in 1915, Kafka, fearful that the cover illustrator "might want to draw the insect itself," wrote the publisher, "Not that, please not that! . . . The insect itself cannot be depicted. It cannot even be shown from a distance." He suggested instead an illustration with "the parents and the chief clerk in front of the closed door or, even better, the parents and the sister in the illuminated room while the door to the entirely dark adjoining room stands open."

Use the following questions for discussion:

• What is the effect of leaving the door ajar?
Possible response: The open door hints at a mysterious presence in the darkened room that may emerge at any moment.

• What emotions does the man's posture evoke?
Possible response: The man holding his head in his hands evokes a range of emotions, including terror, disgust, and sorrow.

35 **Critical Viewing**

Possible response: Kafka may have thought that the image of Gregor would be more powerful if readers were forced to imagine him; he may have wished to emphasize the symbolic, not literal, meaning of the transformation.

36 **Reading Check**

Answer: The keys have been moved to the outside of the doors so Gregor can be locked inside.

Differentiated Instruction Solutions for All Learners

Strategy for English Learners
In a long selection, students may have an especially difficult time resolving questions about content. Suggest that students use self-sticking notes to mark passages, sentences, idioms, or other elements that are confusing. Encourage students to refer to these notes and ask their questions during class discussions.

Enrichment for Gifted/Talented Students
Have students work independently to create their own illustrations for the cover of "The Metamorphosis." Encourage students to consider the Modernist notions of mystery and uncertainty as well as Kafka's wish that Gregor not be depicted. Ask volunteers to present their book covers to the class and discuss their creative process, detailing the mood they hoped to evoke and citing specific inspirational portions of the text. Students may display their book covers on a class bulletin board.

37 Literary Analysis

Modernism

Modernism Do Gregor's thoughts reflect a realistic viewpoint on his life and prospects? Explain.

37 Literary Analysis

Modernism

- Read aloud the bracketed passage. Tell students that Gregor's shame amplifies his feelings of alienation. Then, **ask:** What are the sources of Gregor's shame?

  Answer: Gregor is ashamed of his insect body; he is embarrassed because he is uneasy in his own room; he is ashamed that he feels comfortable only when hiding under the couch.

- **Ask** students the first Literary Analysis question: Do Gregor's thoughts reflect a realistic viewpoint on his life and prospects? Explain.

  Possible response: Yes; by planning how to adapt to his new condition, Gregor shows that he has begun to accept his life as an insect and no longer expects that he will be able to change back into a human. He recognizes that he must become almost invisible in order to survive.

  ▶ **Monitor Progress** Tell students that Gregor seems to be guessing how to behave. **Ask:** In what way does Gregor's lack of clear guidelines reflect a Modernist point of view?

  Answer: Modernists expect life to be filled with uncertainty.

38 Literary Analysis

Modernism

- Read aloud the bracketed passage.

- **Ask** students: Why has Gregor's sister given him a selection of foods? What might she learn from his decisions?

  Answer: Grete does not know what foods Gregor will eat now that he is an insect. She will learn what to bring him to eat in the future.

- **Ask** students the second Literary Analysis question: What evidence does this passage describing his meal provide for the view that Gregor is more alienated from the world of humans than he realizes?

  Answer: Even though Gregor thinks like a human, his needs and instincts are becoming more and more insectlike.

---

37 the inconvenience which he simply had to cause them in his present condition.

Early in the morning—it was still almost night—Gregor had the opportunity of testing the strength of the resolutions he had just made, for his sister, almost fully dressed, opened the door from the foyer and looked in eagerly. She did not see him right away, but when she caught sight of him under the couch—God, he had to be somewhere, he couldn't just fly away—she became so frightened that she lost control of herself and slammed the door shut again. But, as if she felt sorry for her behavior, she immediately opened the door again and came in on tiptoe, as if she were visiting someone seriously ill or perhaps even a stranger. Gregor had pushed his head forward just to the edge of the couch and was watching her. Would she notice that he had left the milk standing, and not because he hadn't been hungry, and would she bring in a dish of something he'd like better? If she were not going to do it of her own free will, he would rather starve than call it to her attention, although, really, he felt an enormous urge to shoot out from under the couch, throw himself at his sister's feet, and beg her for something good to eat. But his sister noticed at once, to her astonishment, that the bowl was still full, only a little milk was spilled around it; she picked it up immediately—not with her bare hands, of course, but with a rag—and carried it out. Gregor was extremely curious to know what she would bring him instead, and he racked his brains on the subject. But he would never have been able to guess what his sister, in the goodness of her heart, actually did. To find out his likes and dislikes, she brought him a wide assortment of things, all spread out on an old newspaper: old, half-rotten vegetables; bones left over from the evening meal, caked with congealed white sauce; some raisins and almonds; a piece of cheese, which two days before Gregor had declared inedible; a plain slice of bread, a slice of bread and butter, and one with butter and salt. In addition to all this she put down some water in the bowl apparently permanently earmarked for Gregor's use. And out of a sense of delicacy, since she knew that Gregor would not eat in front of her, she left hurriedly and even turned the key, just so that Gregor should know that he might make himself as comfortable as he wanted. Gregor's legs began whirring now that he was going to eat. Besides, his bruises must have completely healed, since he no longer felt any handicap, and marveling at this he thought how, over a month ago he had cut his finger very slightly with a knife and how this wound was still hurting him only the day before yesterday. "Have I become less sensitive?" he thought, already sucking greedily at the cheese, which had immediately and forcibly attracted him ahead of all the other dishes. One right after the

38 other, and with eyes streaming with tears of contentment, he devoured the cheese, the vegetables, and the sauce; the fresh foods, on the other hand, he did not care for; he couldn't even stand their smell and even dragged the things he wanted to eat a bit further away. He had finished with everything long since and was just lying lazily at the same spot when his sister slowly turned the key as a sign for him to withdraw.

Literary Analysis

Modernism What evidence does this passage describing his meal provide for the view that Gregor is more alienated from the world of humans than he realizes?

Enrichment

Kafka's Metamorphosis

A year before Kafka wrote "The Metamorphosis," he watched an artist grimacing and mimicking what he was drawing. That day, Kafka wrote this prophetic comment in his diary:

> [The artist] reminds me that I too have a pronounced talent for metamorphosing myself, which no one notices. . . . Yesterday evening, on the way home, if I had observed myself from the outside I should

have taken myself for Tucholsky [a German writer]. The alien being must be in me, then, as distinctly and invisibly as the hidden object in a picture-puzzle, where too, one would never find anything if one did not know that it is there. When these metamorphoses take place, I should especially like to believe in a dimming of my own eyes.

That immediately startled him although he was almost asleep, and he scuttled under the couch again. But it took great self-control for him to stay under the couch even for the short time his sister was in the room, since his body had become a little bloated from the heavy meal, and in his cramped position he could hardly breathe. In between slight attacks of suffocation he watched with bulging eyes as his unsuspecting sister took a broom and swept up, not only his leavings, but even the foods which Gregor had left completely untouched—as if they too were no longer usable—and dumping everything hastily into a pail, which she covered with a wooden lid, she carried everything out. She had hardly turned her back when Gregor came out from under the couch, stretching and puffing himself up.

This, then, was the way Gregor was fed each day, once in the morning, when his parents and the maid were still asleep, and a second time in the afternoon after everyone had had dinner, for then his parents took a short nap again, and the maid could be sent out by his sister on some errand. Certainly they did not want him to starve either, but perhaps they would not have been able to stand knowing any more about his meals than from hearsay, or perhaps his sister wanted to spare them even what was possibly only a minor torment, for really, they were suffering enough as it was.

Gregor could not find out what excuses had been made to get rid of the doctor and the locksmith on that first morning, for since the others could not understand what he said, it did not occur to any of them, not even to his sister, that he could understand what they said, and so he had to be satisfied, when his sister was in the room, with only occasionally hearing her sighs and appeals to the saints. It was only later, when she had begun to get used to everything—there could never, of course, be any question of a complete adjustment—that Gregor sometimes caught a remark which was meant to be friendly or could be interpreted as such. "Oh, he liked what he had today," she would say when Gregor had tucked away a good helping, and in the opposite case, which gradually occurred more and more frequently, she used to say, almost sadly, "He's left everything again."

But if Gregor could not get any news directly, he overheard a great deal from the neighboring rooms, and as soon as he heard voices, he would immediately run to the door concerned and press his whole body against it. Especially in the early days, there was no conversation that was not somehow about him, if only implicitly. For two whole days there were family consultations at every mealtime about how they should cope; this was also the topic of discussion between meals, for at least two members of the family were always at home, since no one

39 The Modernist Revolution

During the late nineteenth and early twentieth centuries, major scientific, technological, and industrial developments occurred that altered the way people lived. Not only were the automobile, the airplane, the telephone, and the machine gun invented, but also brilliant thinkers and scientists emerged, including Sigmund Freud, Albert Einstein, and Friedrich Nietzsche. This period of rapid change culminated in World War I, a bloody conflict that wiped out almost an entire generation of European men. As a result of these events and developments, many people felt the need to discard the ideas and values of the past and to find new ideas that more appropriately reflected twentieth-century life. Franz Kafka's disturbing fictional world is one of the best literary examples of this new vision, but the Modernist movement affected every creative discipline. The Modernists' vibrant, unsettling, and profound artistic experiments continue to resonate in our culture to this day.

Connect to the Literature

List three examples of artistic experiments like "The Metamorphosis" in contemporary music, fine art, literature, or film.

✓ **Reading Check** 41

What kinds of food does Gregor now prefer?

The Metamorphosis, Part II ■ 1083

39 Themes in World Literature

The Modernist Revolution

Generally, the themes of Modernist writers were subtly implied rather than directly stated in order to force readers to draw their own conclusions. Likewise, writers began abandoning traditional plot structure, omitting the expositions and resolutions that clarified the work. As a result, the Modernist story seems to begin arbitrarily and to end without resolution, leaving the reader with possibilities, not solutions. This technique reflected the uncertainties and questions about life provoked by the intellectual revolutions—and mass destruction—of the time.

Connect to the Literature Point out to students that the human imagination continues to expand today, especially in technology, which has helped artists adapt many fantasy stories into films. Ask students to list examples of such artistic experiments in contemporary film, music, fine art, and literature.

Possible responses: Some examples are the film adaptations of the *Harry Potter* series and of the novel *The Lord of the Rings;* Christo and Jeanne-Claude's public art piece "The Gates" in Central Park, New York City; rap music; and Gabriel García Márquez's stories of magical realism.

40 Literary Analysis

Modernism

• Read aloud the bracketed passage.

• **Ask** students how this scene indicates that another degree of alienation has occurred.
  Answer: Grete treats the food as tainted, showing that she now feels that Gregor is dirty, like any other vermin.

• **Ask** students why food is an especially apt symbol for the Modernist theme of alienation.
  Possible response: The need for food is a basic individual need, and traditions in the choice and sharing of food help define an individual's membership in a family or culture. Not eating the same food as others or not eating with others are basic signs of not belonging.

41 Reading Check

Answer: Gregor prefers half-rotten, smelly foods to fresh foods.

Differentiated Instruction Solutions for All Learners

Support for English Learners
Students may benefit from your help with **Vocabulary Warm-up List** and **Vocabulary Warm-up Practice**, pp. 7–8 in *Unit 8 Resources.* After students have finished, ask them to list new or unfamiliar words from Part II of the selection. If any of these words are not covered in the support material students have completed, post meanings and encourage students to create word journals in which they record newly learned words.

Vocabulary for Advanced Readers
Call students' attention to the word *earmarked* in the following passage: "In addition to all this she put down some water in the bowl apparently permanently *earmarked* for Gregor's use." Have students work with partners to research the etymology of this word. Each pair can prepare a presentation about the origins and meaning of the word and how Kafka uses it in the selection.

probably wanted to stay home alone and it was impossible to leave the apartment completely empty. Besides, on the very first day the maid—it was not completely clear what and how much she knew of what had happened—had begged his mother on bended knees to dismiss her immediately; and when she said goodbye a quarter of an hour later, she thanked them in tears for the dismissal, as if for the greatest favor that had ever been done to her in this house, and made a solemn vow, without anyone asking her for it, not to give anything away to anyone.

Now his sister, working with her mother, had to do the cooking too; of course that did not cause her much trouble, since they hardly ate anything. Gregor was always hearing one of them pleading in vain with one of the others to eat and getting no answer except, "Thanks, I've had enough," or something similar. They did not seem to drink anything either. His sister often asked her father if he wanted any beer and gladly offered to go out for it herself; and when he did not answer, she said, in order to remove any hesitation on his part, that she could also send the janitor's wife to get it, but then his father finally answered with a definite "No," and that was the end of that.

In the course of the very first day his father explained the family's financial situation and prospects to both the mother and the sister. From time to time he got up from the table to get some kind of receipt or notebook out of the little strongbox he had rescued from the collapse of his business five years before. Gregor heard him open the complicated lock and secure it again after taking out what he had been looking for. These explanations by his father were to some extent the first pleasant news Gregor had heard since his imprisonment. He had always believed that his father had not been able to save a penny from the business, at least his father had never told him anything to the con-

▼ **Critical Viewing 43**
In this photograph of Mikhail Baryshnikov as Gregor Samsa, what information do you think Gregor might be overhearing? Explain. **[Hypothesize]**

1084 ■ *The Modern World*

trary, and Gregor, for his part, had never asked him any questions. In those days Gregor's sole concern had been to do everything in his power to make the family forget as quickly as possible the business disaster which had plunged everyone into a state of total despair. And so he had begun to work with special ardor[4] and had risen almost overnight from stock clerk to traveling salesman, which of course had opened up very different money-making possibilities, and in no time his successes on the job were transformed, by means of commissions, into hard cash that could be plunked down on the table at home in front of his astonished and delighted family. Those had been wonderful times, and they had never returned, at least not with the same glory, although later on Gregor earned enough money to meet the expenses of the entire family and actually did so. They had just gotten used to it, the family as well as Gregor, the money was received with thanks and given with pleasure, but no special feeling of warmth went with it any more. Only his sister had remained close to Gregor, and it was his secret plan that she who, unlike him, loved music and could play the violin movingly, should be sent next year to the Conservatory, regardless of the great expense involved, which could surely be made up for in some other way. Often during Gregor's short stays in the city, the Conservatory would come up in his conversations with his sister, but always merely as a beautiful dream which was not supposed to come true, and his parents were not happy to hear even these innocent allusions; but Gregor had very concrete ideas on the subject and he intended solemnly to announce his plan on Christmas Eve.

Thoughts like these, completely useless in his present state, went through his head as he stood glued to the door, listening. Sometimes out of general exhaustion he could not listen anymore and let his head bump carelessly against the door, but immediately pulled it back again, for even the slight noise he made by doing this had been heard in the next room and made them all lapse into silence. "What's he carrying on about in there now?" said his father after a while, obviously turning toward the door, and only then would the interrupted conversation gradually be resumed.

Gregor now learned in a thorough way—for his father was in the habit of often repeating himself in his explanations, partly because he himself had not dealt with these matters for a long time, partly, too, because his mother did not understand everything the first time around—that in spite of all their misfortunes a bit of capital, a very little bit, certainly, was still intact from the old days, which in the meantime had increased a little through the untouched interest. But besides that, the money Gregor had brought home every month—he had kept only a few dollars for himself—had never been completely used up and had accumulated into a tidy principal. Behind his door Gregor nodded emphatically, delighted at this unexpected foresight and thrift. Of course he actually could have paid off more of his father's debt to the

---

4. **ardor** (är′ dər) *n.* emotional warmth.

Reading Strategy
Applying the Author's Biography Kafka's father did not support his son's literary aspirations. How does that information add meaning to this discussion about the Conservatory?

Reading Check 45

What event, five years before, had plunged the family into financial distress?

The Metamorphosis, Part II ■ 1085

44 Reading Strategy
Applying the Author's Biography

• Have a volunteer read aloud the bracketed passage. Then, have the class discuss the value some members of society place on practical skills or academic subjects versus the arts.

• **Ask** students the Reading Strategy question: Kafka's father did not support his son's literary aspirations. How does that information add meaning to this discussion about the Conservatory?
Answer: Kafka identifies with the sister and her love of art, so he symbolically nurtures his own aspirations by having Gregor wish to support Grete despite Mr. and Mrs. Samsa's objections.

• In light of the biographical nature of this passage, **invite** students to speculate on how Kafka felt about his parents' lack of support for his literary aspirations.
Possible response: Kafka may have resented his parents' lack of support.

45 Reading Check
Answer: Mr. Samsa's business collapsed, and he lost nearly everything.

Differentiated Instruction   Solutions for All Learners

Strategy for Less Proficient Readers
Organize students into three groups. Assign each group one of the following characters: father, mother, Grete. Have each group list personality and character traits of its assigned character along with details from the story that illustrate those traits. Have each group share and discuss its list with the class.

Strategy for English Learners
Students may have been in situations in which they were capable of understanding those around them but were not understood by others. Encourage students to discuss their experiences and compare their feelings with Gregor's feelings. Ask students what advice they would give Gregor to help alleviate the stress of his being unable to communicate. On the board, write students' suggestions, and have students use your notes to write a letter of advice or comfort to Gregor.

46 Literary Analysis

Modernism

- Read aloud the bracketed passage. Then, **ask** students the Literary Analysis question: In what ways does this information about their finances and work skills emphasize the entire family's alienation from the world at large?
  Answer: Neither Gregor's parents nor his sister are used to working or contributing to life outside the apartment.

- **Ask** students: Does the Samsa family seem unhappy about, or even aware of, its alienation? Explain.
  Possible response: No; the family seems content with the way things have been. They have established a life of complacency, with Gregor providing for them while they remain sheltered from the world.

47 Reading Strategy

Applying the Author's Biography

- Ask a volunteer to read aloud the bracketed passage.

- Then, **ask** students why being able to look out the window is important to Gregor.
  Answer: Gregor wants to recapture the feeling of freedom he once experienced while looking out the window.

- **Ask** students the Reading Strategy question: How would living in a city have helped Kafka write this description?
  Answer: As a city-dweller, Kafka understood how limited the views are and how a person can get tired of seeing the same thing every day. He also understood the importance of windows when so much time is spent indoors.

boss with this extra money, and the day on which he could have gotten rid of his job would have been much closer, but now things were undoubtedly better the way his father had arranged them.

Now this money was by no means enough to let the family live off the interest; the principal was perhaps enough to support the family for one year, or at the most two, but that was all there was. So it was just a sum that really should not be touched and that had to be put away for a rainy day; but the money to live on would have to be earned. Now his father was still healthy, certainly, but he was an old man who had not worked for the past five years and who in any case could not be expected to undertake too much; during these five years, which were the first vacation of his hard-working yet unsuccessful life, he had gained a lot of weight and as a result had become fairly sluggish. And was his old mother now supposed to go out and earn money, when she suffered from asthma, when a walk through the apartment was already an ordeal for her, and when she spent every other day lying on the sofa under the open window, gasping for breath? And was his sister now supposed to work—who for all her seventeen years was still a child and whom it would be such a pity to deprive of the life she had led until now, which had consisted of wearing pretty clothes, sleeping late, helping in the house, enjoying a few modest amusements, and above all playing the violin? At first, whenever the conversation turned to the necessity of earning money, Gregor would let go of the door and throw himself down on the cool leather sofa which stood beside it, for he felt hot with shame and grief.

Often he lay there the whole long night through, not sleeping a wink and only scrabbling on the leather for hours on end. Or, not balking at the huge effort of pushing an armchair to the window, he would crawl up to the window sill and, propped up in the chair, lean against the window, evidently in some sort of remembrance of the feeling of freedom he used to have from looking out the window. For, in fact, from day to day he saw things even a short distance away less and less distinctly; the hospital opposite, which he used to curse because he saw so much of it, was now completely beyond his range of vision, and if he had not been positive that he was living in Charlotte Street—a quiet but still very much a city street—he might have believed that he was looking out of his window into a desert where the gray sky and the gray earth were indistinguishably fused. It took his observant sister only twice to notice that his armchair was standing by the window for her to push the chair back to the same place by the window each time she had finished cleaning the room, and from then on she even left the inside casement of the window open.

If Gregor had only been able to speak to his sister and thank her for everything she had to do for him, he could have accepted her services more easily; as it was, they caused him pain. Of course his sister tried to ease the embarrassment of the whole situation as much as possible, and as time went on, she naturally managed it better and better, but in time Gregor, too, saw things much more clearly. Even the way she came

1086 ■ *The Modern World*

Literary Analysis
Modernism In what ways does this information about their finances and work skills emphasize the entire family's alienation from the world at large?

Reading Strategy
Applying the Author's Biography How would living in a city have helped Kafka write this description?

in was terrible for him. Hardly had she entered the room than she would run straight to the window without taking time to close the door—though she was usually so careful to spare everyone the sight of Gregor's room—then tear open the casements with eager hands, almost as if she were suffocating, and remain for a little while at the window even in the coldest weather, breathing deeply. With this racing and crashing she frightened Gregor twice a day; the whole time he cowered under the couch, and yet he knew very well that she would certainly have spared him this if only she had found it possible to stand being in a room with him with the window closed.

One time—it must have been a month since Gregor's metamorphosis, and there was certainly no particular reason any more for his sister to be astonished at Gregor's appearance—she came a little earlier than usual and caught Gregor still looking out the window, immobile and so in an excellent position to be terrifying. It would not have surprised Gregor if she had not come in, because his position prevented her from immediately opening the window, but not only did she not come in, she even sprang back and locked the door; a stranger might easily have thought that Gregor had been lying in wait for her, wanting to bite her. Of course Gregor immediately hid under the couch, but he had to wait until noon before his sister came again, and she seemed much more uneasy than usual. He realized from this that the sight of him was still repulsive to her and was bound to remain repulsive to her in the future, and that she probably had to overcome a lot of resistance not to run away at the sight of even the small part of his body that jutted out from under the couch. So, to spare her even this sight, one day he carried the sheet on his back to the couch—the job took four hours—and arranged it in such a way that he was now completely covered up and his sister could not see him even when she stooped. If she had considered this sheet unnecessary, then of course she could have removed it, for it was clear enough that it could not be for his own pleasure that Gregor shut himself off altogether, but she left the sheet the way it was, and Gregor thought that he had even caught a grateful look when one time he cautiously lifted the sheet a little with his head in order to see how his sister was taking the new arrangement.

During the first two weeks, his parents could not bring themselves to come in to him, and often he heard them say how much they appreciated his sister's work, whereas until now they had frequently been annoyed with her because she had struck them as being a little useless. But now both of them, his father and his mother, often waited outside Gregor's room while his sister straightened it up, and as soon as she came out she had to tell them in great detail how the room looked, what Gregor had eaten, how he had behaved this time, and whether he had perhaps shown a little improvement. His mother, incidentally, began relatively soon to want to visit Gregor, but his father and his sister at first held her back with reasonable arguments to which Gregor listened very attentively and of which he wholeheartedly approved. But later she had to be restrained by force, and then when she cried out,

Literary Analysis
Modernism What does Gregor now do, deliberately, to alienate himself? Why does he do this?

Reading Check ㊾
Until now, what had been Grete's main activities?

The Metamorphosis, Part II ■ 1087

What Kind of Insect Is Gregor Samsa? In his lectures on "The Metamorphosis" at Cornell University, Vladimir Nabokov made several observations that raise questions about Gregor's insect identity. First, he observed that Gregor, when trying to get out of bed, is "closing his eyes." Nabokov pointed out that, "a regular beetle has no eyelids and cannot close its eyes." Nabokov also noted that in Part III, the cleaning woman calls Gregor a "dung beetle." Nabokov dismissed this identification as an endearing epithet used "only to be friendly."

Connect to the Literature Point out to students that Nabokov believed Gregor to be a kind of beetle, but one whose "metamorphosis is not quite complete as yet."

These speculations only confirm what is suggested by Kafka's insistence that his publisher not provide illustrations for Gregor the "insect"— Gregor's new identity is not a scientifically classifiable one but is rather a condition in which personal identity flounders, revealing its unpleasant obverse side. Ask students whether they see Gregor in the picture of the insect.

Possible response: Students may say that the insect in the picture looks somewhat like their mental picture of Gregor. The differences, however, are that Gregor seems to be longer with a larger head and many more legs than the insect in the picture.

51 Critical Thinking

Speculate

• Explain to students that in the bracketed passage, Grete intends to remove the furniture as an act of kindness.

• **Ask** students to speculate about what will happen once the furniture is removed.

Possible response: The removal of the furniture will further alienate Gregor from his sister and from the human world. Gregor will want to keep his things but will struggle to communicate this message.

"Let me go to Gregor, he is my unfortunate boy! Don't you understand that I have to go to him?" Gregor thought that it might be a good idea after all if his mother did come in, not every day of course, but perhaps once a week; she could still do everything much better than his sister, who, for all her courage, was still only a child and in the final analysis had perhaps taken on such a difficult assignment only out of childish flightiness.

Gregor's desire to see his mother was soon fulfilled. During the day Gregor did not want to show himself at the window, if only out of consideration for his parents, but he couldn't crawl very far on his few square yards of floor space, either; he could hardly put up with just lying still even at night; eating soon stopped giving him the slightest pleasure, so, as a distraction, he adopted the habit of crawling crisscross over the walls and the ceiling. He especially liked hanging from the ceiling; it was completely different from lying on the floor; one could breathe more freely; a faint swinging sensation went through the body; and in the almost happy absent-mindedness which Gregor felt up there, it could happen to his own surprise that he let go and plopped onto the floor. But now, of course, he had much better control of his body than before and did not hurt himself even from such a big drop. His sister immediately noticed the new entertainment Gregor had discovered for himself—after all, he left behind traces of his sticky substance wherever he crawled—and so she got it into her head to make it possible for Gregor to crawl on an altogether wider scale by taking out the furniture which stood in his way—mainly the chest of drawers and the desk. But she was not able to do this by herself; she did not dare ask her father for help; the maid would certainly not have helped her, for although this girl, who was about sixteen, was bravely sticking it out after the previous cook had left, she had asked for the favor of locking herself in the kitchen at all times and of only opening the door on special request. So there was nothing left for his sister to do except to get her mother one day when her father was out. And his mother did come, with exclamations of excited joy, but she grew silent at the door of Gregor's room. First his sister looked to see, of course, that everything in the room was in order; only then did she let her mother come in. Hurrying as fast as he could, Gregor had pulled the sheet down lower still and pleated it more tightly—it really looked just like a sheet accidentally thrown over the couch. This time Gregor also refrained from spying from under the sheet; he renounced seeing

---

Science Connection

50 *What Kind of Insect Is Gregor Samsa?*

Readers of "The Metamorphsis" have long debated what kind of "vermin" Gregor has become. American novelist John Updike writes: "Popular belief has him a cockroach. . . . But, as Vladimir Nabokov, who knew his entomology, pointed out . . . , Gregor is too broad and convex to be a cockroach. . . . Gregor Samsa, awaking, sees 'numerous legs, which were pitifully thin compared to the rest of his bulk.' If 'numerous' is more than six, then he must be a centipede—not an insect at all. From evidence in the story he is brown in color and about as long as the distance between a doorknob and the floor. He has a kind of voice at first . . . which disappears as the story progresses. His jaws don't work as ours do but he has eyelids, nostrils, and a neck. He is, in short, impossible to picture except when the author wants to evoke his appearance, to bump the reader up against some astounding, poignant new aspect of Gregor's embodiment. . . ."

Connect to the Literature

How does the picture of an insect on this page compare with your mental picture of Gregor as an insect?

Enrichment

Kafka's Language

Critic Walter H. Sokel observed that Kafka's characters are almost universally uncertain about their condition. This uncertainty is reflected in Kafka's language, which creates a mood that affects the reader's response: "Kafka's vocabulary is one of inference and conjecture. . . . Kafka prefers 'it seems' to 'it is.' His sentences often consist of two clauses: the first states a fact or a guess; the second qualifies, questions, negates

it. The conjunction 'but' is, therefore, most characteristic of Kafka's thought structure. The frequent use of 'even if' clauses expresses the tendency to cancel expectations and refute inferences."

One example of this structure is the sentence at the top of this page that begins "Gregor thought that it might be a good idea . . ."

his mother for the time being and was simply happy that she had come after all. "Come on, you can't see him," his sister said, evidently leading her mother in by the hand. Now Gregor could hear the two frail women moving the old chest of drawers—heavy for anyone—from its place and his sister insisting on doing the harder part of the job herself, ignoring the warnings of her mother, who was afraid that she would overexert herself. It went on for a long time. After struggling for a good quarter of an hour, his mother said that they had better leave the chest where it was, because, in the first place, it was too heavy, they would not finish before his father came, and with the chest in the middle of the room, Gregor would be completely barricaded; and, in the second place, it was not at all certain they were doing Gregor a favor by removing his furniture. To her the opposite seemed to be the case; the sight of the bare wall was heart-breaking; and why shouldn't Gregor also have the same feeling, since he had been used to his furniture for so long and would feel abandoned in the empty room. "And doesn't it look," his mother concluded very softly—in fact she had been almost whispering the whole time, as if she wanted to avoid letting Gregor, whose exact where-abouts she did not know, hear even the sound of her voice, for she was convinced that he did not understand the words—"and doesn't it look as if by removing his furniture we were showing him that we have given up all hope of his getting better and are leaving him to his own devices without any consideration? I think the best thing would be to try to keep the room exactly the way it was before, so that when Gregor comes back to us again, he'll find everything unchanged and can forget all the more easily what's happened in the meantime."

When he heard his mother's words, Gregor realized that the monot-ony of family life, combined with the fact that not a soul had addressed a word directly to him, must have addled[5] his brain in the course of the past two months, for he could not explain to himself in any other way how in all seriousness he could have been anxious to have his room cleared out. Had he really wanted to have his warm room, comfortably fitted with furniture that had always been in the family, changed into a cave, in which, of course, he would be able to crawl around unham-pered in all directions but at the cost of simultaneously, rapidly, and totally forgetting his human past? Even now he had been on the verge of forgetting, and only his mother's voice, which he had not heard for so long, had shaken him up. Nothing should be removed; everything had to stay; he could not do without the beneficial influence of the furniture on his state of mind; and if the furniture prevented him from carrying on this senseless crawling around, then that was no loss but rather a great advantage.

But his sister unfortunately had a different opinion; she had become accustomed, certainly not entirely without justification, to adopt with her parents the role of the particularly well-qualified expert whenever Gre-gor's affairs were being discussed; and so her mother's advice was now

---

5. **addled** (ad´ ′ld) *v.* muddled or confused.

Literary Analysis
Modernism What does the removal of the furniture suggest to Gregor's mother about the permanence of her son's alienation from the family?

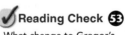 **Reading Check** 53
What change to Gregor's room does Grete decide to make?

The Metamorphosis, Part II ■ 1089

52 Literary Analysis
Modernism

- Have several volunteers take turns reading the bracketed passage aloud.

- Then, **ask** students why Mrs. Samsa is reluctant to let Gregor hear her voice.
  Answer: Mrs. Samsa seems to want to spare Gregor the pain of hearing, and not being able to comprehend, her voice. At the same time, she might be fearful or repulsed by the thought of sharing anything, even the sound of her voice, with this insect.

- **Ask** students the Literary Analysis question: What does the removal of the furniture suggest to Gregor's mother about the permanence of her son's alienation from the family?
  Answer: The removal of the furni-ture suggests to Mrs. Samsa that Gregor will not return to his human form and that his alienation is permanent.

▶ **Monitor Progress Ask:** On the basis of what you know about Modernism, do you think Gregor will return to his human form? Explain.
  Possible response: Gregor will remain an insect. If Gregor were to return to his human form, it would provide a resolution, which is uncharacteristic of Modernist work.

▶ **Reteach** You may wish to give stu-dents who have trouble recognizing elements of Modernism in *The Metamorphosis* the **Literary Analysis** support, p. 11 in *Unit 8 Resources*.

53 Reading Check

Answer: Grete decides to remove the furniture so Gregor can move around more easily.

Differentiated Instruction Solutions for All Learners

Support for Less Proficient Readers
Remind students that point of view is the per-spective from which a story is told. Tell students that if the knowledge of the storyteller is limited to the internal states of one character, then the point of view is *limited*. Ask students the following questions about "The Metamorphosis": Who is telling the story? Is he or she outside the story? Does the narrator know about the feelings and thoughts of all the characters?

Enrichment for Gifted/Talented Students
"The Metamorphosis" is a fantastic tale, yet the reader is willing to accept it without an unusual sense of awe partly because the narrator tells it from the third-person limited point of view. The narrator presents only the thoughts and feelings of Gregor, who remains calm and matter-of-fact throughout. Ask students to consider how readers might respond to this story if it were told from another character's perspective. Challenge them to select a scene and rewrite it from Mr. Samsa's, Mrs. Samsa's, or Grete's perspective.

- Explain to students that in the bracketed passage, the narrator supposes that the removal of the furniture will terrify Gregor. **Ask** students to consider whether this supposition is correct.
Answer: Yes; this supposition is correct. Gregor is already alienated within a strange body, which is very unsettling and frightening. Removing more evidence of his human life will only enhance these feelings of alienation and cause terror.

- **Ask** students the Literary Analysis question: Do you think this explanation for Grete's desire to intensify Gregor's alienation is valid? Explain.
Possible responses: Yes; people like to have a sense of purpose and want to feel needed. No; Grete has shown no sign that she would do anything to hurt, or terrify, Gregor up to this point. It seems unlikely that she would start now.

sufficient reason for her to insist, not only on the removal of the chest of drawers and the desk, which was all she had been planning at first, but also on the removal of all the furniture with the exception of the indispensable couch. Of course it was not only childish defiance and the self-confidence she had recently acquired so unexpectedly and at such a cost that led her to make this demand; she had in fact noticed that Gregor needed plenty of room to crawl around in; and on the other hand, as best as she could tell, he never used the furniture at all. Perhaps, however, the romantic enthusiasm of girls her age, which seeks to indulge itself at every opportunity, played a part, by tempting her to make Gregor's situation even more terrifying in order that she might do even more for him. Into a room in which Gregor ruled the bare walls all alone, no human being besides Grete was ever likely to set foot.

And so she did not let herself be swerved from her decision by her mother, who, besides, from the sheer anxiety of being in Gregor's room, seemed unsure of herself, soon grew silent, and helped her daughter as best she could to get the chest of drawers out of the room. Well, in a pinch Gregor could do without the chest, but the desk had to stay. And hardly had the women left the room with the chest, squeezing against it and groaning, than Gregor stuck his head out from under the couch to see how he could feel his way into the situation as considerately as possible. But unfortunately it had to be his mother who came back first, while in the next room Grete was clasping the chest and rocking it back and forth by herself, without of course budging it from the spot. His mother, however, was not used to the sight of Gregor, he could have made her ill, and so Gregor, frightened, scuttled in reverse to the far end of the couch but could not stop the sheet from shifting a little at the front. That was enough to put his mother on the alert. She stopped, stood still for a moment, and then went back to Grete.

Although Gregor told himself over and over again that nothing special was happening, only a few pieces of furniture were being moved, he soon had to admit that this coming and going of the women, their little calls to each other, the scraping of the furniture along the floor had the effect on him of a great turmoil swelling on all sides, and as much as he tucked in his head and his legs and shrank until his belly touched the floor, he was forced to admit that he would not be able to stand it much longer. They were clearing out his room; depriving him of everything that he loved; they had already carried away the chest of drawers, in which he kept the fretsaw and other tools; were now budging the desk firmly embedded in the floor, the desk he had done his homework on when he was a student at business college, in high school, yes, even in public school—now he really had no more time to examine the good intentions of the two women, whose existence, besides, he had almost forgotten, for they were so exhausted that they were working in silence, and one could hear only the heavy shuffling of their feet.

And so he broke out—the women were just leaning against the desk in the next room to catch their breath for a minute—changed his course four times, he really didn't know what to salvage first, then he saw hang-

Literary Analysis
Modernism Do you think this explanation for Grete's desire to intensify Gregor's alienation is valid? Explain.

Enrichment

Gregor's Picture
In his essay "Gregor Samsa and Modern Spirituality," the critic Martin Greenberg grants that Gregor has been treated badly by his parents but sees his metamorphosis as a fitting punishment for his own shallowness:

He pretends that he will get up and resume his old life. . . . But the human self whose claims he always postponed and continues to postpone, is past being put off, having declared itself negatively by changing him from a human into an insect.

His metamorphosis is a judgment on himself by his defeated humanity. . . .

His mother succinctly describes its deathly aridity as she pleads with the chief clerk: "The only amusement he gets is doing fretwork. For instance, he spent two or three evenings cutting out a little picture frame." That is about what Gregor's "human past" amounts to: a pin-up.

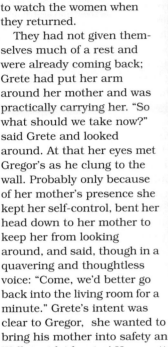

ing conspicuously on the wall, which was otherwise bare already, the picture of the lady all dressed in furs, hurriedly crawled up on it and pressed himself against the glass, which gave a good surface to stick to and soothed his hot belly. At least no one would take away this picture, while Gregor completely covered it up. He turned his head toward the living-room door to watch the women when they returned.

They had not given themselves much of a rest and were already coming back; Grete had put her arm around her mother and was practically carrying her. "So what should we take now?" said Grete and looked around. At that her eyes met Gregor's as he clung to the wall. Probably only because of her mother's presence she kept her self-control, bent her head down to her mother to keep her from looking around, and said, though in a quavering and thoughtless voice: "Come, we'd better go back into the living room for a minute." Grete's intent was clear to Gregor, she wanted to bring his mother into safety and then chase him down from the wall. Well, just let her try! He squatted on his picture and would not give it up. He would rather fly in Grete's face.

But Grete's words had now made her mother really anxious; she stepped to one side, caught sight of the gigantic brown blotch on the flowered wallpaper, and before it really dawned on her that what she saw was Gregor, cried in a hoarse, bawling voice: "Oh, God, Oh, God!"; and as if giving up completely, she fell with outstretched arms across the couch and did not stir. "You, Gregor!" cried his sister with raised fist and piercing eyes. These were the first words she had addressed directly to him since his metamorphosis. She ran into the next room to get some kind of spirits to revive her mother; Gregor wanted to help

Lady in Yellow (Eleanor Reeves), ca. 1905, Susan Watkins, Chrysler Museum of Art, Norfolk, VA

▲ **Critical Viewing** 57
In what ways do you think this portrait is both similar to and different from Gregor's picture of a lady "all dressed in furs"? **[Compare and Contrast]**

✓ **Reading Check** 58
What does Gregor do in reaction to the removal of his furniture?

The Metamorphosis, Part II ■ 1091

55 **Critical Thinking**
Analyze
• Ask a volunteer to read aloud the bracketed passage. Then, read Kafka's earlier description of this picture, which appears in the second paragraph on p. 1066. **Ask** students what this picture might symbolize for Gregor. **Possible response:** The picture symbolizes the personal human relationship Gregor has always wanted and now wants more than ever.

• **Ask:** What might the glass symbolize? Explain. **Possible response:** The glass might symbolize alienation. It separates Gregor from the woman in the picture and represents his inability to achieve human contact.

56 **Humanities**
Lady in Yellow (Eleanor Reeves), by Susan Watkins

Watkins (1875–1913), a California native, trained at the Art Students League in New York City before traveling to Paris to continue her studies. Her skillful portraits and landscape paintings garnered praise in both American and European art circles.

Use the following prompt to stimulate discussion:

Contrast the scene depicted in this painting with Gregor's reality. **Answer:** The woman in the painting looks serene and comfortable. She is seated in a plush setting, surrounded by pillows. Gregor, in contrast, is agitated and uncomfortable in his insect body. His room is being stripped of all its comforts. Unlike the woman shown in this painting, Gregor's reality is fantastical and horrifying.

57 **Critical Viewing**
Answer: Like the woman in Gregor's picture, the lady in the portrait is dressed opulently, but the woman in the portrait does not have fur as a significant part of her clothing.

58 **Reading Check**
Answer: Gregor crawls up the wall and presses himself against a picture that he is determined to keep.

59 too—there was time to rescue the picture—but he was stuck to the glass and had to tear himself loose by force; then he too ran into the next room, as if he could give his sister some sort of advice, as in the old days; but then had to stand behind her doing nothing while she rummaged among various little bottles; moreover, when she turned around she was startled, a bottle fell on the floor and broke, a splinter of glass wounded Gregor in the face, some kind of corrosive medicine flowed around him; now without waiting any longer, Grete grabbed as many little bottles as she could carry and ran with them inside to her mother; she slammed the door behind her with her foot. Now Gregor was cut off from his mother, who was perhaps near death through his fault; he could not dare open the door if he did not want to chase away his sister, who had to stay with his mother; now there was nothing for him to do except wait; and tormented by self-reproaches and worry, he began to crawl, crawled over everything, walls, furniture and ceiling, and finally in desperation, as the whole room was beginning to spin, fell down onto the middle of the big table.

A short time passed; Gregor lay there prostrate; all around, things were quiet, perhaps that was a good sign. Then the doorbell rang. The maid, of course, was locked up in her kitchen and so Grete had to answer the door. His father had come home. "What's happened?" were his first words; Grete's appearance must have told him everything. Grete answered in a muffled voice, her face was obviously pressed against her father's chest; "Mother fainted, but she's better now. Gregor's broken out." "I knew it," his father said. "I kept telling you, but you women don't want to listen." It was clear to Gregor that his father had put the worst interpretation on Grete's all-too-brief announcement and assumed that Gregor was guilty of some outrage. Therefore Gregor now had to try to calm his father down, since he had neither the time nor the ability to enlighten him. And so he fled to the door of his room and pressed himself against it for his father to see, as soon as he came into the foyer, that Gregor had the best intentions of returning to his room immediately and that it was not necessary to drive him back; if only the door were opened for him, he would disappear at once.

But his father was in no mood to notice such subtleties; "Ah!" he cried as he entered, in a tone that sounded as if he were at once furious and glad. Gregor turned his head away from the door and lifted it toward his father. He had not really imagined his father looking like this, as he stood in front of him now; admittedly Gregor had been too absorbed recently in his newfangled crawling to bother as much as before about events in the rest of the house and should really have been prepared to find some changes. And yet, and yet—was this still his father? Was this the same man who in the old days used to lie wearily buried in bed when Gregor left on a business trip; who greeted him **60** on his return in the evening, sitting in his bathrobe in the armchair, who actually had difficulty getting to his feet but as a sign of joy only lifted up his arms; and who, on the rare occasions when the whole family went out for a walk, on a few Sundays in June and on the major hol-

1092 ■ *The Modern World*

Literary Analysis
Modernism How does this scene capture key Modernist themes, especially those of helplessness and alienation?

Literary Analysis
Modernism and Literature of the Fantastic In what ways does Gregor's surprise about his father's changed appearance reflect the fantastic nature of this story?

idays, used to shuffle along with great effort between Gregor and his mother, who were slow walkers themselves, always a little more slowly than they, wrapped in his old overcoat, always carefully planting down his crutch-handled cane, and, when he wanted to say something, nearly always stood still and assembled his escort around him? Now, however, he was holding himself very erect, dressed in a tight-fitting blue uniform with gold buttons, the kind worn by messengers at banking concerns; above the high stiff collar of the jacket his heavy chin protruded; under his bushy eyebrows his black eyes darted bright, piercing glances; his usually rumpled white hair was combed flat, with a scrupulously exact, gleaming part. He threw his cap—which was adorned with a gold monogram, probably that of a bank—in an arc across the entire room onto the couch, and with the tails of his long uniform jacket slapped back, his hands in his pants pockets, went for Gregor with a sullen look on his face. He probably did not know himself what he had in mind; still he lifted his feet unusually high off the floor, and Gregor staggered at the gigantic size of the soles of his boots. But he did not linger over this, he had known right from the first day of his new life that his father considered only the strictest treatment called for in dealing with him. And so he ran ahead of his father, stopped when his father stood still, and scooted ahead again when his father made even the slightest movement. In this way they made more than one tour of the room, without anything decisive happening; in fact the whole movement did not even have the appearance of a chase because of its slow tempo. So Gregor kept to the floor for the time being, especially since he was afraid that his father might interpret a flight onto the walls or the ceiling as a piece of particular nastiness. Of course Gregor had to admit that he would not be able to keep up even this running for long, for whenever his father took one step, Gregor had to execute countless movements. He was already beginning to feel winded, just as in the old days he had not had very reliable lungs. As he now staggered around, hardly keeping his eyes open in order to gather all his strength for the running; in his obtuseness[6] not thinking of any escape other than by running; and having almost forgotten that the walls were at his disposal, though here of course they were blocked up with elaborately carved furniture full of notches and points—at that moment a lightly flung object hit the floor right near him and rolled in front of him. It was an apple; a second one came flying right after it; Gregor stopped dead with fear; further running was useless, for his father was determined to bombard him. He had filled his pockets from the fruit bowl on the buffet and was now pitching one apple after another, for the time being without taking good aim. These little red apples rolled around on the floor as if electrified, clicking into each other. One apple, thrown weakly, grazed Gregor's back and slid off harmlessly. But the very next one that came flying after it literally forced its way into Gregor's back;

---

6. **obtuseness** (äb toʊs′ nəs) *n.* slowness to understand or perceive.

Reading Strategy
Applying the Author's Biography How might Kafka have drawn on personal experience to describe this encounter between Gregor and his father?

 **Reading Check** 62
What objects does Mr. Samsa throw at Gregor?

The Metamorphosis, Part II ■ 1093

61 Reading Strategy
Applying the Author's Biography

• Explain to students that Franz Kafka was thin and short. His father and the other men in his family were generally tall, strong men with loud voices. **Ask** students how Kafka's attitude toward his father's physical presence is reflected in this passage.
Answer: Kafka's intimidation by his father's presence might be reflected in the description of Gregor "stagger[ing] at the gigantic size of the soles of [his father's] boots," and the description of Gregor's need to "gather all his strength for the running."

• **Ask** students the Reading Strategy question: How might Kafka have drawn on personal experience to describe this encounter between Gregor and his father?
Answer: As a child, Kafka might have been frightened by his father, especially if Kafka believed he had done something wrong. We see this anxiety as Gregor attempts to escape his father's anger.

62 Reading Check
Answer: Mr. Samsa throws apples at Gregor.

1. **Possible responses:** Some students will feel sympathy for Gregor because he has become isolated through no fault of his own. He longs for human contact, but it is forever out of his reach. Others will feel disgust for Gregor because he is a filthy and grotesquely huge insect.

2. (a) Gregor learns that his family has money to live on. (b) Gregor is relieved that the family is not destitute but realizes that the day that he could have left his job would have been much closer. (c) The news shows that Gregor was already alienated from his family: The family did not confide in Gregor but kept information secret that would have lessened his burden.

3. (a) Grete hurries straight to the window, opens it, and stands breathing in the fresh air. (b) The room must have a bad odor because of Gregor. (c) Gregor is becoming more insectlike and repulsive; he is intolerable even to his own sister.

4. (a) Gregor is determined to keep the magazine picture of the woman in the fur hat and boa. (b) **Possible response:** The picture might symbolize a relationship with a woman, Gregor's human life, or humanity in general.

5. (a) Grete did little but dress in pretty clothes, sleep late, help around the apartment, enjoy a few amusements, and play her violin. (b) **Possible response:** Grete has become more responsible while caring for Gregor. She has shown courage in entering his room every day. She has shown good judgment and empathy in providing what he needs. (c) **Possible response:** These changes are positive: They demonstrate strength of character and Grete's willingness to care for her isolated and helpless brother.

Go Online For additional information
Author Link about Franz Kafka, have students type in the Web Code, then select *K* from the alphabet, and then select Franz Kafka.

Gregor tried to drag himself away, as if the startling, unbelievable pain might disappear with a change of place; but he felt nailed to the spot and stretched out his body in a complete confusion of all his senses. With his last glance he saw the door of his room burst open, as his mother rushed out ahead of his screaming sister, in her chemise, for his sister had partly undressed her while she was unconscious in order to let her breathe more freely; saw his mother run up to his father and on the way her unfastened petticoats slide to the floor one by one; and saw as, stumbling over the skirts, she forced herself onto his father, and embracing him, in complete union with him—but now Gregor's sight went dim—her hands clasping his father's neck, begged for Gregor's life.

Critical Reading

1. **Respond:** Do you primarily feel sympathy or disgust for Gregor? Explain your answer.

2. **(a) Recall:** What surprising news about the family's finances does Gregor learn? **(b) Interpret:** With what mixed feelings does Gregor react to this news? **(c) Analyze:** What does this news suggest about Gregor's alienation from his family even before his metamorphosis?

3. **(a) Interpret:** Each time Grete enters Gregor's room, how does she react? **(b) Draw Conclusions:** What does her reaction suggest about the condition and smell of the room? **(c) Analyze:** In what ways does this situation emphasize Gregor's isolation from humanity?

4. **(a) Recall:** Which item in his room is Gregor determined to keep? **(b) Interpret:** What emotions, relationships, or desires might this item symbolize to him? Explain.

5. **(a) Generalize:** Why might Grete's parents have seen her as "useless" prior to Gregor's transformation? **(b) Compare and Contrast:** In what ways has Grete changed as a result of Gregor's transformation? **(c) Evaluate:** Are these changes positive or negative? Explain.

Go Online
Author Link
For: More about Franz Kafka
Visit: www.PHSchool.com
Web Code: ete-9801

Enrichment

The Apple

The apple is an important symbol in Western literature. The "forbidden fruit" in the Garden of Eden is traditionally depicted as an apple. When Adam and Eve disobediently eat the fruit, they gain wisdom, but they suffer guilt and are driven from the Garden. Writers often use the apple to symbolize the attainment of wisdom and a subsequent fall from grace. In "The Metamorphosis," the apple functions similarly.

The apple that lodges in Gregor's exoskeleton represents his knowledge that his role in the family has changed. He no longer occupies the role of breadwinner, nor does the family consider him a son and brother.

Now his only role is that of pest. Gregor carries this knowledge—figuratively and literally—with him to his death.

Review and Anticipate

By the end of Part II, Gregor's situation has reached a crisis. His enraged father has attacked Gregor, causing a severe injury. His furious sister has tried both to care for Gregor and to protect her parents. Although the sight of him sickens her, Gregor's mother now pleads for his life. Do you think Gregor can survive in this environment? Do you think the family can tolerate the strain? If not, what does their future hold? Read Part III, in which the story concludes, to find out.

Part III ⑥³

Gregor's serious wound, from which he suffered for over a month—the apple remained imbedded in his flesh as a visible souvenir since no one dared to remove it—seemed to have reminded even his father that Gregor was a member of the family, in spite of his present pathetic and repulsive shape, who could not be treated as an enemy; that, on the contrary, it was the commandment of family duty to swallow their disgust and endure him, endure him and nothing more.

And now, although Gregor had lost some of his mobility probably for good because of his wound, and although for the time being he needed long, long minutes to get across his room, like an old war veteran—crawling above ground was out of the question—for this deterioration of his situation he was granted compensation which in his view was entirely satisfactory: every day around dusk the living-room door—which he was in the habit of watching closely for an hour or two beforehand—was opened, so that, lying in the darkness of his room, invisible from the living room, he could see the whole family sitting at the table under the lamp and could listen to their conversation, as it were with general permission; and so it was completely different from before.

Of course these were no longer the animated conversations of the old days, which Gregor used to remember with a certain nostalgia in small hotel rooms when he'd had to throw himself wearily into the damp bedding. Now things were mostly very quiet. Soon after supper his father would fall asleep in his armchair; his mother and sister would caution each other to be quiet; his mother, bent low under the light, sewed delicate lingerie for a clothing store; his sister, who had taken a job as a salesgirl, was learning shorthand and French in the evenings in order to attain a better position some time in the future. Sometimes his father woke up, and as if he had absolutely no idea that he had been asleep, said to his mother, "Look how long you're sewing again today!" and went right back to sleep, while mother and sister smiled wearily at each other.

Literary Analysis
Modernism Would you consider this after-supper scene a slice of real modern life? Why or why not?

✔ Reading Check ⑥⁵
What does the family now allow Gregor to do every day around dusk?

The Metamorphosis, Part III ■ 1095

- Ask a volunteer to read aloud the bracketed passage. **Ask:** Could a modern American family face similar worries as those of the Samsas?
Possible response: Yes; a modern American family could face the same financial concerns as those of the Samsa family. The Samsa family's concern about moving a giant bug out of the apartment without detection is not one any other family is likely to experience, however.

- **Ask** students the Literary Analysis question: In what ways does this discussion of the family's struggles mix reality and fantasy?
Answer: The discussion involves ordinary things that might happen in modern life, except for the issue of how to relocate Gregor. This topic acts as a reminder of Gregor's fantastic transformation from human to insect.

With a kind of perverse obstinacy his father refused to take off his official uniform even in the house; and while his robe hung uselessly on the clothes hook, his father dozed, completely dressed, in his chair, as if he were always ready for duty and were waiting even here for the voice of his superior. As a result his uniform, which had not been new to start with, began to get dirty in spite of all the mother's and sister's care, and Gregor would often stare all evening long at this garment, covered with stains and gleaming with its constantly polished gold buttons, in which the old man slept most uncomfortably and yet peacefully.

As soon as the clock struck ten, his mother tried to awaken his father with soft encouraging words and then persuade him to go to bed, for this was no place to sleep properly, and his father badly needed his sleep, since he had to be at work at six o'clock. But with the obstinacy that had possessed him ever since he had become a messenger, he always insisted on staying at the table a little longer, although he invariably fell asleep and then could be persuaded only with the greatest effort to exchange his armchair for bed. However much mother and sister might pounce on him with little admonitions,[7] he would slowly shake his head for a quarter of an hour at a time, keeping his eyes closed, and would not get up. Gregor's mother plucked him by the sleeves, whispered blandishments into his ear, his sister dropped her homework in order to help her mother, but all this was of no use. He only sank deeper into his armchair. Not until the women lifted him up under his arms did he open his eyes, look alternately at mother and sister, and usually say, "What a life. So this is the peace of my old age." And leaning on the two women, he would get up laboriously, as if he were the greatest weight on himself, and let the women lead him to the door, where, shrugging them off, he would proceed independently, while Gregor's mother threw down her sewing and his sister her pen as quickly as possible so as to run after his father and be of further assistance.

 Who in this overworked and exhausted family had time to worry about Gregor any more than was absolutely necessary? The household was stinted more and more; now the maid was let go after all; a gigantic bony cleaning woman with white hair fluttering about her head came mornings and evenings to do the heaviest work; his mother took care of everything else, along with all her sewing. It even happened that various pieces of family jewelry, which in the old days his mother and sister had been overjoyed to wear at parties and celebrations, were sold, as Gregor found out one evening from the general discussion of the prices they had fetched. But the biggest complaint was always that they could not give up the apartment, which was much too big for their present needs, since no one could figure out how Gregor was supposed to be moved. But Gregor understood easily that it was not only consideration for him which prevented their moving, for he could easily have been transported in a suitable crate with a few air holes; what mainly

---

7. **admonitions** (ad´ mə nish´ ənz) *n.* mild rebukes; reprimands.

Literary Analysis
Modernism and Literature of the Fantastic
In what ways does this discussion of the family's struggles mix reality and fantasy?

prevented the family from moving was their complete hopelessness and the thought that they had been struck by a misfortune as none of their relatives and acquaintances had ever been hit. What the world demands of poor people they did to the utmost of their ability; his father brought breakfast for the minor officials at the bank, his mother sacrificed herself to the underwear of strangers, his sister ran back and forth behind the counter at the request of the customers; but for anything more than this they did not have the strength. And the wound in Gregor's back began to hurt anew when mother and sister, after getting his father to bed, now came back, dropped their work, pulled their chairs close to each other and sat cheek to cheek; when his mother, pointing to Gregor's room, said, "Close that door, Grete"; and when Gregor was back in darkness, while in the other room the women mingled their tears or stared dry-eyed at the table.

Gregor spent the days and nights almost entirely without sleep. Sometimes he thought that the next time the door opened he would take charge of the family's affairs again, just as he had done in the old days; after this long while there again appeared in his thoughts the boss and the manager, the salesmen and the trainees, the handyman who was so dense, two or three friends from other firms, a chambermaid in a provincial hotel—a happy fleeting memory—a cashier in a millinery store,[8] whom he had courted earnestly but too slowly—they all appeared, intermingled with strangers or people he had already forgotten; but instead of helping him and his family, they were all inaccessible, and he was glad when they faded away. At other times he was in no mood to worry about his family, he was completely filled with rage at his miserable treatment, and although he could not imagine anything that would pique his appetite, he still made plans for getting into the pantry to take what was coming to him, even if he wasn't hungry. No longer considering what she could do to give Gregor a special treat, his sister, before running to business every morning and afternoon, hurriedly shoved any old food into Gregor's room with her foot; and in the evening, regardless of whether the food had only been toyed with or—the most usual case—had been left completely untouched, she swept it out with a swish of the broom. The cleaning up of Gregor's room, which she now always did in the evenings, could not be done more hastily. Streaks of dirt ran along the walls, fluffs of dust and filth lay here and there on the floor. At first, whenever his sister came in, Gregor would place himself in those corners which were particularly offending, meaning by his position in a sense to reproach her. But he could probably have stayed there for weeks without his sister's showing any improvement; she must have seen the dirt as clearly as he did, but she had just decided to leave it. At the same time she made sure—with an irritableness that was completely new to her and which had in fact infected the whole family—that the cleaning of Gregor's room remain her province. One time his mother had submitted Gregor's room to a major housecleaning, which she managed

---

8. **millinery** (mil´ ə ner´ ē) **store** one that sells women's hats.

Literary Analysis
Modernism How do the conditions in which Gregor is now living suggest that his alienation from his family and his former life has reached a new low?

 Reading Check 68
For what reason does the family say they cannot move from their current apartment?

The Metamorphosis, Part III ■ 1097

67 Literary Analysis
Modernism

- Read the first sentence of the bracketed passage aloud. **Ask** students to discuss how Gregor's rage is a symptom of his alienation. **Answer:** Gregor's rage is uncharacteristic and thus demonstrates how alienated from his old self Gregor has become.

- Then, **ask** students the Literary Analysis question: How do the conditions in which Gregor is now living suggest that his alienation from his family and his former life has reached a new low? **Answer:** Gregor's sister no longer gives him the attention that she gave him in the past. Gregor has been abandoned, and, as a result, he has ceased at times to worry about his family.

68 Reading Check

Answer: The family says they do not know how to move Gregor.

Differentiated Instruction   Solutions for All Learners

Strategy for Less Proficient Readers
Explain to students that on this page, Gregor is described as alternately angry and sad. Have students identify the occasions when he is angry and when he is sad. Discuss what Gregor is thinking about and why he is experiencing these intense feelings. Make sure that students understand that these feelings are another sign of Gregor's transformation from his earlier passivity about his career and his responsibilities to his family.

Strategy for Advanced Readers
Have students discuss the dramatic fluctuations in Gregor's thoughts that occur on this page. Then, have students discuss the significance of the images that come to Gregor's mind when he imagines that he is about to take charge of the family's affairs again. Ask students to consider why Gregor is glad when these images fade away.

Analyze

- Have students describe what is happening in the bracketed passage. Then, **ask:** What motivated Gregor's mother to clean Gregor's room when it had been Grete's job?
  Answer: Mrs. Samsa saw the filthy conditions in which Gregor was living and could not allow him to live that way. Even though he has been transformed into something so alien, he is still her son.

- **Ask** students why Grete breaks into tears.
  Answer: Grete has endured the difficult task of taking care of Gregor all this time. When her mother cleans the room, she probably regards it as a criticism. She feels sorry for herself and is overwhelmed.

- **Ask** students why the family gets into such an uproar over Mrs. Samsa's good deed.
  Answer: The stress of the situation has pushed the family to its limits. The family's emotions are brought to the surface with little provocation.

70 Critical Viewing

Answer: The dancer's "antennae" and her buglike facemask emphasize Gregor's physical transformation. The dancer's posture emphasizes the freedom Gregor experienced upon first using his insect legs.

only after employing a couple of pails of water— all this dampness, of course, irritated Gregor too and he lay prostrate, sour and immobile, on the couch— but his mother's punishment was not long in coming. For hardly had his sister noticed the difference in Gregor's room that evening than, deeply insulted, she ran into the living room and, in spite of her mother's imploringly uplifted hands, burst out in a fit of crying, which his parents—his father had naturally been startled out of his armchair—at first watched in helpless amazement; until they too got going; turning to the right, his father blamed his mother for not letting his sister clean Gregor's room; but turning to the left, he screamed at his sister that she would never again be allowed to clean Gregor's room; while his mother tried to drag his father, who was out of his mind with excitement, into the bedroom, his sister, shaken with sobs, hammered the table with her small fists; and Gregor hissed loudly with rage because it did not occur to any of them to close the door and spare him such a scene and a row.

But even if his sister, exhausted from her work at the store, had gotten fed up with taking care of Gregor as she used to, it was not necessary at all for his mother to take her place and still Gregor did not have to be neglected. For now the cleaning woman was there. This old widow, who thanks to her strong bony frame had probably survived the worst in a long life, was not really repelled by Gregor. Without being in the least inquisitive, she had once accidentally opened the door of Gregor's room, and at the sight of Gregor—who, completely taken by surprise, began to race back and forth although no one was chasing him—she had remained standing, with her hands folded on her stomach, marveling. From that time on she never failed to open the door a crack every morning and every evening and peek in hurriedly at Gregor. In the beginning she also used to call him over to her with words she probably considered friendly, like, "Come over here for a minute, you old dung beetle!" or "Look at that old dung beetle!" To forms of address like these Gregor would not respond but remained immobile where he was, as if the door had not been opened. If only they had given this cleaning woman orders to clean up his room every day, instead of letting her disturb him uselessly whenever the mood took her. Once, early in the morning—heavy rain, perhaps already a sign of approaching spring,

1098 ■ *The Modern World*

▲ **Critical Viewing 70**
Which aspects of Gregor's transformation does this ballet adaptation emphasize? Explain.
[Interpret]

Enrichment

Irony
Irony is a contrast between what is stated and what is meant or between what is expected to happen and what actually happens. In *irony of situation,* an event occurs that contradicts the expectations of the characters, of the reader, or of the audience. Point out to students that Gregor's family has often mistakenly viewed his actions as menacing. When Gregor does try to frighten the cleaning woman, he fails miserably, creating a humorous and tragic irony of situation.

was beating on the window panes—Gregor was so exasperated when the cleaning woman started in again with her phrases that he turned on her, of course slowly and decrepitly, as if to attack. But the cleaning woman, instead of getting frightened, simply lifted up high a chair near the door, and as she stood there with her mouth wide open, her intention was clearly to shut her mouth only when the chair in her hand came crashing down on Gregor's back. "So, is that all there is?" she asked when Gregor turned around again, and she quietly put the chair back in the corner.

Gregor now hardly ate anything anymore. Only when he accidentally passed the food laid out for him would he take a bite into his mouth just for fun, hold it in for hours, and then mostly spit it out again. At first he thought that his grief at the state of his room kept him off food, but it was the very changes in his room to which he quickly became adjusted. His family had gotten into the habit of putting in this room things for which they could not find any other place, and now there were plenty of these, since one of the rooms in the apartment had been rented to three boarders. These serious gentlemen—all three had long beards, as Gregor was able to register once through a crack in the door—were obsessed with neatness, not only in their room, but since they had, after all, moved in here, throughout the entire household and especially in the kitchen. They could not stand useless, let alone dirty junk. Besides, they had brought along most of their own household goods. For this reason many things had become superfluous, and though they certainly weren't salable, on the other hand they could not just be thrown out. All these things migrated into Gregor's room. Likewise the ash can and the garbage can from the kitchen. Whatever was not being used at the moment was just flung into Gregor's room by the cleaning woman, who was always in a big hurry; fortunately Gregor generally saw only the object involved and the hand that held it. Maybe the cleaning woman intended to reclaim the things as soon as she had a chance or else to throw out everything together in one fell swoop, but in fact they would have remained lying wherever they had been thrown in the first place if Gregor had not squeezed through the junk and set it in motion, at first from necessity, because otherwise there would have been no room to crawl in, but later with growing pleasure, although after such excursions, tired to death and sad, he did not budge again for hours.

Since the roomers sometimes also had their supper at home in the common living room, the living-room door remained closed on certain evenings, but Gregor found it very easy to give up the open door, for on many evenings when it was opened he had not taken advantage of it, but instead, without the family's noticing, had lain in the darkest corner of his room. But once the cleaning woman had left the living-room door slightly open, and it also remained opened a little when the roomers came in in the evening and the lamp was lit. They sat down at the head of the table where in the old days his father, his mother, and Gregor had eaten, unfolded their napkins, and picked up their knives

Literary Analysis
Modernism Which details in this discussion of the state of his room suggest that Gregor has become useless or disposable? Explain.

 Reading Check ⑦²
To whom has a room in the Samsa apartment been rented?

The Metamorphosis, Part III ■ 1099

Differentiated Instruction Solutions for All Learners

Strategy for Special Needs Students
Call students' attention to the ways Grete's behavior toward Gregor has changed in the course of the story. Students should cite specific examples from the text concerning how Grete feeds, cares for, and protects Gregor. Help students create a comparison and contrast chart to record their observations.

Support for English Learners
The term *boarder* may present a challenge for students because of the multiple meanings of the word *board*. Tell students that the word *board* can mean "daily meals supplied in exchange for pay." Ask students to work in pairs to find the definition for the word *boarder* and to discuss how it relates to the definition for *board* provided above. Then, have each student pair write two sentences using the word *boarder*.

⑦¹ Literary Analysis
Modernism

• Ask students to read the bracketed passage. Then, ask students to discuss the purpose and connotations of a "junk room."

• **Ask** students the Literary Analysis question: Which details in this discussion of the state of his room suggest that Gregor has become useless or disposable? Explain.
Answer: Gregor's family and the cleaning woman have begun placing junk and even trashcans in his room. These details suggest that the room is a place for useless, disposable things and imply that Gregor, too, is useless.

• Call students' attention to the line that describes Gregor's "growing pleasure" with crawling through the trash. **Ask** students how Gregor's response reveals his passage into another stage of alienation from human society.
Answer: Insects are often found crawling through trash. Gregor's adoption and enjoyment of this habit indicates that his metamorphosis is nearly complete.

▶ **Monitor Progress Ask** students how the presence of the three roomers emphasizes Gregor's alienation from society.
Answer: The roomers come from the outside world and want everything very clean and neat. Gregor is confined to his filthy room and has even begun to enjoy roaming through the accumulating trash, which exists because of the roomers.

▶ **Reteach** To assist students who need more help understanding elements of Modernism, review the Literary Analysis instruction on p. 1065.

⑦² Reading Check
Answer: A room has been rented to three gentlemen with long beards.

- Tell students that many Modernists depict the individual as powerless. Read aloud the bracketed passage, and call students' attention to the roomers' behavior toward the Samsa family and remind them of the way Gregor's manager treated Gregor when he came into the home.
Ask students how these parallel incidents reflect a Modernist view of the individual.
Answer: Both examples of behavior show how the outside world looks down on the individual and assumes the right to control and belittle a person who lacks power.

- **Ask** students the Literary Analysis question: In what ways does the family's behavior toward the boarders reveal changes in their sense of identity?
Answer: The family is no longer independent; they have become subservient to these three roomers, who are representatives of the outside world.

and forks. At once his mother appeared in the doorway with a platter of meat, and just behind her came his sister with a platter piled high with potatoes. A thick vapor steamed up from the food. The roomers bent over the platters set in front of them as if to examine them before eating, and in fact the one who sat in the middle, and who seemed to be regarded by the other two as an authority, cut into a piece of meat while it was still on the platter, evidently to find out whether it was tender enough or whether it should perhaps be sent back to the kitchen. He was satisfied, and mother and sister, who had been watching anxiously, sighed with relief and began to smile.

The family itself ate in the kitchen. Nevertheless, before going into the kitchen, his father came into this room and, bowing once, cap in hand, made a turn around the table. The roomers rose as one man and mumbled something into their beards. When they were alone again, they ate in almost complete silence. It seemed strange to Gregor that among all the different noises of eating he kept picking up the sound of their chewing teeth, as if this were a sign to Gregor that you needed teeth to eat with and that even with the best make of toothless jaws you couldn't do a thing. "I'm hungry enough," Gregor said to himself, full of grief, "but not for these things. Look how these roomers are gorging themselves, and I'm dying!"

On this same evening—Gregor could not remember having heard the violin during the whole time—the sound of violin playing came from the kitchen. The roomers had already finished their evening meal, the one in the middle had taken out a newspaper, given each of the two others a page, and now, leaning back, they read and smoked. When the violin began to play, they became attentive, got up, and went on tiptoe to the door leading to the foyer, where they stood in a huddle. They must have been heard in the kitchen, for his father called, "Perhaps the playing bothers you, gentlemen? It can be stopped right away." "On the contrary," said the middle roomer. "Wouldn't the young lady like to come in to us and play in here where it's much roomier and more comfortable?" "Oh, certainly," called Gregor's father, as if he were the violinist. The boarders went back into the room and waited. Soon Gregor's father came in with the music stand, his mother with the sheet music, and his sister with the violin. Calmly his sister got everything ready for playing; his parents—who had never rented out rooms before and therefore behaved toward the roomers with excessive politeness—did not even dare sit down on their own chairs; his father leaned against the door, his right hand inserted between two buttons of his uniform coat, which he kept closed; but his mother was offered a chair by one of the roomers, and since she left the chair where the roomer just happened to put it, she sat in a corner to one side.

His sister began to play. Father and mother, from either side, attentively followed the movements of her hands. Attracted by the playing, Gregor had dared to come out a little further and already had his head in the living room. It hardly surprised him that lately he was showing so little consideration for the others; once such consideration had been

Literary Analysis
Modernism In what ways does the family's behavior toward the boarders reveal changes in their sense of identity?

Enrichment

Kafka's Response to Music
Many people feel that the climax of "The Metamorphosis" is the scene in which Gregor is drawn out of his room by his sister's violin playing. Given the importance of this scene, it seems logical to conclude that Kafka himself had a deep love for music. Yet, in reality, Kafka failed in his attempts to learn to play the violin and the piano as a young man, and he felt unresponsive to music for the rest of his life. In his diary he wrote, "The essence of my unmusicalness consists in my inability to enjoy music connectedly; it only now and then has an effect on me, and how seldom it is a musical one. The natural effect of music on me is to circumscribe me with a wall, and its only constant influence on me is that, confined in this way, I am different from what I am when free. . . . There is, among the public, no such reverence for literature as there is for music."

his greatest pride. And yet he would never have had better reason to keep hidden; for now, because of the dust which lay all over his room and blew around at the slightest movement, he too was completely covered with dust; he dragged around with him on his back and along his sides fluff and hairs and scraps of food; his indifference to everything was much too deep for him to have gotten on his back and scrubbed himself clean against the carpet, as once he had done several times a day. And in spite of his state, he was not ashamed to inch out a little farther on the immaculate living-room floor.

Admittedly no one paid any attention to him. The family was completely absorbed by the violin-playing; the roomers, on the other hand, who at first had stationed themselves, hands in pockets, much too close behind his sister's music stand, so that they could all have followed the score, which certainly must have upset his sister, soon withdrew to the window, talking to each other in an undertone, their heads lowered, where they remained, anxiously watched by his father. It now seemed only too obvious that they were disappointed in their expectation of hearing beautiful or entertaining violin-playing, had had enough of the whole performance, and continued to let their peace be disturbed only out of politeness. Especially the way they all blew the cigar smoke out of their nose and mouth toward the ceiling suggested great nervousness. And yet his sister was playing so beautifully. Her face was inclined to one side, sadly and prob-ingly her eyes followed the lines of music. Gregor crawled forward a little farther, holding his head close to the floor, so that it might be possible to catch her eye. Was he an animal, that music could move him so? He felt as if the way to the unknown nourishment he longed for were coming to light. He was determined to force himself on until he reached his sister, to pluck at her skirt, and to let her know in this way that she should bring her violin into his room, for no one here appreciated her playing the way he would appreciate it. He would never again let her out of his room—at least not for as long as he lived; for once, his nightmarish looks would be of use to him; he would be at all the doors of his room at the same time and hiss and spit at the aggressors; his sister, however, should not be forced to stay with him, but would do so of her own free will; she should sit next to him on the couch, bending her ear down to him, and then he would confide to her that he had had the firm intention of sending her to the Conservatory, and that, if the catastrophe had not intervened, he would have announced this to everyone last Christmas—certainly Christmas had come and gone?—without taking notice of any objections. After this declaration his sister would burst into tears of emotion, and Gregor would raise himself up to her shoulder and kiss her on the neck which, ever since she started going out to work, she kept bare, without a ribbon or collar.

Themes in World Masterpieces

74 Magical Realism

Franz Kafka tells Gregor Samsa's tale by mixing reality and fantasy. Many critics consider Kafka's approach a forerunner of **magical realism,** a literary movement that has gained popularity in the past few decades. Magical realism is strong in Latin America, where its best-known authors include Jorge Luis Borges, Julio Cortázar, Gabriel García Márquez, and Isabel Allende.

Magical realists create worlds that are based in reality and describe everyday settings. However, reality is often punctuated by "magical" elements—fantastic characters, events, or both. For example, in the García Márquez story "A Very Old Man With Enormous Wings," a couple takes captive an elderly, shabby-looking angel. Such magical elements can help readers gain deeper, more vivid insights into the nature of the world and human relationships.

Connect to the Literature

List three "magical" elements in Gregor's metamorphosis.

Literary Analysis

Modernism The music appears to move Gregor to reach out for some meaning to his situation. Do you think he will find that meaning? Explain.

✔ Reading Check 76

What does Gregor's sister do to entertain the boarders?

The Metamorphosis, Part III ■ 1101

74 Themes in World Literature

Magical Realism For Gabriel García Márquez, the work of Franz Kafka was the key that opened the door to his own writing. It was the strange combination of fantastic and realistic details in "The Metamorphosis" that most impressed García Márquez: "The first line almost knocked me off the bed. . . . When I read the line I thought to myself that I didn't know anyone was allowed to write things like that. If I had known, I would have started writing a long time ago. So I immediately started writing short stories."

Connect to the Literature Point out to students that here again is an example of the influence of literature across cultures and its capacity to continue to influence writers over many years. Fine literature does not become outdated. Ask students to discuss the magical elements in Gregor's metamorphosis.

Possible responses: He is an insect now but continues to think and feel like a human, while at the same time manifesting insectlike habits such as crawling in the trash in his room. He responds to music. He cannot speak but can understand. He now likes to eat rotten vegetables and old cheese.

75 Literary Analysis

Modernism

- Read the bracketed passage aloud.

- **Ask** students the Literary Analysis question: The music appears to move Gregor to reach out for some meaning to his situation. Do you think that he will find that meaning? Explain.

  Possible response: No, because in Gregor's imagination he sees himself talking to Grete, keeping her with him, and kissing her on the neck. Gregor can't talk, and Grete would never submit to such close contact with him now.

76 Reading Check

Answer: Grete plays her violin for the boarders.

Differentiated Instruction   Solutions for All Learners

Support for Less Proficient Readers

On the board, write the words *score, performance,* and *Conservatory.* Explain to students that these words, which appear above, refer to music. Guide students in using context clues to develop definitions for these terms. Then, have students write sentences using these words.

Support for English Learners

Work with students to use simpler language to paraphrase difficult passages. Use this sentence as a model: "He felt as if the way to the unknown nourishment he longed for were coming to light." Explain to students that in this sentence the phrase "coming to light" is a figure of speech meaning "being revealed."

Strategy for Advanced Readers

Some readers view "The Metamorphosis" as writing in reverse. The story begins with the climax. After this point everything can be considered falling action. Others claim that the climax occurs when Grete plays the violin. Have students offer their interpretations.

Modernism

- After students read the bracketed passage independently, point out that two of the roomers look to the third one for leadership and initiative. Have students discuss why some people need or rely on authorities and trendsetters to tell them what to think and what to do.

- **Ask** students the Literary Analysis question: How do the boarders' words and actions create new uncertainty for the Samsas?
  Answer: The Samsas were relying on the boarders' rent to help the family financially. Now, the rent will not be paid, and the Samsas may face a lawsuit, which will cost them money as well. The Samsas must be wondering what they will do now.

⓻ Critical Thinking

Analyze

- Have a volunteer read aloud the bracketed passage.

- Call students' attention to the words *groping, staggered,* and *collapsed,* and list the words on the board.

- Remind students that a connotation is an association that a word calls to mind in addition to its dictionary meanings. Words can have positive and negative connotations. **Ask:** Do the listed words have positive or negative connotations?
  Answer: The listed words have negative connotations.

- **Ask:** How does Kafka's word choice in this passage lend to the characterization of Mr. Samsa?
  Possible response: The words *groping, staggered,* and *collapsed*—with their negative connotations—reinforce the physical and mental toll Gregor's transformation has taken on Mr. Samsa. These words suggest physical struggle, one which has left Mr. Samsa drained.

"Mr. Samsa!" the middle roomer called to Gregor's father and without wasting another word pointed his index finger at Gregor, who was slowly moving forward. The violin stopped, the middle roomer smiled first at his friends, shaking his head, and then looked at Gregor again. Rather than driving Gregor out, his father seemed to consider it more urgent to start by soothing the roomers although they were not at all upset, and Gregor seemed to be entertaining them more than the violin-playing. He rushed over to them and tried with outstretched arms to drive them into their room and at the same time with his body to block their view of Gregor. Now they actually did get a little angry—it was not clear whether because of his father's behavior or because of their dawning realization of having had without knowing it such a next door neighbor as Gregor. They demanded explanations from his father; in their turn they raised their arms, plucked excitedly at their beards, and, dragging their feet, backed off toward their room. In the meantime his sister had overcome the abstracted mood into which she had fallen after her playing had been so suddenly interrupted; and all at once, after holding violin and bow for a while in her slackly hanging hands and continuing to follow the score as if she were still playing, she pulled herself together, laid the instrument on the lap of her mother—who was still sitting in her chair, fighting for breath, her lungs violently heaving—and ran into the next room, which the roomers, under pressure from her father, were nearing more quickly than before. One could see the covers and bolsters on the beds, obeying his sister's practiced hands, fly up and arrange themselves. Before the boarders had reached the room, she had finished turning down the beds and had slipped out. Her father seemed once again to be gripped by his perverse obstinacy to such a degree that he completely forgot any respect still due his tenants. He drove them on and kept on driving until, already at the bedroom door, the middle boarder stamped his foot thunderingly and thus brought him to a standstill. "I herewith declare," he said, raising his hand and casting his eyes around for Gregor's mother and sister too, "that in view of the disgusting conditions prevailing in this apartment and family"—here he spat curtly and decisively on the floor—"I give notice as of now. Of course I won't pay a cent for the days I have been living here, either; on the contrary, I shall consider taking some sort of action against you with claims that—believe me—will be easy to substantiate." He stopped and looked straight in front of him, as if he were expecting something. And in fact his two friends at once chimed in with the words, "We too give notice as of now." Thereupon he grabbed the door knob and slammed the door with a bang.

Gregor's father, his hands groping, staggered to his armchair and collapsed into it; it looked as if he were stretching himself out for his usual evening nap, but the heavy drooping of his head, as if it had lost all support, showed that he was certainly not asleep. All this time Gregor had lain quietly at the spot where the roomers had surprised him. His disappointment at the failure of his plan—but perhaps also the weakness caused by so much fasting—made it impossible for him to

Literary Analysis
Modernism How do the boarders' words and actions create new uncertainty for the Samsas?

move. He was afraid with some certainty that in the very next moment a general <u>debacle</u> would burst over him, and he waited. He was not even startled by the violin as it slipped from under his mother's trembling fingers and fell off her lap with a reverberating clang.

"My dear parents," said his sister and by way of an introduction pounded her hand on the table, "things can't go on like this. Maybe you don't realize it, but I do. I won't pronounce the name of my brother in front of this monster, and so all I say is: we have to try to get rid of it. We've done everything humanly possible to take care of it and to put up with it; I don't think anyone can blame us in the least."

"She's absolutely right," said his father to himself. His mother, who still could not catch her breath, began to cough dully behind her hand, a wild look in her eyes.

His sister rushed over to his mother and held her forehead. His father seemed to have been led by Grete's words to more definite thoughts, had sat up, was playing with the cap of his uniform among the plates which were still lying on the table from the roomers' supper, and from time to time looked at Gregor's motionless form.

"We must try to get rid of it," his sister now said exclusively to her father, since her mother was coughing too hard to hear anything. "It will be the death of you two, I can see it coming. People who already have to work as hard as we do can't put up with this constant torture at home, too. I can't stand it anymore either." And she broke out crying so bitterly that her tears poured down onto her mother's face, which she wiped off with mechanical movements of her hand.

"Child," said her father kindly and with unusual understanding, "but what can we do?"

Gregor's sister only shrugged her shoulders as a sign of the bewildered mood that had now gripped her as she cried, in contrast with her earlier confidence.

"If he could understand us," said her father, half questioning; in the midst of her crying Gregor's sister waved her hand violently as a sign that that was out of the question.

"If he could understand us," his father repeated and by closing his eyes, absorbed his daughter's conviction of the impossibility of the idea, "then maybe we could come to an agreement with him. But the way things are——"

79 "It has to go," cried his sister. "That's the only answer, Father. You just have to try to get rid of the idea that it's Gregor. Believing it for so long, that is our real misfortune. But how can it be Gregor? If it were Gregor, he would have realized long ago that it isn't possible for human beings to live with such a creature, and he would have gone away of his own free will. Then we wouldn't have a brother, but we'd be able to go on living and honor his memory. But as things are, this animal persecutes us, drives the roomers away, obviously wants to occupy the whole apartment and for us to sleep in the gutter. Look, Father," she suddenly shrieked, "he's starting in again!" And in a fit of terror that was completely incomprehensible to Gregor, his sister abandoned even her

Literary Analysis
Modernism Do you agree with Grete that Gregor could have gone away of his own free will? Why or why not?

**Reading Check 80**
What action against Gregor does Grete insist the family take?

79 Literary Analysis
Modernism

• Read aloud the bracketed passage.

• Discuss the plan that Grete and Mr. Samsa are formulating. **Ask:** What can you infer from Mr. Samsa's "half questioning" whether or not Gregor can understand them? Is this questioning consistent with Mr. Samsa's previous behavior?
Answer: Mr. Samsa half questions his own assumption that Gregor is unable to communicate with the family. This questioning is somewhat inconsistent with Mr. Samsa's behavior because he has previously acted as though Gregor could understand nothing. However, it is Mr. Samsa's own selfish interests that now cause this questioning of his prior assumptions. Mr. Samsa's longing for communication with Gregor is not based on any desire to repair the relationship with his son but rather to rid the family of Gregor altogether.

• Then, **ask** students the Literary Analysis question: Do you agree with Grete that Gregor could have gone away of his own free will? Why or why not?
Possible responses: Yes; no one would have stopped Gregor, and he could have survived like any other insect. No; Gregor is so huge and helpless that someone surely would have killed him. Besides, Gregor was injured and probably could not have fed himself.

80 Reading Check

Answer: Grete insists that they get rid of Gregor.

Support for English Learners
Read aloud to students the first full paragraph above. Call students' attention to Grete's use of the pronoun *it* when referring to Gregor. Explain that *it* is a gender-neutral pronoun that indicates that the object to which it refers is neither male nor female. Help students understand that Grete's use of the pronoun *it* depersonalizes Gregor, making it easier for the family to take action against him. Guide them to the conclusion that the Samsas see Gregor's metamorphosis as complete. He is no longer human; he is a thing.

Enrichment for Gifted/Talented Students
The scene describing Gregor's slow movement toward the violin, his discovery by the roomers, Mr. Samsa's response, and Grete's tears and rejection is especially vivid and intense. Organize students into groups, and have them study the scene. Then, ask students to assign characters to members of their group, each assuming the identity of his or her assigned character. Each student should write a journal entry describing the scene. Groups can then share their journals with the class.

- Remind students that Modernists attempt to capture the realities of modern life. Emphasize that these realities often are conveyed through descriptions.

- Have students read the bracketed passage.

- Then, **ask** students the Literary Analysis question: How does this description of Gregor's struggles reveal that his family no longer regards him as even remotely human? Explain.

Answer: Gregor struggles greatly to turn around and walk the few feet back to his room. He is in pain, and yet no one makes an effort to help him.

mother, literally shoved herself off from her chair, as if she would rather sacrifice her mother than stay near Gregor, and rushed behind her father, who, upset only by her behavior, also stood up and half-lifted his arms in front of her as if to protect her.

But Gregor had absolutely no intention of frightening anyone, let alone his sister. He had only begun to turn around in order to trek back to his room; certainly his movements did look peculiar, since his ailing condition made him help the complicated turning maneuver along with his head, which he lifted up many times and knocked against the floor. He stopped and looked around. His good intention seemed to have been recognized; it had only been a momentary scare. Now they all watched him, silent and sad. His mother lay in her armchair, her legs stretched out and pressed together, her eyes almost closing from exhaustion; his father and his sister sat side by side, his sister had put her arm around her father's neck.

81 Now maybe they'll let me turn around, Gregor thought and began his labors again. He could not repress his panting from the exertion, and from time to time he had to rest. Otherwise no one harassed him, he was left completely on his own. When he had completed the turn, he immediately began to crawl back in a straight line. He was astonished at the great distance separating him from his room and could not understand at all how, given his weakness, he had covered the same distance a little while ago almost without realizing it. Constantly intent only on rapid crawling, he hardly noticed that not a word, not an exclamation from his family interrupted him. Only when he was already in the doorway did he turn his head—not completely, for he felt his neck stiffening; nevertheless he still saw that behind him nothing had changed except that his sister had gotten up. His last glance ranged over his mother, who was now fast asleep.

He was hardly inside his room when the door was hurriedly slammed shut, firmly bolted, and locked. Gregor was so frightened at the sudden noise behind him that his little legs gave way under him. It was his sister who had been in such a hurry. She had been standing up straight, ready and waiting, then she had leaped forward nimbly. Gregor had not even heard her coming, and she cried "Finally!" to her parents as she turned the key in the lock.

"And now?" Gregor asked himself, looking around in the darkness. He soon made the discovery that he could no longer move at all. It did not surprise him; rather, it seemed unnatural that until now he had actually been able to propel himself on these thin little legs. Otherwise he felt relatively comfortable. He had pains, of course, throughout his whole body, but it seemed to him that they were gradually getting fainter and fainter and would finally go away altogether. The rotten apple in his back and the inflamed area around it, which were completely covered with fluffy dust, already hardly bothered him. He thought back on his family with deep emotion and love. His conviction that he would have to disappear was, if possible, even firmer than his sister's. He remained in this state of empty and peaceful reflection until

Literary Analysis
Modernism How does this description of Gregor's struggles reveal that his family no longer regards him as even remotely human? Explain.

Enrichment

Grete Samsa
In a letter to a woman named Grete Bloch, Kafka discussed the role of Gregor's sister in "The Metamorphosis." He wrote, "Whether you should be looking forward to the 'story' ['The Metamorphosis'], I don't know. . . . Incidentally, the heroine's name is Grete and she doesn't discredit you, at least not in the first section. Later on, though, when the agony becomes too great, she withdraws, embarks on a life of her own, and leaves the one who needs her."

the tower clock struck three in the morning. He still saw that outside the window everything was beginning to grow light. Then, without his consent, his head sank down to the floor, and from his nostrils streamed his last weak breath.

When early in the morning the cleaning woman came—in sheer energy and impatience she would slam all the doors so hard although she had often been asked not to, that once she had arrived, quiet sleep was no longer possible anywhere in the apartment—she did not at first find anything out of the ordinary on paying Gregor her usual short visit. She thought that he was deliberately lying motionless, pretending that his feelings were hurt; she credited him with unlimited intelligence. Because she happened to be holding the long broom, she tried from the doorway to tickle Gregor with it. When this too produced no results, she became annoyed and jabbed Gregor a little, and only when she had shoved him without any resistance to another spot did she begin to take notice. When she quickly became aware of the true state of things, she opened her eyes wide, whistled softly, but did not dawdle; instead, she tore open the door of the bedroom and shouted at the top of her voice into the darkness; "Come and have a look, it's croaked; it's lying there, dead as a doornail!"

The couple Mr. and Mrs. Samsa sat up in their marriage bed and had a struggle overcoming their shock at the cleaning woman before they could finally grasp her message. But then Mr. and Mrs. Samsa hastily scrambled out of bed, each on his side, Mr. Samsa threw the blanket around his shoulders, Mrs. Samsa came out in nothing but her nightgown; dressed this way, they entered Gregor's room. In the meantime the door of the living room had also opened, where Grete had been sleeping since the roomers had moved in; she was fully dressed, as if she had not been asleep at all; and her pale face seemed to confirm this. "Dead?" said Mrs. Samsa and looked inquiringly at the cleaning woman, although she could scrutinize everything for herself and could recognize the truth even without scrutiny. "I'll say," said the cleaning woman, and to prove it she pushed Gregor's corpse with her broom a good distance sideways. Mrs. Samsa made a movement as if to hold the broom back but did not do it. "Well," said Mr. Samsa, "now we can thank God!" He crossed himself, and the three women followed his example. Grete, who never took her eyes off the corpse, said, "Just look how thin he was. Of course he didn't eat anything for such a long time. The food came out again just the way it went in." As a matter of fact, Gregor's body was completely flat and dry; this was obvious now for the first time, really, since the body was no longer raised up by his little legs and nothing else distracted the eye.

82

▲ **Critical Viewing** **83**
Compare and contrast this depiction of the scene in which the cleaning woman discovers Gregor's body with Kafka's description of the event. [Compare and Contrast]

 **Reading Check** **85**
Before he dies, what final thoughts about his family does Gregor have?

The Metamorphosis, Part III ■ 1105

82 **Humanities**

Promena, by Otto Coester

Coester's illustration juxtaposes bold lines, grotesque figures, and distorted perspectives with realistic elements to capture the bizarre and horrifying nature of Gregor's transformation.

Use the following questions for discussion:

• What images from the story does the artist evoke?
Answer: The artist evokes the cleaning woman's shocked reaction, the family's conflicted attitude, and the cramped living conditions.

• What is the mood of this illustration?
Possible responses: The illustration is comical because of the exaggerated figures and whimsical details, such as the cleaning woman's patterned clothing. The illustration is nightmarish because of Gregor's gruesome position and the family's disturbed expressions.

83 **Critical Viewing**

Answer: The description and illustration are similar. The picture depicts the moment when the cleaning woman is standing over Gregor's body with her broom, apparently explaining his death to Mr. and Mrs. Samsa and Grete, who stand in the doorways.

84 **Critical Thinking**
Infer

• Call students' attention to Mr. Samsa's words "'now we can thank God!'" **Ask:** Is he relieved to be rid of Gregor, or is he grateful that Gregor is now free of pain and misery? Explain.
Possible response: Mr. Samsa is relieved to be rid of Gregor.

• When the cleaning woman reaches out with her broom to push Gregor, Mrs. Samsa starts to hold back the broom, but then does not. **Ask** students what they can infer about Mrs. Samsa from this scene.
Possible response: Mrs. Samsa wants to protect her son in his death, but she is alienated by his insect form.

85 **Reading Check**

Answer: Gregor thinks about his family with "deep emotion and love."

1105

86 Literary Analysis

Modernism and Literature of the Fantastic

- After reading aloud the bracketed passage, point out to students that Kafka presents an image of Gregor's "corpse" in the same paragraph as descriptions of spring, the "mildness," the "fresh air," and the "already very bright room." **Ask:** What does the description of this bright room imply has happened now that Gregor is dead? Explain.
Answer: This description implies renewal. Now that Gregor is gone, the world is bright again.

- Review with students the important combination of imaginative and realistic details in "literature of the fantastic." Then, **ask** students the first Literary Analysis question: Does this scene following Gregor's death strike you as realistic? Explain.
Possible response: The family's shock at the unexpected death is realistic. They are quiet and polite and want to spend a few moments alone together to comfort one another. Families in mourning often act like this—and yet they are mourning the death of a giant insect who burdened their lives, a fantastic aspect of the scene.

87 Literary Analysis

Modernism

- Call students' attention to the description of the Samsas marching arm-in-arm toward the roomer. **Ask** students what Kafka, as a Modernist writer, might have intended with this image.
Answer: Kafka wanted to present these three characters as united against the outside world, which the roomers represent.

- **Ask** students the second Literary Analysis question: What is surprising about the effects of Gregor's death on the family?
Answer: The family seems stronger. The Samsas are no longer willing to act servile toward the roomers or even to have them in their home.

"Come in with us for a little while, Grete," said Mrs. Samsa with a melancholy smile, and Grete, not without looking back at the corpse, followed her parents into their bedroom. The cleaning woman shut the door and opened the window wide. Although it was early in the morning, there was already some mildness mixed in with the fresh air. After all, it was already the end of March.

The three boarders came out of their room and looked around in astonishment for their breakfast; they had been forgotten. "Where's breakfast?" the middle roomer grumpily asked the cleaning woman. But she put her finger to her lips and then hastily and silently beckoned the boarders to follow her into Gregor's room. They came willingly and then stood, their hands in the pockets of their somewhat shabby jackets, in the now already very bright room, surrounding Gregor's corpse.

At that point the bedroom door opened, and Mr. Samsa appeared in his uniform, his wife on one arm, his daughter on the other. They all looked as if they had been crying; from time to time Grete pressed her face against her father's sleeve.

"Leave my house immediately," said Mr. Samsa and pointed to the door, without letting go of the women. "What do you mean by that?" said the middle roomer, somewhat nonplussed, and smiled with a sugary smile. The two others held their hands behind their back and incessantly rubbed them together, as if in joyful anticipation of a big argument, which could only turn out in their favor. "I mean just what I say," answered Mr. Samsa and with his two companions marched in a straight line toward the roomer. At first the roomer stood still and looked at the floor, as if the thoughts inside his head were fitting themselves together in a new order. "So, we'll go, then," he said and looked up at Mr. Samsa as if, suddenly overcome by a fit of humility, he were asking for further permission even for this decision. Mr. Samsa merely nodded briefly several times, his eyes wide open. Thereupon the roomer actually went immediately into the foyer, taking long strides; his two friends had already been listening for a while, their hands completely still, and now they went hopping right after him, as if afraid that Mr. Samsa might get into the foyer ahead of them and interrupt the contact with their leader. In the foyer all three took their hats from the coatrack, pulled their canes from the umbrella stand, bowed silently, and left the apartment. In a suspicious mood which proved completely unfounded, Mr. Samsa led the two women out onto the landing; leaning over the banister, they watched the three roomers slowly but steadily going down the long flight of stairs, disappearing on each landing at a particular turn of the stairway and a few moments later emerging again; the farther down they got, the more the Samsa family's interest in them wore off, and when a butcher's boy with a carrier on his head came climbing up the stairs with a proud bearing, toward them and then up on past them, Mr. Samsa and the women quickly left the banister and all went back, as if relieved, into their apartment.

Literary Analysis
Modernism and Literature of the Fantastic
Does this scene following Gregor's death strike you as realistic? Explain.

Literary Analysis
Modernism What is surprising about the effects of Gregor's death on the family?

They decided to spend this day resting and going for a walk; they not only deserved a break in their work, they absolutely needed one. And so they sat down at the table and wrote three letters of excuse, Mr. Samsa to the management of the bank, Mrs. Samsa to her employer, and Grete to the store owner. While they were writing, the cleaning woman came in to say that she was going, since her morning's work was done. The three letter writers at first simply nodded without looking up, but as the cleaning woman still kept lingering, they looked up, annoyed. "Well?" asked Mr. Samsa. The cleaning woman stood smiling in the doorway, as if she had some great good news to announce to the family but would do so only if she were thoroughly questioned. The little ostrich feather which stood almost upright on her hat and which had irritated Mr. Samsa the whole time she had been with them swayed lightly in all directions. "What do you want?" asked Mrs. Samsa, who inspired the most respect in the cleaning woman. "Well," the cleaning woman answered, and for good-natured laughter could not immediately go on, "look, you don't have to worry about getting rid of the stuff next door. It's already been taken care of." Mrs. Samsa and Grete bent down over their letters, as if to continue writing; Mr. Samsa, who noticed that the cleaning woman was now about to start describing everything in detail, stopped her with a firmly outstretched hand. But since she was not going to be permitted to tell her story, she remembered that she was in a great hurry, cried, obviously insulted, "So long, everyone," whirled around wildly, and left the apartment with a terrible slamming of doors.

"We'll fire her tonight," said Mr. Samsa, but did not get an answer from either his wife or his daughter, for the cleaning woman seemed to have ruined their barely regained peace of mind. They got up, went to the window, and stayed there, holding each other tight. Mr. Samsa turned around in his chair toward them and watched them quietly for a while. Then he called, "Come on now, come over here. Stop brooding over the past. And have a little consideration for me, too." The women obeyed him at once, hurried over to him, fondled him, and quickly finished their letters.

Then all three of them left the apartment together, something they had not done in months, and took the trolley into the open country on the outskirts of the city. The car, in which they were the only

▼ **Critical Viewing** 90
Which aspects of this model of Prague, Kafka's home, reflect the mood of this story? Explain.
[Connect]

89

✔ **Reading Check** 91
After Gregor's death, what does Mr. Samsa tell the boarders?

The Metamorphosis, Part III ■ 1107

88 **Critical Thinking**
Draw Conclusions
• Read the bracketed passage aloud. Then, **ask:** Why is the cleaning woman in such a good humor?
Answer: The cleaning woman has evidently disposed of Gregor in a manner that might be particularly gruesome but which she finds satisfying and humorous.

• **Ask:** Why are the Samsas uninterested in hearing about how the cleaning woman disposed of Gregor's body?
Answer: It would be an awful story for the family to hear.

89 **Humanities**
Model of Prague,
by Antonín Langweil

Langweil (1791–1837) created this 20-square-foot model of Prague between 1826 and 1837. It is currently on exhibit in The City of Prague Museum.

Use the following questions for discussion:
• What does this model indicate about living conditions in Prague?
Possible response: Residents of Prague had to live in very close quarters. There appear to be no parks, yards, or gardens; only buildings, streets, and squares.

• On the basis of this model, does Prague look like a place you would like to live? Why or why not?
Possible response: With its red roofs and intricate architecture, Prague looks like a very charming place to live. However, the cramped arrangement of the buildings and lack of natural, open spaces is unappealing.

90 **Critical Viewing**
Answer: Like Kafka's story, the photograph suggests a feeling of isolation and detachment. The buildings of the city seem to loom over the empty city square.

91 **Reading Check**
Answer: Mr. Samsa tells the boarders to leave his home.

1107

1. **Possible responses:** Some students will say that Gregor's family treated him very badly. They should have supported and cared for him. After all, he supported them for a long time. Other students will have more sympathy for the family, recognizing the stress the metamorphosis put on them.

2. (a) Gregor inches closer to be near Grete. (b) When he emerges from his room, Gregor explains to himself that he is indifferent to everything, including the feelings of others. As he moves closer, roused by the music, he feels that the music is the nourishment he craves. (c) Gregor's sudden passion for his sister's music, which was once so important to him, and his desire to seize and protect her while warding off his enemies, show an intense desire for human companionship and a will to assert himself.

3. (a) The family talks about their future and their prospects. (b) **Possible response:** The family is better off without Gregor. His death removes stress and worry from their lives, permits them more flexibility in where and how they live, and results in their taking responsibility for themselves.

4. (a) Gregor's body is thin and wasted away from lack of food. (b) **Possible response:** Gregor was neglected both physically and emotionally. Grete no longer tried to find food that Gregor would eat. He toyed with his food or left it entirely untouched. Gregor's room was scarcely cleaned. He was not welcomed when he tried to listen to his sister's music.

5. The Samsas' uplifted mood is a direct result of Gregor's death. Their happiness is at the expense of Gregor's happiness.

6. **Possible response:** The author might simply portray Gregor as a deeply depressed man who has emotionally and physically separated himself from his family.

passengers, was completely filled with warm sunshine. Leaning back comfortably in their seats, they discussed their prospects for the time to come, and it seemed on closer examination that these weren't bad at all, for all three positions—about which they had never really asked one another in any detail—were exceedingly advantageous and especially promising for the future. The greatest immediate improvement in their situation would come easily, of course, from a change in apartments; they would now take a smaller and cheaper apartment, but one better situated and in every way simpler to manage than the old one, which Gregor had picked for them. While they were talking in this vein, it occurred almost simultaneously to Mr. and Mrs. Samsa, as they watched their daughter getting livelier and livelier, that lately, in spite of all the troubles which had turned her cheeks pale, she had blossomed into a good-looking, shapely girl. Growing quieter and communicating almost unconsciously through glances, they thought that it would soon be time, too, to find her a good husband. And it was like a confirmation of their new dreams and good intentions when at the end of the ride their daughter got up first and stretched her young body.

Critical Reading

1. **Respond:** How do you feel about the Samsa family's treatment of Gregor? Explain.

2. **(a) Recall:** What does Gregor do when he hears Grete playing the violin? **(b) Interpret:** How does he explain his own actions to himself? **(c) Analyze:** In what ways might this scene represent Gregor's desire to hold onto his humanity?

3. **(a) Recall:** What do Gregor's parents and sister discuss when they leave the apartment at the end of the story? **(b) Make a Judgment:** Is the family better off without Gregor? Explain.

4. **(a) Describe:** At the story's end, what is the state of Gregor's body? **(b) Support:** Which details in the story support the statement that Gregor suffers from a profound lack of nourishment, both physically and emotionally?

5. **Analyze:** The early spring setting and the Samsas' uplifted mood seem to set up a traditional happy ending. What makes this ending neither traditional nor happy?

6. **Modify:** How might an author portray similar relationship problems in a fictional family without the use of fantastic or supernatural details?

Go **Online**
Author Link

For: More about Franz Kafka
Visit: www.PHSchool.com
Web Code: ete-9801

Go **Online** For additional information about
Author Link Franz Kafka, have students type in the Web Code, then select *K* from the alphabet, and then select Franz Kafka.

Apply the Skills

The Metamorphosis

Literary Analysis

Modernism

1. Before the rise of **Modernism**, works of fiction often began with expositions, or background information. Why would an exposition make this story less effective?
2. Using a chart like the one shown, discuss two details from Part I of "The Metamorphosis" that show the realities of modern life.

Detail	What It Reveals About Modern Life
1.	
2.	

3. In a typical Modernist work, the narrator neither judges characters nor interprets events. Is this true of "The Metamorphosis"? Explain.
4. **(a)** How do Gregor's perceptions shape the portrayal of other characters? **(b)** Is Gregor's point of view reliable? Why or why not?

Connecting Literary Elements

5. **(a)** Which details in the opening scene, in which Gregor's parents and the office manager speak through the closed door, are realistic? **(b)** Which details are fantastic? **(c)** In what ways is this scene an example of **literature of the fantastic**?
6. **(a)** How does Gregor feel about his job? **(b)** Might his transformation be something he unconsciously wanted? Explain.

Reading Strategy

Applying the Author's Biography

7. Kafka's father was a domineering man who instilled in his son a sense of duty, as well as feelings of fear and guilt. **(a)** Apply the **author's biography** by stating whether Kafka's father served as a model for Mr. Samsa. **(b)** Which details support your point of view?
8. Kafka's father took a dim view of his son's literary aspirations. Does this story symbolically express this conflict? Explain.

Extend Understanding

9. Cultural Connection: Stories in which humans are changed into animals abound in mythology, literature, and popular culture. Select one such story, and discuss the emotions and personality traits that are associated with the transformation.

QuickReview

Modernism was a literary movement that expressed the uncertainties of modern life. Modernists used experimental techniques, avoided traditional plot structures, and drew no final conclusions or meaning.

Literature of the fantastic mixes imaginative and realistic elements to entertain and challenge readers.

When you **apply the author's biography** to his or her work, you think about the writing as an expression of the author's life and times.

Go Online
Assessment
For: Self-test
Visit: www.PHSchool.com
Web Code: eta-6801

The Metamorphosis ■ *1109*

Answers

1. **Possible response:** The first sentence in the story is extremely startling. To precede this sentence with exposition would destroy its impact.

2. **Possible response:** Detail One: grueling job; people must make compromises. Detail Two: boss would come with the health-insurance doctor; employers do not trust their employees.

3. Yes; the narrator makes few direct statements about the characters and allows the events to unfold without drawing conclusions about their meaning.

4. (a) **Possible response:** Because the story uses the third-person limited point of view, Gregor's thoughts shape the portrayals of the other characters. For example, Gregor's affection for Grete results in an appealing portrayal of her. (b) **Possible response:** The point of view is not reliable because it is influenced by Gregor's personal biases.

5. (a) **Possible response:** Realistic details include the plea with Gregor to get up, the boss's threats, and his mother's excuses and her concerns for his health. (b) **Possible response:** Fantastic details include the transformation of Gregor into an insect and his inability to talk and stand up. (c) Some of the details given are imaginative, while others are realistic. Fantastic literature mixes the two, as is done here.

6. (a) Gregor hates his job and wants to quit. (b) Gregor may have wanted a metamorphosis to occur because it provides him with an escape from a situation that he abhors. He can do nothing about this change, so he is free and absolved of guilt.

7. (a) It seems likely that Kafka's father served as a model for Mr. Samsa. (b) Like Kafka's father, Mr. Samsa is strict and domineering. He has instilled in Gregor a sense of duty.

8. The story addresses the conflict through Grete's love of music. Despite his father's disapproval, Gregor encourages and supports Grete's interest and wants to send her to the Conservatory.

Answers continued

9. **Possible response:** Odysseus visits the island of the witch Circe, who turns his men into pigs. The men retain their human intelligence and suffer more because they know they are pigs.

Go Online
Assessment
Students may use the **Self-test** to prepare for **Selection Test A** or **Selection Test B.**

❶ Vocabulary Lesson

Word Analysis

1. not patient
2. a migrating, or moving, into a new place
3. bearing the mark of something pressed into the mind; strongly affected in mind or feelings
4. a state of not being balanced

Spelling Strategy

1. correct
2. correct
3. chuckle

Vocabulary Builder

1. obstinacy
2. pallid
3. imminent
4. exuded
5. gyration
6. rectify
7. debacle
8. impracticable

❷ Grammar and Style Lesson

1. If I didn't hold back for my parents' sake; under what circumstances
2. since my train leaves at five; why
3. When he reached the edge; when
4. as you know; under what circumstances
5. wherever he wanted to go; where

Writing Application

Sample sentences: *When Gregor woke up,* he realized he was an insect. *As soon as he struggled out of bed,* Gregor looked through the door into the living room. He was hurting *because the apple had begun to rot. If he did not get food,* he would go hungry.

₩G Writing and Grammar Platinum Level

For support in teaching the Grammar and Style Lesson, use Chapter 20, Section 2.

Build Language Skills

❶ Vocabulary Lesson

Word Analysis: Latin Prefix *im-*

The Latin prefix *im-* means "not," as in *immature,* or "into" or "toward," as in *impact.* Use your knowledge of this prefix to define each of the following words.

1. impatient
2. immigration
3. impressed
4. imbalance

Spelling Strategy

When words end in *-le* or *-el,* their ending sound is the same. When a *k* sound precedes the ending, as in *debacle, -le* usually is the correct spelling. For each word below, write the correct spelling. If the spelling is correct, write *correct.*

1. tickle
2. excel
3. chuckel

Vocabulary Builder: Analogies

In each item below, match the relationship between the first two words by selecting a word from the vocabulary list on page 1065.

1. *Wisdom* is to *owl* as ___?___ is to *donkey.*
2. *Dull* is to *sparkling* as ___?___ is to *colorful.*
3. *Near* is to *place* as ___?___ is to *time.*
4. *Exhaled* is to *breath* as ___?___ is to *sweat.*
5. *Spiral* is to *shape* as ___?___ is to *movement.*
6. *Offend* is to *insult* as ___?___ is to *apology.*
7. *Achievement* is to *success* as ___?___ is to *failure.*
8. *Improbable* is to *true* as ___?___ is to *possible.*

❷ Grammar and Style Lesson

Adverb Clauses

Adverb clauses are subordinate clauses—groups of words containing a subject and a verb that cannot stand by themselves as sentences—that modify verbs, adjectives, or adverbs. Adverb clauses often begin with conjunctions such as *when, where, if, as if, as, because,* or *since* and explain *how, where, when, why, to what extent,* or *under what circumstances.*

> CONJ.   S   V
> **Example:** *When Gregor Samsa awoke one morning from unsettling dreams,* he found himself changed into a monstrous vermin. **[Tells when]**

Practice Identify the adverb clause in each item below. Indicate whether it tells *how, where, when, why, to what extent,* or *under what circumstances.*

1. If I didn't hold back for my parents' sake, I would have quit long ago.
2. I'd better go, since my train leaves at five.
3. When he reached the edge, he stopped.
4. I'm obligated to the firm, as you know.
5. His little legs strained to carry him away wherever he wanted to go.

Writing Application Write four sentences about Gregor Samsa. Use an adverb clause in each one.

₩G *Prentice Hall Writing and Grammar Connection: Platinum Level, Chapter 20, Section 2*

Assessment Practice

Comparing and Contrasting Texts (For more practice, see *Test Preparation Workbook,* p. 45.)

Have students read the following passage and the first sentence on p. 1066.

> Seated on the bucket, my hands on the handle, the simplest kind of bridle, I propel myself with difficulty down the stairs; but once downstairs my bucket ascends, superbly, superbly . . .
>
> —"The Bucket Rider" by Franz Kafka

Both passages feature—

A allusions.
B sensory details.
C fantastical scenarios.
D figurative language.

The correct answer is *C.* Both passages feature fantastical scenarios.

❸ Writing Lesson

Timed Writing: Essay Responding to a Critical Perspective

In an essay about "The Metamorphosis," Vladimir Nabokov wrote: "Kafka's art consists in accumulating on the one hand, Gregor's insect features, all the sad detail of his insect disguise, and on the other hand, in keeping vivid and limpid before the reader's eyes Gregor's sweet and subtle human nature." Write an essay in response to this statement. Agree or disagree with Nabokov, but defend your view. **(40 minutes)**

Prewriting
(10 minutes)

Review the story. Make one list of details that describe Gregor's insectlike traits. Make a second list that suggests Gregor's human qualities. Decide whether you agree or disagree with Nabokov.

Drafting
(20 minutes)

Express and defend your opinion. Include details from the text that support your view.

Model: Elaborating to Add Support

Gregor Samsa looks like an insect, but he still has human compassion. For example, when the office manager criticizes Gregor's work, Gregor fears for his parents. He calls out, "Sir! Spare my parents!"

> Using quotations from the story can strengthen your ideas.

Revising
(10 minutes)

As you reread your essay, make sure that your supporting details are accurate and easy to follow. Remove any ideas or details that stray from the main purpose of each paragraph.

 Prentice Hall Writing and Grammar Connection: Platinum Level, Chapter 13, Section 3

❹ Extend Your Learning

Listening and Speaking Memorial services often include a **eulogy**, or speech of praise, about the deceased. Use these tips to write a eulogy about Gregor Samsa:

- Skim the story and make notes about an traits in Gregor that you find praiseworthy.
- Decide how, if at all, you will refer to his transformation.

Present the eulogy for the class.

Research and Technology In a small group, research Modernism in the visual arts, music, drama, and architecture. Prepare a **multimedia classroom presentation** that identifies similarities among various expressions of Modernism. **[Group Activity]**

Go Online
Research

For: An additional research activity
Visit: www.PHSchool.com
Web Code: etd-7801

The Metamorphosis ■ 1111

Assessment Resources

The following resources can be used to assess students' knowledge and skills.

Unit 8 Resources
Selection Test A, pp. 18–20
Selection Test B, pp. 21–23

General Resources
Rubrics for Response to Literature,
pp. 55–56

Go Online
Assessment

Students may use the **Self-test** to prepare for **Selection Test A** or **Selection Test B**.

---

❸ Writing Lesson

You may use this Writing Lesson as a timed-writing practice, or you may allow students to develop the essay as a writing assignment over several days.

- To guide students in writing this essay, give them the **Support for Writing Lesson**, p. 15 in *Unit 8 Resources.*

- Explain to students that an essay responding to a critical perspective is a response to literature that is focused on showing whether a given opinion of the work is well founded.

- Use the Writing Lesson to guide students in developing their essays. Have each student begin by writing a thesis sentence that states his or her opinion.

- Use the Response to Literature rubrics in *General Resources,* pp. 55–56, to evaluate students' essays.

Writing and Grammar
Platinum Level
For support in teaching the Writing Lesson, use Chapter 13, Section 3.

❹ Listening and Speaking

- Explain that a eulogy usually describes the deceased's best qualities. Tell students to think about Gregor's intentions as well as his actions, considering what he did not do as well as what he did do.

- Remind students that their audience consists of Gregor's relatives, friends, and co-workers. Have students practice their speeches with partners.

- The **Support for Extend Your Learning** page (*Unit 8 Resources,* p. 16) provides guided note-taking opportunities to help students complete the Extend Your Learning activities.

Go Online
Research

Have students type in the Web Code for another research activity.

Standard Course of Study

IR.2.01.5	Summarize key events and/or points from research text.
IR.2.01.11	Analyze elements of informational environment in informing audience.
CT.4.03.3	Analyze how writers relate the organization to the ideas.

See Teacher Express™/Lesson View for a detailed lesson for Reading Informational Material.

About Scientific Texts

- Point out to students that scientific texts describe experiments, hypotheses, and theories. These texts often include diagrams or illustrations that support the text.

- **Ask** why students might want to analyze scientific texts.
Possible response: Students can use scientific reports in school for classes and reports.

- Have students read "About Scientific Texts."

- **Ask** students why each type of listed information is important.
Answer: Each type of factual information about theories, hypotheses, and experiments explains how scientists reach conclusions.

- Explain to students that reading about experiments allows them to follow the steps of a scientific process through to a hypothesis. Diagrams allow students to picture scientific details without reading lengthy descriptions.

Reading Strategy

Analyzing Text Features

- Have students read "Analyzing Text Features."

- **Ask** how students can use this information to read scientific texts more efficiently.
Answer: Students can preview specific materials to know what information is most important.

- Point out the graphic organizer at the bottom of the page. Have students copy the organizer on a sheet of paper to use later.

Scientific Texts

About Scientific Texts

Science is systematic knowledge, acquired through observation and experimentation, of the structure and behavior of our physical world. **Scientific texts** contain detailed information about science for those who wish to study it.

The typical scientific text contains the following:

- Facts about a variety of science topics
- *Hypotheses*, or theories, to explain scientific facts
- Descriptions of experiments conducted to verify these hypotheses
- Opportunities to duplicate these experiments in other environments
- Diagrams of relevant scientific details

In the section of a scientific text that you are about to read, you can expect to learn facts and details about insects and the process of metamorphosis.

Reading Strategy

Analyzing Text Features

Textbook reading is a complex process. Because your goal as you read a textbook is to understand, to learn, and to remember what you have read, you should read more carefully and more thoughtfully than when you are reading for other purposes.

Analyzing text features will help you meet your goal. Here are some tips to help you analyze text features:

- Find and preview the major headings, charts, diagrams, and pictures.
- Read the introductory and summary paragraphs.
- Study the review questions.
- Note any text that is printed in bold or italics.

As you read this excerpt from a biology textbook, use a chart like the one shown to help you record each text feature, describe its use, and determine how it helps you learn.

Text Feature	How It Is Used	How It Helps Me Learn
Checkpoint	Asks questions about the content	Checks to see that I remember and have understood what I have read

1112 ■ *The Modern World*

Instruction — Solutions for All Learners

Reading Support
Give students reading support with the appropriate version of the **Reader's Notebooks:**

Reader's Notebook: [**L2, L3**]
Reader's Notebook: Adapted Version [**L1, L2**]
Reader's Notebook: English Learner's Version [**EL**]

What Is an Insect?

Like all arthropods, insects have a segmented body, an exoskeleton, and jointed appendages. They also have several features that are specific to insects. **Insects have a body divided into three parts—head, thorax, and abdomen. Three pairs of legs are attached to the thorax.** The beetle in **Figure 28–15** exhibits these characteristics. In many insects such as ants, the body parts are clearly separated from each other by narrow connections. In other insects, such as grasshoppers, the divisions between the three body parts are not as sharply defined. A typical insect also has a pair of antennae and a pair of compound eyes on the head, two pairs of wings on the thorax, and tracheal tubes that are used for respiration.

The essential life functions in insects are carried out in basically the same ways as they are in other arthropods. However, insects have a variety of interesting adaptations that deserve a closer look.

CHECKPOINT *What are the names of the three parts of an insect's body?*

Responses to Stimuli Insects use a multitude of sense organs to respond to stimuli. Compound eyes are made of many lenses that detect minute changes in color and movement. The brain assembles this information into a single, detailed image. Compound eyes produce an image that is less detailed than what we see. However, eyes with multiple lenses are far better at detecting movement—one reason it is so hard to swat a fly!

Insects have chemical receptors for taste and smell on their mouthparts, as might be expected, and also on their antennae and legs. When a fly steps in a drop of water, it knows immediately whether the water contains salt or sugar. Insects also have sensory hairs that detect slight movements in the surrounding air or water. As objects move toward insects, the insects can feel the movement of the displaced air or water and respond appropriately. Many insects also have well-developed ears that hear sounds far above the human range. These organs are located in what we would consider odd places—behind the legs in grasshoppers, for example.

Guide for Reading

Key Concepts
- What are the distinguishing features of insects?
- What two types of development can insects undergo?
- What types of insects form societies?

Vocabulary
incomplete metamorphosis
nymph
complete metamorphosis
pupa

> An italicized question helps readers check their understanding of what they have read.

> This diagram shows the three divisions of an insect's body.

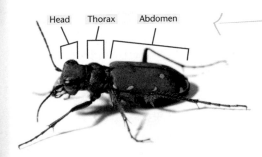

Head   Thorax   Abdomen

◀ **Figure 28–15** Insects have a body divided into three parts—head, thorax, and abdomen. Three pairs of legs are attached to the thorax. In addition to these features, this green tiger beetle has other characteristics of a typical insect—wings, antennae, compound eyes, and tracheal tubes for respiration.

Reading Informational Materials: Scientific Texts ■ 1113

Reading Scientific Texts

- Point out to students that they may find this type of material in a scientific text.
- Direct students' attention to the Guide for Reading at the top of the page. Point out that this guide provides information that readers should gain from the chapter. By reading the guide first, students will know what information to look for as they read the text.
- Point out the Vocabulary text feature. Tell students that they will read these terms in the context of the chapter.
- Have students read the first callout note that corresponds to the Checkpoint feature. Tell students that these questions allow them to test their comprehension. If they cannot answer a question, they need to reread the material. Point out that the answer to a question appears in bold print in the passage and is noted with a key icon, showing that it is a key concept.
- Point out that the second call-out note corresponds to a diagram of the three divisions of an insect's body. Remind students that important concepts are often accompanied by diagrams or other graphics.

continued on p. 1114

Differentiated Instruction   Solutions for All Learners

Strategy for Special Needs Students
Have students create a two-column chart on a poster. In the first column, have them copy each Key Concept question. In the second column, ask them to answer the questions using complete sentences.

Strategy for Less Proficient Readers
Have students work in groups, using the chart to identify several text features as they reread "What Is an Insect?" Remind students to use headings, key icons, boldface text, and diagrams as starting points in their charts. Ask groups to present their findings to the class.

Strategy for English Learners
Provide students with a copy of the chart and colored markers. Ask students to identify several text features in "What Is an Insect?" by writing each feature in a different color. Then, have students complete the "How It Is Used" columns for these text features.

1113

- Point out to students that reading the headings and the material in boldface type will help them scan a page for the most important information. Have students **use** the boldface type to find the definition for *complete metamorphosis*.
  Answer: A complete metamorphosis is defined as a process during which many insects undergo a dramatic change in body form.

- Have students look at Figure 28–18. **Ask** students to explain the purpose of this diagram.
  Answer: The diagram shows the difference between complete metamorphosis and incomplete metamorphosis.

Reading Informational Materials

Metamorphosis The growth and development of insects usually involve metamorphosis, which is a process of changing shape and form. Insects undergo either incomplete metamorphosis or complete metamorphosis. Both complete and incomplete metamorphosis are shown in **Figure 28–18.** The immature forms of insects that undergo gradual or **incomplete metamorphosis,** such as the chinch bug, look very much like the adults. These immature forms are called **nymphs** (NIMFS). Nymphs lack functional sexual organs and other adult structures, such as wings. As they molt several times and grow, the nymphs gradually acquire adult structures. This type of development is characterized by a similar appearance throughout all stages of the life cycle.

Many insects, such as bees, moths, and beetles, undergo a more dramatic change in body form during a process called **complete metamorphosis.** These animals hatch into larvae that look and act nothing like their parents. They also feed in completely different ways from adult insects. The larvae typically feed voraciously and grow rapidly. They molt a few times and grow larger but change little in appearance. Then they undergo a final molt and change into a **pupa** (PYOO-puh; plural: pupae)—the stage in which an insect changes from larva to adult. During the pupal stage, the body is completely remodeled inside and out. The adult that emerges seems like a completely different animal. Unlike the larva, the adult typically can fly and is specialized for reproduction. **Figure 28–18** shows the complete metamorphosis of a ladybug beetle.

> A heading and the definition in boldface type provide basic information about what readers will learn on this page.

Figure 28–18 The growth and development of insects usually involve metamorphosis, which is a process of changing shape and form. Insects undergo incomplete metamorphosis or complete metamorphosis. The chinch bug (left) undergoes incomplete metamorphosis, and the developing nymphs look similar to the adult. The ladybug (right) undergoes complete metamorphosis, and during the early stages the developing larva and pupa look completely different from the adult.

✓**CHECKPOINT** *What is a pupa?*

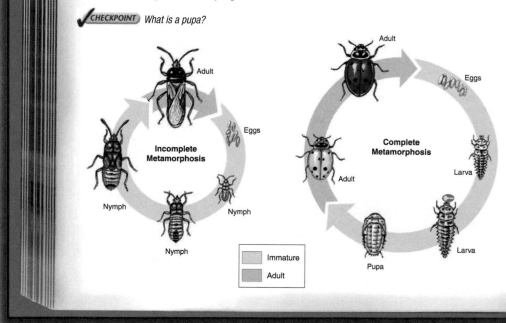

Differentiated Instruction   Solutions for All Learners

Strategy for Less Proficient Readers
Have students work in groups to compare and contrast the two diagrams in Figure 28–18. Ask groups to summarize their findings and present brief oral reports to the class using the diagrams.

Support for English Learners
Review with students the pronunciations and definitions of the vocabulary words in this selection. Encourage students to identify and list other unfamiliar words and phrases, and guide them to use dictionaries to clarify these terms.

Enrichment for Gifted/Talented Students
Instruct each student to draw a diagram that shows a familiar scientific process, such as the seasonal cycles of leaf growth on a tree. Then, have students give brief oral presentations about their diagrams to the class.

Reading: Analyzing Text Feature

Directions: *Choose the letter of the best answer to each question about the scientific article.*

1. How many subheads does the selection have?
   - A two
   - B three
   - C four
   - D five

2. Which of the following best explains why the article's organization is suited to its subject matter?
   - A Dividing complex material makes it easier to understand.
   - B One complete section keeps all of the related ideas in one place.
   - C Limiting sections to one paragraph makes the text more accessible.
   - D Organizing sections in alphabetical order eases reading.

3. Why are some sentences printed in boldface type?
   - A They are vocabulary terms.
   - B They are subtitles.
   - C They are the most important ideas.
   - D They are comprehension questions.

4. What information does Figure 28–18 (page 1114) add to the text above it?
   - A The explanation that all insects follow the same sequence of metamorphosis
   - B A visual aid that allows readers to see each stage of metamorphosis
   - C Colored labels that organize the information
   - D A checkpoint that helps readers understand the text

Reading: Comprehension and Interpretation

Directions: *Write your answers on a separate sheet of paper.*

5. (a) Identify the number of parts into which an insect's body is divided. (b) Explain how the divisions can vary in different kinds of insects.

6. Which type of eye would be better for driving a car: an insect's or a human's? Explain?

7. Define *metamorphosis*, and explain the ways in which the sequence of all insect metamorphosis is the same?

Timed Writing: Summary

Write a paragraph summarizing the main ideas of this science article. Include enough supporting details to make the main ideas clear to your reader. *(15 minutes)*

Reading Informational Materials: Scientific Texts ■ 1115

Reading: Analyzing Text Features

1. A
2. A
3. C
4. B

Reading: Comprehension and Interpretation

5. **Possible response:** (a) An insect's body has three parts: head, thorax, and abdomen. The typical insect has a pair of compound eyes and a pair of antennae on the head, two pairs of wings and tracheal tubes on the thorax, and several legs on the abdomen. (b) Ants are different because the body parts are separated by narrow connections. The grasshopper's body parts are not as clearly defined, and their ears are placed behind their legs.

6. **Possible response:** Human eyes are more appropriate for driving because the compound eyes of an insect produce a less detailed image than human eyes do.

7. **Answer:** Metamorphosis is a process of changing shape and form. The sequence of all insect metamorphosis, whether complete or incomplete, starts with the egg's hatching, then goes through dramatic changes in form, and ends with an adult form.

Timed Writing Summary

- A summary must include all of the main ideas, so check each sentence in boldface type. Then add supporting details for each main idea.

- Suggest that students plan their time to give 5 minutes to planning, 5 minutes to writing, and 5 minutes to revising and editing.

Extend the Lesson

Generating Questions for Research

Tell students that they should follow this process to find out more about insects. Have them prepare a two-column chart with the heads: What I Know and Questions for Research. In the first column, have students record details that they already know about insects. In the second column, students should list questions that they still have about insects.

Tell students to select the two questions that interest them most. Direct them to consult reliable Internet sources, library reference books, and other nonfiction materials to find answers. Then, ask students to record their answers clearly, using complete sentences and paragraphs. Make sure that students cite the sources for their answers.

The Bracelet

Standard Course of Study

Goal 4: CRITICAL THINKING

CT.4.02.2 Use specific references from texts to show theme.

CT.4.02.3 Examine how elements such as irony and symbolism impact theme.

CT.4.03.1 Analyze how writers introduce and develop a main idea.

Goal 5: LITERATURE

LT.5.03.6 Make inferences, predictions, and draw conclusions based on world literature.

LT.5.03.9 Analyze and evaluate the effects of author's craft and style in world literature.

Goal 6: GRAMMAR AND USAGE

GU.6.01.3 Use recognition strategies to understand vocabulary and exact word choice.

Step-by-Step Teaching Guide	Pacing Guide
PRETEACH	
• Administer Vocabulary and Reading Warm-ups as necessary.	5 min.
• Engage students' interest with the motivation activity.	5 min.
• Read and discuss author and background features. **FT**	10 min.
• Introduce the Literary Analysis Skill: Epiphany. **FT**	5 min.
• Introduce the Reading Strategy: Drawing Conclusions. **FT**	10 min.
• Prepare students to read by teaching the selection vocabulary. **FT**	
TEACH	
• Informally monitor comprehension while students read independently or in groups. **FT**	30 min.
• Monitor students' comprehension with the Reading Check notes.	as students read
• Reinforce vocabulary with Vocabulary Builder notes.	as students read
• Develop students' understanding of epiphany with the Literary Analysis annotations. **FT**	5 min.
• Develop students' ability to draw conclusions with the Reading Strategy annotations. **FT**	5 min.
ASSESS/EXTEND	
• Assess students' comprehension and mastery of the Literary Analysis and Reading Strategy by having them answer the Apply the Skills questions. **FT**	15 min.
• Have students complete the Vocabulary Development Lesson and the Grammar and Style Lesson. **FT**	15 min.
• Apply students' ability to analyze an image by using the Writing Lesson. **FT**	45 min. or homework
• Apply students' understanding by using one or more of the Extend Your Learning activities.	20–90 min. or homework
• Administer Selection Test A or Selection Test B. **FT**	15 min.

Resources

Print

Unit 8 Resources

Transparency

Graphic Organizer Transparencies

Print

Reader's Notebook [L2]

Reader's Notebook: Adapted Version [L1]

Reader's Notebook: English Learner's Version [EL]

Unit 8 Resources

Technology

Listening to Literature Audio CDs [L2, EL]

Reader's Notebook: Adapted Version Audio CD [L1, L2]

Print

Unit 8 Resources

General Resources

Technology

Go Online: Research [**L3**]
Go Online: Self-test [**L3**]
ExamView®, Test Bank [**L3**]

Choosing Resources for Differentiated Instruction

[**L1**] Special Needs Students

[**L2**] Below-Level Students

[**L3**] All Students

[**L4**] Advanced Students

[**EL**] English Learners

For Vocabulary and Reading Warm-ups and for Selection Tests, **A** signifies "less challenging" and **B** "more challenging." For Graphic Organizer transparencies, **A** signifies "not filled in" and **B** "filled in."

FT Fast Track Instruction: To move the lesson more quickly, use the strategies and activities identified with **FT**.

Scaffolding for Less Proficient and Advanced Students

The leveled Critical Thinking questions after selections progress in the levels of thinking required to answer them. To address the needs of your different students, you may use the (a) level questions for your less proficient students and the (b) level questions with your on-level and advanced students. The occasional (c) level questions are appropriate for your advanced students.

PRENTICE HALL

TeacherEXPRESS™ Use this complete
Plan · Teach · Assess suite of powerful teaching tools to make lesson planning and testing quicker and easier.

PRENTICE HALL

StudentEXPRESS™ Use the interactive
Learn · Study · Succeed textbook (online and on CD-ROM) to make selections and activities come alive with audio and video support and interactive questions.

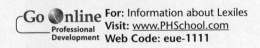

Go Online
Professional Development

For: Information about Lexiles
Visit: www.PHSchool.com
Web Code: eue-1111

Motivation

On the board, write this quotation, the first line from English writer L. P. Hartley's novel *The Go-Between:* "The past is a foreign country: they do things differently there." Discuss with students what Hartley might mean by this statement and whether they agree with it, based on their own experiences. Conclude by explaining that the story they are about to read concerns one woman's encounter with this "foreign country."

❶ Background
More About the Author

Sidonie-Gabrielle Colette (the author's full name) was the first woman president of the Goncourt Academy, an institute established to recognize literary talent. She was also the first woman writer to become a grand officer of the French Legion of Honor.

Geography Note

Draw students' attention to the map at the top of the page. Remind students that Colette was born in the French province of Burgundy. One of twenty-two provincial regions, Burgundy is located in the east-central part of the country and provides both agricultural and industrial resources.

Build Skills *Short Story*

The Bracelet ❶

Colette
(1873–1954)

No other writer captured what it was like to be a woman in France in the late nineteenth and early twentieth centuries better than Colette (kō let'). Yet Colette herself was in no way typical of her time. The women's rights movement was still in its infancy during her lifetime; nevertheless, Colette proved that a woman could be strong, independent, and successful.

First Marriage Colette was born in the small village of St. Sauveur-en-Puisaye (sen' sō vēr' än püē zā) in the French province of Burgundy. As a child, she was taught by her mother to savor the sights, sounds, and textures of country life, an appreciation that her fiction would later reflect. After her twentieth birthday, she married Henri Gauthier-Villars (än rē' gō tyā' vē lär'), a mediocre writer fourteen years her senior. By providing her with encouragement and support and by introducing her to many of the most prominent French writers of the time, Gauthier-Villars played a vital role in launching Colette's literary career. In fact, her husband published her first series of books, known as the "Claudine" novels, under the pseudonym Willy. The "Claudine" novels centered on the misadventures of a teenage girl and became a huge popular success. They inspired numerous related projects and products, including a musical, Claudine clothing, and Claudine soap, perfume, and cigars.

After her marriage ended in 1906, Colette lived alone for several years. During this period, she continued to develop her literary skills while also indulging in a number of other creative endeavors, including singing, dancing, and hairdressing. Colette's experiences during this period of her life inspired two successful books, *The Vagabond* (1910) and *Recaptured* (1913).

Her Star Rises In 1912, Colette married Henri de Jouvenel (də zhōō və nel'), a prominent journalist. The marriage ended in divorce in 1925. As her second marriage failed, however, Colette's fame grew. She published such highly regarded works as *Chéri* (1920), *My Mother's House* (1922), *The Ripening* (1923), *The Last of Chéri* (1926), and *Sido* (1929). Two of these works—*Chéri* and *The Last of Chéri*—focus on a tragic love affair between a young man and an older woman, while the other works deal with the experiences of childhood and adolescence.

Colette married her third husband, Maurice Goudeket (mô rēs' gōō də kā'), another writer, in 1935. Unlike her first two marriages, her marriage to Goudeket brought her great contentment and lasted for the remainder of her life. Unfortunately, her happiness was tainted by the onset of crippling arthritis and by her husband's arrest and imprisonment by the Nazis during World War II. These setbacks did not affect her productivity as a writer, however, and in the 1930s and 1940s she wrote many successful books, including *The Cat* (1933), *Duo* (1934), *Gigi* (1944), and *The Blue Light* (1949).

A Literary Legend By the time of her death in 1954, Colette had written more than fifty novels or novellas and an even greater number of short stories. Among the French public, she had established herself as a literary legend, and she had received a number of distinguished honors, including her induction into both the Royal Belgian Academy and the French Goncourt Academy. During the years since her death, her reputation has continued to grow, and she is now regarded by many as the outstanding French fiction writer of her time.

1116 ■ *The Modern World*

Preview

Connecting to the Literature

If we are unhappy, we sometimes think back with fondness to a better time in our lives. Such is the case of the wealthy but dissatisfied Madame Augelier, whose childhood memory becomes a driving force in her life.

❷ Literary Analysis

Epiphany

An **epiphany** is a sudden flash of insight that a person has about himself or herself, another person, a situation, or life itself. That revelation may be positive, but it may also be negative. In traditional plots, a series of events leads to the resolution of a conflict. However, in many modern stories, the series of events leads to an epiphany that may alter the conflict without resolving it. As you read, use a chart like the one shown to identify details that suggest the nature of the epiphany Madame Augelier experiences. Then, decide whether the conflict is resolved or merely changed.

Connecting Literary Elements

An author's choice of the best words to convey meaning contributes to the power and beauty of a work of writing. Colette's use of precise **descriptive details**—words and phrases that appeal to the senses—is one reason her story is so vivid and clear. Compare these two phrases:

> Apples in a bowl　　　　Calville apples in a silver bowl

While their meaning is essentially the same, the second phrase creates an image, or word picture, that is both more informative and more suggestive of emotion. As you read, notice the many descriptive details Colette employs.

❸ Reading Strategy

Drawing Conclusions

When you **draw conclusions,** you use your reasoning to reach logical decisions on the basis of evidence. For example, if someone comes inside shaking out a wet umbrella, you might draw the conclusion that it is raining. When reading, you draw conclusions by applying your knowledge and experiences to details from the work. As you read "The Bracelet," draw conclusions about Madame Augelier's life and character.

Vocabulary Builder

supple (sup´ əl) *adj.* easily bent; flexible (p. 1118)

connoisseur (kän´ ə sʉr´) *n.* person with expert judgment and taste (p. 1118)

convalescent (kän´ və les´ ənt) *n.* person who is recovering health after illness (p. 1121)

enraptured (en rap´ chərd) *adj.* filled with great pleasure (p. 1121)

iridescent (ir´ i des´ ənt) *adj.* showing rainbowlike shifts in color (p. 1121)

serpentine (sʉr´ pən tēn´) *adj.* resembling a snake (p. 1121)

congealed (kən jēld´) *v.* thickened; solidified (p. 1121)

The Bracelet ■ 1117

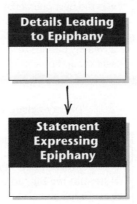

Details Leading to Epiphany

↓

Statement Expressing Epiphany

❷ Literary Analysis

Epiphany

- Read aloud the Literary Analysis instruction. Tell students that both a character and a reader can experience an epiphany.

- Have volunteers share with the class their experiences with epiphanies. Have students discuss what they learned as a result of their epiphanies.

- Then, point out the graphic organizer. Tell students that recognizing significant details or events will help them identify an epiphany in a literary work. Distribute copies of the **Literary Analysis Graphic Organizer A,** p. 184 in *Graphic Organizer Transparencies.* Have students use the organizer as they read the story.

❸ Reading Strategy

Drawing Conclusions

- Have a volunteer read aloud the Reading Strategy instruction.

- Tell students that many literary works are built of layers of meaning. To uncover deeper meanings, a reader must draw conclusions.

- As students read "The Bracelet," have them use details from the selection and their own experiences to draw conclusions about the story's deeper meanings.

Vocabulary Builder

- Pronounce each vocabulary word for students, and read the definitions as a class. Have students identify any words with which they are already familiar.

Differentiated Instruction　Solutions for All Learners

Support for Special Needs Students

Have students read the adapted version of "The Bracelet" in the *Reader's Notebook: Adapted Version.* This version provides basic-level instruction in an interactive format with questions and write-on lines. Completing these pages will prepare students to read the selection in the Student Edition.

Support for Less Proficient Readers

Have students read "The Bracelet" in the *Reader's Notebook.* This version provides basic-level instruction in an interactive format with questions and write-on lines. After students finish the selection in the *Reader's Notebook,* have them complete the questions and activities in the Student Edition.

Support for English Learners

Have students read "The Bracelet" in the *Reader's Notebook: English Learner's Version.* This version provides basic-level instruction in an interactive format with questions and write-on lines. Completing these pages will prepare students to read the selection in the Student Edition.

Facilitate Understanding

Ask students to recall a special gift they cherished in younger years. Have them explain why they think that no new present could ever take its place.

❶ About the Selection

In Colette's story "The Bracelet," a woman of fifty looks back on her life of wealth and privilege to discover a disturbing but unavoidable truth about life, possessions, and the passage of time.

❷ Reading Strategy

Drawing Conclusions

- Remind students that when a reader draws a conclusion, he or she makes a general statement that can be explained or supported with details from the selection.

- Read aloud the bracketed passage. Then, **ask:** What conclusions can you draw about Madame Augelier? **Answer:** She is wealthy, and she must be concerned about aging because she notices the wrinkles around her wrist.

- Then, **ask** students the Reading Strategy question: What conclusions might you draw about the Augeliers' relationship, based on Madame's comment about her husband? **Possible response:** François faithfully buys Madame Augelier an anniversary gift every year, but despite this gesture, or perhaps because of it, Madame Augelier pities her husband.

❸ Reading Check

Answer: She has received a diamond bracelet for her twenty-ninth wedding anniversary.

The Bracelet

Colette

translated by Matthew Ward

Background At the turn of the twentieth century, the women's rights movement was very new. Women in the West were just beginning to enjoy educational and employment opportunities, and marriage generally was the best guarantee of economic security. Like most of Colette's fiction, "The Bracelet" touches on the changing role of women in France in the early twentieth century. The main character, Madame Augelier, is married to a wealthy business executive. In a subtle fashion, the story asks whether the security and predictability of such a marriage is enough for happiness.

". . . Twenty-seven, twenty-eight, twenty-nine . . . There really are twenty-nine . . ."

Madame Augelier mechanically counted and recounted the little *pavé*[1] diamonds. Twenty-nine square brilliants, set in a bracelet, which slithered between her fingers like a cold and <u>supple</u> snake. Very white, not too big, admirably matched to each other—the pretty bijou[2] of a <u>connoisseur</u>. She fastened it on her wrist, and shook it, throwing off blue sparks under the electric candles; a hundred tiny rainbows, blazing with color, danced on the white tablecloth. But Madame Augelier was looking more closely instead at the other bracelet, the three finely engraved creases encircling her wrist above the glittering snake.

"Poor François . . . what will he give me next year, if we're both still here?"

François Augelier, industrialist, was traveling in Algeria at the time, but, present or absent, his gift marked both the year's end and their wedding anniversary. Twenty-eight jade bowls, last year; twenty-seven old enamel plaques mounted on a belt, the year before . . .

"And the twenty-six little Royal Dresden[3] plates . . . And the twenty-four meters of antique Alençon lace[4] . . ." With a slight effort of memory

---

1. *pavé* (pa vā´) jewelry setting in which the gems are placed close together so that no metal shows.
2. **bijou** (bē zhoo´) *n.* jewel.
3. **Royal Dresden** (drez´ dən) fine, decorated porcelain or chinaware made near Dresden, a city in southeast-central Germany.
4. **Alençon** (ə len´ sän´) **lace** needlepoint lace with a solid design on a net background.

1118 ■ *The Modern World*

Vocabulary Builder

supple (sup´ əl) *adj.* easily bent; flexible

connoisseur (kän´ ə sʉr´) *n.* person with expert judgment and taste

Reading Strategy
Drawing Conclusions
What conclusions might you draw about the Augeliers' relationship, based on Madame's comment about her husband?

 **Reading Check** ❸

For what occasion has Madame Augelier received a diamond bracelet from her husband?

Madame Hayden, Amedeo Modigliani

❺ ▲ **Critical Viewing** In what ways is this portrait similar to and different from your image of Madame Augelier? Explain. **[Compare and Contrast]**

❹ Humanities

Madame Hayden,
by Amedeo Modigliani

The Italian painter Amedeo Modigliani (1884–1920) spent most of his artistic life in Paris. He was strongly influenced not only by Picasso and French painters Cézanne and Rousseau but also by the great painters of the Italian Renaissance, especially Sandro Botticelli. Modigliani is best known for his portraits and nudes. The portraits, including the one of Madame Hayden, feature elongated oval shapes. Many of his subjects seem to have melancholy expressions. Modigliani was also a sculptor; his three-dimensional works have many of the characteristics of West African art and masks he had seen displayed in Paris.

Use the following questions for discussion:

• How would you describe the subject's mood?
  Answer: The woman appears resigned and weary.

• What is most striking about the woman's pose?
  Possible response: Students may mention the woman's tilted head and uncomfortable neck position or her long, entwined fingers.

❺ Critical Viewing

Answer: Like Madame Augelier, the woman in the portrait seems melancholy, as if she were assessing her life and the changes that have overtaken her. However, she looks younger than Madame Augelier is described.

Differentiated Instruction   Solutions for All Learners

Strategy for Special Needs Students
Explain to students that "The Bracelet" is rich in sensory details. For example, in the second paragraph, the description of the bracelet as "like a cold and supple snake" appeals to the sense of touch. Tell students that Colette uses vivid imagery. Have students preview the selection to identify and list other sensory details. Then, discuss images and their intended effects on the reader.

Enrichment for Gifted/Talented Students
Many students may be struck by the mood of this story. Have them choose or compose a piece of background music to match the mood of gentle melancholy and resignation in "The Bracelet." Ask students to play the music for the class and explain their choices or compositions. Then, initiate a discussion about the suitability and effectiveness of each musical selection, and have students suggest other music that would be appropriate.

Take a Position

- Draw students' attention to the last sentence in the first paragraph.

- **Ask:** On the basis of this sentence, what can you conclude about the narrator's view of marriage?
Answer: In the absence of love, affection and fidelity can be the basis of a good marriage.

7 Reading Strategy

Drawing Conclusions

- Have a volunteer read the bracketed passage.

- Then, **ask** students the Reading Strategy question: Based on her comments about her husband and her feelings about his gifts, what conclusions can you draw about Madame Augelier's happiness with her life? Explain.
Answer: Madame Augelier is dissatisfied with her life. She acknowledges that her husband is good to her, but she believes that she does not love him enough and knows that the gifts will not satisfy her.

- **Monitor Progress Ask** students: What details from the story did you use to draw your conclusion about Madame Augelier's feelings about her life?
Answer: Students may include the description of her husband as "poor François," her guilt at not loving him enough, and her boredom with the bracelet.

- **Reteach** Direct students' attention to the Reading Strategy instruction on p. 1117. Remind students that when drawing conclusions, a reader must supply textual evidence as support.

8 Critical Viewing

Possible response: François would have given jewels like these later in the marriage; early in their marriage, he could not have afforded such gifts.

1120

Madame Augelier could have gone back as far as four modest silver place settings, as far as three pairs of silk stockings . . .

"We weren't rich back then. Poor François, he's always spoiled me so . . ." To herself, secretly, she called him "poor François," because she believed herself guilty of not loving him enough, underestimating the strength of affectionate habits and abiding fidelity.

Madame Augelier raised her hand, tucked her little finger under, extended her wrist to erase the bracelet of wrinkles, and repeated intently, "It's so pretty . . . the diamonds are so white . . . I'm so pleased . . ." Then she let her hand fall back down and admitted to herself that she was already tired of her new bracelet.

"But I'm not ungrateful," she said naïvely with a sigh. Her weary eyes wandered from the flowered tablecloth to the gleaming window. The smell of some Calville apples in a silver bowl made her feel slightly sick and she left the dining room.

In her boudoir[5] she opened the steel case which held her jewels, and adorned her left hand in honor of the new bracelet. Her ring had on it a black onyx band and a blue-tinted brilliant; onto her delicate, pale, and

5. **boudoir** (bo͞o′ dwär′) *n.* woman's bedroom, dressing room, or private sitting room.

1120 ■ *The Modern World*

▼ **Critical Viewing 8**
Do you think Monsieur Augelier would have given jewels like these to his wife earlier or later in their marriage? Explain.
[Connect]

Enrichment

Glass

Madame Augelier longs to reclaim her glass bangle for its symbolic value, but the beauty and functionality of glass has been treasured for thousands of years.

Glass beads dating from around 2500 B.C. have been found in Egypt and Mesopotamia. Early glass items were made by pouring molten glass over a sand core. The core was removed after the glass hardened, leaving the hollow container behind. The glassblowing technique most likely developed in Syria during the final years of the first century B.C.

At the end of the thirteenth century, Venice, Italy, became a major European center for glassmaking. Venetians might have learned glassmaking from the Near Eastern people they encountered during the Crusades.

Silica, in the form of sand, is the primary ingredient for making glass. Adding various metallic compounds to a mixture of silica and its modifiers and stabilizers produces colored glass. For example, gold, cadmium, or cuprous oxide added to the mixture makes red glass.

somewhat wrinkled little finger, Madame Augelier slipped a circle of dark sapphires. Her prematurely white hair, which she did not dye, appeared even whiter as she adjusted amid slightly frizzy curls a narrow fillet sprinkled with a dusting of diamonds, which she immediately untied and took off again.

"I don't know what's wrong with me. I'm not feeling all that well. Being fifty is a bore, basically . . ."

She felt restless, both terribly hungry and sick to her stomach, like a <u>convalescent</u> whose appetite the fresh air has yet to restore.

"Really now, is a diamond actually as pretty as all that?"

Madame Augelier craved a visual pleasure which would involve the sense of taste as well; the unexpected sight of a lemon, the unbearable squeaking of the knife cutting it in half, makes the mouth water with desire . . .

"But I don't want a lemon. Yet this nameless pleasure which escapes me does exist, I know it does, I remember it! Yes, the blue glass bracelet . . ."

A shudder made Madame Augelier's slack cheeks tighten. A vision, the duration of which she could not measure, granted her, for a second time, a moment lived forty years earlier, that incomparable moment as she looked, <u>enraptured</u>, at the color of the

day, the <u>iridescent</u>, distorted image of objects seen through a blue glass bangle, moved around in a circle, which she had just been given. That piece of perhaps Oriental glass, broken a few hours later, had held in it a new universe, shapes not the inventions of dreams, slow, <u>serpentine</u> animals moving in pairs, lamps, rays of light <u>congealed</u> in an atmosphere of indescribable blue . . .

The vision ended and Madame Augelier fell back, bruised, into the present, into reality.

But the next day she began searching, from antique shops to flea markets, from flea markets to crystal shops, for a glass bracelet, a certain color of blue. She put the passion of a collector, the precaution, the dissimulation[6] of a lunatic into her search. She ventured into what she called "impossible districts," left her car at the corner of strange streets, and in the end, for a few centimes, she found a circle of blue glass which she recognized in the darkness, stammered as she paid for it, and carried it away.

---

6. **dissimulation** (di sim′ yōō lā′ shən) *n.* hiding of one's feelings or motives by pretense.

Literature in Context

⑨ World Events Connection

Algeria and France

At the time of this story, France governed much of western and west-central Africa. Algeria, a French colony since 1834, played an important role in France's economy, partly through its production and export of citrus fruit and wine. Yet the relationship between Algeria and France was never an easy one. Cultural and economic conflicts between the country's poor Muslim majority and wealthy Europeans erupted into armed conflict in 1954, the year of Colette's death. After eight years of struggle, Algeria finally secured its independence from France in July of 1962.

Connect to the Literature

In what way does the reference to Algeria in "The Bracelet" enrich the cultural context of the story?

Vocabulary Builder

convalescent (kän′ və les′ ənt) *n.* person who is recovering health after illness

enraptured (en rap′ chərd) *adj.* filled with great pleasure

iridescent (ir′ i des′ ənt) *adj.* showing rainbowlike shifts in color

serpentine (sur′ pən tēn′) *adj.* resembling a snake

congealed (kən jēld′) *adj.* thickened; solidified

⑪ Reading Check

What object does Madame Augelier long to find?

The Bracelet ■ 1121

Differentiated Instruction — Solutions for All Learners

Enrichment for Less Proficient Readers
Organize students into small groups, and have them discuss whether adults view childhood nostalgically. Tell each group to make a list of five or six interview questions they could ask adults about their views of childhood. Then, have each group interview a parent, grandparent, neighbor, or other adult and record the responses. Have groups present their findings to the class and discuss the results. Then, lead students in a discussion about whether Madame Augelier's feelings about her childhood are realistic.

Enrichment for Advanced Readers
Tell students that in *As You Like It* (II, vii, 139), Shakespeare describes the stages of life. Ask students to read the "All the world's a stage" speech and to discuss it with classmates. Then, have students consider Madame Augelier's changes and speculate on what she must have been like at age ten. Finally, have students explain what stage of life they think Madame Augelier has reached by the end of the story.

---

⑨ Literature in Context

Algeria and France French influences remain in Algeria. Although Arabic was made the only official language in 1996, newspapers and television shows are still produced in both languages. Three radio networks exist; one of them broadcasts in Arabic, one in Berber, and one in French.

France is still the major source of imports to Algeria and the second-largest receiver of exports from Algeria. The French also make up Algeria's largest foreign tourist population.

Connect to the Literature Tell students that 99 percent of the population of present-day Algeria is Arab-Berber, and that Europeans make up less than 1 percent of the population. Algeria is a republic with a legal system based on French and Islamic law. The country has the largest natural gas reserves in the world and is the world's second-largest gas exporter. Ask students to explain how the fact that Madame Augelier's husband is in Algeria creates a broader cultural context for the story.

Possible response: The reference enriches the story's cultural context because it permits the characters to be perceived as being familiar with the culture of Algeria. Monsieur Augelier might have Arab friends, and Madame Augelier could have visited the country as a tourist.

⑩ Vocabulary Builder

Latin Prefix en-

- Draw students' attention to the word *enraptured,* and read its definition.

- Tell students that this word includes the prefix *en-,* which has several meanings, including "to put into or cover," "to cause to be," and "to provide with."

- **Ask** students to list common words that contain the prefix *en-,* and discuss how the prefix helps create the meaning of the word.

Possible responses: Students may suggest *encapsulate, enable, encrypt, encourage, enclose, endear, enjoy, enlarge,* and *enlighten.*

⑪ Reading Check

Answer: She wants to find a blue glass bracelet like one she had in her youth.

⑫ Literary Analysis

Epiphany

• Have a volunteer read aloud the bracketed passage.

• Then, **ask:** Who is the "stranger"?
Answer: The stranger is Madame Augelier at ten years old.

• **Ask:** What insight into herself does Madame Augelier experience at the story's end?
Answer: She learns that she has aged and cannot recapture her youthful feelings.

ASSESS

Answers

1. **Possible response:** Some readers will feel sorry for her loss of childhood innocence; others may think her spoiled and naïve.

2. (a) Madame Augelier is bored. (b) Madame Augelier's boredom reveals that she is jaded both toward the gift and toward her husband's affections. (c) It is safe and secure. Surrounded by wealth, she feels no passion or love.

3. (a) In the third year, Madame Augelier received three pairs of silk stockings; in the fourth, she received four modest silver place settings. (b) The Augeliers have become financially secure and can afford expensive gifts, but their relationship has lost its passion.

4. (a) Madame Augelier remembers a blue glass bracelet. (b) She goes shopping for a bracelet like the one from her youth. (c) She is hoping to recapture the feelings of youth.

5. (a) It is now a trinket worthy of only a "child or savage." (b) Madame Augelier has seen and experienced much since childhood but has lost her passion for life.

6. The title refers to both bracelets. The diamond bracelet is the impetus for Madame Augelier's search for the blue glass bracelet. The blue glass bracelet is the object that leads to her epiphany.

In the discreet light of her favorite lamp she set the bracelet on the dark field of an old piece of velvet, leaned forward, and waited for the shock . . . But all she saw was a round piece of bluish glass, the trinket of a child or a savage, hastily made and blistered with bubbles; an object whose color and material her memory and reason recognized; but the powerful and sensual genius who creates and nourishes the marvels of childhood, who gradually weakens, then dies mysteriously within us, did not even stir.

Resigned, Madame Augelier thus came to know how old she really ⑫ was and measured the infinite plain over which there wandered, beyond her reach, a being detached from her forever, a stranger, turned away from her, rebellious and free even from the bidding of memory: a little ten-year-old girl wearing on her wrist a bracelet of blue glass.

Critical Reading

1. **Respond:** Do you sympathize with Madame Augelier? Why or why not?

2. **(a) Recall:** As the story begins, with what attitude does Madame Augelier count the diamonds in her bracelet? **(b) Analyze:** How does this description show that the bracelet was given and received with little true feeling? **(c) Define:** What does the beginning of the story tell you about the nature of Madame Augelier's world?

3. **(a) Recall:** What gifts did Madame Augelier receive from her husband in their third and fourth years of marriage? **(b) Generalize:** How has the couple's relationship and lifestyle changed since then? Explain.

4. **(a) Recall:** What object does Madame Augelier suddenly remember from her childhood? **(b) Infer:** Why does she go shopping? **(c) Deduce:** What is Madame Augelier truly hoping to find when she goes shopping?

5. **(a) Compare and Contrast:** When Madame Augelier examines the glass bracelet at home, how does it compare with the vision from her childhood? **(b) Interpret:** What has changed since her childhood?

6. **Make a Judgment:** Do you think the title of this story refers to the diamond bracelet or to the blue bracelet? Support your answer.

Go Online
Author Link
For: More about Colette
Visit: www.PHSchool.com
Web Code: ete-9802

Go Online For additional information about
Author Link Colette, have students type in the
Web Code, then select C from the alphabet, and then
select Colette.

Apply the Skills

The Bracelet

Literary Analysis

Epiphany

1. Colette provides an **epiphany** instead of a resolution to the conflict in this story. **(a)** What is the main conflict in "The Bracelet"? **(b)** At the end of the story, Madame Augelier is "resigned." Why is that an important term in understanding Madame Augelier and the conflict?
2. **(a)** What sudden realization does Madame Augelier experience in "The Bracelet"? **(b)** How does she react to that epiphany?
3. Early in the story, how do Madame Augelier's memories of past anniversary presents help prepare readers for her epiphany?
4. Does Madame Augelier's epiphany seem believable? Explain.

Connecting Literary Elements

5. What **descriptive details** about anniversary gifts of the past help draw the reader into the story?
6. **(a)** What details about the blue glass bracelet does Madame Augelier remember? **(b)** In what ways do these details lead to the story's epiphany?

Reading Strategy

Drawing Conclusions

7. Use a chart like the one shown to identify details that allow you to **draw the conclusion** that Madame Augelier is unhappy.

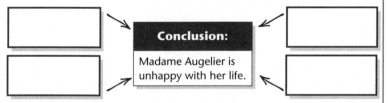

Conclusion:

Madame Augelier is unhappy with her life.

8. **(a)** At the beginning of the story, how does Madame Augelier feel about getting older? **(b)** Do her feelings change at the end of the story? **(c)** Which details led you to draw each of these conclusions?

Extend Understanding

9. Social Studies Connection: What does this story reveal about upper-class life in France in the early twentieth century? Explain.

QuickReview

An **epiphany** is a sudden, profound thought or insight that a character experiences.

Descriptive details are words and phrases that appeal to the senses and create vivid word pictures.

To **draw conclusions** as you read, make decisions about characters and situations by applying your knowledge and experiences to details from the work.

Go Online
Assessment

For: Self-test
Visit: www.PHSchool.com
Web Code: eta-6802

The Bracelet ■ 1123

Answers continued

9. Upper-class people lived lives of comfort and leisure. Women almost never worked outside the home.

Go Online
Assessment Students may use the **Self-test** to prepare for **Selection Test A** or **Selection Test B.**

Answers

1. **(a)** The aging Madame Augelier wants to recapture the freshness and passion of her youth. **(b)** The term implies that Madame Augelier has accepted her age and situation.
2. **(a)** She senses how old she has become and how little is left of the child she was. **(b)** She resigns herself to this realization.
3. She recalls each gift without passion or nostalgia, implying her boredom with life and emphasizing her age.
4. **Possible response:** The epiphany seems believable because a mature, jaded woman would have difficulty rediscovering passion and enthusiasm.
5. The descriptions of the progressively valuable gifts that represent the number of anniversary years provide a history that draws the reader into the story. The reader wants to learn more about this woman who is indifferent to such gifts.
6. **(a)** She remembers the color and iridescence of the bracelet, the distorted image of objects seen through its blue glass, and that it broke within a few hours. **(b)** Madame Augelier's epiphany about her youth mirrors those details provided about the bracelet. Her youth, like the bracelet, is "broken" and gone forever. The distorted image Madame Augelier once saw through the glass parallels the distorted image she now sees of her childhood.
7. Details include her wondering whether she and her husband will still be around in a year; her boredom with the diamond bracelet; her guilt at not loving her husband; her "weary eyes"; her restlessness; and her craving for sensory stimulation.
8. **(a)** She feels that getting older is a bore. **(b)** Her boredom changes to helplessness and resignation. **(c)** At the beginning of the story, Madame Augelier's boredom is revealed by her jaded attitude toward her possessions. At the end of the story, her helplessness and resignation are supported by her recognition of herself as a child—a "stranger," "detached" and unattainable.

1123

❶ Vocabulary Lesson

Word Analysis:
Latin Prefix *en-*

1. to put courage into
2. to put in danger
3. to cause to be larger
4. covered with a robe
5. to provide with light
6. to cause to be cumbered or burdened

Spelling Strategy

1. absent
2. impatient
3. opulent
4. eloquent

Vocabulary Builder

1. convalescent
2. enraptured
3. iridescent
4. connoisseur
5. congealed
6. serpentine
7. supple

❷ Grammar and Style Lesson

1. sat
2. set
3. sitting
4. set
5. sat

Writing Application

Possible response: Yesterday I *sat* in a beautiful iridescent blue sports car. The owner let me *sit* behind the wheel. He was *sitting* beside me so that I wouldn't drive off. Someday, I hope to own one like it. I can just see it *sitting* in my driveway. I even *set* a picture of it on my dresser.

Writing and Grammar
Platinum Level

For support in teaching the Grammar and Style Lesson, use Chapter 26, Section 2.

1124

Build Language Skills

❶ Vocabulary Lesson

Word Analysis: Latin Prefix *en-*

The prefix *en-* has several related meanings, including "to put into or cover," "to cause to be," or "to provide with." The vocabulary word *enraptured* literally means "put into a state of rapture." Use the meanings of *en-* to define each of the following words.

1. encourage
2. endanger
3. enlarge
4. enrobed
5. enlighten
6. encumbered

Spelling Strategy

If a noun ends in *-ence,* the adjective form of the word ends in *-ent.* For example, the noun *iridescence* becomes the adjective *iridescent.* Write the adjective form of each of the following nouns.

1. absence
2. impatience
3. opulence
4. eloquence

Vocabulary Builder: Sentence Completions

Complete each sentence below with a word from the vocabulary list on page 1117.

1. The ___?___ struggled to his feet and, with some assistance, took a few steps.
2. He gave a(n) ___?___ grin at finally being able to walk again.
3. She admired the sparkling, ___?___ beads that decorated the gown.
4. At the five-star restaurant, the ___?___ examined his dessert with a scowl.
5. "This ___?___ chocolate sauce is inedible!" he complained to the waiter.
6. The lioness took a ___?___ path as she followed the herd.
7. Her ___?___ body glided through the grass with ease.

❷ Grammar and Style Lesson

Commonly Confused Words: *sit* and *set*

Be careful to distinguish between *sit* and *set,* two easily confused verbs. *Sit* means "to be seated or resting in a particular spot." *Set* means "to put (something) in a certain place."

> . . . He asked her to *sit* down.
>
> . . . she *set* the bracelet on an old piece of velvet . . .

The main forms of *sit* are *sit, sitting, sat,* and *(have) sat.* The main forms of *set* are *set, setting, set,* and *(have) set.*

Practice Identify the correct verb in each of the following sentences.

1. Twenty-nine square stones (sat, set) in the bracelet.
2. Madame Augelier (sat, set) the bracelet in the box.
3. She was (sitting, setting) in her bedroom.
4. She had (sat, set) the box on the dresser.
5. She paced around the room and then (sat, set) down again.

Writing Application Write a paragraph about things you think you might own someday. Five times in the paragraph, use a form of the verb *sit* or *set* correctly.

*W*G *Prentice Hall Writing and Grammar Connection: Platinum Level, Chapter 22, Section 1*

Assessment Practice

Comparing and Contrasting Texts (For more practice, see *Test Preparation Workbook,* p. 47)

Many tests require students to compare and contrast texts. Use the following sample test item to give students practice at this skill.

Twenty-nine square brilliants, set in a bracelet, which slithered between her fingers like a cold and supple snake. ("The Bracelet" by Colette)

She had started to turn the knob when a hoarse growl, like that of a wild beast surprised in his lair, quickly stopped her. ("A Breath of Air" by Luigi Pirandello)

These passages are similar in that they both use—

A onomatopoeia
B repetition
C simile
D metaphor

Choice C is correct. Both passages feature a simile, or a figure of speech that makes a direct comparison between two subjects, using *like* or *as.* No examples of onomatopoeia, repetition, or metaphor appear in either passage.

❸ Writing Lesson

Timed Writing: Analytical Essay

Write an essay in which you analyze how Colette's use of images—words or phrases that appeal to the senses and create word pictures—helps convey the theme, or message about life, in "The Bracelet." *(40 minutes)*

Prewriting
(10 minutes)

In one sentence, state the story's theme or message. Then, reread the story, listing images that you associate with that theme. Use a chart like the one shown to explore each image.

Drafting
(20 minutes)

Begin with a general statement about the theme, or main idea, of "The Bracelet." Then, cite specific examples of images in the story that suggest or develop that theme or main idea.

Revising
(10 minutes)

As you review your draft, underline your main ideas and check that each one is clearly stated and well supported. Add examples of images as needed to illustrate your points.

W̶G̶ Prentice Hall Writing and Grammar Connection: Platinum Level, Chapter 13, Section 2

❹ Extend Your Learning

Listening and Speaking Adapt "The Bracelet" as a **monologue** given by Madame Augelier. Use these tips to prepare:

- Decide whether Madame Augelier will address the audience or will speak as if she is alone and thinking aloud.
- Determine what confessions Madame Augelier might make.
- Include her epiphany in some way.

Deliver the monologue to a small group or to the class.

Research and Technology "The Bracelet" takes place in France at the turn of the twentieth century. With a partner, research the clothing and decorating styles of that era. Then, prepare a **set and costume design** that accurately reflect Madame Augelier's clothing and home and that could be used for a dramatic performance of the story. [Group Activity]

 Go Online Research
For: An additional research activity
Visit: www.PHSchool.com
Web Code: etd-7802

The Bracelet ■ 1125

❸ Writing Lesson

You may use this Writing Lesson as a timed-writing practice, or you may allow students to develop the analytical essay as a writing assignment over several days.

- To give students guidance in writing this essay, give them the **Support for Writing Lesson**, p. 32 *in Unit 8 Resources.*
- Read aloud the Writing Lesson instruction. Tell students that in an analytical essay, the writer looks critically at various important elements in a work of literature. Explain how the author has used those elements.
- Use the Response to Literature rubrics in *General Resources*, pp. 55–56, to evaluate students' work.

W̶G̶ Writing and Grammar Platinum Level
For support in teaching the Writing Lesson, use Chapter 13, Section 2.

❹ Listening and Speaking

- Explain to students that a monologue is a speech or performance given entirely by one person.
- Have students follow the tips as they prepare their monologues. Encourage students to use an appropriate tone of voice and gestures to emphasize important thoughts or feelings.
- The **Support for Extend Your Learning** page (*Unit 8 Resources*, p. 33) provides guided note-taking opportunities to help students complete the Extend Your Learning activities.

Go Online Research Have students type in the Web Code for another research activity.

Standard Course of Study

Goal 1: WRITTEN LANGUAGE

WL.1.02.5   Demonstrate an understanding of media's impact on analyses and personal reflection.

WL.1.03.2   Identify and analyze text components and evaluate impact on personal reflection.

Goal 4: CRITICAL THINKING

CT.4.03.2   Analyze how writers choose and incorporate significant, supporting details.

Goal 5: LITERATURE

LT.5.01.5   Analyze archetypal characters, themes, and settings in world literature.

LT.5.02.1   Explore works which relate to an issue, author, or theme and show increasing comprehension.

Goal 6: GRAMMAR AND USAGE

GU.6.01.4   Use vocabulary strategies to determine meaning.

Step-by-Step Teaching Guide	Pacing Guide
PRETEACH	
• Administer Vocabulary and Reading Warm-ups as necessary.	5 min.
• Engage students' interest with the motivation activity.	5 min.
• Read and discuss author and background features. **FT**	10 min.
• Introduce the Literary Analysis Skill: Setting. **FT**	5 min.
• Introduce the Reading Strategy: Comparing and Contrasting Characters. **FT**	10 min.
• Prepare students to read by teaching the selection vocabulary. **FT**	
TEACH	
• Informally monitor comprehension while students read independently or in groups. **FT**	30 min.
• Monitor students' comprehension with the Reading Check notes.	as students read
• Reinforce vocabulary with Vocabulary Builder notes.	as students read
• Develop students' understanding of setting with the Literary Analysis annotations. **FT**	5 min.
• Develop students' ability to compare and contrast characters with the Reading Strategy annotations. **FT**	5 min.
ASSESS/EXTEND	
• Assess students' comprehension and mastery of the Literary Analysis and Reading Strategy by having them answer the Apply the Skills questions. **FT**	15 min.
• Have students complete the Vocabulary Development Lesson and the Grammar and Style Lesson. **FT**	15 min.
• Apply students' ability to maintain journalistic objectivity by using the Writing Lesson. **FT**	45 min. or homework
• Apply students' understanding by using one or more of the Extend Your Learning activities.	20–90 min. or homework
• Administer Selection Test A or Selection Test B. **FT**	15 min.

Resources

Print

Unit 8 Resources

Transparency

Graphic Organizer Transparencies

Print

Reader's Notebook [L2]

Reader's Notebook: Adapted Version [L1]

Reader's Notebook: English Learner's Version [EL]

Unit 8 Resources

Technology

Listening to Literature Audio CDs [L2, EL]

Reader's Notebook: Adapted Version Audio CD [L1, L2]

Print

Unit 8 Resources

Technology

Go Online: Research [**L3**]
Go Online: Self-test [**L3**]
ExamView®, Test Bank [**L3**]

Choosing Resources for Differentiated Instruction

[**L1**] Special Needs Students

[**L2**] Below-Level Students

[**L3**] All Students

[**L4**] Advanced Students

[**EL**] English Learners

For Vocabulary and Reading Warm-ups and for Selection Tests, **A** signifies "less challenging" and **B** "more challenging." For Graphic Organizer transparencies, **A** signifies "not filled in" and **B** "filled in."

FT Fast Track Instruction: To move the lesson more quickly, use the strategies and activities identified with **FT.**

Scaffolding for Less Proficient and Advanced Students

The leveled Critical Thinking questions after selections progress in the levels of thinking required to answer them. To address the needs of your different students, you may use the (a) level questions for your less proficient students and the (b) level questions with your on-level and advanced students. The occasional (c) level questions are appropriate for your advanced students.

PRENTICE HALL

Teacher EXPRESS™ Use this complete

Plan · Teach · Assess suite of powerful teaching tools to make lesson planning and testing quicker and easier.

PRENTICE HALL

Student EXPRESS™ Use the interactive

Learn · Study · Succeed textbook (online and on CD-ROM) to make selections and activities come alive with audio and video support and interactive questions.

Go **Online**
Professional
Development

For: Information about Lexiles
Visit: www.PHSchool.com
Web Code: eue-1111

War ❶

Motivation

Explain to students that the characters of Pirandello's story "War" share intimate and painful details about their lives. Discuss with students situations in which perfect strangers might begin talking about their most private matters. Then, invite students to share any experiences they may have had with "sudden familiarity."

❶ Background

More About the Author

The collapse of the sulfur mines in 1903 became a major turning point in Pirandello's life. The resulting financial disaster triggered the onset of his wife's paranoid schizophrenia. Soon after the collapse of the mines, she began having suspicions about her husband's fidelity, which intensified into a frantic jealousy that caused both of them great suffering. In 1919, she was committed to a sanatorium, where she remained until her death in 1959. This dreadful experience caused Pirandello to develop a strong fascination with the complex, hidden world of the human personality—a fascination that is clearly reflected in his later works.

Geography Note

Draw students' attention to the map on this page. Remind students that Pirandello was born in Sicily, the largest island in the Mediterranean Sea. A center for seismic and volcanic activity, the island of Sicily is home to Mount Etna, Europe's highest active volcano.

Luigi Pirandello (1867–1936)

With the completion of his masterpiece, *Six Characters in Search of an Author* (1921)—a play about a group of characters who, in their quest to find an author to tell their story, interrupt a group of actors rehearsing another play—Luigi Pirandello (lōō ē´ jē pir´ ən del´ ō) established himself as one of the most innovative dramatists of his time. Unfortunately, however, Pirandello's success as a playwright has overshadowed his numerous accomplishments as a fiction writer. Today, many people are unaware that in Italy, his native land, Luigi Pirandello is widely recognized as the master of the short story.

Early Trials The son of a successful sulfur merchant, Pirandello was born on the island of Sicily, off the southern tip of Italy. After high school, he attended the University of Rome and later received a doctorate from the University of Bonn in Germany. In 1894, he married the daughter of another sulfur merchant, and with the financial support of both his parents and his in-laws, he devoted the next ten years entirely to writing. When the sulfur mines collapsed in 1903, however, the fortunes of both families were wiped out, and Pirandello became a teacher in order to earn a living. At about the same time, his wife showed symptoms of the mental illness for which she would later be institutionalized.

First Triumphs Despite these setbacks, Pirandello continued to write. Having already established himself as a gifted short-story writer, Pirandello published his best-known novel,

Luigi Pirandello, Primo Conte, Giraudon

The Late Mattia Pascal, in 1904. Like many of his early stories, the novel explored the complexities of personal identity and questioned the distinction between appearance and reality. These themes were also the focus of *It Is So (If You Think So)* (1917), Pirandello's first successful play, and were fully developed in his greatest dramatic works, *Six Characters in Search of an Author* and *Henry IV* (1922).

An International Star Having established a worldwide reputation as a playwright, Pirandello was able to open his own theater company in 1924. At the same time, he continued to write and publish prolifically. Although his later works did not achieve the popularity of his early successful plays, Pirandello received the ultimate recognition for his achievements in 1934 when he was awarded the Nobel Prize in Literature. He died two years later in Rome.

A Great Legacy At the time of his death, it was already clear that Luigi Pirandello's artistic vision had exerted a great influence on the theater, as well as on the literary world in general. However, the full force of his influence did not become clear until the emergence of new generations of playwrights, who found in his work an ideal reflection of modern uncertainties. Perhaps Pirandello summed up his work best when he wrote, "Life is full of infinite absurdities, which, strangely enough, do not even need to appear plausible, since they are true." Because of his originality and his influence on other writers, Luigi Pirandello will be remembered as one of the most important writers of the twentieth century.

Preview

Connecting to the Literature

While war can have a powerful effect upon the soldiers who see combat, it also affects the families who worry about their loved ones on the front lines. This story focuses on those whom the soldiers leave behind.

❷ Literary Analysis

Setting

The **setting** of a literary work is the time and place in which it occurs. Some settings provide a mere backdrop for the action, while others present a force, such as a winter storm or a cultural bias, that affects the characters. In "War," Pirandello establishes the setting with these words:

> At dawn, in a stuffy and smoky second-class carriage . . .

As you read "War," think about the role the setting itself plays in driving the story.

Connecting Literary Elements

Characterization is the art of creating and developing characters. There are two types of characterization:

- **Direct characterization:** The writer simply states what a character is like.
- **Indirect characterization:** The writer reveals what a character is like by describing his or her appearance, words, and actions and by noting what other characters say about him or her.

As you meet the characters in "War," consider not only *what* you learn about them but *how* you learn it.

❸ Reading Strategy

Comparing and Contrasting Characters

"War" is populated by characters who share similar concerns but react in very different ways. Clarify their similarities and differences by **comparing and contrasting the characters.** To do so, use a chart like the one shown.

Vocabulary Builder

plight (plīt) *n.* sad or difficult situation (p. 1129)

paternal (pə tur´ nəl) *adj.* like a father (p. 1129)

discrimination (di skrim´ i nā´ shən) *n.* show of partiality or prejudice (p. 1129)

vitality (vī tal´ ə tē) *n.* energy; life force (p. 1130)

retorted (ri tôrt´ id) *v.* replied, especially in a sharp or challenging way (p. 1130)

stoically (stō´ i klē) *adv.* done with indifference to pain or pleasure (p. 1131)

incongruous (in kän´ grōō əs) *adj.* not fitting a situation; inappropriate (p. 1132)

harrowing (har´ ō iŋ) *adj.* disturbing; frightening (p. 1132)

Character	1	2
Appearance		
Behavior		
Words		
Emotions		
Beliefs		

Standard Course of Study

- Analyze how writers choose and incorporate significant, supporting details. (CT.4.03.2)
- Use strategies for preparation, engagement, and reflection on world literature. (LT.5.01.1)

❷ Literary Analysis

Setting

- Read aloud the Literary Analysis instruction. Emphasize to students that setting includes time as well as place.
- Have students imagine that they are writing a story about their class. Then, have them describe the setting of their classroom. Remind them that the setting of a story helps establish its mood and tone and gives characters context.
- Then, tell students that the setting of "War"—a passenger train during World War I—is crucial to the story. Have students look for the details Pirandello provides to establish this setting.

❸ Reading Strategy

Comparing and Contrasting Characters

- After students have read the Reading Strategy instruction, remind them that the characters are the actors of a story. Some characters do not change in the course of a story. They are known as *static characters.* Others, known as *dynamic characters,* change and learn something from their experiences.
- Encourage students to look for static and dynamic characters as they read "War."
- Give students a copy of *Reading Strategy Graphic Organizer A,* p. 188 in **Graphic Organizer Transparencies.** Have them use it as they read to record details that help distinguish each character.

Vocabulary Builder

- Pronounce each vocabulary word for students, and read the definitions as a class. Have students identify any words with which they are already familiar.

Support for Special Needs Students	Support for Less Proficient Readers	Support for English Learners
Have students read the adapted version of "War" in the *Reader's Notebook: Adapted Version.* This version provides basic-level instruction in an interactive format with questions and write-on lines. Completing these pages will prepare students to read the selection in the Student Edition.	Have students read "War" in the *Reader's Notebook.* This version provides basic-level instruction in an interactive format with questions and write-on lines. After students finish the selection in the *Reader's Notebook,* have them complete the questions and activities in the Student Edition.	Have students read "War" in the *Reader's Notebook: English Learner's Version.* This version provides basic-level instruction in an interactive format with questions and write-on lines. Completing these pages will prepare students to read the selection in the Student Edition.

Facilitate Understanding

Discuss with students the fact that during a tragedy, people do not always think clearly or react normally. Some may rise above the disaster. Others may crumple under the weight of their grief or terror. Still others may put on a mask and deny the tragic circumstance. Have students read "War" to learn how the people on the train deal with their tragedies.

❶ About the Selection

World War I devastated both the landscape and people of Europe. In countries such as Italy, many families had one or more sons who had fought or died in the war. In this story, Pirandello examines the toll such sacrifice took on families.

❷ Literary Analysis

Setting

- Draw students' attention to the Literary Analysis instruction on p. 1127, and emphasize that the setting of a story is sometimes as important as the characters.

- Read the bracketed passage aloud, and point out that it contains the first descriptions of the setting. **Ask:** How does Pirandello create a believable setting? **Possible response:** In the first paragraph, Pirandello provides realistic details about the train, including its destination and the reason for the passengers' wait at the station. Sensory details, such as the description of the carriage as "stuffy" and "smoky," appeal to the reader's senses and thus make the scene familiar.

- **Ask** students the Literary Analysis question: Which details in this description of the setting suggest closeness and discomfort? Explain. **Answer:** Details that suggest closeness and discomfort include the adjectives "stuffy," "smoky," "bulky;" the verbs "hoisted," "puffing," and "moaning;" and the image of the carriage in which five adults have spent the night.

War

Luigi Pirandello *translated by* Samuel Putnam

Background In the late nineteenth and early twentieth centuries, political tensions in Europe led to alliances among several major powers. Germany, Austria-Hungary, and Italy formed the Triple Alliance; Great Britain, France, and Russia formed the Triple Entente. When World War I broke out in 1914, however, Italy did not join in on the side of its allies. Instead, Italian officials made a secret treaty with the Triple Entente, promising Italy's military help in return for land gains at the war's end. Italy then declared war on its former allies. In the years of fighting that followed, approximately 650,000 Italians died—nearly 2 percent of the country's population—and almost 950,000 more were wounded. It is against this bitter cultural landscape that Pirandello's story unfolds.

The passengers who had left Rome by the night express had had to stop until dawn at the small station of Fabriano[1] in order to continue their journey by the small old-fashioned "local" joining the main line with Sulmona.[2]

At dawn, in a stuffy and smoky second-class carriage in which five people had already spent the night, a bulky woman in deep mourning was hoisted in—almost like a shapeless bundle. Behind her—puffing and moaning, followed her husband—a tiny man, thin and weakly, his face death-white, his eyes small and bright and looking shy and uneasy.

Having at last taken a seat he politely thanked the passengers who had helped his wife and who had made room for her; then he turned round to the woman trying to pull down the collar of her coat and politely enquired:

"Are you all right, dear?"

The wife, instead of answering, pulled up her collar again to her eyes, so as to hide her face.

"Nasty world," muttered the husband with a sad smile.

And he felt it his duty to explain to his travelling companions that the poor woman was to be pitied for the war was taking away from her her only son, a boy of twenty to whom both had devoted their entire life,

Literary Analysis
Setting Which details in this description of the setting suggest closeness and discomfort? Explain.

---

1. **Fabriano** (fä´ brē ä´ nō) city in eastern Italy, approximately 100 miles from Rome.
2. **Sulmona** (sōol mō´ na) city in eastern Italy, approximately 75 miles from Rome.

even breaking up their home at Sulmona to follow him to Rome where he had to go as a student, then allowing him to volunteer for war with an assurance, however, that at least for six months he would not be sent to the front and now, all of a sudden, receiving a wire saying that he was due to leave in three days' time and asking them to go and see him off.

The woman under the big coat was twisting and wriggling, at times growling like a wild animal, feeling certain that all those explanations would not have aroused even a shadow of sympathy from those people who—most likely—were in the same <u>plight</u> as herself. One of them, who had been listening with particular attention, said:

"You should thank God that your son is only leaving now for the front. Mine has been sent there the first day of the war. He has already come back twice wounded and been sent back again to the front."

"What about me? I have two sons and three nephews at the front," said another passenger.

"Maybe, but in our case it is our *only* son," ventured the husband.

"What difference can it make? You may spoil your only son with excessive attentions, but you cannot love him more than you would all your other children if you had any. <u>Paternal</u> love is not like bread that can be broken into pieces and spilt amongst the children in equal shares. A father gives all his love to each one of his children without <u>discrimination</u>, whether it be one or ten, and if I am suffering now for my two sons, I am not suffering half for each of them but double. . . ."

"True . . . true . . . " sighed the embarrassed husband, "but suppose (of course we all hope it will never be your case) a father has two sons at the front and he loses one of them, there is still one left to console him . . . while . . . "

"Yes," answered the other, getting cross, "a son left to console him but also a son left for whom he must survive, while in the case of

❻ Critical Viewing ▶
Do you think this painting of a World War I battlefield suggests hope or terror? Explain.

Vocabulary Builder
plight (plīt) *n.* sad or difficult situation
paternal (pə tur´ nəl) *adj.* like a father
discrimination (di skrim´ i nā´ shən) *n.* show of partiality or prejudice

✓ **Reading Check ❸**
According to her husband, why is the woman in the big coat to be pitied?

A Star Shell, exh. 1916, Christopher R.W. Nevinson, Tate Gallery, London

War ■ *1129*

❸ Reading Check
Answer: The woman should be pitied because her only son is being sent to the front.

❹ Vocabulary Builder
Latin Root -*patr*-
• Draw students' attention to the word *paternal,* and ask a volunteer to read its definition.
• On the board, write the following list of words that share the root -*patr*-: *patrician, patriotic, patriarch.*
• Then, have students use dictionaries to find the definitions of the listed words. **Ask** students to infer, on the basis of these definitions, what the Latin root -*patr*- means.
Answer: The root -*patr*- comes from the Latin word *pater,* meaning "father."

❺ Humanities
A Star Shell,
by Christopher R.W. Nevinson
British artist Christopher R.W. Nevinson (1889–1946) experienced the horrors of World War I firsthand as a Red Cross ambulance driver in France. Because of illness, he left active service in 1916, but in 1917, he became an Official War Artist and returned to the front. Like Nevinson's other depictions of war, *A Star Shell* captures the stark and disturbing realities of battle.

Use the following question for discussion.
Nevinson chose not to show a human presence in this painting. What is the effect of this choice?
Answer: The absence of humans not only emphasizes the destruction of the land but also suggests the larger human toll.

❻ Critical Viewing
Possible response: The painting suggests terror. The land, which has been dug up for the trenches, has been decimated. A fiery shell, not a star, provides light. The scene provides little reason for hope.

Differentiated
Instruction — Solutions for All Learners

Strategy for Less Proficient Readers
To give students a context for the story and to model how to compare and contrast characters, distribute copies of **Reading Strategy Graphic Organizer B** (*Graphic Organizer Transparencies,* p. 189). The completed graphic organizer will give students insight into the process of comparing and contrasting. As they read, students can use the organizer for making their own comparisons and contrasts of the characters in this story.

Enrichment for Advanced Readers
In his journal, Pirandello wrote, "There is somebody who is living my life and I know nothing about him." In this statement, the author expresses a theme that he revisits in his plays and fiction. People, he contends, wear social "masks," or facades, and may not be aware of doing so. Ask students to write an essay examining the "masks" they find in "War." Encourage students to answer the following questions as they write: Who in this story is wearing a "mask"? Are these characters aware that they are wearing "masks"?

❼ Critical Thinking

Infer

- Have a volunteer read aloud the bracketed passage. Then, point out that Pirandello describes the "fat, red-faced man" as having "inner violence of an uncontrolled vitality."

- **Ask** students what they think Pirandello is trying to suggest about this character.
 Answer: There is something unhealthy, feverish, or unbalanced about this character.

❽ Humanities

Italian Soldiers,
by Karl Fahringer

This drawing appears in the Heeresgeschichtliches Museum of Military History in Vienna, Austria. The museum is the oldest museum in Vienna and houses a collection of historical artillery as well as an exhibit of World War I uniforms, guns, mortars, and other equipment.

 Use the following questions for discussion:

- How does the style of this drawing reflect the realities of war?
 Possible response: The jumbled and vigorous lines reflect the chaos and tension of battle. The lines almost appear to tie the soldiers together, illustrating their comraderie.

- Is this drawing an appropriate illustration for Pirandello's story? Explain.
 Possible responses: Yes; the drawing is appropriate because it depicts the realities of war about which the families are concerned. No; the drawing is not appropriate because it does not depict the present action of Pirandello's story, and is thus distracting.

❾ Critical Viewing

Possible response: The drawing, with its energetic lines, emphasizes the violence and chaos of combat.

the father of an only son if the son dies the father can die too and put an end to his distress. Which of the two positions is the worse? Don't you see how my case would be worse than yours?"

 "Nonsense," interrupted another traveller, a fat, red-faced man with bloodshot eyes of the palest grey.

 He was panting. From his bulging eyes seemed to spurt inner violence of an uncontrolled <u>vitality</u> which his weakened body could hardly contain.

 "Nonsense," he repeated, trying to cover his mouth with his hand so as to hide the two missing front teeth. "Nonsense. Do we give life to our children for our own benefit?"

 The other travellers stared at him in distress. The one who had had his son at the front since the first day of the war sighed: "You are right. Our children do not belong to us, they belong to the Country. . . ."

 "Bosh," <u>retorted</u> the fat traveller. "Do we think of the Country when we give life to our children? Our sons are born because . . . well, because they must be born and when they come to life they take our own life with them. This is the truth. We belong to them but they never belong to us. And when they reach twenty they are exactly what we were at their age. We too had a father and mother, but there were so many other things as well . . . girls, cigarettes, illusions, new ties . . . and the Country, of course, whose call we would have answered—when we were twenty—even if father and mother had said no. Now, at our age, the love of our Country is still great, of course, but stronger than it is the love for our children. Is there any one of us here who wouldn't gladly take his son's place at the front if he could?"

 There was a silence all round, everybody nodding as to approve.

 "Why then," continued the fat man, "shouldn't we consider the feelings of our children when they are twenty? Isn't it natural that at their age they should consider the love for their Country (I am speaking of decent boys, of course) even greater than the love for us? Isn't it natural that it should be so, as after all they must look upon us as upon old boys who cannot move any more and must stay at home? If Country exists, if Country is a natural necessity like bread, of which each of us must eat in order not to die of hunger, somebody must go to defend it. And our sons go, when they are twenty, and they don't want tears, because if they die, they die inflamed and happy (I am speaking, of

1130 ■ *The Modern World*

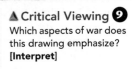

Italian Soldiers Karl Fahringer Heeresgeschichtliches Museum Vienna Austria

▲ **Critical Viewing ❾**
Which aspects of war does this drawing emphasize? **[Interpret]**

Vocabulary Builder
vitality (vī tal´ ə tē) *n.* energy; life force

retorted (ri tôrt´ id) *v.* replied, especially in a sharp or challenging way

Enrichment

The Nobel Prize

In 1934, Luigi Pirandello won the Nobel Prize in Literature, which is awarded to recognize the most distinguished body of literary work. This prize has been beneficial in bringing otherwise little-known writers and their countries into the public light as contributors to world literature.

 At the same time, however, the Nobel Prize in Literature has had its share of controversy. The Nobel committee for literature is made up of four to five members, primarily from Sweden. Some critics suspect a small bias, citing the fact that Scandinavian countries have received the Nobel Prize in Literature most often, monopolizing 14.9 percent of the prizes. France is the runner-up, taking home 12.9 percent of the prizes. The awards have spanned the globe, introducing writers from Guatemala, Czechoslovakia, South Africa, and Iceland.

course, of decent boys). Now, if one dies young and happy, without having the ugly sides of life, the boredom of it, the pettiness, the bitterness of disillusion . . . what more can we ask for him? Everyone should stop crying: everyone should laugh, as I do . . . or at least thank God—as I do—because my son, before dying, sent me a message saying that he was dying satisfied at having ended his life in the best way he could have wished. That is why, as you see, I do not even wear mourning. . . ."

He shook his light fawn[3] coat as to show it; his livid[4] lip over his missing teeth was trembling, his eyes were watery and motionless and soon after he ended with a shrill laugh which might well have been a sob.

"Quite so . . . quite so . . ." agreed the others.

The woman who, bundled in a corner under her coat, had been sitting and listening had—for the last three months—tried to find in the words of her husband and her friends something to console her in her deep sorrow, something that might show her how a mother should resign herself to send her son not even to death but to a probable danger of life. Yet not a word had she found amongst the many which had been said . . . and her grief had been greater in seeing that nobody—as she thought—could share her feelings.

But now the words of the traveller amazed and almost stunned her. She suddenly realized that it wasn't the others who were wrong and could not understand her but herself who could not rise up to the same height of those fathers and mothers willing to resign themselves, without crying, not only to the departure of their sons but even to their death.

She lifted her head, she bent over from her corner trying to listen with great attention to the details which the fat man was giving to his companions about the way his son had fallen as a hero, for his King and his Country, happy and without regrets. It seemed to her that she had stumbled into a world she had never dreamt of, a world so far unknown to her and she was so pleased to hear everyone joining in congratulating that brave father who could so stoically speak of his child's death.

3. **fawn** (fôn) pale, yellowish brown.
4. **livid** (liv′ id) discolored, as from a bruise; black-and-blue.

**Reading Strategy
Comparing and Contrasting Characters** In what ways does the fat man seem different from the other passengers?

Vocabulary Builder
stoically (stō′ i klē) *adv.* done with indifference to pain or pleasure

✓**Reading Check** ⓫
What message did the fat man's son send to him?

⓬

⓭ Critical Viewing ▶ In what ways do you think the couple in this drawing are similar to and different from the couple in this story? **[Compare and Contrast]**

War ■ 1131

Support for English Learners
Draw students' attention to the word *livid* on this page, and read the corresponding footnote. Tell students that people sometimes use the word *livid* to mean "enraged." Have students discuss how this particular use of the word relates to the definition provided in the footnote.

Enrichment for Gifted/Talented Students
In "War," Pirandello offers several physical descriptions of the fat man, including those on these pages. Ask students to use these descriptions to create an illustration of the character. Then, have students consider what these physical, external descriptions suggest about the man's emotions. Ask students to create another illustration—this time depicting the man as he appears in the final paragraph on p. 1132. Have students share their illustrations and discuss how the earlier descriptions of the man prepare for the image of his final collapse.

⓾ **Reading Strategy**
Comparing and Contrasting Characters
- **Ask:** What do the characters in the story have in common?
  Answer: They are saddened by the war and worried about their sons who are fighting.
- Read aloud the bracketed passage. **Ask** students the Reading Strategy question: In what ways does the fat man seem different from the other passengers?
  Answer: Instead of feeling sad and sorry for himself, the fat man energetically justifies the participation of their children in the war.

▶ **Monitor Progress Ask** students to discuss whether they learned about the character of the fat man directly or indirectly.
  Answer: The fat man's character is revealed indirectly through Pirandello's descriptions of his appearance and speech.

▶ **Reteach** Draw a Venn diagram on the board, and guide students as they compare and contrast characters.

⓫ **Reading Check**
Answer: The message was that the fat man's son was proud and satisfied to die in battle.

⓬ **Humanities**
Old Couple, by Käthe Kollwitz
Born in Königsberg, Prussia, Käthe Kollwitz (1867–1945) was known for her dramatic etchings, woodcuts, lithographs, and sculptures.

Use the following question for discussion.

How does lack of color contribute to the mood of this piece?
Possible response: Because the piece and the emotions exhibited by its subjects are not "colored" by connotation, both remain raw and pure.

⓭ **Critical Viewing**
Possible response: The man appears small, and the woman appears shapeless as Pirandello describes. However, the woman in the story is described as bulky, while this woman appears small.

1. **Possible response:** The man inspires pity because he is at last acknowledging his grief.

2. (a) The bulky woman wears a big coat and is dressed for mourning. (b) The woman's clothing reflects her sorrow and her wish to hide and protect herself from the outside world.

3. (a) The son sent a message telling his parents that he was being sent to the front and asking them to see him off. (b) The son assured his parents that he would not go to the front for at least six months. (c) War is unpredictable and takes no heed of promises.

4. (a) The husband claims that his suffering is worse because if he loses his son, he will have no one to console him. (b) The other passengers do not agree because they all believe that their own circumstances are worse. (c) **Possible response:** The argument cannot be won because no external standard exists by which to measure grief.

5. (a) Parents' love for their children is greater than love of their country. (b) Children place their love of country before the love of their parents. (c) The fat man reasons that his son died young and happy, never experiencing the boredom of life and the bitterness of disillusionment.

6. (a) The woman asks whether the fat man's son is really dead. (b) He stares at the woman for a long time and then breaks into uncontrollable sobs. (c) The question shatters the fat man's collected façade and makes him realize for the first time that his son is really dead.

7. **Possible response:** The story helps readers understand manifestations of grief and will cause them to be sympathetic.

Go **O**nline For additional informa-
Author Link tion about Luigi
Pirandello, have students type in the Web
Code, then select *P* from the alphabet,
and then select Luigi Pirandello.

Then suddenly, just as if she had heard nothing of what had been said and almost as if waking up from a dream, she turned to the old man, asking him:

"Then . . . is your son really dead?"

Everybody stared at her. The old man, too, turned to look at her, fixing his great, bulging, horribly watery light grey eyes, deep in her face. For some little time he tried to answer, but words failed him. He looked and looked at her, almost as if only then—at that silly, <u>incongruous</u> question—he had suddenly realized at last that his son was really dead . . . gone for ever . . . for ever. His face contracted, became horribly distorted, then he snatched in haste a handkerchief from his pocket and, to the amazement of everyone, broke into <u>harrowing</u>, heart-rending, uncontrollable sobs.

Vocabulary Builder
incongruous (in kän′ grōō əs) *adj.* not fitting a situation; inappropriate

harrowing (har′ ō in) *adj.* disturbing; frightening

Critical Reading

1. **Respond:** How did you feel about the fat man's emotional breakdown at the end of the story? Explain.

2. (a) **Recall:** What is the "bulky" woman wearing? (b) **Connect:** In what way does her clothing reflect her mental and emotional state?

3. (a) **Recall:** What message did the son send by "wire" to his parents? (b) **Recall:** What assurance had the parents received when their son joined the military? (c) **Draw Conclusions:** What is suggested about the nature of war when this promise is not kept?

4. (a) **Recall:** According to the husband, why is his suffering worse than the suffering of those with more than one child? (b) **Infer:** Do the other passengers agree with him? Explain. (c) **Assess:** Is this an argument that can be won? Why or why not?

5. (a) **Recall:** According to the fat man, what love is greater than the love of country? (b) **Compare and Contrast:** How do the feelings of young people toward their country differ from the feelings of their parents? (c) **Analyze:** How does the fat man use reason to explain away his own personal tragedy? Explain.

6. (a) **Recall:** What question does the mother ask the fat man? (b) **Analyze Cause and Effect:** How does he react to her question? (c) **Draw Conclusions:** Why does he react as he does? Explain.

7. **Synthesize:** In what ways might this story help you react toward people who have suffered a personal loss?

Go **O**nline
Author Link

For: More about Luigi Pirandello
Visit: www.PHSchool.com
Web Code: ete-9803

Apply the Skills

War

Literary Analysis

Setting

1. Using a chart like the one shown below, clarify the **setting** of "War" by naming two details about the time, two details about the place, and two details about the passengers' cultural attitudes.

Time	Place	Attitudes
1.	1.	1.
2.	2.	2.

2. **(a)** How does the historical context—Italy during World War I—affect the characters in this story? **(b)** In what ways does that context help suggest the theme, or message, of the story? Explain.

3. **(a)** In what ways might the setting of this story be similar to a combat zone? **(b)** In what ways might such a setting motivate characters to interact with one another?

Connecting Literary Elements

4. **(a)** Cite two examples of **indirect characterization** that Pirandello uses to present the husband and wife. **(b)** What information about the characters does each of these examples provide? Explain.

5. Write one sentence of **direct characterization** for each of the three main characters—the mother, the father, and the fat traveler.

Reading Strategy

Comparing and Contrasting Characters

6. **(a) Compare and contrast the characters** by examining Pirandello's descriptions of the eyes and the clothes of both the mother and the fat man. **(b)** How do those descriptions suggest similarities and differences between the two characters?

7. **(a)** For which character do you feel the most sympathy? **(b)** What do you think sets him or her apart from the others?

Extend Understanding

8. **Cultural Connection: (a)** According to the fat man, why is the attention of young people "fragmented"? **(b)** Do you see that kind of fragmentation in today's youth culture? Explain.

QuickReview

The **setting** of a literary work is the time and place of the action.

Characterization is the art of creating and developing characters. In **direct characterization**, the author simply states what a character is like. In **indirect characterization**, the author implies what a character is like through details.

When you **compare and contrast characters**, you look for similarities and differences among them.

Go Online
Assessment

For: Self-test
Visit: www.PHSchool.com
Web Code: eta-6803

War ■ 1133

Go Online — Students may use the **Self-test** to Assessment prepare for **Selection Test A** or **Selection Test B.**

Answers

1. **Possible response: Time:** dawn, during World War I; **Place:** carriage of a train, Italy; **Attitudes:** love of country, sadness about the effects of war

2. **(a)** The characters' grown sons serve in the army. **(b)** The historical context suggests that the theme will address the consequences of war.

3. **(a)** All of the characters are placed in immediate contact for a confrontation. **(b)** Because they have spent a long time together in a confined space, the characters talk out of politeness, boredom, or grief.

4. **(a) Possible response:** The wife is described as bulky and her husband as thin and weak. **(b) Possible response:** The first detail suggests that the wife is trying to conceal herself; the second, that the husband's sorrow has caused him to waste away physically.

5. **Possible response:** The mother has begun mourning for her son, even though he is still alive. The father needs to explain his wife's behavior to other travelers. The fat traveler has not fully accepted the reality of his son's death.

6. **(a)** The mother is dressed for mourning and in a big coat, and she looks like a shapeless bundle. She pulls the coat up to her eyes, attempting to hide. In contrast, the fat man's eyes are bulging and bloodshot and openly reflect his distress. **(b)** The woman, although attempting to hide, grieves openly. The fat man is physically exposed but keeps his sorrow and rage hidden.

7. **(a) Possible response:** The fat man inspires sympathy because he has trouble accepting his son's death. **(b) Possible response:** The fat man feels actual loss while the others feel only the possibility of death.

8. **(a)** The attention of young people is fragmented because they have so many interests. **(b) Possible response:** Many young people are pressured to do well in school, to be involved in sports or creative activities, and to participate in community service projects.

Build Language Skills

❶ Vocabulary Lesson

❶ Vocabulary Lesson

**Word Analysis:
Latin Root -patr-**

1. patriarch   3. patrician
2. Patriotic

Spelling Strategy

1. delight   2. foresight

**Vocabulary Builder:
Synonyms**

1. h	3. g	5. d	7. f
2. e	4. a	6. b	8. c

**❷ Grammar and
Style Lesson**

1. who had helped; restrictive;
   modifies *men*

2. whom everyone was watching;
   nonrestrictive; modifies *woman*

3. that grieved her; restrictive;
   modifies *topic*

4. which had claimed many lives;
   nonrestrictive, modifies *war*

5. whose children are in the military;
   restrictive; modifies *parents*

Writing Application

Possible response: The mother,
who needed help getting on the train,
was wrapped in a big coat. She sat
down among the other passengers
who had sons in the war. The sacrifice
that parents make was the main topic
of discussion. The fat traveler, *who had
never shed a tear,* suddenly burst into
uncontrollable sobs.

**Ⓦ𝒢 Writing and Grammar
Platinum Level**
For support in teaching the Grammar
and Style Lesson, use Chapter 20,
Section 2.

Word Analysis: Latin Root -patr-

The root -patr-, found in the word *paternal*,
comes from the Latin word *pater*, which means
"father." Complete each sentence below by filling
in the blank with one of the words listed.

　　patrician　　　patriotic　　　patriarch

1. Grandfather is the family's ___?___.

2. ___?___ people love their homeland.

3. A person of high birth is a ___?___.

Spelling Strategy

Words that contain a long *i* sound followed by a
t are often, but not always, spelled with the letter
combination *ight*. In each pair of words below,
select the word that is spelled correctly.

1. delight/delite　　　2. foresight/foresyte

Vocabulary Builder: Synonyms

Review the vocabulary list on page 1127. Then,
select the word in the right column that is similar in
meaning to the vocabulary word in the left column.

1. plight		a. vigor
2. paternal		b. impassively
3. discrimination		c. distressing
4. vitality		d. retaliated
5. retorted		e. fatherly
6. stoically		f. absurd
7. incongruous		g. favoritism
8. harrowing		h. difficulty

❷ Grammar and Style Lesson

Adjective Clauses

Adjective clauses are subordinate clauses that
modify nouns or pronouns and often begin with
the word *that, which, who, whom,* or *whose.* Restrictive adjective clauses are essential to the meaning
of the sentence and are not set off by commas.
Nonrestrictive adjective clauses are not essential to
the meaning and are set off by commas.

Examples:
Restrictive: The passengers who had left
Rome on the night express had had to stop . . .
[modifies *passengers*]

Nonrestrictive: One of them, who had been
listening with particular attention, said . . .
[modifies *one*]

Practice Identify the adjective clause in each sentence below. Then, indicate whether it is restrictive
or nonrestrictive, and name the word it modifies.

1. He thanked the men who had helped.

2. The unhappy woman, whom everyone was
   watching, listened to the conversation.

3. They discussed a topic that grieved her.

4. The war, which had claimed many lives, soon
   might claim her son.

5. Combat brings grief to many parents whose
   children are in the military.

Writing Application Write a paragraph about the
characters in "War." Include at least two restrictive
and two nonrestrictive adjective clauses.

Ⓦ𝒢 *Prentice Hall Writing and Grammar Connection: Platinum Level, Chapter 20, Section 2*

Assessment Practice

Identify Patterns of Organization (**For more practice, see the** *Test Preparation Workbook*, **p. 48.**)
Many tests require students to identify patterns
of organization. Use the following sample test
item to help students practice this skill.

　　In the late nineteenth and early twentieth
centuries, political tensions in Europe led to
alliances among several major powers.
Germany, Austria-Hungary, and Italy formed
the Triple Alliance; Great Britain, France, and
Russia formed the Triple Entente. When war
broke out in 1914, however, Italy did not
join on the side of its allies.

Which of the following patterns of organiza-
tion is NOT used in the passage?
　A cause and effect
　B specific to general
　C general to specific
　D chronological
The passage uses cause-and-effect, general-
to-specific, and chronological patterns of organ-
ization. It does not provide information in a
specific-to-general pattern. Choice *B* is correct.

❸ Writing Lesson

Newspaper Article

Imagine yourself in the setting of "War." As a journalist on the train, you have witnessed the exchange among the passengers. Write a newspaper article reporting what you observed. Include a general statement about the impact of the war on ordinary people.

Prewriting   Write a rough outline of the events described in the story and the statements the characters make. Review the outline, circling the items that you want to include in the article.

Drafting   Begin with a lead, a strong first paragraph that introduces the subject in an interesting way. Follow with a logically ordered report of the events that you witnessed.

Revising   Review your draft. To maintain objectivity, remove material that is not factual and replace language that suggests a personal bias.

Model: Revising to Maintain Objectivity

Then ~~a foolish old~~ ^{an older} man interrupted. With great animation,

he ~~babbled~~ ^{said} that young men naturally love their country

and want to fight. ~~It was crazy talk.~~

> A newspaper article sticks to the facts and does not express bias.

 Prentice Hall Writing and Grammar Connection: Platinum Level, Chapter 2, Section 2

❹ Extend Your Learning

Listening and Speaking In a small group, prepare a **dramatic reading** of this story. Use these tips to help your planning:

- Select readers for the narrator, the husband, the wife, the fat man, and the two passengers who speak.
- Vary the volume and tone of your voice to capture the characters' emotions.
- Use eye contact and appropriate gestures.

Deliver the dramatic reading in class. **[Group Activity]**

Research and Technology Using print and electronic sources, prepare a **multimedia report** about a typical soldier's experience in battle during World War I. Include information about military technology, trench warfare, standard-issue equipment, and attitudes toward the war. Present the report to the class, using appropriate handouts to clarify information.

Go Online
Research
For: An additional research activity
Visit: www.PHSchool.com
Web Code: etd-7803

War ■ 1135

---

❸ Writing Lesson

- To guide students in writing this newspaper article, give them the **Support for Writing Lesson,** p. 49 in *Unit 8 Resources.*

- Read the Writing Lesson instruction aloud. Then, explain to students that a newspaper article should present information in a factual, objective manner. Information is usually ordered from most important to least important.

- Remind students to answer in their article the questions *who? what? when? where? why?* and *how?*

- Use the Writing Lesson to guide students in developing their articles.

✍ Writing and Grammar
Platinum Level
For support in teaching the Writing Lesson, use Chapter 2, Section 2.

❹ Listening and Speaking

- Tell students that a dramatic reading is an oral presentation that conveys the feelings and mood of a literary work.

- Encourage students to rehearse their presentations individually or with partners several times. Have them experiment with various ways of reading the story. Students might try stressing certain words or passages; changing the tone, volume, and rate at which they speak; and inserting pauses to emphasize meaningful sections.

- The **Support for Extend Your Learning** page (*Unit 8 Resources,* p. 50) provides guided note-taking opportunities to help students complete the Extend Your Learning activities.

Go Online
Research Have students type in the Web Code for another research activity.

CT.4.05.8 Make connections between works, self and related topics in critical texts.

LT.5.01.5 Analyze archetypal characters, themes, and settings in world literature.

LT.5.02.1 Explore works which relate to an issue, author, or theme and show increasing comprehension.

Connections
American Literature

War, whether justified or not, always has the same result: people—especially young people—are killed, and their families are left to grieve for them. Have students reread Pirandello's story "War" on pp. 1128–1132 after they have read "The Corn Planting." What similarities and differences do students notice between the two stories and the ways in which the characters deal with grief?

Journeys of Grief

- **Ask** students to list some ways that people react to grief. Prompt them to consider various reactions to grief that they may have observed in movies, read about in books, observed in person, or experienced personally.

  Possible response: Various reactions to grief include denial, shock, withdrawal, crying, depression, and anger.

- Tell students that the selection they are about to read describes a unique reaction to the news of an only child's death.

CONNECTIONS
American Literature

Journeys of Grief

The mother in Pirandello's short story "War," in this unit, feels desperate and distraught when she thinks of her only son in battle. Human responses to anxiety and grief, however, are individual and unique. On the train with the mother are other travelers who also have sons in combat. These parents have come up with various ways to calm their fears and worries—and even to deal with the ultimate tragedy of losing a child.

Love and Grief The parents of Will Hutchenson in "The Corn Planting" are, like the mother and father in "War," parents of an only son. Their lives revolve around Will, and when they suffer a crushing loss, they have their own special way of dealing with their sorrow. You may notice these parents' similarities to the parents in Pirandello's story, but take note of their differences as well.

The Corn Planting
Sherwood Anderson

1136 ■ *The Modern World*

Enrichment

Chicago

Chicago was already a major city in the Midwest when Will Hutchenson went there to study at the Art Institute. In 1837, when it was incorporated, Chicago had a population of about 4,200. By the time of the Great Fire in 1871, the population had soared to 300,000. By 1893, the city had sufficiently recovered to host the World Columbian Exposition commemorating the four hundredth anniversary of the European discovery of America. With unlimited opportunities to rebuild after the Great Fire, Chicago provided America's finest architects with an unprecedented boost; as a result, the city became filled with decorative and monumental buildings. The Art Institute is one such structure that today houses an impressive collection of artwork.

The farmers who come to our town to trade are a part of the town life. Saturday is the big day. Often the children come to the high school in town.

It is so with Hatch Hutchenson. Although his farm, some three miles from town, is small, it is known to be one of the best-kept and best-worked places in all our section. Hatch is a little gnarled old figure of a man. His place is on the Scratch Gravel Road and there are plenty of poorly kept places out that way.

Hatch's place stands out. The little frame house is always kept painted, the trees in his orchard are whitened with lime halfway up the trunks, and the barn and sheds are in repair, and his fields are always clean-looking.

Hatch is nearly seventy. He got a rather late start in life. His father, who owned the same farm, was a Civil War man and came home badly wounded, so that, although he lived a long time after the war, he couldn't work much. Hatch was the only son and stayed at home, working the place until his father died. Then, when he was nearing fifty, he married a schoolteacher of forty, and they had a son. The schoolteacher was a small one like Hatch. After they married, they both stuck close to the land. They seemed to fit into their farm life as certain people fit into the clothes they wear. I have noticed something about people who make a go of marriage. They grow more and more alike. Then even grow to look alike.

Their one son, Will Hutchenson, was a small but remarkably strong boy. He came to our high school in town and pitched on our town baseball team. He was a fellow always cheerful, bright and alert, and a great favorite with all of us.

For one thing, he began as a young boy to make amusing little drawings. It was a talent. He made drawings of fish and pigs and cows, and they looked like people you knew. I never did know, before, that people could look so much like cows and horses and pigs and fish.

When he had finished in the town high school, Will went to Chicago, where his mother had a cousin living, and he became a student in the Art Institute out there. Another young fellow from our town was also in Chicago. He really went two years before Will did. His name was Hal Weyman, and he was a student at the University of Chicago. After he graduated, he came home and got a job as principal of our high school.

Hal and Will Hutchenson hadn't been close friends before, Hal being several years older than Will, but in Chicago they got together, went together to see plays, and, as Hal later told me, they had a good many long talks.

I got it from Hal that, in Chicago, as at home here when he was a young boy, Will was immediately popular. He was good-looking, so the girls in the art school liked him, and he had a straightforwardness that made him popular with all the young fellows.

Hal told me that Will was out to some party nearly every night, and right away he began to sell some of his amusing little drawings and to make money. The drawings were used in advertisements, and he was well paid.

Thematic Connection
Why do you think the description of Will is so positive?

◀ **Critical Viewing**
In what ways does the farm setting impact the characters in this story? **[Connect]**

The Corn Planting ■ 1137

Thematic Connection

Answer: The Hutchensons' anticipation of and excitement about Will's correspondence shows the pride these parents have in their son's accomplishments. In addition, the voracity with which they consume the letters demonstrates the Hutchensons' curiosity and desire to live vicariously through Will.

He even began to send some money home. You see, after Hal came back here, he used to go quite often out to the Hutchenson place to see Will's father and mother. He would walk or drive out there in the afternoon or on summer evenings and sit with them. The talk was always of Will.

Hal said it was touching how much the father and mother depended on their one son, how much they talked about him and dreamed of his future. They had never been people who went about much with the town folks or even with their neighbors. They were of the sort who work all the time, from early morning till late in the evenings, and on moonlight nights, Hal said, and after the little old wife had got the supper, they often went out into the fields and worked again.

You see, by this time old Hatch was nearing seventy and his wife would have been ten years younger. Hal said that whenever he went out to the farm they quit work and came to sit with him. They might be in one of the fields, working together, but when they saw him in the road, they came running. They had got a letter from Will. He wrote every week.

The little old mother would come running following the father. "We got another letter, Mr. Weyman," Hatch would cry, and then his wife, quite breathless, would say the same thing, "Mr. Weyman, we got a letter."

The letter would be brought out at once and read aloud. Hal said the letters were always delicious. Will larded them with little sketches. There were humorous drawings of people he had seen or been with, rivers of automobiles on Michigan Avenue in Chicago, a policeman at a street crossing, young stenographers hurrying into office buildings. Neither of the old people had ever been to the city and they were curious and eager. They wanted the drawings explained, and Hal said they were like two children wanting to know every little detail Hal could remember about their son's life in the big city. He was always at them to come there on a visit and they would spend hours talking of that.

"Of course," Hatch said, "we couldn't go."

"How could we?" he said. He had been on that one little farm since he was a boy. When he was a young fellow, his father was an invalid and so Hatch had to run things. A farm, if you run it right, is very exacting. You have to fight weeds all the time. There are the farm animals to take care of. "Who would milk our cows?" Hatch said. The idea of anyone but him or his wife touching one of the Hutchenson cows seemed to hurt him. While he was alive, he didn't want anyone else plowing one of his fields, tending his corn, looking after things about the barn. He felt that way about his farm. It was a thing you couldn't explain, Hal said. He seemed to understand the two old people.

It was a spring night, past midnight, when Hal came to my house and told me the news. In our town we have a night telegraph operator at the railroad station and Hal got a wire. It was really addressed to Hatch Hutchenson, but the operator brought it to Hal. Will Hutchenson was dead, had been killed. It turned out later that he was at a party with some other young fellows and there might have been some drinking. Anyway, the car was

Enrichment

Stages of Grief
In her book *On Death and Dying,* Dr. Elisabeth Kübler-Ross, a Swiss-born psychiatrist, details the five stages of grief. Briefly, these stages are as follows:

Stage 1, Denial: The person reacts with a shocked, "No. It's not possible."

Stage 2, Anger: The person wants to blame someone else or even God for what has happened.

Stage 3, Bargaining: The person tries to bargain with God or with another person, as in, "Give me some more time, and I'll . . ."

Stage 4, Depression: The person begins to face what is happening and feels depressed about it.

Stage 5, Acceptance: The person realizes that he or she must accept what cannot be changed.

The Hailstorm, Thomas Hart Benton, Joslyn Art Museum, Omaha, Nebraska

Humanities

The Hailstorm,
by Thomas Hart Benton

Like Will Hutchenson in "The Corn Planting," Thomas Hart Benton (1889–1975) left his small, rural home to attend the Art Institute of Chicago. After a year of study, he traveled to Paris, where he became interested in modern art movements. Benton then returned to the United States and lived in New York City, becoming part of the cutting-edge art scene and experimenting with painting styles. Benton soon abandoned modernism, however, and returned to a more realistic style, painting people and landscapes of the Midwest.

Use the following questions for discussion.

Which details in this painting reflect a realistic style? Which details are unrealistic?
Possible response: The shading and detail of the tree's trunk and leaves are very realistic, as is the shelter shown in the right side of the painting. The stylized, distorted figures and flat, cartoonlike colors are unrealistic.

Critical Viewing

Possible response: The storm—like the news of Will's death—is sudden and violent. The figures depicted in the painting are struggling against the wind, much like the Hutchensons will have to struggle with the reality of their son's death.

Background
Telegraph

"The Corn Planting" is set during the early 1900s, a time when most people did not have telephones. Therefore, the news of Will's death is sent by telegraph. The telegraph was an important means of communication. Morse code, which uses a series of dots and dashes to represent letters of the alphabet, was transmitted over the telegraph wires. After the telegraph operator translated a message, it had to be delivered to the intended recipient.

wrecked, and Will Hutchenson was killed. The operator wanted Hal to go out and take the message to Hatch and his wife, and Hal wanted me to go along.

I offered to take my car, but Hal said no, "Let's walk out," he said. He wanted to put off the moment, I could see that. So we did walk. It was early spring, and I remember every moment of the silent walk we took, the little leaves just coming on the trees, the little streams we crossed, how the moonlight made the water seem alive. We loitered and loitered, not talking, hating to go on.

Then we got out there, and Hal went to the front door of the farmhouse while I stayed in the road. I heard a dog bark, away off somewhere. I heard a child crying in some distant house. I think that Hal, after he got to the front door of the house, must have stood there for ten minutes, hating to knock.

Then he did knock, and the sound his fist made on the door seemed terrible. It seemed like guns going off. Old Hatch came to the door, and I heard Hal tell him. I know what happened. Hal had been trying, all the way out from town, to think up words to tell the old couple in some gentle way, but when it came to the scratch, he couldn't. He blurted everything right out, right into old Hatch's face.

That was all. Old Hatch didn't say a word. The door was opened, he stood there in the moonlight, wearing a funny long white nightgown, Hal told him, and the door went shut again with a bang, and Hal was left standing there.

He stood for a time, and then came back out into the road to me. "Well," he said, and "Well," I said. We stood in the road looking and listening. There wasn't a sound from the house.

And then—it might have been ten minutes or it might have been a half-hour—we stood silently, listening and watching, not knowing what to do—

▲ Critical Viewing
In what ways does the storm in this painting reflect the blow that the Hutchensons are about to receive? **[Connect]**

The Corn Planting ■ 1139

Journeys of Grief

- Read aloud the third paragraph on p. 1139. Then, **ask** students: How will the Hutchensons react to Hal's news?
  Possible responses: The Hutchensons will react with extreme sorrow. They will not fully absorb the news.

- Have students read the first paragraph on page 1141. **Ask** students to predict what the Hutchensons are going to do after they emerge from the house.
  Possible responses: The Hutchensons will begin digging a grave; they will sit somewhere in the field and pray or meditate; or they will bury Will's letters.

Critical Viewing

Possible response: The couple in the picture appears to be similar to the Hutchensons in that they are looking upon the land with great pride. The picture has a contemplative feel, so this couple may be thinking of a child.

1140   The Modern World

Enrichment

Corn

Corn, a member of the grass family, was first cultivated in Central America. In the history of the domestication of plants, corn is actually a latecomer, trailing by a thousand years the cultivation of beans and squash. The original wild corn is small. The much larger size and shape of the modern corncob is a result of centuries of selective breeding.

Corn has long been a staple of Native American societies throughout North America, and different groups have celebrated its cultivation in one way or another. For example, the Pueblo people have traditionally honored their Corn Mothers by providing all newborn children with corn fetishes. Mississippi groups like the Muskogee, Chickasaw, Choctaw, and Cherokee have held Green Corn Dances after each summer's harvest.

we couldn't go away—"I guess they are trying to get so they can believe it," Hal whispered to me. I got his notion all right. The two old people must have thought of their son Will always only in terms of life, never of death.

We stood watching and listening, and then, suddenly, after a long time, Hal touched me on the arm. "Look," he whispered. There were two white-clad figures going from the house to the barn. It turned out, you see, that old Hatch had been plowing that day. He had finished plowing and harrowing a field near the barn.

The two figures went into the barn and presently came out. They went into the field, and Hal and I crept across the farmyard to the barn and got to where we could see what was going on without being seen.

It was an incredible thing. The old man had got a hand corn-planter out of the barn and his wife had got a bag of seed corn, and there, in the moonlight, that night, after they got that news, they were planting corn.

It was a thing to curl your hair—it was so ghostly. They were both in their nightgowns. They would do a row across the field, coming quite close to us as we stood in the shadow of the barn, and then, at the end of each row, they would kneel side by side by the fence and stay silent for a time. The whole thing went on in silence. It was the first time in my life I ever understood something, and I am far from sure now that I can put down what I understood and felt that night—I mean something about the connection between certain people and the earth—a kind of silent cry, down into the earth, of these two old people, putting corn down into the earth. It was as though they were putting death down into the ground that life might grow again—something like that.

They must have been asking something of the earth, too. But what's the use? What they were up to in connection with the life in their field and the lost life in their son is something you can't very well make clear in words. All I know is that Hal and I stood the sight as long as we could, and then we crept away and went back to town, but Hatch Hutchenson and his wife must have got what they were after that night, because Hal told me that when he went out in the morning to see them and to make the arrangements for bringing their dead son home, they were both curiously quiet and Hal thought in command of themselves. Hal said he thought they had got something. "They have their farm and they have still got Will's letters to read," Hal said.

Connecting American Literature

1. **(a)** What do Hatch Hutchenson and his wife have in common with the man and woman who enter the train at Fabriano in Pirandello's "War"? **(b)** In what ways are the two couples' lives different?
2. In what way does nature help Hatch and his wife cope with their devastating loss?
3. **(a)** What do you think the parents in "War" would say to Hatch Hutchenson and his wife? **(b)** What do you think Hatch Hutchenson and his wife would say to the parents in "War"?

Sherwood Anderson (1876–1941)

Born the third of seven children, Sherwood Anderson grew up in a small town in Ohio. His father, a harness maker and house painter, was not always able to earn enough to support the family. Anderson dropped out of school at fourteen to work but finished high school in his twenties, after a year in the army. Much of Anderson's writing, which uses everyday speech to capture the essence of characters, features small-town life in the rural Midwest.

The Corn Planting ■ 1141

- Ask a volunteer to read aloud the first full paragraph. Then, have students **describe** the scene in their own words.
  Possible response: The Hutchensons—dressed only in their nightgowns—plant row upon row of corn, stopping at the end of each row to kneel in silence.

- Ask students to discuss activities that might be comforting to an individual who had just received terrible news.

ASSESS
Answers

1. **(a)** For both the Hutchensons and the couple on the train, their only child, a son, has left home at an early age to study in a faraway city. **(b)** The two couples' lives are different in that the unnamed couple have left their home in Sulmona to follow their son to Rome, whereas the Hutchensons remain on their farm when Will goes to Chicago. Another more profound difference is that the Hutchensons have lost their son in a car accident, whereas the unnamed couple's son is still alive.

2. The Hutchensons take comfort in working the land. Unlike death, this work is something they have some experience with and control over. The act of planting corn not only serves as an example of the solace the land provides but also works symbolically to suggest that the Hutchensons are burying Will's death so that "life might grow again."

3. **(a) Possible response:** The parents in "War" would sympathize with the Hutchensons, offering their condolences. **(b) Possible response:** The Hutchensons might sympathize with the parents in "War," understanding the anguish they must feel as their son goes to the war front. The Hutchensons might advise the couple to focus on another meaningful aspect of their lives as a method of coping with their anxiety and sorrow.

Standard Course of Study

Goal 1: WRITTEN LANGUAGE

WL.1.03.1 Select, monitor, and modify reading strategies appropriate to personal reflection.

Goal 4: CRITICAL THINKING

CT.4.05.2 Analyze text components and evaluate impact on critical interpretation.

Goal 5: LITERATURE

LT.5.01.2 Build knowledge of literary genres, and explore how characteristics apply to literature of world cultures.

LT.5.03.11 Analyze elements of literary environment in world literature.

Goal 6: GRAMMAR AND USAGE

GU.6.01.3 Use recognition strategies to understand vocabulary and exact word choice.

GU.6.01.4 Use vocabulary strategies to determine meaning.

Step-by-Step Teaching Guide	Pacing Guide
PRETEACH	
• Administer Vocabulary and Reading Warm-ups as necessary.	5 min.
• Engage students' interest with the motivation activity.	5 min.
• Read and discuss author and background features. **FT**	10 min.
• Introduce the Literary Analysis Skill: Lyric Poetry and Epiphany. **FT**	5 min.
• Introduce the Reading Strategy: Reading Stanzas as Units of Meaning. **FT**	
• Prepare students to read by teaching the selection vocabulary. **FT**	10 min.
TEACH	
• Informally monitor comprehension while students read independently or in groups. **FT**	30 min.
• Monitor students' comprehension with the Reading Check notes.	as students read
• Reinforce vocabulary with Vocabulary Builder notes.	as students read
• Develop students' understanding of lyric poetry and epiphany with the Literary Analysis annotations. **FT**	5 min.
• Develop students' ability to read stanzas as units of meaning with the Reading Strategy annotations. **FT**	5 min.
ASSESS/EXTEND	
• Assess students' comprehension and mastery of the Literary Analysis and Reading Strategy by having them answer the Apply the Skills questions. **FT**	15 min.
• Have students complete the Vocabulary Lesson and the Grammar and Style Lesson. **FT**	15 min.
• Apply students' ability to reorder paragraphs for coherence by using the Writing Lesson. **FT**	45 min. or homework
• Apply students' understanding by using one or more of the Extend Your Learning activities.	20–90 min. or homework
• Administer Selection Test A or Selection Test B. **FT**	15 min.

Resources

Print

Unit 8 Resources

Transparency

Graphic Organizer Transparencies

Technology

Print

Reader's Notebook [L2]

Reader's Notebook: Adapted Version [L1]

Reader's Notebook: English Learner's Version [EL]

Unit 8 Resources

Technology

Listening to Literature Audio CDs [L2, EL]

Reader's Notebook: Adapted Version Audio CD [L1, L2]

Print

Unit 8 Resources

General Resources

Technology

Go Online: Research [L3]

Go Online: Self-test [L3]

ExamView®, **Test Bank [L3]**

Choosing Resources for Differentiated Instruction

[**L1**] Special Needs Students

[**L2**] Below-Level Students

[**L3**] All Students

[**L4**] Advanced Students

[**EL**] English Learners

For Vocabulary and Reading Warm-ups and for Selection Tests, **A** signifies "less challenging" and **B** "more challenging." For Graphic Organizer transparencies, **A** signifies "not filled in" and **B** "filled in."

FT Fast Track Instruction: To move the lesson more quickly, use the strategies and activities identified with **FT**.

Scaffolding for Less Proficient and Advanced Students

The leveled Critical Thinking questions after selections progress in the levels of thinking required to answer them. To address the needs of your different students, you may use the (a) level questions for your less proficient students and the (b) level questions with your on-level and advanced students. The occasional (c) level questions are appropriate for your advanced students.

PRENTICE HALL

TeacherEXPRESS™ Use this complete
Plan · Teach · Assess suite of powerful
teaching tools to make lesson planning and testing quicker and easier.

PRENTICE HALL

StudentEXPRESS™ Use the interactive
Learn · Study · Succeed textbook (online
and on CD-ROM) to make selections and activities come alive with audio and video support and interactive questions.

 For: Information about Lexiles
Professional **Visit:** www.PHSchool.com
Development **Web Code:** eue-1111

Judith Ortiz Cofer

- You might wish to have students read Judith Ortiz Cofer's introduction to the unit on pages 1050–1051.

- Show Segment 2 on Judith Ortiz Cofer on *From the Author's Desk DVD* to provide insight into why she believes that poetry is so compelling. After students have watched the segment, **ask** how she relates the theme of "Ithaka" to her own life.
  Answer: The poem teaches that journeying towards a goal and overcoming the obstacles on the way to the goal are what matter most—even more than achieving the goal.

- Have students read Cofer's comments on these pages.

- Review briefly with students the main idea of the *Odyssey* and some of the obstacles that Odysseus had to overcome during his return home to Penelope.

- Have students give examples of how difficult situations may make them grow and force them to use their abilities to overcome these situations.

- **Ask** students how Cofer compares the poem's theme to life.
  Answer: Cofer states that people need to be ready to encounter new things and "face the monsters as well as the angels."

 From the Scholar's Desk

JUDITH ORTIZ COFER INTRODUCES
"Ithaka" by Constantine Cavafy

An Interview with Judith Ortiz Cofer
Conducted by Prentice Hall

Judith Ortiz Cofer

Judith Ortiz Cofer has won numerous awards for her work as a poet, an essayist, and a novelist. In 1994, she won the O. Henry Prize for short story. Ortiz is currently a professor of English at the University of Georgia.

What aspect of the ancient Greek epic the *Odyssey* would most help someone reading Cavafy's "Ithaka"? The *Odyssey* contains worlds. It's a love story. It's a story of a man trying to get back home to his wife after fighting and suffering in a long war. It's a story of a king and a story of loyalty. But to Cavafy, I think it was especially a story of the journey in between here and there. He shows you how the journey becomes a symbolic journey, standing for your life and goals and dreams.

Is that why this poem is so often recited at graduations and other ceremonies? Yes, the theme is that, when you go through a passage such as a birthday or a graduation, you should be ready to encounter new things. If life were static and you could predict everything that happens every day, you might feel more secure, but you wouldn't be growing and evolving. In order to learn from living, you have to face the monsters as well as the angels.

For example, on your journey you might come face to face with some "monstrous" problem like the Cyclops, the one-eyed giant from the *Odyssey*. If you don't want to risk running into monsters, then you're the boy or the girl in the bubble: You stay safe, you stay the same day after day.

Do you think "Ithaka" has a dramatic setting, someone talking to someone in a certain place, or is it more abstract? To me, "Ithaka" is more like a letter to a younger person from his or her mentor. If I were writing to my daughter about what she should expect as an adult, I would probably write a letter using the metaphor of the journey.

The greatest teachers were not sermonizers; they did not speak in the abstract. They told a story, a parable, or tale that illustrated their message. Even Einstein, in explaining his theory of relativity, talked about space travelers, who did not exist in his time. So Cavafy, in teaching his lesson about the journey of life, uses Odysseus' story, dramatizing the metaphor.

Teaching Resources

The following resources can be used to enrich or extend the instruction for **From the Scholar's Desk.**

Unit 8 Resources
   Support for Penguin Essay, p. 58
   Listening and Viewing, p. 59

From the Author's Desk DVD
   Judith Ortiz Cofer, Segment 2

◄ Critical Viewing In what ways might the road in this picture symbolize a great journey? [Interpret]

What does "Ithaka" say about facing what you find on your personal journey? Cavafy says you won't encounter monsters that you cannot handle unless you bring them along inside you. What he's saying is that you have to venture out with confidence in the adventure itself, and the Cyclops you may encounter will be the thing that you fear, what you yourself bring to the journey.

I think that this is particularly true for young people and for immigrants, for those who do not feel that they belong to—or who feel powerless in—the world of adults, the mainstream world. Yet the more you learn about your fears, the more you can face with confidence what surprises the world holds in store for you.

Thinking About the Commentary

1. **(a) Recall:** According to Cofer, what must everyone face "in order to learn from living"? **(b) Interpret:** Who or what are the monsters to which Cofer refers? Provide three examples, and explain your choices.

2. **(a) Recall:** What technique does Cofer believe the greatest teachers use to communicate a lesson? **(b) Analyze:** How do listeners use that technique to understand the lesson at hand? **(c) Apply:** What resources or talents do you possess that might help you face the monsters that Cofer mentions?

As You Read "Ithaka". . .

3. Look for images of a journey. Think about what real-life experiences these journey images might represent.

4. Consider whether you share Cavafy's attitude toward the journey.

From the Scholar's Desk: Judith Ortiz Cofer ■ 1143

Critical Viewing

Possible response: Like a great journey, the road in this picture is long, winding, and leads to the unknown.

"Do you think "Ithaka" has dramatic setting . . . ?"

• **Ask** students how Cofer characterizes the setting of "Ithaka."
Answer: She believes that the setting of "Ithaka," a journey, is a metaphor that teaches a lesson about the meaning of life.

• **Ask:** What does Cavafy say about the monsters we face?
Answer: He says that monsters are within us, and that we bring them with us on the journey.

ASSESS

Answers

1. (a) According to Cofer, everyone must face the "monsters" in order to learn from living. (b) **Possible response:** The monsters are the things that people fear. For example, Cofer mentions young people, immigrants, or people who believe that they are outsiders in the mainstream world. These groups of people may believe that they lack power to determine the course of their lives.

2. (a) Cofer believes that great teachers use stories to illustrate their message. (b) The story helps the listener place the message into real-life situations and make it concrete. (c) **Possible response:** Students may reply that they are creative and can adapt to unfamiliar surroundings.

3. **Possible response:** "Ithaka" uses the image of a ship that sails into a strange port, and the speaker wishes that the reader will visit wise people and learn from them. This image might represent me when I arrive at college for the first time and learn from my professors. **Possible responses:** I disagree with Cavafy; although the journey is important, I believe that attaining the goal is most important. I agree with Cavafy; the journey transforms me and prepares me to attain the goal.

Motivation

On the board, write the word *Poetry* in the center of a cluster diagram; around it, write *Music, Death, Life,* and *The Self.* Tell students that this diagram shows some of the major themes of lyric poetry. Emphasize that a lyric poem can express anything a person feels or observes. Tell students that they are going to read five lyric poems. Each is like a snapshot of the poet's feelings.

❶ Background

More About the Authors

Federico García Lorca was especially influenced by the music of the gypsies, which expresses the pain and the happiness of the Andalusian gypsies. The deeply reflective lyrics of these songs influenced García Lorca's tragic and comic vision of life and crystallized the themes that run through his work.

As a boy, Constantine Cavafy helped his father with the family export business. As a young man, however, Cavafy lost interest in the business and became a government clerk.

Gabriela Mistral was the first South American to win the Nobel Prize for Literature. Her book of poems *Desolación* deals primarily with despair, suffering, and death.

Although Juan Ramón Jiménez's poetry is not as dark as Mistral's, much of his work is characterized by a gentle sadness. This melancholy can be seen in "Green."

Geography Note

Draw students' attention to the map on this page. Explain that García Lorca, Cavafy, Mistral, and Jiménez represent a range of cultures. Cavafy was born in Egypt but became a Greek citizen and wrote in Greek. García Lorca and Jiménez were born in Spain and wrote in Spanish. Mistral was born in Chile, which does not appear on this map. Although a great distance separates Chile and Spain, the two countries are united by their official language—Spanish.

❶ The Guitar • Ithaka • Fear • The Prayer • Green

Federico García Lorca (1898–1936)

In August 1936, one month after the start of the Spanish Civil War, the Spanish newspaper *El Diario de Albacete* broke the shocking story that Federico García Lorca had been assassinated. Subsequent reports confirmed that he had been murdered by right-wing Nationalists, who deemed his writings politically offensive.

Ironically, García Lorca did not write explicitly political poetry. His inspiration came from the people and culture of rural Andalusia, where the poet was born. Andalusia is the homeland of the gypsies, or flamencos. With the exception of the poems collected in *Poet in New York,* all of García Lorca's work reflects the dark beauty of Andalusian culture.

Constantine Cavafy (1863–1933)

Constantine Cavafy [kə́ vä́ fē] was born in 1863 in Alexandria, Egypt. Although he lived in Greece only briefly, he became a Greek citizen as soon as he was of age.

In his poems, Cavafy combines two distinct kinds of Greek: demotic Greek, the language of the common people, and purist Greek, the official language of the church and state. Although the distinctions between the two do not translate into English, Cavafy's use of both forms of Greek can be seen as a political statement.

During his lifetime, Cavafy published poems privately. However, when *The Poems of Constantine P. Cavafy* was published posthumously in 1935, Cavafy began to draw the attention of the world.

Gabriela Mistral (1889–1957)

When Chilean poet Gabriela Mistral (gä́ brē ä́ lä mēs träl´) heard the news that she had won the Nobel Prize in Literature in 1945, she declared, "Perhaps it was because I was the candidate of the women and children." Ever since Mistral began writing poetry, women and children were her primary subjects.

A Poet and Teacher Mistral's real name was Lucila Godoy Alcayaga (loō sē´ lə gō doī´ al kī ä´ gə). At fifteen, she began two of her careers—teacher and poet. Fearing that she might lose her teaching jobs because of the content of her poetry, Mistral published her work under pseudonyms. The name Gabriela Mistral came from the archangel Gabriel and the fierce mistral wind that blows over the south of France.

Juan Ramón Jiménez (1881–1958)

Juan Ramón Jiménez is widely viewed as one of Spain's finest poets. Ironically, he spent much of his life in exile from his native land.

Becoming a Poet Jiménez was a law student at the University of Seville when he first published his poems in a magazine. In 1900, he published two volumes of poetry, though he later thought these so awful that he sought out and destroyed every copy he could. Within a few years, however, he had developed a lyrical power more to his liking. That skill is evident in poetry collections like *Pure Elegies* (1908) and in *Platero and I* (1914–1917), his popular prose poems about a man roaming the countryside with his donkey. In 1956, Jiménez was awarded the Nobel Prize in Literature.

Preview

Connecting to the Literature

When traveling, you can journey by car or by plane; you might walk, take a bus, or even ride a horse. If life itself is a journey, how should one travel? These poems look at the long journey of life and express ideas about the best ways to make the trip.

❷ Literary Analysis

Lyric Poetry and Epiphany

Lyric poetry is melodic verse that expresses the observations of a single speaker. Unlike narrative poems, lyric poems do not tell complete stories. Instead, they build to express a moment of insight—an **epiphany,** or revelation. The poet Dante Gabriel Rossetti called the sonnet, which is a type of lyric poem, a "moment's monument." Because of this emphasis on the moment, lyric poems exclude details that a narrative would supply. As you read, look for the moment of insight captured by each poem.

Comparing Literary Works

A **metaphor** is an implied comparison between two seemingly different things. In the example below, García Lorca likens the sound of a guitar to a woeful utterance, and he then characterizes the sky as a kind of building:

> Now begins <u>the cry</u> / <u>Of the guitar,</u> / Breaking <u>the vaults</u> / <u>Of dawn.</u>

While most metaphors are brief, an **extended metaphor** flows throughout a literary work. Several comparisons may be made along the way, combining to create a larger meaning. The poems in this grouping contain metaphors, some of which are extended. As you read, compare the use of metaphor in each poem.

❸ Reading Strategy

Reading Stanzas as Units of Meaning

Many poems take the form of stanzas, or formal groupings of lines. Like a paragraph in a work of prose, a stanza usually expresses one main idea. To aid your understanding of poetry, **read stanzas as units of meaning** in the same way that you read paragraphs. You might pause after each stanza and consider its main thought. Use a chart like the one shown to record statements expressing these ideas.

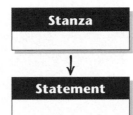

Vocabulary Builder

monotonously (mə nät′n əs lē) *adv.* done in a way that goes on and on without variation (p. 1147)

exalted (eg zôlt′ id) *adj.* lifted high because of dignity or honor (p. 1148)

sensual (sen′ shoo əl) *adj.* pleasing to the senses (p. 1149)

invokes (in vōks′) *v.* calls on (p. 1151)

anoint (ə noint′) *v.* to rub oil or ointment on (p. 1151)

sheaves (shēvz) *n.* bundles of cut stalks of grain (p. 1153)

Poems by García Lorca, Cavafy, Mistral, and Jiménez ■ 1145

> **NC** **Standard Course of Study**
>
> • Select, monitor, and modify reading strategies appropriate to personal reflection. (WL.1.03.1)
>
> • Analyze elements of literary environment in world literature. (LT.5.03.11)

❷ Literary Analysis

Lyric Poetry and Epiphany

• Read the Literary Analysis instruction. Then, remind students that lyric poetry was originally accompanied by music; therefore, musicality is a distinctive feature of this poetry.

• Draw students' attention to the word *epiphany*. Remind them that an epiphany is a sudden flash of recognition or insight that may take the form of disillusionment.

• Encourage students to look for the musical qualities in the poems that follow and to note the details or images that lead to each poem's moment of insight.

❸ Reading Strategy

Reading Stanzas as Units of Meaning

• Point out to students that a stanza, like a paragraph, can be of any length. In many traditional poems, stanzas are unified by a set number of lines in each stanza.

• Preview with students Mistral's "Fear" and Cavafy's "Ithaka." Point out that "Fear" has eight-line stanzas. "Ithaka" combines stanzas of varying lengths, but each stanza is unified primarily by a main idea.

• Explain the use of the graphic organizer on the page. Tell students that noting the main thought of each stanza may help them understand the meaning of a poem as a whole. Give them a copy of the **Reading Strategy Graphic Organizer A** (*Graphic Organizer Transparencies,* p. 192) to use as they read the poems.

Vocabulary Builder

• Pronounce each vocabulary word for students, and read the definitions as a class. Have students identify any words with which they are already familiar.

Differentiated Instruction   Solutions for All Learners

Support for Special Needs Students

Have students use the support pages for these selections in the *Reader's Notebook Adapted Version.* Completing these pages will prepare students to read the selections in the Student Edition.

Support for Less Proficient Readers

Have students use the support pages for these selections in the *Reader's Notebook.* After students finish each selection in the *Reader's Notebook,* have them complete the questions and activities in the Student Edition.

Support for English Learners

Have students use the support pages for these selections in the *Reader's Notebook: English Learner's Version.* Completing these pages will prepare students to read the selections in the Student Edition.

❶ About the Selection

In "The Guitar," the speaker compares the mourning notes of a guitar to a wounded heart.

❷ Humanities

The Old Guitarist, by Pablo Picasso

Spanish-born Pablo Picasso (1881–1973) is considered one of the most important visual artists of the twentieth century. During his long career, Picasso went through numerous periods in which he painted in distinctly different styles. In his Blue Period (c. 1901–1904), his work projects a dark, somber, melan-choly mood. *The Old Guitarist* is from this period.

Discuss this question:

How does Picasso suggest sadness?
Possible response: The angle at which the guitarist is bent suggests that he is defeated or in mourning. The guitarist's gauntness and torn shirt suggest poverty. The colors are dark and opaque.

❸ Critical Viewing

Possible response: Both the painting and the poem evoke melan-choly. The painting does so with its blue-green coloring and the man's anguished face and posture. The poem establishes the same mood with words such as "cry," "weeps," "mourns," and "dead."

❶ The Guitar

Federico García Lorca
translated by
Elizabeth du Gué Trapier

The Old Guitarist, 1903, Pablo Picasso, Spanish, 1881–1973, The Art Institute of Chicago, Estate of Pablo Picasso/Artists Rights Society (ARS), New York

Background García Lorca did not accept the label of "Gypsy Poet." Instead, he insisted, "I could just as well be a poet of sewing needles and hydraulic landscapes. . . ." Never-theless, Gypsy culture pervades García Lorca's work, providing him with images that transcend the local and become universal.

"The Guitar" captures the flamenco music of the Gitanos, the Gypsy popu-lation of Andalusia. Some flamenco music is festive, but García Lorca admired the *cante jondo* (kan′ tä hōn′ dō), a deeper and more somber tradition.

◀ **Critical Viewing ❸**
Does the mood of this painting fit the mood of the poem? Explain.
[Interpret]

Differentiated Instruction Solutions for All Learners

Accessibility at a Glance

	The Guitar	Ithaka	Fear	The Prayer	Green
Language	Syntax: inverted sentences	Syntax: imperative sentences	Straightforward	Formal with capitalized pronouns	Repeated use of color
Concept	Accessible (wounds to the loving heart)	Challenging (the journey through life without fear)	Accessible (mothers' worries about children)	Accessible (the importance of forgiveness)	Accessible (the open gate to love)
Literary Merit	Lyric poem with musical imagery	Lyric poem with advice on how to live	Lyric poem with an emotional message	Lyric poem of intense grief	Lyric poem with vivid visual images
Lexile	NP	NP	NP	NP	NP
Overall Rating	More challenging	Average	More Accessible	Average	Average

Now begins the cry
Of the guitar,
Breaking the vaults
Of dawn.
5 Now begins the cry
Of the guitar.
Useless
To still it.
Impossible
10 To still it.
❹ It weeps monotonously
As weeps the water,
As weeps the wind
Over snow.
15 Impossible
To still it.
It weeps
For distant things,
Warm southern sands
20 Desiring white camellias[1]
It mourns the arrow without a target,
The evening without morning,
And the first bird dead
Upon a branch.
25 O guitar!
A wounded heart,
Wounded by five swords.

1. **camellias** (kə mēl′ yəz) showy, roselike flowers of an ornamental evergreen shrub native to eastern Asia.

Critical Reading

1. **Respond:** Which image in this poem do you find most striking?

2. **(a) Recall:** In lines 3–4, what effect does the guitar's cry have upon the "vaults / Of dawn"? **(b) Interpret:** What does this image suggest about the intensity of emotion expressed by the guitar?

3. **(a) Recall:** In lines 21–24, for what three things does the speaker say the guitar mourns? **(b) Analyze:** How does each of these things capture a sense of unfulfilled promise? Explain.

4. **(a) Recall:** In lines 25–27, which objects wound the guitar?
(b) Interpret: What is your interpretation of this image? Explain.

5. **Extend:** What musical instrument seems most like a person to you? Explain.

Go Online
Author Link

For: More about Federico García Lorca

Visit: www.PHSchool.com
Web Code: ete-9804

The Guitar ■ 1147

Literary Analysis
Lyric Poetry and Epiphany Which words and individual sounds help give lines 7–16 a musical feeling?

Vocabulary Builder
monotonously (me nät′n es lē) *adv.* done in a way that goes on and on without variation

❹ Literary Analysis
Lyric Poetry and Epiphany

- Have a volunteer read the poem aloud. Then, **ask** the Literary Analysis question: Which words and individual sounds help give lines 7–16 a musical feeling?
  Possible response: The repetition of "To still it," and "As weeps" and the repetition of individual sounds, like /s/ in "useless," "Impossible," and "still," create a musical feeling.

- Tell students that elements of a lyric poem build to an epiphany for the speaker, the reader, or both.

- **Ask:** Where does the epiphany of this poem occur?
  Answer: It occurs in the final two lines.

- **Ask:** What elements of the poem point to this revelation?
  Answer: The personification of the guitar, the emphasis on its mournful tune, and the descriptions equating it with a force of nature point to this revelation.

ASSESS

Answers

1. **Possible response:** The most striking image is that of the guitar as a heart, wounded by five swords.

2. (a) It breaks open the vaults of dawn. (b) This image suggests that the emotions are extremely powerful.

3. (a) The guitar mourns for "the arrow without a target, the evening without morning, and the first bird dead upon a branch." (b) All represent incomplete events.

4. (a) Five swords wound the guitar. (b) **Possible response:** The five swords are the five senses, which bring pain and experience to the heart.

5. **Possible response:** The violin may seem most like a person because its tone and expression resemble the human voice.

Go Online For additional informa-
Author Link tion about Federico García Lorca, have students type in the Web Code, then select *L* from the alphabet, and then select Federico García Lorca.

Differentiated Instruction   Solutions for All Learners

Support for English Learners
To help students with the syntax in "The Guitar," tell them that the first sentence has inverted order. Ask students to restate the sentence with the subject first (The cry of the guitar now begins . . .). Then read aloud lines 7–10. Point out that the understood subject and verb in each sentence is *It is*. Ask students to restate lines 26–27 in a complete sentence (You are a heart, wounded by five swords. OR Your heart has been wounded by five swords.). Finally, explain that poets exercise poetic license to phrase ideas in a manner that creates rhythm.

Enrichment for Gifted/Talented Students
Call students' attention to the parallel mood and theme expressed in García Lorca's poem and Picasso's painting. Challenge students to create or locate another piece of art to accompany these two pieces. They may write or find a poem, a piece of music, or a short story. Or students may find or create a painting, drawing, or sculpture. Have each student present his or her piece and discuss how it relates to the works of García Lorca and Picasso.

❺ Scholar's Insight

- Direct students' attention to Cofer's comment about the value of the journey itself.
- Remind students that Odysseus' main goal for twenty years is to return to Ithaka.
- **Ask:** Does Odysseus embody the values that Cofer mentions?
  Answer: Rather than enjoying his journey and learning from his experiences, both good and bad, Odysseus focuses solely on his goal of reaching home.

❻ About the Selection

This poem, in which Cavafy compares the long journey of life to the journey of Odysseus, invites the reader on a spiritual adventure.

❼ Reading Strategy

Reading Stanzas as Units of Meaning

- Remind students that it may be helpful for them to read the stanzas of a poem as they would read paragraphs.
- Read aloud the first stanza. Then, **ask:** What is the main idea of this stanza?
  Answer: The main idea is that one's journey through life will be long and without obstacles if one remains dignified and does not bring on inner strife.
- **Ask:** In the first stanza, what attitude toward their journey does the speaker advise travelers to take?
  Answer: The speaker advises travelers to focus on life as a journey rather than a destination, to be excited by what life has to offer, and to live life with dignity. The speaker encourages travelers to be wary of the figurative monsters that travelers may encounter within themselves.

Ithaka

Constantine Cavafy

translated by
**Edmund Keeley
and Philip Sherrard**

Background

Constantine Cavafy found special inspiration in the Homeric epics—the *Iliad* and the *Odyssey*—and paid tribute to them in at least nine poems and an essay. "Ithaka," published in 1911, is the last of these tributes.

In Homer's *Odyssey*, the hero Odysseus spends twenty years struggling to return to his home, the city of Ithaka. Along the way, he meets monsters and goddesses, suffers losses, and experiences rapture. In this poem, Cavafy uses Odysseus' legendary tale to describe a way to live one's life.

When you set out for Ithaka[1]
Pray that your road's a long one,
full of adventure, full of discovery.
Laistrygonians, Cyclops,
5   angry Poseidon[2]—don't be scared of them:
you won't find things like that on your way
as long as your thoughts are <u>exalted,</u>
as long as a rare excitement
stirs your spirit and your body.
10 Laistrygonians, Cyclops,
wild Poseidon—you won't encounter them
unless you bring them along inside you,
unless your soul raises them up in front of you.

Pray that your road's a long one.
15 May there be many a summer morning when—
full of gratitude, full of joy—
you come into harbors seen for the first time;
may you stop at Phoenician[3] trading centers
and buy fine things,
20 mother of pearl and coral, amber and ebony,

---

1. **Ithaka** often spelled Ithaca; one of a group of islands off the west coast of Greece; the legendary home of Odysseus.
2. **Laistrygonians** (les trə gōn´ ē enz), **Cyclops, angry Poseidon** In Homer's *Odyssey*, the Laistrygonians are a race of giants, the Cyclops is a one-eyed monster, and Poseidon is the sea god. All of these characters pose varying threats to Odysseus and his crew.
3. **Phoenician** of or relating to Phoenicia, the ancient name for a narrow strip of land, now largely modern Lebanon, on the eastern coast of the Mediterranean Sea. The Phoenicians were famous as traders and sailors.

❺ **Judith Ortiz Cofer**
Scholar's Insight
Most of us are in a hurry to get *there*, wherever *there* is, yet most of the time we have only a vague idea of where we want to go or why. In "Ithaka" Cavafy tells us that it is the journey itself, the sights along the way, the wisdom gained, and even the strange characters (or monsters) you may encounter, that teach you about yourself and the world.

Vocabulary Builder
exalted (eg zôlt´ id) *adj.* lifted high because of dignity or honor

Enrichment

Phoenician Trade
The ancient Phoenician trading centers, to which Cavafy's poem refers, were bustling centers of economy. Phoenicia carried on trade by land and sea routes with its colonies and with other trade partners. Most colonies were established to expedite trade by taking advantage of a particular commodity available at that location. For example, Cyprus was colonized as a source of copper and timber. Sardinia and Spain supplied various metals. Phoenicia, in turn, provided the colonies with manufactured goods such as fabrics, pottery, and glass.

Phoenician ships traveled the Mediterranean, Red, and Black Seas; the North Atlantic; the Indian Ocean; and around the west coast of Africa. Some historians believe that Phoenician traders traveled as far as the Americas.

sensual perfumes of every kind,
as many sensual perfumes as you can;
may you visit numerous Egyptian cities
to fill yourself with learning from the wise.

25 Keep Ithaka always in mind.
Arriving there is what you're destined for.
But don't hurry the journey at all.
Better if it goes on for years
so you're old by the time you reach the island,
30 wealthy with all you've gained on the way,
not expecting Ithaka to make you rich.

Ithaka gave you the marvelous journey.
Without her you wouldn't have set out.
She hasn't anything else to give.

35 And if you find her poor, Ithaka won't have fooled you.
Wise as you'll have become, and so experienced,
you'll have understood by then what an Ithaka means.

Critical Reading

1. **Respond:** How do you feel about the journey that this poem describes? Explain your answer.

2. **(a) Recall:** In the first stanza, what three characters from the *Odyssey* does the speaker say the traveler need not fear? **(b) Infer:** According to the speaker in lines 12–13, under what circumstances might such characters appear? **(c) Analyze:** What real-life experiences might these characters represent? Explain.

3. **(a) Infer:** In the second stanza, identify two places that the speaker urges travelers to visit. **(b) Interpret:** What values do these places represent to the speaker? **(c) Evaluate:** Do you think these values are critical to happiness in life? Explain your answer.

4. **(a) Recall:** In line 31, what expectation does the speaker say one should not have of Ithaka? **(b) Draw Conclusions:** What, then, is the value of Ithaka?

5. **Analyze:** In the poem's final line, the poet refers to "an Ithaka," rather than to "Ithaka." In what way does this change suggest that Ithaka has taken on new meaning?

6. **Evaluate:** "Ithaka" was a favorite poem of Jacqueline Kennedy Onassis, the widow of President John F. Kennedy, and it was read at her funeral. In your opinion, is "Ithaka" a good memorial poem? Why or why not?

For: More about Constantine Cavafy
Visit: www.PHSchool.com
Web Code: ete-9805

Ithaka ■ 1149

Vocabulary Builder
sensual (sen′ shoo əl) *adj.*
pleasing to the senses

Literary Analysis
Lyric Poetry and Epiphany In what ways do the details in lines 20–22 help convey the excitement of the journey?

❾ *Judith Ortiz Cofer*
Scholar's Insight
There are trips and there are odysseys. An odyssey is what you will have if, at the end of an experience, life event, or actual journey, you have learned something about the world, human nature, and, most importantly, yourself.

❽ Literary Analysis
Lyric Poetry and Epiphany

• Read aloud the second stanza. Then, reread the bracketed passage. **Ask** students the Literary Analysis question.
Answer: The sensory details about the exotic and rewarding nature of the journey create excitement.

• **Ask:** What kinds of treasures might the items listed in lines 20–22 represent in the journey of life? Explain.
Possible response: The items may represent experience and personal accomplishments. Or they may represent rewarding relationships with friends and family.

❾ Scholar's Insight

• Point out to students the Scholar's Insight in which Cofer comments about the difference between trips and odysseys.

• Note that when Odysseus finally returns to Ithaka things are not as he had envisioned them.

• **Ask:** If Odysseus had not focused solely on reaching home, in which of his experiences might he have found value?
Answer: Rather than concentrating solely on reaching home, Odysseus could have learned a great deal about the other cultures he visited, prized the opportunity to travel the world, and appreciated the adventures he had.

ASSESS

Answers

1. **Possible response:** The journey sounds exciting and rewarding.

2. (a) The speaker tells the traveler not to fear the Laistrygonians, Cyclops, and Poseidon. (b) Such characters might appear if the traveler brings them along in his or her mind or soul. (c) These characters represent negative emotions and evil actions that, like these creatures, can impede or endanger an individual.

3. (a) The speaker urges travelers to visit Phoenician trading centers and Egyptian cities. (b) Phoenicia may represent beauty and sensory experience. Egypt may stand for wisdom. (c) **Possible response:** People can be happy without these values if they have love and personal relationships.

Go Online For additional information about **Author Link** Constantine Cavafy, have students type in the Web Code, then select *C* from the alphabet, and then select Constantine Cavafy.

Answers continued

4. (a) One should not expect Ithaka to provide riches. (b) Ithaka provides a reason for the journey.

5. The change suggests that Ithaka is not a single place but a state of mind. It suggests that each person's Ithaka is different.

6. **Possible response:** "Ithaka" is a good memorial poem because it recalls the joy of life's journey.

Fear

Gabriela Mistral   *translated by* Doris Dana

I don't want them to turn
my little girl into a swallow.
She would fly far away into the sky
and never fly again to my straw bed,
5 or she would nest in the eaves[1]
where I could not comb her hair.
I don't want them to turn
my little girl into a swallow.

I don't want them to make
10 my little girl a princess.
In tiny golden slippers
how could she play on the meadow?
And when night came, no longer
would she sleep at my side.
15 I don't want them to make
my little girl a princess.

And even less do I want them
one day to make her queen.
They would put her on a throne
20 where I could not go to see her.
And when nighttime came
I could never rock her . . .
I don't want them to make
my little girl a queen!

---

1. **eaves** (ēvz) *n.* lower edge(s) of a roof, usually projecting beyond the sides of a building.

Woman and Child, Pablo Picasso, Estate of Pablo Picasso/Artists Rights Society (ARS), New York. Museo Picasso, Barcelona, Spain. Scala

▲ **Critical Viewing ⑫**
Which details in this woman's expression and posture suggest a mother's concern for her child? Explain. **[Interpret]**

The Prayer

Gabriela Mistral
translated by John A. Crowe

Background When Gabriela Mistral was seventeen years old, she met Romelio Ureta, who became the love of her life. Unfortunately, the relationship ended with Ureta's early death, a loss from which Mistral never fully recovered. *Desolación* (1922), the collection in which "Fear" and "The Prayer" appear, reflects her despair over Ureta's death. It is her first great collection of poetry, one that brought her international fame.

Thou knowest, Lord, with what flaming boldness,
my word <u>invokes</u> Thy help for strangers.
I come now to plead for one who was mine,
my cup of freshness, honeycomb of my mouth,

5 lime of my bones, sweet reason of life's journey,
bird-trill to my ears, girdle of my garment.
Even those who are no part of me are in my care.
Harden not Thine eyes if I plead with Thee for this one!

He was a good man, I say he was a man
10 whose heart was entirely open; a man
gentle in temper, frank as the light of day,
as filled with miracles as the spring of the year.

Thou answerest harshly that he is unworthy of entreaty[1]
who did not <u>anoint</u> with prayer his fevered lips,
15 who went away that evening without waiting for Thy sign,
his temples shattered like fragile goblets.

---

1. **entreaty** (en trēt′ ē) *n.* earnest request.

Literary Analysis
Lyric Poetry What attitude toward her subject does the speaker express in the first stanza?

Vocabulary Builder
invokes (in vōks′) *v.* calls on

Vocabulary Builder
anoint (ə noint′) *v.* to rub oil or ointment on

 **Reading Check**
For whom does the speaker say she now comes "to plead"?

The Prayer ■ 1151

---

13 About the Selection
The speaker of "The Prayer" pours out her intense grief over the untimely death of her beloved and asks for God's forgiveness.

14 Literary Analysis
Lyric Poetry
• Read aloud the bracketed passage. Then, point out the images in the stanza's final line. **Ask** students what emotions the images evoke. **Possible response:** The images evoke the sweetness of love.
• **Ask** students the Literary Analysis question: What attitude toward her subject does the speaker express in the first stanza? **Possible response:** The speaker expresses an earnest plea on behalf of her beloved.

15 Reading Strategy
Reading Stanzas as Units of Meaning
• Remind students that restating challenging passages in their own words can enhance their understanding of a work.
• Read aloud the bracketed stanza, and **invite** students to discuss its meaning. Focus the discussion by asking what students think happened to the speaker's beloved. **Possible response:** The speaker's beloved died suddenly or violently.
• Then, **ask** students to restate the stanza in their own words. **Possible response:** You angrily say that my beloved is not worth begging for because he did not pray when he was in trouble and did not wait for divine guidance before dying a violent death.

16 Reading Check
Answer: The speaker says that she comes to plead "for one who was mine," her lost beloved.

The Revolution, Manuel Rodríguez Lozano, Museo Nacional de Arte Moderno, Mexico City

⑰ Humanities

The Revolution,
by Manuel Rodríguez Lozano

Rodríguez Lozano (1897–1971) was born in Mexico City. He studied in Paris from 1912 to 1921 and was influenced by Picasso's purity of craftsmanship. The mysterious shrouded figures and somber colors in *The Revolution* are characteristic of his work, which often addresses themes of death, despair, and ecstasy.

Use the following question for discussion:

Do the colors and figures in the painting reflect the mood of the "The Prayer"? Explain.
Possible response: The mourning colors reflect the speaker's grief, and the supplicatory postures of the figures reflect the speaker's pleas to God.

⑱ Critical Viewing

Possible responses: The women's postures are physical representations of the speaker's grief.

⑲ Reading Strategy

Reading Stanzas as Units of Meaning

• Have a volunteer read aloud the bracketed passage. Discuss challenging words or phrases.

• Then, have students **respond** to the Reading Strategy item: Restate this stanza in your own words.
Possible response: You say he was mean? But, Lord, he knew how completely I loved him. You say he kept me from being happy? It does not matter. Lord, you know that I loved him!

▶ **Monitor Progress** Have students read and explain their restatement of the bracketed stanza.

▶ **Reteach** To help students restate other stanzas in this poem, have them use the **Reading Strategy** support, p. 65 in *Unit 8 Resources*.

But I, my Lord, protest that I have touched,—
just like the spikenard[2] of his brow,—
his whole gentle and tormented heart:
20   and it was silky as a nascent[3] bud!

Thou sayest that he was cruel? Thou forgettest, Lord, that I loved him,
and that he knew my wounded heart was wholly his.
He troubled forever the waters of my gladness?
It does not matter! Thou knowest: I loved him, I loved him!

25   And to love (Thou knowest it well) is a bitter exercise;
a pressing of eyelids wet with tears,
a kissing-alive of hairshirt tresses,[4]
keeping, below them, the ecstatic eyes.

---

2. **spikenard** (spĭk′ nərd) *n.* perennial North American plant with whitish flowers, purplish berries, and fragrant roots.
3. **nascent** (nas′ ənt) *adj.* coming into being.
4. **tresses** (tres′ əz) *n.* woman's or girl's hair.

⑱ ▲ **Critical Viewing**
Do you think these women are expressing the same emotions as the speaker in the poem? Explain. **[Interpret]**

Reading Strategy
Reading Stanzas as Units of Meaning Restate this stanza in your own words.

Enrichment

The Death of Romelio Ureta

"The Prayer," along with many other poems by Gabriela Mistral, was inspired by the death of Mistral's great love, Romelio Ureta. Mistral met Ureta —a pale, dark-haired young man who worked for a railroad company—when she was just seventeen. Not much about their relationship is known for certain, yet Mistral described him as the love of her life.

Their love, however, soon came to a tragic end. To help a friend in dire financial straits, Ureta stole some money from the railroad company. He apparently planned to replace it but was unable to do so. Ureta was caught and charged with embezzlement. This crisis was more than Ureta could bear, and on November 25, 1909, he committed suicide. It is said that when his body was found, he had a card in his pocket inscribed with the name *Lucila Godoy*— Mistral's real name.

30 The piercing iron has a welcome chill,
when it opens, like <u>sheaves</u> of grain, the loving flesh.
And the cross (Thou rememberest, O King of the Jews!)
is softly borne, like a spray of roses.

Here I rest, Lord, my face bowed down
to the dust, talking with thee through the twilight,
35 through all the twilights that may stretch through life,
if Thou art long in telling me the word I await.

I shall weary Thine ears with prayers and sobs;
a timid greyhound, I shall lick Thy mantle's hem,
Thy loving eyes cannot escape me,
40 Thy foot avoid the hot rain of my tears.

Speak at last the word of pardon! It will scatter
in the wind the perfume of a hundred fragrant vials
as it empties; all waters will be dazzling;
the wilderness will blossom, the cobblestones will sparkle.

45 The dark eyes of wild beasts will moisten,
and the conscious mountain that Thou didst forge from stone
will weep through the white eyelids of its snowdrifts;
Thy whole earth will know that Thou hast forgiven!

Vocabulary Builder
sheaves (shēvz) n. bundles
of cut stalks of grain

Critical Reading

1. **Respond:** Which poem did you find more moving? Why?
2. **(a) Recall:** In "Fear," what three things does the speaker say she does not want to happen? **(b) Infer:** What kind of life can you infer the speaker does not want for her child?
3. **(a) Interpret:** Who might "they" be in the poem? **(b) Connect:** In what ways does the title of the poem connect to the speaker's attitude toward "them"?
4. **(a) Recall:** In "The Prayer," for whom is the speaker of the poem pleading? **(b) Analyze:** What does the speaker want?
5. **(a) Interpret:** In stanza six, what two charges against the lost loved one does the speaker attribute to God? **(b) Generalize:** With what single argument does the speaker respond?
6. **(a) Interpret:** What does the speaker say will happen if God does as she asks? **(b) Draw Conclusions:** Why do you think the speaker believes the details noted in the final two stanzas will sway God? Explain.
7. **Make a Judgment:** How important do you think it is to be forgiven and to forgive? Explain your answer.

Go Online
Author Link

For: More about Gabriela Mistral
Visit: www.PHSchool.com
Web Code: ete-9807

The Prayer ■ 1153

20 Critical Thinking
Interpret
• Read aloud the bracketed passage. Discuss with students how the speaker describes herself as a "timid greyhound" at God's foot.
• **Ask** students how this image characterizes the speaker and further clarifies her meaning.
  Possible response: The image presents the speaker as tenacious, yet humble and servile. It conveys her intention to petition for God's pity

ASSESS

Answers

1. **Possible response:** "The Prayer" may be more moving because of the intensity of the speaker's love and grief.
2. (a) The speaker does not want her daughter to be turned into a swallow, made a princess, or made a queen. (b) The speaker does not want a life of privilege, power, and isolation for her daughter.
3. (a) **Possible response:** "They" could refer to humankind or society. (b) The speaker cannot name all the sources of her many fears about her daughter.
4. (a) The speaker pleads on behalf of her deceased lover. (b) The speaker wants God to forgive her lover.
5. (a) The speaker believes that God charges the beloved with cruelty and with being the source of the speaker's unhappiness. (b) The speaker's argument is that she loved the beloved.
6. (a) The speaker says the world will be filled with beauty and emotion. (b) **Possible response:** The speaker knows that she can appeal to God's concern for beauty and peace.
7. **Possible response:** Forgiveness is important because people are imperfect, and forgiveness stimulates spiritual growth.

Go Online For additional informa-
Author Link tion about Gabriela Mistral, have students type in the Web Code, then select *M* from the alphabet, and then select Gabriela Mistral.

Differentiated
Instruction   Solutions for All Learners

Support for Less Proficient Readers
Point out to students the speaker's comparison of herself to a greyhound in line 38. Then, explain that this comparison is a metaphor, or a figure of speech in which one thing is spoken of as though it were something else. A metaphor suggests a comparison between the two things that are identified. Guide students as they review Mistral's poems, and help them identify other metaphors.

Enrichment for Advanced Readers
Tell students that writers throughout history have either written literature to a higher power or pondered humankind's relationship with that higher power. Invite students to seek other literary works addressed to or exploring the divine. Students may begin with the Psalms on pp. 67–70, the selections from the *Qur'an* on pp. 78–80, and the selections from the *Rig Veda* on pp. 180–182. Have each student write a brief analysis about the treatment of the divine in one or more of these selections.

㉑ About the Selection

In this poem, the repetition of "green" emphasizes the power of color. The speaker's lingering passion is expressed by the color that shades his memory.

㉒ Literary Analysis

Lyric Poetry

• Read the poem aloud. **Ask** students to explain to what sense this poem appeals most strongly.
Answer: The poem appeals most strongly to the sense of sight.

• Invite a volunteer to read aloud the final two lines of the poem. Then, **ask** students the Literary Analysis question: What attitude toward the subject does the speaker suggest in the last stanza? Explain.
Possible response: By saying that he will always leave a gate into his life open, it is apparent that the speaker still longs for the maiden.

ASSESS

Answers

1. **Possible response:** Some students will have had an experience like that described in "Green," when a romantic moment has stayed with them for a long time.

2. (a) The maiden's hair is green.
(b) **Possible response:** The speaker is not describing a real person because the maiden is entirely green; however, she may be a real person as seen through the speaker's idealized memory.

3. (a) The speaker leaves open "a small green gate." (b) **Possible response:** The maiden is a memory that the speaker treasures.

4. **Possible response:** Yes; green represents the eternal freshness of the speaker's memory.

Go Online **Author Link** For additional information about Juan Ramón Jiménez, have students type in the Web Code, then select J from the alphabet, and then select Juan Ramón Jiménez.

㉑ Green Juan Ramón Jiménez
translated by J. B. Trend

> Green was the maiden, green, green!
> Green her eyes were, green her hair.
>
> The wild rose in her green wood
> was neither red nor white, but green.
>
> Through the green air she came.
> (The whole earth turned green for her).
>
> The shining gauze of her garment
> was neither blue nor white, but green.
>
> Over the green sea she came.
> (And even the sky turned green then).
>
> **㉒** My life will always leave unlatched
> a small green gate to let her in.

Literary Analysis
Lyric Poetry and Epiphany What attitude toward the subject does the speaker suggest in the last stanza? Explain.

Critical Reading

1. **Respond:** Have you ever had an experience similar to that described in this poem? Explain.

2. **(a) Recall:** In "Green," what color is the maiden's hair?
(b) Interpret: Is the speaker describing a real person? Explain.

3. **(a) Recall:** What does the speaker leave open for the maiden?
(b) Analyze: Why do you think the speaker wants to let the maiden in?

4. **Make a Judgment:** Does Jiménez's symbolic use of color aid your understanding of this poem? Support your answer.

For: More about Juan Ramón Jiménez
Visit: www.PHSchool.com
Web Code: ete-9808

Enrichment

Color

Color, a major element in the poetry of Juan Ramón Jiménez, is a complex phenomenon of light.

Light is actually a kind of electromagnetic vibration. Pure white light is made of vibrations with a certain wavelength. The full range or spectrum of color is contained within that wavelength. This means that white light can be split into all of the different colors. The human eye cannot see the spectrum within white light; however, our eyes can perceive the same colors through different means. For example, red, blue, and green are the primary colors of light. To our eyes, they can be combined to match any color in the spectrum.

Objects get their color from pigments that absorb some of the color in white light. These pigments come in combinations of red, yellow, and blue, called the *subtractive* primary colors because they subtract color from light. Green pigment, for example, absorbs the blue and red in light, so the eye perceives green.

Apply the Skills

The Guitar • Ithaka • Fear • The Prayer • Green

Literary Analysis

Lyric Poetry and Epiphany

1. **(a)** What is the **epiphany,** or moment of perception, that García Lorca explores in his **lyric poem** "The Guitar"? **(b)** What perception does Cavafy share in "Ithaka"?

2. **(a)** In lines 5–8 in "The Prayer," what letter sounds are repeated? **(b)** How do these sounds create a musical feeling?

3. In "Fear," in what ways does Mistral's image of a swallow provide a vivid sense of the mother's worries?

Comparing Literary Works

4. **(a)** Use a chart like the one shown below to examine the meaning of one **metaphor** from each of the poems in this grouping.

Poem	Metaphor	Two Things Compared	Meaning

(b) How does each metaphor express or clarify an abstract, or intangible, idea?

5. **(a)** What is the **extended metaphor** in "Ithaka"? **(b)** What brief comparisons build to create the extended metaphor? **(c)** What does Ithaka itself represent?

Reading Strategy

Reading Stanzas as Units of Meaning

6. Begin to **read stanzas as units of meaning** by writing a one-sentence statement expressing the main idea for each stanza of "The Prayer."

7. Would you recommend this reading strategy to a friend who was struggling with poetry? Why or why not?

Extend Understanding

8. **Geography Connection:** If you were to update "Ithaka," omitting the Homeric references, what modern locations might you use? Why?

QuickReview

Lyric poetry is melodic poetry that expresses the observations and feelings of a single speaker and often contains an **epiphany,** or a sudden moment of insight.

A **metaphor** is an implied comparison between two seemingly dissimilar things.

An **extended metaphor** is a metaphor that is developed throughout a literary work.

To better understand a poem, **read stanzas as units of meaning** by pausing after each stanza to state the main idea.

Assessment
For: Self-test
Visit: www.PHSchool.com
Web Code: eta-6804

Poems by García Lorca, Cavafy, Mistral, and Jiménez ■ 1155

Go Online Students may use the **Self-test** to **Assessment** prepare for **Selection Test A** or **Selection Test B.**

Answers

1. **(a)** The guitar is like a wounded heart. **(b)** Life is a journey that should be long and exciting.

2. **(a)** *Li, s, guh,* and *o* are repeated. **(b)** The repetition of these sounds creates a rhythm.

3. The young bird's leaving the nest embodies the mother's fears of separation from her daughter.

4. **Possible response: "The Guitar"** "O guitar! / A wounded heart"; a guitar is compared to a wounded heart; sound is the best expression of human emotion. **"Ithaka"** "Laistrygonians, Cyclops, / angry Poseidon—don't be scared of them"; the creatures from the *Odyssey* are compared to life's trials; readers should not fear the difficulties they may face. **"Fear"** "I don't want them to make / my little girl a princess. / In tiny golden slippers"; the little girl is compared to a creature of privilege whose status would separate her from her mother. **"The Prayer"** "my cup of freshness, honeycomb of my mouth"; the man the speaker loves is compared to the sweetness of a fresh taste. **"Green"** "My life will always leave unlatched / a small green gate to let her in." The green gate is compared to a heart open to the memory of a loved one.

5. **(a)** The extended metaphor is the comparison of Odysseus' journey home to Ithaka to an individual's journey through life. **(b)** The comparison of Laistrygonians, Cyclops, and Poseidon to life's dangers; the comparison of harbors to pleasant life events; and the comparison of sensual perfumes to life's experiences and pleasures build the metaphor. **(c) Possible response:** Ithaka is a philosophy for living one's life, or life itself.

6. **Sample response: Stanza Three:** This good man had an open heart, a gentle temper, was frank, and was filled with miracles.

7. **Possible response:** The skill may help a reader analyze the poem in small parts.

8. **Possible response:** The Lewis and Clark Expedition or the moon landing might replace Ithaka.

1155

❶ Vocabulary Lesson

Word Analysis:
Greek Prefix *mono-*

1. knowing or using only one language
2. being only one molecule thick
3. consisting of one syllable or mono-syllables
4. consisting of one metal
5. having only one color or hue
6. government by a single person

Spelling Strategy

1. electrician
2. visual
3. patiently
4. expulsion

Vocabulary Builder

1. synonyms
2. synonyms
3. antonyms
4. antonyms
5. antonyms
6. synonyms
7. synonyms
8. antonyms
9. synonyms
10. synonyms

❷ Grammar and Style Lesson

1. Listen to the sound of the guitar.
2. Don't be afraid of its sad melody.
3. While the music plays, hear its grief.
4. Ask the guitarist about the song, but don't be surprised at his answer.
5. Don't hurry the journey at all.

Writing Application

Possible response: Live life to the fullest. Be kind to those around you. Do not be afraid to try new things. Never give up on those you love.

𝒲𝒢 **Writing and Grammar** Platinum Level

For support in teaching the Grammar and Style Lesson, use Chapter 19, Section 2.

Build Language Skills

❶ Vocabulary Lesson

Word Analysis: Greek Prefix *mono-*

The prefix *mono-* means "alone," "one," or "single." Define each of the words below, using your dictionary if necessary.

1. monolingual
2. monomolecular
3. monosyllabic
4. monometallic
5. monochromatic
6. monocracy

Spelling Strategy

The *sh* sound can be spelled with *su (sensual), ti (caution), si (session),* or *ci (delicious).* For each of the words below, spell the *sh* sound correctly.

1. electri__an
2. vi__al
3. pa__ently
4. expul__on

Vocabulary Builder: Synonyms or Antonyms?

Review the vocabulary list on page 1145. Then, classify each of the following pairs of words as either synonyms (words with similar meanings) or antonyms (words with opposite meanings).

1. monotonously, tediously
2. exalted, uplifted
3. sensual, repugnant
4. invokes, dismisses
5. anoint, clean
6. sheaves, bundles
7. invokes, summons
8. exalted, suppressed
9. sensual, luxurious
10. anoint, mark

❷ Grammar and Style Lesson

The Understood *You* in Imperative Sentences

Imperative sentences are sentences that give orders or directions. Often in such sentences, the subject is not stated explicitly but is understood to be *you,* or the person being addressed.

> **Examples:**
>
> Pray that your road's a long one. [*You pray that . . .*]
>
> Keep Ithaka always in mind. [*You keep Ithaka always in mind.*]

Practice Rewrite each sentence below so that it contains the understood *you* as its subject.

1. You listen to the sound of the guitar.
2. Don't you be afraid of its sad melody.
3. While the music plays, you hear its grief.
4. You ask the guitarist about the song, but don't you be surprised at his answer.
5. Don't you hurry the journey at all.

Writing Application Write four imperative sentences of advice. Use the understood *you* as the subject in each sentence.

𝒲𝒢 *Prentice Hall Writing and Grammar Connection: Platinum Level, Chapter 19, Section 2*

Assessment Practice

Identify Patterns of Organization (For more practice, see *Test Preparation Workbook,* p. 51.)

Many writing tests require students to identify patterns of organization. Use the following sample test item to help students practice this skill.

> He was a good man, I say he was a man whose heart was entirely open; a man gentle in temper, frank as the light of day, as filled with miracles as the spring of the year.
> —"The Prayer," lines 9–12

Which of the following best describes the organization of this stanza?

A general to specific
B chronological
C cause and effect
D specific to general

This stanza does not use a chronological, cause-and-effect, or specific-to-general organization. The main idea appears first and is supported by details. Therefore, the correct answer is *A*.

③ Writing Lesson

Timed Writing: Interpretive Essay

In the citation for Gabriela Mistral's Nobel Prize in Literature, the Nobel committee described her work as "poems of love dedicated to death." In an essay, discuss what you think this phrase means and how it applies to one of Mistral's poems. *(40 minutes)*

Prewriting
(10 minutes)
Generate ideas by writing about the quotation for five minutes without stopping. After five minutes, review what you have written, circling ideas you want to develop further.

Drafting
(20 minutes)
To organize your essay, state your main idea in one sentence. Then, list the ideas and details that support it. Elaborate upon each of these ideas in a paragraph. Organize the paragraphs in a logical order, and finish with a strong conclusion.

Revising
(10 minutes)
As you review your essay, check that each paragraph flows logically into the next. Consider reordering paragraphs that seem out of place.

Model: Reordering Paragraphs for Coherence

The speaker admits that her lover was cruel, but then she says it doesn't matter because she loved him. That is reason enough to forgive him.

"The Prayer" is a poem about love and death. The speaker prays to God to forgive her dead lover. She offers God many reasons, but the strongest one is her love.

> In an essay that is coherent, paragraphs flow in a logical order.

 Prentice Hall Writing and Grammar Connection: Platinum Level, Chapter 13, Section 4

④ Extend Your Learning

Listening and Speaking Choose the poem from this grouping that you like best. Then prepare and deliver an **oral interpretation** of the poem. Use these tips to prepare:

- Vary the speed, rhythm, and pitch of your voice.
- Pause to emphasize ideas or add drama.
- Identify words and phrases that should be stressed.

As you deliver the poem for the class, use body language that expresses your feelings.

Research and Technology With a small group, use print and nonprint sources to research the symbolic meanings of colors. Select quotations from visual artists and writers and incorporate them into a **color chart.** Use the chart as the basis of a class discussion about the meaning of color in Jiménez's work. **[Group Activity]**

Go Online
Research

For: An additional research activity
Visit: www.PHSchool.com
Web Code: etd-7805

The Guitar / Ithaka / Fear / The Prayer/ Green ■ 1157

---

③ Writing Lesson

You may use this Writing Lesson as a timed-writing practice, or you may allow students to develop the interpretive essay as a writing assignment over several days.

- To give students guidance in writing this essay, give them **Support for Writing Lesson**, p. 68 in *Unit 8 Resources.*

- Have students complete the Prewriting activity. Then, have them work in pairs to choose main ideas for their essays.

- Have students read aloud their drafts in small groups.

- Use the Response to Literature rubrics in *General Resources*, pp. 55–56, to evaluate students' work.

𝒲𝒢 Writing and Grammar Platinum Level

For support in teaching the Writing Lesson, use Chapter 13, Section 4.

④ Listening and Speaking

- Explain to students that an oral interpretation of a poem is more than a simple reading. Through their speed, rhythm, pitch, pauses, and emphases, students will convey the meaning of the poem.

- Encourage students to record themselves practicing their readings.

- The **Support for Extend Your Learning** page (*Unit 8 Resources*, p. 69) provides guided note-taking opportunities to help students complete the Extend Your Learning activities.

Go Online Have students type in the
Research Web Code for another
research activity.

Assessment Resources

The following resources can be used to assess students' knowledge and skills.

Unit 8 Resources
Selection Test A, pp. 71–73
Selection Test B, pp. 74–76

General Resources
Rubrics for Response to Literature, pp. 55–56

Go Online Students may use the **Self-test** to
Assessment prepare for **Selection Test A** or
Selection Test B.

Background
The Nobel Legacy

Alfred Nobel's dynamite legacy originated in part with his father, Immanuel Nobel. The elder Nobel, an engineer and inventor in his own right, built bridges and buildings in Stockholm and experimented with different methods of blasting rock. Later, in St. Petersburg, Russia, he advised the Russian army to block enemy ships by planting naval mines. He created these devices by filling wooden casks with gunpowder and anchoring the casks on the ocean floor, where they deterred British navy ships during the Crimean War of 1853–1856. Later, Immanuel Nobel worked closely with his son to develop a usable form of nitroglycerine.

Background
Science

Although dynamite can be used in warfare and for other violent purposes, it has an impressive range of industrial applications. It has been used to blast out canal beds, mines, dam sites, and quarries. It also has been used to create or level building sites and passages for roads and railways.

Critical Viewing

Possible response: The photograph of V. S. Naipaul projects a mood of pride and joviality. The photograph of José Saramago, on the other hand, projects a solemn, dignified mood. Both photographs convey the deep significance of the event in the lives of two Nobel laureates.

A Closer Look

The Nobel Prize: A Dynamite Idea

"If I have a thousand ideas a year, and only one turns out to be good, I'm satisfied." Alfred Bernhard Nobel once said. Nobel exceeded his goal many times. The Swedish scientist who invented dynamite is also the founder of the most distinguished of all international honors—the Nobel Prize.

A Scientist with the Soul of a Poet Alfred Nobel was born in Stockholm on October 21, 1833. Although he had a deep interest in literature, he was trained as a chemist and physicist and pursued a successful business career. In the 1850s, Nobel became interested in nitroglycerin, an invention of the Italian chemist Ascanio Sobrero. Nitroglycerine is an extremely volatile liquid that can explode unpredictably under heat or pressure. Nobel wanted to find a way to put it to practical use in construction work.

> " . . . the Nobel Prize in Literature positions literature in the forefront of the human experience and accomplishment. "

Nobel's experiments were often unsuccessful and deadly. In one accident, Nobel's brother Emil and several other people were killed. Yet, Nobel remained undeterred in his quest. In 1866, he finally found a successful formula that stabilized nitroglycerine and allowed it to be shaped into rods. He patented the material under the name of dynamite. He also invented a detonator, or blasting cap, which could be ignited by lighting a fuse. These inventions helped dramatically reduce the cost of construction work, especially where large-scale excavations were required.

A Man of Peace The invention of dynamite made Nobel wealthy, and it transformed the construction industry. A man who valued literature, wrote his own poetry, and held pacifist views, Nobel was deeply disturbed that dynamite was being used in the making of weapons. Nobel held himself responsible for the deaths his invention had caused and would cause. To redeem his legacy, he established a fund of $9 million to fund an annual prize honoring actions promoting peace, as well as achievements in literature, physics, chemistry, medicine, and economics. Nobel died in 1896, and the first prizes were awarded in 1901.

The Literature Prize The Nobel Prize in Literature, which recognizes the most distinguished body of literary work created by a single author, is one of the most highly publicized of all the prizes. The prize represents an international literary standard, and it has helped bring both individual authors and entire countries to the world's attention. For

▼ ▲ **Critical Viewing** While these photographs of Nobel laureates V. S. Naipaul, above, and José Saramago, below, show similar moments in the lives of these two men, they capture very different emotions. Compare and contrast the moods these pictures convey. **[Compare and Contrast]**

Enrichment

Nitroglycerine and Dynamite
To create nitroglycerine, Ascanio Sobrero added glycerol, an alcohol, to nitric and sulfuric acids. When these substances are mixed, a chemical reaction occurs. This reaction is highly exothermic—that is, it generates large amounts of heat. If the mixture cools to below 78° Fahrenheit, it will freeze and form needlelike crystals. If the crystals are heated or broken, they will explode.

Alfred Nobel stabilized nitroglycerine by mixing the thick, oily liquid with a crystalline compound known as silica. The paste that resulted—dynamite—could be kneaded and shaped into explosive rods. The explosive liquid nitroglycerine is mixed with other materials and packed into cylinders. These cylinders, or cartridges, are fitted with a detonating cap and placed into a hole that has been bored in the material to be blasted. The explosion is then set off from a distance by a fuse or an electrical current.

example, Nobel Prizes awarded to Chilean poet Pablo Neruda (1971) and Colombian author Gabriel García Márquez (1982) placed Latin American literature at the forefront of public awareness; Naguib Mahfouz's prize (1988) placed Egyptian literature in the public spotlight. The same has happened for Japanese literature, with awards to Yasunari Kawabata (1968) and Kenzaburo Oe (1994).

Controversies and Criticism At the same time, however, the Nobel Prize in Literature has held its share of controversy. The Nobel committee is made up of four to five members, most of whom are Swedish citizens. Scandinavian countries have received the Nobel Prize in Literature most often, gaining 14.9 percent of the prizes. France is runner-up, taking home 12.9 percent of the prizes. In the past two decades, however, the awards have honored writers from countries around the globe, including Guatemala, the Czech Republic, Poland, Italy, China, and Iceland.

Some critics claim that the decisions of the Nobel committee are politically motivated, honoring the most acceptable rather than the best. These critics cite the omission of some of the greatest writers of the twentieth century, such as Marcel Proust, Franz Kafka, and James Joyce, from the list of prize winners. Imperfect as it may be, the Nobel Prize in Literature positions literature in the forefront of human experience and accomplishment. When the prize is announced, the news makes headlines, stirs debate, and causes celebrations. For a brief moment every year, Nobel achieves his dream of bringing the world together, not for purposes of war or commerce but simply to honor human goodness, creativity, and genius.

Activity

Who is Responsible?

Alfred Nobel's response to the unintended harmful consequences of his invention raises the question: Are scientists and inventors ultimately responsible for the effects that their inventions have on the world, as Nobel believed himself to be?

With a group, discuss this question in the context of modern developments such as the discoveries of DNA and nuclear fission. Use these questions to guide your discussion:

- Who, if anyone, is responsible for the effects of a discovery or an invention?
- Is the inventor responsible for the invention all the time? What later uses or alterations of the idea might lessen the inventor's responsibilities?
- If scientists and inventors profit from their work, do they also have a duty to compensate for the destruction or suffering that their work causes? Explain your response.

Choose a point person to share your thoughts with the class.

Standard Course of Study

Goal 1: WRITTEN LANGUAGE

WL.1.02.5 Demonstrate an understanding of media's impact on analyses and personal reflection.

Goal 2: INFORMATIONAL READING

IR.2.02.1 Summarize situations to examine cause/effect relationships.

IR.2.02.2 Show clear, logical connection among cause/effect events.

Goal 5: LITERATURE

LT.5.02.1 Explore works which relate to an issue, author, or theme and show increasing comprehension.

Goal 6: GRAMMAR AND USAGE

GU.6.01.3 Use recognition strategies to understand vocabulary and exact word choice.

Step-by-Step Teaching Guide	Pacing Guide
PRETEACH	
• Administer Vocabulary and Reading Warm-ups as necessary.	5 min.
• Engage students' interest with the motivation activity.	5 min.
• Read and discuss author and background features. **FT**	10 min.
• Introduce the Literary Analysis Skill: Conflict. **FT**	5 min.
• Introduce the Reading Strategy: Identifying Cause and Effect. **FT**	
• Prepare students to read by teaching the selection vocabulary. **FT**	10 min.
TEACH	
• Informally monitor comprehension while students read independently or in groups. **FT**	30 min.
• Monitor students' comprehension with the Reading Check notes.	as students read
• Reinforce vocabulary with Vocabulary Builder notes.	as students read
• Develop students' understanding of conflict with the Literary Analysis annotations. **FT**	5 min.
• Develop students' ability to identify cause and effect with the Reading Strategy annotations. **FT**	5 min.
ASSESS/EXTEND	
• Assess students' comprehension and mastery of the Literary Analysis and Reading Strategy by having them answer the Apply the Skills questions. **FT**	15 min.
• Have students complete the Vocabulary Lesson and the Grammar and Style Lesson. **FT**	15 min.
• Apply students' ability to address opposing viewpoints by using the Writing Lesson. **FT**	45 min. or homework
• Apply students' understanding by using one or more of the Extend Your Learning activities.	20–90 min. or homework
• Administer Selection Test A or Selection Test B. **FT**	15 min.

Resources

Print

Unit 8 Resources

Transparency

Graphic Organizer Transparencies

Print

Reader's Notebook [L2]

Reader's Notebook: Adapted Version [L1]

Reader's Notebook: English Learner's Version [EL]

Unit 8 Resources

Technology

Listening to Literature Audio CDs [L2, EL]

Print

Unit 8 Resources

General Resources

Technology

Go Online: Research [**L3**]
Go Online: Self-test [**L3**]
ExamView®, Test Bank [**L3**]

Choosing Resources for Differentiated Instruction

[**L1**] Special Needs Students

[**L2**] Below-Level Students

[**L3**] All Students

[**L4**] Advanced Students

[**EL**] English Learners

For Vocabulary and Reading Warm-ups and for Selection Tests, **A** signifies "less challenging" and **B** "more challenging." For Graphic Organizer transparencies, **A** signifies "not filled in" and **B** "filled in."

FT Fast Track Instruction: To move the lesson more quickly, use the strategies and activities identified with **FT**.

Scaffolding for Less Proficient and Advanced Students

The leveled Critical Thinking questions after selections progress in the levels of thinking required to answer them. To address the needs of your different students, you may use the (a) level questions for your less proficient students and the (b) level questions with your on-level and advanced students. The occasional (c) level questions are appropriate for your advanced students.

PRENTICE HALL

TeacherEXPRESS™ Use this complete
Plan · Teach · Assess suite of powerful
teaching tools to make lesson planning and testing quicker and easier.

PRENTICE HALL

StudentEXPRESS™ Use the interactive
Learn · Study · Succeed textbook (online
and on CD-ROM) to make selections and activities come alive with audio and video support and interactive questions.

Benchmark

After students have completed reading *The Artist,* administer **Benchmark Test 10** *(Unit 8 Resources,* **pp. 101–106).** If the Benchmark Test reveals that some of the students need further work, use the **Interpretation Guide** to determine the appropriate reteaching page in the **Reading Kit** and on **Success Tracker.**

 For: Information about Lexiles
Professional **Visit:** www.PHSchool.com
Development **Web Code:** eue-1111

Motivation

Tell students that, like the mother in the story they are about to read, some artists find commercial work distracting and unappealing. Ask students to name some jobs that combine the practical with the aesthetic in a way that is artistically satisfying and financially rewarding.

❶ Background

More About the Author

Tagore's striking appearance helped shape his image as a prophetic sage and teacher. He believed that children should be one with their natural surroundings and that they should be sensitive to the environmental balance of Earth. The school he founded in Bolpur in 1901 was called Santiniketan ("abode of peace"). Many of its classes were held under the campus trees. Even after the school expanded its program in 1921 to become Visva-Bharati University, the curriculum continued to emphasize Tagore's concerns for social reform and international unity.

Geography Note

Point out the map of India on this page. Tell students that India has a long artistic legacy. Among the most notable achievements of Indian art are the frescoes, or wall paintings, found in artificial caves near the village of Ajanta in western India. These caves were created by Buddhist monks during the period from the first century B.C. to the seventh century A.D. The vibrant and colorful paintings on the walls depict Buddhist themes.

The Artist ❶

Rabindranath Tagore (1861–1941)

In 1915, the Indian writer Rabindranath Tagore (rə bēn´ drə nät´ tä´ gôr) was knighted by the British government in recognition of his literary contributions. This was one of the British Empire's highest honors, yet four years later Tagore renounced his title. He did so to protest the Amritsar (əm rit´ sər) Massacre, in which British troops fired on a group of unarmed Indian protesters.

A Gifted Family Tagore was born in Bengal, which was then a province of British India. Tagore's family was highly accomplished. His father was a famous Hindu philosopher and religious reformer. Other members of Tagore's family distinguished themselves in art, music, and finance. A gifted child with a wide range of intellectual and artistic talents, Tagore began writing at the age of eight. He composed both poems and short stories, producing a series of books while he was still in his twenties. This highly productive period culminated with the publication of *Manasi* (mä nä´ sē), one of his finest collections of verse, in 1890.

A Witness to Suffering In 1891, Tagore moved to his father's estate in a rural section of Bengal, where he developed a deep awareness of the poverty and other hardships faced by so many of India's inhabitants. From that point on, his social concerns became the dominant focus of his life. Among the many contributions that he made to Indian society were his establishment of a university and a progressive, open-air school in western Bengal. He was also a vocal supporter of human rights and personal freedom, though he did not press for Indian independence from Britain.

A Prolific Writer Despite involvement in other activities, Tagore remained a productive writer throughout his life. Altogether he produced more than one thousand poems, two dozen plays, eight novels, and several collections of short stories.

Generally, Tagore's poems and stories are considered to be his strongest works. His poems are characterized by a quiet simplicity and dignity, and his short stories are noted for their irony, subtle humor, and social and philosophical themes. Among his most famous collections of poems and short stories are *The Golden Boat* (1894), *Late Harvest* (1896), *Dreams* (1896), *Song Offerings* (1910), and *Bunches of Tales* (1912).

Fame in the West With the publication of the English version of *Gitanjali: Song Offerings* in 1912, Tagore's reputation was firmly established in the West. In his introduction to the English translation, the great Irish poet William Butler Yeats commented, "These lyrics—which are in the original . . . full of subtlety of rhythm, untranslatable delicacies of color, of metrical invention—display in their thought a world I have dreamed of all my life long." The English translation of *Song Offerings*, along with his role in introducing Indian literature to the Western world, earned Tagore the Nobel Prize in Literature in 1913.

A Man of Many Talents Although it is not a well-known fact outside India, Tagore's artistic talents were by no means limited to writing. A gifted musician and composer, he wrote more than two thousand songs and helped create a new style of Indian music. In addition, he was also a talented painter, considered by many art critics to be the finest Indian artist of his time.

Preview

Connecting to the Literature

The struggle between the pursuit of money and the pursuit of happiness is as ancient as civilization itself. In this story, that struggle becomes the dominant theme in the life of one family.

❷ Literary Analysis

Conflict

Conflict, the struggle between opposing forces, is a key element of fiction because most plots develop from conflict. While there are many different types of literary conflict, they can be divided into two general categories:

- *Internal conflict* occurs within the mind of a character and involves a struggle with ideas, beliefs, attitudes, or emotions.
- *External conflict* takes place between a character and an outside force, such as another person, society, nature, fate, or God.

As you read, use a chart like the one shown to examine the conflicts in this story and to categorize them as either internal or external.

Connecting Literary Elements

Characters are the people or animals who take part in the action of a literary work. Like a real person, **round characters** are complex and multifaceted, displaying both good and bad qualities. By contrast, **flat characters** are one-dimensional. As you read, analyze the characters and determine whether they are round and multifaceted or flat and one-dimensional.

❸ Reading Strategy

Identifying Cause and Effect

A **cause** is an event, an action, or a feeling that produces a result. An **effect** is the result that is produced. Sometimes, words like *because, so,* and *therefore* signal causes and effects. However, fiction writers often develop events without presenting such obvious connections. As you read this story, identify the causes and effects of each character's feelings, thoughts, and actions.

Vocabulary Builder

meager (mē´ gər) *adj.* thin; lean (p. 1162)

terminology (tʉr´ mə näl´ ə jē) *n.* terms used in a specific discipline (p. 1162)

frugality (frōō gal´ ə tē) *n.* thrift (p. 1164)

connotations (kän´ ə tā´ shənz) *n.* ideas suggested by a word that go beyond its concrete meaning (p. 1164)

equable (ek´ wə bəl) *adj.* steady; uniform (p. 1164)

squandered (skwän´ dərd) *v.* wasted (p. 1164)

disdain (dis dān´) *n.* strong dislike (p. 1166)

myriad (mir´ ē əd) *adj.* many; varied (p. 1167)

enumerating (ē nōō´ mər āt´ iŋ) *v.* counting; listing (p. 1167)

NC Standard Course of Study

- Summarize situations to examine cause/effect relationships. (IR.2.02.1)

Conflicts	
External	**Internal**
1. Govinda's conflict with Satyabati	1.
2.	2.

The Artist ■ 1161

❷ Literary Analysis

Conflict

- Read aloud the Literary Analysis instruction. Then, tell students that conflict shapes most elements in a story: the characters, the setting, the theme, and particularly the point of view.

- Distribute copies of the **Literary Analysis Graphic Organizer A,** p. 196 in *Graphic Organizer Transparencies.* Have students use the organizer to identify a conflict, record it, and then consider how this conflict shapes the characters' actions.

❸ Reading Strategy

Identifying Cause and Effect

- On the board, write the following sentences: Jean hid Karl's study guide. If she could earn a better score on the test than he could, she would be first in the class.

- **Ask** students what Jean did. Then, ask them what caused Jean to take this particular action and what this action says about Jean's character. **Answer:** Jean hid Karl's study guide so she could earn a better score on the test. This action reveals Jean as a selfish and dishonest person.

- Point out to students that understanding the causes and effects of a character's behavior can uncover the deeper understanding of a literary work.

Vocabulary Builder

- Pronounce each vocabulary word for students, and read the definitions as a class. Have students identify any words with which they are already familiar.

THE ARTIST

Rabindranath Tagore
translated by Mary Lago, Tarun Gupta, and Amiya Chakravarty

Background Rabindranath Tagore is best known as a writer and painter, but he was also a teacher whose theories of education have had an international impact. For Tagore, creativity was the essence of both human beings and the natural world. He believed that traditional education, with its emphasis on uniformity and facts, encouraged children to ignore both their natural creativity and their connections to the world around them. To address this issue, Tagore established a school in Bengal in 1901. Classes were held outdoors. Each day began and ended with an artistic activity. This story reflects these same views about the importance of creativity in people's lives and provides an indictment of modern materialistic values.

Govinda came to Calcutta after graduation from high school in Mymensingh.[1] His widowed mother's savings were <u>meager</u>, but his own unwavering determination was his greatest resource. "I *will* make money," he vowed, "even if I have to give my whole life to it." In his <u>terminology</u>, wealth was always referred to as *pice.*[2] In other words he had in mind a very concrete image of something that could be seen, touched, and smelled; he was not greatly fascinated with fame, only with the very ordinary *pice,* eroded by circulation from market to market, from hand to hand, the tarnished *pice,* the *pice* that smells of copper, the original form of Kuvera,[3] who assumes the assorted guises of silver, gold, securities, and wills, and keeps men's minds in a turmoil.

After traveling many tortuous roads and getting muddied repeatedly in the process, Govinda had now arrived upon the solidly paved embankment of his wide and free-flowing stream of money. He was firmly seated in the manager's chair at the MacDougal Gunnysack Company. Everyone called him MacDulal.

When Govinda's lawyer-brother, Mukunda,[4] died, he left behind a wife, a four-year-old son, a house in Calcutta, and some cash savings.

---

1. **Calcutta** (kal kut′ ə) **. . . Mymensingh** (mī′ mən siŋ′) Calcutta is a seaport in northeastern India; Mymensingh, now in Bangladesh, is about 190 miles northeast of Calcutta.
2. *pice* (pīs) Indian coin.
3. **Kuvera** (kōō ver′ ä) Hindu god of wealth, usually spelled Kubera.
4. **Mukunda** (mə kʊn′ də).

1162 ■ *The Modern World*

Vocabulary Builder
meager (mē′ gər) *adj.* thin; lean

terminology (tʉr′ mə näl′ə jē) *n.* terms used in a specific discipline

Romantic India I, by Gerry Charm

Collage (from the French word meaning "pasting") is an artistic technique in which various decorative elements such as bits of fabric, found materials, printed items, and painting are assembled together on a canvas or other surface. This collage, created in 2000 by American artist Gerry Charm, combines several items and motifs from Indian culture to create a vibrant composition.

Use the following questions for discussion:

• Why might an artist choose to create a collage?
  Possible response: A collage allows an artist to combine different media in one composition. The variety of textures, colors, and motifs in a collage may appeal to an artist who feels limited by one medium.

• How does this collage capture feelings of both tradition and modernity?
  Possible response: The architectural detail and the portrait suggest traditional Indian culture. The postage stamp and the collage format itself are more modern.

❹ **Critical Viewing**

Answer: The images of the postage stamp and the architectural detail suggest that Indian society views many aspects of everyday life—even the most mundane—as works of art.

❹ ▲ **Critical Viewing** This collage includes a postage stamp and an architectural detail. What do these images suggest about the role of art in daily Indian life? Explain. **[Draw Conclusions]**

The Artist ■ 1163

Support for Special Needs Students
Lead a discussion in which students consider what the statement "I *will* make money, even if I have to give my whole life to it" tells the reader about Govinda. Make sure students understand the extent of Govinda's dedication to making money. Then, have students discuss the ways the desire to make money keeps some people's minds in turmoil.

Enrichment for Gifted/Talented Students
As they read, have students note the character traits of Govinda and Satyabati. Then, have students use these traits to create collages to represent each character. Collages should incorporate pictures from magazines, computer clip art, drawings, and objects. Have students display their work in the classroom.

⑤ Themes in World Literature

Obsessions With Wealth Leo Tolstoy's story "How Much Land Does a Man Need"—which appears in this text—deals with a character's relationship with money. In this story, Tolstoy's protagonist Pakhom struggles with his inability to be satisfied with what he has.

Connect to the Literature Point out to students the wisdom of pursuing a career that will bring them financial security, but tell them to remember the saying, "All things in moderation." Ask students to describe the attitude toward money that each character in "The Artist" has.

Possible responses: Before his death, Mukunda was careless about money and spent much of it to encourage his wife's artistic work. Govinda is obsessed with accumulating money and is irritated that Chunilal and Satyabati waste time on art. Satyabati opposes Govinda's values. Even though Satyabati's artistic work earns little income, her passion for art prevails, and she encourages her son's artistic efforts. Chuni cares only for art. Rangalal disdains any concern about money over art.

⑥ Background

A Simple Life

Just as Mukunda chooses to live a life unencumbered by materialism, so have some religious individuals such as Francis of Assisi. In certain traditions, the worship of money led to the vows of poverty taken by those who renounced the pursuit of affluence.

⑦ Critical Thinking

Apply

• Have a volunteer read aloud the bracketed passage. Then, **ask** students to describe what kind of person Mukunda was.

Possible response: Mukunda was affectionate and tolerant, with little desire for control over his household. He defended Satyabati and her art. He was casual about money and enjoyed life.

• Have students **explain** why Mukunda made an ideal husband for Satyabati.

Answer: Mukunda allowed Satyabati to do what she wished and supported her art without worrying about the expense. Mukunda also defended his wife's use of time and was interested in her drawings.

In addition to his property there was some debt; therefore, provision for his family's needs depended upon <u>frugality</u>. Thus his son, Chunilal,[5] was brought up in circumstances that were undistinguished in comparison with those of the neighbors.

Mukunda's will gave Govinda entire responsibility for this family. Ever since Chunilal was a baby, Govinda had bestowed spiritual initiation upon his nephew with the sacred words: "Make money."

The main obstacle to the boy's initiation was his mother, Satyabati.[6] She said nothing outright; her opposition showed in her behavior. Art had always been her hobby. There was no limit to her enthusiasm for creating all sorts of original and decorative things from flowers, fruits and leaves, even food-stuffs, from paper and cloth cutouts, from clay and flour, from berry juices and the juices of other fruits, from *jaba-* and *shiuli*-flower stems. This activity brought her considerable grief, because anything unessential or irrational has the character of flash floods in July: it has considerable mobility, but in relation to the utilitarian[7] concerns of life it is like a stalled ferry. Sometimes there were invitations to visit relatives; Satyabati forgot them and spent the time in her bedroom with the door shut, kneading a lump of clay. The relatives said, "She's terribly stuck-up." There was no satisfactory reply to this. Mukunda had known, even on the basis of his bookish knowledge, that value judgments can be made about art too. He had been thrilled by the noble <u>connotations</u> of the word "art," but he could not conceive of its having any connection with the work of his own wife.

This man's nature had been very <u>equable.</u> When his wife <u>squandered</u> time on unessential whims, he had smiled at it with affectionate delight. If anyone in the household made a slighting remark, he had protested immediately. There had been a singular self-contradiction in Mukunda's makeup; he had been an expert in the practice of law, but it must be conceded that he had had no worldly wisdom with regard to his household affairs. Plenty of money had passed through his hands, but since it had not preoccupied his thoughts, it had left his mind free. Nor could he have tyrannized over his dependents in order to get his own way. His living habits had been very simple; he had never made any unreasonable demands for the attention or services of his relatives.

Mukunda had immediately silenced anyone in the household who cast an aspersion[8] upon Satyabati's disinterest in housework. Now and

---

5. **Chunilal** (chōō´ nē lal).
6. **Satyabati** (sət´ yə bə´ tē).
7. **utilitarian** (yōo til ə ter´ ē ən) *adj.* stressing usefulness.
8. **aspersion** (ə spʉr´ zhən) *n.* damaging or disparaging remark.

𝒯hemes in World Masterpieces

⑤ Obsessions With Wealth

Literature throughout the world expresses the uneasy relationship people have with money.

For Tagore, money is decidedly negative. Wealth and its pursuit is a distraction from the values of creativity and spirituality that really matter. In *The Canterbury Tales*, the English poet Geoffrey Chaucer adopted the biblical viewpoint that love of money is the root of all evil.

Other writers treat the issue more gently. For example, Jane Austen, the English novelist, described characters who marry for love but gain fortune as a bonus. Likewise, Charles Dickens writes of characters who gain wealth without losing their virtue. For example, in his novel Great Expectations, a fortune comes to the kind, loyal, and industrious Pip.

Connect to the Literature

List each of the characters in "The Artist" and describe his or her attitude toward money.

Vocabulary Builder

frugality (frōō gal´ ə tē) *n.* thrift

connotations (kän´ ə tā´ shənz) *n.* ideas suggested by a word that go beyond its concrete meaning

equable (ek´ wə bəl) *adj.* steady; uniform

squandered (skwän´ dərd) *v.* wasted

Enrichment

Tagore's Success

W. B. Yeats introduced Tagore to the English-speaking world after grief forced the Indian poet into retirement from public life in 1907. Writing in 1912, the year before Tagore received the Nobel Prize, Yeats said that "he writes music for his words, and one understands at every moment that he is so abundant, so spontaneous, so daring in his passion, so full of surprise, because he is doing something which has never seemed strange, unnatural, or in need of defense."

then, on his way home from court, he would stop at Radhabazar to buy some paints, some colored silk and colored pencils, and stealthily[9] he would go and arrange them on the wooden chest in his wife's bedroom. Sometimes, picking up one of Satyabati's drawings, he would say, "Well, this one is certainly very beautiful."

One day he had held up a picture of a man, and since he had it upside down, he had decided that the legs must be a bird's head. He had said, "Satu, this should be framed—what a marvelous picture of a stork!" Mukunda had gotten a certain delight out of thinking of his wife's artwork as child's play, and the wife had taken a similar pleasure in her husband's judgment of art. Satyabati had known perfectly well that she could not hope for so much patience, so much indulgence, from any other family in Bengal.[10] No other family would have made way so lovingly for her overpowering devotion to art. So, whenever her husband had made extravagant remarks about her painting, Satyabati could scarcely restrain her tears.

One day Satyabati lost even this rare good fortune. Before his death her husband had realized one thing quite clearly: the responsibility for his debt-ridden property must be left in the hands of someone astute enough to skillfully steer even a leaky boat to the other shore. This is how Satyabati and her son came to be placed completely under Govinda's care. From the very first day Govinda made it plain to her that the *pice* was the first and foremost thing in life. There was such profound degradation in his advice that Satyabati would shrink with shame.

Nevertheless, the worship of money continued in diverse forms in their daily life. If there had been some modesty about it, instead of such constant discussion, it wouldn't have been so bad. Satyabati knew in her heart that all of this lowered her son's standard of values, but there was nothing to do but endure it. Since those delicate emotions endowed with uncommon dignity are the most vulnerable, they are very easily hurt or ridiculed by rude or insensitive people.

The study of art requires all sorts of supplies. Satyabati had received these for so long without even asking that she had felt no reticence[11] with regard to them. Amid the new circumstances in the family she felt terribly ashamed to charge all these unessential items to the housekeeping budget. So she would save money by economizing on her own food and have the supplies purchased and brought in secretly. Whatever work she did was done furtively,[12] behind closed

---

9. **stealthily** (stel´ thə lē) *adv.* secretly or slyly.
10. **Bengal** (ben gôl´) region in northeastern India.
11. **reticence** (ret´ ə sens) *n.* quality or state of being habitually silent or uncommunicative.
12. **furtively** (fur´ tiv lē) *adv.* slyly; secretively.

Literary Analysis
Conflict and Round and Flat Characters Would you describe Mukunda as a round or flat character? Explain.

Literary Analysis
Conflict What is the nature of the conflict between Satyabati and Govinda?

✔ **Reading Check** ❿
To what activity is Satyabati devoted?

The Artist ■ 1165

---

❽ Literary Analysis
Round and Flat Characters

- Remind students that a round character is complex and displays both bad and good characteristics; a flat character is one-dimensional and displays only one dominant trait.
- Have students reread the bracketed passage. **Ask** students the first Literary Analysis question: Would you describe Mukunda as a round or flat character? Explain.
  Possible response: Mukunda is a round character because he has both good and bad qualities. Although he cares for his wife and son, he is ignorant of household affairs and has not been careful with money.

❾ Literary Analysis
Conflict

- Remind students that external conflict often takes place between characters.
- **Ask** students to describe Satyabati's character and Govinda's character.
  Possible response: Satyabati puts her devotion to art above the pursuit of money. Govinda believes that everyone in his household should share his goal of making money.
- Read aloud the bracketed passage. **Ask** students the second Literary Analysis question: What is the nature of the conflict between Satyabati and Govinda?
  Answer: The characters have different priorities: art for Satyabati and money for Govinda.
- ▶ **Monitor Progress Ask** students to explain whether the conflict between Satyabati and Govinda is internal or external.
  Answer: The conflict is primarily external, although each character struggles internally to reconcile his or her own values with those of the other character.
- ▶ **Reteach** If students have difficulty identifying the conflict between Satyabati and Govinda, have them use the **Literary Analysis** support, p. 81 in *Unit 8 Resources*.

❿ Reading Check
Answer: Satyabati is devoted to creating art.

Two Gazelles, from the *Babar Nama*

The *Babar Nama* is an illustrated book created by court painters to commemorate the rule of Babar from 1526 to 1530. Babar, a Turk descended from Genghis Khan, conquered Delhi in 1526, founding the Mogul Empire. The exploits of Babar were told as history and legend, illustrated with active figures.

Rulers of sixteenth-century India were interested in art for its aesthetics as well as its ability to create a sense of history and stability. Note the elegant lines, surface patterns, and decorative details of *Two Gazelles*.

Use the following question for discussion:

What feelings are evoked by *Two Gazelles*?

Possible response: The painting gives the viewer a feeling of peacefulness and abundance.

⑫ Critical Viewing

Possible response: The painting—with its attention to detail and use of color—effectively captures Satyabati's and Chunilal's love of art.

---

doors. She was not afraid of a scolding, but the stares of insensitive observers embarrassed her.

Now Chuni was the only spectator and critic of her artistic activity. Gradually he became a participant. He began to feel its intoxication. The child's offense could not be concealed, since it overflowed the pages of his notebook onto the walls of the house. There were stains on his face, on his hands, on the cuffs of his shirt. Indra,[13] the king of the gods, does not spare even the soul of a little boy in the effort to tempt him away from the worship of money.

On the one hand the restraint increased, on the other hand the mother collaborated in the violations. Occasionally the head of the company would take his office manager, Govinda, along on business trips out of town. Then the mother and son would get together in unrestrained joy. This was the absolute extreme of childishness! They drew pictures of animals that God has yet to create. The likeness of the dog would get mixed up with that of the cat. It was difficult to distinguish between fish and fowl. There was no way to preserve all these creations; their traces had to be thoroughly obliterated before the head of the house returned. Only Brahma, the Creator, and Rudra, the Destroyer, witnessed the creative delight of these two persons; Vishnu,[14] the heavenly Preserver, never arrived.

The compulsion for artistic creation ran strong in Satyabati's family. There was an older nephew, Rangalal, who rose overnight to fame as an artist. That is to say, the connoisseurs of the land roared with laughter at the unorthodoxy of his art. Since their stamp of imagination did not coincide with his, they had a violent scorn for his talent. But curiously enough, his reputation thrived upon <u>disdain</u> and flourished in this atmosphere of opposition and mockery. Those who imitated him most

Two Gazelles, From the Babar Nama, 1530, National Museum, New Delhi, Delhi India

▲ Critical Viewing ⑫

Do you think this painting effectively captures Satyabati's and Chunilal's love of art? **[Evaluate]**

Vocabulary Builder
disdain (dis dān´) *n.* strong dislike

---

13. **Indra** (in´ drə) chief god of the early Hindu religion.
14. **Brahma** (brä´ me) . . . **Rudra** (rōō´ drə) . . . **Vishnu** (vish´ nōō) In the Hindu religion, Brahma is the creator of the universe, Rudra is the god of destruction and reproduction, and Vishnu is the god of preservation.

1166 ■ *The Modern World*

Enrichment

Painting in Ancient India

India has a rich artistic tradition. In his book *The Wonder That Was India,* the historian A. L. Basham offers insights about the art of painting in ancient India.

Painting was a very highly developed art in ancient India. Palaces and the homes of the rich were adorned with beautiful murals, and smaller paintings were made on prepared boards. Not only were there professional artists, but many men and women of the educated classes could ably handle a brush.

Though now all in very bad condition, the surviving remains of ancient Indian painting are sufficient to show its achievement. They consist almost entirely of murals in certain cave temples.

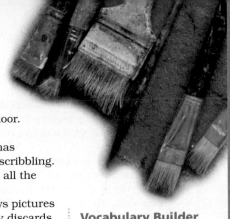

took it upon themselves to prove that the man was a hoax as an artist, that there were obvious defects even in his technique.

This much-maligned artist came to his aunt's home one day, at a time when the office manager was absent. After persistent knocking and shoving at the door he finally got inside and found that there was nowhere to set foot on the floor. The cat was out of the bag.

"It is obvious," said Rangalal, "that the image of creation has emerged anew from the soul of the artist; this is not random scribbling. He and that god who creates form are the same age. Get out all the drawings and show them to me."

Where should they get the drawings? That artist who draws pictures all over the sky in <u>myriad</u> colors, in light and shadow, calmly discards his mists and mirages. Their creations had gone the same way. With an oath Rangalal said to his aunt, "From now on, I'll come and get whatever you make."

There came another day when the office manager had not returned. Since morning the sky had brooded in the shadows of July; it was raining. No one monitored the hands of the clock and no one wanted to know about them. Today Chuni began to draw a picture of a sailing boat while his mother was in the prayer room. The waves of the river looked like a flock of hungry seals just on the point of swallowing the boat. The clouds seemed to cheer them on and float their shawls overhead, but the seals were not conventional seals, and it would be no exaggeration to say of the clouds: "Light and mist merge in the watery waste." In the interests of truth it must be said that if boats were built like this one, insurance companies would never assume such risks. Thus the painting continued; the sky-artist drew fanciful pictures, and inside the room the wide-eyed boy did the same.

No one realized that the door was open. The office manager appeared. He roared in a thunderous voice, "What's going on?"

The boy's heart jumped and his face grew pale. Now Govinda perceived the real reason for Chunilal's examination errors in historical dates. Meanwhile the crime became all the more evident as Chunilal tried unsuccessfully to hide the drawing under his shirt. As Govinda snatched the picture away, the design he saw on it further astonished him. Errors in historical dates would be preferable to this. He tore the picture to pieces. Chunilal burst out crying.

From the prayer room Satyabati heard the boy's weeping, and she came running. Both Chunilal and the torn pieces of the picture were on the floor. Govinda went on <u>enumerating</u> the reasons for his nephew's failure in the history examination and suggesting dire remedies.

Satyabati had never said a word about Govinda's behavior toward them. She had quietly endured everything, remembering that this was the person on whom her husband had relied. Now her eyes were wet with tears, and shaking with anger, she said hoarsely, "Why did you tear up Chuni's picture?"

Vocabulary Builder
myriad (mir´ ē əd) *adj.* many; varied

Vocabulary Builder
enumerating (ē noo´ mər āt´ iŋ) *v.* counting; listing

 **Reading Check** ⑭

Who gradually becomes a participant in Satyabati's artistic activity?

The Artist ■ 1167

⑬ **Critical Thinking**
Speculate
• Tell students to read the bracketed passage.
• **Ask** students why Satyabati calmly discards her artwork. Prompt them to speculate on why a creator would do such a thing.
Possible response: The value of art is in the process, not the product.

⑭ **Reading Check**
Answer: Chunilal gradually becomes a participant in Satyabati's artistic activity.

- Remind students that a cause is an event, an action, or a feeling that produces an effect or result.

- Read aloud the bracketed passage. Then, **ask** students: What causes Satyabati to take Chunilal to her nephew's house?
Answer: Govinda threatens to take Chunilal to boarding school.

ASSESS

Answers

1. **Possible response:** Govinda's perspective is more realistic because without some financial support, Satyabati could not survive.

2. (a) Govinda is determined to obtain money. (b) Govinda regards Satyabati's art as a waste of time and money. (c) Mukunda, unlike Govinda, values art over money.

3. (a) The connoisseurs ridicule Rangalal's art. (b) The art is not appreciated by many. (c) **Possible response:** The author values art as an activity because the characters continue to make art despite others' negative reactions.

4. (a) Brahma, the creator of the universe, is the sky artist. (b) Tagore is suggesting that the creation of art is a spiritual activity.

5. (a) Govinda takes on the responsibility because his brother dies, leaving his wife and son without someone to take care of their finances. (b) **Possible response:** At the time of the story, Indian women did not handle their own affairs.

6. **Possible response:** Satyabati is wise to keep her son from becoming possessed by money; however, Chunilal may have difficulty supporting himself as an adult.

Go Online For additional informa-
Author Link tion about Rabindranath Tagore, have students type in the Web Code, then select *T* from the alphabet, and then select Rabindranath Tagore.

Govinda said, "Doesn't he have to study? What will become of him in the future?"

" Even if he becomes a beggar in the street," answered Satyabati, "he'll be better off in the future. But I hope he'll never be like you. May his pride in his God-given talent be more than your pride in *pices*. This is my blessing for him, a mother's blessing."

"I can't neglect my responsibility," said Govinda. "I will not tolerate this. Tomorrow I'll send him to a boarding school; otherwise, you'll ruin him."

15 The office manager returned to the office. The rain fell in torrents and the streets flowed with water.

Holding her son's hand, Satyabati said, "Let's go, dear."

Chuni said, "Go where, Mother?"

"Let's get out of this place."

The water was knee-deep at Rangalal's door. Satyabati came in with Chunilal. She said, "My dear boy, you take charge of him. Keep him from the worship of money."

Critical Reading

1. **Respond:** Which perspective of the world do you think is more realistic—Satyabati's or Govinda's? Explain.

2. **(a) Recall:** What did Govinda show an "unwavering determination" to obtain? **(b) Interpret:** How does he regard Satyabati's art? **(c) Compare and Contrast:** Compare and contrast Mukunda's attitude toward both money and art with Govinda's.

3. **(a) Recall:** How do "the connoisseurs of the land" regard Rangalal's art? **(b) Connect:** In what ways are Rangalal's art and that of Satyabati and Chunilal similar? **(c) Analyze:** Based on these descriptions, do you think the author values art more as a product or as an activity? Explain.

4. **(a) Interpret:** Who is the sky-artist? **(b) Analyze:** What is Tagore suggesting about the relationship between artistic expression and spirituality?

5. **(a) Interpret:** Why does Govinda take on the responsibility for Satyabati and Chunilal? **(b) Evaluate:** What does this arrangement suggest about Indian culture, particularly the roles of women, at the time of the story?

6. **Make a Judgment:** Do you think Satyabati's actions at the end of the story are wise? Explain.

Go Online
Author Link
For: More about Rabindranath Tagore
Visit: www.PHSchool.com
Web Code: ete-9809

Apply the Skills

The Artist

Literary Analysis
Conflict

1. **(a)** What values does Govinda try to instill in Chunilal? **(b)** In what ways do his values create an **external conflict** with Satyabati?

2. What **internal conflicts** does Satyabati experience as a result of her external conflict with Govinda?

3. **(a)** When does the conflict between Govinda and Satyabati reach its point of greatest intensity? **(b)** How is the conflict resolved?

4. Both Govinda and Satyabati embody specific values. **(a)** What values does each character represent? **(b)** Based on these values, what conflict in society as a whole does this story express? Explain.

Connecting Literary Elements

5. **(a)** When he was alive, how did Mukunda manage his work, his relationship with Satyabati, and his dealings with their relatives? **(b)** Is Mukunda a **flat** or a **round character**? Explain.

6. Both Govinda and Satyabati have obsessions. **(a)** Compare and contrast the effects these obsessions have on their lives. **(b)** Do you think either Govinda or Satyabati is a flat character? Explain.

Reading Strategy
Identifying Cause and Effect

7. **(a)** Use a chart like the one shown to **identify causes and effects** in this story, beginning with Mukunda's death.

Mukunda's Death		
Effect	Effect	Effect

(b) Choose one of these effects and describe how it, in turn, becomes the cause of another series of events.

8. **(a)** What is the cause of Satyabati's decision to practice her art in secret? **(b)** What effect does this secrecy have on her son?

Extend Understanding

9. **Cultural Connection:** How might this story be different if it were set in contemporary America? Explain your answer.

QuickReview

A **conflict** is a struggle between opposing forces. Conflicts can be internal or external.

Flat characters are one-dimensional, possessing a single dominant trait. Like real people, **round characters** are multidimensional, possessing many complex traits.

To **identify cause and effect**, note the circumstances that cause characters' actions and the effects their actions have on others.

Go Online
Assessment

For: Self-test
Visit: www.PHSchool.com
Web Code: eta-6806

The Artist ■ 1169

Go Online Students may use the **Self-test** to
Assessment prepare for **Selection Test A** or
Selection Test B.

Answers

1. (a) Govinda tries to persuade Chunilal that only money is important. (b) Satyabati believes that artistic expression is important, and she does not want her son cut off from art in order to pursue only money.

2. Satyabati's love of art conflicts with her reliance on Govinda to provide for her and Chunilal and causes her to question how to raise her son.

3. (a) The conflict is most intense when Govinda destroys Chunilal's artwork. (b) The conflict is resolved by Satyabati's taking her son to Rangalal.

4. (a) Govinda represents materialism. Satyabati represents artistic expression and spirituality. (b) The story expresses the conflict between materialism and art and spirituality.

5. (a) Mukunda was an expert lawyer who encouraged Satyabati, demanded little of others, and lived very simply. (b) Mukunda is a round character because despite his good characteristics, he was not careful with money.

6. (a) Govinda and Satyabati are both controlled by their passions. Govinda focuses on economic gain whereas Satyabati focuses on the joy and beauty of creation. (b) Govinda is a flat character because he is guided by a single obsession. He has no conflicting character traits.

7. (a) **Possible response:** Govinda's taking over the family, Satyabati's inability to pursue her art freely, and Govinda's attempt to control Chunilal are all effects of Mukunda's death. (b) Govinda's attempt to control Chunilal leads Satyabati to take Chunilal to Rangalal.
   Another sample answer can be found on **Reading Strategy Graphic Organizer B**, p. 199 in *Graphic Organizer Transparencies.*

8. (a) Satyabati has been ridiculed for her art. (b) Chunilal begins to draw.

9. **Possible response:** In contemporary America, Satyabati would not be placed under the legal authority of her brother-in-law.

❶ Vocabulary Lesson

Word Analysis:
Greek Word Part *-logy*

1. c   2. b   3. a

Spelling Strategy

1. certainly

2. claimed

Vocabulary Builder: Context

1. terminology   6. equable

2. meager   7. connotations

3. enumerating   8. frugality

4. disdain   9. myriad

5. squandered

❷ Grammar and Style Lesson

1. Govinda, the villain, worshipped money.

2. He tried to influence his nephew Chunilal.

3. Satyabati, an artist, pursued her dream.

4. Rangalal, a painter, encouraged Satyabati.

5. Satyabati turned to her nephew Rangalal for help.

Writing Application

Possible response: Govinda, *a company manager,* values money, but his brother *Mukunda* did not. Satyabati, *Govinda's sister-in-law,* is an artist like her nephew *Rangalal.* Chunilal, *the son of Mukunda and Satyabati,* also loves art.

𝒲𝒢 **Writing and Grammar**
Platinum Level

For support in teaching the Grammar and Style Lesson, use Chapter 20, Section 1.

1170

Build Language Skills

❶ Vocabulary Lesson

Word Analysis: Greek Word Part *-logy*

The Greek word part *-logy* means "the science, theory, or study of." Therefore, *terminology* means the "system of words used in a specific field." Match the word containing the word part *-logy* in the left column with its definition in the right column.

1. theology   **a.** study of life

2. geology   **b.** study of Earth's physical history

3. biology   **c.** study of religion

Spelling Strategy

In words ending in a consonant preceded by two vowels, do not double the final consonant before adding a suffix: *disdain + -ed = disdained.* Add the indicated suffix to each of the words below.

1. certain + *-ly*   2. claim + *-ed*

Vocabulary Builder: Context

Review the vocabulary list on page 1161. Then, fill in the blanks in the paragraph with the appropriate words from the list.

The book was so successful, it created a whole new __?__. Kids used their __?__ funds to buy copies, __?__ the many reasons why such a purchase was a wise one. While some adults looked on with __?__, believing that their kids had __?__ their money, others had more __?__ feelings. They felt that the book fostered good values and had no negative __?__. They encouraged __?__, but they also knew that their children would find a __?__ of products they wanted to buy.

❷ Grammar and Style Lesson
Appositives and Appositive Phrases

An **appositive** is a noun or pronoun placed near another noun or pronoun to provide additional information about it. When an appositive is accompanied by its own modifiers, it forms an **appositive phrase.**

If an appositive is essential to the meaning of a sentence, commas are not used. If an appositive can be omitted without affecting the meaning, it is set off with commas.

> **Nonessential:** Indra, <u>the king of the gods</u>, does not spare even the soul of a little boy . . .
>
> **Essential:** The story "<u>The Artist</u>" condemns materialism.

Practice Rewrite each sentence below, incorporating the information given as an appositive.

1. Govinda worshipped money. *(the villain)*

2. He tried to influence his nephew. *(Chunilal)*

3. Satyabati pursued her dream. *(an artist)*

4. Rangalal encouraged Satyabati. *(a painter)*

5. Satyabati turned to her nephew for help. *(Rangalal)*

Writing Application Write a paragraph in which you use an appositive or an appositive phrase to describe each character from "The Artist."

𝒲𝒢 *Prentice Hall Writing and Grammar Connection: Platinum Level, Chapter 20, Section 1*

Assessment Practice

Identify Patterns of Organization   (For more practice, see *Test Preparation Workbook,* p. 54.)

Many tests require students to identify patterns of organization. Use this sample test item to give students practice with this skill.

> After traveling many tortuous roads and getting muddied repeatedly in the process, Govinda had now arrived upon the solidly paved embankment of his wide and free-flowing stream of money. He was firmly seated in the manager's chair at the MacDougal Gunnysack Company.

Which of the following best describes the pattern of organization found in this passage?

  A cause and effect

  B specific to general

  C chronological

  D comparison and contrast

A and *B* are not applicable to this passage. *D* is not the best choice, as the passage is organized chronologically. *C* is the best choice.

❸ Writing Lesson

Newspaper Editorial

Newspaper editorials provide a public forum for citizens to express their opinions about pressing issues. As Satyabati, write an editorial in which you argue for a different emphasis in society's values.

Prewriting   Reread the story, taking notes about the values that Satyabati holds dear. Identify experiences in her life that demonstrate the importance of these values. Note ways in which Govinda's worship of money is damaging to himself, his family, and society as a whole.

Drafting   Write an introduction with a vivid anecdote or quotation. Then, clearly state Satyabati's thesis. As you build your body paragraphs, anticipate and address opposing viewpoints.

Model: Drafting to Address Opposing Viewpoints

Of course, we need a strong economy. We need

people who can run businesses successfully. However, we

also need creative people. Art does not detract from our

financial success. Rather, it helps us be successful.

> Anticipating and addressing opposing viewpoints strengthens an argument.

Revising   Read your editorial to identify sections that could be more persuasive. Add or eliminate details to strengthen the overall impression.

 Prentice Hall Writing and Grammar Connection: Platinum Level, Chapter 7, Section 7

❹ Extend Your Learning

Research and Technology In this story, Govinda assumes responsibility for his brother's family after the brother's death. With a small group, research and deliver a **group report** on the traditions and laws that dictate such after-death arrangements in India. Follow these tips to prepare:

- Use photographs, illustrations, or other visual aids.
- Organize the material so that ideas flow smoothly between speakers.

If necessary, do additional research to fill in gaps in your information. [**Group Activity**]

Listening and Speaking Find a collection of Tagore's poetry, and select two or three poems that share a similar theme. Write an introduction and conclusion, and deliver a **themed reading.** To prepare, read the poems aloud, stressing different words to emphasize meaning. Find an appropriate tone, and pace your delivery.

Go Online
Research
For: An additional research activity
Visit: www.PHSchool.com
Web Code: etd-7806

The Artist ■ 1171

❸ Writing Lesson

- To give students guidance in writing this editorial, give them the **Support for Writing Lesson,** p. 85 in *Unit 8 Resources.*
- Read aloud the Writing Lesson instruction. Before students begin their editorials, ask them to brainstorm arguments on both sides of the issue.
- Use the Writing Lesson to guide students in developing their editorials. Encourage students to use specific details from the text to support their thesis statements.
- Use the Persuasion: Persuasive Essay rubrics in *General Resources,* pp. 47–48, to evaluate students' editorials.

Writing and Grammar
Platinum Level
For support in teaching the Writing Lesson, use Chapter 7.

❹ Research and Technology

- After students read the Extension Activity instruction, organize them in small groups. Tell students to evaluate Internet sources to make sure that they are reliable.
- The **Support for Extend Your Learning** page (*Unit 8 Resources,* p. 86) provides guided note-taking opportunities to help students complete the Extend Your Learning activities.

Go Online Have students type in the **Research** Web Code for another research activity.

LT.5.01.6 Make connections between historical and contemporary issues in world literature.

LT.5.01.7 Understand the cultural and historical impact on world literature texts.

LT.5.02.1 Explore works which relate to an issue, author, or theme and show increasing comprehension.

Prewriting

- To guide students in developing this assignment, give them the **Writing About Literature** support, pp. 94–95 in *Unit 8 Resources*.

- Point out that *uncertainty, alienation,* and *despair* are human emotions and conditions. As students review the literature in Unit 8, encourage them to find characters or speakers who express these emotions.

- Remind students to choose works from two cultures. Explain that students will identify (a) how the literature from each culture treats a certain theme, such as alienation; and (b) how treatments of these literary themes are similar and different.

- Distribute copies of the **Three-column Chart** on p. 282 in *Graphic Organizer Transparencies*. Have students use the organizer to narrow their searches.

- After students have selected two works, they can collect textual evidence to support their choices.

- If students have trouble limiting their focus statements to one sentence, have them write short paragraphs. Then, have them condense by generalizing or by combining sentences.

Tips for Test Taking

A writing prompt on a standardized test may assess students' abilities to analyze a topic, state a point of view, and support the point of view with evidence. When writing is timed, students need to determine their theses quickly and provide supporting evidence without using written resources.

Compare and Contrast Literary Trends Across Cultures

The Modern Era, from 1890 to 1945, was a period remade by catastrophic wars, economic upheaval, and revolutionary discoveries in science and technology. Both the form and the content of the work of writers around the world reflected these turbulent times.

The literary movement known as Modernism focused on the themes of uncertainty, alienation, and despair. Write an essay that compares the treatment of these themes in selected works in this unit. Details of the assignment are outlined in the box at the right.

Prewriting

Review the selections. Review the works in this unit, answering the following questions:

- Is the theme of alienation or despair stated or strongly implied in this work?
- In what ways does the writer develop this theme?
- Do formal aspects of this work—for example, the lack of exposition, transitions, and resolution or the use of free verse—reflect this theme?
- In what way does the writer's culture affect the treatment of the theme?

Gather evidence. After you have chosen the works you will discuss in your paper, begin comparing and contrasting the selections by filling in a chart similar to the one below. Use your chart to begin sorting similarities and differences among the works by culture. Then, return to the works to select quotations and specific details of content or form to support your analysis.

Model: Charting to Compare and Contrast Treatments of Theme		
Selection	**How Work Demonstrates Theme**	**Cultural Tie**
"Interior of the Rose"	mystery of a rose	rose common subject in poetry of Europe
"Everything Is Plundered"	acknowledges and rejects despair	destruction of homeland caused by war

Write three focus statements. Based on your review of the literature, write three focus statements. In the first, *define the themes* that you will explore in your essay. In the second, *explain the impact of the theme on form* (if any) in the works you have chosen. In the third, *explain the effect of culture on theme* in these works. Build the introduction for your essay around these three focus statements.

Assignment: Alienation Across Cultures

Write an essay comparing the themes of uncertainty, alienation, and despair in works of at least two of the cultures in this unit.

Criteria:

- Include a thesis statement that defines these themes and draws from your analysis of the literature.
- Support your thesis with detailed analyses of at least two works, each from a different culture.
- Cite evidence of each similarity and difference you explore.
- Approximate length: 700 words

Read to Write
As you reread the texts, look for the theme in the setting, the plot, or the characters. In poetry, also look for the theme in symbols and in formal elements, such as the use of fragmented sentences.

Teaching Resources

The following resources can be used to extend or enrich the instruction for **Writing About Literature.**

Unit 8 Resources
  Writing About Literature, pp. 94–95

General Resources
  Exposition: Comparison-and-Contrast Essay, pp. 53–54

Graphic Organizer Transparencies
  Three-column Chart, p. 282
  Outline, p. 279

Drafting

Outline. Use information from your chart to make a working outline. In the major headings, list the similarities and differences you will discuss. In the subheadings, list the evidence from the literature.

Model: Making a Working Outline

I. World is strange, not set up in human terms

    A. "Interior of the Rose"

        1. Interior of the rose changes world

            a. ". . . a room enclosed in a dream"

    B. "Under Reconstruction"

        1. Construction work in hotel represents unsettledness of postwar life

---

Refer to historical events. Be as specific as you can in describing historical events that shaped the writer's perspective and in explaining their significance.

Revising and Editing

Review content: Check for accuracy. Did the character wear a red jacket? Did the speaker say, "Oh, my aching heart" or "Oh, my breaking heart"? Absolute accuracy is essential if you want readers to take your ideas seriously. Check each reference in your paper for accuracy.

Review style: Vary sentence structure. Choose varied sentence structures to add variety to your writing.

Choppy: The love of nature is a universal theme in poetry. It is a theme that appears in all eras. But the tone of Rilke's "Interior of the Rose" is Modernist. The tone of pain and uncertainty in the poem shows this.

Varied: The love of nature is a universal theme in poetry, one that appears in all eras. But the tone of pain and uncertainty in Rilke's "Interior of the Rose" places the poem well within the Modernist camp.

Publishing and Presenting

Give a dramatic reading. Read excerpts for the class from two of the selections you discussed in your essay. Then, explain why you compared these selections.

W̄Ḡ Writing and Grammar Connection: Platinum Level, Chapter 9

Writing About Literature ■ 1173

✎ Write to Learn

Remember that your outline is only a guide. Include information that supports your arguments even if it doesn't fit neatly into your outline.

✎ Write to Explain

Connect your thoughts clearly so that readers can follow your arguments. Do not leave out any logical steps. The more closely your readers can follow your thinking, the more persuasive your ideas will be.

Drafting

- As students create outlines, have them think of each work of literature as an illustration of the theme on which they are focusing.

- Remind students that historical events often shape cultural perspectives. Students can use quotations from historical research to support and explain the significance of literary themes.

Revising and Editing

Explain that varying sentence structure is an important part of revising and editing and that sentence variety makes writing more engaging. Write this sentence on the board: *Jack was tired and cold and wanted to go home.*
Ask students to revise this sentence by relocating the adjectives.
Answer: Tired and cold, Jack wanted to go home.

Publishing and Presenting

Suggest that students draw on the board or on a poster a Venn diagram showing one or two key points that they will compare and contrast in their essays.

W̄Ḡ Writing and Grammar Platinum Level

Students will find additional instruction on writing a comparison-and-contrast essay in Chapter 9.

Writing and Grammar Interactive Textbook CD-ROM

Students can use the following tools as they complete their essay:

- Organizer: Venn Diagram

- Revising: Sentence Opener Variety, Editing

Six Traits Focus

✓	Ideas	✓	Word Choice
✓	Organization	✓	Sentence Fluency
	Voice	✓	Conventions

Assessing the Essay

To evaluate students' essays, use the Exposition: Comparison-and-Contrast Essay rubrics in *General Resources*, pp. 53–54.

Strategy for Less Proficient Writers
Have students limit their subjects to two works of literature. Students can use Venn diagrams to compare and contrast the works they have selected.

Strategy for English Learners
Encourage students to write about the works they found easiest to read and to understand. Before they begin writing, have students explain in their own words what each work is about and what theme(s) it explores.

Strategy for Advanced Writers
In their essays, invite students to focus on a single literary element through which the writers of their chosen works express their themes. For example, students might compare the writers' use of character, setting, imagery, symbolism, or poetic form in two or more works.

1173

Standard Course of Study

IR.2.02.4 Develop appropriate strategies to illustrate points about cause/effect relationships.

IR.2.03.1 Access cultural information from media sources.

FA.3.01.5 Present data about controversial issues in multiple forms.

From the Scholar's Desk

Judith Ortiz Cofer

Show students Segment 3 on Judith Ortiz Cofer on *From the Author's Desk DVD.* Discuss revision and how she combines fact and creativity in her fiction. Also, discuss how she uses vivid images and descriptions to help readers visualize the story and involve their senses in reading it. Explain that while Judith Ortiz Cofer involves the imagination and senses of her readers by using words creatively, multimedia presentations are designed to present information by involving the audience's senses and highlighting information through words, art, and sounds.

Writing Genres

Using the Form Point out to students that businesses often use multimedia reports. Point out these examples:

• Multimedia presentations may provide entertainment for a group or convey an idea.

• Sales and informational presentations often are multimedia presentations.

• In the classroom, some teachers use multimedia presentations to present difficult concepts.

Exposition: Multimedia Report

The poetry and short stories in this unit have undoubtedly made an impression on you. However, some kinds of information and ideas are better conveyed through images and sounds than through words. In a **multimedia report,** a presenter adds images and sounds to words. He or she shares information, enhancing narration and explanation with media, such as video images, slides, audiotape recordings, music, and art. Follow the steps outlined in this workshop to create your own multimedia report.

Assignment Plan, draft, revise, and present a multimedia report.

What to Include Your multimedia report should feature the following elements:

• well-integrated, varied audio and visual features
• a clear and logical organization
• interesting use of relevant media to convey key concepts
• effective pacing of media, with smooth transitions between elements to create a comprehensible whole
• an enticing introduction and a memorable conclusion

To preview the criteria on which your multimedia report may be judged, see the rubric on page 1181.

Standard Course of Study

• Develop appropriate strategies to illustrate points about cause/effect relationships. (IR.2.02.4)

• Access cultural information from media sources. (IR.2.03.1)

• Present data about controversial issues in multiple forms. (FA.3.01.5)

Using the Form
You may use elements of a multimedia report in these situations:

• research papers
• biographical profiles
• news reports
• art reviews

1174 ■ *The Modern World*

Teaching Resources

The following resources can be used to enrich or extend the instruction for the Writing Workshop.

Unit 8 Resources
Writing Workshop: Multimedia Presentations, pp. 96–97

General Resources
Rubrics for Multimedia Report, pp. 57–58

Graphic Organizer Transparencies
Outline, p. 279

From the Author's Desk DVD
Judith Ortiz Cofer, Segments 3 and 4

Prewriting

Choosing Your Topic

A good topic for a multimedia report needs to meet two criteria. First, it should interest you. Second, the topic must be easily presented through available and appropriate media. To choose a topic, use one of the following strategies:

- **Conduct a magazine review.** Look through favorite magazines for inspiration. Flag pages that have images or ideas that catch your eye. Make a list of possible topics, and then choose the one that offers the most possibilities for a multimedia presentation.
- **Brainstorm.** Choose a broad subject area that interests you, such as music, sports, or science. Then, brainstorm to generate ideas within that subject area. Jot down your ideas, and choose the one that you think best lends itself to a multimedia treatment.

Narrowing Your Topic

Because of the time limitations of your class, you may need to narrow your topic. Focus on a topic that you can develop thoroughly. For example, *baseball* is too broad a topic, but you might narrow your topic to a particular team, a famous player, or an important event in the history of baseball. As you narrow your topic, make sure that you can find media to support your ideas.

Gathering Details

Create a media checklist. In a chart similar to the one shown here, list the various categories of media that you believe will be available and suitable for your topic. In the right column, note your ideas about how to use the various media.

Research the topic. As you research your topic, jot down ideas about creative ways to engage your audience. Consult your library for audio or video clips of interviews and for documentaries, music, and art resources. Search the Internet for similar resources. Consider using any medium that will help bring your topic to life.

Media Checklist	
☑ Music	Pachelbel *Canon in D*
☑ Videos	democracy flowchart
☑ Art	Rockwell's *Freedom of Speech* painting
☑ Photographs	various government images and symbols
☐ Computer Presentation	

Gauge media variety. After your initial media search, review the media that you have located. If most items fall into one category—for instance, black-and-white photographs—look for additional items to ensure that your report is rich in a variety of media, including sound clips, video, and still images. The use of music is an easy way to build a sense of variety.

Writing Workshop ■ 1175

Tips for Using Rubrics

- Before students begin work on this assignment, have them preview the Rubric for Self-Assessment, p. 1181, to know what is expected.
- Review the Assessment criteria in class. Before students use the Rubric for Self-Assessment, work with them to rate the student model by applying one or two criteria to it.

- If you wish to assess students' multimedia presentations, with either a 4-point, 5-point, or 6-point scoring rubric, see *General Resources*, pp. 57 and 58.

Prewriting

- Give students support for prewriting and drafting with p. 96 from *Unit 8 Resources.*
- Guide students to select topics that support strong exposition and for which different varieties of multimedia materials are available. After students narrow a list of topics, have them write a sentence for each in order to clarify their topics.
- Explain to students that visual spreads in magazines or Web sites may give them more ideas for their presentations but that topics are likely to be too wide.
- Make sure students understand that good media use will not make up for a presentation lacking in substance. Therefore, encourage them to use the same processes as they would for a written essay. Be careful to check that students narrow their topics wisely so that they will not have trouble finding images or other media that may not be widely available.
- Tell students to read the Media Checklist. **Ask** whether they think the presentation described on the checklist will engage an audience. **Possible response:** Because the presentation includes four of the five media listed in the checklist, it probably will engage the audience.
- Encourage students to use a media checklist and to be discriminating as they review materials. Remind them to use resources that are reliable, informative, and interesting.

Six Traits Focus

✓	Ideas		Word Choice
✓	Organization		Sentence Fluency
	Voice		Conventions

Writing and Grammar Platinum Level

Students will find additional instruction on prewriting for a multimedia presentation in Chapter 29, Section 3.

Writing and Grammar Interactive Textbook CD-ROM

Students can use the following tools as they complete their reflective essays:

- Topic Bin
- Customizable Outliner
- Transition Word Revising Tool

1175

Drafting

- Remind students to develop a strong thesis statement, using written and media components for support.

- Explain that, like a written report, a multimedia report must be well organized. Review the Organize Your Report chart with the class.

- **Ask** students what part of the chart they would include in an outline for a written report.
  Answer: Students should include all three parts of the chart.

- After students outline their reports, have them draft their scripts, including a list of corresponding multimedia elements. (Students may want to refer to the Student Model on p. 1180.)

- Allow students who have knowledge about different technologies to conduct in-class workshops for other students to help them choreograph and rehearse their presentations.

Six Traits Focus

✓	Ideas	✓	Word Choice
✓	Organization		Sentence Fluency
	Voice		Conventions

Writing and Grammar Platinum Level

Students will find additional instruction on drafting a multimedia report in Chapter 29, Section 3.

Drafting

Shaping Your Report

Identify a thesis. Review your notes and materials. Develop a statement of the key ideas that you intend to cover. This main idea is your thesis statement. Use your thesis statement as a guide as you draft your report.

Outline your report. Create a broad working outline to organize your ideas in a logical way. Decide which parts will be more effective if presented through visual and aural media. The chart shown here outlines an effective sequence for a multimedia presentation.

Providing Elaboration

Use explicit cues. Use your outline and notes to draft a script and plan your delivery. Write cues in your script to indicate what media elements to use and when to use them. Clear directions will help your presentation flow smoothly.

> **Confusing:** [Cue VIDEO, then ZOOM]
> **Clear:** [Cue VIDEO CHART, pause, then cue TRANSITION ZOOM]

Balance your script. As you write, remember to use media selections evenly throughout your report, not just at the beginning and the end. Strive for a balance among the narrative, audio, and visual elements.

Organize Your Report

Introduction: Present the topic and a thesis statement about it. Include a dramatic or vivid media element to win viewers' interest.

Body: Develop the thesis through exposition and examples, the text of which should be enhanced in places by other media.

Conclusion: Reiterate research that supports thesis.

To read the complete student model, see page 1180.

Student Model: Balancing the Script

[Cue (AUDIO)]: Pachelbel *Canon in D*

(NARRATOR): There are three types of democracy.

[Cue (VIDEO)] VIDEO CHART: A flowchart of democracy branching into different types, drawn out as the audience watches.

> The writer's opening strikes a balance among music, image, and narration.

Prepare the equipment. Assemble all of the equipment that you will need for your presentation. Follow these suggestions for getting organized:

- Plan a logical arrangement of props and technology so that you can reach each type of media easily.
- Cue pieces of equipment so that you can run them with one touch at the appropriate moment in your script.
- Make sure everything is functioning properly.
- Work with an assistant if necessary.

1176 ■ *The Modern World*

Tips for
Organization in Writing

Point out to students that anyone who creates a multimedia report must adhere to time limits in the presentation. Suggest that they establish a tentative time frame once they have established their thesis and then shape their presentation to work within that time frame. This strategy will help them refine what should be included and what must be cut because of time constraints.

Judith Ortiz Cofer

In writing my novel *Call Me María*, I drew on my own memories of the fears I felt when I first came to this country and did not speak much English. Like María, I was afraid of being caught in a difficult situation and of not being able to make myself understood. In this episode, María knows she is innocent, but in her panic, she feels that everyone and everything, even the watches in the display case, are judging her.

"Literature is the human search for meaning."

——Judith Ortiz Cofer

Professional Model:

from *Call Me María: A Novel in Letters, Poems, and Prose*

The minute I step through the electric eye, the drugstore's alarm goes off and several pairs of eyes freeze me inside the cage of their suspicion. I stand on the spiky plastic Welcome mat, waiting for someone to release me, to say "Go on, it is all a mistake." The rotund manager, propelling down the center aisle toward me like a nuclear submarine in his too-tight steel-gray suit, his pudgy finger aimed at me, orders me in a loud voice to come back and empty my purse on the counter. I protest, put my hands up. I have not done anything. But his face—folds of hardened rubbery flesh, mouth curling into a tight smile of scorn, eyes almost slits—tells me to expect no pity. He informs me that he will call security if I do not obey. I turn over my bag on the glass case that displays cheap watches, their plastic faces impassively watching me through safety glass— a jury box of Timex ladies' and men's alarms ready to go off when I am found guilty, none of them showing the right time.

I chose words that would make the reader feel anxious along with Maria as she enters the drugstore and the alarm goes off: *electric eye, freeze, cage, spiky.*

I decided to film the action in my mind, as if it were a movie scene, so the reader could visualize the events and sense the tone of danger.

There is a central, but unstated, metaphor in this narrative: the time bomb or explosive confrontation. It is implied through numerous references to watches, alarms, and time, and through words whose connotations suggest a clash: *propelling, nuclear,* and *aimed.*

Writing Workshop ■ *1177*

Judith Ortiz Cofer

- Show students Segment 4 on Judith Ortiz Cofer on *From the Author's Desk DVD.* Discuss how she creates a bridge between reader and writer.

- Point out that Cofer chose words that would show readers, not tell them, how she felt and would help readers visualize the events and understand the tone of the situation. Urge students to review their work to see whether their words convey tone to the reader.

- Review Cofer's comments about her choice of words in the excerpt from *Call Me María: A Novel in Letters, Poems, and Prose.* Ask students how her words help them visualize what is happening in the story.

- For example, **ask** students to explain the differences between the phrases "propelling down the center aisle to me" and "walked toward me." **Possible answer:** The image is of a plane coming down a runway. Applied to the man in the story, the image suggests speed, force, and authority and perhaps explosion in keeping with the central metaphor.

- Cofer's images convey María's fear, the distrust of the store manager, and the accusatory stare of the watches, and are all appropriate to her theme—an explosive confrontation. Tell students that when selecting media for a presentation, they, too, should select images or sounds that support the point that they wish to make and add a dimension that words alone cannot provide.

Tips for
Improving Word Choice

Give students these suggestions for revising for word choice:

1. Look for places where you can visualize what is happening. Use that visualization to describe the action more realistically.

2. Replace empty or weak words, like *spoke,* with words that help show more specific emotion, like *snarled.* These words not only will make your writing or oral presentation more engaging, they will also help establish the tone you want to create.

3. Make sure enough of your images are visual so that you can adapt them to visual media. Call students' attention to the irony in the Welcome mat and how it would translate into another medium.

Revising

- Point out that the best way to revise a presentation is to practice delivering it and then revise as needed.

- Explain to students that transitions in media presentations are as important as they are in written work and that the presentation needs to flow smoothly and logically. Have students exchange reports with a classmate so that each can check for smooth transitions of text and media.

- Have students read the Model on this page. **Ask** students why Mark decides not to repeat the Direct Democracy slides.
  Possible response: The slides of ancient Greece and colonial New England would confuse his audience and detract from the main idea that direct democracy is not practical at the national level.

- Draw students' attention to the Without variety/With variety examples on this page. Then lead students to explain why variety is important.

Six Traits Focus

✓	Ideas	✓	Word Choice
✓	Organization	✓	Sentence Fluency
	Voice		Conventions

*W*G **Writing and Grammar** Platinum Level

Students will find additional guidance for revising a multimedia presentation in Chapter 29, Section 3.

Writing Workshop

Revising

Revising Your Overall Structure

Revise to clarify transitions and sequence. For each transition you make from script to multimedia, make sure that your audience can understand the connection you make. Where necessary, add phrases such as "This chart shows that . . ." or "As this photograph suggests, . . ." to introduce your media.

Peer Review: With a classmate, clarify your transitions and sequence so that your report will flow smoothly. Follow these steps:

1. Give your partner a copy of your script to follow as you present your report.

2. Ask your partner to place a check mark next to any points that needed clarification, seemed out of order, or required transitions.

3. Rewrite as necessary to clarify your sequence and the connections among your ideas. Eliminate or revise transitions that are not working.

To read the complete student model, see page 1180.

> **Student Model: Revising to Improve Transitions**
>
> Direct democracy, appropriate for a town meeting, is not practical on a national level. ~~[Cue repeat of Direct Democracy SLIDES]~~ [Cue Busy People VIDEO]
>
> ~~Direct Democracy SLIDES~~ *Busy People VIDEO: series of crowd scenes, such as city pedestrians at rush hour*
>
> Mark deletes repetitive images and adds a more appropriate video to match his text.

Revising Your Media Choices

Revise to vary the media. Review your script for overuse of a particular form of media, and revise for variety and balance.

Without variety: Play *audio* of interview with actor.

Play *audio* of interview with artist.

Play *audio* of interview with musician.

With variety: Play *video footage* of actor in performance.

Play *audio* of interview with artist to accompany slides of work.

Play *CD* by musician.

1178 ■ *The Modern World*

Tips for
Using Technology in Writing

Technology resources are useful for preparing and delivering multimedia presentations. If possible, provide students with access to audiocassette players, videocassette and DVD players and monitors, digital cameras and recorders, slide projectors, and compact disc players. Many computers are equipped with slide-show applications. If students are not familiar with the equipment, arrange for audiovisual tutorials or workshops.

Developing Your Style

Keeping Tone Consistent

Integrate tone in media. Tone is usually described in emotional terms—it may be friendly or distant, cheerful or angry. In a multimedia report, tone can be revealed through the author's choice of words and multimedia elements. Choose an overall tone for your multimedia report. Then, make sure that your visuals and sounds work with your words to support this tone. For example, if you want the overall tone of your report to be serious, avoid playful music. If you prefer that your report be funny, include amusing and lively visuals.

The chart shows media choices that might be appropriate for two very different subjects and tones.

Media Choices	
Subject: Baseball: our national pastime.	**Subject:** Alternative energy
Tone: affectionate, lighthearted	**Tone:** serious but informal
Video: great plays, "bloopers," teammates piling up after a win	**Video:** smokestacks with full black smoke, windmills turning
Audio: cheering crowd, crack of the bat, radio play-by-play	**Video Graphic:** web diagram showing various energy alternatives
Stills: legendary players, baseball trading cards and cartoons	**Stills:** smog, traffic jam, hybrid cars, solar panels, global warming chart
Music: "Take Me Out to the Ballgame"	**Music:** theme from *2001: A Space Odyssey*

Find It in Your Reading. Read or review "The Prayer" by Gabriela Mistral on page 1151. This poem uses religious language to develop a reverential and respectful tone. What phrases and images reveal the speaker's attitude toward her subject?

Apply It to Your Writing. You can develop the tone of a multimedia report through images and sounds as well as words. Review the draft of your multimedia report, and follow these steps:

1. Determine what kind of impression you want to convey in your presentation and then decide what your tone should be.

2. Review the narrative text. Circle words and phrases that reveal your attitude toward your subject and that capture the desired tone. Revise circled words to make the tone of the narration consistent.

3. Review your media choices, and replace any material that doesn't support the tone you want to convey.

WG Prentice Hall Writing and Grammar Connection: Platinum Level, Chapter 6, Section 2

Developing Your Style

- Ask students to recall special news broadcasts on television. Have them recall the type of music, film footage, and language the announcer used as well as tone of voice. Then have students reflect on how all of these elements influenced the message of the broadcast.

- Review the Media Choices chart with students. Have students select another topic and write it on the board. Then, have them suggest the different media choices they would make to develop the presentation.

- Have students do the **Find It in Your Reading** activity.
  Possible response: "My cup of freshness," "bird-trill to my ears," and "filled with miracles as the spring of the years" reveal the speaker's attitude toward her subject.

- After students review their own drafts, following the steps in **Apply It to Your Writing,** suggest that they videotape their presentations to see whether their intended tone comes across.

- Assure students that cutting media portions is normal even though they might have spent time on the portion.

WG Writing and Grammar Platinum Level
Students will find additional instruction on keeping tone consistent in Chapter 6, Section 2.

1179

Student Model

- Explain that the Student Model is a sample and that students' presentations may be longer.
- Call students' attention to the first call-out note. Point out that the bracketed cues in the Text column correspond to items in the Audio and Video column. Have students read the model silently. If possible, play a recording of Pachelbel's *Canon in D* while students read.
- As a class, discuss how the music influences the reading. Discuss how other musical selections might change the presentation's tone.
- Tell students to avoid dramatic special effects that detract from the main message and to make sure that any effects clarify and enhance the audience's understanding.
- Explain that a multimedia presentation, like an essay, should summarize and reinforce the thesis in the conclusion.

Writing Genres
Multimedia Presentations in the Workplace:

Explain that multimedia presentations are important tools in many businesses. For example, presentations are used for outlining goals and ideas, selling products and services, and training employees. Ask students whether they have encountered multimedia presentations at theme parks, museums, landmarks, or athletic stadiums. If so, have them discuss how these presentations influenced their experiences.

Writing Workshop

Student Model: Mark Sueyoshi
Palm Springs, California

The Government of the United States

Text
[Cue AUDIO] there are three types of democracy. [Cue VIDEO]

Audio and Video
AUDIO: Pachelbel *Canon in D*
VIDEO CHART: A flowchart of democracy branching into different types, drawn out as the audience watches.

> Classical music establishes a formal tone appropriate to the subject.

[Cue TRANSITION ZOOM] In democratic centralism, leaders (not elected by popular vote) decide what is best for the people. Examples of this form of democracy are the Soviet Union and China. [Cue SLIDES]

TRANSITION ZOOM: Zooms into Democratic Centralism rectangle.
Democratic Centralism SLIDES: Rapid sequence showing flags or national symbols of USSR and China

> Use of zoom technique adds motion and interest to charts on governments. (See *Revising*, p. 1178.)

[Cue VIDEO CHART, pause, then cue TRANSITION ZOOM] In direct democracy, each citizen participates directly in policy making. Governments that have used this form of democracy are ancient Greece and colonial New England. [Cue SLIDES]

TRANSITION ZOOM: Zoom into Direct Democracy rectangle.
Direct Democracy SLIDES: Rapid sequence of images of ancient Athens, Norman Rockwell's *Freedom of Speech* painting of a New England town meeting, colonial Maryland

[Cue VIDEO CHART, pause, then cue TRANSITION ZOOM] And in rep-resentative democracy, citizens elect leaders to create policy. The United States maintains this form of government. [Cue SLIDES]

TRANSITION ZOOM: Zooms into Representative Democracy rectangle

D.C. SLIDES: Rapid sequence of Washington images: Capitol Hill, White House, Lincoln Memorial

> Mark provides clear directions to keep the flow of the presentation smooth.

Direct democracy, appropriate for a town meeting, is not practical on a national level. [Cue VIDEO, AUDIO]

Busy People VIDEO: crowd scenes, such as city pedestrians at rush hour
Crowd AUDIO: roar of a crowd

[Cue Timeline SLIDE] And so, for over 225 years the United States government has protected and served its citizens. [Cue VIDEO]

Timeline SLIDE: show major events in U.S. history
Fireworks VIDEO: images of Fourth of July celebrations

> Audiovisual elements provide a vivid and memorable conclusion.

1180 ■ *The Modern World*

Tips for Test Taking

Explain that few tests ask students to create multimedia presentations, but many writing prompts, such as those in the new SAT, call for students to persuade an audience. In a multimedia presentation, students can use strategies to capture an audience's attention and provide visual examples to support their ideas. For example, if the audience is a group of athletes, the writer can use sports imagery and analogies to persuade them.

Editing and Proofreading

Review your multimedia report to eliminate errors in spelling, grammar, and punctuation.

Focus on Printed Text: Review all text that your audience will see, whether in handouts or projected on slides. Make sure that all words are spelled correctly and that text is formatted to look the way you want it to.

Publishing and Presenting

Consider one of the following ways to share your multimedia report.

Present to classmates. Deliver your multimedia report to your class. Be sure to speak at an appropriate pace and volume, and maintain eye contact. Encourage questions and discussion when you finish your presentation.

Present to a community group. Your topic may appeal to a community group that would be interested in your multimedia report. Contact the appropriate group, and arrange to present your report.

Reflecting on Your Writing

Writer's Journal Jot down your thoughts on the experience of creating a multimedia report. Begin by answering these questions:

- Which aspect of the report did you most enjoy, and why?
- In what ways did incorporating media change the expository writing experience for you?

WG Prentice Hall Writing and Grammar Connection: Platinum Level, Chapter 29, Section 3

Rubric for Self-Assessment

Evaluate your multimedia report *using the following criteria and rating scale, or, with your classmates, determine your own reasonable evaluation criteria.*

NG	Criteria	Rating Scale
		not very very
	Focus: How clearly do you present your topic?	1 2 3 4 5
	Organization: How clear and logical is your organization?	1 2 3 4 5
	Support/Elaboration: How well do you integrate relevant audio and visual features to convey concepts?	1 2 3 4 5
	Style: How smooth are the transitions between elements?	1 2 3 4 5
	Conventions: How correct is the grammar and spelling in your presentation materials?	1 2 3 4 5

Differentiated Instruction   Solutions for All Learners

Strategy for Less Proficient Writers

Some students may find the research required for this process challenging. Guide them to select topics for which they are likely to find ample information. Encourage them to write summaries of the sources that they can easily understand. They can then use this source material to narrow their topics and develop their presentations.

Vocabulary for English Learners

Students may encounter unfamiliar language in media sources, catalogues, labels, and technical instructions. Have students work in groups of mixed skill levels to complete their research and to organize their presentations. Encourage group members to help one another interpret unfamiliar terms and phrases.

Strategy for Advanced Writers

Have students choose a controversial topic as the subject of their reports. Presentations should identify both sides of the issue, articulate the presenter's point of view, and attempt to persuade the audience to adopt the presenter's stance on the topic.

Editing and Proofreading

- Suggest that students record their scripts. Then, have them listen to themselves speak to make sure that they do not include any grammatical errors.

- Point out to students that handouts should be clear and uncluttered so that audiences can use them easily.

Six Traits Focus

Ideas		Word Choice	
Organization		Sentence Fluency	
Voice		Conventions	✓

ASSESS

Publishing and Presenting

- Suggest that students rehearse their reports at least five times before presenting them to the class.

- Students may wish to contact a teacher whose class covers the topic of their papers and offer to present the report to that class.

- After students give their presentations to the class, challenge them to write short analyses of their experiences: What were the most useful things they learned? What were the most effective elements of their presentation? What aspects could they improve?

Reflecting on Your Writing

- Have student volunteers offer to share their writer's journal and lead students in a discussion of their experience.

- As a class, review the assessment criteria.

- Before students proceed with self-assessment, have them score the Student Model in class, using one or more of the rubric categories, to help them see how to apply the criteria. Then, direct students to use the rubric to assess their own presentations.

WG **Writing and Grammar Platinum Level**

Students will find additional guidance for editing and proofreading, publishing and presenting, and reflecting on a multimedia report in Chapter 29, Section 3.

Know Your Terms: Applying Information

Explain that the terms listed under Terms to Learn will be used in standardized-test situations when students are asked to apply information from a reading passage.

Terms to Learn

- Review *conclude* and *conclusion*. Point out to students that *to conclude* means "to infer on the basis of convincing evidence." Tell students that to make a conclusion, they must rely on the information in the passage. If they do not base their conclusion on what the passage says, then the conclusion cannot be supported. Point out that when they conclude, or make a conclusion, students go from particular ideas to a general decision or opinion.

- Review *deduce*. Tell students that when they deduce something, they go logically from something that is generally true to a specific situation. Point out that students must be careful when they deduce because a general truth is not always applicable to a specific situation.

ASSESS

Answers

1. Sánchez Mejías was a gifted man who loved danger and is now deceased.

2. Mejías death may have been tragic, and it has affected the speaker deeply.

Vocabulary Workshop

High-Frequency Academic Words

High-frequency academic words are words that appear often in textbooks and on standardized tests. Though you may already know the meaning of many of these words, they usually have a more specific meaning when they are used in textbooks and on tests.

Know Your Terms: Applying Information

Each of the terms listed is a verb that tells you to show that you can recognize and apply logical relationships among different pieces of information. Some questions may use the noun form of the word.

Terms to Learn

Conclude Tell how you use reasoning to reach a decision or an opinion based on the information provided.

> Sample test item: What can you *conclude* about the author's theme or message?

Deduce Tell what you figure out by using logic to apply general information to a particular situation.

> Sample test item: What can you *deduce* about the fate of the characters caught in the blizzard?

Practice

Directions: *Read this excerpt from "Lament for Ignacio Sánchez Mejías: Absent Soul" by Federico García Lorca. Then, on a separate sheet of paper, answer questions 1–2.*

> Nobody knows you. No. But I sing of you.
> For posterity I sing of your profile and grace.
> Of the signal maturity of your understanding.
> Of your appetite for death and the taste of its mouth.
> 5   Of the sadness of your once valiant gaiety.
>
> It will be a long time, if ever, before there is born
> an Andalusian so true, so rich in adventure.
> I sing of his elegance with words that groan,
> And I remember a sad breeze through the olive trees.

1. What can you *conclude* about Sánchez Mejías from lines 2–5?

2. What can you *deduce* about Mejías's death from such words as *groan* and *sad breeze?*

Tips for Test Taking

Point out to students that because time is so important in a timed, standardized-test, they should first answer all of the questions that they can answer easily. While they are answering the easier questions, their minds can subconsciously work on the more difficult questions. When they return to the more difficult questions, they may find that the answers become clearer. This strategy may apply particularly to questions that require deductions and conclusions.

 For: An Interactive Crossword Puzzle
Visit: www.PHSchool.com
Web Code: etj-5801

This crossword puzzle contains vocabulary that reflects the concepts in Unit 8. After students have completed Unit 8, give students the Web Code and have them complete the crossword puzzle.

Assessment Workshop

Critical Reading: Writer's Point of View

NC Standard Course of Study
• WL.1.01.4
• WL.1.03.9
• CT.4.05.7

In the reading sections of some tests, you may be required to read a passage and interpret the writer's point of view. Use the following strategies to help you answer questions testing this skill.

- As you read, look for clues to come to a conclusion about the writer's attitude toward the subject.
- Remember that a writer can reveal his or her attitude in direct statements or indirectly through word choice or choice of details.
- The writer can reveal his or her attitude through tone. Deduce the writer's tone by carefully examining elements such as characterization, plot, imagery, and mood.
- Look for changes in the writer's point of view.

Practice

Directions: *Read the passages below, and then answer questions 1 and 2.*

Passage A. To me, Mr. Smith exemplifies the quiet heroism that characterizes many of the men of his generation. When he learned of his fatal illness, he carried on with his life, going to the office every day that he was well enough. He celebrated the holidays with his family and enjoyed choosing the perfect gift for each family member. Mr. Smith died shortly after the first of the year on the day after his birthday. He died at home in the early evening—peacefully and with dignity, just as he had lived.

Passage B. We all love wilderness areas, but did you know that Winnebago County already has 4,800 acres of wilderness? Fellow citizens, we will be going to the polls soon to vote on a referendum to add Parker's Bayou in perpetuity to the wilderness areas that remain undeveloped. Our county is having financial problems. Companies are leaving our area, in part because of a lack of land on which to build. Let's open Parker's Bayou to development. We do not need more wilderness areas. Vote NO to additional wilderness areas on Tuesday.

1. In Passage A, what is the writer's attitude toward Mr. Smith?

  A amusement   **C** annoyance

  B amazement   **D** admiration

2. In Passage B, which statement best expresses the writer's point of view?

  A Winnebago County already has enough wilderness areas.

  B Winnebago County is a great place in which to live.

  C Parker's Bayou is an unimportant part of Winnebago County.

  D Winnebago County needs more wilderness areas.

Test-Taking Strategies

- As you read, ask yourself what other viewpoint the writer might have taken.

- Identify slanted language or loaded words that indicate the writer's feelings or opinions.

Assessment Workshop ■ 1183

Standard Course of Study

NC Standard Course of Study

WL.1.01.4 Recreate the mood felt by the author in a reminiscence.

WL.1.03.9 Analyze effects of author's craft and style in reflection.

CT.4.05.7 Identify and analyze influences, contexts, or biases in critical text.

Critical Reading

- Point out to students that sometimes they can identify a writer's attitude toward a subject by paying close attention to the ideas that a writer simply assumes to be true, without offering any supporting evidence. A writer may also provide details that confirm an assumption.

- Remind students that the speaker in a passage and the writer of that passage may not be the same person. In fiction, for instance, the writer may even provide more than one speaker. Emphasize to students that they must be careful not to confuse the writer with a passage's speaker.

- After students have read the Practice passages and have answered the questions, point out that in Passage A, the speaker's word choice shows respect, and the content of the passage outlines how Mr. Smith completed his life in spite of his illness. At no time does the writer express a negative response, surprise, or humor. Therefore, the only reasonable choice is D.

- Point out that in Passage B, the speaker provides facts to show that Winnebago County has a high percentage of wilderness areas and does not need more of them. Therefore, D is incorrect. The speaker also indicates that Parker's Bayou is a good place to develop, so C is incorrect. The problems that the county has encountered as a result of the wilderness areas show that B is incorrect. Therefore, the statement that best expresses the writer's point of view is A.

Tips for Test Taking

In order to identify the speaker's point of view on a standardized test, students should first read the passage and summarize what the author is saying. Then students should carefully look at the techniques that the author is using to convince the reader of the point of the passage. For example, students may look for words that tell directly what the author thinks about the topic. The author might also hint at his or her position by using satire or irony. Remind students that they should be able to point to language in the passage that supports their answer.

ASSESS

Answers

1. D

2. A

 Standard Course of Study

WL.1.02.5 Demonstrate an understanding of media's impact on analyses and personal reflection.

IR.2.03.1 Access cultural information from media sources.

CT.4.01.3 Distinguish fact from fiction and recognize personal bias in interpretation.

Evaluate the Content

- Remind students that many television shows present information in a format that projects an image of objectivity while actually expressing a biased viewpoint.

- The next time students watch a television news show, tell them to identify the apparent main idea of a report and then determine whether an objective message is being conveyed.

- Explain that viewers should look for a balance of evidence. If a report acknowledges or explores only one perspective on an issue, then the report may not be objective.

Evaluate the Presentation

- **Ask** students how each of these images sends a different message: (a) a politician shaking hands with people in a crowd; or (b) a politician riding in a motorcade.
  Possible response: The first image suggests that the politician is in touch with constituents, and the second image suggests that the politician is remote.

- Encourage students to listen closely to word choices in media reports. For example, a reporter might use the word *mislead* rather than *lie,* or the word *situation* rather than *crisis* to influence the audience.

- Challenge students to discover whether the credentials of an "expert" are relevant to the issue at hand. For example, Dr. Jones might offer medical opinions, but he or she may actually hold a Ph.D. in history.

Assess the Activity

To evaluate students' analyses, use the **Listening: Analyzing a Media Presentation** rubric, p. 85 in *General Resources.*

Analyzing a Media Presentation

People are bombarded with information from various media sources daily. How can you wade through this deluge to evaluate the quality, thoroughness, and objectivity of the information that comes your way? The strategies on this page can help you **analyze media presentations.**

 Standard Course of Study

- Distinguish fact from fiction and recognize personal bias in interpretation. (CT.4.01.3)

Evaluate the Content

News reports, documentaries, newsmagazines, editorials, and other types of media presentations have a specific purpose—to inform, to persuade, to entertain, or any combination of these. Consider the following points as you analyze news media presentations:

Identify the main idea. Like a headline in a newspaper, the first line of a broadcast report usually relates the most important idea of a news story. Pay careful attention to the type of story being reported and identify the viewpoint of the reporter.

Evaluate supporting evidence. Facts, statistics, quotations, and other evidence should give a sense of the diverse perspectives on an issue. Remember that so-called "objective" evidence can be used selectively to support a point of view.

Evaluate the Presentation

Following are techniques that can be used to influence audience response:

- **Propaganda** Speakers may use irrelevant or even wrongful information to promote their own cause or damage an opposing one.

- **Images** A photograph captures a moment in time, but an editor can choose among many photographs. The choice of a particular image can strongly influence an audience's feelings about a topic.

- **Slanted language** Commentators can present their views by means of explicit statements of opinion and subtle choices of words. Compare these sentences:

  The City Council approved the budget today. (objective)

  After avoiding the issues for a month, the City Council finally approved the budget today. (implies impatience)

- **"Experts"** The experts chosen to analyze news events have opinions and may present the views of one side of an issue more sympathetically than the views of another. When you listen to an expert, consider that person's qualifications and motivations.

Activity ▸ *Analysis and Discussion* Analyze a television news story using the Feedback Form above as a guide. Share your analysis in a class discussion.

Feedback Form for a Media Presentation

Rating System
+ = Excellent   ✓= Average   – = W

Content
Topic of story _____
Main point _____
Supporting Evidence
Expert interviews (with whom? to what ef

Photographs/video (what is shown? to what e

Language (slanted language? to what effe

What visual aids, if any, are used?

Production Values
Effects of set _____
Effects of graphics_____
Effects of music/sound effects_____
Behavior of anchors/reporters_____

Differentiated Instruction   Solutions for All Learners

Strategies for Less Proficient Readers	**Strategies for English Learners**	**Strategies for Advanced Readers**
Record a brief news report, and create an outline shell that lists the main topic of the report and provides columns for the students to record several images and their reactions to each one. It is a good idea to provide one example for students as a model. Play the news report two or three times.	Record a brief news report, and have students list the main topic of the report and provide examples of the images used. Encourage students to work as a group to record their reactions to each image in the report. Play the news report two or three times.	Have students analyze several news reports that cover a current event. Ask students to record the source of the news report, images used, and experts interviewed. Challenge them to compare and contrast the media reports and present their findings to the class.

Featured Titles:

Siddhartha
Herman Hesse, *translated by Joachim Neugroschel, Penguin Classic, 2002*

Fiction Set in India during the sixth century B.C., this novel tells the tale of the handsome and gifted Siddhartha, whose search for wisdom shapes his life. With his friend Govinda, Siddhartha joins a band of ascetics, called *samanas,* who live in poverty and spend their days in meditation. After they pass several years with the samanas, word of a great teacher—the Buddha—reaches Siddhartha and Govinda. The friends go in search of the Buddha. When they find him, Govinda chooses to follow the Buddha, but Siddhartha departs. Alone, Siddhartha discovers the beauty of the world. He settles in a town, becomes involved with a woman, and works in business. Over the course of many years, he gains wealth, but his success soon turns to decadence. Finally, he abandons his town life and resumes his search for wisdom. Read this book to learn whether he finally discovers the truth he has sought.

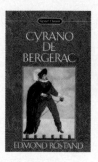

Cyrano de Bergerac
Edmond Rostand, *translated by Lowell Bair, Signet Classic, 2003*

This verse drama in five acts, performed in 1897 and published the following year, is set in seventeenth-century Paris. The action revolves around the noble, swash-buckling Cyrano, who, despite his many gifts, feels that no woman can ever love him because he has an enormous nose.

Secretly in love with the lovely Roxane, Cyrano agrees to help his inarticulate rival, Christian, win her heart by allowing him to present as his own Cyrano's love poems, speeches, and letters. Cyrano's dramatic and beautifully written protestations of love included in letters from the battlefield reinforce Roxane's love for Christian and contribute to a romantic irony that continues to fascinate critics and audiences alike.

Works Presented in Unit Eight:
If sampling a portion of the following texts has built your interest, treat yourself to the full works.

The Transformation and Other Stories
Franz Kafka, *translated by Malcolm Pasley, Penguin Classic, 1995*

Related British Literature:
A Portrait of the Artist as a Young Man
James Joyce, *Signet Classic, 1991*

In a novel closely based on his own life, Joyce describes a young man's coming of age in Catholic Ireland and his rebellion against conventional social values.

Related American Literature:
My Ántonia
Willa Cather, *Pearson Prentice Hall, 2000*

Drawing from her girlhood experiences on a Nebraska ranch, Cather tells the fictional story of a young woman growing up on the prairie in the late 1800s.

Many of these titles are available in the **Prentice Hall Penguin Literature Library. Consult your teacher before choosing one.**

Planning Students' Further Reading

Discussions of literature can raise sensitive and often controversial issues. Before you recommend further reading to your students, consider the values and sensitivities of your community as well as the age, ability, and sophistication of your students. It is also good policy to preview literature before you recommend it to students. The notes below offer some guidance on specific titles.

Siddhartha by Herman Hesse

Siddhartha's quest poses the problem of freedom from earthly desire, and references to sexuality feature significantly. There are also references to gambling and to pregnancy out of wedlock, and Siddartha meets a courtesan. He briefly contemplates suicide. To prepare students to read this work, discuss Buddhist concepts of the wheel of life.

Lexile: Appropriate for high school students

Cyrano de Bergerac by Edmond Rostand

Since adolescents tend to be extremely self-conscious about their physical appearance, the discussion of Cyrano's ugliness should be handled with sensitivity and care.

Lexile: NP

The Transformation and Other Stories by Franz Kafka

Some stories contain minor references to drinking, smoking, and sexual encounters. Other tales, however, describe scenes of death or dying in graphic or emotionally wrenching detail.

Lexile: Appropriate for high school students

A Portrait of the Artist as a Young Man by James Joyce

This book contains offensive language, a main character's obsession with illicit sex and experiences with prostitutes, religious arguments, and rejection of religion.

Lexile: 1120L

My Ántonia by Willa Cather

Racism, prejudice against immigrants, insensitivity toward the mentally retarded and developmentally disabled, and other biased attitudes are expressed in the novel.

Lexile: 1010L

WL.1.02.4 Explain how culture affects personal responses.

FA.3.03.3 Produce responses to literature that emphasize culturally significant events.

CT.4.01.2 Reflect on and show how a real-world event affects viewpoint.

LT.5.01.3 Analyze literary devices and explain their effect on the work of world literature.

LT.5.01.7 Understand the cultural and historical impact on text.

Unit Instructional Resources

In *Unit 9 Resources,* you will find materials to support students in developing and mastering the unit skills and to help you assess their progress.

▶ **Vocabulary and Reading**

Additional vocabulary and reading support, based on Lexile scores of vocabulary words, is provided for each selection or grouping.

• **Word Lists A and B** and **Practices A and B** provide vocabulary-building activities for students reading two grades or one grade below level, respectively.

• **Reading Warm-ups A and B,** for students reading two grades or one grade below level, respectively, consist of short readings and activities that provide a context and practice for newly learned vocabulary.

▶ **Selection Support**

• Reading Strategy
• Literary Analysis
• Vocabulary Builder
• Grammar and Style
• Support for Writing
• Support for Extend Your Learning
• Enrichment

PRENTICE HALL
TeacherEXPRESS™ You may also
Plan · Teach · Assess   access these
resources at TeacherExpress.

Unit 9

Voices of Change

1946–Present

Assessment Resources

Listed below are the resources available to assess and measure students' progress in meeting the unit objectives and your state standards.

Skills Assessment

Unit 9 Resources
    Selection Tests A and B
TeacherExpress™
    ExamView® Test Bank
    Software

Adequate Yearly Progress Assessment

Unit 9 Resources
    Diagnostic Tests 11 and 12
    Benchmark Tests 11 and 12

Standardized Assessment

Standardized Test
    Preparation Workbook

The Contemporary World

Standard Course of Study
In This Unit You Will

- Explain how culture affects personal responses. (WL.1.02.4)
- Produce responses to literature that emphasize culturally significant events. (FA.3.03.3)
- Reflect on and show how a real-world event affects viewpoint. (CT.4.01.2)
- Identify and analyze elements of critical environment. (CT.4.05.11)
- Analyze literary devices and explain their effect on the work of world literature. (LT.5.01.3)
- Understand the cultural and historical impact on world literature texts. (LT.5.01.7)
- Select and modify reading strategies appropriate to reader's purpose. (LT.5.03.1)
- Use vocabulary strategies to determine meaning. (GU.6.01.4)

◄ Umberto Boccioni (1882–1916) painted *Dynamism of a Cyclist* to capture the energy that runs through all objects and people— a basic precept of an artistic movement called Futurism.

Introduce Unit 9

- Direct students' attention to the title of this unit and the art on this spread. **Ask** students: What does this painting suggest about what the contemporary period?
  Possible response: The art depicts a speeding cyclist, suggesting that the contemporary world is fast paced.

- **Ask:** What is the connection between the quotation and the painting?
  Possible response: The quotation defines *liberty* using these present participles: *doubting, making, searching,* and *experimenting*. These active verbs suggest constant motion, action, and effort. When people bicycle, they, too, may feel a sense of freedom or liberty.

- **Ask:** What kinds of literature or themes in literature do you think might come out of this period?
  Possible response: The uses of technology and issues of freedom and self-determination.

Humanities

Dynamism of a Cyclist,
by Umberto Boccioni

Umberto Boccioni (1882–1916) was influenced by the poet Filippo Marinetti, who began the literary movement, Futurism. Boccioni used the ideas of the Futurists in visual arts, and he and other painters stated that the symbols of modern technology should be demonstrated in art through fragmented figures and paintings that show motion and speed.

Use the following question for discussion.

What impression does the painting create of the cyclist?
Possible response: One might see the front wheel of the cycle, but speed and motion fragments the picture so that most of it is a blur.

Unit Features

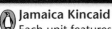 Jamaica Kincaid
Each unit features commentary by a contemporary writer or scholar, under the heading "From the Author's Desk." Author Jamaica Kincaid introduces Unit 9 in Setting the Scene, in which she discusses how she was influenced by contemporary literature. Later in the unit, she introduces a selection from her novel, *Annie John*. In the Writing Workshop, she discusses her approach to revising writing.

Connections
Every unit contains a feature that connects World Literature of the period to British or American Literature. In this unit students will read an excerpt from *Hiroshima,* by John Hersey, on pp. 1318–1321.

Use the information and questions on the Connections pages to help students enrich their understanding of the selections in this unit.

Reading Informational Materials
These selections will help students learn to analyze and evaluate informational texts, such as workplace documents, technical directions, and consumer materials. They will expose students to the organization and features unique to nonnarrative texts.

In this unit, students will read a magazine article called "Holocaust Haggadah," pp. 1274–1277.

Introduce Jamaica Kincaid

- Jamaica Kincaid, who grew up in Antigua, which is part of the British Empire, introduces this unit and provides insight into contemporary literature and her exposure to this literature. "A Walk to the Jetty," an excerpt from her book, *Annie John,* and her commentary about it appear later in the unit on pages 1216–1217.

- Have students read the introductory paragraph about Jamaica Kincaid. Tell them that she learned to read when she was three and a half and was steeped in classical literature before she realized that contemporary world literature existed.

- Use the *From the Author's Desk DVD* to introduce Jamaica Kincaid. Show Segment 1 to provide students with insight into her writing career. After students have watched the segment, **ask:** How did Jamaica Kincaid change from working as a nanny for a family in New York to working as a professional writer?
  Answer: She saved her money, attended college, and became a contributing writer for *The New Yorker.*

Discovering Modern and Contemporary Literature

- Have students read Kincaid's commentary on discovering modern and contemporary literature.

- Point out her explanation of the effect of living under the British Empire as she was growing up.
  Ask: How did living under the rule of the British Empire impact her education?
  Answer: She discovers that her British education limited her horizons. For instance, the only literature she came into contact with was written in the nineteenth century or earlier, and she did not realize that contemporary world literature existed.

- Tell students that they will also read Jamaica Kincaid's introduction to the selection "A Walk to the Jetty" from her book *Annie John,* later in this unit. Kincaid will explain the influences that her early life exercises on her writing.

Setting the Scene

Writers of the contemporary time period experienced two world wars and an unparalleled growth in modern technology. Theirs are the voices of persecution, of freedom, and of hope for a rich future for all of Earth's citizens. In her essay, author Jamaica Kincaid describes her early experiences with contemporary literature and its influence on her writing. In the unit introduction and the works that follow, look for the voices of change, and consider the future direction of contemporary world literature.

Jamaica Kincaid

From the Author's Desk
Jamaica Kincaid Talks About the Time Period

Introducing Jamaica Kincaid (b. 1949) Born in Antigua in the West Indies, Kincaid is widely recognized for an award-winning collection of stories called *At the Bottom of the River* and for her novel, *Annie John.* Kincaid has been granted honorary degrees from a number of colleges, including Colgate University, Amherst College, and Bard College.

Literature of the Empire Was *Not* Contemporary

My literary imagination, which is inseparable from the person sitting before you now writing this essay, was formed by that painful and futile anger-making (to me) historical era known as the British Empire. I was born on the island of Antigua in 1949. I lived there until I was sixteen years of age.

Early Influences of Classic Literature When I was three years old, my mother taught me to read. I can remember even right now the way the letters would bind up together and form words and how the words would leap up to meet my eyes effortlessly. The pleasure of this, the words rushing up to meet my eyes, I have never forgotten.

By the time I was three and a half, I could read quite well and this made me restless, so my mother decided that I should go to school. Children had to be five years old before they were allowed in school and so my mother told me if anyone asked, I should say I was five. At three and a half years of age, I was taught to memorize poems by Shakespeare, Milton, and Keats, and passages from the King James version of the Bible, among other things revered in the British Empire's literary canon.

At the age of five or so, I was in the American equivalent of the second grade and though coping well academically, I was always in trouble socially. It was around then that I was asked to copy Books One and Two of Milton's *Paradise Lost* as a punishment for my bad behavior.

Teaching Resources

The following resources can be used to enrich or extend the instruction for Unit 9 Introduction.

From the Author's Desk DVD
  Jamaica Kincaid, Segment 1

Unit 9 Resources
  Unit Introduction: Names and Terms to Know, p. 5
  Unit Introduction: Focus Questions, p. 6
  Listening and Viewing, p. 25

Voices of Change

Discovering Modern and Contemporary Literature

Until I was nineteen I had never read a book that was written in the twentieth century. At that time, I was living in New York City, working in the home of an American family, serving as a nanny for their children. That family was that now despised American, liberal, and because of that they held opinions which were of great benefit to me, a poor, black young woman from the Third World.

Also, being liberal, they had a great many books, good books, many of them written in the twentieth century. Among them were books written by William Faulkner, Virginia Woolf, James Joyce, Marcel Proust, and Gertrude Stein. I could hardly believe such a thing, that people had continued to write serious literature long after the Brontës (Emily and Charlotte, in particular), Shakespeare, and John Milton.

The Voices of World Literature When I was growing up, I had thought writing, literature, only went as far as Rudyard Kipling and that after him no one wrote any more, that the whole idea, writing, literature, had gone out of style, like some sort of way people wore clothes and no longer do.

I of course had also thought only English people knew how to do this, write serious literature, but finding that not to be so (Faulkner and Stein were Americans, Proust was French) did not shock me at all. What shocked me was finding out that the whole enterprise, writing literature, had continued. It was as if, believing the earth to be round, I was shown evidence that it was not.

Go Online — Author Link

For: A video clip of Jamaica Kincaid
Visit: www.PHSchool.com
Web Code: ete-8901

For: More about Jamaica Kincaid
Visit: www.PHSchool.com
Web Code: ete-9902

Reading the Unit Introduction

Reading for Information and Insight Use the following terms and questions to guide your reading of the unit introduction on pages 1192–1199.

Names and Terms to Know
Cold War
Capitalism
Socialism
United Nations
Sputnik
NATO
European Community

Focus Questions As you read this introduction, use what you learn to answer these questions:
- What is the role of the United Nations regarding human rights?
- In what ways has economic development affected the environment during this period?
- In what ways have the Internet and other modern technologies made an impact on the literature of this period?

From the Author's Desk: Jamaica Kincaid ■ *1189*

Reading the Unit Introduction

Tell students that the terms and questions listed here are the key points in this introductory material. This information provides a context for the selections in this unit. Students should use the terms and questions as a guide to focus their reading of the unit introduction. When students have completed the unit introduction, they should be able to identify or explain each of these terms and answer or discuss the Focus Questions.

Concept Connector

After students have read the unit introduction, return to the Focus Questions to review the main points. For key points, see p. 1199.

Go Online Typing in the Web Codes **Author Link** when prompted will bring students to a video clip and more information on Jamaica Kincaid.

Using the Timeline

The Timeline can serve a number of instructional purposes, as follows:

Getting an Overview

Use the Timeline to help students get a quick overview of themes and events of the period. This approach will benefit all students but may be especially helpful for Visual/Spatial Learners, English Learners, and Less Proficient Readers. (For strategies in using the Timeline as an overview, see the bottom of this page.)

Thinking Critically

Questions are provided on the facing page. Use these questions to have students review the events, discuss their significance, and examine the "so what" behind the "what happened."

Connecting to Selections

Have students refer to the Timeline when they begin to read individual selections. By consulting the Timeline regularly, they will gain a better sense of the period's chronology. In addition, they will appreciate world events that gave rise to these works of literature.

Projects

Students can use the Timeline as a launching pad for projects like these:

- **Author's Publication Timeline**
  Have students select one of the authors listed on the Timeline and research the books the author has written and their dates of publication, as well as any awards the author has received. Then, have each student create a timeline of that author's work, listing the titles and dates of publication, as well as the awards and dates of recognition.

- **Oral Report** Have students select one of the events on the Timeline and research what effect that event had on society and whether the event influenced subsequent literature. Then, have each student prepare an oral report and deliver it to the class. Students may wish to interview older relatives or friends who lived during that time for individual reactions to the event.

World Events

1945   1955   1965

POLITICAL AND CULTURAL EVENTS

- 1947 The transistor is invented.
- 1947 India and Pakistan gain independence.
- 1948 UN approves the Universal Declaration of Human Rights.
- 1948 The state of Israel is born.
- 1949 Communists seize power in China.
- 1950–1953 The Korean War is fought.

- 1952 United States explodes first hydrogen bomb.
- 1953 Watson and Crick discover the chemical basis of DNA. ◄

- 1957 The Russian satellite *Sputnik* goes into orbit. ▼
- 1959 A communist revolution is successful in Cuba.
- 1962 The Cuban missile crisis occurs.

- 1968 Many nations sign the Nuclear Non-Proliferation Treaty.
- 1969 The United States lands a man on the moon. ▼
- 1970s The feminist movement is active in Western countries.
- 1971 The first microprocessor chip is introduced in the United States.

LITERARY EVENTS

- 1947 French author Albert Camus publishes his novel *The Plague.* ▼
- 1947 Italian author Primo Levi publishes *Survival in Auschwitz.*

- 1958 African novelist Chinua Achebe publishes *Things Fall Apart.* ▲
- 1958 Romanian-born Elie Wiesel publishes his Holocaust novel *Night.*
- 1963 The Latin American "Boom" begins with the publication of Julio Cortázar's novel *Hopscotch.*

- 1966 German poet Nelly Sachs receives the Nobel Prize in Literature.
- 1967 Colombian Gabriel García Márquez publishes his novel *One Hundred Years of Solitude.*
- 1968 Japanese novelist Yasunari Kawabata wins the Nobel Prize in Literature.
- 1971 Pablo Neruda wins the Nobel Prize in Literature.
- 1972 Italian author Italo Calvino publishes *Invisible Cities.*

1190 ■ *The Contemporary World*

1975   1985   1995   Present

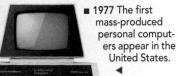

- **1975** After 20 years, the Vietnam War ends.
  - **1977** The first mass-produced personal computers appear in the United States. ◄

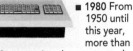

  - **1980** From 1950 until this year, more than 50 new nations have emerged in Africa.
- **1981** The disease known as AIDS is first reported by United States investigators.
- **1982–1983** World music becomes a genre.
- **1980s** More than 50,000 nuclear weapons exist.
- **1980s** European nations form the European Union (EU).

- **1982** Gabriel García Márquez wins the Nobel Prize in Literature.
- **1983** Indian novelist R. K. Narayan publishes *A Tiger for Malgudi.*
- **1983** Caribbean author Jamaica Kincaid publishes her first book, *At the Bottom of the River.*

- **1989** Chinese government suppresses student demonstration in Tiananmen Square. ▼
- **1990–1991** The United States and allies defeat Iraq in first Persian Gulf War.
- **1990s** Apartheid ends in South Africa. ▼
- **1991** Soviet Union collapses.
- **1994** About 500,000 civilians killed in Rwandan ethnic conflicts.

- **1986** Nigerian Wole Soyinka is the first black African to receive the Nobel Prize in Literature.
- **1992** Caribbean writer Derek Walcott wins Nobel Prize in Literature.

- **1997** The Kyoto Protocol is formulated to control global warming.

- **2000** The Internet, a worldwide computer network, thrives.
- **2001** On September 11, hijackers crash planes into the World Trade Center and the Pentagon.
- **2004** The Olympic Games are celebrated in Athens, Greece, home of the games in 776 B.C.

- **1996** Jamaica Kincaid publishes *The Autobiography of My Mother.*
- **1998** Bei Dao publishes a book of poems entitled *Blue House.*
- **1999** Günter Grass receives the Nobel Prize in Literature.
- **2001** R. K. Narayan dies.
- **2004** Nobelist Imre Kertesz publishes *Liquidation.*

Introduction ■ 1191

Critical Viewing

1. What does the illustration of the DNA molecule (1953) suggest about the molecule? **[Infer]**
   Possible response: It suggests that the molecule is complex and may have been difficult to isolate.
2. Compare and contrast the picture of *Sputnik* going into orbit (1957) with the picture of the man on the Moon (1969). **[Compare and Contrast]**
   Possible response: The picture of *Sputnik* is an artist's rendering, but the picture of man on the Moon is an actual photograph. The photo illustrates the progress of technology and space exploration since the time of *Sputnik.*
3. What conclusions can you draw about the Tiananmen Square demonstration (1989) on the basis of the picture provided? **[Draw Conclusions]**
   Possible response: The Chinese government used military tanks to overwhelm the student demonstration.

Analyzing the Timeline

1. (a) What scientific discovery occurred in 1953? (b) What does this discovery indicate about the emphasis on scientific research during this period? **[Deduce]**
   (a) **Possible response:** The DNA molecule was discovered. (b) Scientific research was focused on the basis of life.
2. (a) From 1950 to 1980, how many new nations emerged in Africa? (b) Judging from the Timeline, how did this emergence affect African writers? **[Infer]**
   Answer: (a) Over 50 new nations emerged in Africa during this time period. (b) **Possible response:** African writers began to receive worldwide recognition for their work.
3. (a) What two authors published books about the Holocaust? (b) What is the value of authors using their personal experiences as a basis for writing about world events? **[Evaluate]**
   Answer: (a) Primo Levi and Elie Wiesel wrote about the Holocaust. (b) **Possible response:** By using personal experience, authors provide readers with a more accurate view of what happened and help readers feel what the individuals experienced.
4. (a) What communication method was being used quite successfully in 2000? (b) What influence has this communication network had on the spread of information and the development of communication? **[Interpret]**
   Possible response: (a) The Internet had become a worldwide communication network. (b) Information can be passed almost instantaneously from one area to another throughout the world.
5. (a) What event took place on September 11, 2001? (b) How have the daily lives of Americans changed since this event? **[Apply]**
   Answer: (a) On September 11, 2001, hijackers crashed planes into the World Trade Center and the Pentagon. (b) **Possible response:** There have been changes in security, travel and tourism, and the economy.

Literature of the Period

- In Yehuda Amichai's poem "The Diameter of the Bomb," p. 1313, students will read about the effects of modern weaponry.

- Students will read about the human rights abuses that took place during the Holocaust in the memoirs of Primo Levi and Elie Wiesel, pp. 1254 and 1261.

Critical Viewing

Possible responses: The photograph may remind students of viewing the Moon from Earth, that the Earth is only a tiny part of the Universe, or that there are still places to explore.

Background

Amnesty International

Amnesty International is an independent organization that helps put international pressure on governments that suppress human rights. The organization also strives to set free prisoners of conscience, ensure fair and prompt trials, and end torture and executions throughout the world. Amnesty International has approximately 750,000 members in over 150 countries.

Historical Background

Perhaps the most important photograph of the postwar period is the picture of Earth from the moon. It shows a cloud-wrapped blue jewel of a planet, alone in the darkness of outer space. That jewel is ours. If we—the people of the world—do not learn how to cherish Earth and live in peace with one another, then our treasure will be lost. The history of the contemporary world reveals our failures and successes in this struggle.

The End of Colonialism and the Cold War In the postwar period, the colonial empires built by Western powers during the Age of Imperialism crumbled. In Asia and Africa, people demanded and won freedom. Between 1950 and 1980, more than 50 new nations arose in Africa alone. The new nations emerged into a world dominated and divided by the Cold War, a more than 40-year struggle between the United States and the Soviet Union. Each of these superpowers wanted new countries to adopt its ideology, or system of thought or belief—either capitalism or socialism.

Set up at the end of World War II as a forum for settling disputes, the United Nations (UN) played a vital role in decolonization. It has also tried to act as a peacekeeper and to provide valuable health, educational, and other services for the world's people.

Deadly Weapons Since the United States first exploded two atomic bombs in 1945, nations have been building nuclear weapons. The number of these weapons grew from 3 in 1945 to more than 50,000 in the 1980s. During the Cold War, efforts to curb the arms race had only limited success. Yet, in 1968, many nations signed the Nuclear Non-Proliferation Treaty (NPT), agreeing to halt the spread of nuclear weapons. In 1995, the treaty was renewed, but some nations still refused to sign.

Human Rights and Intervention In 1948, UN members approved the Universal Declaration of Human Rights, which proclaims that all people are entitled to basic freedoms. Nevertheless, human rights abuses, including torture and arbitrary arrest, continue to occur around the world. People have debated whether the world community should intervene to protect individual rights in a sovereign nation. The UN has a mixed record on intervention. In the 1990s, the UN sent peacekeepers to northern Iraq to protect the Kurds from persecution by the Iraqi government. The UN, however, was slow to move against Serbs who persecuted Muslims in Bosnia and did not intervene when Hutus massacred about one million Tutsis in Rwanda.

Terrorism: Deadly Politics Terrorism is the deliberate use of violence, especially against civilians, to achieve political results. Since the 1960s, incidents of terrorism have increased around the world. In 2001, an especially deadly incident occurred on United States soil by suicide bombers opposed to American policies in the Middle East. Thousands were

▲ **Critical Viewing**
This photograph shows Earth as seen from the moon. What thoughts does it inspire in you? Explain. **[Respond]**

Enrichment

The End of Colonialism in Africa

In 1945, the only African nations not ruled by Europeans were Ethiopia and the Kingdom of Egypt. Among the European nations with colonies in Africa were France, Britain, Italy, Belgium, and Portugal. Some key dates in the movement toward African independence are as follows:

1954 Algerian war of independence begins.
1956 Sudan, Tunisia, and Morocco gain independence.

1957 Ghana becomes independent.
1960 Seventeen African states are granted independence.
1963 The Organization of African Unity is created.

killed when several hijacked airplanes crashed into the World Trade Center towers in New York, the Pentagon in Washington, D.C., and a rural field in Pennsylvania.

The Global North and South The Cold War created an ideological split between the communist East and the capitalist West. Today, an economic gulf divides the world into two spheres—the relatively rich nations of the global North and the relatively poor nations of the global South. Nations of the North control much of the world's capital, trade, and technology. Yet, they depend increasingly on low-paid workers in developing states to provide manufactured goods as inexpensively as possible.

The Environment For both rich and poor nations, economic development has taken a heavy toll on the environment. In addition, over the last century, world temperatures have steadily increased. Scientists blame this global warming on the emission of gases into the upper atmosphere. Many warn that unless the world takes action, global warming will continue and cause great harm to the environment.

Old Ways and New In the Western world, industrialization and urbanization began during the Industrial Revolution. In the past fifty years, the rest of the world has experienced similar upheavals. Since 1945, people in the developing world have flocked to cities to find jobs and escape rural poverty. Many, settling in urban slums, have only changed the location of their poverty.

In recent times, religious revivals have swept many religions. Some religious reformers have been called fundamentalists because they stress what they see as the fundamental, or basic, values of their faiths. Many have sought political power to resist changes that they think undermine their beliefs.

Women's Rights After 1945, women's movements brought changes to both the Western and the developing nations. The UN Charter supported "equal rights for men and women." By 1950, women had won the right to vote in many countries. In the industrialized world, more and more women worked outside the home; by the 1970s, the feminist movement sought equal rights for working women.

© 2001 *The Record* (Bergen County, NJ), Thomas E. Franklin, Staff Photographer

▲ **Critical Viewing**
In this photograph, three firemen raise the American flag at Ground Zero, where the World Trade Center had stood on September 11, 2001. What roles did firefighters, police officers, and emergency workers play during and after the terrorist attacks that took place on that day?
[Connect]

Introduction ■ 1193

Background
The Environment
Pollution poses a special problem in Eastern European nations that, now free from Soviet control, are struggling to establish market economies. Years of environmental neglect in these countries have taken a terrible toll. Water and soil have been contaminated by sewage, factory discharge, and toxic waste and acid rain has damaged the forests in Central Europe's industrial belt.

Critical Viewing
Possible response: Emergency workers acted selflessly by rescuing victims of the attack and by trying to keep a sense of calm. In many cases these people gave up their lives trying to save those trapped in the burning buildings while others tirelessly searched for survivors.

Differentiated Instruction Solutions for All Learners

Strategy for Less Proficient Readers
As students read, have them focus on the end of the Cold War and the end of colonialism. Ask students how living with the threat of nuclear war or foreign control might affect the types of literature writers produce. Then, as they read, have students check to see whether their speculations are correct.

Background for English Learners
Students may have a difficult time understanding the terms *Cold War* and *colonialism*. Pair each student with a native English speaker, and have students work together to create a list of ways their lives would be different if they were living in a Cold War or colonial environment.

Enrichment for Advanced Readers
Ask students to use Internet or library resources to investigate one instance of colonialism in Africa or Asia. Have students make a list of the ways in which colonialism affected the people of the colony and how independence affected the people as they formed their new nation.

Background

DNA

In 1953, molecular biologists J. D. Watson and F. H. Crick discovered that DNA was composed of two strands coiled into a double helix configuration. DNA is found in the nucleus of the cell and is the chief material in chromosomes, the cells that control the heredity of living organisms.

Background

Space Exploration

On July 20, 1969, U.S. astronaut Neil Armstrong became the first man to step on the Moon. Edwin Aldrin, Jr., was the second man from the Apollo 11 lunar module, *Eagle,* to walk on the Moon's surface. The *Eagle* was on the Moon for nearly twenty-two hours.

Themes in World Literature

Music in the Historical Context

Point out to students that in a world where there is access to global communication via the Internet, it also makes sense to listen to music from other countries, not only to enrich one's enjoyment but also to develop a greater awareness of cultures that are unknown to us. Suggest that students share their CDs of world music with one another. **Ask** students for examples of their favorite "world music."

Possible response: Some students may mention Panjabi MC, an English rapper of Indian descent who incorporates traditional Indian sounds with hip-hop. Also, they may mention American musician Ry Cooder of the famed "Buena Vista Social Club," and Cuban salsa singer Celia Cruz, who often uses African music to enrich her Caribbean sound. The music of Spanish guitarist Django Reinhart is very popular. Recently, disc jockeys have been combining music and lyrics from various CDs—a musical phenomenon called "mash-up."

Science and Technology Since 1945, the computer has brought an information revolution. By 2000, a huge computer network, the Internet, linked individuals, governments, and businesses around the world, changing the way people learn, shop, and keep in touch with each other. (See Close-up on Culture, page 1198.)

In the field of medicine, vaccines helped prevent the spread of diseases. Recently, however, the spread of new deadly diseases, such as acquired immune deficiency syndrome (AIDS), has challenged researchers. In 1953, James Watson and Francis Crick analyzed the structure of DNA, the chemical underlying genetic inheritance. This discovery made possible the Human Genome Project (1990–present), whose goal is to locate every human gene and identify its chemical makeup.

The space age started in 1957 when the Soviet Union launched *Sputnik,* the first artificial satellite, into orbit. *Sputnik* set off a frantic "space race" between the superpowers. In 1969, the United States landed the first man on the moon. Since the Cold War ended, however, the United States and Russia have cooperated in joint space ventures.

Despite the importance of global issues and trends, not every region experienced the postwar period in the same way. The following summaries focus on specific areas.

Themes in World Masterpieces — Music in the Historical Context

The Growth of "World Music"

Portuguese fado, Brazilian samba, and Pakistani qawwali are diverse musical styles with something important in common. You can probably find all of them at a CD superstore under the category "world music." This grab bag of a genre includes traditional music from every corner of the globe, sometimes spiced with state-of-the-art technology or combined with current Western styles.

Almost every culture has been making music for countless years, but "world music," as such, is only about twenty years old. This genre was the brainchild of store owners and media executives in the United States and Britain who wanted to sell foreign music to Western consumers. Starting out as a marketing idea, it gained momentum with the establishment of a world music chart in 1990 and a world music Grammy Award in 1991.

Today, this category goes beyond CD ratings and sales. Like world literature, world music helps different cultures understand and appreciate one another.

So, if you want to learn about other cultures by adding new flavors to your musical diet, try feasting on Polynesian choirs, the epic songs of Baluchistan bards, or the calypsos of Costa Rica.

Enrichment

The Discovery of DNA

Francis Crick, co-discoverer of DNA, made the following comments on his discovery:

What, then, do Jim Watson and I deserve credit for? If we deserve any credit at all, it is for persistence and the willingness to discard ideas when they became untenable. One reviewer thought that we couldn't have been very clever because we went on so many false trails, but that is the way

discoveries are usually made. Most attempts fail not because of lack of brains but because the investigator gets stuck in a cul-de-sac or gives up too soon. . . .

However, I don't believe all this amounts to much. The major credit I think Jim and I deserve, considering how early we were in our research careers, is for selecting the right problem and sticking to it. . . .

Latin America Despite setbacks, Latin American nations have tried to sustain economic growth and overcome a legacy of poverty and social inequality. Marxism, military rule, and the Roman Catholic Church have been continuing influences in the region. The United States has also exerted a strong influence on Latin American politics. After the communist revolution in Cuba in 1959, the region became the focus of intense Cold War rivalries. Of the larger nations, Mexico enjoyed economic gains, but most of its people remained in poverty. In 2003, Argentina faced a serious economic crisis, and Brazil had just elected a leftist president.

Los Papagayos ("The Parrots") (detail), 1986, Beatriz Gonzalez, Courtesy of the artist, Bogota, Colombia

▲ **Critical Viewing**
The Parrots, a painting by Beatriz Gonzalez, is a commentary on Latin American politics. Judging by the images and colors in this detail from the painting, what statement is the artist making? Explain.
[Interpret]

Europe, West and East Many Western European nations joined with the United States in NATO (North Atlantic Treaty Organization), the alliance that opposed the Soviet Union during the Cold War. Protected by NATO's umbrella, Western Europe enjoyed strong economic growth. Many nations introduced the welfare state, although in the 1980s, economic slowdowns forced cuts in social programs. European nations formed the European Community (EC) in 1957 and the European Union (EU) in the 1980s and 1990s. In 1999, the EU launched a single currency called the euro.

Efforts to reform inefficiencies in government and the economy led to the collapse of the Soviet Union in 1991. After shaking off Soviet domination, nations of Eastern Europe faced economic challenges and ethnic conflicts. Many of them will join the EU. Yugoslavia, a Soviet ally, experienced a breakup into warring nations and ethnic groups, with NATO military pressure resolving crises in Bosnia and Kosovo.

The Middle East Nationalistic and religious struggles have made this region a trouble spot. Israel's declaration of statehood in 1948 represented a rebirth of the Jewish spirit after the Holocaust, the systematic destruction of Jews by the Nazis. Since 1948, however, Israelis and Arabs have engaged in a long struggle punctuated by several wars. In addition, the United States fought two wars against Iraq, in 1990–1991 and again in 2003, when it finally toppled the regime of Saddam Hussein. Both Islamic fundamentalism and pro-democratic movements are significant forces in this region.

Africa Leaders of new African nations set out to build strong central governments, achieve economic growth, and raise standards of living. They have faced a variety of obstacles, including economic dependency and political instability. After independence, a number of new nations experienced military or one-party rule. Many have since introduced multiparty democracy. African nations also experimented with different economic systems, including socialism and mixed economies, which combine capitalism and central control. In the 1990s, after decades of conflict, South Africa abandoned its system of apartheid, or racial separation, and made a transition to democratic rule.

Introduction ■ 1195

Critical Viewing

Possible response: The photograph suggests that contemporary Africa is flourishing. Africans may face the dilemma of moving into the modern world without destroying their traditional and natural heritage.

Historical Background

Comprehension Check

1. What was the Cold War?
   Answer: The Cold War was a forty-year struggle between the United States and the Soviet Union.

2. How has the Internet affected the spread of information?
   Answer: The Internet has provided instantaneous worldwide communication between individuals, governments, and businesses.

3. What event triggered a conflict between Arabs and Israelis in the Middle East?
   Answer: Israel was declared a state in 1948.

4. What political trend in Africa led to many changes in government and economic growth?
   Answer: The end of colonialism led to the establishment of independent countries.

5. How did the Cold War affect Asia?
   Answer: The Cold War led to the Korean War, the Vietnam War, and the deaths of millions.

Critical Thinking

1. Why was the Cold War important politically throughout the world?
   [Apply]
   Answer: Because of the struggle between democracy and communism, conflicts arose in Asia, Europe, and Latin America.

2. Compare the changes in India and Pakistan since independence with the changes in Africa.
   [Compare and Contrast]
   Answer: India and Pakistan have faced rapid urbanization, population growth, and border conflicts. African nations have set out to build and grow strong economies and raise the standard of living.

3. Analyze the reasons for and the problems with the world community intervening in human rights abuses in a sovereign nation.
   [Analyze]
   Possible response: All people should have basic human rights. However, a government has the right to establish its own laws.

▲ Critical Viewing
This photograph was taken in Nairobi National Park, Kenya. What messages does it convey about a contemporary African nation? Explain.
[Interpret]

Asia After its defeat in World War II, Japan introduced democratic reforms and by the 1960s emerged as an economic superpower. Similarly, nations such as Taiwan, Singapore, and South Korea underwent rapid industrialization. In 1949, Mao Zedong led a communist takeover of power in China. Since Mao's death in 1976, communist leaders have attempted to modernize China economically. The violent suppression of student demonstrations in Tiananmen Square (1989), however, showed the regime's determination to keep individual freedoms in check.

Cold War tensions sparked devastating conflicts in Korea, Vietnam, and Cambodia. The Korean War (1950–1953) pitted North Korea and China against South Korea and United Nations forces led by the United States. In the Vietnam War (1955–1975), which was also fought in Cambodia and Laos, the United States failed to prevent communist North Vietnam from taking over South Vietnam. Cambodian communists who seized power after winning a civil war (1975) killed millions of Cambodians.

Since gaining independence in 1947, India and Pakistan have faced rapid urbanization, population growth, and border conflicts with one another. India has built on the legacy of British rule to create the world's largest democracy, although it is still troubled by conflicts between Muslims and Hindus. In Muslim Pakistan, the military has periodically seized power from corrupt civilian regimes, and Islamic parties have gained in recent elections.

Enrichment

Tiananmen Square
In April 1989, Beijing University students protested at Tiananmen Square in Beijing, China, against the government's lagging political reform and suppression of human rights. The "hardline" leaders, with the support of paramount leader Deng Kiaoping, feared the social unrest would pose dangers for China's future. On June 3, 1989, these leaders opted for military suppression of the demonstrators at Tiananmen Square; the crackdown resulted in hundreds of deaths.

Literature

No one knows which of today's works will become tomorrow's classics. (See the Point/Counterpoint feature, below.) What is sure, however, is that writers from many nations are producing exciting and challenging literature.

The Latin American "Boom" The postwar upsurge of literature in Latin America was so dramatic that it was called the "Boom." One of the leading figures of this "Boom" was Argentinian fiction writer Julio Cortázar (hoō´ lē´ ō kôr tə zär´). His experimental novel *Hopscotch* (1963) may be the work that first gained attention for Latin authors. Another landmark novel was *One Hundred Years of Solitude* (1967), by the Colombian Gabriel García Márquez (gäv rē el´ gär sē´ ä mär´ kəs). Poets Pablo Neruda (pä´ blō ne rōō´ də) of Chile and Octavio Paz (ôk tä´ vyô päs´) of Mexico also gained international reputations, and each won the Nobel Prize in Literature.

National and Literary Independence In the newly independent nations of Africa, Asia, and the Caribbean, political independence has gone hand in hand with literary accomplishment. It often seemed as if gifted writers from former British colonies were reconquering the colonizer's language, adding to it the richness of their own traditions.

Nigerians Wole Soyinka (wō´ lā shô yiŋ´ kə), a playwright and poet, and Chinua Achebe (chin´ wä´ ä chā´ bā), a fiction writer, have enhanced their works with African mythology and proverbs.

The Indian writer R. K. Narayan painted a vivid, humorous portrait of everyday Indian life. Nobel Prize-winner Derek Walcott, from the Caribbean, has explored his complex relationship to the West Indies in elegant poetry. Fellow Caribbean author Jamaica Kincaid has written about family relationships and the colonial legacy in Antigua.

Themes in World Masterpieces — Point/Counterpoint

To Preserve or to Change the Literary Canon

Should contemporary multicultural writers be added to the literary canon, the authors accepted for serious study? Two scholars disagree.

Yes! "I'm a cultural historian, and I have been in education all my life. But I didn't know when I began reading for this book [on curriculum] that 'Western Civ' as a subject is as new as it is. The aura it has as the undying, indelible basis of American education is nonsense. . . . There is no final answer, I imagine, to . . . what the curriculum should be."

—Lawrence W. Levine, in
The Chronicle of Higher Education

No! ". . . the Canon's true question remains: What shall the individual . . . read, this late in history? . . . When our English and other literature departments shrink to the dimensions of our current Classics departments . . . we will perhaps be able to return to the study of the inescapable, to Shakespeare and his few peers, who after all, invented all of us."

—Harold Bloom,
The Western Canon

Themes in World Literature
Point/Counterpoint

To Preserve or to Change the Literary Canon Point out that there has been much debate about which authors should be included in the literary canon. Some scholars believe that only those authors whose works are considered classics should be read and studied by American students. Others believe that there is no particular set of authors that should be the basis for education.

1. What do these two viewpoints have in common?
   Possible response: Both scholars believe that books are important for education.

2. In what ways do these viewpoints differ?
   Possible response: Bloom believes that only a few authors have shaped our culture, particularly "Shakespeare and his few peers." Levine believes that there is no final answer as to what the basis for the American school curriculum should be.

3. Point out examples that could support either view.
   Possible response: Bloom's view is supported by the fact that people continue to enjoy Shakespeare and some of his peers. In addition, these works have retained their truth for human kind for hundreds of years, making them an excellent basis for the curriculum. On the other hand, multicultural texts reflect our diverse society, and including literature from other cultures will provide students with a broader understanding of the world.

The Two Europes: Writers Without Illusions The West has produced such outstanding writers as Albert Camus (ka mo͞o′) of France, Günter Grass (go͞on′ tər gräs) of Germany, and Italo Calvino (ē tä′ lō käl vē′ nō) of Italy. These authors are familiar with the ravages of war and the temptations to escape into a material, unreflective existence in postwar society.

Worthy of special mention are Holocaust authors like poet Nelly Sachs and prose writers Primo Levi (prē′ mō lā′ vē) and Elie Wiesel (el′ ē wi zel′). These writers experienced the attempt of the Nazis to exterminate European Jewry and have borne witness to one of history's most terrifying episodes.

Writers from Eastern Europe contended with censorship and the disapproval of authoritarian governments. Their options were few. The Russian poet Yevgeny Yevtushenko (yev gen′ ē yev′ to͞o shenʹ kō) stayed and campaigned for more liberal policies. Another choice, with its own set of problems, was emigration and exile. The Polish poet Czesław Miłosz (chesʹ wäf mē′ wōsh) went into exile, defecting to the West. Russia's Alexander Solzhenitsyn (sōlʹ zhə netʹ sin), however, was forced into exile.

Embattled Writers Eastern Europe was not the only region where writers were censored and harassed. Nadine Gordimer, who is white, stayed in South Africa and attacked the policy of racial segregation and discrimination known as apartheid (ə pär′ tāt′). In China, Bei Dao (bā′ dou) wrote poetry and prose that inspired the student leaders of the Tiananmen Square demonstration. When that demonstration was suppressed, however, Bei Dao went into exile.

Themes in World Masterpieces Close-up on Culture

World Literature and the Internet

World literature, like so much else in today's culture, lives on the Internet. Here are a few ways to pursue foreign authors in the realms of cyberspace:

- **Authors or Works** To find a helpful site, key the name of an author or work into a search engine. The more famous the entry, the greater your chances of finding information. Bypass .com sites that often want to sell you something, and look for those sponsored by universities (.edu) or reputable organizations (.org).
- **Organizations** Two organizations whose sites have information on world literature are the Nobel Foundation and the Academy of American Poets. The Nobel site provides background on winners of the Nobel Prize in Literature. The Academy's site has information on many foreign poets, including Anna Akhmatova, C. P. Cavafy, Czesław Miłosz, and Octavio Paz.
- **Literary Databases** Many literary databases, like the one entitled Literary Resources at Rutgers University, are now available on the Internet. Under "Literary Resources—Other National Literatures," the Rutgers database has links to sites about authors from Australia, France, Germany, Italy, Japan, Russia, and other countries. For additional databases, key "literary databases" into a search engine.

1198 ■ *The Contemporary World*

The Middle East, torn by political and religious conflict, has wounded its writers both literally and figuratively. In 1994, Nobel Prize-winning Egyptian novelist Naguib Mahfouz (nä´ hēb´ mä füz´) was stabbed by an Islamic fundamentalist angered by Mahfouz's portrayal of God in a novel. The Turkish government imprisoned poet Nazim Hikmet (nä zəm´ hik met´) for years because of his leftist political beliefs. Both Palestinian Taha Muhammad Ali and Israeli poet Yehuda Amichai (yə hōō´ də ä´ mi khi) wrote of the pain brought by war.

Another witness to war is Vietnamese poet Nguyen Thi Vinh (nōō´ yin tī vin). She expresses in a few simple words the pain of the Vietnam War, which divided a country, families, and friends: "How can this happen to us / my friend / my foe?"

"The One Great Heart" World literature takes on a new meaning in an era when we can view Earth from the moon. Never before have all the cultures of the world talked to each other so directly and immediately. (See Close-up on Culture, page 1198.) Solzhenitsyn, noting this fact, has called world literature "the one great heart," and he looks to writers as a force for truth and justice.

Solzhenitsyn's vision is menaced in two different ways: by those who would censor or suppress books and by the forces of hunger, poverty, and illiteracy that make it difficult or impossible to read. These warnings aside, however, we should celebrate the achievements of contemporary authors. In few other eras have writers contended with such rapid changes or such breakdowns of traditional ways and truths. In no other era have they searched for identity and meaning with greater persistence or passion. Their spirited, playfully serious poems, essays, and novels are "the one great heart" of our time.

▼ **Critical Viewing**
What links do you see between this painting by Picasso and Solzhenitsyn's concept of world literature as "the one great heart"? **[Connect]**

Round of Friendship . . . , Pablo Picasso, ©2004 Estate of Pablo Picasso/Artists Rights Society (ARS), New York

Introduction ■ *1199*

Humanities

Round of Friendship. . .,
by Pablo Picasso

This painting by Picasso shows people dancing around a central object.

According to Solzhenitsyn's vision, what would the central object represent?
Possible response: World literature.

Critical Viewing

Possible response: Picasso's painting shows a variety of people joined in celebration.

Literature of the Period
Comprehension Check

1. Which Latino poets were awarded the Nobel Prize in Literature?
   Answer: Pablo Neruda and Octavio Paz.

2. How has national independence influenced literature in the nations of Africa, Asia, and the Caribbean?
   Answer: Writers have enhanced their works with themes and traditions of their own nations.

3. What elements threaten Alexander Solzhenitsyn's vision of world literature as "the one great heart?"
   Answer: Censorship, poverty, and illiteracy threaten his vision.

Critical Thinking

1. Why is it important for writers to record the evils of war and protest against a lack of freedom of thought? **[Deduce]**
   Possible response: So that others can work to avoid future problems.

2. Why does Solzhenitsyn call world literature "the one great heart?" **[Infer]**
   Possible response: He views writers and their works as a force for truth and justice.

Concept Connector

Have students return to the Focus Questions on p. 1189. Ask them to summarize the main points in the Unit Introduction. Students' summaries should include the following:

The United Nations and human rights:
- The UN acts provide peacekeeping, health, educational, and other services.
- The UN approved the Universal Declaration of Human Rights, which proclaims that all people are entitled to basic freedoms.
- The UN's record of intervening to stop human rights abuses is mixed.

Ways economic development has affected the environment:
- Economic development has resulted in the emission of gases into the atmosphere.
- The emission of gases has increased world temperatures and could eventually cause great harm to the environment.

Ways the Internet and other modern technologies impact literature:
- Organizations such as the Nobel Foundation have Web sites that give background about writers around the world.
- Literary databases enable people to search for online texts or information about authors.

Standard Course of Study

Goal 2: INFORMATIONAL READING

IR.2.01.9 Analyze and evaluate author's craft and style in research texts.

Goal 5: LITERATURE

LT.5.01.2 Build knowledge of literary genres, and explore how characteristics apply to literature of world cultures.

LT.5.01.5 Analyze archetypal characters, themes, and settings in world literature.

Goal 6: GRAMMAR AND USAGE

GU.6.01.3 Use recognition strategies to understand vocabulary and exact word choice.

GU.6.01.4 Use vocabulary strategies to determine meaning.

GU.6.02.2 Edit for appropriate and correct mechanics.

Step-by-Step Teaching Guide	Pacing Guide
PRETEACH	
• Administer Vocabulary and Reading Warm-ups as necessary.	5 min.
• Engage students' interest with the motivation activity.	5 min.
• Read and discuss author and background features. **FT**	10 min.
• Introduce the Literary Analysis Skill: Magical Realism. **FT**	5 min.
• Introduce the Reading Strategy: Hypothesizing. **FT**	10 min.
• Prepare students to read by teaching the selection vocabulary. **FT**	
TEACH	
• Informally monitor comprehension while students read independently or in groups. **FT**	30 min.
• Monitor students' comprehension with the Reading Check notes.	as students read
• Reinforce vocabulary with Vocabulary Builder notes.	as students read
• Develop students' understanding of magical realism with the Literary Analysis annotations. **FT**	5 min.
• Develop students' ability to hypothesize with the Reading Strategy annotations. **FT**	5 min.
ASSESS/EXTEND	
• Assess students' comprehension and mastery of the Literary Analysis and Reading Strategy by having them answer the Apply the Skills questions. **FT**	15 min.
• Have students complete the Vocabulary Lesson and the Grammar and Style Lesson. **FT**	15 min.
• Apply students' ability to use transitions to clarify order of events by using the Writing Lesson. **FT**	45 min. or homework
• Apply students' understanding by using one or more of the Extend Your Learning activities.	20–90 min. or homework
• Administer Selection Test A or Selection Test B. **FT**	15 min.

Resources

Print

Unit 9 Resources

Transparency

Graphic Organizer Transparencies

Print

Reader's Notebook [L2]

Reader's Notebook: Adapted Version [L1]

Reader's Notebook: English Learner's Version [EL]

Unit 9 Resources

Print

Unit 9 Resources

General Resources

Technology

Go Online: Research [L3]
Go Online: Self-test [L3]
ExamView®, Test Bank [L3]

Choosing Resources for Differentiated Instruction

[L1] Special Needs Students

[L2] Below-Level Students

[L3] All Students

[L4] Advanced Students

[EL] English Learners

For Vocabulary and Reading Warm-ups and for Selection Tests, **A** signifies "less challenging" and **B** "more challenging." For Graphic Organizer transparencies, **A** signifies "not filled in" and **B** "filled in."

FT Fast Track Instruction: To move the lesson more quickly, use the strategies and activities identified with **FT**.

Scaffolding for Less Proficient and Advanced Students

The leveled Critical Thinking questions after selections progress in the levels of thinking required to answer them. To address the needs of your different students, you may use the (a) level questions for your less proficient students and the (b) level questions with your on-level and advanced students. The occasional (c) level questions are appropriate for your advanced students.

Use this complete suite of powerful teaching tools to make lesson planning and testing quicker and easier.

Use the interactive textbook (online and on CD-ROM) to make selections and activities come alive with audio and video support and interactive questions.

Monitoring Progress

Before students read *The Handsomest Drowned Man in the World*, administer **Diagnostic Test 11** (*Unit 9 Resources*, pp. 2–4). This test will determine students' level of readiness for the reading and vocabulary skills.

Go Online
Professional Development

For: Information about Lexiles
Visit: www.PHSchool.com
Web Code: eue-1111

Motivation

Write this statement on the board: *Seeing is believing.* Have students write a paragraph or two in which they agree or disagree with this statement. Use these questions to lead students in a discussion about the nature of reality: Have your perceptions ever misled you? Do important realities sometimes escape your perception? How do people react to the unknown, the mysterious, or the bizarre? What in human nature dictates these reactions?

❶ Background

More About the Author

All of García Márquez's fiction is set in the region of Aracataca, which is, in the words of critic Stephen Minta, a "tropical zone, a world of drama, movement, and light, of endless, and frequently oppressive, heat." The author was deeply influenced by his return to Aracataca in 1950 to sell his grandmother's house after she died. The loss of his childhood home inspired him to recreate in fiction the story of that house and community.

Geography Note

Draw students' attention to the map on the page. Point out that García Márquez's native country is Columbia.

---

❶ The Handsomest Drowned Man in the World

Gabriel García Márquez
(b. 1928)

Colombian author Gabriel García Márquez (gä′ vrē el gär sē′ ä mär′ kes) is one of the originators of magical realism, a literary genre that combines realistic storytelling with elements of folklore and fantasy. In his fiction, he depicts the sharp contrasts of life in Latin America, a continent known not only for its vibrant culture but also for terrible political violence.

Childhood Full of Stories

García Márquez was born in Aracataca, a small village on Colombia's Caribbean coast. Because his parents were poor and struggling, García Márquez lived with his grandparents until he was eight years old. He felt especially close to his grandfather, an impressive man who had fought in the Colombian civil war, called the War of a Thousand Days (1899–1902). García Márquez also had a close relationship with his grandmother. He loved listening to the mysterious fables she recounted and to the tales of military adventure narrated by his grandfather. Later, he adapted for his own work some of these stories he had heard as a child.

After finishing high school, García Márquez decided that he wanted to be a journalist and a novelist. He began working as a reporter only two years later, and he supported himself through newspaper writing until the success of his fiction made him economically independent. Journalism taught him stylistic lessons similar to those he had learned from his grandmother—as he put it, "tricks you need to transform something which appears fantastic, unbelievable, into something plausible, credible."

Beginning by Imitating

In 1955, García Márquez published *Leaf Storm*, the collection of stories that introduced Macondo, a fictional town based on Aracataca. Like many other writers, García Márquez first imitated others in order to find his own true voice. The influence of Faulkner and Hemingway, for example, is evident in *Leaf Storm* and in his other early work. Faulkner taught him the virtues of lush, imaginative writing; in addition, Faulkner's imaginary Mississippi county, described in book after book, probably inspired García Márquez to convert the real Aracataca into the fictional town of Macondo. From Hemingway, García Márquez learned the importance of keen observation. He once recalled his thrill on reading Hemingway's precise description of a bull turning as agilely as a cat rounding a corner.

Later Masterpiece

García Márquez's later masterpiece, *One Hundred Years of Solitude* (1967), chronicles a century of life in Macondo. One of the finest examples of magical realism, the novel earned García Márquez the Nobel Prize in Literature in 1982. On a literal level, this book is the humorous and tragic tale of the Buendía family. Critics have pointed out, however, that the isolation and "solitude" of the Buendías may also symbolize the condition of Colombia or other underdeveloped Latin American countries. García Márquez seemed to confirm this observation in his Nobel acceptance speech when he expressed the hope that "the lineal generations of one hundred years of solitude will have . . . a second chance on earth."

Undoing Death

"The Handsomest Drowned Man in the World" is typical of García Márquez's work in many ways. It marries real events with flights of fantasy. It also presents a dead person as the hero. While death is often lurking in García Márquez's work, the author's vision transforms it. Through the vitality of the story itself, the exuberance of its language, and the sheer power of imagination, death is undone.

Preview

Connecting to the Literature

Reality and dreams are not always opposites. Powerful dreams can have the force of real events, while real events can seem like the product of a dreamer's imagination. In this story, dream and reality come together.

❷ Literary Analysis

Magical Realism

As its name suggests, **magical realism** combines realistic events with elements of myth, magic, and marvels of the natural world. Born out of the conflicts and beauty of Latin American culture, the style mixes reality and fantasy to create a rich sense of life's possibilities and limitations. For example, "The Handsomest Drowned Man in the World" begins with a grimly believable event: a dead body washes up on a beach. Soon, however, García Márquez's descriptions of the body give it mythic proportions:

> Not only was he the tallest, strongest, most virile, and best built man they had ever seen, but even though they were looking at him there was no room for him in their imagination.

As you read these stories, pay close attention to details. Think about which elements are realistic and which are strangely unreal.

Connecting Literary Elements

Magical realist tales often use **archetypes**—universal symbols that evoke deep, even unconscious responses. For example, in "The Handsomest Drowned Man in the World," the archetype of the sea plays a critical role. As you read, identify other archetypes that García Márquez uses and note the ways in which each adds to the mythic feeling of the story.

❸ Reading Strategy

Hypothesizing

When you **hypothesize**, you make informed guesses or propose ideas based on clues in a text. Additional details in the text then prove your hypothesis true or false. As you read this story, use a chart like the one shown to hypothesize.

Vocabulary Builder

bountiful (boun′ tə fəl) *adj.* generous; abundant (p. 1202)

labyrinths (lab′ ə rinths) *n.* structures with an intricate network of winding passages (p. 1203)

haggard (hag′ ərd) *adj.* wasted; worn; gaunt (p. 1203)

resistant (ri zis′ tənt) *adj.* strong; firm (p. 1206)

destitute (des′ tə tōōt′) *adj.* completely poor (p. 1206)

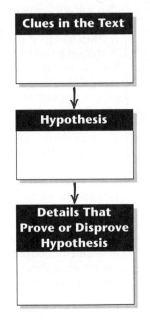

NC Standard Course of Study

- Analyze archetypal characters, themes, and settings in world literature. (LT.5.01.5)
- Use vocabulary strategies to determine meaning. (GU.6.01.4)

Clues in the Text

↓

Hypothesis

↓

Details That Prove or Disprove Hypothesis

The Handsomest Drowned Man in the World ■ 1201

---

❷ Literary Analysis
Magical Realism

- Make sure students understand that Magical Realism describes a combination of realistic and fantastic elements to express the possibilities and limitations of life.

- Invite students to share their memories of Santa Claus, the Easter Bunny, or the Tooth Fairy, for example. Help students understand that these myths combine elements of the real and magical.

- Ask a volunteer to read aloud the first paragraph of the story on p. 1202. Point out that the children easily synthesize elements of the real and the magical. In reality, a drowned man covered with sea debris washes onto the beach. The children use their imaginations to transform the bulge into an enemy ship and then into a whale.

❸ Reading Strategy
Hypothesizing

- Tell students that hypothesizing means proposing ideas based on clues they discover in a text.

- Ask students to use the graphic organizer to form a hypothesis about the content of García Márquez's story on the basis of its title, subtitle, and first paragraph.

- Give students a copy of **Reading Strategy Graphic Organizer A**, p. 201 in *Graphic Organizer Transparencies*. Have them use it to form and test other hypotheses as they read.

Vocabulary Builder

- Pronounce each vocabulary word for students, and read the definitions as a class. Have students identify any words with which they are already familiar.

Differentiated Instruction Solutions for All Learners

Support for Special Needs Students

Have students complete the **Preview** and **Build Skills** pages for "The Handsomest Drowned Man in the World" in the *Reader's Notebook: Adapted Version*. These pages provide a selection summary, an abbreviated presentation of the reading and literary skills, and the graphic organizer on the **Build Skills** page in the student book.

Support for Less Proficient Readers

Have students complete the **Preview** and **Build Skills** pages for "The Handsomest Drowned Man in the World" in the *Reader's Notebook*. These pages provide a selection summary, an abbreviated presentation of the reading and literary skills, and the graphic organizer on the **Build Skills** page in the student book.

Support for English Learners

Have students complete the **Preview** and **Build Skills** pages for "The Handsomest Drowned Man in the World" in the *Reader's Notebook: English Learner's Version*. These pages provide a selection summary, an abbreviated presentation of the skills, additional contextual vocabulary, and the graphic organizer on the **Build Skills** page in the student book.

Facilitate Understanding

Students should find this story very accessible. Have them briefly note the sequence of events after they have finished reading. This technique will help prepare them to analyze the tale.

❶ About the Selection

In this "tale for children," a drowned man washes up on the beach in a small fishing village. The body, shrouded in the mysteries of the sea, is that of a stranger. The women of the village are deeply affected by the drowned man's exceptional size and physical beauty. They name him Esteban and claim him as their own. At first, the men of the village see the drowned man as a bother, but they become affected by his presence as well. The villagers hold a grand funeral for the stranger, pledging to honor his memory.

❷ Literary Analysis

Magical Realism

- Explain that García Márquez combines keen observation and fantastic elements in his fiction.

- Have students read the bracketed passage. Ask them to pay close attention to the details García Márquez describes.

- **Ask** students the Literary Analysis question: Which details in the description of the drowned man are so exaggerated that they seem unreal?
  Answer: The drowned man weighs "almost as much as a horse," "there was barely enough room for him in the house," and the reference to his "ability to keep on growing after death" are exaggerated details.

---

❶ The Handsomest Drowned Man in the World

A Tale for Children

Gabriel García Márquez   translated by **Gregory Rabassa**

Background   This story about an unlikely hero is set in a poor Colombian seaside village that closely resembles the author's home village of Aracataca. In this work and others, García Márquez re-creates and expands upon his grandmother's storytelling style. According to García Márquez, her memorable tales related "things that sounded supernatural and fantastic, but she told them with complete naturalness."

The first children who saw the dark and slinky bulge approaching through the sea let themselves think it was an enemy ship. Then they saw it had no flags or masts and they thought it was a whale. But when it washed up on the beach, they removed the clumps of seaweed, the jelly-fish tentacles, and the remains of fish and flotsam, and only then did they see that it was a drowned man.

❷ They had been playing with him all afternoon, burying him in the sand and digging him up again, when someone chanced to see them and spread the alarm in the village. The men who carried him to the nearest house noticed that he weighed more than any dead man they had ever known, almost as much as a horse, and they said to each other that maybe he'd been floating too long and the water had got into his bones. When they laid him on the floor they said he'd been taller than all other men because there was barely enough room for him in the house, but they thought that maybe the ability to keep on growing after death was part of the nature of certain drowned men. He had the smell of the sea about him and only his shape gave one to suppose that it was the corpse of a human being, because the skin was covered with a crust of mud and scales.

They did not even have to clean off his face to know that the dead man was a stranger. The village was made up of only twenty-odd wooden houses that had stone courtyards with no flowers and which were spread about on the end of a desertlike cape. There was so little land that mothers always went about with the fear that the wind would carry off their children and the few dead that the years had caused among them had to be thrown off the cliffs. But the sea was calm and bountiful and all the men

Literary Analysis
Magical Realism Which details in the description of the drowned man are so exaggerated that they seem unreal?

Vocabulary Builder
bountiful (boun' tə fəl) *adj.* generous; abundant

Differentiated

Instruction   Solutions for All Learners

Accessibility at a Glance

	The Handsomest Drowned Man in the World
Context	A corpse of a drowned man washes up on shore, and the village people give it a remarkable reception.
Language	Syntax: long sentences with embedded clauses
Concept Level	Challenging (Expand your imagination by embracing the different.)
Literary Merit	Breakthrough tale of magical realism
Lexile	1670L
Overall Rating	Average

fit into seven boats. So when they found the drowned man they simply had to look at one another to see that they were all there.

That night they did not go out to work at sea. While the men went to find out if anyone was missing in neighboring villages, the women stayed behind to care for the drowned man. They took the mud off with grass swabs, they removed the underwater stones entangled in his hair, and they scraped the crust off with tools used for scaling fish. As they were doing that they noticed that the vegetation on him came from faraway oceans and deep water and that his clothes were in tatters, as if he had sailed through <u>labyrinths</u> of coral. They noticed too that he bore his death with pride, for he did not have the lonely look of other drowned men who came out of the sea or that <u>haggard</u>, needy look of men who drowned in rivers. But only when they finished cleaning him off did they become aware of the kind of man he was and it left them breathless. Not only was he the tallest, strongest, most virile, and best built man they had ever seen, but even though they were looking at him there was no room for him in their imagination.

They could not find a bed in the village large enough to lay him on nor was there a table solid enough to use for his wake. The tallest men's

Vocabulary Builder

labyrinths (lab´ ə rinths) *n.* structures with an intricate network of winding passages

haggard (hag´ ərd) *adj.* wasted; worn; gaunt

✔**Reading Check** ❸

Who first discovers the drowned man?

4

Waves, 1917, Christopher Nevinson, Phillips, The International Fine Art Auctioneers, UK

5 ▲ **Critical Viewing** Does this painting depict the sea as being "calm and bountiful," as it is described in the story? Why or why not? **[Evaluate]**

The Handsomest Drowned Man in the World ■ 1203

❸ **Reading Check**

Answer: A group of village children first discover the drowned man.

❹ **Humanities**

Waves by Christopher Nevinson

The English painter Christopher Nevinson (1889–1946) was the son of committed social activists. He began to study art in the early part of the twentieth century, spending the years 1909–1912 at the Slade School of Art in London. While in London, Nevinson discovered Futurism, a movement that influenced his early career. After finishing at Slade, he went to Paris, where he continued to study and explore modern art.

World War I was a critical juncture in Nevinson's life. After serving as an ambulance driver and hospital worker for over a year, he fell ill with rheumatic fever. Unable to serve, he began painting his wartime experiences. For some time, he created war paintings for Britain's War Propaganda Bureau, but he grew dissatisfied with this work. Although painted at the height of the war in 1917, *Waves* represents a departure from Nevinson's paintings of the machinery of destruction. After the war, he concentrated on painting cityscapes and, later, pastoral scenes.

Use the following question for discussion:

Do you think this painting is an appropriate illustration for this story? Why or why not?
Possible response: The painting is an appropriate illustration because it suggests the mystery of the ocean and thus parallels the mysterious origins of the drowned man.

❺ **Critical Viewing**

Possible response: The gentle waves and the sense of the sea's vastness depict the sea as being "calm and bountiful."

Differentiated Instruction Solutions for All Learners

Enrichment for Less Proficient Readers
Tell students that critics have described this story as "a Prometheus myth for Latin America." Help students locate and read a version of the Prometheus myth. Invite them to use a Venn diagram to compare and contrast the characters of Prometheus and Esteban.

Enrichment for English Learners
Tell students that critics have described this story as "a Prometheus myth for Latin America." Help students locate and read an illustrated version of this myth. Invite students to compare and contrast the characters of Prometheus and Esteban. Have them use at least five adjectives for each character.

Enrichment for Advanced Readers
Tell students that critics have described this story as "a Prometheus myth for Latin America." Invite students to compare and contrast the characters of Prometheus and Esteban in analytical essays. Tell each student to write a thesis statement in which he or she agrees or disagrees with the critics' statement.

❻ Humanities

Troubled Woman by Egon Schiele

During his brief career, Schiele (1890–1918) became an important and controversial figure in his native Austria. Born outside Vienna, he began studying art in that city at the age of sixteen. The artist Gustav Klimt was an early friend and influence. Schiele's work began to move in different directions, however. Using distorted ink outlines, he began to produce unsettling paintings of contorted figures. His work was at the forefront of Austrian Expressionism. With roots in Germany, Austrian Expressionism as a movement emphasized personal expression through exaggeration and distortion.

Troubled Woman reflects Schiele's emphasis on awkward, uncomfortable figures. But the artist was also known for disturbing images of nudes. Many people were troubled by these paintings—so much so that in 1912, Schiele was arrested. Although he spent little time in prison, the experience was highly dispiriting. Within six years, he died of influenza.

Use the following questions for discussion:

- What elements in this painting suggest that the woman is troubled?
  Possible response: The pose in which the woman is depicted suggests that she is troubled. She crouches uncomfortably and holds her head in her hands. The splotchy color and angularity of her hands and feet add to the impression of trouble.

- What do you imagine is at the root of this woman's troubles? Why?
  Possible response: Her bowed head suggests mourning more than worry. The woman may be grieving over a significant loss.

❼ Critical Viewing

Possible response: The women of the village express enormous sympathy and sorrow for the drowned man, especially after they decide that his name is Esteban. However, the woman depicted in the painting expresses far more pain and anguish than do the women in the story.

❻

❼ ▲ **Critical Viewing** In what ways does this painting reflect the kinds of emotions expressed by the women caring for the drowned man? **[Connect]**

Enrichment

Literature of the Fantastic

Fantasy is a key element of the Magical Realism of Gabriel García Márquez and Julio Cortázar. In literature of the fantastic, writers harness the power of fantasy to challenge, puzzle, discomfort, and entertain readers. Like dreams or daydreams, fantastic stories distort and expand our usual world. They open up passageways into mysterious places. One such story is Jorge Luis Borges's "The Secret Miracle," in which a man facing a firing squad is given a year to finish a play he is writing. The fantastic element of the tale is that the year takes place while the bullets are flying toward him! To everyone in the story, except the man, the year is just a split second.

According to the Argentine critic Alberto Manguel, ". . . fantastic literature deals with what can best be defined as the impossible seeping into the possible, what Wallace Stevens calls 'black water breaking into reality.'"

holiday pants would not fit him, nor the fattest ones' Sunday shirts, nor the shoes of the one with the biggest feet. Fascinated by his huge size and his beauty, the women then decided to make him some pants from a large piece of sail and a shirt from some bridal brabant[1] linen so that he could continue through his death with dignity. As they sewed, sitting in a circle and gazing at the corpse between stitches, it seemed to them that the wind had never been so steady nor the sea so restless as on that night and they supposed that the change had something to do with the dead man. They thought that if that magnificent man had lived in the village, his house would have had the widest doors, the highest ceiling, and the strongest floor, his bedstead would have been made from a midship frame held together by iron bolts, and his wife would have been the happiest woman. They thought that he would have had so much authority that he could have drawn fish out of the sea simply by calling their names and that he would have put so much work into his land that springs would have burst forth from among the rocks so that he would have been able to plant flowers on the cliffs. They secretly compared him to their own men, thinking that for all their lives theirs were incapable of doing what he could do in one night, and they ended up dismissing them deep in their hearts as the weakest, meanest, and most useless creatures on earth. They were wandering through that maze of fantasy when the oldest woman, who as the oldest had looked upon the drowned man with more compassion than passion, sighed:

"He has the face of someone called Esteban."

It was true. Most of them had only to take another look at him to see that he could not have any other name. The more stubborn among them, who were the youngest, still lived for a few hours with the illusion that when they put his clothes on and he lay among the flowers in patent leather shoes his name might be Lautaro. But it was a vain illusion. There had not been enough canvas, the poorly cut and worse sewn pants were too tight, and the hidden strength of his heart popped the buttons on his shirt. After midnight the whistling of the wind died down and the sea fell into its Wednesday drowsiness. The silence put an end to any last doubts: he was Esteban. The women who had dressed him, who had combed his hair, had cut his nails and shaved him were unable to hold back a shudder of pity when they had to resign themselves to his being dragged along the ground. It was then that they understood how unhappy he must have been with that huge body since it bothered him even after death. They could see him in life, condemned to going through doors sideways, cracking his head on crossbeams, remaining on his feet during visits, not

Reading Strategy
Hypothesizing In what ways do you think the arrival of the drowned man will affect life in this village? Explain.

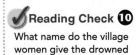

Reading Check ❿
What name do the village women give the drowned man?

---

1. **brabant** (bre bant´) region in Belgium and the Netherlands famous for its textile products.

The Handsomest Drowned Man in the World ■ 1205

Analyze

• Have students pause before they read this page. **Ask** them to summarize the women's thoughts about the drowned man so far in the story. **Answer:** The women are at first impressed with the drowned man's size and good looks, so much so that they imagine him to be superior to their own husbands. This thinking begins to change when one of the older women names the drowned man Esteban.

• Have students read the bracketed passage. Tell them to pay close attention to the way in which the women characterize the drowned man now.

• Point out that although the women have previously expressed admiration for the drowned man, they now show irritation and then sympathy as he becomes like their own men. This transformation breeds a sense of ownership in the women. **Ask** students how this change in attitude is expressed. **Answer:** As they imagine the problems the drowned man's size might have caused him, the women give him words to speak. The drowned man comes to life as a believable, if large, person—at least in the minds of the women.

• Make sure students recognize that in this passage, the drowned man becomes more than just a waterlogged body or a cipher—he becomes a character with his own personality and voice.

⓬ Critical Viewing

Possible response: The coral in the photograph is intricate and mazelike, suggesting a sort of natural labyrinth.

---

knowing what to do with his soft, pink, sea lion hands while the lady of the house looked for her most <u>resistant</u> chair and begged him, frightened to death, sit here, Esteban, please, and he, leaning against the wall, smiling, don't bother, ma'am, I'm fine where I am, his heels raw and his back roasted from having done the same thing so many times whenever he paid a visit, don't bother, ma'am, I'm fine where I am, just to avoid the embarrassment of breaking up the chair, and never knowing perhaps that the ones who said don't go, Esteban, at least wait till the coffee's ready, were the ones who later on would whisper the big boob finally left, how nice, the handsome fool has gone. That was what the women were thinking beside the body a little before dawn. Later, when they covered his face with a handkerchief so that the light would not bother him, he looked so forever dead, so defenseless, so much like their men that the first furrows of tears opened in their hearts. It was one of the younger ones who began the weeping. The others, coming to, went from sighs to wails, and the more they sobbed the more they felt like weeping, because the drowned man was becoming all the more Esteban for them, and so they wept so much, for he was the most <u>destitute</u>, most peaceful, and most obliging man on earth, poor Esteban. So when the men returned with the news that the drowned man was not from the neighboring villages either, the women felt an opening of jubilation in the midst of their tears.

"Praise the Lord," they sighed, "he's ours!"

1206   *The Contemporary World*

Vocabulary Builder
resistant (ri zis′ tənt) *adj.*
strong; firm

Vocabulary Builder
destitute (des′ tə tōōt′) *adj.*
completely poor

⓬ ▼ **Critical Viewing** In what ways does this undersea photograph support the narrator's description of "labyrinths" of coral? **[Support]**

Enrichment

Point of View and Perspective
Point of view is the vantage point from which a story is told. This story is told from an omniscient third-person point of view, meaning that the narrator remains outside the story but has access to the characters' thoughts.

This point of view itself does not change throughout the story. However, there are some surprising shifts in perspective within this point of view. For example, the dead man suddenly comes to life when the narrator gives him imagined dialogue to speak. This shift in perspective is all the more surprising because it takes place in mid-sentence, and Esteban's words are not placed in quotation marks. García Márquez may omit quotation marks from the dialogue to indicate that it is imagined rather than real.

The men thought the fuss was only womanish frivolity. Fatigued because of the difficult nighttime inquiries, all they wanted was to get rid of the bother of the newcomer once and for all before the sun grew strong on that arid, windless day. They improvised a litter with the remains of foremasts and gaffs,[2] tying it together with rigging[3] so that it would bear the weight of the body until they reached the cliffs. They wanted to tie the anchor from a cargo ship to him so that he would sink easily into the deepest waves, where fish are blind and divers die of nostalgia, and bad currents would not bring him back to shore, as had happened with other bodies. But the more they hurried, the more the women thought of ways to waste time. They walked about like startled hens, pecking with the sea charms on their breasts, some interfering on one side to put a scapular[4] of the good wind on the drowned man, some on the other side to put a wrist compass on him, and after a great deal of *get away from there, woman, stay out of the way, look, you almost made me fall on top of the dead man,* the men began to feel mistrust in their lives and started grumbling about why so many main-altar decorations for a stranger, because no matter how many nails and holy-water jars he had on him, the sharks would chew him all the same, but the women kept piling on their junk relics, running back and forth, stumbling, while they released in sighs what they did not in tears, so that the men finally exploded with *since when has there ever been such a fuss over a drifting corpse, a drowned nobody, a piece of cold Wednesday meat.* One of the women, mortified by so much lack of

2. **gaffs** poles that are part of a ship's mast.
3. **rigging** ropes and other gear used to control the sails of a vessel.
4. **scapular** (skap´ yə lər) religious medal.

✓ **Reading Check** 🄸

Why do the women cover the drowned man's face with a handkerchief?

The Handsomest Drowned Man in the World   1207

🄭 **Literary Analysis**
Magical Realism

• Explain to students that realistic elements ground fantasy, and the fantastic elements reveal unimagined possibilities—unrecognized limitations—within real life.

• Have students read the bracketed passage. Then, **ask** them to identify the realistic and the fantastic elements in it.
Answer: The materials the men use in the litter and their irritation at the women are realistic elements. The description of the deepest part of the sea is a fantastic element. The women's fantasy of the drowned man's life as Esteban is also present in this passage, but it is seen through the realistic lens of the men's annoyance.

• **Ask** students to describe how the fantastic elements in this passage affect its realism.
Possible response: The fantastic elements reveal the limitations of the men's realistic and irritable view of their world, hinting at a possibility for transformation with the arrival of the drowned man that the men do not see.

• Encourage students to continue to pay attention to the interaction of realistic and fantastic elements in the remainder of the story, as well as to the differences between the behavior of the men and the women with regard to Esteban.

▶ **Reteach** If students have difficulty identifying the interactions of realistic and fantastic elements in this story, have them use the **Literary Analysis** support, p. 11 in *Unit 9 Resources.*

🄸 **Reading Check**

Answer: The women cover the drowned man's face with a handkerchief "so that the light would not bother him."

Differentiated
Instruction   Solutions for All Learners

Strategy for Less Proficient Students
To model how to hypothesize, give students a copy of **Reading Strategy Graphic Organizer B** (*Graphic Organizer Transparencies,* p. 202). The completed graphic organizer will give students insight into the process of hypothesizing. They can use it as a model for making their own hypotheses as they read the story.

Support for English Learners
Some students may have difficulty with bracketed passage 11 because quotation marks are not used for the dialogue. Point out that this is so because it is an imagined dialogue. Have students work in pairs and write the dialogue, using quotation marks. Post the first sentence. When students have finished, have volunteers post the rest of the dialogue.

Enrichment for Advanced Readers
Students may take special notice of the burial rituals undertaken on behalf of the drowned man by the people of the village. Encourage students to research burial traditions in South American seaside villages. How much of García Márquez's description is realistic and how much is fantasy?

⑮ Humanities

Sunset on the Sea

Artist Unknown

The archetype of the sea can be felt as one views this lush nineteenth century oil painting of the sunset glimmering colorfully on the water's surface. The ship in the distance looks very fragile in the midst of the tumbling waves. Still, the beauty of the rich blue sky and the clouds reflecting the invisible setting sun all suggest the power and beauty of nature.

Use the following questions for discussion:

• Do you think this painting is appropriate for the burial scene?
Possible response: Yes, the beautiful sunset would be a wonderful setting for the burial, and the painting suggests that the beautiful sea is an appropriate place to receive Esteban's corpse.

• How would you describe the feeling this painting evokes?
Possible response: Because so many of the village men work as fishermen and the women worry about them, the painting is very evocative of the mixed emotions the villagers must have about the fearful yet beautiful sea.

⑯ Critical Viewing

Possible response: The lone ship and the rough seas reflect the mysterious and adventurous past that the women imagine Esteban to have had.

⑮

⑯ ▲ **Critical Viewing** Which details in this painting reflect Esteban's imagined past? **[Interpret]**

Enrichment

The Death of Sir Walter Raleigh

Students may be puzzled by the reference to Sir Walter Raleigh. Why is this English explorer a figure of such significance that he would so impress the villagers in this story? When James I succeeded to the throne and became King of England in 1603, he regarded Raleigh as an enemy. The new king had Raleigh stripped of many of his privileges and possessions. Eventually, Raleigh was found guilty of treason.

However, in 1616, the aging explorer was released to make a voyage into Guiana in search of the fabled golden city of El Dorado. This would be his second such voyage—he had already hunted for the legendary city in 1595. Raleigh was warned not to interfere with any Spanish ships or possessions. During the course of the journey, however, one of his fellow explorers captured a Spanish town. This was a violation of Raleigh's order. On his return to England, he was executed. His boldness in South America cost him his life.

care, then removed the handkerchief from the dead man's face and the men were left breathless too.

He was Esteban. It was not necessary to repeat it for them to recognize him. If they had been told Sir Walter Raleigh,[5] even they might have been impressed with his gringo accent, the macaw on his shoulder, his cannibal-killing blunderbuss, but there could be only one Esteban in the world and there he was, stretched out like a sperm whale, shoeless, wearing the pants of an undersized child, and with those stony nails that had to be cut with a knife. They had only to take the handkerchief off his face to see that he was ashamed, that it was not his fault that he was so big or so heavy or so handsome, and if he had known that this was going to happen, he would have looked for a more discreet place to drown in, seriously, I even would have tied the anchor off a galleon around my neck and staggered off a cliff like someone who doesn't like things in order not to be upsetting people now with this Wednesday dead body, as you people say, in order not to be bothering anyone with this filthy piece of cold meat that doesn't have anything to do with me. There was so much truth in his manner that even the most mistrustful men, the ones who felt the bitterness of endless nights at sea fearing that their women would tire of dreaming about them and begin to dream of drowned men, even they and others who were harder still shuddered in the marrow of their bones at Esteban's sincerity.

That was how they came to hold the most splendid funeral they could conceive of for an abandoned drowned man. Some women who had gone to get flowers in the neighboring villages returned with other women who could not believe what they had been told, and those women went back for more flowers when they saw the dead man, and they brought more and more until there were so many flowers and so many people that it was hard to walk about. At the final moment it pained them to return him to the waters as an orphan and they chose a father and mother from among the best people, and aunts and uncles and cousins, so that through him all the inhabitants of the village became kinsmen. Some sailors who heard the weeping from a distance went off course and people heard of one who had himself tied to the mainmast, remembering ancient fables about sirens. While they fought for the privilege of carrying him on their shoulders along the steep escarpment[6] by the cliffs, men and women became aware for the first time of the desolation of their streets,

---

5. **Sir Walter Raleigh** English explorer (1552–1618) known for his charm and boldness; organized expeditions to North and South America.
6. **escarpment** (e skärp´ mənt) slope.

 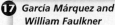

Themes in World Masterpieces

⑰ García Márquez and William Faulkner

The fictional world of Gabriel García Márquez was strongly influenced by the American author William Faulkner, who wrote many stories and novels set in the imaginary Mississippi county of Yoknapatawpha (yōk´ nə´ pə tô´ fə). Inspired by Faulkner's rich and intimate descriptions of Yoknapatawpha and its residents, García Márquez created his own fictional village of Macondo. He also decided that his earlier works had been "simply intellectual elaborations, nothing to do with my reality." To address this flaw, he changed his writing style, incorporating personal imagery, details, and knowledge.

While Macondo is clearly modeled on García Márquez's hometown of Aracataca, it is not merely the product of Márquez's observant eye. Rather, as a fictional setting, the town rests on a deep undercurrent of fantasy and magic, which frequently erupts. As it does, readers travel to a haunting landscape, where reality still holds sway but dream and imagination are equally powerful.

Connect to the Literature

In what ways does the description of Macondo remind you of a dream?

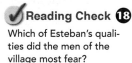

Reading Check ⑱

Which of Esteban's qualities did the men of the village most fear?

The Handsomest Drowned Man in the World ■ 1209

- Reemphasize to students that hypothesizing must be based on the details in a text.

- Have students read the bracketed passage. Instruct them to pay close attention to the details.

- **Ask** students the Reading Strategy question: Do you think the village will remember Esteban after his funeral? Explain.
Possible response: The villagers will remember Esteban because of the feeling of kinship that sweeps the village and because of the decision to bury Esteban at sea without an anchor, "so that he could come back if he wished."

ASSESS

Answers

1. **Possible response:** The most surprising aspect of the story is the normalcy with which the villagers treat the appearance of the drowned man. They even compare Esteban with other drowned men.

2. (a) The men observe that the drowned man is larger and heavier than any other dead man they have carried. (b) Esteban is larger than life, whereas the village is remarkably small. (c) The drowned man is very important.

3. (a) The women wash the drowned man, make him new clothes for his burial, and give him the name Esteban. (b) The women first notice the drowned man's size and good looks. After they name him, the women perceive his innocent, sincere, and piteous qualities.

4. (a) The men are irritated by the women's fuss, dismissing it as "womanish frivolity." (b) The men change their minds when one of the women reveals the drowned man's face. The men are awed by the same qualities the women have perceived in the drowned man.

5. (a) The villagers decide to build larger, more colorful houses and plant flowers to attract and accommodate those who are different from themselves. (b) Esteban brings a new dimension into the lives of the villagers, enlarging their hearts.

1210

---

the dryness of their courtyards, the narrowness of their dreams as they faced the splendor and beauty of their drowned man. They let him go without an anchor so that he could come back if he wished and whenever he wished, and they all held their breath for the fraction of centuries the body took to fall into the abyss. They did not need to look at one another to realize that they were no longer all present, that they would never be. But they also knew that everything would be different from then on, that their houses would have wider doors, higher ceilings, and stronger floors so that Esteban's memory could go everywhere without bumping into beams and so that no one in the future would dare whisper the big boob finally died, too bad, the handsome fool has finally died, because they were going to paint their house fronts gay colors to make Esteban's memory eternal and they were going to break their backs digging for springs among the stones and planting flowers on the cliffs so that in future years at dawn the passengers on great liners would awaken, suffocated by the smell of gardens on the high seas, and the captain would have to come down from the bridge in his dress uniform, with his astrolabe[7] his pole star, and his row of war medals and, pointing to the promontory of roses on the horizon, he would say in fourteen languages, look there, where the wind is so peaceful now that it's gone to sleep beneath the beds, over there, where the sun's so bright that the sunflowers don't know which way to turn, yes, over there, that's Esteban's village.

7. **astrolabe** (as′ trō lāb′) old-fashioned instrument used in navigating a ship.

Critical Reading

1. **Respond:** Which aspect of this story do you find most surprising? Explain.

2. **(a) Recall:** As the village men carry the drowned man from the beach, what do they observe about his size and weight?
(b) Contrast: How does the drowned man's size contrast with the size of the village? **(c) Interpret:** What does this size relationship suggest about the importance of the drowned man?

3. **(a) Recall:** After the men bring the body to town, what do the women do with it? **(b) Analyze Cause and Effect:** As a result of their actions, what qualities do the women notice about the dead man?

4. **(a) Interpret:** With what emotions do the men first react to the women's fuss over the body? Explain. **(b) Analyze Cause and Effect:** What happens to change their minds? Explain.

5. **(a) Generalize:** In what ways does the town change as a result of its encounter with Esteban? **(b) Analyze:** What do these changes suggest about Esteban's symbolic value to the town?

6. **Evaluate:** Do you think that García Márquez intends his subtitle, "A Tale for Children," to be interpreted literally? Why or why not?

7. **Apply:** Philosophers have sometimes expressed the idea that the key to releasing human potential is to expand people's imagination. Explain how this story supports that notion.

1210 ■ *The Contemporary World*

For: More about Gabriel
García Márques
Visit: www.PHSchool.com
Web Code: ete-9901

Answers continued

6. **Possible response:** The subtitle is not meant literally because the story is too complex for children. Rather, the subtitle is intended to suggest that adults need to work to retain the childlike quality of acceptance of that which is different, just as the village children include Esteban in their play without judgment.

7. **Possible response:** The change in attitude and style that comes to the villagers is a result of their imaginative ability to embrace Esteban's difference within their hearts, their minds, and the village itself.

Go Online For additional information about **Author Link** Gabriel García Márquez, have students type in the Web Code, then select *M* from the alphabet, and then select Gabriel García Márquez.

Apply the Skills

The Handsomest Drowned Man in the World

Literary Analysis

Magical Realism

1. **(a)** Use a chart like the one shown to identify realistic and fantastic details in "The Handsomest Drowned Man in the World."

	Realistic Details	**Fantastic Details**
Characters		
Setting		
Events		

   (b) Describe specific ways in which the story begins firmly rooted in the real and slowly develops a fantastic dimension. **(c)** Why do you think this structure is common in works of **magical realism**?

2. In "The Handsomest Drowned Man in the World," how do the children's actions suggest that the world of the story is not quite the world of reality?

3. Besides Esteban, the drowned man, no other character in the story has a name. What effect does this detail have on the magical nature of this story?

Connecting Literary Elements

4. **(a)** Which details in "The Handsomest Drowned Man in the World" present the **archetype** of the sea as the source of life? **(b)** Which details suggest the sea is a taker of life?

5. **(a)** In what ways is Esteban an archetypal character? **(b)** Which details make him seem very human and not archetypal at all? Explain your answers.

Reading Strategy

Hypothesizing

6. **(a)** State one **hypothesis** you formed as you began to read "The Handsomest Drowned Man in the World." **(b)** In what ways did the events of the story prove or disprove your hypothesis?

7. In what ways can hypothesizing increase your involvement in a work of literature? Explain.

Extend Understanding

8. **Psychology Connection:** One writer believed that ". . . the fantastic dimension, and the unexpected" are important in both literature and life. Do you agree? Explain your answer.

QuickReview

Magical realism is a literary style that combines realistic events with elements of myth, magic, and other marvels of the natural world.

An **archetype** is a universal symbol that evokes deep, even unconscious responses.

When you **hypothesize**, you make informed guesses or propose ideas based on clues in a text. As you read further, use details to prove or disprove your hypothesis.

Go Online
Assessment
For: Self-test
Visit: www.PHSchool.com
Web Code: eta-6901

The Handsomest Drowned Man in the World ■ 1211

Go Online Students may use the **Self-test** to
Assessment prepare for **Selection Test A** or
Selection Test B.

1211

❶ Vocabulary Lesson

Word Analysis: Latin Prefix *re-*

1. reabsorb: to take in and make part of again

2. reoccurrence: a repeated appearance or happening

3. recurrent: returning from time to time

4. reanimate: to revive

5. reappraisal: a new evaluation

6. reconstruction: the action of building again

Spelling Strategy

1. heredity   3. scarcity

2. society   4. generosity

Vocabulary Builder

1. synonyms   4. antonyms

2. antonyms   5. antonyms

3. synonyms

❷ Grammar and Style Lesson

1. "Who is it?" asked the children.

2. "We must bury him," said the men.

3. "Don't go, Esteban," said the women.

4. "If they have come, " said Irene, "we must leave at once."

5. I looked at my sister and said, "Yes."

Writing Application

Possible response:

"Well," I said, "here we are."

"Yes, and the village looks so different," Maria marveled, "with all those large homes and gardens!"

"Do you think Esteban ever returned?" I whispered.

Maria murmured, "He's here now in my heart."

Build Language Skills

❶ Vocabulary Lesson

Word Analysis: Latin Prefix *re-*

The Latin prefix *re-* can mean "again" or "back." The word *resistant,* which means "strong or firm," combines this prefix with the Latin root *-sistere,* which means "to stand." Add the prefix *re-* to each word below. Then, write a definition for each new word.

1. absorb
2. occurrence
3. current
4. animate
5. appraisal
6. construction

Spelling Strategy

The suffix *-ety /-ity* means "the state or quality of," but *-ity* is the more common variation in English. Add *-ety* or *-ity* to complete each word below.

1. hered_____
2. soci_____
3. scarc_____
4. generos_____

Vocabulary Builder: Synonyms or Antonyms?

Review the vocabulary words and definitions on page 1201, and notice the way the words are used in the context of each selection. Then, identify each of the following pairs of words as either synonyms (words with similar meanings) or antonyms (words with opposite meanings).

1. labyrinths, mazes
2. resistant, frail
3. haggard, exhausted
4. bountiful, scarce
5. destitute, prosperous

❷ Grammar and Style Lesson

Punctuating Dialogue

In "The Handsomest Drowned Man in the World," García Márquez includes dialogue without punctuation, allowing the story to shift seamlessly from the observations of the villagers to those of the dead man. However, in most pieces of writing, correct **punctuation of dialogue** is essential. To correctly punctuate dialogue, place quotation marks around the speaker's exact words. Locate periods and commas inside the quotation marks.

> **Examples:**
>
> "In that case," she said, picking up her needles again, "we'll have to live on this side."
>
> "Did you have time to bring anything?" I asked hopelessly.

WG Prentice Hall Writing and Grammar Connection: Platinum Level, Chapter 28, Section 4

Practice Rewrite each item below, using correct punctuation.

1. Who is it asked the children
2. We must bury him said the men
3. Don't go, Esteban said the women
4. If they have come said Irene we must leave at once
5. I looked at my sister and said Yes

Writing Application Suppose that two of the women of the village return ten years later. Write a short dialogue that they share as they look over their old home and remember the drowned man. Punctuate each line of dialogue correctly.

Assessment Practice

Analyzing an Author's Meaning and Style

Many standardized tests require students to read literary passages and identify the author's meaning or style.

Use this example from "The Handsomest Drowned Man in the World" to demonstrate:

. . . they noticed that the vegetation on him came from faraway oceans and deep water and that his clothes were in tatters, as if he had sailed through labyrinths of coral.

(For more practice, see *Test Preparation Workbook,* p. 55.)

Why does the author include that the vegetation came from faraway oceans and deep water?

A to emphasize the realism of the situation

B to appeal to readers interested in sea life

C to appeal to sensory perceptions

D to emphasize the foreignness of the body

D is supported by the detail about the vegetation and reflects the author's intent.

❸ Writing Lesson

Timed Writing: Essay Tracing the Development of a Character

In García Márquez's masterful story, the drowned man undergoes a surprising transformation from a less-than-human thing into a fully realized character. Write an essay in which you describe how the author achieves this unlikely feat of characterization. *(40 minutes)*

Prewriting
(10 minutes)
As you reread the story, collect details about the drowned man that appear in the beginning, middle, and end. Identify points at which the drowned man's character takes on new shades of personality and identity.

Drafting
(20 minutes)
Write an introduction that describes the subject of the essay and includes a statement expressing your main idea. Then, in your body paragraphs, follow the chronology of the story to present your insights.

Model: Using Transitions to Clarify Order of Events

At the beginning of the story, the children treat the

body as a toy. Then, the village men carry the body

to town. There, the women clean and care for the

body and make an amazing discovery—they realize

that this is not a typical drowned man but a hero.

> Transitions like *at the beginning* and *then* help readers follow the order of events.

Revising
(10 minutes)
Reread your essay, making sure that you have clearly shown the development of the drowned man's character. Consider adding transitional words and phrases to clarify the logical flow of your ideas.

W_G Prentice Hall Writing and Grammar Connection: Platinum Level, Chapter 10, Section 4

❹ Extend Your Learning

Listening and Speaking Storytellers often use ideas from their listeners when they spin stories. Follow García Márquez's model by creating and delivering an **interactive story** of your own.

- Begin by describing characters, a setting, and a conflict.
- At key moments, pause and ask for suggestions from your audience.

Continue telling your story until the conflict is resolved. **[Group Activity]**

Research and Technology Using old magazines or the Internet, collect both large and small images that evoke the emotions and details in "The Handsomest Drowned Man in the World." Then, create a **collage** that represents Esteban's story. Present your final work to the class.

Go Online
Research
For: An additional research activity
Visit: www.PHSchool.com
Web Code: etd-7901

The Handsomest Drowned Man in the World ■ 1213

Assessment Resources

The following resources can be used to assess students' knowledge and skills.

Unit 9 Resources
Selection Test A, pp. 18–20
Selection Test B, pp. 21–23

General Resources
Rubrics for Response to Literature, pp. 55–56
Rubric for Speaking: Narrative Account, p. 88

Go Online
Assessment
Students may use the **Self-test** to prepare for **Selection Test A** or **Selection Test B**.

---

❸ Writing Lesson

You may use this Writing Lesson as timed-writing practice, or you may allow students to develop the essay as a writing assignment over several days.

- To give students guidance for writing this essay, give them the **Support for Writing Lesson**, p. 15 in *Unit 9 Resources.*

- Tell students that their essays should explain how García Márquez develops the title character of "The Handsomest Drowned Man in the World" from a waterlogged body into the fully realized character of Esteban.

- Tell students to examine the author's style choices—word choice, punctuation, juxtaposition of images, and sensory language—to determine how he creates this transformation.

- Use the Response to Literature rubrics in *General Resources*, pp. 55–56, to evaluate students' work.

W_G Writing and Grammar Platinum Level
For support in teaching the Writing Lesson, use Chapter 10, Section 4.

❹ Listening and Speaking

- Tell students that their interactive stories should be stories told out loud that incorporate suggestions from the audience into the plot.

- Explain to students that they should have key elements of the story—setting, major characters, conflict—planned in advance.

- Use the Speaking: Narrative Account rubric in *General Resources*, p. 88, to evaluate students' work.

- The **Support for Extend Your Learning** page (*Unit 9 Resources*, p. 16) provides guided note-taking opportunities to help students complete the Extend Your Learning activities.

Go Online
Research
Have students type in the Web Code for another research activity.

IR.2.03.2	Prioritize and organize information to construct an explanation to answer a question.
FA.3.04.6	Make inferences and draw conclusions based on argumentative text.
LT.5.01.2	Build knowledge of literary genres, and exploring how characteristics apply to literature of world cultures.

Background

Solzhenitsyn's World Literature

The writings of Alexander Solzhenitsyn celebrate the concept of world literature, and depend on it in very concrete ways. Between the mid-1960s and late 1989, when the Soviet Union collapsed, Solzhenitsyn's works were banned in the Soviet Union and could be published only in foreign nations. The writer himself was eventually forced to leave the Soviet Union after being tried in 1974 for treason. As a resident of Switzerland, Solzhenitsyn was finally able to receive the Nobel Prize.

Background

Goethe's World Literature

"I am more and more convinced," Goethe said in 1827, "that poetry is the universal possession of mankind.... National literature is now a rather unmeaning term; the epoch of world literature is at hand. . . ." And indeed, Goethe's notion of *Weltliteratur* both recognized and helped catalyze a broadening cultural and literary perspective among people of the modern world. For Goethe, the sharing of literature among nations had both social and philosophical implications. He hoped, on the one hand, that it would further civilization by encouraging respect and understanding among peoples; on the other hand, he believed it would help human beings accommodate the divisive polarities of reason and passion, heart and mind, and stability and change.

A Closer Look

I, Witness

In 1970, Alexander Solzhenitsyn, whose writing testified to the tyranny of the government of the Soviet Union, wrote a Nobel Prize acceptance speech called "The One Great Heart." In his speech, the author declared that "world literature is no longer an abstraction or a generalized concept invented by literary critics, but a common body and common spirit, a living, heartfelt unity reflecting the growing spiritual unity of mankind." More and more, Solzhenitsyn believed, readers and writers in even remote countries were connecting with people around the globe through literature. Where once there was sporadic communication, now there is dialogue and community.

New World Literature The concept of world literature is not new. In fact, the German writer Goethe used the phrase some 200 years ago. However, not until the twentieth century did two essential factors—decolonization and globalization—make the concept of world literature a reality. With decolonization, former colonies declared independence from colonial powers. As decolonization occurred, new forms of literature arose that emphasized the voices of former colonial subjects who had traditionally been ignored or silenced.

With globalization, new technologies such as television, the movies, the Internet, and rapid forms of travel have made the disparate cultures of the world increasingly accessible. The cultural cross-pollination that enriches our lives today allows new literary voices to spread far beyond their original geographical borders. For example, the Antiguan writer Jamaica Kincaid is lauded for her autobiographical novels about a girl growing up on a Caribbean island and leaving home for the United States.

❝ *Some of the most powerful works of literature bear witness for those who can no longer speak.* **❞**

Witnesses to History Although the twentieth century ushered in a glorious parade of technological innovations, it also saw bloodshed on an unprecedented scale. Writers from all over the world have borne witness to these evils. From the battlefields of World War I came the frank, anguished voices of young poets turned soldiers, many of whom were killed in the conflict. Their work did not glorify the bloody battles, nor did it flinch from representing the human cost of the first truly modern war. Following World War II, European writers like Primo Levi, an Italian Jewish chemist who survived Auschwitz, and Paul Celan, a Romanian Jewish poet whose parents were deported and killed, documented the destruction of Europe's Jews at the hands of the Nazis.

Enrichment

Globalization

Although technologies such as the Internet, satellite television, and rapid travel have exposed people to new cultures and ideas, some social scientists worry that globalization will yield not a richer world, but a flatter, more homogenous one—one in which most people think the same thoughts, eat the same foods, and wear the same clothes. Other experts dismiss as extreme the idea of a single world culture. They point to local experiences and customs that thrive despite the ubiquity of American fast food chains and media, claiming that the overwhelming majority of people do not belong to a disconnected global culture, as many have mistakenly asserted.

One thing sociologists do agree on, though, is that globalization is still in its early stages—and that no one can predict with certainty what the "global village" of the future will look like.

Subjectivity and Truth Perhaps we look to writers to bear witness because they have the power to convey deeply emotional truths that fact can only suggest. Some of the most powerful works of literature bear witness for those who can no longer speak. When we read Elie Wiesel's account of his father's death in a concentration camp and his own survival, we are reminded of the millions murdered by the Nazis, 9 million who took their stories to the grave. Reading the Misty Poets, we think of the Chinese writers who have been imprisoned or killed for criticizing the Communist government.

Italian Landscape, Ben Shahn © Estate of Ben Shahn/Licensed by VAGA, New York, NY

Somewhere Somebody is Writing Because good writers tell the truth even when it is unwelcome, many of them are forced to write in secret or in exile. At this very moment, someone may be scribbling forbidden words that tell the truth of his or her experience. Some writers risk their lives to share what they have witnessed. The words of writers like Vaclav Havel in Czechoslovakia and Leopold Sedar Senghor in Senegal carry such weight that the authors are chosen for political leadership, enabling them to embody the ideas they express. Wherever it is written, wherever it is read, world literature serves to remind us of our common humanity; in its pages, we hear the steady beat of "One Great Heart."

▲ **Critical Viewing**
How can literature help refugees like those depicted in this painting? **[Synthesize]**

Activity

Witness to the Twenty-first Century

In the twentieth century, new forms of literature gave voice to the victim and empowered the powerless. As the twenty-first century begins, such literature remains vitally important as people around the globe continue to suffer from violence and repression.

With a group, discuss what situations might inspire or generate writing that bears witness in the twenty-first century. Use these questions to guide your discussion:

- What conflicts in the world today deserve their own literature? Who should write it?
- What can literature tell us about war and repression that news and government reports cannot?
- Besides victims of war, what other victims deserve a voice in today's literature?

Choose a point person to share your ideas with the class.

I, Witness ■ 1215

Standard Course of Study

Goal 1: WRITTEN LANGUAGE

WL.1.01.1 Produce reminiscences that use specific and sensory details with purpose.

Goal 4: CRITICAL THINKING

CT.4.01.2 Reflect on and show how a real-world event affects viewpoint.

CT.4.05.9 Analyze and evaluate the effects of craft and style in critical text.

Goal 5: LITERATURE

LT.5.03.1 Select and modify reading strategies appropriate to reader's purpose.

Goal 6: GRAMMAR AND USAGE

GU.6.02.1 Edit for agreement, tense choice, pronouns, antecedents, case, and complete sentences.

Step-by-Step Teaching Guide	Pacing Guide
PRETEACH	
• Administer Vocabulary and Reading Warm-ups as necessary.	5 min.
• Engage students' interest with the motivation activity.	5 min.
• Read and discuss author, background, and From the Author's Desk features. **FT**	10 min.
• Introduce the Literary Analysis Skill: Point of View. **FT**	5 min.
• Introduce the Reading Strategy: Understanding Spatial Relationships. **FT**	
• Prepare students to read by teaching the selection vocabulary. **FT**	10 min.
TEACH	
• Informally monitor comprehension while students read independently or in groups. **FT**	30 min.
• Monitor students' comprehension with the Reading Check notes.	as students read
• Reinforce vocabulary with Vocabulary Builder notes.	as students read
• Develop students' understanding of point of view with the Literary Analysis annotations. **FT**	5 min.
• Develop students' ability to understand spatial relationships with the Reading Strategy annotations. **FT**	5 min.
ASSESS/EXTEND	
• Assess students' comprehension and mastery of the Literary Analysis and Reading Strategy by having them answer the Apply the Skills questions. **FT**	15 min.
• Have students complete the Vocabulary Lesson and the Grammar and Style Lesson. **FT**	15 min.
• Apply students' ability to brainstorm for details by using the Writing Lesson. **FT**	45 min. or homework
• Apply students' understanding by using one or more of the Extend Your Learning activities.	20–90 min. or homework
• Administer Selection Test A or Selection Test B. **FT**	15 min.

Resources

Print

Unit 9 Resources

Transparency

Graphic Organizer Transparencies

Technology

From the Author's Desk DVD . . . . Jamaica Kincaid, Segment 2

Print

Reader's Notebook [L2]
Reader's Notebook: Adapted Version [L1]
Reader's Notebook: English Learner's Version [EL]

Unit 9 Resources

Technology

Listening to Literature Audio CDs [L2, EL]
Reader's Notebook: Adapted Version Audio CD [L1, L2]

Print

Unit 9 Resources

General Resources

Technology

Go Online: Research [L3]
Go Online: Self-test [L3]
***ExamView®*, Test Bank [L3]**

Choosing Resources for Differentiated Instruction

[L1] Special Needs Students

[L2] Below-Level Students

[L3] All Students

[L4] Advanced Students

[EL] English Learners

For Vocabulary and Reading Warm-ups and for Selection Tests, **A** signifies "less challenging" and **B** "more challenging." For Graphic Organizer transparencies, **A** signifies "not filled in" and **B** "filled in."

FT Fast Track Instruction: To move the lesson more quickly, use the strategies and activities identified with **FT**.

Scaffolding for Less Proficient and Advanced Students

The leveled Critical Thinking questions after selections progress in the levels of thinking required to answer them. To address the needs of your different students, you may use the (a) level questions for your less proficient students and the (b) level questions with your on-level and advanced students. The occasional (c) level questions are appropriate for your advanced students.

PRENTICE HALL

TeacherEXPRESS™ Use this complete
Plan · Teach · Assess suite of powerful teaching tools to make lesson planning and testing quicker and easier.

PRENTICE HALL

StudentEXPRESS™ Use the interactive
Learn · Study · Succeed textbook (online and on CD-ROM) to make selections and activities come alive with audio and video support and interactive questions.

Go Online **For:** Information about Lexiles
Professional **Visit:** www.PHSchool.com
Development **Web Code:** eue-1111

Jamaica Kincaid

- You might wish to have students reread Jamaica Kincaid's introduction to the unit on pages 1188–1189.

- Show Segment 2 on Jamaica Kincaid on *From the Author's Desk DVD* to provide insight into Jamaica Kincaid's novel *Annie John*. After students have watched the segment, **ask:** Upon what was *Annie John* based?
Answer: *Annie John* was based on Kincaid's experiences of growing up and on her relationships with her mother and with the British Empire.

The Influence of Autobiography

- After students have read Kincaid's comments on these pages, explain that children very often learn their early memories from the stories that older relatives narrate, as in the case of Jamaica Kincaid. Invite students to tell how they learned some of their early memories from others.

- **Ask** students to explain the parallels between one's mother and the term "mother country."
Possible response: A mother gives birth to her children, and a mother country is the country in which people are born or from which they originate.

- **Ask** students why peoples' youthful years might exercise a great influence on what they write later in life.
Possible response: Youthful experiences shape peoples' identities and the ways in which they view the world. Therefore, these experiences may have a great impact on what they write later.

Critical Viewing

Answer: Annie John might hesitate to leave such an island nation because it is so beautiful and warm; it is what many would consider paradise.

JAMAICA KINCAID INTRODUCES
from Annie John: A Walk to the Jetty

Making Memories and Stories

I come from a small island in the Caribbean that was part of the British Empire until the early 1970s when it gained political independence. Everyone I knew was literate and everyone I knew told stories.

My mother, in particular, not only knew how to read, she did so for sheer pleasure. At the time, she was the only person I ever saw do this, sit and read just for the sake of reading.

She also told me stories but these stories were not folk tales or stories about revered ancestors; they were stories about what she was like as a child, what her mother and father did, what had happened to her before I was born, what the world into which I was born was like before I was born, what the day was like when I took my first steps, the first words I said, the things I liked to eat. I was too young then to make proper memories for myself and so the memories I have of that time are the memories she created for me.

It was at that time, the time before I could make my own memories, that she taught me to read. I believe now that this set of circumstances, my mother telling me stories and teaching me to read, led to my own obsession with literature and writing and especially writing about her.

The Influence of Autobiography

"A Walk to the Jetty" is the final chapter in a novel called *Annie John*. The novel traces the life of a girl growing up on an island in the Caribbean, her ups and downs with the many people in her world; especially it focuses on her relationship with her mother.

It is a work of fiction made up entirely of my own autobiography. It also holds in it the seeds of all that I would later write. Annie's mother could be said to represent the Mother Country, England, and her turbulent relationship with the mother is not unlike my own turbulent relationship with England, whose language, English, is the only language I know how to speak.

As Annie walks towards the jetty, saying goodbye to the familiar and solid world she has so confidently known, the suspicion grows that the future, the world she has so longed to be part of, is much like the sea towards which she is heading: endless and strange horizons, bottomless depths.

Jamaica Kincaid

Jamaica Kincaid won the Morton Dauwen Zabel Award for *At the Bottom of the River* (1983) and she was a finalist for the PEN Faulkner Award for *The Autobiography of My Mother* (1995). Kincaid's stories often focus on the development of relationships between women, especially between mothers and daughters.

1216 ■ *The Contemporary World*

Teaching Resources

The following resources can be used to enrich or extend the instruction for From the Author's Desk.

Unit 9 Resources
　　Support for Penguin Essay, p. 24
　　Listening and Viewing, p. 25

From the Author's Desk DVD
　　Jamaica Kincaid, Segment 2

Thinking About the Commentary

1. (a) Recall: What kind of stories did Kincaid's mother tell her as a child?
(b) Analyze Cause and Effect: In what way might these stories have influenced Kincaid's writing? **(c) Interpret:** What might Kincaid mean when she writes that "[*Annie John*] is a work of fiction made up entirely of my own autobiography"?

2. (a) Recall: According to Kincaid, what does Annie's mother represent in *Annie John*? **(b) Interpret:** Based on Kincaid's essay, who might the character of Annie represent?

As You Read "A Walk to the Jetty" from *Annie John* . . .

3. Note similarities between the life Kincaid describes in this essay and the details in "A Walk to the Jetty."

4. Identify moments that might be fictionalized pieces of Kincaid's experiences, and consider why Kincaid chose to fictionalize them.

5. Look for details of the mother/daughter relationship in "A Walk to the Jetty" that represent Kincaid's feelings about the British Empire.

▲ Critical Viewing
For what reasons might Annie John hesitate to leave an island nation like the one pictured here? **[Speculate]**

From the Author's Desk: Jamaica Kincaid ■ 1217

Motivation

Tell students that they will be reading a story about a dramatic event that establishes a young woman's independence in the adult world. Invite students to share some of the ways they have asserted their own identity and independence as they have grown toward adulthood.

❶ Background

More About the Author

Jamaica Kincaid first appeared in the pages of *The New Yorker* as a subject rather than a contributor. Her friend George W. S. Trow sometimes quoted her in the short nonfiction pieces about life in New York City that he wrote for the magazine. One day, Kincaid went to a West Indian carnival with Trow. Afterward, she wrote her impressions of the carnival and gave the notes to Trow. He passed them on to William Shawn, the legendary editor of *The New Yorker*, who published the notes without editing them at all. According to Kincaid, this appreciation of her writing changed her life forever. "When I saw it [the magazine piece], and it was just what I had put on paper, that is when I realized what my writing was. My writing was the thing that I thought. Not something else. Just what I thought."

Geography Note

Draw students' attention to the map on this page. Antigua won its independence from England in 1981. Until then, Antigua was a British colony, so many Antiguans have grown up speaking English, using British currency, and playing British games such as cricket.

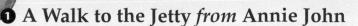
❶ A Walk to the Jetty *from* Annie John

Jamaica Kincaid
(b. 1949)

"I've never really written about anyone except myself and my mother," says author Jamaica Kincaid. Drawn from her childhood experiences on the Caribbean island of Antigua, Kincaid's fiction explores the complex relationship between mother and daughter and the ways in which it changes, sometimes painfully, during a daughter's passage into adulthood.

Rural Childhood Jamaica Kincaid was born Elaine Potter Richardson on May 25, 1949, in St. John's, Antigua. Like most rural Antiguans, Kincaid grew up in a home without electricity or running water. Nonetheless, her early childhood was happy, primarily because of the deep connection she felt to her mother. That attachment changed, however, when Kincaid was nine years old and the first of her three younger brothers was born. The writer was devastated by this threat to a mother's love that she perceived as hers alone.

Salvation in Books Kincaid was highly intelligent, but her intellectual gifts went largely unrecognized by her teachers. Today, she attributes this oversight to the colonial system under which she grew up. At the time, Antigua was a British dependency. It became an independent nation in 1981. Racism and economic oppression ensured that expectations for young black women remained low. In the face of indifference both at home and at school, Kincaid retreated into the world of books, where she discovered a passion that was missing in other areas of her life. One of her favorite novels was Charlotte Brontë's *Jane Eyre*.

Struggle for Education By the time she was a teenager, Kincaid was determined to leave Antigua. At the age of sixteen, she secured a job as a nanny for a wealthy family living in a New York City suburb. From that position she moved on to a series of unskilled jobs and later to an unsuccessful attempt at getting a college degree. Despite educational and career setbacks, Kincaid made a number of connections in the New York City publishing world, and by the early 1970s she was publishing articles in several magazines for teens.

Hard-Won Success Eventually, Kincaid became a staff writer for *The New Yorker*, in which many of her stories first appeared. In 1983, she published *At the Bottom of the River*, a collection of short stories. While its imaginative metaphors seemed too obscure to some reviewers, others praised the book's lyrical prose and keen insights. Kincaid admits that the stories in the collection may be difficult to grasp; in writing them, she says she sometimes fell into a kind of hallucinatory state. Her later works demonstrate a more traditional narrative style.

Fictionalizing Her Life Kincaid's critically acclaimed novels *Annie John* (1985) and *Lucy* (1990) are both clearly autobiographical. *Annie John* relates the experiences of a young girl growing up on a Caribbean island. "A Walk to the Jetty," in which Annie leaves her childhood home—and, by inference, her childhood self—serves as the book's final scene. *Lucy* picks up the same story by relating the tale of a young Caribbean girl who travels to the United States to take a job caring for the children of a wealthy American couple. Both books are classic Jamaica Kincaid, rich in memories and charged with emotional intensity.

Preview

Connecting to the Literature

If you have ever made a big change, such as moving across the country or even to another town, you will understand how the main character in this story feels. As Annie John prepares to leave her childhood home, she follows a road of bittersweet memories.

❷ Literary Analysis

Point of View

All works of fiction are related by a narrator who speaks from a distinct perspective, or **point of view.** Most stories are told from either a first-person or one of two types of third-person point of view. These are defined by the narrator's relationship to the action and by his or her knowledge of other characters' thoughts and feelings. This story is told from the first-person point of view, which has the following characteristics:

- The narrator is a character who is involved in the story.
- The narrator uses the pronouns "I," "we," "me," "our," and "us."

Point of view controls the information the reader receives. For example, the first-person point of view allows Annie John to share her thoughts and feelings, but it prevents other characters from doing the same. As you read, notice the ways in which the point of view shapes your understanding of the story.

Connecting Literary Elements

The first-person point of view lends itself to the use of **flashback**—a section of a literary work that relates an incident from the past. Flashbacks may take the form of dreams, memories, stories, or actual shifts in time. As you read, identify the details that spark Annie John's flashbacks, and notice the ways in which her memories suggest reasons for her decision to leave the island.

❸ Reading Strategy

Understanding Spatial Relationships

As Annie John walks to the jetty, landmarks along the way trigger her memories. In order to better appreciate Annie John's experience, it is helpful to **understand spatial relationships**—the arrangement of physical features within a setting. As you read, use a chart like the one shown to gain a clear picture of Annie John's walk.

Vocabulary Builder

jetty (jet′ ē) *n.* wall or barrier built into a body of water to protect a harbor (p. 1221)

loomed (lo͞omd) *v.* appeared in a large or threatening form (p. 1221)

wharf (wôrf) *n.* structure built as a landing place for boats (p. 1225)

scorn (skôrn) *n.* contempt; open dislike or derision (p. 1225)

stupor (sto͞op′ ər) *n.* mental dullness, as if drugged (p. 1226)

cue (kyo͞o) *n.* prompt or reminder (p. 1226)

 Standard Course of Study

- Produce reminiscences that use specific and sensory details with purpose. (WL.1.01.1)
- Select and modify reading strategies appropriate to reader's purpose. (LT.5.03.1)

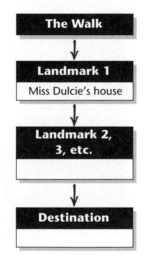

A Walk to the Jetty from *Annie John* ■ 1219

❷ Literary Analysis
Point of View

- Remind students that the narrator, or person who tells a story, has a specific point of view, or perspective.
- On the board, rewrite the first five sentences of the selection in the third person. Suggest that students use a Venn diagram to compare and contrast the point of view of the original version with that of the new version.

❸ Reading Strategy
Understanding Spatial Relationships

- Explain that settings are likely to affect characters in a work of literature. Remind students that a setting includes the arrangement of physical objects as well as time and geography.
- Tell students that creating charts or diagrams can help them envision a setting. Point out the graphic organizer that begins to note the landmarks that Annie passes on her walk to the jetty.
- Give students a copy of the **Reading Strategy Graphic Organizer A,** p. 205 in *Graphic Organizer Transparencies.* As they read, have students use it to record landmarks that help them envision the setting.

Vocabulary Builder

- Pronounce each vocabulary word for students, and read the definitions as a class. Have students identify any words with which they are already familiar.

1219

Facilitate Understanding

Prepare students for the selection by having them draw maps of their neighborhoods and then asking them to annotate their maps with reminiscences.

❶ About the Selection

Fear, excitement, nostalgia, resentment, confusion—this autobiographical story captures all the emotions a young adult feels when taking the first steps toward independence. For Annie John, the emotions associated with leaving home are complicated by her conflicted relationship with her mother and her island home, as well as her need to rise above the low expectations for girls in her culture.

❷ Humanities

Vista II by Hughie Lee-Smith

Of his generation, Hughie Lee-Smith was considered one of the most important painters of African American subjects. Born in 1915 in Eustis, Florida, he studied in Cleveland, Ohio, and graduated from the Cleveland School of Art in 1938. He tried to include art in everything he did during his life and is known especially for drawing attention to social issues.

Use the following question for discussion:

What sensory details might Annie John describe if she were the girl in the painting?
Possible response: She might describe the smell of the water, the warmth of the sun, the coolness of the wind, and the sounds of the sea life around her.

❸ Critical Viewing

Possible response: The woman in this picture seems to be waiting because she is not dressed for travel, and she does not have a bag or a suitcase with her.

❶ A Walk to the Jetty
from Annie John
Jamaica Kincaid

Background At the beginning of *Annie John*, the novel from which "A Walk to the Jetty" is excerpted, Annie John is a happy ten-year-old. She loves both her parents, but she is especially close to her mother. However, when Annie is almost twelve, her mother's affections mysteriously sour. In front of Annie's father, "We were politeness and kindness and love and laughter." Alone, the enmity between the two deepens. When she is sixteen years old, Annie John decides to move to England. The final section of the novel, "A Walk to the Jetty" begins as she prepares to leave the island of her childhood.

❸ ▼ **Critical Viewing**
Does the woman in this painting seem to be departing, like the narrator in the story, or does she seem to be waiting? Explain. **[Make a Judgment]**

Vista II, 1987, Hughie Lee-Smith, Art © Estate of Hughie Lee-Smith/Licensed by VAGA, New York, NY

1220 ■ *The Contemporary World*

Differentiated Instruction   Solutions for All Learners

Accessibility at a Glance

	A Walk to the Jetty *from* Annie John
Context	A 16-year-old's departure for England from her Caribbean island home
Language	First-person narration with words of emotional force
Concept Level	Accessible (The rite of passage may be difficult but is necessary to move on to a new life and new experiences.)
Literary Merit	A narrative that effectively captures the emotional conflicts an adolescent feels when approaching independence
Lexile	1290L
Overall Rating	More accessible

My mother had arranged with a stevedore[1] to take my trunk to the <u>jetty</u> ahead of me. At ten o'clock on the dot, I was dressed, and we set off for the jetty. An hour after that, I would board a launch that would take me out to sea, where I then would board the ship. Starting out, as if for old time's sake and without giving it a thought, we lined up in the old way: I walking between my mother and my father. I <u>loomed</u> way above my father and could see the top of his head. We must have made a strange sight: a grown girl all dressed up in the middle of a morning, in the middle of the week, walking in step in the middle between her two parents, for people we didn't know stared at us. It was all of half an hour's walk from our house to the jetty, but I was passing through most of the years of my life. We passed by the house where Miss Dulcie, the seamstress that I had been apprenticed to for a time, lived, and just as I was passing by, a wave of bad feeling for her came over me, because I suddenly remembered that the months I spent with her all she had me do was sweep the floor, which was always full of threads and pins and needles, and I never seemed to sweep it clean enough to please her. Then she would send me to the store to buy buttons or thread, though I was only allowed to do this if I was given a sample of the button or thread, and then she would find fault even though they were an exact match of the samples she had given me. And all the while she said to me, "A girl like you will never learn to sew properly, you know." At the time, I don't suppose I minded it, because it was customary to treat the first-year apprentice with such scorn, but now I placed on the dustheap of my life Miss Dulcie and everything that I had had to do with her.

We were soon on the road that I had taken to school, to church, to Sunday school, to choir practice, to Brownie meetings, to Girl Guide meetings, to meet a friend. I was five years old when I first walked on this road unaccompanied by someone to hold my hand. My mother had placed three pennies in my little basket, which was a duplicate of her bigger basket, and sent me to the chemist's shop to buy a pennyworth of senna leaves, a pennyworth of eucalyptus leaves, and a pennyworth of camphor.[2] She then instructed me on what side of the road to walk, where to make a turn, where to cross, how to look carefully before I crossed, and if I met anyone that I knew to politely pass greetings and keep on my way. I was wearing a freshly ironed yellow dress that had printed on it scenes of acrobats flying through the air and swinging on a trapeze. I had just had a bath, and after it, instead of powdering me with my baby-smelling talcum powder, my mother had, as a special favor, let me use her own talcum powder, which smelled quite perfumy and came in a can that had painted on it people going out to dinner in nineteenth-century London and was called Mazie. How it pleased me to walk out the door and bend my head down to sniff at myself and see

---

1. **stevedore** (stē′ və dôr) *n.* person whose job is the loading and unloading of ships.
2. **chemist's shop . . . camphor** (kam′ fər) *chemist's shop* is the British term for *pharmacy*; the items mentioned are small amounts of plant matter that are used in remedies.

Reading Check **6**

Why is the narrator going to the jetty?

A Walk to the Jetty ■ 1221

---

that I smelled just like my mother. I went to the chemist's shop, and he had to come from behind the counter and bend down to hear what it was that I wanted to buy, my voice was so little and timid then. I went back just the way I had come, and when I walked into the yard and presented my basket with its three packages to my mother, her eyes filled with tears and she swooped me up and held me high in the air and said that I was wonderful and good and that there would never be anybody better. If I had just conquered Persia, she couldn't have been more proud of me.

We passed by our church—the church in which I had been christened and received[3] and had sung in the junior choir. We passed by a house in which a girl I used to like and was sure I couldn't live without had lived. Once, when she had mumps, I went to visit her against my mother's wishes, and we sat on her bed and ate the cure of roasted, buttered sweet potatoes that had been placed on her swollen jaws, held there by a piece of white cloth. I don't know how, but my mother found out about it, and I don't know how, but she put an end to our friendship. Shortly after, the girl moved with her family across the sea to somewhere else. We passed the doll store, where I would go with my mother when I was little and point out the doll I wanted that year for Christmas. We passed the store where I bought the much-fought-over shoes I wore to church to be received in. We passed the bank. On my sixth birthday, I was given, among other things, the present of a sixpence.[4] My mother and I then went to this bank, and with the sixpence I opened my own savings account. I was given a little gray book with my name in big letters on it, and in the balance column it said "6d." Every Saturday morning after that, I was given a sixpence—later a shilling, and later a two-and-sixpence piece—and I would take it to the bank for deposit. I had never been allowed to withdraw even a farthing from my bank account until just a few weeks before I was to leave; then the whole account was closed out, and I received from the bank the sum of six pounds ten shillings and two and a half pence.

We passed the office of the doctor who told my mother three times that I did not need glasses, that if my eyes were feeling weak a glass of carrot juice a day would make them strong again. This happened when I was eight. And so every day at recess I would run to my school gate and meet my mother, who was waiting for me with a glass of juice from carrots she had just grated and then squeezed, and I would drink it and then run back to meet my chums. I knew there was nothing at all

---

3. **received** v. accepted into the congregation as a mature Christian.
4. **sixpence** n. former monetary unit in the British commonwealth, worth six pennies (about 12 U.S. cents). A shilling was worth two sixpence, a two-and-sixpence was two and one-half shillings (two shillings and one sixpence), a pound was twenty shillings, and a farthing was a "fourthing": one fourth of a penny.

San Antonio de Oriente, Collection of the Art Museum of the Americas. Organization of American States

wrong with my eyes, but I had recently read a story in *The Schoolgirl's Own Annual* in which the heroine, a girl a few years older than I was then, cut such a figure to my mind with the way she was always adjusting her small, round, horn-rimmed glasses that I felt I must have a pair exactly like them. When it became clear that I didn't need glasses, I began to complain about the glare of the sun being too much for my eyes, and I walked around with my hands shielding them—especially in my mother's presence. My mother then bought for me a pair of sunglasses with the exact horn-rimmed frames I wanted, and how I enjoyed the gestures of blowing on the lenses, wiping them with the hem of my uniform, adjusting the glasses when they slipped down my nose, and just removing them from their case and putting them on. In three weeks, I grew tired of them and they found a nice resting place in a drawer, along with some other things that at one time or another I couldn't live without.

We passed the store that sold only grooming aids, all imported from England. This store had in it a large porcelain dog—white, with black spots all over and a red ribbon of satin tied around its neck. The dog sat in front of a white porcelain bowl that was always filled with fresh water, and it sat in such a way that it looked as if it had just taken a long drink. When I was a small child, I would ask my mother, if ever we were near this store, to please take me to see the dog, and I would stand in front of it, bent over slightly, my hands resting on my knees, and stare at it and stare at it. I thought this dog more beautiful and more real than any actual dog I had ever seen or any actual dog I would ever see. I must have outgrown my interest in the dog, for when it disappeared I never asked what became of it. We passed the library, and if there was anything on this walk that I might have wept over leaving, this most surely would have been the thing. My mother had been a member of the library long before I was born. And since she took me everywhere with her when I was quite little, when she went to the library she took me along there, too. I would sit in her lap very quietly as she read books that she did not want to take home with her. I could not read the words yet, but just the way they looked on the page was interesting to me. Once, a book she was reading had a large picture of a man in it, and when I asked her who he was she told me that he was Louis Pasteur[5] and that the book was about his life. It stuck in my mind, because she said it was because of him that she boiled my milk to purify it before I was allowed to drink it, that it was his idea, and that that was why the process was called pasteurization. One of the things I had put away in my mother's old trunk in which she kept all my childhood things was my library card. At that moment, I owed sevenpence in overdue fees.

5. **Louis Pasteur** (pas tʉr´) French chemist and bacteriologist (1822–1895) who developed pasteurization, the process for using heat to kill disease-causing bacteria in milk.

Literary Analysis
Point of View In what ways does the first-person point of view allow the narrator to share specific private thoughts and feelings?

Jamaica Kincaid
Author's Insight
I think of hair lotion, shaving cream, and other such things as meant to make someone think themselves beautiful when used.

✓**Reading Check**
Which landmark from her childhood does the narrator almost weep over leaving?

A Walk to the Jetty ■ 1223

---

⑪ Literary Analysis
Point of View
- Remind students that a first-person narrator can share only his or her thoughts and feelings.
- **Ask** students the Literary Analysis question: In what ways does the first-person point of view allow the narrator to share specific private thoughts and feelings?
  Possible response: A first-person narrator is capable of relaying events and his or her thoughts and feelings about these events. Additionally, a first-person narrator can leap across time within a particular event to give the event depth.

▶**Monitor Progress Ask** students to record any statements that show the narrator's point of view about her mother.
  Possible response: Although she reports several instances when her mother was very nurturing, she also says ". . . but she put an end to our friendship." This suggests a certain bitterness about her mother.

▶**Reteach** To assist students who are having trouble with first-person point of view, have them use the **Literary Analysis** support, p. 30 in *Unit 9 Resources.*

⑫ Author's Insight
- Point out Kincaid's comment about toiletries and to the fact that Annie describes the items in this store as being untouchable.
- **Ask:** Why do you think Kincaid includes the detail that all of the bathing products were imported from England?
  Answer: Annie is on her way to England and may view England as being more sophisticated. England may represent that which is opposite of what she knows.

⑬ Critical Thinking
Infer
- Read aloud the bracketed sentence.
- **Ask:** Why is the library such an important part of Annie's childhood?
  Possible response: It might have been important to Annie because it was important to her mother and because the books allowed Annie a wider view of the world outside her island home.

⑭ Reading Check
Answer: Annie almost weeps over leaving the library.

1223

Humanities Connection

The Landscape and Climate of Antigua A drought is a longer than average time with very little or no rainfall that persists long enough to cause crop damage, water supply shortages, and other serious problems. Even two or three weeks without rain can be damaging to an area like Antigua that depends, in part, on crop production for its economy.

Connect to the Literature Point out that American and European tourists have often been accused of insensitivity to the rampant poverty that plagues many natives of the Caribbean islands. Note how it must feel to be working at a public market hoping to sell your products, only to see a mass of tourists descend from a ship and hurry by without a glance because they are eager to reach a luxurious hotel and beach. Ask students how they think Annie John feels as she leaves home.

Possible response: Clearly, she has very mixed feelings and alarm that she will never again see the hot sun, blue sea, white sand, houses cluttered on the beach, and beautiful blue sky.

16 Reading Strategy

Understanding Spatial Relationships

- Remind students that a character's emotional state often mirrors the setting of the story.

- Ask students whether they have ever felt anxious during a storm or felt content while sitting beneath a tree on a warm day.

- **Ask** students the Reading Strategy question: What is the connection between Annie's physical location and her emotions?

Possible response: Annie has an old fear of slipping between the boards of the jetty into the dark-green water. The emotions Annie associates with this setting are mirrored in her feelings about leaving home. She is suddenly frightened about exchanging the familiar people and surroundings of her childhood for the unknown.

As I passed by all these places, it was as if I were in a dream, for I didn't notice the people coming and going in and out of them, I didn't feel my feet touch ground, I didn't even feel my own body—I just saw these places as if they were hanging in the air, not having top or bottom, and as if I had gone in and out of them all in the same moment. The sun was bright; the sky was blue and just above my head. We then arrived at the jetty.

My heart now beat fast, and no matter how hard I tried, I couldn't keep my mouth from falling open and my nostrils from spreading to the ends of my face. My old fear of slipping between the boards of the jetty and falling into the dark-green water where the dark-green eels lived came over me. When my father's stomach started to go bad, the doctor had recommended a walk every evening right after he ate his dinner. Sometimes he would take me with him. When he took me with him, we usually went to the jetty, and there he would sit and talk to the night watchman about cricket[6] or some other thing that didn't interest me, because it was not personal; they didn't talk about their wives, or their children, or their parents, or about any of their likes and dislikes. They talked about things in such a strange way, and I didn't see what they found funny, but sometimes they made each other laugh so much that their guffaws would bound out to sea and send back an echo. I was always sorry when we got to the jetty and saw that the night watchman on duty was the one he enjoyed speaking to; it was like being locked up in a book filled with numbers and diagrams and what-ifs. For the thing about not being able to understand and enjoy what they were saying was I had nothing to take my mind off my fear of slipping in between the boards of the jetty.

Now, too, I had nothing to take my mind off what was happening to me. My mother and my father—I was leaving them forever. My home on an island—I was leaving it forever. What to make of everything? I felt a familiar hollow space inside. I felt I was being held down against my will. I felt I was burning up from head to toe. I felt that someone was tearing me up into little pieces and soon I would be able to see all the little pieces as they floated out into nothing in the deep blue sea. I didn't know whether to laugh or cry. I could see that it would be better not to think too clearly about any one thing. The launch was being made ready to take me, along with some other passengers, out to the ship that was anchored in the sea. My father paid our fares, and we joined a line of people waiting to board. My mother checked my bag to make sure that I had my passport, the money she had given me, and a

---

6. **cricket** *n.* British game, similar to baseball but played with a flat bat and eleven players on each team.

15 Humanities Connection

The Landscape and Climate of Antigua

White sand beaches, spectacular coral reefs, and an average temperature of 80 degrees make Antigua a popular vacation spot. There are 365 beaches on Antigua—one for each day of the year! The island is approximately 14 miles long and 11 miles wide, covering 108 square miles. With an average rainfall of only 40 inches per year, the island is one of the sunniest in the eastern Caribbean. While the steady supply of sunshine is a pleasure for tourists, the constant threat of drought can be devastating to the property and livelihoods of native Antiguans.

Connect to the Literature

Describe what you think the narrator's feelings are as she leaves such a beautiful place.

Reading Strategy
Understanding Spatial Relationships What is the connection between Annie's physical location and her emotions?

Enrichment

British English

Students may be unfamiliar with such Anglicisms as *chemist* (druggist or pharmacist), *cricket* (a game with some resemblance to baseball), and *sixpence* (a unit of money).

There are differences in pronunciation and vocabulary between British and American English. Viewing language as a process explains these differences. Three factors influence language development: inheritance, innovation, and isolation.

First, people acquire language from the society in which they are raised and from exposure to other languages. Second, new inventions and activities give rise to new words. Finally, geographical features like mountains or rivers separate people, so languages may develop differently.

sheet of paper placed between some pages in my Bible on which were written the names of the relatives—people I had not known existed—with whom I would live in England. Across from the jetty was a <u>wharf</u>, and some stevedores were loading and unloading barges. I don't know why seeing that struck me so, but suddenly a wave of strong feeling came over me, and my heart swelled with a great gladness as the words "I shall never see this again" spilled out inside me. But then, just as quickly, my heart shriveled up and the words "I shall never see this again" stabbed at me. I don't know what stopped me from falling in a heap at my parents' feet.

When we were all on board, the launch headed out to sea. Away from the jetty, the water became the customary blue, and the launch left a wide path in it that looked like a road. I passed by sounds and smells that were so familiar that I had long ago stopped paying any attention to them. But now here they were, and the ever-present "I shall never see this again" bobbed up and down inside me. There was the sound of the sea-gull diving down into the water and coming up with something silverish in its mouth. There was the smell of the sea and the sight of small pieces of rubbish floating around in it. There were boats filled with fishermen coming in early. There was the sound of their voices as they shouted greetings to each other. There was the hot sun, there was the blue sea, there was the blue sky. Not very far away, there was the white sand of the shore, with the run-down houses all crowded in next to each other, for in some places only poor people lived near the shore. I was seated in the launch between my parents, and when I realized that I was gripping their hands tightly I glanced quickly to see if they were looking at me with <u>scorn</u>, for I felt sure that they must have known of my never-see-this-again feelings. But instead my father kissed me on the forehead and my mother kissed me on the mouth, and they both gave over their hands to me, so that I could grip them as much as I wanted. I was on the verge of feeling that it had all been a mistake, but I remembered that I wasn't a child anymore, and that now when I made up my mind about something I had to see it through. At that moment, we came to the ship, and that was that.

The goodbyes had to be quick, the captain said. My mother introduced herself to him and then introduced me. She told him to keep an eye on me, for I had never gone this far away from home on my own. She gave him a letter to pass on to the captain of the next ship that I would board in Barbados.[7] They walked me to my cabin, a small space that I would share with someone else—a woman I did not know. I had never before slept in a room with someone I did not know. My father kissed me goodbye and told me to be good and to write home often. After he said this, he looked at me, then looked at the floor and

---

7. **Barbados** (bär bā´ dōs) easternmost island in the West Indies, southeast of Antigua.

Vocabulary Builder
wharf (wôrf) *n.* structure built as a landing place for boats
scorn (skôrn) *n.* contempt; open dislike or derision

Jamaica Kincaid
Author's Insight
A launch was a little motorized boat meant to ferry passengers back and forth from the large ships to the jetty. At the time, the harbor was too shallow to accommodate big passenger ships.

⓴ ▼ Critical Viewing In what ways does this painting of a ship express the kinds of emotions the narrator experiences as she leaves her home? **[Connect]**

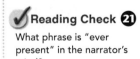

✓ Reading Check ㉑
What phrase is "ever present" in the narrator's mind?

A Walk to the Jetty ■ 1225

⓱ Critical Thinking
Interpret
• Ask a volunteer to read aloud the bracketed passage.
• Then, **ask** students why the words "I shall never see this again" first cause Annie's heart to swell with gladness and then shrivel up.
Possible response: She has mixed emotions about leaving the people and places she knows. She longs for wider experience and opportunities, but she loves much of her past and fears her uncertain future.

⓲ Author's Insight
• Have students read the Author's Insight.
• Point out that Annie notices the water left behind the launch looks like a road. **Ask:** What part do roads play in Annie's remembrance of her youth?
Answer: Annie recalls memories of her youth as she and her parents walk down the road to the jetty. The water left in the wake of the launch looks like a road, and Annie recalls youthful memories related to the sea.

⓳ Critical Thinking
Analyze
• Read aloud the second bracketed passage.
• **Ask** students how Annie's parents surprise her on the launch.
Answer: Annie expects them to note her weakness, but instead they kiss her and offer their hands to her.
• Encourage students to **explain** what this scene suggests about Annie's relationship with her parents.
Possible response: Annie discovers how much her parents love her and how much she depends on them.

⓴ Critical Viewing
Answer: The huge ship is overwhelming, and Annie feels overwhelmed by the idea of leaving home.

㉑ Reading Check
Answer: Annie keeps thinking, "I shall never see this again."

Differentiated
Instruction   **Solutions for All Learners**

Support for Special Needs Students
Students might benefit from working with flash cards that stimulate them to experience flashbacks. Prepare flashcards with the following prompts: *When I was a baby, . . . , The first thing I remember is. . . , Before I started school, . . . , and Last summer, I. . .* Hold up a card, and encourage each student to share or describe in his or her journal a memory prompted by the card.

Enrichment for Gifted/Talented Students
Students may enjoy thinking about how this story could be adapted into a play or movie format. Because so much of the "action" takes place inside the narrator's head, challenge students to think of ways they can *show* an audience what Annie is thinking and feeling. Ask students to rewrite this story as a play. Remind them to pay special attention to creating a setting and including physical details that will convey the emotions evoked in the story.

1225

The Latin Root -stup-

- Draw students' attention to the word *stupor,* and read its definition. Tell students that the word derives from the Latin root *-stup-,* meaning "stunned or amazed."

- **Ask:** How does understanding the root of the word *stupor* enhance your understanding of Annie's feelings about leaving?
Possible response: The root *-stup-* means "stunned or amazed." Annie is literally on the border between childhood and adulthood. This passage generates in her a feeling of stunned amazement. She does not feel like the girl she used to be, and she has not yet become comfortable in the skin of the woman she will become.

ASSESS

Answers

1. **Possible response:** Annie John is admirable for overcoming her fear and for seeking her own identity and independence.

2. (a) **Possible response:** Annie John passes Miss Dulcie's store, the library, the chemist's shop, and the church. (b) She relives formative events as she walks past the landmarks of her town.

3. (a) She experiences the old fear of slipping between the boards of the jetty, falling into the water, and being eaten by eels. (b) **Possible response:** Annie is afraid of losing herself in the unknown world she is about to enter.

4. (a) She compares the sound of the waves with the sound of liquid flowing from a vessel turned on its side. (b) **Possible response:** Annie is emptying herself of all her previous experiences and becoming an empty vessel ready for a new life and new experiences.

5. **Possible response:** Yes; although fate will play a role in Annie's future, her determination and curiosity should serve her well in her new life.

---

swung his left foot, then looked at me again. I could see that he wanted to say something else, something that he had never said to me before, but then he just turned and walked away. My mother said, "Well," and then she threw her arms around me. Big tears streamed down her face, and it must have been that—for I could not bear to see my mother cry—which started me crying, too. She then tightened her arms around me and held me to her close, so that I felt that I couldn't breathe. With that, my tears dried up and I was suddenly on my guard. "What does she want now?" I said to myself. Still holding me close to her, she said, in a voice that raked across my skin, "It doesn't matter what you do or where you go, I'll always be your mother and this will always be your home."

㉒ I dragged myself away from her and backed off a little, and then I shook myself, as if to wake myself out of a <u>stupor</u>. We looked at each other for a long time with smiles on our faces, but I know the opposite of that was in my heart. As if responding to some invisible <u>cue</u>, we both said, at the very same moment, "Well." Then my mother turned around and walked out the cabin door. I stood there for I don't know how long, and then I remembered that it was customary to stand on deck and wave to your relatives who were returning to shore. From the deck, I could not see my father, but I could see my mother facing the ship, her eyes searching to pick me out. I removed from my bag a red cotton handkerchief that she had earlier given me for this purpose, and I waved it wildly in the air. Recognizing me immediately, she waved back just as wildly, and we continued to do this until she became just a dot in the matchbox-size launch swallowed up in the big blue sea.

I went back to my cabin and lay down on my berth. Everything trembled as if it had a spring at its very center. I could hear the small waves lap-lapping around the ship. They made an unexpected sound, as if a vessel filled with liquid had been placed on its side and now was slowly emptying out.

Critical Reading

1. **Respond:** Do you admire Annie John? Why or why not?

2. (a) **Recall:** Identify four places that Annie John passes.
   (b) **Interpret:** In what ways is Annie John walking through time as well as through space?

3. (a) **Recall:** As Annie John approaches the jetty, what old feeling does she experience? (b) **Analyze:** Why does she experience this feeling as she prepares to leave the island?

4. (a) **Recall:** In the story's final image, to what does Annie John compare the sound of the waves? (b) **Analyze:** In what ways does this image mirror her emotional state? Explain.

5. **Speculate:** Do you think Annie John will be successful in her new life? Why or why not?

Vocabulary Builder
stupor (stoo̅p´ ər) *n.* mental dullness, as if drugged

cue (kyoo̅) *n.* prompt or reminder

Go Online
Author Link
For: More about Jamaica Kincaid
Visit: www.PHSchool.com
Web Code: ete-9902

Go Online For additional information about
Author Link Jamaica Kincaid, have students type
in the Web Code, then select *K* from the alphabet,
and then select Jamaica Kincaid.

Apply the Skills

A Walk to the Jetty from *Annie John*

Literary Analysis

Point of View

1. Which elements of the text show that "A Walk to the Jetty" is narrated from the first-person **point of view**? Explain.
2. **(a)** Cite three passages in the text in which you learn something about Annie John's parents. **(b)** What do you learn? **(c)** In what specific ways does the first-person point of view limit information about characters other than the narrator?
3. Why might the first-person point of view generate more sympathy for the narrator than would another point of view?

Connecting Literary Elements

4. Each **flashback** in this excerpt is triggered as Annie John passes a familiar place. Use a chart like the one shown to analyze four of her flashbacks.

Place	Triggered Memory	What We Learn

5. What information do the flashbacks provide about Annie John's reasons for leaving home?

Reading Strategy

Understanding Spatial Relationships

6. **(a)** Describe the ways in which the **spatial relationships** between Annie John and her parents change as they begin their journey, travel on the launch, board the ship, and say goodbye. **(b)** In what ways do their spatial relationships express their emotional relationships?
7. In what ways does Annie John's physical journey relate to her emotional journey?

Extend Understanding

8. **Social Studies Connection:** While not a formal ceremony, Annie John's departure from home is a rite of passage—an event signifying that a child has become an adult. What rites of passage exist in American culture?

A Walk to the Jetty from *Annie John* ■ 1227

QuickReview

Point of view is the perspective from which a story is told. With a **first-person** point of view, a story is told by a narrator who is part of the action and uses the pronouns "I," "me," "we," "our," and "us."
A **flashback** is a section of a literary work that interrupts the sequence of events to relate an incident from the past.

To **understand spatial relationships** as you read, pay attention to details that describe the physical arrangements of elements in a setting.

Go Online
Assessment
For: Self-test
Visit: www.PHSchool.com
Web Code: eta-6902

Answers

1. **Possible response:** The narrator uses pronouns like "my," and "I."
2. **(a) Possible response:** The reader learns about Annie's parents in the following flashbacks: Annie's mother sending her to run errands, the passage about the carrot juice and the sunglasses, and the moment in which her father seems about to tell her something and then does not. **(b)** The first passage explains that Annie is happy to do things that make her mother happy. The second passage shows that when Annie really wants something, her mother makes sacrifices so that Annie can have it. The description of Annie saying goodbye to her father shows that they care deeply about each other, even if their feelings are unspoken. **(c)** Readers get no insight into Annie's parents' thoughts; they are presented with only Annie's interpretation of characters and events.
3. **Possible response:** Readers are more likely to sympathize with the character through whose eyes they see the events of the narrative.
4. **Possible response: Place:** shoe store; church **Triggered Memory:** fighting with her mother over shoes; her christening and the choir **What We Learn:** Sometimes Annie wins arguments with her mother; Annie has been raised as a Christian.
   Another sample answer can be found on **Literary Analysis Graphic Organizer B**, p. 208 in *Graphic Organizer Transparencies.*
5. **Possible response:** They suggest that she feels limited by the people and circumstances of her childhood home.
6. **(a)** Annie begins her journey walking between her parents; when they reach the jetty, the physical arrangement changes so that she moves away from them. **(b) Possible response:** At first, the mother and father surround Annie, but in the end, she moves beyond their protection.
7. **Possible response:** Annie revisits her childhood as she walks past the physical landmarks; then, she leaves both the memories and the landmarks behind. Fittingly, on the ship, she feels empty.

Answers continued

8. **Possible response:** A bar or bat mitzvah, getting a job, attending a prom, obtaining a driver's license, or graduating from school are American rites of passage.

Go Online Students may use the **Self-test** to **Assessment** prepare for **Selection Test A** or **Selection Test B.**

❶ Vocabulary Lesson

Word Analysis: Latin Root -stup-

1. b   2. c   3. a

Spelling Strategy

1. curiosity   3. vacuum
2. occupant   4. concur

Vocabulary Builder: Analogies

1. scorn   4. stupor
2. cue   5. loomed
3. jetty   6. wharf

❷ Grammar and Style Lesson

1. "which reminded her of her mother"; modifies *store*
2. "whose chores involved sweeping"; modifies *Annie*
3. "that they had traveled many times before"; modifies *road*
4. "who often talked with her father"; modifies *watchman*
5. "that lapped against the boat"; modifies *waves*

Writing Application

Possible response:

Annie walked down the road <u>that she used to get to church and school</u>. Annie thought about the store <u>that sold only imported grooming aids</u>.

Writing and Grammar Platinum Level

For support in teaching the Grammar and Style Lesson, use Chapter 20, Section 2.

Build Language Skills

❶ Vocabulary Lesson

Word Analysis: Latin Root -stup-

The word *stupor* contains the Latin root *-stup-*, which means "stunned or amazed." Use the meaning of this root to match each numbered word to its synonym.

1. stupefy   a. bewilderment
2. stupendous   b. numb
3. stupefaction   c. astonishing

Spelling Strategy

In most English words, when a *c* comes before the vowel *u*, it has a *k* sound, as in the word *cue*. In some words, the *c* before a *u* is doubled. Correctly complete the spelling of each word below with letters representing the *k* sound.

1. ___uriosity   3. va___uum
2. o___upant   4. con___ur

❷ Grammar and Style Lesson

Adjective Clauses

An **adjective clause** is a type of subordinate clause—one that contains a subject and a verb but cannot stand alone as a sentence. Adjective clauses modify nouns or pronouns and are introduced with relative pronouns, such as *who* or *whom, whose, which,* or *that.*

> **Example:**
>
> We were soon on the road *that* I had taken to school . . . (*modifies road*)
>
> My mother had placed three pennies in my little basket, *which* was a duplicate of her bigger basket . . . (*modifies basket*)

Prentice Hall Writing and Grammar Connection: Platinum Level, Chapter 20, Section 2

Vocabulary Builder: Analogies

Analogies present words in pairs to emphasize their relationships. Common links include synonym, antonym, degree of intensity, and part to whole. For each numbered item below, study the relationship presented in the first pair. Then, use the vocabulary words on page 1219 to complete word pairs that express the same relationship.

1. *Strength* is to *weakness* as __?__ is to *admiration.*
2. *Advice* is to *guidance* as __?__ is to *prompt.*
3. *Bumper* is to *automobile* as __?__ is to *harbor.*
4. *Frenzy* is to *calmness* as __?__ is to *lucidity.*
5. *Encouraged* is to *supported* as __?__ is to *threatened.*
6. *Hangar* is to *airplane* as __?__ is to *boat.*

Practice Identify the adjective clause and the word it modifies in each of the following sentences.

1. Annie walked past the store, which reminded her of her mother.
2. Miss Dulcie did not respect Annie, whose chores included sweeping.
3. The family walked down the road that they had traveled many times before.
4. Annie remembered the watchman who often talked with her father.
5. The waves that lapped against the boat made a sad sound.

Writing Application Write a paragraph to describe Annie's memories on the day she leaves home. Include one adjective clause in each sentence.

Assessment Practice

Analyzing an Author's Meaning and Style

Use the following sample test item to demonstrate an author's meaning and style:

> I went back to my cabin and lay down on my berth. Everything trembled as if it had a spring at its very center. I could hear the small waves lap-lapping around the ship. They made an unexpected sound, as if a vessel filled with liquid had been placed on its side and now was slowly emptying out.

(For more practice, see *Test Preparation Workbook,* p. 57.)

Why does Kincaid choose to use the word *berth* instead of a synonym like *bunk?*

A *Berth* is a homophone for *birth.*
B The words *berth* and *back* create alliteration.
C Kincaid's writing style is extremely formal.
D Annie wants to sound like an adult.

A is the correct answer. There are many references to birth in the passage: Annie's body position, trembling, water, and emptying out.

❸ Writing Lesson

A Reminiscence

Imagine that you are walking through a familiar landscape, such as your neighborhood, a shopping mall, or your school. Write a reminiscence—a narrative that relates events from the past—in which memories are triggered by elements of the setting. You may write as yourself or as a fictional character.

Prewriting Brainstorm for memories and sensory details—elements that relate to the senses—by using a cluster diagram like the one shown. Try to identify larger themes or ideas that the memories capture.

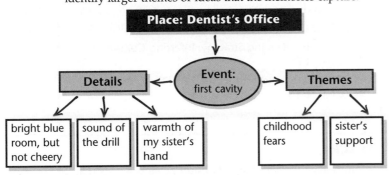

Drafting Begin by describing the purpose of your journey. Then, use the landscape itself to order the narrative. Describe each place you pass, and explain the memory it triggers.

Revising As you review your writing, make sure that you have used vivid sensory details. Consider adding details to enliven your reminiscence.

WG Prentice Hall Writing and Grammar Connection: Platinum Level, Chapter 4, Section 2

Extend Your Learning

❹ Listening and Speaking Conduct a **discussion** about the benefits and challenges of traveling or schooling abroad. Use these tips to prepare:

- Invite someone in your school to speak to your class about travel or education in another country.
- Generate a list of questions in advance.

You may wish to take notes about the discussion and write a report or interview for your school newspaper. **[Group Activity]**

Research and Technology Using details from the text, create a **map** showing Annie's walk to the jetty. Include landmarks, illustrations, and other references to help make your map a vivid representation of Kincaid's narrative. Include a key so that viewers can connect the illustrations with the related site on Annie's journey.

For: An additional research activity
Visit: www.PHSchool.com
Web Code: etd-7902

A Walk to the Jetty from Annie John ■ 1229

Assessment Resources

The following resources can be used to assess students' knowledge and skills.

Unit 9 Resources
Selection Test A, pp. 37–39
Selection Test B, pp. 40–42

General Resources
Rubrics for Narration: Autobiographical
Narrative, pp. 43–44

Go **O**nline Students may use the **Self-test** to —Assessment prepare for **Selection Test A** or **Selection Test B**.

---

❸ Writing Lesson

You may use this Writing Lesson as timed-writing practice, or you may allow students to develop their reminiscences as a writing assignment over several days.

- To give students guidance in writing this reminiscence, give them the **Support for Writing Lesson**, p. 34 in *Unit 9 Resources.*

- Students may need help extracting themes from their memories. Use the following key questions to help students make the leap from literal to thematic thinking: What did you learn from this event? Why are your memories of this event so vivid? Why do you remember this event when other memories have slipped away? Did this event change you in some way? Did this event affect your worldview in some way?

- Use the Narration: Autobiographical Narrative rubrics in *General Resources,* pp. 43–44, to evaluate students' work.

WG **Writing and Grammar Platinum Level**
For support in teaching the Writing Lesson, use Chapter 4, Section 2.

❹ Listening and Speaking

- Help students research the school system in the country where the guest speaker was educated or the country in which the speaker has traveled.

- Tell students to use their research to write informed and insightful questions for the speaker in advance.

- The **Support for Extend Your Learning** page (*Unit 9 Resources,* p. 35) provides guided note-taking opportunities to help students complete the Extend Your Learning activities.

Go **O**nline Have students type in the —Research Web Code for another research activity.

Goal 3: FOUNDATIONS OF ARGUMENT

FA.3.01.5 Present data about controversial issues in multiple forms.

FA.3.03.3 Produce responses to literature that emphasize culturally significant events.

FA.3.04.7 Identify and analyze influences, contexts, or biases in argument.

Goal 5: LITERATURE

LT.5.01.7 Understand the cultural and historical impact on world literature texts.

LT.5.03.6 Make inferences, predictions, and draw conclusions based on world literature.

Step-by-Step Teaching Guide	Pacing Guide
PRETEACH • Administer Vocabulary and Reading Warm-ups as necessary.	5 min.
• Engage students' interest with the motivation activity.	5 min.
• Read and discuss author and background features. **FT**	10 min.
• Introduce the Literary Analysis Skill: Existentialism. **FT**	5 min.
• Introduce the Reading Strategy: Inferring Cultural Attitudes. **FT**	
• Prepare students to read by teaching the selection vocabulary. **FT**	10 min.
TEACH • Informally monitor comprehension while students read independently or in groups. **FT**	30 min.
• Monitor students' comprehension with the Reading Check notes.	as students read
• Reinforce vocabulary with Vocabulary Builder notes.	as students read
• Develop students' understanding of existentialism with the Literary Analysis annotations. **FT**	5 min.
• Develop students' ability to infer cultural attitudes with the Reading Strategy annotations. **FT**	5 min.
ASSESS/EXTEND • Assess students' comprehension and mastery of the Literary Analysis and Reading Strategy by having them answer the Apply the Skills questions. **FT**	15 min.
• Have students complete the Vocabulary Lesson and the Grammar and Style Lesson. **FT**	15 min.
• Apply students' ability to compare fiction to philosophy by using the Writing Lesson. **FT**	45 min. or homework
• Apply students' understanding by using one or more of the Extend Your Learning activities.	20–90 min. or homework
• Administer Selection Test A or Selection Test B. **FT**	15 min.

Resources

Print

Unit 9 Resources

Transparency

Graphic Organizer Transparencies

Print

Reader's Notebook [L2]

Reader's Notebook: Adapted Version [L1]

Reader's Notebook: English Learner's Version [EL]

Unit 9 Resources

Technology

Listening to Literature Audio CDs [L2, EL]

Print

Unit 9 Resources

General Resources

Technology

Go Online: Research [L3]

Go Online: Self-test [L3]

ExamView®, **Test Bank [L3]**

Choosing Resources for Differentiated Instruction

[L1] Special Needs Students

[L2] Below-Level Students

[L3] All Students

[L4] Advanced Students

[EL] English Learners

For Vocabulary and Reading Warm-ups and for Selection Tests, **A** signifies "less challenging" and **B** "more challenging." For Graphic Organizer transparencies, **A** signifies "not filled in" and **B** "filled in."

FT Fast Track Instruction: To move the lesson more quickly, use the strategies and activities identified with **FT**.

Scaffolding for Less Proficient and Advanced Students

The leveled Critical Thinking questions after selections progress in the levels of thinking required to answer them. To address the needs of your different students, you may use the (a) level questions for your less proficient students and the (b) level questions with your on-level and advanced students. The occasional (c) level questions are appropriate for your advanced students.

PRENTICE HALL

TeacherEXPRESS™ Use this complete
Plan · Teach · Assess   suite of powerful
teaching tools to make lesson planning and testing quicker and easier.

PRENTICE HALL

StudentEXPRESS™ Use the interactive
Learn · Study · Succeed   textbook (online
and on CD-ROM) to make selections and activities come alive with audio and video support and interactive questions.

Go Online For: Information about Lexiles
Professional Visit: www.PHSchool.com
Development Web Code: eue-1111

Motivation

Ask students to imagine the following situation: You move to a new neighborhood just as simmering disagreement has split neighbors into two hostile sides. As tensions rise and arguments become increasingly bitter, even violent, you struggle to keep your distance. Soon, however, your neighbors begin to look at you suspiciously and wonder which side you are on.

Tell students that the main character in "The Guest" is in a position like this. He is caught up, not in a neighborhood dispute, but in the beginnings of a fierce war, and his life may depend on the choices he makes.

❶ Background

More About the Author

During World War II, Albert Camus wrote unsigned editorials for a Parisian underground newspaper called *Combat*. Readers of these much-admired editorials did not know until after the liberation of Paris that their author was the man who wrote *The Stranger*. The following is an excerpt from an editorial Camus wrote as Allied and German troops fought in the streets of Paris:

> This huge Paris, all black and warm in the summer night, with a storm of bombers overhead and a storm of snipers in the streets, seems to us more brightly lighted than the City of Light the whole world used to envy us. It is bursting with all the fires of hope and suffering, it has the flame of lucid courage and all the glow, not only of liberation, but of tomorrow's liberty.

Geography Note

Draw students' attention to the map on this page. Point out the location of Algeria, Camus's birthplace, and tell students that the country contains large sections of the Sahara desert. Explain that in most of Algeria the heat of the sun is so intense that, during the middle of the day, people must wear clothes that cover most of their skin.

Build Skills *Short Story*

The Guest ❶

Albert Camus
(1913–1960)

When a now-famous Polish writer was an unknown student in Paris, he often wandered around the city at all hours. Late one night, he met a solitary man in a cheap café and the two shared a stimulating philosophical discussion. Only later, when he was home in bed, did he realize that he had been talking with the celebrated French author Albert Camus (ka mōō´). This remarkable anecdote illustrates several of Camus's most endearing qualities: his modesty, his searching intelligence, and his restless night-owl habits.

Early Hardship Camus was born in Mondovi, Algeria, to parents of European descent. His family was desperately poor and his mother was deaf. Camus's childhood became even more difficult when his father died in World War I.

Despite his poverty, Camus's intelligence shone; his teachers recognized his gifts and encouraged him in his studies. Although Camus had to work at odd jobs while attending the University of Algiers, he was an excellent scholar. In addition to his main studies in literature, he also helped found a small theater group that staged plays of interest to working-class people. Years later, when he wrote plays such as *Caligula* (1944), the drama of a Roman emperor who resembles modern dictators like Hitler and Mussolini, Camus drew on this early theatrical experience.

Tests of Integrity A man of strong moral principles, Camus sometimes suffered for his convictions. For instance, when he publicly criticized the French colonial government of Algiers, he was forced to leave the country. He emigrated to France, where he worked as an investigative reporter for a Parisian newspaper.

Camus's integrity was tested again when the Germans occupied France during World War II. At the risk of his life, Camus supported the French Resistance Movement by serving as the principal editor of *Combat*, an illegal newspaper. As an underground journalist, he won recognition for his independent views and the emphasis he placed on moral behavior.

First Important Works Despite the turmoil of World War II, Camus published two of his most influential works, the novel *The Stranger* (1942) and the essay "The Myth of Sisyphus" (1942), during the war years. The novel describes a man who realizes that conventional values are ultimately senseless and absurd—humans are uninvited guests in an indifferent universe. In 1947, Camus published another novel that deals with similar themes but in a more positive way. Set in the Algerian city of Oran, *The Plague* describes an epidemic that symbolizes both the German Occupation of France and all the other evils that beset humankind. In combating the plague, several of the characters learn the importance of honor and compassion.

Acknowledged as a major twentieth-century writer, Camus spent part of the late 1940s touring and lecturing in North and South America. On returning to Paris, he withdrew from public life and continued to produce essays and plays. In 1957, he received the Nobel Prize in Literature. Camus's death in an auto accident three years later cut short his brilliant career. However, in 1994, *The First Man*, a manuscript that had been found in the wreckage of his car, was published in France. English publication of the book followed in 1995. An autobiographical work-in-progress, the book reveals Camus in all his brilliance, modesty, and humanity.

Preview

Connecting to the Literature

If you have ever resisted pressure to do something you felt was wrong, you will understand how the main character in this story feels. Caught between hostile parties as a revolution begins, Daru stands alone.

❷ Literary Analysis

Existentialism

Existentialism is a philosophy that teaches the importance of personal choice, not universal codes, in creating values. The various forms of Existentialism agree on these essential points:

- The universe is indifferent and can provide no answers.
- Our lives matter because of our own actions, not because we are part of a greater plan.
- The individual has total freedom to choose and to act.
- Human life is inherently valuable; freedom is an end in itself.

Although Camus did not accept the label of Existentialist, he is widely regarded as one of its foremost literary practitioners. As you read this story, look for details that suggest an Existentialist outlook.

Connecting Literary Elements

The **setting** of a story is the time and place of the action. In many stories, the setting is merely a context, like a painted backdrop on a stage. Sometimes, however, the setting adds meaning. For example, in "The Guest," the stark, windswept vistas reflect the **theme**—the story's central message. As you read, think about how the setting and theme are intertwined.

❸ Reading Strategy

Inferring Cultural Attitudes

Cultural attitudes are the customs, values, and beliefs that are held by people living in a distinct place and time. In most literary works, the author does not spell out these attitudes. Instead, he or she provides details, such as dialogue, actions, and descriptions, that allow readers to infer cultural attitudes. As you read, use a chart like the one shown to identify details and to infer the cultural attitudes they express.

Vocabulary Builder

plateau (pla tō´) *n.* elevated tract of relatively level land (p. 1233)

siege (sēj) *n.* the surrounding of a fortified place by an opposing force, such as an army (p. 1234)

foretaste (fôr´ tāst´) *n.* slight experience or hint of something that is still to come (p. 1235)

mobilized (mō´ bə līzd´) *v.* ready for action or battle (p. 1237)

denounce (dē nouns´) *v.* accuse publicly (p. 1239)

fraternized (frat´ ər nīzd´) *v.* associated in a brotherly way; socialized (p. 1242)

furtive (fur´ tiv) *adj.* done in a secret or sneaky way (p. 1242)

NC Standard Course of Study

- Produce responses to literature that emphasize culturally significant events. (FA.3.03.3)
- Understand the cultural and historical impact on world literature texts. (LT.5.01.7)

Detail

Daru offers mint tea to the visitors.

↓

Cultural Attitude

Hospitality is important.

The Guest ■ 1231

❷ Literary Analysis

Existentialism

- Tell students that Existentialists recognize the absurdity of looking for meaning in an indifferent universe, yet they also believe that life is inherently valuable and that people are free to choose their own actions. Tell students that they will see evidence of the Existentialist viewpoint as they read this story.

- Read aloud the Literary Analysis instruction. Focus on the list of Existentialism's essential points. Remind students of the importance this philosophy places on individuals, not on larger constructs like society.

- As students read "The Guest," encourage them to consider how various elements of the story such as setting, plot, and characters present an Existentialist viewpoint.

❸ Reading Strategy

Inferring Cultural Attitudes

- Remind students that an inference is a logical assumption made by carefully considering evidence and one's previous experience.

- Tell students that readers find clues about the beliefs, values, and customs of characters by comparing them with other characters or by drawing on their own real-life experiences.

- Give students a copy of the **Reading Strategy Graphic Organizer A**, p. 209 in *Graphic Organizer Transparencies.* As they read, have students use it to record story details or descriptions that reveal cultural attitudes.

- Remind students that they will have to read between the lines to make inferences about cultural attitudes. Suggest that they try to assume a character's perspective in order to learn more about the culture of which the character is a part.

Vocabulary Builder

- Pronounce each vocabulary word for students, and read the definitions as a class. Have students identify any words with which they are already familiar.

Facilitate Understanding

Ask students to jot down questions as they read. Questions should relate to the action, setting, and theme of the story. For example: Will the Arab try to hurt Daru? Will the Arab escape? In such an isolated place, can anyone help the Arab, hurt Daru, or help Daru? Is it better for Daru to do what the authorities expect or for him to try to help the Arab?

❶ About the Selection

This short story resembles a parable on the futility of human action. In a time of growing conflict between French settlers and the colonized Algerians, a French schoolteacher named Daru struggles to act on his conscience in a time when brutality reigns and good intentions seem to count for very little.

❷ Humanities

Album de voyage: Spain, Morocco, Algeria, by Eugène Delacroix

The Romantic artists were interested in the natural world—in contrast to the sophisticated life of modern cities—and in the theme of a person's solitary position in the universe. Both of these concerns can be found in Camus's story. Encourage students to find these motifs in this painting.

Use the following question for discussion:

How would you describe the feelings this painting evokes?
Possible response: It evokes loneliness, peacefulness, and happiness in the midst of beauty, but it also evokes a sense of weariness during a long journey.

❸ Critical Viewing

Possible response: The vast landscape seems to hold no one but the man on horseback. An individual might feel alone in the vastness of the natural world.

❶ The Guest   Albert Camus

translated by Justin O'Brien

❷

Album de voyage: Spain, Morocco, Algeria, 1834, Eugène Delacroix, Musée Condé, Chantilly, France

❸ ▲ **Critical Viewing** What details of this image capture the isolation of the setting Camus describes? **[Connect]**

1232 ■ *The Contemporary World*

Differentiated Instruction   Solutions for All Learners

Accessibility at a Glance

	The Guest
Context	Algeria in 1954 during the war for independence from France
Language	Vivid adjectives build a setting and create strong, convincing characters.
Concept Level	Accessible (Choices have consequences for which we must take responsibility.)
Literary Merit	Moving tale that reflects Existential principles
Lexile	770L
Overall Rating	More challenging

Background

Background In 1954, a war for independence began in the North African country of Algeria, which had been a colony of France since 1848. More than a century of colonialism had created a deeply divided society with a wealthy European elite, a small European working class, and a large Muslim majority that was mostly poor. The independence struggle began with terrorist attacks on police posts by a radical Muslim group, the National Liberation Front (FLN). As the revolt spread, the French military retaliated with severe reprisals. The early stages of the rebellion provide the historical context for this story.

❹

❺

The schoolmaster was watching the two men climb toward him. One was on horseback, the other on foot. They had not yet tackled the abrupt rise leading to the schoolhouse built on the hillside. They were toiling onward, making slow progress in the snow, among the stones, on the vast expanse of the high, deserted <u>plateau</u>. From time to time the horse stumbled. Without hearing anything yet, he could see the breath issuing from the horse's nostrils. One of the men, at least, knew the region. They were following the trail although it had disappeared days ago under a layer of dirty white snow. The schoolmaster calculated that it would take them half an hour to get onto the hill. It was cold; he went back into the school to get a sweater.

Literary Analysis
Existentialism; Setting and Theme Why might this setting be appropriate in a story expressing Existentialist views?

Vocabulary Builder
plateau (pla tō´) *n.* elevated tract of relatively level land

**Reading Check** ❻
Why is the trail to the schoolhouse difficult for the men to follow?

The Guest ■ 1233

---

❼ Literary Analysis

Existentialism

- Have a volunteer read aloud the bracketed passage. **Ask** students to paraphrase its meaning.
  Possible response: Daru is better off now than during the three-day snowstorm because he no longer has to stay in his room when he is not feeding the chickens or getting coal. He had received supplies shortly before the storm and expects another delivery in two days.

- **Ask** students the Literary Analysis question: In what ways does the description of Daru's circumstances during the blizzard reflect Existentialist ideas?
  Possible response: Daru is alone and at the mercy of nature, which is indifferent to his plight. Still, he makes meaningful choices, such as feeding the chickens and burning coal to stay warm.

❽ Reading Strategy

Inferring Cultural Attitudes

- Have students read the bracketed passage and then **find** phrases that apply to poverty and the land the poor population tries to cultivate and phrases that apply to Daru.
  Possible response: Phrases that apply to poverty and the land include "ragged ghosts," "plateaus burned to a cinder," "earth shriveled up," "literally scorched," and "sheep had died." Phrases that apply to Daru include "satisfied with the little he had," "felt like a lord," "white-washed walls," "narrow couch," "unpainted shelves," "his well," and "weekly provision of water and food."

- **Ask** students the Reading Strategy question: What cultural attitudes toward wealth are suggested by this discussion of drought and poverty?
  Possible response: Wealth is associated with a comfortable dwelling and a detachment from the difficulties of the terrain and weather. The administration trusts the wealthy to store and distribute their rations to the poor; the wealthy are expected to cooperate.

He crossed the empty, frigid classroom. On the blackboard the four rivers of France, drawn with four different colored chalks, had been flowing toward their estuaries for the past three days. Snow had suddenly fallen in mid-October after eight months of drought without the transition of rain, and the twenty pupils, more or less, who lived in the villages scattered over the plateau had stopped coming. With fair weather they would return. Daru now heated only the single room that was his lodging, adjoining the classroom and giving also onto the plateau to the east. Like the class windows, his window looked to the south too. On that side the school was a few kilometers[1] from the point where the plateau began to slope toward the south. In clear weather could be seen the purple mass of the mountain range where the gap opened onto the desert.

Somewhat warmed, Daru returned to the window from which he had first seen the two men. They were no longer visible. Hence they must have tackled the rise. The sky was not so dark, for the snow had stopped falling during the night. The morning had opened with a dirty light which had scarcely become brighter as the ceiling of clouds lifted. At two in the afternoon it seemed as if the day were merely beginning. But still this was better than those three days when the thick snow was falling amidst unbroken darkness with little gusts of wind that rattled the double door of the classroom. Then Daru had spent long hours in his room, leaving it only to go to the shed and feed the chickens or get some coal. Fortunately the delivery truck from Tadjid,[2] the nearest village to the north, had brought his supplies two days before the blizzard. It would return in forty-eight hours.

Besides, he had enough to resist a <u>siege</u>, for the little room was cluttered with bags of wheat that the administration left as a stock to distribute to those of his pupils whose families had suffered from the drought. Actually they had all been victims because they were all poor. Every day Daru would distribute a ration to the children. They had missed it, he knew, during these bad days. Possibly one of the fathers or big brothers would come this afternoon and he could supply them with grain. It was just a matter of carrying them over to the next harvest. Now shiploads of wheat were arriving from France and the worst was over. But it would be hard to forget that poverty, that army of ragged ghosts wandering in the sunlight, the plateaus burned to a cinder month after month, the earth shriveled up little by little, literally scorched, every stone bursting into dust under one's foot. The sheep had died then by thousands and even a few men, here and there, sometimes without anyone's knowing.

In contrast with such poverty, he who lived almost like a monk in his remote schoolhouse, nonetheless satisfied with the little he had and with the rough life, had felt like a lord with his white-washed walls, his

---

---

1. **kilometers** (kil′ ə mēt′ ərz) *n.* measures of distance, each of which is equal to 1,000 meters, or about five eighths of a mile.
2. **Tadjid** (tä jēd′)

narrow couch, his unpainted shelves, his well, and his weekly provision of water and food. And suddenly this snow, without warning, without the foretaste of rain. This is the way the region was, cruel to live in, even without men—who didn't help matters either. But Daru had been born here. Everywhere else, he felt exiled.

He stepped out onto the terrace in front of the schoolhouse. The two men were now halfway up the slope. He recognized the horseman as Balducci, the old gendarme[3] he had known for a long time. Balducci was holding on the end of a rope an Arab who was walking behind him with hands bound and head lowered. The gendarme waved a greeting to which Daru did not reply, lost as he was in contemplation of the Arab dressed in a faded blue jellaba,[4] his feet in sandals but covered with socks of heavy raw wool, his head surmounted by a narrow, short chèche.[5] They were approaching. Balducci was holding back his horse in order not to hurt the Arab, and the group was advancing slowly.

Within earshot, Balducci shouted: "One hour to do the three kilometers from El Ameur!"[6] Daru did not answer. Short and square in his thick sweater, he watched them climb. Not once had the Arab raised his head. "Hello," said Daru when they got up onto the terrace. "Come in and warm up." Balducci painfully got down from his horse without letting go the rope. From under his bristling mustache he smiled at the schoolmaster. His little dark eyes, deep-set under a tanned forehead,

---

3. **gendarme** (zhän därm´) *n.* French police officer.
4. **jellaba** (je lä´ be) *n.* roomy, capelike outer garment worn in the Middle East.
5. *chèche* (shesh) *n.* cloth wrap worn as headware, common in rural Algeria.
6. **El Ameur** (el äm yoor´)

Arab at the Door of His House, Eugène Delacroix, Rijksmuseum, Amsterdam

The Guest ■ 1235

Vocabulary Builder
foretaste (fôr´ tāst´) *n.* slight experience or hint of something that is still to come

Reading Strategy
Inferring Cultural Attitudes
What can you infer about Daru based on his interest in the Arab's clothing?

✓ **Reading Check**
Who are the two men who approach Daru's schoolhouse?

◀ **Critical Viewing**
How is this dwelling similar to or different from your image of Daru's schoolhouse? **[Compare and Contrast]**

---

⑨ Vocabulary Builder
Anglo-Saxon Prefix *fore*-
- Draw students' attention to the word *foretaste.* Tell students that the Anglo-Saxon prefix *fore*- means "before in time, place, order, or rank."
- Have students **suggest** other words with the prefix *fore*-.
  Answer: Words with the prefix *fore*- include *forearm, forebode,* and *forecast.*

⑩ Reading Strategy
Inferring Cultural Attitudes
- Read aloud the bracketed sentence, and **ask** students to use their own words to describe the Arab.
  Answer: The Arab is wearing a faded blue robe, heavy socks with sandals, and a head wrap.
- **Ask** students the Reading Strategy question: What can you infer about Daru based on his interest in the Arab's clothing?
  Answer: Daru is trying to figure out the relationship between the two men. The Arab's clothing indicates to Daru the man's social standing. Daru can also determine that the Arab is a native of the area, whereas the gendarme is not.

⑪ Reading Check
Answer: The two men are an old French police officer named Balducci and an unnamed Arab.

⑫ Humanities
Arab at the Door of His House,
by Eugène Delacroix

A major influence on Eugène Delacroix's work was an 1832 trip to North Africa. Like other Romantics, he found vitality in the natural world and the cultures of non-Europeans.

Use this question for discussion:
Why would a painter from Paris in the 1830s paint this picture?
Possible response: He might have wanted to show his viewers an unusual, exotic scene.

⑬ Critical Viewing
Possible response: The dwelling is similar to Daru's schoolhouse in that it is simple, spare, and modest.

Differentiated
Instruction Solutions for All Learners

Strategy for Special Needs Students
Have students use the Internet or library sources to research traditional clothing worn by people in North Africa. Have students create a list of reasons such garments might be better suited for life in North Africa than typical western clothes.

Strategy for English Learners
Draw students' attention to this passage: "But Daru had been born here. Everywhere else, he felt exiled." Explain the meaning of the word *exiled,* and ask students whether they have a similar attachment to their birthplaces or whether it is easy or difficult to live there. Ask volunteers to discuss the possible reasons for Daru's feelings toward Algeria, such as having family nearby or being part of the culture.

⑭ Humanities

The Ear of Grain (L'espiga de blat),
by Joan Miró

Joan Miró is best known as one of the foremost Surrealist painters of the twentieth century. This work, not typical of his mature style, is one of a series of severe still life paintings done in 1922 and 1923. After this series, his style changed quite abruptly and no longer included realistic and recognizable objects.

This painting shows a lidded pitcher, a strainer, and an ear of grain. The background is a plain table with no cloth. All the objects are painted realistically, if somewhat two-dimensionally, and suggest a clean and simple way of life.

Use the following question for discussion:

In what way does this painting remind you of the life led by Daru?
Answer: Daru's life, like the life suggested in the painting, is stark and simple with few luxuries.

⑮ Critical Viewing

Possible response: With its clean lines and careful rendering of details, the image conveys a feeling of simplicity. The table and the objects on it do not look worn out or poorly crafted, as they would if the painting conveyed a feeling of poverty.

⑯ Reading Strategy

Inferring Cultural Attitudes

- Have a pair of students read aloud the bracketed passage, with each taking a role of one of the characters and using appropriate intonations to express the character's emotions.

- **Ask** the Reading Strategy question: Based on Daru's response to Balducci's instruction, what inference can you draw about his attitudes toward authority? Explain.

Possible response: Daru apparently does not believe authority should be obeyed unquestioningly. He is compelled to question authority when told to do something that is not one of his duties or when he has an ethical argument against it.

---

and his mouth surrounded with wrinkles made him look attentive and studious. Daru took the bridle, led the horse to the shed, and came back to the two men, who were now waiting for him in the school. He led them into his room. "I am going to heat up the classroom," he said. "We'll be more comfortable there." When he entered the room again, Balducci was on the couch. He had undone the rope tying him to the Arab, who had squatted near the stove. His hands still bound, the *chèche* pushed back on his head, he was looking toward the window. At first Daru noticed only his huge lips, fat, smooth, almost Negroid; yet his nose was straight, his eyes were dark and full of fever. The *chèche* revealed an obstinate forehead and, under the weathered skin now rather discolored by the cold, the whole face had a restless and rebellious look that struck Daru when the Arab, turning his face toward him, looked him straight in the eyes. "Go into the other room," said the schoolmaster, "and I'll make you some mint tea." "Thanks," Balducci said. "What a chore! How I long for retirement." And addressing his prisoner in Arabic: "Come on, you." The Arab got up and, slowly, holding his bound wrists in front of him, went into the classroom.

With the tea, Daru brought a chair. But Balducci was already enthroned on the nearest pupil's desk and the Arab had squatted against the teacher's platform facing the stove, which stood between the desk and the window. When he held out the glass of tea to the prisoner, Daru hesitated at the sight of his bound hands. "He might perhaps be untied." "Sure," said Balducci. "That was for the trip." He started to get to his feet. But Daru, setting the glass on the floor, had knelt beside the Arab. Without saying anything, the Arab watched him with his feverish eyes. Once his hands were free, he rubbed his swollen wrists against each other, took the glass of tea, and sucked up the burning liquid in swift little sips.

"Good," said Daru. "And where are you headed?"

Balducci withdrew his mustache from the tea. "Here, son."

"Odd pupils! And you're spending the night?"

"No. I'm going back to El Ameur. And you will deliver this fellow to Tinguit.[7] He is expected at police headquarters."

⑯ Balducci was looking at Daru with a friendly little smile.

"What's this story?" asked the schoolmaster. "Are you pulling my leg?"

"No, son. Those are the orders."

"The orders? I'm not . . ." Daru hesitated, not wanting to hurt the old Corsican.[8] "I mean, that's not my job."

---

7. **Tinguit** (ting´ wēt)
8. **Corsican** (kôr´ si kən) native of Corsica, a Mediterranean island.

The Ear of Grain (L'espiga de blat), 1922–1923, Joan Miró

▲ Critical Viewing ⑮
Does this image convey a feeling of poverty, like that suffered by Daru's students, or merely a feeling of simplicity? Explain. **[Make a Judgment]**

Reading Strategy
Inferring Cultural Attitudes
Based on Daru's response to Balducci's instruction, what inference can you draw about his attitudes toward authority? Explain.

Enrichment

Arabic
Balducci speaks to the Arab prisoner in Arabic. This is a Semitic language spoken in most of the Arabian Peninsula and other parts of the Middle East and in North Africa. The language used in the *Qur'an* (the sacred book of Islam), it is used as the language of religion by all Muslims. Arabic sounds very different from languages that originated in Europe, including English. It has many guttural sounds and some consonants that are pronounced by constricting the pharynx and raising the back of the tongue. There are three vowels (*a, i,* and *u*), each of which has a short and a long sound. A single consonant followed by a vowel begins every Arabic word, and long vowels are almost always followed by a single consonant. The language does not have any sound made by more than two consonants. All Arabic words have two parts: the root and the pattern of vowels used with the root. The root is usually three consonants, and the pattern of vowels determines the specific meaning of the root.

"What! What's the meaning of that? In wartime people do all kinds of jobs."

"Then I'll wait for the declaration of war!"

Balducci nodded.

17 "O.K. But the orders exist and they concern you too. Things are brewing, it appears. There is talk of a forthcoming revolt. We are <u>mobilized</u>, in a way."

Daru still had his obstinate look.

"Listen, son," Balducci said. "I like you and you must understand. There's only a dozen of us at El Ameur to patrol throughout the whole territory of a small department[9] and I must get back in a hurry. I was told to hand this guy over to you and return without delay. He couldn't be kept there. His village was beginning to stir; they wanted to take him back. You must take him to Tinguit tomorrow before the day is over. Twenty kilometers shouldn't faze a husky fellow like you. After that, all will be over. You'll come back to your pupils and your comfortable life."

18 Behind the wall the horse could be heard snorting and pawing the earth. Daru was looking out the window. Decidedly, the weather was clearing and the light was increasing over the snowy plateau. When all the snow was melted, the sun would take over again and once more would burn the fields of stone. For days, still, the unchanging sky would shed its dry light on the solitary expanse where nothing had any connection with man.

"After all," he said, turning around toward Balducci, "what did he do?" And, before the gendarme had opened his mouth, he asked: "Does he speak French?"

"No, not a word. We had been looking for him for a month, but they were hiding him. He killed his cousin."

"Is he against us?"

"I don't think so. But you can never be sure."

"Why did he kill?"

"A family squabble, I think. One owed the other grain, it seems. It's not at all clear. In short, he killed his cousin with a billhook.[10] You know, like a sheep, *kreezk!*"

Balducci made the gesture of drawing a blade across his throat and the Arab, his attention attracted, watched him with a sort of anxiety. Daru felt a sudden wrath against the man, against all men with their rotten spite, their tireless hates, their blood lust.

But the kettle was singing on the stove. He served Balducci more tea, hesitated, then served the Arab again, who, a second time, drank avidly. His raised arms made the jellaba fall open and the schoolmaster saw his thin, muscular chest.

"Thanks, kid," Balducci said. "And now, I'm off."

He got up and went toward the Arab, taking a small rope from his pocket.

---

9. **department** administrative district in France and certain other countries, similar to a state.
10. **billhook** tool with a carved or hooked blade, used for pruning or cutting.

✓**Reading Check** **19**

What crime has the Arab prisoner committed?

The Guest ■ 1237

Literary Analysis
Existentialism How does Balducci's statement that "the orders exist" represent a choice for Daru?

Vocabulary Builder
mobilized (mō′ bə līzd′) *v.* ready for action or battle

Differentiated Instruction   Solutions for All Learners

Strategy for Less Proficient Readers
To model how to infer cultural attitudes, give students a copy of **Reading Strategy Graphic Organizer B**, in *Graphic Organizer Transparencies*, p. 210. The completed graphic organizer will give students insight into the process of inference. They can use it as a tool to make their own inferences about cultural attitudes as they read.

Support for English Learners
Direct students' attention to Daru's question on page 1236: "Are you pulling my leg?" Explain to students that this is an English idiom, an expression that is not to be taken literally. Tell them that to "pull someone's leg" is to get him or her to accept a ridiculous story as true. Have students brainstorm other English idioms.

Strategy for Advanced Readers
Ask students to keep a log of the communications between Balducci and Daru and between Daru and the Arab. Have students track the information and feelings the characters convey to each other as well as the important failures of communication that occur. Then, have students write essays about how these failures are important to the story.

---

17 **Literary Analysis**
Existentialism

- Read aloud the bracketed passage. Point out to students that Balducci tries to convince Daru that he has no choice but to take the Arab to Tinguit the next day.

- **Ask** the Literary Analysis question: How does Balducci's statement that "the orders exist" represent a choice for Daru?
   Possible response: Balducci's orders are vague in that he does not tell Daru who expects him to take the Arab nor what will happen to him if he disobeys; Daru is able to choose what is meant by the word "exist" and then to act accordingly.

▶ **Monitor Progress** Ask students which points of Existentialism the story has presented so far.
   Answer: Daru's independent lifestyle, his kindness to poor students and their families, and his certainty about making his own decisions about the Arab all involve principles of Existentialism.

▶ **Reteach** If students are having difficulty recognizing elements of Existentialism in "The Guest," have them use the **Literary Analysis** support, p. 47 in *Unit 9 Resources*.

18 **Critical Thinking**
Infer

- Have students review the dialogue between Balducci and Daru, looking for clues about their relationship.
   Ask: Are these two men friendly with each other? Explain.
   Possible response: The men seem to be friendly. They talk in an informal manner, and Balducci calls Daru "son" and says "I like you."

- **Ask** students what they can infer about Daru and Balducci from this dialogue.
   Answer: Daru does not want to get involved; Balducci seems to think that Daru faces few difficulties because he says, "After that, all will be over. You'll come back to your pupils and your comfortable life."

19 **Reading Check**

Answer: The Arab prisoner has killed his cousin.

20

② Humanities

Album Afrique 1835–1845. Arab of Constantine by Auguste Raffet

Auguste Raffet was an artist of the Romantic period who, although popular in his own time, is now much less known than his contemporaries Géricault and Delacroix. He was an expert in watercolors and in lithographs, which were used for book illustrations.

Like the Romantic artists, many scholars, writers, and musicians of the nineteenth century began to study non-Western and pre-industrial cultures around the world. Examples are the German folk stories collected by the Grimm brothers and the folk music used by composers in many countries.

Use the following question for discussion:

Why is it significant that the Arab in "The Guest," like the one in this painting, is wearing traditional clothing?
Possible response: He would be seen as a member of the traditional group in the colony and someone who has not joined the French settlers by adopting their style of dress.

② Critical Viewing

Possible response: The prisoner probably wonders whether he should trust Daru and whether Daru trusts him; he is likely preoccupied with the thought of going to prison.

② Reading Strategy

Inferring Cultural Attitudes

• After reading aloud the bracketed passage, have students **compare** Balducci's and Daru's attitudes about the importance of being armed.
Possible response: They agree that it is important to have a weapon, but they disagree on the importance of keeping the weapon close at hand. Balducci thinks that Daru should keep his shotgun near his bed, but Daru says that he keeps it in the trunk because he has "nothing to fear."

• **Ask** the Reading Strategy question: What does Balducci mean when he says, "we're all in the same boat"? Explain.
Answer: Balducci means that all the non-Arabs in the area will be threatened by the native Arab population.

20

Album Afrique 1835–1845. Arab of Constantine, Auguste Raffet, Musée Condé, Chantilly, France

21 ◀ **Critical Viewing**
Imagine that this Arab is Balducci's prisoner. What might he be thinking? **[Speculate]**

"What are you doing?" Daru asked dryly.

Balducci, disconcerted, showed him the rope.

"Don't bother."

The old gendarme hesitated. "It's up to you. Of course, you are armed?"

"I have my shotgun."

"Where?"

"In the trunk."

"You ought to have it near your bed."

"Why? I have nothing to fear."

"You're crazy, son. If there's an uprising, no one is safe, we're all in the same boat."

"I'll defend myself. I'll have time to see them coming."

Balducci began to laugh, then suddenly the mustache covered the white teeth.

"You'll have time? O.K. That's just what I was saying. You have always been a little cracked. That's why I like you, my son was like that."

At the same time he took out his revolver and put it on the desk.

"Keep it; I don't need two weapons from here to El Ameur."

The revolver shone against the black paint of the table. When the gendarme turned toward him, the schoolmaster caught the smell of leather and horseflesh.

"Listen, Balducci," Daru said suddenly, "every bit of this disgusts me, and first of all your fellow here. But I won't hand him over. Fight, yes, if I have to. But not that."

The old gendarme stood in front of him and looked at him severely.

1238 ■ *The Contemporary World*

Reading Strategy
Inferring Cultural Attitudes
What does Balducci mean when he says, "we're all in the same boat"? Explain.

"You're being a fool," he said slowly. "I don't like it either. You don't get used to putting a rope on a man even after years of it, and you're even ashamed—yes, ashamed. But you can't let them have their way."

"I won't hand him over," Daru said again.

"It's an order, son, and I repeat it."

"That's right. Repeat to them what I've said to you: I won't hand him over."

Balducci made a visible effort to reflect. He looked at the Arab and at Daru. At last he decided.

"No, I won't tell them anything. If you want to drop us, go ahead; I'll not <u>denounce</u> you. I have an order to deliver the prisoner and I'm doing so. And now you'll just sign this paper for me."

"There's no need. I'll not deny that you left him with me."

"Don't be mean with me. I know you'll tell the truth. You're from hereabouts and you are a man. But you must sign, that's the rule."

Daru opened his drawer, took out a little square bottle of purple ink, the red wooden penholder with the "sergeant-major" pen he used for making models of penmanship, and signed. The gendarme carefully folded the paper and put it into his wallet. Then he moved toward the door.

"I'll see you off," Daru said.

"No," said Balducci. "There's no use being polite. You insulted me."

He looked at the Arab, motionless in the same spot, sniffed peevishly, and turned away toward the door. "Good-by, son," he said. The door shut behind him. Balducci appeared suddenly outside the window and then disappeared. His footsteps were muffled by the snow. The horse stirred on the other side of the wall and several chickens fluttered in fright. A moment later Balducci reappeared outside the window leading the horse by the bridle. He walked toward the little rise without turning around and disappeared from sight with the horse following him. A big stone could be heard bouncing down. Daru walked back toward the prisoner, who, without stirring, never took his eyes off him. "Wait," the schoolmaster said in Arabic and went toward the bedroom. As he was going through the door, he had a second thought, went to the desk, took the revolver, and stuck it in his pocket. Then, without looking back, he went into his room.

For some time he lay on his couch watching the sky gradually close over, listening to the silence. It was this silence that had seemed painful to him during the first days here, after the war. He had requested a post in the little town at the base of the foothills separating the upper plateaus from the desert. There, rocky walls, green and black to the north, pink and lavender to the south, marked the frontier of eternal summer. He had been named to a post farther north, on the plateau itself. In the beginning, the solitude and the silence had been hard for him on these wastelands peopled only by stones. Occasionally, furrows suggested cultivation, but they had been dug to uncover a certain kind of stone good for building. The only plowing here was to harvest rocks. Elsewhere a thin layer of soil accumulated in the hollows would be

Vocabulary Builder
denounce (dē nouns´)
v. accuse publicly

Reading Strategy
Inferring Cultural Attitudes
What cultural attitudes are suggested by Balducci's statement, "I know you'll tell the truth. You're from hereabouts and you are a man"?

**Reading Check** **24**
What order does Daru refuse to follow?

The Guest ■ 1239

Literary Analysis

Existentialism; Setting and Theme

- Have a volunteer read aloud the bracketed passage. Then, **ask** this question: What is suggested by this description of the setting?
Possible response: The harsh land supports a harsh way of life. Human life and society mean little in the face of the inhospitable immensity of the desert. This encourages Daru's pessimism in the face of apparently pointless human actions.

- **Ask** students the first Literary Analysis question: In what ways does the statement that "no one in this desert . . . mattered" reflect Existentialist thought?
Possible response: The statement reflects the Existentialist view that the universe is indifferent to human life.

26 Literary Analysis

Existentialism

- Read aloud the bracketed passage. **Ask** students to speculate about why Daru puts the revolver in the desk drawer.
Possible response: He realizes the incongruity of protecting himself from the hungry man with whom he will soon share a meal.

- **Ask** students the second Literary Analysis question: Which personal choices and values does Daru's replacing the revolver demonstrate? Explain.
Possible response: When Daru replaces the revolver, he demonstrates that he has made his own decision regarding the Arab. It is clear that Daru does not intend to follow every bit of advice that Balducci has given him.

---

scraped out to enrich paltry village gardens. This is the way it was: bare rock covered three quarters of the region. Towns sprang up, flourished, then disappeared; men came by, loved one another or fought bitterly, then died. No one in this desert, neither he nor his guest, mattered. And yet, outside this desert neither of them, Daru knew, could have really lived.

When he got up, no noise came from the classroom. He was amazed at the unmixed joy he derived from the mere thought that the Arab might have fled and that he would be alone with no decision to make. But the prisoner was there. He had merely stretched out between the stove and the desk. With eyes open, he was staring at the ceiling. In that position, his thick lips were particularly noticeable, giving him a pouting look. "Come," said Daru. The Arab got up and followed him. In the bedroom, the schoolmaster pointed to a chair near the table under the window. The Arab sat down without taking his eyes off Daru.

"Are you hungry?"

"Yes," the prisoner said.

Daru set the table for two. He took flour and oil, shaped a cake in a frying-pan, and lighted the little stove that functioned on bottled gas. While the cake was cooking, he went out to the shed to get cheese, eggs, dates, and condensed milk. When the cake was done he set it on the window sill to cool, heated some condensed milk diluted with water, and beat up the eggs into an omelette. In one of his motions he knocked against the revolver stuck in his right pocket. He set the bowl down, went into the classroom, and put the revolver in his desk drawer. When he came back to the room, night was falling. He put on the light and served the Arab. "Eat," he said. The Arab took a piece of the cake, lifted it eagerly to his mouth, and stopped short.

"And you?" he asked.

"After you. I'll eat too."

The thick lips opened slightly. The Arab hesitated, then bit into the cake determinedly.

The meal over, the Arab looked at the schoolmaster. "Are you the judge?"

"No, I'm simply keeping you until tomorrow."

"Why do you eat with me?"

"I'm hungry."

The Arab fell silent. Daru got up and went out. He brought back a folding bed from the shed, set it up between the table and the stove, perpendicular to his own bed. From a large suitcase which, upright in a corner, served as a shelf for papers, he took two blankets and arranged them on the camp bed. Then he stopped, felt useless, and sat down on his bed. There was nothing more to do or to get ready. He had to look at this man. He looked at him, therefore, trying to imagine his face bursting with rage. He couldn't do so. He could see nothing but the dark yet shining eyes and the animal mouth.

"Why did you kill him?" he asked in a voice whose hostile tone surprised him.

The Arab looked away.

1240 ■ *The Contemporary World*

Literary Analysis
Existentialism; Setting and Theme In what ways does the statement that "no one in this desert . . . mattered" reflect Existentialist thought?

Literary Analysis
Existentialism Which personal choices and values does Daru's replacing the revolver demonstrate? Explain.

Enrichment

Algerian Cuisine
The meal Daru serves the Arab is a simple but typical version of Algerian cuisine. French, Turkish, Arab, and Berber traditions are all found in the Algerian kitchen. Unleavened bread and couscous, a semolina-based pasta, are dietary staples, often served with a meat, chickpea and vegetable stew often highly spiced.

Other common dishes include mutton, lamb, and poultry. Desserts often use native-grown figs, dates, almonds, and locally produced honey. Mint tea, which Daru offers to his guests, is a favorite drink in Algeria, as is strong, sweet, Turkish-style coffee.

Arabe assis de face, les mains croisses (Seated Arab), Eugène Delacroix, Réunion des Musées Nationaux

28 ◄ **Critical Viewing**
Is this man's clothing appropriate for the setting Camus describes? Why or why not? **[Assess]**

"He ran away. I ran after him."

He raised his eyes to Daru again and they were full of a sort of woeful interrogation. "Now what will they do to me?"

"Are you afraid?"

He stiffened, turning his eyes away.

"Are you sorry?"

The Arab stared at him openmouthed. Obviously he did not understand. Daru's annoyance was growing. At the same time he felt awkward and self-conscious with his big body wedged between the two beds.

"Lie down there," he said impatiently. "That's your bed."

The Arab didn't move. He called to Daru:

"Tell me!"

The schoolmaster looked at him.

"Is the gendarme coming back tomorrow?"

"I don't know."

"Are you coming with us?"

"I don't know. Why?"

The prisoner got up and stretched out on top of the blankets, his feet toward the window. The light from the electric bulb shone straight into his eyes and he closed them at once.

"Why?" Daru repeated, standing beside the bed.

The Arab opened his eyes under the blinding light and looked at him, trying not to blink.

"Come with us," he said.

In the middle of the night, Daru was still not asleep. He had gone to bed after undressing completely; he generally slept naked. But when he suddenly realized that he had nothing on, he hesitated. He felt vulnerable and the temptation came to him to put his clothes back on. Then he shrugged his shoulders; after all, he wasn't a child and, if need be,

Reading Strategy
Inferring Cultural Attitudes
Does the prisoner fail to grasp Daru's question ("Are you sorry?") because he holds different cultural attitudes, or is it simply a matter of his personality? Explain.

✓**Reading Check** **30**
How does Daru feel at the thought his prisoner might have fled?

The Guest ■ *1241*

27 **Humanities**

Arabe assis de face, les mains croisses (Seated Arab),
by Eugène Delacroix

In 1832, Delacroix (1798–1863) spent four months in North Africa, where he was inspired to paint images like this one. The man's simple clothing and meditative posture suggest quiet contemplation.

Use the following question for discussion:

What Existentialist attitude does the minimalist background of the painting suggest?
Possible response: The plain background emphasizes the man, not his surroundings.

28 **Critical Viewing**

Possible response: The man's clothing covers his body completely, protecting him from the harsh sun and whipping winds. Therefore, it is appropriate for the setting.

29 **Reading Strategy**

Inferring Cultural Attitudes

- Have a volunteer read aloud the bracketed passage. Then, **ask** students to describe the mood of the scene and the characters' interactions.
Possible response: The mood is one of discomfort between the characters as they try to communicate. Daru asks the Arab a few questions to try to understand him, but the Arab seems wary and frightened.

- **Ask** the Reading Strategy question: Does the prisoner fail to grasp Daru's question ("Are you sorry?") because he holds different cultural attitudes, or is it simply a matter of his personality? Explain.
Possible response: Perhaps it does not occur to the man that being sorry for a crime is relevant in Daru's culture. On the other hand, the man may simply be uncomfortable, taken aback by Daru's personal questions.

30 **Reading Check**

Answer: Daru feels glad at the thought that the Arab might have fled.

Differentiated Instruction   Solutions for All Learners

Support for Less Proficient Readers
Read aloud with students from "'Are you hungry?'" on p. 1240 to "'Come with us,' he said" above. Help students focus on the actions that Daru performs—setting the table, cooking, putting the revolver away, putting on the light, serving the Arab, eating, talking, retrieving and setting up the folding bed, and so on—as well as the behavior of the Arab. Then, lead students in a discussion that compares the way Daru treats the Arab with the way Balducci treated him. Finally, discuss the reasons that the Arab asks Daru to travel with him and Balducci.

Enrichment for Gifted/Talented Students
Have students reread the scene between Daru and the Arab, beginning with the second paragraph on p. 1240. Invite them to create works of art based on the scene. For example, they might create a musical composition appropriate for a dramatized version of the scene. Other possibilities include paintings, drawings, sculptures, or poems based on the scene. Encourage students to share their finished works with classmates.

The Existentialist Three: Camus, Sartre, and de Beauvoir Jean Paul Sartre did not shy away from the label "Existentialist," as did other like-minded thinkers. He did, however, reject another label: that of Nobel Prize winner. In 1964, he refused to accept this prestigious award for work characterized by the Nobel organization as ". . . rich in ideas and filled with the spirit of freedom and the quest for truth, [which] has exerted a far-reaching influence on our age."

Connect to the Literature Note that Simone de Beauvoir's contribution to the feminist movement in the middle of the twentieth century is as well known as her contribution to Existentialist thought. She and Sartre were at the center of the intellectual community of the Left Bank in Paris just after World War II. Have students discuss how Daru treats his guest in a socially responsible manner.

Possible response: Daru treats the Arab like a guest, suggesting that Balducci untie his prisoner's hands so that he can drink tea, refusing to turn him over to the authorities, sharing a meal with him, offering him the comfort of a bed, and asking him about his feelings about the killing. Later, he offers the Arab money and the choice to turn himself in or flee.

32 Critical Thinking

Interpret

- Read with students the bracketed passage. Discuss Daru's mental state.
- **Ask** students why Daru is bothered by the man's presence.
  Possible response: Daru is bothered by the man's presence because he has grown accustomed to solitude; the man's presence reminds Daru of the community of friends he no longer has.

- **Ask** students to explain Daru's attitude toward the prisoner and toward the situation in which he finds himself.
  Possible response: Daru has mixed feelings toward the prisoner. He is angry that the prisoner has killed someone in what was probably a squabble over grain, yet he tries to establish a connection with the prisoner by treating him decently and asking him about his feelings. Despite his anger toward the prisoner, he does not want to be the one to turn him over to the police.

---

he could break his adversary in two. From his bed he could observe him, lying on his back, still motionless with his eyes closed under the harsh light. When Daru turned out the light, the darkness seemed to coagulate all of a sudden. Little by little, the night came back to life in the window where the starless sky was stirring gently. The schoolmaster soon made out the body lying at his feet. The Arab still did not move, but his eyes seemed open. A faint wind was prowling around the schoolhouse. Perhaps it would drive away the clouds and the sun would reappear.

During the night the wind increased. The hens fluttered a little and then were silent. The Arab turned over on his side with his back to Daru, who thought he heard him moan. Then he listened for his guest's breathing, become heavier and more regular. He listened to that breath so close to him and mused without being able to go to sleep. In this room where he had been sleeping alone for a year, this presence bothered him. But it bothered him also by imposing on him a sort of brotherhood he knew well but refused to accept in the present circumstances. Men who share the same rooms, soldiers or prisoners, develop a strange alliance as if, having cast off their armor with their clothing, they <u>fraternized</u> every evening, over and above their differences, in the ancient community of dream and fatigue. But Daru shook himself; he didn't like such musings, and it was essential to sleep.

A little later, however, when the Arab stirred slightly, the schoolmaster was still not asleep. When the prisoner made a second move, he stiffened, on the alert. The Arab was lifting himself slowly on his arms with almost the motion of a sleep-walker. Seated upright in bed, he waited motionless without turning his head toward Daru, as if he were listening attentively. Daru did not stir; it had just occurred to him that the revolver was still in the drawer of his desk. It was better to act at once. Yet he continued to observe the prisoner, who, with the same slithery motion, put his feet on the ground, waited again, then began to stand up slowly. Daru was about to call out to him when the Arab began to walk, in a quite natural but extraordinarily silent way. He was heading toward the door at the end of the room that opened into the shed. He lifted the latch with precaution and went out, pushing the door behind him but without shutting it. Daru had not stirred. "He is running away," he merely thought. "Good riddance!" Yet he listened attentively. The hens were not fluttering; the guest must be on the plateau. A faint sound of water reached him, and he didn't know what it was until the Arab again stood framed in the doorway, closed the door carefully, and came back to bed without a sound. Then Daru turned his back on him and fell asleep. Still later he seemed, from the depths of his sleep, to hear <u>furtive</u> steps around the schoolhouse. "I'm dreaming! I'm dreaming!" he repeated to himself. And he went on sleeping.

Themes in World Masterpieces

31 *The Existentialist Three: Camus, Sartre, and de Beauvoir*
When Albert Camus moved to France at the age of twenty-five, he entered a dynamic literary world in which other writers and philosophers were already exploring theories of individual freedom and morality. He became intimate friends with two of them: Jean-Paul Sartre (1905–1980) and Simone de Beauvoir (1908–1986). Together, they became leaders of the Existentialist movement, influencing French literature and philosophical thought through much of the twentieth century.

Sartre was the most prominent of the three. In books like *No Exit* (1946) and *Being and Nothingness* (1956), he popularized the Existentialist view of individual freedom, human dignity, and social responsibility.

De Beauvoir met Sartre in 1929, and they became lifelong companions. Today, she is best known as a pioneering feminist whose 1949 book, *The Second Sex*, influenced the changing roles of women.

Connect to the Literature

In what specific ways does Daru respect his guest's human dignity?

Vocabulary Builder
fraternized (frat´ ər nīzd´) *v.* associated in a brotherly way; socialized

furtive (fur´ tiv) *adj.* done in a secret or sneaky way

When he awoke, the sky was clear; the loose window let in a cold, pure air. The Arab was asleep, hunched up under the blankets now, his mouth open, utterly relaxed. But when Daru shook him, he started dreadfully, staring at Daru with wild eyes as if he had never seen him and such a frightened expression that the schoolmaster stepped back. "Don't be afraid. It's me. You must eat." The Arab nodded his head and said yes. Calm had returned to his face, but his expression was vacant and listless.

The coffee was ready. They drank it seated together on the folding bed as they munched their pieces of the cake. Then Daru led the Arab under the shed and showed him the faucet where he washed. He went back into the room, folded the blankets and the bed, made his own bed and put the room in order. Then he went through the classroom and out onto the terrace. The sun was already rising in the blue sky; a soft, bright light was bathing the deserted plateau. On the ridge the snow was melting in spots. The stones were about to reappear. Crouched on the edge of the plateau, the schoolmaster looked at the deserted expanse. He thought of Balducci. He had hurt him, for he had sent him off in a way as if he didn't want to be associated with him. He could still hear the gendarme's farewell and, without knowing why, he felt strangely empty and vulnerable. At that moment, from the other side of the schoolhouse, the prisoner coughed. Daru listened to him almost despite himself and then, furious, threw a pebble that whistled through the air before sinking into the snow. That man's stupid crime revolted him, but to hand him over was contrary to honor. Merely thinking of it made him smart with humiliation. And he cursed at one and the same time his own people who had sent him this Arab and the Arab too who had dared to kill and not managed to get away. Daru got up, walked in a circle on the terrace, waited motionless, and then went back into the schoolhouse.

The Arab, leaning over the cement floor of the shed, was washing his teeth with two fingers. Daru looked at him and said: "Come." He went back into the room ahead of the prisoner. He slipped a hunting-jacket on over his sweater and put on walking-shoes. Standing, he waited until the Arab had put on his *chèche* and sandals. They went into the classroom and the schoolmaster pointed to the exit, saying: "Go ahead." The fellow didn't budge. "I'm coming," said Daru. The Arab went out. Daru went back into the room and made a package of pieces of rusk,[11] dates, and sugar. In the classroom, before going out, he hesitated a second in front of his desk, then crossed the threshold and locked the door. "That's the way," he said. He started toward the east, followed by the prisoner. But, a short distance from the schoolhouse, he thought he heard a slight sound behind them. He retraced his steps and examined the surroundings of the house; there was no one there. The Arab watched him without seeming to understand. "Come on," said Daru.

---

11. **rusk** (rusk) *n.* sweet bread or cake, toasted or baked until crisp.

Literary Analysis
Existentialism; Setting and Theme In what ways does Daru's throwing the pebble into the desert reflect Existentialist views?

 **Reading Check** ❸❹
What does Daru hear "from the depths of his sleep"?

The Guest ■ 1243

❸❸ **Literary Analysis**
Existentialism; Setting and Theme

• Have a volunteer read aloud the bracketed passage. Then, **ask** students why Daru feels "empty and vulnerable" at this time.
Possible response: Daru probably feels both the loss of his friend and the possibility of needing allies in case circumstances turn dangerous. He also feels alone in grappling with his decision about what to do with the Arab.

• **Ask** students the Literary Analysis question: In what ways does Daru's throwing the pebble into the desert reflect Existentialist views?
Possible response: Daru expresses his anger by throwing the pebble, but nature answers with an indifferent response—it simply swallows up the pebble silently without even allowing it to reverberate.

❸❹ **Reading Check**
Answer: Daru seems to hear furtive steps around the schoolhouse.

Differentiated Instruction   Solutions for All Learners

Support for Less Proficient Readers
Discuss with students the two times Daru thinks he hears someone lurking around the schoolhouse (during the night "from the depths of his sleep," and the next morning when he and the prisoner are starting out). Ask students whether they think someone might really be there and if so, for what reason. Point out that Camus might have a dual purpose in including these incidents: to foreshadow coming events and to show that Daru is subject to fears based on his situation.

Strategy for Advanced Readers
Suggest that students discuss this question before going on with the story: Should Daru be angrier with "his own people" who have given him the responsibility of dealing with the Arab or with the Arab for not escaping? Point out that this question presents Daru's basic problem: He deals with forces beyond his control, yet he must decide his best course of action under these circumstances.

③⑤ Literary Analysis

Existentialism; Setting and Theme

• Read aloud the bracketed passage. **Ask** students to explain what is happening in the natural setting Camus describes.
Answer: As the snow melts, puddles evaporate quickly in the morning sun, leaving the plateau dry. The occasional bird sings out suddenly.

• **Ask** students the Literary Analysis question: In what ways does the setting reflect both a change in Daru's mood and Existentialist ideas about personal freedom?
Possible response: When Daru feels "a sort of rapture before the vast familiar expanse," he feels that he is not completely overwhelmed by his difficulties. Despite the dilemma he faces, he can feel joy at the beauty of nature, knowing that he does have a choice.

③⑥ Critical Viewing

Possible response: The man may be thinking about what he has done, wondering what his family and friends will do without him, and hoping that his punishment will be light.

③⑤ They walked for an hour and rested beside a sharp peak of limestone. The snow was melting faster and faster and the sun was drinking up the puddles at once, rapidly cleaning the plateau, which gradually dried and vibrated like the air itself. When they resumed walking, the ground rang under their feet. From time to time a bird rent the space in front of them with a joyful cry. Daru breathed in deeply the fresh morning light. He felt a sort of rapture before the vast familiar expanse, now almost entirely yellow under its dome of blue sky. They walked an hour more, descending toward the south. They reached a level height made up of crumbly rocks. From there on, the plateau sloped down, eastward, toward a low plain where there were a few spindly trees and, to the south, toward outcroppings of rock that gave the landscape a chaotic look.

Daru surveyed the two directions. There was nothing but the sky on the horizon. Not a man could be seen. He turned toward the Arab, who was looking at him blankly. Daru held out the package to him. "Take it," he said. "There are dates, bread, and sugar. You can hold out for two days. Here are a thousand francs[12] too." The Arab took the package and the money but kept his full hands at chest level as if he didn't

---

12. **a thousand francs** (fraŋks) *n.* at that time, monetary units of France and certain other countries, 1,000 francs being enough money for a few days' food and travel.

Literary Analysis
Existentialism; Setting and Theme In what ways does the setting reflect both a change in Daru's mood and Existentialist ideas about personal freedom?

③⑥ ▼ **Critical Viewing**
Imagine that this man is the prisoner, walking toward the police station. What might he be thinking as he turns himself in? **[Speculate]**

1244 ▪ *The Contemporary World*

Enrichment

Algerian Culture

Algeria's two main ethnic groups are the Berbers and the Arabs. The Berbers, who have been in Algeria since at least 3000 B.C., generally live in rural villages, farming and herding. Traditional Berber households include an extended family. Each married couple has its own home, opening onto the family courtyard in the back. Family is so important to the Berbers that their village governments are based on it.

Arab culture became influential in Algeria in the A.D. 600s, when the Arabs began to conquer North Africa. Arab traditions are like Berber traditions in many ways. Both groups, for example, traditionally live with extended families. However, whereas Berbers tend to be farmers, some Arabs favor a nomadic lifestyle.

Over the centuries, Arabs and Berbers have had many conflicts. France's colonization of the area resulted in even more conflicts. Still, there have been long periods during which these different groups have lived peacefully and have learned from one another.

know what to do with what was being given him. "Now look," the schoolmaster said as he pointed in the direction of the east, "there's the way to Tinguit. You have a two-hour walk. At Tinguit you'll find the administration and the police. They are expecting you." The Arab looked toward the east, still holding the package and the money against his chest. Daru took his elbow and turned him rather roughly toward the south. At the foot of the height on which they stood could be seen a faint path. "That's the trail across the plateau. In a day's walk from here you'll find pasturelands and the first nomads. They'll take you in and shelter you according to their law." The Arab had now turned toward Daru and a sort of panic was visible in his expression. "Listen," he said. Daru shook his head: "No, be quiet. Now I'm leaving you." He turned his back on him, took two long steps in the direction of the school, looked hesitantly at the motionless Arab, and started off again. For a few minutes he heard nothing but his own step resounding on the cold ground and did not turn his head. A moment later, however, he turned around. The Arab was still there on the edge of the hill, his arms hanging now, and he was looking at the schoolmaster. Daru felt something rise in his throat. But he swore with impatience, waved vaguely, and started off again. He had already gone some distance when he again stopped and looked. There was no longer anyone on the hill.

Reading Strategy
Inferring Cultural Attitudes
Based on Daru's statement about the nomads, what can you infer about their cultural attitudes?

 Reading Check 38
What items does Daru give the prisoner before he departs?

The Guest ■ 1245

37 Reading Strategy
Inferring Cultural Attitudes

• Ask a volunteer to read aloud the bracketed passage. Then, **ask** this question: Why does Daru present a choice to the Arab, without stating directly that the Arab is getting a chance to escape?
Possible response: Daru wants the Arab to make his own decision, free from outside influence.

• Ask students the Reading Strategy question: Based on Daru's statement about the nomads, what can you infer about their cultural attitudes?
Possible response: Nomads believe it is important to help anyone who needs it, regardless of background or social class.

38 Reading Check

Answer: Daru gives the prisoner a package that has enough dates, bread, and sugar to last two days. He also gives him a thousand francs.

- Read aloud the bracketed passage, and **ask** students: What does the Arab decide to do?
  Answer: He decides to turn himself in.

- Then, **ask:** Why might he make this decision?
  Possible response: The Arab realizes he must take responsibility for his crime.

- Guide students to see that the Arab's decision means a loss of freedom. Have students draw a conclusion about Existentialist views of freedom from this fact.
  Possible response: For Existentialists, choices have consequences for which we must take responsibility—we are "imprisoned" by freedom.

ASSESS

Answers

1. **Possible response:** Yes; Daru acted kindly toward the Arab and did not turn him in.

2. (a) Balducci and his Arab prisoner arrive at Daru's home. (b) Balducci is on a horse and an Arab with bound hands is walking behind him. (c) **Possible response:** Balducci is in charge and the Arab is powerless.

3. (a) Balducci demands that Daru deliver the prisoner to the police in Tinguit. (b) Daru is thought to be loyal to the French. (c) **Possible response:** Daru wants to remain neutral.

4. (a) The police believed that the villagers would not punish the Arab. (b) **Possible response:** The villagers will blame Daru for handing the Arab over to the authorities.

5. (a) **Possible response:** Daru is disgusted with the Arab for having killed a man and for not escaping. (b) No; Daru treats him as an equal.

6. (a) Daru gives the Arab the choice of turning himself in or escaping. (b) **Possible response:** Yes; Daru gave the man a choice. No; Daru should not turn a murderer loose.

7. **Possible response:** Daru would not have acted differently. If he turned the prisoner over to his Arab friends, he would risk the wrath of the French colonials; if he turned the prisoner over to the police, he would risk the wrath of the Arab's friends.

Daru hesitated. The sun was now rather high in the sky and was beginning to beat down on his head. The schoolmaster retraced his steps, at first somewhat uncertainly, then with decision. When he reached the little hill, he was bathed in sweat. He climbed it as fast as he could and stopped, out of breath, at the top. The rock-fields to the south stood out sharply against the blue sky, but on the plain to the east a steamy heat was already rising. And in that slight haze, Daru, with heavy heart, made out the Arab walking slowly on the road to prison.

A little later, standing before the window of the classroom, the schoolmaster was watching the clear light bathing the whole surface of the plateau, but he hardly saw it. Behind him on the blackboard, among the winding French rivers, sprawled the clumsily chalked-up words he had just read: "You handed over our brother. You will pay for this." Daru looked at the sky, the plateau, and, beyond, the invisible lands stretching all the way to the sea. In this vast landscape he had loved so much, he was alone.

Critical Reading

1. **Respond:** Did you find the end of the story surprising? Why or why not?

2. (a) **Recall:** Who are the two men who arrive at Daru's home? (b) **Interpret:** As the men approach, what details in their appearance and behavior does Daru observe? (c) **Analyze:** What do these details suggest about the characters and status of the men?

3. (a) **Recall:** What demand does Balducci make of Daru with regard to the Arab prisoner? (b) **Infer:** Why is Daru expected to take orders delivered to him by Balducci? (c) **Analyze:** Why do you think Daru refuses to comply?

4. (a) **Recall:** Why did the police feel it necessary to remove the Arab prisoner from custody in his village? (b) **Draw Conclusions:** How does this situation emphasize the danger of Daru's position?

5. (a) **Infer:** What is Daru's opinion of the Arab? Support your answer. (b) **Interpret:** Do Daru's feelings about the Arab affect his treatment of the man? Explain.

6. (a) **Interpret:** How does Daru resolve his dilemma over the Arab? (b) **Make a Judgment:** Do you think this was a good resolution?

7. **Speculate:** Would Daru have acted differently if he had known the Arab's friends might seek revenge? Why or why not?

For: More about Albert Camus
Visit: www.PHSchool.com
Web Code: ete-9903

Go Online For additional information about **Author Link** Albert Camus, have students type in the Web Code, then select *C* from the alphabet, and then select Albert Camus.

Apply the Skills

The Guest

Literary Analysis

Existentialism

1. Daru shows the Arab two paths and leaves him to make his own choice. In what ways does this decision reflect **Existentialist** ideas?

2. **(a)** How does Daru feel about the Arab's crime? **(b)** How does he treat the Arab? **(c)** What values do Daru's feelings and actions reflect? Explain.

3. What does the end of the story suggest about the difficulties of living one's life according to Existentialist principles? Explain.

Connecting Literary Elements

4. **(a)** Use a chart like the one shown to identify details about the climate, the landscape, and the cultural conflict in this story.

Weather	Location	Cultural Conflict

   (b) Discuss the ways in which these details of the **setting** reflect ideas that are central to the story's meaning, or **theme**.

5. **(a)** Why do you think Daru feels that "outside this desert neither of them [Daru or the Arab] . . . could have really lived"? **(b)** In what ways does this statement contribute to the story's theme?

6. Who is the guest in this story—the Arab prisoner in Daru's house or Daru in Algeria? Explain.

Reading Strategy

Inferring Cultural Attitudes

7. Daru's blackboard shows the four rivers of France. **Infer cultural attitudes** by describing what this statement reveals about the mind-set of Europeans living in Algeria.

8. What cultural attitudes can you infer from the message the Arab's supporters leave on Daru's blackboard? Explain.

Extend Understanding

9. **Literature Connection:** Camus believed that he had a responsibility to serve humanity through his writing. In what ways do you think that literature can accomplish this goal?

QuickReview

Existentialism is a philosophy that emphasizes the value of personal choice in an indifferent world.

The **setting** is the time and the place in which a story occurs. The **theme** is the central message or insight about life that is communicated in a literary work.

To **infer cultural attitudes** when reading, look for clues about the values and customs of a group of people.

Go Online
Assessment
For: Self-test
Visit: www.PHSchool.com
Web Code: eta-6903

The Guest ■ 1247

Answers continued

8. **Possible response:** They believe that matters arising in their community should be kept there; the message also suggests that revenge is part of their culture.

9. **Possible response:** Literature can serve humanity by raising questions of ethics, conscience, and meaning.

Go Online
Assessment Students may use the **Self-test** to prepare for **Selection Test A** or **Selection Test B.**

Answers

1. **Possible response:** Daru's decision gives the Arab the opportunity to choose his own action, just as Daru has had to do.

2. **(a)** Daru is disgusted and angry about the Arab's crime. **(b)** He treats the Arab as an equal. **(c) Possible response:** Daru's feelings and actions reflect his attitude that despite people's shortcomings, they share a common humanity and should be treated with dignity and respect.

3. **Possible response:** Living one's life according to Existentialist principles is difficult because others may not understand one's choices and may, in fact, oppose them. No ultimate authority tells individuals what to do—they make their own decisions using only conscience as a guide.

4. (a) **Sample response: Weather:** Extreme cold and heat; **Location:** Algeria; **Cultural Conflict:** The native population resents the French colonials.
   Another sample answer can be found on **Literary Analysis Graphic Organizer B,** p. 212 in *Graphic Organizer Transparencies.*
   (b) **Possible response:** The details reflect the isolation that characters face as they make choices, take stands, and risk danger.

5. (a) **Possible response:** The Arab is a part of the native group in the desert, finding his identity there; Daru finds the desert well suited to his belief in the individual's acting autonomously. (b) **Possible response:** This statement emphasizes the dilemma both characters face. The Arab and Daru cannot escape their situations, nor can they look to others for guidance.

6. **Possible response:** Each character can be seen as a guest. Although he serves as host to the Arab prisoner, Daru is a guest in Algeria. Even though he was born there, his ancestors are not among the native peoples of Algeria.

7. **Possible response:** This lesson implies that knowledge about France, the mother country, may be more valuable to the students' futures than knowledge about Algeria.

❶ Vocabulary Lesson

Word Analysis: Anglo-Saxon Prefix *fore-*

1. foreword: an introduction to a book
2. foresight: the act or power of looking ahead
3. forerunner: a warning or sign of something that is yet to arrive

Spelling Strategy

1. grief
2. brief
3. relieve
4. thief
5. achieve

Vocabulary Builder

1. mobilized
2. plateau
3. foretaste
4. denounce
5. siege
6. fraternized
7. furtive

❷ Grammar and Style Lesson

1. along the trail, modifies *walked*, adverb phrase
2. with the jellaba, modifies *man*, adjective phrase
3. With quick movements, modifies *served*, adverb phrase
4. in a hurt tone, modifies *said*, adverb phrase
5. from the village, modifies *Arabs*, adjective phrase

Writing Application

Daru's home is a single (room) off *his classroom*. (adjective phrase) The (walls) *of the room* are white washed. (adjective phrase) Daru's room (is furnished) *in a simple manner*. (adverb phrase)

WG Writing and Grammar Platinum Level

For support in teaching the Grammar and Style Lesson, use Chapter 20, Section 1.

Build Language Skills

❶ Vocabulary Lesson

Word Analysis: Anglo-Saxon Prefix *fore-*

The prefix *fore-*, as in *foretaste*, means "before in time, place, order, or rank." Add the prefix *fore-* to each of the words below. Then, write a definition for each new word.

1. word   2. sight   3. runner

Spelling Strategy

When *i* and *e* spell the long *e* sound, the letters usually appear as *ie*, as in *siege*. For each sentence below, write the correct spelling of the underlined word.

1. The Arab did not feel any <u>greef</u>.
2. Balducci stayed for a <u>breef</u> time.
3. Balducci wanted Daru to <u>releeve</u> him.
4. The Arab was not a <u>theef</u>.
5. Daru did not <u>acheeve</u> peace.

Vocabulary Builder: Sentence Completion

Review the vocabulary list on page 1231. Then, complete the sentences below with words from the list.

1. As the battle neared, the village ___?___ its forces.
2. The house overlooked a vast ___?___.
3. The clash between Daru and the officer gave a ___?___ of conflicts to come.
4. The criminal feared that his friend would ___?___ him.
5. He had enough food to survive a ___?___.
6. He had never befriended his neighbor or ___?___ with him.
7. Because he distrusted the prisoner, he kept a ___?___ eye on him all night.

❷ Grammar and Style Lesson

Prepositional Phrases as Adjectives and Adverbs

A **prepositional phrase** is a group of words made up of a preposition and a noun or pronoun. When a prepositional phrase modifies a noun or pronoun, it is called an adjective phrase; when it modifies a verb, adjective, or adverb, it is called an adverb phrase.

> **Adverb:** Snow had suddenly fallen . . . <u>after eight months</u>. (modifies *fallen*)
>
> **Adjective:** It had disappeared under a layer <u>of dirty white snow</u>. (modifies *layer*)

Practice Identify the prepositional phrase in each sentence below, note the word it modifies, and state whether it is an adjective or adverb phrase.

1. The prisoner walked along the trail.
2. Daru studied the man with the jellaba.
3. With quick movements, Daru served tea.
4. Balducci said goodbye in a hurt tone.
5. The Arabs from the village were angry.

Writing Application Write a paragraph describing Daru's home. Identify adjective phrases and adverb phrases, circling the word each phrase modifies.

WG Prentice Hall Writing and Grammar Connection: Platinum Level, Chapter 20, Section 1

Assessment Practice

Analyzing an Author's Meaning and Style

(For more practice, see *Test Preparation Workbook*, p. 58.)

In "The Guest," what does Camus mean by having Daru struggle as he does only to find the following message on the blackboard?

"You handed over our brother. You will pay for this."

A In French colonies, anyone harboring criminals must pay their legal fees, whether they are guilty or innocent.

B One should always seek professional advice before making decisions that have social and political implications.

C Action is always absurd; whatever one's intentions, every choice is a "bad" one in the sense that it has unforeseen consequences—for which one still must take responsibility.

D Indecisiveness regarding right versus wrong is punishable even if one ultimately makes the right decision.

The correct answer is C. It refers to an existential paradox central to the story.

❸ Writing Lesson

Timed Writing: Essay Evaluating Fiction as an Expression of Philosophy

Although Camus refused the label of Existentialist, his work has often been read as an expression of that philosophy. Write an essay in which you discuss the ways in which Daru's situation, thoughts, and actions in "The Guest" do or do not reflect an Existentialist stance. **(40 minutes)**

Prewriting (10 minutes) Scan the story for details describing Daru's circumstances, actions, thoughts, and statements. Use a chart like the one shown to analyze how each detail does or does not reflect Existentialist views.

Model: Using a Chart to Compare Fiction to Philosophy

Details	Existentialist Ideas
Daru's Situation: Daru is isolated and alone.	Human beings are alone in an indifferent universe.
Daru's Thoughts:	
Daru's Actions:	

Drafting (20 minutes) Choose point-by-point or block organization for your essay. With the former, introduce each detail and discuss it in relationship to Existentialism. With the latter, discuss all the details that reflect Existentialist ideas. Then, discuss all of those that do not.

Revising (10 minutes) As you reread your draft, underline your main ideas. If a paragraph lacks a clear main idea, add one or combine it with another paragraph. If a paragraph has more than one main idea, create two paragraphs.

 Prentice Hall Writing and Grammar Connection: Platinum Level, Chapter 9, Section 2

❹ Extend Your Learning

Listening and Speaking With a small group, adapt and perform "The Guest" as a **play.** Use these tips to prepare:

- Reread the story, listing details about the characters.
- Write roles for the three characters, a narrator, and a director.
- Include stage directions.

Rehearse the play and then perform it for the class. **[Group Activity]**

Research and Technology Conduct research on the Internet to learn about the history and culture of Algeria. Then, create a **timeline** that identifies important events and people. In a brief explanation, draw conclusions about the authenticity of Camus's portrayal of this culture.

Go Online
Research

For: An additional research activity
Visit: www.PHSchool.com
Web Code: etd-7903

The Guest ■ 1249

Assessment Resources

The following resources can be used to assess students' knowledge and skills.

Unit 9 Resources
 Selection Test A, pp. 54–56
 Selection Test B, pp. 57–59

General Resources
 Rubrics for Exposition, Comparison-and-Contrast Essay, pp. 53–54
 Rubric for Speaking: Narrative Account, p. 88

Go Online
Assessment Students may use the **Self-test** to prepare for **Selection Test A** or **Selection Test B.**

---

❸ Writing Lesson

You may use this Writing Lesson as timed-writing practice, or you may allow students to develop the essay as a writing assignment over several days.

- To give students guidance in writing this essay, give them the **Support for Writing Lesson,** p. 51 in *Unit 9 Resources.*

- Tell students that in their evaluative essays, they will use evidence to support a view. In this case, they will evaluate whether Camus's story "The Guest" expresses an Existentialist attitude.

- Tell students that a good essay has an introduction that makes a strong statement of the writer's position. The introduction is followed by the body of the essay and a conclusion. Each part of the essay is connected to and supports the others.

- Point out that the body of the essay uses details to support the theme, or main point, of the essay. Tell students that using a chart is one way to organize their thoughts and keep the essay coherent.

- Adapt the Exposition: Comparison-and-Contrast Essay rubrics in *General Resources,* pp. 53–54, to evaluate students' work.

Writing and Grammar
Platinum Level
For support in teaching the Writing Lesson, use Chapter 9, Section 2.

❹ Listening and Speaking

- Organize students into small groups, and have them follow the tips as they prepare their presentations.

- Allow time for students to rehearse before presenting their plays to the class.

- Use the Speaking: Narrative Account rubric in *General Resources,* p. 88, to evaluate students' work.

- The **Support for Extend Your Learning** page (*Unit 9 Resources,* p. 52) provides guided note-taking opportunities to help students complete the Extend Your Learning activities.

Go Online
Research Have students type in the Web Code for another research activity.

1249

❶ Types of Nonfiction

• Tell students that they will study nonfiction in Unit 9. **Ask** students: What types of nonfiction have you read previously?
Possible responses: Students may say that they have read newspapers, sports magazines, biographies, emails, or school-related Web sites.

• Remind students that most of them have probably read stories of people's lives as well as textbooks containing nonfiction.

• Review the types of nonfiction with students, and point out that when students write about actual events or people or write in their journal or diary, they are writing nonfiction.

❷ Categories of Nonfiction

• Review the categories of nonfiction with students, and emphasize that nonfiction includes everything from recipes to instructions to food labels. **Ask** students: How many categories of nonfiction do you use in a single day, in a week, or in a month? Allow time for students to think and respond.
Possible response: Students may say that they read several forms of nonfiction every day for each subject they take at school, including Language Arts, which requires that they read literary criticism. They also read nonfiction at home when they prepare food or use the Internet.

• Point out that these categories listed in the book are only some of the common categories of nonfiction. **Ask** students: What categories of nonfiction do you use most frequently?
Possible response: Students will most likely say that they read informational texts most frequently.

Defining Nonfiction

Nonfiction is prose writing that presents and explains ideas or that tells about real people, places, objects, or events. To be considered nonfiction, a work must be true.

𝓘 LIKE IT BEST WHEN A PIECE FEELS AS IF IT HAS WRITTEN ITSELF, AS IF IT HAS FOUND IN ME ONLY A DUTIFUL SCRIBE, A WILLING INSTRUMENT. —*Rebecca Walker on nonfiction*

❶ Types of Nonfiction

The label *nonfiction* includes many genres and styles of writing. Here are some of the most common kinds of writing that are classified as nonfiction:

• **Autobiography:** a person's life story, written by himself or herself. Autobiographies include a writer's thoughts, feelings, and insights about events.
 Example: *Dust Tracks on a Road* by Zora Neale Hurston

• **Memoir:** a form of autobiography in which the writer focuses on part of his or her own life. Memoirs often reveal the personal side of public or historical events.
 Example: *Survival in Auschwitz* by Primo Levi, page 1254

• **Biography:** a person's life story, written by someone else. Biographers usually choose subjects whose lives and experiences can be a model or serve as a lesson for others.
 Example: *Galileo's Daughter* by Dava Sobel

• **Speech:** a nonfiction work that is delivered orally to an audience. Speeches are often tailored to specific, formal events such as debates, graduations, or presidential inaugurations.
 Example: *Nobel Lecture* by Alexander Solzhenitsyn, page 1291

• **Essay or Article:** a short nonfiction work on a single subject. Articles usually appear in magazines or newspapers. The audience for both essays and articles varies greatly, depending on the subject matter.
 Example: "Holocaust Haggadah" from *Duke Magazine*, page 1274

• **Diary, Journal, or Letter:** an autobiographical record of daily events, personal thoughts, and observations. Diaries and journals are usually not written for a broad audience. Journals, however, are usually less intimate than diaries. Unlike diaries and journals, letters are communications intended to be read by someone else.
 Example: *The Pillow Book* by Sei Shōnagon, page 317

> Letters, diaries, and journals are considered **primary source documents**, nonfiction works that offer firsthand accounts of historical periods or events.

1250 ■ *The Contemporary World*

Extend the Lesson

Writing a Journal Entry

• Choose a recent, well-known event that occurred in the students' community or at school, and have students write a journal entry about the event, describing what happened, why it happened, and what its significance is for the school or community. Then have several volunteers read aloud their journal entries. Point out that the volunteers differ on what they included in their entries, how they perceived what happened, and the importance to which they gave the event.

Ask students the following questions:
1. Why do the accounts differ?
 Possible response: Not everyone sees an event in the same way, and authors' personal feelings may affect what they write.
2. What does this tell you about journals, diaries, and letters, as well as other nonfiction?
 Possible response: Students may say that although nonfiction is grounded in reality, personal biases or other subjective influences may still affect nonfiction writing.

❷ Categories of Nonfiction

Because nonfiction is grounded in reality, the topics of nonfiction are as diverse as the world around us. Here are some of the most common categories of nonfiction by topic:

- history
- literary criticism
- travel
- science and technology

- politics
- philosophy
- informational texts—such as how-to books, cookbooks, and guidebooks

❸ Purposes of Nonfiction

Nonfiction is generally written with at least one, and often more than one, specific purpose in mind. Here are some common purposes of nonfiction:

Author's Purpose	Example
To inform	*Hiroshima*, an account of the dropping of the first atomic bomb, by John Hersey, page 1318
To persuade	"I Have A Dream," a speech by Martin Luther King, Jr.
To teach	"Leonardo: The Eye, the Hand, the Mind," a feature article about Leonardo Da Vinci, by Holland Cotter, page 810
To entertain	*Something to Declare*, a collection of autobiographical essays by Julia Alvarez
To explain	"Astronomical Messages," an essay by Galileo Galilei, page 758
To describe	"Flood," an essay by Annie Dillard

❹ Strategies for Reading Nonfiction

Use these strategies as you read nonfiction.

Recognize the Main Idea and Supporting Details In nonfiction, the *main idea* is the central point that the author wishes to convey. The *supporting details* consist of the facts, examples, or reasons that explain or justify the central point. Look for topic sentences that state the main idea, and note supporting details that relate to the main idea.

Analyze the Author's Purpose An author's purpose is the reason why he or she is writing—for example, to inform, to describe, or to entertain. Look for language that teaches, persuades, or amuses to determine why the work was written.

Distinguish Between Fact and Opinion Nonfiction is usually a mixture of facts and opinions. As you read, take note of the facts a writer uses to support ideas and opinions, and decide whether you agree with the writer's opinion. Look for charged words or phrases, and consider why the writer made such choices.

Focus on Literary Forms: Nonfiction ■ 1251

❸ Purposes of Nonfiction

- Tell students that the author's purpose will usually influence the type of nonfiction writing that he or she chooses to write.

- Review with students the purposes of nonfiction. Clarify the purposes, and suggest that students refer back to this material when they are trying to determine an author's purpose. **Ask** students to think of other purposes for writing nonfiction and give an example of a nonfiction category for each purpose.
Possible response: Students may say the following purposes: to criticize, as in a letter to the editor or an editorial in a newspaper; and to declare, as in a list of ingredients.

❹ Strategies for Reading Nonfiction

- Tell students that they must analyze nonfiction to determine whether the author offers full support for the main idea.

- Point out that readers should look for the details the author provides to explain or justify the central point. If supporting details are lacking, the main idea becomes less believable.

- An author may have more than one purpose for writing, and students may not know the author's purpose until they read some of the work. Tell students to identify the main idea or thesis statement. By doing so, they can usually determine the author's purpose for writing.

- Tell students to read carefully to identify an author's assumptions. An *assumption* is an idea that someone takes for granted as being true. Assumptions may indicate the presence of bias, and students should not take an author's claims at face value. Students must determine whether the claims are supported by reasoning or evidence.

Standard Course of Study

Goal 1: WRITTEN LANGUAGE

WL.1.02.3 Exhibit an awareness of cultural context of text in a personal reflection.

Goal 2: INFORMATIONAL READING

IR.2.01.7 Analyze influences, contexts, or biases in research texts.

Goal 3: FOUNDATIONS OF ARGUMENT

FA.3.01.4 Compile response and research data to organize argument about controversial issues.

Goal 4: CRITICAL THINKING

CT.4.01.2 Reflect on and show how a real-world event affects viewpoint.

Goal 5: LITERATURE

LT.5.01.6 Make connections between historical and contemporary issues in world literature.

LT.5.01.7 Understand the cultural and historical impact on world literature texts.

Goal 6: GRAMMAR AND USAGE

GU.6.01.3 Use recognition strategies to understand vocabulary and exact word choice.

Step-by-Step Teaching Guide	Pacing Guide
PRETEACH	
• Administer Vocabulary and Reading Warm-ups as necessary.	5 min.
• Engage students' interest with the motivation activity.	5 min.
• Read and discuss author and background features. **FT**	10 min.
• Introduce the Literary Analysis Skill: Autobiography. **FT**	5 min.
• Introduce the Reading Strategy: Connecting to Historical Context. **FT**	10 min.
• Prepare students to read by teaching the selection vocabulary. **FT**	
TEACH	
• Informally monitor comprehension while students read independently or in groups. **FT**	30 min.
• Monitor students' comprehension with the Reading Check notes.	as students read
• Reinforce vocabulary with Vocabulary Builder notes.	as students read
• Develop students' understanding of autobiography with the Literary Analysis annotations. **FT**	5 min.
• Develop students' ability to connect to historical context with the Reading Strategy annotations. **FT**	5 min.
ASSESS/EXTEND	
• Assess students' comprehension and mastery of the Literary Analysis and Reading Strategy by having them answer the Apply the Skills questions. **FT**	15 min.
• Have students complete the Vocabulary Lesson and the Grammar and Style Lesson. **FT**	15 min.
• Apply students' ability to revise for audience and purpose by using the Writing Lesson. **FT**	45 min. or homework
• Apply students' understanding by using one or more of the Extend Your Learning activities.	20–90 min. or homework
• Administer Selection Test A or Selection Test B. **FT**	15 min.

Resources

Print
Unit 9 Resources

Transparency
Graphic Organizer Transparencies

Print
Reader's Notebook [L2]

Reader's Notebook: Adapted Version [L1]

Reader's Notebook: English Learner's Version [EL]

Unit 9 Resources

Technology
Listening to Literature Audio CDs [L2, EL]

Reader's Notebook: Adapted Version Audio CD [L1, L2]

Print
Unit 9 Resources

General Resources

Technology
Go Online: Research [L3]
Go Online: Self-test [L3]
ExamView®, **Test Bank [L3]**

Choosing Resources for Differentiated Instruction

[**L1**] Special Needs Students

[**L2**] Below-Level Students

[**L3**] All Students

[**L4**] Advanced Students

[**EL**] English Learners

For Vocabulary and Reading Warm-ups and for Selection Tests, **A** signifies "less challenging" and **B** "more challenging." For Graphic Organizer transparencies, **A** signifies "not filled in" and **B** "filled in."

FT Fast Track Instruction: To move the lesson more quickly, use the strategies and activities identified with **FT**.

Scaffolding for Less Proficient and Advanced Students

The leveled Critical Thinking questions after selections progress in the levels of thinking required to answer them. To address the needs of your different students, you may use the (a) level questions for your less proficient students and the (b) level questions with your on-level and advanced students. The occasional (c) level questions are appropriate for your advanced students.

TeacherEXPRESS™ Use this complete
Plan · Teach · Assess   suite of powerful
teaching tools to make lesson planning and testing quicker and easier.

StudentEXPRESS™ Use the interactive
Learn · Study · Succeed   textbook (online
and on CD-ROM) to make selections and activities come alive with audio and video support and interactive questions.

Benchmark

After students have completed reading these selections, administer **Benchmark Test 11** *(Unit 9 Resources,* **pp. 77–82).** If the Benchmark Test reveals that some of the students need further work, use the **Interpretation Guide** to determine the appropriate reteaching page in the **Reading Kit** and on **Success Tracker.**

 For: Information about Lexiles
Visit: www.PHSchool.com
Web Code: eue-1111

Motivation

To acquaint students with the trauma of the Nazi concentration camps, assign a number to each seat in the classroom before class begins. When students arrive, begin addressing them by their seat numbers rather than their names. Be certain to maintain a somber classroom atmosphere during this exercise. After students are settled and the daily classroom start-up procedures are completed, lead students in a discussion about having their names replaced with numbers. Help students understand that removing a person's identity is a first step in dehumanization. Genocide is possible only after oppressors succeed in stripping victims of their humanity.

❶ Background

More About the Authors

Primo Levi had little sense of his own Judaism growing up: "Religion did not count for much in my family." Yet, Judaism counted for an enormous amount as Nazism swept Europe. The Italian government enacted "racial laws" that placed heavy restrictions on Jews.

Unlike Levi, Elie Wiesel grew up in a devoutly religious family. Wiesel remains a man committed to Judaism. He wrote for a Yiddish newspaper and has authored books on the Holocaust and on the role of Jewish faith in the modern world.

Nelly Sachs grew up in a middle-class family and studied dance and music as well as literature. However, her comfortable life was obliterated by the Holocaust. During the war, she earned money translating German poetry into Swedish. Over the years, her own poetry brought her international recognition.

Geography Note

Draw students' attention to the map. Remind them that the enormous tragedy of the Holocaust was concentrated in this highlighted area of Europe.

Build Skills — *Nonfiction • Poem*

❶ *from* Survival in Auschwitz • *from* Night • When in early summer . . .

Primo Levi
(1919–1987)

Both a chemist and a writer, Primo Levi had more than one side. Yet his fate hinged on a single fact: He was Jewish. This fact alone was enough to send Levi, like millions of other Jews in the 1930s and 1940s, to a brutal concentration camp.

Captured When the Nazis occupied Italy in 1943, Levi, a native of Turin, joined a resistance group. In December, the Nazis captured the young chemist and deported him to the camp at Auschwitz, in Poland. Levi was freed when the Allies liberated the camp in 1945. He achieved fame when his early memoir of the experience, *Survival in Auschwitz* (1947), was republished in 1958.

Writer and Chemist Levi worked as a chemist until 1977, when he retired to write full time. In books such as *The Periodic Table* (1975), he explores science, literature, and history. In his last book, *The Drowned and the Saved* (1986), he returns to the Holocaust with a darker, less hopeful eye.

Elie Wiesel (b. 1928)

Convinced that he had survived the Holocaust in order to "bear witness" to its horrors, Elie Wiesel nonetheless waited a decade to relate his experiences. "I didn't want to use the wrong words," he recalls. Finally, in 1956, Wiesel published *Night*, his renowned memoir of the Holocaust.

A Family Broken Wiesel grew up in the small Romanian town of Sighet. As World War II raged, the Nazis shipped Sighet's Jews to Auschwitz. The family was split up. The sixteen-year-old Wiesel ended up with his father in Buchenwald, a concentration camp in Germany.

Remembering In 1945, American troops liberated the camp. Orphaned by the war, Wiesel went to France, where he began his career as a journalist and spokesperson against oppression. Over the decades, he has spoken out against apartheid in South Africa, "ethnic cleansing" in Bosnia, and other practices he found to resemble Nazism. For his humanitarian efforts, Wiesel was awarded the Nobel Peace Prize in 1986.

Nelly Sachs
(1891–1970)

As a teenager in Berlin, Germany, Nelly Sachs wrote a letter to a favorite author, Sweden's Selma Lagerlöf. That fateful letter began a correspondence that eventually saved Sachs's life.

History Interrupts By the 1920s, Sachs, with Lagerlöf's encouragement, was publishing her poetry in a Berlin newspaper. She might have continued on to moderate literary success, but history intervened. The Nazis came to power in 1933, and Sachs, who was Jewish, watched as the world turned dark. In 1940, threat became reality: She learned that she was to be sent to a concentration camp.

A Friend Helps When Lagerlöf heard of her friend's danger, she lobbied Sweden's royalty for the permission Sachs and her mother needed to move to Sweden. The Swedish government issued visas to Sachs and her mother, and the two escaped Germany. Haunted by friends and relatives killed in the Holocaust, Sachs devoted much of her poetry to the event. Though she eventually became a Swedish citizen, she continued to write in German. In 1966, Sachs, like Selma Lagerlöf before her, was awarded the Nobel Prize in Literature.

Preview

Connecting to the Literature

Being somebody looks easy: "I'm somebody who jogs." "I'm somebody who likes rock music." Watch a former friend ignore you, though, and it's not hard to feel like a nobody. In the 1940s, a nation tried to turn the writers in this unit into nobodies. Their words speak for the nobody in all of us.

❷ Literary Analysis

Autobiography

An **autobiography** is a nonfiction work in which a person tells his or her own life story. An autobiography may be written for a number of reasons:

- Famous people may write autobiographies to satisfy readers' curiosity and to ensure accuracy about their lives.
- People who have shaped or witnessed historic events may write autobiographies to give insight into those events.

In their autobiographical writings, Primo Levi and Elie Wiesel give readers insight into the Holocaust. As you read, note ways in which the writers' purposes shape their autobiographies.

Comparing Literary Works

One form of autobiography is the **memoir,** a first-person account that focuses on one person or series of events in the writer's life, rather than telling the writer's full life story. Like many memoirs, Levi's and Wiesel's works offer an understanding of the meaning of events.

Use a chart like the one shown to compare the writers' insights.

❸ Reading Strategy

Connecting to Historical Context

Holocaust narratives offer universal truths, but they are also rooted in history. To understand these works fully, **connect to historical context,** linking the work to events of the time. For instance, to understand why Levi, an Italian, is a prisoner of the Germans, you need to know that the Nazis occupied Italy in 1943. As you read, connect the background information on pages 1254 and 1261 with events and images in the selections.

Vocabulary Builder

sordid (sôr′ did) *adj.* filthy; depressingly wretched (p. 1259)

prophetic (prō fet′ ik) *adj.* giving a prediction of the future (p. 1259)

intuition (in′ tōō ish′ ən) *n.* instinctive understanding (p. 1259)

affinity (ə fin′ i tē) *n.* close relationship; natural liking (p. 1259)

plaintive (plān′ tiv) *adj.* expressing sorrow; mournful (p. 1263)

beseeching (bē sēch′ iŋ) *adj.* asking for something earnestly (p. 1263)

liquidated (lik′ wi dāt′ id) *adj.* disposed of; ended; killed (p. 1268)

deportees (dē′ pôr tēz′) *n.* people ordered to leave a country (p. 1268)

from *Survival in Auschwitz* / from *Night* / *When in early summer . . .* ■ 1253

Standard Course of Study

- Exhibit an awareness of cultural context. (WL.1.02.3)
- Reflect on and show how a real-world event affects viewpoint. (CT.4.01.2)

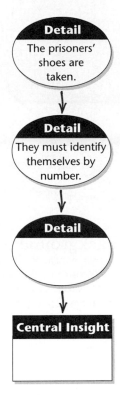

Detail
The prisoners' shoes are taken.

Detail
They must identify themselves by number.

Detail

Central Insight

❷ Literary Analysis

Autobiography

- Read aloud the Literary Analysis instruction. Make sure that students understand that in an autobiography, the author tells his or her own life story. Have students create quick timelines of the significant events in their lives, beginning with birth and ending with the present.

- After reading the Comparing Literary Works instruction, tell students to circle one memorable timeline event. Tell students that a memoir of this event would focus on specific details and would offer some insight into the event's significance.

- Give students a copy of the **Literary Analysis Graphic Organizer A,** p. 213 in *Graphic Organizer Transparencies.* Have them use it to record three key details about the event they circled on their timeline.

- Then, help students complete their graphic organizers by adding central insights that the details suggest, given the vantage point of time and history.

❸ Reading Strategy

Connecting to Historical Context

- Ask a volunteer to read aloud the Reading Strategy instruction.

- Lead students in a discussion about the importance of historical context when reading memoirs. Tell students that memoirs like *Survival in Auschwitz* and *Night* present readers with in-depth, personal depictions of world-changing events. They offer universal truths, but they are also rooted in specific historical contexts.

Vocabulary Builder

- Pronounce each vocabulary word for students, and read the definitions as a class. Have students identify any words with which they are already familiar.

Differentiated Instruction   Solutions for All Learners

Support for Special Needs Students	**Support for Less Proficient Readers**	**Support for English Learners**
Have students use the support pages for these selections in the *Reader's Notebook: Adapted Version.* Completing these pages will prepare students to read the selections in the Student Edition.	Have students use the support pages for these selections in the *Reader's Notebooks.* After students finish each selection in the *Reader's Notebooks,* have them complete the questions and activities in the Student Edition.	Have students use the support pages for these selections in the *Reader's Notebooks: English Learner's Version.* Completing these pages will prepare students to read the selections in the Student Edition.

te Understanding

❶ About the Selection

This harrowing selection depicts Primo Levi's arrival at Auschwitz, the notorious Nazi concentration camp. Arriving with a group of Italian Jews, Levi immediately recognizes Auschwitz as hell, the very bottom of human experience. Through interpreters, German SS officers mock the prisoners, order them to strip naked, and leave them standing and waiting for hours. Eventually, they are washed and shaved bare. They are issued prison clothing but forced to run naked through the cold before they can dress. Finally, Levi describes being tattooed with an identification number.

❷ Critical Viewing

Possible response: Some prisoners might imagine that the message communicates a sense of hope that they might be able to preserve themselves through work. However, Levi is highly perceptive, recognizing the true nature of what is happening while those around him attempt to deny it. A prisoner like Levi will probably note the irony of a sign about freedom placed above the gates of a prison.

from Survival ❶ in Auschwitz

Primo Levi
translated by Stuart Woolf

❷ ▲ **Critical Viewing**
Explain how a prisoner such as Levi might react to the sight of this sign, "Work Gives Freedom," over the gate of Auschwitz. **[Connect]**

Background The Holocaust was the systematic persecution and murder of millions of Jews and others deemed unfit by Germany's Nazi party. The Nazis came to power in Germany in 1933. During World War II (1939–1945), Nazi forces rounded up Jews throughout German-occupied lands and shot them or shipped them to concentration camps. Here, the prisoners were worked or starved to death or killed, often by poison gas. In this excerpt, Primo Levi describes his arrival at the complex of three camps at Auschwitz, in Poland.

On the Bottom

The journey did not last more than twenty minutes. Then the lorry[1] stopped, and we saw a large door, and above it a sign, brightly illuminated (its memory still strikes me in my dreams): *Arbeit Macht Frei*,[2] work gives freedom.

---

1. **lorry** (lor´ ē) *n.* British term for "truck."
2. ***Arbeit Macht Frei*** (ar´ bĭt mäkt frī)

Differentiated Instruction   Solutions for All Learners

Accessibility at a Glance

	from Survival at Auschwitz	*from* Night	When in Early Summer . . .
Context	The Holocaust	The Holocaust	The Holocaust
Language	Personal recollections	Personal recollections with gripping dialogue	Symbolic language
Concept Level	Accessible (the hideous effects of oppression)	Accessible (the conflict between self-survival and helping others)	Challenging (Nature's beauty distracts the world from remembering the Holocaust.)
Literary Merit	Levi's harrowing memoir of the Holocaust is a historical gem.	Wiesel's heartrending memoir offers vivid details of the horrors of the Holocaust.	Moving poetic juxtaposition of images of nature's beauties and the Holocaust
Lexile	1010L	510L	NP
Overall Rating	Average	Average	More challenging

We climb down, they make us enter an enormous empty room that is poorly heated. We have a terrible thirst. The weak gurgle of the water in the radiators makes us ferocious; we have had nothing to drink for four days. But there is also a tap—and above it a card which says that it is forbidden to drink as the water is dirty. Nonsense. It seems obvious that the card is a joke, "they" know that we are dying of thirst and they put us in a room, and there is a tap, and *Wassertrinken Verboten*.[3] I drink and I incite my companions to do likewise, but I have to spit it out, the water is tepid and sweetish, with the smell of a swamp.

This is hell. Today, in our times, hell must be like this. A huge, empty room: we are tired, standing on our feet, with a tap which drips while we cannot drink the water, and we wait for something which will certainly be terrible, and nothing happens and nothing continues to happen. What can one think about? One cannot think anymore, it is like being already dead. Someone sits down on the ground. The time passes drop by drop.

We are not dead. The door is opened and an SS[4] man enters, smoking. He looks at us slowly and asks, *"Wer kann Deutsch?"*[5] One of us whom I have never seen, named Flesch, moves forward; he will be our interpreter. This SS man makes a long calm speech; the interpreter translates. We have to form rows of five, with intervals of two yards between man and man; then we have to undress and make a bundle of the clothes in a special manner, the woolen garments on one side, all the rest on the other; we must take off our shoes but pay great attention that they are not stolen.

Stolen by whom? Why should our shoes be stolen? And what about our documents, the few things we have in our pockets, our watches? We all look at the interpreter, and the interpreter asks the German, and the German smokes and looks him through and through as if he were transparent, as if no one had spoken.

I had never seen old men naked. Mr. Bergmann wore a truss[6] and asked the interpreter if he should take it off, and the interpreter hesitated. But the German understood and spoke seriously to the interpreter pointing to someone. We saw the interpreter swallow and then he said: "The officer says, take off the truss, and you will be given that of Mr. Coen." One could see the words coming bitterly out of Flesch's mouth; this was the German manner of laughing.

---

3. *Wassertrinken Verboten* (väs´ ər trink´ 'n fer bōt´ 'n) German: "It is forbidden to drink the water."
4. **SS** abbreviation for the *Shutzstaffel* (shoōtz´ shtäf el), a quazi-military unit of the Nazi party, used as a secret police.
5. *Wer kann Deutsch?* (ver kän doich) German: "Who knows German?"
6. **truss** *n.* padded strap worn to support a hernia (an abdominal muscle rupture).

Literary Analysis
Autobiography Why does Levi tell some of his autobiography in the first-person plural (we)?

4 ▼ Critical Viewing
What does this image of wedding rings taken from concentration camp prisoners suggest about the treatment Levi will receive? **[Interpret]**

☑ Reading Check 5
Why are the men tormented by the tap and the sound of dripping water in the room?

from *Survival in Auschwitz* ■ 1255

---

❸ Literary Analysis
Autobiography

- Explain that in an autobiography, the author relates, generally in the first person, his or her own experiences. In *Survival in Auschwitz*, for example, Primo Levi presents his own experiences during the Holocaust and in the Nazi concentration camps.

- Have students read the bracketed passage independently. **Ask** them to point out anything unusual they notice about the way Levi narrates the events he describes. **Answer:** Levi primarily uses the first person plural (*we*) to narrate, rather than the first person singular (*I*).

- **Ask** students the Literary Analysis question: Why does Levi tell some of his autobiography in the first person plural (*we*)? **Possible response:** Levi is describing not only his own experiences but also historical events. The use of the first person plural conveys his understanding that what is happening to him is also happening to others. Additionally, because many Jews did not survive the Holocaust, Levi uses the first person plural to connect their untold stories with his own.

- Encourage students to note the points at which Levi's collective and individual stories converge and separate. Discuss why these convergences and separations occur at the points where they do.

▶ **Reteach** Should students have trouble with this autobiographical account, have them use the **Literary Analysis** support, p. 64 in *Unit 9 Resources*.

❹ Critical Viewing

Possible response: The huge pile of wedding rings shows the huge number of people upon whom the Nazi crimes were perpetrated and suggests that the Nazis will take everything—even the most personal of belongings—from their prisoners. The Nazis will attempt to strip Levi of his identity.

❺ Reading Check

Answer: The prisoners are ordered to put all the shoes in one corner. From here, the shoes are swept out of the room in one big jumble.

❻ Humanities

Concentration Camp Inmates,
by Hellmut Bachrach-Barée

Although virtually no information about Hellmut Bachrach-Barée exists, the extraordinary emotional impact of *Concentration Camp Inmates* suggests that the artist witnessed what he depicts. The date of this work—February 1945, within a month of the liberation of Auschwitz—hints that the memory was fresh in the artist's mind.

Use the following question for discussion:

What elements of this painting suggest that the artist was in a concentration camp?
Possible response: The subjects' pain and hopelessness is so vivid that the artist must have had first-hand experience of the camps.

❼ Critical Viewing

Possible response: The dull, drab colors and rough texture capture the grim experience of the prisoners as do the sorrowful facial expressions and hunched postures of the figures.

Now another German comes and tells us to put the shoes in a certain corner, and we put them there, because now it is all over and we feel outside this world and the only thing is to obey. Someone comes with a broom and sweeps away all the shoes, outside the door in a heap. He is crazy, he is mixing them all together, ninety-six pairs, they will be all mixed up. The outside door opens, a freezing wind enters and we are naked and cover ourselves up with our arms. The wind blows and slams the door; the German reopens it and stands watching with interest how we writhe[7] to hide from the wind, one behind the other. Then he leaves and closes it.

Now the second act begins. Four men with razors, soapbrushes and clippers burst in; they have trousers and jackets with stripes, with a number sewn on the front; perhaps they are the same sort as those others of this evening (this evening or yesterday evening?); but these are robust[8] and flourishing. We ask many questions but they catch hold of us and in a moment we find ourselves shaved and sheared. What comic faces we have without hair! The four speak a language which does not seem of this world. It is certainly not German, for I understand a little German.

Finally another door is opened: here we are, locked in, naked, sheared and standing, with our feet in water—it is a shower-room. We are alone. Slowly the astonishment dissolves, and we speak, and everyone asks questions and no one answers. If we are naked in a shower-room, it means that we will have a shower. If we have a shower it is because they are not going to kill us yet. But why then do they keep us standing, and give us nothing to drink, while nobody explains anything, and we have no shoes or clothes, but we are all naked with our feet in the water, and we have been traveling five days and cannot even sit down.

And our women?

Mr. Levi asks me if I think that our women are like us at this moment, and where they are, and if we will be able to see them again. I say yes, because he is married and has a daughter; certainly we will see them again. But by now my belief is that all this is a game to mock and

Concentration Camp Inmates, February 1945. Pencil and watercolor on paper, Hellmut Bachrach-Barée, Gift of the artist. Courtesy of the Yad Vashem Art Museum, Jerusalem

▲ **Critical Viewing** ❼
What details of style—color, texture, clarity, line—help this drawing of concentration camp prisoners convey a sad or even grim mood? Explain. **[Analyze]**

---

7. **writhe** (rīth) v. twist the body about, as in pain.
8. **robust** (rō bust′) adj. strong and healthy; full of vigor.

Enrichment

Terezin—"The Waiting Room for Hell"
The town of Terezin lies outside Prague, the capital of Czechoslovakia from 1918 to 1993. During the Holocaust, the Nazis used Terezin as a "model" concentration camp they could present to the world to hide the fact that they were systematically murdering the Jews of Europe. Jewish leaders and cultural figures were sent here. The shops were stocked with food, at least when Nazi cameras rolled to create propaganda films. The Red Cross was allowed to visit Terezin on one occasion. Even this international relief organization was apparently fooled, concluding that life in Terezin was as decent as might be expected in wartime.

But Terezin was not what it seemed. Although the Jews here were not treated as harshly as they were at such camps as Auschwitz, countless thousands died of hunger and disease. Large numbers of families and the elderly were sent to Terezin and then moved to other camps. Terezin became known as the "waiting room for hell."

sneer at us. Clearly they will kill us, whoever thinks he is going to live is mad, it means that he has swallowed the bait, but I have not; I have understood that it will soon all be over, perhaps in this same room, when they get bored of seeing us naked, dancing from foot to foot and trying every now and again to sit down on the floor. But there are two inches of cold water and we cannot sit down.

We walk up and down without sense, and we talk, everybody talks to everybody else, we make a great noise. The door opens, and a German enters; it is the officer of before. He speaks briefly, the interpreter translates. "The officer says you must be quiet, because this is not a rabbinical school."[9] One sees the words which are not his, the bad words, twist his mouth as they come out, as if he was spitting out a foul taste. We beg him to ask what we are waiting for, how long we will stay here, about our women, everything; but he says no, that he does not want to ask. This Flesch, who is most unwilling to translate into Italian the hard cold German phrases and refuses to turn into German our questions because he knows that it is useless, is a German Jew of about fifty, who has a large scar on his face from a wound received fighting the Italians on the Piave.[10] He is a closed, taciturn[11] man, for whom I feel an instinctive respect as I feel that he has begun to suffer before us.

The German goes and we remain silent, although we are a little ashamed of our silence. It is still night and we wonder if the day will ever come. The door opens again, and someone else dressed in stripes comes in. He is different from the others, older, with glasses, a more civilized face, and much less robust. He speaks to us in Italian.

By now we are tired of being amazed. We seem to be watching some mad play, one of those plays in which the witches, the Holy Spirit and the devil appear. He speaks Italian badly, with a strong foreign accent. He makes a long speech, is very polite, and tries to reply to all our questions.

We are at Monowitz, near Auschwitz, in Upper Silesia, a region inhabited by both Poles and Germans. This camp is a work-camp, in German one says *Arbeitslager*,[12] all

---

Reading Strategy
Connecting to Historical Context In what way do these difficulties over language reflect the actions and policies of the Nazis in Europe?

▼ **Critical Viewing** ❿
Explain which aspect of Levi's experience the faceless figures in this image capture. **[Connect]**

Guard with Stick, a collage of paper cut from an office ledger, Soña Spitzova, Jewish Museum in Prague, Courtesy of the United States Holocaust Memorial Museum

---

9. **rabbinical school** school for the training of rabbis (scholars and teachers of Jewish law). The comment is a negative reference to the practice in such schools of orally disputing issues of law.
10. **Piave** (pyä′ vā) river in northeastern Italy, located between Padua and Venice.
11. **taciturn** (tas′ ə tʉrn′) *adj.* habitually silent; uncommunicative.
12. ***Arbeitslager*** (är′ bïts läg′ r)

from *Survival in Auschwitz* ■ 1257

There was a class of people in the camps designated as criminals. These prisoners probably included common criminals, who had a higher status than Jews. In Levi's account, however, the nature of the Hungarian doctor's crime is unclear.

❷ Humanities

Drawing for the Transportation Bas Relief, by Dee Clements

Colorado-based artist Dee Clements specializes in sculpture. He belongs to the National Sculptor's Guild and has created numerous public sculptures. Among these is the Desert Holocaust Memorial in Palm Desert, California, dedicated in 1995. The centerpiece of this memorial is a bronze sculpture of seven figures, European Jews whose lives were torn apart by the Holocaust. Also part of the memorial are eleven bas-reliefs—sculpted images that project outward from flat backgrounds—portraying various aspects of the great tragedy. Clements's _Drawing for the Transportation Bas Relief_ depicts one of the trains the Nazis used to bring Jews from all over Europe to concentration camps such as Auschwitz.

Use the following questions for discussion:

• What does this image suggest about the nature of the Holocaust?
Possible response: The train is a potent symbol of industry, suggesting that the mass murders of the Holocaust were carried out in an industrial, mechanical, and impersonal manner.

• Imagine a completed bas-relief of this image. How do you think the bas-relief would affect you as a viewer?
Possible response: The solidity and permanence of the bas-relief might make the image even more powerful.

❸ Critical Viewing

Possible response: The group of people, reaching almost as far as the eye can see, suggests that the human spirit is being crushed. These people are about to be packed together in the train's boxcars as if they were inhuman cargo and are about to undergo an experience that will be inhuman.

the prisoners (there are about ten thousand) work in a factory which produces a type of rubber called Buna, so that the camp itself is called Buna.

We will be given shoes and clothes—no, not our own—other shoes, other clothes, like his. We are naked now because we are waiting for the shower and the disinfection, which will take place immediately after the reveille, because one cannot enter the camp without being disinfected.

Certainly there will be work to do, everyone must work here. But there is work and work: he, for example, acts as doctor. He is a Hungarian doctor who studied in Italy and he is the dentist of the Lager.[13] He has been in the Lager for four and a half years (not in this one: Buna has only been open for a year and a half), but we can see that he is still quite well, not very thin. Why is he in the Lager? Is he Jewish like us? "No," he says simply, "I am a criminal."

We ask him many questions. He laughs, replies to some and not to others, and it is clear that he avoids certain subjects. He does not speak of the women: he says they are well, that we will see them again soon, but he does not say how or where. Instead he tells us other things, strange and crazy things, perhaps he too is playing with us. Perhaps he is mad—one goes mad in the Lager. He says that every Sunday there are concerts and football matches. He says that whoever boxes well can become cook. He says that whoever works well receives prize-coupons with which to buy tobacco and soap. He says that the water is really not drinkable, and that instead a coffee substitute is distributed every day, but generally nobody drinks it as the soup itself is sufficiently watery to quench thirst. We beg him to find us something to drink, but he says that he cannot, that he has come to see us secretly, against SS orders, as we still have to be disinfected, and that he must leave at once; he has come because he has a liking for Italians, and because, he says, he "has a little heart." We ask him if there are other Italians in the camp and he says there are some, a few, he does not know how many; and he at once changes the subject. Meanwhile a bell

13. **Lager** (läg' r) German: "camp."

Drawing for the Transportation Bas Relief, Dee Clements

▼ Critical Viewing ❸
In what way does this image capture the "demolition of a man" discussed by Levi? **[Connect]**

Enrichment

The Holocaust in Italy
Italy had encouraged the Nazis' rise to power. But Italian dictator Benito Mussolini originally had little interest in persecuting Italy's Jews. In fact, the Italian Fascist party included a small number of Jewish members. Yet, as Germany and Italy drew closer together, Mussolini decided that Italy, too, needed to preserve its "racial purity." In November 1938, Italy's "racial laws" went into effect.

However, until the German invasion of 1943, Italian Jews such as Primo Levi were seldom deported to camps. Even after the German invasion, many Italians hid their Jewish neighbors or smuggled them to freedom. For this reason, about 85 percent of the 45,200 Italian Jews survived to the end of the war. Yet almost 7,000 were captured, loaded onto cattle cars, and sent to concentration camps. Primo Levi was one of the tiny minority who returned home to tell their stories.

rang and he immediately hurried off and left us stunned and disconcerted. Some feel refreshed but I do not. I still think that even this dentist, this incomprehensible person, wanted to amuse himself at our expense, and I do not want to believe a word of what he said.

At the sound of the bell, we can hear the still dark camp waking up. Unexpectedly the water gushes out boiling from the showers—five minutes of bliss; but immediately after, four men (perhaps they are the barbers) burst in yelling and shoving and drive us out, wet and steaming, into the adjoining room which is freezing; here other shouting people throw at us unrecognizable rags and thrust into our hands a pair of broken-down boots with wooden soles; we have no time to understand and we already find ourselves in the open, in the blue and icy snow of dawn, barefoot and naked, with all our clothing in our hands, with a hundred yards to run to the next hut. There we are finally allowed to get dressed.

When we finish, everyone remains in his own corner and we do not dare lift our eyes to look at one another. There is nowhere to look in a mirror, but our appearance stands in front of us, reflected in a hundred livid faces, in a hundred miserable and <u>sordid</u> puppets. We are transformed into the phantoms glimpsed yesterday evening.

Then for the first time we became aware that our language lacks words to express this offense, the demolition of a man. In a moment, with almost <u>prophetic</u> <u>intuition</u>, the reality was revealed to us: we had reached the bottom. It is not possible to sink lower than this; no human condition is more miserable than this, nor could it conceivably be so. Nothing belongs to us anymore; they have taken away our clothes, our shoes, even our hair; if we speak, they will not listen to us, and if they listen, they will not understand. They will even take away our name: and if we want to keep it, we will have to find in ourselves the strength to do so, to manage somehow so that behind the name something of us, of us as we were, still remains.

⑭ We know that we will have difficulty in being understood, and this is as it should be. But consider what value, what meaning is enclosed even in the smallest of our daily habits, in the hundred possessions which even the poorest beggar owns: a handkerchief, an old letter, the photo of a cherished person. These things are part of us, almost like limbs of our body; nor is it conceivable that we can be deprived of them in our world, for we immediately find others to substitute the old ones, other objects which are ours in their personification and evocation of our memories.

Imagine now a man who is deprived of everyone he loves, and at the same time of his house, his habits, his clothes, in short, of everything he possesses: he will be a hollow man, reduced to suffering and needs, forgetful of dignity and restraint, for he who loses all often easily loses himself. He will be a man whose life or death can be lightly decided with no sense of human <u>affinity</u>, in the most fortunate of cases, on the basis of a pure judgment of utility. It is in this way that one can understand

from Survival in Auschwitz ■ 1259

⑭ Literary Analysis
Autobiography

- Remind students that in an autobiography, an author tells his or her own life story and can offer personal insight into historical events.

- Have students read the first sentence in the bracketed passage, and call their attention to the phrase "the demolition of a man." **Ask** them to explain what Levi means by this.
  Possible response: The Nazis will destroy Levi and his comrades spiritually, emotionally, and physically.

- Suggest to students that for Levi, "the demolition of a man" is what the Nazis did to Jews beginning with their arrival at Auschwitz. It is a central focus of Levi's autobiography.

- **Ask** students the Literary Analysis question: Identify one technique Levi uses to put "the demolition of a man" into words.
  Possible response: Levi lists the things the Nazis have taken from the prisoners, including their clothes, their hair, the capacity to be understood, and their names; he describes the importance of "the smallest of [the individual's] daily habits" and possessions, all of which have been taken away; and he describes a person robbed of everything as "a hollow man" whom others will not consider human.

- Make sure that students recognize that in these paragraphs, Levi uses language, which he first denounces as lacking, to describe his experiences. Discuss the impact of this strategy on the reader.

⑮ Reading Check
Answer: Levi says that the prisoners are left with nothing at all.

- Point out that *Survival in Auschwitz* is a memoir because it focuses on Levi's experiences during the Holocaust. Rather than telling his entire life story, he offers insight into this historical event.

- Have students read the bracketed passage. Then, **ask** the Reading Strategy question: By telling the reader about his number, what insight does Levi suggest? Explain. **Possible response:** Levi suggests that the process of being numbered and tattooed is a "baptism" for death rather than for life.

ASSESS

Answers

1. **Possible response:** This work could be recommended to anyone interested in the Holocaust. Anyone who believes that he or she is superior to any other group of human beings might benefit from reading Levi's narrative. It might force such readers to recognize the destruction of elitism and racism.

2. (a) **Possible responses:** The prisoners are deprived of water; their clothes are taken away; they are forced to stand and wait indefinitely while naked and cold; they are sheared; they are insulted by Nazi officers; and they are denied information. (b) Hell is the worst experience humanly imaginable. The treatment by the Nazis is worse than anything Levi has previously imagined. Therefore, the room with the water replaces any predetermined notions of hell, because the water, essential for life, is undrinkable.

3. (a) Flesch is a selective translator. He translates most, but not all, of the German words. (b) **Possible response:** Flesch is reluctant to be a conduit for oppression by inflicting the cruelty of the words and actions on his fellow prisoners.

4. (a) The prisoners are "renamed" when they are tattooed with numbers they must show to get food. (b) Levi describes the renaming as a baptism for death.

---

the double sense of the term "extermination camp," and it is now clear what we seek to express with the phrase: "to lie on the bottom."

Häftling:[14] I have learnt that I am a Häftling. My number is 174517; we have been baptized, we will carry the tattoo on our left arm until we die.

The operation was slightly painful and extraordinarily rapid: they placed us all in a row, and one by one, according to the alphabetical order of our names, we filed past a skillful official, armed with a sort of pointed tool with a very short needle. It seems that this is the real, true initiation: only by "showing one's number" can one get bread and soup. Several days passed, and not a few cuffs and punches, before we became used to showing our number promptly enough not to disorder the daily operation of food-distribution; weeks and months were needed to learn its sound in the German language. And for many days, while the habits of freedom still led me to look for the time on my wristwatch, my new name ironically appeared instead, its number tattooed in bluish characters under the skin.

16

14. *Häftling* (heft´ lin) German: "prisoner."

Literary Analysis
Autobiography and Memoir By telling the reader about his number, what insight does Levi suggest? Explain.

Critical Reading

1. **Respond:** To what audience would you recommend Levi's autobiography? Why?

2. **(a) Recall:** Describe three ways in which the prisoners are mistreated when they arrive at Auschwitz. **(b) Interpret:** What do you think Levi means when he writes "Today, in our times, hell must be like this"?

3. **(a) Recall:** Describe the way in which Flesch fulfills his role as translator. **(b) Infer:** Why is he reluctant to translate the German officer's comments into Italian?

4. **(a) Recall:** Explain the way in which the prisoners are "renamed" at the camp. **(b) Analyze:** What does Levi feel is the significance of this renaming?

5. **(a) Infer:** According to Levi, what makes up human identity? **(b) Draw Conclusions:** What does Levi suggest are the primary goals of the concentration camp?

6. **Draw Conclusions:** Referring to the Nazi treatment of the prisoners, Levi writes that "our language lacks words to express this offense, the demolition of a man." What does this remark imply about Levi's task of writing a memoir of this experience?

For: More about Primo Levi
Visit: www.PHSchool.com
Web Code: ete-9904

Answers continued

5. (a) Levi believes that family and home as well as many small things, like hair, clothes, minor possessions, and personal habits make up human identity. (b) Levi suggests that the concentration camp's goal is to strip away everything that makes up the human identities of its prisoners. Levi says a person robbed of identity is one "whose life or death can be lightly decided with no sense of human affinity."

6. **Possible response:** Levi acknowledges the inadequacy of words to convey the demolition of a man; yet, he writes his narrative anyway. His act suggests that storytelling is the only means he has to rebuild a man.

Go Online For additional information about **Author Link** Primo Levi, have students type in the Web Code, then select *L* from the alphabet, and then select Primo Levi.

from Night

Elie Wiesel

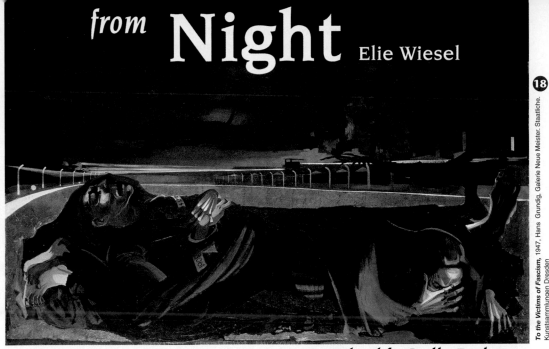

To the Victims of Fascism, 1947, Hans Grundig, Galerie Neue Meister. Staatliche. Kunstsammlungen Dresden

⑱

translated by Stella Rodway

Background Toward the end of World War II (1939–1945), as the Allied armies fighting the Germans gained territory, German forces evacuated the inmates of the concentration camps in forced "death marches" and in "death trains." They hoped to send the prisoners deeper into Germany to prevent their liberation. In this excerpt from *Night,* Wiesel describes his experiences as a sixteen-year-old sent on such a journey with his father.

⑲ ▲ **Critical Viewing**
What does this painting suggest about the mood of Wiesel's memoir? **[Predict]**

That same evening, we reached our destination.

It was late at night. The guards came to unload us. The dead were abandoned in the train. Only those who could still stand were able to get out.

Meir Katz stayed in the train. The last day had been the most murderous. A hundred of us had got into the wagon. A dozen of us got out—among them, my father and I.

We had arrived at Buchenwald.[1]

⑳ **Reading Check**
What happened to many of the narrator's fellow passengers?

---

1. **Buchenwald** (book´ 'n wôld´) village in Germany that was the site of a Nazi concentration camp and extermination center.

from Night ■ 1261

Infer

- Have students read the bracketed line. Then, ask them to consider the image of the teenage Eliezer holding his father's hand. Students may observe that this act may not be common in our society today.

- **Ask** students what inferences they can make about the relationship between Eliezer and his father from the image of the boy holding his father's hand.
  Possible response: Eliezer's experience in the camps has in some ways thwarted his rite of passage into adulthood; therefore, he clings, childlike, to his father, who is the last link with Eliezer's life before the camps.

- Tell students to bear this inference in mind as they read more about the complicated relationship between Eliezer and his father.

22 **Literary Analysis**

Autobiography

- Remind students that an autobiography is an author's telling of his or her life story.

- Explain to students that although it is very different in style from Primo Levi's *Survival in Auschwitz, Night* is also an autobiography that focuses on its author's experiences in the Nazi concentration camps.

- Point out that one of the key differences between Wiesel's and Levi's autobiographies is that Wiesel makes extensive use of dialogue.

- Have students read the bracketed passage independently. Then, have them read it a second time, with different students taking turns reading the dialogue aloud.

- **Ask** students the Literary Analysis question: In what way does Wiesel's use of dialogue enrich his autobiography?
  Possible response: The suffering of Wiesel's father and the young Wiesel's frustration with his father are clearly conveyed through dialogue. The first-person narrator cannot relay his father's thoughts and feelings in any other way.

At the gate of the camp, SS[2] officers were waiting for us. They counted us. Then we were directed to the assembly place. Orders were given us through loudspeakers:

"Form fives!" "Form groups of a hundred!" "Five paces forward!"

21 I held onto my father's hand—the old, familiar fear: not to lose him.

Right next to us the high chimney of the crematory oven[3] rose up. It no longer made any impression on us. It scarcely attracted our attention.

An established inmate of Buchenwald told us that we should have a shower and then we could go into the blocks. The idea of having a hot bath fascinated me. My father was silent. He was breathing heavily beside me.

"Father," I said. "Only another moment more. Soon we can lie down—in a bed. You can rest. . . ."

He did not answer. I was so exhausted myself that his silence left me indifferent. My only wish was to take a bath as quickly as possible and lie down in a bed.

But it was not easy to reach the showers. Hundreds of prisoners were crowding there. The guards were unable to keep any order. They struck out right and left with no apparent result. Others, without the strength to push or even to stand up, had sat down in the snow. My father wanted to do the same. He groaned.

"I can't go on. . . . This is the end. . . . I'm going to die here. . . ."

He dragged me toward a hillock of snow from which emerged human shapes and ragged pieces of blanket.

"Leave me," he said to me. "I can't go on. . . . Have mercy on me. . . . I'll wait here until we can get into the baths. . . . You can come and find me."

I could have wept with rage. Having lived through so much, suffered so much, could I leave my father to die now? Now, when we could have a good hot bath and lie down?

"Father!" I screamed. "Father! Get up from here! Immediately! You're killing yourself. . . ."

22 I seized him by the arm. He continued to groan.

"Don't shout, son. . . . Take pity on your old father. . . . Leave me to rest here. . . . Just for a bit, I'm so tired . . . at the end of my strength. . . ."

He had become like a child, weak, timid, vulnerable.

"Father," I said. "You can't stay here."

I showed him the corpses all around him; they too had wanted to rest here.

"I can see them, son. I can see them all right. Let them sleep. It's so long since they closed their eyes. . . . They are exhausted . . . exhausted. . . ."

His voice was tender.

I yelled against the wind:

---

2. **SS** quasi-military unit of the Nazi party, used as a special police.
3. **crematory oven** large oven in which the corpses of Holocaust victims were burned. In some cases, victims were burned while still alive.

1262 ■ *The Contemporary World*

Literary Analysis
Autobiography In what way does Wiesel's use of dialogue enrich his autobiography?

Enrichment

Life and Death in the Nazi Concentration Camps

The first concentration camps were established as early as 1933. By the time World War II had started, more than 20,000 people were imprisoned in the camps. The numbers grew tremendously over the next six years. Upon arrival at the camps, those who were not strong enough to work were gassed to death; their bodies were then burned in crematoriums. Those who could work were forced into slave labor and simply worked to death.

Countless prisoners died of starvation and disease and from the awful living conditions. Millions were gassed or shot. The Nazis often killed the sick. Nazi doctors performed medical experiments on the healthy. By the war's end—which was rapidly approaching in this excerpt from *Night*—the Nazis had killed about six million Jews—nearly two-thirds of Europe's entire Jewish population.

22 "They'll never wake again! Never! Don't you understand?"

For a long time this argument went on. I felt that I was not arguing with him, but with death itself, with the death that he had already chosen.

The sirens began to wail. An alert. The lights went out throughout the camp. The guards drove us toward the blocks. In a flash, there was no one left on the assembly place. We were only too glad not to have had to stay outside longer in the icy wind. We let ourselves sink down onto the planks. The beds were in several tiers. The cauldrons of soup at the entrance attracted no one. To sleep, that was all that mattered.

It was daytime when I awoke. And then I remembered that I had a father. Since the alert, I had followed the crowd without troubling about him. I had known that he was at the end, on the brink of death, and yet I had abandoned him.

I went to look for him.

23 But at the same moment this thought came into my mind: "Don't let me find him! If only I could get rid of this dead weight, so that I could use all my strength to struggle for my own survival, and only worry about myself." Immediately I felt ashamed of myself, ashamed forever.

I walked for hours without finding him. Then I came to the block where they were giving out black "coffee." The men were lining up and fighting.

A <u>plaintive</u>, <u>beseeching</u> voice caught me in the spine:

"Eliezer . . . my son . . . bring me . . . a drop of coffee. . . ."

I ran to him.

"Father! I've been looking for you for so long. . . . Where were you? Did you sleep? . . . How do you feel?"

He was burning with fever. Like a wild beast, I cleared a way for myself to the coffee cauldron. And I managed to carry back a cupful. I had a sip. The rest was for him. I can't forget the light of thankfulness in his eyes while he gulped it down—an animal gratitude. With those few gulps of hot water, I probably brought him more satisfaction than I had done during my whole childhood.

24 He was lying on a plank, livid,[4] his lips pale and dried up, shaken by tremors. I could not stay by him for long. Orders had been given to

---

4. **livid** (liv´ id) *adj.* here, bruised; grayish blue or pale.

25 ▲ **Critical Viewing**
Does Wiesel's memoir suggest any possibility of understanding why a group of people reduced others to the condition of these inmates? Explain. **[Apply]**

Vocabulary Builder
plaintive (plān´ tiv) *adj.* expressing sorrow; mournful

beseeching (bē sēch´ iŋ) *adj.* asking for something earnestly

 **Reading Check** **26**
What problem with his father does Eliezer have to confront?

from Night ■ 1263

---

23 **Reading Strategy**
Connecting to Historical Context

• Have a volunteer read aloud the bracketed passage. Then, **ask** students whether they think Eliezer's thoughts and feelings about finding his father are selfish.
Possible response: The reality of the camp would make such thoughts unavoidable.

• Remind students of the unimaginable pressure on Eliezer and the difficulty of surviving in the camps. Read aloud the Enrichment note on the previous page.

• **Ask** students whether, given the historical context, Eliezer's feelings are understandable.
Possible response: Eliezer's conflicted feelings are understandable. His efforts to suppress his darkest thoughts are even heroic.

24 **Critical Thinking**
Analyze

• **Ask** students what comparison the author uses to describe his actions and his father's response in this passage.
Answer: He compares himself to a wild beast in the way that he pushes himself through the crowd of men to get coffee for his father. He compares his father's thankfulness to animal gratitude.

• Then, **ask** students what the author's purpose is in making comparisons between human and animal behavior.
Answer: The author wanted to show how dehumanized the prisoners had become. Humans had become like animals—all actions focused on survival.

25 **Critical Viewing**

Possible response: Wiesel's memoir emphasizes the humanity and suffering of concentration camp inmates. By allowing the reader to identify with Eliezer's problems and his pain, the memoir makes it difficult to comprehend why a group would inflict such suffering on others.

26 **Reading Check**

Answer: Eliezer struggles—against his father's lack of will and his own survival instinct—to keep his father alive. Eliezer also struggles with his desire to be rid of this burden.

㉗ Humanities

1943 A.D., by Ben Shahn

Ben Shahn (1898–1969) did not witness the Holocaust. Nonetheless, he had a long history of addressing social issues in his work. His first solo exhibition was held in New York City in 1930. *The Passion of Sacco and Vanzetti,* scenes from the controversial murder trial of Italian-American anarchists painted between 1931 and 1932, made Shahn famous. He went on to create images of the Great Depression for the United States government.

1943 A.D. suggests the intense thoughtfulness characteristic of Shahn's work.

Use the following question for discussion:

What elements of this painting indicate that its subject is the Holocaust?
Possible response: The man in the foreground faces barbed wire, a piece of which appears to bind his forehead. His emaciated appearance and the laborers behind him also suggest the Holocaust. Finally, the title of the painting is the year the Holocaust was at its peak.

㉘ Critical Viewing

Possible response: This prisoner may be struggling with moral conflicts as he tries to survive.

㉙ Critical Thinking

Infer

- Ask a volunteer to read the bracketed passage aloud.

- Then, **ask** students to explain what the author means when he says that his father spoke as if he were afraid he would not have time.
Answer: The father talks faster and faster because he is afraid he will die before he can tell his son where to find the gold and money.

---

clear the place for cleaning. Only the sick could stay.

We stayed outside for five hours. Soup was given out. As soon as we were allowed to go back to the blocks, I ran to my father.

"Have you had anything to eat?"

"No."

"Why not?"

"They didn't give us anything . . . they said that if we were ill we should die soon anyway and it would be a pity to waste the food. I can't go on any more. . . ."

I gave him what was left of my soup. But it was with a heavy heart. I felt that I was giving it up to him against my will. No better than Rabbi Eliahou's son[5] had I withstood the test.

He grew weaker day by day, his gaze veiled, his face the color of dead leaves. On the third day after our arrival at Buchenwald, everyone had to go to the showers. Even the sick, who had to go through last.

On the way back from the baths, we had to wait outside for a long time. They had not yet finished cleaning the blocks.

Seeing my father in the distance, I ran to meet him. He went by me like a ghost, passed me without stopping, without looking at me. I called to him. He did not come back. I ran after him:

"Father, where are you running to?"

He looked at me for a moment, and his gaze was distant, visionary; it was the face of someone else. A moment only and on he ran again.

㉙ Struck down with dysentery,[6] my father lay in his bunk, five other invalids with him. I sat by his side, watching him, not daring to believe that he could escape death again. Nevertheless, I did all I could to give him hope.

Suddenly, he raised himself on his bunk and put his feverish lips to my ear:

"Eliezer . . . I must tell you where to find the gold and the money I buried . . . in the cellar. . . . You know. . . ."

He began to talk faster and faster, as though he were afraid he would not have time to tell me. I tried to explain to him that this was not the

---

5. **Rabbi Eliahou's son** Earlier in the book, Elie has witnessed a son abandoning his father, Rabbi Eliahou, by pretending not to notice when his father falls behind on a forced march.
6. **dysentery** (dis´ ən ter´ ē) *n.* disease of the intestines.

1264 ■ *The Contemporary World*

1943 A.D., c.1943, Ben Shahn, Courtesy of the Syracuse University Art Collection, © Estate of Ben Shahn/Licensed by VAGA, New York, NY

㉘ ▲ **Critical Viewing** Given what you have read in Wiesel's memoir, explain what thoughts might preoccupy this prisoner. **[Apply]**

Enrichment

The Holocaust's Other Victims

The elimination of the Jews of Europe was the goal of the Holocaust, and Jews were the main targets of the Nazi concentration camps. But they were not the only victims of the Nazis. Communists, Gypsies, and others whom the Nazi party believed did not exemplify German purity were imprisoned in concentration camps. Many suffered the same hideous treatment the Nazis meted out to their Jewish victims.

Many Jews have written remembrances of the atrocities they suffered during the Holocaust.

But just as Jews were not the only victims, they have not been the only ones to bear witness. A great deal of powerful writing—for both adults and children—has come from the memoirs of non-Jews living in occupied Italy, Norway, Poland, Holland, and even within Germany itself. You may wish to recommend to students martyred Lutheran theologian Dietrich Bonhoeffer's *Letters and Papers from Prison.* Bonhoeffer wrote this work during his incarceration in a Nazi prison during the war.

end, that we would go back to the house together, but he would not listen to me. He could no longer listen to me. He was exhausted. A trickle of saliva, mingled with blood, was running from between his lips. He had closed his eyes. His breath was coming in gasps.

For a ration of bread, I managed to change beds with a prisoner in my father's bunk. In the afternoon the doctor came. I went and told him that my father was very ill.

"Bring him here!"

I explained that he could not stand up. But the doctor refused to listen to anything. Somehow, I brought my father to him. He stared at him, then questioned him in a clipped voice:

"What do you want?"

"My father's ill," I answered for him. "Dysentery . . ."

"Dysentery? That's not my business. I'm a surgeon. Go on! Make room for the others."

Protests did no good.

"I can't go on, son. . . . Take me back to my bunk. . . ."

I took him back and helped him to lie down. He was shivering.

"Try and sleep a bit, father. Try to go to sleep. . . ."

His breathing was labored, thick. He kept his eyes shut. Yet I was convinced that he could see everything, that now he could see the truth in all things.

Another doctor came to the block. But my father would not get up. He knew that it was useless.

Besides, this doctor had only come to finish off the sick. I could hear him shouting at them that they were lazy and just wanted to stay in bed. I felt like leaping at his throat, strangling him. But I no longer had the courage or the strength. I was riveted to my father's deathbed. My hands hurt, I was clenching them so hard. Oh, to strangle the doctor and the others! To burn the whole world! My father's murderers! But the cry stayed in my throat.

When I came back from the bread distribution, I found my father weeping like a child:

"Son, they keep hitting me!"

"Who?"

I thought he was delirious.

"Him, the Frenchman . . . and the Pole . . . they were hitting me."

Another wound to the heart, another hate, another reason for living lost.

"Eliezer . . . Eliezer . . . tell them not to hit me. . . . I haven't done anything . . . . Why do they keep hitting me?"

I began to abuse his neighbors. They laughed at me. I promised them bread, soup. They laughed. Then they got angry; they could not stand

Cultural Connection

 Wiesel's Nobel Prize

On December 10, 1986, Elie Wiesel was presented with the Nobel Prize for his contributions to world peace. The president of the Nobel Committee mentioned Wiesel's father in his introductory address. He said, "You were with your father when he passed away; it was the darkest hour of your life. And this is the most glorious. It is therefore fitting that your own son be with you as you receive the highest distinction humanity can bestow upon one of its own." In his memoir *All Rivers Run to the Sea*, Wiesel describes his response to the president's unexpected words: "I was shaken by the linking of my father and my son. I saw them standing together. My lips moved, but no sound came out. Tears filled my eyes, the tears I couldn't shed so long ago."

Connect to the Literature

Why do you think Wiesel was able to shed tears in 1986 that he could not shed in the camps?

 **Reading Check** 32

Give an example of a way in which Eliezer takes care of his father.

from *Night* ■ 1265

---

30 **Literature in Context**
Cultural Connection

Wiesel's Nobel Prize Wiesel titled his Nobel acceptance speech "Keep Memory Alive." In it, he contemplated his own memories of the Holocaust, his childhood, and his father. "I remember:" he spoke. "It happened yesterday, or eternities ago. A young Jewish boy discovered the Kingdom of Night. I remember his bewilderment, I remember his anguish. It all happened so fast. The ghetto. The deportation. The sealed cattle car.

"I remember he asked his father: 'Can this be true? Who would allow such crimes to be committed? How could the world remain silent?'"

Connect to the Literature Tell students that Wiesel continued his speech with a moving account of how the boy inside him asks, "What have you done with your life?" Wiesel then explains that he has tried to keep the memory of the Holocaust alive, "Because if we forget, we are guilty, we are accomplices."

Have students explain why Wiesel cried in 1986 so many years after his imprisonment.
Possible response: In camp, he repressed all of his rage in order to survive. Years later, during the ceremony when he heard the reference to his son and his father, his grief came to the surface freely.

31 **Critical Thinking**
Connect

• Have students pause before reading the bracketed passage. **Ask** them to describe Eliezer's feelings toward his father.
Answer: Eliezer loves his father. However, Eliezer has a desperate, guilty desire to be free of the burden of caring for him.

• Have students read the bracketed passage independently. **Ask** them to connect the emotions Eliezer reveals with their previous impressions
Possible response: Eliezer's outpouring of rage illuminates the depth of his love for, and urge to protect, his father.

32 **Reading Check**

Possible responses: Eliezer shares his rations with his father and trades some of his bread to get a bunk near his father.

my father any longer, they said, because he was now unable to drag himself outside to relieve himself.

The following day he complained that they had taken his ration of bread.

"While you were asleep?"

"No. I wasn't asleep. They jumped on top of me. They snatched my bread . . . and they hit me . . . again. . . . I can't stand any more, son . . . a drop of water. . . ."

33 I knew that he must not drink. But he pleaded with me for so long that I gave in. Water was the worst poison he could have, but what else could I do for him? With water, without water, it would all be over soon anyway. . . .

"You, at least, have some mercy on me. . . ."

Have mercy on him! I, his only son!

A week went by like this.

"This is your father, isn't it?" asked the head of the block.

"Yes."

"He's very ill."

"The doctor won't do anything for him."

"The doctor *can't* do anything for him, now. And neither can you."

He put his great hairy hand on my shoulder and added:

"Listen to me, boy. Don't forget that you're in a concentration camp. Here, every man has to fight for himself and not think of anyone else. Even of his father. Here, there are no fathers, no brothers, no friends. Everyone lives and dies for himself alone. I'll give you a sound piece of advice—don't give your ration of bread and soup to your old father. There's nothing you can do for him. And you're killing yourself. Instead, you ought to be having his ration."

34 I listened to him without interrupting. He was right, I thought in the most secret region of my heart, but I dared not admit it. It's too late to save your old father, I said to myself. You ought to be having two rations of bread, two rations of soup. . . .

Only a fraction of a second, but I felt guilty. I ran to find a little soup to give my father. But he did not want it. All he wanted was water.

"Don't drink water . . . have some soup. . . ."

"I'm burning . . . why are you being so unkind to me, my son? Some water. . . ."

I brought him some water. Then I left the block for roll call. But I turned around and came back again. I lay down on the top bunk. Invalids were allowed to stay in the block. So I would be an invalid myself. I would not leave my father.

There was silence all round now, broken only by groans. In front of the block, the SS were giving orders. An officer passed by the beds. My father begged me:

"My son, some water. . . . I'm burning. . . . My stomach. . . ."

"Quiet, over there!" yelled the officer.

"Eliezer," went on my father, "some water. . . ."

1266 ■ *The Contemporary World*

Reading Strategy
Connecting to Historical Context Using facts about life in the concentration camps, explain why Wiesel was led to such dark thoughts.

The officer came up to him and shouted at him to be quiet. But my father did not hear him. He went on calling me. The officer dealt him a violent blow on the head with his truncheon.

I did not move. I was afraid. My body was afraid of also receiving a blow.

Then my father made a rattling noise and it was my name: "Eliezer."

I could see that he was still breathing—spasmodically.[7]

I did not move.

When I got down after roll call, I could see his lips trembling as he murmured something. Bending over him, I stayed gazing at him for over an hour, engraving into myself the picture of his blood-stained face, his shattered skull.

Then I had to go to bed. I climbed into my bunk, above my father, who was still alive. It was January 28, 1945.

I awoke on January 29 at dawn. In my father's place lay another invalid. They must have taken him away before dawn and carried him to the crematory. He may still have been breathing.

There were no prayers at his grave. No candles were lit to his memory. His last word was my name. A summons, to which I did not respond.

I did not weep, and it pained me that I could not weep. But I had no more tears. And, in the depths of my being, in the recesses of my weakened conscience, could I have searched it, I might perhaps have found something like—free at last!

I had to stay at Buchenwald until April eleventh. I have nothing to say of my life during this period. It no longer mattered. After my father's death, nothing could touch me any more.

I was transferred to the children's block, where there were six hundred of us.

The front was drawing nearer.

I spent my days in a state of total idleness. And I had but one desire—to eat. I no longer thought of my father or of my mother.

7. **spasmodically** (spaz mäd′ ik ə lē) *adv.* in spasms; intermittently; irregularly.

 ▲ **Critical Viewing**
Explain what Wiesel's memoir adds to your reaction to this image of a young prisoner of Buchenwald. **[Respond]**

Literary Analysis
Autobiography and Memoir By focusing on his father, what basic human concerns does Wiesel dramatize?

 **Reading Check**
What eventually happens to Eliezer's father?

from Night ■ 1267

35 Literary Analysis
Autobiography and Memoir
• Have students discuss Wiesel's depiction of his relationship with his father up to this point. Guide students to understand that Eliezer has struggled to remain loyal to his dying father, even when his loyalty threatens his own survival.
• Have students bear this in mind as they read the bracketed passage. Then, **ask** them the Literary Analysis question: By focusing on his father, what basic human concerns does Wiesel dramatize?
Possible response: Wiesel focuses on his father to dramatize the importance of family, even under such inhuman circumstances as the concentration camps. Wiesel also dramatizes his own struggle to remain human in an inhuman world.
• Point out to students that the style of Wiesel's memoir will change now that one of its central focuses—Eliezer's father—is gone.

36 Critical Viewing
Possible response: Wiesel's memoir has given readers a strong sense of what the boy in the photograph has endured and what he has yet to endure. It is also possible that the child may be waiting in line to be put to death. The young rarely survived the camps. If Eliezer had been this age, he may not have lived.

37 Reading Check
Answer: Eliezer's father is taken away during the night of January 28, 1945, presumably to the crematory. Wiesel speculates that he might have been barely alive when the guards took him.

Differentiated Instruction   Solutions for All Learners

Support for Special Needs Students
Although students should be able to follow the sequence of events Wiesel describes on these pages, they may have difficulty understanding his themes. Through discussion, lead students to understand that by caring for his father, Eliezer rejects the block head's advice: "Everyone lives and dies for himself alone."

Strategy for English Learners
The straightforward, accessible language of *Night* may offer students an ideal opportunity to practice speaking. Organize students into small groups. Within each group, have students take turns reading aloud, one or two paragraphs at a time. As groups read aloud, monitor student progress.

Enrichment for Gifted/Talented Students
When his father finally dies, Eliezer is drastically changed: "nothing could touch me any more." Encourage students to write a story or poem that depicts this transformation. Tell students to describe what Eliezer is like before his father's death—and what he becomes.

From time to time I would dream of a drop of soup, of an extra ration of soup. . . .

On April fifth, the wheel of history turned.

It was late in the afternoon. We were standing in the block, waiting for an SS man to come and count us. He was late in coming. Such a delay was unknown till then in the history of Buchenwald. Something must have happened.

Two hours later the loudspeakers sent out an order from the head of the camp: all the Jews must come to the assembly place.

38 This was the end! Hitler was going to keep his promise.

The children in our block went toward the place. There was nothing else we could do. Gustav, the head of the block, made this clear to us with his truncheon. But on the way we met some prisoners who whispered to us:

"Go back to your block. The Germans are going to shoot you. Go back to your block, and don't move."

We went back to our block. We learned on the way that the camp resistance organization had decided not to abandon the Jews and was going to prevent their being <u>liquidated</u>.

As it was late and there was great upheaval—innumerable Jews had passed themselves off as non-Jews—the head of the camp decided that a general roll call would take place the following day. Everybody would have to be present.

The roll call took place. The head of the camp announced **41** that Buchenwald was to be liquidated. Ten blocks of <u>deportees</u> would be evacuated each day. From this moment, there would be no further distribution of bread and soup. And the evacuation began. Every day, several thousand prisoners went through the camp gate and never came back.

Vocabulary Builder
liquidated (lik′ wi dāt′ id) *adj.* disposed of; ended; killed

deportees (dē′ pôr tēz′) *n.* people ordered to leave a country

40 ▼ **Critical Viewing**
What does Wiesel's account of daily life in Buchenwald add to your appreciation of the spirit of an inmate (see photograph) in drawing this portrait of another inmate? **[Interpret]**

1268 ■ *The Contemporary World*

Enrichment

The End of Elie Wiesel's War
Buchenwald, the concentration camp that Elie Wiesel describes in this section of *Night,* was located near the city of Weimar, Germany. More than 80,000 people were imprisoned there. Then, things changed: "On April fifth," Wiesel writes, "the wheel of history turned."

World War II was nearing its end in Europe. By April 1, Allied forces were in Germany. American troops were closing in on the Nazi's key industrial region, moving from the west. Weimar and Buchenwald were on the path to Berlin, the Nazi's capital.

The chaotic events Wiesel describes unfolded as Allied troops swept through Germany. The Nazi effort to evacuate the camp could have been stimulated only by the pressure of the imminent arrival of the Allies. American troops liberated the camp on April 11, according to Wiesel, after the Nazis had fled. By the end of that day, American forces were at the Elbe River. As April came to an end, Nazi resistance dwindled to virtually nothing. Hitler committed suicide on April 30. On May 8, 1945, the Nazis officially surrendered.

On April tenth, there were still about twenty thousand of us in the camp, including several hundred children. They decided to evacuate us all at once, right on until the evening. Afterward, they were going to blow up the camp.

So we were massed in the huge assembly square, in rows of five, waiting to see the gate open. Suddenly, the sirens began to wail. An alert! We went back to the blocks. It was too late to evacuate us that evening. The evacuation was postponed again to the following day.

We were tormented with hunger. We had eaten nothing for six days, except a bit of grass or some potato peelings found near the kitchens.

At ten o'clock in the morning the SS scattered through the camp, moving the last victims toward the assembly place.

Then the resistance movement decided to act. Armed men suddenly rose up everywhere. Bursts of firing. Grenades exploding. We children stayed flat on the ground in the block.

The battle did not last long. Toward noon everything was quiet again. The SS had fled and the resistance had taken charge of the running of the camp.

At about six o'clock in the evening, the first American tank stood at the gates of Buchenwald.

Critical Reading

1. **Respond:** Describe your reaction when sixteen-year-old Wiesel was liberated.

2. **(a) Recall:** In what ways does Wiesel change during his time in the camp? **(b) Analyze Cause and Effect:** What causes these changes?

3. **(a) Recall:** How does Wiesel respond to his father's illness? **(b) Compare and Contrast:** Contrast Wiesel's response with those of the doctor and his father's blockmates. **(c) Generalize:** What does this contrast show about basic human values in the camp?

4. **(a) Analyze:** While Wiesel's father is alive, what conflicting feelings does Wiesel experience? **(b) Infer:** Citing details, explain what Wiesel feels, in addition to sorrow, at his father's death.

5. **Evaluate:** Do you think Wiesel's complicated feelings about his father show selfishness, or might anyone have experienced them? Explain.

6. **Extend:** Why might guilt be a common emotion experienced by the survivors of a tragedy? In your answer, draw on details from Wiesel's memoir.

Go Online
Author Link

For: More about Elie Wiesel
Visit: www.PHSchool.com
Web Code: ete-9905

from *Night* ■ 1269

ASSESS

Answers

1. **Possible response:** Students may be torn between feelings of relief and lingering sorrow over the degree to which Eliezer's experiences have devastated his character.

2. (a) Although he clearly loves his father, Eliezer becomes hardened and unable to experience fully the grief of losing his father. (b) The dehumanizing conditions and daily brutality of the concentration camps cause these changes.

3. (a) Wiesel struggles to care for his father and, against all odds, to keep him from dying. (b) Eliezer is willing to risk his own survival for his father; others are not. The doctor and the blockmates see Eliezer's father as an annoyance to be eliminated. (c) The contrast shows that the camp is meant to destroy basic human values. Only through great struggle can inmates keep these values alive.

4. (a) Wiesel is torn between his desire to care for his father and his instinct to preserve his own life at all costs. (b) Wiesel feels free from having to care for and worry about his father. Wiesel thinks, "Free at last!" upon his father's death.

5. **Possible response:** Wiesel's feelings reveal a degree of selfishness. However, given the horrific conditions of the camps, Wiesel's complicated feelings are to be expected. Wiesel's effort to focus on caring for his father in such conditions is even heroic.

6. **Possible response:** Survivors of tragedies must deal with the fact that they have survived while many others—including those closest to them—have died. Survivors often wonder why they were spared when others were not.

Go Online For additional informa-
Author Link tion about Elie Wiesel, have students type in the Web Code, then select *W* from the alphabet, and then select Elie Wiesel.

Differentiated Instruction Solutions for All Learners

Strategy for Special Needs Students
Students may find Wiesel's depiction of the final days of the Buchenwald concentration camp confusing. Explain that the Nazis were losing the war at this point. Allied troops—in this case, Americans—were getting closer and closer to the camp. The Nazis did not want the camp to be discovered or its prisoners to be liberated. Have students read or reread these facing pages, pausing at key moments to review what has happened.

Enrichment for Advanced Readers
Encourage students to research the liberation of the concentration camps at the end of World War II. Students can begin by reading the rest of *Night*. Then, they should conduct research: When were the camps liberated and by which armies? How did people react when news of the Nazis' camps reached the rest of the world? What became of the prisoners? Have students share their findings with the class.

About the Selection

The speaker describes the beauty of early summer and the enchantment of dreams. However, the reverie is interrupted by memory. Children have been thrown to fiery deaths. How can the world go on, the speaker asks? Earth has not been discarded, and the sun and moon pretend they "have seen nothing."

ASSESS

Answers

1. **Possible response:** The image of children "thrown like butterflies, / wings beating into the flames" may evoke powerful feelings of rage and sorrow.

2. (a) The speaker describes moonbeams and the blooming of lilies. (b) The opening lines suggest that the speaker is amazed by the beauty of nature and in awe of its mysteries.

3. (a) The voice accuses the world of playing games and "cheating time." (b) The children "thrown like butterflies" into fire—a reference to the Holocaust—should stop the world from its games. (c) **Possible response:** The memory of the Holocaust's horror interrupts the speaker's enchantment with the world, making it impossible to find pleasure in a world where such things have happened.

4. **Possible response:** The speaker might chastise poets who, after the Holocaust, write nature poems as if nothing has happened, calling them "witnesses who have seen nothing."

Go Online
Author Link   For additional information about Nelly Sachs, have students type in the Web Code, then select *S* from the alphabet, and then select Nelly Sachs.

1270

When in early summer...

Nelly Sachs

translated by
Ruth and Matthew Mead

When in early summer the moon sends out secret signs,
the chalices of lilies scent of heaven,
some ear opens to listen
beneath the chirp of the cricket
5   to earth turning and the language of spirits set free.

But in dreams fish fly in the air
and a forest takes firm root in the floor of the room.

But in the midst of enchantment a voice speaks clearly and amazed:
World, how can you go on playing your games
10   and cheating time—
World, the little children were thrown like butterflies,
wings beating into the flames—

and your earth has not been thrown like a rotten apple
into the terror-roused abyss—

15   And sun and moon have gone on walking—
two cross-eyed witnesses who have seen nothing.

Critical Reading

1. **Respond:** Which image evoked your strongest response? Why?

2. **(a) Recall:** What natural events does the speaker describe in the first two lines? **(b) Interpret:** Describe the relationship between the poet and nature that is suggested by these opening lines.

3. **(a) Recall:** What does the "voice" accuse the world of doing in lines 9–10? **(b) Infer:** According to the voice, what event should prevent the world from doing these things? **(c) Interpret:** In what sense does the voice break the enchantment of the opening?

4. **Speculate:** What might Sachs's speaker say to a poet who, after the Holocaust, continued to write poetry about nature?

Go Online
Author Link

For: More about Nelly Sachs
Visit: www.PHSchool.com
Web Code: ete-9906

Apply the Skills

from *Survival in Auschwitz* • from *Night* • When in early summer . . .

Literary Analysis

Autobiography

1. **(a)** What might Levi's purpose be in writing an **autobiography**? Cite supporting details. **(b)** Identify one example of a way in which Levi draws the reader into events.
2. **(a)** What do you think Wiesel's purpose is in writing an **autobiography**? Cite supporting details. **(b)** Explain two ways in which Wiesel's report of his difficulties with his father helps readers understand concentration camp life.
3. Imagine that another writer has written an account of the lives of Levi and Wiesel. Identify two ways in which this account would differ from these autobiographies.

Comparing Literary Works

4. Compare and contrast the central insights of Levi's and Wiesel's **memoirs,** using a chart like the one shown.

	Events	Insights	Similarities/ Differences
Levi			
Wiesel			

5. **(a)** Explain Levi's insight into ways the concentration camp stripped people of words. **(b)** In Sachs's poem, what point is made about consequences of the Holocaust for poetry? **(c)** Using these insights, explain why it is difficult but important to put the Holocaust into words.

Reading Strategy

Connecting to Historical Context

6. Explain the way in which **historical context** adds to your understanding of the different nationalities of the people Levi first meets.
7. What historical facts help you understand the conclusion of the selection from *Night*? Explain.

Extend Understanding

8. **Social Studies Connection:** In today's world, what steps might people take to prevent governments from treating people in dehumanizing ways? Explain your answer.

QuickReview

An **autobiography** is a form of nonfiction in which a person tells his or her own life story.

A **memoir** is a first-person account that focuses on a person or series of events in the writer's life, offering insight into the person or the events.

To **connect works to their historical context,** link the details to the events and ideas of the writer's time.

Go Online
Assessment
For: Self-test
Visit: www.PHSchool.com
Web Code: eta-6904

from Survival in Auschwitz / from Night / When in early summer . . . ■ 1271

Answers

1. **(a) Possible responses:** Levi's purpose is to make clear the impact of the camps on the human psyche. The steps taken by the Nazis to prepare the prisoners and Levi's description of the effect of these preparations on individuals emphasize this purpose. **(b) Possible response:** Levi allows the reader to experience the same unsettling confusion as the prisoners.

2. **(a) Possible responses:** Wiesel's purpose in writing an autobiography is to bear witness to the Holocaust: to illustrate how the camps made the prisoners mistreat and abandon one another. Eliezer's efforts to help his father and his descriptions of the abuses prisoners endured from one another support this purpose. **(b) Possible response:** Wiesel's difficulties with his father convey the daily struggle between life and death and how the camps destroyed human sentiment.

3. **Possible response:** The author would not be able to convey the inner thoughts and emotions of Levi and Wiesel. The biographies would also lack some of the eyewitness accounts.

4. **Possible responses: Levi: Events:** New prisoners at Auschwitz are stripped of clothing, hair, and names; **Insights:** The prisoners lose their identities; **Similarities/ Differences:** Both authors focus on the loss of identity; however, Levi ties identity to small things. **Wiesel: Events:** In the last days, Wiesel loses his father; **Insights:** Without his father, Wiesel loses his humanity; **Similarities/Differences:** Both authors focus on the loss of humanity, but Wiesel struggles much longer to prevent this loss.

5. **(a) Possible responses:** The abuse of the camps was so profound that language cannot describe it. Also, the Germans do not speak Italian, so the prisoners are stripped of their ability to communicate with their captors. **(b)** After the Holocaust, poetry can no longer embrace the beauty of the world. **(c)** It is important to find language to describe the Holocaust to prevent the world from acting as though nothing had happened.

6. From every nation the Nazis occupied, they deported Jews.

Answers continued

7. The Allies liberated the concentration camps, as the Nazis fled in defeat. This situation helps explain the chaos at the conclusion of *Night.*

8. **Possible response:** Powerful nations or international organizations can encourage governments that oppress their citizens to change their policies, using diplomacy or economic threats.

Go Online Students may use the **Self-test** to
Assessment prepare for **Selection Test A** or
Selection Test B.

1271

Build Language Skills

❶ Vocabulary Lesson

❶ Vocabulary Lesson

**Word Analysis:
Latin Root -port-**

1. An *importer* carries items into one country or region from another.

2. Something that is *portable* can be carried or moved easily.

3. A person's *deportment* is the manner in which that person carries himself or herself.

Spelling Strategy

1. liquidation   3. succession

2. indecision

Vocabulary Builder: Antonyms

1. b	4. a	7. b
2. b	5. a	8. c
3. c	6. a	

❷ Grammar and Style Lesson

1. its number tattooed in bluish characters under the skin

2. none

3. his lips [being] pale and dried up

4. none

5. wings beating into the flames

Writing Application

Possible response: The Nazis fled the concentration camp, *the officers stopping for nothing.* The prisoners waited throughout the day. The Americans arrived that evening, *tanks bearing the promise of food and shelter.*

✍ Writing and Grammar
Ⓖ Platinum Level
For support in teaching the Grammar and Style Lesson, use Chapter 20, Section 1.

Word Analysis: Latin Root -port-

The Latin root -port- means "carry" or "move." The word *deportees* means "people who are moved away," or expelled from a country. Explain what -port- adds to the meaning of these words:

1. importer   2. portable   3. deportment

Spelling Strategy

The -tion ending, found in *intuition*, makes the *shun* sound. The ending -sion is generally pronounced *zhun*, as in *diversion*. The ending -ssion, pronounced *shun*, is common with base words that end in -ss—for example, *possess, possession*. Complete each word with the correct ending: -tion, -sion, or -ssion.

1. liquida____   2. indeci____   3. succe____

Vocabulary Builder: Antonyms

In each item, choose the antonym, or word opposite in meaning, of the first word.

1. affinity: **(a)** similarity, **(b)** hatred, **(c)** friendliness

2. deportees: **(a)** teachers, **(b)** immigrants, **(c)** promises

3. intuition: **(a)** payment, **(b)** thoughtfulness, **(c)** incomprehension

4. liquidated: **(a)** made, **(b)** destroyed, **(c)** ate

5. prophetic: **(a)** commemorative, **(b)** intelligent, **(c)** strong

6. beseeching: **(a)** answering, **(b)** asking, **(c)** wondering

7. sordid: **(a)** ugly, **(b)** clean, **(c)** jumbled

8. plaintive: **(a)** old, **(b)** fancy, **(c)** cheerful

❷ Grammar and Style Lesson

Absolute Phrases

An **absolute phrase,** or nominative absolute, consists of a noun or a pronoun modified by a participle or a participial phrase. Unlike a participial phrase, an absolute phrase does not modify a subject or an object elsewhere in the sentence. It has no grammatical relationship to the rest of the sentence. Study this example from *Night*, noting how the phrase adds descriptive detail in few words.

> **Absolute Phrase:** My father grew weaker day
>   NOUN PART.
> by day, <u>his gaze *veiled*.</u>
>
> **Participial (Not Absolute) Phrase:**
> <u>Having lived through so much,</u> . . . could I leave my father to die now?

✍ Ⓖ *Prentice Hall Writing and Grammar Connection: Platinum Level, Chapter 20, Section 1*

Practice Identify the absolute phrase in each item, or write *none* if the item lacks such a phrase.

1. . . . my new name ironically appeared instead, its number tattooed in bluish characters under the skin.

2. Imagine now a man who is deprived of everyone he loves. . . .

3. He was lying on a plank, livid, his lips [being] pale and dried up. . . .

4. Seeing my father in the distance, I ran to meet him.

5. . . . the little children were thrown like butterflies, / wings beating into the flames . . .

Writing Application Use two absolute phrases in a description of Wiesel's liberation.

Assessment Practice

Analyzing an Author's Meaning and Style

Many standardized tests require students to read literary passages to identify the author's deepest meaning. Use the following sample test item to demonstrate.

> When we finish, everyone remains in his corner and we do not dare lift our eyes to look at one another. There is nowhere to look in a mirror, but our appearance stands in front of us, reflected in a hundred livid faces, in a hundred miserable and sordid puppets.

(For more practice, see
***Test Preparation Workbook*, p. 60.)**

In the context of *Survival in Auschwitz*, what theme does the author imply in this passage?

  A The prisoners are upset.

  B The prisoners have lost their identities.

  C The prisoners have been badly mistreated.

  D The prisoners do not want to look at each other.

A, C, and *D* are all expressed by this passage, but they are not themes. The correct answer is *B.*

❸ **Writing Lesson**

Timed Writing: Persuasive Essay

Imagine that your school is planning a curriculum unit to teach students about the Holocaust. Write an essay supporting the inclusion in the unit of Levi's or Wiesel's autobiographical works or Sachs' poem. In your essay, explain your choice, using reasons suited to your audience—the teachers at your school. *(40 minutes)*

Prewriting
(10 minutes)
First, choose the selection you will propose. You might choose a work on the basis of its emotional impact or its strong historical insight. Then, list at least three reasons that this selection should be included in a unit about the Holocaust.

Drafting
(20 minutes)
Begin your draft with a clear statement of your opinion. Then, provide supporting arguments in a logical order. Use strong, direct language that will reinforce your points.

Revising
(10 minutes)
Review your essay to ensure that you have included details and used language appropriate to your audience and purpose. Replace words that are weak or that might not be suitable. Add details that your audience will find persuasive.

> **Model: Revising for Audience and Purpose**
>
> Finally, ~~I thought~~ what Levi says about identity is ~~cool.~~ profound. He shows
> how important respect for the identity of others is. In addition to learning
> history, students reading the memoir will reflect on basic values.

 Prentice Hall Writing and Grammar Connection: Platinum Level, Chapter 7, Section 4

❹ Extend Your Learning

Research and Technology Using the Internet, research Holocaust memorials around the world. Then, create a **multimedia presentation,** using a slide-show program. Compare the following aspects of each memorial:

• main purpose, including commemoration or documentation, and any specific focus
• distinctive features, including art, architecture, exhibits, and archives

Give your presentation to the class. Express your opinions and questions as you view your classmates' presentations.

Listening and Speaking Hold a **group discussion** in which you compare Wiesel's and Levi's works. For instance, you might compare their use of certain types of sentences for effect, as well as their themes. In your discussion, listen actively to build on the contributions of others. **[Group Activity]**

Go Online **For:** An additional research activity
Research **Visit:** www.PHSchool.com
Web Code: etd-7904

from Survival in Auschwitz / from Night / When in early summer . . . ■ 1273

Assessment Resources

The following resources can be used to assess students' knowledge and skills.

Unit 9 Resources
Selection Test A, pp. 71–73
Selection Test B, pp. 74–76
Benchmark Test 11, pp. 77–82

General Resources
Rubrics for Persuasion: Persuasive Essay, pp. 47–48

Go Online Students may use the **Self-test** to **Assessment** prepare for **Selection Test A** or **Selection Test B.**

Benchmark
Administer **Benchmark Test 11.** If some students need further work, use the **Interpretation Guide** to determine the appropriate reteaching page in the **Reading Kit** and on **Success Tracker.**

---

❸ **Writing Lesson**
You may use this Writing Lesson as a timed-writing practice, or you may allow students to develop the persuasive essay as a writing assignment over several days.

• To give students guidance in writing this essay, give them the **Support for Writing Lesson,** p. 68 in *Unit 9 Resources.*
• Remind students that their arguments should be aimed at the audience—in this case, the teachers who will decide what to include in the Holocaust unit. Help students brainstorm a list of criteria teachers might consider when developing curriculum.
• After they have chosen the selections about which they will write, tell students to develop at least three reasons for including their choice in the unit.
• Use the Persuasion: Persuasive Essay rubrics in *General Resources,* pp. 47–48, to evaluate students' essays.

Writing and Grammar Platinum Level
For support in teaching the Writing Lesson, use Chapter 7, Section 4.

❹ **Research and Technology**

• Tell students that their multimedia presentations should combine images of Holocaust memorials around the world with explanations and descriptions of each one.
• Monitor students as they research memorials. To avoid anti-Semitic Web sites, make sure that students conduct their searches from the official website of the United States Holocaust Memorial Museum.
• The **Support for Extend Your Learning** page (*Unit 9 Resources,* p. 69) provides guided note-taking opportunities to help students complete the Extend Your Learning activities.

Go Online Have students type in the **Research** Web Code for another research activity.

See Teacher Express™/Lesson View for a detailed lesson plan for Reading Informational Materials.

About Magazine Articles

- After students have read "About Magazine Articles," explain to students that magazines cover an almost endless variety of topics ranging from news, video games, lives of celebrities, ideas, or products.

- Show students examples of magazines from the school's library.

- Have students discuss their reasons for reading magazines and the particular types of information they can get from magazines.

- Explain to students that libraries catalog magazines in hardcopy form or in digital format. Therefore, students can access magazine articles from many years ago.

Reading Strategy

Establishing a Purpose for Reading

- Tell students that when they read magazines for academic information, their purpose for reading must be more focused that it would be for reading for entertainment, for instance, or for reading to pass the time in a doctor's office.

- Direct students to the graphic organizer on this page. Point out that they will gain much more from their reading if they determine what they want to know before they read. Then, as they read, they can watch for the information they wish to gain from the article. If they record the information that they have gained, they can go back and review whatever they may have missed in the article. Instruct students to copy and fill in the chart as they read the selection.

Reading Informational Materials

Magazine Articles

About Magazine Articles

Today, people turn to a variety of sources for information. In a single day, citizens may check newspapers, television, radio, and the Internet to keep up with the news. Despite the popularity of television and electronic media, magazines remain an important source of news, information, and entertainment. Magazines articles appeal to their readers for many reasons:

- **Focused topics for a targeted audience:** Specialty magazines reach out to readers interested in such specific subjects as tennis, fine dining, or skateboarding. They also can target readers of a specific age group, geographical area, or writing or reading ability.

- **Depth of Reporting:** Magazines are usually published weekly or monthly, allowing writers to treat topics in more depth than is possible for journalists working in a daily news cycle. Magazine articles may offer readers a broader perspective than other sources of "breaking news" can.

Reading Strategy

Establishing a Purpose for Reading

People turn to reading material with a variety of purposes, or reasons for reading. Readers may pick up a newspaper to gather information, and they may enjoy a short story to be entertained or to experience new cultures. Film buffs might read a movie review to decide which film to see.

To **establish a purpose for reading** a magazine article:

- Scan the title and the first few paragraphs to identify the topic.

- Then, focus on a specific idea, concept, or goal as you begin reading an article. Decide what you want to explore, learn about, or experience as you read.

- As you read, complete a chart like the one shown with details related to your reading purpose.

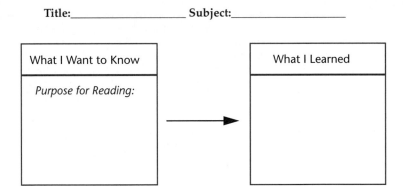

Title:_____ Subject:_____

What I Want to Know	What I Learned
Purpose for Reading:	

Differentiated Instruction   Solutions for All Learners

Reading Support

Give students reading support with the appropriate version of the *Reader's Notebooks:*

Reader's Notebook: [L1, L2]

Reader's Notebook: Adapted Version [L3]

Reader's Notebook: English Learner's Version [EL]

THE HOLOCAUST HAGGADAH

Selections from the Rare Book, Manuscript, and Special Collections Library

> The opening paragraph identifies the subject and tells why it is significant.

Zygfryd and Helene Wolloch of New York commissioned a Passover Haggadah in 1981 in memory of their parents, who died in the Holocaust. What began as a personal tribute was soon recognized as an unparalleled contribution to Jewish art and history. The Rare Book, Manuscript, and Special Collections Library at Duke owns an original portfolio of the limited published edition of the Wollochs' Pessach Haggadah in Memory of the Holocaust.

> This paragraph provides important background information on the Haggadah.

The Haggadah (plural, Haggadot) is the Jewish book of ritual used at Passover Seders in the celebration of the Exodus from Egypt. Religious scholar Cecil Roth has referred to the Haggadah, comparing it to other books in the Jewish tradition, as one of the most amenable to adaptation and artistic

expression. The "Holocaust Haggadah," as the Wollochs' Haggadah is commonly called, illustrated by David Wander with calligraphy by Yonah Weinreb, makes the point beautifully.

Wander and Weinreb juxtapose the themes of the Exodus and the Holocaust by emphasizing the shared histories of slavery, destruction, and redemption. Wander's art is powerful in its simplicity and directness. He depicts crematoria, burning books, and the Star of David alongside the traditional Hebrew text

> Here the writer presents an overview of the Holocaust Haggadah, explaining that David Wander has intertwined the themes of the Exodus and the Holocaust.

of the Haggadah. He also includes brilliant borders, flowers, and the Israeli flag to symbolize the eventual freedom of the Jewish people. His drawings are devoid of human figures, signifying the absence of those who perished during the Holocaust.

Reading Magazine Articles

- Tell students that they are likely to encounter magazine articles when they are researching a topic for school, or for personal interest, or when they are waiting somewhere. They may even choose to subscribe to a magazine or magazines that match their interests.
- Have students read "The Holocaust Haggadah."
- **Ask** students to identify why the Holocaust Haggadah was commissioned.
  Answer: It was commissioned by Zygfryd and Helene Wolloch of New York in memory of their parents, who died during the Holocaust.
- Remind students that it is important to first identify the definition of the subject of an article.
  Ask: What is a *Haggadah*?
  Answer: A *Haggadah* is the book of Jewish ritual used at Passover Seders, or feasts in the celebration of the Exodus from Egypt.
- **Ask** students how the Holocaust Haggadah combines the themes of the Exodus and the Holocaust.
  Answer: The artist uses images of crematoria, burning books, and the Star of David alongside the traditional text. The calligraphy and illustrations emphasize the shared histories of slavery, destruction, and redemption that Jewish people experienced during their time in Egypt and under Nazi rule.

continued on p. 1276

Differentiated Instruction — Solutions for All Learners

Strategy for Less Proficient Readers
Ask students to list their favorite activities. Then have them list something they would like to learn about each activity. Point out that this is one purpose for reading a magazine article. Then have students go to the library and use the online catalogue or database to search for their interests and an article that will answer a question about those interests. Have students copy the chart from the text and fill it in as they read the article. Then have them share their findings with the class.

Strategy for Advanced Readers
Have students go to the library and search the online database for a magazine article and a journal article on an academic topic that interests them. Have students establish a purpose for reading each article and then read each article. Then have students compare the ways in which the journal article and the magazine article treat the topic. Have students make a list of the similarities and differences of purpose for reading each article. Then have them write a statement explaining the purposes for reading the two articles on the same topic.

Reading Magazine Articles (cont.)

Direct students' attention to the paragraph in which the author discusses two particularly striking images in the Holocaust Haggadah. **Ask:** How does the Holocaust Haggadah help exemplify the meaning of the quotation?

Possible response: The quotation means that each generation of Jewish people must see themselves and their lives as a participation in the Exodus story of liberation from slavery in Egypt. The Holocaust Haggadah can help contemporary Jews to see the experience of the Holocaust as a participation in this same liberation story.

Two of Wander's drawings are particularly striking and well-known. One, a concentration-camp uniform placed within a passage reading, "In each generation one is obligated to regard himself as though he personally left Egypt." In the second image, four books illustrate the portion of the Haggadah text in which four children question the leader of the Seder. For the wise child, Judaism is an open book to be studied; for the wicked child the book is on fire; for the simple child the book is open but blank; and for the fourth child, who does not yet know to ask about the Exodus, the book is closed.

The Wollochs exhibited their Holocaust Haggadah at the Milton J. Weill Art Gallery at the 92nd Street Y in New York, where it received such wide public attention that they agreed to its publication in a limited edition to benefit the International Society for Yad Vashem. Herbert Goldman's Art Gallery in Haifa, Israel, was the publisher, and David Wander himself prepared the plates and oversaw the printing of his artwork at the Burston Graphic Center in Jerusalem.

Each hand-printed portfolio consists of twelve full-page prints signed and numbered by the artist, thirty-one illuminated pages, and thirteen black-and-white pages. A total of 290 Haggadot were produced: 250 were numbered 1 to 250; and 31 were numbered I to XXXI. Duke's copy is number 70 of 250. Nine artists' proofs were reserved for the publisher, the artists, and their colleagues.

Duke's Holocaust Haggadah is one of many impressive Haggadot within the Special Collections Library's extensive Abram and Frances Pascher Kanof Collection of Jewish Art, Archeology, and Symbolism. According to Eric Meyers, Bernice and Morton Lerner Professor of religion, Duke's Haggadah Collection, containing originals and facsimiles representing more than 1,000 years of Jewish experience, is a rich resource for students and scholars of Jewish history. Meyers says that the Duke Center for Judaic Studies intends to publish an online catalog of the collection, as well as a booklet highlighting selected holdings.

Pessach Haggadah in Memory of the Holocaust
Original portfolio, 1981
Illustrated by David Wander
Calligraphy by Yonah Weinreb
Hand printed on Velin Cuvé Rives, 250-gram paper

Here the writer offers details about two especially striking images.

This passage focuses on factual details about how the Haggadah came to be published in a limited edition.

In the conclusion, the writer cites an expert, who places the subject of the article in the broader context of the resources offered by the Duke Center for Judaic Studies. Note that the article originally appeared in a magazine published for Duke University alumni.

Reading: Establishing a Purpose

Directions: *Choose the letter of the best answer to each question about the magazine article.*

1. To understand the article, which of the following questions does a reader need answered?
   A How did Duke University acquire the Holocaust Haggadah?
   B What are some of David Wander's other works?
   C What is a Haggadah?
   D What is the traditional date of the Exodus from Egypt?

2. For what purpose might a historian read this article?
   A to learn how the Haggadah was made
   B to learn where the Hagaddah is being exhibited
   C to learn how old the Haggadah is
   D to learn how past events influenced the design of the Haggadah

3. Which of the following purposes for reading is most appropriate for this article as a whole?
   A for entertainment
   B for information
   C for reflection
   D for instruction

4. Which of the following groups of readers would not have an obvious purpose for reading the Haggadah article?
   A scholarly experts on sacred texts
   B alumni of Duke with an interest in art and Jewish studies
   C collectors of David Wander's illustrations
   D readers with a special interest in Middle Eastern political affairs

Reading: Comprehension and Interpretation

Directions: *Write your answers on a separate sheet of paper.*

5. **(a)** What themes do the illustrators of the Holocaust Haggadah—David Wander and Yonah Weinreb—develop in their work? **(b)** In what way do the illustrations support these themes?

6. Which two drawings does the author single out as especially effective? Based on the descriptions, why do you think these illustrations are particularly moving to readers of the Haggadah?

Timed Writing: Evaluation

In the opening paragraph, the author of this article expresses this opinion about the Holocaust Haggadah: "What began as a personal tribute was soon recognized as an unparalleled contribution to Jewish art and history." How effectively does the article support this claim, in your view? Explain your answer, using specific references to the text of the article to support your response. *(25 minutes)*

Reading Informational Materials: Magazine Articles ■ 1277

Answers

Reading: Establishing a Purpose

1. C
2. D
3. B
4. D

Reading: Comprehension and Interpretation

5. (a) David Wander and Yonah Weinreb develop the themes of the Exodus and the Holocaust by focusing on the shared histories of slavery, destruction, and redemption. (b) Their illustrations support these themes through the use of crematoria, burning books, and the Star of David alongside the traditional text. They also include brilliant borders, flowers, and the flag of Israel. The illustrations also have no human figures, indicating those who perished during the Holocaust.

6. The two drawings that the author sees as particularly effective are the concentration camp uniform placed within a quote about each generation and the illustration with the four children who question the leader of the Seder.
   Possible response: These are particularly moving because they represent the sacrifices of the Exodus and the Holocaust as well as the importance of the history of the Exodus.

Timed Writing Evaluation

- Read the instruction aloud with students, and then have students review the article, jotting down information that they can use to support either position.

- Tell students to choose a position based on the information they have found.

- As students write, have them support their views with specific examples from the text.

- Suggest that students allow five minutes for reading the article and determining a position, fifteen minutes for writing, and five minutes for reviewing and revising.

Extend the Lesson

Magazine Articles

To provide students with more practice with establishing a purpose for reading magazine articles, have students select a news article from a magazine. Then have them list people in four different categories, such as students, people waiting in the checkout line at a grocery store, people in a bookstore, or teachers, who might read the magazine article for different purposes. Next to each category of people, have students write a sentence explaining the reasons that group might read the article and what they might hope to learn from it. Then have students share their lists with the class.

Standard Course of Study

Goal 1: WRITTEN LANGUAGE

WL.1.03.7 Analyze influences, contexts, or biases in expressive texts.

Goal 4: CRITICAL THINKING

CT.4.02.3 Examine how elements such as irony and symbolism impact theme.

CT.4.05.9 Analyze and evaluate the effects of craft and style in critical text.

Goal 5: LITERATURE

LT.5.01.3 Analyze literary devices and explain their effect on the work of world literature.

Goal 6: GRAMMAR AND USAGE

GU.6.02.1 Edit for agreement, tense choice, pronouns, antecedents, case, and complete sentences.

Step-by-Step Teaching Guide	Pacing Guide
PRETEACH	
• Administer Vocabulary and Reading Warm-ups as necessary.	5 min.
• Engage students' interest with the motivation activity.	5 min.
• Read and discuss author and background features. **FT**	10 min.
• Introduce the Literary Analysis Skill: Irony. **FT**	5 min.
• Introduce the Reading Strategy: Evaluating the Writer's Statement of Philosophy. **FT**	10 min.
• Prepare students to read by teaching the selection vocabulary. **FT**	
TEACH	
• Informally monitor comprehension while students read independently or in groups. **FT**	30 min.
• Monitor students' comprehension with the Reading Check notes.	as students read
• Reinforce vocabulary with Vocabulary Builder notes.	as students read
• Develop students' understanding of irony with the Literary Analysis annotations. **FT**	5 min.
• Develop students' ability to evaluate the writer's statement of philosophy with the Reading Strategy annotations. **FT**	5 min.
ASSESS/EXTEND	
• Assess students' comprehension and mastery of the Literary Analysis and Reading Strategy by having them answer the Apply the Skills questions. **FT**	15 min.
• Have students complete the Vocabulary Lesson and the Grammar and Style Lesson. **FT**	15 min.
• Apply students' ability to list relevant details by using the Writing Lesson. **FT**	45 min. or homework
• Apply students' understanding by using one or more of the Extend Your Learning activities.	20–90 min. or homework
• Administer Selection Test A or Selection Test B. **FT**	15 min.

Resources

Print

Unit 9 Resources

Transparency

Graphic Organizer Transparencies

Print

Reader's Notebook [L2]

Reader's Notebook: Adapted Version [L1]

Reader's Notebook: English Learner's Version [EL]

Unit 9 Resources

Technology

Listening to Literature Audio CDs [L2, EL]

Print

Unit 9 Resources

General Resources

Technology

Go Online: Research [**L3**]

Go Online: Self-test [**L3**]

ExamView®, Test Bank [**L3**]

Choosing Resources for Differentiated Instruction

[**L1**] Special Needs Students

[**L2**] Below-Level Students

[**L3**] All Students

[**L4**] Advanced Students

[**EL**] English Learners

For Vocabulary and Reading Warm-ups and for Selection Tests, **A** signifies "less challenging" and **B** "more challenging." For Graphic Organizer transparencies, **A** signifies "not filled in" and **B** "filled in."

FT Fast Track Instruction: To move the lesson more quickly, use the strategies and activities identified with **FT**.

Scaffolding for Less Proficient and Advanced Students

The leveled Critical Thinking questions after selections progress in the levels of thinking required to answer them. To address the needs of your different students, you may use the (a) level questions for your less proficient students and the (b) level questions with your on-level and advanced students. The occasional (c) level questions are appropriate for your advanced students.

PRENTICE HALL

Teacher EXPRESS™ Use this complete
Plan · Teach · Assess   suite of powerful
teaching tools to make lesson planning and testing quicker and easier.

PRENTICE HALL

Student EXPRESS™ Use the interactive
Learn · Study · Succeed   textbook (online
and on CD-ROM) to make selections and activities come alive with audio and video support and interactive questions.

Monitoring Progress

Before students read these selections, administer **Diagnostic Test 12** (*Unit 9 Resources,* **pp. 83–85**). This test will determine students' level of readiness for the reading and vocabulary skills.

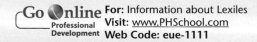

Go **Online** **For:** Information about Lexiles
Professional **Visit:** www.PHSchool.com
Development **Web Code:** eue-1111

Motivation

Ask students to recall books, movies, or news stories in which people faced crisis situations. Have students describe those situations, and the people's reactions, in vivid detail. Then, explain to students that they may be surprised by the way these poets describe desperate situations.

❶ Background

More About the Authors

When Czesław Miłosz was a young man, he admired his uncle, Oscar Miłosz, who had sold his family's estate and become a well-known poet in Paris. A reader of many languages, Oscar Miłosz became a role model for his nephew.

Wisława Szymborska has said, "No questions are of such significance as those that are naive." Her poetry asks direct questions about the meaning of life and death. Upon granting her the 1996 Nobel Prize for Literature, the Swedish Academy called her the "Mozart of poetry."

Geography Note

Draw students' attention to the map on this page. Explain that both poets have played important roles in Polish culture. Both Miłosz and Szymborska show appreciation for the history of a nation that has many times faced the kinds of crises described in these poems.

Build Skills [*Poems*]

❶ A Song on the End of the World • The End and the Beginning

Czesław Miłosz
(1911–2004)

Poet, essayist, and novelist Czesław Miłosz (chez´ wäf mē´ wōsh) has lived as many lives as the legendary cat. From a young writer haunted by "gloomy visions" to a diplomat in Washington, D.C., to a university professor in California, Miłosz is widely known today as a distinguished Nobel Prize winner.

Born in the Lithuanian city of Wilno (also known as Vilna), young Miłosz decided to study law. Hitler had just seized control in Germany, and Miłosz rejected the Nazi glorification of the state. Communism seemed like an antidote, yet Miłosz questioned the rigidity of its doctrines. His early poetry captures the violence-haunted atmosphere of the 1930s.

Defiance and Resignation After World War II broke out, Miłosz moved to Warsaw, Poland, where he participated in underground publishing activities carried on in defiance of the Nazi occupiers. After the war, when the Communist U.S.S.R. dominated Poland, Miłosz served as a diplomat for Poland in Washington, D.C. Miłosz was not a hard-line Communist; he hoped for reform. In 1951, though, he gave up hopes of working for change from within and broke with the Communist government. Moving first to France, he later became a professor of literature at the University of California at Berkeley.

Leading by Example Although he says he is uncomfortable in the role of moral leader, Miłosz's independence of mind has been widely admired by younger generations of Poles. His poems have carried a great deal of moral authority in Poland. In 1980, his international stature was confirmed when he received the Nobel Prize in Literature.

Wisława
Szymborska (b. 1923)

For Wisława Szymborska (vis wa´ va shim boor´ ska), inspiration begins when a poet says "I don't know." Her work centers around the rediscovery of astonishment. "[I]n the language of poetry," she said in her 1996 Nobel Prize acceptance speech, "where every word is weighed, nothing is usual or normal. Not a single stone or a single cloud above it."

Born in the small town of Bnin, Poland (now a part of Kórnik), Szymborska moved in 1931 to Krakow, where she still lives today. In 1945, her first published poem appeared in a daily newspaper. In 1953, she became the poetry editor at a literary magazine.

Privacy and Politics Unlike her fellow Pole Miłosz, Szymborska has led much of her life out of the public eye. Still, politics left an inevitable mark on her work.

In the early 1950s, Szymborska wrote in the government-permitted style of the time. A relaxation of government regulations allowed her to publish in her own voice, but in the 1980s, the government again cracked down on dissent. During that time, Szymborska contributed to underground and exile periodicals. The triumph of Poland's Solidarity movement in 1989 brought an end to strict government oversight of culture.

A Distinguished Honor Szymborska has published more than sixteen collections of poetry, as well as a collection of essays. She has refused to give readings, however, out of her dislike for publicity. When told she had won the 1996 Nobel Prize in Literature, Szymborska said it felt as if the world "came crashing down on me." Although she valued the honor, she told Miłosz at the time, "I am a private person."

Preview

Connecting to the Literature

If you have ever rediscovered your first-grade class picture or revisited a long-forgotten childhood playground, then you know that, as these poets show, time is measured by how much we forget more than by what we remember.

❷ Literary Analysis

Irony

Irony occurs when writers create a contrast between what is stated and what is meant or between what is expected to happen and what actually happens. Irony can take the following forms:

- **Situational irony** is an opposition between events and expectations. In his poem, Miłosz insists that the day the world ends will be like any other, although we expect it to be more dramatic.
- **Verbal irony** is a clash between the words used for a thing and its reality. Szymborska writes "After every war / someone has to tidy up," ironically understating the damage caused by war.

As you read, note the poets' use of verbal and situational irony.

Comparing Literary Works

These poets use irony to challenge our ideas of history. They take **history as a theme,** looking for a meaning or a pattern in historical events.

- Miłosz's irony makes us reconsider just what an ordinary day is.
- Szymborska's irony suggests that progress means forgetting, not learning from, the past.

As you read, compare the lessons about history in these poems. Consider whether history appears as a cycle that repeats itself or as a straight line.

❸ Reading Strategy

Evaluating the Writer's Statement of Philosophy

To **evaluate a writer's philosophy,** first identify the writer's view of life. Begin by analyzing patterns in the work, such as similarities in details that point to a common meaning. Then, decide whether the writer's view is supported by your own ideas and experiences.

As you read, evaluate each poet's philosophy, using a chart like this one.

Vocabulary Builder

glimmering (glim′ ər iŋ) v. flickering; giving a faint, unsteady light (p. 1280)

prophet (präf′ ət) n. inspired person who speaks great truths or foretells the future (p. 1281)

shards (shärdz) n. sharp fragments (p. 1282)

glaze (glāz) v. fit glass to a window; cover with a shiny finish (p. 1282)

gawking (gôk′ iŋ) v. staring foolishly; gaping (p. 1284)

NC	**Standard Course of Study**

- Analyze influences, contexts, or biases in expressive texts. (WL.1.03.7)
- Examine how elements such as irony and symbolism impact theme. (CT.4.02.3)

Details

"A Song on the End of the World"
"A bee circles clover . . ."
"A fisherman mends a glimmering net."

↓

Meanings They Suggest

Ordinary events seem extraordinary on the day the world ends.

↓

Philosophy

Ordinary life is precious; we just forget how precious.

↓

Evaluation

A Song on the End of the World / The End and the Beginning ■ 1279

❷ Literary Analysis

Irony

- Read with students the Literary Analysis instruction, and ask students to give examples of situational and verbal irony. Prompt them with a real-life example of situational irony, such as the many people who survived the September 11, 2001, World Trade Center attacks because they were late to work that day. Typically, being late causes problems rather than prevents them.

- As students read, urge them to relate to the situations in these poems by visualizing the many scenes of war that play out daily in the current news. Discuss the irony in the contrast between our distant image of war and its reality.

❸ Reading Strategy

Evaluating the Writer's Statement of Philosophy

- After reading aloud the Reading Strategy instruction, remind students that a philosophy is a way of looking at the world. People often filter their descriptions or experiences through a central philosophy, for example, that "all people are essentially good."

- Review the graphic organizer, read aloud each box, and discuss each entry. As a class, agree on an entry for the "Evaluation" cell, such as "This makes sense to me because . . ." or "I agree because. . . ." Then, give students a copy of **Reading Strategy Graphic Organizer A,** p. 217 in *Graphic Organizer Transparencies.* As they read each poem, have students use it to record recurring images or descriptions that suggest the writer's view of life.

Vocabulary Builder

- Pronounce each vocabulary word for students, and read the definitions as a class. Have students identify any words with which they are already familiar.

Facilitate Understanding

Help students imagine the situations to which these poems respond. Inspire their historical imaginations by locating and reading excerpts from *Emanuel Ringelblum's Notes from the Warsaw Ghetto.*

❶ About the Selection

This poem contrasts the everyday experiences of people and animals amidst war and devastation in the Warsaw Ghetto. Miłosz makes the powerful argument that continuing with everyday tasks despite war's horrors reflects heroism.

❷ Literary Analysis

Irony

• Have a volunteer read aloud the bracketed stanzas. **Ask** students what they would expect the world to be like on the day it ends. **Possible response:** The world might be full of portentous signs of disaster, such as those described in biblical accounts.

• Then, **ask** students to respond to the Literary Analysis item: Explain why the details in these two stanzas are ironic, given the situation. **Answer:** Given that the world is ending, one would expect more unpleasant events to be occurring, not the ordinary, everyday events described in these stanzas.

❸ Vocabulary Builder

Related Words: *glaze* and *glimmering*

• Point out the word *glimmering* on this page and the word *glaze* on p. 1282. Read the definitions for both words.

• Tell students that both words come from a root meaning "to shine or to glow." **Ask** students how this meaning is reflected in the word *glimmer.* **Possible response:** Something that glimmers appears to shine.

1280

---

❶A Song on the End of the World

Czesław Miłosz   *translated by Anthony Miłosz*

Background Written in 1944, this poem reflects historical events: A world *did* come to an end in the Polish capital of Warsaw during World War II. In 1939, Nazi Germany and the Soviet Union invaded Poland and divided the country between them. In the summer of 1944, as the Polish resistance movement rebelled against Nazi rule, Warsaw was nearly leveled.

Miłosz thought it unlikely that he would survive the war, but he found wisdom in the advice of Martin Luther, a leader of the Protestant movement for religious reform: "[W]hen asked what he would do if he knew tomorrow was going to be the end of the world, he said, 'I would plant apple trees.'"

The calm conviction of Miłosz's poem reflects this insight into the value of the ordinary. It also reflects Poland's long history as the target of invasion and occupation, a history that also echoes in Szymborska's poem "The End and the Beginning."

On the day the world ends
A bee circles a clover,
A fisherman mends a glimmering net. ❸
Happy porpoises jump in the sea,
5   By the rainspout young sparrows are playing
And the snake is gold-skinned as it should always be.

❷

On the day the world ends
Women walk through the fields under their umbrellas,
A drunkard grows sleepy at the edge of a lawn,
10   Vegetable peddlers shout in the street
And a yellow-sailed boat comes nearer the island,
The voice of a violin lasts in the air
And leads into a starry night.

1280 ■ *The Contemporary World*

Vocabulary Builder
glimmering (glim′ ər iŋ) *v.*
flickering; giving a faint, unsteady light

Literary Analysis
Irony Explain why the details in these two stanzas are ironic, given the situation.

Differentiated Instruction   Solutions for All Learners

Accessibility at a Glance

	A Song on the End of the World	The End and the Beginning
Context	Warsaw Ghetto in WWII	WWII: Destruction in Poland
Language	Rhythmic repetitions of clauses and phrases	Matter-of-fact observations in straightforward, simple terms
Concept Level	Accessible (the heroism of doing everyday tasks in the face of disaster)	Accessible (the danger of forgetting the causes and effects of war)
Literary Merit	The poem celebrates the value of the ordinary in the face of horror.	The poem cautions against forgetting the causes and effects of war.
Lexile	NP	NP
Overall Rating	Average	Average

And those who expected lightning and thunder
15 Are disappointed.
And those who expected signs and archangels' trumps[1]
Do not believe it is happening now.
As long as the sun and the moon are above,
As long as the bumblebee visits a rose,
20 As long as rosy infants are born
No one believes it is happening now.

Only a white-haired old man, who would be a <u>prophet</u>
Yet is not a prophet, for he's much too busy,
Repeats while he binds his tomatoes:
25 There will be no other end of the world,
There will be no other end of the world.

Warsaw, 1944

---

1. **trumps** *n.* trumpets.

Critical Reading

1. **Respond:** Are you disturbed or comforted by Miłosz's poem? Explain.
2. **(a) Recall:** With what phrase do the first two stanzas begin? **(b) Compare:** What do the details that follow each phrase have in common? **(c) Analyze:** What is surprising about them?
3. **(a) Recall:** In the third stanza, what does the speaker say that some people are expecting? **(b) Infer:** What traditional views about the end of the world do these expectations reflect? **(c) Draw Conclusions:** Why do these people not believe that the world is ending?
4. **(a) Infer:** Why do you think the old man binds tomatoes if he believes the world is ending? **(b) Interpret:** What is the meaning of the poem's last line? **(c) Analyze:** What is the effect of repeating this line?
5. **(a) Generalize:** In what sense might one appreciate every day as if it were the last day? **(b) Draw Conclusions:** What point does the poet make about the value of ordinary things?
6. **(a) Compare:** What do the speaker and the white-haired "prophet" have in common? **(b) Evaluate:** Prophets are said to foresee fateful events, such as the end of the world. In what sense does the writer of this poem play the role of a prophet?

Go Online
Author Link
For: More about
Czesław Miłosz
Visit: www.PHSchool.com
Web Code: ete-9907

A Song on the End of the World ■ 1281

In this prosaic yet moving poem, Wisława Szymborska describes the everyday tasks people must accomplish to repair their world after war. As windows are replaced and bridges rebuilt, the speaker acknowledges that the crisis passes. Time moves forward, and those who do not remember the crisis begin to outnumber those who lived it, demonstrating the relentlessness of time and progress.

❻ Critical Viewing

Possible response: The woman in the painting does not represent the "someone" in the poem. The "someone" from the poem has an indomitable spirit—or an ability to forget horror—that enables the "someone" to repair the destruction, whereas the woman in the painting seems overwhelmed and despairing of accomplishing repairs.

❼ Reading Strategy

Evaluating the Writer's Statement of Philosophy

- After students silently read the bracketed stanzas, **invite** them to define "sound bites" and "photo opportunities."
  Answer: Sound bites are small snippets of a speech that create a particular image of a person or situation. Photo opportunities are apparently spontaneous situations that lend themselves to photographs.

- **Ask** students the Reading Strategy question: What view of modern life does the speaker express in these lines?
  Answer: The speaker suggests that modern life reflects an interest in the superficial.

❽ Critical Thinking

Analyze

- Ask a volunteer to read aloud the bracketed sentence.

- Then, have students **explain** the meaning of the sentence.
  Possible response: Those participating in the rebuilding will roll up their shirtsleeves so many times during the course of the work that they will become tattered and torn.

- In what way does this image reflect the emotions of those rebuilding?
  Possible response: The work is so demanding and relentless that those rebuilding feel emotionally shredded.

❺The End and the Beginning

Wisława Szymborska

translated by Stanislaw Baranczak and Clare Cavanagh

After every war
someone has to tidy up.
Things won't pick
themselves up, after all.

5   Someone has to shove
the rubble to the roadsides
so the carts loaded with corpses
can get by.

Someone has to trudge
10   through sludge and ashes,
through the sofa springs,
the shards of glass,
the bloody rags.

Someone has to lug the post
15   to prop the wall,
someone has to glaze the window,
set the door in its frame.

❼   No sound bites, no photo opportunities,
and it takes years.
20   All the cameras have gone
to other wars.

The bridges need to be rebuilt,
the railroad stations, too.
Shirtsleeves will be rolled
❽ 25   to shreds.

1282 ■ *The Contemporary World*

❻ **Critical Viewing** ▶
Might this woman represent the "someone" in the poem, or does that "someone" have a different spirit? Explain. **[Connect]**

Vocabulary Builder
shards (shärdz) *n.* sharp fragments
glaze (glāz) *v.* fit glass to a window; cover with a shiny finish

Reading Strategy
Evaluating the Writer's Statement of Philosophy
What view of modern life does the speaker express in these lines?

Enrichment

War in Poland

Poland has many times faced the wartime destruction both Miłosz and Szymborska describe. In particular, during World War II, Poland saw terrible devastation. German Nazis invaded on September 1, 1939, and quickly took over. Within two weeks, Germany had made a deal with the Soviet Union—which had invaded from the east—to divide the occupied lands.

The Nazis hated Christian Poles as much as they despised the Jews, whom they did not regard as Polish citizens even though Jews had lived in Poland for a thousand years. All Poles were subject to brutal treatment. They could be rounded up at a moment's notice for dangerous work details, or they could be tortured and killed at the Nazis' whim.

The Polish Resistance movement mounted its own rebellion against Nazi rule in the summer of 1944. In the course of this uprising, which ultimately failed, Warsaw was nearly leveled.

Aftermath, 1945, Karl Hofer, Hamburg Kunsthalle, Hamburg, Germany

❾ Humanities

Aftermath, by Karl Hofer

Karl Hofer (1878–1955) knew of Nazi discrimination and destruction first-hand. Hofer was both figuratively cast out by the Nazis for what they called his "degenerative art" and physically cast out when they ransacked his art studio. Many of Hofer's works reflect despair and emotional isolation, as does this image of an old woman surrounded by debris.

Use the following question for discussion:

How does this painting capture the emotions that rebuilding after war might bring?

Possible response: The woman's posture and expression reflect the overwhelming feelings of sorrow and helplessness of those faced with rebuilding. In addition, the dark colors and angular figures create a feeling of confinement.

The End and the Beginning ■ *1283*

Differentiated Instruction   Solutions for All Learners

Support for Special Needs Students

In order to discern the alliteration in the poem, students may benefit from hearing the poem read aloud. Refer them to the **Listening to Literature Audio CDs.** Encourage students to listen to the recording several times. Then, present examples of alliteration, such as "the rubble to the roadsides" or "the carts loaded with corpses." Discuss how the repeated sounds create an almost chantlike effect that suggests the numbness a war survivor might feel.

Strategy for English Learners

Review multiple meanings in the poem's details so that students can better appreciate the text. For example, the word *springs* refers to the coils inside the sofa, not to the time of year, and the word *bites* refers to small selections of sound, not to the bites a person takes of food. Have students refer to dictionaries to search for multiple meanings of these and other words.

• Have students read the bracketed stanzas.

• Then, **ask** students the Literary Analysis question: According to the speaker, what pattern does history follow after a war?
Possible response: In time, people who lived through the war die, and succeeding generations grow up knowing less and less about it.

ASSESS

Answers

1. **Possible response:** Some readers will say that their views have changed because Szymborska emphasizes the importance of recognizing and understanding history.

2. (a) A war has taken place before the poem begins. (b) The aftermath requires survivors to rebuild both physical and emotional structures. (c) People forget about the war as those who know little or nothing of the war outnumber those who do, as referenced in the lines "Those who knew/what this was all about/must make way for those/who know little."

3. (a) The word "someone" indicates who must do the work. (b) The speaker is referring to any individual who takes up the tasks of repair. (c) **Possible response:** The word suggests the nameless many who historically have taken up the task of rebuilding.

4. (a) The "others" are busy and find the war memories boring. (b) The attitude of the "others" encourages poeple to forget or to ignore the causes and effects of war.

5. **Possible response:** The end of the poem may suggest healing, as people move beyond war's damage; however, it also suggests that forgetting about war's causes and effects will allow it to recur. Therefore, the conclusion represents a superficial healing and conceals danger.

Someone, broom in hand,
still remembers how it was.
Someone else listens, nodding
his unshattered head.
30   But others are bound to be bustling nearby
who'll find all that
a little boring.

From time to time someone still must
dig up a rusted argument
35   from underneath a bush
and haul it off to the dump.

Those who knew
what this was all about
must make way for those
40   who know little.
And less than that.
And at last nothing less than nothing.

Someone has to lie there
in the grass that covers up
45   the causes and effects
with a cornstalk in his teeth,
gawking at clouds.

Literary Analysis
Irony and History as a Theme According to the speaker, what pattern does history follow after a war?

Vocabulary Builder
gawking (gôk´ iŋ) *v.* staring foolishly; gaping

Critical Reading

1. **Respond:** Does this poem cause you to rethink your own feelings about history, or does it leave them unchanged? Explain.

2. **(a) Recall:** What event has taken place before the poem begins? **(b) Generalize:** Identify what kinds of tasks the aftermath of this event requires. **(c) Interpret:** What is the ultimate result of this work? Cite details to support your answer.

3. **(a) Recall:** What repeated word indicates who must do this work? **(b) Infer:** To whom is the speaker referring? **(c) Interpret:** What does the use of this word indicate about the reason that people do the work and, eventually, forget the event?

4. **(a) Interpret:** What is the attitude of the "others" in line 30? **(b) Connect:** In what way does the attitude of the "others" allow "someone" to just lie in the grass?

5. **Make a Judgment:** Does the conclusion of the poem represent a healing of society or does it conceal a danger? Explain.

For: More about Wisława Szymborska
Visit: www.PHSchool.com
Web Code: ete-9908

Go Online
Author Link For additional information about Wisława Szymborska, have students type in the Web Code, then select *S* from the alphabet, and then select Wisława Szymborska.

Apply the Skills

A Song on the End of the World •
The End and the Beginning

Literary Analysis

Irony

1. **(a)** Identify an example of **verbal irony** in lines 22–26 of "A Song on the End of the World." **(b)** Explain what the irony in your example involves.
2. In what way is the central idea of the poem—that the day the world ends will be an ordinary day—an example of **situational irony**?
3. **(a)** Explain one verbal irony in the first stanza of "The End and the Beginning." **(b)** Explain the irony in the last stanza. **(c)** In what way does the irony in the first and last stanzas relate to the poem's title?
4. Explain the way in which each poem might be different if its message were stated directly, without irony.

Comparing Literary Works

5. **(a)** Compare **history as a theme** in each poem, using a chart like the one shown.

Events Described	"Final" Event	Pattern of History	Optimistic/ Pessimistic

   (b) In your opinion, which poem presents the more optimistic view? Explain.
6. **(a)** In what sense does the speaker in each poem remember something that others forget or ignore? **(b)** What role in history does each poem suggest that poets have? Explain.

Reading Strategy

Evaluating the Writer's Statement of Philosophy

7. **(a)** What **philosophical statement** does Miłosz make about the value of an ordinary day? Give details from the poem in support. **(b)** What philosophical statement does Szymborska make about our ability to learn from the past? Support your answer with details.
8. With which philosophy do you agree? Explain.

Extend Understanding

9. **Social Studies Connection:** In the early twentieth century, many believed progress was making the world a better place. How do these late-twentieth-century poems challenge that idea?

QuickReview

Irony occurs when writers create a contrast between appearance or expectation and reality. **Situational irony** involves an opposition between expectations and actual events. **Verbal irony** is a clash between the words used for a thing and its reality.

When writers take **history as a theme,** they look for a meaning or a general pattern in events, such as a repeating cycle.

To **evaluate the writer's statement of philosophy,** decide whether your own experiences and ideas support the view of life suggested by the work.

Assessment
For: Self-test
Visit: www.PHSchool.com
Web Code: eta-6905

A Song on the End of the World / The End and the Beginning ■ 1285

Answers

1. (a) The man is described both as a "white-haired old man" and a "prophet." (b) Miłosz seems at once to ridicule and revere the man.
2. The poem plays on the difference between the drama expected at the end of the world and the ordinary events that are occurring on that day.
3. (a) Szymborska understates the damage caused by war by writing "After every war/someone has to tidy up." (b) Someone who forgets the war lies on grass that covers up the causes and effects of that war. (c) In both the first and last stanzas, the speaker includes an end and a beginning. History is cyclical; the end of the war and its results will be the beginning of the next one.
4. **Possible response:** Without irony, the poems might have an angrier tone.
5. (a) **Sample response: Events Described:** war; **"Final" Event:** the end of the world, the end of the war; **Pattern of History:** everyday events continue amid horror; everyday events in time cover up horror; **Optimistic/Pessimistic:** optimistic; pessimistic (b) **Possible response:** The Miłosz poem is more optimistic because it shows the persistence of the human spirit in the face of disaster. Another sample answer can be found on **Literary Analysis Graphic Organizer B,** p. 220 in *Graphic Organizer Transparencies.*
6. (a) The speaker in Miłosz's poem recognizes signs of the end of the world that others ignore. The speaker in Szymborska's poem remembers the war that others forget. (b) **Possible response:** A poet's role is to remember and record history.
7. (a) Miłosz states that an ordinary day is valuable. For example, he describes the prophet who is busy with his tomatoes in the face of the world's end. (b) Szymborska's poem suggests that life continues and limits one's ability to learn from the past. An example is the boredom felt by those who come after the war.

Answers continued

8. **Possible response:** Miłosz's philosophy is appealing because people must go on living their daily lives, regardless of what happens in the world.
9. **Possible response:** These poems suggest that technology has created devastating weapons.

Go Online Students may use the **Self-test** to **Assessment** prepare for **Selection Test A** or **Selection Test B.**

❶ Vocabulary Lesson

Related Words: *glaze* and *glimmering*

1. A glimpse is a quick look at something or a flicker of light.
2. Gold is a shiny metal.
3. If an object glints, it shines in the light.

Spelling Strategy

1. short   3. long
2. long

Vocabulary Builder: Analogies

1. prophet   4. shards
2. glaze   5. gawking
3. glimmering

❷ Grammar and Style Lesson

1. No one, I
2. Someone, I
3. others, I; that, D
4. Those, D; this, D; those, D
5. that, D

Writing Application

Sample sentences: *No one* (I) who survived the terrorist attack of September 11, 2001, will ever forget that day. An event like *that* (D) can haunt *someone* (I) forever. *Those* (D) who perished will never be forgotten. *Many* (I) will remember the event as a challenge to stand by American ideals.

𝘞𝘎 Writing and Grammar Platinum Level

For support in teaching the Grammar and Style Lesson, use Chapter 16, Section 2.

Build Language Skills

❶ Vocabulary Lesson

Related Words: *glaze* and *glimmering*

Glaze and *glimmering* are related to the Indo-European root *ǵhel*, meaning "to shine or to glow." To *glaze* is to fit glass, a shiny substance, to a window. A *glimmering* is a faint shining. Explain how the root meaning "to shine" adds to the meaning of each of these related words:

   1. glimpse   **2.** gold   **3.** glint

Spelling Strategy

If a word is spelled with a doubled consonant preceded by a single vowel, the vowel sound is short. *Glimmering* has a short *i* sound. In contrast, if a single consonant appears between two vowels, the first vowel sound is often long. *Glaze* has a long *a* sound. Explain whether the boldface vowel in each of these words is short or long.

   1. d**a**pper   **2.** v**a**cate   **3.** p**o**tential

Vocabulary Builder: Analogies

For each item below, study the relationship presented in the first pair. Then, complete the analogies by using the vocabulary words on page 1279 to build word pairs expressing the same relationship.

1. *Storyteller* is to *tale* as __?__ is to *prediction*.
2. *Upholster* is to *cloth* as __?__ is to *glass*.
3. *Drizzling* is to *rain* as __?__ is to *light*.
4. *Rocks* are to *stones* as __?__ are to *fragments*.
5. *Yelling* is to *whispering* as __?__ is to *peeking*.

❷ Grammar and Style Lesson

Indefinite and Demonstrative Pronouns

An **indefinite pronoun** is used to refer to persons, places, or things without specifying which one. Indefinite pronouns include such words as *each, everything,* and *someone.* A **demonstrative pronoun** is used to point out a specific person, place, or thing. These pronouns include *this, that, these,* and *those.*

> **Indefinite:** <u>Someone</u> has to shove / the rubble to the roadsides. . . .
>
> **Demonstrative:** . . . <u>those</u> who expected thunder and lightning . . .

Practice For each item, identify the indefinite or demonstrative pronouns, and label each *I* or *D.*

1. No one believes it is happening now.
2. Someone, broom in hand, / still remembers how it was.
3. But others are bound to be bustling nearby / who'll find all that / a little boring.
4. Those who knew / what this was all about / must make way for those / who know little.
5. And less than that.

Writing Application Write four sentences about an event from history, using at least one indefinite and one demonstrative pronoun.

𝘞𝘎 *Prentice Hall Writing and Grammar Connection: Platinum Level, Chapter 16, Section 2*

Assessment Practice

Strategy

Many standardized tests require students to recognize various writing strategies. Use the following sample test item to demonstrate this skill.

    The destruction of Warsaw during World War II certainly explains why Miłosz was thinking about the world's end. However, the reaction to these events expressed in the poem is at first puzzling. Miłosz evokes a peaceful, almost lyrical world, ending with a description of a man binding tomatoes.

(For more practice, see *Test Preparation Workbook*, p. 61.)

Which of the following would be the best addition to the end of this paragraph?

  A Miłosz's writing is very powerful.
  B The tomato captures the readers' attention.
  C This quality of the poem invites serious thought.
  D The old man in Miłosz's poem is heroic.

C is the correct answer. Miłosz wants readers to think differently about the world's end.

❸ Writing Lesson

Narrative About a Quiet Hero

The old man in Miłosz's poem shows heroic devotion to ordinary pursuits in the midst of danger. Write an account of a person, real or fictional, with such a devotion, showing why he or she deserves your admiration.

Prewriting Begin by listing details that describe the dangerous situation and the way in which your subject managed to keep a sense of quiet dignity. Circle those that are most vivid or significant.

Model: Listing Relevant Details

(tornado alarm)	She said, "We will be fine."
kids yelling in the hall	
Mrs. Clark stayed calm.	She reminded us where to go in the building.
(She moved slowly.)	
She touched me on the shoulder as I passed by.	

Details about the situation and the hero will help bring the event to life.

Drafting As you draft, remember that understatement is often more effective than exaggeration. Choose precise verbs and adjectives to *show* the quiet heroism of your character, rather than announcing it.

Revising As you revise your account, add specific details that will help the reader imagine the scene.

W̶G Prentice Hall Writing and Grammar Connection: Platinum Level, Chapter 6, Section 2

❹ Extend Your Learning

Listening and Speaking With a partner, present a **multimedia reading** of one of the poems. Accompany your reading with appropriate audiovisuals, such as music or slides. Use these tips to prepare:

- Select musical and visual qualities of the poem to emphasize, such as repetition.
- Practice the timing of your presentation before you perform it for the class.

After your presentation, ask audience members to evaluate the effectiveness of each of its elements. **[Group Activity]**

Research and Technology In their poems, Miłosz and Szymborska respond to Poland's difficult history. Create a **map or set of maps** showing Poland's shifting boundaries over time. Clearly indicate which nations have ruled Poland, as well as the birthplace or main city of residence of each poet.

 Go Online Research

For: An additional research activity
Visit: www.PHSchool.com
Web Code: etd-7905

A Song on the End of the World / The End and the Beginning ■ 1287

Assessment Resources

The following resources can be used to assess students' knowledge and skills.

Unit 9 Resources
  Selection Test A, pp. 97–99
  Selection Test B, pp. 100–102

General Resources
  Rubrics for Narration: Short Story,
    pp. 63–64

Go Online Assessment Students may use the **Self-test** to prepare for **Selection Test A** or **Selection Test B**.

---

❸ Writing Lesson

You may use this Writing Lesson as a timed-writing practice, or you may allow students to develop the narrative essay as a writing assignment over several days.

- To give students guidance in writing this narrative, give them the **Support for Writing Lesson**, p. 94 in *Unit 9 Resources.*

- Narratives usually recount a specific event or events and how the central figures respond to the events. This narrative should focus on how the central figure responds to danger.

- Explain that an effective narrative should begin by introducing the central figure and situation. Writers often do this by using dialogue or by describing the central figure in action. The narrative should then develop toward its crisis or climax. In this case, the crisis could be the presentation of danger.

- In selecting the central figure for their narratives, students should review fictional characters from recent reading or focus on real characters from personal experience or news stories.

- Use the Narration: Short Story rubrics in *General Resources*, pp. 63–64, to evaluate students' work.

W̶G Writing and Grammar Platinum Level

For support in teaching the Writing Lesson, use Chapter 6, Section 2.

❹ Research and Technology

- Clarify the difference between using one map and using a set of maps. If using one map, students will need multiple layers or colors. If using a set of maps, students can show each time period separately.

- Discuss likely information sources with students, such as historical atlases and Internet sites that focus on Polish history.

- The **Support for Extend Your Learning** page (*Unit 9 Resources*, p. 95) provides guided note-taking opportunities to help students complete the Extend Your Learning activities.

Go Online Research Have students type in the Web Code for another research activity.

1287

Standard Course of Study

Goal 1: WRITTEN LANGUAGE

WL.1.03.2 Identify and analyze text components and evaluate impact on personal reflection.

Goal 3: FOUNDATIONS OF ARGUMENT

FA.3.04.10 Analyze connections between ideas, concepts, characters and experiences in argumentative work.

Goal 5: LITERATURE

LT.5.01.1 Use strategies for preparation, engagement, and reflection on world literature.

LT.5.03.6 Make inferences, predict, and draw conclusions based on world literature.

Goal 6: GRAMMAR AND USAGE

GU.6.01.4 Use vocabulary strategies to determine meaning.

GU.6.01.7 Use language effectively to create mood and tone.

GU.6.02.2 Edit for appropriate and correct mechanics.

Step-by-Step Teaching Guide	Pacing Guide
PRETEACH	
• Administer Vocabulary and Reading Warm-ups as necessary.	5 min.
• Engage students' interest with the motivation activity.	5 min.
• Read and discuss author and background features. **FT**	10 min.
• Introduce the Literary Analysis Skill: Speaker. **FT**	5 min.
• Introduce the Reading Strategy: Inferring the Speaker's Attitude. **FT**	
• Prepare students to read by teaching the selection vocabulary. **FT**	10 min.
TEACH	
• Informally monitor comprehension while students read independently or in groups. **FT**	30 min.
• Monitor students' comprehension with the Reading Check notes.	as students read
• Reinforce vocabulary with Vocabulary Builder notes.	as students read
• Develop students' understanding of the speaker with the Literary Analysis annotations. **FT**	5 min.
• Develop students' ability to infer the speaker's attitude with the Reading Strategy annotations. **FT**	5 min.
ASSESS/EXTEND	
• Assess students' comprehension and mastery of the Literary Analysis and Reading Strategy by having them answer the Apply the Skills questions. **FT**	15 min.
• Have students complete the Vocabulary Lesson and the Grammar and Style Lesson. **FT**	15 min.
• Apply students' ability to choose effective persuasive language by using the Writing Lesson. **FT**	45 min. or homework
• Apply students' understanding by using one or more of the Extend Your Learning activities.	20–90 min. or homework
• Administer Selection Test A or Selection Test B. **FT**	15 min.

Resources

Print

Unit 9 Resources

Transparency

Graphic Organizer Transparencies

Print

Reader's Notebook [L2]

Reader's Notebook: Adapted Version [L1]

Reader's Notebook: English Learner's Version [EL]

Unit 9 Resources

Technology

Listening to Literature Audio CDs [L2, EL]

Print

Unit 9 Resources

General Resources

Technology

Go Online: Research [L3]

Go Online: Self-test [L3]

ExamView®, **Test Bank [L3]**

Choosing Resources for Differentiated Instruction

[**L1**] Special Needs Students

[**L2**] Below-Level Students

[**L3**] All Students

[**L4**] Advanced Students

[**EL**] English Learners

For Vocabulary and Reading Warm-ups and for Selection Tests, **A** signifies "less challenging" and **B** "more challenging." For Graphic Organizer transparencies, **A** signifies "not filled in" and **B** "filled in."

FT Fast Track Instruction: To move the lesson more quickly, use the strategies and activities identified with **FT**.

Scaffolding for Less Proficient and Advanced Students

The leveled Critical Thinking questions after selections progress in the levels of thinking required to answer them. To address the needs of your different students, you may use the (a) level questions for your less proficient students and the (b) level questions with your on-level and advanced students. The occasional (c) level questions are appropriate for your advanced students.

PRENTICE HALL
Teacher EXPRESS™ Use this complete
Plan · Teach · Assess   suite of powerful
teaching tools to make lesson planning and testing quicker and easier.

PRENTICE HALL
Student EXPRESS™ Use the interactive
Learn · Study · Succeed   textbook (online
and on CD-ROM) to make selections and activities come alive with audio and video support and interactive questions.

Go Online **For:** Information about Lexiles
Professional **Visit:** www.PHSchool.com
Development **Web Code:** eue-1111

❶ Freedom to Breathe • *from* Nobel Lecture • Visit

Motivation

Ask students to imagine that they have suddenly been stricken with amnesia. They can still speak and function, but they have no memories of the past. Discuss with them how they would be different people. Lead them to see that remembering the past—both the good and the bad—is an essential part of self-understanding. Tell them that the two authors they are about to read show the importance of memory and reflection on the past.

❶ Background

More About the Authors

During World War II, Solzhenitsyn served in the Red Army where he rose to the rank of artillery captain and was decorated for bravery. After completing his eight-year prison sentence, he was exiled to Kazakhstan. His citizenship was restored in 1956, three years after Soviet leader Josef Stalin's death.

Yevtushenko grew up in the open spaces of central Asia, a region not unlike western Colorado. Ironically, this most Russian of writers was not Russian by birth. His mother came from Latvia. His father's family was Ukranian and had been exiled to Siberia by the czar in the 1800s. As a member of the Congress of People's Deputies, he supported what he calls "revolution from below"—a reform of Soviet society directed by the Soviet people.

Geography Note

Draw students' attention to the map on this page. Tell them that the former Soviet Union was the world's largest nation. It consisted of fifteen republics, comprised more than one hundred nationalities, covered 8,650,000 square miles, and had the longest coastline of any nation.

Alexander Solzhenitsyn
(b. 1918)

Alexander Solzhenitsyn (sōl′ zhə nēt′ sin) spent years in Soviet prison camps. There, he resolved to survive as a witness to oppression. His unsparing accounts of the camps are among the most important documents of the twentieth century.

Early Imprisonment Born in Kislovodsk, a city in southern Russia, Solzhenitsyn served in the Soviet army during World War II. While a soldier, he was convicted of treason—he had written letters critical of Josef Stalin, the Soviet leader. Solzhenitsyn found himself in a windswept camp in central Asia, where prisoners did backbreaking work on a meager diet.

Released in 1953, Solzhenitsyn eventually wrote a novel about life in the camps, *One Day in the Life of Ivan Denisovich* (1962). Although the government encouraged this novel's publication, the political tide soon shifted. After 1963, the government banned further publication of Solzhenitsyn's books.

Exile Officially rejected in Russia, Solzhenitsyn began to publish his novels in the West. The faster his prestige grew abroad, the worse his fortunes were at home. When he was awarded the Nobel Prize in Literature in 1970, Solzhenitsyn would not travel to accept it, fearing that the Soviet government would not let him return. Finally, in 1973, Solzhenitsyn published the first volume of *The Gulag Archipelago, 1918–1956*, a chronicle of the prison camps. Within months, he was deported by the Soviet government.

Solzhenitsyn eventually settled in the United States, where he continued to speak out on behalf of freedom. He returned to Russia in 1994. His life and work bear witness to the power of words—a power mighty enough to upset a nation.

Yevgeny Yevtushenko
(b. 1933)

Perhaps the best introduction to Russian poet Yevgeny Yevtushenko (yev gen′ ē yev′ tōō shen′ kō) is one of his recordings. Yevtushenko is a remarkable performer, his voice fit to calm a child or storm a barricade. He has not been afraid to raise this voice against injustice.

The Celebrity Poet Born in 1933 in Zima Junction, along the Trans-Siberian Railroad, Yevtushenko published his first book, *Prospectors of the Future* (1952), while he was still in college. Over the next nine years, his poems and his public readings made him a celebrity in the Soviet Union, as popular as any movie star in the West. Yevtushenko did not merely read his poems: He acted them, lived them—lowering his voice to a whisper, then breaking out in a mighty roar, all the while gesturing dramatically.

Breaking Silence In 1961, Yevtushenko's fame became international with the poem "Babi Yar." It was at Babi Yar, near Kiev, that German troops murdered 34,000 Jews during two days in 1941. In his poem, Yevtushenko boldly referred to Russian anti-Semitism, a forbidden subject in Soviet Russia. The editor of the Russian *Literary Gazette* agonized over the poem, knowing that printing it could cost him his job. As the magazine's presses began to roll, and after consulting with his wife, he decided to take the risk. The poem's passionate attack on prejudice won Yevtushenko admirers in the West.

Elected in 1989 to the Congress of People's Deputies, Yevtushenko supported Mikhail Gorbachev's *perestroika*, or restructuring of Soviet society. His most recent work is *Don't Die Before You're Dead* (1993), a novel concerning life after the dismantling of the Soviet Union.

Preview

Connecting to the Literature

Perhaps you have awakened early on a spring morning and, in the unfamiliar stillness, found the person you have always been. Perhaps you felt then how far a day might carry you—how large the future is. Literature, as these writers show, is also a moment to rediscover freedom and the future.

❷ Literary Analysis

Speaker

The **speaker** of a work is the character who "says" its words, or the voice of the work. There are various types of speaker. A speaker may be

- a distinctive fictional character.
- a character bearing a close resemblance to the writer.
- a writer's representation of himself or herself.
- a generalized, impersonal voice, as in a factual essay.

In Yevtushenko's poem "Visit," the speaker has an intimate, personal voice and uses details from the poet's experience. In this poem, the speaker is the poet's representation of himself. Solzhenitsyn himself is the speaker in his Nobel Lecture, yet he carefully crafts a particular public voice for himself. As you read, note the qualities of the speaker in each work.

Comparing Literary Works

As each of these works develops, the speaker takes on a new role, ensuring a dramatic conclusion. In Solzhenitsyn's Nobel Lecture, for example, the speaker turns from his role as award recipient to a role as spokesperson for truth. In Yevtushenko's poem, the speaker shifts from one who remembers the past to one who is confronted by it. As you read, compare the speakers' changes, noting ways in which they add drama to the works.

❸ Reading Strategy

Inferring the Speaker's Attitude

To fully understand a work, use the details to **infer the speaker's attitude,** determining the speaker's views of ideas and events. Use a chart like the one shown to list and interpret clues to the speaker's attitude.

Vocabulary Builder

glistens (glis´ enz) v. shines or sparkles with reflected light (p. 1290)

reciprocity (res´ ə präs´ ə tē) n. mutual exchange (p. 1291)

assimilate (ə sim´ ə lāt´) v. absorb; incorporate into a greater body (p. 1292)

inexorably (in eks´ ə rə blē´) adv. relentlessly (p. 1293)

oratory (ôr´ ə tôr´ ē) n. skillful public speaking (p. 1293)

fungus (fuŋ´ gəs) n. mildew; any of a group of plants lacking leaves and roots (p. 1296)

clenched (klencht) v. gripped firmly or tightly (p. 1296)

NC **Standard Course of Study**

- Analyze connections between ideas, concepts, characters and experiences in argumentative work. (FA.3.04.10)

- Identify and analyze elements of critical environment. (CT.4.05.11)

Clue
Describes each detail of Zima Junction as familiar

Inference
Place has not changed

↓

Clue
Remembers a "sudden thought" from childhood

Inference
Visit confronts him with past hopes

↓

Speaker's Attitude
The speaker realizes how much he has changed.

Freedom to Breathe / from *Nobel Lecture* / *Visit* ■ 1289

❷ Literary Analysis

Speaker

- On the board, list works from other units, and ask students to identify the speakers or narrators: for example, "How Much Land Does a Man Need?" (a distinctive fictional character); from *Annie John* (a character bearing a close resemblance to the writer); from *History of the Peloponnesian War* (a generalized, impersonal voice).

- Remind students that the speaker is not necessarily the writer. In some cases, the speaker and the writer may be one and the same, but they are often different.

❸ Reading Strategy

Inferring the Speaker's Attitude

- Remind students that an inference is a conclusion made from hints and implications in a text.

- Direct students' attention to the graphic organizer. Explain that identifying detailed clues from a text allows readers to make conclusions about the speaker's thoughts and, in turn, his or her attitude. Understanding a speaker's attitude can lead to more accurate interpretations of a text. Then, give students a copy of **Reading Strategy Graphic Organizer A,** p. 221 in *Graphic Organizer Transparencies.* As students read each selection, have them use it to record clues to the speaker's attitude.

Vocabulary Builder

- Pronounce each vocabulary word for students, and read the definitions as a class. Have students identify any words with which they are familiar.

Differentiated Instruction Solutions for All Learners

Support for Special Needs Students

Have students complete the **Preview** and **Build Skills** pages for these selections in the *Reader's Notebook: Adapted Version.* These pages provide a selection summary, an abbreviated presentation of the reading and literary skills, and the graphic organizer on the **Build Skills** page in the student book.

Support for Less Proficient Readers

Have students complete the **Preview** and **Build Skills** pages for these selections in the *Reader's Notebook.* These pages provide a selection summary, an abbreviated presentation of the reading and literary skills, and the graphic organizer on the **Build Skills** page in the student book.

Support for English Learners

Have students complete the **Preview** and **Build Skills** pages for these selections in the *Reader's Notebook: English Learner's Version.* These pages provide a selection summary, an abbreviated presentation of the reading and literary skills, additional contextual vocabulary, and the graphic organizer on the **Build Skills** page in the student book.

Facilitate Understanding

These essays and the poem may be difficult for students. Read sections aloud, periodically stopping to clarify points and ask questions.

❶ About the Selection

In the essay "Freedom to Breathe," Solzhenitsyn reflects on how imprisonment altered his appreciation of the simple act of breathing.

❷ Critical Thinking

Infer

- Have students read the last two paragraphs on this page.
- **Ask** students what they can infer about the speaker from this passage. **Possible response:** The speaker's prison confinement has stripped away a focus on material values and distractions and replaced them with an appreciation for the simple pleasures of nature and of life. The speaker's return to elemental pleasures gives him hope for humanity.
- Then, **ask:** Do you think most people in the United States would have the same experience while standing under an apple tree? Explain why or why not. **Possible response:** Most Americans would probably appreciate the beauty of the experience to a lesser degree because they often take their freedom for granted.

❸ Literary Analysis

Speaker and Dramatic Conclusion

- Remind students that setting is often an integral part of a literary work.
- Read aloud the bracketed passage. Then, **ask** the Literary Analysis question: Why is it surprising to learn these details about the setting at the conclusion? **Possible response:** It is surprising because the reader has been led to believe that the setting is pastoral when, in reality, it is urban.

❶ *Freedom to Breathe*

Alexander Solzhenitsyn
translated by Michael Glenny

Background In this brief essay and in his Nobel Lecture, Alexander Solzhenitsyn argues for the power of freedom and of truth. During the Soviet period in Russia, freedom of speech was curtailed. Writers could publish legally only with the approval of the state. Dissenting opinions and alternative literature circulated secretly, as typewritten manuscript, in a literary underground. Solzhenitsyn himself was exiled for his dissent. Clearly, the Soviet government would have agreed with Solzhenitsyn's assessment—freedom is our truth, and truth is dangerous to an oppressive government.

A shower fell in the night and now dark clouds drift across the sky, occasionally sprinkling a fine film of rain.

I stand under an apple tree in blossom and I breathe. Not only the apple tree but the grass round it <u>glistens</u> with moisture; words cannot describe the sweet fragrance that pervades the air. I inhale as deeply as I can, and the aroma invades my whole being; I breathe with my eyes open, I breathe with my eyes closed—I cannot say which gives me the greater pleasure.

This, I believe, is the single most precious freedom that prison takes away from us: the freedom to breathe freely, as I now can. No food on earth, no wine, not even a woman's kiss is sweeter to me than this air steeped in the fragrance of flowers, of moisture and freshness.

❷ No matter that this is only a tiny garden, hemmed in by five-story houses like cages in a zoo. I cease to hear the motorcycles backfiring, radios whining, the burble of loudspeakers. As long as there is fresh air to breathe under an apple tree after a shower, we may survive a little longer.

1290 ■ The Contemporary World

Vocabulary Builder
glistens (glis′ enz) *v.* shines or sparkles with reflected light

Literary Analysis
Speaker and Dramatic Conclusion Why is it surprising to learn these details about the setting at the conclusion?

Differentiated Instruction — Solutions for All Learners

Accessibility at a Glance

	Freedom to Breathe	*from* Nobel Lecture	Visit
Context	Reflections on freedom	Acceptance speech	A return home after Stalin's death
Language	Syntax: compound sentences	Syntax: long sentences embedded with clauses	Syntax: sentences with implied subjects and participial phrases
Concept Level	Accessible (the value of the freedom to breathe in a free society)	Accessible (Writers must reveal a government's lies.)	Accessible (Memories can stimulate an analysis of one's past hopes and current potential.)
Literary Merit	Essay that posits the value of a free society	Famous speech about the importance of world literature	Nostalgic poem that confronts the speaker's past, present, and future
Lexile	1020L	1350L	NP
Overall Rating	Average	Average	More challenging

from Nobel Lecture

Alexander Solzhenitsyn
translated by F. D. Reeve

I am, however, encouraged by a keen sense of WORLD LITERATURE as the one great heart that beats for the cares and misfortunes of our world, even though each corner sees and experiences them in a different way.

In past times, also, besides age-old national literatures there existed a concept of world literature as the link between the summits of national literatures and as the aggregate[1] of reciprocal literary influences. But there was a time lag: readers and writers came to know foreign writers only belatedly, sometimes centuries later, so that mutual influences were delayed and the network of national literary high points was visible not to contemporaries but to later generations.

Today, between writers of one country and the readers and writers of another, there is an almost instantaneous <u>reciprocity</u>, as I myself know. My books, unpublished, alas, in my own country, despite hasty and often bad translations have quickly found a responsive world readership. Critical analysis of them has been undertaken by such leading Western writers as Heinrich Böll.[2] During all these recent years, when both my work and my freedom did not collapse, when against the laws of gravity they held on seemingly in thin air, seemingly ON NOTHING, on the invisible, mute surface tension of sympathetic people, with warm gratitude I learned, to my complete surprise, of the support of the world's writing fraternity. On my fiftieth birthday I was astounded to receive greetings from well-known European writers. No pressure put on me now passed unnoticed. During the dangerous weeks when I was

---

1. **aggregate** (ag´ rə git) *n.* group of things gathered together and considered as a whole.
2. **Heinrich Böll** (hin´ riH böl) German novelist (1917–1985) and winner of the Nobel Prize in Literature.

Vocabulary Builder
reciprocity (res´ ə präs´ ə tē)
n. mutual exchange

✓ **Reading Check** ❽

According to Solzhenitsyn, what is the main difference between world literature in the past and in the present?

---

from *Nobel Lecture* ■ 1291

---

being expelled from the Writers' Union,[3] THE PROTECTIVE WALL put forward by prominent writers of the world saved me from worse persecution, and Norwegian writers and artists hospitably prepared shelter for me in the event that I was exiled from my country. Finally, my being nominated for a Nobel Prize was originated not in the land where I live and write but by François Mauriac[4] and his colleagues. Afterward, national writers' organizations expressed unanimous support for me.

As I have understood it and experienced it myself, world literature is no longer an abstraction or a generalized concept invented by literary critics, but a common body and common spirit, a living, heartfelt unity reflecting the growing spiritual unity of mankind. State borders still turn crimson, heated red-hot by electric fences and machine-gun fire; some ministries of internal affairs still suppose that literature is "an internal affair" of the countries under their jurisdiction; and newspaper headlines still herald, "They have no right to interfere in our internal affairs!" Meanwhile, no such thing as INTERNAL AFFAIRS remains on our crowded Earth. Mankind's salvation lies exclusively in everyone's making everything his business, in the people of the East being anything but indifferent to what is thought in the West, and in the people of the West being anything but indifferent to what happens in the East. Literature, one of the most sensitive and responsive tools of human existence, has been the first to pick up, adopt, and <u>assimilate</u> this sense of the growing unity of mankind. I therefore confidently turn to the world literature of the present, to hundreds of friends whom I have not met face to face and perhaps never will see.

Bust of Soviet leader V. I. Lenin.

My friends! Let us try to be helpful, if we are worth anything. In our own countries, torn by differences among parties, movements, castes, and groups, who for ages past has been not the dividing but the uniting force? This, essentially, is the position of writers, spokesmen of a national language, of the chief tie binding the nation, the very soil which the people inhabit, and, in fortunate circumstances, the nation's spirit too.

I think that world literature has the power in these frightening times to help mankind see itself accurately despite what is advocated by partisans[5] and by parties. It has the power to transmit the condensed experience of one region to another, so that different scales of values

---

3. **Writers' Union** official Soviet writers' organization. In addition to being expelled from this union, Solzhenitsyn was forbidden to live in Moscow.
4. **François Mauriac** (frän swä´ mô´ rē ak´) French novelist and essayist (1885–1970).
5. **partisans** (pärt´ i zenz) *n.* emotional supporters of a party or viewpoint.

1292

are combined, and so that one people accurately and concisely knows the true history of another with a power of recognition and acute awareness as if it had lived through that history itself—and could thus be spared repeating old mistakes. At the same time, perhaps we ourselves may succeed in developing our own WORLD-WIDE VIEW, like any man, with the center of the eye seeing what is nearby but the periphery[6] of vision taking in what is happening in the rest of the world. We will make correlations[7] and maintain world-wide standards.

Who, if not writers, are to condemn their own unsuccessful governments (in some states this is the easiest way to make a living; everyone who is not too lazy does it) as well as society itself, whether for its cowardly humiliation or for its self-satisfied weakness, or the lightheaded escapades of the young, or the youthful pirates brandishing knives?

We will be told: What can literature do against the pitiless onslaught of naked violence? Let us not forget that violence does not and cannot flourish by itself; it is inevitably intertwined with LYING. Between them there is the closest, the most profound and natural bond: nothing screens violence except lies, and the only way lies can hold out is by violence. Whoever has once announced violence as his METHOD must <u>inexorably</u> choose lying as his PRINCIPLE. At birth, violence behaves openly and even proudly. But as soon as it becomes stronger and firmly established, it senses the thinning of the air around it and cannot go on without befogging itself in lies, coating itself with lying's sugary <u>oratory</u>. It does not always or necessarily go straight for the gullet; usually it demands of its victims only allegiance to the lie, only complicity in the lie.

The simple act of an ordinary courageous man is not to take part, not to support lies! Let *that* come into the world and even reign over it, but not through me. Writers and artists can do more: they can VANQUISH LIES! In the struggle against lies, art has always won and always will. Conspicuously, incontestably for everyone. Lies can stand up against much in the world, but not against art.

Once lies have been dispelled, the repulsive nakedness of violence will be exposed—and hollow violence will collapse.

That, my friends, is why I think we can help the world in its red-hot hour: not by the nay-saying of having no armaments, not by abandoning oneself to the carefree life, but by going into battle!

---

6. **periphery** (pə rif′ ər ē) surrounding area; boundary; perimeter.
7. **correlations** (kôr′ ə lā′ shənz) analysis of relationships or connections.

⑪

Literary Analysis
Speaker In addition to the role of award recipient, what other role does Solzhenitsyn assume through this speech?

Vocabulary Builder
inexorably (in eks′ ə rə blē) *adv.* relentlessly

oratory (ôr′ ə tôr′ ē) *n.* skillful public speaking

⑫ ▼ Critical Viewing
What do stamps such as the ones on these pages suggest about the role of modern communications in creating a world literature? **[Draw a Conclusion]**

✔ Reading Check ⑬
Identify one reason that, according to Solzhenitsyn, writers have the power to serve justice.

from *Nobel Lecture* ■ 1293

Differentiated Instruction
Solutions for All Learners

Strategy for Less Proficient Readers
Play appropriate selections from the **Listening to Literature Audio CDs.** Tell students that listening to a recording of the speech may enhance their comprehension or help them appreciate the urgency of Solzhenitsyn's message. After students listen to the reading, have them reread the text above and work in groups to summarize key points.

Enrichment for Gifted/Talented Students
Play appropriate selections from the **Listening to Literature Audio CDs** so that students can listen to the text above. Then, ask students to write a short story that portrays an "ordinary courageous man," or woman, like the one Solzhenitsyn mentions. Have them describe a situation in which it would be easier to ignore events or a lie than to act. Students' stories should illustrate simple, ordinary situations in which telling the truth about a lie might create positive change.

---

⑪ Literary Analysis
Speaker

• Have students reread Solzhenitsyn's biography on p. 1288. **Ask** them how he describes the Soviet government in his writings.
Answer: Solzhenitsyn wrote letters critical of Stalin and accounts of Stalin's oppressive labor camps.

• Why would Solzhenitsyn have the moral authority to call on writers to "condemn their own unsuccessful governments"?
Possible response: Solzhenitsyn himself "condemned" Stalinism and suffered for his beliefs.

• **Ask** students the Literary Analysis question: In addition to the role of award recipient, what other role does Solzhenitsyn assume through this speech?
Possible response: Solzhenitsyn serves as a model of what writers can accomplish if they continue to speak the truth and resist governments that are unfair or repressive. He also takes on the role of one who thanks his benefactors (the writers who aided him) and that of a political orator, who speaks to persuade others to a course of action.

▶ **Monitor Progress Ask** students to describe Solzhenitsyn's view of a writer's role.
Possible response: Solzhenitsyn views the writer as a social or political activist.

▶ **Reteach** If students have difficulty with the Literary Analysis skill, have them use the **Literary Analysis** support, p. 107 in *Unit 9 Resources.*

⑫ Critical Viewing
Possible response: The images of these stamps illustrate that countries around the world proudly display their great writers on postage stamps. The stamps are placed on letters that will travel the globe and spread information about literatures of the world.

⑬ Reading Check
Answer: Writers can vanquish lies in literature, conspicuously serving justice.

In Russian, proverbs about TRUTH are favorites. They persistently express the considerable, bitter, grim experience of the people, often astonishingly:

ONE WORD OF TRUTH OUTWEIGHS THE WORLD.

On such a seemingly fantastic violation of the law of the conservation of mass and energy[8] are based both my own activities and my appeal to the writers of the whole world.

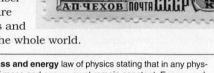

8. **the law of the conservation of mass and energy** law of physics stating that in any physical or chemical change, the sum of mass and energy must remain constant: Energy and matter are not created by nature from nothing.

Critical Reading

1. **Respond:** Have you found that your own readings in world literature have broadened your understanding of the world? Explain.

2. **(a) Recall:** In the first paragraph of "Freedom to Breathe," what details does the writer use to set the scene? **(b) Interpret:** Describe the mood of this setting. **(c) Evaluate:** Does the description of the surrounding area help you appreciate the speaker's delight? Explain.

3. **(a) Recall:** What fundamental freedom does prison take away, according to "Freedom to Breathe"? **(b) Compare:** With what does the speaker contrast this freedom?

4. **Evaluate:** Do you agree that "freedom to breathe" is a basic necessity? Explain.

5. **(a) Recall:** Name two ways in which, according to Solzhenitsyn's Nobel Lecture, European writers showed support for Solzhenitsyn. **(b) Connect:** How does Solzhenitsyn's own career exemplify his idea of a modern world literature?

6. **(a) Infer:** Why does Solzhenitsyn say in his Nobel Lecture that a nation's literature is a "uniting force"? **(b) Interpret:** In what sense does he call world literature "the one great heart"?

7. **Evaluate:** Is Solzhenitsyn's claim about the power of literature to contest violence valid? Explain.

8. **Apply:** Give a modern instance in which people are discouraged from speaking their minds, and explain what Solzhenitsyn might say about this situation.

Enrichment

Russian Writers and Social Reform

Russia has a long tradition of viewing the writer as someone who searches for the truth and speaks out against social injustice. Poets and novelists have played a highly influential part in Russian life.

Alexander Pushkin began the tradition of the writer as public spokesman in the early nineteenth century by speaking out against the mistreatment of the Russian poor. His example inspired the novelist Leo Tolstoy to take even stronger action later in the century.

In Tolstoy's day, most work in Russia was done by peasants who were desperately poor, and most of the wealth was held by a few rich families. Believing this situation to be immoral, Tolstoy, a wealthy man, gave everything he owned away, even the copyrights of his highly successful books. He lived simply and took a leading role in social reform or, as the Russians call it, "community action."

Visit

⑭

Yevgeny Yevtushenko
translated by
Robin Milner-Gulland
and Peter Levi, S.J.

⑭ About the Selection

"Visit" describes Yevtushenko's return home from Moscow to Zima Junction in Central Asia in the summer of 1953. That year was a pivotal one in Soviet history: Stalin had died that spring, after twenty-four years of tyrannical rule, and the nation looked forward to what might lie ahead with a mixture of hope and concern.

⑮ Background

Yevgeny Yevtushenko wrote and directed a film about his World War II experiences in his hometown of Zima Junction. He called the film *Kindergarten* because, he said, the war was a "classroom" in which his generation first learned about life's difficulties.

⑯ Reading Check

Answer: The speaker knows the place well and seems fond of it. The speaker probably grew up there.

⑮ Going to Zima Junction,[1] quiet place.
Watching out for it in the distance
with the window of the carriage wide open,
familiar houses, ornamental carving.
5 The jump down from the train before it stops,
crunching along on the warm slag;[2]
the linesman working with a hose
cursing and swearing in the stifling heat.
The ducks in midstream with their heads buried,
10 the perches where the poultry crow at dawn,
along the sidings ornamental stars
of white and colored bricks set in the wall.
Walking along the dusty paving-boards,
passing the clock that sits on the town hall,
15 hearing behind the fence of the old market
rustle of oats and clink of weights and measures:
and there the painted wooden fruit-baskets,
the cranberries wet on the low counters,
and the bright yellow butter-balls afloat
20 in basins made of flower-painted china.
Same cranny where the birds are still nesting,
and, most familiar, the faded gate.
And the house is exactly the same size,
the log fence still mended with boards,
25 the same broom leaning upon the stove,

---

1. **Zima** (zē´ mə) **Junction** town in the Asian part of Russia (formerly part of the Soviet Union), just west of Lake Baikal and north of Mongolia.
2. **slag** (slag) refuse separated from a metal in the process of smelting.

⑯ 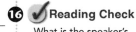 **Reading Check**
What is the speaker's likely connection to the place he describes?

Visit ■ 1295

Differentiated Instruction — Solutions for All Learners

Strategy for Special Needs Students
Have students create a word web for "Visit." In the center, have students write *Zima Junction* and on the web's rays, list areas described in the poem: town hall, market, speaker's house, river, and woods. Ask students to record the details that describe the speaker's hometown.

Strategy for English Learners
Point out that a sudden change in chronology occurs in line 29. Explain that up to this point, the speaker is describing the return home. At line 29, the speaker begins to remember events that happened when the speaker was younger. Ask students to make a timeline of the poem's events.

Enrichment for Advanced Students
Tell students that the idea of returning home is a durable theme in world literature. Have students read *The Epic of Gilgamesh* or "My Old Home" by Lu Hsun. Direct students to write an analytical essay in which they discuss the treatment of this theme in two or more works.

- **Ask** students what role memory plays when they return to a special place they have not seen in some time.
Possible response: Memory can allow one to revisit a special time, and it can measure how a place or a person has changed.

- Have students **describe** the mood of the poem during the description of the boys playing in the river.
Possible response: The mood is one of happy recollection.

- Have students reread the poem. Then, **ask** the Reading Strategy question: Confronted by this concluding memory, what questions might the speaker ask about his present life?
Possible response: The speaker might ask himself how he is different from the boy he sees in his memory; how his present life reflects this boy; and how he can reconcile the boy and the man.

ASSESS

Answers

1. **Possible response:** Readers may enjoy visiting places that hold happy memories but may shy away from places that hold troubling memories.

2. (a) The speaker describes walking from the train station, past the town hall, and through the marketplace. (b) When the speaker reaches the house (line 29), the poem shifts into memories of the past. The ellipses and the next line indicate a flashback.

3. **Possible response:** The speaker remembers his realization as a boy that he had a future full of possibility. By remembering this realization, he may be brought to ask himself, "What use have I made of my possibilities to date? What should I do to realize them in the future?"

4. **Possible response:** Memories of events ten years in the past may evoke the same reaction in the reader as they do in the author—nostalgia, regret, and hope.

---

the same tinned mushrooms on the window-sill,
the crack in the stairs is not different,
darkening deeply down, feeding <u>fungus</u>. . . .
Some nut or bolt or other I'd picked up
30   just as I always picked something up
was <u>clenched</u> happily in my hand
and dropped again as I went hurrying
down to the river and the river-mist,
and wandering sometimes in the woods
35   by a path choked in a tangle of tall weeds
in search of some deep-colored country flower,
and working with the freckled ferry girl,
heaving the glossy hawser hand by hand.
Trying the quality of "old honey"
40   where the beehives rear up above the pond,
rocking along slow-motion in the cart,
slow rhythms of the whip's lazy flicking.
Wandering through the cranberry patches
with a casual crowd of idle lads,
45   and fishing beneath bridges with the noise
of trains thundering above your head,
joking, throwing your shirt off in the grass,
and diving in high from the river-bank,
with one sudden thought, how little I
50   have done in life, how much I can do.

⑰

Critical Reading

1. **Respond:** Do you like revisiting places where you once spent a great deal of time? Why or why not?

2. **(a) Recall:** Identify three scenes described by the speaker as he moves through the town toward his old home. **(b) Infer:** At what point does the poem shift from the speaker's present visit to his memories of the past? Explain your response.

3. **Interpret:** In what sense do the speaker's memories of the past lead him to confront his present and his future?

4. **Relate:** Imagine that, ten years from now, you are remembering today, as the adult speaker remembers his childhood. What reactions might you have?

1296 ■ *The Contemporary World*

Go ●nline For additional information about
Author Link Yevgeny Yevtushenko, have students
type in the Web Code, then select *Y* from the alphabet,
and then select Yevgeny Yevtushenko.

Vocabulary Builder
fungus (fuŋ´ gəs) *n.* mildew; any of a group of plants lacking leaves and roots

clenched (klencht) *v.* gripped firmly or tightly

Reading Strategy
Inferring the Speaker's Attitude Confronted by this concluding memory, what questions might the speaker ask about his present life?

For: More about Yevgeny Yevtushenko
Visit: <u>www.PHSchool.com</u>
Web Code: ete-9910

Apply the Skills

Freedom to Breathe • from *Nobel Lecture* • *Visit*

Literary Analysis

Speaker

1. **(a)** For each of the three works, identify statements in the following categories: personal details, public facts, generalizations, and exclamations. **(b)** Characterize each **speaker,** explaining whether he speaks in a personal voice, a public voice, or a mixed voice.

2. **(a)** Identify two ways in which Solzhenitsyn's Nobel Lecture links general themes to personal experience. **(b)** Why does this link add authority to the speaker's general points?

3. In "Visit," what contrast does the speaker suggest between his present and his past? Explain your answer, citing details.

Comparing Literary Works

4. **(a)** Compare the dramatic endings created by the call to action in the Nobel Lecture and the turn from *I* to *we* in "Freedom to Breathe." **(b)** In what way do these endings extend the speakers' preceding points?

Speaker's Role		Meaning of Events	
Beginning	End	Beginning	End

5. Compare the shift in the speaker's role in "Freedom to Breathe" and in "Visit," analyzing details with a chart like the one shown.

Reading Strategy

Inferring the Speaker's Attitude

6. What is the **speaker's attitude** toward city life in "Freedom to Breathe"? Give details in support.

7. What is Solzhenitsyn's attitude toward literature in his Nobel Lecture? Identify two details supporting your answer.

8. From images and direct statements in Yevtushenko's "Visit," what can you infer about the speaker's attitude toward his visit?

Extend Understanding

9. **Science Connection:** Explain why Solzhenitsyn thinks literature "violates" the law of the conservation of mass and energy.

QuickReview

The **speaker** is the character or voice that "says" the words of a literary work. A change in the speaker's role or purpose in a work can add drama.

To **infer the speaker's attitude,** look for details that suggest how a speaker views his or her subject.

Go Online
Assessment

For: Self-test
Visit: www.PHSchool.com
Web Code: eta-6906

Freedom to Breathe/ from *Nobel Lecture / Visit* ■ 1297

Answers

1. **(a) Possible response: Nobel: Personal:** "I was astounded to receive greetings. . . ."; **Public:** "Critical analysis . . . by Heinrich Böll." **Generalization:** first paragraph; **Exclamation:** "My friends!" **(b)** "**Freedom**" mixed; **Nobel** public; "**Visit**" personal

2. **(a) Possible response:** The speaker links both his own fame and his evasion of worse persecution to the fact that today writers can easily follow the work and fate of writers in another country. **(b)** These links add authority by providing specific examples and by adding the weight of firsthand experience.

3. **Possible response:** The speaker suggests that as a child he would lose himself in the present but was also seized by the sense of his own immeasurable future: "one sudden thought, how little I / have done in life, how much I can do." As an adult, he has a past and now faces the question of what he has done with his possibilities.

4. **(a) Possible response:** The lecture builds Solzhenitsyn's own experiences into a matter of urgent concern for his audience. The transition from *I* to *we* in "Freedom" turns the speaker's private experience into a universal truth. **(b)** In the lecture, the call to expose the truth builds on the preceding points that violence depends on lies. In "Freedom," the descriptions move the reader to better appreciate his claim that we need such experiences to survive.

5. **Possible response:** "Freedom to Breathe": Speaker's Role—**Beginning** describes his own particular experience; **End** makes a universal claim about survival **Meaning—Beginning** shows the deep value of peace of mind; **End** shows that even in a noisy city, freedom enables us to survive. "Visit": Speaker's Role—**Beginning** also describes a particular experience; **End** asks a specific question about his own life **Meaning—Beginning** depicts personal experiences that readers can relate to; **End** shows that ordinary experiences can lead to deep and important questions.

6. **Possible response:** The speaker describes the noises of city life as minor distractions.

Answers continued

7. **Possible response:** He presents literature as our conscience when he says that it can "help mankind see itself accurately. . . ." He presents it as a savior when he notes its power to vanquish tyranny.

8. **Possible response:** Pleasant recollections suggest that the speaker takes pleasure in the visit. The end suggests it makes him think.

9. Using words, which have negligible "mass" or "energy," literature can change the world. In this sense, literature creates "energy" out of nothing.

❶ Vocabulary Lesson

Usage: Forms of *reciprocity*

1. b	3. a
2. c	

Spelling Strategy

1. stimulus	3. adventurous
2. campus	

Vocabulary Builder

1. b	3. a	5. a	7. b
2. b	4. c	6. c	

❷ Grammar and Style Lesson

1. Solzhenitsyn—whose; readers—writes

2. speaker—and; part—is

3. road—each

4. future—but

5. writers—Pushkin; Solzhenitsyn—have

Writing Application

Possible response: The garden—tiny though it is—provides peace and comfort to the neighborhood. People of all ages—from babies to grandparents—love to sit near the cool fountain. Such green spaces are a model for other communities—and even other nations—that want to promote peace.

Writing and Grammar
Platinum Level
For support in teaching the Grammar and Style Lesson, use Chapter 28, Section 5.

Build Language Skills

❶ Vocabulary Lesson

Usage: Forms of *reciprocity*

The noun *reciprocity*, meaning "mutual exchange," has adjective, adverb, and verb forms. Complete each item with a form of *reciprocity*.

a. reciprocally   **b.** reciprocal   **c.** reciprocate

1. Pen pals have a ___?___ arrangement.
2. Although he could not ___?___, he appreciated the support of other writers.
3. Just as others supported his rights, he acts ___?___ to support the rights of others.

Spelling Strategy

In some nouns derived from Latin, such as *fungus*, the final sound *us* is spelled *us*. In an adjective, this final sound is usually spelled *ous*. For each word below, add the correct ending.

1. stimul__   2. camp__   3. adventur__

Vocabulary Builder: Synonyms

Review the vocabulary list on page 1289. Then, for each numbered vocabulary word listed below, select the letter of its synonym, the word closest to it in meaning.

1. assimilate: **(a)** calculate, **(b)** absorb, **(c)** compare
2. glistens: **(a)** glides, **(b)** shines, **(c)** speaks
3. oratory: **(a)** eloquence, **(b)** radiance, **(c)** benevolence
4. clenched: **(a)** kissed, **(b)** soaked, **(c)** gripped
5. inexorably: **(a)** relentlessly, **(b)** endlessly, **(c)** bluntly
6. fungus: **(a)** rash, **(b)** shrub, **(c)** mildew
7. reciprocity: **(a)** suburb, **(b)** exchange, **(c)** cookery

❷ Grammar and Style Lesson

Using Dashes

A **dash** (—) indicates a longer, more emphatic pause than a comma does. A dash usually signals an interruption in the sequence of ideas and may be used to indicate an abrupt shift of focus, a dramatic exclamation, or a break from listing details to generalizing about them. Review this sentence from "Freedom to Breathe":

> . . . I breathe with my eyes open, I breathe with my eyes closed—I cannot say which gives me the greater pleasure.

Writers can use dashes to set up distinctive rhythms in their writing, achieving the feeling of a living voice that wanders off or bursts into digressions, exclamations, and explanations.

Practice Insert dashes where necessary in the following sentences.

1. Solzhenitsyn whose life was saved by his readers writes of the power of literature.
2. The speaker and this is the strange part is actually in a small inner-city garden.
3. Scenes at the railroad station, scenes along the road each is as familiar as the next.
4. The speaker remembers discovering that he had a future but now he *is* that future!
5. Three Russian writers Pushkin, Pasternak, and Solzhenitsyn have all believed in the writer's role as social critic.

Writing Application Write a brief description of a garden, using dashes correctly in three sentences.

Prentice Hall Writing and Grammar Connection: Platinum Level, Chapter 28, Section 5

Assessment Practice

Style   (For more practice, see *Test Preparation Workbook,* p. 62.)

Style questions on standardized tests often focus on understanding the author's purpose on the basis of his or her effective use of language. Read this paragraph from Solzhenitsyn's Nobel lecture:

> Once lies have been dispelled, the repulsive nakedness of violence will be exposed—and hollow violence will collapse.

Why does Solzhenitsyn isolate this sentence as a stand-alone paragraph?

A to emphasize the word *nakedness*
B to describe Russian politics
C to describe how lies function
D to draw attention to an idea

A, B, and *C* do not reflect the stylistic purpose of the paragraph. *D* is the correct answer: A one-sentence paragraph amidst longer paragraphs stands out.

③ Writing Lesson

Persuasive Speech

The written word may seem without force, but in his Nobel Lecture, Solzhenitsyn argues that the word can conquer violence. Write a persuasive speech in which you support or refute Solzhenitsyn's view of the power of words and truth. To persuade your readers, use precise and powerful language.

Prewriting   Reread the Nobel Lecture, jotting down each important point Solzhenitsyn makes. Write a one-sentence summary of his idea of truth, and decide whether or not you agree with it. Then, list reasons, examples, and other details to support your position.

Drafting   Begin your essay with a statement of your position. As you draft, make sure you use charged, precise words to add persuasive force.

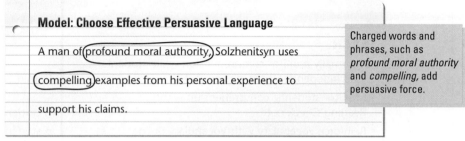

Model: Choose Effective Persuasive Language

A man of ⟨profound moral authority,⟩ Solzhenitsyn uses

⟨compelling⟩ examples from his personal experience to

support his claims.

> Charged words and phrases, such as *profound moral authority* and *compelling,* add persuasive force.

Revising   Review your speech. Identify any weak or unclear wording, and replace it with stronger phrasing.

WG Prentice Hall Writing and Grammar Connection: Platinum Level, Chapter 7, Section 3

④ Extend Your Learning

Listening and Speaking Using "Freedom to Breathe" or "Visit" as a model, present an **oral description** of the sights and smells of one of your favorite places. Use these tips to prepare:

- Before you write, brainstorm for vivid imagery appealing to the five senses.
- As you practice, pay special attention to your tempo, speaking slowly enough to be understood, but not dragging.
- Give a dress rehearsal for a small audience.

Present your description to the class.

Research and Technology Solzhenitsyn is a famous Nobel Prize winner. Working in a small group, compile an **annotated list** of Nobel Prize winners in literature. For each writer, include a capsule biography and a brief description of his or her works. Post your list in the classroom. **[Group Activity]**

Go Online
Research

For: An additional research activity
Visit: www.PHSchool.com
Web Code: etd-7906

Freedom to Breathe / from *Nobel Lecture* / *Visit* ■ 1299

Assessment Resources

The following resources can be used to assess students' knowledge and skills.

Unit 9 Resources
    Selection Test A, pp. 114–116
    Selection Test B, pp. 117–118

General Resources
    Rubrics for Persuasion: Persuasive Essay,
      pp. 47–48

Go Online Students may use the **Self-test** to
Assessment prepare for **Selection Test A** or **Selection Test B.**

---

③ Writing Lesson

You may use this Writing Lesson as a timed-writing practice, or you may allow students to develop the persuasive speech as a writing assignment over several days.

- To give students guidance in writing this persuasive essay, give them the **Support for Writing Lesson,** p. 102 in *Unit 9 Resources.*

- Encourage students to reread Solzhenitsyn's *Nobel Lecture,* making sure that they clearly understand his argument that literature can overcome violence.

- Review the definition of a persuasive speech. Discuss with students how strong, specific language convinces readers that an author's opinion is sound.

- Use the Persuasion: Persuasive Essay rubrics in *General Resources,* pp. 47–48, to evaluate students' work.

WG Writing and Grammar
Platinum Level
For support in teaching the Writing Lesson, use Chapter 7, Section 3.

④ Research and Technology

- Encourage English learners to research Nobel Prize winners from countries where they or their families have lived. Suggest that students read excerpts from the Nobel Prize winners' speeches aloud to the class.

- Encourage students to include Internet links in their annotated lists. The links will allow class members to read more about Nobel winners whom they want to research individually.

- The **Support for Extend Your Learning** page (*Unit 9 Resources,* p. 112) provides guided note-taking opportunities to help students complete the Extend Your Learning activities.

Go Online Have students type
Research in the Web Code for another research activity.

Goal 1: WRITTEN LANGUAGE

WL.1.03.11   Identify and analyze elements of expressive environment in personal reflections.

Goal 2: INFORMATIONAL READING

IR.2.01.11   Analyze elements of informational environment in informing audience.

Goal 5: LITERATURE

LT.5.03.8   Make connections between works, self and related topics in world literature.

LT.5.03.11   Analyze elements of literary environment in world literature.

Goal 6: GRAMMAR AND USAGE

GU.6.02.3   Edit for parallel structure.

Step-by-Step Teaching Guide	Pacing Guide
PRETEACH	
• Administer Vocabulary and Reading Warm-ups as necessary.	5 min.
• Engage students' interest with the motivation activity.	5 min.
• Read and discuss author and background features. **FT**	10 min.
• Introduce the Literary Analysis Skill: Surrealism. **FT**	5 min.
• Introduce the Reading Strategy: Determining the Author's Purpose. **FT**	10 min.
• Prepare students to read by teaching the selection vocabulary. **FT**	
TEACH	
• Informally monitor comprehension while students read independently or in groups. **FT**	30 min.
• Monitor students' comprehension with the Reading Check notes.	as students read
• Reinforce vocabulary with Vocabulary Builder notes.	as students read
• Develop students' understanding of Surrealism with the Literary Analysis annotations. **FT**	5 min.
• Develop students' ability to determine the author's purpose with the Reading Strategy annotations. **FT**	5 min.
ASSESS/EXTEND	
• Assess students' comprehension and mastery of the Literary Analysis and Reading Strategy by having them answer the Apply the Skills questions. **FT**	15 min.
• Have students complete the Vocabulary Lesson and the Grammar and Style Lesson. **FT**	15 min.
• Apply students' ability to add descriptive detail by using the Writing Lesson. **FT**	45 min. or homework
• Apply students' understanding by using one or more of the Extend Your Learning activities.	20–90 min. or homework
• Administer Selection Test A or Selection Test B.	15 min.

Resources

Print
Unit 9 Resources

Transparency
Graphic Organizer Transparencies

Print
Reader's Notebook [L2]
Reader's Notebook: Adapted Version [L1]
Reader's Notebook: English Learner's Version [EL]
Unit 9 Resources

Technology
Listening to Literature Audio CDs [L2, EL]
Reader's Notebook: Adapted Version Audio CD [L1, L2]

Print
Unit 9 Resources

General Resources

Technology
Go Online: Research [L3]
Go Online: Self-test [L3]
ExamView®, **Test Bank [L3]**

Choosing Resources for Differentiated Instruction

[L1] Special Needs Students

[L2] Below-Level Students

[L3] All Students

[L4] Advanced Students

[EL] English Learners

For Vocabulary and Reading Warm-ups and for Selection Tests, **A** signifies "less challenging" and **B** "more challenging." For Graphic Organizer transparencies, **A** signifies "not filled in" and **B** "filled in."

FT Fast Track Instruction: To move the lesson more quickly, use the strategies and activities identified with **FT**.

Scaffolding for Less Proficient and Advanced Students

The leveled Critical Thinking questions after selections progress in the levels of thinking required to answer them. To address the needs of your different students, you may use the (a) level questions for your less proficient students and the (b) level questions with your on-level and advanced students. The occasional (c) level questions are appropriate for your advanced students.

PRENTICE HALL

Teacher EXPRESS™ Use this complete
Plan · Teach · Assess suite of powerful
teaching tools to make lesson planning and testing quicker and easier.

PRENTICE HALL

Student EXPRESS™ Use the interactive
Learn · Study · Succeed textbook (online
and on CD-ROM) to make selections and activities come alive with audio and video support and interactive questions.

Go Online **For:** Information about Lexiles
Professional **Visit:** www.PHSchool.com
Development **Web Code:** eue-1111

Motivation

Play for students a recording of the Joni Mitchell song "The Circle Game." Have students listen several times, writing down phrases and images from the song that catch their attention. Then, ask them to summarize its message. (Time passes quickly, and people grow older before they know it.) Conclude by telling them that the story they are about to read has a similar message, although it is presented in a different way and comes from a different culture.

❶ Background

More About the Author

Mahfouz's novels have been considered the "Baedeker guide" to Gamaliya, the Cairo neighborhood where Mahfouz grew up. His vivid depiction of the alleys, houses, palaces, mosques, and people is one of the most outstanding characteristics of his work. He captures the soul of Egypt as he describes the Egyptian family, which is at the core of the country. In his description of the Egyptian family, he draws heavily on autobiography; like one of his characters, Mahfouz was the youngest son of a merchant family.

Geography Note

Draw students' attention to the map on this page. Tell students that many of Mahfouz's stories are set in Cairo, the capital of Egypt and the largest city on the African continent. Cairo, which means "the victorious" in Arabic, has stood on the banks of the Nile for more than one thousand years. Although Cairo is located in the foothills of the Arabian Desert, irrigation from the Nile gives the city lush vegetation.

Build Skills   *Short Story*

❶ Half a Day

Naguib Mahfouz (b. 1911)

A writer may become so closely associated with a place that the two seem inseparable. Charles Dickens seems to have created Victorian England just for his novels; the American Dust Bowl itself seems to speak through John Steinbeck's works. Novelist Naguib Mahfouz (nä´ heb´ mä fōōz´) has just such a special relationship with Egypt. For his vivid depictions of twentieth-century Cairo, the Egyptian capital, Western literary critics have compared him to Dickens and to Honoré de Balzac, the great chronicler of French life. Strangely, the very country for which Mahfouz is a voice forced him to find new, indirect ways to speak his mind.

Dangerous Times Mahfouz was born in 1911 in an old quarter of Cairo. In 1930, he entered the University of Cairo, where he studied philosophy. Throughout his undergraduate career, he contributed essays on philosophical subjects to various magazines. Although his readings in literature were slim, classes at the University of Cairo were in English and French, and Mahfouz's access to those languages increased the scope of his reading. Among his favorite authors were Tolstoy, Chekhov, Kafka, and Ibsen.

Mahfouz began his career as a novelist in a politically dangerous, repressive period. In 1930, Ismail Sidki, the new prime minister, had suspended Egypt's 1923 constitution. Once in power, Sidki brutally crushed any attempt to question his authority. Two of Mahfouz's main influences, the writers Taha Hussein and Abbas al-Akkad, were persecuted during this time: Hussein was accused of heresy, and al-Akkad was imprisoned.

Telling the Truth The harsh treatment of Hussein, al-Akkad, and others made Mahfouz realize the futility of direct criticism of the government. He turned instead to narrative. During World War II, he wrote three historical novels set in ancient Egypt.

Mixing history with symbolism, Mahfouz's tales of tyrannical rule and foreign occupation had strong contemporary implications. At the time Mahfouz was writing, Egypt was ruled by a despot, dominated by an aristocracy of foreign (largely Turkish) origins, and occupied by British troops. Yet because the novels were not "about" the present, telling instead of ancient history, Mahfouz escaped censorship. In the end, these novels express a tragic vision that extends beyond their specific political implications.

Master of Many Styles Mahfouz wrote prolifically through the 1940s, withdrew from writing for much of the 1950s, and returned to literature in the 1960s. During his career, he has experimented widely with style. Some of his short stories of the 1960s are surrealistic. Later novels, such as *Arabian Nights and Days* (1982), have an open-ended structure reminiscent of traditional Arabic narratives.

Mahfouz is perhaps most celebrated, though, for mastering the novel, a Western genre, and making it relevant to Egyptian life. He also modernized the literary language of the Arab tradition. By shaping classical Arabic into a vehicle of popular speech, he created an authoritative voice in which to tell of the lives of ordinary Egyptians.

The Master Honored In 1988, Mahfouz won the Nobel Prize. The award, he remarked, made way for a new international recognition of Arab literature: "Egypt and the Arab world also get the Nobel Prize with me. . . . [I]n the future, literate people will look for Arab literature, and Arab literature deserves that recognition." Now almost deaf and partially blind, Mahfouz claims to live only to write; he has said, "If the urge should ever leave me, I want that day to be my last."

Preview

Connecting to the Literature

"If you take out the trash every day, then we'll talk about getting a dog." Sometimes, life seems like one big detour. But what if all of life really *is* a detour, and we can never get to what we wanted in the first place? In this story, Mahfouz plays a trick with time to confront us with this question.

❷ Literary Analysis

Surrealism

Surrealism, meaning "beyond realism," refers to works that use realism to create a dreamlike world. Surrealist works generally portray people and objects in realistic detail. By connecting realistic elements in strange ways, though, surrealistic works break rules of logic and sequence. In this passage from "Half a Day," for example, realistic details create a dream-like situation—in one day, the world has changed:

> I proceeded a few steps, then came to a startled halt. . . . Where was the street lined with gardens? Where had it disappeared to?

As you read, use a chart like this one to note realistic elements and the ways they become dreamlike.

Connecting Literary Elements

By causing confusion and surprise, Mahfouz's surrealism pushes the reader to see life from a shocking new angle. In this way, Mahfouz uses surrealism to convey his **theme,** or message about life. As you read, note ways in which your reactions to events help you better appreciate the theme.

❸ Reading Strategy

Determining the Author's Purpose

To **determine the author's purpose** in writing, think about the effect the work is meant to have on readers. For example, in "Half a Day," Mahfouz includes details that make readers think about the way life works. His purpose is to convey an insight into life. To fully understand Mahfouz's purpose, connect his choice of details to possible insights as you read.

Vocabulary Builder

unmarred (un märd´) *adj.* unspoiled; unimpaired (p. 1303)

intimacy (in´ tə mə sē) *n.* familiarity; warmth (p. 1303)

intricate (in´ tri kit) *adj.* complicated; elaborate (p. 1304)

presumed (prē zoomd´) *v.* expected; supposed (p. 1304)

throngs (thrônz) *n.* crowds (p. 1305)

hordes (hôrdz) *n.* large moving crowds; wandering tribes (p. 1305)

hastened (hās´ ənd) *v.* hurried; moved swiftly (p. 1306)

Standard Course of Study

• Make connections between works, self and related topics in world literature. (LT.5.03.8)

• Analyze elements of literary environment in world literature. (LT.5.03.11)

Realistic Details

Surrealistic Connections

Half a Day ■ 1301

---

❷ Literary Analysis

Surrealism

• Tell students that as they read, they will encounter details that may not seem to make sense in the story's context. Discuss how the narrative of a surrealistic story does not follow a logical pattern.

• Give students a copy of **Literary Analysis Graphic Organizer A,** p. 225 in *Graphic Organizer Transparencies.* Have them use it to identify realistic details and surrealistic elements as they read the story.

❸ Reading Strategy

Determining the Author's Purpose

• Ask students whether they have ever read a story or seen a program that made them feel confused about what was going on. Have them discuss why an author might want to throw readers off guard and leave them wondering about events.

• Remind students that the surrealism of Mahfouz's story is designed to keep readers guessing what is real and what is not.

• Ask students to discuss whether things in life must always make sense and whether there are always good reasons for the way things in life happen.

Vocabulary Builder

• Pronounce each vocabulary word for students, and read the definitions as a class. Have students identify any words with which they are familiar.

Facilitate Understanding

Ask students to write a one-page journal entry about a time when they started school—either for the first time or at a new school. Have them explain the significance of beginning school and their feelings about the event.

❶ About the Selection

A young Egyptian boy fearfully begins his first day of school, gradually overcomes his fears, and learns to enjoy the resources and opportunities school offers. As if by magic, time passes, the boy is grown, and the world he returns to at the end of "half a day" is very different from the one he woke up to that morning.

❶ Half a Day

Naguib Mahfouz

translated by Denys Johnson-Davies

1302 • *The Contemporary World*

Differentiated Instruction   Solutions for All Learners

Accessibility at a Glance

	Half a Day
Context	The streets of Cairo, Egypt
Language	Syntax: first-person narrative with long sentences embedded with verbal phrases
Concept Level	Accessible (In maturity, you cannot return to the paradise of your youth.)
Literary Merit	Clever surrealistic tale of time's passing
Lexile	860L
Overall Rating	Average

Background

"Half a Day" is set in Cairo, the capital of Egypt and the city in which Naguib Mahfouz grew up. Cairo itself embodies the mysteries of time that Mahfouz explores in the story. Ancient and modern exist there side by side. Along the skyline, contemporary hotels rub shoulders with the ancient pyramids. Narrow, twisting streets where camels, horses, and pedestrians once jostled are now choked with vehicular traffic. Modern Western influences are visible in people's clothing and in the fast-food restaurants, alongside traditional garb and open-air markets. As you read Mahfouz's story, you will encounter hints of the changes that brought the modern world to ancient Cairo.

I proceeded alongside my father, clutching his right hand, running to keep up with the long strides he was taking. All my clothes were new: the black shoes, the green school uniform, and the red tarboosh.[1] My delight in my new clothes, however, was not altogether <u>unmarred</u>, for this was no feast day but the day on which I was to be cast into school for the first time.

My mother stood at the window watching our progress, and I would turn toward her from time to time, as though appealing for help. We walked along a street lined with gardens; on both sides were extensive fields planted with crops, prickly pears, henna trees, and a few date palms.

"Why school?" I challenged my father openly. "I shall never do anything to annoy you."

"I'm not punishing you," he said, laughing. "School's not a punishment. It's the factory that makes useful men out of boys. Don't you want to be like your father and brothers?"

I was not convinced. I did not believe there was really any good to be had in tearing me away from the <u>intimacy</u> of my home and throwing me into this building that stood at the end of the road like some huge, high-walled fortress, exceedingly stern and grim.

When we arrived at the gate we could see the courtyard, vast and crammed full of boys and girls. "Go in by yourself," said my father, "and join them. Put a smile on your face and be a good example to others."

I hesitated and clung to his hand, but he gently pushed me from him. "Be a man," he said. "Today you truly begin life. You will find me waiting for you when it's time to leave."

I took a few steps, then stopped and looked but saw nothing. Then the faces of boys and girls came into view. I did not know a single one of them, and none of them knew me. I felt I was a stranger who had lost his way. But glances of curiosity were directed toward me, and one boy approached and asked, "Who brought you?"

---

1. **tarboosh** (tär boosh´) *n.* brimless cap of felt or other cloth shaped like a truncated cone.

Vocabulary Builder
unmarred (un märd´) *adj.* unspoiled; unimpaired

Literary Analysis
Surrealism What ordinary details give the opening descriptions a realistic quality?

Vocabulary Builder
intimacy (in´ tə mə sē) *n.* familiarity; warmth

❸ ◀ **Critical Viewing**
What does this photograph suggest about contrasts between ancient and modern in the setting of the story? **[Connect]**

❹ ✔ **Reading Check**
Why is the day an important one for the boy?

Half a Day ■ 1303

---

❷ **Literary Analysis**
Surrealism

- **Ask** students what small children might think or worry about on their first day of school.
  Possible answer: They might be concerned about their clothing and school supplies, leaving home for the first time, the appearance of the classroom, the demeanor of their classmates, and the attitude of the teacher.

- Read aloud the bracketed passage. Then, **ask** the Literary Analysis question: What ordinary details give the opening descriptions a realistic quality?
  Answer: The boy's new clothes, the different types of trees lining the street, the mother standing at the window, the boy's exchange with his father, the boy's hesitation on entering the courtyard, and the other students' curiosity give the opening scene a realistic quality.

❸ **Critical Viewing**

Answer: The photograph suggests that the ancient and the modern will clash or that time will alternate between them. Because the modern features are in the foreground, readers may expect them to dominate.

❹ **Reading Check**

Answer: The day is important for the boy because he is starting school.

Differentiated Instruction   Solutions for All Learners

Strategy for Special Needs Students
Help students follow both the story's literal narrative and its surreal narrative by mapping events in the text. Give students a copy of the **Plot Diagram** in *Graphic Organizer Transparencies,* p. 280, to use as they read.

Support for English Learners
In the first sentence, point out the participial phrases *clutching his right hand* and *running to keep up.* Explain that both of these phrases serve as adjectives modifying the subject *I.* Advise students that not all words ending in *-ing* are participles, and then point out the main verb *am punishing* in the fourth paragraph.

Enrichment for Gifted/Talented Students
Ask students to depict the passing of time in artistic works of their own creation. These artistic responses can be in the form of paintings, drawings, sculptures, musical compositions, poems or stories, dances, videos, or any other media.

- Review with students the relationship that the narrator appears to have with his father.

- Draw students' attention to the two bracketed lines, and read them aloud.

- **Ask** students what they think the effect of the boy's statement might be on the narrator.
  Possible response: It might serve as his introduction to the real world, where people die and other people's experiences differ greatly from the ones he has had.

6 Literature in Context

Surrealism in Art Surrealism in art and literature was popular in Europe between World War I and World War II. Surrealism was a reaction against the European "rationalism" in culture and politics. André Breton's *Manifesto* described Surrealism as "the real process of thought . . . free from any control by the reason and of any aesthetic or moral preoccupation."

Connect to the Literature Point out to students that Surrealist paintings could be designed to shock viewers. For example, one work by René Magritte illustrated a table setting with a slice of ham on a plate—and a human eye looking out from the ham. Ask students to discuss surrealistic elements in this story that are intended to shock readers.
Possible response: The sudden appearance of a familiar middle-aged man, the change in the environment of the streets, the surging crowds, and the lad who addresses the narrator as "Grandpa" are all surrealistic elements.

7 Humanities

The Persistence of Memory,
by Salvador Dalí

Salvador Dalí's *The Persistence of Memory* includes a representative image of the coast of Catalonia, Spain, his home. The drooping watches, however, are part of a Surrealist landscape. The timepieces droop like soft cheese; indeed, Dalí called the image "the camembert of time."

Use this question for discussion:

What does the shape of the watches in the picture imply about the passage of time?
Possible response: The drooping watches imply that time has lost its meaning.

---

5 "My father," I whispered.
"My father's dead," he said quite simply.
   I did not know what to say. The gate was closed, letting out a pitiable screech. Some of the children burst into tears. The bell rang. A lady came along, followed by a group of men. The men began sorting us into ranks. We were formed into an <u>intricate</u> pattern in the great courtyard surrounded on three sides by high buildings of several floors; from each floor we were overlooked by a long balcony roofed in wood.
   "This is your new home," said the woman. "Here too there are mothers and fathers. Here there is everything that is enjoyable and beneficial to knowledge and religion. Dry your tears and face life joyfully."
   We submitted to the facts, and this submission brought a sort of contentment. Living beings were drawn to other living beings, and from the first moments my heart made friends with such boys as were to be my friends and fell in love with such girls as I was to be in love with, so that it seemed my misgivings had had no basis. I had never imagined school would have this rich variety. We played all sorts of different games: swings, the vaulting horse, ball games. In the music room we chanted our first songs. We also had our first introduction to language. We saw a globe of the Earth, which revolved and showed the various continents and countries. We started learning the numbers. The story of the Creator of the universe was read to us, we were told of His present world and of His Hereafter, and we heard examples of what He said. We ate delicious food, took a little nap, and woke up to go on with friendship and love, play and learning.

The Persistence of Memory, Salvador Dali, 1931,
The Museum of Modern Art / Artists Rights Society (ARS), New York

   As our path revealed itself to us, however, we did not find it as totally sweet and unclouded as we had <u>presumed.</u> Dust-laden winds and unexpected accidents came about suddenly, so we had to be watchful, at the ready, and very patient. It was not all a matter of playing and fooling around. Rivalries could bring about pain and hatred or give rise to fighting. And while the lady would sometimes smile, she would often scowl and scold. Even more frequently she would resort to physical punishment.
   In addition, the time for changing one's mind was over and gone and there was no question of ever returning to the paradise of home. Nothing lay ahead of us but exertion, struggle, and perseverance. Those who

---

6 Humanities Connection

Surrealism in Art

   Surrealism is a movement in art and literature that favors mysterious, dreamlike imagery and rejects convention and reason. The French writer André Breton first described the movement's goals in his *Manifesto of Surrealism* (1924). He and other surrealists aimed to give the unconscious mind a voice through art. Their ideas of the unconscious were influenced by the writings of the psychoanalyst Sigmund Freud, whose work Breton had read and whom he had met in 192... One method the Surrealists used was automatic writing, a technique similar to Freud's free association.
   Surrealist painters included Salvador Dali, Max Ernst, René Magritte, and Joan Miró. In more recent times, Surrealism has influenced Latin American writers such as Julio Cortázar.

Connect to the Literature

What characteristics of surrealism do you notice in this ...

Vocabulary Builder
intricate (in´ tri kit) *adj.*
complicated; elaborate

presumed (prē zōōmd´) *v.*
expected; supposed

were able took advantage of the opportunities for success and happiness that presented themselves amid the worries.

The bell rang announcing the passing of the day and the end of work. The <u>throngs</u> of children rushed toward the gate, which was opened again. I bade farewell to friends and sweethearts and passed through the gate. I peered around but found no trace of my father, who had promised to be there. I stepped aside to wait. When I had waited for a long time without avail, I decided to return home on my own. After I had taken a few steps, a middle-aged man passed by, and I realized at once that I knew him. He came toward me, smiling, and shook me by the hand, saying, "It's a long time since we last met—how are you?"

With a nod of my head, I agreed with him and in turn asked, "And you, how are you?"

"As you can see, not all that good, the Almighty be praised!"

Again he shook me by the hand and went off. I proceeded a few steps, then came to a startled halt. . . . Where was the street lined with gardens? Where had it disappeared to? When did all these vehicles invade it? And when did all these <u>hordes</u> of humanity come to rest upon its surface? How did these hills of refuse come to cover its sides? And where were the fields that bordered it? High buildings had taken over, the street surged with children, and disturbing noises shook the air. At various points stood conjurers showing off their tricks and making snakes appear from baskets. Then there was a band announcing

8 ▲ Critical Viewing
Explain which part of the story this image illustrates—the world before or the world after the narrator's day at school. **[Connect]**

Vocabulary Builder
throngs (thrônz) *n.* crowds

hordes (hôrdz) *n.* large moving crowds; wandering tribes

✓ Reading Check 11
What is the reason for the narrator's confusion?

Half a Day ■ 1305

8 Critical Viewing
Answer: The image illustrates the world after the narrator's day at school. The world has changed and become crowded and modern.

9 Vocabulary Builder
Connotations: Words for Crowds
• Remind students that words with similar meanings can have different connotations, or associations.
• Point out the word *throngs* in the bracketed line, and read its definition. Have students **suggest** other words that mean "crowd." **Possible responses:** Words that mean "crowd" include *group, clique, gang, team, multitude, mob,* and *party.*
• Ask students to use each word for "crowd" in a sentence and discuss its connotation. Have students identify whether each word's connotation is positive or negative.

10 Reading Strategy
Determining the Author's Purpose
• Have students read aloud the bracketed passage.
• **Ask** students: Which details in these paragraphs suggest that Mahfouz's purpose is to play tricks with time? **Possible response:** The narrator's father never comes, probably because time has passed and he has died. When the narrator knows and greets a middle-aged person, he is probably middle-aged himself.

▶ **Monitor Progress** Ask students to discuss what insight into life Mahfouz is offering.

▶ **Reteach** If students have difficulty determining the author's purpose, have them use the **Reading Strategy** support, p. 125 in *Unit 9 Resources.*

11 Reading Check
Answer: The narrator is confused because the world has changed while he was in school. He does not realize how quickly time has passed.

12 Reading Strategy

Determining the Author's Purpose

- **Ask** students whether the story has offered any explanations for the changes the narrator sees. **Possible response:** The story has not offered explanations.

- **Ask** the Reading Strategy question: What does the final sentence suggest about the writer's purpose? **Possible response:** The writer wants to convey that life is so brief that in what seems like only "half a day" people pass from youth to old age.

ASSESS

Answers

1. **Possible response:** Yes; the narrator cannot comprehend the world around him.

2. (a) The father takes the narrator to school. (b) He is hesitant but gains confidence as he greets the children.

3. (a) The narrator learns that the boy's father has died. (b) The narrator does not know what to say. (c) At the end, the narrator's father never arrives.

4. (a) The narrator and his classmates find that they can be hurt both physically and emotionally. (b) The passage indicates that pain and change are certainties.

5. (a) The narrator meets a middle-aged man he knows. (b) The person might be a friend of the narrator. The narrator doesn't recognize him at first because the friend and the narrator have aged.

6. (a) The narrator has aged. He does not recognize the modern world around him, and a young man calls him "Grandpa." (b) **Possible response:** People can become accustomed to one view of themselves and not realize that change and aging are inevitable.

7. **Possible response:** Both can be fulfilling. Childhood may seem easier because children have few responsibilities. Yet adulthood might offer direction, satisfaction, and understanding.

---

the opening of a circus, with clowns and weight lifters walking in front. A line of trucks carrying central security troops crawled majestically by. The siren of a fire engine shrieked, and it was not clear how the vehicle would cleave its way to reach the blazing fire. A battle raged between a taxi driver and his passenger, while the passenger's wife called out for help and no one answered. . . . I was in a daze. My head spun. I almost went crazy. How could all this have happened in half a day, between early morning and sunset? I would find the answer at home with my father. But where was my home? I could see only tall buildings and hordes of people. I <u>hastened</u> on to the crossroads between the gardens and Abu Khoda. I had to cross Abu Khoda to reach my house, but the stream of cars would not let up. The fire engine's siren was shrieking at full pitch as it moved at a snail's pace, and I said to myself, "Let the fire take its pleasure in what it consumes." Extremely irritated, I wondered when I would be able to cross. I stood there a long time, until the young lad employed at the ironing shop on the corner **12** came up to me. He stretched out his arm and said gallantly, "Grandpa, let me take you across."

Vocabulary Builder
hastened (hās' ənd) v. hurried; moved swiftly

Reading Strategy
Determining the Author's Purpose What does the final sentence suggest about the writer's purpose?

Critical Reading

1. **Respond:** At the story's conclusion, did you feel sympathy for the narrator? Why or why not?

2. **(a) Recall:** Where does the father take the narrator?
   (b) Interpret: How does the narrator feel as he faces this change?

3. **(a) Recall:** What does the narrator learn from the first boy with whom he speaks? **(b) Infer:** What is the effect of the boy's statement on the narrator? **(c) Connect:** In what sense does this statement point to the end of the story?

4. **(a) Recall:** What discovery does the narrator make in the paragraph beginning, "As our path revealed itself . . . "? **(b) Interpret:** What view of people's paths through life underlies this passage?

5. **(a) Recall:** After the bell rings and the narrator goes outside the gates, whom does he meet? **(b) Hypothesize:** Who might this person be? Explain your answer.

6. **(a) Analyze:** What has happened to the narrator by the end of the story? Give two details in support of your answer.
   (b) Draw Conclusions: What does the story suggest about people's ability to make a home for themselves in the world?

7. **Make a Judgment:** Explain whether you think adulthood can be fulfilling or whether you agree with Mahfouz's suggestion that adulthood cannot replace the lost paradise of childhood.

For: More about Naguib Mahfouz
Visit: www.PHSchool.com
Web Code: ete-9911

Go Online For additional information about
Author Link Naguib Mahfouz, have students type in the Web Code, then select *M* from the alphabet, and then select Naguib Mahfouz.

Apply the Skills

Half a Day

Literary Analysis

Surrealism

1. **(a)** What everyday event does "Half a Day" explore? **(b)** At what point in the story do events turn **surreal**? Explain.

2. **(a)** Identify two dreamlike details, descriptions, or events in the story. **(b)** For each example, explain the way in which an ordinary, realistic context adds to its dreamlike quality.

3. Is the ending of the story realistic, surreal, or both? Explain your answer.

Connecting Literary Elements

4. **(a)** Explain in what way the following passage reflects the story's **theme**: "[T]he time for changing one's mind was over and gone and there was no question of ever returning to the paradise of home." **(b)** What insight about life is expressed in the narrator's final attempt to return home?

5. Do you think the surprise ending of the story helps a reader grasp the story's insight into time? Explain why or why not.

Reading Strategy

Determining the Author's Purpose

6. How does the story's title, repeated in the last paragraph, help you **determine the author's purpose**?

7. Use a chart like the one below to list three details that serve as clues to the author's purpose. For each, explain what the detail indicates about that purpose.

Detail	What It Shows About the Author's Purpose

Extend Understanding

8. **Cultural Connection:** What lesson does the story suggest about modern times, when new technology may change the world dramatically during one person's lifetime?

QuickReview

Surrealism is the use of realistic elements to create a dreamlike effect, often by breaking the rules of logic or sequence.

The **theme** of a work is its central message about life.

To **determine the author's purpose,** think about the effect the work, including its use of details, is meant to have on readers.

Go Online
Assessment
For: Self-test
Visit: www.PHSchool.com
Web Code: eta-6907

Half a Day ■ 1307

 Students may use the **Self-test** to prepare for **Selection Test A** or **Selection Test B.**

Answers

1. (a) "Half a Day" explores a boy's first day of school. (b) The events turn surreal when the boy leaves school and finds that the world has changed.

2. (a) **Possible response:** One event is the rush of people leaving school while the narrator waits for his father. Another event is his attempt to walk home through a street that has been transformed. (b) **Possible response:** The scenario of the boy waiting for his father is realistic, but the boy's transformation into an old man adds a dreamlike quality. The realistic act of walking home after school emphasizes the dreamlike quality of the narrator's not recognizing what was once familiar.

3. Both; the ending is surreal because the narrator has aged without realizing it. It is realistic because it depicts a young person helping an elderly man.

4. (a) The passage reflects the story's theme that life passes quickly, and the "paradise of home" cannot be recaptured. (b) **Possible response:** People cannot return to the homes or the times of their youth.

5. **Possible response:** Yes; the surprise ending emphasizes the writer's theme about the passage of time.

6. **Possible response:** The title emphasizes the passage of time. A half day is brief, but it cannot be regained when lost.

7. **Possible responses: Detail:** The narrator meets a child whose father is dead. **Shows:** The boy faces mortality. **Detail:** The boy's father does not appear. **Shows:** The boy's youth has passed and his father is gone. **Detail:** Young man calls narrator "Grandpa." **Shows:** The narrator has become old in an astonishingly short time. Another sample answer can be found on **Reading Strategy Graphic Organizer B**, p. 228 in *Graphic Organizer Transparencies.*

8. **Possible response:** New technology introduces change and removes familiar touchstones.

1307

❶ Vocabulary Lesson

Connotations: Words for Crowds

1. *Masses* connotes a large number of average people.

2. *Throngs* connotes an uncomfortable, crowded group.

3. *Swarms* connotes people congregating and moving as a group of bees might.

Spelling Strategy

1. occurred   3. repelled
2. benefited

Vocabulary Builder: Context

1. Yes; an *unmarred* piece would not be damaged and would cost more than a marred piece.

2. No; one would feel comfortable.

3. No: an *intricate* dance step might be difficult to learn.

4. No; a person *presumed* innocent should not be found guilty or be punished.

5. No; a desert island would likely be uninhabited.

6. Feeding *hordes* would require large amounts of food.

7. No; one would not wait long for a person who hurried to one's side.

❷ Grammar and Style Lesson

1. There were many moments . . .
2. Here were a few students . . .
3. correct
4. There was the boy's father . . .
5. From the street come loud noises.

Writing Application

Possible response:

There is usually a great deal of activity in my neighborhood. People stop to visit with neighbors. On the sidewalk are parents pushing baby strollers.

Build Language Skills

❶ Vocabulary Lesson

Connotations: Words for Crowds

The word *throngs* is one of several words meaning "crowds." Each of these words has different connotations, or associations. For example, *horde* has negative associations, suggesting a destructive crowd, whereas *assembly* has positive ones, suggesting an orderly decision-making group. Identify the connotations of each of the following "crowd" words.

   1. masses   2. throngs   3. swarms

Spelling Strategy

When adding the suffix -ed to a word ending "consonant + vowel + consonant," double the final consonant only if the last syllable is stressed. For example, *re fer´* + -ed becomes *refe̱rred*. If the last syllable is not stressed, make no change. For example, *has´ ten* + -ed becomes *hastened*. Copy the following words, adding the suffix -ed to each.

   1. occur   2. benefit   3. repel

Vocabulary Builder: Context

Use your knowledge of the italicized words to answer the following questions:

1. Is an *unmarred* piece of furniture likely to cost more than a marred piece? Explain.

2. Would you feel "on guard" in an atmosphere of *intimacy*? Why or why not?

3. Is an *intricate* dance step easy to learn? Explain.

4. If someone is *presumed* to be innocent, should he or she be punished? Explain.

5. Would you be likely to see *throngs* on a desert island? Why or why not?

6. If *hordes* are coming to dinner, how much food will you have to make? Explain.

7. If a person *hastened* to your side, would you have to wait a long time? Explain.

❷ Grammar and Style Lesson

Agreement in Inverted Sentences

In an **inverted sentence,** the subject follows the verb. As in any sentence, the subject and verb must agree. Common examples are sentences beginning with *here* or *there*, such as this model from "Half a Day":

> **Example:** . . . there <u>was</u> a <u>band</u> announcing the opening of a circus . . .

Writers may choose to invert sentences to create emphasis or vary the rhythm of their prose. When Mahfouz writes, "At various points stood conjurers . . .", he creates a small build-up to the word *conjurers*, adding a sense of surprise.

Practice Rewrite each sentence below to correct errors in subject-verb agreement. For any sentence without an error, write *correct*.

1. There was many moments when the boy enjoyed school.

2. Here was a few students he had not met yet.

3. There were lessons in geography and science.

4. There were the boy's father, outside the school.

5. From the street comes loud noises.

Writing Application Write a paragraph about your neighborhood. Include at least two inverted sentences. Check that subjects and verbs agree.

WG Prentice Hall Writing and Grammar Connection: Platinum Level, Chapter 24, Section 1

Assessment Practice

Organization   (For more practice, see *Test Preparation Workbook*, p. 63.)

To give students practice responding to test items on organization, use the following test item.

(1) When he won the Nobel Prize, Mahfouz became known in the West. (2) *The Cairo Trilogy* was published in 1956–1957. (3) However, *The Cairo Trilogy* was not available in translation for many years. (4) Because his fiction is now widely available, readers in the West can understand why Mahfouz is considered the finest modern writer in the Arabic language. (5) Mahfouz published his first novel more than fifty years ago.

Choose the sequence of sentence numbers that makes the structure most logical.

A 2, 3, 1, 5, 4
B 1, 2, 3, 5, 4
C 1, 2, 3, 4, 5
D 5, 2, 3, 1, 4

The best organization for this information is chronological. *D* is the correct answer.

❸ Writing Lesson

Surrealistic Descriptive Essay

In "Half a Day," Mahfouz writes about ordinary life using the logic of a dream. Using this surrealistic logic, write a description of an object or event. Make sure to provide enough precise details to support your surrealistic effects.

Prewriting Once you have a topic, make a T-chart, listing realistic details on the left and surrealistic connections between them on the right.

Drafting As you draft, focus on providing complete, vividly realistic descriptions to support your surrealistic flights of fantasy.

Revising Reread your description. Mark passages in which your descriptions are vague. Consider adding specific details to those passages.

Model: Revising to Add Descriptive Detail

The giraffe unclipped its long nose and left it _{freckled} , bending its neck with a queen's grace,

hanging on the tree. The modest tree shed three _{piercing}

musical notes, bringing the night to peer out from

the cracks in its _{crystal} mountain. Soon, the world was

plunged into gloom.

> Adding vivid, descriptive details supports the surrealistic logic of this description.

Prentice Hall Writing and Grammar Connection: Platinum Level, Chapter 6, Section 4

❹ Extend Your Learning

Listening and Speaking Mahfouz's story suggests that change makes it impossible to reach what one wants. Form a **discussion panel** with classmates to talk about the effects of change.

- Have one member moderate, ensuring that all have a fair chance to contribute.
- Appoint a notetaker.
- Listen actively to other panelists' ideas, responding with questions for clarification.

Post a summary of your discussion in class.
[Group Activity]

Research and Technology Prepare and present a **multimedia presentation** on the culture of Egypt, Mahfouz's homeland, including daily life, religion, and the arts, using photographs, videos, maps, and music. Familiarize yourself beforehand with the equipment you will use, and test it to make sure it works properly.

 Go Online **Research**

For: An additional research activity
Visit: www.PHSchool.com
Web Code: etd-7907

Half a Day ■ 1309

Assessment Resources

The following resources can be used to assess students' knowledge and skills.

Unit 9 Resources
Selection Test A, pp. 131–133
Selection Test B, pp. 134–136

General Resources
Rubrics for Descriptive Essay, pp. 67–68

Go Online **Assessment** Students may use the **Self-test** to prepare for **Selection Test A** or **Selection Test B.**

❸ Writing Lesson

You may use this Writing Lesson as a timed-writing practice, or you may allow students to develop the descriptive essay as a writing assignment over several days.

- To give students guidance in writing this descriptive essay, give them the **Support for Writing Lesson,** p. 128 in *Unit 9 Resources.*

- Tell students that their surrealistic descriptive essays will leave behind the logic and reason of the everyday world and will make impossible, magical connections unimaginable in real life.

- Tell students that they can choose a topic by asking themselves questions beginning with "What if," such as "What if trees could talk?" or "What if you could start a day over again?"

- Use the Descriptive Essay rubrics in *General Resources,* pp. 67–68, to evaluate students' work.

WG Writing and Grammar Platinum Level
For support in teaching the Writing Lesson, use Chapter 6, Section 4.

❹ Research and Technology

- Organize the class into small groups for the presentations, and make sure that all of the listed elements of Egyptian culture are covered by at least one group.

- Discuss potential research sources, such as Web sites for online encyclopedias, as well as the Egyptian Museum in Cairo and the Bibliotheca Alexandrina.

- Invite students to present their reports to the class as part of a celebration of Egyptian history and culture.

- The **Support for Extend Your Learning** page (*Unit 9 Resources,* p. 129) provides guided note-taking opportunities to help students complete the Extend Your Learning activities.

Go Online **Research** Have students type in the Web Code for another research activity.

Standard Course of Study

Goal 1: WRITTEN LANGUAGE

WL.1.03.5 Summarize key events and points from personal reflection.

WL.1.03.10 Analyze connections between ideas, concepts, characters and experiences in reflection.

Goal 2: INFORMATIONAL READING

IR.2.01.4 Demonstrate comprehension of main idea and supporting details in answering research questions.

Goal 5: LITERATURE

LT.5.01.3 Analyze literary devices and explain their effect on the work of world literature.

LT.5.03.9 Analyze and evaluate the effects of author's craft and style in world literature.

Goal 6: GRAMMAR AND USAGE

GU.6.01.3 Use recognition strategies to understand vocabulary and exact word choice.

Step-by-Step Teaching Guide	Pacing Guide
PRETEACH	
• Administer Vocabulary and Reading Warm-ups as necessary.	5 min.
• Engage students' interest with the motivation activity.	5 min.
• Read and discuss author and background features. **FT**	10 min.
• Introduce the Literary Analysis Skill: Imagery. **FT**	5 min.
• Introduce the Reading Strategy: Evaluating a Writer's Message. **FT**	
• Prepare students to read by teaching the selection vocabulary. **FT**	10 min.
TEACH	
• Informally monitor comprehension while students read independently or in groups. **FT**	30 min.
• Monitor students' comprehension with the Reading Check notes.	as students read
• Reinforce vocabulary with Vocabulary Builder notes.	as students read
• Develop students' understanding of imagery with the Literary Analysis annotations. **FT**	5 min.
• Develop students' ability to evaluate a writer's message with the Reading Strategy annotations. **FT**	5 min.
ASSESS/EXTEND	
• Assess students' comprehension and mastery of the Literary Analysis and Reading Strategy by having them answer the Apply the Skills questions. **FT**	15 min.
• Have students complete the Vocabulary Lesson and the Grammar and Style Lesson. **FT**	15 min.
• Apply students' ability to revise to strengthen a central image by using the Writing Lesson. **FT**	45 min. or homework
• Apply students' understanding by using one or more of the Extend Your Learning activities.	20–90 min. or homework
• Administer Selection Test A or Selection Test B. **FT**	15 min.

Resources

Print

Unit 9 Resources

Transparency

Graphic Organizer Transparencies

Print

Reader's Notebook [L2]

Reader's Notebook: Adapted Version [L1]

Reader's Notebook: English Learner's Version [EL]

Unit 9 Resources

Technology

Listening to Literature Audio CDs [L2, EL]

Print

Unit 9 Resources

Technology

Go Online: Research [L3]

Go Online: Self-test [L3]

***ExamView®*, Test Bank [L3]**

Choosing Resources for Differentiated Instruction

[**L1**] Special Needs Students

[**L2**] Below-Level Students

[**L3**] All Students

[**L4**] Advanced Students

[**EL**] English Learners

For Vocabulary and Reading Warm-ups and for Selection Tests, **A** signifies "less challenging" and **B** "more challenging." For Graphic Organizer transparencies, **A** signifies "not filled in" and **B** "filled in."

FT Fast Track Instruction: To move the lesson more quickly, use the strategies and activities identified with **FT**.

Scaffolding for Less Proficient and Advanced Students

The leveled Critical Thinking questions after selections progress in the levels of thinking required to answer them. To address the needs of your different students, you may use the (a) level questions for your less proficient students and the (b) level questions with your on-level and advanced students. The occasional (c) level questions are appropriate for your advanced students.

PRENTICE HALL

TeacherEXPRESS™ Use this complete suite of powerful teaching tools to make lesson planning and testing quicker and easier.

Plan · Teach · Assess

PRENTICE HALL

StudentEXPRESS™ Use the interactive textbook (online and on CD-ROM) to make selections and activities come alive with audio and video support and interactive questions.

Learn · Study · Succeed

Go Online For: Information about Lexiles
Professional Visit: www.PHSchool.com
Development Web Code: eue-1111

Motivation

Display pictures with bold headlines from newspapers and magazines, depicting the effects of life-changing events, such as natural disasters, accidents, or violence. Then, guide students to recognize that disturbing or painful events can be turning points for those who experience or witness them. Such events may have so deep an emotional impact on people that they are changed forever. Suggest that students keep the emotional power of the images in mind as they read.

❶ Background

More About the Authors

Ravikovitch is known for her translations of children's literature—including *Mary Poppins* and "Cinderella"—as well as the works of William Butler Yeats, Edgar Allan Poe, and T. S. Eliot. She has been awarded the Bialik Prize for literature and received the 1990 Israel Prize, Israel's highest honor.

Amichai's poems are extremely popular in Israel. Each of his books of poems sells about 15,000 copies. This may not sound like a large number until the relative proportions are calculated. There are only three million readers of Hebrew in Israel, which means that one out of every 200 of these readers buys his books. If Israel were the size of the United States and had 36 million readers, each of Amichai's books would sell 180,000 copies!

Geography Note

Draw students' attention to the map on this page. Tell students that Israel developed from the desire for a Jewish homeland. The State of Israel came into being in 1948 and has been plagued by tension and war with its neighbors.

Build Skills | *Poems*

❶ Pride • The Diameter of the Bomb • From the Book of Esther I Filtered the Sediment

Dahlia Ravikovitch
(b. 1936)

"Can't you write about me without me?" poet Dahlia Ravikovitch once asked an interviewer. Painfully shy, Ravikovitch has always shunned the limelight. Yet her poems are filled with intense feeling, fusing emotional revelation with images of history, religion, and mythology. Ravikovitch is probably Israel's most prominent female poet.

A Traumatic Childhood Ravikovitch was born in Ramat Gan, a suburb of Tel Aviv, twelve years before Israel became a nation. When she was six, her father was killed in a hit-and-run accident, and she moved with the rest of her family to an Israeli communal farm, or kibbutz. Her father's death left a lifelong scar, but it also made her deeply sympathetic to the suffering of others. "Because I know what it is like to be hurt," she explains, "I try not to hurt anyone."

Turning Pain to Poetry Poetry became the means by which Ravikovitch expressed her deepest feelings. Drawing on the Bible as well as the English literature she had studied in college, she published her first full volume of poetry in 1959. Two collections, *A Dress of Fire* (1978) and *The Window* (1989), have been translated into English.

Working for Peace Ravikovitch's compassion also marks her involvement in the Israeli peace movement. Israel has an uneasy, sometimes violent, relationship with the Palestinian inhabitants of the region. In 1997, when uprisings drove many Israelis away from Palestinian areas, the sixty-year-old Ravikovitch continued to visit the city of Hebron, bringing chocolates and cheer to a ten-year-old Palestinian boy she had met there.

Yehuda Amichai
(1924–2000)

In modern Israel, the language of the streets and shops is Hebrew, the ancient language of the Bible. As the Israeli poet Yehuda Amichai observes, "Every word we use carries in and of itself connotations from the Bible. . . . Every word reverberates through the halls of Jewish history." Amichai's genius lay in his ear for both the traditional and modern resonances of the language.

Rebellion and Loss Amichai was born in Germany. Before the outbreak of World War II, however, his Orthodox Jewish family emigrated to Palestine, the region in which Israel was later (1948) to be established. Eventually, the family settled in Jerusalem. The young Amichai rebelled against his father's strict religious practices, yet his great love for his father survived the conflict.

Apprenticeships As a young man, Amichai served in World War II and in Israel's War of Independence. An early collection of short stories is based in part on his wartime experiences. During this period, he began reading the English poets W. H. Auden and T. S. Eliot. Both poets, especially Auden, inspired him to use colloquial language in his work.

Speaking for Others Amichai published his first collection of poems in 1955, but it was with his second book of poetry, *Two Hopes Away* (1958), that Amichai was embraced as the spokesperson for his generation, capturing its disillusionment. In this book, Amichai introduced what one critic called the characteristic themes of his subsequent work: "love, war, the passage of time, his relationship with his father, his father's death, and his own undefined guilt."

Preview

Connecting to the Literature

"What would I do if I had total control?" Most people have a quick answer—they would win every time. These poems ask a trickier question: "What happens when we want to control life—but find we can't?"

❷ Literary Analysis

Imagery

Imagery is descriptive language that re-creates sensory experience. An **image** is a specific word picture created using such language. For example, "Pride" contains powerful images of movement and rest:

> And so the moss flourishes, the seaweed / whips around, / the sea pushes through and rolls back—/ the rocks seem motionless.

A **sustained image** is one that is extended over a number of lines. As you read, note the effects of both brief and sustained images.

Comparing Literary Works

Poets often use imagery to develop **figurative language,** or language that is not meant to be taken literally. Figures of speech include

- **metaphor,** in which one thing is spoken of as if it were another kind of thing
- **simile,** in which one thing is compared to another using *like* or *as*
- **personification,** in which a nonhuman subject is given human characteristics.

For example, in "From the Book of Esther . . . ," the poet speaks of numbing oneself to the pains and joys of life as "filtering sediment." In this metaphor, a habit of mind is described as if it were a physical act. As you read, compare the poets' uses of figurative language to probe life.

❸ Reading Strategy

Evaluating a Writer's Message

To **evaluate a writer's message,** identify the work's main insight. Then, consider whether the insight makes sense and whether it is well supported. For example, in "The Diameter of the Bomb," Amichai's message concerns the effects of a single act. He supports his message with a vivid, sustained image. As you read, use a chart like this one to evaluate the writers' messages.

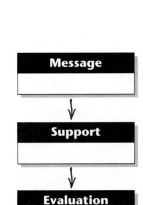

Vocabulary Builder

flourishes (flûr′ ish ez) *v.* thrives; grows vigorously (p. 1312)

considerably (kən sid′ er ə blē) *adv.* to a great degree (p. 1313)

solitary (säl′ ə ter′ ē) *adj.* lone; single; sole (p. 1313)

sediment (sed′ ə mənt) *n.* waste material that settles to the bottom of a liquid (p. 1314)

vulgar (vul′ gər) *adj.* coarse; common (p. 1314)

NC **Standard Course of Study**

- Summarize key events and points from personal reflection. (WL.1.03.5)
- Analyze literary devices and explain their effect on the work of world literature. (LT.5.01.3)

❷ Literary Analysis

Imagery

- Explain to students that using imagery is the same as using descriptive or figurative language to create word pictures for readers. These word pictures employ language that appeals to the senses of sight, hearing, touch, taste, and smell to help readers imagine and experience, to some extent, the image.

- Have groups of students choose an item and describe it. Challenge each group to see how many sensory details they can generate for each item.

❸ Reading Strategy

Evaluating a Writer's Message

- Remind students that strong, powerful images can be convincing support for a writer's insight.

- Give students a copy of **Reading Strategy Graphic Organizer A,** p. 229 in *Graphic Organizer Transparencies.* During their initial reading of the poems, have students use it to jot down notes about the poems' messages and supporting details. Instruct students to fill in the graphic organizer's "Evaluation" box by using these notes to assess how effectively each poem's message is conveyed.

Vocabulary Builder

- Pronounce each vocabulary word for students, and read the definitions as a class. Have students identify any words with which they are already familiar.

Support for Special Needs Students

Have students complete the **Preview** and **Build Skills** pages for these selections in the *Reader's Notebook: Adapted Version.* These pages provide a selection summary, an abbreviated presentation of the reading and literary skills, and the graphic organizer on the **Build Skills** page in the student book.

Support for Less Proficient Readers

Have students complete the **Preview** and **Build Skills** pages for these selections in the *Reader's Notebook.* These pages provide a selection summary, an abbreviated presentation of the reading and literary skills, and the graphic organizer on the **Build Skills** page in the student book.

Support for English Learners

Have students complete the **Preview** and **Build Skills** pages for these selections in the *Reader's Notebook: English Learner's Version.* These pages provide a selection summary, an abbreviated presentation of the reading and literary skills, additional contextual vocabulary, and the graphic organizer on the **Build Skills** page in the student book.

Facilitate Understanding

Tell students that a conversation with a friend whom you have not seen for a while can be like a ride on a city bus. You "get on" the conversation at one topic, go a short distance, and then make a sudden stop at another topic. With each stop, a new rush of memories and stories boards the bus, only to disembark at the next stop as another bunch pushes through the doors.

Point out to students that this description of a conversation involves a sustained comparison—it compares a conversation to a bus ride in a number of respects, not just one. For example, the comparison refers to the frequent stops made by a bus; the press of passengers pushing their way on and off the bus; and so on. Explain that in these poems, Ravikovitch and Amichai use sustained comparisons, elaborating on a central image.

❶ About the Selections

Rich in imagery, "Pride" addresses a fateful moment for people.

"The Diameter of the Bomb" alludes to a terrorist attack that killed four people and wounded eleven.

❷ Literary Analysis

Imagery and Figurative Language

- Have students read aloud the first eight lines of "Pride."
- Then, have students **respond** to the Literary Analysis item: Identify two words or phrases that personify the rocks, giving them human qualities. **Possible response:** The rocks "lie on their backs"; they seem "peaceful" and "don't move."

▶ **Monitor Progress Ask** students to infer how the rocks in this poem are like people.
Possible response: With people, as with rocks, a crack that starts small can become a complete break under pressure.

▶ **Reteach** If students have trouble with imagery, have them use the **Literary Analysis** support, p. 141 in *Unit 9 Resources.*

Pride

❶

Dahlia Ravikovitch

translated by Chana Bloch *and* Ariel Bloch

Background Before the onset of World War II, Jews had begun to return to Palestine, the Jewish homeland in biblical times. Violence flared up between the Arab inhabitants of Palestine and the new immigrants. In 1948, the United Nations divided Palestine, creating the state of Israel for Jewish settlers, who now included refugees from the Holocaust. Palestinians and their Arab allies were outraged, and the region was plunged into a series of wars and uprisings. The work of these poets suggests that, exposed day after day to threats and horrors, people in the region face a kind of moral weariness.

❷

I tell you, even rocks crack,
and not because of age.
For years they lie on their backs
in the heat and the cold,
5   so many years,
it almost seems peaceful.
They don't move, so the cracks stay hidden.
A kind of pride.
Years pass over them, waiting.
10 Whoever is going to shatter them
hasn't come yet.
And so the moss <u>flourishes</u>, the seaweed
whips around,
the sea pushes through and rolls back—
15 the rocks seem motionless.
Till a little seal comes to rub against them,
comes and goes away.
And suddenly the rock has an open wound.
I told you, when rocks break, it happens by surprise.
20 And people, too.

Literary Analysis
Imagery and Figurative Language Identify two words or phrases that personify the rocks, giving them human qualities.

Vocabulary Builder
flourishes (flʉrʹ ish ez) v. thrives; grows vigorously

1312   *The Contemporary World*

Differentiated Instruction   Solutions for All Learners

Accessibility at a Glance

	Pride	The Diameter of the Bomb	From the Book of Esther / I Filtered the Sediment
Context	Arab-Jewish conflict	A terrorist bombing in Israel	Effects of Arab-Jewish conflict
Language	Figurative language with personification	Syntax: long sentences embedded with clauses	Syntax: long sentences embedded with elliptical clauses
Concept Level	Accessible (One's pride can crack like a rock.)	Accessible (Violence has widespread repercussions.)	Accessible (A life without feelings is a dead life.)
Literary Merit	Poem with a sustained metaphor for pride	Poem with metaphor of the circle of violence	Poem with metaphor of sediment for damaged emotions
Lexile	NP	NP	NP
Overall Rating	Average	More Challenging	Average

The Diameter of the Bomb

Yehuda Amichai
translated by Chana Bloch *and* Stephen Mitchell

The diameter of the bomb was thirty centimeters
and the diameter of its effective range about seven meters,
with four dead and eleven wounded.
And around these, in a larger circle
5 of pain and time, two hospitals are scattered
and one graveyard. But the young woman
who was buried in the city she came from,
at a distance of more than a hundred kilometers,
enlarges the circle <u>considerably</u>,
10 and the <u>solitary</u> man mourning her death
at the distant shores of a country far across the sea
includes the entire world in the circle.
And I won't even mention the crying of orphans
that reaches up to the throne of God and
15 beyond, making
a circle with no end and no God.

Critical Reading

1. **Respond:** In each poem, what most surprised you? Explain.
2. **(a) Recall:** What happens to the rocks at the end of "Pride"?
   (b) Analyze Cause and Effect: Compare the apparent cause of this event with its deeper causes.
3. **(a) Interpret:** What does the expansion of the circle in the poem suggest about human suffering? **(b) Draw Conclusions:** What lesson about justice does the poem suggest?

Literary Analysis
Imagery How does the visual image of the circle change in lines 1–6?

Vocabulary Builder
considerably (kən sid′ er ə blē) *adv.* to a great degree

solitary (säl′ ə ter′ ē) *adj.* lone; single; sole

Go Online
Author Link

For: More about Dahlia Ravikovitch and Yehuda Amichai
Visit: www.PHSchool.com
Web Code: ete-9912

The Diameter of the Bomb ■ 1313

❸ About the Translation
Compare the translation of "The Diameter of the Bomb" here with that of Ted Hughes:

> The diameter of the bomb was
>   thirty centimeters
> and the diameter of its effective
> range—about seven meters.
> And in it four dead and eleven
>   wounded.
> And around them in a greater circle
> of pain and time are scattered
> two hospitals and one cemetery.
> But the young woman who was
> buried where she came from
> over a hundred kilometers away
> enlarges the circle greatly.
> And the lone man who weeps over
>   her death
> in a far corner of a distant country
> includes the whole world in the
>   circle.
> And I won't speak at all about the
>   crying of orphans
> that reaches to the seat of God
> and from there onward, making
> the circle without end and without
>   God.

❹ Literary Analysis
Imagery
- Tell students that concentric circles share a common center.
- **Ask** the Literary Analysis question.
  Answer: It changes from a crater to a "circle" of people and places.

ASSESS
Answers

1. **Possible response:** The last line of "Pride" surprises readers by stating that humans break like rocks. The last line of "The Diameter of the Bomb" surprises readers by showing how far one act of violence reaches.

2. (a) The rocks suddenly break.
   (b) The rocks break because they have not been able to change.

3. (a) Human suffering is shared.
   (b) The poem suggests that it is foolish to seek justice by revenge.

Go Online For additional information
Author Link about Dahlia Ravikovitch, have students type in the Web Code, then select *R* from the alphabet, and then select Dahlia Ravikovitch.

❺ Vocabulary Builder

Latin Word Origins: *vulgar*

- Draw students' attention to the word *vulgar* and its definitions.
- **Ask** students which definition fits best in the context of the poem. **Answer:** "Common" joy makes the most sense in the poem.

❻ Critical Thinking

Interpret

- Tell students to analyze the nature of the "peace" the poet has gained.
- **Ask:** Does the word *peace* have its usual positive connotations in this context? **Possible response:** In this context, *peace* is synonymous with spiritual death.

❼ Reading Strategy

Evaluating a Writer's Message

- Discuss with students how those who allow themselves to feel great joy may also feel great pain.
- Then, **ask** students the Reading Strategy question: What do these lines suggest about the speaker's reason for living a life "censored and pasted and limited and in peace"? **Answer:** The speaker is tired of sadness and has drained all emotion from life to avoid pain.

ASSESS

Answers

1. **Possible response:** The poem's hopelessness makes it difficult to empathize with the speaker's weariness.

2. (a) The speaker filters vulgar joy, pain, and the search for love. (b) The "sediment" includes human experience. The sanitized "new Bible" will be emotionally sterile, granting the speaker emotional freedom.

3. (a) The "great weariness" leads him or her to lie. (b) The phrases "another woman," "already died," and "before her time" indicate that the friend died an untimely death.

4. **Possible response:** Without joy and pain, life will mean little.

From the Book of Esther I Filtered the Sediment

Yehuda Amichai
translated by Chana Bloch

❺ From the Book of Esther I filtered the <u>sediment</u>
of <u>vulgar</u> joy, and from the Book of Jeremiah
the howl of pain in the guts. And from
the Song of Songs the endless
5 search for love, and from Genesis the dreams
and Cain, and from Ecclesiastes
the despair, and from the Book of Job: Job.
And with what was left, I pasted myself a new Bible.
❻ Now I live censored and pasted and limited and in peace.

10 A woman asked me last night on the dark street
how another woman was
❼ who'd already died. Before her time—and not
in anyone else's time either.
Out of a great weariness I answered,
15 "She's fine, she's fine."

Vocabulary Builder

sediment (sed´ ə mənt) *n.* waste material that settles to the bottom of a liquid

vulgar (vul´ gər) *adj.* coarse; common

Reading Strategy
Evaluating a Writer's Message What do these lines suggest about the speaker's reason for living a life "censored and pasted and limited and in peace"?

Critical Reading

1. **Respond:** How did you react to the speaker's "weariness"?

2. **(a) Recall:** List three examples of the "sediment" that the speaker filters from the Bible. **(b) Connect:** Explain the connection between the "sediment" the speaker removes and the type of life mapped out in his "new Bible."

3. **(a) Analyze:** What does the speaker's "great weariness" lead him to do in the last line? **(b) Infer:** What is the probable source of his attitude? Cite details to support your answer.

4. **Apply:** What advice might you offer someone in the speaker's position?

Go Online
Author Link

For: More about Yehuda Amichai
Visit: www.PHSchool.com
Web Code: ete-9912

Go Online For additional information about
Author Link Yehuda Amichai, have students type in the Web Code, then select *A* from the alphabet, and then select Yehuda Amichai.

Apply the Skills

Pride • The Diameter of the Bomb • From the Book of Esther I Filtered the Sediment

Literary Analysis

Imagery

1. **(a)** Identify three **images** in "Pride," explaining to which sense each one appeals. **(b)** Explain the connection between each image and the "pride" to which the title refers.
2. **(a)** What **sustained image** is central to "The Diameter of the Bomb"? **(b)** Using a chart like this one, explain how the development of this image moves from a specific event to a general idea.

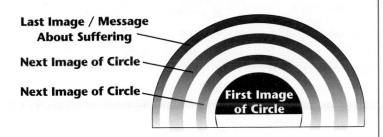

Last Image / Message About Suffering

Next Image of Circle

Next Image of Circle

First Image of Circle

3. **(a)** How is the image of "sediment" in "From the Book of Esther . . . " contradicted by the experiences it symbolizes? **(b)** In using this image, what attitude does the speaker reveal? Explain.

Comparing Literary Works

4. Identify the types of **figurative language** used in "Pride" and "The Diameter of the Bomb."
5. Compare the image of the circle in "The Diameter of the Bomb" with the image of sediment in "From the Book of Esther . . . ." **(a)** Which image expands the reader's vision of the world? Explain. **(b)** Which gives more insight into the poem's speaker? Explain.

Reading Strategy

Evaluating a Writer's Message

6. **(a)** Identify the **writer's message** in each of the three poems. **(b)** For each one, identify the way in which the poet supports it (makes it understandable and compelling).
7. In your judgment, which message is best supported? Explain.

Extend Understanding

8. **Math Connection: (a)** Using the terms *circumference* and *diameter*, describe the last circle in Amichai's poem. **(b)** Do you think such a circle can be defined using a mathematical equation? Explain.

Pride / The Diameter of the Bomb / From the Book of Esther I Filtered the Sediment ■ 1315

QuickReview

Imagery is descriptive language that re-creates sensory experience. An **image** is a specific word picture created using such language. A **sustained image** is an image that extends over several lines or throughout an entire work.

Figurative language is language that is not meant to be taken literally. Figures of speech include: **metaphor, simile,** and **personification.**

To **evaluate a writer's message,** identify the work's main insight and consider whether it is well supported.

Go Online
Assessment
For: Self-test
Visit: www.PHSchool.com
Web Code: eta-6908

Go Online Students may use the **Self-test** to
Assessment prepare for **Selection Test A** or
Selection Test B.

Answers

1. **(a) Possible response:** Sight: rocks lying on their backs; Touch: the seal rubbing against the rocks; the rocks in the heat and cold. **(b) Sample response:** The description of rocks exposed to the elements shows how people are exposed to the "weathering" of emotions.

2. **(a)** The sustained image of concentric circles is central to the poem. **(b) Possible response: First Image:** bomb leaves four dead and eleven wounded; **Second Image:** two hospitals and a graveyard; **Third Image:** a woman buried in a distant city; **Fourth Image:** a man in a foreign country mourning the woman's death; **Last Image:** crying orphans; **Message:** Violence has widespread effects. Another sample answer can be found on **Literary Analysis Graphic Organizer B,** p. 232 in *Graphic Organizer Transparencies.*

3. **(a)** The image of "sediment" is a negative one, like an impurity that must be cleansed. However, the "sediment" represents positive, human emotions. **(b)** By using the negative image of "sediment," the speaker demonstrates emotional distance.

4. In "Pride," the poet uses personification. In "The Diameter of the Bomb," the poet uses a metaphor.

5. **(a) Possible response:** The circle in "The Diameter of the Bomb" expands the reader's vision of the world by expanding outward. **(b) Possible response:** The sediment in "From the Book of Esther. . ." gives more insight into the poem's speaker by showing the speaker's damaged, restricted emotional range.

6. **(a) Sample response:** The message of "The Diameter of the Bomb" is that one act of violence spreads pain worldwide. **(b) Sample response:** "The Diameter of the Bomb" supports the message by providing an ever-widening map of suffering.

7. **Possible response:** The message of "The Diameter of the Bomb" is best supported because it depicts many layers of pain.

Answers continued

8. **(a)** The diameter of the poem connects the center of the bomb to the throne of God. The last circle of the poem has the largest circumference, including the entire universe. **(b) Possible response:** The circle could be defined using the algebraic equation for a circle ($x^2+y^2-r^2=0$) and setting the radius equal to infinity.

Build Language Skills

❶ Vocabulary Lesson

❶ Vocabulary Lesson

Latin Word Origins: *vulgar*

Latin Word Origins: *vulgar*

1. Priests in the Middle Ages spoke Latin, but farmers used vulgar languages.

2. A feast is a vulgar affair; it invites unchecked gluttony.

3. Only a vulgar person would yawn loudly throughout a performance.

The word *vulgar*, meaning "common" or "coarse," is related to the Latin word *vulgus*, meaning "the common people" or "the public." Historically, *vulgar* also came to refer to the spoken language of a country (as opposed to Latin, used by the church and in government). Today, *vulgar* is often used to mean "improper." The original meaning of the root -*vulg*- can be detected, though, in words such as *divulge*, meaning "to make public."

For each item below, write a sentence that includes the word *vulgar*.

1. the language spoken by medieval farmers

2. a common pleasure, such as sharing a meal

3. an audience member who sniffs, yawns, and stretches loudly throughout a performance

Vocabulary Builder

1. antonyms   4. synonyms
2. antonyms   5. antonyms
3. synonyms

Vocabulary Builder: Synonyms and Antonyms

Synonyms are words that are the same or nearly the same in meaning. Antonyms are opposites. Identify each synonym or antonym pair below.

1. flourishes / withers
2. considerably / slightly
3. solitary / sole
4. sediment / residue
5. vulgar / courtly

Spelling Strategy

1. comfortably   3. agreeably
2. miserably

Spelling Strategy

When adding the suffix -*ly* to a word ending in a consonant + *le*, drop the *le*. Add -*ly* to each of the following words.

1. comfortable   2. miserable   3. agreeable

❷ Grammar and Style Lesson

1. and [they crack] not because of age

2. and from the Book of Jeremiah [I filtered] the howl of pain in the guts.

3. Ravikovitch's [images are] more concrete.

4. Ravikovitch [writes] with a large heart

5. great art [is born] of great suffering

❷ Grammar and Style Lesson

Elliptical Clauses

Elliptical comes from the word *ellipsis*, meaning "omission." In an **elliptical clause,** some words are left out, but the clause is understood as if they were present. Review the following example:

> **Elliptical Clause:** The diameter of the bomb was thirty centimeters / and the <u>diameter of its effective range</u> [. . .] <u>about seven meters</u>, . . . (*was* is understood)

Practice For each item below, write the elliptical clauses and the understood words.

1. "I tell you, even rocks crack, / and not because of age."

2. "From the Book of Esther I filtered the sediment / of vulgar joy, and from the Book of Jeremiah / the howl of pain in the guts."

3. Amichai's images are more abstract; Ravikovitch's, more concrete.

4. Amichai writes with a keen eye; Ravikovitch, with a large heart.

5. They might agree on this idea: Art is born of suffering; great art, of great suffering.

Writing Application

Possible response: People respond to suffering in different ways. Some people show their grief, *others not.* Some people view emotional display as a sign of weakness, *others of hysteria.*

Writing Application Write a paragraph about people's responses to misfortune. Include two sentences with elliptical clauses.

𝒲𝒢 *Prentice Hall Writing and Grammar Connection: Platinum Level, Chapter 23, Section 2*

𝒲𝒢 **Writing and Grammar** Platinum Level

For support in teaching the Grammar and Style Lesson, use Chapter 23, Section 2.

Assessment Practice

Style   (For more practice, see *Test Preparation Workbook*, p. 64.)

Style questions on standardized tests focus on the writer's point of view and effective use of language. Use the following passage and question to help students assess their understanding of style.

> And so the moss flourishes, the seaweed whips around,
> the sea pushes through and rolls back—
> the rocks seem motionless.

The author's description of the rocks in the sea relies mostly on the reader's sense of—

A touch.   C taste.
B sound.   D smell.

The poet does not use language in the passage that appeals to the reader's sense of taste, sound, or smell, so answers *B, C,* and *D* are not correct. The writer's use of words like *whips* and *pushes* appeals to the reader's sense of touch, so *A* is the correct answer.

❸ Writing Lesson

Poem with a Strong Central Image

Following the examples of Ravikovitch and Amichai, write a poem with a strong central image that conveys a message about life. For the best effect, make sure that your poem is focused, with each detail supporting your central image.

Prewriting Select a topic, such as *kindness,* and write several sentences about it. Use these sentences to develop a message for your poem. Next, list images that will help convey this message. Circle the strongest one.

Drafting As you draft, keep your central image and message in mind. Bring the image to life by using words that appeal to the senses.

Revising Underline in one color those details in your poem that develop the central image. Use another color to underline details that distract from it. Consider eliminating distracting details and elaborating on those that strengthen the central image.

Model: Revising to Strengthen Your Central Image

A smile, a word of kindness, a needed hug—

(a seed), planted in the soil of someone's day

it holds a <u>waiting flower,</u>

<u>unfurling it sunward</u>

~~leaving its mark~~ after you have gone.

> Eliminating distracting details and providing additional support help clarify the central image.

Prentice Hall Writing and Grammar Connection: Platinum Level, Chapter 6, Section 4

❹ Extend Your Learning

Listening and Speaking The speaker in "From the Book of Esther . . ." has a sharp, ironic understanding of his own "weariness." Give an **oral interpretation** of the poem, using these tips:

- Jot down notes on the speaker's attitude toward life.
- Identify the reaction to that attitude—does the speaker feel self-contempt? Resignation?
- Experiment with various tones of voice and pacing to convey the speaker's personality.

Present your interpretation to the class.

Research and Technology The rocks in "Pride" lie along the ocean shore. In a group, produce a **multimedia presentation** on seaside geology. Divide tasks and conduct research on the following subtopics: Types of Rocks, Rock Formation, and Erosion. Use visuals to present your information to the class. **[Group Activity]**

 Go Online
Research

For: An additional research activity
Visit: www.PHSchool.com
Web Code: etd-7908

Pride / The Diameter of the Bomb / From the Book of Esther I Filtered the Sediment ■ 1317

---

❸ Writing Lesson

- To give students guidance in writing this poem, give them the **Support for Writing Lesson,** p. 145 in *Unit 9 Resources.*
- Point out to students that their successful completion of a poem using imagery depends on their choice of subject matter. Tell students that they will need to select a central image that can represent a larger idea or theme.

𝒲𝒢 Writing and Grammar Platinum Level
For support in teaching the Writing Lesson, use Chapter 6, Section 4.

❹ Listening and Speaking

- Have students paraphrase each line (in its entirety) for a listener as part of the preparation process. Any line that they cannot paraphrase—or that the listener fails to comprehend—indicates a passage that needs further study.
- The **Support for Extend Your Learning** page (*Unit 9 Resources,* p. 146) provides guided note-taking opportunities to help students complete the Extend Your Learning activities.

Go Online Have students type in the **Research** Web Code for another research activity.

Assessment Resources

The following resources can be used to assess students' knowledge and skills.

Unit 9 Resources
Selection Test A, pp. 148–150
Selection Test B, pp. 151–153

Go Online Students may use the **Self-test** to **Assessment** prepare for **Selection Test A** or **Selection Test B.**

Standard Course of Study

CT.4.04.1 Identify clear criteria for evaluation of work of others.

CT.4.05.8 Make connections between works, self and related topics in critical texts.

LT.5.01.2 Build knowledge of literary genres, and explore how characteristics apply to literature of world cultures.

Connections

American Literature

War everywhere and in every time creates havoc in people's lives. Individuals are killed, injured, left to grieve, and made homeless. Through poetry or nonfiction journalism, war descriptions bring these vivid images alive in reader's minds. Have students reread Yehuda Amichai's "The Diameter of the Bomb" on p. 1313 after they have read the excerpt from John Hersey's *Hiroshima*. Discuss how the results of these two wars are similar and different, and how the authors' reactions to war overlap or differ.

In the Shadows of Destruction

- Explain that John Hersey's reporting recorded a turning point in the history of modern warfare. After nearly six years of fighting, American President Harry Truman chose to use new technology with the hope of bringing an end to World War II. An atomic bomb was dropped on Hiroshima, killing tens of thousands of people. A second bomb was dropped on Nagasaki.

- Point out that both Amichai's poem and Hersey's account focus on how bombs affect individual people rather than descriptions of buildings or military activities.

- Discuss how details narrow the focus of both of these accounts, giving the reader more accessibility to the characters. For example, Amichai describes the size of the bomb, and Hersey describes the daily activities of survivors.

CONNECTIONS
American Literature

United States

In the Shadows of Destruction

In Yehuda Amichai's poem "The Diameter of the Bomb" (p. 1313), the circle of devastation that is described extends physically and metaphorically in all directions and for eternal distances. Modern and contemporary literature has all too often had occasion to address issues related to war, bombing, and destruction, as well as their dramatic effect on the everyday lives of individuals.

The Ultimate Weapon John Hersey's account of the dropping of the atomic bomb on Hiroshima in 1945 provides a deceptively calm and objective account of horror. In this excerpt from *Hiroshima*, the specific details of Miss Toshiko Sasaki's normal morning activities form the story of a step-by-step journey toward disaster. In this nonfiction account, as in the fiction, poetry, and other nonfiction in this unit, similar mundane details serve as reminders that ordinary lives can become extraordinary in an instant and that those directly affected by violence and tragedy are—up to that moment—just like everyone else.

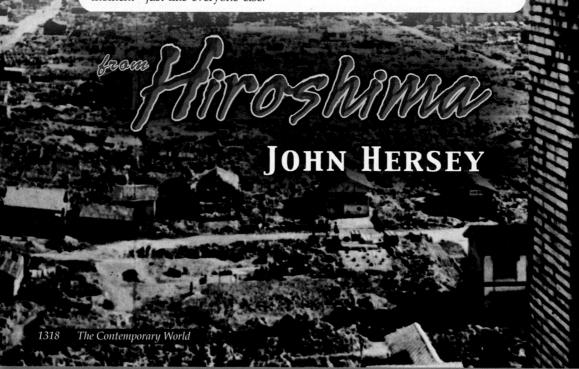

from *Hiroshima*

JOHN HERSEY

1318   *The Contemporary World*

Enrichment

Hiroshima and Nagasaki

Familiarize students with the geography and history of the Japanese cities of Hiroshima and Nagasaki. Explain that Japan, as a chain of islands, can be attacked only by air or by sea. Its western neighbors are North and South Korea, Russia, and China. The four main islands of Japan are Hokkaido, Honshu, Shikoku, and Kyushu.

Hiroshima is a port city on the southwest coast of Honshu. Nagasaki is a port city on the west coast of Kyushu. During World War II, both of these cities had military installations and a certain amount of industry. The cities were mostly destroyed by the bombs but were reconstructed in the 1950s. Today, both house important tourist sites and monuments that attract antiwar and antinuclear supporters from around the world.

Critical Viewing

Possible response: The impact of the image is greater without people because the bomb appears to have erased all signs of life.

In the Shadows of Destruction

- Ask a volunteer to read aloud the last five sentences on this page.

- Explain that Hersey chooses to tell the story of the dropping of the bomb through the lives of four survivors. **Ask** students why they think Hersey chose these four survivors as his focus.
  Possible response: These survivors were chosen for their ordinariness. By describing typical people living in Hiroshima at the time of the bombing, Hersey makes the point that the victims of the bomb were helpless civilians.

- Point out that Hersey notes that small acts and decisions made the difference between life and death for the survivors. **Ask** students what they can infer about war from these details.
  Possible response: The details of everyday life for the survivors suggest the arbitrariness and senselessness of war.

At exactly fifteen minutes past eight in the morning, on August 6, 1945, Japanese time, at the moment when the atomic bomb flashed above Hiroshima, Miss Toshiko Sasaki, a clerk in the personnel department of the East Asia Tin Works, had just sat down at her place in the plant office and was turning her head to speak to the girl at the next desk. At that same moment, Dr. Masakazu Fujii was settling down cross-legged to read the Osaka *Asahi* on the porch of his private hospital, overhanging one of the seven deltaic rivers which divide Hiroshima; Mrs. Hatsuyo Nakamura, a tailor's widow, stood by the window of her kitchen, watching a neighbor tearing down his house because it lay in the path of an air-raid-defense fire lane; . . . and the Reverend Mr. Kiyoshi Tanimoto, pastor of the Hiroshima Methodist Church, paused at the door of a rich man's house in Koi, the city's western suburb, and prepared to unload a handcart full of things he had <u>evacuated</u> from town in fear of the massive B-29 raid which everyone expected Hiroshima to suffer. A hundred thousand people were killed by the atomic bomb, and these [four] were among the survivors. They still wonder why

▲ Critical Viewing
There are no people shown in this photograph—nor in many others depicting the devastation wrought by the Hiroshima bomb. Does the lack of humanity lessen or intensify the power of the image? **[Assess]**

Vocabulary Builder
evacuated (e vak´ yoo āt´ əd) v. made empty; withdrawn

Differentiated Instruction Solutions for All Learners

Strategy for Less Proficient Readers
Explain that *Hiroshima* is a work of nonfiction that discusses actual events. Help students track the events in the excerpt by creating a chart with these headings: *Person, Description, Before the Bomb, After the Bomb.* Encourage volunteers to share and discuss their charts with the class.

Strategy for English Learners
Clarify the chronology of the excerpt by explaining that the excerpt from *Hiroshima* begins with the actions of four people and then jumps back to before the bomb struck. Ask students to make a timeline of events on the board.

Enrichment for Advanced Readers
Stress that this excerpt from *Hiroshima* describes actual events in a way that affects readers' emotions. Challenge students to look for details and literary devices that move the account beyond a typical news article and into the realm of literature. Have students write a paragraph showing how Hersey achieves his emotional impact.

they lived when so many others died. Each of them counts many small items of chance or <u>volition</u>—a step taken in time, a decision to go indoors, catching one streetcar instead of the next—that spared him. And now each knows that in the act of survival he lived a dozen lives and saw more death than he ever thought he would see. At the time, none of them knew anything. . . .

Miss Toshiko Sasaki, the East Asia Tin Works clerk, . . . got up at three o'clock in the morning on the day the bomb fell. There was extra housework to do. Her eleven-month-old brother, Akio, had come down the day before with a serious stomach upset; her mother had taken him to the Tamura Pediatric Hospital and was staying there with him. Miss Sasaki, who was about twenty, had to cook breakfast for her father, a brother, a sister, and herself, and—since the hospital, because of the war, was unable to provide

1320 ■ *The Contemporary World*

1320

food—to prepare a whole day's meals for her mother and the baby, in time for her father, who worked in a factory making rubber earplugs for artillery crews, to take the food by on his way to the plant. When she had finished and had cleaned and put away the cooking things, it was nearly seven. The family lived in Koi, and she had a forty-five-minute trip to the tin works, in the section of town called Kannonmachi. She was in charge of the personnel records in the factory. She left Koi at seven, and as soon as she reached the plant, she went with some of the other girls from the personnel department to the factory auditorium. A prominent local Navy man, a former employee, had committed suicide the day before by throwing himself under a train—a death considered honorable enough to warrant a memorial service, which was to be held at the tin works at ten o'clock that morning. In the large hall, Miss Sasaki and the others made suitable preparations for the meeting. This work took about twenty minutes.

Miss Sasaki went back to her office and sat down at her desk. She was quite far from the windows, which were off to her left, and behind her were a couple of tall bookcases containing all the books of the factory library, which the personnel department had organized. She settled herself at her desk, put some things in a drawer, and shifted papers. She thought that before she began to make entries in her lists of new employees, discharges, and departures for the Army, she would chat for a moment with the girl at her right. Just as she turned her head away from the windows, the room was filled with a blinding light. She was paralyzed by fear, fixed still in her chair for a long moment (the plant was 1,600 yards from the center).

Everything fell, and Miss Sasaki lost consciousness. The ceiling dropped suddenly and the wooden floor above collapsed in splinters and the people up there came down and the roof above them gave way; but principally and first of all, the bookcases right behind her swooped forward and the contents threw her down, with her left leg horribly twisted and breaking underneath her. There, in the tin factory, in the first moment of the atomic age, a human being was crushed by books.

John Hersey (1914–1993)

Born in China to American parents and raised there until age ten, John Hersey returned repeatedly to East Asia during his long career as a war correspondent, novelist, and essayist. During the 1940s, Hersey traveled to China and Japan as a correspondent for *The New Yorker* and *Time* magazines. He also used these visits to gather material for his most famous and acclaimed book, *Hiroshima*. This remarkable report of the devastation caused by the atomic bomb first appeared in *The New Yorker*, when Wallace Shawn, the editor at that time, made the unprecedented decision to bump all of the magazine's other editorial content to publish Hersey's work as a four-part article.

Connecting American Literature

1. **(a)** In what way are the everyday details that Hersey provides about Miss Toshiko Sasaki's life similar to those provided in Amichai's poem "The Diameter of the Bomb"? **(b)** How do they differ?

2. Which has a stronger impact on you: the poetic account of a terrorist's bomb or this nonfiction account of a wartime bombing? Explain using details from the selection to support your response.

3. In what other literary works that you have read have tiny, ordinary decisions made the difference between life and death? Explain.

Connections: from *Hiroshima* ■ 1321

Standard Course of Study

Goal 4: CRITICAL THINKING

CT.4.05.10 Analyze connections between ideas, concepts, characters and experiences in critical text.

Goal 5: LITERATURE

LT.5.01.3 Analyze literary devices and explain their effect on the work of world literature.

LT.5.01.4 Analyze the importance of tone and mood in world literature.

LT.5.01.5 Analyze archetypal characters, themes, and settings in world literature.

LT.5.03.7 Analyze influences, contexts, or biases in world literature.

Step-by-Step Teaching Guide	Pacing Guide
PRETEACH	
• Administer Vocabulary and Reading Warm-ups as necessary.	5 min.
• Engage students' interest with the motivation activity.	5 min.
• Read and discuss author and background features, including From the Author's Desk. **FT**	10 min.
• Introduce the Literary Analysis Skill: Atmosphere. **FT**	5 min.
• Introduce the Reading Strategy: Identifying With a Character. **FT**	
• Prepare students to read by teaching the selection vocabulary. **FT**	10 min.
TEACH	
• Informally monitor comprehension while students read independently or in groups. **FT**	30 min.
• Monitor students' comprehension with the Reading Check notes.	as students read
• Reinforce vocabulary with Vocabulary Builder notes.	as students read
• Develop students' understanding of atmosphere with the Literary Analysis annotations. **FT**	5 min.
• Develop students' ability to identify with a character with the Reading Strategy annotations. **FT**	5 min.
ASSESS/EXTEND	
• Assess students' comprehension and mastery of the Literary Analysis and Reading Strategy by having them answer the Apply the Skills questions. **FT**	15 min.
• Have students complete the Vocabulary Lesson and the Grammar and Style Lesson. **FT**	15 min.
• Apply students' ability to introduce examples by using the Writing Lesson. **FT**	45 min. or homework
• Apply students' understanding by using one or more of the Extend Your Learning activities.	20–90 min. or homework
• Administer Selection Test A or Selection Test B. **FT**	15 min.

Resources

Print

Unit 9 Resources

Transparency

Graphic Organizer Transparencies

Print

Reader's Notebook [L2]

Reader's Notebook: Adapted Version [L1]

Reader's Notebook: English Learner's Version [EL]

Unit 9 Resources

Technology

Listening to Literature Audio CDs [L2, EL]

Reader's Notebook: Adapted Version Audio CD [L1, L2]

Print

Unit 9 Resources

Technology

Go Online: Research [L3]

Go Online: Self-test [L3]

ExamView®, **Test Bank [L3]**

Choosing Resources for Differentiated Instruction

[L1] Special Needs Students

[L2] Below-Level Students

[L3] All Students

[L4] Advanced Students

[EL] English Learners

For Vocabulary and Reading Warm-ups and for Selection Tests, **A** signifies "less challenging" and **B** "more challenging." For Graphic Organizer transparencies, **A** signifies "not filled in" and **B** "filled in."

FT Fast Track Instruction: To move the lesson more quickly, use the strategies and activities identified with **FT**.

Scaffolding for Less Proficient and Advanced Students

The leveled Critical Thinking questions after selections progress in the levels of thinking required to answer them. To address the needs of your different students, you may use the (a) level questions for your less proficient students and the (b) level questions with your on-level and advanced students. The occasional (c) level questions are appropriate for your advanced students.

PRENTICE HALL

TeacherEXPRESS™ Use this complete
Plan · Teach · Assess   suite of powerful teaching tools to make lesson planning and testing quicker and easier.

PRENTICE HALL

StudentEXPRESS™ Use the interactive
Learn · Study · Succeed   textbook (online and on CD-ROM) to make selections and activities come alive with audio and video support and interactive questions.

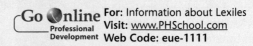 **For:** Information about Lexiles
Professional **Visit:** www.PHSchool.com
Development **Web Code:** eue-1111

Motivation

Tell students that the two selections in this grouping provide a look at Africa during a time in which strong traditional values were giving way to new ideas of freedom and justice. Ask students to discuss a time in their lives when an established way of doing things changed.

❶ Background

More About the Authors

South African writer Nadine Gordimer once described herself as "not a politically minded person by nature." She said, "I don't suppose if I had lived elsewhere, my writing would have reflected politics much, if at all." Nonetheless, her novels and story collections do reflect politics, like an unforgiving mirror held up to South African society; the images have sometimes been so ugly that three of her books were banned by the South African government.

In addition to directing a radio station and serving as a diplomat in Nigerian politics, Chinua Achebe has worked as a teacher. Today, he earns his living as an instructor in Nigeria and the United States, teaching courses at such universities as Northwestern and the City University of New York.

Geography Note

Draw students' attention to the map on this page. Point out that the Federal Republic of Nigeria is today the most populous African nation and one of the most diverse. The Republic of South Africa is larger than Nigeria, but its location at the tip of the African continent isolates it from other countries.

Build Skills $\boxed{\textit{Short Stories}}$

❶ Comrades • Marriage Is a Private Affair

Nadine Gordimer
(b. 1923)

Most of Nadine Gordimer's fiction is set in her native country of South Africa. During the years of apartheid—South Africa's official policy of racial segregation that ended in 1990—Gordimer wrote passionately in favor of racial justice. In her fiction, she demonstrates how institutionalized racism damages everyone in a society. It harms the oppressed by denying their rights to health, education, economic security, and political determination; it harms the oppressors by distorting their deepest human feelings.

Early Bloomer Born in Springs, South Africa, Gordimer grew up in a profoundly segregated society. Like most other white middle-class children in South Africa at the time, she attended private, all-white schools and lived in all-white neighborhoods. Her mother believed her daughter had a delicate constitution and often kept her home. As a result, Gordimer turned to writing to occupy herself. Her literary gifts bore fruit, and by the time she was fifteen years old, Gordimer was publishing regularly. As she grew older and became more aware of her country's problems, she applied her talents to describing the damage suffered by all South Africans under apartheid.

International Stardom Today, Gordimer is one of the most successful writers in the world. Her many literary works include *The Soft Voice of the Serpent* (1952), *Not for Publication* (1965), *The Conservationist* (1974), *The Essential Gesture: Writing, Politics, and Place* (1988), *Jump and Other Stories* (1991), and *The House Gun* (1998). In 1991, Gordimer added the Nobel Prize in Literature to her long list of honors.

Chinua Achebe
(b. 1930)

During the Nigerian civil war, which lasted from 1967 to 1970, Chinua Achebe (chin wä´ ə cheb´ ā) survived the bombing of his house by fleeing for his life, leaving behind an unpublished manuscript. When Achebe eventually returned home, he found one remaining copy, which someone had managed to save. This manuscript—*How the Leopard Got His Claws*, Achebe's parable about Nigeria—was published in 1972.

Living in Two Worlds Achebe was born in the Ibo village of Ogidi, Nigeria. His parents named him Albert, after Prince Albert, the husband of England's Queen Victoria. As a university student, Achebe later abandoned his English name in favor of Chinua, his Ibo name. The duality reflected in Achebe's names permeates his work, which describes the effects of Western customs and values on traditional African society.

Writing in English One legacy of British colonialism in Nigeria is the widespread use of English in education and government. As an educated Nigerian, Achebe writes in English, but he uses Ibo parables, words, and attitudes to convey a distinctly Nigerian sensibility. His keen ear and satiric sensibility have made him one of the most highly esteemed African writers in English.

A Landmark Work Achebe's signature work, the novel *Things Fall Apart*, was published to international acclaim in 1958. Many critics consider the book to be the first major work of fiction to emerge from Africa. Both a critical and popular success, the novel has been translated into more than fifty languages and has exerted a major influence on other African writers.

Preview

Connecting to the Literature

Most people who have known only peace and comfort develop a view of reality quite different from that of those who have known war and suffering. In these selections, characters struggle to bridge their differences.

❷ Literary Analysis

Atmosphere

In literature, **atmosphere**—or **mood**—refers to the emotional quality of the world the author creates. Atmosphere arises from descriptive details, setting, or plot and often mirrors the emotions of the characters themselves. In "Marriage Is a Private Affair," for example, descriptions of the weather reflect the pain and confusion in an old man's heart:

> He leaned against a window and looked out. The sky was overcast with heavy black clouds and a high wind began to blow. . . .

As you read these stories, look for descriptive details that reflect the characters' emotions and create distinctive atmospheres.

Comparing Literary Works

Both of these selections explore the ways in which intense cultural tensions can distort the kind feelings and good intentions of well-meaning people. As you read, identify the cultural tensions each story examines. Then, compare the ways in which both stories show that the damage caused by such tensions can be private and subtle but still devastating.

❸ Reading Strategy

Identifying With a Character

You may better appreciate each of these stories if you **identify with a character** who appears in the work. To do so, imagine yourself in the character's situation. Think about what you would do and feel. As you read, use a chart like the one shown to explore similarities between yourself and a key character.

Vocabulary Builder

assent (ə sent′) *n.* expression of agreement (p. 1325)

euphemisms (yōō′ fə miz′ əmz) *n.* words or phrases that are less expressive or direct but considered less distasteful or offensive than others (p. 1327)

furtively (fʉr′ tiv lē) *adv.* in a sneaky manner, as if to hinder observation (p. 1328)

revelation (rev′ ə lā′ shən) *n.* striking disclosure of something (p. 1328)

disposed (di spōzd′) *adj.* inclined; tending toward (p. 1330)

vehemently (vē′ ə mənt lē) *adv.* forcefully; intensely (p. 1331)

deference (def′ ər əns) *n.* submission to the desires or opinions of another; courteous respect (p. 1333)

perfunctorily (pər fuŋk′ tôr i lē) *adv.* indifferently; with little interest or care (p. 1334)

Standard Course of Study

- Analyze the importance of tone and mood in world literature. (LT.5.01.4)
- Analyze influences, contexts, or biases in world literature. (LT.5.03.7)

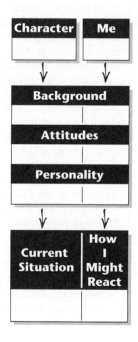

Comrades / Marriage Is a Private Affair ■ 1323

---

❷ Literary Analysis

Atmosphere

- Read aloud the Literary Analysis instruction. Explain that the term *atmosphere* in the context of literature (and film) often communicates to the reader or audience one or more characters' emotional patterns.

- Have students reread the example from "Marriage Is a Private Affair." Then, point out that writers evoke a story's atmosphere not only through setting or character but also through language. **Ask** students to identify the words in the example that reinforce the atmosphere of pain and confusion. **Possible responses:** The words *overcast, heavy, black, clouds,* and *wind* create this atmosphere.

- Read aloud the Comparing Literary Works instruction. Explain to students that cultural tensions can contribute to a work's atmosphere. Encourage students to consider how cultural tensions create or contribute to each selection's atmosphere.

❸ Reading Strategy

Identifying With a Character

- Call students' attention to the graphic organizer. Then, give them a copy of the **Reading Strategy Graphic Organizer A**, p. 233 in *Graphic Organizer Transparencies*. Have them use it to analyze each character in the selections to assess his or her situation and also to show how they identify with each character.

- Point out that an analysis and assessment of a character will help students see how complex well-written characters can be—just as real people are complex.

Vocabulary Builder

- Pronounce each vocabulary word for students, and read the definitions as a class. Have students identify any words with which they are already familiar.

Facilitate Understanding

Read aloud the Background information. Then, draw students' attention
to the image. Point out that this
photograph shows a protest against
discrimination in South Africa. Ask
students to discuss how these citizens
of South Africa might feel.

❶ About the Selection

In "Comrades," a white, middle-
class woman activist engaged in the
struggle against apartheid finds herself
confronted with the reality of the lives
of young black men who live under
that system of injustice.

❷ Literary Analysis

Atmosphere

• Remind students that atmosphere
is the emotional quality of a work.
Then, read aloud the bracketed
passage.

• **Ask** students the Literary Analysis
question: In the first paragraph,
which descriptive details contribute
to an atmosphere of tension?
Answer: Opposites (the "city
street" and the "enclave of learning";
the "tended flowerbeds" and the
"guards and dogs"; the "people to
be educated" and the "committee";
the "white and black activists"; and
the "leftists secular and Christian")
create a sense of tension.

❸ Reading Strategy

Identifying With a Character

• After students have read the bracketed passage, have them discuss
how both Mrs. Telford and the boys
feel during this initial encounter.

• **Ask** students the Reading Strategy
question: Can you identify with
Mrs. Telford's mixed feelings as she
agrees to take the youths to town?
Why or why not?
Possible response: Students may
identify with how Mrs. Telford is
torn between doing the right thing
(giving the youths a ride) and her
desire to get home.

Comrades

Nadine Gordimer

Background From 1948 until 1990, the country of South Africa
operated under the apartheid system—the government policy that called
for strict racial segregation and political and economic discrimination
against nonwhites. Many South Africans, both white and black, fought
against the apartheid system. While much of the dissent was political and
peaceful, the tensions sometimes boiled over into violence. It is against this
backdrop of painful political and cultural divisions that this story takes place.

---

❷ As Mrs. Hattie Telford pressed the electronic gadget that deactivates
the alarm device in her car a group of youngsters came up behind her.
Black. But no need to be afraid; this was not a city street. This was a
non-racial enclave of learning, a place where tended flowerbeds and
trees bearing botanical identification plates civilized the wild reminder
of campus guards and dogs. The youngsters, like her, were part of the
crowd loosening into dispersion after a university conference on People's Education. They were the people to be educated; she was one of
the committee of white and black activists (convenient generic for revolutionaries, leftists secular and Christian, fellow-travelers and liberals)
up on the platform.

—Comrade . . . — She was settling in the driver's seat when one so
slight and slim he seemed a figure in profile came up to her window. He
drew courage from the friendly lift of the woman's eyebrows above blue
eyes, the tilt of her freckled white face: —Comrade, are you going to
town?—

❸ No, she was going in the opposite direction, home . . . but quickly, in
the spirit of the hall where these young people had been somewhere,
somehow present with her (ah no, she with them) stamping and singing
Freedom songs, she would take them to the bus station their spokesman named. —Climb aboard!—

The others got in the back, the spokesman beside her. She saw the
nervous white of his eyes as he glanced at and away from her. She
searched for talk to set them at ease. Questions, of course. Older people
always start with questioning young ones. Did they come from Soweto?

They came from Harrismith, Phoneng Location.

1324 ■ *The Contemporary World*

Literary Analysis
Atmosphere In the first
paragraph, which descrip-
tive details contribute to
an atmosphere of tension?

Reading Strategy
**Identifying With a Char-
acter** Can you identify
with Mrs. Telford's mixed
feelings as she agrees to
take the boys to town?
Why or why not?

She made the calculation: about two hundred kilometers distant. How did they get here? Who told them about the conference?

—We are Youth Congress in Phoneng.—

A delegation. They had come by bus; one of the groups and stragglers who kept arriving long after the conference had started. They had missed, then, the free lunch?

At the back, no one seemed even to be breathing. The spokesman must have had some silent communication with them, some obligation to speak for them created by the journey or by other shared experience in the mysterious bonds of the young—these young. —We are hungry.— And from the back seats was drawn an <u>assent</u> like the suction of air in a compressing silence.

She was silent in response, for the beat of a breath or two. These large gatherings both excited and left her overexposed, open and vulnerable to the rub and twitch of the mass shuffling across rows of seats and loping up the aisles, babies' fudge-brown soft legs waving as their napkins are changed on mothers' laps, little girls with plaited loops on their heads listening like old crones, heavy women swaying to chants, men with fierce, unreadably black faces breaking into harmony tender and deep as they sing to God for his protection of Umkhonto weSizwe,

Reading Strategy
Identifying With a Character What do you think the boys are feeling as they sit in the back of Mrs. Telford's car?

Vocabulary Builder
assent (ə sent´) *n.* expression of agreement

✔ **Reading Check ⑤**

What gathering have Mrs. Telford and the group of boys just attended?

⑥ ▲ Critical Viewing How might this scene of an anti-apartheid demonstration resemble the event attended by Mrs. Telford and the students? Explain. **[Connect]**

Comrades ■ 1325

④ Reading Strategy
Identifying With a Character

• Have a volunteer read aloud the bracketed passage.

• **Ask** students the Reading Strategy question: What do you think the boys are feeling as they sit in the back of Mrs. Telford's car?
Possible response: The boys are probably feeling nervous or uncomfortable riding in a car with a white woman.

▶ **Monitor Progress Ask** students to discuss how they know what the boys are feeling. Remind them that in order to identify with a character, the reader must imagine himself or herself in the character's situation.
Possible response: Evidence from the text—such as the description of the group collectively holding its breath and the "silent communication"—and personal experiences with discomfort help readers infer what the boys are feeling.

▶ **Reteach** Point out to students that the boys may feel uncomfortable with Mrs. Telford not only because of their difference in race but also because of their difference in age. Ask students to discuss experiences when they felt a "generational gap" or a moment of awkwardness caused by a difference in age.

⑤ Reading Check

Answer: Mrs. Telford and the boys have just attended a university conference on People's Education.

⑥ Critical Viewing

Answer: This scene and the conference have the same spirit—in both, people share the goal of abolishing apartheid.

- Have a volunteer read aloud the bracketed passage. Then, **ask** students to explain the "historical slight" to which the text alludes.
Answer: Historically, the back door served as the servants' entrance and the entrance for all blacks regardless of their employment. Mrs. Telford recognizes that many would misconstrue the act of bringing the boys in through the back as a "slight" or an insult.
- **Ask** students: Why does Mrs. Telford, despite her understanding of the social implications of using the back entrance, bring the boys in through the back door?
Answer: Mrs. Telford usually enters her house through the back door and she knows that the boys will not misconstrue this act.

❽ Humanities

This South African sculpture of a leopard and cub probably was carved from Mukwa wood, also known as African teak. This wood, prized for its attractive wide grain and warm range of colors, is considered by many one of the best furniture woods in existence.

Use the following question for discussion.

How does the inclusion of this piece contribute to the story?
Possible responses: The carving helps readers visualize Mrs. Telford's carving, despite the differences between them. Also, the sculpture emphasizes the importance of maintaining South African culture.

❾ Literary Analysis

Atmosphere

- Have students read the bracketed passage independently.
- **Ask** students the Literary Analysis question: Which details contribute to an atmosphere of tension or suspense in Mrs. Telford's house? Explain.
Possible response: The obvious class differences between Mrs. Telford and the boys, the boys' silence and extreme hunger, and Mrs. Telford's self-conscious chatter all create tension.

as people on both sides have always, everywhere, claimed divine protection for their soldiers, their wars. At the end of a day like this she wanted a drink, she wanted the depraved luxury of solitude and quiet in which she would be restored (enriched, oh yes! by the day) to the familiar limits of her own being.

Hungry. Not for iced whiskey and feet up. It seemed she had scarcely hesitated: —Look. I live nearby, come back to my house and have something to eat. Then I'll run you into town.—

—That will be very nice. We can be glad for that.— And at the back the tight vacuum relaxed.

They followed her in through the gate, shrinking away from the dog—she assured them he was harmless but he was large, with a fancy collar by which she held him. She trooped them in through the kitchen because that was the way she always entered her house, something she would not have done if they had been adult, her black friends whose sophistication might lead them to believe the choice of entrance was an unthinking historical slight. As she was going to feed them, she took them not into her living-room with its sofas and flowers but into her dining-room, so that they could sit at table right away. It was a room in confident taste that could afford to be spare: bare floorboards, matching golden wooden ceiling, antique brass chandelier, reed blinds instead of stuffy curtains. An African wooden sculpture represented a lion marvelously released from its matrix in the grain of a Mukwa tree-trunk. She pulled up the chairs and left the four young men while she went back to the kitchen to make coffee and see what there was in the refrigerator for sandwiches. They had greeted the maid, in the language she and they shared, on their way through the kitchen, but when the maid and the lady of the house had finished preparing cold meat and bread, and the coffee was ready, she suddenly did not want them to see that the maid waited on her. She herself carried the heavy tray into the dining-room.

They are sitting round the table, silent, and there is no impression that they stopped an undertone exchange when they heard her approaching. She doles out plates, cups. They stare at the food but their eyes seem focused on something she can't see; something that overwhelms. She urges them—Just cold meat, I'm afraid, but there's chutney[1] if you like it . . . milk everybody? . . . is the coffee too strong, I have a heavy hand, I know. Would anyone like to add some hot water?—

They eat. When she tries to talk to one of the others, he says *Ekskuus?* And she realizes he doesn't understand English, of the white man's languages knows perhaps only a little of that of the Afrikaners in the rural town he comes from. Another gives his name, as if in some delicate acknowledgement of the food. —I'm Shadrack Nsutsha.— She repeats the surname to get it right. But he does not speak again. There

---

1. **chutney** (chut´ nē) *n.* relish or sauce of Indian origin, typically combining sweet and sour ingredients, such as fruit and vinegar, with sugar and spices.

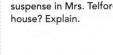

Literary Analysis
Atmosphere Which details contribute to an atmosphere of tension or suspense in Mrs. Telford's house? Explain.

is an urgent exchange of eye-language, and the spokesman holds out the emptied sugar-bowl to her. —Please.— She hurries to the kitchen and brings it back refilled. They need carbohydrate, they are hungry, they are young, they need it, they burn it up. She is distressed at the inadequacy of the meal and then notices the fruit bowl, her big copper fruit bowl, filled with apples and bananas and perhaps there is a peach or two under the grape leaves with which she likes to complete an edible still life. —Have some fruit. Help yourselves.—

They are stacking their plates and cups, not knowing what they are expected to do with them in this room which is a room where apparently people only eat, do not cook, do not sleep. While they finish the bananas and apples (Shadrack Nsutsha had seen the single peach and quickly got there first) she talks to the spokesman, whose name she has asked for: Dumile. —Are you still at school, Dumile?— Of course he is not at school—*they* are not at school; youngsters their age have not been at school for several years, they are the children growing into young men and women for whom school is a battleground, a place of boycotts and demonstrations, the literacy of political rhetoric, the education of revolt against having to live the life their parents live. They have pompous titles of responsibility beyond childhood: he is chairman of his branch of the Youth Congress, he was expelled two years ago—for leading a boycott? Throwing stones at the police? Maybe burning the school down? He calls it all—quietly, abstractly, doesn't know many ordinary, concrete words but knows these <u>euphemisms</u>— "political activity." No school for two years? No. —So what have you been able to do with yourself, all that time?—

She isn't giving him a chance to eat his apple. He swallows a large bite, shaking his head on its thin, little-boy neck. —I was inside. Detained from this June for six months.—

She looks round the others. —And you?—

Shadrack seems to nod slightly. The other two look at her. She should know, she should have known, it's a common enough answer from youths like them, their color. They're not going to be saying they've been selected for the 1st Eleven at cricket or that they're off on a student tour to Europe in the school holidays.

The spokesman, Dumile, tells her he wants to study by correspondence, "get his matric" that he was preparing for two years ago; two years ago when he was still a child, when he didn't have the hair that is now appearing on his face, making him a man, taking away the childhood. In the hesitations, the silences of the table, where there is nervously spilt coffee among plates of banana skins, there grows the certainty that he will never get the papers filled in for the correspondence college, he will never get the two years back. She looks at them all and cannot believe what she knows: that they, suddenly here in her house, will carry the AK-47s[2] they only sing about, now, miming death as they sing. They will have a career of wiring explosives to the

---

2. **AK-47s** military assault rifles.

Reading Strategy
Identifying With a Character With whom do you identify more strongly—the students or Mrs. Telford? Explain.

Vocabulary Builder
euphemisms (yo͞o′ fə miz′ əmz) *n.* words or phrases that are less expressive or direct but considered less distasteful or offensive than others

Reading Check 12

For how long have the boys not attended school?

Comrades ■ 1327

---

❿ Reading Strategy
Identifying With a Character
- Review with students the Reading Strategy instruction on p. 1323. Remind them that a reader must use his or her imagination and experience to understand a situation and to appreciate what a character must be feeling.
- Then, **ask** students what this passage tells the reader about the experiences of the young men.
  Possible response: The young men live—without much sustenance—in one-room houses in which all residents eat, cook, and sleep.
- **Ask** students the Reading Strategy question: With whom do you identify more strongly—the students or Mrs. Telford? Explain.
  Possible responses: Some readers may identify with Mrs. Telford because they have no experience living in dire poverty. Others may relate to the youths, having lived in such a house or having experienced a situation in which they did not know what was expected of them or in which they experienced a communication breakdown.

⓫ Vocabulary Builder
Greek Prefix *eu-*
- Draw students' attention to the word *euphemisms,* and read its definition.
- Tell students that *euphemisms* contains the Greek prefix *eu-,* which means "good" or "well." Then, have students **discuss** how the meaning of this prefix relates to the word *euphemisms.*
  Answer: A euphemism is a "good" way of conveying information that would otherwise be considered unpleasant or crass.
- Have students **suggest** other words that use the prefix *eu-,* and **discuss** how the meaning of the prefix relates to the meaning of each word.
  Possible responses: *Euphoria, eugenic,* and *euphony* all feature *eu-.*
  Sample response: In *euphony,* the prefix *-eu* with *phone* (sound or voice) means "sweet-voiced, musical."

⓬ Reading Check
Answer: The boys have not attended school for two years.

1. **Possible responses:** Readers may have hoped for an ending in which the boys are not revealed to be future killers. Others may have hoped that Mrs. Telford would offer to help the boys finish school.

2. (a) The university conference on People's Education has just ended. (b) Mrs. Telford was on the committee of activists who sat on the stage. The students attended the conference. (c) Mrs. Telford's participation suggests that she is active in the movement against apartheid.

3. (a) The boy draws courage from Mrs. Telford's friendly uplifted eyebrows and tilted face. (b) Mrs. Telford's expression suggests that she is open, friendly, and approachable. (c) The student is black, and it is illegal for the races to mix under apartheid.

4. (a) The boys are hungry, and Mrs. Telford intends to feed them. (b) The boys' physical hunger might represent the spiritual depravity induced by apartheid.

5. (a) The wooden floors and ceilings, the antique chandelier, and carved wooden statue suggest Mrs. Telford's affluence. (b) Mrs. Telford lives in a safe, comfortable environment; the students live in a violent, unstable environment. (c) Mrs. Telford lives alone in a house with many rooms and has plenty of food on hand. The students probably live with many people in one room and must struggle to survive. She enjoys freedom of movement and association and the right to vote; the students do not.

6. (a) They were expelled for participating in "political activity." (b) Mrs. Telford realizes that education is not in the boys' future but that violence and death certainly are. (c) **Possible response:** Violence is all that the boys know, and so their future immersion in it is inevitable but not justified.

7. **Possible response:** Political struggles often bring together people of different backgrounds and beliefs because they share ideals.

undersides of vehicles, they will go away and come back through the bush to dig holes not to plant trees to shade home, but to plant land-mines. She can see they have been terribly harmed but cannot believe they could harm. They are wiping their fruit-sticky hands <u>furtively</u> palm against palm.

She breaks the silence; says something, anything.

—How d'you like my lion? Isn't he beautiful? He's made by a Zim-babwean artist, I think the name's Dube.—

But the foolish interruption becomes <u>revelation</u>. Dumile, in his gaze—distant, lingering, speechless this time—reveals what has over-whelmed them. In this room, the space, the expensive antique chande-lier, the consciously simple choice of reed blinds, the carved lion: all are on the same level of impact, phenomena undifferentiated, undecipher-able. Only the food that fed their hunger was real.

Vocabulary Builder
furtively (fur´ tiv lē) *adv.* in a sneaky manner, as if to hinder observation
revelation (rev´ ə lā´ shən) *n.* striking disclosure of something

Critical Reading

1. **Respond:** As you read the story, what outcome did you hope for?

2. **(a) Recall:** When the students approach Mrs. Telford, what event has just ended? **(b) Distinguish:** What different roles did Mrs. Telford and the students play at the event? **(c) Infer:** What does her participation in the event reveal about Mrs. Telford's politics?

3. **(a) Recall:** When the student first approaches Mrs. Telford in her car, which details in her appearance give him courage? **(b) Generalize:** What do these details suggest about her character? Explain. **(c) Analyze:** Why do you think the student needs courage to speak with Mrs. Telford?

4. **(a) Recall:** Why does Mrs. Telford take the students to her house instead of to town? **(b) Interpret:** What emotion or idea might the students' physical hunger represent? Explain.

5. **(a) Classify:** Which details in the description of Mrs. Telford's home suggest her affluence? **(b) Infer:** In what ways does Mrs. Telford's home stand in sharp contrast to the environment in which the students live? **(c) Support:** Which details in the text support your answer? Explain.

6. **(a) Deduce:** Why do the boys no longer attend school? **(b) Infer:** What realization does Mrs. Telford have about the students' futures? **(c) Take a Position:** Do you think the harm the boys have suffered jus-tifies any harm they will do in the future? Explain.

7. **Synthesize:** Why might shared political struggles involve groups with otherwise very different backgrounds and beliefs?

For: More about Nadine Gordimer
Visit: www.PHSchool.com
Web Code: ete-9913

Go Online For additional information about
Author Link Nadine Gordimer, have students type in the Web Code, then select *G* from the alphabet, and then select Nadine Gordimer.

Marriage Is a Private Affair

Chinua Achebe

Background The main characters in this story belong to two different Nigerian ethnic groups, the Ibo (ē′ bō′) (also called the Igbo) and the Ibibio (ib′ ə bē′ ō′). The Ibo are the largest ethnic group in southeastern Nigeria and one of the largest in the nation. During Britain's colonial rule of Nigeria, many Ibo were educated in British missionary schools, and today most of the Ibo population is Christian. The Ibo strongly supported the independence of southeastern Nigeria during the civil war of 1967–1970, and as a result, they earned the resentment of powerful Nigerian ethnic groups in the north. The Ibibio, also of southeastern Nigeria, are a smaller but nevertheless powerful group. Conflict between traditional Ibo values and those of modern life are at the center of this story.

"Have you written to your dad yet?" asked Nene[1] one afternoon as she sat with Nnaemeka[2] in her room at 16 Kasanga Street, Lagos.[3]

"No. I've been thinking about it. I think it's better to tell him when I get home on leave!"

"But why? Your leave is such a long way off yet—six whole weeks. He should be let into our happiness now."

Nnaemeka was silent for a while, and then began very slowly as if he groped for his words: "I wish I were sure it would be happiness to him."

"Of course it must," replied Nene, a little surprised. "Why shouldn't it?"

"You have lived in Lagos all your life, and you know very little about people in remote parts of the country."

---

1. **Nene** (nā′ nā′)
2. **Nnaemeka** ('n nē′ mə kə)
3. **Lagos** (lā′ gäs′) former capital city of Nigeria.

  Reading Check

What has Nnaemaka been thinking about doing?

Marriage Is a Private Affair ■ 1329

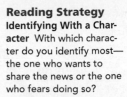

⑯ Reading Strategy

Identifying With a Character

- Remind students that readers cannot identify with a character until they understand the character's motives and actions.

- Read aloud the bracketed passage. Then, **ask** students to describe the action each character wants to take and the motives behind these actions.
  Answer: Nene is happy about her impending marriage to Nnaemeka; consequently, she wants Nnaemeka to tell his father the news of their engagement. She probably thinks that Nnaemeka's father has a right to know about the marriage. Nnaemeka, fearing his father's disapproval, does not want to share the news.

- **Ask** students the Reading Strategy question: With which character do you identify most—the one who wants to share the news or the one who fears doing so?
  Possible responses: Readers may identify with Nene's happiness and her desire to share the news. Others may identify with Nnaemeka's desire to avoid confrontation.

⑰ Critical Thinking

Infer

- Ask a volunteer to read aloud the bracketed passage. Remind students that this letter reveals the father's own words and ideas about his son's marriage.

- **Ask** students: On the basis of this letter, what can you infer about Nnaemeka's father? What is he like? What does he value?
  Possible response: Nnaemeka's father is a Christian who believes in the tradition of arranged marriage. He believes that a wife should have little or no education and proper religious training.

⑱ Critical Viewing

Possible response: The painting, with its presentation in two parts, captures the separation between Nnaemeka and his father and between tradition and modern life. The figures in each box look similar but not harmonious.

---

⑯ "That's what you always say. But I don't believe anybody will be so unlike other people that they will be unhappy when their sons are engaged to marry."

"Yes. They are most unhappy if the engagement is not arranged by them. In our case it's worse—you are not even an Ibo."

This was said so seriously and so bluntly that Nene could not find speech immediately. In the cosmopolitan atmosphere of the city it had always seemed to her something of a joke that a person's tribe could determine whom he married.

At last she said, "You don't really mean that he will object to your marrying me simply on that account? I had always thought you Ibos were kindly <u>disposed</u> to other people."

"So we are. But when it comes to marriage, well, it's not quite so simple. And this," he added, "is not peculiar to the Ibos. If your father were alive and lived in the heart of Ibibio-land he would be exactly like my father."

"I don't know. But anyway, as your father is so fond of you, I'm sure he will forgive you soon enough. Come on then, be a good boy and send him a nice lovely letter . . ."

"It would not be wise to break the news to him by writing. A letter will bring it upon him with a shock. I'm quite sure about that."

"All right, honey, suit yourself. You know your father."

As Nnaemeka walked home that evening he turned over in his mind the different ways of overcoming his father's opposition, especially now that he had gone and found a girl for him. He had thought of showing his letter to Nene but decided on second thoughts not to, at least for the moment. He read it again when he got home and couldn't help smiling to himself. He remembered Ugoye[4] quite well, an Amazon[5] of a girl who used to beat up all the boys, himself included, on the way to the stream, a complete dunce at school.

⑰ *I have found a girl who will suit you admirably—Ugoye Nweke,[6] the eldest daughter of our neighbor, Jacob Nweke. She has a proper Christian upbringing. When she stopped schooling some years ago her father (a man of sound judgment) sent her to live in the house of a pastor where she has received all the training a wife could need. Her Sunday School teacher has told me that she reads her Bible very fluently. I hope we shall begin negotiations when you come home in December.*

On the second evening of his return from Lagos Nnaemeka sat with his father under a cassia tree. This was the old man's retreat where he went to read his Bible when the parching December sun had set and a fresh, reviving wind blew on the leaves.

⑲ "Father," began Nnaemeka suddenly, "I have come to ask forgiveness."

"Forgiveness? For what, my son?" he asked in amazement.

"It's about this marriage question."

---

4. **Ugoye** (yōō gō´ ye)
5. **Amazon** (am´ ə zän) large, strong, masculine woman. In Greek mythology, the Amazons were a race of female warriors.
6. **Nweke** ('n wā´ kā)

1330 ■ *The Contemporary World*

Reading Strategy
Identifying With a Character With which character do you identify most—the one who wants to share the news or the one who fears doing so?

Vocabulary Builder
disposed (di spōzd´) *adj.* inclined; tending toward

⑱ **Critical Viewing** ▶
Do you think this painting captures the characters and mood of this story? Why or why not?
[Generalize]

Enrichment

Nigeria

Nigeria, the setting for "Marriage Is a Private Affair," has had a long history. In the late 1800's, the British annexed lands in west Africa, eventually setting up the colony of Nigeria. Local rulers resisted British domination, and in 1960, Nigeria finally achieved independence.

Religious, economic, and ethnic divisions flared after independence. The Ibo in the southeast felt that the Muslim Huasa-Fulani of the north dominated Nigeria. The Ibo seceded from Nigeria, setting up the independent Republic of Biafra. A brutal civil war followed, and in 1970, a defeated Biafra rejoined Nigeria.

"Which marriage question?"

"I can't—we must—I mean it is impossible for me to marry Nweke's daughter."

"Impossible? Why?" asked his father.

"I don't love her."

"Nobody said you did. Why should you?" he asked.

"Marriage today is different . . ."

"Look here, my son," interrupted his father, "nothing is different. What one looks for in a wife are a good character and a Christian background."

Nnaemeka saw there was no hope along the present line of argument.

"Moreover," he said, "I am engaged to marry another girl who has all of Ugoye's good qualities, and who . . ."

His father did not believe his ears. "What did you say?" he asked slowly and disconcertingly.

"She is a good Christian," his son went on, "and a teacher in a Girls' School in Lagos."

"Teacher, did you say? If you consider that a qualification for a good wife I should like to point out to you, Emeka, that no Christian woman should teach. St. Paul in his letter to the Corinthians[7] says that women should keep silence." He rose slowly from his seat and paced forwards and backwards. This was his pet subject, and he condemned <u>vehemently</u> those church leaders who encouraged women to teach in their

---

7. **St. Paul . . . Corinthians** reference to the Bible's New Testament (1 Corinthians 14:34), in which Paul writes, "Let your women keep silent in the churches."

Literary Analysis
Atmosphere What atmosphere do Nnaemeka's disturbed emotions create?

Vocabulary Builder
vehemently (vē´ ə mənt lē) *adv.* forcefully; intensely

✓ **Reading Check** ❷⓿
What arrangement has Nnaemeka's father made for his son's marriage?

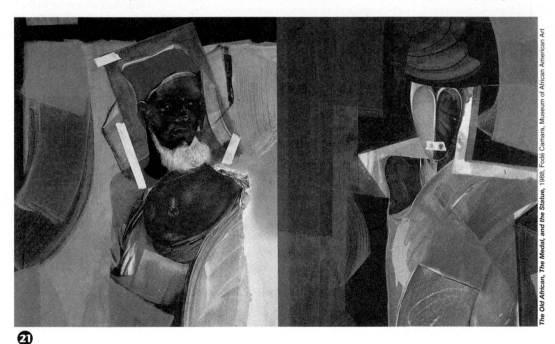

The Old African, The Medal, and the Statue, 1988, Fodé Camara, Museum of African American Art

Marriage Is a Private Affair ■ 1331

❶⓿ Literary Analysis
Atmosphere
• Review with students the Literary Analysis instruction on p. 1323. Make sure students understand that the emotions of the characters tinge the overall atmosphere of a work.
• Ask a volunteer to read aloud the bracketed passage. Then, have students **cite** examples from the passage that reveal Nnaemeka's unease.
Answer: Uncertain of how to approach his father, Nnaemeka stammers, "I can't—we must—I mean it is impossible for me to marry Nweke's daughter." It is clear that Nnaemeka is reluctant and uncomfortable.
• **Ask** students the Literary Analysis question: What atmosphere do Nnaemeka's disturbed emotions create?
Answer: Nnaemeka's emotions create an atmosphere of tension and conflict.

❷⓿ Reading Check
Answer: Nnaemeka's father has planned to start negotiations for his son to marry the daughter of a neighbor.

❷❶ Humanities
The Old African, The Medal, and the Statue, by Fodé Camara
Contemporary artist Fodé Camara, a native of Dakar, Sénégal, studied at the Institut National des Arts du Sénégal and in Paris at the École Nationale Supérieure des Arts Décoratifs. His bright, abstract paintings provide an expressive insight into the issues of colonialism and colonial identity.
Use the following question for discussion.
What adjectives describe the figure on the left side of the painting?
Possible response: The figure looks serious, pondering, and attentive.

Differentiated Instruction Solutions for All Learners

Strategy for Special Needs Students
As students read the story, explain that its events take place over the course of eight years. Guide students to create a four-box flowchart with the headings *As the Story Begins, A Few Weeks Later* (p. 1332), *Six Months Later* (p. 1333), and *Eight Years Later* (p. 1333). Have students use the organizer to record notable events for each time period. Then, after students have finished reading the entire story, lead a class discussion in which they consider why the story's resolution takes as long as it does.

Enrichment for Advanced Readers
Tell students that Achebe once said, "Stories are not just meant to make people smile . . . our life depends on them." Encourage students to keep this quotation in mind as they read "Marriage Is a Private Affair" and to take notes on specific examples in the text that support or refute this assertion. Then, have students use their notes to write brief essays in which they discuss the relevance of this quotation to the story. Encourage volunteers to share their work with the class.

1331

② Themes in World Literature

Arranged Marriages The custom of arranged marriages is practiced to some degree in the United States today, most often within small communities of immigrants from countries such as India or Iraq, where arranged marriage is an established tradition. Although many Americans consider an arranged marriage an infringement on personal choice, cultures for which this practice is a custom defend it for its focus on family and roots in traditional culture.

Connect to the Literature Some students may be products of arranged marriages or have relatives who favor this arrangement, so advise students that the discussion of this sensitive topic should be respectful of cultural differences. Ask students to suggest why Nnaemeka's father is so committed to the custom of arranged marriage.

Possible response: His father may believe that an arranged marriage avoids societal and religious conflicts and honors age-old traditions.

② Literary Analysis

Atmosphere

• After students have read the bracketed passage, **ask** the Literary Analysis question.

Answer: In this paragraph, it becomes clear that the men believe that Nnaemeka will be the first and only Ibo man to marry outside his cultural group. Therefore, Nnaemeka faces the rejection of not only his father but also his entire culture.

▶ **Monitor Progress** What does Nnaemeka's ignorance of the elder's verdict and of the depth of his father's grief add to the atmosphere of the story?

Possible response: His ignorance contributes to an atmosphere of suspense or of looming disaster.

▶ **Reteach** If students have difficulty answering questions about atmosphere, have them use the **Literary Analysis** support, p. 149 in *Unit 9 Resources*.

---

schools. After he had spent his emotion on a long homily[8] he at last came back to his son's engagement, in a seemingly milder tone.

"Whose daughter is she, anyway?"

"She is Nene Atang."

"What!" All the mildness was gone again. "Did you say Neneataga, what does that mean?"

"Nene Atang from Calabar.[9] She is the only girl I can marry." This was a very rash reply and Nnaemeka expected the storm to burst. But it did not. His father merely walked away into his room. This was most unexpected and perplexed Nnaemeka. His father's silence was infinitely more menacing than a flood of threatening speech. That night the old man did not eat.

When he sent for Nnaemeka a day later he applied all possible ways of dissuasion. But the young man's heart was hardened, and his father eventually gave him up as lost.

"I owe it to you, my son, as a duty to show you what is right and what is wrong. Whoever put this idea into your head might as well have cut your throat. It is Satan's work." He waved his son away.

"You will change your mind, Father, when you know Nene."

"I shall never see her," was the reply. From that night the father scarcely spoke to his son. He did not, however, cease hoping that he would realize how serious was the danger he was heading for. Day and night he put him in his prayers.

Nnaemeka, for his own part, was very deeply affected by his father's grief. But he kept hoping that it would pass away. If it had occurred to him that never in the history of his people had a man married a woman who spoke a different tongue, he might have been less optimistic. "It has never been heard," was the verdict of an old man speaking a few weeks later. In that short sentence he spoke for all of his people. This man had come with others to commiserate with Okeke[10] when news went round about his son's behavior. By that time the son had gone back to Lagos.

"It has never been heard," said the old man again with a sad shake of his head.

"What did Our Lord say?" asked another gentleman. "Sons shall rise against their Fathers; it is there in the Holy Book."

"It is the beginning of the end," said another.

The discussion thus tending to become theological, Madubogwu, a highly practical man, brought it down once more to the ordinary level.

"Have you thought of consulting a native doctor about your son?" he asked Nnaemeka's father.

"He isn't sick," was the reply.

"What is he then? The boy's mind is diseased and only a good

---

8. **homily** (häm´ ə lē) *n.* religious speech.
9. **Calabar** (kal´ ə bär) seaport in southeast Nigeria.
10. **Okeke** (o kā´ kā)

Until the twentieth century, arranged marriages were common in almost all cultures of the world. It is no surprise, then, that this nuptial custom has been both chronicled and critiqued by countless writers throughout history. The author of the Old Testament book of Genesis, for example, describes the arranged marriage between Isaac, son of Abraham, and Rebekah. Two millennia later, Shakespeare treats the same theme—but far less objectively—in his tragedy *Romeo and Juliet* (1595). More recently, writers from India and other parts of Asia have tackled this difficult subject, most notably Chitra Divakaruni in her collection of short stories *Arranged Marriage* (1995).

Connect to the Literature

Why do you think Nnaemeka's father is so committed to the custom of arranged marriages?

Literary Analysis
Atmosphere In what ways does this paragraph intensify the sense of Nnaemeka's isolation?

Enrichment

Writing in English
Although Achebe writes in English, he recognizes the pitfalls of doing so. In an article in *Nigeria* magazine (June 1964), Achebe discussed some of the problems he faced in using English.

For an African, writing in English is not without its serious setbacks. He often finds himself describing situations or modes of thought which have no direct equivalent in the English way of life. Caught in that situation he can do one of two things. He can try and contain what he wants to say within the limits of conventional English or he can try to push back those limits to accommodate his ideas. The first method produces competent, uninspired and rather flat work. The second method can produce something new and valuable to the English language as well as to the material he is trying to put over.

herbalist can bring him back to his right senses. The medicine he requires is *Amalile*, the same that women apply with success to recapture their husbands' straying affection."

"Madubogwu is right," said another gentleman. "This thing calls for medicine."

"I shall not call in a native doctor." Nnaemeka's father was known to be obstinately ahead of his more superstitious neighbors in these matters. "I will not be another Mrs. Ochuba. If my son wants to kill himself let him do it with his own hands. It is not for me to help him."

"But it was her fault," said Madubogwu. "She ought to have gone to an honest herbalist. She was a clever woman, nevertheless."

"She was a wicked murderess," said Jonathan who rarely argued with his neighbors because, he often said, they were incapable of reasoning. "The medicine was prepared for her husband, it was his name they called in its preparation and I am sure it would have been perfectly beneficial to him. It was wicked to put it into the herbalist's food, and say you were only trying it out."

Six months later, Nnaemeka was showing his young wife a short letter from his father:

It amazes me that you could be so unfeeling as to send me your wedding picture. I would have sent it back. But on further thought I decided just to cut off your wife and send it back to you because I have nothing to do with her. How I wish that I had nothing to do with you either.

When Nene read through this letter and looked at the mutilated picture her eyes filled with tears, and she began to sob.

"Don't cry, my darling," said her husband. "He is essentially good-natured and will one day look more kindly on our marriage." But years passed and that one day did not come.

For eight years, Okeke would have nothing to do with his son, Nnaemeka. Only three times (when Nnaemeka asked to come home and spend his leave) did he write to him.

"I can't have you in my house," he replied on one occasion. "It can be of no interest to me where or how you spend your leave—or your life, for that matter."

The prejudice against Nnaemeka's marriage was not confined to his little village. In Lagos, especially among his people who worked there, it showed itself in a different way. Their women, when they met at their village meeting, were not hostile to Nene. Rather, they paid her such excessive <u>deference</u> as to make her feel she was not one of them. But as time went on, Nene gradually broke through some of this prejudice and even began to make friends among them. Slowly and grudgingly they began to admit that she kept her home much better than most of them.

The story eventually got to the little village in the heart of the Ibo country that Nnaemeka and his young wife were a most happy couple. But his father was one of the few people who knew nothing about this.

Literary Analysis
Atmosphere How does the discussion among the old men show that Nnaemeka's conflict with his father is part of a much larger societal conflict?

Reading Strategy
Identifying With a Character Can you identify with Nene's reaction to the letter and photograph? Explain.

Vocabulary Builder
deference (def' ər əns) *n.* submission to the desires or opinions of another; courteous respect

**Reading Check 26**
For how long does Okeke avoid all contact with his son?

---

24 Literary Analysis
Atmosphere

- After students have read the bracketed passage independently, **ask** them to identify words that describe the atmosphere, or mood, in the village when the old men meet to talk.
Possible response: The atmosphere is somber as the men consider the cultural ramifications of Nnaemeka's marriage, but it is also a little comical as the men hyperbolize and speculate on Nnaemeka's "sickness."

- **Ask** students the Literary Analysis question: How does the discussion among the old men show that Nnaemeka's conflict with his father is part of a larger societal conflict?
Answer: It is clear from the men's discussion that not only tribal but also religious conflicts—between ancient paganism, Christianity, and modern secularism—exist in the community.

25 Reading Strategy
Identifying With a Character

- Read aloud the bracketed sentence. Then, **ask** students the Reading Strategy question: Can you identify with Nene's reaction to the letter and photograph? Explain.
Possible response: Some readers may identify with Nene's frustration at being prejudged by Okeke.

26 Reading Check
Answer: Okeke avoids contact with Nnaemeka for eight years.

1333

• Have a volunteer read aloud the bracketed passage. Then, **ask** students to consider the atmosphere of the story prior to this letter.
Possible response: The atmosphere of the story up to this point has been one of sorrow and hopelessness.

• Then, **ask** students the Literary Analysis question: In what ways does Nene's letter change the story's atmosphere?
Answer: The atmosphere becomes hopeful as Nene's letter melts Okeke's resolve to continue to shun his son and daughter-in-law.

1. **Possible responses:** Some readers may want to shame Okeke for wasting eight years of his life by being angry at his son. Others may want to commend Okeke for sticking to his principles.

2. (a) A suitable wife should be a good Christian and poorly educated. She should also be an Ibo. (b) Nnaemeka chooses Nene because she is a good person, well educated, a respected teacher, and a good Christian. Also, he loves her. (c) By making Nene so sympathetic and likeable, it is clear that the author favors Nnaemeka's criteria.

3. (a) Reading the letter from Nene triggers the father's emotional trauma. (b) **Possible response:** The father, overcome with remorse, will reconcile with his son and meet his grandsons as soon as possible.

4. **Possible responses:** Readers may say that choosing a mate is a very personal decision and that the opinions of others should play no role. Others may suggest that it is important to consider the opinions of friends and relatives because their experience—and resulting advice—may prove useful.

He always displayed so much temper whenever his son's name was mentioned that everyone avoided it in his presence. By a tremendous effort of will he had succeeded in pushing his son to the back of his mind. The strain had nearly killed him but he had persevered, and won.

Then one day he received a letter from Nene, and in spite of himself he began to glance through it <u>perfunctorily</u> until all of a sudden the expression on his face changed and he began to read more carefully.

㉗

> . . . Our two sons, from the day they learnt that they have a grandfather, have insisted on being taken to him. I find it impossible to tell them that you will not see them. I implore you to allow Nnaemeka to bring them home for a short time during his leave next month. I shall remain here in Lagos . . . .

The old man at once felt the resolution he had built up over so many years falling in. He was telling himself that he must not give in. He tried to steel his heart against all emotional appeals. It was a re-enactment of that other struggle. He leaned against a window and looked out. The sky was overcast with heavy black clouds and a high wind began to blow filling the air with dust and dry leaves. It was one of those rare occasions when even Nature takes a hand in a human fight. Very soon it began to rain, the first rain in the year. It came down in large sharp drops and was accompanied by the lightning and thunder which mark a change of season. Okeke was trying hard not to think of his two grandsons. But he knew he was now fighting a losing battle. He tried to hum a favorite hymn but the pattering of large rain drops on the roof broke up the tune. His mind immediately returned to the children. How could he shut his door against them? By a curious mental process he imagined them standing, sad and forsaken, under the harsh angry weather—shut out from his house.

That night he hardly slept, from remorse—and a vague fear that he might die without making it up to them.

Critical Reading

1. **Respond:** What would you like to say to Nnaemeka's father at the end of the story? Explain.
2. **(a) Recall:** What criteria does Nnaemeka's father use to judge the suitability of a wife? **(b) Infer:** What criteria has Nnaemeka used to choose Nene? **(c) Evaluate:** Does the author seem to favor one set of criteria over the other? Explain.
3. **(a) Analyze Cause and Effect:** Which event triggers the father's emotional trauma at the end of the story? **(b) Predict:** Based on the story's final scene, what do you think the father will do?
4. **Take a Position:** Should marriage be an entirely private affair or should the opinions of friends and relatives play a role? Explain.

Vocabulary Builder
perfunctorily (pər fuŋk´ tôr i lē) *adv.* indifferently; with little interest or care

Literary Analysis
Atmosphere In what ways does Nene's letter change the story's atmosphere?

Go Online
Author Link
For: More about Chinua Achebe
Visit: www.PHSchool.com
Web Code: ete-9914

Go Online For additional information about
Author Link Chinua Achebe, have students type in the Web Code, then select *A* from the alphabet, and then select Chinua Achebe.

Apply the Skills

Comrades • Marriage Is a Private Affair

Literary Analysis

Atmosphere

1. **(a)** How would you describe the **atmosphere** in the opening paragraph of "Comrades"? **(b)** Use a chart like the one shown to identify descriptive details that contribute to this atmosphere.

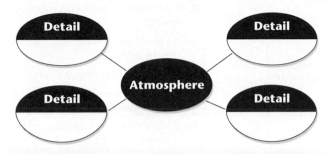

2. **(a)** After Mrs. Telford carries the tray into the dining room, how does the story's verb tense change? **(b)** What is the effect of this change on the story's atmosphere?
3. **(a)** In "Marriage Is a Private Affair," which details contribute to the story's atmosphere of intense but restrained emotion? Explain. **(b)** At what point does the atmosphere change, and why?

Comparing Literary Works

4. Which specific cultural pressures or tensions are at work in each of these stories?
5. **(a)** In what ways do both Mrs. Telford and Nnaemeka's father try to behave honorably? **(b)** Do they succeed? Why or why not?
6. What does each story say about the cruelties of prejudice? Explain.

Reading Strategy

Identifying With a Character

7. With which character or situation in each story do you most strongly **identify**? Explain.
8. At which point in each story would you have felt or acted differently than the character did? Explain.

Extend Understanding

9. **Career Connection:** Mediators are professionals who help people settle disputes peacefully. If you were a mediator, what advice would you give to Nnaemeka and his father?

QuickReview

Atmosphere is the emotional quality of the world the author creates in a work of literature.

To **identify with a character** as you read, imagine yourself in the place of a character and try to experience events through his or her eyes.

Go Online
Assessment
For: Self-test
Visit: www.PHSchool.com
Web Code: eta-6909

Comrades / Marriage Is a Private Affair ■ 1335

Answers

1. **(a)** The atmosphere is tense. **(b) Possible response:** Mrs. Telford is aware that the young men are approaching her from behind; Mrs. Telford has just unlocked her car, making her vulnerable; Mrs. Telford is aware that the young men are black; Mrs. Telford has to remind herself that she is not in the city and probably not in danger. Another sample answer can be found on **Literary Analysis Graphic Organizer B**, p. 236 in *Graphic Organizer Transparencies.*

2. **(a)** The verb tense changes from past tense to present tense. **(b)** The change in tense makes the scene at the table seem as if it were happening at the present moment, creating a paradoxical atmosphere of immediacy and suspense.

3. **(a)** The use of letters to communicate, Nnaemeka's aversion to talking to his father, and Okeke's refusal to talk to his son all indicate restrained emotion. **(b)** The atmosphere changes immediately after Okeke reads the letter from Nene. When he learns about his grandsons, Okeke's anger and prejudices are washed away.

4. In "Comrades," Mrs. Telford feels pressure to be friendly and open toward the young men. In "Marriage Is a Private Affair," Nnaemeka resists pressure from his father and his culture. His refusal to follow tradition causes tension between him and his father.

5. **(a)** Mrs. Telford tries to behave honorably by giving the young men a ride and by feeding them. Nnaemeka's father tries to behave honorably by adhering to his cultural traditions. **(b)** Mrs. Telford feeds the young men, but she has no way of connecting with them. Nnaemeka's father succeeds for eight years in upholding his tradition, but denying love to a son in favor of a tradition has no honor.

6. In "Comrades," the young men have suffered as a result of prejudice. In "Marriage Is a Private Affair," Okeke's prejudice costs him a relationship with his son's family.

7. **Possible response:** Readers may identify with the young characters because they are breaking traditions that they feel do not work.

Answers continued

8. **Possible response:** Readers may suggest that they would not disown a son because he chose to marry a member of another ethnic group.

9. **Possible response:** A mediator might suggest the need for a concession from each character.

Go Online Students may use the **Self-test** to
Assessment prepare for **Selection Test A** or
Selection Test B.

❶ Vocabulary Lesson

**Word Analysis:
Greek Prefix *eu-***

1. a speech that praises someone
2. sweet sounding or melodious

Spelling Strategy

1. apostrophe   3. sorrowful
2. megaphone   4. graphite

Vocabulary Builder: Context

1. Yes; those inclined to eat fish would try salmon.
2. Yes; one should show a queen courteous respect.
3. No; Lee would need to give the materials more attention.
4. Yes; you will be busy completing those tasks that you agreed to do.
5. No; a phone call conducted in a sneaky manner would be difficult to hear.
6. No; Mike will not play a game he intensely dislikes.
7. Yes; the disclosure of a password would make access easier.
8. Yes; such indirect phrases would not offend.

❷ Grammar and Style Lesson

1. what was in the refrigerator; direct object
2. how nicely she kept her home; direct object
3. what she knows; direct object
4. that the letter would change his feelings; direct object
5. why she was upset; direct object

Writing Application

Possible response: Nnaemeka knew *that his father would be upset by the news of his marriage to Nene.* Later, Nene wrote in a letter *that her sons wanted to meet their grandfather.*

Build Language Skills

❶ Vocabulary Lesson

Word Analysis: Greek Prefix *eu-*

The prefix *eu-* means "good" or "well." Use the clues in parentheses and your knowledge of the meaning of the prefix *eu-* to write a definition of both words below.

1. eulogy (*-logy* = word or speech)
2. euphonious (*-phonious* = sounding)

Spelling Strategy

In many English words of Greek origin, *ph* is used to spell the *f* sound, as in *euphemism, telephone,* and *graph.* For each of the following pairs, choose the correct spelling.

1. apostrofe/apostrophe
2. megafone/megaphone
3. sorrowful/sorrowphul
4. grafite/graphite

Vocabulary Builder: Context

Answer *yes* or *no* to each question below. Explain each response.

1. If you are *disposed* to eating fish, would you try salmon?
2. Is *deference* proper when meeting a queen?
3. If Lee studies *perfunctorily,* can she expect to earn an A?
4. If you *assent* to more, will you be busier?
5. Could a phone call made *furtively* be easily overheard?
6. If Mike *vehemently* dislikes soccer, will he choose to play the game?
7. Would the *revelation* of a password help you gain access to something?
8. Could you use *euphemisms* to avoid disturbing someone?

❷ Grammar and Style Lesson

Noun Clauses

A subordinate clause is a group of words with a subject and a verb that cannot stand by itself as a complete sentence. A **noun clause** is a subordinate clause that functions as a noun. It can serve as the subject of a verb, a direct object, or the object of a preposition. Noun clauses are often introduced by the words *that, what, which, how,* and *why.*

> **Subject:** "<u>What one looks for in a wife</u> are a good character and a Christian background."
>
> **Direct Object:** They're not going to be saying . . . <u>that they're off on a student tour in Europe</u>.

Practice For each item below, identify the noun clause and explain its function in the sentence.

1. She went to the kitchen to see what was in the refrigerator.
2. The women saw how nicely she kept her home.
3. She cannot believe what she knows.
4. She did not know that the letter would change his feelings.
5. He understood why she was upset.

Writing Application Write a summary of the events in one of these stories. Include at least two noun clauses.

W͞G *Prentice Hall Writing and Grammar Connection: Platinum Level, Chapter 20, Section 2*

Assessment Practice

Using Context Clues to Determine Meanings

(For more practice, see *Test Preparation Workbook,* p. 3.)

The reading sections of many tests require students to use context clues to determine the appropriate meaning of a word in a given passage. Use the following sample test item to demonstrate.

These large gatherings both excited and left her overexposed, open and <u>vulnerable</u> to the rub and twitch of the mass shuffling across rows of seats and loping up the aisles. . . .

In this passage, the word <u>vulnerable</u> most nearly means—

A impolite.   C respected.
B sensitive.   D strong.

Answers *A, C,* and *D* do not make sense within the context of the sentence. Two words— *overexposed* and *open*—suggest a sensitivity to being hurt and act as clues to the meaning of *vulnerable. B* is the correct answer.

❸ Writing Lesson

Manual on How to Change a Story's Atmosphere

Gordimer uses precise descriptive details to create an intense and vivid atmosphere in "Comrades." Using her story as an example, write a manual for young authors on how to create various types of atmosphere in a story.

Prewriting Reread "Comrades" and list details Gordimer uses to create a tense atmosphere. Then, brainstorm for other types of atmosphere that a story might create and the kinds of details that would be effective.

Drafting Explain the concept of atmosphere. Follow with three sections, each of which describes how to create a different type of atmosphere and provides examples. Introduce each example.

Model: Drafting to Introduce Example Text

For example, notice how altered details change the

atmosphere from one of tension to one of friendliness:

Original Text: The others got in the back, the spokesman

beside her. She saw the nervous white of his eyes.

New Text: The others tumbled into the back, the

spokesman beside her. She saw weary gratitude in his

eyes as he sent her a silent *thanks*.

> A clear introduction to an example clarifies its purpose.

Revising As you review your work, make sure that your examples clearly evoke the types of atmospheres you specify. Consider altering details as needed to create the desired effect.

W̶G Prentice Hall Writing and Grammar Connection: Platinum Level, Chapter 6, Section 2

❹ Extend Your Learning

Listening and Speaking With a small group, write and perform a **dramatization** of a scene from "Comrades." Use these tips to prepare:

- As a group, choose a scene to dramatize.
- Review the scene, noting details that suggest characters' posture and attitudes.
- Write the dramatization in script form.

Use both dialogue and body language to re-create the story's tension. [**Group Activity**]

Research and Technology Conduct research on the nation of Nigeria. Focus your research by organizing it into the following categories: geography; population; economy; art and culture; and history. Share your findings in a five-minute **presentation** for the class.

Go Online
Research

For: An additional research activity
Visit: www.PHSchool.com
Web Code: etd-7909

Comrades / Marriage Is a Private Affair ■ 1337

---

❸ Writing Lesson

- To give students guidance in writing this manual, give them the **Support for Writing Lesson**, p. 162 in *Unit 9 Resources*.

- Remind students that a manual should give directions in a logical, step-by-step fashion. Each set of instructions should be followed by clear examples.

- If students have difficulty brainstorming types of atmosphere, get them started by listing moods and atmospheres such as joyful, mysterious, and sorrowful.

W̶G Writing and Grammar Platinum Level

For support in teaching the Writing Lesson, use Chapter 6, Section 2.

❹ Listening and Speaking

- Organize students into groups of three or four. Consider assigning sequential scenes to the groups so that they can recreate the narrative of the story.

- Remind students as they review their scenes to consider dialogue separately from action. Suggest that students act out the scenes without spoken dialogue in order to hone their body language.

- The **Support for Extend Your Learning** page (*Unit 9 Resources*, p. 163) provides guided note-taking opportunities to help students complete the Extend Your Learning activities.

Go Online Have students type in the
Research Web Code for another research activity.

Assessment Resources

The following resources can be used to assess students' knowledge and skills.

Unit 9 Resources
Selection Test A, pp. 165–167
Selection Test B, pp. 168–170

Go Online Students may use the **Self-test** to
Assessment prepare for **Selection Test A** or
Selection Test B.

Chinua Achebe

- Have students read Achebe's comments on these pages.

- Point out that Chinua Achebe lived in Nigeria prior to Nigeria's independence from Great Britain.

- **Ask** students why many Nigerians might have wanted British colonial rule to end.
  Possible response: The British imposed European values and culture on Nigeria without respecting Nigeria's people and their ways of life.

- **Ask:** What does Nnaemeka underestimate in the story?
  Answer: He underestimates the strength of the opposition of his people toward his marriage.

A Generation That Changed

- Point out that people in any culture may have a variety of opinions about a treasured cultural tradition.

- **Ask** students why the grandchildren were able to change the mind of Nnaemeka's father about the excommunication of his family.
  Possible response: Nnaemeka's father may have realized that the grandchildren bear no responsibility for the family conflict and may suffer from the excommunication.

CHINUA ACHEBE DISCUSSES
"Marriage Is a Private Affair"

A Generation That Changed

This short story is one of the two earliest works of fiction I ever published. Reading it again today, half a century later, I can recognize myself and my generation in the raw energy and unwavering conviction of the plot. I hope at least some of my fellow students at the University would have recognized something of themselves and their times in Nnaemeka and Nene and their story. Change was in the air because the country was on the threshold of freedom from British colonial rule. Young, educated people in particular were eagerly and confidently awaiting the event. They saw themselves as the "new people" who would right the many wrongs of the past. "Marriage Is a Private Affair" is more than the title of a story; it is like a proclamation emblazoned on the placard of the new generation, "marching as to war."

On Understanding Culture The strength of the opposition Nnaemeka encountered from his people on his marriage caught him unawares because he and Nene did not understand how complex their society really was. This is particularly true of Nene, as the reader can see clearly in her lighthearted remarks at the beginning of the story. Nnaemeka is much better grounded in their culture, but even he is still something of an alien in his father's village. Although the story does not raise it we may reasonably marvel at the kind of education they must have received under colonial rule.

A "Conflict of Cultures" A story like "Marriage Is a Private Affair" is sometimes described as a "conflict of cultures" story. But we must be careful not to be misled into thinking in a simple way of two antagonistic cultures facing each other, one ancient, the other modern; or one African and the other European. Such a view would be simplistic and would miss the rich complexity before us in the story. We would miss the fact, for instance, that the small crowd of fellow villagers who assemble to commiserate with Nnaemeka's father in his grief are not all of one heart and one mind, but reveal an amazing variety of beliefs and attitudes. Nnaemeka's father himself is a combination of conservative Christian persuasion and traditional African beliefs.

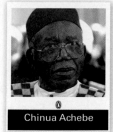
Chinua Achebe

Nominated for the Nobel Prize in Literature in 2000, Achebe has written the celebrated *Things Fall Apart* (1958) and *Anthills of the Savannah* (1987).

Change of Heart and Mind After many bitter years and much suffering caused largely by ignorance and rigidity, Nnaemeka's father suddenly withdraws his excommunication of his son, daughter-in-law, and grandchildren. The irony of the old man's change of mind is that it is not brought about by either of the primary combatants but by totally innocent parties—the grandchildren, assisted by the weather! This surprising resolution of the conflict may well reflect the power attributed to grandchildren in African culture. This power, in turn, may derive from the belief that a parent cannot be reincarnated in his or her children but in the grandchildren

I hope nobody is going to tell me that this is nothing but African superstition. For me it is one more example of mankind's attempt through metaphor and symbol to understand and account for the mysteries of our existence. One of the best jokes I have heard in America is about an elderly man playing in the front yard of his suburban home with two lively grandchildren and pausing, breathless, to say to a neighbor: "If I'd known grandchildren were this fun I'd have had them first."

One hopes that Nnaemeka's father would be saying similar words to his neighbors.

▲ **Critical Viewing**
What messages about life and love are symbolized in this simple image?
[Interpret]

Thinking About the Commentary

1. **(a) Recall:** According to Achebe, which characters did he hope his fellow university students would recognize? **(b) Infer:** In what way does Achebe's essay reveal a tenderness for Nnaemeka's father? **(c) Speculate:** Why might Achebe now identify with Nnaemeka's father?

2. **(a) Recall:** According to the essay, in what form might a parent be reincarnated? **(b) Make a Judgment:** Does this cultural belief make Nnaemeka's father more worthy of the sympathy of readers? Explain.

As You Think About "Marriage is a Private Affair"...

3. **(a) Recall:** What hope does Achebe hold for Nnaemeka's father? **(b) Take a Stand:** Do you share Achebe's optimism? Why or why not?

From the Author's Desk: Chinua Achebe ■ *1339*

Critical Viewing

Possible response: The image of clasped hands symbolizes the strength and mutual support offered in love and friendship, and it is often a gesture that represents the resolution of conflict.

ASSESS
Answers

1. (a) He hopes that they would recognize something of themselves in the characters of Nnaemeka and Nene. (b) Achebe respectfully depicts the father as both loving his son and struggling with the pull of cherished cultural traditions. (c) **Possible response:** Achebe may be a grandfather at this point and may have gained similar wisdom as he has matured.

2. (a) A parent might be reincarnated in a grandchild. (b) This cultural belief may correspond with some readers' views of grandchildren. Consequently, readers can identify with the father and applaud his withdrawal of the excommunication.

3. (a) He hopes that the old man will fully embrace the lives of his grandchildren, son, and daughter-in-law. (b) **Possible response:** Students may say that they share Achebe's optimism. The father has already experienced a profound change and most likely will be involved in the lives of his grandchildren for the remainder of his life.

Standard Course of Study

Goal 1: WRITTEN LANGUAGE

WL.1.02.4 Explain how culture affects personal responses.

Goal 2: INFORMATIONAL READING

IR.2.01.7 Analyze influences, contexts, or biases in research texts.

Goal 4: CRITICAL THINKING

CT.4.02.1 Show an understanding of cultural context in analyzing thematic connections.

Goal 5: LITERATURE

LT.5.01.2 Build knowledge of literary genres, and explore how characteristics apply to literature of world cultures.

LT.5.01.6 Make connections between historical and contemporary issues in world literature.

Goal 6: GRAMMAR AND USAGE

GU.6.02.3 Edit for parallel structure.

Step-by-Step Teaching Guide	Pacing Guide
PRETEACH	
• Administer Vocabulary and Reading Warm-ups as necessary.	5 min.
• Engage students' interest with the motivation activity.	5 min.
• Read and discuss author and background features. **FT**	10 min.
• Introduce the Literary Analysis Skill: Political Poetry. **FT**	5 min.
• Introduce the Reading Strategy: Connecting to Historical Context. **FT**	
• Prepare students to read by teaching the selection vocabulary. **FT**	10 min.
TEACH	
• Informally monitor comprehension while students read independently or in groups. **FT**	30 min.
• Monitor students' comprehension with the Reading Check notes.	as students read
• Reinforce vocabulary with Vocabulary Builder notes.	as students read
• Develop students' understanding of political poetry with the Literary Analysis annotations. **FT**	5 min.
• Develop students' ability to connect to historical context with the Reading Strategy annotations. **FT**	5 min.
ASSESS/EXTEND	
• Assess students' comprehension and mastery of the Literary Analysis and Reading Strategy by having them answer the Apply the Skills questions. **FT**	15 min.
• Have students complete the Vocabulary Lesson and the Grammar and Style Lesson. **FT**	15 min.
• Apply students' ability to combine sentences for variety by using the Writing Lesson. **FT**	45 min. or homework
• Apply students' understanding by using one or more of the Extend Your Learning activities.	20–90 min. or homework
• Administer Selection Test A or Selection Test B. **FT**	15 min.

Resources

Print
Unit 9 Resources
Transparency
Graphic Organizer Transparencies

Print
Reader's Notebook [L2]

Reader's Notebook: Adapted Version [L1]

Reader's Notebook: English Learner's Version [EL]

Unit 9 Resources
Technology
Listening to Literature Audio CDs [L2, EL]

Print
Unit 9 Resources
General Resources
Technology
Go Online: Research **[L3]**
Go Online: Self-test **[L3]**
ExamView®, Test Bank **[L3]**

Choosing Resources for Differentiated Instruction

[L1] Special Needs Students

[L2] Below-Level Students

[L3] All Students

[L4] Advanced Students

[EL] English Learners

For Vocabulary and Reading Warm-ups and for Selection Tests, **A** signifies "less challenging" and **B** "more challenging." For Graphic Organizer transparencies, **A** signifies "not filled in" and **B** "filled in."

FT Fast Track Instruction: To move the lesson more quickly, use the strategies and activities identified with **FT**.

Scaffolding for Less Proficient and Advanced Students

The leveled Critical Thinking questions after selections progress in the levels of thinking required to answer them. To address the needs of your different students, you may use the (a) level questions for your less proficient students and the (b) level questions with your on-level and advanced students. The occasional (c) level questions are appropriate for your advanced students.

PRENTICE HALL
Teacher EXPRESS™ Use this complete
Plan · Teach · Assess suite of powerful
teaching tools to make lesson planning and testing quicker and easier.

PRENTICE HALL
Student EXPRESS™ Use the interactive
Learn · Study · Succeed textbook (online
and on CD-ROM) to make selections and activities come alive with audio and video support and interactive questions.

Benchmark

After students have completed reading these selections, administer **Benchmark Test 12 (*Unit 9 Resources,* pp. 195–200).** If the Benchmark Test reveals that some of the students need further work, use the **Interpretation Guide** to determine the appropriate reteaching page in the **Reading Kit** and on **Success Tracker.**

 For: Information about Lexiles
Professional **Visit:** www.PHSchool.com
Development **Web Code:** eue-1111

Motivation

Discuss with students what they know about the United States Civil War. Then, tell them that Nguyen Thi Vinh describes a civil war in Vietnam that split families and forced brothers to fight brothers. To draw students into the selections from China, tell them about the 1989 Tiananmen Square massacre, in which students in Beijing protested government tactics. In response, the Chinese government shot hundreds of young people. With the class, compare and contrast civil wars and protest movements students have heard of, such as the civil rights movement in the United States and the anti-apartheid movement in South Africa.

❶ Background

More About the Authors

Until 1975, Nguyen Thi Vinh served as editor-in-chief of the journal *New Wind* and director of the magazine *The East.* She is a well-educated poet writing in an accessible style and about accessible subjects.

Bei Dao's family was from the region of Shanghai and the lower Chang River valley, which was both a center of traditional Chinese civilization and a region under the influence of the West. Bei Dao draws on Chinese and Western traditions in his work.

Shu Ting is the pen name of Gong Peiyu. In 1981 and 1983, she received China's National Poetry Award.

Geography Note

Draw students' attention to the map on this page, and point out China and Vietnam. The Vietnamese literary tradition grew from Chinese influences. Thus, early Vietnamese poetry often reflected Confucian beliefs and was considered an exercise for rulers and scholars.

Thoughts of Hanoi • All • Also All • Assembly Line ❶

Nguyen Thi Vinh (b. 1924)

Nguyen Thi Vinh (nōō´ yin tǐ vin) was born in Ha Dong Province in the Red River Delta of North Vietnam. She is a novelist, poet, and editor, but most of all she is a writer of short stories. Her first and most famous work is the novel *Two Sisters,* published in 1953. She is also the author of six other books of fiction, as well as a collection of poetry.

In 1954, the country of Vietnam was divided into two independent countries: communist North Vietnam and democratic South Vietnam. Prior to the installation of the communist government in the North, nearly one million North Vietnamese fled south. Among these was Nguyen Thi Vinh. In 1975, North Vietnam defeated South Vietnam and invaded Saigon, the country's capital. Up until that moment, Nguyen had been a prominent member of the Saigon community of writers. After the fall of Saigon, she remained in Vietnam but refused to play any public role. In 1983, Nguyen joined her family in Norway, thus becoming a refugee once again.

Bei Dao (b. 1949)

Bei Dao (bā dou) was born just two months before China's communists founded the People's Republic. He attended one of China's best schools and seemed destined for a position in the communist bureaucracy. Instead, in 1965, he became a member of the Red Guard, the quasi-military group that enforced the Cultural Revolution. At first, this movement sought to revitalize revolutionary fervor, but it soon degenerated into wholesale persecution of artists, teachers, and intellectuals.

Disillusioned, Bei Dao turned to poetry. Bold, questioning, and vivid, his poems express a deep dissatisfaction with Chinese society. Eventually, he became associated with a like-minded group of writers called the Misty Poets.

When a new wave of discontent swept China in 1976, Bei Dao's poem "Answer" became a rallying cry for change. In 1978, students set up large bulletin boards in public spaces, where they posted dissident writings. This unusual form of publication became known as the Democracy Wall Movement, and it brought Bei Dao's work to a wide audience.

During the Tiananmen Square massacre in 1989, Bei Dao was traveling abroad. The period of repression that followed the massacre prevented his return home. Today, he lives and works in the West, separated from his wife and daughter, who remain in China.

Shu Ting (b. 1952)

Shu Ting (shōō tin) was born in Jinjiang County of Fujian Province. Still in middle school during China's Cultural Revolution, she was forced to leave her home, abandon her education, and go to live in a small, impoverished peasant village. When she returned to Fujian in 1973, she worked on construction sites and in factories. In spite of these experiences, she began writing poetry and, while still in her twenties, gained nationwide fame as a poet. Shu Ting became associated with the Misty Poets when her work appeared in the underground literary magazine *Today.* Shu Ting still lives in China, in the seaport city of Xiamen.

1340 ■ *The Contemporary World*

Preview

Connecting to the Literature

If you are like most American students, you had no direct experience of political violence before September 11, 2001. Think of what life must be like for people who face the ravages of war daily, whose right to free speech is stifled. The authors of these poems offer some insights.

❷ Literary Analysis

Political Poetry

Political poetry connects the realm of private emotion to the political or social arena. While political poems often tell stories and express personal feelings, they are written in reaction to political events or as commentary about a political situation. For example, in "Thoughts of Hanoi," the speaker expresses the personal pain caused by the Vietnam War:

> Brother, I am afraid
> that one day I'll be with the March-North Army
> meeting you on your way to the South.
> I might be the one to shoot you then. . . .

As you read these poems, think about how each one examines the effects of political events or conditions on the private lives of individuals.

Comparing Literary Works

People respond to the suffering caused by war or repression in different ways. Some become hopeless, while others hold on to a belief in the human spirit. As you read these poems, compare each speaker's attitude toward both the sufferings of the present and the promise of the future.

❸ Reading Strategy

Connecting to Historical Context

Political poems will carry deeper meaning for you if you **connect to the historical context** that they reflect. Use a chart like the one shown to list details from each poem that pertain to the historical situation from which it arose. Then, form an overall sense of the writer's message. Use the poets' biographies and the background notes to help you as you read.

Vocabulary Builder

jubilant (jo͞oʹ bə lənt) *adj.* extremely happy; exultant (p. 1344)

obsolete (äbʹ sə lētʹ) *adj.* out of date; out of use (p. 1345)

lamentation (lamʹ ən tāʹ shən) *n.* outward expression of grief; weeping or wailing (p. 1346)

heralds (herʹ əldz) *v.* announces; introduces (p. 1346)

reverberates (ri vʉrʹ bə rātzʹ) *v.* echoes; sounds again (p. 1346)

chasm (kazʹ əm) *n.* deep crack in Earth's surface (p. 1347)

monotony (mə nätʹ ʹn ē) *n.* tedious sameness (p. 1348)

tempo (temʹ pō) *n.* rate of speed; pace (p. 1348)

Standard Course of Study

- Explain how culture affects personal responses. (WL.1.02.4)
- Show an understanding of cultural context in analyzing thematic connections. (CT.4.02.1)

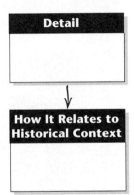

Thoughts of Hanoi / All / Also All / Assembly Line ■ 1341

---

❷ Literary Analysis

Political Poetry

- After reading aloud the Literary Analysis instruction, remind students that political poetry often protests injustice or oppression. Explain that political poetry may protest specific government policies, such as the oppression of free speech, or more general cultural injustices, such as racism or sexism.

- Tell students that political speech is dangerous in some countries. Students may find the political criticism within poems such as "All" indirect, because the poems use images and allusions instead of direct speech.

❸ Reading Strategy

Connecting to Historical Context

- Have a volunteer read aloud the Reading Strategy instruction. Explain that knowing historical context can help a reader understand the thoughts, feelings, and images presented in a work.

- Present students with these lines from "Thoughts of Hanoi": "Brother, I am afraid / that one day I'll be with the March-North Army / meeting you on your way to the South."

- Set the historical context for these lines by explaining that the poem refers to Vietnam's division into democratic South Vietnam and communist North Vietnam.

- Explain the use of the graphic organizer. Then, give students a copy of **Reading Strategy Graphic Organizer A**, p. 237 in *Graphic Organizer Transparencies.* Encourage students to use it to make connections between a poem's details and the historical situation from which it arose.

Vocabulary Builder

- Pronounce each vocabulary word for students, and read the definitions as a class. Have students identify any words with which they are familiar.

Facilitate Understanding

Ask students to discuss which of the visual images in "Thoughts of Hanoi" is most memorable, vivid, and realistic. Lead students to see why an image is memorable or vivid so that they can apply this knowledge in their own writing.

❶ About the Selection

In "Thoughts of Hanoi," a speaker who has fled North Vietnam for South Vietnam asks a former peacetime friend about beloved places in Hanoi, and wonders whether the war will force him or her to face this friend as an enemy.

❷ Humanities

Morning Rain, by Bich Nguyet

With its intense use of color and aggressive brush strokes, this painting by Vietnamese artist Bich Nguyet (b. 1956) creates a bold image of figures caught in a downpour.

Use the following questions to stimulate discussion.

How would you describe the mood of this painting? What details or techniques create this mood?
Possible response: The mood of this painting is melancholy. The varying hues of blue and obscured background create this mood.

❸ Critical Viewing

Possible response: Yes; the scene might recall a happy memory for the speaker. The speaker fondly remembers ordinary events before the war.

THOUGHTS OF HANOI
❶

— Nguyen Thi Vinh

translated by Nguyen Ngoc Bich *with* Burton Raffel *and* W. S. Merwin

❷

Morning Rain, 2001, Bich Nguyet, Courtesy of Galeria La Vong Ltd.

❸ ▲ **Critical Viewing** Does this scene of people in the morning rain seem like a memory for which the speaker of this poem might yearn? Why or why not? **[Connect]**

1342 ■ *The Contemporary World*

Differentiated Instruction   Solutions for All Learners

Accessibility at a Glance

	Thoughts of Hanoi	All	Also All	Assembly Line
Context	Civil War in Vietnam	Chinese Cultural Revolution	Chinese Cultural Revolution	Chinese Cultural Revolution
Language	Words of personal pain and yearning	Adjectives that describe emotions	Words negating the message of "All" and suggesting hope	Words suggesting monotony and drudgery
Concept Level	Accessible (burdens of war)	Accessible (Oppression leads to hopelessness.)	Accessible (the value of hope)	Accessible (the effects of treating workers like machines)
Literary Merit	Political poem	Political poem	Political poem	Political poem
Lexile	NP	NP	NP	NP
Overall Rating	Average	More Challenging	More Accessible	Average

Background Vietnam was a colony of France until 1954, when the French suffered a major defeat at the hands of Vietnamese insurgent leader Ho Chi Minh. A cease-fire agreement divided the country into communist North Vietnam and democratic South Vietnam, with Ho ruling the North from Hanoi. The cease-fire called for elections to determine the fate of the country, but they were never held. Ho Chi Minh's troops, who were supported by Russia and China, battled the South Vietnamese government and its American backers. In the war that ensued, members of the same family sometimes fought on different sides. It was in this climate that Nguyen Thi Vinh wrote "Thoughts of Hanoi," her personal lyric about the Vietnam War from the perspective of a North Vietnamese living in the South.

The night is deep and chill
as in early autumn. Pitchblack,
it thickens after each lightning flash.
I dream of Hanoi:
5   Co-ngu[1] Road
ten years of separation
the way back sliced by a frontier of hatred.

❹ I want to bury the past
to burn the future
10   still I yearn
still I fear
those endless nights
waiting for dawn.

Brother,
15   how is Hang Dao[2] now?
How is Ngoc Son[3] temple?
❺ Do the trains still run
each day from Hanoi
to the neighboring towns?
20   To Bac-ninh, Cam-giang, Yen-bai,[4]
the small villages, islands
of brown thatch in a lush green sea?

The girls
     bright eyes
25   ruddy cheeks
     four-piece dresses

---

1. **Co-ngu** (cô gōō)
2. **Hang Dao** (häŋ dou)
3. **Ngoc Son** (nōk sōn)
4. **Bac-ninh** (bäk nin), **Cam-giang** (käm gyäŋ), **Yen-bai** (ēŋ bǐ)

Reading Strategy
Connecting to Historical Context What "past" do you think the speaker wishes to "bury"?

❻ 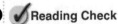 **Reading Check**
For how many years has the speaker been away from Hanoi?

Thoughts of Hanoi ■ 1343

❹ Reading Strategy
Connecting to Historical Context

- Explain that Nyugen's reference in line 6 to "ten years of separation" (the separation between North Vietnam and South Vietnam) indicates that this poem was written in the early 1970s.

- Have students read the bracketed line independently. Then, **ask** the Reading Strategy question: What "past" do you think the speaker wishes to "bury"?
Possible response: The speaker wants to bury Vietnam's internal conflict.

▶ **Monitor Progress Ask** students to explain the speaker's probable situation in the first stanza, given the historical context.
Answer: Because of the war between North and South Vietnam, the speaker cannot return to Hanoi, the capital of the North.

▶ **Reteach** To help students understand the connections between historical context and a work's larger meaning, have them use the **Reading Strategy** support, p. 176 in *Unit 9 Resources.*

❺ Critical Thinking
Infer

- Read aloud the bracketed passage. Then, **ask** students to make an inference about the poem's speaker.
Answer: The speaker is a Vietnamese person familiar with Hanoi. Because of the war, the speaker can no longer return to this familiar city and its people.

- **Ask** students: To whom does the speaker direct questions? Why does the speaker call the person "Brother"?
Answer: The person addressed is someone living in North Vietnam. The person is called "Brother" because the two are from the same place or are related either literally or symbolically.

❻ Reading Check
Answer: The speaker has been away from Hanoi for ten years.

❼ Humanities

Peacefulness, by Tran Nguyen Dan

Hanoi painter Tran Nguyen Dan (b. 1941) specializes in woodcuts depicting traditional Vietnamese scenes, such as festivals and temples. A graduate of the Hanoi College of Industrial Fine Arts, Tran Nguyen Dan has won numerous awards and has work exhibited in the Fine Arts Museum of Vietnam and the Asia-Pacific Museum of Poland.

Use the following questions for discussion:

• What elements of the poem does this woodcut illustrate?
Answer: The woodcut captures the tranquillity and beauty described in the poem. It also captures the sense of safety that the speaker describes prior to the war.

• What elements of the woodcut create a feeling of peace?
Possible response: The muted colors, harmonious figures, and sense of symmetry all create a feeling of peace.

❽ Critical Viewing

Possible response: The painting depicts serenity before the war.

❾ Critical Thinking

Analyze

• Ask a volunteer to read aloud the bracketed passage. Then, point out to students that in this passage, the speaker refers to several generations. Have students **identify** the words and phrases that indicate these generations.
Answer: The speaker refers to "children," "village graybeards," and "grandmothers."

• **Ask** students why the speaker includes these references.
Possible response: These references reinforce the feeling of community in Hanoi and the image the speaker has created. The speaker suggests that all—young and old—have been affected by the war.

❼

Peacefulness, Tran Nguyen Dan, Indochina Arts Project

❽ ◀ Critical Viewing
What image of Vietnamese society does this painting convey? **[Interpret]**

```
                    raven-bill scarves
               sowing harvesting
                    spinning weaving
30          all year round,
        the boys
               plowing
                    transplanting
        in the fields
35               in their shops
               running across
                    the meadow at evening
        to fly kites
                    and sing alternating songs.

40      Stainless blue sky,
                jubilant voices of children
        stumbling through the alphabet,
                village graybeards strolling to the temple,
        grandmothers basking in twilight sun,
45              chewing betel leaves
        while the children run—
```

Vocabulary Builder
jubilant (jo͞o′ bə lənt) *adj.* extremely happy; exultant

1344 ■ *The Contemporary World*

Enrichment

Hanoi

Originally called Long Bien, Hanoi was founded in the sixth century and briefly served as the country's capital. It became the capital again in the eleventh century. In 1831, the Nguyen dynasty renamed the city Hanoi, and in 1902 France made it the seat of the French Indochinese government.

When Vietnam was divided in 1954, Hanoi became the capital of North Vietnam. From 1965 to 1972, Hanoi was the target of frequent bombings that wiped out most of the city's factories and resources. Although most of

Hanoi was destroyed, the Vietnamese rebuilt the city, and it again became the capital when the country was reunited in 1976.

Located in the north on the Red River, Hanoi is the country's cultural center. It has been the hub of the country for decades, with rail connections to Saigon.

Before the war, Saigon was the capital of South Vietnam. Now a major industrial port of the Socialist Republic of Vietnam, Saigon was renamed Ho Chi Minh City in 1976.

Brother,
how is all that now?
Or is it <u>obsolete</u>?
50 Are you like me,
reliving the past,
imagining the future?
Do you count me as a friend
or am I the enemy in your eyes?
55 Brother, I am afraid
that one day I'll be with the March-North Army
meeting you on your way to the South.
I might be the one to shoot you then
or you me
60 but please
not with hatred.

For don't you remember how it was,
you and I in school together,
plotting our lives together?
65 Those roots go deep!

Brother, we are men,
conscious of more
than material needs.
How can this happen to us
70 my friend
my foe?

Vocabulary Builder
obsolete (äb′ sə lēt′) *adj.*
out of date; out of use

Literary Analysis
Political Poetry What truth about the people fighting the Vietnam War does this stanza express?

Critical Reading

1. **Respond:** Which images do you find the most vivid? Explain.
2. **(a) Recall:** In the first three lines, which details describe the night in which the speaker is dreaming? **(b) Generalize:** How would you describe the mood the speaker establishes in these lines?
3. **(a) Recall:** By what boundary does the speaker say the "way back" is sliced? **(b) Interpret:** Is this a physical boundary, an emotional boundary, or both? Explain.
4. **(a) Interpret:** Which experiences has the speaker shared with the "Brother"? Explain. **(b) Infer:** What emotional bond do these experiences suggest? **(c) Analyze:** How has that bond been tested by war?
5. **Take a Position:** While all war is terrible, do you think that civil war, like the one in Vietnam, is especially devastating? Why or why not?

Go Online
Author Link
For: More about Nguyen Thi Vinh
Visit: www.PHSchool.com
Web Code: ete-9915

Thoughts of Hanoi ■ 1345

❿ Literary Analysis
Political Poetry

- Have a volunteer read aloud the bracketed passage. Then, **ask:** How does Nguyen focus on the individual in this passage?
  Possible response: The question format suggests a personal exchange between the speaker and the "Brother." The use of "me" and "I" emphasizes individual identity.
- **Ask** students the Literary Analysis question: What truth about the people fighting the Vietnam War does this stanza express?
  Answer: Friends, neighbors, and family members often fought on opposing sides. Despite political differences, these people continued to care about one another.

ASSESS
Answers

1. **Possible response:** The image of two friends, or brothers, marching toward one another in battle depicts the personal anguish of war.
2. (a) The "night is deep and chill"; the season is autumn. Lightning strikes in a "pitchblack" sky.
   (b) **Possible response:** The speaker establishes a foreboding mood.
3. (a) The "way back" is sliced "by a frontier of hatred." (b) Both; the geographical boundary reflects the ideological differences within Vietnam.
4. (a) The two attended school and planned their lives together. (b) The two shared childhood experiences and have the emotional bond of siblings. (c) The war calls into question whether they are personal friends or political enemies.
5. **Possible response:** Yes; instead of uniting against a common enemy, friends and families may become political enemies.

Go Online For additional information
Author Link about Nguyen Thi Vinh, have students type in the Web Code, then select *V* from the alphabet, and then select Nguyen Thi Vinh.

Differentiated Instruction   Solutions for All Learners

Support for Less Proficient Readers
Read aloud the last two stanzas of the poem as students follow along. Help students identify the four complete sentences that make up these stanzas by pointing out that the author asks two questions, makes one exclamation, and makes one statement. Remind students that political poetry connects the realm of private emotion to the political or social arena. On the board, write the four sentences, and ask students to consider what emotion is behind each.

Enrichment for Advanced Readers
Tell students that Vietnamese literature is continually being translated from French and Vietnamese into English. Challenge them to read other Vietnamese selections. Then, ask students to share in oral presentations their readings and their discoveries about Vietnam and Vietnamese culture.

⓫ About the Selections

In "All," Bei Dao criticizes a repressive Chinese regime for taking away its citizens' hope and joy.

Shu Ting counters Bei Dao in "Also All." Her poem argues that China's people will succeed. It defends the power of hope and the promise of tomorrow.

⓬ Background
Gu Cheng

Gu Cheng was the youngest of the so-called Misty Poets. Because his father, Gu Gong, was a prominent poet, his family was forced to leave Beijing during the Cultural Revolution in the late 1960s. When Gu Cheng returned there in 1974, he earned his living as a carpenter and wrote poetry in his spare time.

Five years later, his first poems appeared in print, and he subsequently became one of the most respected poets writing in Chinese. In the years before his death, he lived in New Zealand; however, in 1992, he gave a series of readings in the United States.

⓭ Literary Analysis
Political Poetry

- Tell students that at the time the poem was written, China was ruled by a totalitarian government. The Communist party wielded absolute control over all aspects of Chinese citizens' lives and suppressed political and cultural expression.

- Explain to students how, in a country where private feelings are suspect, the expression of personal feelings in poetry could be viewed as a political act.

- Have students read the bracketed line. Then, **ask** the Literary Analysis question: Within the context of a repressive government, why might "every speech" be a "repetition"? **Possible response:** If people are not allowed to express their feelings or to disagree with government policy, every speech might praise the government and thus sound like a repetition of the same speech.

1346

All

⓫ Bei Dao   *translated by* Donald Finkel *and* Xueliang Chen

⓬ Background

In 1980, a Chinese poet named Gu Cheng published a poem that depicted two children in bright colors emerging from a world of gray. At that time, Chinese life was very regimented: People's jobs and even their style of dress were dictated by the state. Gu Cheng's poem seemed to criticize the dull grayness of that life and of the kind of literature the state prescribed: realistic, supportive of communism, and not subjective or personal. When a state literary critic attacked Gu Cheng's poem as "misty," Gu Cheng and some of his fellow poets adopted the term as a badge of honor, calling themselves the Misty Poets. Bei Dao and Shu Ting are two of the best known of the Misty Poets.

All is fated,
all cloudy,

all an endless beginning,
all a search for what vanishes,

5 all joys grave,
all griefs tearless,

⓭ | every speech a repetition,
every meeting a first encounter,

all love buried in the heart,
10 all history prisoned in a dream,

all hope hedged with doubt,
all faith drowned in <u>lamentation.</u>

Every explosion <u>heralds</u> an instant of stillness,
every death <u>reverberates</u> forever.

1346 ■ *The Contemporary World*

Literary Analysis
Political Poetry Within the context of a repressive government, why might "every speech" be a "repetition"?

Vocabulary Builder
lamentation (lam ən tā′ shən) *n.* outward expression of grief; weeping or wailing

heralds (her′ əldz) *v.* announces; introduces

reverberates (ri vʉr′ bə rātz′) *v.* echoes; sounds again

Enrichment

The Misty Poets

The Misty Poets, including Bei Dao and Shu Ting, took as their model neither traditional Chinese poetry nor the "gray" literature of communism. Instead, they patterned their work after Western poets like Baudelaire and Sylvia Plath, writers known for their surprising images and highly personal emotions.

In the late 1980s, people in China challenged totalitarian rule and demanded a say in their government, as they had in 1976. The new poets fueled these yearnings—even though,

to a North American reader, some of their poems may not seem openly political. Living in a society that places a high value on conformity, the Misty Poets continued to find a way to express their individuality through vivid images that convey raw emotions. The inclusion of these elements alone would be enough to place the poets in conflict with their country's rulers; however, they continue to challenge—directly or indirectly—the communist bureaucracy.

Also All
In Answer to Bei Dao's "All"

Shu Ting   *translated by* Donald Finkel *and* Jinsheng Yi

Not all trees are felled by storms.
Not every seed finds barren soil.
Not all the wings of dream are broken,
nor is all affection doomed
5   to wither in a desolate heart.

No, not all is as you say.

Not all flames consume themselves,
shedding no light on other lives.
Not all stars announce the night
10   and never dawn. Not every song
will drift past every ear and heart.

No, not all is as you say.

Not every cry for help is silenced,
nor every loss beyond recall.
15   Not every chasm spells disaster.
Not only the weak will be brought to their knees,
nor every soul be trodden under.

It won't all end in tears and blood.
Today is heavy with tomorrow—
20   the future was planted yesterday.
Hope is a burden all of us shoulder
though we might stumble under the load.

Literary Analysis
Political Poetry Which people in Chinese society might the speaker be describing as "flames"? Explain.

Vocabulary Builder
chasm (kaz´ əm) *n.* deep crack in Earth's surface

Critical Reading

1. **(a) Recall:** In lines 5–6 of "All," which adjective describes "joys"? **(b) Recall:** Which adjective describes "griefs"? **(c) Analyze:** What is the speaker saying about the kinds of emotions that are possible in a repressive society? Explain.

2. **(a) Recall:** According to the subtitle of "Also All," to whom and to what is the speaker responding in this poem? **(b) Generalize:** Which repeated line suggests the poet's motivation for writing this poem?

3. **Make a Judgment:** Do you think "Also All" can be read independently of "All" and still carry the same meaning? Why or why not?

Author Link

For: More about Bei Dao and Shu Ting
Visit: www.PHSchool.com
Web Code: ete-9916

Also All ■ 1347

Differentiated Instruction   Solutions for All Learners

Strategy for Special Needs Students
On the board, draw a two-column chart, labeling one column *Resignation* and one *Hope.* Have students choose a line from "All" that shows resignation, such as "all cloudy" and explain what the line means. Record comments in the first column. Then, have students choose a line from "Also All" that offers hope, such as "Not all the wings of dream are broken" and explain what the line means. Record comments in the second column.

Strategy for Gifted/Talented Students
Have students work in pairs to act out an exchange between Bei Dao and Shu Ting in which the poets explain their reasons for writing "All" and "Also All" and their reasons for presenting images of discouragement and hope. Encourage students to base their statements on what they have learned about this historical period so that they can speak knowledgeably about Chinese politics and political poetry of the time. Then, ask volunteers to to present short "debates" between the two authors.

---

⑭ Literary Analysis
Political Poetry

• Read aloud the bracketed passage. Make sure that students understand that the image of the flame is a metaphor for certain kinds of people. **Ask:** What kind of person would shed light "on other lives"? **Possible response:** Someone whose behavior is inspiring would shed light on other lives.

• **Ask** students the Literary Analysis question: Which people in Chinese society might the speaker be describing as "flames"? Explain. **Possible response:** "Flames" might be student leaders, protesters, or even poets who inspire action.

⑮ Critical Thinking
Compare and Contrast

• Have students read independently the last four lines of "All." Then, have them read the second bracketed passage on this page.

• Have students **compare** and **contrast** the messages in the two passages. **Answer:** Bei Dao says that life is hopeless; Shu Ting says that everyone must have hope for the sake of the future.

ASSESS
Answers

1. (a) The adjective "grave" describes "joys." (b) The adjective "tearless" describes "griefs." (c) The speaker says that even ordinary emotions are distorted in a repressive society.

2. (a) The speaker is responding to Bei Dao's poem "All." (b) The line "No, not all is as you say" suggests Shu Ting's motivation.

3. **Possible responses:** Yes; "Also All" could stand alone because the negatives can be seen as poetic devices rather than refutations. No; Shu Ting's vision requires the contrast of Bei Dao's bleak hopelessness.

Go Online Author Link For additional information about Bei Dao and Shu Ting, have students type in the Web Code, then select the letter of the author's last name from the alphabet, and then select the author's name.

1347

1348

17 Reading Strategy

Connecting to Historical Context

• Have students read the bracketed passage independently. Then, have students **describe** assembly lines and suggest images associated with them.
Possible response: Assembly lines require workers to perform the same task in repetition. Assembly lines evoke images of monotony, boredom, drudgery, and conformity.

• **Ask** the Reading Strategy question: What does the first stanza suggest about the lives of Chinese citizens at this time?
Answer: Chinese citizens work long hours at dehumanizing jobs that dull the senses.

18 Vocabulary Builder

Latin Root *-temp-*

• Point out the word *tempo* and its definition. Tell students that *tempo* contains the Latin root *-temp-*, which is based on the Latin word meaning "time."

• Have students **use** dictionaries to find other words with the root *-temp*.
Possible responses: *Temporary, contemporary, temper,* and *temperance* all feature this root.

ASSESS

Answers

1. **Possible response:** Students may picture factory images or a foreboding night.

2. (a) The speaker notices stars and trees. (b) The speaker sees the trees and stars positioned as if on assembly lines. Adjectives that could apply to assembly lines and workers describe the stars and trees.

3. (a) **Possible response:** The speaker's fate is "manufactured" because it is controlled by the assembly line. (b) The speaker's humanity has been lost because the speaker thinks of himself or herself as a part of a machine.

---

16 Assembly Line

Shu Ting *translated by* Carolyn Kizer

In time's assembly line
Night presses against night.
We come off the factory night-shift
In line as we march towards home.
17 5   Over our heads in a row
The assembly line of stars
Stretches across the sky.
Beside us, little trees
Stand numb in assembly lines.

10   The stars must be exhausted
After thousands of years
Of journeys which never change.
The little trees are all sick,
Choked on smog and monotony,
15   Stripped of their color and shape.
It's not hard to feel for them;
18 │ We share the same tempo and rhythm.

Yes, I'm numb to my own existence
As if, like the trees and stars
20   —perhaps just out of habit
—perhaps just out of sorrow,
I'm unable to show concern
For my own manufactured fate.

Vocabulary Builder
monotony (mə nät´ 'n ē) *n.* tedious sameness

tempo (tem´ pō) *n.* rate of speed; pace

Critical Reading

1. **Respond:** Describe the mental picture you formed while reading this poem.
2. **(a) Recall:** In lines 6–9, what natural objects does the speaker notice?
   (b) Analyze: How are the speaker and the natural objects alike?
3. **(a) Analyze:** Why is the speaker's fate "manufactured"?
   (b) Analyze Cause and Effect: What is the speaker saying about the ways in which an "assembly line" existence harms the human spirit?

Go Online
Author Link
For: More about Shu Ting
Visit: www.PHSchool.com
Web Code: ete-9916

Go Online For additional information about
Author Link Shu Ting, have students type in the Web Code, then select *T* from the alphabet, and then select Shu Ting.

Apply the Skills

Thoughts of Hanoi • All • Also All • Assembly Line

Literary Analysis

Political Poetry

1. **(a)** Use a chart like the one shown to identify personal and political details in each poem. **(b)** Which poem speaks to a specific political event most directly? Explain.

	Thoughts of Hanoi	All	Also All	Assembly Line
Personal details				
Political details				

2. **(a)** How does each of these examples of **political poetry** express the speaker's powerlessness in the face of terrible circumstances? **(b)** How do these examples suggest the power of a single voice?

Comparing Literary Works

3. In lines 10–11 of "Thoughts of Hanoi," the speaker describes both yearning and fear. Which emotion is stronger in the poem? Explain.

4. **(a)** Cite images in "Also All" that present a balance between hope and destruction. **(b)** How are the emotions of yearning and fear that Nguyen expresses also expressed in the poems by Shu Ting? **(c)** Does Bei Dao convey a similar mix of emotions? Explain.

Reading Strategy

Connecting to Historical Context

5. What information in the poet's biography or the background helps you **connect to the historical context** of "Thoughts of Hanoi"? Explain.

6. Choose a single line from "All" or "Also All" that you think best expresses the historical context of China's repressive rule. Explain your choice.

Extend Understanding

7. **Social Studies Connection:** In what ways do you think works of literature can affect political or social change? Explain.

QuickReview

Political poetry is verse that is written in response to or as commentary about political events or circumstances.

To **connect to the historical context** as you read, decide how details in the poem reflect the specific circumstances of the political climate in which they were written.

Assessment
For: Self-test
Visit: www.PHSchool.com
Web Code: eta-6910

Go Online Students may use the **Self-test** to **Assessment** prepare for **Selection Test A** or **Selection Test B.**

Answers

1. (a) **Possible response:** **Thoughts: Personal:** going to school with "Brother"; **Political:** separation of North and South Vietnam; **All: Personal:** hopelessness; **Political:** oppressive government; **Also All: Personal:** hope; **Political:** activists working against the regime; **Assembly Line: Personal:** dehumanization of workers; **Political:** communist regime's control over citizens (b) "Thoughts of Hanoi" directly addresses the civil war in Vietnam. Another sample answer can be found on **Literary Analysis Graphic Organizer B,** p. 240 in *Graphic Organizer Transparencies.*

2. (a) "Thoughts of Hanoi" describes how the speaker may face a friend in war. "All" describes how a repressive government regulates the display of private emotions. "Also All" says that everyone bears the burden of hope. "Assembly Line" illustrates how people lose their humanity when they are treated like machines. (b) All voice discontent with political situations and call for change.

3. Yearning is stronger. The speaker spends most of the poem yearning for things and people.

4. (a) Images include "trees . . . felled by storms," "seed finds barren soil," "wings of dream," and "affection doomed." (b) **Possible response:** In "Also All," Shu Ting yearns when she refers to not "every loss beyond recall." In "Assembly Line," she expresses fear of dehumanization. (c) Bei Dao's poem argues that "all" hope and faith are beyond recovery.

5. **Possible response:** Like the poem's speaker, Nguyen was forced to leave North Vietnam and live in South Vietnam.

6. **Possible response:** The line "every speech a repetition" best expresses the historical context of China's repression. Every speech could be only a "repetition" of accepted policies.

7. **Possible response:** Literature encourages citizens to see that others share their dissatisfaction and calls them to action.

1349

❶ Vocabulary Lesson

**Word Analysis:
Latin Root -temp-**

1. c   2. a   3. b

Spelling Strategy

1. chemistry   2. chaotic

**Vocabulary Builder:
Synonyms or Antonyms?**

1. antonyms   5. synonyms
2. synonyms   6. synonyms
3. antonyms   7. antonyms
4. antonyms   8. antonyms

❷ Grammar and Style Lesson

1. parallel construction and repetition of "still I"

2. parallel construction and repetition of "perhaps just out of"

3. parallel construction of phrases using present participles ("strolling," "basking")

4. parallel construction with parallel use of past participles ("buried, prisoned") and repetition of "all"

5. parallel construction with participial phrases using past participles ("choked," "stripped")

Writing Application

Possible response:
We remember our country united and free, then:
We pause and smile.
We pause and weep.

〽️ Writing and Grammar
Platinum Level

For support in teaching the Grammar and Style Lesson, use Chapter 21, Section 4.

Build Language Skills

❶ Vocabulary Lesson

Word Analysis: Latin Root -temp-

Some time-related words in English contain the root -temp-, which is based on the Latin word *tempus,* meaning *time.* Thus, *tempo* refers to a rate of speed. Use your knowledge of the root to match each word below with its definition.

1. temporal   a. delay; evade

2. temporize   b. done without preparation

3. extemporaneous   c. worldly

Spelling Strategy

In many words of Greek origin that begin with a *k* sound, the sound is spelled *ch,* as in *chasm.* Complete the spelling of the words in each sentence below.

1. She took courses in __emistry.

2. His life was busy and __aotic.

Vocabulary Builder: Synonyms or Antonyms?

Review the vocabulary list on page 1391 and notice the way each word is used in the context of the selections. Then, determine whether the words in each pair below are synonyms (words with similar meanings) or antonyms (words with opposite meanings).

1. monotony/excitement
2. heralds/greets
3. chasm/mountaintop
4. jubilant/distressed
5. reverberates/echoes
6. tempo/pace
7. obsolete/new
8. lamentation/rejoicing

❷ Grammar and Style Lesson

Parallelism

Parallelism is the repeated expression of similar ideas in a similar grammatical form—words, phrases, clauses, or whole sentences. Parallelism is used to emphasize equal relationships between ideas and to create a smooth, musical flow of language.

Examples:

Not every cry for help is silenced,
nor every loss beyond recall. (parallel repetition of similar words)

the boys / plowing / transplanting / in the fields (parallel use of participles)

Practice Identify and explain the uses of parallelism in each item below

1. still I yearn / still I fear /

2. —perhaps just out of habit / —perhaps just out of sorrow,

3. village greybeards strolling . . . / grandmothers basking . . .

4. all love buried in the heart, / all history prisoned in a dream,

5. Choked on smog and monotony, / Stripped of their color and shape.

Writing Application Write a few lines of poetry. Include at least two examples of parallelism.

〽️ *Prentice Hall Writing and Grammar Connection: Platinum Level, Chapter 21, Section 4*

Assessment Practice

Using Context Clues to Determine Meanings

(For more practice, see *Test Preparation Workbook,* p. 6.)

Use the following sample test item to demonstrate how to use context clues to determine word meanings.

Although the Misty Poets are alike in their struggle to bring democracy to China, the poets express these ideas quite differently. In fact, Shu Ting's poem "Also All" provides a direct rebuttal of Bei Dao's "All."

In this passage, rebuttal means
A confirmation   C defense
B refutation   D explanation

The context clues *although* and *quite differently* indicate that "All" and "Also All" are poems with contradictory messages. A *confirmation* is an affirmation; a *defense* is an argument in support of something; and an *explanation* makes something understandable. Therefore, *B* is the best choice because a *rebuttal* is a refutation.

❸ Writing Lesson

Timed Writing: Literary Analysis

Write a literary analysis of one of the poems in this group. In your literary analysis, explore how elements of the poem work together to support its overall theme. *(40 minutes)*

Prewriting
(10 minutes)
Choose a poem and reread it carefully. As you read, jot down details that seem especially important or powerful. Identify ways in which the details combine to express a single message, or theme.

Drafting
(20 minutes)
Begin with an introduction stating your thesis—a brief statement summarizing the poem's overall effect or theme and the elements that contribute to it. In the body of the paper, support your thesis with specific details from the poem.

Revising
(10 minutes)
As you reread your work, double-check the structure of your sentences. If you have too many short, choppy sentences, combine them to achieve variety.

Model: Revising Sentences to Create Variety and Interest

In "Thoughts of Hanoi,"
∧ Nguyen uses images like a series of frames in a film

~~in "Thoughts of Hanoi." She does this~~ to re-create a

untroubled
sense of the life of the past. ~~That life was untroubled.~~
∧

> Combining short, repetitive sentences creates a more interesting flow.

 Prentice Hall Writing and Grammar Connection: Platinum Level, Chapter 21, Section 3

❹ Extend Your Learning

Listening and Speaking With a partner, prepare a **dialogue** that might have occurred between the speaker in "Thoughts of Hanoi" and her friend after the war. Use these tips to prepare:

- Make a list of questions the two might ask each other and their likely responses.
- Decide whether the two will rediscover their friendship or will remain hostile.

Practice until your dialogue sounds natural and spontaneous. Then, present it to the class.

Research and Technology With a small group, prepare a **multimedia report** on the events that occurred at Tiananmen Square in 1989. Use books, magazines, and the Internet to gather information about government leaders, leaders of the democracy movement, and the Democracy Wall. **[Group Activity]**

Go Online
Research

For: An additional research activity
Visit: www.PHSchool.com
Web Code: etd-7910

Thoughts of Hanoi / All / Also All / Assembly Line ■ 1351

Assessment Resources

The following resources can be used to assess students' knowledge and skills.

Unit 9 Resources
Selection Test A, pp. 182–184
Selection Test B, pp. 185–187
Benchmark Test 12, pp. 195–200

General Resources
Rubrics for Response to Literature, pp. 55–56

Go Online
Assessment
Students may use the **Self-test** to prepare for **Selection Test A** or **Selection Test B**.

Benchmark
Administer **Benchmark Test 12.** If some students need further work, use the **Interpretation Guide** to determine the appropriate reteaching page in the **Reading Kit** and on **Success Tracker.**

---

❸ Writing Lesson

You may use this Writing Lesson as timed-writing practice, or you may allow students to develop the literary analysis as a writing assignment over several days.

- To give students guidance in writing this essay, give them the **Support for Writing Lesson,** p. 179 in *Unit 9 Resources.*

- Remind students that in a literary analysis, a writer takes a critical look at important elements in a work. The writer then explains how the work uses those elements and how they work together to convey the message.

- Use the Response to Literature rubrics in *General Resources,* pp. 55–56, to evaluate students' essays.

Writing and Grammar
Platinum Level

For support in teaching the Writing Lesson, use Chapter 21, Section 3.

❹ Listening and Speaking

- Remind students to consider the political positions held by the speaker and his or her friend.

- Encourage students to research North and South Vietnam to provide details for their dialogues and settings. They may want to consult maps to include local landmarks or find information about the two countries' leaders and ideologies.

- The **Support for Extend Your Learning** page (*Unit 9 Resources,* p. 180) provides guided note-taking opportunities to help students complete the Extend Your Learning activities.

Go Online
Research
Have students type in the Web Code for another research activity.

Standard Course of Study

WL.1.02.3 Exhibit an awareness of cultural context of text in a personal reflection.

WL.1.03.9 Analyze effects of author's craft and style in reflection.

LT.5.01.5 Analyze archetypal characters, themes, and settings in world literature.

Prewriting

- To give students guidance in developing this assignment, give them the **Writing About Literature** support, pp. 188–189 in *Unit 9 Resources.*

- Have a volunteer read aloud the boxed Assignment. Clarify that students are to write about two selections from two cultures, for a total of four selections.

- Organize students into small groups to review the unit selections and share their views on how each selection addresses the relationship between society and the individual. Encourage students to choose selections that speak strongly about this relationship.

- Review the Model Chart at the bottom of the page, and discuss its use.

- Emphasize the importance of developing a working thesis statement before beginning to draft. It is critical to plan for effective writing, even if the thesis statement needs to be modified as students revise.

Tips for
Test Taking

A writing prompt on the SAT or ACT test may assess students' ability to analyze a topic, state a point of view regarding the topic, and support the point of view with evidence. When writing under timed circumstances, students will need to quickly clarify a point of view (their thesis statement) and the evidence that supports it. Because they won't be able to refer to a text, their evidence must be based on their own experiences, readings, or observations.

Compare and Contrast Literary Themes Across Cultures

For many writers, the world wars, totalitarian states, and consumer economy of our era mark the failure of society to give meaningful form to life. The individual seems left on his or her own to make sense of the world, as in Camus's "The Guest." Yet the global scale of current events emphasizes the interconnections among lives. In this spirit, some writers chart the ways individual lives are shaped by the history of a group, as Derek Walcott does in *Omeros.* Camus, Walcott, and others share a general insight: The place where individual and society meet is haunted by unsettled—and unsettling—questions.

Write an essay in which you compare this theme across cultures. Refer to the box at right for details of the assignment.

Prewriting

Choose selections. Review the selections to identify those with themes that relate to the individual's place in society. Choose at least two works from two cultures for your analysis. Ask questions such as the following to help guide your search:

- What does this selection suggest about the relationship between society and the individual?

- How is this theme revealed: through the plot, setting, characterization, language, or a combination of elements?

- In what ways is the relationship between individual and society in this selection like or unlike their relationship in other works?

Drawing on your notes, fill out a chart like the one shown. Then, review the chart and choose four or more selections, at least two from each of two cultures. To ensure that your essay will be interesting and rich in detail, choose works that show striking similarities or contrasts.

Model: Charting to Compare and Contrast Themes

Selection	Theme	Evidence of Theme
"The Handsomest Drowned Man in the World"	Individuals perceive and imagine together, collectively.	Women agree the drowned man's name is Esteban.

Write a working thesis. After you have decided which aspects of the theme appear in the works you have chosen, write a working thesis. Introduce the selections you will compare and contrast and the specific ways they present the individual in society.

1352 ■ *The Contemporary World*

Assignment: Who Am I? The Individual Across Cultures

Write an analytical essay that compares the theme of the individual in society in works from two of the following cultures included in this unit: the Americas, Western Europe, Eastern Europe, the Middle East, Africa, and Asia.

Criteria:
- Include a thesis statement drawn from your analysis of the literature of the two cultures.
- Support your thesis with detailed comparisons and contrasts of at least two selections from each culture.
- Cite several examples from each work.
- Approximate length: 700 words

Read to Write

As you reread the texts, analyze the tone. Tone, the author's attitude toward the subject and the reader, can help you understand the theme of a work.

Teaching Resources

The following resources can be used to extend or enrich the instruction for **Writing About Literature.**

Unit 9 Resources
　Writing About Literature, pp. 188–189

General Resources
　Exposition: Comparison-and-Contrast Essay rubrics, pp. 53–54

Graphic Organizer Transparencies
　Three-column Chart, p. 282
　Outline, p. 279

Drafting

Prepare an outline. Make an outline to help you organize your essay. Each main heading preceded by a Roman numeral should stand for an important idea that you plan to explore in its own paragraph. Under each subheading, list supporting examples.

> **Model: Using a Working Outline**
>
> I. Writers of the Americas emphasize family and heritage
> > A. "Handsomest Drowned Man in the World"
> > > 1. Groups of men and women think alike
> > > 2. Village agrees on what to do with drowned man
> > B. "House Taken Over"
> > > 1. Brother and sister live in family house

Refer to history. To strengthen your arguments, support them with references to historical events or cultural movements. Explain, where appropriate, the effect of historical circumstances on the works.

Revising and Editing

Review content: Reformulate points for accuracy. Reread your draft. Circle each sentence in which you state a main point. Then, review your circled points. For each, consider whether it accurately sums up an insight to which your paper leads. Rewrite as necessary to ensure that you have used just the right terms to explain your ideas.

Review style: Delete unnecessary words. Make sure that you have communicated your ideas in the simplest, most straightforward way possible. Take out any unnecessary words that you may have used.

Wordy: Very obviously, the title of the story gives a strong hint about its nature and tone. From the very first sentence, the reader knows that the story will not be completely realistic and will probably include elements of fantasy.

Revised: The title gives a strong hint about the tone of the story. From the first sentence, the reader knows that the story will include elements of fantasy.

Publishing and Presenting

Have a discussion. Gather with classmates who wrote about the same selections you did. Compare group members' interpretations of the literature.

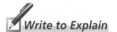 *Writing and Grammar Connection: Platinum Level, Chapter 9*

Write to Learn

As you write your first draft, you may notice that some examples from the selections do not adequately support your ideas. Look back at the selections to make sure you have chosen the details or quotations that best illustrate the theme of the individual in society.

Write to Explain

Use parallel construction to make your comparisons and contrasts as clear as possible to readers.

Drafting

- Review sources of cultural information. Remind students to support any references to historical events or cultural movements with accurate information.
- Point out how the working outline model addresses each selection under its own heading.
- Students should list page references in their outlines so that they will be able to find text examples more easily as they draft.

Revising and Editing

- Have students compare their drafts with their outlines. They should confirm that they have included each main point and item of supporting evidence.
- Stress the importance of the style review. Work through the provided models, identifying unnecessary words. Have a volunteer read aloud the Revised example. Point out that it conveys the point concisely and effectively.

Publishing and Presenting

As an alternative, create groups in which all the selections are represented. Students can then share ideas about how each selection addresses the issue of the relationship between individuals and societies.

WG Writing and Grammar Platinum Level

Students will find additional instruction on writing a comparison-and-contrast essay in Chapter 9.

Writing and Grammar Interactive Textbook CD-ROM

Students can use the following tools as they complete their essay:

- Organizers: Customizable outline
- Revising Tools: Unity and Coherence, Troublesome Adjectives and Adverbs, Editing

Six Traits Focus

✓	Ideas	✓	Word Choice
✓	Organization	✓	Sentence Fluency
	Voice	✓	Conventions

Assessing the Essay

To evaluate students' essays, use the Exposition: Comparison-and-Contrast Essay rubrics in *General Resources*, pp. 53–54.

1353

Differentiated Instruction   Solutions for All Learners

Support for Less Proficient Writers
To help students make comparisons and contrasts, review comparative and superlative transition words and adjectives. Explain that words and phrases such as *similarly, also, on the other hand,* and *instead* can help show comparison and contrast. Words such as *more* and *most* can help create degrees of description.

Strategy for English Learners
Invite students to share knowledge from their native cultures about the relationship between society and the individual. In particular, if students share cultural origins with writers from the unit selections, ask them to share that knowledge with the class as a whole.

Strategy for Advanced Writers
Encourage students to include significant historical and cultural references in their essays. Students may do this through research. Remind students that it is not enough to provide only background, however. Students must clearly link the historical events or cultural movements to their essays' themes.

IR.2.02.4	Develop appropriate strategies to illustrate points about cause/effect relationships.
GU.6.01.6	Use correct format for writing.
GU.6.02.4	Edit for clichés/trite expressions.
GU.6.02.5	Edit for spelling.

 From the Author's Desk

Jamaica Kincaid

Show students Segment 3 on **Jamaica Kincaid** on *From the Author's Desk DVD.* Discuss how Jamaica Kincaid deals with writer's block.

Writing Genres

Using the Form Tell students that job portfolios are often used in the business world. Point out these examples:

• Job applications require job portfolios.

• Requests for promotions or raises may require the applicant to submit a job portfolio.

• Scholarship applications may also require a résumé or list of the applicant's experiences and skills.

 Online Essay Scorer

A writing prompt for this mode of writing can be found on the *PH Online Essay Scorer* at PHSuccessNet.com.

Writing Workshop

Workplace Writing:
Job Portfolio and Résumé

Several of the authors in this unit have held unusual jobs. Shu Ting worked on construction sites and in factories; Czesław Miłosz was a diplomat; John Hersey was a war correspondent. People seeking jobs usually compile a **job portfolio**—a collection of materials a job candidate submits to a potential employer. Most job portfolios include a **résumé**, which is a summary of qualifications and experience, and a **cover letter**, which introduces the job seeker. Other materials may include references and writing samples. Follow the steps in this workshop to write your own résumé.

Assignment Write a résumé presenting your qualifications for employment.

What to Include Your résumé should feature the following elements:

• prominently displayed name, address, and contact information
• summaries of work history, education, and related experience, all specifically tailored to the job under consideration
• consistent style and precise language, including active verbs
• easy-to-follow, consistent résumé format

To preview the criteria on which your résumé may be assessed, refer to the rubric on page 1361.

 Standard Course of Study

• Use correct format for writing. (GU.6.01.6)
• Edit for clichés/trite expressions. (GU.6.02.4)
• Edit for spelling. (GU.6.02.5)

Using the Form
You may use elements of workplace writing in these types of writing:

• memorandums (memos)
• cover letters
• job applications
• forms

1354 ■ *The Contemporary World*

Teaching Resources

The following resources can be used to enrich or extend the instruction for the Writing Workshop.

Unit 9 Resources
Writing Workshop: Job Portfolios, pp. 190–191

General Resources
Rubrics for Job Portfolios, pp. 59 and 60

From the Author's Desk DVD
Jamaica Kincaid, Segments 3 and 4

Prewriting

Gathering Information

List information. Begin by listing all of your work experience. Include exact dates of employment, employers' names and addresses, and your duties in each job. Also write down relevant extracurricular, volunteer, and educational experiences. Include any special skills you may have, such as word processing or other computer skills, and special achievements or awards.

Choosing Prospective Employers

Conduct a job and career study. Decide what type of job you would like to obtain, and apply to suitable employers. To conduct a thorough, well-informed job search, follow these steps:

- **Learn about available jobs.** Consult library resources, visit employment agencies, and speak with guidance counselors, friends, and family to familiarize yourself with key responsibilities and job skills that various types of jobs require.

- **Research local businesses.** Review print or Web guides to local businesses, and list employers of interest to you.

- **Consult job listings.** Consult job listings at your school, at an employment agency, and in the Help Wanted section of the newspaper.

Target your résumé. Determine which of your experiences are most relevant to a specific job. Emphasize those experiences in your résumé. For example, a store advertising for help with displays might look for evidence of creativity. A store with an opening for a cashier might be more interested in accuracy and mathematical skills. Matching your experience to the job will give you a better chance of success.

> **Type of Job:**
> working with or supervising children
>   –summer camp
>   –crafts and activities
> **Experience to Emphasize:**
> camp counselor assistant
> mother's helper
> **Skills to Emphasize:**
> sports
> arts and crafts experience
> **Other Accomplishments:**
> baby-sitting certification
> teen character award

Writing Workshop ■ 1355

Tips for Using Rubrics

- Before students begin work on this assignment, have them preview the Rubric for Self-Assessment, p. 1361, to know what is expected.

- Review the Assessment criteria in class. Before students use the Rubric for Self-Assessment, work with them to rate the student model by applying one or two criteria to it.

- If you wish to assess students' job portfolios with a 4-point, 5-point, or 6-point scoring rubric, see *General Resources,* pp. 59 and 60.

Prewriting

- Have students share the criteria they might look for when searching for a job. For example, a job applicant may want to know how much experience is required, whether the job has flexible hours, or whether he or she could work outdoors. Tell students that it is as important to think about a job's environment—for example, large office or small shop—as it is to consider the job's actual tasks. Choosing a job that fits with one's interests and strengths increases an applicant's chances of being hired.

- Have students brainstorm a list of Internet job search resources. Students might identify local companies through a city's Web site and then visit the companies' Web sites for additional information.

- Also, help students identify people-based resources, such as family, friends, or businesses.

- Encourage students to list their work experiences creatively. For example, if a student has regularly prepared family meals, this work is important experience. It has taught the student to plan, organize, and execute in a position of responsibility. Assure students that employers generally recognize that students have had limited paid job experience.

- Encourage students to review the Self-Assessment Rubric on p. 1361 so that they will know what is expected of their job portfolios.

Six Traits Focus

✓	Ideas		Word Choice
✓	Organization		Sentence Fluency
	Voice		Conventions

Writing and Grammar Platinum Level
Students will find additional instruction on prewriting for a job portfolio in Chapter 15, Section 1.

Writing and Grammar Interactive Textbook CD-ROM
Students can use the following tools as they complete their job portfolios:

- List Organizer
- Character Trait Word Bin
- Editing Tool
- Vague Adjectives Tool

Drafting

- Explain that there are may correct styles for résumés. The critical point is that any résumé must be consistent within its own style. Inconsistency will distract the reader from the résumé's content and weaken the portfolio.

- Try to dissuade students from using hard to read italic fonts and highly ornate or unusual formats. Tell them that employers might not read anything that is difficult to decipher and might react negatively to unusual formats.

- Remind students to use the Résumé Conventions checklist as they draft. No matter which format they use, the résumé should contain all the features listed.

- Point out to students that they should never list their Social Security number on a résumé, as this number needs to be protected to prevent identity theft. If they are hired, their employer will ask for their Social Security number at that time.

- Stress again the importance of accuracy in a résumé. Remind students to work slowly and carefully.

Six Traits Focus

✓	Ideas	✓	Word Choice
✓	Organization		Sentence Fluency
	Voice		Conventions

 Writing and Grammar Platinum Level

Students will find additional instruction on drafting a job portfolio in Chapter 15, Section 1.

Drafting

Shaping Your Résumé

Select a Format. One key to an effective résumé is an easy-to-follow organization. Résumés can follow several possible formats, including the one modeled on page 1360. Résumé information is typically organized by category, such as education and work experience.

The checklist shows the standard categories. No matter what format you choose for your résumé, follow it consistently.

Include essential information. Certain information is essential on a résumé. Always include these features:

- Name, address, phone number, e-mail address, and other contact information, displayed prominently at the top of the document
- List of work and other applicable experiences and accomplishments, starting with the most recent
- Names and addresses of employers in boldface or otherwise set off
- Dates of terms of employment with each employer
- Brief description of responsibilities for each job listing

Styling Your Résumé

Select a style Choose a résumé style, and apply it consistently as you draft your résumé. For example, you may choose to use either sentences or phrases in the descriptions of your job history. Select one of these styles, and use it consistently.

Whole sentences: Responsibilities included routing copy, running errands, and assisting reporters.

Phrases: Routed copy; ran errands; assisted reporters.

Follow résumé language conventions. Do not use the pronoun *I*. Use the present tense to describe your responsibilities in a job you currently hold. Otherwise use the past tense.

> ### Résumé Conventions
>
> ❑ **Heading** includes the candidate's name, address, and contact information.
>
> ❑ **Objective** or **Summary** provides a brief statement about the candidate and his or her professional goals.
>
> ❑ **Experience** lists details of work and other relevant history.
>
> ❑ **Education** provides a history of the candidate's schooling and other training.
>
> ❑ **Skills** section notes special abilities, such as computer training or fluency in a foreign language.
>
> ❑ **Honors/Activities/Memberships** is a flexible category that includes applicable activities that do not fit into other sections of the résumé.

Reading **Writing** *Connection*

To read the complete student model, see page 1360.

Student Model: Following Résumé Conventions

2000 to Present	**Baby Sitter**
	Hickory, NC
	Care for several different children; regular duties include feeding, bathing, playing games, and reading bedtime stories.

The writer began with complete sentences, but then removed the pronoun *I*. Note the use of the present tense.

1356 ■ *The Contemporary World*

From the Author's Desk
Jamaica Kincaid on the Revision Process

This excerpt is from a book I wrote called *Among Flowers: A Walk in the Himalaya.* In October of 2002, I went on a seed collecting expedition in Nepal. I was in the company of three botanists who were also in the plant selling business. The book gives an account of our daily life as we walked through the remote Nepalese countryside, in the foothills of the mountains Everest, Makalu, and Kangchenjunga.

Jamaica Kincaid

Professional Model:

from *Among Flowers: A Walk in the Himalaya*

The first version, showing changes:
The∧Those two days off had renewed us. It is true ~~that in those two days~~ Dan and Bleddyn had ~~gone off and~~ gathered a lot of seeds but ~~it was agreed that~~ they wouldn't have gone ~~through all this~~ ∧out of their way ~~just~~ to ∧make this collection, what ~~only the things~~ they had collected∧is the sort of thing you collect on your way to real garden treasure. ~~, that the real, serious, desirable things were to come.~~

The final version:
Those two days off had renewed us. It is true Dan and Bleddyn had gathered a lot of seeds but they wouldn't have gone out of their way to make this collection, what they had collected is the sort of thing you collect on your way to real garden treasure.

"It takes me a long time to put down my words on paper and so when I finally let them go, I almost never can see how to change them."
—— Jamaica Kincaid

I made this change because it had a better sound to me. I never change for technical reasons or for any other reason than the sound or the feel of the sentence itself.

- Show students Segment 4 on Jamaica Kincaid on *From the Author's Desk DVD*. Discuss Kincaid's view of writing as a psychological journey.

- Have students read Kincaid's quotation about her writing. Then point out that many people make some of their revisions mentally before they actually write them on paper.

- Point out that Jamaica Kincaid revises only because the writing does not "sound right." Tell students that writers often know what "sounds right" and are not satisfied with their writing until they are convinced that it sounds the way they want it to sound. Urge students to listen to how their writing sounds and to revise accordingly.

- Have students look at Kincaid's revisions and her comments about the revisions. Ask students to read both versions. Ask volunteers to explain why one version sounds better than the other.

Tips for
Improving Word Choice

Give students these suggestions for revising word choice.

1. Read your paper to see how it "sounds." If it does not "sound" right, circle the areas that are weak and revise it to say what you want to say. Although you should "sound like yourself," make sure your writing voice does not sound timid or boastful. Make sure you don't understate or overstate your abilities and experience.

2. Circle the verbs and adverbs in your writing. Try to replace adverbs with stronger verbs that capture what the adverb added to the sentence.

3. Choose adjectives carefully. If an adjective does not add to the writing, drop it or replace it with a more precise word.

4. As Kincaid does, delete all words that are useless in that they add nothing to the meaning of the sentence.

Revising

- Point out that proofreading may be the most important step in writing a résumé. First impressions are vital in a job search, and mistakes are difficult to undo after the résumé has been delivered. Mention to students that many employers will not consider hiring anyone whose résumé contains errors.

- Emphasize that revising for consistency is important as is making sure to correct all spelling, grammar, and punctuation mistakes. Punctuation as well as style and format should be consistent throughout. Remind students to use parallelism in listing résumé entries.

- Once students have completed their résumés, suggest that they allow them to sit for a day or two and then go back and look them over. Distancing themselves from their work for a few days may help them spot errors.

- Encourage students to review the language in their résumés. They should ask: Is the language precise? Is it vivid? Does it portray experiences effectively? Is it varied, using different verbs and adjectives? Is it concise?

Six Traits Focus

✓	Ideas	✓	Word Choice
✓	Organization	✓	Sentence Fluency
✓	Voice	✓	Conventions

 Writing and Grammar
Platinum Level
Students will find additional guidance for revising a job portfolio in Chapter 15, Section 1.

Writing Workshop

Revising

Revising Your Overall Structure

Revise for consistency. Make sure that you have followed a consistent organizational strategy, as well as a consistent format and style.

1. Check that the entries are aligned consistently.
2. Confirm that the headings are boldfaced and capitalized.
3. Make sure that all of the information in a section is organized following the same pattern.

Reading Writing Connection

To read the complete student model, see page 1360.

Student Model: Revise for Consistency

August 2001 (to) Present   **St. Stephen High School,**
                            Hickory, NC
2000 —(to)— Present   **Baby Sitter**

> The use of *to* in the first entry and the dash in the second are inconsistent. Choose one style or the other.

Peer Review: Ask a classmate to scan your résumé for consistency in format and wording. Correct any inconsistencies that your partner notes.

Revising Your Word Choice

Use specific, active language. Let precise, active words carry your message.

- Avoid vague terms and passive verbs.

  Vague: Was assigned work on brochures.
  Specific: Researched and wrote copy for four-color brochures for advertising agency.

- Use brief explanations to describe the essentials of the work you have done.

  Wordy: Make sure that surfaces were clean; disposed of fixer used in printing and processing.
  Concise: Maintained darkroom

- Use strong verbs to emphasize mastery of tasks and responsibilities.

  Weak: *Looked after* patients and *helped* with email.
  Strong: *Monitored* patient diets and *communicated* with nurses.

1358 ■ *The Contemporary World*

Tips for
Using Technology in Writing

Some word processing programs offer résumé templates that students may find useful. If these programs are not available, students can use auto-format features such as bulleted lists and hanging indents to create a layout like the Student Model. Remind students to use these features carefully because auto-formatting can contain hidden settings. Students can modify these settings under "AutoCorrect" or other similar features in the Tools menu of many programs. Encourage students to choose a simple, readable typeface, such as Times or Helvetica but to experiment with variations in type size and use of boldface to highlight important features.

Students can also use the organizing tools and revision checkers on the **Writing and Grammar Interactive Textbook CD-ROM.**

Developing Your Style

Active vs. Passive Voice

Express yourself. A résumé should be more than simply a list of jobs and activities. It should reflect who you are and convey pride in your accomplishments. You can project this confidence through the strong words you use to describe the work you have done. Especially in résumé writing, choose words in the active voice.

Defining the active voice. Verbs in the active voice express the action that the subject performs. In contrast, verbs in the passive voice receive the action of the verb.

> **Passive:** I am employed by a mother of a child.
> **Active:** I assist mother of severely handicapped daughter. I help with feeding and medications and supervise the child when the mother does errands.

Find It in Your Reading Read or review the student model of a résumé on page 1360. Note how Megan describes her work experience and achievements.

1. Find three examples of active verb constructions. Explain what the active voice conveys about Megan.

2. Choose one job description from the résumé. Identify the powerful verbs that convey responsibility and confidence. Explain the effect these words have on your impression of Megan and her skills.

Apply it to Your Writing Review the draft of your résumé and follow these steps:

1. Circle all verbs, and make sure they are active. Replace passive verbs with active verbs.

> **Passive:** Was given correspondence to type.
> **Active:** Typed correspondence.

2. Review descriptions for clarity and detail. Replace vague or generic terms with specific, vivid language.

> **Vague:** camp
> **Specific:** nonprofit camp for city children

3. Your résumé should fit on a single page. Edit lengthy descriptions, keeping key points and cutting unnecessary words. Consider breaking descriptions longer than a sentence into a bulleted list.

WG *Prentice Hall Writing and Grammar Connection: Platinum Level, Chapter 22, Section 2*

Developing Your Style

- Point out that the active voice stresses the doer, or the one who performs the action. Using the active voice makes the subject the focus of the sentence, and because the writers are the subject, the active voice brings attention to them.

- Tell students that the active voice emphasizes action and that the passive voice emphasizes reaction. Without necessarily being aware of language, employers may react more favorably to the more "active" or action-oriented writing.

- Remind students to use the active voice wherever possible in all of their writing, not just in their résumés.

- Allow students a few minutes to find the answers to **Find It in Your Reading.**
  Sample response: 1. Examples of active verbs are "help," "assist," and "received." The active voice suggests that Megan is an outgoing person. 2. As a "part-time mother's helper," the verbs "assist," "help," and "watch" suggest that Megan is caring and competent.

- As students complete **Appy It to Your Writing,** point out that they can help a short résumé look better on the page by slightly increasing the font size and margins. They can make a résumé that is long fit the page by using an eleven point font size and slightly shrinking the margins.

WG **Writing and Grammar**
Platinum Level
Students will find additional instruction on active and passive voice in Chapter 22, Section 2.

Student Model

- Explain that the Student Model is a sample and that students' own résumés may be shorter or longer. Note that as a rule, résumés should not exceed two pages. At this point in their working lives, students' résumés should be only one page.

- Point out to students that the Student Model uses layout to enhance readability. For example, Megan positioned her name prominently at the top of the page and used labels for education, work experience, skills, and special achievements. Megan did not use special typefaces, italics, or underlining. This format allows employers to scan the document into a computer.

- Point out the shorthand format of a résumé. Megan began her sentences with a verb rather than with a first-person pronoun. Students should take care, however, to keep their verb tenses consistent within an entry.

- Emphasize that the goal of a résumé is to present experience pertinent to a particular job. This goal may mean writing different versions of a résumé if students apply for different types of jobs. Tell students that it is not unusual to have a version that highlights experience with children and another that focuses on work with computers.

- Review the bulleted items at the bottom of Megan's résumé. Students can list skills here that paint an overall picture. These help employers gain a sense of the applicant's potential, especially when the applicant is a high school student with limited work experience.

Writing Genres

Job Portfolios in the Workplace

Students will almost certainly need to create a job portfolio at least once in their lives. Both paying and volunteer positions usually require the presentation of work experience. Often the portfolio is a potential employer's first introduction to the applicant. It must be effective, or the applicant may never get the chance to present himself or herself in person. Discuss what qualities of a portfolio might impress employers and increase students' chances of getting a job interview.

1360

Writing Workshop

Student Model: Megan Mary Mahoney
Hickory, North Carolina

Megan Mary Mahoney
1234 Anystreet
Hickory, NC 28601
(888)555-5555
e-mail@e-mail.com

> Name and contact information are placed prominently at the top of the page and set in a larger font size.

OBJECTIVE
To obtain a position as a camp counselor in order to work with children.

EDUCATION
August 2001 to Present — **St. Stephen High School**, Hickory, NC
Expected graduation date: June 2005. Honor student.
Special courses; Journalism; Advanced Placement English
Extracurricular activities: Beta Club, yearbook staff, varsity tennis, JV soccer, and JV basketball

> Megan uses clear headings to label her education, work, and other relevant experiences. (See *Revising*, p. 1358.)

WORK EXPERIENCE
Summer 2002 and 2003 — **Counselor's Assistant**
Camp Joy, Hickory, NC
Helped campers with arts, sports, games, and social interaction at this nonprofit camp for underprivileged children.

2002 to Present — **Part-time Mother's Helper**
Sue Smith, Hickory, NC
Assist mother of severely handicapped daughter. Help with feeding and medications and watch over the child when the mother does errands.

> Megan provides specific details about experiences related to her objective.

2000 to Present — **Baby Sitter**
Hickory, NC
Care for several different children; regular duties include feeding, bathing, playing games, and reading bedtime stories.

SKILLS
- Sports: tennis, soccer, basketball, volleyball
- Arts and crafts, piano
- Computer skills: word processing, Internet research

SPECIAL ACHIEVEMENTS
- Received Baby-Sitting Certification at Frye Regional Hospital in December 2001. Was trained in basic first aid and baby-sitting.
- Received the Teen Character Award from the local YMCA in May 2001. Nominated for this award by teachers.

> Bullets and boldface headings make Megan's information clear and easy to follow. Headings, dates, and bulleted items are aligned consistently.

Differentiated Instruction   Solutions for All Learners

Strategy for Less Proficient Writers
Have students review their work and life experiences in time order. They may use the **Timeline Tool** on the **Writing and Grammar Interactive Textbook CD-ROM** as an aid. Have students think back to each school year and ask: What responsibilities did I have? What skills did I learn? In which activities did I participate?

Vocabulary for English Learners
Stress that accuracy and consistency in a résumé are far more important than elaborate language. Students should feel comfortable using basic language, provided that it is used correctly. Verb tenses must be consistent, punctuation must be correct, and spelling must be accurate. Encourage English learners to refer to a dictionary and grammar handbook.

Vocabulary for Advanced Writers
Encourage students to use powerful and descriptive verbs to describe their experiences. For example, Megan might have added the word *Sole* before her Baby Sitter description. This word would highlight the responsibility that she had for the children. Students should choose specific verbs and occasional adjectives for their résumés.

Editing and Proofreading

Review your résumé to make sure that it is free from errors in grammar, punctuation, and spelling.

Focus on Spelling: Use a dictionary to make sure that you have spelled all words correctly, especially proper names and technical terms.

Publishing and Presenting

Consider one of the following ways to share your writing.

Prepare a cover letter. In a letter, state your interest in the position and briefly identify your qualifications. Address your letter to the person who is in charge of reviewing the company's applications.

- Follow standard business letter format by including a heading, the inside address, the date, and an appropriate salutation and closing.
- Explain that your résumé is attached, and indicate your availability for an interview.
- Thank the recipient in advance for his or her consideration.

Build a job portfolio. A résumé serves as the centerpiece of your job application. To complete your job portfolio, attach samples of your work, letters of recommendation, citations, and other information that might help a prospective employer.

Reflecting on Your Writing

Writer's Journal Jot down your thoughts on the experience of writing a résumé. Begin by answering these questions:

- What was the hardest part of writing a résumé, and why?
- What insights about yourself did you gain from writing your résumé?

WG *Prentice Hall Writing and Grammar Connection: Platinum Level, Chapter 15*

Rubric for Self-Assessment

Evaluate your résumé using the following criteria and rating scale, or, with your classmates, determine your own reasonable evaluation criteria.

Criteria	Rating Scale
	not very very
Focus: How well do you state your qualifications and experience?	1 2 3 4 5
Organization: How well do you employ an easy-to-follow résumé format?	1 2 3 4 5
Support/Elaboration: How appropriately do you present your work history and education for the type of work sought?	1 2 3 4 5
Style: How consistent and precise is your use of language?	1 2 3 4 5
Conventions: How correct is your grammar and spelling?	1 2 3 4 5

Writing Workshop ■ *1361*

Tips for Test Taking

Tell students that because résumés require such careful proofreading, standardized tests might include them on proofreading items. When presented with such questions, students should remember résumé conventions such as the use of phrases that are punctuated as sentences and the importance of consistency in format, in addition to mechanical errors. Students should quickly review the résumé examples to identify its chosen format before looking for any deviations or errors.

Editing and Proofreading

- Suggest that students read their drafts aloud and listen for awkward usage as they read. This can be done alone or in pairs. They should make revisions after they have finished reading aloud.

Six Traits Focus

	Ideas		Word Choice
	Organization		Sentence Fluency
✓	Voice	✓	Conventions

ASSESS

Publishing and Presenting

- Show students a variety of résumés. You might find these on the Internet or in a book on the topic. Point out that résumés should be printed on high-quality, neutral-color paper. Direct students to stationery stores for appropriate paper.

- Remind students to save their completed résumés to a disk that they will keep. Point out that it is usually much easier to update an existing résumé than it is to start over from scratch.

- Review the features of a business letter, and have students include a specific follow-up proposal, such as a plan to call the employer in a week's time.

Reflecting on Your Writing

- In their journals have students imagine that they are an employer looking at the student's résumé. Have students write about the impression the résumé creates.

- Encourage students to read the assessment criteria before finalizing their résumés. Make sure that they understand how each of the criteria is reflected in the Student Model.

- Agree as a class on an acceptable score, such as at least two 4s and no score less than a 3. This will give students a benchmark for acceptability.

WG **Writing and Grammar** **Platinum Level**
Students will find additional guidance for editing and proofreading, publishing and presenting, and reflecting on a job portfolio in Chapter 15.

 Standard Course of Study

CT.4.04.1 Identify clear criteria for evaluation of work of others.

CT.4.05.2 Analyze text components and evaluate impact on critical interpretation.

CT.4.05.3 Provide evidence to support understanding of and response to critical interpretation.

Know Your Terms: Thinking Critically About Text

Explain that the terms listed under Terms to Learn will be used in standardized-test situations when students are asked to think critically about a reading passage.

Terms to Learn

• Review *evaluate* and *evaluation*. Tell students that an evaluation requires them to look critically at an idea or topic and decide its level of value. When students evaluate, have them ask themselves, "What importance does this idea or topic have in the work?" Remind students that they must form their evaluations based on information in the passage.

• Review *judge*. Tell students that to judge means to make an estimation or a decision about something after looking at it critically. Point out that judgments about an issue can vary from person to person because judging requires a person to form an opinion.

ASSESS

Answers

1. The writer's choice of the title "Comrades" for this selection is a good choice because it shows both the tie between the individuals and the leftist leanings of the characters involved.

2. The most telling thought or action is her attempt to put the boys at ease as she is going completely out of her way to take them to the bus station.

 SAT **PREP** ACT

High-Frequency Academic Words

High-frequency academic words are words that appear often in textbooks and on standardized tests. Although you may already know the meaning of many of these words, they usually have a more specific meaning when they are used in textbooks and on tests.

Know Your Terms: Thinking Critically About Texts

Each of the terms listed below is a verb that prompts you to weigh the merits of material. The terms indicate the kind of details and information you should provide in your answer.

Terms to Learn

Evaluate Determine the value or importance of something.

> Sample test item: *Evaluate* the author's thesis.

Judge Assess or form an opinion about something.

> Sample test item: What do you *judge* to be the most telling anecdote that the writer includes in this memoir?

Practice

Directions: *Read the following passage from "Comrades," a short story by Nadine Gordimer. Then, answer the questions that follow.*

—Comrade . . . —[Mrs. Telford] was settling into the driver's seat when one so slight and slim he seemed a figure in profile came up to her window. He drew courage from the friendly life of the woman's eyebrows above blue eyes, the tilt of her freckled white face: —Comrade, are you going to town?—

No, she was going in the opposite direction, home . . . but quickly, in the spirit of the hall where these young people had been somewhere, somehow present with her (ah no, she with them) stamping and singing Freedom songs, she would take them to the bus station their spokesman named.— Climb aboard!—

The others got in the back, the spokesman beside her. She saw the nervous white of his eyes as he glanced at and away from her. She searched for talk to set them at ease. Questions, of course. Older people always start with questioning young ones. Did they come from Soweto?

They came from Harrismith, Phoneng Location.

1. *Evaluate* the writer's choice of the title "Comrades" for this passage.

2. What do you *judge* to be the most telling thought or action of Mrs. Telford?

1362 ■ *The Contemporary World*

 Standard Course of Study

• Identify clear criteria for evaluation of work of others. (CT.4.04.1)

• Select, monitor, and modify reading strategies appropriate to critical interpretation. (CT.4.05.1)

• Analyze text components and evaluate impact on critical interpretation. (CT.4.05.2)

Tips for Test Taking

• It can be very difficult to set aside one's preconceived notions or prejudices. As students answer questions dealing with evaluation and judging in standardized-test situations, remind them to deal only with the material presented in the reading passage.

• Students very often have difficulty answering certain types of questions on a standardized test, such as evaluation and judging questions. Remind students not to spend too much time on a difficult question but to skip the question and return to it after they complete the rest of the test.

Go Online **For:** An Interactive Crossword Puzzle
Vocabulary **Visit:** www.PHSchool.com
Web Code: etj-5901
This crossword puzzle contains vocabulary that reflects the concepts in Unit 9. After students have completed Unit 9, give students the Web Code and have them complete the crossword puzzle.

Critical Reading:
Analyzing an Author's Meaning

Standard Course of Study

- FA.3.04.4
- FA.3.04.5
- FA.3.04.6

In the reading sections of some tests, you may be required to read a passage and interpret the author's ideas or opinions. The following strategies will help you answer such test questions.

- Identify the main idea and the supporting details of the passage.
- Select the correct answers to questions about the passage, based on your own knowledge and the information in the passage.
- Eliminate answer choices that are unrelated to the passage.

Practice

Directions: *Read the passages below, and then answer the questions.*

Passage A. America is experiencing an epidemic of obesity. Assign much of the blame to our frenetic lifestyles. We are too busy to prepare and eat home-cooked meals very often, and, besides, fast food is delicious. Hamburgers, which used to weigh 4 ounces, now weigh 8, 12, or even 16 ounces. Popcorn sold in movie theaters, which used to come in small bags or dainty boxes, is now served in huge vats. This trend is wreaking havoc on Americans' waistlines and health.

Passage B. The mayor's plan to drain the swamp behind the Mayville town park is a sound one, but you may be surprised to learn the strongest reason for it. You might think at first of the mosquitoes that breed in the swamp. You might think of the town's need for land on which to build a new school. The truth is that our town has hit hard times. A project such as draining the swamp, financed in part by state grants, is just what Mayville's unemployed need to find temporary work until there is a full economic recovery.

1. With which statement would the writer of Passage A most likely agree?

   A We need to make fast food more tasty.

   B We need to eat less fast food.

   C We need to close down fast-food restaurants.

   D We need to install gyms in fast-food restaurants.

2. In Passage B, the author's main point is that

   A the mosquitoes should be killed.

   B Mayville has hit hard times.

   C the swamp should be drained to give Mayville's unemployed work.

   D the swamp should be drained for many reasons.

Test-Taking Strategies

- To interpret parts of a passage, restate the ideas in your own words.

- Read all of the words in a passage carefully. Even small details may give clues to correct answers.

- Evaluate the main ideas in a passage. Do you agree or disagree with these ideas?

Critical Reading

- Remind students that the main idea of a passage is what a passage is mostly about.

- Point out that students always must support their answers with information in the passage.

- After students have read the Practice passage and have answered the questions, point out that for question 1, the correct answer is B. Although the writer believes that people should eat less fast food, the writer does not seem opposed to fast-food in principle, so C is incorrect. The writer does not discuss option D, and A is contradicted in the passage.

- Point out that for question 2, the writer names another means for killing the mosquitoes, so A is incorrect. While B is supported in the essay, it is not the main point, and the real reason that the swamp should be drained is to provide employment, so C is correct; D is not the main point.

ASSESS

Answers

1. B
2. C

Tips for Test Taking

In order to interpret the meaning of a writer's ideas or opinions in a passage on a standardized-test question, students need to read the passage carefully and pay close attention to what type of writing the passage is. Cause-and-effect passages, for example, will express a writer's ideas or opinions differently than a persuasive passage will express. Identifying the type of writing that a passage is will help students understand what a test question is asking them to do and determine which answer choice *best* answers the question.

Prepare Your Content

- Review with students the features and tools of a multimedia presentation. Make sure that they understand the function of each component. List this information on the board.

- Discuss the items in the bulleted list. Invite students to share examples of different media from effective presentations they have viewed. Prompt students by recalling such presentations at museums or libraries.

- Remind students to vary the media in their presentations where possible. A presentation that smoothly incorporates both visual and auditory media can reach more people effectively. Students should avoid presenting competing media simultaneously.

Prepare Your Delivery

- Students should practice their presentations several times, preferably with an audience and in a room similar to that of the actual presentation. This allows students to become familiar with equipment and conditions.

- Give students the opportunity to examine audiovisual equipment. Offer a demonstration, or invite an experienced student or teacher to model equipment use.

- Remind students that they may want—or need, in the event of technology failure—to deliver parts of the presentation live. Students should therefore have note cards prepared for a speech and should practice delivering that speech.

Assess the Activity

To evaluate students' delivery, use the Listening: Evaluating a Media Presentation rubric, p. 86 in *General Resources*.

1364

Delivering a Multimedia Presentation

Many presentations can be enhanced through the use of sounds and visuals. When you give a **multimedia presentation**, you might use an overhead projector, a slide projector, a video or audio player, a computer, or another electronic device. The following strategies will help you develop and deliver an effective multimedia presentation.

Prepare Your Content

The suggestions below will help you develop your multimedia presentation:

- Outline your presentation, and decide which parts can be effectively presented through, or with the support of, visual or sound media.
- Choose media that suit your topic. For example, if your topic is American life during World War II, you might play popular music of the time as background.
- Use audio or visual support throughout your presentation, not just at the beginning or at the end.

Prepare Your Delivery

Multimedia presentations can be wonderful experiences for presenter and audience alike—but only if all the technology functions as intended. These tips may help you prepare to use audio and visual technology in your presentation:

- Rehearse your presentation with the multimedia equipment you will use. Become familiar with the equipment, and learn how to make volume, focus, and other adjustments to it.
- Before the presentation, double-check the equipment to make sure that all of it is functioning properly.
- Make sure visuals will be seen and the audio portion will be heard by the entire audience.
- Have a backup plan, in case the equipment fails. For example, you might have on hand photocopies of charts and graphs to pass out to the audience in case the overhead projector fails.

Activity **Presentation and Feedback** Prepare a multimedia presentation in which you explain how to make or do something at which you excel. Practice your presentation with a partner, using the Feedback Form shown to evaluate your content and delivery. Use the evaluation to help you polish your presentation, and then deliver it to the class.

1364 ■ *The Contemporary World*

Feedback Form for Multimedia Presentation

Rating System
+ = Excellent   ✓= Average   – = Weak

Content
Match of media and topic _____
Media enhance topic _____
Media used at appropriate points_____

Delivery
Smoothness of presentation _____
Ability to adjust equipment _____
Ability to work around glitches in equipment
_____

Differentiated Instruction   Solutions for All Learners

Support for Special Needs Students
Offer students additional time to practice with the multimedia equipment. If possible, arrange for one-on-one direction from a knowledgeable guide. Explain that multimedia presentations need not be complex in order to be effective. In fact, the choice of media allows students to draw on their strengths and minimize any weaknesses. Work with students to identify those strengths and weaknesses, and then brainstorm for which media will fit closely with these.

Support for English Learners
Stress the opportunity that multimedia presentations offer. Much of the spoken component can be prerecorded in an environment where the student does not feel the pressure of an audience. Further, the visual and audio components offer students an opportunity to extend creativity without concern about language. Ask students to present elements of their presentations in their native language if it is appropriate to the topic.

Suggestions for Further Reading

Featured Titles:

Things Fall Apart
Chinua Achebe, *Anchor Books, 1959*

Fiction Set in Umofia, a small Ibo village in Nigeria, this novel explores the destructive effects of European values on African culture. The story centers on Okonkwo, one of the most honored men of his village. Okonkwo is wealthy, industrious, and brave, but he also has a violent temper and is overly concerned about his status. When he accidentally kills a member of his tribe, he is sent into exile for seven years. During Okonkwo's exile, a Christian missionary arrives in Umofia and converts many of the Ibo. This development is set within the context of an escalating British presence, which includes a new government and the threat of vast military might. Under these pressures, traditional Ibo society simply collapses. When Okonkwo returns to Umofia, he tries to fight the British presence, a decision that leads to disastrous consequences.

One Day in the Life of Ivan Denisovich
Alexander Solzhenitsyn, *translated by Ralph Parker, Signet Classic, 1998*

Fiction This powerful work of fiction exposes the brutality and inhumanity of the former Soviet Union's political oppression. Set in a Siberian forced-labor prison camp, the novel details the events of an ordinary day in January 1951 as seen through the eyes of a political prisoner, Ivan Denisovich Shukhov. The prisoner, wrongfully convicted of treason during World War II and sentenced to ten years in the labor camp, manages to maintain his humanity and dignity despite the camp's relentless dehumanization. His strength and his determination to survive are moving tributes to the human spirit.

Work Presented in Unit Nine:
If sampling a portion of the following text has built your interest, treat yourself to the full work.

Night
Elie Wiesel, *translated by Stella Rodway, Pearson Prentice Hall, 2000*

Related British Literature:
Lord of the Flies
William Golding, *Perigee, 1987*

This novel about British schoolboys stranded on an island is both an adventure story and a parable about the nature of evil.

Related American Literature:
Something to Declare
Julia Alvarez, *Plume, 1999*

In this collection of amusing and insightful essays, Alvarez discusses her life as a Dominican immigrant in America and her struggles to become a writer.

Many of these titles are available in the Prentice Hall/Penguin Literature Library. Consult your teacher before choosing one.

Suggestions for Further Reading ■ 1365

Planning Students' Further Reading

Discussions of literature can raise sensitive and often controversial issues. Before you recommend further reading to your students, consider the values and sensitivities of your community as well as the age, ability, and sophistication of your students. It is also good policy to preview literature before you recommend it to students. The notes below offer some guidance on specific titles.

Things Fall Apart, by Chinua Achebe

Achebe's novel of the conflict in Nigeria between European and African cultures features polygamy, war-time violence, alcohol, and overt sexual references.

Lexile: Appropriate for high school students

One Day in the Life of Ivan Denisovich, by Alexander Solzhenitsyn

Throughout this novel, Solzhenitsyn graphically portrays life at a Soviet labor camp in the 1950s. Some readers might be offended by the profanity used by the characters and by the inhumane, unsanitary conditions they live in. Also, the prisoners frequently mention tobacco and smoking, one of the few pleasures they have in the camp.
Lexile: 900L

Night, by Elie Wiesel

The book chronicles anti-Semitism and the enslavement, oppression, and genocide of European Jews during World War II, as well as the author's temporary loss of faith. Sexual abuse is also touched on, and offensive language is used.
Lexile: 590L

Lord of the Flies, by William Golding

Sensitive issues include the violence that occurs and the sexual imagery that is used when the pig is slaughtered.
Lexile: 770L

Something to Declare, by Julia Alvarez

This work includes accounts of racial and gender stereotyping. It also refers to the use of illegal substances.

Lexile: Appropriate for high school students

RESOURCES

■ Reading and Vocabulary Handbook

■ Literary Handbook

■ Writing Handbook

■ Communications Handbook

■ Grammar, Usage, and Mechanics Handbook

■ Indexes

GLOSSARY

High utility and academic words appear in green.

abases (ə bās´ əz) v. lowers; brings down

abhor (ab hôr´) v. feel disgust for; hate

accordance (ə kôrd´ 'ns) n. agreement; harmony

accrue (ə krōō´) v. come to as an advantage or a right

adjured (a joord´) v. ordered solemnly

adroit (ə droit´) adj. skillful in a physical or mental way

affably (af´ ə blē) adv. in a friendly manner

affidavit (af´ ə dā´ vit) n. legal document containing sworn testimony

affinity (ə fin´ i tē) n. close relationship; natural liking

affliction (ə flik´ shən) n. something that causes pain or distress

alters v. changes

analyze (an´ ə līz) v. break down a topic or issue into parts and explain them

ancestral (an ses´ trəl) adj. inherited, as from an ancestor

anguish (aŋ´ gwish) n. great suffering; agony

anoint (ə noint´) v. to rub oil or ointment on

anticipate (an tis´ ə pāt´) v. expect

antiquity (an tik´ wə tē) n. early period of history

apply (ə plī´) v. tell how you use information in a specific situation

appropriate (ə prō´ prē āt´) v. take for one's own use

assent (ə sent´) n. expression of agreement

assimilate (ə sim´ ə lāt´) v. absorb; incorporate into a greater body

avenged (ə venjd´) v. took revenge on behalf of

avenger (ə venj´ ər) n. one who takes revenge

awe (ô) n. feelings of reverence, fear, and wonder

babel (bab´ əl) n. confusion of voices or sounds

bashful (bash´ fəl) adj. shy

beneficent (bə nef´ ə sənt) adj. kind; helpful; charitable

benevolent (bə nev´ ə lənt) adj. doing or inclined to do good; kindly; charitable

bereft (bē reft´) adj. deprived or robbed

beseeching (bē sēch´ iŋ) adj. asking for something earnestly

bewildered (bē wil´ dərd) adj. puzzled; confused

bias (bī´ əs) n. prejudice; partiality

bland (bland) adj. mild

blaspheming (blas fēm´ iŋ) adj. irreverent

blasphemous (blas´ fə məs) adj. showing disrespect toward God or religious teachings

blight (blīt) n. destructive disease

bountiful (boun´ tə fəl) adj. generous; abundant

brazen (brā´ zən) adj. literally, of brass; shamelessly bold

buffeted (buf´ it id) v. struck sharply

calamity (kə lam´ ə tē) n. deep trouble

calculating (kal´ kyōō lāt´ iŋ) adj. shrewd or cunning

candor (kan´ dər) n. open honesty and frankness

caricature (kar´ i kə chər) n. likeness or imitation that is so distorted or inferior as to seem ridiculous

chasm (kaz´ əm) n. deep crack in Earth's surface

chastised (chas´ tīzd) v. punished

chastisements (chas´ tiz mənts) n. punishments

chide (chīd) v. scold

clemency (klem´ ən sē) n. mercy toward an enemy or offender

clenched (klencht) v. gripped firmly or tightly

commiserate (kə miz´ ər āt´) v. share grief or sorrow

compare (kəm per´) v. tell the important similarities and explain why they are important

compassionate (kəm pash´ ən it) adj. feeling or showing sympathy or pity

competence (käm´ pə təns) n. ability

comprised (kəm prīzd´) v. included; consisted of

conclude (kən klood´) v. tell how you use reasoning to reach a decision or opinion based on the information provided

conduits (kän´ dōō itz) n. channels or pipes

conflagration (kän´ flə grā´ shən) n. large, destructive fire

congealed (kən jēld´) v. thickened; solidified

conjectures (kən jek´ chərz) n. guesses

connoisseur (kän´ ə sur´) n. person with expert judgment and taste

connotations (kän´ ə tā´ shənz) n. ideas suggested by a word that go beyond its concrete meaning

consecrate (kän´sə krāt´) v. cause to be revered or honored

considerably (kən sid´ er ə blē) adv. to a great degree

consonant (kän´ sə nənt) adj. in harmony or agreement

conspicuous (kən spik´ yōō əs) adj. easy to see or perceive

constitution (kän´ stə tōō´ shən) n. structure or makeup of a person or thing

consummation (kän´ sə mā´ shən) n. state of supreme perfection, skillfulness, and expertise

contention (kən ten´ shən) n. disputing; quarreling

contraband (kän´ trə band´) n. unlawful or forbidden goods

contrast (kən trast´) v. tell the important differences and explain why they are important

convalescent (kän´ və les´ ənt) n. person who is recovering health after illness

corrupt (kə rupt´) adj. spoiled by sin or dishonesty; rotten

countenance (koun´ tə nəns) n. the look on a person's face

courtly (kôrt´ lē) adj. dignified; polite; elegant

covenant (kuv´ ə nənt) n. serious, binding agreement

crone (krōn) n. very old woman

cue (kyōō) n. prompt or reminder

culmination (kul´ mə nā´ shən) n. highest point or climax

debacle (di bäk´ əl) n. overwhelming failure or defeat

deduce (dē dōōs´) v. tell what you figure out by using logic to apply general information to a particular situation

deference (def´ ər əns) n. submission to the desires or opinions of another; courteous regard or respect

define (dē fīn´) v. tell the specific qualities or features that make something what it is

degree (di grē´) n. step; stage; level

demarcation (dē´ mär kā´ shən) n. boundary

demonstrate (dəm´ ən strāt´) v. use examples to show that you understand how the information works in a specific situation

denounce (dē nouns´) v. accuse publicly

deportees (dē´ pôr tēz´) n. people ordered to leave a country

derive (di rīv´) v. to get or receive from a source

describe (di skrīb´) v. show that you know and understand something by explaining it in detail

desecrating (des´ i krāt´ iŋ) v. treating as not sacred

despicable (dəs´ pi kə bəl) adj. deserving to be despised; contemptible

despondent (di spän´ dənt) adj. dejected; hopeless

destitute (des´ tə tōōt´) adj. extremely poor

diabolical (dī ə bäl´ ik əl) adj. devilish; wicked

differentiate (dif´ ər en´ shē āt) v. identify and explain the qualities that distinguish two items or ideas

diffidence (dif´ ə dəns) n. lack of confidence in oneself

discord (dis´ kôrd) n. dissension; conflict

discrimination (di skrim´ i nā´ shən) n. show of partiality or prejudice

disdain (dis dān´) n. strong dislike

dispatch (di spach´) v. kill

dispel (di spel´) v. cause to vanish

disposed (di spōzd´) adj. inclined; tending toward

disreputable (dis rep´ yōō tə bəl) adj. not fit to be seen or approved

distinguishing (di stiŋ´ gwish iŋ) adj. serving to mark as separate or different

dominion (də min´ yən) n. kingdom; area of rule

duped (dōōpt) v. tricked; fooled

earnest (ur´ nist) adj. serious; not joking

ecstasy (ek´ stə sē) n. great joy

eddies (ed´ ēz) n. waters moving in circles against the main current

elated (ē lāt´ əd) adj. extremely happy; joyful

elixir (ē liks´ ir) n. magical potion that cures all ailments

eloquence (el´ ə kwəns) n. fluent, persuasive speech

endeavor (en dev´ ər) n. earnest attempt at achievement

endowed (en doud´) v. given, or provided with

enmity (en´ mə tē) n. state of being enemies; antagonism; hostility

enraptured (en rap´ chərd) adj. completely delighted; spellbound; filled with great pleasure

enumerating (ē nōō´ mər āt´ iŋ) v. counting; listing

envoys (än´ voiz´) n. messengers

epidemic (ep´ ə dem´ ik) n. rapidly and widely spreading disease

equable (ek´ wə bəl) adj. steady; uniform

esteemed (e stēmd´) v. valued; respected

estranged (e strānjd´) adj. isolated and unfriendly; alienated

euphemisms (yōō´ fə miz´ əmz) n. words or phrases that are less expressive or direct but considered less distasteful or offensive than others

evacuated (e vak´ yōō at əd) v. made empty; withdrawn

evaluate (ē val´ yōō āt´) v. determine the value or importance of something

evasions (ē vā´ zhənz) n. attempts to avoid duties or questions

exalted (eg zôlt´ id) adj. lifted high because of dignity or honor

excruciating (eks krōō´ shē āt´ iŋ) adj. causing intense mental or bodily pain

exhorting (eg zôrt´ iŋ) v. urging

expanse (ek spans´) n. very large open area

extirpate (ek´ stər pāt´) v. exterminate; destroy or remove completely

extortions (eks tôr´ shənz) n. acts of obtaining money or something else through threats, violence, or misuse of authority

exuded (ig zōōd´ id) v. discharged a liquid through the skin

exulting (eg zult´ iŋ) v. rejoicing

exults (eg zults´) v. rejoices greatly

fasting (fast´ iŋ) v. eating very little or nothing

fathom (fa*th*´ əm) v. probe the depths of; understand

fathomless (fa*th*´ əm les) adj. immeasurably deep

fervent (fur´ vənt) adj. intensely devoted or earnest

fervor (fur´ vər) n. strong or heated feeling; zeal

fettered (fet´ ərd) adj. shackled; chained

fetters (fet´ ərz) n. shackles; chains

flounders (floun´ dərz) v. struggles to move

flourish (flu' ish) n. fanfare, as of trumpets

flourishes (flur´ ish ez) v. thrives; grows vigorously

foretaste (fôr´ tāst´) n. slight experience or hint of something that is still to come

fraternized (frat´ ər nīzd´) v. associated in a brotherly way; socialized

frivolous (friv´ ə ləs) adj. silly and light-minded; not sensible

frugality (frōō gal´ ə tē) n. thrift

frugally (frōō´ gə lē) adv. thriftily; economically

fungus (fuŋ´ gəs) n. mildew; any of a group of plants lacking leaves and roots

furtive (fur´ tiv) adj. done in a secret or sneaky way

furtively (fur´ tiv lē) adv. in a sneaky manner, as if to hinder observation

gawking (gôk´ iŋ) v. staring foolishly; gaping

glaze (glāz) v. fit glass to a window; cover with a shiny finish

glean (glēn) v. collect grain left by reapers

glimmering (glim´ ər iŋ) v. flickering; giving a faint, unsteady light

glistens (glis´ enz) v. shines or sparkles with reflected light

grafter (graft´ ər) n. someone who takes advantage of his or her position to gain money or property dishonestly

gratify (grat´ i f ī) v. please

grotesque (grō tesk´) adj. strangely distorted

guile (gīl) n. trickery

gyration (jī rā´ shən) n. circular or spiral motion

haggard (hag´ ərd) adj. wasted; worn; gaunt

hallow (hal´ ō) v. make holy or sacred

harrowed (har´ ōd) v. distressed; tormented

harrowing (har´ ō iŋ) adj. disturbing; frightening

hastened (hās´ ənd) v. hurried; moved swiftly

hazards (haz´ ərdz) n. dangers

heralds (her´ əldz) v. announces; introduces

homage (häm´ ij) n. act of reverence and respect

hordes (hôrdz) n. large moving crowds; wandering tribes

hypocrite (hip´ ə krit´) n. someone who merely pretends to be virtuous

identify (ī den´ tə fī) v. name or show that you recognize something

illustrate (il´ ə strāt´) v. give examples that show what information means

illustrious (i lus´ trē əs) adj. distinguished or outstanding

imminent (im´ ə nənt) adj. ready to happen at any moment

immolation (im´ ə lā´ shən) n. offering or killing made as a sacrifice

immortality (im´ môr tal´ i tē) n. quality or state of being exempt from death; unending existence

impediments n. obstacles

impelled (im peld´) v. used here as adj. pushed or driven forward

imperceptibly (im´ pər sep´ tə blē) adv. without being noticed

impertinence (im purt´ 'n əns) n. insolence; impudence

impervious (im pur´ vē əs) adj. not affected by, or unable to be damaged

importunity (im´ pôr tōōn´ i tē) n. persistence

impracticable (im prak´ ti kə bəl) adj. not capable of being put into practice

impudence (im´ pyōō dəns) n. rashness; boldness

impulsive (im pul´ siv) adj. sudden and unthinking

incantation (in´ kan tā´ shən) n. chant

incensed (in senst´) adj. very angry; enraged

incongruous (in käŋ´ grōō əs) adj. inconsistent; lacking in harmony; not fitting a situation; inappropriate

incredulous (in krej´ oo ləs) adj. disbelieving; doubtful; skeptical

incurred (in kurd´) v. brought about through one's own actions

indefinitely (in def´ ə nit lē) adv. without a specified limit

indictment (in dīt´ mənt) n. formal accusation

indignantly (in dig´ nənt lē) adv. in a way showing righteous anger or scorn

indiscreet (in´ di skrēt´) adj. unwise or not careful

induced (in dōōst´) v. persuaded; caused

inexorably (in eks´ ə rə blē) adv. relentlessly

infamous (in´ fə məs) adj. disgraceful

infatuation (in fach´ ōō ā´ shən) n. foolish or shallow feelings of affection

infer (in fur´) v. show that you have used text details to figure out what it not stated

infirmity (in fur´ mə tē) n. weakness; illness

ingenuity (in´ je nōō´ ə tē) n. cleverness; inventiveness

innuendo (in´ yōō en´ dō) n. indirect remark or gesture that hints at something bad; sly suggestion

insatiableness (in sā´ shə bəl nəs) n. the quality of being impossible to fill

interpret (in tur´ prət) v. explain the underlying meaning of a phrase, a passage, or an entire work by examining words, images, and events

intimacy (in´ tə mə sē) n. familiarity; warmth

intolerable (in täl´ ər ə bəl) adj. unbearable; painful; cruel

intrepid (in trep´ id) adj. brave; fearless

intricate (in´ tri kit) adj. complicated; elaborate

intuition (in´ tōō ish´ ən) n. instinctive understanding

inverted (in vurt´ id) adj. upside down

invoke (in vōk´) v. summon; cause to appear; call on

invoked (in vōkt´) v. called on for help

iridescent (ir´ i des´ ənt) adj. showing rainbow-like shifts in color

jetty (jet´ ē) n. wall or barrier built into a body of water to protect a harbor

jubilant (jōō´ bə lənt) adj. extremely happy; exultant

judge (juj) v. assess or form an opinion about something

label (lā´ bəl) v. attach the correct name to something

labyrinths (lab´ ə rinths) n. structures with an intricate network of winding passages

lamentation (lam´ ən tā´ shən) n. outward expression of grief; weeping or wailing

lamented (lə ment´ id) v. felt deep sorrow for

languishing (laŋ´ gwish iŋ) v. becoming weak

liquidated (lik´ wi dāt´ id) adj. disposed of; ended; killed

loathsome (lō*th*´ səm) adj. detestable

loomed (lōōmd) v. appeared in a large or threatening form

lucid (lōō´ sid) adj. clear; apparent

malice (mal´ is) n. ill will; evil intent; spite

malicious (mə lish´ əs) adj. intending harm; spiteful

malignant (mə lig′ nənt) adj. very harmful

manifest (man′ ə fest) adj. clear; evident

manifestations (man′ ə fes tā′ shənz) n. material forms

manifested (man′ ə fest′ id) v. proved or revealed

manifold (man′ ə fōld′) adj. many; various

meager (mē′ gər) adj. thin; lean

mediocre (mē′ dē ō′ kər) adj. not good enough; inferior

mitigated (mit′ ə gāt′ id) v. moderated; eased

mobilized (mō′ bə līzd′) v. ready for action or battle

monotone (män ə tōn) n. sound or song that repeats a single note

monotonously (mə nät′ ′n əs lē) adv. done in a way that goes on and on without variation

monotony (mə nät′ ′n ē) n. tedious sameness

morose (mə rōs′) adj. gloomy; in a bad or sullen mood

multitude (mul′ tə tōōd) n. a great number

munificence (myōō nif′ ə səns) n. great generosity

murmur (mur′ mər) n. low, indistinct, continuous sound

mutely (myōōt′ lē) adv. silently; without the capacity to speak

myriad (mir′ ē əd) adj. many; varied

myriads (mir′ ē ədz) n. great numbers of persons or things

naturalistic (nach′ ər əl is′ tik) adj. faithful to nature

navigated (nav′ i gāt′ əd) v. piloted; steered (a boat)

nimble (nim′ bəl) adj. able to move quickly and lightly; agile

nonchalantly (nän′ shə länt′ lē) adv. in a casually indifferent manner

notions (nō′ shənz) n. ideas

obsequiously (əb sē′ kwē əs lē) adj. in a manner that shows too great a willingness to serve

obsolete (äb′ sə lēt′) adj. out of date; out of use

obstinacy (äb′ stə nə sē) n. stubbornness

obstinate (äb′ stə nət) adj. determined to have one's way; stubborn

ominous (äm′ ə nəs) adj. hinting at bad things to come

oratory (ôr′ ə tôr′ ē) n. skillful public speaking

painstakingly (pānz′ tāk iŋ lē) adv. using great diligence or care

pallid (pal′ id) adj. pale

palpable (pal′ pə bəl) adj. able to be touched, felt, or handled

paternal (pə tur′ nəl) adj. like a father

pathos (pā′ thäs′) n. quality in something that evokes sorrow or compassion

perfunctorily (pər fuŋk′ tôr ə lē) adv. indifferently; with little interest or care

perilous (per′ ə ləs) adj. dangerous

perjured (pur′ jərd) adj. purposely false

pervades (pər vādz′) v. spreads throughout

pestilence (pes′ tə lens) n. plague

piety (pī′ ə tē) n. devotion to religious duties or practices; respect for the gods

pillaging (pil′ ij iŋ) v. plundering; looting

placidly (plas′ id lē) adv. calmly

plaintive (plān′ tiv) adj. expressing sorrow; mournful

plateau (pla tō′) n. elevated tract of relatively level land

plight (plīt) n. sad or difficult situation

plunder (plun′ dər) v. to rob by force in warfare

poised (poizd) adj. balanced and steady, as though suspended

pomp (pämp) n. ceremonial splendor; magnificence

portents (pôr′ tents′) n. signs that suggest what is about to occur

precepts (prē′ septs) n. rules of conduct

precipitous (prē sip′ ə təs) adj. steep like a precipice; sheer

predict (prē dikt′) v. tell what you think will happen based on details in the text

presumed (prē zōōmd′) v. expected; supposed

primal (prī′ məl) adj. original; fundamental

pristine (pris′ tēn′) adj. unspoiled; uncorrupted

proclaiming (prō klām′ iŋ) v. announcing publicly and loudly

prodigal (präd′ i gəl) n. person who spends money wastefully

prodigy (präd′ ə jē) n. person of very great ability

proffering (präf′ ər iŋ) v. offering

prone (prōn) adj. lying face downward

prophecy (präf′ ə sē) n. prediction of the future

prophet (präf′ ət) n. inspired person who speaks great truths or foretells the future

prophetic (prō fet′ ik) adj. giving a prediction of the future

proprieties (prō prī′ ə tēz) n. conformities with what is considered fitting, suitable, or proper

prostrate (präs′ trāt) adj. lying with one's face down

prowess (prou′ is) n. ability

putrid (pyōō′ trid) adj. rotten; stinking

rank (raŋk) adj. foul; odorous

rebuked (ri byōōkt′) v. scolded sharply

recall (ri kôl′) v. tell the details as you remember them

reciprocity (res′ ə präs′ ə tē) n. mutual exchange

recompense (rek′ əm pens′) n. payment of what is owed; reward

rectify (rek′ tə fī′) v. to set things right or restore balance

redeem (ri dēm′) v. buy back; fulfill a promise

renown (ri noun′) n. fame

repentance (ri pen′ təns) n. sorrow for wrongdoing; remorse

reposes (ri pōz′ əz) v. puts to rest

reprimand (rep′ rə mand′) v. chastise; blame

reprobate (rep′ rə bāt′) n. scoundrel

repulse (ri puls′) v. drive back; repel, as an attack

resistant (ri zis′ tənt) adj. strong; firm

resolutely (rez′ ə loot′ lē) adv. in a determined way

resplendent (ri splen′ dənt) adj. brightly shining; dazzling

retorted (ri tôrt′ id) v. replied, especially in a sharp or challenging way

retribution (re′ trə byōō′ shən) n. punishment; revenge

revelation (rev′ ə lā′ shən) n. striking disclosure of something

reverberates (ri vur′ bə rātz′) v. echoes; sounds again

reverence (rev′ rəns) v. show great respect

ritual (rich′ ōō əl) n. observance of prescribed rules

sacrosanct (sak′ rō saŋkt′) adj. very holy; sacred

sated (sāt′ ed) v. completely satisfied

scope (skōp) n. range of perception or understanding

scorn (skôrn) n. contempt; open dislike or derision

scorn (skôrn) v. reject

scruples (skrōō′ pəlz) n. feelings of doubt over what is ethical

scurry (skur′ ē) v. to run hastily; to scamper

sediment (sed′ ə mənt) n. waste material that settles to the bottom of a liquid

sensual (sen′ shōō əl) adj. pleasing to the senses

sequence (sē′ kwəns) n. order; succession

serene (sə rēn′) adj. clear; calm; peaceful

serenity (sə ren′ ə tē) n. peace; tranquillity

serpentine (sur′ pən tēn′) adj. resembling a snake

shards (shärdz) n. sharp fragments

sheaves (shēvz) n. bundles of cut stalks of grain

shrewdest (shrōōd′ est) adj. most cunning or clever

siege (sēj) n. the surrounding of a fortified place by an opposing force, such as an army

sinister (sin′ is tər) adj. wicked; threatening harm

skulks (skulks) v. lurks in a cowardly way

sleek (slēk) adj. smooth; glossy

sojourn (sō′ jurn) n. visit

solitary (säl′ ə ter′ ē) adj. lone; single; sole

solitude (säl′ ə tōōd′) n. isolation

somber (säm′ bər) adj. dark; gloomy

sordid (sôr′ did) adj. filthy; depressingly wretched

sovereign (säv′ rən) n. monarch or ruler

sovereign (säv′ rən) adj. chief; superior; highest

spendthrift (spend′ thrift′) n. person who spends money carelessly

squander (skwän′ dər) v. spend or use wastefully

squandered (skwän′ dərd) v. wasted

squandering (skwän′ dər iŋ) v. spending money wastefully

steadfast (sted′ fast′) adj. firm; not changing

stems (stemz) v. stops or dams up (as a river)

stoically (stō′ i klē) adv. done with indifference to pain or pleasure

strains (strānz) n. pl. passages of music; tunes; airs

stupor (stōōp′ ər) n. mental dullness, as if drugged

submissive (sub mis′ iv) adj. yielding; giving in without resistance

subordinate (sə bôr′ də nit) adj. inferior; ranking under or below

subsided (səb sīd′ ed) v. settled; lessened; died down

succor (suk′ ər) n. aid; relief

suffuses (sə fyōō′ zəz) v. overspreads; fills with a glow

sullen adj. gloomy; dismal

summarize (sum′ ə rīz′) v. briefly state the most important information and ideas in the text

sumptuous (sump′ chōō əs) adj. costly; lavish

superimposed (sōō′ pər im pōzd′) v. placed on top of something else

supple (sup′ əl) adj. easily bent; flexible

sustained (sə stānd′) v. maintained; supported

taciturn (tas′ ə turn) adj. almost always silent; not given to talking

tactless (takt′ lis) adj. unskilled in dealing with people

tangible (tan′ jə bəl) adj. definite; objective

tardily (tär′ də lē) adv. late

teemed (tēmd) v. was full of; swarmed

tempest (tem′ pist) n. storm

tempo (tem′ pō) n. rate of speed; pace

tenacity (tə nas′ ə tē) n. persistence; stubbornness

tenuous (ten′ yōō əs) adj. slender or fine, as a fiber

terminology (tur′ mə näl′ ə jē) n. terms used in a specific discipline

throngs (thrôŋz) n. crowds

thwarted (thwôrt′ əd) v. hindered; frustrated

tremulous (trem′ yōō ləs) adj. quivering; shaking

tumult (tōō′ mult′) n. commotion; confusion

unfettered (un fet′ ərd) adj. unrestrained

unhampered (un ham′ pərd) adv. freely; without interference

unmarred (un märd′) adj. unspoiled; unimpaired

unrestrained (un ri strānd′) v. not checked or controlled

vassal (vas′ əl) n. person who holds land under the feudal system, pledging loyalty to an overlord

vehemently (vē′ ə mənt lē) adv. forcefully; intensely

veiled (vāld) v. covered

vitality (vī tal′ ə tē) n. energy; life force

vivacity (vī vas′ ə tē) n. liveliness or animation

void (vɔid) n. empty space; total emptiness

volition (vo lish′ ən) n. act of using the will

vulgar (vul′ gər) adj. coarse; common

wharf (wôrf) n. structure built as a landing place for boats

writhes (rīthz) v. twists and turns the body, as in agony

zeal (zēl) n. ardor; fervor

TIPS FOR IMPROVING READING FLUENCY

When you were younger, you learned to read. Then, you read to expand your experiences or for pure enjoyment. Now, you are expected to read to learn. As you progress in school, you are given more and more material to read. The tips on these pages will help you improve your reading fluency, or your ability to read easily, smoothly, and expressively. Use these tips as you read daily.

Keeping Your Concentration

One common problem that readers face is the loss of concentration. When you are reading an assignment, you might find yourself rereading the same sentence several times without really understanding it. The first step in changing this behavior is to notice that you do it. Becoming an active, aware reader will help you get the most from your assignments. Practice using these strategies:

- Cover what you have already read with a note card as you go along. Then, you will not be able to reread without noticing that you are doing it.

- Set a purpose for reading beyond just completing the assignment. Then, read actively by pausing to ask yourself questions about the material as you read. Check the accuracy of your answers as you continue to read.

- Use the Reading Strategy instruction and notes that appear with each selection in this textbook.

- Look at any art or illustrations that accompany the reading and use picture clues to help your comprehension.

- Stop reading after a specified period of time (for example, 5 minutes) and summarize what you have read. To help you with this strategy, use the Reading Check questions that appear with each selection in this textbook. Reread to find any answers you do not know.

Reading Phrases

Fluent readers read phrases rather than individual words. Reading this way will speed up your reading and improve your comprehension. Here are some useful ideas:

- Experts recommend rereading as a strategy to increase fluency. Choose a passage of text that is neither too hard nor too easy. Read the same passage aloud several times until you can read it smoothly. When you can read the passage fluently, pick another passage and keep practicing.

- Read aloud into a tape recorder. Then, listen to the recording, noting your accuracy, pacing, and expression. You can also read aloud and share feedback with a partner.

- Use the *Prentice Hall Listening to Literature* audiotapes or CDs to hear the selections read aloud. Read along silently in your textbook, noticing how the reader uses his or her voice and emphasizes certain words and phrases.

- Set a target reading rate. Time yourself as you read and work to increase your speed without sacrificing the level of your comprehension.

Understanding Key Vocabulary

If you do not understand some of the words in an assignment, you may miss out on important concepts. Therefore, it is helpful to keep a dictionary nearby when you are reading. Follow these steps:

- Before you begin reading, scan the text for unfamiliar words or terms. Find out what those words mean before you begin reading.
- Use context—the surrounding words, phrases, and sentences—to help you determine the meanings of unfamiliar words.
- If you are unable to understand the meaning through context, refer to the dictionary.

Paying Attention to Punctuation

When you read, pay attention to punctuation. Commas, periods, exclamation points, semicolons, and colons tell you when to pause or stop. They also indicate relationships between groups of words. When you recognize these relationships you will read with greater understanding and expression. Look at the chart below.

Punctuation Mark	Meaning
comma	brief pause
period	pause at the end of a thought
exclamation point	pause that indicates emphasis
semicolon	pause between related but distinct thoughts
colon	pause before giving explanation or examples

Using the Reading Fluency Checklist

Use the checklist below each time you read a selection in this textbook. In your Language Arts journal or notebook, note which skills you need to work on and chart your progress each week.

Reading Fluency Checklist

- ☐ Preview the text to check for difficult or unfamiliar words.
- ☐ Practice reading aloud.
- ☐ Read according to punctuation.
- ☐ Break down long sentences into the subject and its meaning.
- ☐ Read groups of words for meaning rather than reading single words.
- ☐ Read with expression (change your tone of voice to add meaning to the word).

Reading is a skill that can be improved with practice. The key to improving your fluency is to read. The more you read, the better your reading will become.

HIGH FREQUENCY ACADEMIC WORDS

Academic vocabulary is the specialized vocabulary that appears frequently throughout academic texts in all content areas, including standardized tests and textbooks. The words on this page are culled from a variety of academic vocabulary word lists, including the work of Averil Coxhead, Jim Burke, and Xue Guoyi and I.S.P. Nation. Words in green are featured in the Vocabulary Workshops in this book.

abstract
affect
alter
analogy
analyze
anticipate
apply
approach
appropriate
approximate
aspects
assemble
assert
assess
assume
brief
category
chart
cite
clarify
code
coherent
compare
compile
complement
conceive
conclude
conduct
confirm
consequence
consist
constant
constitutes
consult
contend
context
contradict
contrast
correlate
correspond
credible
credit
criteria
crucial
debate
deduce
define
demonstrate
derive
describe

detect
devise
differentiate
dimension
diminish
discriminate
domain
draft
edit
elements
emphasize
equivalent
establish
estimate
evaluate
exclude
exhibit
extract
factor
feature
focus
format
formulate
fragment
graph
highlight
hypothesize
identify
illustrate
imply
incorporate
indicate
infer
integrate
interact
interpret
investigate
involve
isolate
judge
label
locate
margin
metaphor
method
modify
monitor
notation
objective
occur

participation
perspective
plot
predict
presume
previous
primary
prior
process
project
quote
reaction
recall
relevant
require
respond
reveal
revise
score
series
significance
source
spatial
specific
speculate
strategy
structure
style
subjective
subsequent
substitute
sum
summarize
summary
survey
technique
theme
thesis
tone
topic
trace
trait
transition
unique
utilize
valid
vary
verify

THE LIFE OF THE ENGLISH LANGUAGE

The life of every language depends on the people who use it. Whenever you use English by asking a question, talking on the phone, going to a movie, reading a magazine, or writing an e-mail, you keep it healthy and valuable.

What's in a Word?

Using a Dictionary

Use a **dictionary** to find the meaning, the pronunciation, and the part of speech of a word. Consult a dictionary also to trace the word's *etymology*, or its origin. Etymology explains how words change, how they are borrowed from other languages, and how new words are invented, or "coined."

Here is an entry from a dictionary. Notice what it tells about the word *anthology*.

anthology (an thäl´ə jē) *n., pl.* **–gies** [Gr. *anthologia*, a garland, collection of short poems < *anthologos*, gathering flowers < *anthos*, flower + *legein*, to gather] a collection of poems, stories, songs, excerpts, etc., chosen by the compiler

Dictionaries provide the denotation of each word, or its objective meaning. The symbol < means "comes from" or "is derived from." In this case, the Greek words for "flower" and "gather" combined to form a Greek word that meant a garland, and then that word became an English word that means a collection of literary flowers—a collection of literature like the one you are reading now.

Using a Thesaurus

Use a **thesaurus** to increase your vocabulary. In a thesaurus, you will find synonyms, or words that have similar meanings, for most words. Follow these guidelines to use a thesaurus:

- Do not choose a word just because it sounds interesting or educated. Choose the word that expresses exactly the meaning you intend.

- To avoid errors, look up the word in a dictionary to check its precise meaning and to make sure you are using it properly.

Here is an entry from a thesaurus. Notice what it tells about the word *book*.

book *noun*

A printed and bound work: tome, volume. See WORDS.

book *verb* **1.** To register in or as if in a book: catalog, enroll, inscribe, list, set down, write down. See REMEMBER. **2.** To cause to be set aside, as for one's use, in advance: bespeak, engage, reserve. *See* GET.

If the word can be used as different parts of speech, as *book* can, the thesaurus entry provides synonyms for the word as each part of speech. Many words also have *connotations*, or emotional associations that the word calls to mind. A thesaurus entry also gives specific synonyms for each connotation of the word.

> **Activity:** Look up the words *behemoth* and *caravan* in a dictionary. (a) What are their etymologies? (b) Explain what their etymologies reveal about the development of English.
>
> Then, check the word *behemoth* in a thesaurus. (c) What are two synonyms for this word? (d) In what way do the connotations of the synonyms differ?

The Origin and Development of English

OLD ENGLISH English began about the year 500 when Germanic tribes from the middle of Europe traveled west and settled in Britain. These peoples—the Angles, Saxons, and Jutes—spoke a Germanic language that combined with Danish and Norse when Vikings attacked Britain and added some Latin elements when Christian missionaries arrived. The result was Old English, which looked like this:

Hwaet! We Gar-Dena	in gear-dagum,
peod-cyninga,	prym gefrunon,
hu da aepelingas	ellen fremedon!

These words are the opening lines of the Old English epic poem *Beowulf*, probably composed in the eighth century. In modern English, they mean: "Listen! We know the ancient glory of the Spear-Danes, and the heroic deeds of those noble kings!"

MIDDLE ENGLISH The biggest change in English took place after the Norman Conquest of Britain in 1066. The Normans spoke a dialect of Old French, and Old English changed dramatically when the Normans became the new aristocracy. From about 1100 to 1500, the people of Britain spoke what we now call Middle English.

> A Knyght ther was, and that a worthy man,
>
> That fro the tyme that he first bigan
>
> To riden out, he loved chivalrie,
>
> Trouthe and honour, fredom and curtesie.

These lines from the opening section of Geoffrey Chaucer's *Canterbury Tales* (c. 1400) are much easier for us to understand than the lines from *Beowulf*. They mean: "There was a knight, a worthy man who, from the time he began to ride, loved chivalry, truth, honor, freedom, and courtesy."

MODERN ENGLISH During the Renaissance, with its emphasis on reviving classical culture, Greek and Latin languages exerted a strong influence on the English language. In addition, Shakespeare added about two thousand words to the language. Grammar, spelling, and pronunciation continued to change. Modern English was born.

> But soft! What light through yonder window breaks?
>
> It is the East, and Juliet is the sun!

These lines from Shakespeare's *Romeo and Juliet* (c. 1600) need no translation, although it is helpful to know that "soft" means "speak softly." Since Shakespeare's day, conventions of usage and grammar have continued to change. For example, the *th* at the ends of many verbs has become *s*. In Shakespeare's time, it was correct to say "Romeo *hath* fallen in love." In our time, it is right to say "he *has* fallen in love." However, the changes of the past five hundred years are not nearly as drastic as the changes from Old English to Middle English, or from Middle English to Modern English. We still speak Modern English.

Old Words, New Words

MODERN ENGLISH has a larger vocabulary than any other language in the world. The *Oxford English Dictionary* contains about a half million words, and it is estimated that another half million scientific and technical terms do not appear in the dictionary. Here are the main ways that new words enter the language:

- **War**—Conquerors introduce new terms and ideas—and new vocabulary, such as *anger*, from Old Norse.

- **Immigration**—When large groups of people move from one country to another, they bring their languages with them, such as *boycott*, from Ireland.

- **Travel and Trade**—Those who travel to foreign lands and those who do business in faraway places bring new words back with them, such as *shampoo*, from Hindi.

- **Science and Technology**—In our time, the amazing growth of science and technology adds multitudes of new words to English, such as *Internet*.

English is also filled with **borrowings**, words taken directly from other languages. Sometimes borrowed words keep basically the same meanings they have in their original languages: *pajamas* (Hindi), *sauna* (Finnish), *camouflage* (French), *plaza* (Spanish). Sometimes borrowed words take

on new meanings. *Sleuth*, for example, an Old Norse word for trail, has come to mean the person who follows a *trail* —a detective.

Mythology contributed to our language too. Some of the days of the week are named after Norse gods—Wednesday was Woden's Day, Thursday was Thor's Day. Greek and Roman myths have given us many words, such as *jovial* (from Jove), *martial* (from Mars), *mercurial* (from Mercury), and *herculean* (from Hercules).

Americanisms are words, phrases, usages, or idioms that originated in American English or that are unique to the way Americans speak. They are expressions of our national character in all its variety: *easy as pie, prairie dog, bamboozle, panhandle, halftime, fringe benefit, bookmobile, jackhammer, southpaw, lickety split*.

Activity: Look up the following words in a dictionary. Describe the ways in which you think these words entered American English.

cafeteria   piano   umbrella   tycoon   boss

The Influence of English

English continues to have an effect on world cultures and literature. There are about three hundred million native English speakers, and about the same number who speak English as a second language. Although more people speak Mandarin Chinese, English is the dominant language of trade, tourism, international diplomacy, science, and technology.

Language is a vehicle of both communication and culture, and the cultural influence of English in the twenty-first century is unprecedented in the history of the world's languages. Beyond business and science, English spreads through sports, pop music, Hollywood movies, television, and journalism. A book that is translated into English reaches many more people than it would in its native language alone. Perhaps most significantly, English dominates the Internet. The next time you log on, notice how many websites from around the world also have an English version. The global use of English is the closest the world has ever come to speaking an international language.

Activity: Choose one area of culture—such as sports, fashion, the arts, or technology—and identify three new words that English has recently added to the world's vocabulary. (a) How do you think non-English speakers feel about the spread of English? (b) Do you think English helps to bring people together? Why or why not?

LITERARY TERMS

ALLEGORY An *allegory* is a literary work with two or more levels of meaning—a literal level and one or more symbolic levels. The events, settings, objects, or characters in an allegory—the literal level—stand for ideas or qualities, such as goodness, tyranny, salvation, and so on. Dante's *Divine Comedy* (p. 657) is an allegory written in the Middle Ages, when allegorical writing was common. Many works can be read allegorically as well as literally, requiring a reader's effort to match every element at the literal level with a corresponding element at the symbolic level. Allegories are also written in the form of parables.

See also Fable *and* Parable.

ALLITERATION *Alliteration* is the repetition of initial consonant sounds in accented syllables. Derek Walcott uses alliteration in these lines from "Omeros:"

. . . higher than those hills / of infernal anthracite.

Especially in poetry, alliteration is used to emphasize and to link words, as well as to create musical sounds.

ALLUSION An *allusion* is a reference to a well-known person, place, event, literary work, or work of art. Writers often make allusions to the Bible, classical Greek and Roman myths, plays by Shakespeare, historical events, and other material with which they expect their readers to be familiar. Canto V of the *Inferno* by Dante (p. 675) contains an allusion to the story of Lancelot.

AMBIGUITY *Ambiguity* is the effect created when words suggest and support two or more divergent interpretations. Ambiguity may be used in literature to express experiences or truths that are complex or even contradictory.

See also Irony.

ANALOGY An *analogy* is an extended comparison of relationships. It is based on the idea or insight that the relationship between one pair of things is like the relationship between another pair. Unlike a metaphor, another form of comparison, an analogy involves an explicit comparison, often using the word *like* or *as*.

See also Metaphor *and* Simile.

ANAPEST See Meter.

ARCHETYPAL LITERARY ELEMENTS *Archetypal literary elements* are patterns in literature found around the world. For instance, the occurrence of events in threes is an archetypal element of fairy tales. *The Epic of Gilgamesh* (p. 17) presents an archetypal battle between the forces of good and the forces of evil. Certain character types, such as mysterious guides, are also archetypal elements of traditional stories. According to some critics, these elements express in symbolic form truths about the human mind.

ASSONANCE *Assonance* is the repetition of vowel sounds in stressed syllables containing dissimilar consonant sounds.

See also Consonance.

BALLAD A *ballad* is a song that tells a story, often about adventure or romance, or a poem imitating such a song. Most ballads are divided into four- or six-line stanzas, are rhymed, use simple language, and depict dramatic action. Many ballads employ a repeated refrain. Some use incremental repetition, in which the refrain is varied slightly each time it appears.

BLANK VERSE *Blank verse* is unrhymed poetry usually written in iambic pentameter (see Meter). Occasional variations in rhythm are introduced in blank verse to create emphasis, variety, and naturalness of sound. Because blank verse sounds much like ordinary spoken English, it is often used in drama, as by Shakespeare, and in poetry.

See also Meter.

CARPE DIEM A Latin phrase, *carpe diem* means "seize the day" or "make the most of passing time." Many great literary works have been written with the *carpe diem* theme.

CHARACTER A person (though not necessarily a human being) who takes part in the action of a literary work is known as a character. Characters can be classified in different ways. A character who plays an important role is called a *major character*. A character who does not is called a *minor character*. A character who plays the central role in a story is called the *protagonist*. A character who opposes the *protagonist* is called the *antagonist*. A *round character* has many aspects to his or her personality. A *flat character* is defined by only a few qualities. A character who changes is called *dynamic*; a character who does not change is called *static*.

See also Characterization *and* Motivation.

CHARACTERIZATION *Characterization* is the act of creating and developing a character. A writer uses *direct characterization* when he or she describes a character's traits explicitly. Writers also use *indirect characterization*. A character's traits can be revealed indirectly in what he or she says, thinks, or does; in a description of his or her appearance; or in the statements, thoughts, or actions of other characters.

See also Character *and* Motivation.

CHOKA A traditional Japanese verse form, *choka* are poems that consist of alternating lines of five and seven syllables, with an additional seven-syllable line at the end. There is no limit to the number of lines in a choka. Choka frequently end with one or more *envoys* consisting of five lines of five, seven, five, seven, and seven syllables. Generally, the envoys elaborate or summarize the theme of the main poem.

CLIMAX The *climax* is the high point of interest or suspense in a literary work. Often, the climax is also the crisis in the plot, the point at which the protagonist changes his or her understanding or situation. Sometimes, the climax coincides with the *resolution*, the point at which the central conflict is ended.

See also Plot.

COMEDY A *comedy* is a literary work, especially a play, that has a happy ending. A comedy often shows ordinary characters in conflict with their society. Types of comedy include *romantic comedy*, which involves problems between lovers, and the *comedy of manners*, which satirically challenges the social customs of a sophisticated society. Comedy is often contrasted with tragedy, in which the protagonist meets an unfortunate end.

See also Drama *and* Tragedy.

CONCEIT A *conceit* is an unusual and surprising comparison between two very different things. This special kind of metaphor or complicated analogy is often the basis for a whole poem. *Petrarchan conceits* make extravagant claims about the beloved's beauty or the speaker's suffering, with comparisons to divine beings, powerful natural forces, and objects that contain a given quality in the highest degree. See Petrarch's "Laura" (p. 730) for an example.

See also Metaphor.

CONFLICT A *conflict* is a struggle between opposing forces. Sometimes, this struggle is internal, or within a character. At other times, the struggle is external, or between the character and some outside force. The outside force may be another character, nature, or some element of society, such as a custom or a political institution. Often, the conflict in a work combines several of these possibilities.

See also Plot.

CONNOTATION *Connotation* refers to the associations that a word calls to mind in addition to its dictionary meaning. For example, the words *home* and *domicile* have the same dictionary meaning. However, the first has positive connotations of warmth and security, whereas the second does not.

See also Denotation.

CONSONANCE Consonance is the repetition of final consonant sounds in stressed syllables containing dissimilar vowel sounds. Following are some examples of consonance: *black/block; slip/slop; creak/croak; feat/fit; slick/slack*. When each word in the pair is used at the end of a line, the effect is one form of *slant rhyme*.

See also Assonance.

COUPLET A *couplet* is a pair of rhyming lines written in the same meter. A *heroic couplet* is a rhymed pair of iambic pentameter lines. In a *closed couplet*, the meaning and grammar are completed within the two lines.

See also Sonnet.

DACTYL *See* Meter.

DENOTATION *Denotation* is the objective meaning of a word—that to which the word refers, independent of other associations that the word calls to mind. Dictionaries list the denotative meanings of words.

See also Connotation.

DIALECT *Dialect* is the form of a language spoken by people in a particular region or group. Dialects differ from one another in grammar, vocabulary, and pronunciation.

DIALOGUE *Dialogue* is a conversation between characters. Writers use dialogue to reveal character, to present events, to add variety to narratives, and to interest readers. Dialogue in a story is usually set off by quotation marks and paragraphing. Dialogue in a play script generally follows the name of the speaker.

DIARY A *diary* is a personal record of daily events, usually written in prose. Most diaries are not written for publication; sometimes, however, interesting diaries or diaries written by influential people are published.

DICTION *Diction* is a writer's word choice. It can be a major determinant of the writer's style. Diction can be described as formal or informal, abstract or concrete, plain or ornate, ordinary or technical.

See also Style.

DIMETER *See* Meter.

DRAMA A *drama* is a story written to be performed by actors. It may consist of one or more large sections, called acts, which are made up of any number of smaller sections, called scenes.

Drama originated in the religious rituals and symbolic reenactments of primitive peoples. The ancient Greeks, who developed drama into a sophisticated art form, created such dramatic forms as tragedy and comedy.

Oedipus the King (p. 468) is a definitive example of Greek tragedy. The classical dramas of the Greeks and the Romans faded away as the Roman empire declined.

Drama revived in Europe during the Middle Ages. The Renaissance produced a number of great dramatists, most notably England's William Shakespeare. Molière's *Tartuffe* is a comedy of manners, a form of drama popular in the seventeenth century. Goethe's tragic *Faust* (p. 846) represents a peak of nineteenth-century Romanticism. Henrik Ibsen's *A Doll House* (p. 942) began a trend toward realistic prose drama and away from drama in verse form. Most of the great plays of the twentieth century are written in prose.

Among the many forms of drama from non-Western cultures are the Nō plays of Japan, such as Zeami's *The Deserted Crone.*

See also Comedy *and* Tragedy.

DRAMATIC MONOLOGUE A *dramatic monologue* is a poem in which an imaginary character speaks to a silent listener. During the monologue, the speaker reveals his or her personality, usually at a moment of crisis.

ELEGY An *elegy* is a solemn and formal lyric poem about death. It may mourn a particular person or reflect on a serious or tragic theme, such as the passing of youth or beauty.

See also Lyric Poem.

END-STOPPED LINE An *end-stopped line* is a line of poetry concluding with a break in the meter and in the meaning. This pause at the end of a line is often punctuated by a period, comma, dash, or semicolon.

See also Run-on Line.

EPIC An *epic* is a long narrative poem about the adventures of gods or of a hero. A *folk epic* is one that was composed orally and passed from storyteller to storyteller. The ancient Greek epics attributed to Homer—the *Iliad* (p. 363) and the *Odyssey*—are folk epics. The *Aeneid* (p. 533), by the Roman poet Virgil, and *The Divine Comedy* (p. 658), by the Italian poet Dante Alighieri, are examples of literary epics from the Classical and Medieval periods, respectively. An epic presents an encyclopedic portrait of the culture in which it was produced.

Epic conventions are traditional characteristics of epic poems, including an opening statement of the theme; an appeal for supernatural help in telling the story (an invocation); a beginning *in medias res* (Latin: "in the middle of things"); catalogs of people and things; accounts of past events; and descriptive phrases.

EPIGRAM An *epigram* is a brief statement in prose or in verse. The concluding couplet in a sonnet may be epigrammatic. An essay may be written in an epigrammatic style.

EPIPHANY *Epiphany* is a term introduced by James Joyce to describe a moment of insight in which a character recognizes a truth. In Colette's "The Bracelet" (p. 1117), the main character's epiphany comes at the end of the story when she realizes she cannot recapture her past.

EPITAPH An *epitaph* is an inscription written on a tomb or burial place. In literature, epitaphs include serious or humorous lines written as if intended for such use.

ESSAY An *essay* is a short nonfiction work about a particular subject. Essays are of many types but may be classified by tone or style as formal or informal. An essay is often classed by its main purpose as descriptive, narrative, expository, argumentative, or persuasive.

EXTENDED METAPHOR *See* Metaphor.

FABLE A *fable* is a brief story, usually with animal characters, that teaches a lesson or moral. The earliest known fables are those attributed to Aesop, a Greek writer of the sixth century B.C. Jean de La Fontaine continued this tradition during the Age of Rationalism with such fables as "The Fox and the Crow" (p. 790) and "The Oak and the Reed" (p. 792).

See also Allegory *and* Parable.

FICTION *Fiction* is prose writing about imaginary characters and events. Some writers of fiction base their stories on real events, whereas others rely solely on their imaginations.

See also Narration *and* Prose.

FIGURATIVE LANGUAGE *Figurative language* is writing or speech not meant to be interpreted literally. Poets and other writers use figurative language to paint vivid word pictures, to make their writing emotionally intense and concentrated, and to state their ideas in new and unusual ways.

Figurative language is classified into various *figures of speech*, including hyperbole, irony, metaphor, metonymy, oxymoron, paradox, personification, simile, and synecdoche.

See also the entries for individual figures of speech.

FOLKLORE The stories, legends, myths, ballads, riddles, sayings, and other traditional works produced orally by a culture are known as *folklore*. Folklore influences written literature in many ways. "The Fisherman and the Jinnee," from *The Thousand and One Nights* (p. 85), is an example of folklore.

FOOT *See* Meter.

FREE VERSE *Free verse* is poetry not written in a regular, rhythmical pattern, or meter. Instead of having metrical feet and lines, free verse has a rhythm that suits its meaning and that uses the sounds of spoken language in lines of different lengths. Free verse has been widely used in twentieth-century poetry. An example is this stanza from Nguyen Thi Vinh's "Thoughts of Hanoi" (p. 1342):

Brother, we are men,
conscious of more
than material needs.
How can this happen to us
my friend
my foe?

GOTHIC *Gothic* is a term used to describe literary works that make extensive use of primitive, medieval, wild, mysterious, or natural elements.

HEPTAMETER *See* Meter.

HEXAMETER *See* Meter.

HYPERBOLE *Hyperbole* is a deliberate exaggeration or overstatement. In Candide (p. 802), Voltaire turns a philosophical idea into this figure of speech:

> Pangloss taught metaphysico-theologo-cosmolonigology. He proved admirably that there is no effect without a cause and that in this best of all possible worlds, My Lord the Baron's castle was the best of castles and his wife the best of all possible Baronesses.

Hyperbole may be used for heightened seriousness or for comic effect.

See also Figurative Language.

IAMBIC PENTAMETER *See* Meter.

IMAGE An *image* is a word or phrase that appeals to one or more of the senses—sight, hearing, touch, taste, or smell. In a famous essay on *Hamlet*, T. S. Eliot explained how a group of images can be used as an "objective correlative." By this phrase, Eliot meant that a complex emotional state can be suggested by images that are carefully chosen to evoke this state.

See also Imagery.

IMAGERY *Imagery* is the descriptive language used in literature to re-create sensory experiences. Imagery enriches writing by making it more vivid, setting a tone, suggesting emotions, and guiding readers' reactions.

IRONY *Irony* is the general name given to literary techniques that involve surprising, interesting, or amusing contradictions. In *verbal irony*, words are used to suggest the opposite of their usual meaning. In *dramatic irony*, there is a contradiction between what a character thinks and what the reader or audience knows to be true. In *irony of situation*, an event occurs that directly contradicts expectations.

LEGEND A *legend* is a widely told story about the past that may or may not be based in fact. A legend often reflects a people's identity or cultural values, generally with more historical truth than that in a myth. *The Epic of Gilgamesh* (p. 18) from Sumeria and the *Shah-nama* from Persia are both based in part on legends. In Europe, the well-known German legend of Johann Faust inspired novels and plays, including Goethe's *Faust* (p. 845).

See also Fable *and* Myth.

LYRIC POEM A *lyric poem* is a poem expressing the observations and feelings of a single speaker. Unlike a narrative poem, it presents an experience or a single effect, but it does not tell a full story. Early Greeks defined a lyric poem as that which was expressed by a single voice accompanied by a lyre. The poems of Archilochus, Callinus, Sappho (p. 414), and Pindar (p. 418) are lyric. Although they are no longer designed to be sung to the accompaniment of a lyre, lyric poems retain a melodic quality that results from the rhythmic patterns of rhymed or unrhymed verse. Modern forms of lyric poems include the elegy, the ode, and the sonnet.

METAPHOR A *metaphor* is a figure of speech in which one thing is spoken of as though it were something else, as in "death, that long sleep." Through this identification of dissimilar things, a comparison is suggested or implied.

An *extended metaphor* is developed at length and involves several points of comparison. A mixed metaphor occurs when two metaphors are jumbled together, as in "The thorns of life rained down on him."

A *dead metaphor* is one that has been so overused that its original metaphorical impact has been lost. Examples of dead metaphors include "the foot of the bed" and "toe the line." *See also* Figurative Language.

METER *Meter* is the rhythmical pattern of a poem. This pattern is determined by the number and types of stresses, or beats, in each line. To describe the meter of a poem, you must scan its lines. Scanning involves marking the stressed and unstressed syllables, as follows in this line from "Sonnet 29" by Shakespeare (p. 740):

> That then | Ĭ scórn | tŏ chánge | mў státe | wĭth kíngs

As you can see, each stressed syllable is marked with a slanted line (´) and each unstressed syllable with a horseshoe symbol (˘). The stresses are then divided by vertical lines into groups called feet. The following types of feet are common in English poetry:

1. *Iamb:* a foot with one unstressed syllable followed by one stressed syllable, as in the word *afraid*
2. *Trochee:* a foot with one stressed syllable followed by one unstressed syllable, as in the word *heather*
3. *Anapest:* a foot with two unstressed syllables followed by one stressed syllable, as in the word *disembark*
4. *Dactyl:* a foot with one stressed syllable followed by two unstressed syllables, as in the word *solitude*
5. *Spondee:* a foot with two stressed syllables, as in the word *workday*
6. *Pyrrhic:* a foot with two unstressed syllables, as in the last foot of the word *unspeak | ably*
7. *Amphibrach:* a foot with an unstressed syllable, one stressed syllable, and another unstressed syllable, as in the word *another*
8. *Amphimacer:* a foot with a stressed syllable, one unstressed syllable, and another stressed syllable, as in *up and down*

A line of poetry is described as *iambic, trochaic, anapestic,* or *dactylic* according to the kind of foot that appears most often in the line. Lines are also described in terms of the number of feet that occur in them, as follows:

1. *Monometer:* verse written in one-foot lines
2. *Dimeter:* verse written in two-foot lines
3. *Trimeter:* verse written in three-foot lines
4. *Tetrmeter:* verse written in four-foot lines
5. *Pentameter:* verse written in five-foot lines
6. *Hexameter:* verse written in six-foot lines
7. *Heptameter:* verse written in seven-foot lines

A complete description of the meter of a line tells both how many feet there are in the line and what kind of foot is most common. Thus, the translated stanza from Horace's ode quoted at the beginning of this entry would be described as being made up of iambic pentameter lines. Poetry that does not have a regular meter is called *free verse*.

See also Free Verse.

METONYMY *Metonymy* is a figure of speech that substitutes something closely related for the thing actually meant. For example, in Genesis (p. 38), it is said, "By the sweat of your brow / Shall you get bread to eat." Here the word *sweat* represents hard labor.

See also Figurative Language.

MOCK EPIC A *mock epic* is a poem about a trivial matter written in the style of a serious epic. The incongruity of style and subject matter produces comic effects.

MODERNISM *Modernism* describes an international movement in the arts during the early twentieth century. Modernists rejected old forms and experimented with the new. Literary Modernists used images as symbols. They presented human experiences in fragments, rather than as a coherent whole, which led to new experiments in the forms of poetry and fiction.

MONOLOGUE A *monologue* is a speech or performance given entirely by one person or by one character.

See also Dramatic Monologue *and* Soliloquy.

MOOD *Mood*, or atmosphere, is the feeling created in the reader by a literary work or passage. Mood may be suggested by the writer's choice of words, by events in the work, or by the physical setting.

See also Setting *and* Tone.

MOTIVATION *Motivation* is a reason that explains or partially explains a character's thoughts, feelings, actions, or speech. Characters may be motivated by their physical needs; by their wants, wishes, desires, or dreams; or by their beliefs, values, and ideals. Effective characterization involves creating motivations that make characters seem believable.

MYTH A *myth* is a fictional tale, originally with religious significance, that explains the actions of gods or heroes, the causes of natural phenomena, or both. Allusions to characters and motifs from Greek, Roman, Norse, and Celtic myths are common in English literature. In addition, mythological stories are often retold or adapted.

See also Fable *and* Legend.

NARRATION *Narration* is writing that tells a story. The act of telling a story is also called narration. The *narrative*, or story, is told by a character or speaker called the *narrator*. Biographies, autobiographies, journals, reports, novels, short stories, plays, narrative poems, anecdotes, fables, parables, myths, legends, folk tales, ballads, and epic poems are all narratives, or types of narration.

See also Point *of* View.

NARRATIVE POEM A *narrative poem* is a poem that tells a story in verse. Three traditional types of narrative poems are ballads, epics, and metrical romances. The *Shahnama*, the *Iliad* (p. 363), the *Aeneid* (p. 534), and the *Song of Roland* (p. 628) are epic narrative poems. Poets who have written narrative poems include Alexander Pushkin, Victor Hugo, and Wole Soyinka.

NATURALISM *Naturalism* was a literary movement among writers at the end of the nineteenth century and during the early decades of the twentieth century. The Naturalists depicted life in its grimmer details and viewed people as hopeless victims of natural laws.

See also Realism.

NEOCLASSICISM *Neoclassicism* was a literary movement of the late seventeenth and the eighteenth centuries in which writers turned to classical Greek and Roman literary models. Like the ancients, many Neoclassical writers dealt with themes related to proper human conduct. The most popular literary forms of the day—essays, letters, early novels, epigrams, parodies, and satires—reflected this emphasis.

See also Romanticism.

NOVEL A *novel* is an extended work of fiction that often has a complicated plot, many major and minor characters, a unifying theme, and several settings. Novels can be grouped in many ways, based on the historical periods in which they are written (such as Victorian), on the subjects and themes that they treat (such as Gothic or regional), on the techniques used in them (such as stream of consciousness), or on their part in literary movements (such as in Naturalism or Realism). A *novella* is not as long as a novel but is longer than a short story.

OBJECTIVE CORRELATIVE *See* Image.

OCTAVE *See* Stanza.

ODE An *ode* is a long, formal lyric poem with a serious theme. It may have a traditional structure with stanzas grouped in threes, called the *strophe*, the *antistrophe*, and the *epode*. Odes often honor people, commemorate events, or respond to natural scenes. The ancient Greek poet Pindar is famous for odes such as "Olympia 11" (p. 418), praising victorious athletes.

See also Lyric Poem.

ONOMATOPOEIA *Onomatopoeia* is the use of words that imitate sounds. Examples of such words are *buzz, hiss, murmur,* and *rustle.* Onomatopoeia creates musical effects and reinforces meaning.

ORAL TRADITION *Oral tradition* is the body of songs, stories, and poems preserved by being passed from generation to generation by word of mouth. Folk epics, ballads, myths, legends, folk tales, folk songs, proverbs, and nursery rhymes are all products of the oral tradition.

See also Ballad, Folklore, Legend, *and* Myth.

OXYMORON An *oxymoron* is a figure of speech that fuses two contradictory ideas, such as "freezing fire" or "happy grief," thus suggesting a paradox in just a few words.

See also Figurative Language *and* Paradox.

PARABLE A *parable* is a short, simple story from which a moral or religious lesson can be drawn. The most famous parables are those in the New Testament. Leo Tolstoy's "How Much Land Does a Man Need?" (p. 913) echoes a biblical parable.

PARADOX A *paradox* is a statement that seems to be contradictory but that actually presents a truth. Because a paradox is surprising or even shocking, it draws the reader's attention to what is being said.

See also Figurative Language *and* Oxymoron.

PARODY A *parody* is a humorous imitation of another work or of a type of work.

PASTORAL *Pastoral* refers to literary works that deal with the pleasures of a simple rural life or with escape to a simpler place and time. The tradition of pastoral literature began in ancient Greece with the poetic idylls of Theocritus. The Roman poet Virgil also wrote a famous collection of pastoral poems, the *Eclogues.*

PENTAMETER *See* Meter.

PERSONA *Persona* means, literally, "a mask." A persona is a fictional self created by an author—a self through whom the narrative of a poem or story is told.

See also Speaker.

PERSONIFICATION *Personification* is a figure of speech in which a nonhuman subject is given human characteristics. Effective personification of things or ideas makes their qualities seem unified, like the characteristics of a person, and their relationship with the reader seem closer.

See also Figurative Language *and* Metaphor.

PLOT *Plot* is the sequence of events in a literary work. The two primary elements of any plot are characters and a conflict. Most plots can be analyzed into many or all of the following parts:

1. The *exposition* introduces the setting, the characters, and the basic situation.
2. The *inciting incident* introduces the central conflict.
3. During the *development*, the conflict runs its course and usually intensifies.
4. At the *climax*, the conflict reaches a high point of interest or suspense.
5. The *denouement* ties up loose ends that remain after the climax of the conflict.
6. At the *resolution*, the story is resolved and an insight is revealed.

There are many variations on the standard plot structure. Some stories begin in *medias res* ("in the middle of things"), after the inciting incident has already occurred. In some stories, the expository material appears toward the middle, in flashbacks. In many stories, there is no denouement. Occasionally, the conflict is left unresolved.

POETRY *Poetry* is one of the three major types, or genres, of literature, the others being prose and drama. Poetry defies simple definition because there is no single characteristic that is found in all poems and not found in all nonpoems.

Often, poems are divided into lines and stanzas. Poems such as sonnets, odes, villanelles, and sestinas are governed by rules regarding the number of lines, the number and placement of stressed syllables in each line, and the rhyme scheme. In the case of villanelles and sestinas, the repetition of words at the ends of lines or of entire lines is required. However, some poems are written in free verse. Most poems make use of highly concise, musical, and emotionally charged language. Many also use imagery, figurative language, and devices of sound like rhyme.

Types of poetry include *narrative poetry* (ballads, epics, and metrical romances); *dramatic poetry* (dramatic monologues and dramatic dialogues); *lyric poetry* (sonnets, odes, elegies, and love poems); and *concrete poetry* (a poem presented on the page in a shape that suggests its subject).

POINT OF VIEW The perspective, or vantage point, from which a story is told is its *point of view.* If a character within the story narrates, then it is told from the *first-person point of view.* If a voice from outside the story tells it, then the story is told from the third-person point of view. If the knowledge of the storyteller is limited to the internal states of one character, then the storyteller has a *limited point of view.* If the storyteller's knowledge extends to the internal states of all the characters, then the storyteller has an *omniscient point of view.*

PROSE *Prose* is the ordinary form of written language and one of the three major types of literature. Most writing that is not poetry, drama, or song is considered prose. Prose occurs in two major forms: fiction and nonfiction.

PROTAGONIST The *protagonist* is the main character in a literary work.

PYRRHIC *See* Meter.

QUATRAIN *See* Stanza.

REALISM *Realism* is the presentation in art of details from actual life. During the last part of the nineteenth century and the first part of the twentieth, Realism enjoyed considerable popularity among writers in the English-speaking world. Novels often dealt with grim social realities and presented realistic portrayals of the psychological states of characters.

See also Symbolism.

REFRAIN A *refrain* is a regularly repeated line or group of lines in a poem or song.

See also Ballad.

REGIONALISM *Regionalism* is the tendency to confine one's writing to the presentation of the distinct culture of an area, including its speech, customs, and history.

RHYME *Rhyme* is the repetition of sounds at the ends of words. *End rhyme* occurs when rhyming words appear at the ends of lines. *Internal rhyme* occurs when rhyming words fall within a line. *Exact rhyme* is the use of identical rhyming sounds, as in *love* and *dove*. *Approximate,* or *slant, rhyme* is the use of sounds that are similar but not identical, as in *prove* and *glove.*

RHYME SCHEME *Rhyme scheme* is the regular pattern of rhyming words in a poem or stanza. To indicate a rhyme scheme, assign a different letter to each final sound in the poem or stanza. The following lines from Morris Bishop's translation of Petrarch's "Laura" (p. 730) have been marked.

She used to let her golden hair fly free	a
For the wind to toy and tangle and molest;	b
Her eyes were brighter than the radiant west.	b
(Seldom they shine so now.) I used to see	a
Pity look out of those deep eyes on me.	a

RHYTHM *See* Meter.

ROMANCE A *romance* is a story that presents remote or imaginative incidents rather than ordinary, realistic experience. The term *romance* was originally used to refer to medieval tales of the deeds and loves of noble knights and ladies. From the eighteenth century on, the term *romance* has been used to describe sentimental novels about love.

ROMANTICISM *Romanticism* was a literary and artistic movement of the eighteenth and nineteenth centuries. In reaction to Neoclassicism, the Romantics emphasized imagination, fancy, freedom, emotion, wildness, the beauty of the untamed natural world, the rights of the individual, the nobility of the common man, and the attractiveness of pastoral life. Important figures in the Romantic Movement include Johann Wolfgang von Goethe, Victor Hugo, and Heinrich Heine.

RUN-ON LINE A *run-on line* is a line that does not contain a pause or a stop at the end. The flow of words carries the reader to the following line. A poet may use run-on lines to avoid creating a sing-song effect, in which each line is separated from the next by a pause.

See also End-Stopped Line.

SATIRE *Satire* is writing that ridicules or holds up to contempt the faults of individuals or groups. Although a satire is often humorous, its purpose is not simply to make readers laugh but also to correct the flaws and shortcomings that it points out.

SCANSION *Scansion* is the process of analyzing the metrical pattern of a poem.

See also Meter.

SESTET *See* Stanza.

SETTING The *setting* is the time and place of the action of a literary work. A setting can provide a backdrop for the action. It can be the force that the protagonist struggles against and thus the source of the central conflict. It can also be used to create an atmosphere. In many works, the setting symbolizes a point that the author wishes to emphasize. In Albert Camus's short story "The Guest" (p. 1231), the setting is a lonely desert plateau in an Arab country occupied by France. Fearing an Arab insurrection, and unable to spare anyone for a long trip, the local French police ask a schoolteacher to take an Arab suspect to the authorities. Such a situation would only arise in an isolated colonial area. The setting also adds a grim atmosphere and conveys a theme—human freedom. In the following scene, a character must choose between two directions:

> They reached a level height made up of crumbly rocks. From there on, the plateau sloped down, eastward, toward a low plain where there were a few spindly trees and, to the south, toward outcroppings of rock that gave the landscape a chaotic look.
> Daru surveyed the two directions. There was nothing but the sky on the horizon. Not a man could be seen.

See also Mood *and* Symbol.

SHORT STORY A *short story* is a brief work of fiction. The short story resembles the longer novel, but it generally has a simpler plot and setting. In addition, a short story tends to reveal a character at a crucial moment, rather than to develop a character through many incidents.

SIMILE   A *simile* is a figure of speech that compares two apparently dissimilar things using *like* or *as*. Many similes appear in the *Iliad* (p. 363), including the following:

> And swift Achilles kept on coursing Hector, nonstop
> as a hound in the mountains starts a fawn from its lair,
> hunting him down the gorges, down the narrow glens.

By comparing apparently dissimilar things, the writer of a simile surprises the reader into an appreciation of the hidden similarities of the things being compared.

See also Figurative Language.

SOLILOQUY   A *soliloquy* is a long speech in a play or in a prose work made by a character who is alone and thus reveals private thoughts and feelings to the audience or reader.

See also Monologue.

SONNET   A *sonnet* is a fourteen-line lyric poem with a single theme. Sonnets are usually written in iambic pentameter. The *Petrarchan*, or *Italian*, *sonnet* is divided into two parts, an eight-line octave and a six-line sestet. The octave rhymes *abba abba*, while the sestet generally rhymes *cde cde* or uses some combination of *cd* rhymes. The octave raises a question, states a problem, or presents a brief narrative, and the sestet answers the question, solves the problem, or comments on the narrative.

The *Shakespearean*, or *English*, *sonnet* has three four-line quatrains plus a concluding two-line couplet. The rhyme scheme of such a sonnet is usually *abab cdcd efef gg*. Each of the three quatrains usually explores a different variation of the main theme. Then, the couplet presents a summarizing or concluding statement.

See also Lyric Poem *and* Sonnet Sequence.

SONNET SEQUENCE   A *sonnet sequence* is a series or group of sonnets, most often written to or about a beloved. Although each sonnet can stand alone as a separate poem, the sequence lets the poet trace the development of a relationship or examine different aspects of a single subject.

See also Sonnet.

SPEAKER   The *speaker* is the imaginary voice assumed by the writer of a poem; the character who "says" the poem. This character is often not identified by name but may be identified otherwise.

Recognizing the speaker and thinking about his or her characteristics are often central to interpreting a lyric poem.

See also Persona *and* Point of View.

SPONDEE   *See* Meter.

STANZA   A *stanza* is a group of lines in a poem, which is seen as a unit. Many poems are divided into stanzas that are separated by spaces. Stanzas often function like paragraphs in prose. Each stanza states and develops one main idea.

Stanzas are commonly named according to the number of lines found in them, as follows:

1. *Couplet:* a two-line stanza
2. *Tercet:* a three-line stanza
3. *Quatrain:* a four-line stanza
4. *Cinquain:* a five-line stanza
5. *Sestet:* a six-line stanza
6. *Heptastich:* a seven-line stanza
7. *Octave:* an eight-line stanza

See also Sonnet.

STYLE   *Style* is a writer's typical way of writing. Determinants of a writer's style include formality, use of figurative language, use of rhythm, typical grammatical patterns, typical sentence lengths, and typical methods of organization. For example, Yehuda Amichai's colloquial style in a poem such as "From the Book of Esther I Filtered the Sediment" (p. 1314), is an innovation in Hebrew literature.

See also Diction.

SURREALISM   *Surrealism* is a movement in art and literature that uses realism to create a dreamlike world. Surrealist works generally portray people and objects in realistic detail. By connecting realistic elements in strange ways, they break rules of logic and sequence. Originating in France following World War I, Surrealism was a protest against the so-called Rationalism that led the world into catastrophic war. Surrealism can be found in Naguib Mahfouz's "Half A Day" (p.1301).

SYMBOL   A *symbol* is a sign, word, phrase, image, or other object that stands for or represents something else. Thus, a flag can symbolize a country, a spoken word can symbolize an object, a fine car can symbolize wealth, and so on. In literary criticism, a distinction is often made between traditional or conventional symbols—those that are part of our general cultural inheritance—and *personal symbols*—those that are created by particular authors for use in particular works.

Conventional symbolism is often based on elements of nature. For example, youth is often symbolized by greenery or springtime, middle age by summer, and old age by autumn or winter. Conventional symbols are also borrowed from religion and politics. For example, a cross may be a symbol of Christianity, or the color red may be a symbol of Marxist ideology.

SYMBOLISM *Symbolism* was a literary movement of nineteenth-century France. The Symbolist writers reacted against Realism and stressed the importance of emotional states, especially by means of symbols corresponding to these states. The Symbolists were also concerned with using sound to achieve emotional effects. Arthur Rimbaud and Paul Verlaine are among the best-known Symbolist poets. Many twentieth-century writers around the world were influenced by the Symbolist movement.

See also Realism.

SYNECDOCHE *Synecdoche* is a figure of speech in which a part of something is used to stand for the whole. For example, one might speak of "hands" to refer to the crew of a ship, "wheels" to refer to a car, or "the law" to refer to the whole criminal justice system.

See also Figurative Language.

TANKA *Tanka* is a form of Japanese poetry consisting of five lines of five, seven, five, seven, and seven syllables. Tanka is the most prevalent verse form in traditional Japanese literature. Tanka often tell a brief story or express a single feeling or thought.

TETRAMETER *See* Meter.

THEME *Theme* is the central idea, concern, or purpose in a literary work. In an essay, the theme might be directly stated in what is known as a thesis statement. In a serious literary work, the theme is usually expressed indirectly rather than directly. A light work, one written strictly for entertainment, may not have a theme.

TONE *Tone* is the writer's attitude toward the readers and toward the subject. It may be formal or informal, friendly or distant, personal or pompous. The tone of Gabriela Mistral's poem "Fear" (p. 1150) is, not surprisingly, fearful.

See also Mood.

TRADITION In literary study and practice, a *tradition* is a past body of work, developed over the course of history. A literary tradition may be unified by form (the tradition of the sonnet), by language (literature in Spanish), or by nationality (Japanese literature). A tradition develops through the acknowledgment of works, forms, and styles as classic. Writers participate in a tradition if only by following conventions about the suitable forms and subjects for literature. They make conscious use of the tradition when they use references, stories, or forms from old literature to give authority to their work.

TRAGEDY *Tragedy* is a type of drama or literature that shows the downfall or destruction of a noble or outstanding person, traditionally one who possesses a character weakness called a *tragic flaw*. The *tragic hero* is caught up in a sequence of events that inevitably results in disaster. Because the protagonist is neither a wicked villain nor an innocent victim, the audience reacts with mixed emotions—both pity and fear, according to the Greek philosopher Aristotle, who defined tragedy in the *Poetics*. The outcome of a tragedy, in which the protagonist is isolated from society, contrasts with the happy resolution of a comedy, in which the protagonist makes peace with society. Sophocles' *Oedipus the King* (p. 467) is a Greek tragedy.

See also Comedy *and* Drama.

TRIMETER *See* Meter.

TROCHEE *See* Meter.

TIPS FOR DISCUSSING LITERATURE

As you read and study literature, discussions with other readers can help you understand, enjoy, and develop interpretations of what you read. Use the following tips to practice good speaking and listening skills in group discussions of literature.

- **Understand the purpose of your discussion.**
  Your purpose when you discuss literature is to broaden your understanding and appreciation of a work by testing your own ideas and hearing the ideas of others. Be sure to stay focused on the literature you are discussing and to keep your comments relevant to that literature. Starting with one focus question will help to keep your discussion on track.

- **Communicate effectively.**
  Effective communication requires thinking before speaking. Plan the points that you want to make and decide how you will express them. Organize these points in logical order and cite details from the work to support your ideas. Jot down informal notes to help keep your ideas focused.

    Remember to speak clearly, pronouncing words slowly and carefully so that your listeners will understand your ideas. Also, keep in mind that some literature touches readers deeply—be aware of the possibility of counterproductive emotional responses and work to control them.

- **Make relevant contributions.**
  Especially when responding to a short story or a novel, avoid simply summarizing the plot. Instead, consider *what* you think might happen next, *why* events take place as they do, or *how* a writer provokes a response in you. Let your ideas inspire deeper thought or discussion about the literature.

- **Consider other ideas and interpretations.**
  A work of literature can generate a wide variety of responses in different readers—and that can make your discussions really exciting. Be open to the idea that many interpretations can be valid. To support your own ideas, point to the events, descriptions, characters, or other literary elements in the work that led to your interpretation. To consider someone else's ideas, decide whether details in the work support the interpretation he or she presents. Be sure to convey your criticism of the ideas of others in a respectful and supportive manner.

- **Ask questions and extend the contributions of others.**
  Get in the habit of asking questions to help you clarify your understanding of another reader's ideas. You can also use questions to call attention to possible areas of confusion, to points that are open to debate, or to errors in the speaker's points.

    In addition, offer elaboration of the points that others make by providing examples and illustrations from the literature. To move a discussion forward, summarize and evaluate tentative conclusions reached by the group members.

When you meet with a group to discuss literature, use a chart like the one shown to analyze the discussion.

Work Being Discussed:	
Focus Question:	
Your Response:	**Another Student's Response:**
Supporting Evidence:	**Supporting Evidence:**
One New Idea That You Considered About the Work During the Discussion:	

TYPES OF WRITING

NARRATION

Whenever writers tell any type of story, they are using **narration.** Although there are many kinds of narration, most narratives share certain elements, such as characters, a setting, a sequence of events, and, often, a theme. Following are some types of narration:

Autobiographical Writing Autobiographical writing tells a true story about an important period, experience, or relationship in the writer's life. An autobiographical narrative can be as simple as a description of a recent car trip or as complex as the entire story of a person's life. Effective autobiographical writing includes

- A series of events that involve the writer as the main character
- Details, thoughts, feelings, and insights from the writer's perspective
- A conflict or an event that affects the writer
- A logical organization that tells the story clearly
- Insights that the writer gained from the experience

A few types of autobiographical writing are autobiographical incidents, personal narratives, autobiographical narratives or sketches, reflective essays, eyewitness accounts, anecdotes, and memoirs.

Short Story A short story is a brief, creative narrative—a retelling of events arranged to hold a reader's attention. Most short stories include

- Details that establish the setting in time and place
- A main character who undergoes a change or learns something during the course of the story
- A conflict or a problem to be introduced, developed, and resolved
- A plot, the series of events that make up the action of the story
- A theme or generalization about life

A few types of short stories are realistic stories, fantasies, historical narratives, mysteries, thrillers, science-fiction stories, and adventure stories.

DESCRIPTION

Descriptive writing is writing that creates a vivid picture of a person, place, thing, or event. Descriptive writing can stand on its own or be part of a longer work, such as a short story. Most descriptive writing includes

- Sensory details—sights, sounds, smells, tastes, and physical sensations
- Vivid, precise language

- Figurative language or comparisons
- Adjectives and adverbs that paint a word picture
- An organization suited to the subject

Some examples of descriptive writing include description of ideas, observations, travel brochures, physical descriptions, functional descriptions, remembrances, and character sketches.

PERSUASION

Persuasion is writing or speaking that attempts to convince people to accept a position or take a desired action. When used effectively, persuasive writing has the power to change people's lives. As a reader and a writer, you will find yourself engaged in many forms of persuasion. Here are a few of them:

Persuasive Essay A persuasive essay presents your position on an issue, urges your readers to accept that position, and may encourage them to take an action. An effective persuasive essay

- Explores an issue of importance to the writer
- Addresses an issue that is arguable
- Uses facts, examples, statistics, or personal experiences to support a position
- Tries to influence the audience through appeals to the readers' knowledge, experiences, or emotions
- Uses clear organization to present a logical argument

Persuasion can take many forms. A few forms of persuasion include editorials, position papers, persuasive speeches, grant proposals, advertisements, and debates.

Advertisements An advertisement is a planned communication meant to be seen, heard, or read. It attempts to persuade an audience to buy a product or service, accept an idea, or support a cause. Advertisements may appear in printed form—in newspapers and magazines, on billboards, or as posters or flyers. They may appear on radio or television, as commercials or public-service announcements. An effective advertisement includes

- A memorable slogan to grab the audience's attention
- A call to action, which tries to rally the audience to do something
- Persuasive and/or informative text
- Striking visual or aural images
- Details that provide such information as price, location, date, and time

Several common types of advertisements are public-service announcements, billboards, merchandise ads, service ads, online ads, product packaging, and political campaign literature.

EXPOSITION

Exposition is writing that informs or explains. The information you include in expository writing is factual or based on fact. Effective expository writing reflects a well-thought-out organization—one that includes a clear introduction, body, and conclusion. The organization should be appropriate for the type of exposition you are writing. Here are some types of exposition:

Comparison-and-Contrast Essay A comparison-and-contrast essay analyzes the similarities and differences between two or more things. You may organize your essay either point by point or subject by subject. An effective comparison-and-contrast essay

- Identifies a purpose for comparison and contrast
- Identifies similarities and differences between two or more things, people, places, or ideas
- Gives factual details about the subjects being compared
- Uses an organizational plan suited to its topic and purpose

Types of comparison-and-contrast essays are product comparisons, essays on economic or historical developments, comparison and contrast of literary works, and plan evaluations.

Cause-and-Effect Essay A cause-and-effect essay examines the relationship between events, explaining how one event or situation causes another. A successful cause-and-effect essay includes

- A discussion of a cause, event, or condition that produces a specific result
- An explanation of an effect, outcome, or result
- Evidence and examples to support the relationship between cause and effect
- A logical organization that makes the explanation clear

Some appropriate subjects for cause-and-effect essays are science reports, current-events articles, health studies, historical accounts, and cause-and-effect investigations.

Problem-and-Solution Essay A problem-and-solution essay describes a problem and offers one or more solutions to it. It describes a clear set of steps to achieve a result. An effective problem-and-solution essay includes

- A clear statement of the problem, with its causes and effects summarized for the reader

- The most important aspects of the problem
- A proposal of at least one realistic solution
- Facts, statistics, data, or expert testimony to support the solution
- Language appropriate to the audience's knowledge and ability levels
- A clear organization that makes the relationship between problem and solution obvious

Some types of issues that might be addressed in a problem-and-solution essay include consumer issues, business issues, time-management issues, and local issues.

RESEARCH WRITING

Research writing is based on information gathered from outside sources, and it gives a writer the power to become an expert on any subject. A research paper—a focused study of a topic—helps writers explore and connect ideas, make discoveries, and share their findings with an audience. Effective research writing

- Focuses on a specific, narrow topic, which is usually summarized in a thesis statement
- Presents relevant information from a wide variety of sources
- Structures the information logically and effectively
- Identifies the sources from which the information was drawn

Besides the formal research report, there are many other specialized types of writing that depend on accurate and insightful research, including multimedia presentations, statistical reports, annotated bibliographies, and experiment journals.

Documented Essay A documented essay uses research gathered from outside sources to support an idea. What distinguishes this essay from other categories of research is the level and intensity of the research. In a documented essay, the writer consults a limited number of sources to elaborate an idea. In contrast, a formal research paper may include many more research sources. An effective documented essay includes

- A well-defined thesis that can be fully discussed in a brief essay
- Facts and details to support each main point
- Expert or informed ideas gathered from interviews and other sources
- A clear, coherent method of organization
- Full internal documentation to show sources of information

Subjects especially suited to the documented essay format include health issues, current events, and cultural trends.

Research Paper A research paper presents and interprets information gathered through an extensive study of a subject. An effective research paper has

- A clearly stated thesis statement
- Convincing factual support from a variety of outside sources, including direct quotations whose sources are credited
- A clear organization that includes an introduction, body, and conclusion
- A bibliography, or works-cited list, that provides a complete listing of research sources

Some research formats you may encounter include lab reports, annotated bibliographies, and multigenre research papers.

RESPONSE TO LITERATURE

When you write a **response-to-literature essay,** you give yourself the opportunity to discover *what, how,* and *why* a piece of writing communicated to you. An effective response

- Contains a reaction to a poem, story, essay, or other work of literature
- Analyzes the content of a literary work, its related ideas, or the work's effect on the reader
- Presents a thesis statement to identify the nature of the response
- Focuses on a single aspect of the work or gives a general overview
- Supports opinion with evidence from the work addressed

The following are just a few of the ways you might respond in writing to a literary work: reader's response journals, character analyses, literary letters, and literary analyses.

WRITING FOR ASSESSMENT

One of the most common types of school **assessment** is the written test. Most often, a written test is announced in advance, allowing you time to study and prepare. When a test includes an essay, you are expected to write a response that includes

- A clearly stated and well-supported thesis or main idea
- Specific information about the topic derived from your reading or from class discussion
- A clear organization

In your school career, you will probably encounter questions that ask you to address each of the following types of writing: explain a process; defend a position; compare, contrast, or categorize; and show cause and effect.

WORKPLACE WRITING

Workplace writing is probably the format you will use most after you finish school. It is used in offices and factories and by workers on the road. Workplace writing includes a variety of formats that share common features. In general, workplace writing is fact-based writing that communicates specific information to readers in a structured format. Effective workplace writing

- Communicates information concisely to make the best use of both the writer's and the reader's time
- Includes a level of detail that provides necessary information and anticipates potential questions
- Reflects the writer's care if it is error-free and neatly presented

Some common types of workplace writing include business letters, memorandums, résumés, forms, and applications.

WRITING PERSONAL LETTERS

A personal letter is a letter to a friend, a family member, or anyone with whom the writer wants to communicate in a personal, friendly way. Most personal or friendly letters are made up of five parts:

- the heading
- the salutation, or greeting
- the body
- the closing
- the signature

The purpose of a personal letter is often one of the following:

- to share personal news and feelings
- to send or to answer an invitation
- to express thanks

Model Personal Letter

In this personal letter, Betsy thanks her grandparents for a birthday present and gives them some news about her life.

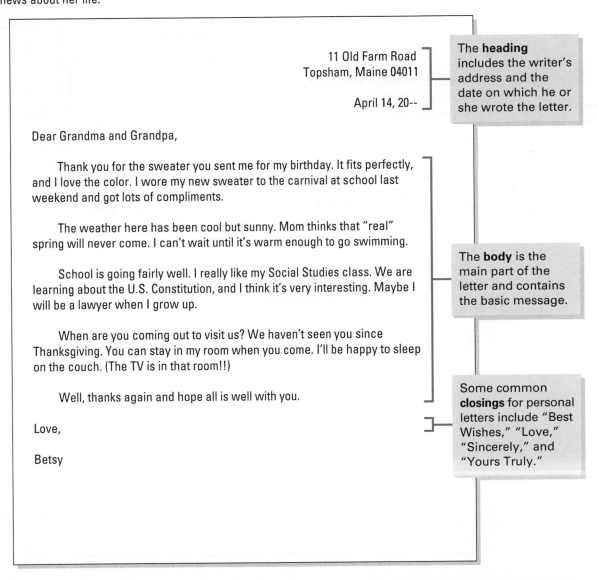

11 Old Farm Road
Topsham, Maine 04011

April 14, 20--

Dear Grandma and Grandpa,

Thank you for the sweater you sent me for my birthday. It fits perfectly, and I love the color. I wore my new sweater to the carnival at school last weekend and got lots of compliments.

The weather here has been cool but sunny. Mom thinks that "real" spring will never come. I can't wait until it's warm enough to go swimming.

School is going fairly well. I really like my Social Studies class. We are learning about the U.S. Constitution, and I think it's very interesting. Maybe I will be a lawyer when I grow up.

When are you coming out to visit us? We haven't seen you since Thanksgiving. You can stay in my room when you come. I'll be happy to sleep on the couch. (The TV is in that room!!)

Well, thanks again and hope all is well with you.

Love,

Betsy

The **heading** includes the writer's address and the date on which he or she wrote the letter.

The **body** is the main part of the letter and contains the basic message.

Some common **closings** for personal letters include "Best Wishes," "Love," "Sincerely," and "Yours Truly."

WRITING BUSINESS LETTERS

Business letters follow one of several acceptable formats. In **block format** each part of the letter begins at the left margin. A double space is used between paragraphs. In **modified block format,** the headings, the closings, and the signature are indented to the center of the page. No matter which format is used, all letters in business format have a heading, an inside address, a salutation, or greeting, a body, a closing, and a signature. These parts are shown and annotated on the model business letter below, formatted in modified block style.

Model Business Letter

In this letter, Yolanda Dodson uses modified block format to request information.

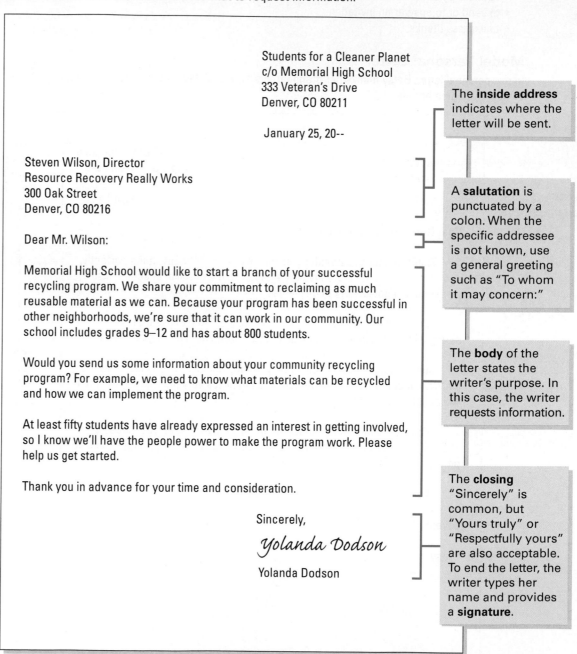

Students for a Cleaner Planet
c/o Memorial High School
333 Veteran's Drive
Denver, CO 80211

January 25, 20--

The **inside address** indicates where the letter will be sent.

Steven Wilson, Director
Resource Recovery Really Works
300 Oak Street
Denver, CO 80216

Dear Mr. Wilson:

A **salutation** is punctuated by a colon. When the specific addressee is not known, use a general greeting such as "To whom it may concern:"

Memorial High School would like to start a branch of your successful recycling program. We share your commitment to reclaiming as much reusable material as we can. Because your program has been successful in other neighborhoods, we're sure that it can work in our community. Our school includes grades 9–12 and has about 800 students.

Would you send us some information about your community recycling program? For example, we need to know what materials can be recycled and how we can implement the program.

The **body** of the letter states the writer's purpose. In this case, the writer requests information.

At least fifty students have already expressed an interest in getting involved, so I know we'll have the people power to make the program work. Please help us get started.

Thank you in advance for your time and consideration.

Sincerely,

Yolanda Dodson

Yolanda Dodson

The **closing** "Sincerely" is common, but "Yours truly" or "Respectfully yours" are also acceptable. To end the letter, the writer types her name and provides a **signature**.

RESEARCH AND TECHNOLOGY GUIDE

Using the Internet for Research

Key Word Search

Before you begin a search, you should identify your specific topic. To make searching easier, narrow your subject to a key word or a group of key words. These are your search terms, and they should be as specific as possible. For example, if you are looking for the latest concert dates for your favorite musical group, you might use the band's name as a key word. However, if you were to enter the name of the group in the query box of the search engine, you might be presented with thousands of links to information about the group that is unrelated to what you want to know. You might locate such information as band member biographies, the group's history, fan reviews of concerts, and hundreds of sites with related names containing information that is irrelevant to your search. Because you used such a broad key word, you might need to navigate through all that information before you could find a link or subheading for concert dates. In contrast, if you were to type in "Duplex Arena and [band name]," you would have a better chance of locating pages that contain this information.

How to Narrow Your Search

If you have a large group of key words and still do not know which ones to use, write out a list of all the words you are considering. Once you have completed the list, scrutinize it. Then, delete the words that are least important to your search, and highlight those that are most important.

These **key search connectors** can help you fine-tune your search:

AND: Narrows a search by retrieving documents that include both terms. For example: *baseball* AND *playoffs*

OR: Broadens a search by retrieving documents including any of the terms. For example: *playoffs* OR *championships*

NOT: Narrows a search by excluding documents containing certain words. For example: *baseball* NOT *history of*

Tips for an Effective Search

1. Remember that search engines can be case-sensitive. If your first attempt at searching fails, check your search terms for misspellings and try again.

2. If you are entering a group of key words, present them in order from the most important to the least important key word.

3. Avoid opening the link to every single page in your results list. Search engines present pages in descending order of relevancy. The most useful pages will be located at the top of the list. However, read the description of each link before you open the page.

4. Some search engines provide helpful tips for specializing your search. Take the opportunity to learn more about effective searching.

Other Ways to Search

Using Online Reference Sites How you search should be tailored to what you are hoping to find. If you are looking for data and facts, use reference sites before you jump onto a simple search engine. For example, you can find reference sites to provide definitions of words, statistics about almost any subject, biographies, maps, and concise information on many topics. Here are some useful online reference sites:

Online libraries

Online periodicals

Almanacs

Encyclopedias

You can find these sources using subject searches.

Conducting Subject Searches As you prepare to go online, consider your subject and the best way to find information to suit your needs. If you are looking for general information on a topic and you want your search results to be extensive, consider the subject search indexes on most search engines. These indexes, in the form of category and subject lists, often appear on the first page of a search engine. When you click on a specific highlighted word, you will be presented with a new screen containing subcategories of the topic you chose.

Evaluating the Reliability of Internet Resources

Just as you would evaluate the quality, bias, and validity of any other research material you locate, check the source of information you find online. Compare these two sites containing information about the poet and writer Langston Hughes:

Site A is a personal Web site constructed by a college student. It contains no bibliographic information or links to sites that he used. Included on the site are several poems by Langston Hughes and a student essay about the poet's use of symbolism. It has not been updated in more than six months.

Site B is a Web site constructed and maintained by the English Department of a major university. Information on Hughes is presented in a scholarly format, with a bibliography and credits for the writer. The site includes links to other sites and indicates new features that are added weekly.

For your own research, consider the information you find on Site B to be more reliable and accurate than that on Site A. Because it is maintained by experts in their field who are held accountable for their work, the university site will be a better research tool than the student-generated one.

Tips for Evaluating Internet Sources

1. Consider who constructed and who now maintains the Web page. Determine whether this author is a reputable source. Often, the URL endings indicate a source.
   - Sites ending in *.edu* are maintained by educational institutions.
   - Sites ending in *.gov* are maintained by government agencies (federal, state, or local).
   - Sites ending in *.org* are normally maintained by nonprofit organizations and agencies.
   - Sites ending in *.com* are commercially or personally maintained.
2. Skim the official and trademarked Web pages first. It is safe to assume that the information you draw from Web pages of reputable institutions, online encyclopedias, online versions of major daily newspapers, or government-owned sites produce information as reliable as the material you would find in print. In contrast,

unbranded sites or those generated by individuals tend to borrow information from other sources without providing documentation. As information travels from one source to another, it could have been muddled, misinterpreted, edited, or revised.

3. You can still find valuable information in the less "official" sites. Check for the writer's credentials, and then consider these factors:
   - Do not be misled by official-looking graphics or presentations.
   - Make sure that the information is updated enough to suit your needs. Many Web pages will indicate how recently they have been updated.
   - If the information is borrowed, notice whether you can trace it back to its original source.

Respecting Copyrighted Material

Because the Internet is a relatively new and quickly growing medium, issues of copyright and ownership arise almost daily. As laws begin to govern the use and reuse of material posted online, they may change the way that people can access or reprint material.

Text, photographs, music, and fine art printed online may not be reproduced without acknowledged permission of the copyright owner.

CITING SOURCES AND PREPARING MANUSCRIPT

In research writing, cite your sources. In the body of your paper, provide a footnote, an endnote, or an internal citation, identifying the sources of facts, opinions, or quotations. At the end of your paper, provide a bibliography or a Works Cited list, a list of all the sources you cite. Follow an established format, such as Modern Language Association (MLA) Style or American Psychological Association (APA) Style.

Works Cited List (MLA Style)

A Works Cited list must contain accurate information sufficient to enable a reader to locate each source you cite. The basic components of an entry are as follows:

- Name of the author, editor, translator, or group responsible for the work
- Title
- Place and date of publication
- Publisher

For print materials, the information required for a citation generally appears on the copyright and title pages of a work. For the format of Works Cited list entries, consult the examples at right and in the chart on page R29.

Parenthetical Citations (MLA Style)

A parenthetical citation briefly identifies the source from which you have taken a specific quotation, factual claim, or opinion. It refers the reader to one of the entries on your Works Cited list. A parenthetical citation has the following features:

- It appears in parentheses.
- It identifies the source by the last name of the author, editor, or translator.
- It gives a page reference, identifying the page of the source on which the information cited can be found.

Punctuation A parenthetical citation generally falls outside a closing quotation mark but within the final punctuation of a clause or sentence. For a long quotation set off from the rest of your text, place the citation at the end of the excerpt without any punctuation following.

Special Cases

- If the author is an organization, use the organization's name, in a shortened version if necessary.
- If you cite more than one work by the same author, add the title or a shortened version of the title.

Sample Works Cited Lists

Carwardine, Mark, Erich Hoyt, R. Ewan Fordyce, and Peter Gill. *The Nature Company Guides: Whales, Dolphins, and Porpoises.* New York: Time-Life Books, 1998.

Whales in Danger. "Discovering Whales." 18 Oct 1999. <http://whales.magna.com.au/DISCOVER>

Neruda, Pablo. "Ode to Spring." *Odes to Opposites.* Trans. Ken Krabbenhoft. Ed. and illus. Ferris Cook. Boston: Little, Brown and Company, 1995.

The Saga of the Volsungs. Trans. Jesse L. Byock. London: Penguin Books, 1990.

> List an anonymous work by title.

> List both the title of the work and the collection in which it is found.

Sample Parenthetical Citations

It makes sense that baleen whales such as the blue whale, the bowhead whale, the humpback whale, and the sei whale (to name just a few) grow to immense sizes (Carwardine, Hoyt, and Fordyce 19–21). The blue whale has grooves running from under its chin to partway along the length of its underbelly. As in some other whales, these grooves expand and allow even more food and water to be taken in (Ellis 18–21).

> Author's last name

> Page numbers where information can be found

MLA Style for Listing Sources

Book with one author	Pyles, Thomas. *The Origins and Development of the English Language.* 2nd ed. New York: Harcourt Brace Jovanovich, Inc., 1971.
Book with two or three authors	McCrum, Robert, William Cran, and Robert MacNeil. *The Story of English.* New York: Penguin Books, 1987.
Book with an editor	Truth, Sojourner. *Narrative of Sojourner Truth.* Ed. Margaret Washington. New York: Vintage Books, 1993.
Book with more than three authors or editors	Donald, Robert B., et al. *Writing Clear Essays.* Upper Saddle River, NJ: Prentice Hall, Inc., 1996.
Single work from an anthology	Hawthorne, Nathaniel. "Young Goodman Brown." *Literature: An Introduction to Reading and Writing.* Ed, Edgar V. Roberts and Henry E. Jacobs. Upper Saddle River, NJ: Prentice Hall, Inc., 1998. 376–385. [Indicate pages for the entire selection.]
Introduction in a published edition	Washington, Margaret. Introduction. *Narrative of Sojourner, Truth.* By Sojourner Truth. Ed. Margaret Washington. New York: Vintage Books, 1993, pp. v–xi.
Signed article in a weekly magazine	Wallace, Charles. "A Vodacious Deal." *Time* 14 Feb. 2000: 63.
Signed article in a monthly magazine	Gustaitis, Joseph. "The Sticky History of Chewing Gum." *American History* Oct. 1998: 30–38.
Unsigned editorial or story	"Selective Silence." Editorial. *Wall Street Journal* 11 Feb. 2000: A14. [If the editorial or story is signed, begin with the author's name.]
Signed pamphlet or brochure	[Treat the pamphlet as though it were a book.]
Pamphlet with no author, publisher, or date	*Are You at Risk of Heart Attack?* n.p. n.d. [n.p. n.d. indicates that there is no known publisher or date.]
Filmstrips, slide programs, videotape, DVDs, and other audiovisual material	*The Diary of Anne Frank.* Dir. George Stevens. Perf. Millie Perkins, Shelly Winters, Joseph Schildkraut, Lou Jacobi, and Richard Beymer. Twentieth Century Fox, 1959.
Radio or television program transcript	"The First Immortal Generation." *Ockam's Razor.* Host Robyn Williams. Guest Damien Broderick. National Public Radio. 23 May 1999. Transcript.
Internet	"Fun Facts About Gum." NACGM site. National Association of Chewing Gum Manufacturers. 19 Dec. 1999 <http://www.nacgm.org/consumer/funfacts.html> [Indicate the date you accessed the information. Content and addresses at Web sites change frequently.]
Newspaper	Thurow, Roger. "South Africans Who Fought for Sanctions Now Scrap for Investors." *Wall Street Journal* 11 Feb. 2000: A1+ [For a multipage article, write only the first page number on which it appears, followed by a plus sign.]
Personal interview	Smith, Jane. Personal interview. 10 Feb. 2000.
CD (with multiple publishers)	Simms, James, ed. *Romeo and Juliet.* By William Shakespeare. CD-ROM. Oxford: Attica Cybernetics Ltd.; London: BBC Education; London: HarperCollins Publishers, 1995.
Signed article from an encyclopedia	Askeland, Donald R. (1991). "Welding." *World Book Encyclopedia.* 1991 ed.

APA Style for Listing Sources

Book with one author	Pyles, T. (1971). *The Origins and Development of the English Language.* (2nd ed.). New York: Harcourt Brace Jovanovich, Inc.
Book with two or three authors	McCrum, R., Cran, W., & MacNeil, R. (1987). *The Story of English.* New York: Penguin Books.
Book with an editor	Truth, S. (1993). *Narrative of Sojourner Truth* (M. Washington, Ed.). New York: Vintage Books.
Book with more than three authors or editors	Donald, R. B., Morrow, B. R., Wargetz, L. G., & Werner, K. (1996). *Writing Clear Essays.* Upper Saddle River, New Jersey: Prentice Hall, Inc. [With six or more authors, abbreviate all authors after sixth as "et al."]
Single work from an anthology	Hawthorne, N. (1998) Young Goodman Brown. In E. V. Roberts, & H. E. Jacobs (Eds.), *Literature: An Introduction to Reading and Writing* (pp. 376–385). Upper Saddle River, New Jersey: Prentice Hall, Inc.
Introduction in a published edition	Washington, M. (1993). Introduction. In M. Washington (Ed.), *Narrative of Sojourner Truth* (v–xi). New York: Vintage Books.
Signed article in a weekly magazine	Wallace, C. (2000, February 14). A Vodacious Deal. *Time, 155,* 63. [The volume number appears in italics before the page number.]
Signed article in a monthly magazine	Gustaitis, J. (1998, October). The sticky history of chewing gum. *American History, 33,* 30–38.
Unsigned editorial or story	Selective Silence [Editorial]. (2000, February 11). *Wall Street Journal,* p. A14.
Signed pamphlet	Pearson Education. (2000). *LifeCare* (2nd ed.) [Pamphlet]. New York: Smith, John: Author.
Pamphlet with no author, publisher, or date	[No style is offered under this heading.]
Filmstrips, slide programs, videotape, DVDs, and other audiovisual material	Stevens, G. (Producer & Director). (1959). *The Diary of Anne Frank.* [Videotape]. United States: Twentieth Century Fox. [If the producer and the director are two different people, list the producer first and then the director, with an ampersand (&) between them.]
Radio or television program transcript	Broderick, D. (Speaker). (1999, May 23). The First Immortal Generation. (R. Williams, Radio Host). *Ockam's Razor* [Radio transcript]. New York: National Public Radio.
Internet	National Association of Chewing Gum Manufacturers. (1999). Retrieved December 19th, 1999 from http://www.nacgm.org/consumer/ funfacts.html [References to Websites should begin with the author's last name, if available. Indicate the site name and the available path or URL address.]
Newspaper	Thurow, R. (2000, February 11). South Africans who fought for sanctions now scrap for investors. *Wall Street Journal,* pp. A1, A4.
Personal interview	[APA states that, since interviews (and other personal communications) do not provide "recoverable data," they should only be cited in text.]
CD (with multiple publishers)	[No style is offered under this heading.]
Signed article from an encyclopedia	Askeland, D. R. (1991). Welding. In *World Book Encyclopedia.* (Vol. 21 pp. 190–191). Chicago: World Book, Inc.

WRITING ABOUT LITERATURE

By writing **criticism**—writing that analyzes literature—readers share their responses to a written work. Criticism is also a way for a reader to deepen his or her own understanding and appreciation of the work, and to help others to deepen theirs.

The information in this handbook will guide you through the process of writing criticism. In addition, it will help you to refine your critical perceptions to ensure that you are ready to produce work at the college level.

Understanding Criticism

There are a few different types of criticism. Each can enhance understanding and deepen appreciation of literature in a distinctive way. All types share similar functions.

The Types of Criticism

Analysis Students are frequently asked to analyze, or break into parts and examine, a passage or a work. When you write an analysis, you must support your ideas with references to the text, as in this example:

> **Conclusion:** In "Heat," the poet H.D. creates an enduring image of heat. There is no deeper meaning here; her task is to commemorate physical experience in words.
>
> **Support:** The poem's imagery gives heat solidity and depth. In the first stanza, the speaker asks the wind to "cut apart the heat" and, in the third stanza, to "plow through it," as if heat were a thick substance like earth.

Biographical Criticism Biographical criticism uses information about a writer's life to shed light on his or her work, as in this passage by Kenneth Silverman:

> Much of [Poe's] later writing, despite its variety of forms and styles, places and characters, is driven by the question of whether the dead remain dead. . . .
> [C]hildren who lose a parent at an early age, as Edgar lost Eliza Poe [his mother], invest more feeling in and magnify the parent's image. . . . The young child . . . cannot comprehend the finality of death. . . .

Historical Criticism Historical criticism traces connections between an author's work and the events, circumstances, or ideas that shaped the writer's historical era. For example, Jean H. Hagstrum analyzes William Blake's character of Urizen by showing how the character symbolizes the Enlightenment ideas of the scientist Isaac Newton and the philosopher John Locke:

> Urizen is also an active force. Dividing, partitioning, dropping the plummet line, applying Newton's compasses to the world, he creates abstract mathematical forms. Like Locke, he shrinks the senses, narrows the perceptions, binds man to the natural fact.

The Functions of Criticism

In each of the previous examples of criticism, you can find evidence of the following critical functions:

Making Connections All criticism makes connections between two or more things. For instance, the analysis of H.D.'s poetry connects different parts of a poem (the images of heat being cut or parted by a plow).

Making Distinctions Criticism must make distinctions as well as connections. In the analysis of "Heat," the critic distinguishes between two possible purposes for poetry: first, to create an enduring image and, second, to present a deeper meaning.

Achieving Insight By making connections and distinctions, criticism achieves insight. The analysis of H.D.'s poem reaches the insight that the poem stands on its own as a work of beauty apart from any deeper meaning.

Making a Judgment Assessing the value of a work is an important function of criticism. A critic may assess a work by comparing it with other works and by using a standard such as enjoyment, insight, or beauty.

"Placing" the Work Critics guide readers not by telling them *what* to think but by giving them *terms in which to think.* In the passage quoted above, Hagstrum helps us "place" Urizen. We cannot respond to Urizen, she reminds us, as if he were an individual like Macbeth or Holden Caufield. Instead, we respond to him best by perceiving him as a historical force—the pursuit of reason—personified. The terms on which we appreciate and understand each of these characters are different.

Writing Criticism

Like all solid writing, a work of criticism presents a thesis (a central idea) and supports it with arguments and evidence. Follow the strategies below to develop a critical thesis and gather support for it.

Formulate a Working Thesis

Once you have chosen a work or works on which to write, formulate a working thesis. First, ask yourself questions like these:

- What strikes you most about the work or the writer that your paper will address? What puzzles you most?

- In what ways is the work unlike others you have read?

- What makes the techniques used by the writer so well-suited to (or so poorly chosen for) conveying the theme of the work?

Jot down notes answering your questions. Then, reread passages that illustrate your answers, jotting down notes about what each passage contributes to the work. Review your notes, and write a sentence that draws a conclusion about the work.

Gather Support

Taking Notes From the Work Once you have a working thesis, take notes on passages in the work that confirm it. To aid your search for support, consider the type of support suited to your thesis, as in the chart.

Conducting Additional Research If you are writing biographical or historical criticism, you will need to consult sources on the writer's life and era. Even if you are writing a close analysis of a poem, you should consider consulting the works of critics to benefit from their insights and understanding. For a more detailed explanation of the research process, see pages 942–947.

Take Notes

Consider recording notes from the works you are analyzing, as well as from any critical works you consult, on a set of note cards. A good set of note cards enables you to recall details accurately, to organize your ideas effectively, and to see connections between ideas.

If your thesis concerns . . .	look for support in the form of . . .
Character	• dialogue • character's actions • writer's descriptions of the character • other characters' reactions to the character
Theme	• fate of characters • patterns and contrasts of imagery, character, or events • mood • writer's attitude toward the action
Style	• memorable descriptions, observations • passages that "sound like" the writer • examples of rhetorical devices, such as exaggeration and irony
Historical Context	• references to historical events and personalities • evidence of social or political pressures on characters • socially significant contrasts between characters (for example, between the rich and the poor)
Literary Influences	• writer's chosen form or genre • passages that "sound like" another writer • events or situations that resemble those in other works • evidence of an outlook similar to that of another writer

One Card, One Idea If you use note cards while researching, record each key passage, theme, critical opinion, or fact on a separate note card. A good note card includes a brief quotation or summary of an idea and a record of the source, including the page number, in which you found the information. When copying a sentence from a work, use quotation marks and check to make sure you have copied it correctly.

Coding Sources Keep a working bibliography, a list of all works you consult, as you conduct research. Assign a code, such as a letter, to each work on the list. For each note you take, include the code for the source.

Coding Cards Organize your note cards by labeling each with the subtopic it concerns.

Present Support Appropriately

As you draft, consider how much support you need for each point and the form that support should take. You can provide support in the following forms:

- **Summaries** are short accounts in your own words of important elements of the work, such as events, a character's traits, or the writer's ideas. They are appropriate for background information.

- **Paraphrases** are restatements of passages from a work in your own words. They are appropriate for background and for information incidental to your main point.

- **Quotations of key passages** are direct transcriptions of the writer's words, enclosed in quotation marks or, if longer than three lines, set as indented text. If a passage is crucial to your thesis, you should quote it directly and at whatever length is necessary.

Quotations of multiple examples are required to support claims about general features of a work, such as a claim about the writer's ironic style or use of cartoonlike characters.

Stage of the Writing Process	The Developing Thesis Statement
Prewriting: A student rereads Sarte's story "The Wall" to find passages that support her thesis.	**First formulation:** "In his short story 'The Wall,' Sartre illustrates the belief that human life is ruled by inescapable fate."
Drafting: As the student summarizes the story's ending, she is struck by the fact that the narrator's final act has exactly the opposite effect from what he intended. She revises her thesis statement.	**Second formulation:** "In his short story 'The Wall,' Sartre demonstrates the power of fate by showing how the effects of a person's actions can completely contradict the person's intentions."
Revising: As the student rereads her first draft, she grows dissatisfied with her explanation of the story's ending. Why does the writer spend so much time showing the narrator's resignation to fate, only to to have fate strike unexpectedly? She reworks her paper to support a new thesis statement.	**Final formulation:** "In his short story 'The Wall,' Sartre shows that 'fate' is a myth: However hard we try to resign ourselves to fate, we can never eliminate our responsibility for our own actions."

Revise Ideas as You Draft

When writing criticism, do not be afraid to revise your early ideas based on what you learn as you research or write further. As you draft, allow the insights—or the difficulties—that emerge to guide you back to the writer's works or other sources for clarification or support. What you discover may lead you to modify your thesis.

The chart above presents an example of the way this circular process can work.

DO's and DON'T's of Academic Writing

Avoid gender and cultural bias. Certain terms and usages reflect the bias of past generations. To eliminate bias in any academic work you do, edit with the following rules in mind:

- **Pronoun usage** When referring to an unspecified individual in a case in which his or her gender is irrelevant, use forms of the pronoun phrase *he or she.* Example: "A lawyer is trained to use <u>his or her</u> mind."

- **"Culture-centric" terms** Replace terms that reflect a bias toward one culture with more generally accepted synonyms. For instance, replace terms such as *primi-*

tive (used of hunting-gathering peoples), *the Orient* (used to refer to Asia), and *Indians* (used of Native Americans), all of which suggest a view of the world centered in Western European culture.

Avoid plagiarism. Presenting someone else's ideas, research, or exact words as your own is plagiarism, the equivalent of stealing or fraud. Laws protect the rights of writers and researchers in cases of commercial plagiarism. Academic standards protect their rights in cases of academic plagiarism.

To avoid plagiarism, follow these practices:

- Read from several sources.

- Synthesize what you learn.

- Let the ideas of experts help you draw your own conclusions.

- Always credit your sources properly when using someone else's ideas to support your view.

By following these guidelines, you will also push yourself to think independently.

GUIDE TO RUBRICS

What is a rubric?

A rubric is a tool, often in the form of a chart or a grid, that helps you assess your work. Rubrics are particularly helpful for writing and speaking assignments.

To help you or others assess, or evaluate, your work, a rubric offers several specific criteria to be applied to your work. Then the rubric helps you or an evaluator indicate your range of success or failure according to those specific criteria. Rubrics are often used to evaluate writing for standardized tests.

Using a rubric will save you time, focus your learning, and improve the work you do. When you know what the rubric will be before you begin writing a persuasive essay, for example, you will be aware as you write of specific criteria that are important in that kind of an essay. As you evaluate the essay before giving it to your teacher, you will focus on the specific areas that your teacher wants you to master— or on areas that you know present challenges for you. Instead of searching through your work randomly for any way to improve it or correct its errors, you will have a clear and helpful focus on specific criteria.

How are rubrics constructed?

Rubrics can be constructed in several ways.
- Your teacher may assign a rubric for a specific assignment.
- Your teacher may direct you to a rubric in your textbook.
- Your teacher and your class may construct a rubric for a particular assignment together.
- You and your classmates may construct a rubric together.
- You may create your own rubric with criteria you want to evaluate in your work.

How will a rubric help me?

A rubric will help you assess your work on a scale. Scales vary from rubric to rubric but usually range from 6 to 1, 5 to 1, or 4 to 1, with 6, 5, or 4 being the highest score and 1 being the lowest. If someone else is using the rubric to assess your work, the rubric will give your evaluator a clear range within which to place your work. If you are using the rubric yourself, it will help you make improvements to your work.

What are the types of rubrics?

- A **holistic rubric** has general criteria that can apply to a variety of assignments. See p. R35 for an example of a holistic rubric.
- An **analytic rubric** is specific to a particular assignment. The criteria for evaluation address the specific issues important in that assignment. See p. R34 for examples of analytic rubrics.

Rubric With a 4-point Scale

The following analytic rubric is an example of a rubric to assess a persuasive essay.
It will help you evaluate focus, organization, support/elaboration, and style/convention.

	Focus	Organization	Support/Elaboration	Style/Convention
4	Demonstrates highly effective word choice; clearly focused on task.	Uses clear, consistent organizational strategy.	Provides convincing, well-elaborated reasons to support the position.	Incorporates transitions; includes very few mechanical errors.
3	Demonstrates good word choice; stays focused on persuasive task.	Uses clear organizational strategy with occasional inconsistencies.	Provides two or more moderately elaborated reasons to support the position.	Incorporates some transitions; includes few mechanical errors.
2	Shows some good word choices; minimally stays focused on persuasive task.	Uses inconsistent organizational strategy; presentation is not logical.	Provides several reasons, but few are elaborated; only one elaborated reason.	Incorporates few transitions; includes many mechanical errors.
1	Shows lack of attention to persuasive task.	Demonstrates lack of organizational strategy.	Provides no specific reasons or does not elaborate.	Does not connect ideas; includes many mechanical errors.

Rubric With a 6-point Scale

The following analytic rubric is an example of a rubric to assess a persuasive essay.
It will help you evaluate presentation, position, evidence, and arguments.

	Presentation	Position	Evidence	Arguments
6	Essay clearly and effectively addresses an issue with more than one side.	Essay clearly states a supportable position on the issue.	All evidence is logically organized, well presented, and supports the position.	All reader concerns and counterarguments are effectively addressed.
5	Most of essay addresses an issue that has more than one side.	Essay clearly states a position on the issue.	Most evidence is logically organized, well presented, and supports the position.	Most reader concerns and counterarguments are effectively addressed.
4	Essay adequately addresses issue that has more than one side.	Essay adequately states a position on the issue.	Many parts of evidence support the position; some evidence is out of order.	Many reader concerns and counterarguments are adequately addressed.
3	Essay addresses issue with two sides but does not present second side clearly.	Essay states a position on the issue, but the position is difficult to support.	Some evidence supports the position, but some evidence is out of order.	Some reader concerns and counterarguments are addressed.
2	Essay addresses issue with two sides but does not present second side.	Essay states a position on the issue, but the position is not supportable.	Not much evidence supports the position, and what is included is out of order.	A few reader concerns and counterarguments are addressed.
1	Essay does not address issue with more than one side.	Essay does not state a position on the issue.	No evidence supports the position.	No reader concerns or counterarguments are addressed.

Sample Holistic Rubric

Holistic rubrics such as this one are sometimes used to assess writing assignments on standardized tests. Notice that the criteria for evaluation are focus, organization, support, and use of conventions.

Points	Criteria
6 Points	• The writing is strongly focused and shows fresh insight into the writing task. • The writing is marked by a sense of completeness and coherence and is organized with a logical progression of ideas. • A main idea is fully developed, and support is specific and substantial. • A mature command of the language is evident, and the writing may employ characteristic creative writing strategies. • Sentence structure is varied, and writing is free of all but purposefully used fragments. • Virtually no errors in writing conventions appear.
5 Points	• The writing is clearly focused on the task. • The writing is well organized and has a logical progression of ideas, though there may be occasional lapses. • A main idea is well developed and supported with relevant detail. • Sentence structure is varied, and the writing is free of fragments, except when used purposefully. • Writing conventions are followed correctly.
4 Points	• The writing is clearly focused on the task, but extraneous material may intrude at times. • Clear organizational pattern is present, though lapses may occur. • A main idea is adequately supported, but development may be uneven. • Sentence structure is generally fragment free but shows little variation. • Writing conventions are generally followed correctly.
3 Points	• Writing is generally focused on the task, but extraneous material may intrude at times. • An organizational pattern is evident, but writing may lack a logical progression of ideas. • Support for the main idea is generally present but is sometimes illogical. • Sentence structure is generally free of fragments, but there is almost no variation. • The work generally demonstrates a knowledge of writing conventions, with occasional misspellings.
2 Points	• The writing is related to the task but generally lacks focus. • There is little evidence of organizational pattern, and there is little sense of cohesion. • Support for the main idea is generally inadequate, illogical, or absent. • Sentence structure is unvaried, and serious errors may occur. • Errors in writing conventions and spellings are frequent.
1 Point	• The writing may have little connection to the task and is generally unfocused. • There has been little attempt at organization or development. • The paper seems fragmented, with no clear main idea. • Sentence structure is unvaried, and serious errors appear. • Poor word choice and poor command of the language obscure meaning. • Errors in writing conventions and spelling are frequent.
Unscorable	The paper is considered unscorable if: • The response is unrelated to the task or is simply a rewording of the prompt. • The response has been copied from a published work. • The student did not write a response. • The response is illegible. • The words in the response are arranged with no meaning. • There is an insufficient amount of writing to score.

Guide to Rubrics ■ *R35*

STUDENT MODEL

Persuasive Writing

This persuasive letter, which would receive a top score according to a persuasive rubric, is a response to the following writing prompt, or assignment:

Write a letter to a government official strongly supporting an environmental issue that is important to you and urging the official to take a specific action that supports your cause.

Dear Secretary of the Interior:

It's a normal carefree day in the forest. The birds are singing and all of the animals are relaxing under the refreshing glow of the sun. But suddenly the thunderous sound of a chainsaw echoes throughout the woodlands, and trees fall violently. The creatures of the forest run in terror. Many of these beautiful creatures will starve to death slowly and painfully as their homes are destroyed, and this precious ecosystem will not be able to regrow to its previous greatness for many years to come.

> A descriptive and interesting introduction grabs the reader's attention and shows a persuasive focus.

This sad story is a true one in many places around the globe. We must slow deforestation and replant trees immediately to save our breathable air, fertile soil, and fragile ecosystems.

If entire forests continue to be obliterated, less oxygen will be produced and more CO_2 emitted. In fact, deforestation accounts for a quarter of the CO_2 released into the atmosphere each year: about 1–2 billion tons. Forests provide the majority of the oxygen on earth, and if these forests disappear our air will soon be unbreathable.

Second, deforestation results in a loss of topsoil. Many of the companies who are involved in deforestation claim that the land is needed for farms, but deforestation makes the land much less fertile because it accelerates the process of erosion. According to the UN Food and Agriculture Organization, deforestation has damaged almost 6 million square kilometers of soil.

Finally, if cutting doesn't slow, many species will die off and many ecosystems will be destroyed. The 2000 UN Global Environment Outlook says that forests and rain forests have the most diverse plant and animal life in the world. The GEO also notes that there are more than 1,000 threatened species living in the world's forests. Imagine someone destroying all the houses in your neighborhood and leaving all of the residents homeless. This is how it is for the organisms that live in the forests.

> The writer supports the argument with facts and evidence, and also uses the persuasive technique to the reader's emotions.

In conclusion, deforestation must slow down and trees must be replanted immediately, or we will lose clean air, topsoil, and many precious organisms. Furthermore, a loss in forests will result in a generation that knows very little about nature. So, to prevent the chaotic disturbance of peace in the forests, please do whatever you can to prevent deforestation. Vote YES on any UN bills that would help the condition of our world's forests.

> The conclusion restates the argument and presents a call to action.

Sincerely Yours,
Jamil Khouri

CRITICAL COMMUNICATION SKILLS

You use communication every day in writing, speaking, listening, and viewing. Having strong communication skills will benefit you both in and out of school. Many of the assignments accompanying the literature in this textbook involve speaking, listening, and viewing. This handbook identifies some of the terminology related to the oral and visual communication you experience every day and the assignments you may do in conjunction with the literature in this book.

You use speaking and listening skills everyday. When you talk with your friends, teachers, or parents, or when you interact with store clerks, you are communicating orally. In addition to everyday conversation, oral communication includes class discussions, speeches, interviews, presentations, debates, and performances. When you communicate, you usually use more than your voice to get your message across. For example, you use one set of skills in face-to-face communication and another set of skills in a telephone conversation. In all types of communication, be sure to be polite, accept praise graciously, and say thank you as necessary.

The following terms will give you a better understanding of the many elements that are part of communication and help you eliminate barriers to listening by managing any distractions:

BODY LANGUAGE refers to the use of facial expressions, eye contact, gestures, posture, and movement to communicate a feeling or an idea.

CONNOTATION is the set of associations a word calls to mind. The connotations of the words you choose influence the message you send. For example, most people respond more favorably to being described as "slim" rather than as "skinny." The connotation of *slim* is more appealing than that of *skinny.*

EYE CONTACT is direct visual contact with another person's eyes.

FEEDBACK is the set of verbal and nonverbal reactions that indicate to a speaker that a message has been received and understood.

GESTURES are the movements made with arms, hands, face and fingers to communicate.

LISTENING is understanding and interpreting sound in a meaningful way. You listen differently for different purposes.

Listening for key information: For example, when a teacher gives an assignment, or when someone gives you directions to a place, you listen for key information.

Listening for main points: In a classroom exchange of ideas or information, or while watching a television documentary, you listen for main points.

Listening critically: When you evaluate a performance, song, or a persuasive or political speech, you listen critically, questioning and judging the speaker's message.

MEDIUM is the material or technique used to present a visual image. Common media include paint, clay, and film.

NONVERBAL COMMUNICATION is communication without the use of words. People communicate nonverbally through gestures, facial expressions, posture, and body movements. Sign language is an entire language based on nonverbal communication. Be aware of your nonverbal communication and make sure that your gestures and facial expressions do not conflict with your words.

PROJECTION is speaking in such a way that the voice carries clearly to an audience. It's important to project your voice when speaking in a large space like a classroom or an auditorium.

VIEWING is observing, understanding, analyzing, and evaluating information presented through visual means. You might use the following questions to help you interpret what you view:

- What subject is presented?
- What is communicated about the subject?
- Which parts are factual? Which are opinion?
- What mood, attitude, or opinion is conveyed?
- What is your emotional response?

VOCAL DELIVERY is the way in which you present a message. Your vocal delivery involves all of the following elements:

Volume: the loudness or quietness of your voice

Pitch: the high or low quality of your voice

Rate: the speed at which you speak; also called pace

Stress: the amount of emphasis placed on different syllables in a word or on different words in a sentence

All of these elements individually, and the way in which they are combined, contribute to the meaning of a spoken message.

Speaking, Listening, and Viewing Situations

Here are some of the many types of situations in which you apply speaking, listening, and viewing skills:

AUDIENCE Your audience in any situation refers to the person or people to whom you direct your message. An audience can be a group of people observing a performance or just one person. When preparing for any speaking situation, it's useful to analyze your audience, so that you can tailor your message to them.

CHARTS AND GRAPHS are visual representations of statistical information. For example, a pie chart might indicate how the average dollar is spent by government, and a bar graph might compare populations in cities over time.

DEBATE A debate is a formal public-speaking situation in which participants prepare and present arguments on opposing sides of a question, stated as a **proposition.**

The two sides in a debate are the *affirmative* (pro) and the *negative* (con). The affirmative side argues in favor of the proposition, while the negative side argues against it. Each side has an opportunity for *rebuttal,* in which they may challenge or question the other side's argument.

DOCUMENTARIES are nonfiction films that analyze news events or other focused subjects. You can watch a documentary for the information on its subject.

GRAPHIC ORGANIZERS summarize and present information in ways that can help you understand the information. Graphic organizers include charts, outlines, webs, maps, lists, and diagrams. For example, a graphic organizer for a history chapter might be an outline. A Venn diagram is intersecting circles that display information showing how concepts are alike and different.

GROUP DISCUSSION results when three or more people meet to solve a common problem, arrive at a decision, or answer a question of mutual interest. Group discussion is one of the most widely used forms or interpersonal communication in modern society.

INTERVIEW An interview is a form of interaction in which one person, the interviewer, asks questions of another person, the interviewee. Interviews may take place for many purposes: to obtain information, to discover a person's suitability for a job or a college, or to inform the public of a notable person's opinions.

MAPS are visual representations of Earth's surface. Maps may show political boundaries and physical features and provide information on a variety of other topics. A map's titles and its key identify the content of the map.

ORAL INTERPRETATION is the reading or speaking of a work of literature aloud for an audience. Oral interpretation involves giving expression to the ideas, meaning, or even the structure of a work of literature. The speaker interprets the work through his or her vocal delivery. **Storytelling,** in which a speaker reads or tells a story expressively, is a form of oral interpretation.

PANEL DISCUSSION is a group discussion on a topic of interest common to all members of a panel and to a listening audience. A panel is usually composed of four to six experts on a particular topic who are brought together to share information and opinions.

PANTOMIME is a form of nonverbal communication in which an idea or a story is communicated completely through the use of gesture, body language, and facial expressions, without any words at all.

POLITICAL CARTOONS are drawings that comment on important political or social issues. Often, these cartoons use humor to convey a message about their subject. Viewers use their own knowledge of events to evaluate the cartoonist's opinion.

READERS THEATRE is a dramatic reading of a work of literature in which participants take parts from a story or play and read them aloud in expressive voices. Unlike a play, however, sets and costumes are not part of the performance, and the participants remain seated as they deliver their lines.

ROLE PLAY To role-play is to take the role of a person or character and act out a given situation, speaking, acting, and responding in the manner of the character.

SPEECH A speech is a talk or address given to an audience. A speech may be **impromptu** or **extemporaneous**—delivered on the spur of the moment with no preparation—or formally prepared and delivered for a specific purpose or occasion.

- *Purposes:* the most common purposes of speeches are to persuade, to entertain, to explain, and to inform.

- *Occasions:* Different occasions call for different types of speeches. Speeches given on these occasions could be persuasive, entertaining, or informative, as appropriate.

VISUAL REPRESENTATION refers to informative texts, such as newspapers and advertisements, and entertaining texts, such as magazines. Visual representations use elements of design—such as texture and color, shapes, drawings, and photographs—to convey the meaning, message, or theme.

GRAMMAR, USAGE, AND MECHANICS HANDBOOK

Summary of Grammar

Nouns A **noun** names a person, place, or thing. A **common noun**, such as *country*, names any one of a class of people, places, or things. A **proper noun**, such as *Great Britain*, names a specific person, place, or thing.

Pronouns are words that stand for nouns or for words that take the place of nouns. **Personal pronouns** refer to the person speaking; the person spoken to; or the person, place, or thing spoken about.

	Singular	Plural
First Person	I, me, my, mine	we, us, our, ours
Second Person	you, your, yours	you, your, yours
Third Person	he, him, his, she, her, hers, it, its	they, them, their, theirs

A **reflexive pronoun** ends in *-self* or *-selves* and names the person or thing receiving an action when that person or thing is the same as the one performing the action.

> I pray you, school *yourself*. (Shakespeare, p. 355)

An **intensive pronoun** also ends in *-self* or *-selves*. It adds emphasis to a noun or pronoun.

> ". . . I should like to take breakfast with you this morning, together with my companion here, but you must not put *yourself* to any trouble." (reflexive) (Boccaccio, p. 747)

Demonstrative pronouns—such as *this, that, these,* and *those*—single out specific people, places, or things.

A **relative pronoun** begins a subordinate clause and connects it to another idea in the sentence.

> "Did you imagine I should not observe the crafty scheme *that* stole upon me. . .?" (Sophocles, p. 487)

Interrogative pronouns are used to begin questions.

> "*Who* sent you to us?" (Sophocles, p. 504)

Indefinite pronouns refer to people, places, or things, often without specifying which ones.

> *One* ate whatever one could get. (Maupassant, p. 906)

Verbs A **verb** is a word or group of words that express an action, a condition, or the fact that something exists, while indicating the time of the action, condition, or fact. An **action verb** tells what action someone or something is performing. An action verb is **transitive** if it directs action

toward someone or something named in the same sentence.

> On his airy perch among the branches
> Master Crow was *holding* cheese in his beak.
> (La Fontaine, p. 790)

An action verb is **intransitive** if it does not direct action toward something or someone named in the same sentence.

> No smoke *came* now from the chimney of the cabin.

A **linking verb** expresses the subject's condition by connecting the subject with another word.

> She *felt* restless. . . . (Colette, p. 1121)

Helping verbs are verbs added to another verb to make a single verb phrase. They indicate the time at which an action takes place or whether it actually happens, could happen, or should happen.

> "It *can be stopped* right away." (Kafka, p. 1100)

Adjectives An **adjective** is a word used to describe what is named by a noun or pronoun or to give a noun or pronoun a more specific meaning. Adjectives answer these questions:

> What kind? *purple* hat, *happy* face
> Which one? *this* bowl, *those* cameras
> How many? *three* cars, *several* dishes
> How much? *less* attention, *enough* food

The **articles** *the, a,* and *an* are adjectives. *An* is used before a word beginning with a vowel sound. *This, that, these,* and *those* are used as **demonstrative adjectives** when they appear directly before a noun.

A noun may sometimes be used as an adjective:

> *language* lesson   *chemistry* book

Adverbs An **adverb** is a word that modifies a verb, an adjective, or another adverb. Adverbs answer the questions *where, when, how,* or *to what extent.*

> She will answer *soon*. (modifies verb *will answer*)
> I was *extremely* sad. (modifies adjective *sad*)
> You called *more* often than I. (modifies adverb *often*)

Prepositions A preposition is a word that relates a noun or pronoun that appears with it to another word in the sentence. It can indicate relations of time, place, causality, responsibility, and motivation. Prepositions are almost always followed by nouns or pronouns.

around the fire　　　　　*for* us
in sight　　　　　　　　*till* sunrise

Conjunctions A conjunction is used to connect other words or groups of words.

Coordinating conjunctions connect similar kinds or groups of words:

bread *and* wine　　　　brief *but* powerful

Correlative conjunctions are used in pairs to connect similar words or groups of words:

both Luis *and* Rosa　　*neither* you *nor* I

Subordinating conjunctions indicate the connection between two ideas by placing one below the other in rank or importance:

When the man's speech returned once more, he told him of his adventure. (Marie de France, p. 648)

Interjections An **interjection** is a word or phrase that expresses feeling or emotion and functions independently of a sentence.

"*Oh,* what an awful awakening!" (Ibsen, p. 1013)

Sentences A **sentence** is a group of words with a subject and predicate, expressing a complete thought. A sentence fragment is a group of words that does not express a complete thought. Sentence fragments should be avoided in writing, unless used for effect, as in realistic dialogue.

Phrases A **phrase** is a group of words without a subject and verb that functions as one part of speech. A **prepositional phrase** includes a preposition and a noun or pronoun.

before dawn　　　　　*as a result of* the rain

An **adjective phrase** is a prepositional phrase that modifies a noun or pronoun.

The likeness *of the dog* would get mixed up with that *of the cat.* (Tagore, p. 1166)

An **adverb phrase** is a prepositional phrase that modifies a verb, an adjective, or an adverb.

From every side men ran to *the succor of the dame.* (Marie de France, p. 647)

An **appositive phrase** is a noun or pronoun with modifiers, placed next to a noun or pronoun to add information and details.

And Icarus, *[Daedalus'] son,* stood by and watched him, . . . (Ovid, p. 551)

A **participial phrase** is a participle that is modified by an adjective or adverb phrase or that has a complement (a group of words that completes the participle's meaning). The entire phrase acts as an adjective.

Her mother seemed *drained of strength.* . . .

A **gerund** is a noun formed from the present participle of a verb (ending in -ing). A **gerund phrase** is a gerund with modifiers or a complement (words that complete its meaning), all acting together as a noun.

"This *getting up so early,*" he thought, "makes anyone a complete idiot." (Kafka, p. 1067)

An **infinitive phrase** is an infinitive with modifiers, complements (words completing its meaning), or a subject, all acting together as a single part of speech. (In the example, the second infinitive phrase is part of the complement of the first.)

And he felt it his duty <u>to *explain* to his traveling companions that the poor woman was *to be* pitied</u>. . . . (Pirandello, p. 1128)

Clauses A **clause** is a group of words with its own subject and verb. An **independent clause** can stand by itself as a complete sentence. A **subordinate clause** cannot stand by itself as a complete sentence.

An **adjective clause** is a subordinate clause that modifies a noun or pronoun by telling *what kind* or *which one.*

The more stubborn among them, who were the youngest, still lived for a few hours with the illusion that . . . his name might be Lautaro. (García Márquez, p. 1205)

Subordinate adverb clauses modify verbs, adjectives, adverbs, or verbals by telling *where, when, in what way, to what extent, under what condition,* or *why.*

The room fell silent, and all eyes were on him, As Father Aeneas from his high couch began . . . (Virgil, p. 535)

Subordinate noun clauses act as nouns.

. . . she said, in order to remove any hesitation on his part, *that she could also send the janitor's wife to get it* . . . (Kafka, p. 1084)

Summary of Capitalization and Punctuation

Capitalization

Capitalize the first word in sentences, interjections, and complete questions. Also, capitalize the first word in a quotation if the quotation is a complete sentence.

> Daru shook his head: "No, be quiet. Now I'm leaving you." (Camus, p. 1245)

Capitalize all proper nouns and adjectives.

> Trinidadian   Thames River

Capitalize titles showing family relationships when they refer to a specific person unless they are preceded by a possessive noun or pronoun.

> Uncle Oscar   Mangan's sister

Capitalize the first word and all other key words in the titles of books, periodicals, poems, stories, plays, songs, and other works of art.

> *Faust*   "Two Friend"

Punctuation

End Marks Use a **period** to end a declarative sentence, an imperative sentence, an indirect question, and most abbreviations.

> She never talked to anyone.
> I wonder what she would have done without her dog.

Use a **question mark** to end an interrogative sentence.

> What did you say?
> Which route should we take?

Use an **exclamation mark** after an exclamatory sentence, a forceful imperative sentence, or an interjection expressing strong emotion.

> Oh, you and your cats!

Commas Use a **comma** before the conjunction to separate two independent clauses in a compound sentence.

> The youth began his journey from the castle, and the daytime whole he did not meet one living soul. . . . (Chrétien de Troyes, p. 630)

Use commas to separate three or more words, phrases, or clauses in a series.

> Kendall's tool kit contained a hammer, three screw-drivers, a tape measure, and a box of band-aids.

Use commas to separate adjectives unless they must stay in a specific order.

> Her grandmother was a kind woman and they lived a quiet, happy life.

Use a comma after an introductory word, phrase, or clause.

> As soon as Pakhom and his family reached their new abode, he applied for admission into the commune of a large village. (Tolstoy, p. 918)

Use commas to set off nonessential expressions.

> Sasha Uskov, the young man of twenty-five who was the cause of all the commotion, had arrived some time before. . . . (Chekhov, p. 929)

Use commas with places, dates, and titles.

> Cairo, Egypt
> September 1, 1939
> Reginald Farrars, M. P.

Use commas after items in addresses, after the salutation in a personal letter, after the closing in all letters, and in numbers of more than three digits.

> Paris, France
> Dear Randolph,
> Yours faithfully,
> 9,744

Use a comma to indicate words left out of parallel clauses, to set off a direct quotation, and to prevent a sentence from being misunderstood.

> In Rimbaud's poetry, I admire the music; in Pasternak's, the deep emotion.

> "I will never believe it," replied the fisherman, "until I see you enter this bottle with my own eyes!" (N. J. Dawood, translator, p. 89)

Semicolons Use a **semicolon** to join independent clauses that are not already joined by a conjunction.

> She fastened it on her wrist, and shook it, throwing off blue sparks under the electric candles; a hundred tiny rainbows, blazing with color, danced on the white tablecloth. (Colette, p. 1118)

Use semicolons to avoid confusion when independent clauses or items in a series already contain commas.

> I enjoy reading ancient authors: Homer, for the action; Catullus, for his bluntness; and Plato, for his ideas.

Colons Use a **colon** before a list of items following an independent clause.

> When the greatest of French poetry is discussed, the following names are certain to be mentioned: Charles Baudelaire, Arthur Rimbaud, Paul Valéry, and Victor Hugo.

Use a colon to introduce a formal or lengthy quotation.

> Finally M. Sauvage pulled himself together: "Come on! On our way! But let's go carefully." (Maupassant, p. 909)

Use a colon to introduce an independent clause that summarizes or explains the sentence before it.

> One empty bier is decorated and carried in the procession: this is for the missing, whose bodies could not be recovered. (Thucydides, p. 424)

Quotation Marks A **direct quotation** represents a person's exact speech or thoughts and is enclosed within quotation marks.

> "We are in trouble," repeated Maria.

An **indirect quotation** reports only the general meaning of what a person said or thought and does not require quotation marks.

> A woman asked me last night on the dark street how another woman was who'd already died. . . . (Amichai, p. 1314)

Always place a comma or a period inside the final quotation mark.

> Out of a great weariness I answered, "She's fine, she's fine." (Amichai, p. 1314)

Always place a question mark or an exclamation mark inside the final quotation mark if the end mark is part of the quotation; if it is not part of the quotation, place it outside the final quotation mark.

> "Why school?" I challenged my father openly. (Mahfouz, p. 1303)

Use single quotation marks for a quotation within a quotation.

> Pointing out clues about character in dialogue, the teacher told her students, "We can infer that

Margaret Atwood's mother did not approve of swearing by the fact that she substitutes 'blankety-blank' for stronger language."

Use quotation marks around the titles of short written works, episodes in a series, songs, and titles of works mentioned as parts of collections.

> "An Astrologer's Day"   "Boswell Meets Johnson"

Italics Italicize the titles of long written works, movies, television and radio shows, lengthy works of music, paintings, and sculpture. Also, italicize foreign words not yet accepted into English and words you wish to stress.

If you are writing by hand or working in some other format that does not allow you to italicize text, underline such titles and words.

> <u>Oedipus the King</u>   <u>60 Minutes</u>
> <u>Guernica</u>   <u>déjà vu</u>

Parentheses Use **parentheses** to set off asides and explanations only when the material is not essential or when it consists of one or more sentences.

> And to love (Thou knowest it well) is a bitter exercise. . . . (Mistral, p. 1152)

Hyphens Use a **hyphen** with certain numbers, after certain prefixes, with two or more words used as one word, with a compound modifier, and within a word when a combination of letters might otherwise be confusing.

> twenty-nine   re-create
> pre-Romantic   brother-in-law

Apostrophe Add an **apostrophe** and an *s* to show the possessive case of most singular nouns and of plural nouns that do not end in *-s* or *-es*.

> Rilke's poems   the mice's whiskers

Add an apostrophe to show the possessive case of plural nouns ending in *-s* and *-es*.

> the girls' songs   the Ortizes' car

Use an apostrophe in a contraction to indicate the position of the missing letter or letters.

> that's all I'd have to try with my boss; I'd be fired on the spot. (Kafka, p. 1067)

Use an apostrophe and an *-s* to write the plurals of symbols, letters, and words used to name themselves.

> five *a's*   no *if's* or *but's*

Glossary of Common Usage

among, between

Among is generally used with three or more items. *Between* is generally used with only two items.

> *Among* Ibsen's characters, my favorite has always been Nora in *A Doll House*.

> The main character is at first torn *between* social conventions and her own moral principles.

amount, number

Amount refers to quantity or a unit, whereas *number* refers to individual items that can be counted. *Amount* generally appears with a singular noun, and *number* appears with a plural noun.

> The *amount* of attention that great writers have paid to the Faust legend is remarkable.

> A considerable *number* of important writers have been fascinated by the legend of Joan of Arc.

as, because, like, as to

To avoid confusion, use *because* rather than *as* when you want to indicate cause and effect.

> *Because* he felt he had fulfilled himself as a poet, Arthur Rimbaud set down his pen and pursued a life of adventure.

Do not use the preposition *like* to introduce a clause that requires the conjunction *as*.

> *As* we might expect from the verse of Baudelaire, the tone of "Invitation to the Voyage" is sultry and musical.

The use of *as to* for *about* is awkward and should be avoided.

bad, badly

Use the predicate adjective *bad* after linking verbs such as *feel, look,* and *seem*. Use *badly* when an adverb is required.

> In "The Handsomest Drowned Man in the World," the men of the village feel *bad* that the women are attracted to a stranger.

> At the end of *A Doll House,* Nora chooses to leave her husband, realizing just how *badly* she'd been affected by seven years in a loveless marriage.

because of, due to

Use *due to* if it can logically replace the phrase *caused by*. In introductory phrases, however, *because of* is better usage than *due to*.

> The resurgence of interest in Ibsen's *A Doll House* in recent decades may be *due to* its feminist themes.

> *Because of* the expansion of the reading public, writers during the eighteenth century became less dependent on wealthy patrons for support.

compare, contrast

The verb *compare* can involve both similarities and differences. The verb *contrast* always involves differences. Use *to* or *with* after *compare*. Use *with* after *contrast*.

> Harvey's report *compared* the bohemian lifestyle of Baudelaire *to* that of Rimbaud, noting parallels in their writing styles as well.

> The Greeks *contrasted* inner vision *with* physical vision; thus, the legend that Homer was a blind bard indicates how highly they esteemed introspection.

continual, continuous

Continual means "occurring again and again in succession (but with pauses or breaks)," whereas *continuous* means "occurring without interruption."

> In the poem "Invitation to the Voyage," Baudelaire's *continual* use of a two-line refrain creates a feeling of the rolling ocean waves.

> Though critics assert that Pablo Neruda spent many painstaking hours shaping his verse, the exuberant voice of the speaker in "Ode to My Socks" suggests that he may have written this poem in a single *continuous* burst of inspiration.

different from, different than

The preferred usage is *different from*.

> Colette's third marriage was very different from her previous ones simply because it brought her great happiness and satisfaction.

farther, further

Use *farther* when you refer to distance. Use *further* when you mean "to a greater degree" or "additional."

> Discontented with his new life in Paris, the young French poet Rimbaud traveled *farther* east to quench his thirst for adventure.

> In Ibsen's *A Doll House,* Nora realizes that staying in her unhappy marriage will only bring *further* psychological abuse.

fewer, less

Use *fewer* for things that can be counted. Use *less* for amounts or quantities that cannot be counted.

> When asked to compare the two versions of the Faust legend they had read, *fewer* students preferred Christopher Marlowe's version. Most found it to be *less* dramatic than Goethe's.

just, only

Only should appear directly before the word it modifies. *Just,* used as an adverb meaning "no more than," also belongs directly before the word it modifies.

> The form of the villanelle allows a poet to use *just* two rhymes.

> Poet Arthur Rimbaud was *only* fifteen years old when he was first published.

lay, lie

Lay is a transitive verb meaning "to set or put something down." Its principal parts are *lay, laying, laid, laid.*

Lie is an intransitive verb meaning "to recline." Its principal parts are *lie, lying, lay, lain.*

> In Shakespeare's *The Tempest,* Prospero has the power to *lay* strange curses and spells on his enemies.

> According to Blaise Pascal, an individual *lies* somewhere in the midst of a paradoxical universe, unable to comprehend the extremes of nature.

plurals that do not end in *-s*

The plurals of certain nouns from Greek and Latin are formed as they were in their original language. Words such as *data, criteria, media,* and *phenomena* are plural and should be treated as such. Each has its own distinctive singular form: *datum, criterion, medium, phenomenon.*

> Are the electronic *media* of the twentieth century contributing to the death of literature?

raise, rise

Raise is a transitive verb that usually takes a direct object. *Rise* is intransitive and never takes a direct object.

> In "On an Autumn Evening in the Mountains," poet Wang Wei *raises* an allegorical question about mortality.

> As the poets in Dante's *Inferno* pass the Gates of Hell, they hear the anguished cries of the opportunists *rise* within.

that, which, who

Use the relative pronoun *that* to refer to things. Use *which* only for things and *who* only for people. Use *that* when introducing a subordinate clause that singles out a particular thing or person.

> The Ibsen play that I most enjoy is *A Doll House.*

Which is usually used to introduce a subordinate clause that is not essential to identifying the thing or person in question:

> World War II, *which* disrupted Colette's personal life, did not affect her literary output.

Who can be used to introduce either essential or non-essential subordinate clauses:

> Derek Walcott, *who* is deeply admired by many critics, won the Nobel Prize in Literature.

when, where

Do not directly follow a linking verb with *when* or *where.* Also, be careful not to use *where* when your context requires *that.*

> Evaluation is ~~when you make~~ the *process of making* a judgment about the quality or value of something.

> Colin read ~~where~~ *that* even though he was a physician, Anton Chekhov was plagued by poor health.

who, whom

Remember to use *who* only as a subject in clauses and sentences and *whom* only as an object.

> Goethe, *who* spent more than sixty years writing his masterpiece, first encountered the Faust story in a puppet show at a country fair.

> Alexander Pushkin, *whom* critics perceive as a man of plain words, wove magical tales with his simple dialogue.

INDEX OF AUTHORS AND TITLES

Note: Nonfiction selections and informational text appear in red. Page numbers in *italic text* refer to background or biographical information.

INDEX OF SKILLS

Note: Page numbers in **boldface** refer to pages where terms are defined.

Reading Strategies

Writing Strategies

INDEX OF FEATURES

Note: Page numbers in **boldface** refer to pages where terms are defined.

ACKNOWLEDGMENTS

American University in Cairo Press."Haiku: "Clouds come from time to time...," and "The sun's way...," two haikus by Matsuo Basho from *An Introduction to Haiku* by Harold G. Henderson, copyright © 1958 by Harold G. Henderson. Used by permission of Doubleday, a division of Random House, Inc.

Dutton Signet, a division of Penguin Group (USA), Inc. "A Doll House," from *The Complete Major Prose Plays of Henrik Ibsen* by Henrik Ibsen, translated by Rolf Fjelde, copyright © 1965, 1970, 1978 by Rolf Fjelde. Used by permission of Dutton Signet, a division of Penguin Group (USA), Inc.

Everyman's Library "The Lay of the Werewolf," (originally titled "VIII: The Lay of the Werewolf"), by Marie de France, translated by Eugene Mason from *Lays of Marie de France and Other French Legends*.

Farrar, Straus & Giroux, Inc. "When in early summer," by Nelly Sachs translated by Ruth and Matthew Mead from The Seeker and Other Poems. Copyright © 1970 by Farrar, Straus & Giroux, Inc. "Freedom to Breathe," by Alexander Solzhenitsyn translated by Michael Glenny from Alexander Solzhenitsyn: Stories and Prose Poems. Translation copyright © 1970, 1971 by Michael Glenny. "The Grownup," by Ranier Maria Rilke, translated by Randall Jarrell from *An Anthology of German Poetry from Hoderine to Rilke in English Translation*. "Comrades" from *Jump and Other Stories* by Nadine Gordimer. Copyright © 1991 by Felix Licensing B.V. All rights reserved. "from Annie John: from A Walk to the Jetty," from *Annie John* by Jamaica Kincaid. © 1985 by Jamaica Kincaid. "Also All" and "Assembly Line" by Shu Ting, translated by Donald Finkel and Jinsheng Yi. "All" by Bei Dao, translated by Donald Finkel and Xueliang Chen from *A Splintered Mirror, Chinese Poetry from the Democracy*. Translation copyright © 1991 by Donald Finkel. Excerpt from Nobel Lecture by Alexander Solzhenitsyn, translated by F.D. Reeve. Copyright © 1972 by the Nobel Foundation. Translation copyright © 1972 by Farrar, Straus & Giroux. "The Bracelet" from *The Collected Stories of Colette* by Colette. Translation copyright © 1957, 1966, 1983 by Farrar, Straus & Giroux, Inc. "from The Expiation: Russia 1812," from Imitations translated by Robert Lowell. Copyright © 1958, 1959, 1960, 1961 by Robert Lowell.

The Estate of Angel Flores c/o The Permissions Company "Ophelia," translated by Daisy Alden, from Angel Flores, ed., *An Anthology of French Poetry from Nerval to Valery in English Translation with French* Originals (New York: Anchor Books, 1958). Copyright © 1958 and renewed 1986 by Angel Flores. Reprinted with permission of the Estate of Angel Flores, c/o The Permissions Company, High Bridge, New Jersey.

David R. Godine, Publisher, Inc. "The Albatross," from *Les Fleurs Du Mal* by Charles Baudelaire, translated from the French by Richard Howard, illustrations by Michael Mazur. Copyright © 1982 by Charles Baudelaire. Reprinted by permission of David R. Godine, Publisher, Inc.

Grove/Atlantic, Inc. "I Built My House Near Where Others Dwell," by T'ao Ch'ien, translated by William Acker from *Anthology of Chinese Literature: From early times to the fourteenth century*. Copyright © 1965 by Grove Press, Inc. All rights reserved. Used by permission of Grove/Atlantic, Inc.

Harcourt, Inc. "Invitation to the Voyage," (originally titled "Charles Baudelaire: L'Invitation au Voyage"), from *Things of this World*, English translation, copyright © 1956 and renewed 1984 by Richard Wilbur. "The End and the Beginning," from *View with a Grain of Sand*, copyright © 1993 by Wislawa Szymborska, English translation by Stanislaw Baranczak and Clare Cavanagh, copyright © 1995 by Harcourt, Inc. This material may not be reproduced in any form or by any means without prior written permission of the publisher. Reprinted by permission of the publisher.

HarperCollins Publishers, Ltd. "The Handsomest Drowned Man in the World," from *Leaf Storm and Other Stories* by Gabriel Garcia Marquez. Copyright © 1971 by Gabriel Garcia Marquez. "A Song on the End of the World," from *The Collected Poems, 1931-1987* by Czeslaw Milosz and translated by Robert Hass. Copyright © 1988 by Czeslaw Milosz Royalties, Inc. Reprinted by permission of HarperCollins Publishers, Inc. "From The Gulistan: From The Matter of Kings," by Sa´di, translated by Edward Rehatsek from *The Gulistan, or Rose Garden, of Sa´di*. Reprinted by permission of HarperCollins Publishers.

Hill and Wang, an imprint of Farrar, Straus & Giroux, Inc. From *Night* by Elie Wiesel translated by Stella Rodway. Copyright © 1960 by MacGibbon & Kee; originally published in French by Les Eiditions de Minuit, copyright © 1958.

Hispanic Society of America "The Guitar," by Federico Garica Lorca from Translations from Hispanic Poets. Copyright © 1938 by The Hispanic Society of America. Reprinted with the permission of The Hispanic Society of America.

Barbara Hogenson Agency, Inc. "The Tiger Who Would Be King," by James Thurber from *Further Fables for Our Time*. Copyright © 1956 by James Thurber. Copyright © renewed 1984 by Rosemary A. Thurber.

Houghton Mifflin Company "Sent to Li Po as a Gift," by Tu Fu, translated and edited by Amy Lowell and Florence Ayscough from *Fir-Flower Tablets, Poems translated from the Chinese*. Copyright © 1921, copyright renewed 1949 by Ada D. Russell. Reprinted by permission of Houghton Mifflin Co. All rights reserved.

Indiana University Press "from Metamorphoses: The Story of Daedalus and Icarus," (originally titled "from Book 8: The Story of Daedalus and Icarus") by Ovid from *Ovid: Metamorphoses*, translated by Rolfe Humphries. Copyright © 1955 by Indiana University Press. Reprinted by permission of Indiana University Press.

International African Institute "African Proverbs: Liberia: The Jabo: "The one who listens . . ."," "Children are the wisdom . . ."," "Daring talk . . ."," "One who cannot pick up an ant . . ."," "The butterfly that flies among . . ."," "A man's ways are good . . ."," from *Jabo Proverbs from Liberia: Maxims in the Life of Native Tribe*. Published for the International Institute of African Languages & Cultures by Oxford University Press, London: Humphrey Milford, 1936.

The Estate of Alta Jablow "African Proverbs: Nigeria: The Yoruba: "One does not set. . ."," from *Yes and No: The Intimate Folklore of Africa: Dilemma Tales, Proverbs and Stories of Love, and Adult Riddles* by Alta Jablow. Copyright © 1961 by Alta Jablow.

The Jewish Publication Society "from The Bible: Genesis: 1-3: The Creation and the Fall," (originally titled "Genesis: 1-3"), "from The Bible: Genesis 6-9: The Story of the Flood," (originally titled "Genesis: 6-9"), "The Book of Ruth," (originally titled "Ruth: 1-4"), "Psalm 8," "Psalm 19," "Psalm 23," and "Psalm 137," reprinted from the *Tanakh: A New Translation of the Holy Scriptures According to the Hebrew Text*. Copyright date © 1985, by the Jewish Publication Society. Reprinted by permission.

John & Alcock Ltd. "I have visited again," by Alexander Pushkin, translation © 1982 by D.M. Thomas, from *The Bronze Horseman: Selected Poems of Alexander Pushkin*, The Viking Press, New York, 1982. Used with permission of Johnson & Alcock Ltd.

Kensington Publishing Corp. "The Lorelei" by Heinrich Heine from The Poetry and Prose of Heinrich Reine, edited by Frederic Ewen. Copyright © 1948, 1976 by The Citadel Press. All rights reserved. Reprinted by arrangement with Kensington Publishing Corp. www.kensingtonbooks.com.

Alfred A. Knopf, Inc, a division of Random House, Inc. "The Guest," from *Exile and the Kingdom* by Albert Camus, translated by Jusin O'Brien, copyright © 1957, 1958 by Alfred A. Knopf, Inc. a division of Random House, Inc. "from *Hiroshima*," by John Hersey, copyright © 1946 and renewed 1974 by John Hersey. "Ancestral Voices" and "Substance" from *The Vixen* by W.S. Merwin, copyright © 1995 by W.S. Merwin. Used by permission of Alfred A. Knopf, a division of Random House, Inc.

L. R. Lind "from Canzoniere: Laura," "from Canzoniere: Spring," by Francesco Petrarch, translated by Morris Bishop, reprinted by permission of L.R. Lind, Editor, from *Lyric Poetry of the Italian Renaissance*, copyright 1954. Used by permission.

Macmillan Education Christopher Marlowe, *The Tragical History of Doctor Faustus*. Text of 1604, with Introduction and Notes by William Modlen (London: Macmillan & Co., repr. 1966).

Maypop Books "The Guest House," "Elephant in the Dark," "Two Kinds of Intelligence," "Which is Worth More" by Coleman Barks translated from *The Essential Rumi*. Copyright © 1995 by Coleman Barks. All rights reserved. Reprinted by permission.

The Modern Library, an imprint of Random House, Inc. "from Candide: Chapter I and Chapter II," (originally titled "from Candide: Chapter I: How Candide was brought up in a noble castle and how he was expelled from the same and Chapter II: What Happened to Candide among the Bulgarians") from *Candide; And Philosophical Letters* by Voltaire, translated by Richard Aldington, copyright © 1928, 1956, 1984 by Random House, Inc.

Jonathan Musere "African Proverbs: Uganda: The Bagada: "A small deed out of friendship . . .," "Two people can keep the words a secret . . .," "One who loves you, warns you . . .," "The one who is hopeful . . .," "The one who has not made the journey . . .," "The one who travels is the one who sees things . . .," "Words are easy, but friendship is difficult . . .," and "Where there are no dogs . . ." from *African Proverbs and Proverbial Names* by Jonathan Musere. Copyright © 1999 by Ariko Publications. Reprinted by permission.

New Directions Publishing Corporation "Jade Flower Palace," by Tu Fu, translated by Kenneth Rexroth, from *One Hundred Poems from the Chinese*, copyright © 1971 by Kenneth Rexroth. "The River-Merchant's Wife: A Letter," by Ezra Pound, from *Personae*, copyright © 1926 by Ezra Pound. "The Prayer," by Gabriella Mistral, translated by Donald Devenish Walsh, from *Anthology of Contemporary Latin-American Poetry*, copyright © 1942, 1947 by New Directions Publishing Corp. Reprinted by permission of New Directions Publishing Corp.

New York Times Co. "Leonardo: The Eye, the Hand, the Mind" by Holland Cotter from *The New York Times*, January 24, 2003. Copyright © 2003 by the New York Times Co. Reprinted by permission.

Harold Ober Associates, Incorporated "Marriage is a Private Affair," from *Girls at War and Other Stories* by Chinua Achebe, copyright © 1972, 1973 by Chinua Achebe. Reprinted by permission of Harold Ober Associates, Incorporated.

Oxford University Press, Inc. and David Higham Associates Ltd. "from Faust: from The First Part of the Tragedy: Night," and "from Faust: Prologue in Heaven," (originally titled "from *Faust, Part 1 & 2*"), by Johann Wolfgang von Goethe, translated by Louis MacNeice, copyright © 1951, 1954 by Federick Louis MacNeice; renewed 1979 by Hedi MacNeice. Used by permission of Oxford University Press, Inc.

Oxford University Press, UK "How Much Land Does a Man Need?" by Leo Tolstoy from *The Raid and Other Stories*, translated by Louise an Aylmer Maude (1935). Reprinted by permission of Oxford University Press.

Oxford University Press, UK and Columbia University Press "from The Pillow Book of Sei Shonagon: The Cat Who Lived in the Palace," "Things That Arouse a Fond Memory of the Past," "I Remember a Clear Morning," from *The Pillow Book of Sei Shonagon* by Sei Shonagon, translated and edited by Ivan Morris. Copyright (c) Ivan Morris 1967. Reprinted by permission.

Pearson Education, Inc. publishing as Pearson Prentice Hall "What is an Insect?" from *Prentice Hall Biology* by Kenneth R. Miller, Ph.D., and Joseph Levine, Ph.D. © 2002 Pearson Education, Inc. publishing as Pearson Prentice Hall. Used by permission.

Pearson Education Ltd. "from Sundiata: An Epic of Old Mali: from The Lion's Awakening," from *Sundiata: An Epic of Old Mali* by D.T. Niane, translated by G.D. Pickett. Copyright © Presence Africaine, 1960(original French version: *Soundjata, ou L'Epopee Mandingue*). © 1965 Longman Group Ltd. (English). Reprinted by permission of Pearson Education Limited. "from Sundiata: An Epic of Old Mali: Childhood," from *Sundiata: An Epic of Old Mali* by D.T. Niane, translated by G.D. Pickett. Copyright © Presence Africaine, 1960(original French version: *Soundjata, ou L'Epopee Mandingue*). © 1965 Longman Group Ltd. (English).

Penguin Books Ltd., London "from The Annals: from The Burning of Rome," from *The Annals of Imperial Rome* by Tacitus, translated by Michael Grant(Penguin Classics 1956, Sixth revised edition 1989) copyright © Michael Grant Publications Ltd., 1969. "From Tales from the Thousand and One Nights: The Fisherman and the Jinnee," from *Tales from the Thousand and One Nights* translated by N.J. Dawood (Penguin Classics 1954, Revised edition 1973) translation copyright © N.J. Dawood, 1954, 1973. "from The Rig Veda: "Creation Hymn" and "Night,"" from *The Rig Veda, An Anthology* translated by Wendy Doniger O'Flaherty (Penguin Classics, 1981). Copyright © Wendy Doniger O'Flaherty, 1981. "Visit," by Yevgeny Yevtushenko from *Yevtushenko: Selected Poems*, translated by Robin Milner-Gulla and Peter Levi, S.J. (Penguin Books, 1962) copyright © Robin Milner-Gulla and Peter Levi, 1962. "The Qur'an," (originally titled "from The Koran) from *The Koran*, translated by N.J. Dawood (Penguin Classics, 1956, Fifth revised edition 1990). Copyright © N.J. Dawood, 1956, 1959, 1966, 1968, 1974, 1990. "Prayer to Masks," by Leopold Sedar Senghor, translated by Gerald Moore and Ulli Beier from *The Penguin Book of Modern African Poetry* edited by Gerald Moore and Ulli Beier, first published as *Modern Poetry from Africa*, 1963 (Penguin Books, 1984). Copyright © Gerald Moore and Ulli Beier, 1963, 1968, 1984. "from The Decameron: Federigo's Falcon," (originally titled "Ninth Story") by Giovanni Boccaccio from *The Decameron*, translated by G.H. McWilliam (Penguin Classics, 1972 Second Edition, 1995). Copyright © G.H. McWilliam, 1972, 1995. "From History of the Peloponnesian War: Pericles' Funeral Oration," by Thucydides from *History of the Peloponnesian Wars*, translated by Rex Warner (Penguin Classics, 1954). Translation copyright © Rex Warner, 1954. "from The Epic of Gilgamesh: Prologue," (originally titled "from Prologue: Gilgamesh King in Uruk"), "The Battle with Humbaba," (originally titled "from The Forest Journey"), "The Death of Enkidu," (originally titled "from

The Death of Enkidu"), "The Story of The Flood," and "The Return," from *The Epic of Gilgamesh*, translated by N.K. Sanders (Penguin Classics 1960, Third Edition 1972). Copyright © N.K. Sanders, 1960, 1964, 1972. "from the Tao Te Ching: I, III, IX & XLIII," from *Tao Te Ching: The Book of Meaning and Life* by Lao Tzu, translated by Richard Wilhelm, translated by H.G. Ostwald (Arkana, 1989) copyright © Eugen Diederichs Verlag GmBh & Co, Koln, 1985. English translation copyright © Routeledge & Kegan Paul, 1985. "from **The Nibelungentilied:** How Siegfried Was Slain," (originally titled "Chapter 16. How Siegfried Was Slain") from *The Nibelungenlied* translated by A.T. Hatto (Penguin Classics, 1965, revised edition 1969) copyright © A.T. Hatto, 1965, 1969. Reproduced by permission of Penguin Books Ltd.

Peter Pauper Press, Inc. "African Proverbs: Nigeria: The Yoruba: "The day on which one starts out . . .," "He who is being carried does not realize . . .," "Time destroys all things." and "Little is better than nothing."" Reprinted by permission. "African Proverbs: Ghana: The Ashanti: "Rain beats a leopard skin . . .," "If you are in hiding . . .," "One falsehood . . .," and "No one tests the depth of a river . . . "" from *African Proverbs*, compiled by Charlotte and Wolfe Leslau. Copyright © 1962, Peter Pauper Press.

Princeton University Press "Ithaka," by C.P. Cavafy, from *C.P. Cavafy: Selected Poems*, translated by Edmund Keeley and Philip Sherrard. Copyright © 1972 by Edmund Keeley and Philip Sherrard. Reprinted by permission of Princeton University Press.

Random House, Inc. "from The Aeneid: from Book II: How They Took the City," by Virgil from *The Aenid*, translated by Robert Fitzgerald, copyright © 1980, 1982, 1983 by Robert Fitzgerald. Used by permission of Random House, Inc.

Rupert Crew Limited on behalf of Steve and Megumi Biddle From "The Origins of Origami" by Steve and Megumi Biddle from *Origami: Inspired by Japanese Prints*. Copyright © 1998 by The Metropolitan Museum of Art. Introduction, instructions, diagrams and models © 1998 by Steve and Megumi Biddle. All rights reserved. Reprinted by permission.

The Sheep Meadow Press "Pride," by Dahlia Ravikovitch from A Dress of Fire translated by Chana Bloch, The Sheep Meadow Press, Riverdale-on-Hudson. Reprinted by permission.

Simon & Schuster Adult Publishing Group "The Wooden People," (originally titled "from Popol Vuh"), reprinted with permission of Simon & Schuster Adult Publishing Group from *Popol Vuh: The Definative Edition of the Mayan Book of the Dawn of Life and the Glories of Gods and Kings* translated by Dennis Tedlock. Copyright © Dennis Tedlock, 1985, 1996.

William Jay Smith "The Sleeper in the Valley," by Arthur Rimbaud, translated by William Jay Smith, in *Collected Translations: Italian, French, Spanish, Portuguese*, published by New Rivers Press, copyright © 1985 by William Jay Smith. Reprinted by permission.

Elyse Sommer "CurtainUp Review: A Doll's House," copyright April 1997, Elyse Sommer. Reprinted courtesy of www.curtainup.com, online theater magazine.

David Spencer "A Doll's House by Henrik Ibsen, a new version by Frank McGuinness," reviewed by David Spencer from www.aislesay.com. Reprinted by permission of the author, David Spencer.

Story Line Press "Autumn Song," by Paul Verlaine, translated by Louis Simpson from *Modern Poets of France, A Bilingual Anthology*. Copyright © 1997, 1998 by Louis Simpson. Reprinted by permission of the author and Story Line Press.

Tufts University, Perseus Project, Classics Department "from The Perseus Digital Library (http://www.perseus.tufts.edu/Olympics/)," reproduced by kind permission of Tufts University, Perseus Project.

Charles E. Tuttle Co, Inc. of Boston, Massachussetts and Tokyo, Japan "Zen Parables: "A Parable," "The Taste of Banzo's Sword" and "Publishing the Sutras," from *Zen Flesh, Zen Bones: A Collection of Zen & Pre-Zen Writings* compiled by Paul Reps. Reprinted by permission.

The University of California Press "He is More Than a Hero," and "You Know the Place: Then," by Sappho from *Sappho: A New Translation*, translated by Mary Barnard. Copyright © 1958, by The Regents of the University of California. "Green" by Juan Ramon Jimenez from *Juan Ramon Jimenez: Fifty Spanish Poems*, translated by J. B. Trend. "The Diameter of the Bomb," and "From The Book of Esther I Filtered the Sediment," by Yehuda Amichai from *The Selected Poetry of Yehuda Amichai*, translated by Chana Boch and Stephen Mitchell. English translation copyright © 1986 by Chana Boch and Stephen Mitchell. Reprinted by permission.

The University of Chicago Press "Olympia 11," by Pindar from *The Odes of Pindar, Second Edition*, translated by Richmond Lattimore. Copyright © 1947, 1976 by The University of Chicago Press. "He is More Than a Hero," by Sappho from Greek Lyrics, translated by Richmond Lattimore. Copyright © 1949 and 1955 by Richmond Lattimore. "from The Panchatantra: Numskull and the Rabbit," from *The Panchatantra*, translated by Arthur W. Ryder. Copyright © 1925 by The University of Chicago. Copyright renewed 1953 by Mary E. Ryder and Winifred Ryder. "Oedipus the King," by Sophocles, D. Grene, translator, from *The Complete Greek Tragedies: Oedipus the King, Oedipus at Colonus, Antigone, Volume II*, D. Grene and Richmond Lattimore, editors, pp. 11-76. Copyright © 1942 by The University of Chicago. All rights reserved. Reprinted by permission of The University of Chicago Press.

The University of Georgia Press from "Perceval or The Story of the Grail" translated by Ruth Harwood Cline. Copyright © 1983 by Ruth Harwood Cline. Used by permission of the University of Georgia Press.

Vedanta Society of Southern California "from The Bhagavad-Gita: The Yoga of Knowledge," from *The Song of God: Bhagavad-Gita*, translated by Swami Prabhavananda and Christopher Isherwood. Copyright © 1944, 1951 by The Vedanta Society of Southern California. Reprinted by permission.

Viking Penguin, a division of Penguin Group (USA) Inc. "from Book 1: The Quarrel (originally titled "from Book 1: The Rage of Achilles")," "from Book 6: The Meeting of Hector and Andromache (originally titled "from Book 6: Hector Returns to Troy")," "from Book 24: Achilleus and Priam," "from Book 22: The Death of Hector," from *The Iliad* by Homer, translated by Robert Fagles, copyright © 1990 by Robert Fagles. "The Fox and the Crow," copyright © 1952 by Marianne Moore, renewed © 1980 by Lawrence E. Brinn and Louise Crane, Executors of the Estate, "The Oak and the Reed," from *The Fables of La Fontaine*, translated by Marianne Moore, copyright © 1952, 1953, 1954, © 1964 by Marianne Moore, renewed © 1980, 1981, 1982 by Lawrence Brinn and Louise Crane, Executors of the Estate. "On the Bottom," from *If This is a Man (Survival in Auschwitz)*," by Primo Levi, translated by Stuart Woolf, copyright © 1959 by Orion Press, Inc., © 1958 by Giulio Einaudi editore, s.p.a. "from The Ingenious Gentleman Don Quixote de la Mancha," (originally titled "from The Ingenious Gentleman Don Quixote de la Mancha, Part 1, Chapter 1") from *Don Quixote* by Miguel de Cervantes Saavedra, translated by Samuel Putnam, copyright © 1949 by The Viking Press, Inc. "from The Ramayana: Rama and Ravana in the Battle," from *The Ramayana* by R.K. Narayan, copyright © 1972 by R.K. Narayan. Used by permission of Viking Penguin, a division of Penguin Group (USA), Inc.

Visva-Bharati Publishing Department, Visva Bharati University "The Artist," by Rabindranath Tagore from *The Housewarming and Other Selected Writings*, translated by Amiya Chakravarty, Mary Lago and Tarun Gupta. Copyright © 1965 Amiya Chakravarty. All rights reserved. Used by permission.

W. W. Norton & Company, Inc. From *The Song of Roland*, translated by Frederick Goldin. Copyright © 1978 by W.W. Norton & Company, Inc. "from The Inferno: Cantos I: The Dark Wood of Error," "from The Inferno: Cantos III: Vestibule of Hell / The Opportunists," "from The Inferno: Cantos V: Circle Two / The Carnal," "from The Inferno: Cantos XXXIV: Circle Nine / Cocytus," from *The Divine Comedy* by Dante Alighieri, translated by John Ciardi. Copyright © 1954, 1957, 1959, 1960, 1965, 1967, 1970 by the Ciardi Family Publishing Trust. This selection may not be reproduced, stored in a retrieval system or transmitted in any form or by any means without prior written permission of the publisher. Used by permission of W.W. Norton & Company, Inc.

The Arthur Waley Estate "from The Book of Songs: 34," "from The Book of Songs: 24," from *Translations from the Chinese* and "from *The Analects of Confucius*," translated by Arthur Waley, George Allen & Unwin, Ltd. London. All rights reserved. Reprinted by permission of the Arthur Waley Estate.

Washington Post Writers Group "A Lot of Baggage for Nora to Carry: After a History of Misinterpretation, Ibsen's Leave-Taking Heroine Finally Gets Her Due," by Lloyd Rose from *The Washington Post*, April 20, 1997. Copyright © 1997, The Washington Post. Reprinted with permission.

Gwendoline Mary Watkins "Comme on void sur la branche ("Roses")," by Pierre Ronsard, translated by Vernon Watkins. Reprinted by permission.

Witswatersrand University Press "African Proverbs: South Africa: The Zulu: "You cannot chase two gazelles.","" "The one offended never forgets . . .","" "No dew ever competed . . .","" "It never dawns in the same way.","" "Look as you fell a tree.","" "Do not speak of rhinoceros . . .","" "Eyes do not see all.","" "There is no foot . . .","" "What has happened before . . .","" from *Zulu Proverbs* edited by C.L. Sibusiso Nyembezi, M.A. Copyright 1954 Witswaterarand University Press. All rights reserved. Reprinted by permission.

Yale University Press "To Helene," (originally titled "Le Second Livre des Sonnets pour Helene, XLIII"), by Pierre de Ronsard from *Lyrics of the French Renaissance: Marot, Du Bellay, Ronsard*, translated by Norman R. Shapiro. Copyright © 2002 by Yale University. All rights reserved. This book may not be reproduced in whole or in part, in any form (except by reviewers for the public press) without written permission from the publishers. Reprinted by permission.

CREDITS

Cover: Werner Forman/Art Resource, NY; **i:** Werner Forman/Art Resource, NY; **iv: t.** Christopher Felver/CORBIS; **iv: m (1).** Prentice Hall; **iv: m (2).** Prentice Hall; **iv: m (3).** Getty Images; **iv: b.** Prentice Hall; **v: t.** Prentice Hall; **v: m (1).** Prentice Hall; **v: m (2).** Miriam Berkley/Authorpix; **v: m (3).** Photo © Sigrid Estrada; **v: b.** Reuters Pictures; **vii:** Royalty-Free/CORBIS; **viii:** Christopher Felver/CORBIS; **ix:** *The Creation of Adam,* (detail), 1510, Fresco, 280x570 cm. Michelangelo de Lodovico Buonarroti Simoni (Italian, 1475–1564). Cappella Sistina, Vatican. Canali Photobank Milan/Superstock; **x:** Prentice Hall; **xi: t.** Prentice Hall; **xi: b.** Arjuna and Krishna in the Chariot, Between the Two Armies, Illustration from Bhagavad-Gita, Photo by Lynn Saville; **xii:** © Matthias Kulka/CORBIS; **xiii:** Getty Images; **xiv:** Sei Shonagon, Heibonsha/Pacific Press Service; **xv:** Prentice Hall; **xvi:** Prentice Hall; **xvii:** © Dorling Kindersley; **xviii:** Prentice Hall; **xix:** Corel Professional Photos CD-ROM™; **xx:** Miriam Berkley/Authorpix; **xxi:** © Dorling Kindersley; **xxii:** Photo © Sigrid Estrada; **xxiii:** © Sylvain Grandadam/Photo Researchers, Inc.; **1:** The Art Archive/Archaeological Museum Istanbul/Dagli Orti; **2: t.** Christopher Felver/CORBIS; **2: b.** The Art Archive/Bodleian Library Oxford/The Bodleian Library; **4: m.l.** Head of an Acadion Ruler, Nineveh, 2300–2200 B.C., Bhagdad Museum, Scala/Art Resource, New York; **4: m.r.** Boltin Picture Library; **4: t.r.** Araldo de Luca/CORBIS; **4: b.l.** Founders Society purchase, General Membership Fund/Bridgeman Art Library, London/New York; **4: b.r.** The Palma Collection/Getty Images; **4: t.l.** Astrolabe, Museum fur Kunst und Gewerbe, Hamburg; **5: m.** Art Resource, New York; **5: t.** The Art Archive/Ethnic Jewellery Exhibition Milan/Dagli Orti; **5: b.** Senegalese glass painting used on Sundiata, from the collection of Professor Donal Cruise-O'Brien, Courtesy of Longman International Education; **6: b.** Babylonian globe, c. 5000 B.C., The British Museum, Bridgeman/Art Resource, New York; **6: t.** Astrolabe, Museum fur Kunst und Gewerbe, Hamburg; **8: b.** Page from the Book of the Dead, c. 1100 B.C., Egyptian, The British Museum, Photo by Michael Holford; **8: t.** Astrolabe, Museum fur Kunst und Gewerbe, Hamburg; **9:** Will and Deni McIntyre/Getty Images; **10: b.** Mary Evans/Edwin Wallace; **10: t.** Astrolabe, Museum fur Kunst und Gewerbe, Hamburg; **11:** Bojan Brecelj/CORBIS; **12:** Astrolabe, Museum fur Kunst und Gewerbe, Hamburg; **13:** The Simurgh Brings Zal to Sam, Leaf from Shah-nameh by Ferdowsi, 14th century, The Metropolitan Museum of Art, Rogers Fund, 1969, © Copyright by The Metropolitan Museum of Art; **15:** Erich Lessing/Art Resource, NY; **16:** Colossus of the King holding a lion (Gilgamesh), relief from the Palace of Sargon II at Khorsabada. Assyrian, ca. 725 BCE. Inv.: AO 19861-16. Photo: Herve Lewandowski. Louvre, Paris, France. Reunion des Musees Nationaux/Art Resource, NY **18:** Colossus of the King holding a lion (Gilgamesh), relief from the Palace of Sargon II at Khorsabada. Assyrian, ca. 725 BCE. Inv.: AO 19861-16. Photo: Herve Lewandowski. Louvre, Paris, France. Reunion des Musees Nationaux/Art Resource, NY; **20-21:** Yann Arthus-Bertrand/CORBIS; **22:** Scala/Art Resource, NY; **23:** Kabul Museum, Afghanistan/Bridgeman Art Library, London/New York; **26:** Front of lyre from tomb of Queen Pu-abi, Early Dynastic period, c. 2685–2290 B.C., British Museum, London; **28-29:** Erich Lessing/Art Resource, NY; **30-31:** Academy of Natual Sciences of Philadelphia/CORBIS; **38:** *The Creation of Adam* (detail), 1510, Fresco, 280x 570 cm. Michelangelo de Lodovico Buonarroti Simoni (Italian, 1475–1564). Cappella Sistina, Vatican. Canali Photobank Milan/Superstock; **40-41:** *The Creation of Adam,* 1510, Fresco, 280x 570 cm. Michelangelo de Lodovico Buonarroti Simoni (Italian, 1475–1564). Cappella Sistina, Vatican. Canali Photobank Milan/Superstock; **42:** Scala/Art Resource, NY; **44:** Bettmann/CORBIS; **47:** Corel Professional Photos CD-ROM™; **48:** *Noah's Ark,* Aaron Douglas, Fisk University Fine Art Galleries, Nashville, Tennessee; **54:** Harvey Lloyd/Getty Images; **55:** Dick S. Ramsay Fund, The Brooklyn Museum; **56:** Werner Forman Archive, Liverpool Museum, Liverpool/Art Resource, NY; **60:** Corel Professional Photos CD-ROM™; **62:** Historical Picture Archive/CORBIS; **65:** Chaim Gross (1904–1991). "Ketubbah, (Marriage Contract)", New York, ca. 1970, silkscreen on paper, 24 1/4 x 20 3/4 in. © Chaim Gross Studio Museum. Photo: John Parnell. Photo Credit: The Jewish Museum of New York/Art Resource, NY. The Chaim Gross Studio Museum, New York, NY, USA; **67:** *Il Buon Pastore* (The Good Shepherd), Early Christian, 4th century, Vatican Museum, Scala/Art Resource, New York; **69:** David Composing the Psalms, Illustrated by Paris Psalter, 10th century, Photo Bibliotheque Nationale, Paris; **75:** The Granger Collection, New York; **78:** CORBIS; **79:** Arabic Manuscript: 30,60. Page from a Koran, 8th–9th century. Kufic script H: 23.8 x W: 35.5 cm. Courtesy of the Freer Gallery of Art, Smithsonian Institution, Washington, D.C.: Purchase, F1930.60r; **84:** Scheherazade and King Shahriyar, (detail), Anton Pieck. Illustration from Stories of the Arabian Nights. Retold by Naomi Lewis. Illus. © 1984 by B.V. Elsevier. Uitgeversmaatschappij, Amsterdam. Photo by Rex Joseph.; **86:** Nick Koudis/Getty Images; **89:** Illustration from Arabian NIghts, for the story "The Fisherman and the Genie", Edmund Dulac, NY, Scribner's & Sons: 1907, Photo courtesy of the New York Public Library, Astor, Lenox and Tilden Foundations/Art Resource, NY; **90:** Monique le Luhandre/© Dorling Kindersley; **93:** George Hood/The Palma Collection/Getty Images; **94-95:** Christie's Images/CORBIS; **100: l.** Bettmann/CORBIS; **100: r.** Courtesy of the Freer Gallery of Art, Smithsonian Institution, Washington, D.C.: Gift of the Art and History Trust in honor of Ezzat-Malek Soudavar, F1998.5.6a; **103:** *Rubáiyát of Omar Khayyám,* Edmund Dulac, Photo by John Lei/Omni-Photo Communications, Inc.; **104:** *Rubáiyát of Omar Khayyám,* Edmund Dulac, Photo by John Lei/Omni-Photo Communications, Inc.; **107:** National Gallery Collection; By kind permission of the Trustees of the National Gallery, London/CORBIS; **109:** The Art Archive/Biblioteca Nazionale Marciana Venice/Dagli Orti; **114: b.** Scala/Art Resource, NY; **114: t.** Christopher Felver/CORBIS; **115:** Courtesy of the Trustees of British Library; www.bl.uk/imagesonline.; **116:** The Art Archive/Dagle Orti (A); **118:** Pococke 400 folio 99r/The Art Archive/Bodleian Library Oxford/The Bodleian Library; **120:** The Art Archive/Museum of Islamic Art Cairo/Dagli Orti; **123:** Bildarchiv Preussischer Kulturbesitz/Art Resource, NY; **124:** The Art Archive/Bodleian Library Oxford/The Bodleian Library; **128:** Private Collection/Heine Schneebeli/Bridgeman Art Library, London/New York; **130:** Werner Forman/Art Resource, NY; **133:** Pearson Education/PH School Division; **134:** Cover of SUNDIATA by David Wisniewski. Copyright © 1992 by David Wisniewski. Reprinted by permission of Clarion Books/Houghton Mifflin Company. All rights reserved.; **137:** © Michael Melford; **139:** Monique le Luhandre/© Dorling Kindersley; **145: t.** Photograph by J.D. Dallet, (c) 2002 Board of Trustees, National; Gallery of Art, Washington; **145: m.** The Art Archive/Egyptian Museum, Cairo/Dagli Orti; **150:** Bananastock/PictureQuest; **153:** Christopher Felver/CORBIS; **162-163:** The Art Archive/Victoria and Albert Museum London/Eileen Tweedy; **164: m.** Prentice Hall; **164: b.** Bildarchiv Preussisher Kulturbesitz/Art Resource, NY; **164: t.** Astrolabe, Museum fur Kunst und Gewerbe, Hamburg; **166 m.m.** Kanch Mandir/B.P.S. Walia/© Dorling Kindersley; **166: m.l.** The Granger Collection, New York; **166: m.r.** Buddha Standing, bronze, 1st half of 7th century, The Metropolitan Museum of Art, Purchase, Bequest of Florance Waterbury, 1969, © Copyright by The Metropolitan Museum of Art; **166: b.l.** Bridgeman Art Library, London/New York; **166: b.r.** Attic Red Figure Nolan Amphora: Hephaestus Making Armor for Achilles, The Dutuit painter, Francis Bartlett Fund, Courtesy, Museum of Fine Arts, Boston; **166: t.** Astrolabe, Museum fur Kunst und Gewerbe, Hamburg; **167: t.r.** © Christie's Images., 2004; **167: t.l.** Scala/Art Resource, New York; **167: b.** Werner Forman/Art Resource, NY; **168: t.** Astrolabe, Museum fur Kunst und Gewerbe, Hamburg; **170: t.** Astrolabe, Museum fur Kunst und Gewerbe, Hamburg; **171: r.** Scala/Art Resource, NY; **171: l.** David Buffington/Getty Images; **172: r.** *Zero,* 1980–1996, Robert Indiana, Morgan Art Foundation Limited/Art Resource, NY, © Copyright ARS, NY; **172: l.** Astrolabe, Museum fur Kunst und Gewerbe, Hamburg; **173:** Rama and Lakshman Confer with the Animal Armies, from the Adventures of Rama, Courtesy of the Freer Gallery of Art, Smithsonian Institution, Washington, D.C., fol. 194v, full view. Gift of Charles Lang Freer, F1907.271.194; **174: b.** Dinodia/Omni-Photo Communications, Inc.; **174: t.** Astrolabe, Museum fur Kunst und Gewerbe, Hamburg; **176: b.** Victoria & Albert Museum, London/Art Resource, NY; **176: t.** Prentice Hall; **177:** Lindsay Hebberd/CORBIS; **178:** Ann and Bury Peerless Picture Library/Bridgeman Art Library, London/New York; **180:** © Matthias Kulka/CORBIS; **180-181:** © Matthias Kulka/CORBIS; **182:** © Otto Rogge/Stock Photos/CORBIS; **187:** Bibliotheque National, Paris, France, Flammarion; Giraudon/The Bridgeman Art Library, London/New York; **188: b.** Victoria and Albert Museum, London/Art Resource, NY; **188: t.** Astrolabe, Museum fur Kunst und Gewerbe, Hamburg; **190:** Krishna on a Swing, Scala/Art Resource, NY; **192:** Indra, engraved by Marlet et Cie, 1841. Private Collection/The Stapleton Collection/Bridgeman Art Library, London/New York; **194:** Vishnu and Lakshmi Riding on Garuda, Ann & Bury Peerless Picture Library/Bridgeman Art Library, London/New York; **197:** A Hawk, Indian Mughal, 18th century miniature, Victoria and Albert Museum, Photo by Michael Holford; **198:** King Sibi's Sacrifice to the God Indra, Gandharan Art, c. 2nd century, Courtesy of the Trustees of the British Museum; **200:** © Art Resource, New York; **202:** Arjuna and Krishna in the Chariot, Between the Two Armies, Illustration from Bhagavad-Gita, Photo by Lynn Saville; **205:** © Werner Forman/Art Resource, NY; **211:** Corel Professional Photos CD-ROM™; **212:** Ingo Jezierski/Getty Images; **213:** Rama and Lakshmana shooting arrows at the demon Ravana. gouache on paper. Dehle of Jaipur school. 19th century, © Victoria & Albert Museum, London/Art Resource, NY; **214:** Lyndsay Hebberd/CORBIS; **220:** Kangra Valley Painting, New York Public Library; **223:** *A Lion at Rest,* The Metropolitan Museum of Art, The Alice and Nasli Heeramaneck Collection, Gift of Alice Heeramaneck, 1985. (1985.221); **225:** Monique le Luhandre/© Dorling Kindersley; **230:** Royalty-Free/CORBIS; **231:** Bettmann/CORBIS; **234:** © Dorling Kindersley; **238:** Gary Conner/PhotoEdit Inc.; **241:** Prentice Hall; **250-251:** Katsusika Hokusai (1760–1849). *The Great Wave of Kanagawa,* from 36 Views of Mount Fuji. Private Collection. Art Resource, NY.; **252: m.** Prentice Hall; **252: b.** Bettmann/CORBIS; **252: t.** Astrolabe, Museum fur Kunst und Gewerbe, Hamburg; **254: m.r.** Mary Evans Picture Library; **254: b.** Pawel Kumelowski/Omni-Photo Communications, Inc.; **254: m.l.** Pearson Education EMG Education Management Group; **254: t.** Astrolabe, Museum fur Kunst und Gewerbe, Hamburg; **255: t.** *First Landing at Kurihama,* July 14, 1853, Gessan Ogata, Courtesy of United States Naval Academy Museum; **255: b.** Reuters NewMedia Inc./CORBIS; **255: m.** © Will and Deni McIntyre/Photo Researchers, Inc.; **256:** Astrolabe, Museum fur Kunst und Gewerbe, Hamburg; **257:** Dallas and John Heaton/CORBIS; **258: b.** Tokyo National Museum; **258: t.** Astrolabe, Museum fur Kunst und Gewerbe, Hamburg; **259:** Pearson Education Corporate Digital Archive; **260: b.** *The Poet Li Po Admiring a Waterfall,* Hokusai, Honolulu Academy of Arts, Gift of James A. Michener (21,892); **260: t.** Astrolabe, Museum fur Kunst und Gewerbe, Hamburg; **262:** Astrolabe, Museum fur Kunst und Gewerbe, Hamburg; **263:** Asian Art & Archaeology, Inc./CORBIS; **264: r.** The Granger Collection, New York; **264: l.** Foto Marburg/Art Resource, NY; **267:** *Poet on a Mountain Top,* Shen Chou, The Nelson-Atkins Museum of Art, Kansas City, Missouri; **268:** *Old Trees by Cold Waterfall,* 1470–1559, Wen Zhengming. Ming dynasty, dated 1531, hanging scroll, ink and colored paper, 86 1/2 x 17 1/8 in. The Los Angeles County Museum of Art, The Ernest Larsen Blancok Memorial Fund. Museum No. 55.67.1. Photograph © 2004 Museum Associates/LACMA; **274:** The Granger Collection, New York; **275:** *Benjamin Franklin* (detail), c.1790, Pierre Michel Alix, National Portrait Gallery, Smithsonian Institution, Washington, D.C./Art Resource, New York; **278: b.l.** T'ao Ch'ien, Collection of the National Palace Museum, Taipei, Taiwan, Republic of China; **278: t.** © New York Public Library/Art Resource, NY; **278: b.r.** New York Public Library Picture Collection; **281:** *Fishing Village in the Wind and Rain,* hanging scroll painting, 1955, Li K'e-jan, Werner Forman/Art Resource, NY; **283:** *A Myriad of Trees on Strange Peaks,* Yen Wen-Kuei (Northern Sung Dynasty), The Granger Collection, New York; **285:** *River and Mountains in Autumn Color,* 1120–1182, Zhao Boju, Imerial Palace Museum, Beijing, China.; **287:** *River Village in a Rainstorm,* Hanging scroll, ink and slight color on silk, 169.2 x 103.5 cm, Lü Wenying, Chinese, active ca. 1490–1507, © The Cleveland Museum of Art, John L. Severance Fund, 70.76; **288-289:** Eyewire/Getty Images; **290:** Corel Professional Photos CD-ROM™; **294: b.** *Landscape with a Solitary Traveler,* c. 1780. Japan, Edo Period (1615–1868) Hanging Scroll, ink and light colors on silk 40 x 14 3/8 in. (101.5x36.4 cm), Copyright © 2005 by Kimbell Art Museum; **294: t.** Prentice Hall; **296: m.r.** Yosa Buson, Heibonsha/Pacific Press Service; **296: b.r.** Kobayashi Issa, Heibonsha/Pacific Press Service; **296: t.r.** Basho, The Granger Collection, New York; **296: m.l.** Onono-komachi, Heibonsha/Pacific Press Service; **296: t.l.** Kino Tsurayuki, Heibonsha/Pacific Press Service; **296: b.l.** Jakuren Houshi, Heibonsha/Pacific Press Service; **298:** *Snow at Senso-ji Temple in Asakusa,* Victoria and Albert Museum, London/Art Resource, NY; **300:** *The Monkey Bridge in Koshu Province,* 1841, Hiroshige Hitsu, © Christie's Images, Inc., 2004; **301:** *Sudden Shower on Ohashi Bridge,* Hiroshige, Art Resource, New York; **302:** Artville/Getty Images; **306:** Sei Shonagon, Heibonsha/Pacific Press Service; **309:** *Triptych of Snow, Moon, and Flower* (Center Panel), c.1780's, Shunsho, Museum of Art, Tami, Japan; **311:** Sei Shonagon, Heibonsha/Pacific Press Service; **316:** Astrolabe, Museum fur Kunst und Gewerbe, Hamburg; **317:** *The Celebrated Beauty of the Teahouse, Kagiya, at Kasamori Shrine,* Suzuki Harunobu, 18th century, The Metropolitan Museum of Art, the Henry L. Phillips Collection, Bequest of Henry L. Phillips, 1940, © Copyright by The Metropolitan Museum of Art; **318:** Large Enso, hanging scroll, Torei Enji, Gitter-Yelen Art Center; **320:** CORBIS; **321:** Monique le Luhandre/© Dorling Kindersley; **327-330:** Instructions, diagram and models © 1998 by Steve and Megumi Biddle. Models photograph by Les Morsillo. Photograph ©1998 The Metropolitan Museum; **334:** John Neubauer/PhotoEdit Inc.; **337:** Prentice Hall; **346-347:** *Aeneas at Delos,* Claude Lorrain, © National Gallery Collection; By kind permission of the Trustees of the National Gallery, London/CORBIS; **348: t.** Getty Images; **348: b.** Photo by Janine Norton; **350: m.l.** Mimmo Jodice/CORBIS; **350: b.l.** Ann & Bury Peerless Picture Library/Bridgeman Art Library, London/New York; **350: b.r.** Seattle Art Museum/CORBIS; **350: t.r.** Antonio M. Rosario/Getty Images; **350: t.l.** Astrolabe, Museum fur Kunst und Gewerbe, Hamburg; **351: t.l.** Roman Mosaic: Gladiator with Leopard, Galleria Borghese, Scala/Art Resource, New York; **351: t.r.** Bettmann/CORBIS; **351: b.** Michael S. Yamashita/CORBIS; **352:** Astrolabe, Museum fur Kunst und Gewerbe, Hamburg; **354: r.** The Apollo Belvedere, Roman marble copy probably of Greek original of late 4th (or 1st) century BC, Vatican Museums, Rome, Scala/Art Resource, New York; **354: l.** Astrolabe, Museum fur Kunst und Gewerbe, Hamburg; **355:** Erich Lessing/Art Resource, NY; **356: b.** Richard Quataert/Folio, Inc.; **356: t.** Astrolabe, Museum fur Kunst und Gewerbe, Hamburg; **357:** *Circe Meanwhile Had Gone Her Ways...,* 1924, From THE ODYSSEY by Homer, William Russell Flint, Collection of the New York Public Library; Astor, Lenox and Tilden Foundations; **358: b.** The Art Archive/Biblioteca Braidense Milan/Dagli Orti; **358: t.** Astrolabe, Museum fur Kunst und Gewerbe, Hamburg; **359:** The Art Archive/Dagli Orti; **360:** Bettmann/CORBIS; **363:** Mimmo Jodice/CORBIS; **364:** Mimmo Jodice/CORBIS; **365:** Historical Picture Archive/CORBIS; **366:** Kimbell Art Museum/CORBIS; **369:** Hirmer Verlag Munchen; **370:** *Minerva restrains Achilles from killing Agamemnon,* Giambattista Tiepolo, Scala/Art Resource, New York; **372:** Liz McAulay/© Dorling Kindersley; **374:** Mimmo Jodice/CORBIS; **377:** *Hector Taking Leave of Andromache,* Angelica Kauffmann, Tate Gallery, London/Art Resource, New York; **379:** Odysseus' Mission to Achilles, Cleophrades Painter, 485–475 B.C., Staatliche Antikensammlungen und Glyptothek, Munich; **383:** Mimmo Jodice/CORBIS; **386:** Araldo de Luca/CORBIS; **389:** Monique le Luhandre/© Dorling Kindersley; **391:** *Achilles defeating Hector,* Peter Paul Rubens, Musee des Beaux-Arts, Giraudon/Art Resource, New York; **392:** *Achilles Deciding to Resume Fighting Upon the Death of Patroclus,* 1620, Dirck van Baburen/Bridgeman Art Library, London/New York; **395:** *Andromache and Astyanax,* 1789, Richard Cosway, Courtesy of the Trustees of Sir John Soane's Museum, London/Bridgeman Art Library, London/New York; **397: t.** Mimmo Jodice/CORBIS; **397: b.** "*Achilles*" detail from the fresco "*Thetis consoling Achilles*", Giovanni Battista Tiepolo, Scala/Art Resource, New York; **401:** The Granger

R60 ■ *Credits*

MAP AND ART CREDITS

All graphic organizers: In-House Pros; all maps by Mapping Specialist, except where noted

STAFF CREDITS

ADDITIONAL CREDITS

Zlata Filipovic
John Phillip Santos
Anita Desai
Gary Soto
Julius Lester
Coleman Barks
William L. Andrews
Laurence Yep
Judith Ortiz Cofer
Susan Power
Gretel Ehrlich
David Mamet
Jane Yolen
Richard Peck
Jon Scieszka
Jamaica Kincaid
Burton Raffel
Susan Vreeland
Jacqueline Woodson
Wayson Choy
Charles Johnson
Andrew Mishkin
Cherie Bennett
David Henry Hwang
Walter Dean Myers
Nell Irvin Painter
Chinua Achebe
Elizabeth McCracken
Gretel Ehrlich
James Berry
Frank Kermode
Anita Desai
C.J. Cherryh
Patricia McKissack
Zlata Filipovic
Elizabeth McCracken
Gary Blackwood
Jean Craighead George
Jon Scieszka
Julius Lester
Walter Dean Myers
Dean Smith
Richard Mühlberger
Pat Mora
Jamaica Kincaid
Gretel Ehrlich
Gary Blackwood
Cornelius Eady
Pat Mora
Eric Weihenmayer
Joao Magueijo
Joseph Bruchac
Samantha Chang
Frank Kermode
Walter Dean Myers
Patricia MᶜKissack
Richard Rodriguez
Wendy Doniger
Seamus Heaney
Anne Tyler
Cornelius Eady
Tim O'Brien
Arthur Miller
Rebecca Wakefield
Marilyn Nelson
John Kilgo
Jean Craighead George